THE
LONGMAN ANTHO
OLD ENGL
OLD ICELAND
ANGLO-NORMAN
LITERATURES

* * *

CW01310138

THE LONGMAN ANTHOLOGY OF OLD ENGLISH, OLD ICELANDIC AND ANGLO-NORMAN LITERATURES

* * *

Richard North
Joe Allard
and
Patricia Gillies

Routledge
Taylor & Francis Group
LONDON AND NEW YORK

First published 2011 by Pearson Education Limited

Published 2014 by Routledge
2 Park Square, Milton Park, Abingdon, Oxon OX14 4RN
711 Third Avenue, New York, NY 10017, USA

Routledge is an imprint of the Taylor & Francis Group, an informa business

Copyright © 2011, Taylor & Francis.

The rights of Richard North, Joe Allard and Patricia Gillies to be identified as authors of this work have been asserted by them in accordance with the Copyright, Designs and Patents Act 1988.

All rights reserved. No part of this book may be reprinted or reproduced or utilised in any form or by any electronic, mechanical, or other means, now known or hereafter invented, including photocopying and recording, or in any information storage or retrieval system, without permission in writing from the publishers.

Notices
Knowledge and best practice in this field are constantly changing. As new research and experience broaden our understanding, changes in research methods, professional practices, or medical treatment may become necessary.

Practitioners and researchers must always rely on their own experience and knowledge in evaluating and using any information, methods, compounds, or experiments described herein. In using such information or methods they should be mindful of their own safety and the safety of others, including parties for whom they have a professional responsibility.

To the fullest extent of the law, neither the Publisher nor the authors, contributors, or editors, assume any liability for any injury and/or damage to persons or property as a matter of products liability, negligence or otherwise, or from any use or operation of any methods, products, instructions, or ideas contained in the material herein.

ISBN 13: 978-1-4082-4770-9 (pbk)

British Library Cataloguing in Publication Data
A CIP catalogue record for this book can be obtained from the British Library

Library of Congress Cataloging in Publication Data
The Longman anthology of Old English, Old Icelandic and Anglo-Norman literatures/
Richard North, Joe Allard and Patricia Gillies.
p. cm.
Includes index.
ISBN 978-1-4082-4770-9 (pbk.)
1. English literature–Old English, ca. 450-1100. 2. Old Norse literature.
3. Anglo-Norman literature. I. North, Richard, 1961– II. Allard, Joe, 1948–
III. Gillies, Patricia.
PR1505.L66 2011
808.8–dc22
2011003914

Runic font created by Daniel Smith
Set by 35 in 10/12pt Minion

In memory of John D. North
(1934–2008)

In memory of Margaret S. Harris
(1916–2010)

CONTENTS

PREFACE xiv

Heroic Poems 1

Beowulf 5

Scyld Scefing's funeral 6

Beowulf and the Danish coastguard 10

Beowulf greets King Hrothgar 15

Beowulf's fight with Grendel 20

Funeral at Finnsburh: Hildeburh and Wealhtheow 27

Future foretold: the fall of Hygelac 35

King Hrothgar on Grendel's Mere 37

Beowulf's fight with Grendel's Mother 39

King Hrothgar's sermon 45

Beowulf on Princess Freawaru 52

The lament of the last survivor 56

King Beowulf fights the Dragon 59

Wiglaf helps King Beowulf 63

History related: the rise of Hygelac 69

King Beowulf's funeral 74

Finnsburh Fragment 82

Warriors attack the hall 82

Y Gododdin 86

The fight at Catterick 87

Widsith 91

Deor 101

The Lay of Wayland 106

Prose introduction 107

Vǫlundr's lost marriage 108

Níðuðr binds Vǫlundr 109

Vǫlundr's revenge 113

Sayings of the High One 118

Óðinn and the wife of Billingr 118

Fragment of The Lay of Hildebrand 122

Hildebrand pleads with Hadubrand 123

Bragi's *Eulogy on Ragnarr* 128

Vengeance on Jǫrmunrekkr 129

Heðinn's everlasting battle 131

The Exile of the Sons of Uisliu 134
The flight of Deirdre and Noisiu 135

Waldere 145
I. Hildegyth rouses Waldere to battle 146
II. Hagena stands down before Waldere 148

The Lay of Attila 150
Gunnarr accepts the summons 151
The death of Gunnarr and Hǫgni 154
The vengeance of Guðrún 160

Poems on the Meaning of Life **163**

The Wanderer 167

Egill's *Hard Loss of Sons* 176

The Seafarer 186

Vainglory 196

Maxims I 203
A. The spirit of exchange 204
B. God, the world and women 205

Sayings of the High One 210
What it's like when you get there 211
Friendship and exchange 213
How to get on 215
Love and trust 218

The Rhyming Poem 223

Wulf and Eadwacer 232

Riddles 236
No. 1 'Wind' 237
No. 5 'Shield' 238
No. 7 'Swan' 239
No. 9 'Cuckoo' 240
No. 12 'Ox' 241
No. 22 'Wagon of stars' 242
No. 25 'Onion' 243
No. 30a 'The Cross' 244
No. 46 'Lot and family' 245
No. 47 'Bookworm' 246
No. 54 'Churn' 247

The Wife's Lament 248

The Husband's Message 253

The Lay of Hamðir 259
Guðrún's lament 260
The Exile of the Sons of Uisliu 262
Deirdre of the Sorrows 262
The Ruin 269

Poems of Devotion 273

Cædmon's *Hymn* 276
Northumbrian text 277
The Cross speaks 279
The Ruthwell *Crucifixion Poem* 280
The Brussels Cross Riddle 283
The Dream of the Rood 283
Exodus 295
The Lord's pact with Moses 296
The Israelites sail to the Red Sea 300
Moses puts heart into the Israelites 305
The drowning of the Egyptians 308
Cynewulf's *Elene* 314
Constantine's Vision of the Cross 315
Elene's discovery of the nails of the Cross 324
Cynewulf's signed Epilogue 330
Cynewulf's *Christ II* 336
Thoughts on the final harbour 336
Genesis B 341
Lucifer the rebel 342
Satan chafes in Hell 346
Satan's demon tempts Adam 354
Satan's demon tempts Eve 359
Eve, deceived, deceives Adam 363
Rejoicing and despair 368
Andreas 376
Matthew and the Mermedonians 377
Andrew talks with the Lord 382
Andrew frees Matthew 387
Andrew calls forth a flood 393
Judith 401
The feast of Holofernes 402
Judith wields the sword 406
Vengeance on the Assyrians 409

The Earliest English Prose 421

Anglo-Saxon Chronicle 424
The coming of the Saxons 424
Cynewulf and Cyneheard 426

King Alfred's *Prefaces* 430
Preface to the translation of Gregory's *Pastoral Care* 431
Preface to the translation of Boethius' *Consolation of Philosophy* 436
Preface to the translation of Augustine's *Soliloquies* 437

The West Saxon *Boethius* 440
Orpheus and Eurydice 441
Ulysses and Circe 446
Fate and Providence 449

The West Saxon *Bede* 454
The conversion of King Edwin 454
The miracle of Cædmon 459

Viking Wars 467

Anglo-Saxon Chronicle 470
The Battle of Brunanburh (937) 470
Edmund's Capture of the Five Boroughs (942) 475

The English poems of Egill Skalla-Grímsson 477
Eulogy on Æthelstan (*c.* 937) 477
Head-Ransom (*c.* 952) 478

The Lay of Eiríkr Bloodaxe (*c.* 954) 488

Eyvindr's *Lay of King Hákon the Good* (*c.* 961) 492

The Battle of Maldon (*c.* 991) 499
Byrhtnoth and the Viking herald 501
Byrhtnoth gives Vikings ground 504
The Vikings take out Byrhtnoth 508
Englishmen fight to the end 512

Gods of the Vikings 519

Snorri's *Edda* (*c.* 1220–30) 523
The Old Norse myth of Creation 524
The death of Baldr the Beautiful 527

Bragi's *Eulogy on Ragnarr* (*c.* 850) 532
Gefjun drags land from Sweden 532
Þórr fishes for the World Serpent 532

The Lay of Skírnir 534

Þjóðólfr's *Harvest-Long* (*c.* 900) 548
Þjazi steals Iðunn from the gods 549
Þórr duels with Hrungnir 553

Einarr's *Gold-Shortage* (*c.* 980) 558
Proem on the Mead of Poetry 559
Óðinn helps Earl Hákon win Norway 560
Earl Hákon restores the sacrifices 560
The gods guide Earl Hákon 562

The Thunderclap Ballad 564

Eilífr's *Eulogy on Þórr* (*c.* 985) 573
Þórr sets off without Loki 574
Þórr and Þjalfi cross the river 575
Þórr in Geirrøðr's cave 577

Úlfr's *Eulogy on the House* (early 990s) 583
Proem on the Mead of Poetry 584
Heimdallr beats Loki to Freyja's necklace 584
Þórr fishes for the World Serpent 585
The gods ride to Baldr's funeral pyre 586
A summation 587

Hallfreðr's *Eulogy on Earl Hákon* (*c.* 994) 588
Hákon the Mighty at Hjǫrungavágr 588
The earl goes to bed with Norway 589

The Sibyl's Prophecy 591
The Creation 592
The Æsir-Vanir cult-war 596
Þórr's blunder and Baldr's death 597
Visions of the End 599
Ragnarǫk: the Day of Judgement 602
World's rebirth: the New Jerusalem 606

Loki's Truth-Game 609
Loki crashes the party 610
Loki toasts all the gods 614
Enter Þórr, exit Loki 627

Sagas of Icelanders **633**

Ari's *Book of Icelanders* 638
Greenland and America 638
The conversion of Iceland 639

The Saga of Eiríkr the Red 643
Vikings in America 643

The Saga of Egill Skalla-Grímsson 651
Egill and King Æthelstan 651
Eiríkr Bloodaxe and the *Head-Ransom* 655
In the backwoods: Egill and Ármóðr 658
Bǫðvarr and the *Hard Loss of Sons* 664
The Saga of the People of Laxdale 669
Hǫskuldr buys Melkorka 670
The birth of Óláfr the Peacock 673
Hjarðarholt and *Eulogy on the House* 677
Bolli kills Kjartan 682
The Saga of the Burned Njáll 689
Hallgerðr wins Gunnarr 690
Gunnarr's last stand 693
The burning of Njáll 697
The Saga of Grettir the Strong 702
Grettir's fight with Glámr 702
Grettir fights the cave-trolls 709

Writers of the Benedictine Reform 715

Alexander's Letter to Aristotle 719
Alexander's address to Aristotle 720
A meeting with King Porus 723
The Prophecy of the trees of Sun and Moon 726
The Blickling Homilies 733
No. 16 'The Feast of St Michael the Archangel' 734
Abbot Ælfric of Eynsham 740
Preface to Genesis 740
The Life of St Edmund 746
Archbishop Wulfstan of York 756
De Falsis Deis 757
Secundum Marcum 759
Sermo Lupi 765

Early Chivalry 777

Apollonius of Tyre 781
The Princess falls in love 783
The Song of Roland 792
The dreams of Charlemagne 793
The trial of Ganelon 796
Gaimar's *History of the English* 802
Havelok the Dane 802
Hereward the Wake 806

The Poem of My Cid 810
Exile of the Campeador 812

Lyrics of William IX 815
A suitable poem 816
Feeling sleepy 818

Fin'amor from Orkney: Rǫgnvaldr kali 824

Wace's *Brut* 827
Arthur fights the giant of Mont St Michel 827

Thomas of Britain's *Tristan* 835
Sailing towards England 836
Tristan disguised as a leper 838
Love and images 841

Marie de France's *The Nightingale* 845
The husband finds the nightingale 847

The Play of Adam 852
The devil talks to Eve 853
Adam takes the apple 857

INDEX 860

CONTENTS OF THE CUSTOM VERSION 865

PREFACE

✳

To those who know the price of everything and the value of nothing, this anthology will be a reminder that some culture isn't dead yet and still needs putting down. Other people believe that the culture of the Middle Ages can have no price, but presently we seem to be on the margin. Soon the price may be too high for the managers of our modern 'universities' to sustain, like the intellectual level of the age that created the institution of the university itself. In the meantime, however, as politically if not culturally we all move into a new middle ages, we might remind ourselves of the value the old one had. My invitation to do so is extended to the very top. Bankers have to get their bonuses from somewhere, so why not here? Even the Neros of high finance, fiddling while our culture burns, might be surprised to learn that the Middle Ages invented banking, football and Modern Europe, as well as science and the Liberal Arts. It is medieval literature that gives the best impression of what our ancestors thought, how close they were to us in some ways, and how, in others, they understood more of the world both here and beyond. Not long ago, in a cheerful attempt to upsize the community that reads this kind of literature, Joe Allard and I, and some like-minded scholars including Patricia Gillies, spoke up for it in *'Beowulf' & Other Stories: A New Introduction to Old English, Old Icelandic and Anglo-Norman Literatures* (Harlow, 2007). Now, like the Blues Brothers with an orphanage to save, a full tank and on a mission from God (but so far without incident in tunnels or railway hotels), we aim to go further and let literature speak for itself.

Laid out here in this anthology are many selections of works, entirely or in extract, in the order in which we discussed them in *'Beowulf' & Other Stories* (all references to *B&OS* in this volume are to the first edition). We are starting this volume with significant excerpts from the great epic poem *Beowulf*, then with the text and translation of a range of excerpts in poetry and prose from Old English and Old Icelandic and Anglo-Norman literatures. One principle that has guided the selection and presentation of these texts is that Old English and Old Icelandic and Anglo-Norman are cognate parts of a larger Germanic and Scandinavian culture which emerged from the years of the Great Migration in the third and fourth centuries during the decline and dissolution of the Roman Empire. 'Old English' (OE) is English literature written in the language of its time in England from around the year 600 to 1100; 'Old Icelandic' (OIce) is poems and prose works from around 850 to 1400 and composed, spoken, and then written in Norway and Iceland in the twelfth and thirteenth centuries: the 'Anglo-Norman' in this book will cover literature in England, the Celtic Atlantic and France in the period 1066 to about 1200, and leads into the better-known works of Middle English literature such as *The Canterbury Tales* of Geoffrey Chaucer. There again, the Anglo-Saxons who spoke Old English fought, settled down and intermarried with Vikings, Danes and Norwegians who spoke Old Scandinavian, or 'Old Norse', a language that was written down in Iceland and so is also called 'Old Icelandic'. Many of the Icelandic sagas, which are rather like historical novels, tell stories about the Vikings in England. The Normans who invaded England in 1066 were themselves of Norwegian origin and spoke a French that changed the English language into its present form. They also cleared the way for new forms of literature from France, such as rhyming octosyllabic poetry and 'Romance'. Because Old English, Old Icelandic and Anglo-Norman overlap in this way we are putting them together in this book, with *Beowulf* at their head.

As can be seen from the table of Contents we have arranged our material thematically, as well as by chronology. Broadly speaking we have followed patterns established in *'Beowulf' & Other Stories*. We begin, of course, with *Beowulf* itself and other **Heroic Poems**, not only from Old English but also from Old Norse, Old High German, Welsh and Irish. Next are what we call **Poems on the Meaning of Life**, which include elegies, eulogies, laments, riddles, maxims and wisdom verse in the same sequence as the source of many of these items, the Exeter Book. The real benefit of combining the Old English and Old Icelandic and Old Irish works will be clear here. The section **Poems of Devotion** gives a good idea of the range of religious literature from our long period. Here, moreover, are examples of different Old English dialects. The biblical, both Old and New Testament, is well represented, as well as ancient and idiosyncratic poetic meditations such as *The Dream of the Rood* (also in its runic form). In the works excerpted in **The Earliest English Prose** we have a combination of motives. On the one hand we can see the historical and religious concerns of the writers. On the other hand, and of special interest to us now, we get a clear idea of the development of the English written language itself (there is a lucid introduction to Old English by Peter Baker in Chapter 10 in *'Beowulf' & Other Stories*). From here on in, Old Icelandic is given a more prominent billing. **Viking Wars** would not be complete without the literature of both sides, and, as the selections make clear, England in this period was anything but a monolingual entity resisting an alien threat ('Notes on the Old Norse language' can be found in the like-named chapter in *'Beowulf' & Other Stories*). **Gods of the Vikings** gives vivid images in mostly Norse poetic form of the heathen mythology and religion of Scandinavia and England. **Sagas of Icelanders** presents a variety of narrative forms: the saga, the history and the *þáttr* 'short tale'. A range of saga material is included, starting with material relating to the Viking adventure in North America around the turn of the first millennium. We also give examples of histories (an abiding passion in Iceland) of the Norwegian kings, Iceland's settlement and adoption of Christianity, and the voyages of discovery to North America. **Writers of the Benedictine Reform** brings us into better documented history, in which we can see further development and refinement of the language. The final section, **Early Chivalry**, takes us through Edward the Confessor's England into the Norman Conquest in 1066 and beyond into the heady period of early Plantagenet rule. The texts here, an Old English prose romance, Norse troubadour lyrics and a Castillian *chanson de geste*, as well as poems in Occitan and dialects of French, show how with the Normans there came a flood of ideas and images, forms and modes, from the Francophone zones of Europe. These influences further helped to form our language and led to the emergence of the 'Middle English' of Geoffrey Chaucer in his *Canterbury Tales*. But that, of course, is another story.

The layout of this anthology has been achieved with certain rules of presentation. Each section has its headnote, and thereafter each text or associated group of texts has its own smaller headnote. In most cases each headnote and smaller note has a small bibliography appended to enable closer reading, with the guidance of the endnotes for each text, which are usually laid out at the foot of the page beneath the text. The bibliographies are intended wherever possible to be adjacent to the texts on which they have a bearing, and to be longer than the reading lists of *'Beowulf' & Other Stories*, the older sister volume to this. Repetition of entries is kept to a minimum, and sometimes the references in the section headnote may apply later on in the smaller introductions. The principle is that custom texts can be added at will without the complications and potential errors of fishing out bibliographies from other locations.

In formatting texts, unbold line numbers are used where possible, in both original and translation, to find the place in long passages of non-stanzaic verse, and occasionally also for Anglo-Norman *laisses* 'verse passages' as well. Where the poetry is stanzaic, bold numbers to the left are used to indicate stanza numbers, not lines. In the case of riddles, the abbreviation for 'Riddle' will be followed by a point and then the number, all in bold. Endnote entries for poems are generally introduced with quotation of the words that will be discussed, in both original and translated form, although the quoted words may not be exactly the whole phrase that appears in the main text. Where prose is cited and translated, the relevant chapter numbers are used again in bold and followed by a point. The correlation of notes to the original text and translation is accomplished in prose not with numbers, but with the aid of having the relevant words of the text in bold in both original and translation and then in the note. Cross-references are made throughout the anthology not to the number of the section (there is none), but to the title of the section, which is always given in bold. Again, this is to enable a selection of the additional texts of the Custom Version to be dropped into place with the minimum reworking of notes.

The policy on translations is always to prefer literal to elegant or poetic forms wherever such a choice must be made. A translation is a guide to the original, not a substitute for it. Sometimes, in this spirit of deference, we have made an attempt to replicate the word order of the original (as when the object is placed first or the verb is postponed for rhetorical effect) in a way that does not interfere with Modern English clarity or understanding. The policy with foreign-language titles, such as from Latin or Old Icelandic or Anglo-Norman poetry or prose, is to keep these wherever possible, but to lead into them by having solely the Modern English translations of these titles in the Contents, then the latter above the original titles each on the opening page of its text. Roman numerals are usually expanded to words in original, but not translated, texts. The policy with terms for the Deity is to use capitals for the leading epithet in the original, for this and associated words in the translation, and mostly (where this does not interfere with literary effects) to use capitals for the Deity's He-pronoun in both original and translated texts. One book abbreviation is *B&OS*, for '*Beowulf*' *& Other Stories*. Another is ÍF for 'Íslenzk Fornrit'. Otherwise m. is for 'masculine, f. for 'feminine', n. for 'neuter', sg. for 'singular', pl. for 'plural'; vs. for 'verse' in Snorri's *Edda*, ed Faulkes (1998).

To end this preface, I would like to give special thanks to my co-editors with whom I share the blame: to Joe Allard, for editing and translating the texts in Icelandic prose in **Gods of the Vikings** and **Sagas of Icelanders**, and for helping with the proofing and editing of the whole book from beginning to end; and to Patricia Gillies, for editing and translating the French and Occitan texts in **Early Chivalry**, a chapter that was also edited by Joe and myself. With Joe, I thank Philip Langeskov for initiating this Anthology four summers ago, as a sequel to *B&OS*, just before leaving us the bill in *The Anchor & Hope*; Gavin Phipps, for showing us his erection (= Heron Tower, ed.); Jane Roberts for commenting upon my notes and translation of *Vainglory*; Stewart Brookes for advising me on early medieval Jewry; Lezmur der Thèref for his help with impressing the Government; my wife Inma Ridao for choosing the passage from the *Poema del Mio Cid*; Kate Ahl at Pearson for arranging to give us permission to produce this book, and patiently putting up with our squabbles and demands; Colin Reed for reading the runes and for talking to us about formatting; Josephine Bryan and Barbara Massam their for eagle-eyed attention to copy-editing and proofing the final text; and Helen Savill and Josie O'Donoghue for steering this volume from harbour to open sea.

Richard North

HEROIC POEMS

* * *

HEROIC POEMS

✳ ✳ ✳

The flagship of this section is *Beowulf*, from which as many as 15 passages may be read (more in the Custom Version) here as a means of getting to know this eventually tragic poem. The shorter heroic poems follow: catalogues, mysterious squibs and fragments in the case of Old English, Old High German and Icelandic; extracts from longer works and sometimes whole lays in the case of the relevant Welsh, Irish and other Icelandic literature. By reading these poems one may make comparisons. Hildegyth for example helps her lover escape from a tyrant in *Waldere*, rather as Deirdre does her lover in *The Exile of the Sons of Uisliu*. There again, we might wonder how these women compare with Hildr in Bragi's *Eulogy on Ragnarr*, whose response to her father's pursuit of herself and her lover is to cast a spell that sets the two armies fighting each other in an endless battle. Does this myth make a comment on male as opposed to female heroics? The men in the Finnsburh Episode, or in Freawaru's Danish Heathobard marriage, will go on fighting whatever the cost, even when this destroys family life. Does the poet of *Beowulf* deplore this tendency as well as admire it, or is he more in the world of Aneirin on the glory of Gododdin against overwhelming odds in Catterick, or the *Fragment* on Hnæf's stout defence in Finnsburh?

The ethos of this wide range of poetry is broadly heroic, but there are differences worthy of study. Where the ethics of these poets are based on religion, it can be seen that the Christianity of many of these poems sets the struggles and achievements of their heroes and heroines in a context of God or destiny which determines the individual's fate. The selection ends with a Norwegian poem, however, *The Lay of Attila*, where this rule does not apply. Here there is no power but the will of King Gunnarr to shape his own end, and that of his sister Guðrún to avenge him, in ways so terrible that it is clear that aesthetics rather than morals governed this heathen poet's understanding of heroic conduct. Whereas Beowulf honours one God, sacrificing himself in order to save and enrich his people, Gunnarr sacrifices his people in order to turn his death into a godless work of art. The difference is starker than ever, yet the need for comparison remains. Most of the works on offer in this section were composed in the same period, from the early ninth to the late tenth century, either in the British Isles or nearby in Norway. By reading them here we can compare the Christians and heathens who often traded with each other when they did not yet live side by side. For many readers, the point of mixing up the poems in this selection may be to see the larger context in which Old English heroic poems such as *Beowulf* were composed.

General bibliography

Baker, P. S., 'The Old English language', *B&OS* 272–300

Bjork, R. E., and J. D. Niles, ed., *A Beowulf Handbook* (Exeter, 1997)

Chambers, R. W., *Beowulf: an Introduction to the Study of the Poem*, 3rd ed., with supplement by C. L. Wrenn (Cambridge, 1959), 68–88

Dronke, U., ed., trans. and comm., *The Poetic Edda, vol. I: Heroic Poems* (Oxford, 1969)

Garmonsway, G. N., and J. Simpson, trans., *Beowulf and its Analogues*, including 'Archaeology and *Beowulf*' by H. R. Ellis Davidson (London and New York, 1968)

Hill, J., ed., *Old English Minor Heroic Poems*, Durham and St Andrews Medieval Texts 4 (Durham, 1983)

Larrington, C., trans., *The Poetic Edda* (Oxford, 1996)

Mitchell, B., and F. C. Robinson, ed., *Beowulf: An Edition with Relevant Shorter Texts*, including 'Archaeology and *Beowulf*', by L. Webster (Oxford, 1998)

North, R., *Heathen Gods in Old English Literature*, Cambridge Studies in Anglo-Saxon England 22 (Cambridge, 1997)

North, R., *The Origins of 'Beowulf': From Vergil to Wiglaf* (Oxford, 2006)

North, R., 'Old English minor heroic poems', *B&OS* 95–129

North, R., 'Notes on the Old Norse language', *B&OS* 323–9

Orchard, A., *A Critical Companion to Beowulf* (Woodbridge, 2003)

Orchard, A., 'Beowulf and other battlers: an introduction to *Beowulf*', *B&OS* 63–94

Beowulf

HWÆT WE GARDEna in geardagum
þeodcyninga þrym gefrunon,
hu ða æþelingas ellen fremedon!
(*Beowulf*, lines 1–3)

We have heard of the glory of the nation-kings
of the Spear-Danes in days of yore,
how those princelings carried out deeds of courage!

Beowulf is preserved in only one copy, in the Nowell Codex, which was bound to the back of another codex to make the present manuscript, 'British Library, Cotton Vitellius A.XV'. This manuscript is dated very approximately to the year 1000. It was nearly burned but survived with staining and damaged edges in the Cotton Library fire of 1731. Luckily two brief excerpts of *Beowulf* had already been printed, and in 1787–9 two copies of the poem (Thorkelin A and B) were made before worse damage set in. The manuscript was rebound in 1845 in a process that caused more damage. In the Nowell Codex, *Beowulf* follows *The Passion of St Christopher*, *The Wonders of the East* and the Old English *Alexander's Letter to Aristotle*, and is followed by the headless poem *Judith*. It has been suggested that the compiler wanted *Beowulf* because he was making a collection of monster literature. His compilation was copied by two scribes, now named 'A' and 'B', with B taking over from A at the beginning of the third line on folio 172 verso (the rear of the page), on *Beowulf*, line 1939. It has been suggested that Scribe B wrote in a hand of the late tenth century, Scribe A in one of the early eleventh. Not only a high number of garbled spellings, but also some likely textual lacunae in *Beowulf* show that both scribes were probably copying from an exemplar (a copy text) which was itself defective. The poem *Beowulf*, then, was probably composed some time before its manuscript.

Beowulf is divided into cantos named 'fitts', which are numbered in sequence beginning one fitt late, but later with corrections, and then incompletely. These textual divisions are also probably older than the manuscript. When it comes to dating this great work, all dates possible for the Anglo-Saxon period have been considered at some time, and for all kinds of reasons, and sometimes for no reason but personal conviction. The seventh century went out in favour of the eighth, the reign of Offa (757–96), when Dorothy Whitelock wrote *The Audience of Beowulf* (Oxford, 1951). The eighth century was gladly dropped in favour of a range of later periods in the Toronto Symposium, whose proceedings were edited by Colin Chase (Toronto, 1981). Here Roberta Frank promoted the late ninth-century Alfredian period (pp. 123–39), Walter Goffart the tenth-century Æthelstanian (pp. 83–100), Kevin Kiernan the reign of Cnut, 1016–35 (pp. 9–21 and then *Beowulf and the Beowulf Manuscript*, 2nd ed., Ann Arbor, MI, 1996). The pendulum swung back to the early eighth century, however, when R. D. Fulk set a (southern) Mercian metrical-morphological *terminus ad quem* (latest possible date) of *c.* 725 in *A History of Old English Meter* (Philadelphia,

PA, 1992) and Sam Newton launched his dashing case in *The Origins of Beowulf and the Pre-Viking Kingdom of East Anglia* (Cambridge, 1993). Since then North has argued for 826–7 in the Mercia of King Wiglaf (827–39), in *The Origins of Beowulf: From Vergil to Wiglaf* (Oxford, 2006). But there will be more attempts on this question, of that there is no doubt. With this anthology, it is hoped that more readers will be able to judge for themselves.

The following excerpts give an idea of the character of Beowulf as temperamentally ambitious rather than modest or temperate, endlessly loyal to his bad-lot uncle Hygelac while less concerned with what his true friend Hrothgar has to say to him about 'eternal rewards' in the textual heart of *Beowulf*, lines 1700–84. Beowulf's three fights with monsters show how the poet could command swift action as easily as reflect on an unknown future, lost ages or the slow pace of time. While the poet is an advocate for good heathens, he never forgets that they are probably damned and he makes this clear in the curse on the treasure which Beowulf wins from the Dragon's hoard. The genre appears to be 'epic', but 'elegy' has always seemed nearer the mark, and in view of the moral darkness in which Beowulf leaves the world, as the emblem of not an individual's but a culture's heroic failure, 'tragedy' might come the closest of all.

Bjork, R. E., and J. D. Niles, ed., *A Beowulf Handbook* (Exeter, 1997)

Mitchell, B., and F. C. Robinson, ed., *Beowulf: An Edition with Relevant Shorter Texts*, including 'Archaeology and *Beowulf*', by L. Webster (Oxford, 1998)

Orchard, A., *Pride and Prodigies: Studies in the Monsters of the Beowulf-Manuscript* (Woodbridge, 1995)

Orchard, A., *A Critical Companion to Beowulf* (Woodbridge, 2003)

Scyld Scefing's funeral

Through Scyld Scefing at the head of the royal Danish family, the poet seems determined to construct an agrarian ideology as well as a foundation narrative for the heathen Danes. Scyld's funeral at the end of this fitt (unnumbered but really Fitt I) also allows the poet to give his heathen subjects the saving grace of ignorance in the religion they follow. This passage has often been discussed in relation to the genealogy of King Alfred's father, Æthelwulf, in the *Anglo-Saxon Chronicle* for 855, in which the old man claimed descent from Beaw son of Scyldwa son of Sceaf. It seems likely to the present editors that Æthelwulf's men plundered this part of *Beowulf* in their search for a genealogy to beat all others.

Chambers, R. W., *Beowulf: An Introduction to the Study of the Poem*, 3rd ed., with supplement by C. L. Wrenn (Cambridge, 1959), 68–88

Meaney, A., 'Scyld Scefing and the dating of *Beowulf* – again', *Bulletin of the John Rylands University Library of Manchester* 71 (1989), 1–40

Tolley, C., '*Beowulf*'s Scyld Scefing episode: some Norse and Finnish analogues', *Arv* 52 (1996), 7–48

HWÆT WE GARDEna in geardagum
þeodcyninga þrym gefrunon,
hu ða æþelingas ellen fremedon!
Oft Scyld Scefing sceaþena þreatum,
monegum mægþum, meodosetla ofteah,
egsode eorl[as], syððan ærest wearð
feasceaft funden. He þæs frofre gebad,
weox under wolcnum, weorðmyndum þah,
oð þæt him æghwylc þara ymbsittendra
ofer hronrade hyran scolde,
gomban gyldan. Þæt wæs god cyning!
Ðæm eafera wæs æfter cenned
geong in geardum, þone God sende

LISTEN, WE HAVE HEArd of the glory
of the nation-kings of Spear-Danes in days of yore,
how those princelings carried out deeds of courage!
Often Shield of Sheaf took the meadbenches
off bands of assailants, off many tribes,
put fear into noblemen, since first he was
found with no shaft. He experienced solace for that,
grew under the clouds, received honours,
until each of the peoples around him
were obliged to obey him over the whale-road,
pay him tribute. That was a good king!
To him thereafter was an heir produced,
young in the world's yard, whom God sent

---

1 *HWÆT WE GARDEna* 'LISTEN, WE HAVE HEArd' etc. The first three lines of *Beowulf* prime the audience for the theme, one which is known to them all. This is like Homeric openings in *Iliad* and *Odyssey*, and unlike the laying out of a programme in Vergil's *Aeneid* (19 BC) or John Milton's *Paradise Lost* (1656). The audience knows the Scylding story, or most of it, already. The scribe failed to mark this fitt with 'I', which he uses at the beginning of the next fitt, on line 53. For this reason, many people refer to this fitt as the 'prologue' of *Beowulf*.

4 *Scyld Scefing* 'Shield of Sheaf'. The Scyldings derives from Scyld through the generations that follow. The following translation tries to capture the poet's stylisation of Scyld's warlike progress as the growth of harvest bounty in the fields of Scandinavia, with sheaf, shaft, growing under clouds, and springing blades of barley.

6 *eorl[as]* 'noblemen'. Manuscript *eorl* needs –*e*, if *Eorle* means 'Heruli' as was once thought, a Danish tribe which was famous for being defeated in European migrations in the fifth century. However, no other *eorle* is attested, and *eorlas* seems more straightforward.

7 *feasceaft funden* 'found with no shaft'. OE *feasceaft* here also means 'destitute', its primary meaning, although the panoply later put aboard Scyld's funeral ship is said to be no smaller than that in the boat on which he arrived as a baby. This contradiction may be resolved by taking *feasceaft* literally as the image of a seedling from the wheatsheaf.

folce to frofre. Fyrenðearfe ongeat,
þæt hie ær drugon aldorlease
lange hwile. Him þæs lif-Frea,
wuldres Wealdend, woroldare forgeaf.
Beow wæs breme (blæd wide sprang),
Scyldes eafera Scedelandum in.
Swa sceal geong guma gode gewyrcean,
fromum feohgiftum on fæder bearme,
þæt hine on ylde eft gewunigen
wilgesiþas, þonne wig cume,
leode gelæsten: lofdædum sceal
in mægþa gehwære man geþeon!
Him ða Scyld gewat to gescæphwile

---

to comfort the masses. He knew the dire distress
which they had suffered before, leaderless
for a long while. To them for that did life-Lord,
Wielder of Glory, give worldly bounty.
Barley was famous (his blade sprang widely),
offspring of Shield in the lands of Skåne.
So shall a young man ensure by giving good things,
bold gifts of cash in his father's bosom,
that in old age he be attended once again
by joy's companions when war may come,
be obeyed by his men: doing deeds of praise
is how a man shall prosper in any tribe!
Shield then set off at his destined time

---

14 *Fyrenðearfe ongeat* 'He knew the dire distress' etc. This leaderless period follows the death of Heremod, whose Macbeth-like story is subject of allusions in lines 901–15 (the poet's, mediating a Danish bard) and 1709–22 (King Hrothgar's).

18 Beow *wæs breme (blæd wide sprang)* 'Barley was famous (his blade sprang widely)'. The manuscript says *Beowulf* for the son of Scyld, both here and on line 53. However, the genealogy for King Alfred's father Æthelwulf in the *Anglo-Saxon Chronicle*, year 855, which has probably borrowed the first three Scylding names from a text of *Beowulf*, has them as *Sceaf*, *Scyldwa*, *Beaw*. The last form suggests that *Beow* in an earlier *Beowulf* text was confused by a scribe with the name of the Geatish 'Beowulf' whose career dominates the poem as a whole. OE *beow* means 'barley', the offspring of a sheaf. The line's second half appears to pun on OE *blæd* (long vowel) 'renown' and *blæd* (short vowel) 'blade', once again conceiving triumph in war as the successful growth of barley in Scandinavian fields.

23 *wilgesiþas* 'joy's companions'. Men who share the good times, and the bad, with their prince who then becomes a king.

24–5 *lofdædum* 'doing deeds of praise is how' etc. The last word of *Beowulf*, on line 3182, hails or blames its hero as *lofgeornost* 'most eager to win praise', with a word which may also mean 'most prodigal (for praise's sake)' (the first is the Geats' perspective, the second perhaps the poet's). This opening comment with the same initial word gives us a taste of the ideology that drives Beowulf to his final hour.

felahror feran   on Frean wære.
Hi hyne þa ætbæron   to brimes faroðe
swæse gesiþas   swa he selfa bæd
þenden wordum weold   wine Scyldinga,
leof landfruma   lange ahte.
Þær æt hyðe stod   hringedstefna,
isig ond utfus,   æþelinges fær.
Aledon þa   leofne þeoden,
beaga bryttan,   on bearm scipes,
mærne be mæste.   Þær wæs madma fela
of feorwegum   frætwa gelæded,
ne hyrde ic cymlicor   ceol gegyrwan
hildewæpnum   ond heaðowædum,
billum ond byrnum.   Him on bearme læg
madma mænigo   þa him mid scoldon
on flodes æht   feor gewitan.

---

moving very strong into the Lord's covenant.
Carried him then to the sea's edge
his sweet companions, as he himself had bidden
for as long as the word of the Scyldings' friend,
of their land's beloved prince, held sway.
There at the jetty stood the ringed prow,
glinting, keen to go, a chieftain's vessel.
They then laid down a king beloved,
ring-dispenser, in the ship's hold,
splendid by the mast. Many treasures there,
many ornaments were loaded from long roads,
nor did I hear of a keel in more comely fashion
adorned with weapons of war, battle garments,
axes and coats of mail. In her hold there lay
a mass of treasures which was going to travel
with him far into the flood's possession.

---

27 *felahror* 'very strong'. Not the most obvious epithet for a corpse, so Mitchell and Robinson (1998: 257) say 'having done much'. However, if the funeral is also imagined as a shield ritual with sheaf inside, we have a heathen agrarian perspective on this scene as not the end but the fruition of Scyld's reign. [*on Frean wære* 'into the Lord's covenant'. The Danes and most other tribes in this poem are heathens. The poet, however, encourages us to see them like the tribes of Israel before Jesus, with the same intermittently failing monotheism and the same chance of salvation in the hereafter. Hence the term *wær* 'covenant' for the Danish bond with God, which may be compared with that of the Israelites in *Exodus*, line 306 and elsewhere (see **Poems of Devotion**).

33 *isig* 'glinting'. Literally 'icy', which is obscure, unless 'ice' connotes the glint of metal (here of treasure on board), as in OIce *ímun-fǫlr íss* 'war-pale ice' for 'shield-boss' in *Haustlǫng* 'harvest-long' (*c.* 900), stanza 17 (see **Gods of the Vikings**) and *blóðíss* 'blood-ice' for steel weapons in *Liðsmannaflokkr* 'Soldiers' Song' (1016), stanza 8 (see **Viking Wars**, Custom Version).

Nalæs hi hine læssan lacum teodan
þeodgestreonum þon þa dydon
þe hine æt frumsceafte forð onsendon
ænne ofer yðe umborwesende.
Þa gyt hie him asetton segen gyldenne
heah ofer heafod, leton holm beran,
geafon on garsecg. Him wæs geomor sefa,
murnende mod. Men ne cunnon
secgan to soðe, selerædende,
hæleð under heofenum, hwa þam hlæste onfeng.

In no way with lesser offerings, lesser tribal
treasures did they adorn him than those did
who sent him forth in the first shaft of creation
alone over waves as an infant child.
Still at this time they set a golden standard
high over his head, let ocean carry him,
gave him to the spear-man. Their feelings were sad,
their minds in mourning. Men do not know,
retainers, hall-advisers, heroes under heaven,
how to say in truth who received that cargo.

Beowulf and the Danish coastguard

More effectively than if the poet did this, Beowulf is described to us carefully through the coastguard's eyes. The wit of the older man is worth noting as he deals with the young foreign hot-head. He allows that what is left of Beowulf, if not the living Beowulf himself, may make the journey back, and offers to look after the ship in the meantime.

Shippey, T. A., *Beowulf*, Studies in English Literature 70 (London, 1978)

---

45 *æt frumsceafte* 'in the first shaft of creation'. This translation attempts to capture the pun in the noun for 'first things' with the 'shaft' of a seedling (see note to line 7).

49 *geafon on garsecg* 'gave him to the spear-man'. OE *garsecg* is a common poetic term for the ocean (other examples are in *Beowulf*, line 437, *Exodus*, lines 281 and 490, *Andreas*, line 530). Its elements define the meaning as 'spear-man', which looks like a taboo coinage to avoid danger at sea (but which may come from a fifth-century 'Saxon' practice of sacrificing captives to the deep after a successful raid).

50–1 *Men ne cunnon secgan* 'Men do not know how to say' etc. The poet does his best for the heathens he loves, making it clear that, although they have superstition (*garsecg*, see above; and even devil-worship on lines 175–83), they sin from ignorance.

Gewat þa ofer wægholm,   winde gefysed,
flota famiheals   fugle gelicost,
oðþæt ymb antid   oþres dogores
wundenstefna   gewaden hæfde
þæt ða liðende   land gesawon,
brimclifu blican,   beorgas steape,
side sænæssas.   Þa wæs sund liden,
eoletes æt ende.   Þanon up hraðe
Wedera leode   on wang stigon,
sæwudu sældon,   syrcan hrysedon,
guðgewædo,   Gode þancedon
þæs þe him yþlade   eaðe wurdon.

Þa of wealle geseah   weard Scildinga,
se þe holmclifu   healdan scolde,
beran ofer bolcan   beorhte randas,

Passed then over ocean wave, made keen by winds,
the foamy-necked vessel most like a bird,
until around the prime on the second day
the curved prow had moved along
to where the sailors could see land,
sea-cliffs gleaming, headlands steep,
long sea promontories. Sound was now sailed,
briny at its end. Rapidly up from there
Weather-Geat tribesmen climbed on shore,
moored up the sea-wood, shook mailcoats,
their war-garments, gave thanks to God
that the roller-road was easy on them.

Then from the wall the Scyldings' watchman,
whose duty it was to keep the ocean-cliffs,
saw them bearing down the gangway bright shields,

---

219 *ymb antid* 'around the prime'. 6 a.m., by monastic liturgical time: one of the signs that the poet is himself of monastic background.

222 *brimclifu blican* 'sea-cliffs gleaming'. Cliffs of Dover or Dorset, rather than the fjord outside Roskilde in Denmark. Landscape needs no authenticity in this or other Old English poems; what matters is the mood, which is here exuberant.

226 *syrcan hrysedon* 'shook mailcoats'. As Professor Bruce Mitchell used to say in his lectures, the chained mail folds up in a small space.

fyrdsearu fuslicu.   Hine fyrwyt bræc
modgehygdum,   hwæt þa men wæron.
Gewat him þa to waroðe   wicge ridan
þegn Hroðgares,   þrymmum cwehte
mægenwudu mundum,   meþelwordum frægn:
'Hwæt syndon ge   searohæbbendra,
byrnum werede,   þe þus brontne ceol
ofer lagustræte   lædan cwomon,
hider ofer holmas?   Hwile ic wæs
endesæta,   ægwearde heold,
þe on land Dena   laðra nænig
mid scipherge   sceðþan ne meahte.
No her cuðlicor   cuman ongunnon
lindhæbbende,   ne ge leafnesword
guðfremmendra   gearwe ne wisson,
maga gemedu.   Næfre ic maran geseah
eorla ofer eorþan   ðonne is eower sum,
secg on searwum.   Nis þæt seldguma,
wæpnum geweorðad,   næfne him his wlite leoge,

---

armour ready for campaign. Curiosity penetrated
his mind's thoughts as to what these men were.
Moved then down to shore riding his steed
Hrothgar's thegn, majestically brandished
mighty wood in hand, asking in assembly-speech:
'What kind of men in armour are you,
with coats of chained mail, who your tall keel thus
along sea's highway have come bringing
here across the deep? For some time I have been
a border guard, kept coast watch to sea
that no hostile men on the Danish shore
might inflict damage with raiding ships.
Never have men with shields more openly
made as if to come here, nor have you had surety
given readily with words of leave for warriors,
or relatives' pass. Not once have I seen a bigger
gentleman on this earth than is a certain man
bearing arms among you. No hall-retainer he,
honoured in weapons, unless his look, his peerless

232–4 *Hine fyrwyt bræc modgehygdum* 'Curiosity pentrated his mind's thoughts'. An ironic understatement (litotes) for a man observing a war-party disembarking.

236 *meþelwordum* 'in assembly-speech'. Politeness. What follows is a masterpiece of understatement, often ironic, in which flowery language defuses great tension: 'the wary politeness of men who habitually go about armed'.

247 *Næfre ic maran geseah* 'Not once have I seen a bigger' etc. The poet's use of a stranger's perspective on Beowulf, here and in lines 249–51, begins to characterise him for us.

ænlic ansyn.   Nu ic eower sceal
frumcyn witan,   ær ge fyr heonan
leassceaweras   on land Dena
furþur feran.   Nu ge feorbuend,
mereliðende,   minne gehyrað
anfealdne geþoht: ofost is selest
to gecyðanne   hwanan eowre cyme syndon.'

Him se yldesta   ondswarode,
werodes wisa,   wordhord onleac:
'We synt gumcynnes   Geata leode
ond Higelaces   heorðgeneatas.
Wæs min fæder   folcum gecyþed,
æþele ordfruma,   Ecgþeow haten.
Gebad wintra worn,   ær he on weg hwurfe,
gamol of geardum.   Hine gearwe geman
witena welhwylc   wide geond eorþan.
We þurh holdne hige   hlaford þinne,
sunu Healfdenes,   secean cwomon,

---

appearance, deceives me. Now I must know
your genealogy, before far from here
as spies into the land of Danes
you go any further. So then, men from afar
who sail the sea, you listen to my
single simple maxim: haste is best for
making the motive of your coming known.'

Him the most senior gave an answer,
guide to the troop, wordhoard unlocked:
'We are tribesmen of manly Geatish kindred
and hearth-companions to Hygelac.
My father's name became famous to people
as Ecgtheow, frontline captain of noble birth.
He got through a few winters, before he moved on,
worn out from the world's yard. He is readily remembered
widely across the earth by just about every wise man.
It is with loyal purpose that we have come to visit
your personal lord, the son of Healfdene,

---

253 *leassceaweras* 'as spies'. The coastguard's words become less polite the more he goes on.

265 *Hine gearwe geman* 'He is readily remembered' etc. Beowulf puts a spin on the truth. Ecgtheow, so we learn in snatches later in the poem, was a liability whose life Hrothgar saved by paying off the relatives of Heatholaf, whom he had killed with bare hands in northern Sweden. His name, however, gives him out as a Swedish royal, probably kin to King Ongentheow.

leodgebyrgean.   Wes þu us larena god!
Habbað we to þam mæran   micel ærende,
Deniga frean,   ne sceal þær dyrne sum
wesan þæs ic wene.   Þu wast (gif hit is
swa we soþlice   secgan hyrdon)
þæt mid Scyldingum   sceaðona ic nat hwylc,
deogol dædhata,   deorcum nihtum
eaweð þurh egsan   uncuðne nið,
hynðu ond hrafyl.   Ic þæs Hroðgar mæg
þurh rumne sefan   ræd gelæran,
hu he frod ond god   feond oferswyðeþ
(gyf him edwenden   æfre scolde
bealuwa bisigu,   bot eft cuman),
ond þa cearwylmas   colran wurðaþ,
oððe a syþðan   earfoðþrage,
þreanyd þolað,   þenden þær wunað
on heahstede   husa selest.'

---

protector of his tribe. Be generous at teaching us how!
We are on a great mission for that renowned man,
lord of the Danes, nor do I suppose that may be a place
where something stays secret for long. You know
(if the story goes as we genuinely heard it said)
that among the Scyldings some assailant I know not who,
some hidden tyranniser on dark nights,
through acts of terror reveals unheard-of violence,
humiliation and slaughter. I can give Hrothgar,
from my great heart, instructions on how,
experienced and generous, he will overpower the foe
(that is, if he should ever again expect a reversal
of fortune, any cure, for this affliction of evil),
and how either those waves of care will grow cooler,
or he will always henceforth endure a period
of trouble, dire necessity, for as long as it stays there,
the best of houses in its lofty place.'

---

269 *leodgebyrgean* 'protector of his tribe'. Beowulf begins to show his young anger at the coastguard's presumption, with an increasingly ironic commentary on King Hrothgar's helplessness.

272 *gif hit is* 'if the story goes' etc. Compare *gyf him* 'that is, if' etc. on line 280. Beowulf uses if-clauses parenthetically apparently to be polite, but actually to undermine Hrothgar's power as a king.

285 *husa selest* 'the best of houses'. Beowulf puts his finger on the cause of Grendel's attacks, indicating that Hrothgar's Danish 'house', his family, is no longer equal to the building he commissioned.

Weard maþelode ðær on wicge sæt,
ombeht unforht: 'Æghwæþres sceal
scearp scyldwiga gescad witan,
worda ond worca, se þe wel þenceð.
Ic þæt gehyre, þæt þis is hold weorod
frean Scyldinga. Gewitaþ forð beran
wæpen ond gewædu, ic eow wisige.
Swylce ic maguþegnas mine hate
wið feonda gehwone flotan eowerne,
niwtyrwydne nacan on sande
arum healdan, oþðæt eft byreð
ofer lagustreamas leofne mannan
wudu wundenhals to Wedermearce.
Godfremmendra swylcum gifeþe bið
þæt þone hilderæs hal gedigeð.'

The watchman spoke where he sat on his steed,
officer without fear: 'Between word and deed
is a difference which a shieldsman who is sharp,
who thinks properly, must see in every case.
This is how I hear it, that the troop here is loyal
to the Scyldings' lord. Move out and carry onwards
your weapons and gear, I will guide you.
Likewise, I will command my young thegns
to keep the vessel of you all against all foes,
the newly tarred longship on the sand
with all due respect, until back again she bears
over sea's currents a man beloved,
a wood with curved neck to the Weather-march.
Such a prince among benefactors will be fated
to survive this rush of battle in one piece.'

Beowulf greets King Hrothgar

How soon generosity is ungratefully reinterpreted, as repayment for earlier services rendered, is the theme of this exchange, in which Hrothgar's careful test of the hero's conviction begins with a deceptively absent-minded reply to Beowulf's grand self-promotion and offer of help.

---

290 *Ic þæt gehyre* 'This is how I hear it'. A performative use of OE *gehyran* 'to hear', one which grants Beowulf the visa he failed to apply for.

295–6 *on sande arum healdan* 'keep on the sand with all due respect'. Beowulf's surety for good behaviour. The ship will be hauled ashore, making it hard for the Geats to escape in it.

299 *Godfremmendra swylcum* 'Such a prince among benefactors' etc. The coastguard's closing irony is conceived to make it clear to Beowulf that he may not survive Grendel after all.

Beowulf maðelode (on him byrne scan,
searonet seowed smiþes orþancum):
'Wæs þu, Hroðgar, hal! Ic eom Higelaces
mæg ond magoðegn, hæbbe ic mærða fela
ongunnen on geogoþe. Me wearð Grendles þing
on minre eþeltyrf undyrne cuð.
Secgað sæliðend þæt þæs sele stande,
reced selesta, rinca gehwylcum
idel ond unnyt, siððan æfenleoht
under heofenes hador beholen weorþeð.
Þa me þæt gelærdon leode mine
þa selestan, snotere ceorlas,
þeoden Hroðgar, þæt ic þe sohte,
forþan hie mægenes cræft minne cuþon,
selfe ofersawon, ða ic of searwum cwom,
fah from feondum, þær ic fife geband,
yðde eotena cyn ond on yðum slog
niceras nihtes, nearoþearfe dreah,
wræc Wedera nið (wean ahsodon),

Beowulf spoke (on him the mailcoat shone,
a net of cunning sewn with smith's deep skill):
'Greetings to you, Hrothgar! I am Hygelac's
young kinsman and thegn, many exploits have I
undertaken in youth. The Grendel affair became
known to me in detail on my home turf.
Seafarers are saying that this hall, a building
finer than all others, stands for all men at arms
idle and unprofitable when the evening light
beneath heaven's vault becomes concealed.
My tribesmen instructed me, from
the highest in rank to wise churls,
Lord Hrothgar, that I should find you,
for they knew the skill in my power,
themselves had surveyed me when I unarmed,
bloody from the foe where I bound five,
wiped out a family of giants and in the waves
killed monsters by night, endured severe distress,
avenged the war on Weather-Geats (they asked for woe),

407–8 *Ic eom Higelaces mæg* 'I am Hygelac's young kinsman'. Beowulf's king, mother's brother and best friend. Beowulf always puts him first. Hygelac's death in Frisia (lines 1205–7, 2201, 2355–9, 2910–21) is the big tragedy of Beowulf's life.

415 *me þæt gelærdon leode mine* 'My tribesmen instructed me'. The *snotere ceorlas* 'wise churls' to whom Beowulf refers a line later have already been seen encouraging him on line 202. Of more interest is the absence of Hygelac from this list of people urging Beowulf on (see his petulance in lines 1994–7).

forgrand gramum, ond nu wið Grendel sceal,
wið þam aglæcan, ana gehegan
ðing wið þyrse. Ic þe nu ða,
brego Beorhtdena, biddan wille,
eodor Scyldinga, anre bene,
þæt ðu me ne forwyrne, wigendra hleo,
freowine folca, nu ic þus feorran com,
þæt ic mote ana ond minra eorla gedryht,
þes hearda heap, Heorot fælsian!
Hæbbe ic eac geahsod þæt se æglæca
for his wonhydum wæpna ne recceð.
Ic þæt þonne forhicge (swa me Higelac sie,
min mondrihten, modes bliðe),
þæt ic sweord bere oþðe sidne scyld,
geolorand to guþe, ac ic mid grape sceal
fon wið feonde ond ymb feorh sacan,
lað wið laþum. Ðær gelyfan sceal
Dryhtnes dome se þe hine deað nimeð.

---

destroyed the hostiles, and shall now with Grendel,
that monstrous adversary, alone set up
a deal with the ogre. You I now
want to ask, prince of Bright-Danes,
defence of Scyldings, just one request,
that you do not refuse me, protector of warriors,
liberal friend of peoples, now I have come from so far,
that I alone with my retinue of gentlemen,
this hardened band, may cleanse Heorot!
I have also found out that the monster
in his rashness has no care for weapons.
So I despise the idea (may the heart of Hygelac,
my man and master thus be happy with me)
that I bear a sword or broad shield,
a yellow rim to war, rather with my grip I shall
take on the enemy and contend for life,
one foe against the other. There he will believe
in the Lord's verdict, the man whom death takes.

425–6 *ana gehegan ðing wið þyrse* 'alone set up a deal with the ogre'. The import of OE *gehegan þing*, literally 'fence off an assembly', is a little obscure, but it seems that Beowulf is making light of his forthcoming battle by describing it as a session in the local assembly.

431 *ana ond minra eorla gedryht* 'I alone with my retinue of gentlemen'. This formulation has posed problems for our logical way of thinking, but makes sense if we understand that the leader always takes credit for his men's achievements, whether or not he slays the adversary himself (Hygelac is called *bonan Ongenþioes* 'Ongentheow's slayer' on line 1968, although it is his champions Wulf and Eofor who actually kill him on lines 2961–81).

Wen' ic þæt he wille, gif he wealdan mot,
in þam guðsele Geotena leode
etan unforhte, swa he oft dyde,
mægen Hreðmanna. Na þu minne þearft
hafalan hydan, ac he me habban wile
dreore fahne, gif mec deað nimeð,
byreð blodig wæl, byrgean þenceð,
eteð angenga unmurnlice,
mearcað morhopu. No ðu ymb mines ne þearft
lices feorme leng sorgian.
Onsend Higelace, gif mec hild nime,
beaduscruda betst, þæt mine breost wereð,
hrægla selest; þæt is Hrædlan laf,
Welandes geweorc. Gæð a wyrd swa hio scel.'

Hroðgar maþelode, helm Scyldinga:
'For werefyhtum þu, wine min Beowulf,

I expect that he will, if permitted to win,
eat Geatish tribesmen without fear of them
in that hall of war, as he often did with others,
the flower of Triumph-Men. Never will you need
to hide my head, rather he will hold on to my
body smeared in gore, if death takes me,
will carry the bloody carrion, think of tasting it,
the lone stalker will eat without proper mourning,
stain his moor-refuge. Never will you need to trouble
longer where the feeding of my body is concerned.
Send to Hygelac, if the battle takes me,
this best of war-shrouds that guards my breast,
the finest shirt, for that is Hrethel's inheritance,
Wayland's work. Fate ever goes as she must.'

Hrothgar spoke, refuge of the Scyldings:
'For manly fighting, Beowulf my friend,

---

445 *mægen Hreðmanna* 'the flower of Triumph-Men'. The *Hreð*-prefix (literally 'triumph') denotes Geats, as in *Hreðel*, their main king before Hygelac.

450 *No ðu ymb mines ne þearft* 'Never will you need to trouble' etc. This varies *Na þu minne þearft* 'Never will you need' etc. on line 445. Beowulf's colourful image of his own dismemberment is proof to all of his intention to go through with this, but it also becomes clear that he takes Hrothgar's consent for granted.

457 *For werefyhtum* 'For manly fighting' etc. The first impression with these words and *arstafum* is that Hrothgar refers to Beowulf's deeds and kindness, but in fact he means his own, in having saved Ecgtheow's life from the Wylfings. Beowulf's offer of help is thus reinterpreted as the repayment of a debt. The ambiguity of Hrothgar's first two lines thus pays Beowulf back for his momentary arrogance, while leaving his decision open.

ond for arstafum usic sohtest.
Gesloh þin fæder fæhðe mæste.
Wearþ he Heaþolafe to handbonan
mid Wilfingum. Đa hine Wedera cyn
for herebrogan habban ne mihte.
Þanon he gesohte Suðdena folc
ofer yða gewealc, ar-Scyldinga.
Đa ic furþum weold folce Deniga
ond on geogoðe heold ginne rice,
hordburh hæleþa. Đa wæs Heregar dead,
min yldra mæg unlifigende,
bearn Healfdenes. Se wæs betera ðonne ic!
Siððan þa fæhðe feo þingode,
sende ic Wylfingum ofer wæteres hrycg
ealde madmas. He me aþas swor.
Sorh is me to secganne on sefan minum
gumena ængum hwæt me Grendel hafað
hynðo on Heorote mid his heteþancum,
færniða gefremed. Is min fletwerod,
wigheap gewanod, hie wyrd forsweop

---

and for kindness have you sought us out.
Your father's fighting started the greatest feud.
With his bare hands he killed Heatholaf
among the Wylfings. Then the Weather-Geatish family
could not have him for their terror of raids.
From there he sought the folk of Denmark southwards
over waves' rolling, the kindness-Scyldings.
I was then ruling Danish folk for the first time
and in my youth held down an ample kingdom,
a heroes' hoard-town. Heorogar was dead by then,
my older kinsman no longer living,
son of Healfdene. He was a better man than I!
After that, this feud was settled with money,
over water's back I sent the Wylfings
ancient treasures. He swore oaths to me.
It is a sorrow for me in my heart to tell
any kind of man what humiliations, what
sudden acts of violence Grendel has done to me
with his thoughts of hate. My household brigade,
my war-band has waned, fate swept them off

---

469 *Se wæs betera ðonne ic!* 'He was a better man than I!'. He seems to mean that Hrothgar's brother was too strong to need Ecgtheow, and that Hrothgar's need to build a good retinue dictated his acceptance of Beowulf's father all those years ago.

on Grendles gryre. God eaþe mæg
þone dolsceaðan dæda getwæfan!
Ful oft gebeotedon beore druncne
ofer ealowæge oretmecgas
þæt hie in beorsele bidan woldon
Grendles guþe mid gryrum ecga.
Đonne wæs þeos medoheal on morgentid,
drihtsele dreorfah, þonne dæg lixte,
eal bencþelu blode bestymed,
heall heorudreore. Ahte ic holdra þy læs,
deorre duguðe, þe þa deað fornam.
Site nu to symle ond onsæl meoto,
sigehreð secgum, swa þin sefa hwette.'

---

in the Grendel horror. God can easily
put a stop to the deeds of this mad assailant!
Full often did the champions drink beer
and then promise over their ale-cups
that in the beerhall they would wait for
war with Grendel with the terror of their blades.
Then was this meadhall in the morning hour,
this lordly palace at day's gleam, smeared with gore,
all the benchboards spattered in blood,
the hall, with terrible gore. I had fewer loyal men
from my precious guard for death having seized them.
Sit at the feast now and reveal your capacity,
such triumphs to the men as your sense tells you.'

Beowulf's fight with Grendel

As one of the most exciting parts of *Beowulf*, this passage conveys the terror of the unknown as Grendel approaches; the speed and resolution with which Beowulf wrestles him, holding on while Grendel pulls to the door; the ways in which Grendel thinks and feels as he meets Beowulf; his likely fate in hell in the hereafter; and the strange term *ealuscerwen*, here interpreted as the reflex of the old runic **alu**: a term which marks the Danes' change of fortune for the better. The passage as a whole may stand comparison with King Arthur's battle with the giant of Mont St Michel in Wace's *Brut* of *c.* 1155 (see **Early Chivalry**); also, as a potential loan, in the fight at Sandhaugar in *The Saga of Grettir the Strong* of *c.* 1400 (see **Sagas of Icelanders**).

---

489 *onsæl meoto, sigehreð* 'reveal your capacity, such triumphs' etc. OE *meoto* occurs only here, but must mean 'measure, capacity' in comparison with *metan* 'to measure' and *Meotud* 'Measurer (God)'. Hrothgar imagery of slaughter has just outdone Beowulf's. Now he invites the young man to carry on boasting to the company there, mocking Beowulf's claimed indifference to his safety. The way is clear for Unferth to test Beowulf's resolution further.

Greenfield, S. B., 'Grendel's approach to Heorot: syntax and poetry', in *Old English Poetry: Fifteen Essays*, ed. R. P. Creed (Providence, RI, 1967), 275–84

Lapidge, M., '*Beowulf* and the psychology of terror', in *Heroic Poetry in the Anglo-Saxon Period: Studies in Honor of Jess B. Bessinger*, ed. H. Damico and J. Leyerle, Studies in Medieval Culture 32 (Kalamazoo, MI, 1993), 373–402

North, R., ' "Wyrd" and "wearð ealuscerwen" in *Beowulf*', *Leeds Studies in English* New Series 25 (1994), 69–82

XI

Ða com of more under misthleoþum
Grendel gongan, Godes yrre bær.
Mynte se manscaða manna cynnes
sumne besyrwan in sele þam hean,
wod under wolcnum to þæs þe he winreced,
goldsele gumena, gearwost wisse,
fættum fahne. Ne wæs þæt forma sið
þæt he Hroþgares ham gesohte.
Næfre he on aldordagum ær ne siþðan
heardran hæle healðegnas fand.
Com þa to recede rinc siðian,
dreamum bedæled. Duru sona onarn,
fyrbendum fæst, syþðan he hire folmum æthran.
Onbræd þa bealohydig, ða he gebolgen wæs,
recedes muþan. Raþe æfter þon
on fagne flor feond treddode,

XI

Then off the moor beneath misty slopes came
Grendel walking, bore the wrath of God.
Minded was the criminal assailant of mankind
to ensnare one man in that lofty palace,
moved beneath the clouds until he could most readily
make out the wine-building, men's golden palace,
ornamented with plate. Nor was that the first time
that he had sought out Hrothgar's home.
Never in the days of his life before or since
did he find hall-thegns bringing harder fortune.
Came then to the building a man on his journey
deprived of happiness. At once the door rushed open,
made firm with fired bonds, when his hands touched it.
With evil purpose he swung it open, now he was enraged,
the building's mouth. Swiftly after that
did the fiend tread on the stained floor,

---

719 *healðegnas* 'hall-thegns'. Here read as accusative plural, although this word could be a late spelling for genitive singular in *–es*, in which case *hæle* 'fortune' would be accusative, rather than an instrumental dative. 'Fortune' is a major theme in this passage.

721 *Duru sona onarn* 'At once the door rushed open'. See *Andreas*, line 999 for an apparently mocking quotation of this half line (**Poems of Devotion**).

eode yrremod. Him of eagum stod
ligge gelicost leoht unfæger.
Geseah he in recede rinca manige,
swefan sibbegedriht samod ætgædere,
magorinca heap. Þa his mod ahlog,
mynte þæt he gedælde ær þon dæg cwome
atol aglæca anra gehwylces
lif wið lice, þa him alumpen wæs
wistfylle wen. Ne wæs þæt wyrd þa gen
þæt he ma moste manna cynnes
ðicgean ofer þa niht. Þryðswyð beheold
mæg Higelaces, hu se manscaða
under færgripum gefaran wolde.
Ne þæt se aglæca yldan þohte,
ac he gefeng hraðe forman siðe
slæpendne rinc, slat unwearnum,
bat banlocan, blod edrum dranc,
synsnædum swealh, sona hæfde
unlyfigendes eal gefeormod,

---

walked in wrathful of mind. From his eyes appeared
most like a flame a light of no beauty.
He could see in the building many warriors,
a kindred retinue sleeping mustered together,
a young war-band. Then his heart laughed,
the terrifying monster was minded to part
before day came each and every man's
life from his body, now the hope had arrived
of feasting his fill. Yet it was not his fate now
to be allowed to consume any more of
mankind after that night. Hygelac's mighty
kinsman watched to see how the criminal assailant
would behave when held in a sudden grip.
Nor did the monster think of delaying,
but he swiftly seized as his first enterprise
a warrior asleep, tore him open ceaselessly,
bit the bone-locks, drank blood from arteries,
swallowed sinful morsels, at once had
used up the provender of all the dead man,

---

727 *leoht unfæger* 'a light of no beauty'. One of the few details that the poet allows us, as part of his means of instilling terror (Lapidge 1993).

734 *wistfylle wen* 'hope of feasting his fill'. The poet uses f. *wist* 'feast' with irony as a metaphor of royal itineration: Grendel enjoying his rights.

743 *synsnædum* 'sinful morsels'. Cannibalism is not only wrong; it is a sin to eat meat without the blood first drained.

fet ond folma. Forð near ætstop,
nam þa mid handa higeþihtigne
rinc on ræste, ræhte ongean
feond mid folme. He onfeng hraþe
inwitþancum ond wið earm gesæt.
Sona þæt onfunde fyrena hyrde
þæt he ne mette middangeardes,
eorþan sceata, on elran men
mundgripe maran. He on mode wearð
forht on ferhðe, no þy ær fram meahte.
Hyge wæs him hinfus, wolde on heolster fleon,
secan deofla gedræg, ne wæs his drohtoð þær
swylce he on ealderdagum ær gemette.
Gemunde þa se goda, mæg Higelaces,
æfenspræce, uplang astod
ond him fæste wiðfeng, fingras burston.
Eoten wæs utweard, eorl furþur stop.
Mynte se mæra, þær he meahte swa,
widre gewindan ond on weg þanon
fleon on fenhopu, wiste his fingra geweald
on grames grapum. Þæt wæs geocor sið
þæt se hearmscaþa to Heorute ateah.
Dryhtsele dynede. Denum eallum wearð,

---

down to feet and hands. Nearer he advanced,
seized then with hands a stout-hearted
warrior on his bed, the fiend reached
with palm towards him. The other quickly took up
hostile intentions and sat against his arm.
At once the guardian of wickedness discovered
that he had not met in the Middle World
on the surface of the earth in any other man
a handgrip greater than this. His mind, his spirit
became frightened, nor could he leave the sooner for that.
His aim was to light out, would flee into darkness,
seek the devils' mob, nor was his state in that place
such as he had met before in the days of his life.
The capable kinsman of Hygelac recalled
his evening speech, stood away his whole length
and firmly took his hold, his fingers cracked.
The giant was for out, the gentleman advanced further.
The infamous was minded, if he could do so,
to twist away wider and on the road out of there
to flee to fen-retreats, knew his fingers' power
in a hostile's grip. That was a melancholy mission
the harmful assailant embarked on to Heorot.
The lordly hall resounded. To all the Danes was,

ceasterbuendum, cenra gehwylcum,
eorlum ealuscerwen. Yrre wæron begen,
reþe renweardas. Reced hlynsode.
Þa wæs wundor micel þæt se winsele
wiðhæfde heaþodeorum, þæt he on hrusan ne feol,
fæger foldbold; ac he þæs fæste wæs
innan ond utan irenbendum
searoþoncum besmiþod. Þær fram sylle abeag
medubenc monig, mine gefræge,
golde geregnad, þær þa graman wunnon.
Þæs ne wendon ær witan Scyldinga
þæt hit a mid gemete manna ænig,
betlic ond banfag, tobrecan meahte,
listum tolucan, nymþe liges fæþm
swulge on swaþule. Sweg up astag
niwe geneahhe. Norð-Denum stod
atelic egesa, anra gehwylcum
þara þe of wealle wop gehyrdon,

---

to city-dwellers, to each brave man, to nobles,
good fortune prescribed. Both were wrathful,
fierce the house-janitors. The building boomed.
It was then a great miracle that the wine-palace
withheld the risk-takers, that it did not fall to earth,
dazzling building, rather it was firmly
within and without with iron bonds
cunningly fashioned. There left the boards
many a meadbench, from what I have heard,
forged with gold, where those hostiles fought.
No Scylding wise men had before supposed
that any man ever even at full capacity
could break up this stately antler-crowned place,
destroy it with skill, unless the flame's embrace
would swallow it up in fire. A melody arose,
a new one, constantly. Danes in Norway were struck
with a terrible fear, any one of them was,
who heard this weeping from his sea-wall,

---

769 *ealuscerwen* 'good fortune prescribed'. Runic ᚨᛚᚢ **alu** in ancient bracteates meant 'good fortune'. OE *ealu* 'ale' is a homophone, as the poet probably knew, who seems to misread this compound for comic effect in his *meoduscerwen* 'serving of mead' in *Andreas*, line 1526 (North 1994).

770 *renweardas* 'house-janitors'. The poet of *Beowulf* has its own sense of humour, too, though a conservative one based on understatement.

783 *Norð-Denum* 'Danes in Norway'. This is the only way this makes sense, given the emptiness of the Roskildefjord, unless we assume that the poet's words are chosen sometimes for no more than metrical reasons (see North 2006: 87).

gryreleoð galan   Godes ondsacan,
sigeleasne sang,   sar wanigean
helle hæfton.   Heold hine fæste
se þe manna wæs   mægene strengest
on þam dæge   þysses lifes.

XII
Nolde eorla hleo   ænige þinga
þone cwealmcuman   cwicne forlætan,
ne his lifdagas   leoda ænigum
nytte tealde.   Þær genehost brægd
eorl Beowulfes   ealde lafe,
wolde freadrihtnes   feorh ealgian,
mæres þeodnes,   ðær hie meahton swa.
Hie þæt ne wiston,   þa hie gewin drugon,
heardhicgende   hildemecgas,
ond on healfa gehwone   heawan þohton,
sawle secan,   [þæt] þone synscaðan
ænig ofer eorþan   irenna cyst,
guðbilla nan,   gretan nolde,
ac he sigewæpnum   forsworen hæfde,

---

a litany of horror sung by God's adversary,
a song with no victory, an anguish keened
by hell's captive. He held him fast
who was physically the strongest
of all men in that day of this life.

XII
The shield of nobles would not for anything
leave the death-dealing visitor alive,
nor did he count the days of his life to be useful
for any tribesman. There most incessantly would one man
of Beowulf's and then another draw his old heirloom,
wishing to protect the lifeblood of his first lord,
his renowned prince, where they might do so.
They did not know as they engaged in that fighting,
tough-minded champions of war,
and meant to cut into each part of him,
seek out his soul, [that] the sinning assailant
by no choice iron on the face of the earth,
by no war-blade, could be touched,
for he had cast a spell on victorious weapons,

---

786 *gryreleoð* 'litany of horror'. Grendel seems to know that he is damned, unlike the humans in the poem.

790 *on þam dæge þysses lifes* 'in that day of this life'. This phrase reiterates the transience of Beowulf's powers, as shown when we first meet him, on line 197.

ecga gehwylcre. Scolde his aldorgedal
on ðæm dæge þysses lifes
earmlic wurðan, ond se ellorgast
on feonda geweald feor siðian.
Ða þæt onfunde se þe fela æror
modes myrðe manna cynne,
fyrene gefremede (he wæs fag wið god),
þæt him se lichoma læstan nolde,
ac hine se modega mæg Hygelaces
hæfde be honda. Wæs gehwæþer oðrum
lifigende lað. Licsar gebad
atol æglæca, him on eaxle wearð
syndolh sweotol, seonowe onsprungon,
burston banlocan. Beowulfe wearð
guðhreð gyfeþe, scolde Grendel þonan
feorhseoc fleon under fenhleoðu,
secean wynleas wic. Wiste þe geornor
þæt his aldres wæs ende gegongen,
dogera dægrim. Denum eallum wearð
æfter þam wælræse willa gelumpen.

---

on any kind of edge. His parting from life would
of necessity on that day of this life
be a wretched one, and the alien spirit
would have to journey far into the power of fiends.
Then he discovered, who had in former times
done many things, much evil to the injury
of the mind of mankind (he was God's outlaw),
that his bodily vessel would not obey him,
for the wild-hearted kinsman of Hygelac
had him by the hand. Each one to the other was
hateful while he lived. A body wound was what
the terrifying monster experienced, on his shoulder
appeared a clear lasting wound, sinews sprang apart,
bone-lockers burst. To Beowulf was
war-triumph granted, Grendel from there should
flee mortally wounded under fenland cliffs,
seek a joyless abode. He knew the more eagerly
that the end had arrived for his life on earth,
the count of all his days. All the Danes found
that after the slaughtering battle their desire was attained.

---

819 *guðhreð gyfeþe* 'war-triumph granted'. Fate's operation is highlighted in this passage (see note to line 769).

823–4 *wearð willa gelumpen* 'desire was attained'. A variant for the construction *wearð . . . ealuscerwen* on line 769.

Hæfde þa gefælsod se þe ær feorran com,
snotor ond swyðferhð, sele Hroðgares,
genered wið niðe. Nihtweorce gefeh,
ellenmærþum.

He who had just come from afar, wise and strong of spirit,
had now cleansed Hrothgar's palace,
saved it from big evil. He rejoiced in the night's work,
in courageous exploits.

Funeral at Finnsburh: Hildeburh and Wealhtheow

The Finnsburh 'Episode', as it is known, has been a notorious source of puzzlement over the years. The tactical moves of the heroes in the Finnsburh story, to which the poet alludes in foreshortened style, are sinuous and allusive, yet capable of elucidation. The *Finnsburh Fragment* shows that the Half-Danes are mercenaries, not visitors, in Finn's household (see below). The Episode shows how Finn, having killed Hnæf, his brother-in-law, allows the latter's lieutenant Hengest to take command of the Half-Dane survivors in a treaty that is shameful to none but the kinsmen of Hnæf. These are prevented from avenging their dead captain by Hengest and his Jutes. Hengest is the key: he will not betray Finn's new arrangement, at least not until the Danes approach him with the idea of transferring command and the oath-liability to themselves, so that he may avenge himself on Jutish traitors who fought with Finn on the Frisian side, while they may avenge Hnæf. The poet's true focus, however, is on Hildeburh, for as the innocent victim of the violent men around her, Hildeburh is the harbinger of Wealhtheow in Heorot at a later date. Wealhtheow is smart enough to see the resemblance. Vainly as it turns out, she is determined to keep Heorot from becoming a Finnsburh of its own, especially now that Hrothgar has promised Beowulf a place in the royal family.

Fry, D. K., ed., *Finnsburh: Fragment and Episode* (London, 1974)

North, R., 'Tribal loyalties in the *Finnsburh Fragment* and Episode', *Leeds Studies in English* new series 21 (1990), 13–43

Taylor, P. B., '*Beowulf* 1130, 1875 and 2006: in defence of the manuscript', *Neuphilologische Mitteilungen* 82 (1981), 357–61

Tolkien, J. R. R., *Finn and Hengest: The Fragment and the Episode*, ed. A. Bliss (London, 1982)

Þær wæs sang ond sweg samod ætgædere
fore Healfdenes hildewisan,
gomenwudu greted, gid oft wrecen,

There was song and music in combination
before the war-captains of Healfdene,
mirthboard touched, a song often performed

ðonne healgamen   Hroþgares scop
æfter medobence   mænan scolde
[be] Finnes eaferum,   ða hie se fær begeat,
hæleð Healfdena,   Hnæf Scyldinga
in Freswæle   feallan scolde.
Ne huru Hildeburh   herian þorfte
Eotena treowe,   unsynnum wearð
beloren leofum   æt þam lindplegan,
bearnum ond broðrum.   Hie on gebyrd hruron,
gare wunde.   Þæt wæs geomuru ides!
Nalles holinga   Hoces dohtor
meotodsceaft bemearn,   syþðan morgen com,
ða heo under swegle   geseon meahte
morþorbealo maga,   þær he[o] ær mæste heold
worolde wynne.   Wig ealle fornam
Finnes þegnas   nemne feaum anum,
þæt he ne mehte   on þam meðelstede
wig Hengeste   wiht gefeohtan,

---

when Hrothgar's poet was asked to relate
a hall-entertainment along the meadbench
[about] Finn's heirs, when swift attack got them,
Half-Dane heroes, when Hnæf of the Scyldings
in the Frisian slaughter was doomed to fall.
Nor indeed did Hildeburh have need to praise
Jutish pledges, for no blame of hers was she
made to lose her loved ones in play of lindenshields,
children and brothers. They moved into destiny,
wounded with the spear. That was a melancholy lady!
Not at all in vain did Hoc's daughter
mourn fate's decree when morning came,
when under the sun she could see
the terrible murder of kinsmen, where once she held
her greatest joy in the world. Combat took all
Finn's thegns except a few ones here and there
in that he could not in that assembly place
fight a battle with Hengest even close to the finish,

1068 *[be] Finnes eaferum* '[about] Finn's heirs'. Something is probably missing here, perhaps a line or two.

1069 *hæleð Healfdena* 'Half-Dane heroes'. Perhaps the poet's own formulation, as it occurs nowhere else: a term for intertribal mercenaries in which the Danes amount to half.

1071–2 Hildeburh had reason to loathe the pledges of the Jutes: when these were broken.

1080 *worolde wynne* 'joy in the world'. One's children, as seen also from the monastic point of view, in which spiritual joys are higher.

ne þa wealafe   wige forþringan
þeodnes ðegna.   Ac hig him geþingo budon,
þæt hie him oðer flet   eal gerymdon,
healle ond heahsetl,   þæt hie healfre geweald
wið Eotena bearn   agan moston,
ond æt feohgyftum   Folcwaldan sunu
dogra gehwylce   Dene weorþode,
Hengestes heap   hringum wenede
efne swa swiðe   sincgestreonum
fættan goldes,   swa he Fresena cyn
on beorsele   byldan wolde.
Ða hie getruwedon   on twa healfa
fæste frioðuwære.   Fin Hengeste
elne, unflitme   aðum benemde
þæt he þa wealafe   weotena dome
arum heolde,   þæt ðær ænig mon
wordum ne worcum   wære ne bræce,
ne þurh inwitsearo   æfre gemænden

---

nor dislodge the woeful remnant in a battle
with the lord's thegn. Rather they offered him terms,
so that the Frisians cleared out a whole other floor for them,
a hall and high seat, that control of half might
the Half-Danes have with the sons of Jutes,
and in gifts of wealth the son of Folcwalda
day in day out would honour the Danes,
would present Hengest's band with rings,
with ornaments and treasures of plated gold,
just as extensively as he would encourage
the tribe of Frisians in their beerhall.
Then on the two sides they pledged
a firm pact of peace. Finn to Hengest
zealously, free from flyting, pronounced in oaths
that by the verdict of wise men he would keep
that woeful remnant in favour, that none of them
in word or deed should break the treaty,
nor ever with malicious cunning complain,

1085 The Danes make their Half-Dane brethren secure a deal from Finn whereby they all remain together in a hall of their own.

1090 Finn agrees to reincorporate the Half-Danes in his army, where they were before he decided to remove his brother-in-law Hnæf.

1097 *unflitme* 'free from flyting (insults)'. Some emend, but the word makes sense as a sign of the care with which Finn draws up his treaty.

ðeah hie hira beaggyfan   banan folgedon
ðeodenlease,   þa him swa geþearfod wæs.
Gyf þonne Frysna hwylc   frecnan spræce
ðæs morþorhetes   myndgiend wære,
þonne hit sweordes ecg   s*e*ðan scolde.
Að wæs geæfned   ond i[n]cge-gold
ahæfen of horde.   here-Scyldinga
betst beadorinca   wæs on bæl gearu.
Æt þam ade wæs   eþgesyne
swatfah syrce,   swyn ealgylden,
eofer irenheard,   æþeling manig
wundum awyrded.   Sume on wæle crungon!
Het ða Hildeburh   æt Hnæfes ade
hire selfre sunu   sweoloðe befæstan,
banfatu bærnan   ond on bæl don
e*a*me on eaxle.   Ides gnornode,
geomrode giddum.   Guðrinc astah.
Wand to wolcnum   wælfyra mæst,
hlynode for hlawe.   Hafelan multon,
bengeato burston,   ðonne blod ætspranc,

---

though they followed their ring-giver's killer
without a lord, since this need lay upon them.
If then any Frisian with dangerous expressions
continued to recall the murderous hatred,
then the sword's edge would settle this.
The oath was carried out and the Ing-gold
lifted from the hoard. The best fighting man
of raiding Scyldings was ready on the bier.
At that pyre it was easy to see
a bloodstained war-shirt, an all-gold swine,
an iron-hard boar, many a prince sent by wounds
to his maker. A few men died in that slaughter!
Hildeburh then had at Hnæf's pyre
her own son committed to the flames,
his bone-vessel burned and put on the fire
by his uncle's shoulder. The lady mourned,
keened with songs. The war-hero went up.
Wound to the clouds the greatest carrion-fire,
roared before the mound. Heads melted,
wound-gates burst, when blood sprang up,

1106 *seðan* 'settle', as in 'verify' (OE *soð* 'true'), emended from *syððan* 'then'.

1107 *Að wæs geæfned* 'The oath was carried out'. That is what the manuscript says, although *ad* 'pyre' is further down. The treaty is sealed tight with oaths. [*i[n]cge gold* 'the Ing-gold'. The name of their god, and Hengest's god too on whom he swears, is Ingui or Ing (North 1997: 44 and 70–1). The treaty is watertight.

laðbite lices.   Lig ealle forswealg,
gæsta gifrost,   þara ðe þær guð fornam
bega folces.   Wæs hira blæd scacen.

XII   Gewiton him ða wigend   wica neosian,
freondum befeallen,   Frysland geseon,
hamas ond heaburh.   Hengest ða gyt
wælfagne winter   wunode mid Finne
eal unhlitme   (eard gemunde),
þeah þe he meahte   on mere drifan
hringedstefnan.   Holm storme weol,
won wið winde,   winter yþe beleac
isgebinde,   oþðæt oþer com
gear in geardas,   swa nu gyt deð,
þa ðe syngales   sele bewitiað,
wuldortorhtan weder.   Đa wæs winter scacen,
fæger foldan bearm.   Fundode wrecca,

hateful body-bite. Flame swallowed all,
greediest of spirits, all those whom war took
of both sides of the people. Their glory had moved on.

XII   The fighters then moved off to spy out their dwellings,
their kinmen fallen from them, to see Frisian lands,
homes and high forts. Hengest then still
stayed a slaughter-stained winter with Finn
without casting lots (he was mindful of a homeland),
although he could launch upon the sea
a ring-prowed ship. The ocean welled with gales,
fought with the wind, winter locked the waves
with ice-binding, until there came another
year into the world's yard, as they do even now,
years which continually observe the seasons,
the glory-brilliant weather. Then winter had moved on,
dazzling was the landscape's bosom. The exile hastened,

1124 *bega folces* 'of both sides of the people'. The people who appear to be on both sides of this feud are the Jutes, according to Tolkien (1982: 113–15).

1127 *hamas ond heaburh* 'homes and high forts'. An accurate vision of the undyked Frisian landscape at this time. The dispersal of Finn's men is a sign that his treaty has made him completely safe under Hengest's protection.

1129 *unhlitme* 'without casting lots'. Casting lots is a procedure that opens a voyage, as with that of the Saxons who set sail for Kent in Gildas' *On the Ruin of Britain* (*c.* 550, ch. 23); see North (1990: 26–7).

1130 *þeah þe he meahte* 'although he could' etc. The temptation to add *ne* 'not' should be avoided. See Taylor (1981: 257–8).

gist of geardum,   he to gyrnwræce
swiðor þohte   þonne to sælade,
gif he torngemot   þurhteon mihte
þæt he Eotena bearn   inne gemunde.
Swa he ne forwyrnde   woroldrædenne,
þonne him Hunlafing   hildeleoman,
billa selest,   on bearm dyde.
Þæs wæron mid Eotenum   ecge cuðe.
Swylce ferhðfrecan   Fin eft begeat
sweordbealo sliðen   æt his selfes ham,
siþðan grimne gripe   Guðlaf ond Oslaf
æfter sæsiðe   sorge mændon,
ætwiton weana dæl.   Ne meahte wæfre mod
forhabban in hreþre.   Ða wæs heal roden
feonda feorum,   swilce Fin slægen,
cyning on corþre,   ond seo cwen numen.
Sceotend Scyldinga   to scypon feredon
eal ingesteald   eorðcyninges,
swylce hie æt Finnes ham   findan meahton
sigla, searogimma.   Hie on sælade

---

the guest, to leave the courts, he thought harder
of revenge for his injury than of taking the sea-road,
to see if he might set up an angry encounter
that he might remember the sons of Jutes in this country.
So he did not refuse worldly counselling
when Hunlaf's son put a battle-flash,
finest of blades, into his lap.
Its edges were not strange to the tall Jutish men.
Caught later, likewise, was the savage-tempered Finn
by sword-bale of cruel sharpness in his own home,
after Guthlaf and Oslaf lamented the fierce
attack, sorrow after sea-voyage, laid blame
for their share of woes. The restless mood could not
be restrained within the breast. Then the hall was reddened
with the lifeblood of foes, such as Finn being slain,
a king in his bodyguard, and the queen abducted.
Scyldings shooting missiles to ships ferried
all Ing's household goods that the earth-king owned
such as they could find in Finn's home,
jewels, exquisite gems. They on the sea-road

1141 *Eotena bearn inne* 'sons of Jutes in this country'. See North (1990: 19–20).

1145 *mid Eotenum* 'to the tall Jutish men'. Literally 'to the giants', who would have reason to fear this sword if it were Freyr's in *The Lay of Skírnir*, stanza 8 (see **Gods of the Vikings**). The poet may blend these terms for descriptive effect.

drihtlice wif to Denum feredon,
læddon to leodum. Leoð wæs asungen,
gleomannes gyd.

Gamen eft astah,
beorhtode bencsweg, byrelas sealdon
win of wunderfatum. Þa cwom Wealhþeo forð
gan under gyldnum beage, þær þa godan twegen
sæton suhtergefæderan. Þa gyt wæs hiera sib ætgædere,
æghwylc oðrum trywe. Swylce þær Unferþ þyle
æt fotum sæt frean Scyldinga. Gehwylc hiora his ferhþe treowde,
þæt he hæfde mod micel, þeah þe he his magum nære
arfæst æt ecga gelacum. Spræc ða ides Scyldinga:
'Onfoh þissum fulle, freodrihten min,
sinces brytta! Þu on sælum wes,
goldwine gumena, ond to Geatum spræc
mildum wordum, swa sceal man don.
Beo wið Geatas glæd, geofena gemyndig
nean ond feorran þu nu hafast.

---

ferried the lordly woman to the Danes,
led her to her tribe. The lay was sung,
song of the entertainer.

The fun rose up again,
bench-melody intensified, cup-servers poured
wine from wondrous vessels. Forth then came Wealhtheow
walking beneath a golden necklace to where the two generous men
were sitting, uncle and nephew. Still at this time was their kindred together,
each man true to the other. Likewise Unferth there, the spokesman,
sat at the feet of the Scylding lord. Each of them trusted his spirit,
that he had a great courage, though to his kinsmen he may not have been
gracious in the play of blades. Spoke then the lady of the Scyldings:
'Receive this cup, my liberal lord,
dispenser of treasure! You be happy,
gold-giving friend of men, and speak to the Geats
with generous words as a man must do.
Be gracious to the Geats, mindful of the gifts
from near and far that you now have.

1160 One of *Beowulf*'s great contrasts, in light and mood, between the dismal and the ecstatic.

1163–8 *Beowulf*'s first great burst of hypermetric lines, a means of adverting us to something significant: the treachery from Hrothulf to come? Wealhtheow is betting on Hrothulf.

1173–4 *geofena nean ond feorran þu nu hafast* 'of the gifts from far and near that you now have'. The queen reminds the king that some things he is entrusted with, indeed the kingdom and succession, are not his to give away to non-blood relatives. Portable gifts only for the Geats, she means.

Me man sægde   þæt þu ðe for sunu wolde
hereri[n]c habban.   Heorot is gefælsod,
beahsele beorhta.   Bruc þenden þu mote
manigra medo,   ond þinum magum læf
folc ond rice,   þonne ðu forð scyle
metodsceaft seon.   Ic minne can
glædne Hroþulf,   þæt he þa geogoðe wile
arum healdan,   gyf þu ær þonne he,
wine Scildinga,   worold oflætest.
Wene ic þæt he mid gode   gyldan wille
uncran eaferan,   gif he þæt eal gemon,
hwæt wit to willan   ond to worðmyndum
umborwesendum ær   arna gefremedon.'

Hwearf þa bi bence   þær hyre byre wæron,
Hreðric ond Hroðmund,   ond hæleþa bearn,
giogoð ætgædere.   Þær se goda sæt,
Beowulf Geata,   be þam gebroðrum twæm. [*end of fitt*]

It has been said to me that you would have as a son
this raiding man. Heorot is cleansed,
the bright ring-hall. Use, while you may,
the rewards of the many, and leave your kinsmen
your people and kingdom when you must go hence
to see fate's decree. I know my
Hrothulf is well-disposed, that he will keep
these youths in favour, if you, the friend
of Scyldings, depart the world sooner than he.
I expect it is with advantage that he will repay
our heirs, if he remembers everything
the two of us for his will and honour
performed for him before, while he was a child.'

Then she passed by the bench where her boys were,
Hrethric and Hrothmund, and the sons of men,
the youths together. There sat the good man,
Beowulf of the Geats, between the brothers.

1176 *hereri[n]c* 'raiding man'. Wealhtheow's term for *Beowulf* is not a happy one, given that Beowulf has just delivered them from a true raider. She is focused on stopping Beowulf's adoption to the place of royal son-in-law, then king, of the Danes.

1191 The seating arrangement promises to make Beowulf into another 'brother', by dint of marrying the boys' sister Freawaru. Can Wealhtheow stop the match in time?

Future foretold: the fall of Hygelac

The poet moves into his first reference to King Hygelac's future death on the Frisian raid (the others are on lines 2200–1, 2354–66 and 2913–20). While they continue to be ignorant of this blow to come, Wealhtheow addresses Beowulf in public for the first time, offering him portable treasures and the status of adviser (as in *lareow* 'teacher') to her sons. The fear unspoken in Wealhtheow is that Beowulf will be offered her daughter Freawaru's hand in marriage, thereafter the throne: Denmark could fall apart. She is hard-headed enough to bet her sons' survival on Hrothulf.

Damico, H., *Beowulf's Wealhtheow and the Valkyrie Tradition* (Madison, WI, 1984)

Damico, H., and Olsen, A. H., *New Readings on Women in Old English Literature* (Bloomington, IN, 1990)

Overing, G. R., *Language, Sign, and Gender in 'Beowulf'* (Carbondale and Edwardsville, IL, 1990)

XVIII Him wæs ful boren   ond freondlaþu
wordum bewægned   ond wunden gold
estum geeawed,   earm[h]reade twa,
hrægl ond hringas,   healsbeaga mæst
þara þe ic on foldan   gefrægen hæbbe.
Nænigne ic under swegle   selran hyrde
hordmaðum hæleþa   syþðan Hama ætwæg
to *þæ*re byrhtan byrig   Br*e*singa mene,
sigle ond sincfæt.   Searoniðas *flea*h
Eormenrices,   geceas ecne ræd.
Þone hring hæfde   Higelac Geata

XVIII To him a cup was passed and friendly invitation
conveyed in words and twisted gold
offered with favours, two arm-rings,
garments and bracelets, the greatest necklace
that I have ever learned of on the earth.
Never under firmament did I hear of a better
hoard-object for heroes since Hama carried off
the necklace of the Bresings to the bright city,
jewel and precious setting. Cunning enmities he fled
of Eormanric, chose an eternal reward.
Hygelac of the Geats had that ring,

1192 The poem continues, with the queen ensuring that Beowulf is offered portable wealth (see note to lines 1173–4).

1199 The size of the necklace may be intended to satisfy Beowulf, in lieu of Hrothgar's rash offer of adoption on lines 946–50. [*Bresinga mene* 'necklace of the Bresings'. Emended from *Brosinga*, in alignment with Brísinga men 'necklace of the Brísingar', which is Freyja's necklace (see **Gods of the Vikings**). Hama gives his treasure away for eternal rewards. Will Beowulf learn to do the same, when the moment comes?

nefa Swertinges   nyhstan siðe
siðþan he under segne   sinc ealgode,
wælreaf werede.   Hyne wyrd fornam
syþðan he for wlenco   wean ahsode
fæhðe to Frysum.   He þa frætwe wæg
eorclan stanes   ofer yða ful
rice þeoden.   He under rande gecranc.
Gehwearf þa in Francna fæþm   feorh cyninges,
breostgewædu   ond se beah somod.
Wyrsan wigfrecan   wæl reafed*on*
æfter guðsceare,   Geata leode
hreawic heoldon.   Heal swege onfeng.

Wealhðeo maþelode,   heo for þæm werede spræc:
'Bruc þisses beages,   Beowulf leofa,
hyse mid hæle,   ond þisses hrægles neot,
þeodgestreona,   ond geþeoh tela,
cen þec mid cræfte,   ond þyssum cnyhtum wes
lara liðe!   Ic þe þæs lean geman.
Hafast þu gefered,   þæt ðe feor ond neah

Swerting's nephew, on his last expedition,
when he guarded his treasure beneath a banner,
defended deadly spoil. Fate seized him
when through pride he asked for woe,
a feud with Frisia. He carried that ornament
of precious stone over the cup of the waves,
the powerful king. He perished beneath a targe.
Passed then into the Franks' clutches the king's life,
his breast-covering and the necklace all in one.
Lower-ranking war-braves plundered the slain
after the war-squadron, Geatish tribesmen
held the corpse encampment. The hall received applause.

Wealhtheow spoke, pronounced before the host:
'Commute this necklace, dear Beowulf,
young man, for your fortune, and enjoy these garments,
treasures of our nation, and prosper well,
play your cards right, and to these boys
be a kind tutor! I will remember you with a reward for this.
You have brought it to pass that far and wide

1205 *wælreaf werede* 'defended deadly spoil'. The meaning is also that Hygelac's lust for spoil has been deadly to him. This is a calamity for his people, and the big tragedy of Beowulf's life.

1214 Another extraordinary jump from the dark to the bright, but this time backwards across a gulf of time. The temporal liberties of this poet surpass those of a Joseph Conrad.

1220 *lara liðe* 'kind tutor'. Literally 'kind in teachings', but the meaning is clear: Beowulf may stay on as their mentor, but not as their new brother-in-law.

ealne wideferhþ weras ehtigað,
efne swa side swa sæ bebugeð
windgeard, weallas. Wes þenden þu lifige
æþeling eadig! Ic þe an tela
sincgestreona. Beo þu suna minum
dædum gedefe, dreamhealdende!
Her is æghwylc eorl oþrum getrywe,
modes milde, mandrihtne hol*d*,
þegnas sindon geþwære, þeod ealgearo,
druncne dryhtguman doð swa ic bidde.'

---

men will respect you for ever and always,
just as far as the sea, the wind-enclosure,
surrounds coast-walls. Be, for all your lifetime,
a prince of good fortune! I will, as is right,
grant you treasure. Be gracious
to my son in your deeds, O joyful one!
In this place each gentleman is true to the other,
generous of heart, loyal to man and master,
thegns are in harmony, the nation all prepared,
drunk men of the retinue do as I ask them.'

King Hrothgar on Grendel's Mere

This passage has drawn the attention of scholars for two reasons: one, that it closely resembles the language of St Paul's vision of hell, in the final section of Blickling Homily No. 16, for the Feast of St Michael; the other, that it may or may not be indebted also to Vergil's description of Avernus (the Roman underworld) in Vergil's *Aeneid*, Book VI (*inter alia* for North 2006: 8–10; against Renoir 1974).

North, R., *The Origins of 'Beowulf': From Vergil to Wiglaf* (Oxford, 2006), 8–10

Renoir, A., 'The terror of the dark waters: a note on Virgilian and Beowulfian techniques', in *The Learned and the Lewed: Studies in Chaucer and Medieval Literature*, ed. L. D. Benson, Harvard English Studies 5 (Cambridge, MA, 1974), 147–60

Wright, C. D., *The Irish Tradition in Old English Literature*, Cambridge Studies in Anglo-Saxon England 6 (Cambridge, 1993)

1224–5 *þenden þu lifige æþeling* 'for all your life-time a prince'. But not a king, not as far as Wealhtheow is concerned.

1230 *þeod ealgearo* 'nation all prepared'. Prepared for what? is the question. For the moment of Hrothgar's succession, is probably the answer. This speech from Wealhtheow to Beowulf could be read as a covert threat.

1231 *druncne dryhtguman* 'drunk men of the retinue'. The meaning of *druncne* may include 'men who have drunk something', but the idea is twofold: on the face of it, that Wealhtheow can stop even the most unruly behaviour; and underneath, that the warriors, because she pours for them, all owe her. Beowulf take note.

'Ic þæt londbuend, leode mine,
selerædende, secgan hyrde
þæt hie gesawon swylce twegen
micle mearcstapan moras healdan,
ellorgæstas. Ðæra oðer wæs,
þæs þe hie gewislicost gewitan meahton,
idese onlicnæs, oðer earmsceapen
on weres wæstmum wræclastas træd,
næfne he wæs mara þonne ænig man oðer.
Þone on geardagum Grendel nemdon
foldbuende. No hie fæder cunnon,
hwæþer him ænig wæs ær acenned
dyrnra gasta. Hie dygel lond
warigeað, wulfhleoþu, windige næssas,
frecne fengelad, ðær fyrgenstream
under næssa genipu niþer gewiteð,
flod under foldan. Nis þæt feor heonon
milgemearces þæt se mere standeð.
Ofer þam hongiað hri*m*de bearwas,

'I have heard the inhabitants of this land,
my tribesmen, hall-advisers, say
that they have seen two such as these
two great boundary powlers haunt the moors,
alien spirits. One of these was,
from the clearest they could make it out,
in the likeness of a woman, the other misshapen
in man's outline trod the paths of exile,
save that he was bigger than any other man.
Him in days of yore the peasants called
Grendel. If he had a father, they never knew,
whether any such was once bought forth
by powers of darkness. A secret land
they inhabit, wolf-slopes, windy bluffs,
savage fenland roads, where the mountain stream
passes down beneath the mists of headlands,
a river under the earth. It is not far from here,
in a measure of miles, that the lake stands;
above it there hang frost-rimed groves,

1355 *No hie fæder cunnon* 'If he had a father, they never knew'. Some (film director Robert Zemeckis among them) think that Hrothgar might be the father, though without any sign of this in the poem; others, that it could be the devil.

1357–63 The language here resembles that of Blickling Homily No. 16, probably through a vernacular source that was common to both texts (Wright 1993: 106–36; see **Writers of the Benedictine Reform**).

wudu wyrtum fæst   wæter oferhelmað.
Þær mæg nihta gehwæm   niðwundor seon,
fyr on flode.   No þæs frod leofað
gumena bearna,   þæt þone grund wite;
ðeah þe hæðstapa   hundum geswenced,
heorot hornum trum,   holtwudu sece,
feorran geflymed,   ær he feorh seleð,
aldor on ofre,   ær he in wille
hafelan hydan.   Nis þæt heoru stow!
Þonon yðgeblond   up astigeð
won to wolcnum,   þonne wind styreþ,
lað gewidru,   oðþæt lyft drysmaþ,
roderas reotað.'

---

a wood made fast by its roots overshadows the water.
There each night a fearful wonder may be seen,
fire on the flood. No man lives so wise
of the sons of men that he may know the bottom.
Though the heath-stepper by hounds afflicted,
a stag strong in antlers, may seek the woods
put to flight from afar, he will give his life,
his very existence on the bank before in there
he hides his head. That is no pleasant place!
From there a mingling of waves rises up,
dark towards the clouds, when stirred by wind,
a hostile storm, until the sky grows gloomy,
the heavens weep.'

Beowulf's fight with Grendel's Mother

This monster-fight seems to be more traditional to the Beowulf archetype than his contest with Grendel. Both the hero's (*beadwe heard*, *freca Scyldinga*) and Grendel's Mother's epithets (*brimwylf*, *grundwyrgen*) better recall his analogue name *Bǫðvarr* 'battle ready' and Danish hireling status against a she-wolf (*ylgr*) in *Beowulf*'s Skjǫldung analogues. In addition, these scenes may or may not (Fjalldal: 1998: 39–44) have been known to the author of *The Saga of Grettir the Strong* as the fight between Beowulf and Grendel (see **Sagas of Icelanders**).

Fjalldal, M., *The Long Arm of Coincidence: The Frustrated Connection between 'Beowulf' and 'Grettis saga'* (Toronto, 1998)

Beowulf maðelode, bearn Ecgþeowes:
'Geþenc nu, se mæra maga Healfdenes,
snottra fengel, nu ic eom siðes fus,
goldwine gumena, hwæt wit geo spræcon,
gif ic æt þearfe þinre scolde
aldre linnan, þæt ðu me a wære
forðgewitenum on fæder stæle.
Wes þu mundbora minum magoþegnum,
hondgesellum, gif mec hild nime.
Swylce þu ða madmas þe þu me sealdest,
Hroðgar leofa, Higelace onsend.
Mæg þonne on þam golde ongitan Geata dryhten,
geseon sunu Hrædles, þonne he on þæt sinc starað,
þæt ic gumcystum godne funde
beaga bryttan, breac þonne moste.
Ond þu Unferð læt ealde lafe,
wrætlic wægsweord, widcuðne man
heardecg habban. Ic me mid Hruntinge
dom gewyrce, oþðe mec deað nimeð.'

Beowulf spoke, son of Ecgtheow:
'Think now, renowned son of Healfdene,
clever lord, now I am keen for the mission,
men's gold-giving friend, of what the two of us earlier said,
if I, in the service of your need, was going to
give up my life, that you would always be
to me, once I was gone hence, like a father.
Be as the protecting hand over my young thegns,
my close comrades, if battle takes me.
Likewise, those treasures which you granted me,
dear Hrothgar, please send to Hygelac.
The lord of the Geats, Hrethel's son, will then be able
to see in that gold, when he looks at the treasure,
that I met a man of virtue, a generous dispenser
of rings, made good use of them while I might.
And let Unferth have the ancient heirloom,
the splendid patterned sword, let the man widely
known have the hard edge. I will work with Hrunting
for my reputation, or death will take me.'

1478–9 *me forðgewitenum* 'to me once I was gone hence'. It is possibly double-edged of Beowulf to say this. Hrothgar had meant 'in this life' when he offered to love Beowulf as a son (lines 946–9), not when he might be killed; or the meaning could be that he will do so when Beowulf is safely returned home; but in neither case as the hero's father-in-law. Hrothgar seems not to have followed up on his earlier promise. For that, we must wait until the opening of his 'sermon' below.

Æfter þam wordum Wedergeata leod
efste mid elne, nalas ondsware
bidan wolde. Brimwylm onfeng
hilderince. Đa wæs hwil dæges
ær he þone grundwong ongytan mehte.
Sona þæt onfunde se[o] ðe floda begong
heorogifre beheold hund missera,
grim ond grædig, þæt þær gumena sum
ælwihta eard ufan cunnode.
Grap þa togeanes, guðrinc gefeng
atolan clommum. No þy ær in gescod
halan lice, hring utan ymbbearh,
þæt heo þone fyrdhom ðurhfon ne mihte
locene leoðosyrcan laþan fingrum.
Bær þa seo brimwylf, þa heo to botme com,
hringa þengel to hofe sinum,
swa he ne mihte, no he þæs modig wæs,
wæpna gewealdan, ac hine wundra þæs fela
swencte on sunde, sædeor monig
hildetuxum heresyrcan bræc,
ehton aglæcan. Đa se eorl ongeat

After these words the Weater-Geatish noble
sped off with courage, not at all for answer
would he wait. Brimming billows received
the man of war. Then it was the length of a day
before he could make out the lake-floor.
Straightaway she who had occupied the flood's extent
with monstrous hunger for a hundred half-years,
grim and greedy, perceived that some human there
was exploring the alien world from above.
She grasped then at him, seized the man of battle
with terrifying talons. Not once the sooner for that
did they harm his body, for outward rings preserved it safe,
so that she could not penetrate the campaign-coat,
the interlinked mail-shirt with her hostile fingers.
Then the she-wolf of the sea, when she got to the bottom,
carried the ring-prince into her courtyard,
as he could not, no matter how spirited he was,
command his weapons, for a lot of freaks so
afflicted him as they swam, many a sea-beast
broke its war-tusks on his raiding-shirt,
hunted their adversary. Then the hero knew

1506 *seo brimwylf* 'the she-wolf of the sea'. This is a kenning. Nonetheless, Grendel's Mother may be developed here out of a wolfish monster such as we meet in the *Bjarkarímur* 'rhymes of Bjarki' from the fifteenth century (*ylgrin* 'the she-wolf'; North 2006: 48).

þæt he in niðsele   nathwylcum wæs,
þær him nænig wæter   wihte ne sceþede,
ne him for hrof sele   hrinan ne mehte
færgripe flodes.   Fyrleoht geseah,
blacne leoman,   beorhte scinan.
Ongeat þa se goda   grundwyrgenne,
merewif mihtig.   Mægenræs forgeaf
hildebille,   hond sweng ne ofteah,
þæt hire on hafelan   hringmæl agol
grædig guðleoð.   Ða se gist onfand
þæt se beadoleoma   bitan nolde,
aldre sceþðan,   ac seo ecg geswac
ðeodne æt þearfe.   Ðolode ær fela
hondgemota,   helm oft gescær,
fæges fyrdhrægl.   Ða wæs forma sið
deorum madme,   þæt his dom alæg.
Eft wæs anræd,   nalas elnes læt,
mærða gemyndig   mæg Hylaces.
Wearp ða wundenmæl   wrættum gebunden
yrre oretta,   þæt hit on eorðan læg
stið ond stylecg.   Strenge getruwode,

---

that he was in a palace of evil of some kind
where no water could harm him in any way,
nor for the roof of this palace could he be touched
by flood's feared attack. He could see firelight,
a gleaming light that was brightly shining.
Then the good man felt the monster of the abyss,
the mighty mere-wife. A mighty stroke he gave
with his war-blade, his hand not restraining the swing,
that on her head the ring-pattern sang out
a greedy battle hymn. Then the visitor discovered
that this battle-flash would not bite,
harm her life, but the edge went weak
in its lord's need. It had once endured many
encounters hand-to-hand, often sliced a helmet,
campaign-apparel of the doomed. First time, then,
for this precious object to fail its test of renown.
He revived his resolve, by no means slow in valour,
mindful of his exploits was Hygelac's kinsman.
Then he threw away his wire-bound damascened,
did the wrathful soldier, so that it lay on the ground,
stiff and steel-edged. In his strength he trusted,

1523 *bitan nolde* 'would not bite'. Just as with Grendel earlier, so Beowulf's men discover on line 803.

mundgripe mægenes. Swa sceal man don,
þonne he æt guðe gegan þenceð
longsumne lof, na ymb his lif cearað.
Gefeng þa be eaxle (nalas for fæhðe mearn)
guð-Geata leod Grendles modor,
brægd þa beadwe heard, þa he gebolgen wæs,
feorhgeniðlan, þæt heo on flet gebeah.
Heo him eft hraþe andlean forgeald
grimman grapum ond him togeanes feng.
Oferwearp þa werigmod wigena strengest,
feþecempa, þæt he on fylle wearð.
Ofsæt þa þone selegyst ond hyre seax geteah,
brad ond brunecg, wolde hire bearn wrecan,
angan eaferan. Him on eaxle læg
breostnet broden. Þæt gebearh feore,
wið ord ond wið ecge ingang forstod.
Hæfde ða forsiðod sunu Ecgþeowes
under gynne grund, Geata cempa,

---

in his mighty hand-grip. Thus must a man do
when in warfare he intends to gain
long-lasting praise, he never cares about his life.
By her shoulder then (not once he mourned the feud)
the tribesman of war-Geats seized Grendel's Mother,
the battle-hard then twisted, now swollen with rage,
his deadly opponent so that she hit the floor.
Back once more she quickly gave him payment
with fierce grip and with him grappled.
Stumbled then the strongest fighter, his mind exhausted,
infantry champion, so that he took a fall.
Straddling the palace-visitor then, she drew bowie knife,
broad and burnished, would avenge her child,
her only heir. On his upper body lay
a woven breast-net. That saved his life,
withstood the entry of point and blade.
He would have perished then, son of Ecgtheow,
beneath the ample ground above, Geatish champion,

1536 *na ymb his lif cearað* 'he never cares about his life'. the poet's expectations are seemingly high, rather as those of the *c.* 700 poet of *The Dream of the Rood*, lines 112–14 (see **Poems of Devotion**).

1545 *Ofsæt* 'Straddling'. An erotic meaning seems a tad out of place, given that this is a fight to the death, with seconds to spare before Grendel's Mother finds a way of gutting the stranger in her cave. She is deadlier than the male. [*seax* 'bowie knife'. This weapon has been studied alongside Hrunting the *hæftmece* 'hafted-sword' on line 1457, in that Grettir has a *sax* 'knife' and fights a cave-troll with a *heptisax* in *The Saga of Grettir the Strong* (see **Sagas of Icelanders**). The latter occurs nowhere else in Icelandic literature; the chances of this being a coincidence, rather than a borrowing, seem too great (*pace* Fjalldal).

nemne him heaðobyrne helpe gefremede,
herenet hearde, ond halig God
geweold wigsigor. Witig Drihten,
rodera Rædend, hit on ryht gesced
yðelice, syþðan he eft astod.
Geseah ða on searwum sigeeadig bil,
eald sweord eotenisc, ecgum þyhtig,
wigena weorðmynd. Þæt wæs wæpna cyst,
buton hit wæs mare ðonne ænig mon oðer
to beadulace ætberan meahte,
god ond geatolic, giganta geweorc.
He gefeng þa fetelhilt, freca Scyldinga
hreoh ond heorogrim hringmæl gebrægd,
aldres orwena, yrringa sloh,
þæt hire wið halse heard grapode,
banhringas bræc. Bil eal ðurhwod
fægne flæschoman, heo on flet gecrong.
Sweord wæs swatig, secg weorce gefeh.
Lixte se leoma, leoht inne stod,
efne swa of hefene hadre scineð
rodores candel.

---

if his skirmish-mail had not given him help,
the hard raiding-net, and if Holy God
had not governed victory in combat. The Wise Lord,
Ruler of the Skies, determined this rightly
with ease, whereupon he stood up again.
He saw then among the panoplies a blade rich
in victories, an old sword of giant make, edges
powerful, an honour for warriors. The finest weapon,
but that it was bigger than any other man
could carry away as a trophy of battle,
good and splendid, the work of titans.
Then he seized the swordhilt, Scylding brave,
savage and ferocious drew back the ring-pattern,
with no hope of life struck with rage,
that the hard thing locked into her neck,
broke the bone-rings. The whole blade passed through
the doomed flesh-cover, dead she dropped to the floor.
Sword was bloodied, the man rejoiced at his deed.
The gleam shone, a light appeared within,
just as from heaven's vault shines
the candle of the sky.

1556 *syþðan* 'whereupon'. This meaning is possible in the subordinating conjunction, and necessary if the Lord's power is to be recognised as the cause, not the consequence, of Beowulf's sudden spurt of energy.

King Hrothgar's sermon

At the heart of *Beowulf* is a poignant speech delivered in honour and aid of Beowulf by Hrothgar, old king of the Danes. Beowulf has just returned, against expectations, with the head of Grendel and the evidence, in the sword-hilt from Grendel's Mother's cave, that he has killed this older monster as well. Hrothgar looks at the hilt of the sword (the blade melted in her blood) but does not necessarily understand its writing or the story that it contains: the survival of Cain's progeny in Noah's flood through Cham, Noah's evil magician son, for whom it seems the sword was made (Orchard 1995: 69–75). Nonetheless, Hrothgar feels its huge antiquity and represents himself as the best repository of knowledge that the Danes might have as a means of understanding this.

Studying the sword for a moment, Hrothgar turns to Beowulf and gives him a long warning against pride. Some people call this speech a 'sermon', given that it is full of parental wisdom, like a father advising his son. It does not rehearse a story in the way of several earlier digressions, but rather delivers an argument based on: (a) the bad case of King Heremod, a Macbeth of Hrothgar's past who started well and then went to the bad, dying in exile (compare him in lines 901–15); (b) a generalised story of the rake's progress, a king whose success leads him to forget his mortality and focus too much on wealth, so that an arrow of the devil's temptation may one day pierce the armour of his Conscience; (c) an injunction to Beowulf to avoid this course, to think of *ece rædas* 'eternal rewards' (line 1760) and not pride; (d) a personal reflection on how Hrothgar, having ruled successfully for 50 years, was still surprised by the sudden twist of fate when Grendel came, by a 'reversal' (*edwenden*, line 1774). The language of this speech is heavily influenced by the Psalms and by Christian sermons and patristic commentaries (Atherton 1993: 653–7; Wright 1993: 260–1; Orchard 2003: 160–1). That is why scholars so often call it a sermon. Yet Hrothgar is a heathen king who intuits rather than knows the Christian theology to which he cannot have any access. As Hrothgar is heathen, and his great speech is stimulated by the mysterious runic lettering on the hilt of Grendel's Mother's sword, this sermon of his could just as easily be known as the 'sword-hilt speech'.

Atherton, M., 'The Figure of the Archer in *Beowulf* and the Anglo-Saxon Psalter', *Neophilologus* 77 (1993), 653–7

Clemoes, P., *Interactions of Thought and Language in Old English Literature*, Cambridge Studies in Anglo-Saxon England 12 (Cambridge, 1995)

Lapidge, M., '*Beowulf* and Perception', *Proceedings of the British Academy* 111 (2001), 61–97

Mitchell, B., and F. C. Robinson, ed., *Beowulf: An Edition with Relevant Shorter Texts*, including 'Archaeology and *Beowulf*', by L. Webster (Oxford, 1998)

North, R., *The Origins of 'Beowulf': From Vergil to Wiglaf* (Oxford, 2006)

Orchard, A., *Pride and Prodigies: Studies in the Monsters of the Beowulf-Manuscript* (Woodbridge, 1995)

Orchard, A., *A Critical Companion to Beowulf* (Woodbridge, 2003)

Wright, C. D., *The Irish Tradition in Old English Literature*, Cambridge Studies in Anglo-Saxon England 6 (Cambridge, 1993)

Đa wæs gylden hilt gamelum rince
harum hildfruman on hand gyfen
enta ærgeweorc. Hit on æht gehwearf
æfter deofla hryre Denigea frean,
wundorsmiþþa geweorc; ond þa þas worold ofgeaf
gromheort guma, Godes andsaca,
morðres scyldig ond his modor eac,
on geweald gehwearf woroldcyninga
ðæm selestan be sæm tweonum
ðara þe on Scedenigge sceattas dælde.
Hroðgar maðelode, hylt sceawode,
ealde lafe. On ðæm wæs or writen
fyrngewinnes, syþðan flod ofsloh,
gifen geotende, giganta cyn.
Frecne geferdon! Þæt wæs fremde þeod
ecean Dryhtne, him þæs endelean
þurh wæteres wylm Waldend sealde.
Swa wæs on ðæm scennum sciran goldes

Then was the golden hilt given into the hand
of the aged warrior, the grey-haired war-leader,
an ancient work of giants. It passed into the keeping
of the lord of the Danes after the ruin of devils,
this work of the smiths of wonders; and when the wild hearted man,
God's adversary, gave up this world
guilty of murder, and his mother also,
into the power it passed of the best
of worldly kings between the seas
who ever shared out coins in the isles of Scania.
Hrothgar made a speech, looked at the hilt,
the old heirloom. On that was written the beginning
of the ancient strife, when the flood,
the rushing ocean, killed the race of giants.
Terribly they fared! That was a nation estranged
from the eternal Lord. Them the Ruler gave
final payment with a surge of water.
So it was marked on the swordguard

1679 *enta ærgeweorc* 'an ancient work of giants'. OE *eald enta geweorc* ('old works of giants') is a phrase that refers to Roman and other ancient ruins in *The Wanderer*, line 87 and also (without the *eald*) in *The Ruin*, line 2, of the Exeter Book.

1686 *on Scedenigge* 'in the isles of Scania'. Compare *Scedelandum in* ('in the lands of Scania') on line 19, a term for Denmark's possessions around the southern Swedish peninsula. These names are older in form than *Sconeg*, a term for 'Scandinavia' in Alfred's reign in the 890s. Consequently, it can be argued that *Beowulf* was composed before Alfred's time (lived 849–99).

þurh runstafas rihte gemearcod,
geseted ond gesæd, hwam þæt sweord geworht,
irena cyst, ærest wære,
wreoþenhilt ond wyrmfah. Đa se wisa spræc,
sunu Healfdenes (swigedon ealle):

'Þæt la mæg secgan se þe soð ond riht
fremeð on folce, feor oft gemon,
eald eðelweard, þæt se eorl wære
geboren betera! Blæd is aræred
geond widwegas, wine min Beowulf,
ðin ofer þeoda gehwylce. Eal þu hit geþyldum healdest,
mægen mid modes snyttrum. Ic sceal mine gelæstan
freoðe, swa wit furðum spræcon. Đu scealt to frofre weorþan

---

of bright gold, with the right runic letters,
set down and made clear, for whom that sword
of the finest iron had first been made
with hilt twisted, and patterning serpentine. Then the wise man spoke,
son of Healfdene (they all fell silent):

'Lo, he may say who furthers truth and justice
in the people, who remembers always from long ago,
old guardian of his homeland, that this nobleman was
born to be of better rank! Fame is raised up
on roads through distant regions, my friend Beowulf,
your fame over each and every nation. All this power you are keeping
with patience, with wisdom of mind. I shall fulfil
my agreement, just as the two of us spoke earlier. You shall become a comfort

---

1695 *þurh runstafas rihte gemearcod* 'marked with the right runic letters'. The ancient Germanic alphabet was mostly, but not entirely, superseded by the Roman letters of Christian literacy. Compare with the runes in which the carvers of the Ruthwell Cross wrote down an old form of *The Dream of the Rood* (see **Poems of Devotion**).

1699 *sunu Healfdenes* 'son of Healfdene'. Hrothgar's father is the son of Beow ('barley'; miswritten in the manuscript as 'Beowulf'), son of Scyld ('shield'), son of Scef ('sheaf'). This is an epic epithet such as may be expected in heroic poems at the beginning of a speech.

1700–1 *se þe soð ond riht fremeð on folce* 'who furthers truth and justice in the people'. A term for the king of Denmark, here chosen by himself. The word *riht* can mean more specifically 'law', such as the *ealde riht* ('old laws', line 2330) which King Beowulf believes he has transgressed when the Dragon burns Geatland towards the end of *Beowulf.*

1705–7 Hypermetric lines, the second of three groups of such lines in *Beowulf* (the others are on lines 1162–8 and 2995–6). Hypermetric lines are held together by six stressed syllables rather than the four of ordinary lines. They are commoner in other poems such as *The Dream of the Rood* and *Judith.* Their relative rarity in *Beowulf* presupposes that something very important in them is being said. In this case, the message appears to be that Beowulf can expect a (contractual) reward from Hrothgar in keeping with his new fame. Is this the *niwe sibb* 'new kinship' which Hrothgar promised him the day before, on line 949, pointing to marriage with Freawaru? Unfortunately not. Hrothgar immediately says that Beowulf will be king of the Geats, not of the Danes.

eal langtwidig leodum þinum,
hæleðum to helpe. Ne wearð Heremod swa
eaforum Ecgwelan, Ar-Scyldingum,
ne geweox he him to willan ac to wælfealle
ond to deaðcwalum Deniga leodum.
Breat bolgenmod beodgeneatas,
eaxlgesteallan, oþþæt he ana hwearf,
mære þeoden, mondreamum from,
ðeah þe hine mihtig God mægenes wynnum,
eafeþum stepte, ofer ealle men
forð gefremede. Hwæþere him on ferhþe greow
breosthord blodreow, nallas beagas geaf
Denum æfter dome. Dreamleas gebad,
þæt he þæs gewinnes weorc þrowade,
leodbealo longsum. Đu þe lær be þon,
gumcyste ongit. Ic þis gid be þe
awræc wintrum frod. Wundor is to secganne,

---

all long-lasting to your people,
an aid to men. Not so was Heremod
to the sons of Ecgwela, to the Favour-Scyldings!
He did not grow up as a joy for them, but as the slaughter
and destruction of the Danish people.
Swollen with wrath, he struck down his table companions,
comrades of his shoulder, until, alone, he moved away,
infamous chieftain, from the joys of man,
though Mighty God had raised him up in the bliss
of strength and power, before all men
God advanced him. In Heremod's breast, however,
the hoarded thoughts grew bloody and cruel. No more did he give rings
to Danes to match an honour earned. Without joy he lived
to suffer pain for the strife this caused,
a long-lasting torment. You learn from this,
take note of a man's excellence. It is for you that I,
made wise by winters, composed this song. Wonder is to tell

1707 *freoðe* 'agreement'. This word is usually read as *freode* ('love') despite the form of the letter *ð* being visible in the manuscript, but the meaning is much the same.

1709 *Heremod.* Heremod is earlier the subject of the poet's allusion on the Danes' triumphal ride back from the Mere (lines 901–14). The unnamed Danish thegn who sings Beowulf's praises on this occasion seems to contrast him with Heremod, a bad example to follow. Heremod is the king whose exile and death leads to the kingless period for the Danes, which the Almighty relieves by sending them Scyld Scefing as a baby in the 'Prologue' of *Beowulf* (lines 12–16).

1710 *Ecgwelan.* Ecgwela is unknown from other sources.

1723 *gumcyste ongit* 'take note of a man's excellence'. Hrothgar refers to his own, one which must be visible in his aged splendour as king of Denmark. The meaning 'to perceive, notice' is the only one *ongietan* has in *Beowulf* (Lapidge 2001: 90–1; who regards this use, however, as an exception).

hu mihtig God   manna cynne
þurh sidne sefan   snyttru bryttað,
eard ond eorlscipe.   He ah ealra geweald.
Hwilum he on lufan   læteð hworfan
monnes modgeþonc   mæran cynnes,
seleð him on eþle   eorþan wynne
to healdanne,   hleoburh wera,
gedeþ him swa gewealdene   worolde dælas,
side rice,   þæt he his selfa ne mæg
for his unsnyttrum   ende geþencean.
Wunað he on wiste,   no hine wiht dweleð
adl ne yldo,   ne him inwitsorh
on sefan sweorceð,   ne gesacu ohwær
ecghete eoweð,   ac him eal worold
wendeð on willan,   he þæt wyrse ne con.

XXV   Oð þæt him on innan   oferhygda dæl
weaxeð ond wridað,   þonne se weard swefeð,
sawele hyrde;   bið se slæp to fæst,

---

how Mighty God to mankind
in His wide heart shares out wisdom,
land and rank. He has power over all!
Sometimes He gives free rein
to the cherished thoughts of a man of renowned family,
gives him in his homeland earthly bliss,
an estate of dependent men to keep as his own,
brings him regions of the world, a wide kingdom,
to rule with such power that the man himself cannot,
in all his lack of wisdom, imagine any end to it.
The man lives on in satiety, neither is he touched
by illness or old age, nor does conscience
grow dark in the face of his mind, nor does enmity anywhere
reveal its sharp hatred, but the whole world
turns to his will. Of worse things he knows nothing!

XXV   And then within him a measure of prideful thoughts
increases and flourishes, when the keeper sleeps,
the guardian of the soul. That sleep is too sound,

1740 XXV *Oð þæt* 'And then'. A new fitt (manuscript section) begins just here. Those who see the fitt numbers as a scribal imposition on *Beowulf*, later than the poem, translate *oð þæt* here as 'until', linking this to the previous sentence as a subordinate clause (see, however, Mitchell and Robinson 1998: 105).

1742 *sawele hyrde* 'the guardian of the soul'. This term is also used of St Michael the Archangel (Orchard 1995: 51). Here it (also) refers to the *inwitsorh* just mentioned ('conscience', line 1736).

bisgum gebunden,   bona swiðe neah,
se þe of flanbogan   fyrenum sceoteð.
Þonne bið on hreþre   under helm drepen
biteran stræle   – him bebeorgan ne con –
wom wundorbebodum   wergan gastes;
þinceð him to lytel   þæt he lange heold,
gytsað gromhydig,   nalles on gylp seleð
fætte beagas   ond he þa forðgesceaft
forgyteð ond forgymeð   þæs þe him ær God sealde,
wuldres waldend,   weorðmynda dæl.
Hit on endestæf   eft gelimpeð
þæt se lichoma   læne gedreoseð,
fæge gefealleð,   fehð oþer to,
se þe unmurnlice   madmas dæleþ
eorles ærgestreon,   egesan ne gymeð.
Bebeorh þe þone bealonið,   Beowulf leofa,
secg betsta,   ond þe þæt selre geceos,

---

bound with cares, the slayer very close,
who shoots wickedly from a fiery bow.
Then in his heart is he struck beneath his armour
with a bitter arrow (he knows not how to protect himself!),
with the crooked miraculous commands of the accursed spirit.
It seems too little to him, what he long held,
wild at heart he grows greedy, not any more does he nobly
give plated rings, and then the world to come
he forgets and neglects, the portion of worldly honours
which God, the Ruler of Glory, once gave him.
Finally it happens at the end of his appointed day
that the body, on loan to him, declines and falls,
marked for to death. Another man takes over,
who ungrudgingly shares out his treasures,
the old man's ancient wealth, without fear of calamity.
Save yourself from that grievous enmity, dear Beowulf,
best of men, and choose for yourself the better course,

1743–4 *bona se þe of flanbogan fyrenum sceoteð* 'the slayer who shoots wickedly from a fiery bow'. Hrothgar's words recall St Paul's Letter to the Ephesians, in which new converts are urged to shield themselves against 'all the flaming arrows of the evil one' (*omnia tela nequissimi ignea*, 6:16; Atherton 1993: 655).

1751 *forgyteð ond forgymeð* 'he forgets and neglects'. See line 1767.

1753 *Hit on endestæf* 'at the end of his appointed day' etc. This phrase is found elsewhere, particularly in the Blickling 'Homily for Easter Sunday' (No. 7), *æt endestæfe* 'at His appointed end', used by the devils of Jesus before the Harrowing of Hell.

1754 *læne* 'on loan'. The standard OE metaphor for transience, with an economic basis. This word is also in *The Wanderer*, line 108 (see **Poems on the Meaning of Life**).

ece rædas, oferhyda ne gym,
mære cempa. Nu is þines mægnes blæd
ane hwile. Eft sona bið
þæt þec adl oððe ecg eafoþes twæfeð
oððe fyres feng oððe flodes wylm
oððe gripe meces oððe gares fliht
oððe atol yldo, oððe eagena bearhtm
forsiteð ond forsworceð; semninga bið
þæt ðec, dryhtguma, deað oferswyðeð.
Swa ic Hring-Dena hund missera
weold under wolcnum ond hig wigge beleac
manigum mægþa geond þisne middangeard,
æscum ond ecgum, þæt ic me ænigne
under swegles begong gesacan ne tealde.
Hwæt me þæs on eþle edwenden cwom,
gyrn æfter gomene, seoþðan Grendel wearð,
ealdgewinna, ingenga min.

---

eternal rewards! Have no regard for prideful thoughts,
renowned champion! The fame of your power now will last
only for a little while. Soon there will come a time
when either disease or the blade parts you from your strength,
or the fire's grip, or the flood's surge,
or the sword's bite, or the spear's flight,
or terrible old age, or the brightness of your eyes
will fail and grow dim. In the end it shall happen
that death, man of the retinue, will overpower you.
So it was I ruled the Ring-Danes for a hundred six-months
beneath the skies, while with war I enclosed them
safe from many tribes throughout this middle world,
with spears and swords, in such a way that no man
would be counted as my adversary beneath the compass of the sun.
Well then, to me in my home there came a reversal,
affliction after festivity, when Grendel,
an ancient foe, became the intruder of my house.

1760 *ece rædas* 'eternal rewards'. Using this phrase at the heart of the poem, Hrothgar intuits the heavenly salvation of Christianity without having knowledge of it. Will Beowulf follow this advice? Only if he masters his big disappointment.

1763–7 *oððe* (× 7) 'or'. Alternative noun-pairs (polysyndeton) are a feature of Christian homilies.

1767 *forsiteð ond forsworceð* 'will fail and grow dim'. This doublet, just as *forgyteð ond forgymeð* on line 1751, is frequent in OE homilies (Clemoes 1995: 42–6).

1776 *ealdgewinna* 'ancient foe'. Otherwise a term for the devil, as in Latin *antiquus hostis* of the same meaning.

Ic þære socne singales wæg
modceare micle. Þæs sig Metode þanc,
ecean Dryhtne, þæs ðe ic on aldre gebad,
þæt ic on þone hafelan heorodreorigne
ofer eald gewin eagum starige!
Ga nu to setle, symbelwynne dreoh,
wiggeweorþad. Unc sceal worn fela
maþma gemænra siþðan morgen bið.'

I from that persecution have borne constantly
great cares of mind. Thanks be to Providence,
to the eternal Lord, that I have lived long enough
to behold that battle-bloodied head,
the old fight over, with my own eyes!
Go now to your seat, enjoy the pleasures of feasting,
honoured for combat. From me to you shall pass
a heap of many treasures when tomorrow comes.'

Beowulf on Princess Freawaru

The poet juxtaposes Beowulf with Ingeld here, though they never meet. With clearer vehemence than motive, Beowulf predicts to his uncle Hygelac the outcome of Ingeld's marriage with Freawaru in lines 2021–69. This prediction has been connected to the Finnsburh Episode, in that Freawaru will shortly be married to Ingeld in an attempt to heal an old feud (Shippey 1978: 32–3; Irving 1989: 34–8). Yet Beowulf's mind is of more interest. It is puzzling that he should present Freawaru's wedding plans in such detail as the prelude to his report for Hygelac when he comes home. Just when we expect to hear of his glory with the Grendels, Beowulf diverts us for 48 lines with a prediction about Hrothgar's daughter. Did Beowulf expect to receive her as his? If we match this speech with Hrothgar's offer of a *niwe sibbe* 'new kinship' on line 949, it seems likely that he did.

Irving, E. B., Jr., *Rereading Beowulf* (Philadelphia, PA, 1989)

North, R., 'Boethius and the Mercenary in *The Wanderer*', in *Pagans and Christians: the Interplay between Christian Latin and Traditional Germanic Cultures in Early Medieval Europe*, ed. T. Hofstra, L. A. J. R. Houwen and A. A. MacDonald, Germania Latina II (Groningen, 1995), 71–98

Shippey, T. A., *Beowulf*, Studies in English Literature 70 (London, 1978)

'Weorod wæs on wynne,   ne seah ic widan feorh
under heofones hwealf   healsittendra
medudream maran.   Hwilum mæru cwen,
friðusibb folca,   flet eall geondhwearf,
bædde byre geonge,   oft hio beahwriðan
secge sealde   ær hie to setle geong.
Hwilum for duguðe   dohtor Hroðgares
eorlum on ende   ealuwæge bær
þa ic Freaware   fletsittende
nemnan hyrde,   þær hio nægled sinc
hæleðum sealde.   Sio gehaten is,
geong, goldhroden,   gladum suna Frodan.
Hafað þæs geworden   wine Scyldinga,
rices hyrde,   ond þæt ræd talað,
þæt he mid ðy wife   wælfæhða dæl
sæcca gesette.   Oft seldan hwær
æfter leodhryre   lytle hwile
bongar bugeð,   þeah seo bryd duge!
Mæg þæs þonne ofþyncan   ðeod*ne* Heaðo-Beardna

'The troops were joyful, nor did I see in all my life
among banqueting heroes under heaven's vault
a greater mead-rejoicing. At times the splendid queen,
treaty-pledge of peoples, crossed all the hall,
exhorted the young lads, often a bracelet she
would give to the chaps before going to her settle.
At times before the veterans Hrothgar's daughter
carried an ale-cup for warriors in turn,
she whom I heard called Freawaru by men
sitting on the benches, where she gave
heroes the studded vessel. She is promised,
young and gold-adorned, to Froda's gracious son.
Concerning him it has occurred to the friend of Scyldings,
their kingdom's guardian, and he rates it a plan,
that with this woman a share of deadly feuds
and conflicts he may settle. Often anywhere
after a nation's defeat, even for a little while,
the death-spear rests seldom, though the bride may do!
All can seem emotional to the lord of the Heathobards,

2017 *friðusibb folca* 'treaty-pledge of peoples'. With this summation of what Wealhtheow is in Heorot, Beowulf reveals that in her time, too, she was given as a bride to unite peoples.

2022–3 *þa ic Freaware nemnan hyrde* 'whom I heard called Freawaru'. It follows from this that Beowulf was not presented to Freawaru while in Denmark.

2025 *suna Frodan* 'Froda's son'. Ingeld, a Heathobard (from Hadeland, in SE Norway).

2029–31 With this cluttered sentence, Beowulf tries to take account of all cases, in any of which the outcome would be the same.

ond þegna gehwam   þara leoda
þonne he mid fæmnan   on flett gæð.
Dryhtbearn Dena,   duguða biwenede,
on him gladiað   gomelra lafe,
heard ond hringmæl   Heaða-Bear[d]na gestreon
þenden hie ðam wæpnum   wealdan moston.

[XXX] ‘Oð ðæt hie forlæddan   to ðam lindplegan
swæse gesiðas   ond hyra sylfra feorh!
Þonne cwið æt beore   se ðe beah gesyhð,
eald æscwiga,   se ðe eall geman,
garcwealm gumena   (him bið grim sefa),
onginneð geomormod   geongum cempan
þurh hreðra gehygd   higes cunnian,
wigbealu weccean,   ond þæt word acwyð:

“Meaht ðu, min wine,   mece gecnawan
þone þin fæder   to gefeohte bær
under heregriman   hindeman siðe,

---

and to each of the thegns of those tribesmen,
when he walks with the woman into the hall.
Sons of the Danish retinue he has lavishly entertained,
on them gleam ancestors’ heirlooms,
strong and ring-patterned treasures which Heathobards
had while it was granted them to wield their weapons.

[XXX] ‘And then in the play of shields they led to destruction
their dear companions and their own life-blood!
Then he speaks at beer who sees a precious ornament,
an old spear-fighter who remembers everything,
the lance-killing of men (his disposition is fierce),
sad-hearted he begins to test out the courage
of a young champion through the thoughts of his mind,
to rouse the evil of war, and these are the words he says:

“Can you recognise that sword, my friend,
an expensive iron which your father was carrying
while he wore his war-mask for the last time

2039 The manuscript page was crowded here, with the scribe’s attempt to fit in his text before running out of pages further along, so no fitt number was written in. [*Oð ðæt* ‘And then’. See Mitchell and Robinson, ed. *Beowulf* (1998: 105, note to lines 1739–41).

2042 *eald æscwiga* ‘an old spear-fighter’. This is a prediction, so Beowulf cannot give (real persons’) names, but in this case he has got the man right: Old Norse legend calls the disrupter figure Starkaðr, an old Odinic mercenary in the service of Fróði and his son Ingjaldr (North 1995: 78–84).

dyre iren, þær hyne Dene slogon,
weoldon wælstowe, syððan Wiðergyld læg,
æfter hæleþa hryre, hwate Scyldungas?
Nu her þara banena byre nathwylces
frætwum hremig on flet gæð,
morðres gylpeð ond þone maðþum byreð
þone þe ðu mid rihte rædan sceoldest."

Manað swa ond myndgað mæla gehwylce
sarum wordum oð ðæt sæl cymeð
þæt se fæmnan þegn fore fæder dædum
æfter billes bite blodfag swefeð,
ealdres scyldig. Him se oðer þonan
losað lifigende, con him land geare.
Þonne bioð abrocene on ba healfe
aðsweord eorla, syððan Ingelde
weallað wælniðas ond him wiflufan
æfter cearwælmum colran weorðað.
Þy ic Heaðo-Bear[d]na hyldo ne telge,
dryhtsibbe dæl Denum unfæcne,
freondscipe fæstne.

---

to the fight where the Danes slew him, where they took
possession of the killing ground once Withergyld lay dead,
fierce Scyldings after these heroes were fallen?
Here now some boy or other of one those killers,
swaggering in adornments, walks into the hall,
boasts of the murder and bears the treasure
which you by right should have in your power."

He admonishes thus and reminds at each opportunity
with grievous words until the time comes
when for the deeds of his father, the bride's thegn
sleeps blood-stained after the bite of a blade,
forfeiting his life. From that place the other man
escapes with his life, the land he knows well.
Then there is a total breach on both sides
of gentlemen's oaths, whereupon in Ingeld
deadly enmities will well up and his wife-love
will grow cooler after these surges of care.
So I do not rate the loyalty of Heathobards,
their part, as untreacherous in a Danish alliance,
this friendship as secure.

2051 *Wiðergyld*. This name is allegorical, 'Recompense', though skilfully suffixed in *–gield* like Ingeld, as if to mark the tribe. Beowulf wants to illustrate the reason why the feud continues through its agents.

Ic sceal forð sprecan
gen ymbe Grendel þæt ðu geare cunne
sinces brytta to hwan syððan wearð
hondræs hæleða' . . .

I shall speak on,
about Grendel again, so that you clearly know,
dispenser of the treasure, where next the heroes'
unarmed combat led them' . . .

The lament of the last survivor

The ultimate in the poet's imaginative forays into the past, this passage delves into a time one thousand years before the narrative present (line 3050). That the man depositing his treasure is also the last of a kind, is a clear sign of the poet's wish to stress the glory of Beowulf and his tribe *sub specie aeternitatis* as quite insignificant. Moreover, the last survivor is also the author of a curse, an anathema that damns a grave-robber to hell. By not revealing this here, the poet might wish to put us in a category similar to that of Beowulf and the others, who have no idea of the man-traps such as this one that lie in wait for them. For the time being, the ancient's highly patterned language (Orchard 2003: 227–8) gives him out to be an intelligent man without comfort in God. Unlike the Wise Man who can see Providence in *The Wanderer*, line 107, this speaker invokes the despair of pre-Christian materialism to its fullest extent. The objects by which he measures his and his culture's merits have no future except to crumble into dust. He can see nothing more than that he will go the same way.

Orchard, A., *A Critical Companion to Beowulf* (Woodbridge, 2003)

Þær wæs swylcra fela
in ðam eorðhuse ærgestreona,
swa hy on geardagum gumena nathwylc,
eormenlafe æþelan cynnes,

There were many such
treasures of ancient times in that earth-house
as some man in days of yore, I know not who,
hid there while thinking carefully,

2067–9 Presumably Beowulf pretends to advise his uncle about the strengths and weaknesses of the Danes.

2070 *gen ymbe Grendel* 'about Grendel again'. This wording tells us that Beowulf treats his prediction as a digression, not as part of what he was supposed to be saying.

þanchycgende þær gehydde,
deore maðmas. Ealle hie deað fornam
ærran mælum, ond se an ða gen
leoda duguðe, se ðær lengest hwearf,
weard winegeomor, wende þæs ylcan,
þæt he lytel fæc longgestreona
brucan moste. Beorh eallgearo
wunode on wonge wæteryðum neah,
niwe be næsse, nearocræftum fæst.
Þær on innan bær eorlgestreona
hringa hyrde hordwyrðne dæl,
fættan goldes, fea worda cwæð:

'Heald þu nu, hruse, nu hæleð ne moston,
eorla æhte! Hwæt, hyt ær on ðe
gode begeaton. Guðdeað fornam,
feorhbealo frecne, fyra gehwylcne
leoda minra, þara ðe þis lif ofgeaf,

---

the immense bequests of a noble race,
precious objects. Death took them all
at even earlier times, and the one man still
of the tribe's veterans who moved there the longest,
keeper missing friends, he expected the same,
that but little space would he be granted to enjoy
treasures of time back yonder. A barrow all prepared
stood on a level near the waves of the deep,
new by a headland, secure with confining devices.
There a hoard-worthy share of noble treasures
and plated gold was carried inside
by the shepherd of rings, whose words were few:

'O earth, hold to you, now that heroes may not,
the possessions of noblesse! Listen, it was once in you
that good men obtained it. Death in war took them,
savage harm of lifeblood took each individual
from the men of my tribe who gave up this life,

2243 *nearocræftum fæst* 'secure with confining devices'. Locks perhaps, or intangible spells that hide the place from passers-by. The escaped slave finds the mound because he is himself trying to hide.

2245 *hringa hyrde* 'shepherd of rings'. A sterile occupation unless rings breed like sheep.

2247 *hruse* 'O earth'. Since he addresses the earth, perhaps we are encouraged to think of him worshipping the earth as a deity.

gesawon seledream. Ic nah hwa sweord wege
oððe feormie fæted wæge,
dryncfæt deore. Duguð ellor sceoc.
Sceal se hearda helm hyrsted golde
fætum befeallen, feormynd swefað,
þa ðe beadogriman bywan sceoldon,
ge swylce seo herepad, sio æt hilde gebad
ofer borda gebræc bite irena,
brosnað æfter beorne. Ne mæg byrnan hring
æfter wigfruman wide feran,
hæleðum be healfe. Næs hearpan wyn,
gomen gleobeames, ne god hafoc
geond sæl swingeð, ne se swifta mearh
burhstede beateð. Bealocwealm hafað
fela feorhcynna forð onsended!'

Swa giomormod giohðo mænde
an æfter eallum, unbliðe hwearf
dæges ond nihtes, oððæt deaðes wylm
hran æt heortan.

---

they saw palatial merriment. There is no one left to me
who may carry a sword or polish the plated vessel,
the precious drinking cup. The host moved elsewhere.
The hard helmet adorned with gold will lose
its plates as they fall away, the men who polish them
are sleeping, whose job was to maintain the battle-mask,
and likewise the war-coat which in the fighting endured
across the smash of boards the bite of iron blades,
that crumbles alongside the man. The mail-shirt
cannot travel far on its combat captain,
alongside the heroes. No joy was there of lyre-play,
pleasure of music-tree, nor does a good hawk
swing through the chamber, nor does the swift stallion
beat the building floor. Terrible execution has
sent on many mortal races that once had life!'

So sad in heart did he lament his sorrows
one man in memory of them all, unhappily moved
about by day and night, until death's surge
touched his heart.

2258 As Orchard notes (2003: 288), this line carries an internal rhyme, which links war-coat (*herepad*) with endurance (*gebad*), while the latter OE word introduces six more all alliterating on *b*.

2265 *Bealocwealm* 'Terrible execution'. This is how the speaker sees his own death: not with the guarded hopes of a believer who may hope for grace in heaven.

King Beowulf fights the Dragon

In this passage, Beowulf stands down his small elite troop on the grounds that he is stronger than they are. The question raised by this decision, how mentally competent he now is, must be a little like the suspicion the Geats seem to have of King Hrothgar as they leave, on lines 1886–7. There is also a chance that Beowulf has been seduced by the Dragon's treasure, having seen a cup from this on lines 2403–5. The fight itself is a study in heroic failure. The poet prepares us for this on line 2574.

Greenfield, S. B., 'Beowulf and the judgement of the righteous', in *Learning and Literature in Anglo-Saxon England: Studies Presented to Peter Clemoes on the Occasion of his 65th Birthday* (Cambridge, 1985), 393–407

Leyerle, J., 'Beowulf the hero and the king', *Medium Ævum* 34 (1965), 89–102

'Gebide ge on beorge   byrnum werede
secgas on searwum   hwæðer sel mæge
æfter wælræse   wunde gedygan
uncer twega.   Nis þæt eower sið
ne gemet mannes   nefne min anes
þæt he wið aglæcean   eofoðo dæle,
eorlscype efne.   Ic mid elne sceall
gold gegangan   oððe guð nimeð
feorhbealu frecne   frean eowerne!'

Aras ða bi ronde   rof oretta,
heard under helme,   hiorosercean bær
under stancleofu,   strengo getruwode
anes mannes.   Ne bið swylc earges sið!

'You may bide on the barrow armed in chained mail,
men in your panoplies, to see which one may better
after deadly combat live through his wounds
of the two of us. It is neither your mission
nor the capacity of any man except myself
to deal in strength against the monstrous enemy,
carry out a noble act. I with courage shall
get the gold, or warfare will take me,
savage harm of lifeblood take your lord!'

Arose then by shield-rim the strong champion,
hard under helmet, bore his battle shirt
in under rock-cliff, trusted in the strength
of one man. Such is no coward's mission!

2536 *gold gegangan* 'get the gold'. Is the treasure now Beowulf's first or secondary motive for facing the Dragon?

Geseah ða be wealle   se ðe worna fela,
gumcystum god,   guða gedigde,
hildehlemma,   þonne hnitan feðan,
stondan stanbogan,   stream ut þonan
brecan of beorge.   Wæs þære burnan wælm
heaðofyrum hat,   ne meahte horde neah
unbyrnende   ænige hwile
deop gedygan   for dracan lege.
Let ða of breostum,   ða he gebolgen wæs,
Weder-Geata leod   word ut faran,
stearcheort styrmde.   Stefn in becom
heaðotorht hlynnan   under harne stan.
Hete wæs onhrered,   hordweard oncniow
mannes reorde,   næs ðær mara fyrst
freode to friclan.   From ærest cwom
oruð aglæcean   ut of stane,
hat hildeswat.   Hruse dynede.

He could see along the wall, the man good in virtues
who had lived through battles in great number
and skirmishes when the foot-troops clashed,
stone arches standing, a stream out from there
breaking from the mound. The welling of that spring
was hot from deadly fires, nor could he
free of burning for any while near the hoard
venture deep and live against the dragon's flames.
Let then from his chest, now he was enraged,
the Weather-Geatish tribesman some words pass out
with toughened heart he yelled. His voice came
vault-bright reverberating in under the grey rock.
Hate had been stirred, hoard-keeper knew
it was a human voice, nor was there more time
to ask for friendship. Bold came and instantly
the monster's breath from out of the rock,
a hot sweat of battle. The ground was rumbling.

2545 *stondan stanbogan* 'stone arches standing'. Not the style of megalithic tombs, but rather that of church crypts. However, the poet does create an atmosphere.

2554–5 *hordweard oncniow mannes reorde* 'hoard-keeper knew it was a human voice'. The monster's sentience is an interest here, as it was with Grendel or his Mother earlier, but the Dragon's seems more basic, as that of an implacable enemy of man.

Biorn under beorge   bordrand onswaf
wið ðam gryregieste,   Geata dryhten.
Đa wæs hringbogan   heorte gefysed
sæcce to seceanne.   Sweord ær gebræd
god guðcyning,   gomele lafe,
ecgum unslaw,   æghwæðrum wæs
bealohycgendra   broga fram oðrum.
Stiðmod gestod   wið steapne rond
winia bealdor,   ða se wyrm gebeah
snude tosomne.   He on searwum bad.
Gewat ða byrnende   gebogen scriðan,
to gescipe scyndan.   Scyld wel gebearg
life ond lice   læssan hwile
mærum þeodne   þonne his myne sohte,
ðær he þy fyrste,   forman dogore
wealdan moste   swa him wyrd ne gescraf
hreð æt hilde.   Hond up abræd
Geata dryhten,   gryrefahne sloh
incgelafe,   þæt sio ecg gewac

The warrior beneath the barrow, lord of Geats,
swung his shield-face towards that terrible stranger.
Then was the heart of the coiled bow made keen
to seek battle. First the good king of battle
drew his sword, the ancient heirloom
no dullard in its edges, in each opponent
intending to do harm was a terror of the other.
Stern-minded he took position with shield held high,
doomed lord of friends, as the serpent curved round
swiftly in one move. In panoply he waited.
Coiled one then came sliding with burning fire,
speeding into destiny. The shield well saved
the life and body of the splendid king
for a lesser time than he found to his liking,
where for the first day in all the time of his life
he must command with fate not prescribing him
triumph in battle. His arm up he drew,
warlord of Geats, so struck the gleaming horror
with the Ing-inheritance that the edge went weak,

2559–62 This passage should be read alongside Þórr's fight with the World Serpent in Bragi's *c.* 850 *Eulogy on Ragnarr*, stanzas '14–15' (see **Gods of the Vikings**) by anyone who thinks the poet of Beowulf would understand Skaldic verse.

2570–5 This sentence inverts and extends the pronouncment on Beowulf's victory in lines 818–19.

2577 *incgelafe* 'with the Ing-inheritance'. As with Hengest's sword on line 1145, this one appears stylised as if it were Freyr's in *The Lay of Skírnir*, stanza 8 (see **Gods of the Vikings**), but at the moment of failure perhaps because it is a heathen sword.

brun on bane, bat unswiðor
þonne his ðiodcyning þearfe hæfde,
bysigum gebæded. Þa wæs beorges weard
æfter heaðuswenge on hreoum mode,
wearp wælfyre, wide sprungon
hildeleoman. Hreðsigora ne gealp
goldwine Geata, guðbill geswac,
nacod æt niðe, swa hyt no sceolde,
iren ærgod. Ne wæs þæt eðe sið,
þæt se mæra maga Ecgðeowes
grundwong þone ofgyfan wolde.
Sceolde ofer willan wic eardian
elles hwergen, swa sceal æghwylc mon
alætan lændagas. Næs ða long to ðon
þæt ða aglæcean hy eft gemetton.
Hyrte hyne hordweard (hreðer æðme weoll)
niwan stefne. Nearo ðrowode,
fyre befongen, se ðe ær folce weold.
Nealles him on heape handgesteallan
æðelinga bearn ymbe stodon
hildecystum, ac hy on holt bugon,
ealdre burgan.

---

burnished on the bone, bit less hard
than served its emperor's need, impelled
as he was by anxieties. The mound-keeper then
was in savage mood after that deadly swing,
cast murderous fire, flash sprang widely
upon war-flash. No boasts of triumphal glory
for Geats' gold-giving friend, his war-blade weakened
vulnerable in violence as it never should have,
an iron good from before. It was no easy mission
in which the renowned son of Ecgtheow
should want to give up that level ground.
Against his will he was obliged to take up abode
in some place else, as indeed every man must
abandon the days of his life. It was not long then
before the monstrous adversaries met again.
The hoard-guardian spurred himself (his chest welled
with vapour) to a second attempt. Confined in agony,
enveloped in fire, was he who once ruled his people.
In no body-ring did his hand-picked comrades,
the sons of princes, stand about him
with the virtues of war, but made for the woods
to save their lives.

2592 *ða aglæcean* 'those monstrous adversaries'. The meaning of *aglæcea* is not quite clear, but the poet may be saying something about Beowulf's appearance when enveloped in flames.

Wiglaf helps King Beowulf

The failure of Beowulf's elite troop to help him throws the success of his reign (see lines 20–5) or the loyalties of his day into doubt, yet Wiglaf is the noble exception. The following passage introduces Wiglaf as Beowulf's distant relative, and then in the first fitt in a row of four that have Wiglaf at their head. Sharing the limelight thus with Beowulf for the last 580 lines of this work, for the last fifth of *Beowulf*, Wiglaf is significant in more than the role attributed to Bǫðvarr's Hjalti in the Norse analogues.

Farrell, R. T., '*Beowulf*, Swedes and Geats', *Saga-Book of the Viking Society* 18 (1972), 227–86

Lehmann, R. P. M., 'Ecgþeow the Wægmunding: Swede or Geat?', *English Language Notes* 31.3 (1994), 1–5

Wardale, E. E., '*Beowulf*: the nationality of Ecgþeow', *Modern Language Review* 24 (1929), 322

Hiora in anum weoll
sefa wið sorgum. Sibb' æfre ne mæg
wiht onwendan þam ðe wel þenceð.

XXXVI Wiglaf wæs haten, Weoxstanes sunu,
leoflic lindwiga, leod Scylfinga,
mæg Ælfheres. Geseah his mondryhten
under heregriman hat þrowian.
Gemunde ða ða are, þe he him ær forgeaf,

In one of them welled up
common sense with sorrows. Nothing can ever in any way
change kinship in the man who thinks straight.

XXXVI Wiglaf he was called, son of Weohstan,
admirable shield warrior, prince of Scylfings,
kinsman of Ælfhere. He saw his man and lord
enduring hot agony beneath his war mask.
He recalled then the favours he once gave him,

2601 The kinship of this unknown with Beowulf is emphasised even before we learn of Wiglaf's details in the next fitt.

2602 Weohstan has a named analogue (Vésteinn of the Swedes), unlike his son whose name is found nowhere except in early English history and charters. The leading example of a historical Wiglaf, successor to a Ludeca who ruled with Beornwulf, was king of Mercia in 827–9 and again in 830–9. For an attempt to date *Beowulf* (to 826–7) on the basis of this history, see North (2006).

2603–4 *leod Scylfinga* 'prince of Scylfings' etc. Wiglaf is a Swede, but on his mother's side. His father is a Wægmunding. The name Ælfhere looks Swedish, with the initial vowel alliteration and *-here* suffix of Ohthere, father of Eadgils and Eanmund. It seems likely that Ælfhere is Wiglaf's mother's brother.

wicstede weligne Wægmundinga,
folcrihta gehwylc, swa his fæder ahte.
Ne mihte ða forhabban, hond rond gefeng,
geolwe linde, gomel swurd geteah.
Þæt wæs mid eldum Eanmundes laf,
suna Ohthere[s]. Þam æt sæcce wearð
wræccan wineleasum Weohstan bana
meces ecgum ond his magum ætbær
brunfagne helm, hringde byrnan,
ealdsweord etonisc. Þæt him Onela forgeaf,
his gædelinges guðgewædu,
fyrdsearo fuslic. No ymbe ða fæhðe spræc,
þeah ðe he his broðor bearn abredwade.
He [ða] frætwe geheold fela missera,
bill ond byrnan, oð ðæt his byre mihte
eorlscipe efnan swa his ærfæder.
Geaf him ða mid Geatum guðgewæda,
æghwæs unrim, þa he of ealdre gewat
frod on forðweg. Þa wæs forma sið

---

the wealthy estate of the Wægmundings,
each tribal entitlement his father had had.
He could not then hold back, one hand grabbed shield,
the yellow linden-board, another drew his old sword.
That was among men the legacy of Eanmund,
Ohthere's son. This man in conflict,
a friendless exile, was killed by Weohstan
by edge of blade, who presented next of kin
with bloody burnished helmet, shirt of chained mail,
ancient sword of giant make. This Onela gave him,
with his kinsman's battle-dress, his ready
panoply of campaign. Never did he talk of feud,
though Weohstan struck down his brother's son.
He then held this gear for many seasons,
blade and mail-shirt, until his own boy could
carry out nobility like his father before him.
Weohstan then gave Wiglaf the panoply in Geatland,
everything in countless supply, when he passed from life
wise on the way hence. This was now the first time

2611 Rebels against their uncle King Onela, Eadgils and Eanmund are taken in by Heardred, Hygelac's son, who pays for this decision with his life when Onela comes after them. Weohstan then fights for Onela and kills Eanmund, keeping the dead man's weapons and passing these on to Wiglaf. For a suggstion that 'Eanmund' is also the name of the poet of *Beowulf*, with this line as his aural signature, see North (2006: 321–31).

geongan cempan   þæt he guðe ræs
mid his freodryhtne   fremman sceolde.
Ne gemealt him se modsefa,   ne his mæg*es* laf
gewac æt wige.   Þæt se wyrm onfand
syððan hie togædre   gegan hæfdon!

Wiglaf maðelode, wordrihta fela
sægde gesiðum   (him wæs geomor sefa):
'Ic ðæt mæl geman   þær we medu þegon,
þonne we geheton   ussum hlaforde
in biorsele   ðe us ðas beagas geaf
þæt we him ða guðgetawa   gyldan woldon,
gif him þyslicu   þearf gelumpe,
helmas ond heard sweord.   Đe he usic on herge geceas
to ðyssum siðfate   sylfes willum,
onmunde usic mærða   ond me þas maðmas geaf,
þe he usic garwigend   gode tealde,
hwate helmberend,   þeah ðe hlaford us
þis ellenweorc   ana aðohte
to gefremmanne   folces hyrde,

---

the young champion was going to join battle
in armed combat alongside his liberal lord.
Neither did his mind melt, nor his father's heirloom
go weak on him in battle. This the serpent found
once the two of them had come together!

Wiglaf spoke, many were the duties he spelled out
in words to his companions (his heart was sad):
'I recall the occasion when we consumed mead,
when we made vows to this our lord
in the beerhall, to him who gave us those rings,
that we would repay him for that war-gear
if any need of this kind should befall him,
for helmets and hard swords. That is why he chose us
for his outfit on this raid, of his own free will,
considered us good for the deed, and why he gave me
these objects, because he rated us good spearmen,
sharp men in helmets, even if this lord of ours,
shepherd of the people, decided to carry out
this deed of courage completely on his own,

2630 Wiglaf's pause for a 28-line speech is a necessary act of dramatic licence.

2633 *þær we medu þegon* 'when we consumed mead'. These words may be compared with Ælfwine's in *The Battle of Maldon*, line 211 (see **Viking Wars**).

2642–4 Wiglaf is critical of Beowulf's decision to fight alone, not only here but also in his epitaph for the king on lines 3079–83.

for ðam he manna mæst   mærða gefremede,
dæda dollicra.   Nu is se dæg cumen
þæt ure mandryhten   mægenes behofað
godra guðrinca.   Wutun gongan to,
helpan hildfruman   þenden hyt sy
gledegesa grim!   God wat on mec
þæt me is micle leofre   þæt minne lichaman
mid minne goldgyfan   gled fæðmie!
Ne þynceð me gerysne   þæt we rondas beren
eft to earde   nemne we æror mægen
fane gefyllan,   feorh ealgian
Wedra ðeodnes.   Ic wat geare
þæt næron ealdgewyrht   þæt he ana scyle
Geata duguðe   gnorn þrowian,
gesigan æt sæcce.   Urum sceal sweord ond helm,
byrne ond b*ea*duscrud   bam gemæne!'

Wod þa þurh þone wælrec,   wigheafolan bær
frean on fultum,   fea worda cwæð:
'Leofa Biowulf,   læst eall tela,
swa ðu on geoguðfeore   geara gecwæde

---

for he has carried out glory which in all others
would be acts of folly. Now is the day come
that our man and lord needs the strength
of good fighting men. Let us go to,
help the war-captain for as long as the grim
fiery terror may last! God knows in me,
that rather than run I would have the blaze
embrace my body as well as my gold-giver!
It does not seem right to me that we should carry shields
back to our country unless first of all we can
fell down our foe, protect the lifeblood
of the king of Weather-Geats. I readily know
that his deeds of old were not such that he alone
of the Geatish brigade should suffer agony,
sink down in battle. Both of us shall share
sword and helmet, mail-shirt and battle-shroud!'

He waded then through the deadly smoke,
gave his king cover, spoke a few words:
'Beloved Beowulf, do it all magnificently,
just as long ago in your youth you said

2646 *dæda dollicra* 'acts of folly'. An acknowledgement of Beowulf's superhuman strength in the past.

þæt ðu ne alæte   be ðe lifigendum
dom gedreosan.   Scealt nu dædum rof,
æðeling anhydig,   ealle mægene
feorh ealgian;   ic ðe fullæstu!'

Æfter ðam wordum   wyrm yrre cwom,
atol inwitgæst,   oðre siðe
fyrwylmum fah   fionda niosian,
laðra manna.   Ligyðum for.
Born bord wið rond,   byrne ne meahte
geongum garwigan   geoce gefremman,
ac se maga geonga   under his mæges scyld
elne geeode,   þa his agen wæs
gledum forgrunden.   Þa gen guðcyning
mærða gemunde,   mægenstrengo sloh
hildebille,   þæt hyt on heafolan stod
niþe genyded.   Nægling forbærst,
geswac æt sæcce   sweord Biowulfes,
gomol ond grægmæl.   Him þæt gifeðe ne wæs
þæt him irenna   ecge mihton

---

that as long as you still lived you would not let
your reputation perish. Now brave in your deeds,
prince of faultless purpose, you must defend your life
with all vigour. I will help you!'

After these words, the serpent came in wrath,
terrifying malign spirit, for the second time,
stained black with its welling flames to spy out
its hated human enemies. In waves of fire it moved.
Shield-board charred to rim, mail-shirt could not
extend assistance to the young spear-fighter,
but the young lad under his kinsman's shield
performed acts of courage, since his own was
incinerated by the blaze. Still then the war-king
remembered his glories, with main strength struck
with his war-blade so that it stood in the head
by hatred driven in. Nægling shattered,
Beowulf's sword went weak in combat,
old and patterned grey. It was not to be granted
that the edges of his iron blade could

2665–6 *ðu ne alæte dom gedreosan* 'would not let your reputation perish'. This may be Beowulf's main motive, above the practical, for facing the Dragon single-handed. Or it may be Wiglaf's understanding of his old king's motive.

helpan æt hilde.   Wæs sio hond to strong,
se ðe meca gehwane,   mine gefræge,
swenge ofersohte,   þonne he to sæcce bær
wæpen wundrum heard.   Næs him wihte ðe sel.

Þa wæs þeodsceaða   þriddan siðe,
frecne fyrdraca,   fæhða gemyndig,
ræsde on ðone rofan,   þa him rum ageald,
hat ond heaðogrim,   heals ealne ymbefeng
biteran banum.   He geblodegod wearð
sawuldriore,   swat yðum weoll.

XXXVII Ða ic æt þearfe gefrægn   þeodcyninges
andlongne eorl   ellen cyðan,
cræft ond cenðu,   swa him gecynde wæs.
Ne hedde he þæs heafolan,   ac sio hand gebarn
modiges mannes,   þær he his mæges healp,
þæt he þone niðgæst   nioðor hwene sloh,
secg on searwum,   þæt ðæt sweord gedeaf,
fah ond fæted,   þæt ðæt fyr ongon

---

help him in battle. The hand was too strong
which overtaxed, from what I have heard,
any blade in the blow, when to strife he bore
the weapon wondrously hard. It did not help him.

Then the huge assailant, dangerous firedrake
mindful of its feuds, for the third time
raced at the strong man when time allowed,
white-hot and warlike fierce, clamped his whole neck
with teeth biting sharp. The man was bloodied
with heart's dark blood, his gore welled in waves.

XXXVII Then, I have heard that in the great king's need
his upright nobleman made known his courage,
strength and bravery, as befitted the kin they had in common.
He did not hide his head, but the brave man's
hand burned where this man in armour
helped his kinsman by striking the hostile demon
somewhere further down, so that the sword plunged,
bloody and ornamented and made the fire

2696 *swa him gecynde wæs* 'as befitted the kin they had in common'. Meanings of kindred and nature (Middle English *kynde*) are fused in *gecynde* here, with the assumption that aristocracy produces courage. Once again, however, the poet is keen to show that Wiglaf is related to Beowulf.

sweðrian syððan. Þa gen sylf cyning
geweold his gewitte, wællseaxe gebræd
biter ond beaduscearp, þæt he on byrnan wæg.
Forwrat Wedra helm wyrm on middan.
Feond gefyldan (ferh ellen wræc),
ond hi hyne þa begen abroten hæfdon,
sibæðelingas. Swylc sceolde secg wesan,
þegn æt ðearfe! Þæt ðam þeodne wæs
siðast sigehwila sylfes dædum,
worlde geweorces.

---

thereafter begin to cease. The king himself then still
mastered his wits, drew a deadly knife,
bitter and battle-sharp, which he carried on his coat of mail.
The shelter of Weather-Geats carved the serpent in half.
They felled the fiend (courage drove out its life)
and by then, they had both destroyed him,
these kindred princes. So should a man be,
a thegn at need! For the king that was
the last moment of victory which came from his deeds,
his last work in the world.

History related: the rise of Hygelac

The following is taken from the speech of the unnamed Geatish Messenger, who tells his people of their king's death. The poet uses the Messenger to reflect on the tribal doom that follows. The more the Messenger says, the further back in time he goes in search of causes for the present calamity. It is perhaps characteristic of the poet's chronological daring that he relates Hygelac's glorious beginning here, near the end; whereas he first gave us the end of Hygelac's life in lines 1202–14, closer to the beginning of the poem. Both digressions are proofs of Hygelac's prodigality and his constant need to replenish this. What starts with the great (heathen) treasure of Uppsala in his case will end (or has ended) with ignominy under a shield on the mouth of the Rhine. Moreover, there is an indication in the hypermetric sequence below, the third and last in the poem, that Hygelac dispossessed Weohstan, Wiglaf's father, of his lands in order to reward Wulf and Eofor.

Green, A., 'An episode in Ongentheow's fall (*Beowulf* ll. 2957–2960)', *Modern Language Review* 12 (1917), 340–3

2708 *sibæðelingas* 'kindred princes'. See the above note. [*Swylc sceolde secg wesan* 'So should a man be'. Praise for a man who fights like Wiglaf, or praise for Wiglaf? In all events, the poet seems to expect a lot from warriors of his day.

'Ne ic to Sweoðeode   sibbe oððe treowe
wihte ne wene,   ac wæs wide cuð
þætte Ongenðio   ealdre besnyðede
Hæðcen Hreþling   wið Hrefnawudu,
þa for onmedlan   ærest gesohton
Geata leode   guð-Scilfingas.
Sona him se froda   fæder Ohtheres,
eald ond egesfull,   ondslyht ageaf,
abreot brimwisan,   bryd ahredde,
gomela iomeowlan   golde berofene,
Onelan modor   ond Ohtheres,
ond ða folgode   feorhgeniðlan,
oððæt hi oðeodon   earfoðlice
in Hrefnesholt   hlafordlease.
Besæt ða sinherge   sweorda lafe,
wundum werge,   wean oft gehet
earmre teohhe   ondlonge niht,
cwæð, he on mergenne   meces ecgum
getan wolde,   sum on galgtreowum

'Neither peace nor pledge from the Swedes do I have
the slightest reason to expect, for it is common knowledge
that Ongentheow snipped short the life-span
of Hæthcyn son of Hrethel at Ravens' Wood,
when, in their presumption, Geatish tribesmen
were the first to attack the battle-Scylfings.
Straightaway did Ohthere's experienced father,
ancient and terrifying, hand down the onslaught,
wiped out the sea-captain, rescued his bride,
his old lady once a girl, despoiled of gold,
Onela's mother and also Ohthere's,
and then pursued his mortal enemies
until with great hardship they escaped
into Raven's Woodland without a lord.
With standing army he besieged the leavings of swords,
by their wounds made weary, woe often promised
to that wretched parcel the livelong night,
said that in the morning with sword's edge
he would cut them open, some on gallows-trees

2926 *for onmedlan* 'in their presumption'. The whole tribe appears to be blamed for this early version of *desmesure* 'lack of measure'. The Messenger's term resembles *for wlenco* 'though pride', which the poet uses of Hygelac himself on line 1206. The Geats under the foolish Hæthcyn, Hrethel's son, kidnap the Swedish queen for a ransom. Here we have the poet's third allusion to the Swedish wars in *Beowulf*, with an account of the first one.

2940 *getan wolde* 'would cut them open'. Not only an Odinic frame of reference, with the gallows, but a sacrificial aspect is given to this line with *getan* 'to make pour', which the old Ongentheow sardonically promises to his *Geatas* here.

[fuglum] to gamene. Frofor eft gelamp
sarigmodum somod ærdæge,
syððan hie Hygelaces horn ond byman,
gealdor ongeaton, þa se goda com
leoda dugoðe on last faran.

XLI Wæs sio swatswaðu Sweona ond Geata,
wælræs weora wide gesyne,
hu ða folc mid him fæhðe towehton.
Gewat him ða se goda mid his gædelingum,
frod, felageomor, fæsten secean,
eorl Ongenþio, ufor oncirde;
hæfde Higelaces hilde gefrunen,
wlonces wigcræft, wiðres ne truwode,
þæt he sæmannum onsacan mihte,
heaðoliðendum hord forstandan,
bearn ond bryde, beah eft þonan
eald under eorðweall. Þa wæs æht boden

---

as fun [for the birds]. Solace once more arrived
for the anxious minded gathered in early day
when they made out the magic of Hygelac's
horn and trumpets, when the generous one
came marching in the rear of his tribesmen's brigade.

XLI That swathe of blood of Swedes and Geats,
the death-charge of men, was widely to be seen,
how those peoples had worked out the feud between them.
With his troops the generous one pulled back then,
wise, much saddened, to find his fortress,
nobleman Ongentheow moved further away,
had heard of Hygelac's ability in warfare,
tactics of this dashing one, trusted in no resistance
by which he then could attack the seamen,
stand up for his hoard, his son and bride
against warring seafarers, so moved higher up,
old under earthwall. Then the prize was advertised,

2944 *gealdor ongeaton* 'made out the magic' etc. Probably drums as well as trumpets are assigned to the charismatic Hygelac, whose first entry into history is also his most glorious. The poet wants Hygelac as a latter-day Heremod of the Geats.

2945 Hygelac is Hrethel's youngest son and so comes with reinforcements after his brother's defeat.

2954 *sæmannum* 'seamen'. The Geats, whose passage to Sweden is partly over large inland waters (of Vänern and Vättern).

Sweona leodum, segn Higelace[s]
freoðowong þone forð ofereodon,
syððan Hreðlingas to hagan þrungon.
Þær wearð Ongenðiow ecgum sweorda,
blondenfexa, on bid wrecen,
þæt se þeodcyning ðafian sceolde
Eafores anne dom. Hyne yrringa
Wulf Wonreding wæpne geræhte,
þæt him for swenge swat ædrum sprong
forð under fexe. Næs he forht swa ðeh,
gomela Scilfing, ac forgeald hraðe
wyrsan wrixle wælhlem þone,
syððan ðeodcyning þyder oncirde.
Ne meahte se snella sunu Wonredes
ealdum ceorle ondslyht giofan,
ac he him on heafde helm ær gescer,
þæt he blode fah bugan sceolde,
feoll on foldan. Næs he fæge þa git,

---

from Swedish tribesmen, Hygelac's standards
moved straight across that sacred ground,
when Hrethel's people drove him into his lair.
There was Ongentheow with sword-blades,
grey-haired man, driven into a corner
so that the great king was obliged to consent
to Eofor's only judgement. Him did Wulf
son of Wonred smite wrathfully with his weapon,
that for that swing the blood in his veins sprang
from under his hair. Nor did that scare him, however,
the old Scylfing, but rapidly he repaid
the deadly crack with a worse exchange,
the nation's king, once he got to his feet.
Nor could the valiant son of Wonred
give onslaught to the ancient carl,
for sooner this one sheared the helmet on his head
so that covered in blood he had to crouch,
fell to the ground. Nor was the Swede as yet a goner,

2958 *segn Higelace[s]* 'Hygelac's standards'. The meaning of this line is problematic (Green 1917), but the Swedish treasure is probably to be seen in the *æht* 'prize', which Hygelac announces to his troops.

2959 *freoðowong þone* 'that sacred ground'. OE *freoðo* 'treaty' suggests a religious sanctuary here such as we might expect in Uppsala from Adam of Bremen's later reference to Uppsala as the site of a major temple (North 1997: 100–1).

2962 *on bid wrecen* 'driven into a corner'. Like an animal at bay, although Ongentheow's assailants have the names 'wolf' and 'boar'. The following fight is ferocious enough for animals.

ac he hyne gewyrpte, þeah ðe him wund hrine.
Let se hearda Higelaces þegn
bradne mece, þa his broðor læg,
eald sweord eotonisc, entiscne helm
brecan ofer bordweal. Ða gebeah cyning,
folces hyrde, wæs in feorh dropen.
Ða wæron monige þe his mæg wriðon,
ricone arærdon, ða him gerymed wearð
þæt hie wælstowe wealdan moston.
Þenden reafode rinc oðerne,
nam on Ongenðio irenbyrnan,
heard swyrd hilted ond his helm somod,
hares hyrste Higelace bær.
He ðam frætwum feng ond him fægre gehet
leana mid leodum, ond gelæste swa.
Geald þone guðræs Geata dryhten,
Hreðles eafora, þa he to ham becom,
Iofore ond Wulfe mid ofermaðmum,
sealde hiora gehwæðrum hund þusenda

---

but had recovered, though the wound touched him,
Then the hardened thegn of Hygelac let
his broadsword, an old blade of giant make,
now his brother lay there, split the Swede's titan helmet
over the wall of his shield. Knelt then the king,
guardian of his people, had been mortally hit.
Then there were many who bandaged Eofor's kinsman,
raised up the powerful man, when they had the space
once they might possess the killing ground.
While one warrior was despoiling the other,
Eofor took from Ongentheow his iron coat of mail,
the hard hilted sword together with his helmet,
the greyhair's harness he carried to Hygelac.
He received those treasures and in fair language
promised them tribal rewards and performed it thus.
The lord of Geats, Hrethel's heir, rewarded
that war-charge when he came to his home-seat
with an excess of treasure for Eofor and Wulf,
gave each of them one hundred and twenty thousand

2993 *mid ofermaðmum* 'with an excess of treasure'. There is no other instance of this word, which seems thus coined in order to show a streak of prodigality in young Hygelac.

landes ond locenra beaga (ne ðorfte him ða lean oðwitan
mon on middangearde syððan hie ða mærða geslogon),
ond ða Iofore forgeaf angan dohtor,
hamweorðunge, hyldo to wedde.'

---

in land and linked rings (nor need any man in the Middle World begrudge
them that reward, since they had won those glories by fighting for them)
and then he gave Eofor his only daughter
as an ennobler of his estate, as a pledge of his loyalty.'

King Beowulf's funeral

To say the end of *Beowulf* is morally complicated is to begin to acknowledge the baroque skill of its poet, who has planted doubts about the hero's motivations at intervals from the moment we see Beowulf studying the stolen cup. Perhaps we should ask whether Beowulf was tempted by this gold. The Dragon, who guards but does not own it, has flown out and set fire to Geatland, so surely must be stopped, except that Wiglaf tells us that he and Beowulf's other advisers urged him not to go (lines 3079–83). If the Dragon were to stop eventually, it is not clear why Beowulf should still wish to face him. Nor is it clear whether he stands down his guards to win renown or the gold for himself (lines 2535–6). Perhaps he really meant this gold to be for his people, as he later says (lines 2797–8). However, his people do not want it. That they bury it all back with him without more ado, as if sending him to the dead in imperial style, darkens the picture further. The treasure is cursed and will send its robber to hell; Beowulf is the man who has robbed it, and so Beowulf will be in yet more danger of hell than his paganism allows. These questions disturb the mood of Beowulf's funeral. Doubtless the poet would like us to remember King Hrothgar's warning to Beowulf against pride some 50 years earlier. The deepest question here is whether Beowulf understood the old man about *ece rædas* 'eternal rewards' on line 1760. That arrow shot by the devil while Conscience lies sleeping – could that be the poet's meaning in the imagery of Wiglaf's final epitaph below?

Bliss, A. J., '*Beowulf* lines 3074–3075', in *J. R. R. Tolkien, Scholar and Storyteller*, ed. M. Salu and R. T. Farrell (Ithaca, NY, 1979), 41–63

Gretsch, M., *The Intellectual Foundations of the English Benedictine Reform*, Cambridge Studies in Anglo-Saxon England 25 (Cambridge, 1999)

Smithers, G. V., 'Five notes on Old English texts', *English and Germanic Studies* 4 (1951–2), 65–85

Stanley, E. G., 'Hæthenra Hyht in *Beowulf*', in *Studies in Old English Literature in Honour of Arthur G. Brodeur*, ed. S. B. Greenfield (New York, 1963), 136–51; repr. in E. G. Stanley, *A Collection of Papers* (Toronto, 1987), 192–208

2995–6 These hypermetric lines are evasive, but imply that some people did begrudge the champions their reward; that their new great tracts of land have come at the price of dispossessing other nobles; and that Weohstan leaves the Geats at this point, to take service with the Swedes, as a man dispossessed by Hygelac.

XLII Þa wæs gesyne, þæt se sið ne ðah
þam ðe unrihte inne gehydde
wræte under wealle, weard ær ofsloh
feara sumne, þa sio fæhð gewearð
gewrecen wraðlice. Wundur hwar þonne
eorl ellenrof ende gefere
lifgesceafta þonne leng ne mæg
mon mid his magum meduseld buan.
Swa wæs Biowulfe þa he biorges weard
sohte searoniðas, seolfa ne cuðe
þurh hwæt his worulde gedal weorðan sceolde.
Swa hit oð domes dæg diope benemdon
þeodnas mære, þa ðæt þær dydon,
þæt se secg wære synnum scildig
hergum geheaðerod hellbendum fæst
wommum gewitnad se ðone wong strude;

XLII Then it was clear the adventure had brought no gain
to him who unlawfully kept those treasures hidden
inside beneath the wall. Their guardian, however,
by the time the feud was savagely avenged, had slain
a man more distinguished than any other. It is a wonder where
a courageous warrior may reach the end of his life
predestined, when he, a man, may no longer
inhabit the mead-building with his kinsmen.
So it was with Beowulf, when he sought the barrow's guardian,
sought cunning enmities. He himself did not know
how his parting from the world should come about.
So the renowned princes who put it there
solemnly declared that until the Day of Judgement
that man would be guilty of crimes,
closed up in heathen shrines, firmly bound in the bonds of hell,
punished with defilements, who plundered this place.

3059 *þam ðe unrihte inne gehydde* 'to him who unlawfully kept hidden inside'. This is ambiguous about the concealer, whether the Dragon or the man who, having laid the gold in the ground, has now lost it to Geatish plunderers. The law in question must accord with Christian custom, which would not approve of wealth if hoarded for its own sake.

3062 *Wundur* 'a wonder'. Something not to be foreseen by the likes of us, the manner in which a man leaves the world. The poet comments with more humour on human foresight on lines 1059–60.

3063–5 This euphemism for dying repeats one earlier for Beowulf in lines 2589–91.

3067 *sohte searoniðas* 'sought cunning enmities'. The same expression is used by Beowulf himself, who flatly denies seeking these in his last speech, on line 2738. The poet's version is the one to trust.

3069–73 The poet's first intimation of the hoard's Pharaonic curse.

næs he goldhwæte   gearwor hæfde
agendes est   ær gesceawod.

Wiglaf maðelode,   Wihstanes sunu:
'Oft sceall eorl monig   anes willan
wræc adreogan,   swa us geworden is.
Ne meahton we gelæran   leofne þeoden,
rices hyrde   ræd ænigne,
þæt he ne grette   goldweard þone,
lete hyne licgean   þær he longe wæs,
wicum wunian   oð woruldende;
heoldon heahsceap.   Hord ys gesceawod,
grimme gegongen.   Wæs se gifeðe to swið,
þe ðone [þeodcyning]   þyder ontyhte.
Ic wæs þær inne   ond þæt eall geondseh,
recedes geatwa,   þa me gerymed wæs,
nealles swæslice   sið alyfed

Not once before this time had he been more prepared
to see an owner's gold-bestowing favour.

Wiglaf spoke, the son of Weohstan:
'Often through the will of one man must many a nobleman
endure exile, as has happened to us now.
Nor could we teach the beloved chief,
shepherd of the commonwealth, with any counsel,
not to approach that gold guardian,
but to let him lie where he had long been,
inhabit his place until the end of the world.
They held to a high destiny; the hoard has been seen,
fiercely won as it was; that fate was too powerful
which impelled [the king of the people] to go there.
I was inside there and surveyed it all,
riches of the house, when the way was cleared for me,
though not at all gently was I granted entry

3074–5 A *locus desperatus* 'desperate place' in literary criticism, if only because most critics will not have their Beowulf potentially damned. Smithers (1951–2: 75–80) solves *goldhwæte* as 'gold-bestowing', placing this with *est* 'favour'. Bliss (1979: 53–4) tries to make *agend* 'owner' into a term for God, but heathen gold is unlikely to be the favour of God. Stanley keeps his bets open (1963: 145), allowing for God in *agend* but also acknowledging this word's more likely temporal sense. So in short, it looks as if the poet has come clean about Beowulf's love of treasure, increased as it is by old age. For a heathen like Beowulf, rather than Hrothgar, this treasure is an accident waiting to happen.

3084 *heoldon heahsceap* 'They held to a high destiny'. This is probably better than *heold on heahsceap* 'he held to a high destiny', or *heoldon* [for *healdan*] *heahsceap* '(leave the Dragon) to hold to his high destiny'. Wiglaf's point is that Beowulf and the Dragon were predestined to meet.

inn under eorðweall. Ic on ofoste gefeng
micle mid mundum mægenbyrðenne
hordgestreona, hider ut ætbær
cyninge minum. Cwico wæs þa gena,
wis ond gewittig. Worn eall gespræc
gomol on gehðo ond eowic gretan het,
bæd þæt ge geworhton æfter wines dædum
in bælstede beorh þone hean,
micelne ond mærne, swa he manna wæs
wigend weorðfullost wide geond eorðan,
þenden he burhwelan brucan moste.
Uton nu efstan oðre [siðe]
seon ond secean searo[gimma] geþræc,
wundur under wealle. Ic eow wisige,
þæt ge genoge neon sceawiað
beagas ond brad gold. Sie sio bær gearo,
ædre geæfned, þonne we ut cymen,
ond þonne geferian frean userne,
leofne mannan, þær he longe sceal
on ðæs Waldendes wære geþolian.'

---

in under the earth-wall. In haste I took
great hold in my arms of the main load
of hoard-treasures, carried them out here
to my king. Living was he still at that time,
conscious and clear in mind. Many things
did the old man say all in grief, and ordered me to greet you,
commanding that you build the high barrow,
in memory of your friend's deeds, in the place of the pyre,
as big a barrow and splendid, as surely he was of all men
the most honoured fighter far throughout the earth
while he was permitted to enjoy the wealth of his citadel.
Let us now hasten a second [time]
to seek out and see the pile of cunningly wrought [gems],
a wonder beneath the wall. I will guide you
so that you see at close hand sufficient quantity
of rings and massive gold. Let that pyre be prepared,
swiftly appointed for when we come out,
and then let us bring our lord,
the beloved man, to where he shall long
endure in the keeping of the Lord.'

3108–9 *longe on ðæs Waldendes wære geþolian* 'long endure in the keeping of the Lord'. The language resembles that of Christian sermons. With this moral translation of Wiglaf's untutored belief-system, the poet gives his young hero the unwitting vision of Beowulf in hell, figuratively waiting for rescue like *þam þe þær bryne þolodan* 'those who suffering burning there', Adam and Eve before the harrowing in *The Dream of the Rood*, line 149 (see **Poems of Devotion**).

Het ða gebeodan byre Wihstanes,
hæle hildedior, hæleða monegum,
boldagendra, þæt hie bælwudu
feorran feredon, folcagende,
godum togenes: 'Nu sceal gled fretan,
weaxan wonna leg, wigena strengel
þone ðe oft gebad isernscure
þonne stræla storm strengum gebæded
scoc ofer scildweall, sceft nytte heold
fæðergearwum fus, flane fulleode'.

Huru se snotra sunu Wihstanes
acigde of corðre cyninges þegnas
syfone tosomne, þa selestan,
eode eahta sum under inwithrof
hilderinca. Sum on handa bær
æledleoman, se ðe on orde geong.
Næs ða on hlytme hwa þæt hord strude,
syððan orwearde ænigne dæl
secgas gesegon on sele wunian,
læne licgan. Lyt ænig mearn

Then Weohstan's boy, a hero brave in battle,
bade them announce to many warriors
and owners of homesteads that tribal leaders
should bring pyre-wood from afar, converging
on the generous man: 'Now fire must consume,
the dark flame engulf, the ruler of men
who often endured showers of iron
when a storm of arrows propelled by bowstrings
passed over shieldwall, when arrow-shaft made itself useful,
hastening with feather-gear assisted the arrow-head.'

Indeed the clever son of Weohstan
called from the guard the king's thegns
seven together, men the highest ranking,
himself the eighth warrior walked with them
under the malign roof. One in his hand bore
a kindled light he who walked in the lead.
There was no allotting who should plunder the hoard
when without their keeper the men could see
just any part of it inhabiting the chamber,
lying there on loan. Little did any mourn

3115–19 Wiglaf's image of flames and arrows captures, again without his knowing it, Hrothgar's of the devil shooting a fiery arrow of temptation past the guard of sleeping Conscience, on lines 1744–6. Wiglaf thus seems to have more in common with Hrothgar than Beowulf ever did.

þæt hi ofostlice   ut geferedon
dyre maðmas.   Dracan ec scufun,
wyrm ofer weallclif,   leton weg niman,
flod fæðmian   frætwa hyrde.
Þa wæs wunden gold   on wæn hladen,
æghwæs unrim,   æþeling boren,
har hilderinc   to Hronesnæsse.

XLIII Him ða gegiredan   Geata leode
ad on eorðan   unwaclicne,
helmum behongen,   hildebordum,
beorhtum byrnum,   swa he bena wæs.
Alegdon ða tomiddes   mærne þeoden
hæleð hiofende,   hlaford leofne.
Ongunnon þa on beorge   bælfyra mæst
wigend weccan,   wudurec astah,
sweart ofer swioðole,   swogende leg
wope bewunden   (windblond gelæg),
oðþæt he ða banhus   gebrocen hæfde,
hat on hreðre.   Higum unrote
modceare mændon,   mondryhtnes cwealm.

---

the haste with which they ferried out
these costly objects. The Dragon too they shoved,
serpent, over the cliff wall, let the wave take him,
the flood envelop the treasure's guardian.
Then was the twisted gold loaded on a wagon,
all in countless quantity, the chieftain laid in,
grey warrior borne in state to Whale's Ness.

XLIII For him then the Geatish tribesmen prepared
a pyre on earth of no mean stature,
hung about with helmets, war-boards,
bright-glinting mailcoats, as was his request.
In the midst of it the grieving heroes laid
their renowned king, their beloved lord.
On a mound then men at arms began to coax
the biggest bonfire. The wood smoke climbed,
black over the blaze, roaring flame
encircled by weeping (buffeting wind lay still),
until it had broken up the bone-house,
burned hot in the body. Men unhappy in mind
bewailed the care of their hearts, the killing of their lord.

3140 *swa he bena wæs* 'as was his request'. The poet is not clear on this, but it is possible that Beowulf is understood to have asked for the hoard to accompany him to his final resting place.

Swylce giomorgyd [Geatisc] meowle
æfter Beowulf bundenheorde
song sorgcearig swiðe geneahhe
þæt hio hyre heofungdagas hearde ondrede,
wælfylla worn, werudes egesan,
hynðo ond hæftnyd. Heofon rece swealg.
Geworhton ða Wedra leode
hleo on hoe, se wæs heah ond brad,
wægliðendum wide gesyne,
ond betimbredon on tyn dagum
beadurofes becn, bronda lafe
wealle beworhton, swa hyt weorðlicost
foresnotre men findan mihton.
Hi on beorg dydon beg ond siglu,
eall swylce hyrsta, swylce on horde ær
niðhedige men genumen hæfdon,
forleton eorla gestreon eorðan healdan,
gold on greote, þær hit nu gen lifað
eldum swa unnyt swa hit æror wæs.
Þa ymbe hlæw riodan hildediore,

Likewise a mournful dirge in Beowulf's memory
a [Geatish] lady with her hair bound up
sorrowing most constantly sang,
of dreading for herself cruel days of grief,
mass killings in number, fearing battalions,
humiliation and captivity. Heaven swallowed the smoke.
Weather-Geatish tribesmen then built
a shelter on the spur which was high and broad,
one widely visible to travellers on the wave,
and in ten days they carpentered a beacon
for the war-champion, around firebrand remnants
built him a wall, in the most prestigious way
the men of highest intellect could find.
In the barrow they put necklaces and jewels,
all such trappings as in the hoard before
the men disposed to warfare had seized,
let the earth keep the treasures of nobility,
gold in the ground where now it lives still
as useless to mankind as it was long before.
Then around the mound rode the daring in war,

3150 *[Geatisc] meowle* '[Geatish] lady'. Presumably Beowulf's concubine, unless he stayed single. Her lack of queenly status would pose no problem, for some Mercian kings before Offa (ruled 757–96) took women only as concubines for entirely political reasons.

3168 *eldum swa unnyt* 'as useless to mankind' etc. Gold must be circulated.

æþelinga bearn, ealra twelfe,
woldon ceare cwiðan ond kyning mænan,
wordgyd wrecan ond ymb wer sprecan;
eahtodan eorlscipe ond his ellenweorc
duguðum demdon. Swa hit gedefe bið
þæt mon his winedryhten wordum herge,
ferhðum freoge, þonne he forð scile
of lichaman læded weorðan.
Swa begnornodon Geata leode
hlafordes hryre, heorðgeneatas,
cwædon þæt he wære wyruldcyninga
manna mildust ond monðwærust,
leodum liðost ond lofgeornost.

---

sons of princes, twelve of them in all,
wished to pronounce their care and lament the king,
recite a dirge in words and speak about the man,
they rated his nobility, and his acts of courage
proclaimed before the hosts. So it is right
for a man to praise in words his friend and lord,
cherish him in mind, when he must forth
be conveyed from the covering of his body.
So Geatish tribesmen mourned and keened
for the fall of their lord, companions of his hearth,
said that he was of the kings of this world
the most generous of men and gentlest,
kindest to his people and most eager to win praise.

3171–2 The repetition in the four verbal infinitives in these lines announces the coming end of the poem.

3182 *lofgeornost* 'most eager to win praise'. The approving Geatish point of view. However, OE *lofgeorn* may also mean 'prodigal', as in a butler (who gives too much of his master's wealth in order to win men's approval; Gretsch 1999: 418–19). Has Beowulf done this with his soul?

Finnsburh Fragment

The Battle of Finnsburg was transcribed and published by George Hickes, an early antiquarian and philologist scholar, in his *Thesaurus* of 1703–5, from just one surviving leaf which he had found in a homiliary in the Lambeth Palace Library. Then the manuscript leaf was lost, and with it any prospect of correcting Hickes' readings where the text is clearly in doubt. Yet we should look on the bright side. It was a stroke of luck to find part of the story which is also represented in *Beowulf*, lines 1063–1159. It is not a problem that the *Fragment* covers the opening of this story up to a point before the story resumes, as it were, in Beowulf's Finnsburh Episode. The *Fragment* gives enough information to show that the Hnæf's band, the Half-Danes as they are known in *Beowulf*, are mercenaries formerly in the service of King Finn, their captain's brother-in-law. For the rest of the tale, see 'Funeral at Finnsburh: Hildeburh and Wealhtheow' (under *Beowulf*). From its late spellings, the *Fragment* was probably copied in the early eleventh century, as part of a longer poem (perhaps from Canterbury, if celebrating Hengest's invasion of Kent). The poem proceeds with the utmost energy and speed, given the poet's sudden five-day temporal advance, yet with time to show the pathos of an untried warrior's death, and it appears to be lining up Hengest, on line 17, for his role as saviour of the doomed Hnæf's men.

Fry, D. K., ed., *Finnsburh: Fragment and Episode* (London, 1974)

North, R., 'Tribal loyalties in the *Finnsburh Fragment* and Episode', *Leeds Studies in English* new series 21 (1990), 13–43

Tolkien, J. R. R., *Finn and Hengest: The Fragment and the Episode*, ed. A. Bliss (London, 1982)

Warriors attack the hall

0 ['[. . .] ðis dagað eastan, her draca fleogeð,
1 her ðisse healle hor]nas byrnað?'

[H]næ*f* hleoþrode ða, hea*þ*ogeong cyning:
'Ne ðis ne dagað east*an*, ne her draca ne fleogeð,

---

0 ['[. . .] is this the eastern dawning, does a dragon fly here,
1 of this hall here are the hor]ned gables burning?'

Hnæf gave voice then, king young in battle:
'This is not the eastern dawning, no dragon flies here,

---

0 This line, though it cannot be numbered as part of the poem, is supplied on the basis of Hnæf's reply to the speaker asking the question.

2 *[H]næf* 'Hnæf'. George Hickes' transcript has *næfre* 'never', presumably a mistake, given that the leader speaks. Hnæf is known to be the leader, so Hnæf must be speaking here.

ne her ðisse healle hornas ne byrnað.
Ac her forþ berað, fugelas singað,
gylleð græghama, guðwudu hlynneð,
scyld scefte oncwyð. Nu scyneð þes mona
waðol under wolcnum. Nu arisað weadæda
ðe ðisne folces nið fremman willað.
Ac onwacnigeað nu, wigend mine,
habbað eowre l*i*nda, hi*c*geaþ on ellen,
winnað on orde, wesað onmode!'

Ða aras mænig goldhladen ðegn, gyrde hine his swurde.
Ða to dura eodon drihtlice cempan,
Sigeferð and Eaha, hyra sword getugon,
and æt oþrum durum Ordlaf and Guþlaf,
and Hengest sylf hwearf him on laste.
Ða gyt Garulf Guðere styrde

---

nor in this hall here are the horned gables burning!
But here the attack comes on, birds sing,
the grey-corslet rings, war-wood resounds,
shield answers shaft. Now shines the moon
wandering beneath the clouds. Now arise deeds of woe
that will further this tribal enmity.
So awaken now, my men at arms,
have your linden-shields, think of valour,
fight in the vanguard, be of good heart!'

Then arose many a gold-laden thegn, girt on his sword.
Then to the doors went the noble champions
Sigeferth and Eaha, drew their swords,
and at the other doors Ordlaf and Guthlaf,
and Hengest himself moved up behind them.
Still then did Guthere hold back Garulf, saying

---

5 *her forþ berað* 'here the attack comes on' etc. Hnæf's speech is lively, as befits this moment, consisting of a verb in almost each half-line, here in the present tense, later in second person plural imperative form. [*fugelas singað* 'birds sing'. The beasts and birds of battle topos, to be found in most Old English (and Norse) poems that show battles.

14 *drihtlice cempan* 'noble champions'. A champion by definition is a special member of any retinue. That Hnæf's has at least two *cempan* shows the presence of the Half-Danes, an elite troop of mercenaries, as they appear in Frisia in *Beowulf*, line 1069.

17 *Hengest sylf* 'Hengest himself'. The officer who takes command of the Half-Danes after Hnæf's death, according to the Finnsburh Episode in *Beowulf*. Also likely to be the Hengistus who leads his brother Horsa with their (Jutish) tribesmen to Kent in sources that start with Bede's *Ecclesiastical History*, Book I, ch. 15.

18 *Ða gyt Garulf Guðere styrde* 'Still then did Guthere hold back Garulf'. In syntax, these names could be transposed, but it seems Garulf is the younger man, given the emphatic notice of his death on line 31. Garulf is probably on the Frisian side (see note for line 32). His name makes him likely to be a Jute, according to the Jutish designation of *Gefwulf* in *Widsith*, line 26.

ðæt he swa freolic feorh forman siþe
to ðære healle durum hyrsta ne bære,
nu hyt niþa heard anyman wolde,
ac he frægn ofer eal undearninga,
deormod hæleþ, hwa ða duru heolde.

'Sigeferþ is min nama,' cweþ he, 'ic eom Secgena leod,
wreccea wide cuð. Fæla ic weana gebad,
he*a*rdra hilda. Đe is gyt her witod
swæþer ðu sylf to me secean wylle!'

Đa wæs on healle wælslihta gehlyn,
sceolde cel*lod* bord *c*enu*m* on handa,
banhelm berstan (buruhðelu dynede),
oð æt ðære guðe Garulf gecrang,
ealra ærest eorðbuendra,

---

that so noble a life for the first time to those
hall doors in harness he should not bear,
now that a man battle hardened would take it from him,
but he asked before all of them quite openly,
dare-devil hero, who held those doors.

'Sigeferth is my name', the other said, 'I'm a Secgan prince,
an exile widely heard of. Many woes, harsh
wars, have I suffered. For you one fate is granted,
whichever outcome you would seek from me!'

Then in the hall was the clamour of cruel slaughters,
the rounded boards had to be on brave men's arms,
bone-helmets would burst (the fortress floorboards rumbled)
until in that battle Garulf perished,
pre-eminent of all settlers in that country,

---

22 *ac he frægn* 'but he asked'. The subject change indicates young Garulf, if we take Guthere to do the restraining on line 18. It turns out that the young man (a Jute living in Frisia) has fatally risked his life.

24 Sigeferth. *Secgena leod* 'Secgan prince' is close enough to Sæferth, king of the *Sycgan* in *Widsith*, line 31, for the men to be understood as related. This tribal designation means that the Half-Danes are so called because they consist of many tribes.

25 *Fæla ic weana gebad* 'Many woes have I suffered' etc. This is like Beowulf's own career summary before fighting the Dragon, in *Beowulf*, lines 2426–7: *Fela ic on gioguðe guðræsa genæs, orleghwila* 'many combats in war did I survive in my youth, many times of conflict'.

32 *ealra ærest eorðbuendra* 'pre-eminent of all settlers in that country'. King Finn's designation as *eorðcyning* 'earth-king' in *Beowulf*, line 1155, tells us that these 'settlers' or 'farmers' are on the Frisian side, although Garulf's name suggests that he may be of Jutish origin.

Guðlafes sunu,   ymbe hyne godra fæla,
hwearfl*ic*ra hr*æw*.   Hræfen wandrode,
sweart and sealobrun.   Swurdleoma stod,
swylce eal Finn[e]sburuh   fyrenu wære.
Ne gefrægn ic næfre wurþlicor   æt wera hilde
sixtig sigebeorna   sel gebærann,
ne nefre sw*e*tne medo   sel forgyldan
ðonne Hnæfe guldan   his hægstealdas.

Hig fuhton fif dagas,   swa hyra nan ne feol
drihtgesiða,   ac hig ða duru heoldon.
Đa gewat him wund hæleð   on wæg gangan,
sæde þæt his byrne   abrocen wære,
heresceorp u*n*hror,   and eac wæs his helm ðyr[e]l,
ða hine sona frægn   folces hyrde,
hu ða wigend hyra   wunda genæson,
oððe hwæþer ðæra hyssa   [. . .

Guthlaf's son, and many good men about him,
corpses of the valiant. The raven circled,
dusky and shiny black. Sword-gleam appeared
as if all Finnsburh was was on fire.
Nor did I ever hear of sixty victorious warriors more
worthily bearing themselves up better in men's war,
nor of men ever requiting their sweet mead better
than when Hnæf's companions paid for theirs with him.

They fought for five days in such a way than not one fell
of the comrades of the troop, but they held those doors.
As soon as a wounded hero fell back to the wall,
said that his chained mail was all broken,
his war-gear not fresh and his helmet, too, shot through,
then would the shepherd of the people ask him immediately
how those men at arms were surviving their wounds,
or which of those lads [. . .

---

36 *Finn[e]sburuh* 'Finnsburh'. The conventional title is based on *Finnsburg*, Hickes' likely misspelling of the name in the title of the story.

39 The men's requital of their mead to Hnæf is similar to that of the Welsh Gododdin to their king Mynyddog Mwynfawr in *Y Gododdin*, although perhaps not for a whole year where Hnæf is concerned. This topos indicates that Hnæf has taken his band around with him, or at least commands it within the Frisian domain of Finn, his brother-in-law.

43 *Đa gewat him wund hæleð* 'As soon as a wounded hero fell back'. This man may be taken as a general type, rather than as someone later named in the story, simply because Finn, the more important person, is asking the same question to all who fall back.

46 *folces hyrde* 'shepherd of the people'. See previous note. This must be Finn, the only true king in the story, also the son of *Folcwald* according to *Beowulf* (line 1089) and other sources (North 1990: 34).

Y Gododdin

(attributed to Aneirin)

⁂

The early medieval literature of Wales is preserved in manuscripts of the later Middle Ages. This state of survival mirrors that of the bulk of Old Icelandic literature. Both traditions differ from Old English poetry and prose, nearly all of which pre-dates the Norman Conquest and survives in manuscripts of the tenth and eleventh centuries. Yet some Welsh poetry, as with the Icelandic which is more plentifully represented in this book, has roots that extend to much earlier times. The Welsh poem excerpted below, *Y Gododdin*, is a poem of this kind. Although the text survives in two incomplete versions in a manuscript of the thirteenth century (Cardiff MS 2.81), it celebrates a battle in Catraeth, or Catterick in Yorkshire, which must have taken place very roughly in *c.* 600 (though a different and earlier battle has been suggested, in *c.* 570; Koch 1997). The earliest linguistic forms of the poem take some parts of the text back to the tenth, or even the ninth century, with the remainder composed in later times, but the theme is as old as the battle itself. Although it is a poem which originates from a northern Welsh dialect, it may also be regarded as the oldest extant poem from Scotland.

Y Gododdin runs to 1480 lines, a series of elegies (*englynion*) to the men of the *Gododdin* tribe (known as *Votadini* in the Roman era) who lived north of the Cheviot Hills and south of Edinburgh (*Eiddyn*), in *Hen Ogledd* 'the old north'. The poem also contains the earliest literary allusion to Arthur, on line 1241, in stanza 99, where a warrior named Gwawrddur is said to be good 'though he was no Arthur'. For King Arthur, glory of western European romance in the twelfth to fifteenth centuries, see Wace's *Brut* in **Early Chivalry**. The poet's focus, however, is on the men of the Gododdin and other groups. Three hundred of them are said to have been invited by King Mynyddog Mwynfawr for a year's mead-drinking and feasting, before launching an attack against overwhelming odds against the Bernicians (*Brenneich*) in the more northerly of the two Anglian kingdoms of Northumbria (the southern one was Deira). The Bernicians had taken lands that the Gododdin wanted back. The Gododdin warriors, who are not really 'drunk' (the stylisation of their feasting in stanza 9) are said to die a heroic death.

The manuscript of *Y Gododdin* is named the 'Book of Aneirin' after the poet who is alleged to have composed the work, according to the *Historia Brittonum* 'History of the Britons' (*c.* 829). If we credit this anonymous early Welsh history, both Aneirin and the Battle of Catterick, the poet and the disaster he sings of, may be placed in the era of Anglian invasion in northern Yorkshire. *Y Gododdin* resembles two Germanic texts which may be traced to the same era. The *Finnsburh Fragment* appears to have been copied in the early eleventh century, though its manuscript is lost, and tells the story of an attack by overwhelming forces on a group of Half-Dane mercenaries in a hall in Frisia in *c.* 449. The *Bjarkamál* 'Lay of Bjarki', secondly, is traceable to the early eleventh century at the earliest and celebrates the last stand of King Hrólfr and his heroes in Lejre, Denmark, perhaps a generation later. As with these much smaller and fragmentary texts, *Y Gododdin* is essentially a theme, rather than a text. It has been reworked in succeeding incarnations from perhaps the very late sixth century into the thirteenth. Its Welsh heroic ethos is similar to the Germanic, except that the heroes of *Y Gododdin* are mourned as good Christians, with some rather more ironic reflection and injections of anger than may be found in the more vigorous *Finnsburh Fragment.* The text below is from Williams, the translation from Skene.

Bromwich, R., and A. O. H. Jarman and B. F. Roberts, ed., *The Arthur of the Welsh: The Arthurian Legend in Medieval Welsh Literature* (Cardiff, 1991)

Dumville, D. N., 'Sub-Roman Britain: history and legend', *History* 62 (1977), 173–92

Hope-Taylor, B., *Yeavering: An Anglo-Saxon Centre of Early Northumbria*, Department of the Environment Archaeological Reports 7 (London, 1977)

Jackson, K. H., trans., *The Gododdin: The Oldest Scottish Poem* (Edinburgh, 1969)

Jarman, A. O. H., ed. and trans., *Aneirin: Y Gododdin, Britain's Oldest Heroic Poem* (Llandysul, 1988)

Koch, J. T., *The Gododdin of Aneurin: Text and Context from Dark-Age North Britain* (Cardiff, 1997)

Rowlands, J., *Early Welsh Saga Poetry* (Cambridge, 1990)

Rowlands, J., 'OE *Ealuscerwen/Meoduscerwen* and the concept of "paying for mead"', *Leeds Studies in English* new series 21 (1990), 1–12

Skene, W. F., trans., *The Four Ancient Books of Wales*, 2 vols (Edinburgh, 1868)

Williams, I., ed., *Canu Aneirin: gyda rhagymadrodd a nodiadau* (Aberystwyth, 1938)

Wood, I., 'An historical context for Hope-Taylor's *Yeavering*', in *Yeavering: People, Power and Place*, ed. P. Frodsham and C. O'Brien (Stroud, 2005), 185–9

The fight at Catterick

8 Gwyr a aeth Gatraeth oed fraeth eu llu.
glasved eu hancwyn a gwenwyn vu.
trychant trwy beiryant en cattau.
a gwedy elwch tawelwch vu.
ket elwynt e lanneu e benydu.
dadyl dieu agheu y eu treidu.

---

8 The men went to Catraeth, loquacious was their host;
Fresh mead was their feast, and also their poison.
Three hundred were contending with weapons;
And after sportive mirth, stillness ensued!
Though they went to churches to do penance,
The inevitable strife of death was to pierce them.

9 Gwyr a aeth Gatraeth veduaeth uedwn.
fyryf frwythlawn oed cam nas kymhwyllwn.
e am lavnawr coch gorvawr gwrmwn.
dwys dengyn ed emledyn aergwn.
ar deulu Brenneych beych barnasswn.
dilyw dyn en vyw nys adawsswn.
kyueillt a golleis diffleis oedwn.
rugyl en emwrthryn rynn riadwn.
ny mennws gwrawl gwadawl chwergrwn.
maban y Gian o Vaen Gwynngwn.

10 Gwyr a aeth Gatraeth gan wawr
trauodynt eu hed eu hovnawr.
milcant a thrychant a emdaflawr.
gwyarllyt gwynnodynt waewawr.
ef gorsaf yng gwryaf. eggwryawr.
rac gosgord Mynydawc Mwynvawr.

---

9 The men went to Catraeth, fed with mead, and drunk,
Firm and vigorous; it were wrong if I neglected to praise them.
Around the red, mighty, and murky blades
Obstinately and fiercely fought the dogs of war.
If I had judged you to be on the side of the tribe of Brenneich,
Not the phantom of a man would I have left alive.
A friend I have lost, myself being unhurt;
He openly opposed the terrible chief –
The magnanimous hero did not seek the dowry of his father-in-law;
The son of Cian of Maen Gwyngwn.

10 The men went to Catraeth with the dawn;
They dealt peaceably with those who feared them.
A hundred thousand and three hundred engaged in mutual overthrow.
Drenched in gore they served as butts for lances;
Their post they most manfully defended
Before the retinue of Mynyddawg Mwynfawr.

---

9 *veduaeth uedwn* 'fed with mead, and drunk'. 'Having drunk mead' is the correct sense, not any absurd idea that the Gododdin went into battle so. [*Brenneych*. The Bernicians, a tribe of Angles which moved into the Gododdin lands in the Cheviot Hills and further south in the sixth century. Their interaction with the indigenous was not always warlike, and the archaeology of Yeavering, which was their (originally Celtic) sacred site at *Ad Gefin*, may give evidence that the two communities coexisted peacefully for a while (Hope-Taylor 1977: 16–27; Wood 2005).

10 *Mynydawc Mwynvawr* 'Mynyddawg (Mynyddog) Mwynfawr'. King of the Gododdin, whose hospitality obliges the Gododdin to attack Catraeth at odds of 333 to 1.

11 Gwyr a aeth Gatraeth gan wawr
dygmyrrws eu hoet eu hanyanawr.
med evynt melyn melys maglawr.
blwydyn bu llewyn llawer kerdawr.
coch eu cledyuawr na phurawr.
eu llain. gwyngalch a phedryollt bennawr
rac gosgord Mynydawc Mwynvawr.

12 Gwyr a aeth Gatraeth gan dyd.
neus goreu o gadeu gewilid.
wy gwnaethant en geugant gelorwyd.
a llavnavr llawn annawd em bedyd.
goreu yw hwnn kyn kystlwn kerennyd.
enneint creu ac angeu oe hennyd.
rac bedin Ododin pan vudyd.
neus goreu deu bwyllyat neirthyat gwychyd?

---

11 The men went to Catraeth with the dawn;
Regretted are their absence and their disposition;
Mead they drank, yellow, sweet, ensnaring.
In that year many a minstrel fell.
Redder were their swords than their plumes.
Their blades were white as lime, their helmets split into four parts,
Before the retinue of Mynyddawg Mwynfawr.

12 The men went to Catraeth with the day:
Have not the best of battles their disgrace?
They made biers a matter of necessity.
With blades full of vigour in defence of Baptism.
This is best before the alliance of kindred.
Exceedingly great was the bloodshed and death, of which they were the cause,
Before the army of Gododdin, when the day occurred.
Is not a double quantity of discretion the best strengthener of a hero?

---

12 *annawd em bedyd* 'in defence of Baptism'. The Bernicians are heathens (and remained so until the dramatic success of Bishop Paulinus in 627; see 'The Conversion of King Edwin' in **The Earliest English Prose**). [*neus goreu deu* 'Is not a double quantity of discretion' etc. The discretion of the Gododdin lies in their attack against overwhelming odds. This is the Welsh version of understatement (litotes), here for an act of insane courage.

13 Gwyr a aeth Gatraeth gan dyd.
ne llewes ef vedgwyn vei noethyd.
bu truan gyuatcan gyvluyd.
e neges ef or drachwres drenghidyd.
ny chryssyws Gatraeth
mawr mor ehelaeth
e aruaeth uch arwyt.
ny bu mor gyffor
o Eidyn ysgor
e esgarei oswyd.
Tutvwlch Hir ech e dir ae dreuyd.
ef lladei Saesson seithuet dyd.
perheit y wrhyt en wrvyd
ae govein gan e gein gyweithyd.
pan dyvu Dutvwlch dut nerthyd.
oed gwaetlan gwyaluan vab Kilyd.

---

13 The man went to Catraeth with the day:
Truly he quaffed the foaming mead on serene nights;
He was unlucky, though proverbially fortunate:
His mission, through ambition, was that of a destroyer.
There hastened not to Catraeth
A chief so magnificent
As to his design on the standard.
Never was there such a host
From the fort of Eiddyn,
That would scatter abroad the mounted ravagers.
Tudvwlch Hir, near his land and towns,
Slaughtered the Saxons for seven days.
His valour remained until he was overpowered;
And his memory will remain among his fair associates.
When Tudvwlch, the supporter of the land, arrived,
The station of the son of Cilydd became a plain of blood.

---

13 *o Eidyn ysgor* 'From the fort of Eiddyn'. Edinburgh, the place to which the Gododdin had been forced to retreat from their old homelands. [*Saesson* 'Saxons'. This is the general name for 'Angles', or English, forms of which are still current in Celtic languages today. [*seithuet dyd* 'for seven days'. A notional number indicating great time. Compare with *Hi fuhton fif dagas* 'they fought for five days' in the *Finnsburh Fragment*, line 41.

Widsith

✳

The Exeter Book, compiled in *c.* 980 or a little later, preserves a catalogue poem now known as *Widsith* 'Far Traveller'. It is variously regarded as a rambling curiosity, as an example of a template for Anglo-Saxon *scopas* on heroic themes, as a scholars' trove for nuggets of information about heroic figures better known in *Beowulf* or in Old Norse literature, and even as a poem with some literary merit concerning the troubadour's self-characterisation. Perhaps it could be called a version before Johnny Cash of 'I've been everywhere'. The poet's persona is ruined gentry: he must recover his father's lands at any cost, and eventually buys these back from his king with a necklace of terrifying value, one given him by King Eormanric of the Goths. In what may be a foretaste of twelfth-century *fin'amor* (see **Early Chivalry**) Widsith loves the latter's wife, Ealhhild, as his patron. She is possibly to be seen as enjoying her last days of happiness before her aged husband descends into madness (see note to line 97). Thus there is an unexpected note of pathos in *Widsith*.

The poet's persona seems to be developed from that of the Old English standard *scop* 'minstrel'. One thing worth noting, however, with this idea is that this Old English word *scop* is never found in the poem. This self-referential template concludes with some remarks about singing in courts of the Age of Migrations, but otherwise presents a picture of international eulogists more in keeping with what is known of Norse *skáld* 'scolds' of the Viking Age. Notwithstanding this apparently late cultural frame, the best date to put on *Widsith* is the ninth century, probably in the middle. That is because King Offa of Mercia (ruled 757–96), and most likely a poem composed on him near the end of his reign, appears to be the inspiration for the poet's first riff on a Germanic king of old, in lines 35–44. Another thing that may be of interest is that the poet of *Widsith* seems not to know *Beowulf*.

Dronke, U., ed., trans. and comm., *The Poetic Edda, vol. I: Heroic Poems* (Oxford, 1969)

Foulke, W. D., trans., ed. E. Peters, *History of the Lombards, by Paul the Deacon* (Pennsylvania, PA, 1974)

Hill, J., ed., *Old English Minor Heroic Poems*, Durham and St Andrews Medieval Texts 4 (Durham, 1983)

North, R., 'Tribal loyalties in the *Finnsburh Fragment* and Episode', *Leeds Studies in English* new series 21 (1990), 13–43

North, R., *Heathen Gods in Old English Literature*, Cambridge Studies in Anglo-Saxon England 22 (Cambridge, 1997)

North, R., *The Origins of 'Beowulf': From Vergil to Wiglaf* (Oxford, 2006)

Orchard, A., *Pride and Prodigies: Studies in the Monsters of the Beowulf-Manuscript* (Woodbridge, 1995)

Tolkien, C. [J. R. R.], ed. and trans., *The Saga of King Heidrek the Wise* (London, 1960)

Wolfram, H., *History of the Goths*, trans. T. J. Dunlap, 2nd ed. (Berkeley, CA, 1988)

Widsið maðolade, wordhord onleac,
se þe monna mæst mægþa ofer eorþan,
folca geondferde. Oft he on flette geþah
mynelicne maþþum. Him from Myrgingum
æþele onwocon. He mid Ealhhilde,
fælre freoþuwebban, forman siþe
Hreðcyninges ham gesohte
eastan of Ongle, Eormanrices,
wraþes wærlogan.

Ongon þa worn sprecan:
'Fela ic monna gefrægn mægþum wealdan!
Sceal þeodna gehwylc þeawum lifgan,
eorl æfter oþrum eðle rædan,
se þe his þeodenstol geþeon wile.
Þara wæs Hwala hwile selast,
ond Alexandreas ealra ricost

Widsith spoke, unlocked his word-hoard,
he who of men had travelled in most nations
and peoples on earth. Often in the hall did he receive
a desirable treasure. His noble ancestry awoke
from Myrging stock. He with Ealhhild,
faithful treaty-weaver, for the first time
came seeking the home east of Angeln
of Goth-king Eormanric, savage-hearted
breaker of covenants.

He began to speak of much:
'Many are the men, so I hear, who rule nations!
Every people's king must live virtuously,
noble upon noble must govern his inheritance,
who wants his royal seat to prosper.
Of these was Hwala for a while the highest-ranking,
and Alexander the mightiest of all

5–6 *Ealhhilde fælre freoþuwebban* 'Ealhhild, faithful treaty-weaver'. The thought that Ealhhild might be an English version of Norse Svanhildr, murdered by Jǫrmunrekkr on suspicion of adultery, gives her epithet here a special edge. See note to line 97.

14 *Hwala hwile selast* 'Hwala for a while the highest-ranking'. Possibly Emperor Valens, the first emperor of the Eastern Empire (ruled 364–78), who brought the romanised Goths into revolt (Wolfram 1988: 124–8).

15 *ond Alexandreas ealra ricost* 'and Alexander the mightiest' etc. On the *–andreas* suffix, 'the garbled form of the name, which contaminates Alexander (the Great) with Andreas (the Saint) suggests ignorance rather than knowledge' (Hill 1983: 78). Or it could be the scribe's, in the Exeter Book. At any rate, the Old English translation of *Letter of Alexander to Aristotle*, and two citations in *The Wonders of the East*, are but two of many cases of a lively interest in Alexander (356–323 BC) in Anglo-Saxon England (Orchard 1995: 116–20; see **Writers of the Benedictine Reform**).

monna cynnes, ond he mæst geþah
þara þe ic ofer foldan gefrægen hæbbe.
Ætla weold Hunum, Eormanric Gotum,
Becca Baningum, Burgendum Gifica.
Casere weold Creacum ond *Cælic* Finnum,
Hagena Holmrygum ond Heoden Glommum.
Witta weold Swæfum, Wada Hælsingum,
Meaca Myrgingum, Mearchealf Hundingum.
Þeodric weold Froncum, Þyle Rondingum,
Breoca Brondingum, Billing Wernum.
Oswine weold Eowum ond Ytum Gefwulf,

---

mankind, while he took the most tribute
of any I have heard of on earth.
Attila ruled the Huns, Eormanric the Goths,
Becca the Banings, Gifica the Burgundians.
Caesar ruled the Greeks and Caelic the Lapps,
Hagena the Island-Rugians, and Heoden the Glommas.
Witta ruled the Swabians, Wada the Hælsings,
Meaca the Myrgings, Mearchealf the Hundings.
Theodric ruled the Franks, Thyle the Rondings,
Breoca the Brondings, Billing the Wernas.
Oswine ruled the Eowas, and Gefwulf the Jutes,

---

18 Attila (434–53): see *The Lay of Attila*. Ermanaric (died *c.* 375), Norse Jǫrmunrekkr: see Bragi's *Eulogy on Ragnarr*. Ermanaric is thought to have died by suicide before the Huns first arrived from the steppes, pushing Goths and other Germanic nomads across the Danube in 376 (Dronke 1969: 192–4; Wolfram 1988: 117–31).

19 Gifica is King Gibicha who ruled the Burgundians towards the end of the fifth century; Norse Gjúki, the father of Gunnarr and Hǫgni in *The Lay of Attila* (Dronke 1969: 30–1).

21 For Heoden's tribe, 'Heodeningas', see *Deor*, line 36, in which the eponymous poet laments losing his post to Heorrenda, possibly because the latter helps Heoden in a mission to win a princess (North 1997: 168–9).

24 Frankish Theodric is otherwise known as Hug-Dietrich, to distinguish him from Theodric the Goth, subject of *Deor*, lines 18–19, also the namesake king of legend in the Old Norwegian *Saga of Þiðrekr of Bern* (*c.* 1260).

25 This is the Breca to whom Beowulf refers in *Beowulf*, lines 530–86, his opponent in the primeval Baltic swimming contest. Billing may or may not be connected with the 'Billingr' whose wife (or daughter) thwarts Óðinn's amatory intentions in *Sayings of the High One*, stanzas 96–101. The Wernas or Werne appear to be Varini, a tribe associated with the Anglii in Tacitus' *Germania*, ch. 40 (*c.* 98).

26 Gefwulf, king of the *Yte* 'Jutes', looks related to the Garulf who appears to be killed in the first attack on Hnæf's hall in the *Finnsburh Fragment*, line 31. Given that Hengest on the inside team is probably a Jute as well, the solution seems to be that this conflict has Jutes on both sides, some of them (such as Garulf) settled in Frisia.

Fin Folcwalding   Fresna cynne.
Sigehere lengest   Sæ-Denum weold,
Hnæf Hocingum,   Helm Wulfingum,
Wald Woingum,   Wod Þyringum,
Sæferð Sycgum,   Sweom Ongendþeow,
Sceafthere Ymbrum,   Sceafa Longbeardum,
Hun Hætwerum   ond Holen Wrosnum.
Hringweald wæs haten   Herefarena cyning.
Offa weold Ongle,   Alewih Denum,
se wæs þara manna   modgast ealra,
no hwæþre he ofer Offan   eorlscype fremede,
ac Offa geslog   ærest monna,
cnihtwesende,   cynerica mæst.

Finn son of Folcwald the Frisian race.
Sigehere ruled the Sea-Danes for the longest time,
Hnæf the Hocings, Helm the Wulfings,
Wald the Wō-ings, Wōd the Thuringians,
Sæferth the Sycgan, Ongendtheow the Swedes,
Scefthere the Ymbras, Sceafa the Lombards,
Hun the Hetware and Holen the Wrosnas.
Hringweald was the name of the Raiders' king.
Offa ruled Angeln, Alewih the Danes,
who was the bravest of all these men,
but that he did not outmatch Offa in courage,
for Offa, first among men, fought for and won
the greatest of kingdoms even while a youth.

27–9 On Finn and Hnæf, see the *Finnsburh Fragment* and *Beowulf*'s Finnsburh Episode (North 1990).

31 Sæferth the Sycgan looks like Sigeferth of the Secgan who speaks for the Half-Danes in the *Finnsburh Fragment*, lines 24–7, and probably kills the young Garulf on line 31 of that poem. Ongen(d)theow is a terrifying old king who dies in combat with Hygelac's two champions in the first of the three Swedish Wars in *Beowulf*, in lines 2946–98.

32 Sceafa looks similar to the father of Scef, father of Scyld (Scefing) who is the founder of King Hrothgar's Scylding dynasty in *Beowulf*, lines 1–52. The absence of the Scandinavian aspect here in *Widsith* provides one reason to suggest that Beowulf was unknown to the poet of *Widsith* (another is that Hygelac and Beowulf are missing).

33 Hun's 'Hætware' are the 'Hetware' who turn up as part of the Merovingian battle-group which wipes out King Hygelac on his ill-fated Frisian raid, named in *Beowulf*, lines 2363 and 2916.

35 Offa of Angeln figures in the Mercian royal genealogies in the Anglian Collection of *c.* 812 onwards, as the ancestor of King Offa (ruled 757–96). This duel-story may hail Offa's Dyke. This Offa is also in *Beowulf*, lines 1944–62, in which he is said to tame a princess (some scholars call her 'Thryth') who has all her other suitors killed. Offa's exposure in this part of *Widsith* suggests that (a) the poem is of Mercian origin, (b) more tenuously, that there was at least one great poem in *Widsith*'s background that celebrated the Mercian Offa on the basis of his alleged north German ancestor. Offa also figures in the *Lives of the Two Offas* (*Vitae duorum Offarum*) of St Albans, from the thirteenth century (*B&OS* 239–41; North 2006: 226–39).

Nænig efeneald him eorlscipe maran
on orette. Ane sweorde
merce gemærde wið Myrgingum
bi Fifeldore. Heoldon forð siþþan
Engle ond Swæfe, swa hit Offa geslog.
Hroþwulf ond Hroðgar heoldon lengest
sibbe ætsomne suhtorfædran,
siþþan hy forwræcon wicinga cynn
ond Ingeldes ord forbigdan,
forheowan æt Heorote Heaðobeardna þrym.

'Swa ic geondferde fela fremdra londa
geond ginne grund. Godes ond yfles
þær ic cunnade, cnosle bidæled,
freomægum feor, folgade wide.
Forþon ic mæg singan ond secgan spell,
mænan fore mengo in meoduhealle
hu me cynegode cystum dohten.
Ic wæs mid Hunum ond mid Hreðgotum,

No one of like age was warrior enough to achieve
greater deeds of valour. With one special sword
he fixed a boundary against the Myrgings
on the Eider. From then on Angles and Swabians kept
it just as Offa, by fighting, had established it.
Hrothulf and Hrothgar, uncle and nephew,
had kept their family united for the longest time
when they drove off the tribe of Vik-pirates,
crushed Ingeld's front line, and at Heorot
cut down the glory of the Heathobards.

'So it was I crossed many foreign lands
through the wide world. Of good and evil
I learned things there, cut off from family,
far from noble kinsmen, and served widely.
And so I can sing and say tidings,
recite before the troop in mead-hall of how
generous royals availed me with choice gifts.
I was with the Huns and Baltic Goths,

45–9 Ingeld, briefly husband of Freawaru, before he invades her father Hrothgar's country in repudiation of that match, is a major background figure in *Beowulf* (*B&OS* 106–8; North 2006: 101–31; see 'Beowulf on Princess Freawaru').

53 *freomægum feor* 'far from noble kinsmen'. This formula is also part of the Wanderer's lament in *The Wanderer*, line 21 (see **Poems on the Meaning of Life**).

mid Sweom ond mid Geatum   ond mid Suþ-Denum,
mid Wenlum ic wæs ond mid Wærnum   ond mid wicingum,
mid Gefþum ic wæs ond mid Winedum   ond mid Gefflegum,
mid Englum ic wæs ond mid Swæfum   ond mid Ænenum,
mid Seaxum ic wæs ond Sycgum   ond mid Sweordwerum,
mid Hronum ic wæs ond mid Deanum   ond mid Heaþo-Reamum,
mid Þyringum ic wæs   ond mid Þrowendum,
ond mid Burgendum,   þær ic beag geþah.
Me þær Guðhere forgeaf   glædlicne maþþum
songes to leane.   Næs þæt sæne cyning!
Mid Froncum ic wæs ond mid Frysum   ond mid Frumtingum,
mid Rugum ic wæs ond mid Glommum   ond mid Rumwalum.
Swylce ic wæs on Eatule   mid Ælfwine,
se hæfde moncynnes,   mine gefræge,
leohteste hond   lofes to wyrcenne,
heortan unhneaweste   hringa gedales,
beorhtra beaga,   bearn Eadwines.
Mid Sercingum ic wæs   ond mid Seringum;

---

with the Swedes and with the Geats and the South-Danes,
with the Wendle I was and with the Werne and with the men of Vik,
with the Gefthas I was and with the Wends and with the Gefflegas,
with the Angles I was and with Swabians and with the Ænenas,
with the Saxons I was and with Sycgan and with Swordsmen,
with the Hronas I was and with Danes and with Battle-Romerikians,
with Thuringians I was and with the Throwendas,
and with Burgundians, where I accepted a ring.
To me there Guthere gave a glittering treasure
in reward for my song. That king was forthcoming!
With the Franks I was and with Frisians and with Frumtings,
with Rugians I was and with Glommas and with Rumwalas.
Likewise I was in Italy with Ælfwine,
who, from what I heard, of all mankind
the lightest hand with which to win his praise,
his heart the least grudging to dispense rings,
bright necklaces, son of Eadwine.
With the Saracens I was and with the Serings,

58–64 The tribes in this and later bursts of hypermetric lines are largely named earlier, proof if more were needed that *Widsith* is a composite catalogue for working poets. The Geats are named only here in the poem. The 'Wendle' are Vandals, who named Andalusia on their way to Carthage in the fifth century; 'Gefthas' are fourth-century Gepids ('Sluggards'), a tribe in the Gothic group; Wends are Poles, a force to be reckoned with in the later tenth century (King Cnut's mother was a Wend).

60 *Gefflegum* 'Gefflegas'. Bizarrely or not, this name resembles *Gifteleia* 'Iffley' (Oxon.). 'Men of Iffley'?

70–4 Alboin (ruled 565–72), son of Audoin (ruled 546–65), kings of northern Italy who are celebrated (Alboin for being murdered by his Gepid wife) in *The History of the Lombards* of Paul the Deacon (790s; Foulke and Peters 1974: 81–3; Hill 1983: 79, 81).

mid Creacum ic wæs ond mid Finnum   ond mid Casere,
se þe winburga   geweald ahte,
wiolena ond wilna,   ond Wala rices.
Mid Scottum ic wæs ond mid Peohtum   ond mid Scridefinnum,
mid Lidwicingum ic wæs ond mid Leonum   ond mid Longbeardum,
mid hæðnum ond mid hæleþum   ond mid Hundingum.
Mid Israhelum ic wæs   ond mid Exsyringum,
mid Ebreum ond mid Indeum   ond mid Egyptum.
Mid Moidum ic wæs ond mid Persum   ond mid Myrgingum,
ond Mofdingum   ond ongend Myrgingum,
ond mid Amothingum.   Mid East-Þyringum ic wæs
ond mid Eolum ond mid Istum   ond Idumingum.

'Ond ic wæs mid Eormanrice   ealle þrage.
Þær me Gotena cyning   gode dohte,
se me beag forgeaf,   burgwarena fruma,
on þam siex hund wæs   smætes goldes,
gescyred sceatta   scillingrime.
Þone ic Eadgilse   on æht sealde,

---

with the Greeks I was and with Lapps, and with Caesar,
who had the rule over the cities of wine,
riches and desirable things, and the Welsh kingdom.
With the Irish and Scots I was and with the Picts and the Skiing-Lapps,
with the Lidwicings I was and with the Lions and the Lombards,
with heathens and with heroes and with the Hundings.
With Israelites I was and with the Assyrians,
with the Hebrews and with the Indians and with the Egyptians.
With the Medes I was and the Persians and the Myrgings,
and Mofdings and back with the Myrgings again,
and with Amothings. With the East-Thuringians I was,
and with the Eolas and the Iste and the Idumings.

'And I was with Eormanric all this time.
There the king of Goths availed me with good things,
prince of townsfolk, who gave me a necklace
which was valued at six hundred pieces
of refined gold in the count of shillings.
This I gave into the keeping of Eadgils,

---

82 It is no problem that the Israelites and Assyrians are ancient (the Greeks are presumably Byzantines). The Anglo-Saxons made heroic poems on warlike biblical themes such as *Exodus* and *Judith* (see **Poems of Devotion**).

85 *ongend Myrgingum* 'back with the Myrgings again'. Widsith's family, from whom he cannot bear to be separated (line 52).

91 *smætes goldes* 'of refined gold'. Cynewulf uses this as a metaphor for the top layer of heaven-bound souls in *Elene*, line 1308–14 (his Epilogue; see **Poems of Devotion**).

minum hleodryhtne,   þa ic to ham bicwom,
leofum to leane,   þæs þe he me lond forgeaf,
mines fæder eþel,   frea Myrginga.
Ond me þa Ealhhild   oþerne forgeaf,
dryhtcwen duguþe,   dohtor Eadwines.
Hyre lof lengde   geond londa fela,
þonne ic be songe   secgan sceolde
hwær ic under swegle   selast wisse
goldhrodene cwen   giefe bryttian.
Đonne wit Scilling   sciran reorde
for uncrum sigedryhtne   song ahofan
(hlude bi hearpan   hleoþor swinsade),
þonne monige men,   modum wlonce,
wordum sprecan,   þa þe wel cuþan,
þæt hi næfre song   sellan ne hyrdon.
Đonan ic ealne geondhwearf   eþel Gotena,
sohte ic a gesiþa   þa selestan,
þæt wæs innweorud   Earmanrices.

great king of Myrgings, my protecting lord,
when I came home, as payment to a dear man
for giving me lands, my father's inheritance.
And then Ealhhild gave me another necklace,
lordly queen of the company, Eadwine's daughter.
Praise of her reached through many lands,
when it came to me to tell stories in song
of where beneath the sun I best knew
of any gold-laden queen dispensing gifts.
When Shilling and I with bright voice
raised a song for our victorious lord
(loud with the lyre did the melody echo),
then many were the men, proud at heart,
knowing this business, who said in speeches
that they had never heard a better song.
From there I wandered all Gothic homelands,
always sought the noblest companions,
and that was Eormanric's hearth-troop.

97 Ealhhild's role with Eormanric, as a young and perhaps ill-starred wife, resembles that of Svanhildr in the Norse poems, whose fate is to be trampled by Jǫrmunrekkr's horses for an alleged affair with Randvér, her new stepson (see here Bragi's *Eulogy on Ragnarr*; *B&OS* 114–15).

98 If this Eadwine is the same as before, i.e. Audoin of the Lombards (see note to lines 70–4), then Ealhhild is a Lombard princess. The fact that she would thus be living in *c.* 550, though married to Eormanric the Goth who died in *c.* 375, is certainly of no consequence to a reader of heroic lays (*pace* Hill 1983: 81).

103 *Scilling* is either a fellow minstrel, or the name of Widsith's lyre. The latter may be true, given Widsith's shilling-count of his works on line 92; see also *The Rhyming Poem*, line 27 for *scyl wæs hearpe* 'shrill was the lyre' (**Poems on the Meaning of Life**).

'Heðcan sohte ic ond Beadecan ond Herelingas,
Emercan sohte ic ond Fridlan ond Eastgotan,
frodne ond godne fæder Unwenes.
Seccan sohte ic ond Beccan, Seafolan ond Þeodric,
Heaþoric ond Sifecan, Hliþe ond Incgenþeow.
Eadwine sohte ic ond Elsan, Ægelmund ond Hungar,
ond þa wloncan gedryht Wiþ-Myrginga.
Wulfhere sohte ic ond Wyrmhere. Ful oft þær wig ne alæg,
þonne Hræda here heardum sweordum
ymb Wistlawudu wergan sceoldon
ealdne eþelstol ætlan leodum.
Rædhere sohte ic ond Rondhere, Rumstan ond Gislhere,
Wiþergield ond Freoþeric, Wudgan ond Haman.
Ne wæran þæt gesiþa þa sæmestan,
þeah þe ic hy anihst nemnan sceolde.
Ful oft of þam heape hwinende fleag
giellende gar on grome þeode.

'Hethca I sought, and Beadeca and the Harlings,
Emerca I sought and Fridla and Eastgota
the wise and generous father of Unwene.
Secca I sought and Becca, Seafola and Theodric,
Heathoric and Sifeca, Hlithe and Incgentheow.
Eadwine I sought and Elsa, Ægelmund and Hungar,
and the proud retinue of the Vid-Myrgings.
Wulfhere I sought and Wyrmhere. Very often no war was lacking
when the Gothic armies with cruel swords
were said to defend their ancient inherited seat
against Attila's people by the Vistula woods.
Rædhere I sought and Rondhere, Rumstan and Gislhere,
Withergield and Frederic, Wudga and Hama.
Nor were these the meanest of companions,
though I have had to name them last of all.
Very often from that band the whistling spear
flew with a shriek into the enemy nation.

116 The complex of legends to which Heathoric and Sifeca, Hlithe and Incgentheow belong derives from the Gothic history of the Carpathians and the river Vistula in the fourth century. The major analogue is with Heiðrekr, Hlǫðr and Angantýr in the Norse *Saga of Heiðrekr and Hervǫr* (*Heiðreks saga ok Hervarar*), whose subject King Heiðrekr, a peripatetic monogamist with princesses, preserves the story presumably lost with Heathoric (Tolkien 1960).

119 Wyrmhere is matched by 'Ormarr' in the *Saga of Heiðrekr* (see note to line 116). Lines 119–22 allude to the grand battle between Goths and Huns which features in ch. 10 of this saga.

124 Withergield is Beowulf's imagined name for a dead Heathobard warrior, whose son, he says, will be incited to vengeance during the ill-fated wedding of Freawaru and Ingeld (*Beowulf*, line 2051). Wudga and Hama are popular elsewhere in *Beowulf* and in the minor Old English heroic poems (*B&OS* 111–21).

Wræccan þær weoldan   wundnan golde
werum ond wifum,   Wudga ond Hama.
Swa ic þæt symle onfond   on þære feringe,
þæt se biþ leofast   londbuendum
se þe him God syleð   gumena rice
to gehealdenne,   þenden he her leofað.'

Swa scriþende   gesceapum hweorfað
gleomen gumena   geond grunda fela,
þearfe secgað,   þoncword sprecaþ,
simle suð oþþe norð   sumne gemetað
gydda gleawne,   geofum unhneawne,
se þe fore duguþe wile   dom aræran,
eorlscipe æfnan,   oþþæt eal scæceð,
leoht ond lif somod;   lof se gewyrceð,
hafað under heofonum   heahfæstne dom.

Wudga and Hama, men in exile, ruled there
the men and women with their twisted gold.
So what I ever found in all my faring is
that the king most popular to countrymen
is he to whom God gives a kingdom of men
to dispose over while living in this world.'

Just so do the people's gleemen go wandering
according to their destinies through many countries,
say what they need, speak words of thanks.
Always will they meet some man, north or south,
with taste in songs and no meanness in giving,
who wishes to raise his reputation, make visible
his nobility to the troop, until all things pass,
light and life together: he who performs praise
keeps a high renown fast under heaven.

Deor

✻

Deor, copied into six little prose blocks in the Exeter Book, is clearly a poem that refers to heroic legends. It is usually read as a sad poem, in line with the four named and one unnamed melancholy situations that are cited by Deor, the persona: Weland's captivity, Beadohild's pregnancy, Geat's frustrated love, Theodric's 30-year exile and the sufferings of mad King Eormanric's many subjects; and then a man who looks like the prisoner Boethius, waiting for Philosophy rather than death in his cell. Each time, however, we are assured (unusually in a refrain) that this suffering will pass.

Scholarly consensus runs out early in *Deor* studies, but it remains true that all of the named people in this parsimoniously allusive poem are Goths or connected to the Goths of heroic legend; Boethius, too, of course, if he is the unnamed man in lines 28–30. Everyone has this relation except, apparently, Deor himself. His name is apparently a Welsh loanword (Breeze 1997) and his situation is that he was court poet to the Heodenings until the king, let's call him Heoden, gave Deor's job and lands to a new poet by the name of Heorrenda. The odd thing about this scrap of legend is that it places Deor in a time before Heorrenda's story begins: to judge by the Middle High German analogue in *Kutrun* (*c.* 1200), Heorrenda's singing will help Heoden elope with a new bride (a story in which Chaucer's *Wades boot* is also involved). For a view of this poem as comic, as a *jeu d'esprit*, composed to mock Alfred's father on his return with a young bride from Francia in 856, composed with satirical reference to his Gothic genealogy in the *Anglo-Saxon Chronicle* for 855 (with Geat, founder of the Gothic race), see North (1988, 1997: 160–71). For those who prefer to keep an open mind, Hill's edition is well rounded and good. This poem has also been read as a begging poem from a minstrel seeking new appointment.

Breeze, A., 'A Celtic etymology for Old English *Deor* "Brave" ', in *Alfred the Wise: Studes in Honour of Janet Bately on the Occasion of her Sixty-Fifth Birthday*, ed. J. Roberts and J. L. Nelson, with M. Godden (Cambridge, 1997), 1–4

Hill, J., ed., *Old English Minor Heroic Poems*, Durham and St Andrews Medieval Texts 4 (Durham, 1983)

Kiernan, K. S., '*Deor*: the consolations of an Anglo-Saxon Boethius', *Neuphilologische Mitteilungen* 79 (1978), 333–40

Mostert, M., 'Remembering the Barbarian past: oral traditions about the distant past in the Middle Ages', in *The Medieval Chronicle IV*, ed. E. Kooper (Amsterdam, 2006), 113–25

North, R., '*Jeux d'Esprit* in "Deor" 14–16: Geat and Mæðhild', *Amsterdamer Beiträge zur älteren Germanistik* 27 (1988), 11–24

North, R., *Heathen Gods in Old English Literature*, Cambridge Studies in Anglo-Saxon England 22 (Cambridge, 1997)

Welund him be *wif*man wræces cunnade,
anhydig eorl earfoþa dreag,
hæfde him to gesiþþe sorge ond longaþ,
wintercealde wræce. Wean oft onfond,
siþþan hine Niðhad on nede legde,
swoncre seonobende on syllan monn.
Þæs ofereode, þisses swa mæg.

Beadohilde ne wæs hyre broþra deaþ
on sefan swa sar swa hyre sylfre þing,
þæt heo gearolice ongieten hæfde
þæt heo eacen wæs. Æfre ne meahte

Welund by a woman got to know wretchedness,
single-minded nobleman, endured hardships,
had for companionship sorrow and longing,
winter-cold revenge. He often found woe
after Nithad laid constraints upon him,
supple sinew-bonds on a higher-ranking man.
Sorrow went from that, so it can from this.

To Beadohild the death of her brothers
Was not so grievous in mind as her own condition,
that she had suddenly discovered
that she was pregnant. Never could she

---

1 *be wifman* 'by a woman'. The manuscript has the less intelligible *be wurman* 'by worms', or 'by serpents'. However, the text before *Deor* in the Exeter Book, *Soul and Body II*, refers to *wyrmas* '(grave's) worms' on lines 22, 67, 78, 105, 110, 117 and 119 (just before the end), enough times for the scribe to have thought of *wyrmum* and copied it by ear in a late West Saxon spelling *wurman* for *be *wifman* here. The woman is Nithad's queen, if *wræces cunnade* means 'got to know wretchedness'; Beadohild, their daughter, if it means 'tried out revenge'.

5 *hine Niðhad on nede legde* 'Nithad laid constraints on him'. OE *nede* here is close to *hǫfgar nauðir* 'heavy chains' which Vǫlundr (Wayland) finds on him when he awakes in *The Lay of Wayland*, stanza 12.

6 *swoncre seonobende* 'supple sinew-bonds'. This resembles the *besti . . síma* 'bast-rope cords' which Wayland seems to mention in *The Lay of Wayland*, stanza 13.

7 'Sorrow' is supplied, as the idea understood to cover the genitives of the pronouns in *Deor*'s refrain.

10 *gearolice ongieten* 'suddenly discovered'. An unsual perspective, to show this moment for Beadohild some time down the line.

11 *eacen* 'pregnant'. OIce *aukin* of the same (elsewhere unattested) meaning in *The Lay of Wayland*, stanza 36, shows once more that there is an earlier source comon to both this and *Deor*, probably in England.

þriste geþencan,   hu ymb þæt sceolde.
Þæs ofereode,   þisses swa mæg.

We þæt Mæðhilde   monge gefrugnon
(wurdon grundlease   Geates frige)
þæt hi[m] seo sorglufu   slæp ealle binom.
Þæs ofereode,   þisses swa mæg.

Ðeodric ahte   þritig wintra
Mæringa burg;   þæt wæs monegum cuþ.
Þæs ofereode,   þisses swa mæg.

think with boldness how that should turn out.
Sorrow went from that, so it can from this.

We heard this of Mæthild's love-trade
(Geat's affections went without fulfilment)
that this sorrowful love deprived him of sleep completely.
Sorrow went from that, so it can from this.

Theodric ruled for thirty winters
the city of the Mærings. That was known to many.
Sorrow went from that, so it can from this.

12 *þriste geþencan* 'think with boldness'. OE *þristhycgende* 'boldly thinking' is used of the Virgin Mary planning to give her maidenhead to God in Advent Lyrics No. 9, *Christ* I, 288. It is worth noting that the Franks Casket panel (*B&OS*, plate 4) which depicts Beodohild visiting Welund on its left half, has on its right the Visitation of the Magi to Mary. [*hu ymb þæt sceolde* 'how that should turn out'. Beadohild gives birth, so we deduce from the Norse and other analogues, to the (Gothic) hero Widia.

14 *Mæðhilde* 'Mæthild's'. The manuscript has *mæð hilde*, which led some to look for a sense 'moderation' in the first element, but it seems more likely that this is an early OE form of the name *Matilda*. [*monge* 'love-trade'. The 'trade' word survives in the stem of Modern English *monger*. 'Love' is supplied for the context.

15 *Geates frige* 'Geat's affections'. Geat, if he is Gapt or Gautr, is the founder of the Gothic race. The poet seems to cast him in failed lover's role, which we see with Óðinn (also known as Gautr) and Billingr's wife in *The Sayings of the High One*, stanzas 96–102.

16 *hi[m]* 'him' (dative). This reading takes the scribe to have omitted a macron on the *hi* of the manuscript here, which could otherwise be read as 'her' (for *hie*), changing the meaning completely.

18 *Ðeodric ahte þritig wintra* 'Theodric ruled for thirty winters'. If the legendary 30-year exile of Dietrich, which forms part of the *Hildebrandslied*, is part of this allusion, the city of the Mærings must refer to a region in the Balkans. This story was widespread. The poem in the Rök runestone incription of Gotland, from the late ninth century, presents Þioðrekr as *skati Mæringja* 'prince of Mærings'. His name is recorded in *Widsith*, line 115, something of his exile in *Waldere* II, 4–9, while Alfred's scholars cite him in a historical context in the West Saxon *Boethius* (see **The Earliest English Prose**).

We geascodan Eormanrices
wylfenne geþoht; ahte wide folc
Gotena rices. Þæt wæs grim cyning!
Sæt secg monig sorgum gebunden,
wean on wenan, wyscte geneahhe
þæt þæs cynerices ofercumen wære.
Þæs ofereode, þisses swa mæg.

Siteð sorgcearig, sælum bidæled,
on sefan sweorceð, sylfum þinceð
þæt sy endeleas earfoða dæl.
Mæg þonne geþencan, þæt geond þas woruld
witig Dryhten wendeþ geneahhe,
eorle monegum are gesceawað,
wislicne blæd, sumum weana dæl.
Þæt ic bi me sylfum secgan wille
þæt ic hwile wæs Heodeninga scop,

We have heard about Eormanric's
wolvish intention. He had power over the wide nation
of the Goths. That was a fierce king!
Many a man sat bound up with sorrows,
with woe all he could hope for, wished constantly
that this man's kingdom might be overcome.
Sorrow went from that, so it can from this.

He sits with sorrowful care, deprived of fortunes,
his mind darkens, to the man himself it seems
that his share of hardship may be endless.
He can then consider that through this world
the mighty Lord changes constantly,
shows his grace to many a nobleman,
an established fame, to others a share of woe.
This about myself I wish to say,
that at one time I was the Heodenings' poet,

---

23 *Þæt wæs grim cyning!* 'That was a fierce king!'. Eormanric has a supporting role as Hama's pursuer in *Beowulf*, lines 1200–1, as husband of the poet's lady patron in *Widsith*, lines 8, 18 and 88, and as Jǫrmunrekkr, doomed magician king, in Bragi's *Eulogy on Ragnarr* (*c.* 850), stanzas '1–6', and in *Hamðismál* 'The Lay of Hamðir'.

28 *Siteð sorgcearig* 'He sits with sorrowful care'. This looks rather like Boethius, but could be anyone.

36 *Heodeninga scop* 'Heodenings' poet'. Heoden is king of the *Glomme* or *Glommas* in *Widsith*, line 21. As Heðinn, he takes part in an everlasting battle (alongside Hjarrandi) for a princess named Hildr in Bragi's *Eulogy on Ragnarr* (*c.* 850), stanzas '7–10' and refrain. For an argument that Heorrenda is, or will be, Heoden's accomplice in securing a princess as bride, see North (1997: 168–9). This is how Hêtele and Hôrant proceed in *Kutrun* (*c.* 1200).

dryhtne dyre. Me wæs Deor noma.
Ahte ic fela wintra folgað tilne,
holdne hlaford, oþþæt Heorrenda nu,
leoðcræftig monn londryht geþah,
þæt me eorla hleo ær gesealde.
Þæs ofereode, þisses swa mæg!

---

dear to my master. 'Dear' was my name.
For many winters I had an excellent following,
a loyal lord, until Heorrenda now,
a man skilled in songs, received those titles to land
that the shield of nobles once gave to me.
Sorrow went from that, so it can from this.

---

37 *Me wæs Deor noma* '"Dear" was my name'. OE *deor*, a word which may be of Welsh origin (Breeze 1997), means 'valiant', but a pun is clearly intended with *dyre* 'dear' just before.

The Lay of Wayland

Vǫlundarkviða

Vǫlundarkviða is the most haunting poem of the Poetic *Edda*, also the most battered and obscure (Dronke 1997). The story is set in unidentified northern wastes which are probably near Finnmark in sub-arctic Norway, a region that was described by a Norwegian to King Alfred in the 890s (see 'The voyages of Ohthere' in **The Earliest English Prose**, custom version). The poem's characteristic minimal style, partly a consequence of poor preservation, intensifies the emotions of a story about different forms of loss. First Wayland and his two brothers meet their wives. The men are hunters and apparently Sámi (or Lapps). The women are supernatural, swan-women caught by the temporary loss of their feathered shapes (ultimately this is thought to be a Siberian motif; Tolley 2009: 553–4). Whether or not this episode was added on later as a prelude, as some believe, it is certain that a redactor has written in the verses that connect the swan-women with heroic dynasties in Europe. Married life is happy, but the women long to become the swans they once were, and after eight years of marriage they suddenly leave and migrate south.

Egill and Slagfinn go after their women, while Wayland stays behind for his. It is hard to say whether this is from pride at not running after, or from a hope that waiting will bring her back. But Wayland loses his brothers too, and after a period of solitude in which he crafts ring after ring possibly to lure his wife back, he finds himself made captive by Níðuðr, king of the 'Niárar'. Here the story enters the phase known also in *Deor* and on the Frank's Casket. Wayland is classed as a wild animal by Níðuðr's unnamed queen, his sinews are cut so that he cannot escape, and he is placed in a smithy on an island in a lake in order to fashion trinkets for the king and queen and their two sons and daughter. The daughter's name is Bǫðvildr, identical with Beadohild in *Deor*. The children grow curious, and one day Níðuðr's two sons overcome their fears and come to the *álfa ljóði* 'prince of demons' in his secluded smithy, accepting his invitation to return on a second, this time utterly secret, visit. He kills them, making bowls, jewels and brooches out of respectively their skulls, eyes and teeth, which he passes on as *objets d'art* to the unwitting parents. True wealth lies in human not material resource. This message is to be found not only in Wayland's warning rattle to the king in stanza 15, but less cruelly also in *Sayings of the High One*, stanza 47 (see **Poems on the Meaning of Life**). Bǫðvildr then visits Wayland, drawn to the lonely recluse by emotional curiosity as well as for the apparent reason that her ring, the one that Wayland had once made for his bride, needs a repair. Wayland repairs himself by making Bǫðvildr his new bride. He rapes her, taking advantage after plying her with beer. She proceeds home pregnant while Wayland, now magically empowered it seems by the return of his ring, lifts himself laughing into the sky like a Lappish shaman.

It is possible that Bǫðvildr loves Wayland even after this. As the poet reveals, in an expression for her feelings that may not be sarcastic, Bǫðvildr *tregði fǫr friðils* 'grieved for lover's parting' (stanza 29). Wayland tells all to the king, after securing oaths to protect the princess from her parents, for she will give birth to his child. The scene between father and daughter has emotional delicacy, the obverse of the cruelty of vengeance which the poet so well understands. Wayland's cruelty is the product of an education by the king whom he punishes with the loss of true wealth, his sons. However, Wayland also leaves Níðuðr with a grandson after teaching him to cherish his family in the way that he once might have respected Wayland's. From another point of view, *Vǫlundarkviða* also tells the tale of the birth of Widia or Viðia, a great hero of the Germanic 'age of migrations'. This is the perspective of *Deor*, and it may seem that this poem has more in common with *Deor* than names or heroic formulae. It has been suggested that in respect of Wayland, *Deor* and *Vǫlundarkviða* were based on one poem, and that this was composed in the Danelaw, in England, in the late ninth or early tenth century (McKinnell 2001).

Dronke, U., ed., trans. and comm., *The Poetic Edda, vol. II: Mythological Poems* (Oxford, 1997)

McKinnell, J., 'The Context of *Vǫlundarkviða*', *Saga-Book of the Viking Society* 23 (1990), 1–27

McKinnell, J., 'Eddic poetry in Anglo-Scandinavian northern England', in *Vikings and the Danelaw: Select Papers from the Proceedings of the Thirteenth Viking Congress, Nottingham and York, 21–30 August 1997*, ed. J. Graham-Campbell, R. Hall, J. Jesch and D. N. Parsons (Oxford, 2001), 327–44

Motz, L., 'New thoughts on *Vǫlundarkviða*', *Saga-Book of the Viking Society* 22 (1986), 50–68

Taylor, P. Beekman, 'The structure of *Vǫlundarkviða*', *Neophilologus* 47 (1963), 228–36

Tolley, C., *Shamanism in Norse Myth and Magic*, 2 vols, Folklore Fellows' Communications 296 (Helsinki, 2009)

Prose introduction

Níðuðr hét konungr í Svíþjóð. Hann átti tvá sonu ok eina dóttur. Hon hét Bǫðvildr. Brœðr váru þrír, synir Finnakonungs. Hét einn Slagfiðr, annarr Egill, þriði Vǫlundr. Þeir skriðu ok veiddu dýr. Þeir kómu í Úlfdali ok gerðu sér þar hús. Þar er vatn, er heitir Úlfsjár. Snemma of morgin fundu þeir á vatnsstrǫndu konur þrjár, ok spunnu lín. Þar váru hjá þeim álptarhamir þeira. Þat váru valkyrjur. Þar váru tvær dœtr Hlǫðvés konungs, Hlaðguðr svanhvít ok Hervǫr alvítr, in þriðja var Ǫlrún Kjársdóttir af Vallandi. Þeir hǫfðu þær heim til skála með sér. Fekk Egill Ǫlrúnar, en Slagfiðr Svanhvítrar, en Vǫlundr Alvitrar. Þau bjuggu sjau vetr. Þá flugu þær at vitja víga ok kómu eigi aptr. Þá skreið Egill at leita ǫlrúnar, en Slagfiðr leitaði Svanhvítrar, en Vǫlundr sat í Úlfdǫlum. Hann var hagastr maðr, svá at menn viti, í fornum sǫgum. Níðuðr konungr lét hann hǫndum taka, svá sem hér er um kveðit:

There was a king in Sweden called Níðuðr. He had two sons and one daughter, whose name was Bǫðvildr. There were three brothers, sons of the king of Lapps. One was called Slagfinn, the other one Egill, Wayland the third. They went skiing and hunting deer, came into Wolfdale and built themselves a house. There is a lake there called Wolf Water. Early one morning they found on the lakeside three women spinning linen. Their swan-shapes were lying near them and they were valkyries, two daughters of King Louis named Hlaðgunn Swanwhite and Hervǫr Allwhite, while the third was Ale-rune the daughter of King Kjárr of France. The men took the women home with them to their cabin. Egill married

Ale-rune, and Slagfinn Swanwhite, and Wayland Allwhite. They all lived as man and wife for seven years. Then the women flew away to seek battles and didn't come back. Egill then skied off to look for Ale-rune, while Slagfinn looked for Swanwhite, but Wayland sat in Wolfdale. He was the most skilled craftsman known to anyone in stories of the past. Níðuðr had his arms bound as a prisoner, as is said in this poem:

Vǫlundr's lost marriage

1 Meyjar flugu sunnan myrkvið í gǫgnum,
alvítr unga[r], ǫrlǫg drýgja;
þær á sævarstrǫnd settusk at hvílask
drósir suðrœnar, dýrt lín spunnu.

Girls flew from south, right across Mirkwood,
Young foreign beings, to live their destiny.
They settled down to rest on the lakeside,
Southern maidens, spun precious linen.

2 Ein nam þeira Egil at verja,
fǫgr mær fira, faðmi ljósum;
ǫnnur var Svanhvít, svanfjaðrar dró,
en in þriðja þeira systir
varði hvítan hals Vǫlundar.

One of them did clasp Egill,
Fair maiden of men, to her dazzling breast.
The other, Swanwhite, drew in her swanfeathers,
While the third sister of those three
Clasped the white neck of Wayland.

3 Sátu síðan sjau vetr at þat,
en inn átta allan þráðu,
en inn níunda nauðr of skilði;
meyjar fýstusk á myrkvan við,
alvítr unga[r], ǫrlǫg drýgja.

So they stayed for seven winters,
But all the eighth they were yearning,
And need split them up in the ninth.
The girls made haste to Mirkwood,
Young foreign beings, to live their destiny.

---

1 The prose introduction in the manuscript, Codex Regius, succeeds in setting the story, but like the editorial interventions subsequent to the poet, attaches too much importance to the women's identity as daughters of imperial Europe. Vǫlundr's wife may not be named in the poem as it was composed, but as 'Alhvítr' (probably an adaptation of *alvítr* 'alien being', or even related to *álpt* 'swan'), she is the daughter of a King Hlǫðvér (Ludwig or Louis) like her sister 'Hlaðgunn', while the third women's father is Kiár (Caesar) of France.

4 Kom þar af veiði veðreygr skyti,
[Vǫlundr, líðandi um langan veg],
Slagfiðr ok Egill, sali fundu auða,
gengu út ok inn ok um sáusk.

Came from the hunt a weather-eyed marksman,
[Wayland, ranging over a great expanse,]
Slagfinn and Egill, rooms found deserted,
Went outside and inside and looked around.

5 Austr skreið Egill at ǫlrúnu,
en suðr Slagfiðr at Svanhvítu,
en einn Vǫlundr sat í Ulfdǫlum.

East skied Egill for Ale-rune,
And Slagfinn south for Swanwhite,
But Wayland sat alone in Wolfdales.

6 Hann sló gull rautt við gim fastan,
lukði hann alla lindbauga vel;
svá beið hann sinnar ljós[s]ar
kvánar, ef hánum koma gerði.

He beat a gem its casing from burnished red gold,
Closed all his rings well to thread on linden rope.
Thus did he wait for his own dazzling
Wife, did she only come to him.

Níðuðr binds Vǫlundr

7 Þat spyrr Níðuðr, Níára dróttinn,
at einn Vǫlundr sat í Ulfdǫlum;
nóttum fóru seggir, neglðar váru brynjur,
skildir bliku þeira við inn skarða mána.

Níðuðr hears this, lord of the Níárar,
That Wayland sat alone in Wolfdales.
Men went by night, with studded mailcoats,
Their shields glinted against the waning moon.

4 As may be deduced from the formulaic style, lines appear to be missing here and in stanza 16, which are supplied in square brackets from the stanzas which resemble them.

6 *gim fastan* 'a gem its casing'. The word *gim* is probably loaned from OE *gimm* 'gem'.

8 Stigu ór sǫðlum at salar gafli,
gengu inn þaðan endlangan sal;
sáu þeir á bast bauga dregna,
sjau hundruð allra, er sá seggr átti.

Climbed off the saddle by the house gable,
From there they walked in down the hall.
They saw rings drawn up on bast-rope,
Seven hundred in all which that man owned.

9 Og þeir af tóku ok þeir á létu,
fyr einn útan, er þeir af létu.

And they took them off and they put them on,
All except one which they kept off.

10 Kom þar af veiði veðreygr skyti,
Vǫlundr, líðandi um langan veg.
Gekk hann brúnni [beru] hold steikja,
hár brann hrísi allþurr fura,
viðr inn vindþurri, fyr Vǫlundi.

Came from the hunt a weather-eyed marksman,
Wayland, ranging over a great expanse.
He went to roast the flesh of a brown [she-bear],
High burned the all-dry brushwood of pinetree,
The wind-dried wood before Wayland.

11 Sat á berfjalli, bauga talði,
alfa ljóði, eins saknaði;
hugði hann, at hefði Hlǫðvés dóttir,
alvítr unga væri hon aptr komin.

Sat on the bear-skin, counted rings,
Prince of demons, found one missing.
He believed that Hlǫðvér's daughter had it,
That the young foreign being had come back.

12 Sat hann svá lengi, at hann sofnaði,
ok hann vaknaði viljalauss;
vissi sér á hǫndum hǫfgar nauðir,
en á fótum fjǫtur of spenntan.

He sat so long that he fell asleep,
And he awakened without joy.
He felt heavy chains on his hands,
And a fetter stretched around his feet.

---

10 *beru* 'of a she-bear'. Supplied where the text has nothing.

12 *á hǫndum hǫfgar nauðir* 'heavy chains on his hands'. The poet's use of *nauðir* in this unusual way resembles that of OE *nede* 'constraints' on Welund in *Deor*, line 5.

13 'Hverir ro jǫfrar, þeir er á lǫgðu
besti byr síma ok mik bundu?'

'Who are the warriors who laid these on,
Bast-rope cords, and bound me?'

14 Kallaði nú Níðuðr Níara dróttinn:
'Hvar gaztu, Vǫlundr, vísi alfa,
vára aura í Ulfdǫlum?'
Gull var þar eigi á Grana leiðu?
Fjarri hugða ek várt land fjǫllum Rínar!'

Called out now Níðuðr, lord of the Níárar,
'Where did you, Wayland, prince of demons,
In Wolfdales win this money of ours?
Was there no gold on Grani's path?
Our land, I thought, lay far from Rhine mountains!'

'Grani's path': the Rhineland, which Sigurðr crosses on Grani, his horse, after slaying Fáfnir the dragon.

15 'Man ek, at vér meiri mæti áttum,
er vér heil hjú heima várum.'

[spurious additional text: see note]

'I remember that we owned a greater treasure,
When we were all one family at home.'

16 [Úti stóð kunnig kván Níðaðar,]
hon inn of gekk endlangan sal,
stóð á golfi, stillti rǫddu:
'Era sá nú hýrr, er ór holti ferr.'

[Standing outside was the knowing wife of Níðuðr,]
She walked in down the hall,
Stopped on the floor and lowered her voice:
'The man from the woods won't be easy on us now.'

---

13 *besti byr síma* 'Bast-rope cords'. The element *byr* is doubtless corrupt, as it makes no sense.

15 The stanza's second half (*Hlaðguðr ok Hervǫr, borin var Hlǫðvé, / kunn var Ǫlrún, Kiárs dóttir* 'Hlaðguðr and Hervǫr, she was born to Hlǫðvér, Ǫlrún was famous, Caesar's daughter') introduces genealogy into this charged emotional context without the slightest regard for what Vǫlundr is saying.

Níðuðr konungr gaf dóttur sinni, Bǫðvildi, gullhring þann, er hann tók af bastinu at Vǫlundar, en hann sjálfr bar sverðit, er Vǫlundr átti. En dróttning kvað:

King Níðuðr gave his daughter Bǫðvildr the golden ring he took from Wayland off the bast-rope, while himself he wore the sword that had been Wayland's. The queen, however, said:

17 'Tenn hánum teygjask, er hánum er tét sverð,
ok hann Bǫðvildar baug of þekkir;
ámun eru augu ormi þeim inum frána.
Sníðið ér hann sina magni
ok setið hann síðan í Sævarstǫð.'

'The teeth on him extend when the sword is displayed,
And Bǫðvildr's ring he knows by sight.
His eyes are like those of the gleaming serpent.
Cut him, you men, from the strength of his sinews
And put him then in the House on the Lake.'

Svá var gert, at skornar váru sinar í knésfótum, ok settr í hólm einn, er þar var fyrir landi, er hét Sævarstaðr. Þar smíðaði hann konungi alls kyns gǫrsimar. Engi maðr þorði at fara til hans nema konungr einn. Vǫlundr kvað:

So it was done, the sinews in the hollows of his knees were cut and he was placed on an island off shore called the House on the Lake. There he fashioned all kinds of treasures for the king. No one dared to go to him except the king himself. Wayland said:

18 'Skínn Níðaði sverð á linda,
þat er ek hvessta, sem ek hagast kunna
ok ek herðak, sem mér hœgst þótti.

'Shines for Níðuðr a sword on the linden belt,
The one I did sharpen with the greatest skill I knew
And tempered as seemed to me most fitting.

19 'Sá er mér fránn mækir æ fjarri borinn,
sékka ek þann Vǫlundi til smiðju borinn.
Nú berr Bǫðvildr brúðar minnar
(bíðka ek þess bót) bauga rauða.'

'That gleaming sword is carried forever far from me,
I never see it carried to Wayland in his smithy.
Now Bǫðvildr wears my bride's burnished
(I wait for no recompense) red rings.'

Vǫlundr's revenge

20 Sat hann, né hann svaf, ávallt ok hann sló hamri;
vél gørði hann heldr hvatt Níðaði.
Drifu ungir tveir á dýr sjá
synir Níðaðar, í Sævarstǫð.

He sat constantly, nor did he sleep, and beat his hammer,
A magic he was making, rather quickly, for Níðuðr.
Two young ones rushed to see riches,
Sons of Níðuðr to the House on the Lake.

21 Kómu þeir til kistu, krǫfðu lukla,
opin var illúð er þeir í sáu;
fjǫlð var þar menja, er þeim mǫgum sýndisk
at væri gull rautt ok gǫrsimar.

They came to a chest, craved keys,
Open lay evil when they looked inside.
There were many necklaces which seemed to those boys
To be burnished red gold and jewelled treasures.

22 'Komið einir tveir, komið annars dags;
ykkr læt ek þat gull of gefit verða;
segiða meyjum né salþjóðum,
manni engum, at it mik fyndið.'

'Come just the two of you, come another day,
I will have that gold given both of you.
Don't tell any of the girls or hall people,
Don't tell anyone that you have met me.'

23 Snemma kallaði seggr annan,
bróðir á bróður: 'Gǫngum baug séa!'
Kómu til kistu, krǫfðu lukla,
opin var illúð, er þeir í litu.

Early it was when one man called the other,
Brother to brother: 'Let's go see rings!'
They came to the chest, craved keys,
Open lay evil when they looked inside.

---

20 *á dýr sjá* 'to see riches'; but also 'to see the beast'.

21 *er þeim mǫgum sýndisk* 'which seemed to those boys'. Treasure does not exist in itself, but as a medium of good or bad will. The poet does not mean that this is not treasure within the chest, for it is, but rather that the boys fail to see the malice behind it.

24 Sneið af hǫfuð húna þeira
ok und fen fjǫturs fœtr of lagði;
en þær skálar, er und skǫrum váru,
sveip hann útan silfri, seldi Níðaði.

He cut off the heads of those cubs
And laid their feet under the mud of the forge,
While the bowls that lay under their hair
He swathed in silver, gave to Níðuðr.

25 En ór augum jarknasteina
sendi hann kunnigri konu Níðaðar,
en ór tǫnnum tveggja þeira
sló hann brjóstkringlur, sendi Bǫðvildi.

And from the eyes, gemstones
He sent to the knowing wife of Níðuðr,
And from the teeth of those two
He forged brooches, sent them to Bǫðvildr.

26 Þá nam Bǫðvildr baugi at hrósa,
[bar hann Vǫlundi], er brotit hafði:
'Þoriga ek at segja nema þér einum.'

It was then that Bǫðvildr did praise her ring,
[Bore it to Wayland], which had broken:
'I dare not reveal it, save only to you.'

27 'Ek bœti svá brest á gulli
at feðr þínum fegri þykkir
ok mœðr þinni miklu betri
ok sjalfri þér at sama hófi.'

'I will mend the break in the gold
So that to your father it seems fairer,
And to your mother much better,
And to yourself like it was before.'

28 Bar hann hana bjóri, því at hann betr kunni,
svá at hon í sessi of sofnaði.
'Nú hef ek hefnt harma minna
allra, *né* einna, íviðgi*rna*!

He overcame her with beer, in that he knew better,
So that she fell asleep in her chair.
'Now I have avenged my injuries,
Not one, but all of the envious snares!

---

24 *þær skálar, er und skǫrum váru* 'the bowls that lay under their hair'. As Dronke points out, the poet's term for the boys' skulls is 'cruelly anticipatory' (1997: 318). But this also shows his daring in describing things metonymously, at one remove, as with *illúð* 'evil' in stanzas 21 and 23, and possibly *fjǫturs* 'of the fetter', 'forge', in stanzas 24 and 34.

26 *bar hann Vǫlundi* 'Bore it to Wayland'. This half-line is supplied where the text has nothing.

29 'Vél [á] ek,' kvað Vǫlundr, 'verða ek á fitjum
þeim er mik Níðaðar námu rekkar.'
Hlæjandi Vǫlundr hófsk at lopti,
grátandi Bǫðvildr gekk ór eyju,
tregði fǫr friðils ok fǫður reiði.

'I have the magic,' said Wayland, 'may I be on those webbed feet
That the heroes of Níðuðr took from me!'
Laughing, Wayland lifted into the sky,
Weeping, Bǫðvildr left the island,
Grieved for lover's parting, father's wrath.

30 Úti stendr kunnig kván Níðaðar,
ok hon inn of gekk endlangan sal,
en hann á salgarð settisk at hvílask:
'Vakir þú, Níðuðr Níara dróttinn?'

Standing outside was the knowing wife of Níðuðr,
And she walked inside and down the hall,
While he sat down to rest by the chamber wall:
'Are you awake, Níðuðr, lord of the Níarar?'

31 'Vaki ek ávallt viljalauss,
sofna ek minnst síz mína sonu dauða;
kell mik í hǫfuð, kǫld eru mér ráð þín,
vilnumk ek þess nú, at ek við Vǫlund dœma.

'I lie awake constantly, without any joy,
Least likely to sleep since the death of my sons.
There's a chill in my head, your advice is cold to me,
What now I desire is to talk with Wayland.

32 'Seg þú mér þat, Vǫlundr, vísi alfa,
af heilum hvat varð húnum mínum?'

'Tell me, Wayland, prince of demons,
What became of my healthy young cubs?'

---

28 *allra, né einna, íviðgirna*! 'Not one, but all of the envious snares!' This line barely makes sense, even after emending MS *nema* 'but for' to *né* 'not' and *ivið giarira* to 'íviðgiarnra' 'of malicious (harms)'.

29 *Vél [á] ek* 'I have the magic'. Usually *vél* is 'device' or 'scheme', but when Wayland takes off, it appears to be magic that helps him fly. The poet introduces elements of Lappish shamanism, in which spiritual flights were possible, without making his smith hero into a shaman (Tolley 2009: 552–8). The thirteenth-century *Velents þáttr* 'Tale of Velent', within *Þiðreks saga af Bern* 'The saga of Theoderic of Verona', a Norse translation of a Low German story of Wielandt, shows Wayland at this point making a flying shape out of feathers. But this cannot be his escape mechanism here. There is an apparent use of *vél* earlier, in stanza 20, with *vél gørði* 'a magic he was making', to express Wayland's magic (implicit in his name).

33 'Eiða skaltu mér áðr alla vinna,
at skips borði ok at skjaldar rǫnd,
at mars bœgi ok at mækis egg,
at þú kveljat kván Vǫlundar
né brúði minni at bana verðir,
þótt vér kván eig[i]m, þá er ér kunnið,
eða íoð eigim innan hallar.

'Oaths you shall first all swear to me,
By ship's board and by shield's rim,
By stallion's back and by sword's edge,
That you won't kill the queen of Wayland,
Nor be the slayer of my bride,
Though we may have a queen whom you know
And we may have a child inside this hall.

34 'Gakk þú til smiðju, þeirar er þú gørðir,
þar fiðr þú belgi blóði stokkna;
sneið ek af hǫfuð húna þinna,
ok und fen fjǫturs fœtr of lagðak.

'Go to the smithy that you made,
There you will find bellows soaked in blood.
I cut off the heads of your cubs
And laid their feet under the mud of the forge.

35 'En þær skálar, er und skǫrum váru,
sveip ek útan silfri, selda ek Níðaði;
en ór augum jarknasteina
senda ek kunnigri kván Níðaðar.

'And the bowls that lay under their hair
I swathed in silver, gave to Níðuðr,
And from the eyes, gemstones
I sent to the knowing wife of Níðuðr.

36 'En úr tǫnnum tveggja þeira
sló ek brjóstkringlur, senda ek Bǫðvildi;
nú gengr Bǫðvildr barni aukin,
eingadóttir ykkur beggja.'

'And from the teeth of those two
I forged brooches, sent them to Bǫðvildr.
Now Bǫðvildr goes with child,
Only daughter of the two of you.'

---

36 *barni aukin* 'with child'. OIce *aukin* 'increased (f.)' is nowhere else recorded for 'pregnant', the common meaning for OE *eacen* (f.), as with Beadohild in *Deor*, line 11. This is the strongest evidence that *Vǫlundarkviða* was composed in a Norse-speaking region of England.

37 'Mæltira þú þat mál, er mik meir tregi,
né ek þik vilja, Vǫlundr, verr of ní[ó]ta;
erat svá maðr hár, at þik af hesti taki,
né svá ǫflugr, at þik neðan skjóti,
þar er þú skollir við ský uppi.'

'You have spoken no words which could grieve me more,
Nor could I wish you, Wayland, worse joy of them.
There's no man so high he can reach you from horseback,
Nor so powerful that he can shoot you from below,
Where you are dangling up against the clouds.'

38 Hlæjandi Vǫlundr hófsk at lopti,
en ókátr Níðuðr sat þá eptir.

Laughing, Wayland lifted into the sky,
And unhappy now, Níðuðr stayed behind him.

39 'Upp rístu, Þakkráðr, þræll minn inn bezti,
bið þú Bǫðvildi, meyna bráhvítu,
ganga fagrvarið við fǫður rœða.

'Rise up now, Tancred, best of my thralls,
Ask Bǫðvildr, the maiden blond of brow,
To go dressed fair to speak with her father.

40 'Er þat satt, Bǫðvildr, er sǫgðu mér:
Sátuð it Vǫlundr saman í holmi?'

'Is it true, Bǫðvildr, what they said to me:
You and Wayland sat together on the island?'

41 'Satt er þat, Níðuðr, er sagði þér:
Sátum vit Vǫlundr saman í holmi,
eina ǫgurstund – æva skyldi!
ek vætr hánum [vinna] kunnak,
ek vætr hánum vinna máttak.'

'True it is, Níðuðr, what he said to you:
We sat together on the island, Wayland and I,
For one turn of the tide – it should never have happened!
I had no knowledge to fight him,
I had no power to fight him.'

---

41 *eina ǫgurstund* 'For one turn of the tide'. The *ǫgur*-prefix may mean this, the moment before the tide turns, but also 'anguish'. Like the author of *Deor*, this poet spends some time with the feelings of Wayland's victim.

Sayings of the High One

Hávamál

✳

For a note on this large composite poem, see the headnote in **Poems on the Meaning of Life**. The narrative on the woman below appears to have been composed together with a second narrative on Gunnlǫð at the end of the process in which *Hávamál* 'Sayings of the High One' was formed, perhaps with the aid of Ovid's *Amores* 'Love Affairs', and other works as a bridge to confirm the join of the Norwegian Gnomic Poem (stanzas 1–79 and following) with *Hávamál* Proper (stanzas 111–64).

Óðinn and the wife of Billingr

The story in this part of *Hávamál* works on its own terms as an analogue for that of Geat and Mæthild in *Deor* 14–16. The setting is heroic, with an earl on one side and a lady, probably a married woman, with her retinue of armed men in a riverside hall on the other. *Hávamál* has no other footing for this adventure in the 'heroic age', but the early modern ballads of Gaute and Magnild in Norway, and of Gauti and Magnildur in Iceland, tell us that Geat and Mæthild had their story in Scandinavia probably from medieval times (Malone 1961: 8–9), but the story in each ballad, that of a harpist who sings his wife back from the dead, is clearly different. If we take it to have been supplanted by the myth of Orpheus, it is possible that the earlier story was in line with that of Geat and Mæthild. Óðinn is elsewhere known as 'Gautr', which is the Norse form of 'Geat', and in this section of *Hávamál*, at any rate, he is likewise involved with a woman who tricks him into a night of frustrated desire. Of the two possibilities with the 'Billings mær' construction, that *mær* 'girl' plus a male name means 'daughter' or 'wife', the young woman's role as Billingr's wife is the more likely (Nordal 1936). In *Hávamál*, the coveted wife is named only in her relation to a certain 'Billingr'. The fact that Billingr is elsewhere twice as a dwarf's name should not influence a reading of the story in *Hávamál*, which seems to be drawn from a non-mythological tradition. This narrative and its sequel in the tale of Óðinn and Gunnlǫð (stanzas 104–110; see *The Mead of Poetry*, **Gods of the Vikings**, Custom Version) could have been composed in the later twelfth century as a sequence with which to improve an existing bridge between the standard and mystical gnomic parts of *Hávamál*, in stanzas 1–77 and 111–64 respectively (North 1991: 136–8). John McKinnell has also proposed that '*Hávamál B*', as he calls this pair of love stories, was composed at this time in emulation of Ovid's adulterous *Ars amatoria* or other love poetry of the kind that is known to have been read in monasteries in Iceland (2005: 107). These suggestions fit the earlier theory that Óðinn's phrase *hold ok hjarta* 'flesh and blood' in stanza 96 is derived from an expression in French and German romances from the twelfth century (von See 1978).

Clark, D. E. Martin, ed. and trans., *The 'Hávamál': With Selections from other Poems of the Edda, illustrating the Wisdom of the North in Heathen Times* (Cambridge, 1923)

Evans, D. A. H., ed., *Hávamál* (London, 1986)

Faulkes, A., *Glossary and Index* [to *Hávamál*] (London, 1987)

Malone, K., ed., *Deor* (London, 1961)

McKinnell, J., '*Hávamál B*: a poem of sexual intrigue', *Saga-Book of the Viking Society* 29 (2005), 83–114

North, R., *Pagan Words and Christian Meanings* (Amsterdam and Atlanta, GA, 1991)

von See, K., 'Das Herz in Edda und Skaldendichtung', *Skandinavistik* 8 (1978), 16–26

Sigurður Nordal, 'Billings mær', *Bidrag till nordisk filologi tillägnade Emil Olsson* (Lund, 1936), 288–95

95 Hugr einn þat veit er býr hjarta nær:
einn er hann sér um sefa;
øng er sótt verri hveim snotrum manni
en sér øngu at una.

The mind alone knows what lives near the heart,
mind alone is conscious of feelings.
No sickness is worse for any wise man
than to be happy with nothing.

96 Þat ek þá reynda er ek í reyri sat
ok vættak míns munar;
hold ok hjarta var mér in horska mær,
þeygi ek hana at heldr hefik.

This I experienced when I sat in the reeds
and waited for the one I wanted.
Flesh and blood for me that clever girl was,
yet I don't have her the sooner for that.

97 Billings mey ek fann beðjum á
sólhvíta sofa;
jarls ynði þótti mér ekki vera
nema við þat lík at lifa.

Billingr's wife I found on her bed,
sleeping, white as the sun.
No earl's enjoyment seemed real to me
unless to live with that body.

---

96 *hold ok hjarta* 'Flesh and blood'. This doublet looks modelled on either the German *herz und lîp* or French *cor e cors* 'heart and body', or both, from romances of the twelfth or thirteenth century (von See, 1978: 25).

97 *jarls ynði* 'earl's enjoyment'. Óðinn's self-characterisation as an earl is unprecedented, and it implies that the woman has a similar rank. The 'earl' best known for going after other men's wives, though without the intrigue, was the heathen reactionary Hákon Sigurðarson, earl of Trøndelag and Norway (died 995; see **Gods of the Vikings**).

98 'Auk nær apni skaltu, Óðinn, koma,
ef þú vilt þér mæla man:
alt eru óskǫp nema einir viti
slíkan lǫst saman.'

'Once again, Óðinn, you must come towards evening,
if you'll talk your way to a mistress.
It will be a total disaster if more than two know
of such a sin together.'

99 Aptr ek hvarf ok unna þóttumk
vísum vilja frá;
hitt ek hugða, at ek hafa myndak
geð hennar alt ok gaman.

Back I turned and was thinking of making love
with joy guaranteed.
This I believed, that I'd have to myself
all her passion and pleasure.

100 Svá kom ek næst at in nýta var
vígdrótt ǫll um vakin;
með brennandum ljósum ok bornum viði:
svá var mér vilstígr of vitaðr.

The next time I came, it was like her smart bodyguards
were all waiting wide awake,
With burning torches and firewood brought in, that's how
my path to joy was planned.

101 Ok nær morni er ek var enn um kominn,
þá var saldrótt um sofin;
grey eitt ek þá fann innar góðu konu
bundit beðjum á.

And towards morning, when I had come yet again,
and the palace guard was asleep,
I found a bitch on the bed of that worthy woman,
tied there with a leash.

---

98 The use of dialogue is as skilled as any in the *Edda*, particularly in the way this stanza suggests the tail-end of a conversation in which Óðinn does not get everything he wants.

100 *vilstígr* 'path to joy'. Evans (1986: 119) prefers *vílstígr* 'path of misery', as does Faulkes (1987: 37) 'path of wretchedness', because of an instance in *Sverris saga* 'The Saga of King Sverrir', but this context asks for *vilstígr* because of *vísum vilja frá* 'with joy guaranteed' in the stanza directly before. Of course Óðinn is ironic.

102 Mǫrg er góð mær, ef gǫrva kannar,
hugbrigð við hali;
þá ek þat reynda er it ráðspaka
teygða ek á flærðir fljóð;
háðungar hverrar leitaði mér it horska man
ok hafða ek þess vætki vífs!

Many a worthy girl, if you get to know her carefully,
shows a mind that is fickle with men.
This I experienced when I tried to lure that resourceful
lady into acts of deceit.
The clever mistress sought out every humiliation for me,
and I got nothing from that wife at all!

---

102 *vífs* 'wife'. Usually *víf* means '(domestic) woman' in general, but this context supports 'wife'. The emphasis on *lǫst* 'sin' (stanza 98) and on *flærðir* 'acts of deceit', which only the two should know, suggests that adultery is the theme, rather than the seduction of a nobleman's daughter.

Fragment of The Lay of Hildebrand

Hildebrandslied

⁕

That father and son meet on opposing sides is bad; as opposing champions, one for each army, is worse. This stark poem, now in a fragment, presents the worst case in which the father prepares to fight and kill his son. Hildebrand, the father, is the champion of King Dietrich the Ostrogoth, former king of Italy (Theoderic, OE *Þeodric*). Hildebrand has shared a 30-year Balkan exile with his master after they were driven out from Ravenna by a usurper named Odoacer (the same name as OE *Eadwacer*; see **Poems on the Meaning of Life**). Now Dietrich is back in Italy to take his kingdom from Odoacer. The battle will be resolved by a duel between their champions (Norman 1973). The tragic potential of this poem lies in the fact that Hildebrand's son, a baby when his father fled, has grown up to become Odoacer's champion. Hildebrand discovers that his opponent is the same Hadubrand, when he asks him for his genealogy before the battle starts. Hildebrand now tries and fails to persuade his son to put their kinship first and to stand down. Hadubrand refuses to believe that this old warrior is his father, but dismisses him as a Hunnish deceiver. Even if he believes Hildebrand just a little, it all comes too late: Hadubrand cannot abandon his duty to Odoacer, which requires him to defeat Dietrich by killing the enemy. The fragment runs out before we know who kills who, although it seems likely that father will kill son.

Hildebrandslied (Kassel, Landesbibliothek) is thought to contain a tragedy of particular Germanic type in which one system of obligation (to the king) must clash irreconcilably with another (to one's kin). There is a more complex version of this type in the story of Finnsburh in *Beowulf*, lines 1063–159 ('Hildeburh and Wealhtheow: funeral at Finnsburh'), and a quasi-historical version in the *Anglo-Saxon Chronicle*, year 755 (for 786), in 'Cynewulf and Cyneheard' (**The Earliest English Prose**). Later permutations appear in the Norse treatment of the Nibelung cycle, here in *Fragment of The Lay of Sigurðr*, in which Gunnarr must break his oath to Sigurðr, a bloodbrother, against the interests of Guðrún, his sister, in order to satisfy the honour of Brynhildr, his wife. The *Hildebrandslied*, to give this heroic lay its modern name, has been dated to *c.* 700 by Norman (1973) but to *c.* 800 by most others. This poem appeals to the emotions of a Germanic aristocracy, probably in northern Germany and in the reign of Emperor Charlemagne (768–814). It seems to have been copied in Germany in the East Franconian monastery of Fulda in the first third of the ninth century, by a scribe who may have tried to convert its High German Bavarian into a Low German dialect more resembling Old Saxon (Bostock 1977: 75–7; on this language, see *Genesis B*, in **Poems of Devotion**). This copying fits the legend in a biography of Charlemagne, which says that this Franconian emperor ordered the transcription of *barbara et antiquissima carmina quibus veterum regum actus et bella canebantur* 'barbarian (or: 'heathen') and most ancient songs in which the deeds and wars of old kings were sung' (see Dronke and Dronke 1977). Charlemagne's son, Louis the Pious (815–40), is thought to have had these poems destroyed as part of his programme of ecclesiastical reform.

Whether or not it does come from before 814, *Hildebrandslied* is the only legendary heroic poem to have survived in the Old High German vernacular.

Historically, the legend of Theoderic and Odoacer has changed from its historical basis many times over. The Greuthung Goth Theoderic became the Byzantine prefect of Italy in Ravenna in 493. This was after four years' campaign against Odoacer of the Sciri, a rival Germanic chieftain, who was the legitimate ruler of Italy in that he had won this country in 476 from the very last Roman emperor, Romulus Augustulus. Theoderic murdered Odoacer after inviting him to a parley in 493. The fact that in the legend Odoacer usurps Dietrich, exiling him to the Balkans for 30 years, is a later embellishment of Theoderic's success, for Theoderic had earlier been plundering the Balkans, the region that Zeno, the Byzantine emperor, intended to liberate by inviting Theoderic to conquer Italy. Theoderic was the subject of a cycle of heroic lays, most of which have been lost. These were known in England, where he is cited in *Widsith* and *Deor*; and in Bavaria, of course, in the *Nibelungenlied*, from *c.* 1200, where Dietrich is restored to Ravenna only when King Etzel (Attila) has been crowned and when the usurper Odoacer has died. In Scandinavia, the now-lost Low German romance of King Dietrich of Bern (Verona) survives in a Norwegian translation of the late thirteenth century, *Þiðreks saga af Bern*. In this version, Hildibrandr defeats his opponent Álibrandr, spares his life and is reconciled to him on finding that they are father and son. In the fifteenth-century Faroese version, however, *Snjólfskvæði*, Hildebrandur does kill his son. The story is known in scraps of narrative from other sources too. What distinguishes *Hildebrandslied*, apart from its early date, is its lack of the (chivalric) sentiment which seems to have turned the tragic ending into a happy one. Its best-known analogue for the classic tragic form of this story is the Persian tale from *The Shahnameh* 'The Epic of Kings', in which Rostam mortally wounds Sohrab only to find, from an arm ring that he had given his boy at birth, that he is the dying man's father.

Bostock, J. Knight, rev. K. C. King and D. R. McLintock, *A Handbook of Old High German Literature*, 2nd ed. (Oxford, 1976), 43–82

Dronke, U. and P. Dronke, *Barbara et Antiquissima Carmina* (Barcelona, 1977), 27–79

Murdoch, B., *The Germanic Hero: Politics and Pragmatism in Early Medieval Poetry* (London, 1996)

Norman, F., 'Das Lied vom Alten Hildebrand', in F. Norman, *Three Essays on the Hildebrandslied* (London, 1973), 51–82

Steinmeyer, E. von, ed., *Die kleineren althochdeutschen Denkmäler* (Berlin and Zurich, repr. 1963)

Hildebrand pleads with Hadubrand

Ik gihorta ðat seggen,
ðat sih urhettun   ænon muotin,
Hiltibra*n*t enti Haðubrant   untar heriun tuem.
Sunufatarungo   iro saro rihtun,

I heard it said
that the champions met, one against one,
Hildebrand and Hadubrand, between the two armies.
Father and son put their armour straight,

garutun sê iro guðhamun, gurtun sih iro suert ana,
helidos, ubar [h]ringa do sie to dero hiltiu ritun.

Hiltibra*n*t gimahalta, Heribrantes sunu (her uuas heroro man,
ferahes frotoro, her fragen gistuont
fohem uuortum [h]wer sin fater wari
fireo in folche). [. . .

. . .] 'eddo [h]welihhes cnuosles du sis.
Ibu du mi ęnan sages, ik mi de odre uuet,
chind in chunincriche, chud ist m*i* al irmindeot.'

Hadubra*n*t gimahalta, Hiltibrantes sunu:
'Dat sagetun mi usere liuti,
alte anti frote, dea érhina warun,
dat Hiltibrant hætti min fater. Ih heittu Hadubrant.
Forn her ostar gi*w*eit, floh her Otachres nid,
hina miti Theotrihhe enti sinero degano filu.
Her furlaet in lante luttila sitten,
prut in bure, barn unwahsan,

---

readied their war-gear and girded on their swords,
heroes, over ring-mail, when they rode to the battle.

Hildebrand spoke, son of Heribrand, he was the older man,
more experienced in life, who stood up to ask
in few words who the other man's father might be,
from which men in the nation: [. . .

. . .] 'or of which kindred you may be.
If you say me one name, I will know the other
families in the kingdom, I am wise to all the world.'

Hadubrand, spoke son of Hildebrand:
'I have been told by our people,
old and wise, who have lived long,
that my father was called Hildebrand. I am called Hadubrand.
Long ago he moved east, fled the malice of Odoacer
from here with Dietrich and many of his thegns.
He left sitting in poverty in the homeland
a bride in bower, a child not fully grown,

---

18 *Otachres nid* 'the malice of Odocacer'. This formula is also used of the Gothic Ermanaric (died 376) in *Beowulf*, lines 1200–1, where Hama *searoniðas fleah Eormanrices* 'fled the cunning enmities of Eormanric'. Historically Odoacer, who conquered Italy from Romulus Agustulus in 476, was the legitimate ruler whom Theoderic usurped (in 489–93: see below), but the legend has transformed him in order to glorify Theoderic.

19 *hina miti Theotrihhe* 'from here with Dietrich'. Theoderic 'the Ostrogoth', prefect of Ravenna and Italy for the Byzantine Empire 493–526 (see Theodric in *Widsith* and *Deor*, and in 'King Theoderic and Boethius' in the West Saxon *Boethius*, **The Earliest English Prose**).

arbeo laosa.   He[r] raet ostar hina.
Sid Detrihhe   darba gistuontu*n*
fate*re*s mines.   Dat uuas so friuntlaos man!
Her was Otachre   ummett irri,
degano dechisto   *m*iti Deotrichh*e*.
Her was eo folches at ente: imo was eo feh*t*a ti leop.
Chud was her   chonnem mannum.
ni waniu ih iu lib habbe.' [. . .]

'Wettu irmingot', quad Hiltibra*n*t,   'obana ab heuane,
dat du neo dana halt   mit sus sippan man
dinc ni gileitos!' [. . .]

Want her do ar arme   wuntane bauga,
cheisuringu gitan,   so imo se der chuning gap,
Huneo truhtin: 'Dat ih dir it nu bi huldi gibu.'

Hadubra*n*t gima[ha]lta,   Hiltibrantes sunu:
'Mit geru scal man   geba infahan,
ort widar orte. [. . .]

---

bereft of inheritance. He rode further east from here.
From that time forth Dietrich stood in great need
of my father. That was such a friendless man!
To Odoacer he bore a hate without limits,
most beloved of the thegns with Dietrich.
He was ever in the army's vanguard: ever did he love to fight.
Famous he was with courageous men.
I do not think that he is still alive.' [. . .]

'Great God be witness', said Hildebrand, 'high up in heaven,
that never yet did you keep with so close a kinsman
any assembly or company!' [. . .]

Then he unwound from his arm a spiral ring
made of imperial gold, which the king had given him,
lord of the Huns: 'From loyalty I now give you this.'

Hadubrand spoke, son of Hildebrand:
'With a spear must a gift be received,
point towards point [. . .]

---

24 *Dat uuas so friuntlaos man!* 'That was such a friendless man!' The force of this phrase as an encapsulation is similar to OE *Þæt wæs geomuru ides!* 'That was a melancholy lady!', in *Beowulf*, line 1075; *Þæt wæs grim cyning!* 'That was a fierce king!', in *Deor*, line 23.

30 *Wettu irmingot* 'Great God be witness'. These warriors are both Christians, as Dietrich certainly is, but the *irmin*-prefix is also known to have represented that of the Irminsuul, the great Saxon pillar that was destroyed by Charlemagne's troops on the river Weser in 777. In this light, *irmingot* literally 'universal god' is a case of converting a heathen term to Christian usage, possibly by inculturation in the north German plain in the 770s.

Du bist dir, alter Hun, ummet spaher;
spenis mih mit dinem wortun, wili mih dinu speru werpan.
Pist also gialtet man, so du ewin inwit fuortos.
Dat sagetun mi sęolidante
westar ubar Wentilsęo, dat *in*an wic furnam:
tot ist Hiltibrant, Heribrantes suno!'

Hiltibra*n*t gimahalta, Heri*bran*tes suno:
'Wela gisihu ih in dinem hrustim,
dat du habes heme herron goten,
dat du noh bi desemo riche reccheo ni wurti.
[. . .]
Welaga nu, waltant got, wewurt skihit!
Ih wallota sumaro enti wintro sehstic ur lante,

Old Hun, you are cunning without measure,
will lure me with your words, then spear me through.
You have grown old just so, by ever practising such tricks.
Sailors said this to me as they fared
west across the Vandal Sea, that battle took him:
Hildebrand, the son of Heribrand, is dead!'

Hildebrand spoke, son of Heribrand:
'Clearly I can see in your armour
that you serve in the house of a good lord,
that you haven't yet been exiled by this mighty man.
[. . .]
Woe now, O Ruling God, a woeful fate will pass!
I wandered, summer and winter, sixty half-years from this land,

---

39 *alter Hun, ummet spaher* 'Old Hun cunning without measure' etc. The only apparent insult in this text (Bostock 1976: 58–9). Father must thus fight with son for reasons other than insult. Probably this is because Hadubrand insists on fighting, while Hildebrand has his position as Dietrich's champion to think of before the eyes of two armies.

43 *westar ubar Wentilsęo* 'as they fared west across the Vandal Sea'. Merchants putting into northern Italian ports on the Adriatic, en route from the east (the Balkans) where they would have heard news of Hildebrand's death.

48 *bi desemo riche reccheo ni wurti* 'haven't been exiled by this mighty man'. The alliteration *riche-reccheo* is held as proof that the poem was once composed in a dialect of Old High German, such as spoken in Bavaria, on a theme drawn from heroic lays which were composed in Italy, in Lombardic (Bostock 1976: 79). The Low German (Saxon) forms, as *riki-wrekkio*, would not have alliterated.

49 *quad Hiltibrant* 'said Hildebrand'. Cut out here as unmetrical. It is thought a copyist added this and other such formulae, for they break up the alliteration. It is thus uncertain to whom the speech on lines 49–54 should really be assigned, as well as lines 55–7 and 58–62. However, the majority opinion favours Hildebrand in all these cases (Bostock 1976: 55). The poem as we have it seems to focus on the father's plight rather than on the son's.

50 *sumaro enti wintro sehstic* 'summer and winter, sixty half-years'. Thirty years. Understood here is the length of either summer or winter as six months, or half a year (as with OE *missere* and OIce *misseri* 'six months'). Hildebrand thus stresses the seasonal hardship of his 30-years' exile.

dar man mih eo scerita in folc sceotantero.
So man mir at burc ęnigeru banun ni gifasta.
Nu scal mih suasat chind suertu hauwan,
breton mit sinu billiu, eddo ih imo ti banin werdan!
Doh maht du nu aodlihho, ibu dir din ellen taoc,
in sus heremo man hrusti giwinnan,
rauba bi*r*ahanen, ibu du dar enic reht habes.
Der si doh nu argosto ostarliuto,
der dir nu wiges warne, nu dih es so wel lustit,
gudea gimeinun. Niuse de motti
[h]werdar sih [hiutu] dero hregilo hru[o]men muotti,
erdo desero brunnono bedero uualtan!'

Do lęttun se ærist asckim scritan,
scarpen scurim, dat in dem sciltim stont.
Do stoptun to samane staimbort chlu*b*un,
heuwun harmlicco huittę scilti,
unti im iro lintun luttila wurtun,
giwigan miti wabnum [. . .]

---

to where I was always placed against batallions of archers.
At no fort of any kind did death overcome me.
But now my sweet child shall slay me with sword,
break me with blade, or I will become his slayer!
Still, you can find out now if your courage is good enough,
as to which of the two of us will win the mail-shirt,
reckon up the war-booty, if you are in any way right in this.
You will take him now for the cowardliest of Eastern tribesmen
if he refuse you a fight, so fired up you are now
to join battle. Cost what it may,
let combat see who will boast of this armour
and lay claim to these two coats of mail!'

Then they first let the ash-spears fly at each other,
in sharp showers, that each stood into its shield.
From this, they stepped forward to meet, cleaved the jewelled boards,
cut with harm into the white shields,
until their linden-targes became of little use to them,
beaten in by weapons [. . .]

---

58 *Der si doh nu argosto* 'You will take him now for the cowardliest' etc. Hildebrand's sense of honour reasserts itself just ahead of his sense of 'the enormity of the crime he is being forced to commit' (Bostock 1976: 51). [*quad Hiltibrant* 'said Hildebrand'. Cut out here from mid-line, as unmetrical and unnecessary.

65 *staimbort* 'the jewelled boards'. This kenning for 'shield' is perhaps similar to *on stanfate* 'in its jewelled housing', in *Waldere* II, line 3, apparently for 'scabbard'.

68 *giwigan miti wabnum* 'beaten in by weapons'. The fragment runs out here, but the meaning seems clear. It is now one man against another with blades but without shields. It seems more likely that father will kill son.

Bragi's *Eulogy on Ragnarr*

Ragnarsdrápa

Bragi *inn gamli* 'the Old' Boddason, *c.* 850

⁂

Skaldic poetry is occasional Norse verse, from the Viking Age or later, whose authors are usually named. As its metre is the most complex of any surviving, the diction of Skaldic poetry is baroque and so are the arresting kennings that the *skáld* 'scolds, versifiers' construct. This poem cited in extract here, Bragi's *Eulogy on Ragnarr*, is credited with being the oldest Skaldic poem surviving because its alleged dedicatee, Ragnarr *loðbrók* 'Shaggy Breeches', was a Dano-Norwegian Viking from the mid-ninth century who spawned three invaders of England (including the sadistic Hinguar (Ingvarr or Ívarr the Boneless) in Ælfric's *Life of St Edmund*; see **Writers of the Benedictine Reform**). Ragnarr, who has a legendary saga all to himself, is said to have been thrown into a wolf-pit by King Ælle of Northumbria.

Bragi says that he has made the poem as thanks for the gift of a shield. As he bases his stories on the pictures of this shield, his poem is an 'ecphrasis' like Þjóðólfr's *Harvest-Long* (*c.* 900), or Úlfr's *Eulogy on the House* (early 990s), or even Keats' *Ode on a Grecian Urn*. Bragi's poem is preserved only in manuscripts of Snorri's *Edda* (*c.* 1220s–1230s, ed. Faulkes), in sections, in no particular order nor with any real proof of connection with the title that Snorri cites. Among much that remains unknown, the order and disposition of Bragi's stanzas and half stanzas, as below, is a matter of editorial choice.

The *Eulogy on Ragnarr* has four surviving sections. The first one, cited here, tells the tale of Guðrún's sons' attempt on the life of King Jǫrmunrekkr of the Goths in revenge for his murder of their half-sister Svanhildr, whom he put to death on suspicion of adultery with his son. The second section is about Heðinn's elopement with Hildr and his endless battle with Hǫgni, Hildr's father (a certain Hjarrandi is also involved). As the names indicate, these tales are related to stories in *Deor*; the second to a story with Heoden and Heorrenda, which in *Deor* has yet to take place.

Clunies Ross, M., 'Bragi Boddason', in *Medieval Scandinavia*, ed. P. Pulsiano (New York and London, 1993), 55–6

Faulkes, A., ed., *Skáldskaparmál*, 2 vols (London, 1997), vs. = 'verse'

Frank, R., *Old Norse Court Poetry: The Dróttkvætt Stanza*, Islandica 42 (Ithaca and London, 1978)

Turville-Petre, E. O. G., *Scaldic Poetry* (Oxford, 1976)

Vengeance on Jǫrmunrekkr

Proem

1 Vilið Hrafnketill heyra hvé hreingróit steini
Þrúðar skalk ok þengil þjófs ilja blað leyfa? (vs. 237)
Nema svát góð ens gjalla gjǫld baugnafaðs vildi
meyjar hjóls enn mæri mǫgr Sigurðar Hǫgna! (vs. 238)

Will you, Hrafnkell, and your chieftain hear how I shall praise him
And the leaf, grown bright with jewels, of Þrúðr's thief's footsoles?
For none but that renowned kin of Sigurðr would want good payment
For this ringing wheel, disk-hubbed, of the daughter of Hǫgni!

'Þrúðr': apparently Þórr's daughter, whose (would-be) 'thief' is Hrungnir. 'Leaf' of Hrungnir's 'footsoles': shield (see *Haustlǫng* 14–20). 'Kin of Sigurðr': Ragnarr *loðbrók* ('shaggy breeches') Sigurðarson. 'Daughter of Hǫgni': Hildr (valkyrie), whose 'wheel' is a shield (with disk-plated boss).

[. . .]

2 Knátti eðr við illan Íǫrmunrekr at vakna
með dreyrfáar dróttir draum í sverða flaumi;
rósta varð í ranni Randvés haufuðniðja
þás hrafnbláir hefnðu harma Erps of barmar. (vs. 154)

And now did Jǫrmunrekkr amid blood-stained retinues
Awake to an evil dream in the eddying of swords;
There was riot in the building of the head of Randvér's family
When the raven-black bosom-brothers of Erpr avenged their sorrows.

Jǫrmunrekkr: king of the Goths (d. 376; OE *Eormanric*). Randvér: the king's son by a marriage before Svanhildr; head of his family: Jǫrmunrekkr (who has Randvér hanged on suspicion of an affair with Svanhildr). Erpr: Guðrún's stepson, whose 'bosom-brothers' are Guðrún's sons Hamðir and Sǫrli (who kill Erpr on the way there). 'Raven-black': dark-haired; OIce *erpr* means 'brown'.

3 Flaut of set, við sveita, sóknar alfs, á golfi,
hræva dǫgg, þars hǫggnar hendr sem fœtr of kendu;
fell í blóði blandinn brunn ǫlskakki runna
(þats á Leifa landa laufi fátt) at haufði. (vs. 155)

Flowed the corpse-dew through the halls of the dispute demon
Where hewn-off arms knew legs, legs their arms, against the gore;
In a blood-blended fountain fell the ale-server of leavings-trees
(That's painted on the leaf of King Leifi's lands) on his head.

'Corpse-dew': blood. 'Dispute demon': Jǫrmunrekkr. 'Leavings-trees': men who leave food in their bowls (pun on *leifa* from the next line, gen. pl. of *leifar* 'leavings'), whose ale-server is the king. '(King) Leifi': sea-king, whose 'lands' are the sea, whose 'leaf' is a shield (on the gunwale).

4 Þar, svát gerðu gyrðan golfhǫlkvis, sá fylkir
segls Naglfara siglur saums andvanar standa;
urðu snemst ok Sǫrli samráða þeir Hamðir
hǫrðum herðimýlum her-Gauts vinu barðir. (vs. 156)

There the general saw standing unnailed, as they put a girth
On the floor-horse, his masts of the sail of the World's-End Warship;
In an instant and by common accord were Sǫrli and Hamðir
Pelted by the hard shoulder-clods of war-Goth's girlfriend.

'Unnailed': (Goths) as yet uninjured by the attackers. 'Put a girth on': (the Goths) surrounded. 'Floor-horse': hall. 'World's-End Warship': the ship Naglfar(i), whose 'sail' is a shield, whose 'masts' are (Jǫrmunrekkr's) warriors. 'War-Goth': Óðinn, or possibly King Jǫrmunrekkr himself, whose 'girlfriend' is the Gothic earth, whose 'hard shoulder-clods' are stones.

5 Mjǫk lét stála støkkvir styðja Gjúka niðja,
flaums þás fjǫrvi næma fogl-Hildar mun vildu,
ok bláserkjar birkis (ball) fagrgǫtu allir
(ennihǫgg ok eggjar) Íónakrs sonum launa. (vs. 157)

Hugely did the steel-snapper have them anvilled, those Gjúki-descended
Boys who would rob from life the love of the eddy-bird Valkyrie,
And all the men repay Jónakr's sons (blows rang out on foreheads
And on blades likewise) for the shining path of the blue-shirt birch-tree.

'Steel-snapper': sword-breaker: king. 'Have them anvilled': have them beaten on (i.e. with) stones. 'Gjúki-descended boys': Hamðir and Sǫrli, whose mother (Guðrún) is the daughter of King Gjúki of the Burgundians. 'Eddy-bird': swan; swan-'Valkyrie (-Hildr)': Svan-hildr, whose 'love' (ironically enough) is Jǫrmunrekkr. 'Jónakr's sons': Hamðir and Sǫrli. 'Blue-shirt': coat of mail, whose 'birch-tree' is a warrior, whose 'shining path' is the blood which flows from his sword: (Jǫrmunrekkr's) blood.

6 Þat segik fall á fǫgrum flotna randar botni;
Ræs gǫfumk reiðar mána Ragnarr ok fjǫlð sagna. (vs. 158)

This the Vikings' downfall which I show on the shield-rim's dazzling bottom;
Ragnarr gave me the moon of King Rær's chariot and many stories too.

'(King) Rær': sea-king, whose 'chariot' is a ship, whose 'moon' is a shield.

Heðinn's everlasting battle

7 Ok ofþerris æða ósk-Rǫ́n at þat sínum
til fárhuga fœra feðr veðr boga hugði,
þás hristi-Sif hringa hals, en bǫls of fylda
bar til byrjar drǫsla baug ørlygis draugi. (vs. 250)

And after this the Rán who wished to dry up too many veins
Intended to bring her father a storm of bows with hostile intention,
When the Sif of shaking bracelets, the woman filled with malice,
Bore to the wind's steed a neck-ring for the conflict tree.

'Rán who wished to dry up too many veins': predatory woman wanting bloodshed: Hildr. 'Storm of bows': battle. 'Sif of shaking bracelets': marriageable woman: Hildr. 'Wind's steed': ship. 'Conflict tree': warrior: here Hǫgni, father of Hildr.

8 Bauða sú til bleyði bœti-Þrúðr at móti
malma mætum hilmi men dreyrugra benja;
svá lét ey, þótt etti, sem orrostu letti,
jǫfrum ulfs at sinna með algífris lifru. (vs. 251)

Offered not that Valkyrie of the healing of bloody wounds her necklace
To the splendid protector for cowardice's sake at the meeting of metals;
Ever in this way she made as if to hinder warfare, even while inciting
Boar-princes to companionship with the wolf's quite monstrous sister.

'Valkyrie (Þrúðr) of the healing bloody wounds': woman reviving the dead: Hildr. 'Splendid protector': her father Hǫgni. 'Meeting of metals': battle. 'Wolf's sister': the goddess Hel, whose 'companionship' is death.

9 Letrat lýða stillir landa vanr á sandi
(þá svall heipt í Hǫgna) hǫðglamma mun stǫðva,
es þrymregin þremja þróttig Heðin sóttu
heldr an Hildar svíra hringa þeir of fingi. (vs. 252)

The land-lacking people-controller on the sand doesn't hinder
(Hatred then swelled in Hǫgni) the stopping of war-howler's desire,
When the sword-edges' tireless noise-divinities attacked Heðinn
Rather than any throat-rings from Hildr they might accept.

'Land-lacking people-controller': sea-king: Hǫgni. 'War-howler': wolf, whose 'desire' is hunger for dead warriors; 'stopping' this 'desire' means sating wolves with war-dead, which the Viking 'doesn't hinder': Hǫgni encourages the battle. 'Sword-edges' noise-divinities': fighting swordsmen. 'Throat-ring': necklace.

10 Ok fyr hǫnd í holmi Hveðru brynju Viðris
fengeyðandi fljóða fordæða nam ráða;
allr gekk herr und hurðir Hjarranda framm kyrrar
reiðr *af* Reifnis skeiði ráðalfs of mar brǫ́ðum. (vs. 254)

And instead of the Wutherer of the chained-mail ogress, it was,
On the duel-island, women's own spoil-destroying witch who decided;
All the army went forward beneath Hjarrandi's steady doors
Wrathful off the swift track of Reifnir over the decision-demon's mount.

'Chained-mail ogress (Hveðra)': enemy of the mail-shirt: axe, whose 'Wutherer (Óðinn)' is a king: Hǫgni. 'Spoil-destroying': each night she turns the dead warriors' weapons to stone. 'Hjarrandi's doors': sounding-boards (of lyres); 'steady boards': shields. '(King) Reifnir's track': sea. 'Decision-demon': Hildr, whose 'mount (horse)' is the island.

***Refrain* (11)** Þá má sókn á Svǫlnis salpenningi kenna;
Ræs gǫfumk reiðar mána Ragnarr ok fjǫlð sagna. (vs. 253)

That dispute may be made out on Svǫlnir's hall-penny;
Ragnarr gave me the moon of King Rær's chariot and many stories too.

'Svǫlnir's (Óðinn's) hall': Valhǫll, whose 'penny' is a shield. '(King) Rær': sea-king, whose 'chariot' is a ship, whose 'moon' is a shield.

Notes

1 *Vilið Hrafnketill* 'Will you, Hrafnkell, and your' etc. An awkward formulation. It is not clear who or what Hrafnkell is in relation to Ragnarr, whom the title claims as dedicatee. [*ens gjalla meyjar hjóls Hǫgna* 'this ringing wheel of the daughter of Hǫgni'. Hildr's wheel is a shield, for she is a valkyrie. However, this kenning looks forward to the story in stanzas '7–10' and refrain in which Hildr casts a spell on her men by which Heðinn fights Hǫgni for her forever.

2 *Randvés haufuðniðja* 'of the head of Randvér's family'. Ironic, given that Jǫrmunrekkr has executed Randvér, his son, on suspicion of adultery with Svanhildr, his second wife. [*hefnðu harma Erps of barmar* 'bosom-brothers of Erpr avenged their sorrows'. Their mission to avenge Svanhildr conflicts with their killing of Erpr, another half-sibling, earlier.

3 *Flaut hræva dǫgg* 'Flowed the corpse-dew' etc. The imagery of fighting descends into the surrealism of a flood, with blood for waves, in a pattern that is the inverse of the Red Sea drowning of the Egyptians in *Exodus*, lines 447–58 (see **Poems of Devotion**). [*hǫggnar hendr sem fœtr* 'hewn-off arms . . . legs'. The brothers Hamðir and Sǫrli chop off Jǫrmunrekkr's limbs prior to thinking of his head, their big mistake.

4 *Naglfara* 'Word's-End Warship'. The monster Muspell has a self-propelling invasion-ship in Ragnarǫk, end of the Norse world, in *Gylfaginning* 'the beguiling of Gylfi', ch. 43. See also *The Sibyl's Prophecy*, stanza 47 (**Gods of the Vikings**). This kenning identifies Jǫrmunrekkr with the monster, his men with the forces of evil and the brothers as the Norse gods, all about to perish. [*her-Gauts vinu* 'war-Goth's girlfriend'. Gautr (OE *Geat*) founds the Goths, Jǫrmunrekkr's tribe. The god's (and king's consort) is the earth, who accompanies any progenitor king. 'War-Goth' identifies the god as Óðinn.

5 *flaums fogl-Hildar* 'eddy-bird Valkyrie'. For Swan-*hildr* (i.e. Svan-hildr, see above). This type of kenning is known as *ofljóst* 'too lucid' (another joke).

7 *ofþerris æða ósk-Rǫ́n* 'Rán who wished to dry up too many veins'. Rán is the sea-goddess who nets in sailors (see *mægðegsan wyn* 'joy of the terror of nations' for sailor in *Maxims I*, 106, in **Poems on the Meaning of Life**). As avalkyrie, it is Hildr's intention to win all the men in the battle for herself.

8 *lét sem orrostu letti* 'she made as if to hinder warfare'. When her father Hǫgni refuses her necklace, another ring or circle like Bragi's shield, Hildr encourages the battle by cursing him (and forcing her lover Heðinn) into fighting forever. Is this an ironic female commentary on some men's enjoyment of war?

9 The first half of this stanza contains an embellished litotes or understatement for 'encouraged battle'. Compare the more standard Old English expression *swenges ne wyrnde* 'did not withhold the stroke', *The Battle of Maldon* (*c.* 991), line 118 (see **Viking Wars**).

10 *und hurðir Hjarranda kyrrar* 'beneath Hjarrandi's steady doors'. This shield-kenning implicates Hjarrandi (OE *Heorrenda*) as a harpist on the side of Heðinn (*Heoden*). The abduction story which forms part of Kutrun, and which may be Heorrenda's future service to his king in *Deor*, seems to be here as well, in that Hǫgni is the angry father pursuing his daughter's lover (in this case to Hoy, in Orkney; see *Deor*).

Refr. *ok fjǫlð sagna* 'and many stories too'. These may take the form of illustrations on the shield. Bragi's *Eulogy on Ragnarr* is an ecphrasis.

The Exile of the Sons of Uisliu

Longes Mac n-Uislenn

⁜

The *Longes Mac n-Uislenn* or *Loinges Mac n-Uislenn And-so* 'Exile of the Sons of Uisliu' forms an early part of the 'Ulster Cycle', a prelude to the better-known battle sagas of Conchobar and Cú Chulainn in the *Tain bó Cuailnge* 'Cooley's Cattle Raid'. The *Longes* tells a love story, one between the hero Noisiu (Naoise) and Deirdre, the woman whose beauty is prophesied to cause wars between all men who see her. Noisiu is the nephew of Conchobar, the polygamous king of Ulster who has already married a brace of sisters, including the formidable Medbh (Maeve), later queen of Connaught. Shortly after the prophecy concerning Deirdre, even before her birth, Conchobar decides to have her to himself. He brings her up in seclusion solely to be his bride, but Deirdre falls in love with Noisiu. They flee to Scotland, but there more jealousy ensues from the local king, whom Noisiu and his brothers now serve as mercenaries. From this they all take refuge on an island in the Western Isles, where they receive an invitation from Conchobar, who apparently forgives them, to come back home to Ulster. Tired of running, they accept, although against Deirdre's better judgement. Deirdre's lover does not listen to her, and on their arrival in Ireland the trap is sprung. The lovers are artfully separated from the main guarantor of their safety, Fergus mac Roig. This important ally, once king of Ulster himself, tricked out of his throne by Conchobar and now the champion of Ulster, is put in a position where his *geis* or taboo honour tells him to accept an invitation to a feast on the way to the royal hall at Emain Macha (Armagh). The lovers have no choice but to go on without him. There is a public ceremony of welcome when they get there, but then Conchobar has Noisiu and his brothers, and Fergus' son, speared to death in front of Deirdre, whom he then makes captive in the marriage she had tried to avoid. Fergus, in revenge for the death of his son and the loss of his honour, makes war on Ulster, burns down Armagh and, before going into exile in Connaught, slaughters the maidens of Ulster. The grieving Deirdre adds herself to the dead. When Conchobar, in revenge for her unrelenting coldness, passes her on to Eogan mac Durthacht, the vassal who had murdered Noisiu and his friends, Deirdre commits suicide by leaning out of their chariot, smashing her head on a rock.

This powerful Irish story has inspired much Anglo-Irish literature of the early modern period in the twentieth century. No fewer than five plays have been written about Deirdre, including W. B. Yeats' *Deirdre* (1907) and J. M. Synge's *Deirdre of the Sorrows* (1910). The source for all this, *Loinges Mac n-Uislenn And-so*, is visibly an analogue and often thought to be the source for the Brythonic romance of Tristan and Iseult (see Thomas of Britain's *Tristan*, **Early Chivalry**). It survives in two versions from the eleventh century, though with a textual origin as early as the eighth. The older version of the work is cited and annotated here on the basis of Vernam Hull's edition and translation, with the text simplified and the translation modernised. This work is a poem with prose, a sort of prosimetrum rather like *Guðrúnarkviða* I and other heroic poems of the Icelandic Poetic *Edda*. Deirdre's lament, given with chs. 17–19 in **Poems**

on the Meaning of Life, may also be compared thematically in that section with those of Guðrún and other grieving or elegiac women, including the speaker of the Old English poem *The Wife's Lament.*

Hull, V., ed. and trans., *Longes Mac n-Uislenn: The Exile of the Sons of Uisliu* (New York, 1949)
Kinsella, T., trans., *The Táin* (Oxford, 1969)

The flight of Deirdre and Noisiu

1. Cid diamboí longes mac n-Uisnig? Ni ansa. Bátar Ulaid oc ól i taig Feidlimthe maic Daill, scēlaigi Conchobuir. Baī dano ben ind Feidlimthe oc airiuc don t-slúag ōsa cinn is sí thorrach. Tairmchell corn ocus chuibrenn ocus rolāsat gáir mesca. A mbátar do lupthugud, dolluid in ben dia lepaid. Oc dul dī dar lár in taige, rogréch in lenab inna broinn cocloss fon less uile. Atraig cach fer di alailiu is'tig lasin scréich í-sin combátar einn ar chinn isin tig.

Is and adragart Sencha mac Ailella: 'Na cuirid cor díb!' or-se. 'Tucthar cucunn in ben cofestar cid diatá a ndeilim se.'

Tucad ïarum in ben chucu.

2. Is and asbert a cēile Feidlimid:

Cīa deilm dremun derdrethar,
dremnas fot broinn búredaig?
Bruït[h] clūasaib cluinethar
gloim eter do dā thoīb, trēn tormaid.
Mór n-ūath adn-āigethar
mo chride crēchtnaigedar crūaid.

---

1. Why were the sons of Uisliu exiled? The story is not hard to tell. The Ulstermen were drinking in the house of Feidlimid mac Daill, story-teller of Conchobar. Now the wife of Feidlimid was attending upon the host, standing up, and even so she was pregnant. Drinking horns circled and food was shared out and drunkenly they shouted. When they were about to turn in, the woman came to her bed, and as she was crossing the floor of the house, the infant in her womb screamed in such a way that the whole enclosure heard. At that scream there each man rose up, one after the other, so that they stood shoulder to shoulder.

Then Sencha mac Ailella, the seer of Ulster, issued a prohibition. 'Do not make a movement,' he said. 'Let the woman be brought to us in order that the reason may be known for this noise.'

Thereupon the woman was brought to them.

2. Her consort, Feidlimid, then said:

What is that violent noise that resounds,
That rages throughout your bellowing womb?
The clamour between your sides, strongly it sounds,
It crushes any man who has ears.
My heart is in fear
Of the great terror that keenly wounds.

3. Is and rolāsi co Cathbath, ar ba fissid side:

Cluinid Cathbad cóem-ainech
cáin, mál, mind mór mochtaide
mbrogthar tre druidechta drúad,
ōr nadfil lem féin find-focla
frismberad Feidlimid
fursundud fiss,
ar nádfitir ban-scál
cīa fo brú bī,
cid fom chriöl bronn bēcestar.

4. Is and asbert Cathbad:

Fot chriöl bronn bēcestair
bē fuilt buidi buide-chass
ségdailb sūilib sell-glassaib.
Sīan a grúade gorm-chorcrai;
fri dath snechtai samlamar
sét a détnge díänim.
Nīamdai a béoil partuing-deirg –
bé diambiät il-ardbe
eter Ulad erredaib.

---

3. Thereupon she rushed to Cathbad, for he was a soothsayer:

Hear, handsome Cathbad of the comely face,
A prince, a mighty great diadem you are,
One whom the spells of druids do magnify,
Since I myself have not the wise words
By which Feidlimid might obtain
The enlightenment of knowledge,
Seeing as the woman does not know
What is in her womb,
What cried out in the basket of my womb.

4. Then Cathbad said:

What cried out in the basket of your womb
Was a woman of golden hair with golden curls
With comely grey-green irised eyes.
Her purplish-pink cheeks like foxglove;
With the colour of snow I compare
The treasure of her spotless row of teeth.
Lustrous her lips of scarlet red,
A woman for whom there will be much slaughter
Among chariot-fighters of Ulster.

---

4. *Biät īar tur* 'They will be searched out'. The meaning is uncertain. 'They will be in the west' is another possibility, reading *biät īarthur*. Whichever it is, the line appears to predict the flight of Deirdre and Noisiu from one high king to another.

Gēssid fot brú búirethar
bē find fota folt-lebor,
imma curaid cossēnat,
imma n-ard-ríg īarfassat.
Biät īar tur trom-thoraib
fo chlí chóicid Chonchobuir.
Biät a béoil partuing-deirg
imma dēta nēmanda,
fris-mbat formdig ard-rígna,
fria cruth ndīgraiss ndīänim.

5. Dorat īar suidiu in Cathbath a láim fora broinn inna mnā coroderdrestar in lelap foa láim.

'Fir,' ar-se, 'ingen fil and ocus bid Derdriu a hainm ocus biaid olc impe.'

Rogēnair ind ingen īar sin, ocus dixit Cathbad:

A Derdriu

1 A Derdriu, maindēra már,
dia-msa cóem-ainech cloth-bán.
Cēsfaitit Ulaid rit ré,
a ingen fīal Feidlimthe.

What screams in your bellowing womb
Is a woman, fair, tall, long-haired,
For whom champions will enter into duels,
Of whom high kings will beg courtship.
They will be searched out with heavy troops
Supported by the province of Conchobar.
Her lips will scarlet red
About her pearl-white teeth,
Against her high queens will be jealous,
Jealous against her matchless, faultless form!

5. Cathbad then put his hand on the stomach of the woman, so that the infant roared beneath his hand.

'True,' he said, 'it is a girl there, and her name will be Deirdre, and much evil will come of her.'

Afterwards, when the girl was born, Cathbad said:

Deirdre

1 Deirdre, much you will destroy
If you turn out fair of face and fame.
Ulstermen will suffer while you live,
Demure daughter of Feidlimid.

2 Biäid ētach cid īar tain
dot dáig, a bé for lassair.
Is it aimsir – cluinte se –
longes tri mac n-Uislinne.

3 Is it aimsir gním dremuin
gēntar íarum i n-Emuin.
Bid aithrech coll cid īar tain
fo[r] foīsam maic Roig rogmair.

4 Is triüt, a bé co mbail,
longes Fergusa ó Ultaib,
ocus gním ar-coínfed guil
guin Fiachnai maic Conchobuir.

5 Is it chin, a bé co mbail,
guin Gerrci maic Illadain,
ocus gním nat lugu smacht,
orggain Eogain mac Durthacht.

---

2 Even afterwards, jealousy will be
Ablaze, woman, because of you.
In your time will be, and hear this,
The exile of Uisliu's three sons.

3 In your time a violent deed
Will be performed in Emain.
Repented afterwards will be
The ruin wrought by mighty Mac Roig.

4 Woman of destiny, because of you
Fergus will be exiled from Ulster,
Through you will be a lamentable deed,
The slaughter of Fiachnae mac Conchobuir.

5 Woman of destiny, for your crime
Gerrce mac Illadain will be slain,
Through you, the penalty of which is not less,
Eogan mac Durthacht will be killed.

5.2 'Uisliu'. Father of Noisiu, Aindle and Arddan; husband of Conchobar's sister. Noisiu is thus the nephew of Conchobar, as Tristan to King Mark. Cathbad's prophecy signposts the tale to come. As well as outraging any notion of decency, his poem offers the conundrum of a seer who inflicts a disaster on his people by inviting them to escape it. The stories are different, but it is worthwhile comparing Cathbad here with Teiresias in regard to Oedipus.

5.3 *i n-Emuin* 'in Emain'. *Emain Macha* (Armagh), the palace of King Conchobar which will end up in charred ruins when the story has almost worked itself out: a graphic illustration of illicit love. Now Nawan Fort, near Armagh. ['Mac Roig'. Fergus, son of Ro-ech 'Big-Horse'. Fergus avenges the lovers at the story's end.

5.4 'Fiachnae mac Conchobuir'. One of Conchobar's sons, slain in revenge for the death of Noisiu.

5.5 'Gerrce mac Illadain'. A champion of Ulster. ['Eogan mac Durthacht'. King of Fernmag (Farney), Conchobar's vassal.

6 Dogēna gním ngrānda ngarg
ar feirg ri ríg n-Ulad n-ard.
Biaid do lechtán i nnach dú;
bid scél n-airdairc, a Deirdriu.

6. 'Marbthar ind ingen!' ol ind óic.

'Ní-thó!' ol Conchobor. 'Bērthair lim-sa ind ingen i mbārach,' ol Conchobor, 'ocus ailebthair dom réir féin ocus bid sí ben bías im farrad-sa.'

Ocus niralāmatar Ulaid a chocert immi. Dogníther ón dano: Roalt la Conchobor co-mbo sí ingen as mór-áillem roboí i n-Hērinn. Is i llis fo leith roalt conachacced fer di Ultaib cosin n-úair nofoad la Conchobor ocus nibaí duine nolēicthe isin les sin acht a haite-si ocus a mumme ocus dano Lebarcham, ar níéta gabáil di ssidi ar ba ban-cháinte.

7. Fecht n-and didiu baí a haite na ingine oc fennad loíg fothlai for snechtu i-mmaig issin gaimriuth dia funi di-ssi. Con-accasi ní, in fíach oc ól inna fola forsin t-snechtu.

Is and asbert-si fri Lebarchaim, 'Ro-pad inmain ōen-fer forsambetis na tri dath ucut i in folt amal in fiachocus in grúad amal in fuil ocus in corp amal in snechta.'

'Orddan ocus tocad duit!' ar in Lebarcham. 'Ni cían úait. Atá is'taig it arrad i Noísi mac Usnig.'

'Ni-pam slán-sa ám,' ol-si, 'conidn-accur-saide.'

---

6 A fierce horrifying deed you will perform
In anger against the king of noble Ulstermen.
Your little grave will be everywhere,
A famous tale of you, O Deirdre.

6. 'Let the girl be slain!' cried the warriors.

'By no means,' said Conchobar. 'I am going to take the girl with me tomorrow,' Conchobar added, 'and she will be brought up according to my own will and she will be the woman for me.'

And the Ulstermen didn't dare to put him right with regard to that. And it was done, too. She was brought up by Conchobar until she grew up into the most beautiful girl Ireland had ever seen. Except Ireland didn't see her. She was brought up in a remote court where no man of Ulster might see her, right up to the night she was to spend with Conchobar, and no person was allowed to enter that court apart from her fosterfather, her fostermother, and Leborcham, who couldn't be prevented because she was a mocking woman poet.

7. One day, then, the fosterfather of the girl was skinning a weaned calf on the snow, outside in the winter, so as to cook it for her. The girl saw a raven on the snow drinking the blood.

Then she said to Leborcham, 'Dear to me would be one man with the three colours yonder, hair like the raven, cheeks like the blood, a body like the snow.'

'Dignity and fortune attend you,' said Leborcham, 'he isn't far from you. Indeed he is in the grounds nearby, Noisiu son of Uisliu.'

'I will not be well until I see him,' she said.

---

6. *ban-cháinte* 'a mocking woman poet'. Compare the Icelandic and other *skáld* ('scolds'), originally conceived as satirists; especially Steinunn *skáldkona* ('woman poet'), who mocked the German missionary Þangbrandr in Iceland in about 998.

8. Fecht n-and didiu baī-seom int-í Noísi a óenur for dóe inna rrátha i ina Emna, oc andord. Ba bind immurgu a n-andord mac n-Usnig. Cech bó ocus cech míl rochluined, nombligtis dā trian blechtad'immarcraid ūadib. Cech duine rodchluined, ba lór síthcahire ocus airfitiud dóib. Ba maith a ngaisced dano. Cīa nobeth cōiced Ulad i n-ōen-baili impu, acht corrochuired cách díb a triur a druim fri araile, nibertais búaid diib ar febas na ursclaige ocus na imdíten. Bat comlūatha dano fri conaib oc tafonn. Nomarbdais na fīada ar lúas.

9. A mboí-seom didiu a oínur int-í Noísi i-mmaig, mosētlan-si cuci i-mmach amal bid do thecht secha ocus nisn-athgéoin.

'Is cáin,' ol-se-sseom, 'in t-samaisc téte sechunn!'

'Dlegtair,' ol-si-si, 'samaisci móra bale nabít tairb.'

'Atá tarb in chóicid lat,' or-se-sseom, 'i rí Ulad.'

'Notogfainn-se etruib far ndís,' or-si-se, 'ocus nogēbainn tarbín óag amalt-so.'

'Ni-thó!' ol-se-sseom. 'Cid fo bīthin fáitsine Cathbad.'

'In dom fémed-sa adieri sin?'

'Bid dō immurgu,' or-se-ssem.

Lo sodain foceird-si bedg cuci corrogab a dá n-ó fora chinn.

'Dá n-ó mēle ocus cuitbiuda in-so,' ol-si, 'manumbera-su latt.'

'Eirgg ūaim, a ben!' ol-se.

'Rotbia ón', ol-si-si.

Atracht la sodain a andord n-ass. Amail rochūalatar Ulaid in-nunn in n-andord, atraig cech fer díb di alailiu.

---

8. One time after that, when the aforesaid Noisiu was alone on the rampart of the earthwork of Emain, he sang in a tenor. Melodious was the tenor singing of the sons of Uisliu. Each cow and each beast that heard this, two thirds the quantity of their milk was milked of them extra. Each person that heard it, his mind always settled down in harmony to enjoy the music. Good also were the arms of the sons of Uisliu. The province of all Ulster, though it might lie about them, still it would not gain the victory through the excellence of their parrying and self-defence, as long as the three of them fought back to back. As swift as hounds they were at hunting, moreover, through which they used to kill the wild stags.

9. So while the aforesaid Noisiu was standing alone outside, Deirdre quickly stole out, as if to walk past him unrecognised.

'Fair,' he said, 'is the heifer that goes past me.'

'The heifers,' she said, 'are bound to be big where the bulls are not.'

'You have the bull of the province,' he said, 'the king of Ulster.'

'If it was the two of you I had to choose between,' she said, 'I would take a young bullock like you.'

'By no means!' he said. 'Think of Cathbad's prophecy.'

'Do you say that to get rid of me?'

'I most assuredly do,' he said.

At that moment she leapt up at him and clasped both ears on his head.

'This be the ear of shame, this the ear of derision,' she said, 'unless you take me with you.'

'You go away from me, woman,' he said.

'You shall have that,' she said.

Thereupon the tenor voice rose from him in song. As the men of Ulster yonder heard his tenor song, each one of them stood up, one after the other.

10. Lotar maic Uislenn i-mmach do thairmesc a mbrāthar.

'Cid notaí?' ol-seat. 'Na'mmangonad d'Ultaib it chinaid!' Is and atchúaid dóib a ndorónad friss.

'Biaid olc de,' ol ind óicc. 'Cīa beith, nocobia-so fo mebail céin bemmit-ni i mbethaid. Ragmai-ni lee i tír n-aili. Nifil i n-Hērinn ríg natibre fāilti dún.'

Batar eat a comairli. Roimthigsetar in n-aidchi sin i tri coīcait láech dóib, ocus tri coīcait ban, ocus tri coīcait con, ocus tri coīcait gilla, ocus Derdiu i cumusc cáich combaī etarru.'

11. Bātar for fōesamaib céin móir mór-thimchell n-Érenn cotrīallta a ndíth co mmenic tria indleda ocus chelga Conchobuir ō-thá Ess Rúaid timchell síar-des co Beinn Étair sair-thúaid iterum. Ar-aī-de trá conda[t]roīfnetar Ulaid tairis i crích n-Alban. Congabsat i ndīthrub and. Ōnd úair roscáich dóib fíadach in t-slébe, doelsat for cethra fer n-Alban do thabairt chucu. Dochótar side dia ndīlgiund i n-ōen-ló condeochatar dochum ríg Alban condarragaib ina munteras ocus corogabsat amsaini acca ocus rosuidigsitar a tige issind faithchi. Im déigin ina ingine dorónta na tige connahacced nech leo hí ar dáig naromarbtais impe.

---

10. The sons of Uisliu went out to stop their brother.

'What is wrong with you?' they said. 'Let the men of Ulster not slay each other for your crime.' Then he told them what had been done to him.

'Evil will come of it,' the warriors said. 'Although you will not fall into any disgrace as long as we are living. We shall all go with her into another land. There is not a king in Ireland who will give a welcome to us now.'

That was their decision. They set out that night with warriors, women, dogs and servants, three groups of fifty of each, and Deirdre was in the midst of them all.

11. For a long time they came under the protection of other kings, all around Ireland, and often through the snares and wiles of Conchobar their destruction was attempted, from the Falls of Assaroe to south-west round north-east again to the Peak of Étair. The Ulstermen after that, however, chased them across the Irish Sea, into the highlands of Scotland. They settled there in the wilds. When the mountains ran out of game they turned on the cattle of the men of Scotland so as to get this for themselves. When these men one day sought to destroy them in turn, the sons of Uisliu proceeded to the Scottish king and he took them into his household. They took service with him as mercenaries, and set up their houses on common land. Because of the girl, their homes were made so that none of those visiting might see her, so that no one should have to die because of her.

---

11. *Ess Rúaid* 'the Falls of Assaroe'. On the Donegal-Connaught border. [*Beinn Étair* 'Peak of Étair'. The Hill of Howth, NW Dublin Bay. [*i crích n-Alban* 'into the highlands of Scotland'. Britain where Gaelic is spoken.

12. Fecht n-and didiu luid in rechtaire matain moch corralai cor imma techsom. Con-accae in lānamain inna cotluth. Dochūaid īar sin corodúsig in ríg.

'Nifūaramar-ni,' or-se, 'mnaī do dingbāla-so cosin diu. Atá i fail Noísen maic Uislenn ben dingbāla ríg íathair domuin. Marbthat for chét-oir Noīsi ocus foath in ben lat-so,' ol in rechtaire.

'Acc,' ol in rí, 'acht eirg-siu dia guidi dam-sa cech lāa fo chlith.'

Dogníther ón. A n-atbered immurgu in rechtaire frie-si chaidchi, adfeded-si dia cēliu in n-aidchi sin fo chét-óir. Ūair naroétad ní dī, noerálta for maccaib Uislenn dul i ngābthib ocus i cathaib ocus i ndrobēlaib ar dáig corommarbtais. Ar-aī-de natar sonairtisium im cech n-imguin connarétad ní dóib asna amsib sin.

13. Rotinōlta fir Alban dia marbad íarna chomairli frie-si. Atfét-si do Noísin.

'Imthigid ass!' or-si. 'Manidigsid ass in-nocht, nobormairfither i mbárach.'

Lothat ass ind aidchi sin combātar i n-inis mara. Adfiadar do Ultaib an-í-sin.

'Is tróg, a Conchobuir,' ol Ulaid, 'maic Uislenn do thuitim i tírib námat tre chin droch-mná. Ba ferr a comaitecht ocus a mbíathath ocus a nem-guin ocus tuidecht dóib dochum a tiré oldaas a tuitim lia náimtiu.'

'Tecat didiu,' ol Conchobor, 'ocus tíagat commairgi friu.' Benair chucu an-í-sin.

---

12. One day, then, early in the morning, the king's steward came in and made a tour of their house, saw the couple asleep, and went out to wake up the king.

'I haven't found,' he said, 'a woman who was a match for you until this day. In company with Noisiu, son of Uisliu, is a woman worthy of any king of the western world. Have Noisiu killed immediately, let the woman spend the night with you,' the steward added.

'No,' said the king, 'but you shall go each day to court her secretly on behalf of me.'

So it was done. However, whatever the steward said to Deirdre at any time, she would pass on instantly to her bed companion the same night. Since nothing could ever be had from her in this way, the sons of Uisliu were often ordered into all manner of dangers, battles and hazards where they might be killed. Nonetheless, in each slaughter they were so valiant that nothing could ever be had from them with these attempts.

13. Having consulted with Deirdre, the men of Scotland began to assemble in order to kill the sons of Uisliu. She passed this on to Noisiu.

'Leave this place', she said. 'If you don't go from here by tonight, tomorrow you will be killed!'

That night they went away until they found themselves on an island in the sea. News of this was related to the men of Ulster.

'Grievous it is, Conchobar,' said the Ulstermen, 'for the sons of Uisliu to fall in hostile lands through the crime of a bad woman. It were better to go easy with them, and feed them, and not slay them, better for them to come to this land than fall at the hands of their foes.'

'Well then, let them come,' said Conchobar, 'and let guarantors of safe conduct go for them.' The message was brought to them.

---

12. *mnaī do dingbāla-so* 'a woman who was a match for you'. Compare the idea in Freyr's words, on his spying Gerðr the giantess, *mér tíða mey* 'a girl just right for me' (*The Lay of Skírnir*, stanza 6: see **Gods of the Vikings**).

13. Fergus mac Roig, the great champion of Ulster. Dubthach, who slays Mane mac Conchobuir in revenge for Noisiu. Cormac mac Conchobuir, later leader of the exiled Ulstermen.

'Is fo chen linn,' ol-seat. 'Regthair ocus tǽt Fergus frinn i commairgi ocus Dubthach cus Cormac mac Conchobuir.'

Tīgait side congabsat a lláma di muir.

14. Baí immurgu imchosnam im Fergus dia churiud do chormannaib a comairli Chonchobuir, ar asbertatar maic Uislenn nadconístais bíad i n-Hērinn acht bīad Conchobuir i tossuch. Luid īarum Fiachu mac Fergusa leo ocus anaid Fergus ocus Dubthach ocus dollotar maic Uislenn combátar for faithchi na Emna. Is and dano tānic Eogan mac Durthacht rí Fernmaige do chórai fri Conchobor, ar roboí i n-essíd friss i cíana. Is ē-side roherbad dia mmarbad ocus amsaig Conchobuir immi connatīstais cucisium.

15. Bātar maic Uislenn ina sesum for lār na fathche ocus bātar inna mnā inna suidib for dōu na h-Emna. Luid didiu Eogan cuccu inna thur iarsind faithchi. Dolluid immurgu mac Fergusa combaī for lethláim Noísen. Feraid Eogan fāilti friu la béim forgama do gaī mór i n-Noísin corroīmid a druim triit. Foceird la sodain mac Fergusa cotuc a dí láim dar Noīsin cotuc foí ocus cotarliac fair anúas ocus is samlaid robíth Noísiu tre mac Fergusa anūas. Romarbtha īar suidiu sethnón na faithche connatérna ass acht a ndechuid do rind gaī ocus di giun chlaidib; ocus rucad-si in-nunn co Conchobor combaí fora láim ocus rocumrigthe a lláma íarna cúl.

'We welcome this,' they said. 'We shall go, and let Fergus come for us as a guarantor, and Dubthach, and Cormac son of Conchobar.'

These men came and gave escort to the sons of Uisliu from the sea.

14. Conchobar, however, planned it so that Fergus would be invited to ale-feasts by a number of competing hosts, whereas the sons of Uisliu had said that they would not be eating any food in Ireland unless this were first the food of Conchobar. That is how it happened that Fiachu, son of Fergus, escorted them while Fergus and Dubthach remained behind. The sons of Uisliu travelled until they came to the common land of Emain. This, moreover, was when King Eogan mac Durthacht of Fernmag had come to make peace with Conchobar, having been long at war with him. It was he who was suborned to kill them, while Conchobar had himself ringed by mercenaries so that the sons of Uisliu might not approach him.

15. The sons of Uisliu were standing in the middle of the common land, and the women were in their seats on the rampart of Emain. So Eogan went up to these men with his own body of troops along the green. But the son of Fergus stepped up to stand by Noisiu's side. Eogan welcomed them by thrusting his great spear at Noisiu so hard it broke his back to do so. Just then the son of Fergus threw himself into the gap between them, put his arms around Noisiu to bring him under, and cast himself down upon him. And so it was that Noisiu was slain from above through the son of Fergus. The others after that were killed across the common, none of them left that place save through spear's point or sword's edge; and Deirdre was carried off to Conchobar to be beside him, her hands bound behind her back.

---

14. Here, as in the prose elsewhere, the story is abbreviated, but Conchobar tricks Fergus into accepting a separate hospitality on the way to Emain, one which his *geis* 'prohibition' (a kind of Gaelic taboo) prevents him from turning down. Thus he cannot protect the sons of Uisliu from what follows.

16. Atchūas do Fergus īarum an-í-sin ocus do Dubthach ocus do Chormac. Tāncatar side condernsat gníma móra fo chétóiri. Dubthach do marbad Mane maic Conchobuirocus Fiachna mac Fedilme ingine Conchobuir do guin dond ōen-forgab ocus Fergus do marbad Thraigthrēoin maic Traiglethain ocus a brāthar ocus sārugud Conchobuir impu ocus cath do thabairt eturru īar sin isind ōen-lōu cotorchratar tri chét de Ultaib eturru ocus ingenrad Ulad do marbad do Dubthach rīa matain ocus Emain do loscud do Fergus. Is ed lotar īarum eo Ailill ocus co Meidb ar rofetatar is sí lānamain fodarōelsat ocus dano ni-bu cūl serce do Ultaib. Tricha cét ba é lín na lloingse. Co cenn sē mblíadna déc niroan gol na crith leu i n-Ultaib acht gol ocus crith leu cech n-ōen-aidchi.

---

16. News of this was then passed to Fergus and Dubthach and Cormac. They came and at once carried out great deeds. Dubthach killed Mane, son of Conchobar, and with one thrust was Fiachna, son of Feidelm Conchobar's daughter, dispatched. Fergus slew Traigthen son of Traiglethan and his brother as well. Conchobar's honour being outraged by these losses, battle was afterwards joined between him and the guarantors on that day with the deaths of three hundred Ulstermen. Before morning, the girls of Ulster were put to death by Dubthach and the palace of Emain Macha was burned down by Fergus. These men then went over to Ailill and Maeve, knowing that this couple would be able to support them, and it wasn't from misplaced love that the men of Ulster went there. Three thousand was the number of those who went into exile. For sixteen more years neither weeping nor trembling in Ulster ceased, but through them there was weeping and trembling during this time every single night.

---

16. *Thraigthrēoin maic Traiglethain* 'Traigthen son of Traiglethan'. A champion of Ulster, 'Strong-Foot, son of Broad-Foot'. [*Ailill ocus Meidb* 'Ailill and Maeve': King and queen of Connaught, parents of Sencha the Soothsayer. [*Cūl serce*, reading dative *cūl* for 'from misplaced love', rather than *chūl serce* 'a refuge of love'.

Waldere

✻

The two Old English *Waldere* fragments were discovered in 1860 in the Royal Library in Copenhagen: two vellum folds in a pile of old papers and parchments (Ny kongelig Samling 167b). Both were written by the same hand and appeared to have been taken out of the same or two different gatherings of vellum pages in a larger manuscript. No one knows where each fold was once bound in relation to the other. It is likely that this poem suffered the same fate as *Finnsburh* and any number of others, to be used as wrappers or bindings by Tudor printers when Henry VIII dissolved the English monasteries in the 1530s. The *Waldere* text that survives, however, amounts to four pages, representing two parts of one now-lost poem which may have been some 1000 lines long. These parts are named *Waldere* (parts I and II), in an order of play established by convention.

Waldere has been explained best of all with the help of its next oldest analogue, the *Waltharius*, a Latin epic that was probably composed in St Gall, in Switzerland, in the tenth century. Waldere is the son of Ælfhere, king of Aquitaine, who engages him as a child to a Burgundian princess (whose name must be reconstructed as Hildegyth). Waldere and Hildegyth are sent to live as hostages at the court of Ætla (Attila). Waldere becomes the king's champion and befriends Hagena, another Burgundian hostage, whom the Huns later allow to go home. Waldere and Hildegyth make their own escape when Waldere is threatened with a Hunnish marriage. On the west side of the Rhine King Guthere of the Burgundians waits for them in ambush, told to do so by Ætla. Guthere's band includes Hagena, their best but also a reluctant warrior who tries to stop the battle. In the first fragment, Hildegyth rallies her husband's courage. Waldere has already killed some of Guthere's troops. In the second, Waldere tries to stop any further ambush by offering Hagena his prestigious sword, which is called Mimming. Hagena makes it clear that he will stand down without this. Beyond the end, it seems that a reconcilaition will take place.

Hill, J., ed., *Old English Minor Heroic Poems*, Durham and St Andrews Medieval Texts 4 (Durham, 1983)

Norman, F., ed., *Waldere* (London, 1933)

North, R., 'Old English minor heroic poems', *B&OS* 95–129, at 116–23

Zettersten, A., ed., *Waldere* (Manchester, 1979)

I. Hildegyth rouses Waldere to battle

[. . .] hyrde hyne georne:
'Huru Welandes worc ne geswiceð
monna ænigum ðara ðe Mimming can
heardne gehealdan. Oft æt hilde gedreas
swatfag ond sweordwund secg æfter oðrum.
Ætlan ordwyga, ne læt ðin ellen nu gy[t]
gedreosan to dæge, dryhtscipe [. . .]
[. . . Nu] is se dæg cumen
þæt ðu scealt aninga oðer twega:
lif forleosan oððe l[an]gne dom
agan mid eldum, Ælfheres sunu.
Nalles ic ðe, wine min, wordum cide
ðy ic ðe gesawe æt ðam sweord*p*legan
ðurh edwitscype æniges monnes
wig forbugan oððe on weal fleon
lice beorgan ðeah þe laðra fela
ðinne byrnhomon billum heowun.

She eagerly hardened his resolve:
'At least Weland's work will not fail
any man who knows how to hold
the cruel Mimming. Often in battle there fell down
one man after another, blood-bespattered and wounded by that sword.
Front-line man of Attila, don't now let your courage
or your discipline themselves fall down on this day.
[. . . Now] the day has come
when you must do one of two things,
either lose your life or take possession,
son of Ælfhere, of lasting fame among men.
Not at all with these words, my love, do I chide you
as if I had seen you in that sword-play
shame yourself with any man
by shirking battle or fleeing that slaughter,
saving your body, though a lot of enemies
were hacking with blades at your coat of mail.

I, 2 *Welandes worc* 'Weland's work'. A sword of the finest worksmanship.

6 *Ætlan ordwyga* 'Front-line man of Attila'. Waldere has grown up to fight for the Huns as their champion.

11 *Ælfheres sunu* 'son of Ælfhere'. Waldere's Aquitainian father is no relation to the Ælfhere of *Beowulf*, line 2604, who is probably Wiglaf's (Swedish) mother's brother.

12 *Nalles ic ðe, wine min* 'Not at all, my love' etc. Hildegyth pauses in her Spartan mother's discourse to show some wifely concern.

Ac ðu symle furðor feohtan sohtest
mæl ofer mearce, ðy ic ðe metod ondred
þæt ðu to fyrenlice feohtan sohtest
æt ðam ætstealle, oðres monnes,
wigrædenne. Weorða ðe selfne
godum dædum ðenden ðin God recce.
Ne murn ðu for ði mece. Ðe wearð maðma cyst
gifeðe to [g]eoce mid ðy ðu Guðhere scealt
beot forbigan, ðæs ðe he ðas beaduwe ongan
mid unryhte ærest secan.
Forsoc he ðam swurde ond ðam syncfatum
beaga mænigo. Nu sceal bega leas
hworfan from ðisse hilde, hlafurd secan
ealdne eðel oððe her ær swefan
gif he ða [. . .]'

But you were always seeking to fight more,
looking for business on their side of the boundary.
I have been dreading the fate that would see you seeking
to fight too rashly, to the place the other fellow,
your opponent wanted. Make yourself honoured
with good deeds as long as God may care for you!
Nor mourn the loss of your sword: to you was granted
the most costly treasure to help us both. With this you must
punish Guthere's pride for having been the first
to start looking for this battle, with no legal right to do so.
He forsook the sword and the plated treasures,
a mass of rings: ringless he shall now
have to move from this conflict, seek a lord,
his old homeland, or just sleep in his place
if he then [. . .]'

II. Hagena stands down before Waldere

'[. . . me]ce bæteran
buton ðam anum ðe ic eac hafa
on stanfate stille gehided.
Ic wat ðæt [h]*it* ðohte Đeodric Widian
selfum onsendon and eac sinc micel
maðma mid ði mece, monig oðres mid him
golde gegirwan; iulean genam,
þæs ðe hine of nearwum Niðhades mæg
Welandes bearn, Widia ut forlet.
Đurh fifela gewe[a]ld forð onette.'

Waldere mað[e]lode, wiga ellenrof,
hæfde him on handa hildefro[f]re,
guðbilla gripe, gyddode wordum:
'Hwæt, ðu huru wendest, wine Burgenda,
þæt me Hagenan hand hilde gefremede

'[I don't know of any sword among men] that is better,
but for the one that I, too, have
hidden quiet in its jewelled housing.
I know that Theodric thought of sending it to Widia
himself, and also much treasure with that sword,
great riches, and thought of adorning much beside it
with gold. This was a reward which Widia,
Nithad's grandson, Weland's child, received
for a past service, for having released Theodric from captivity.
He hurried him right out of the clutches of giants.'

Waldere spoke, courageous fighter,
held in his hand the war-solace,
battle-axe blade catcher, sang out these words:
'So, friend of Burgundians, were you really expecting
the hand of Hagena to do battle with me

II, 1 *[. . . me]ce bæteran* 'sword . . . better'. The context supports OE *mece* here, in the words of Hagena, who responds here to Waldere's offer to buy him off with his sword. Hagena is the most formidable man in Guthere's ambush party; he is also a friend of Waldere's, and has also spent time with the Huns.

8 *þæs ðe hine of nearwum ut forlet* 'for having released Theodric from captivity'. The Theodric legend is lost, but its situation seems apposite here, in that it is Hagena who holds the key to releasing Waldere. He will do this without accepting Waldere's sword.

14 *wine Burgenda* 'friend of Burgundians'. Guthere, whose Norse counterpart, Gunnarr, is *vin Borgunda* of the same meaning in *The Lay of Attila*, stanza 18.

ond getwæmde [fe]ðewigges; feta, gyf ðu dyrre,
æt ðus heaðuwerigan hare byrnan.
Stand*e*ð me her on eaxelum Ælfheres laf
god ond geapneb golde geweorðod
ealles unscende æðelinges reaf
to habbanne þonne ha[n]d wereð
feorhhord feondum. *H*e bið fah wið me
þonne [me] unmægas eft ongynnað,
mecum gemetað swa ge me dydon.
Đeah mæg sige syllan se ðe symle byð
recon ond rædfest ryhta gehwilces;
se ðe him to ðam halgan helpe gelifeð
to Gode gioce he þær gearo findeð
gif ða earnunga ær geðenceð.
Þonne *m*oten wlance welan britnian,
æhtum wealdan, þæt is [. . .]'

---

and stop the foot-combat? Fetch, if you dare,
the grey coat of mail from a man so weary with battle!
It stands for me ready on my back, left me by Ælfhere,
good and well-bossed, ornamented in gold,
the all-unblemished war-gear that a prince
should have, when his arm defends
his lifehoard from enemies. It won't turn on me,
when [. . .] false kinsmen start on me once more,
or meet me with swords, as you all have done.
And yet He can give victory, He who is ever
in all judgements prompt and resolute.
That man who believes in help from the Holy One,
and from God, will straightaway get it,
if only he thinks of the means of earning that reward.
Only then may proud warriors distribute treasure,
dispose of their wealth, that is [. . .]'

---

18 *Ælfheres laf* 'left me by Ælfhere'. Waldere's father's legacy, his coat of mail. It is a better friend to Waldere than Guthere.

23 *unmægas* 'false kinsmen'. This is probably Waldere's mocking reference to Guthere's (and possibly Hagena's) past murder of Guthere's brother-in-law, whose name, if it had survived clearly in the Old English version of the legend, would be Sigeweard (however, see *The Husband's Message*, **Poems on the Meaning of Life**).

25 *Đeah mæg sige syllan* 'And yet He can give victory'. Above Waldere's father's chained mail is the figure of God. This is more explicit than any statement in *Beowulf*, but follows the same deferential heroic pattern. Waldere is now confident that Hagena will stay out of any fight with Guthere.

The Lay of Attila

Atlakviða

✳

Atlakviða 'The Lay of Attila' is preserved towards the end of the Codex Regius manuscript of Eddic poetry from *c.* 1290, just before *Atlamál* 'The Greenland Lay of Attila'. The two are quite different in style. *The Lay of Attila* is formulaic, tending to the minimalist, a little corrupt and so problematic in what date might be assigned. *The Greenland Lay of Attila* proceeds in contrast like a saga in verse, with swathes of narrative detail and lavish descriptions of dreams through which character can be more easily discussed. Whereas *The Lay of Attila* looks like a poem, or theme, composed in the late tenth century in Norway and thence exported to Iceland, *The Greenland Lay*, as the name suggests, seems to have been composed and copied in the Norse colony in Greenland, probably near the cathedral in Garðar and in the mid-thirteenth century, not too long before the date of Codex Regius.

In the older *Lay*, the great incidents of early central Europe are brought together in time and place, the armies replaced by strong characters and the complex motives by conflicts of love, duty and honour. King Gunnarr of the Burgundians is more memorable than Guthere in *Waldere*. At the end of his career he must decide how to die, whether in battle west in France or east in Hunnish captivity. He chooses the latter in order to thwart Attila in his sole objective, finding the Nibelung hoard. The cost, however, for his kingless children and people will be annihilation in a Hunnish attack. Gunnarr prosecutes his hidden plan at the cost of Hǫgni's life, whose heart is excised at Gunnarr's request, solely so that Gunnarr may take the secret of the hoard's whereabouts with him to his own grave. In a godless way unimaginable to English poetry of this period, Gunnarr turns his, Hǫgni's and his people's death into a work of art. Guðrún finishes the project by taking hideous revenge on Attila for her brothers' death. These brothers of hers are the men whom Brynhildr suborned to kill Sigurðr, Guðrún's earlier husband, yet even so the craving for vengeance takes an absurd priority. The emotions are as extreme. The spirit of this poem is existentialism, heroic ideology in pure form.

Andersson, T. M., 'Did the poet of *Atlamál* know *Atlaqviða*?', in *Edda: A Collection of Essays*, ed. R. J. Glendinning and Haraldur Bessason, University of Manitoba Icelandic Studies 4 (Winnipeg, 1983), 243–57

Dronke, U., ed., trans. and comm., *The Poetic Edda, vol. I: Heroic Poems* (Oxford, 1969)

Finch, R. G., '*Atlakviða*, *Atlamál*, and *Vǫlsunga saga*: a study in combination and integration', in *Speculum Norroenum: Norse Studies in Memory of Gabriel Turville-Petre*, ed. U. Dronke, Guðrún P. Helgadóttir, G. W. Weber and H. Bekker-Nielsen (Odense, 1981), 123–38

North, R., 'Old English minor heroic poems', *B&OS* 95–129, at 116–23

Stephens, J., 'The poet and *Atlakviða*: variation on some themes', in *Iceland and the Medieval World: Studies in Honour of Ian Maxwell*, ed. G. Turville-Petre and J. Stanley Martin (Melbourne, 1974), 56–61

Gunnarr accepts the summons

1 Atli sendi ár til Gunnars,
kunnan segg at ríða, Knéfrøðr var sá heitinn;
at gǫrðum kom hann Gjúka ok at Gunnars hǫllu,
bekkjum aringreypum ok at bjóri svásum.

Attila sent a herald to Gunnarr,
A knowing man to ride, Knéfrøðr he was called.
To Gjúki's courts he came and to Gunnarr's hall,
To hearth-encircling benches and sweet-tasting beer.

2 Drukku þar dróttmegir (en dyljendr þǫgðu)
vín í valhǫllu, vreiði sásk þeir Húna;
kallaði þá Knéfrøðr kaldri rǫddu,
seggr inn suðrœni sat hann á bekk hám:

Drank there the retinues (but silent hid their thoughts)
Wine in a choice hall, they feared the Huns' fury.
Called then Knéfrøðr with a cold voice,
The southern man sat on a high bench:

3 'Atli mik hingat sendi ríða ørendi
mar inum mélgreypa myrkvið inn ókunna,
at biðja y*kk*r, Gunnarr, at it á bekk kœmið
með hjalmum aringreypum at sœkja heim Atla.

'Attila sent me here to ride with his message
On a bit-clenching steed across Mirkwood the unknown,
To ask you Gunnarr, and your brother, to come to our benches
With their hearth-encircling helmets, to visit Attila in his home.

4 'Skjǫldu kneguð þar velja ok skafna aska,
hjalma gullroðna ok Húna mengi,
silfrgyllt sǫðulklæði, serki valr*au*ða,
dafar darrað[a]r, drǫsla mélgreypa.

'Shields you may choose there and shaven ash-spears,
Gold-adorned helmets with a multitude of Huns,
Silver-gilt saddle-cloths, choice red tunics,
Flagged lances, steeds that clench the bit.

---

2 *dyljendr þǫgðu* 'silent hid their thoughts'. The Burgundians can hope for nothing good from Knéfrøðr, as soons happens. Attila, his master, is after the hoard which the Nibelungs, the kings of Burgundy, have inherited from Sigurðr the Dragon-Slayer.

5 ‘Vǫll lézk ykkr ok mundu gefa víðrar Gnitaheiðar,
af geiri gjallanda ok af gylltum stǫfnum,
stórar meiðmar ok staði Danpar,
hrís þat it mæra, er meðr Myrkvið kalla.’

‘The plain he said he’d give you, also, of the wide Knetterheide,
Of shrill spear and of ships’ gilded prows,
A great treasure and homesteads on the Dnieper,
That renowned brushwood which men call Mirkwood.’

6 Hǫfði vatt þá Gunnarr ok Hǫgna til sagði:
‘Hvat ræðr þú okkr, seggr inn œri, alls vit slíkt heyrum?
Gull vissa ek ekki á Gnitaheiði,
þat er vit ættima annat slíkt.

Gunnarr then turned his head and to Hǫgni he said:
‘What do you, young man, advise us, when we hear of such a thing?
I knew of no gold on Knetterheide
That the two of us didn’t have a hoard to match it.

7 ‘Sjau eigum vit salhús sverða full,
hverju eru þeira hjǫlt ór gulli;
minn veit ek mar beztan, en mæki hvassastan,
boga bekksœma, en brynjur ór gulli,
hjalm ok skjǫld hvítastan kominn ór hǫll Kíars,
einn er minn betri en sé allra Húna.’

‘Seven the warehouses filled with swords that we have,
On each one of these is a hilt of gold.
My steed I know for best, and my blade for sharpest,
My bow gives honour to benches, and my mailcoats of gold,
My helmet and shield the whitest come from the Caesar’s hall,
One of mine is better than those of all the Huns.’

---

5 *víðrar Gnitaheiðar* ‘the wide Knetterheide’. Though the location is unknown, this German place-name comes closest (see Dronke 1969: 50–1). The real problem, that Gnitaheiðr does not lie within Attila’s gift but is rather where Sigurðr came by the original dragon-hoard, is soluble if we treat this offer as part of Attila’s cunning plan. His envoy’s reference to this heath allows the Burgundians to see (a) the extent of Attila’s claim of power over them, and (b) that his offer, at best, is really an exchange of their Nibelung hoard for the right to be resettled either in the Ukraine, or in Mirkwood, another trackless interior.

6 Gunnarr’s words here and in the next stanza show Knéfrøðr that he sees Attila’s true reason for inviting him.

8 'Hvat hyggr þú brúði bendu, þá er hon okkr baug sendi,
varinn váðum heiðingja? Hygg ek, at hon vǫrnuð byði.
Hár fann ek heiðingja riðit í hring rauðum,
ylfskr er vegr okkarr at ríða ørendi.'

'What do you think the bride meant when she sent us two a ring
Wrapped in heath-stalker's clothes? I think she offered us warning.
The hair of a heath-stalker I found wound in a red ring,
Wolfish our way is if we ride on this mission.'

'The bride': their sister Guðrún, not long married to Attila. 'Heath-stalker': wolf, whose 'clothes' are a wolf-skin.

9 Niðjargi hvǫttu Gunnar né náungr annarr,
rýnendr né ráðendr né þeir er ríkir váru.
Kvaddi þá Gunnarr, sem konungr skyldi,
mærr í mjǫðranni af móði stórum:

No kinsmen urged Gunnarr nor other close associate,
No advisers nor counsellors nor those who had the power.
Gunnarr then spoke as a king should speak,
Glorious in meadhouse with great heart:

10 'Rístu nú, Fjǫrnir, láttu á flet vaða
greppa gullskálir með gumna hǫndum.

'Rise up now Fjǫrnir, let them pass around the floor
Golden cups for warriors in the hands of men.

11 'Ulfr mun ráða arfi Niflunga,
gamlir, grán*f*erðir, ef Gunnars missir,
birnir blakkfjallir bíta þreftǫnnum,
gamna greystóði, ef Gunnarr né kømrat!'

'The wolf will rule the inheritance of Nibelungs
In old grey divisions if Gunnarr goes missing,
Bears with black pelts will bite with snagging teeth,
Will pleasure the stud of bitches if Gunnarr does not come!'

12 Leiddu landrǫgni lýðar óneisir
grátendr gunnhvata ór garði húna.
Þá kvað þat inn œri erfivǫrðr Hǫgna:
'Heilir farið nú ok horskir, hvars ykkr hugr teygir!'

People without dishonour, they led the land's ruler,
Weeping led the war-sharp from the city of their cubs.
Said then the young inheritor of Hǫgni's estate:
'Go now with fortune and wisdom to where your courage lures you!'

The death of Gunnarr and Hǫgni

13 Fetum lét*u* frœknir um fjǫll at þyrja
mari ina mélgreypu Myrkvið inn ókunna;
hristisk ǫll Húnmǫrk þar er harðmóðgir fóru,
[v]ráku þeir vannstyggva vǫllu algrœna.

With their feet the valiant men spurred on the bit-clenching stallions
To gallop over mountains across Mirkwood the unknown.
All the Huns' march shook where the tough-hearted travelled,
They drove on the whip-shy through the all-green plains.

14 Land sá þeir Atla ok liðskjalfar djúpa,
Bikka greppar standa á borg inni há,
sal of suðrþjóðum sleginn sessmeiðum,
bundnum rǫndum, bleikum skjǫldum,
dafa[r] darrað[a]r, en þar drakk Atli
vín í valhǫllu. Verðir sátu úti
at varða þeim Gunnari, af þeir hér vitja kvæmi
með geiri gjallanda at vekja gram hildi.

They saw the land of Attila and deep-plunging gate-towers,
On the high fortress Bikki's battalion stands,
The palace of southern nations, set out with timber benches,
With rim-girt targes, with gleaming shields,
There were flagged lances, and there Attila drank
Wine in a choice hall. Sentries there sat outside
To watch for Gunnarr's men lest they come calling
With shrill spear to rouse the chief to battle.

15 Systir fann þeira snemst, at þeir í sal kómu
brœðr hennar báðir, bjóri var hon lítt drukkin:
'Ráðinn ertu nú, Gunnarr! Hvat muntu, ríkr, vinna
við Húna harmbrǫgðum? Hǫll gakk þú ór snemma.

Soonest was it their sister who found them entering the palace,
Both her brothers, it was hardly beer she was drunk with:
'You are betrayed now, Gunnarr! What, you mighty king, will you do
Against Huns' harmful moves? Get out of the hall right now!

16 'Betr hefðir þú, bróðir, at þú í brynju fœrir,
sem hjalmum aringreypum at sjá heim Atla.
Sætir þú í sǫðlum sólheiða daga,
nái nauðfǫlva létir nornir gráta,
Húna skjaldmeyjar herfi kanna,
en Atla sjalfan létir þú í ormgarð koma.
Nú er sá ormgarðr ykkr of folginn!'

'Better you had done, brother, to come here in coat of mail,
As if seeing Attila's home with its hearth-encircling helmets.
You should have sat in the saddle for sun-bleached days,
Let Norns bewail the pale corpses' of men you forced to die,
Should have taught Hun shield-maidens to use the harrow,
While Attila himself you should have put in the snake-pit.
Now that snake-pit is prepared for the two of you!'

17 'Seinat er nú, systir, at samna Niflungum;
langt er at leita lýða sinnis til,
of Rosmufjǫll Rínar rekka óneissa.'

'It is too late now, sister, to summon the Nibelungs,
A long way to look for the help of our levies,
For warriors without dishonour from Worms on the Rhine.'

18 Fengu þeir Gunnar ok í fjǫtur settu
vi*n* Borgunda ok bundu fastla.

They took hold of Gunnarr and put into fetters
The friend of Burgundians and bound him fast.

19 Sjau hjó Hǫgni sverði hvǫssu,
en inum átta hratt hann í eld heitan;
svá skal frœkn fjándum verjask
[sem] Hǫgni varði hendr Gunnars.

Seven men did Hǫgni slay with sharp sword,
While the eighth he shoved into a hot fire.
Let a valiant man defend himself from enemies
[The way] Hǫgni defended the body of Gunnarr.

---

17 *Rosmufjǫll Rínar* 'from Worms on the Rhine'. The red sandstone of Worms is connected to the meaning of its name (Dronke 1969: 58–9).

18 *vin Borgunda* 'friend of Burgundians'. This epithet is identical with Guthere's, *wine Burgendra*, in *Waldere* II, line 14.

20 Frágu frœknan ef fjǫr vildi
Gotna þjóðann gulli kaupa.

They asked the valiant man if his life,
Lord of Goths, he would buy with gold.

21 'Hjarta skal mér Hǫgna í hendi liggja
blóðugt ór brjósti skorit baldriða
saxi slíðrbeitu, syni þjóðans.'

'The heart of Hǫgni must lie in my hand,
Cut bleeding from the breast of the bold rider,
Of the king's son, with knife of fearful sharpness.'

22 Skáru þeir hjarta Hjalla ór brjósti
blóðugt ok á bjóð lǫgðu ok báru þat fyr Gunnar.

They cut the heart of Hjalli from its breast,
Laid it bloody on a board and bore it before Gunnarr.

23 Þá kvað þat Gunnarr, gumna dróttinn:
'Hér hefi ek hjarta Hjalla ins blauða,
ólíkt hjarta Hǫgna ins frœkna,
er mjǫk bifask, er á bjóði liggr,
bifðisk halfu meir, er í brjósti lá.'

Then Gunnarr said, lord of men:
'Here I have the heart of Hjalli the cowardly,
Unlike the heart of Hǫgni the valiant.
It trembles too much when it lies on the board,
Twice as much did it tremble when it lay in his breast.'

---

20 *Gotna þjóðann* 'Lord of Goths'. 'Burgundians' and 'Goths' appear to have been interchangeable categories for this poet, whose ideas of difference focus on what is Hunnish and non-Hunnish. The Goth term does serve, however, to stress Gunnarr's royal power in contrast to the potentially degrading position in which he now finds himself.

22 Hjalli is a kitchen-boy conveniently at hand. The poet compresses a longer narrative of which more but variant details survive in *Atlaviða*'s companion piece in Codex Regius, the doubtless thirteenth-century *Atlamál in Grœnlenzku* 'The Greenland Lay of Attila', stanzas 58–61 (Dronke 1969: 60, with 18–19, 88–9, 128). In the present poem, the Huns suspect a trick in what Gunnarr demands, and use Hjalli's heart to try him out. In *The Greenland Lay of Attila*, however, Hjalli begs for mercy with the aid of Hǫgni, who gives his life for Hjalli's to get the business over and done with.

24 Hló þá Hǫgni, er til hjarta skáru
kvikvan kumblasmið, kløkkva hann sízt hugði;
blóðugt þat á bjóð lǫgðu ok báru fyr Gunnar.

Hǫgni was laughing when to his heart they cut
The living craftsman of wounds, to cry out was his last thought.
They laid it bloody on a board and bore it before Gunnarr.

25 Mærr kvað þat Gunnarr, geir-Niflungr:
'Hér hefi ek hjarta Hǫgna ins frœkna,
ólíkt hjarta Hjalla ins blauða,
er lítt bifask, er á bjóði liggr,
bifðisk svági mjǫk, þá er í brjósti lá.

Glorious he said this, Gunnarr the spear-Nibelung:
'Here I have the heart of Hǫgni the valiant,
Unlike the heart of Hjalli the cowardly.
It trembles too little when it lies on the board,
Not even so much did it tremble when in lay in his breast.

26 'Svá skaltu, Atli, augum fjarri,
sem munt menjum [mínum] verða;
er und einum mér ǫll of folgin
hodd Niflunga, lifira nú Hǫgni.

'As far shall you be, Attila, from men's eyes
As you will be from treasures that are mine.
Concealed in the mind of me alone lies all
The Nibelung hoard, now Hǫgni lives no longer.

27 'Ey var mér týja, meðan vit tveir lifðum,
nú er mér engi, er ek einn lifik.
Rín skal ráða rógmalmi skatna,
[á] su *in* áskunna arfi Niflunga.
Í veltanda vatni lýsask valbaugar,
heldr en á hǫndum gull skíni Húna bǫrnum!'

'A doubt was in me always while the two of us lived,
Now there is none, when I am sole survivor.
Rhine shall rule the strife-metal of princes,
That river the god-sprung, the Nibelungs' inheritance.
In the rolling waters the foreign rings shall glint rather
Than the gold may shine on the hands of Huns' children!'

---

27 Gunnarr reveals himself here. He has turned his own death into a masterpiece of deception, a work of art. If there is a heaven for him, it is not Valhǫll or any other supernatural plane, but rather an image in present-time of his treasure dumped into the Rhine.

28 'Ýkvið ér hvélvǫgnum, haptr er nú í bǫndum.'

'Wheel out the wagons, now the captive is in bonds!'

29 Atli inn ríki reið Glaum mǫnum,
sleginn rógþornum, sifjungr þeira.
[Systir þeira] Guðrún [rǫmm] sigtíva,
varnaði við tárum, vaðin í þyshǫllu:

Attila the mighty rode Glaumr of the mane,
Set about with slander-thorns, their own brother-in-law.
Guðrún [mighty sister of those] victorious heroes,
Pushed back the tears, bereaved, in the running hall.

'Glaumr of the mane': Attila's horse. 'Slander-thorns': a hedge of blades for Attila's protection: his bodyguard.

30 'Svá gangi þér, Atli, sem þú við Gunnar áttir
eiða opt of svarða ok ár of nefnda,
at sól inni suðrhǫllu ok at Sigtýs bergi,
hǫlkvi hvílbeðjar ok at hringi Ullar.'

'So may it go for you, Attila, as for the oaths to Gunnarr,
Oaths you often swore and long ago pronounced,
By the south-bending sun and by the mountain of Victory-Deity,
By the steed of sleep's pillows and by the ring of Brilliance.'

'Victory-Deity': Óðinn. 'Ring of Brilliance (Ullr)': the sun.

---

28 This line appears to be Attila's, his only words in the poem. It is worth noting that he does not respond to what Gunnarr has said. As if to save face, his order treats Gunnarr's execution as following on naturally from his arrival and captivity in the Hunnish court.

29 *sleginn rógþornum* 'set about with slander-thorns'. The kenning not only appears to denote blades, as for the warriors holding them, in protective formation, but also to show the same warriors ready to 'slander' their king, that is having thoughts about his family honour. [*[Systir þeira] Guðrún [rǫmm] sigtíva* 'Guðrún [mighty sister of those] victorious heroes'. This hotchpotch, partially reconstructed and unmetrical, might nonetheless show some admixture of a doomsday line from a mythological Eddic poem, such as the refrain in *The Sibyl's Prophecy*, stanzas 43, 46 and 55: *ragna rǫk rǫmm sigtíva* 'the mighty fates of victory-divine powers'. The tradition evidently traced Guðrún's family to a divine origin. [*varnaði við tárum, vaðin í þyshǫllu* 'pushed back the tears, bereaved, in the running hall'. The poet's words contrast Guðrún's tearlessness with the hall's fluidity of movement in a way that suggests a secondary meaning for *vaðin* as 'swept away by flood' (OIce *vaða* 'flow').

30 *hǫlkvi hvílbeðjar* 'the steed of sleep's pillows'. Translation from Dronke, whose note is thorough (1969: 64–5). [*at hringi Ullar* 'by the ring of Brilliance'. *Ullr*, as cognate with OE *wuldor* 'glory', seems himself to represent the sun, whose path towards its midday zenith we see in *at sól inni suðrhǫllu* 'by the south-bending sun'. Why two out of Guðrún's four images of permanence should refer to the sun is less easy to answer than to compare these with the 'sun' as the only reference-point in the oath sworn by the Husband (Sigeweard, as we suggest) in *The Husband's Message*, lines 49–50 (see **Poems on the Meaning of Life**).

31 Ok meir þaðan menvǫrð bituls
dolgrǫgni dró til dauðs skokkr.

And from that place did the trunk with bridle harness draw
The necklace-keeper, prince of hostility, closer to his death.

32 Lifanda gram lagði í garð,
þann er skriðinn var, skatna mengi,
innan ormum, en einn Gunnarr
heiptmóðr hǫrpu hendi kníði,
glumðu strengir; svá skal gulli
frœkn hringdrifi við fira halda.

The living chieftain they laid in the enclosure,
Did the multitude of princes, that was crawling
From within with serpents, while alone Gunnarr
With hate in his heart plucked the lyre with his hand.
The strings resounded. That is how a valiant
Dispenser of rings must keep his gold from men.

33 Atli lét lands síns á vit
ío eyrskán aptr frá morði;
dynr var í garði, drǫslum of þrungit,
vápnsǫngr virða, váru af heiði komnir.

Attila wheeled back towards his lands
His ear-slanted steed from the murder.
A din was in the palace, with chargers it was crowded,
The weapon-song of warriors, from the heath had they come.

---

31 This verse is the most Skaldic of all verses in *The Lay of Attila*, in its courtly convolution of words, as if to stress the ceremony of Gunnarr's tumbril-ride to the pit. In his final role, *menvǫrð* 'necklace-keeper', Gunnarr is celebrated as a king who guards his treasure from others.

32 The poet's closing comment, in the authenticating voice, lets Gunnarr's fate be known as extraordinary. A king normally gives rings. If he ever has to keep them, these are the lengths to which he must go. *Widsith*, lines 66–7, confirms that Gunnarr was normally generous: *me þær Guðhere forgeaf glædlicne maþþum . . . Næs þæt sæne cyning* 'Guthere gave me there a radiant treasure . . . that was no sluggard king!'

The vengeance of Guðrún

34 Út gekk þá Guðrún Atla í gǫgn
með gylltum kálki at reifa gjǫld rǫgnis:
'Þiggja knáttu, þengill, í þinni hǫllu
glaðr at Guðrúnu gnadda niflfarna.'

Out then walked Guðrún to meet Attila,
With gilded chalice, to give the king his payment:
'My liege, you must be of good cheer, when, in your hall,
Guðrún lets you taste these little beasts gone to the shades.'

35 Umðu ǫlskálir Atla vínhǫfgar,
þá er í hǫll saman Húnar tǫlðusk,
gumar gransíðir, gengu inn hvatir.

Echoed the wine-heavy ale-cups of Attila,
When in the hall together Huns assembled,
Men with long moustaches. The keen ones marched in.

36 Skævaði þá in skírleita veigar þeim at bera,
afkár dís jǫfrum ok ǫlkrásir valði
nauðug neffǫlum, en níð sagði Atla:

Skivvied then the bright-faced as she bore the men their cups,
A demon lady she, who chose ale-morsels for the noblemen,
Forcing herself for faces sickly pale, and told Attila his shame:

37 'Sona hefir þinna, sverða deilir,
hjǫrtu hrædreyrug við hunang of tuggin;
melta knáttu, móðugr, manna valbráðir,
eta at ǫlkrásum ok í ǫndugi at senda.

'Sword-dealer, from your own sons you have
Chewed the hearts of their bleeding corpses with honey.
The steaks you digest, brave man, are slaughtered from humans,
Which you eat as ale-morsels and send to the high seats.

---

34 *gnadda niflfarna* 'these little beasts gone to the shades'. Translation based on Dronke (1969: 10). OIce *þiggja* 'receive', 'taste' is related to OE *aþecgan*, 'try in your mouth', in *Wulf and Eadwacer*, lines 2 and 7.

38 Kallaraðu síðan til kníá þinna
Erp né Eitil, ǫlreifa tvá;
séraðu síðan í seti miðju
gulls miðlendr geira skepta,
manar meita né mara keyra.'

'Never again will you call to your knees
Erpr or Eitill, the two beer-flushed boys.
Never again will you see in mid platform
Dispensers of gold fitting shafts to their spears,
Clipping manes or whipping on their stallions.'

39 Ymr varð á bekkjum, afkárr sǫngr virða,
gnýr und guðvefjum, grétu bǫrn Húna;
nema ein Guðrún, er hon æva grét
brœðr sína berharða ok buri svása,
unga, ófróða, þá er hon við Atla gat.

There was a groan on the benches, a demon song of warriors,
A roar beneath finewoven cloaks, the sons of Huns were weeping,
All except Guðrún, for she wept never
For her bear-hard brothers and sweet boys,
The young, ungrown boys that she bore to Attila.

40 Gulli søri in gaglbjarta,
hringum rauðum reifði hon húskarla;
skǫp lét hon vaxa, en skíran malm vaða,
æva fljóð ekki gáði fjarghúsa.

The goose-white woman sowed gold,
With burnished red rings she enriched housecarls,
Destiny she let climb and the bright metal flow,
Not once did the lady heed the shrines of gods.

---

39 *brœðr sína berharða* 'her bear-hard brothers'. Something more than toughness, or dark hair, in the sons of Gjúki is meant here, if we treat Gunnarr's bear-baiting epiphany, earlier in stanza 11, as a sign that the Burgundians claim the animal in their bloodline. The English parallel is *Beowulf* 'wolf of bees: bear'; the Norse, Bǫðvarr *bjarki* 'little bear'.

40 *fjarghúsa* 'shrines of gods'. An implication from the later, Christian, treatment of Norse shrines is that Guðrún cleans out Attila's palace to the extent of flaying his gilded idols for every last ounce of gold. Thereby she annihilates the source of her brothers' death. Perhaps this is as near as the poet, probably a Norwegian heathen of the mid-tenth century, comes to a Christian's denunciation of gold.

41 Óvarr Atl*i* móðan hafði hann sik drukkit,
vápn hafði hann ekki, varnaðit hann við Guðrúnu;
opt var sá leikr betri, þá er þau lint skyldu
optarr um faðmask fyr ǫðlingum.

Attila, unwary, had drunk himself weary,
Weapons he had none, did not push Guðrún back.
Often that play was better when more times than this
They were softly meant to embrace before the chieftains.

42 Hon beð broddi gaf blóð at drekka,
hendi helfússi ok hvelpa leysti,
hratt fyr hallar dyrr ok húskarla vakði
brandi brúðr heitum, þau lét hon gjǫld brœðra.

With a sword-point she gave the bed blood to drink,
With hand hell-bound she also freed the whelps,
Shoved before the hall doors, and roused the housecarls,
The bride, her burning brand: let these things buy her brothers.

43 Eldi gaf hon þá alla, er inni váru
ok frá morði þeira Gunnars komnir váru ór Myrkheimi;
forn timbr fellu, fjarghús ruku,
bœr Buðlunga, brunnu ok skjaldmeyjar
inni aldrstamar, hnigu í eld heitan.

To the fire she gave all those who were inside
And had come from Murkhome where they murdered Gunnarr.
Old timbers fell in, the god-shrines smoked,
Home of the Buðlungs, and shieldmaidens also burned.
Tamed of their lives within, they sank into the hot fire.

44 Fullrœtt er um þetta, ferr engi svá síðan
brúðr í brynju brœðra at hefna;
hon hefir þriggja þjóðkonunga
banorð borit, bjǫrt, áðr sylti.

The tale is fully told. Never from this time forth
Shall chained-mail bride avenge her brothers thus.
Three emperors did she consign
To death, bright, before she died.

---

41 As the alliteration has broken down, so a line or two may have been lost here. *optarr* 'more times than this'. Even their public embraces outdid this one. The implication of *skyldu* 'they were meant to' is that the marriage had been a formality.

44 To judge by its cataloguing style, this stanza looks added on by a redactor who collected *The Lay of Attila* some time before it was copied into the Codex Regius.

POEMS ON THE MEANING OF LIFE

* * *

POEMS ON THE MEANING OF LIFE

* * *

This section is intended as a tribute to the Exeter Book, without which English literature would be far poorer. The Exeter Book was bequeathed to its Cathedral Library by the half-French Bishop Leofric in 1072. Over the Channel and in England during this Klondyke Norman time, a new form of chivalric literature was stirring which would transform love poetry into the *roman courtois* (see **Early Chivalry**). And here we have a book containing many short poems now known as 'elegies', some of which celebrate the pathos of love, as well as Christ's life and works, Saints' Lives, God, fate, nature and nurture, sex and entertainment. The provenance of this book is uncertain, let alone its place of origin, though the hand of the one scribe gives reason to suppose that it was copied in stages in the 960–70s. Leofric appears to have described it in his inventory as *micel englisce boc be gehwilcum þingum on leoðwisan geworht* 'a great English book made up in verse about various things'. Such will be the character, we hope, of this section. Greater poems will here be given in extract, lesser ones usually in their entirety. As with the previous section, however, we intend to mix these poems with others composed in a similar vein. *The Wanderer*, a meditation on bereavement and Providence, is thus followed by *Hard Loss of Sons*, a true elegy to a son who was the light of the poet's life. *The Seafarer* explores the world beyond, inciting ecstasy as a means of approaching God. Yet other poems, Norse as well as English, are less strenuous and reflect on men and women and the everyday. *The Rhyming Poem*, on changes of life, experiments by changing the traditional English for a new Latin-based poetic form. Then there are *Riddles*, which offer surreal perspectives on the things and people we all take for granted. Some of the elegies that follow have been read as Riddles too, so mysterious they are, with their poets using heroic legends as a vehicle for ideas about love.

The genre of these Exeter Book poems 'on various things' remains problematic: 'elegies', 'wisdom' and 'riddles' have been variously accepted as markers for most of the poems here. Yet the OE term *giedd* ('song') is found in most poems of each supposed category. The fact that OIce *geð* ('soul', 'affection', 'spirit'), the formal cognate of OE *giedd*, is also a prominent word in two of the Norse poems quoted here, reveals an archaic common ground between most of the poems in this section which is sufficient for the OE term, at any rate, to be treated as the contemporary name for the genre. Where our terms are concerned, in any case, 'elegies', 'wisdom' and 'riddles' are really different aspects of the same kind of poetry. This is why we decided to call the present section **Poems on the Meaning of Life**.

General bibliography

Bradley, S. A. J., trans., *Anglo-Saxon Poetry: An Anthology of Old English Poems in Prose Translation* (London, 1982)

Conner, P. W., 'The structure of the Exeter Book Codex (Exeter, Cathedral Library, MS. 3501)', *Scriptorium* 40 (1986), 233–42; also in Richards 1994: 301–15

Fulk, R. D., and C. M. Cain, *A History of Old English Literature* (Oxford, 2003)

Gameson, R., 'The origin of the Exeter Book of Old English Poetry', *Anglo-Saxon England* 25 (1996), 135–85

Klinck, A. L., *The Old English Elegies: A Critical Edition and Genre Study* (Montreal and Kingston, 1992)

Larrington, C., trans., *The Poetic Edda* (Oxford, 1996)

Muir, B., ed., *The Exeter Anthology of Old English Poetry: An Edition of Exeter Dean and Chapter MS 3502*, 2nd ed. (Exeter, 2000)

Neville, J., 'Joyous play and bitter tears: the *Riddles* and the Elegies', *B&OS* 130–59

Richards, M. P., ed., *Anglo-Saxon Manuscripts: Basic Readings* (New York and London, 1994)

Swanton, M. J., trans., *The Anglo-Saxon Chronicle* (London, 1996)

Williamson, Craig, *The Old English Riddles of the Exeter Book* (Chapel Hill, NC, 1977)

The Wanderer

The Wanderer was highly regarded by the compiler of the Exeter Book, in which it is now found in folios 76 verso on into 78 recto. Two-thirds of the way into the tenth century, this poem was copied into the first booklet of the manuscript as its fourth poem (after *Azarias*, *The Phoenix* and Cynewulf's *Juliana*), before a new booklet was sewn on to the front with five lengthier poems (*Christ I*, *II* (Cynewulf) and *III* and *Guthlac A* and *B*). *The Wanderer* is a devoutly Christian poem, yet not openly so, for in it Christ's name is not mentioned once. The poem thus marks the beginning of the so-called 'elegies' of the Exeter Book in which Christian concerns are expressed through largely secular forms of wisdom and experience. In keeping with this, the question of who speaks where in this poem is often left to one side as immaterial, and the poem is read as the transformation of a character from long-term sufferer to wise philosopher at the end.

The present text has a more traditional view. Here the poet's unnamed persona introduces an unnamed heroic type whose life, according to his speech from line 8 onwards, is spent moving from one court to another in his search for a new employer. This is the Wanderer. The present text fixes the end of the Wanderer's speech at line 29a. Thereafter the poet's persona describes the lonely Wanderer again and the dreams, disappointments and apparent hallucinations of his dismal life, before speaking as himself at the poem's mid-point, on line 58. Here the poem becomes didactic, a little fabulous, even mystical, as the poet's persona urges a man to be moderate in all things and ready to accept the world's end as surely as he does his own. At this point he creates a new archetype, a Wise Man, whose speech in lines 92–110 reflects on the world's decline. The first difference between Wise Man and Wanderer is that the Wise Man's words are hypermetric, unstable and emotionally turbulent. The second difference is that the Wanderer knows only fate, the impact of events, whereas the Wise Man knows that there is a Providence that fashions them. To say that the first type develops into the second is to describe this religious poem as if it were a psychological novel. A less anachronistic approach would be to see the Wanderer as a heathen stoic, godless and going nowhere in a Christian sense, and the Wise Man as a philosopher whose speech contains an epiphany. Like Boethius in his *De consolatione Philosophiae* 'On the Consolation of Philosophy', the poet of *The Wanderer* reaches enlightenment through stages of teaching, fable and poetry. He is a Christian but never becomes explicit about the Christian message, which is implied, never revealed. Moreover he lays false trails, with one archetype whose narrative identifies him with mercenary heroic life, and with another who seems to sit in a library. The poet's tantalising evasive style brings his work close to a riddle, but never close enough to be classed as one. The meanings one can infer are various, but the compiler was in no doubt about the excellence of this poem. *The Wanderer* may be read for a lifetime and still yield something new.

Cross, J. E., '*Ubi sunt* passages in Old English – sources and relationships', *Vetenskaps-Societetens i Lund Årsbok* (Lund, 1956), 25–44

Diekstra, F. N. M., 'The passion of the mind and the cardinal virtues', *Neophilologus* 55 (1971), 73–88

Dunning, T. P., and A. J. Bliss, ed., *The Wanderer* (London, 1969)

Klinck, A. L., *The Old English Elegies: A Critical Edition and Genre Study* (Montreal and Kingston, 1992)

North, R., 'Boethius and the Mercenary in *The Wanderer*', in *Pagans and Christians: the Interplay between Christian Latin and Traditional Germanic Cultures in Early Medieval Europe*, ed. T. Hofstra, L. A. J. R. Houwen and A. A. MacDonald, Germania Latina II (Groningen, 1995), 71–98

Richardson, J., 'Two notes on the time frame of *The Wanderer* (lines 22 and 73–87)', *Neophilologus* 73 (1989), 158–9

Roberts, J., 'Understanding Hrothgar's humiliation: *Beowulf* lines 144–74 in context', in *Text, Image, Interpretation: Studies in Anglo-Saxon Literature and its Insular Context in Honour of Éamonn Ó Carragáin*, ed. A. Minnis and J. Roberts, Studies in the Early Middle Ages 18 (Turnhout, 2007), 355–67

Oft him anhaga are gebideð,
Metudes miltse, þeah þe he modcearig
geond lagulade longe sceolde
hreran mid hondum hrimcealde sæ,
wadan wræclastas. Wyrd bið ful aræd!

Swa cwæð eardstapa, earfeþa gemyndig,
wraþra wælsleahta, winemæga hryre:
'Oft ic sceolde ana uhtna gehwylce
mine ceare cwiþan. Nis nu cwicra nan

Often a lone survivor experiences grace,
Measurer's mercy, though, sad at heart
across the paths of ocean long has he had to
stir with his arms the rime-cold sea,
travel the roads of exile. Fate is fully determined.

Thus spoke the Wanderer, mindful of hardships,
of cruel savage slaughters, of the ruin of friends and family:
'It is often alone each early dawn I have had to
lament my griefs. There is no one alive

1 *anhaga* 'lone survivor'. See Dunning and Bliss (1969: 37–40). Most probably the same word as *anhoga* in *earmne anhogan* on line 40, especially as in *Beowulf*, line 2368, the bereaved hero swims back to Geatland as an *earm anhaga* 'wretched lone survivor' of Hygelac's Frisian raid. More figurative uses: for the Phoenix, in *The Phoenix*, line 87, and in *Guthlac B*, line 997, *enge anhoga* 'mean lone survivor' for death; and for the subject of *Riddle* 5.1 (shield, or chopping block). [*are gebideð* 'experiences grace'. The *ge*-prefix on *bidan* 'wait, endure' suggests 'getting something by waiting for it', hard to render in Modern English. In addition, the rowing in line 4 makes 'experiences the oar' a momentarily viable meaning for line 1 (f. *ar* means both). Does the poem start by trying to mislead us?

5 *Wyrd bið ful aræd* 'Fate is fully determined'. The poet either invokes predestination, or gives this half-line as the Wanderer's unthinking response to his lot, or both.

6 *Swa cwæð* 'Thus spoke'. A clear rubric which has been taken to look back to lines 1–5 as well as forward to the speech beginning on line 8. See note to line 111, where *Swa cwæð* looks back.

6–7 The words *earfeþa*, *wælsleahta* and *hryre* are all in the genitive, dependent on *gemyndig*. A lifetime's experience is compressed into a small space, as if to capture the workings of memory.

þe ic him modsefan   minne durre
sweotule asecgan.   Ic to soþe wat
þæt biþ in eorle   indryhten þeaw,
þæt he his ferðlocan   fæste binde,
healde his hordcofan,   hycge swa he wille.
Ne mæg werig mod   wyrde wiðstondan,
ne se hreo hyge   helpe gefremman.
Forðon domgeorne   dreorigne oft
in hyra breostcofan   bindað fæste;
swa ic modsefan   minne sceolde,
oft earmcearig,   eðle bidæled,
freomægum feor   feterum sælan,
siþþan geara iu   goldwine minne
hrusan heolstre biwrah,   ond ic hean þonan

---

to whom my thoughts and feelings I dare
say clearly. I know, in truth,
that in a gentleman it is a courtly virtue
that he bind fast his spirit locker,
keep in his hoard-coffer, let him think what he will.
Neither can a weary heart withstand fate,
nor can the angry mind extend any help.
And so men eager for glory often bind fast
their sad minds in their breast-coffers;
Likewise I have had to seal, often wretchedly grieving,
robbed of my inherited land, far from noble kinsmen,
my own thoughts and feelings with fetters,
since long long ago my gold-giving friend
I covered with soil's holster, and disgraced from that place

15–16 An active-passive dichotomy for elements of *mod* 'mind' resists events, while *hyge* tries to extend help against them; futile in either case.

17 *domgeorne dreorigne* '(men) eager for glory . . . sad (minds)'. This poet's diction is elliptical, compressed and ambiguous. The adjective stands for a noun and *hyge* is left out because we have heard it already on line 16. The word *dom* 'glory' may connote Judgement and afterlife in heaven, as entirely Christian, or it may refer to a man's reputation for skill in war, as entirely secular; or in between, depending on the reader's piety (see also Dunning and Bliss 1969: 45).

19–21 The enveloping of three half-lines between *sceolde* 'have had to' and *sælan* 'seal' illustrates the poet's desire to enclose his memories through the very syntax of his line. In between, the compressed 'wretched – deprived – remote' sequence of epithets presents the Wanderer's experiences as worsening each time.

22 *geara iu* 'long long ago'. This expression in all other cases (Richardson 1989: 158) denotes times extending far beyond the human lifespan (about 670 years, in *The Dream of the Rood* 27; see **Poems of Devotion**).

23 *hrusan heolstre biwrah* '[I] covered with soil's holster'. With the darkness of the ground: a periphrasis for 'buried' (see the scene on line 84). OE *heolster*, etymon of *holster*, means a veil or covering that produces darkness. The *ic*-subject of *biwrah* is left out because we have heard it on line 19 and hear it again on 23b. Still, some have emended to *heolster* in order to make the darkness cover the dead lord.

wod wintercearig   ofer waþema gebind,
sohte seledreorig   sinces bryttan,
hwær ic feor oþþe neah   findan meahte
þone þe in meoduhealle   [minne] mine wisse,
oþþe mec freondleasne   frefran wolde,
weman mid wynnum.'

Wat se þe cunnað,
hu sliþen bið   sorg to geferan,
þam þe him lyt hafað   leofra geholena.
Warað hine wræclast,   nales wunden gold,
ferðloca freorig,   nalæs foldan blæd.
Gemon he selesecgas   ond sincþege,
hu hine on geoguðe   his goldwine
wenede to wiste.   Wyn eal gedreas!
Forþon wat se þe sceal   his winedryhtnes

I travelled, grieving in winter, over the waves' binding,
sad in a hall went searching for a dispenser of treasure,
where, far or near, I might be able to find
the man who would know what I like in the mead-hall,
or would want to give me solace in my friendless state,
draw me in with joy.'

He knows, who tries it,
how sharp sorrow is as a travelling companion to the man
who has few dear associates he might call his own.
Exile's road keeps hold of him, not fine-twisted gold,
a frozen mind-locker, not the glory of earth.
He remembers hall-servants and receiving treasure,
how in his youth his gold-giving friend
would accustom him to the banquet. Joy all fell away.
And so he knows, who must long suffer without

---

25 *sohte seledreorig* 'sad in a hall went searching'. Or the manuscript's *sele dreorig*, of the same meaning. Others add 'at the loss of' to the meaning of *seledreorig* (Dunning and Bliss 1969: 65, 137; Klinck 1992: 110). This spoils the sense, for the text does allow the Wanderer to visit new halls in search of a lord to replace the one he has lost.

27 *[minne] mine wisse* 'would know what I like'. OE *myne* 'desire, liking, thought' has a short vowel and cannot take the line's third stress as in the manuscript. OE *mīne* '(of) me' has been proposed, which would have much the same meaning, but the phrase *ne his myne wisse* occurs also in *Beowulf*, line 169, where the intruding Grendel could not approach Hrothgar's gift-throne because of God 'or know His purpose' (Roberts 2007: 358). This, however, could be 'Hrothgar's purpose', as an idiom of the bond between king and thegn. The present reading assumes that the scribe wrote one word (*mine*) for his exemplar's possible two (*minne mine*).

29 *weman mid wynnum* 'draw me in with joy'. Sometimes emended to *wenian* 'accustom' on the basis of *wenede to wiste* 'would accustom . . . to the banquet' on line 36 (see Klinck 1992: 111). But in Ælfric's *Life of St Oswald*, King Oswald asks the Irish (of Iona) to send him *sumne lareow . . . þe his leoda mihte to Gode geweman* 'some teacher who might entice his people to God'.

29b The switch from first-person to third halfway through line 29 is here taken to mark the end of the Wanderer's speech. At 21.5 lines (8–29a), this is comparable to the Wise Man's at 19 (lines 92–110).

leofes larcwidum   longe forþolian,
ðonne sorg ond slæp   somod ætgædre
earmne anhogan   oft gebindað,
þinceð him on mode   þæt he his mondryhten
clyppe ond cysse,   ond on cneo lecge
honda ond heafod,   swa he hwilum ær
in geardagum   giefstolas breac.
Ðonne onwæcneð eft   wineleas guma,
gesihð him biforan   fealwe wegas,
baþian brimfuglas,   brædan feþra,
hreosan hrim ond snaw,   hagle gemenged.
Þonne beoð þy hefigran   heortan benne,
sare æfter swæsne.   Sorg bið geniwad,
þonne maga gemynd   mod geondhweorfeð.
Greteð gliwstafum,   georne geondsceawað

---

the teachings pronounced by his beloved friend and lord,
that when sorrow and sleep, in combination,
often bind up the lone survivor,
it seems to him in his mind that he embraces and kisses
his man and lord, and places on his knee
his hand and his head, just as in former times
in the old days he enjoyed gifts from the throne.
Then the man without friends awakens once more,
sees fallow waves in front of him,
sea-birds bathing, stretching out their wings,
frost and snow falling mingled in with hail.
Heavier to bear then are heart's wounds,
grief for the sweet man. Sorrow is renewed
when feeling moves through memory of kinsmen.
He greets them with their notes of music, with yearning he observes,

---

44 *giefstolas breac* 'enjoyed gifts from the throne'. The scene in the Wanderer's dream is a thegn's personal love for his king stylised within the limits of the ritual of homage.

46 *fealwe wegas* 'fallow waves'. Colours are difficult. There are *fealwe mearas* 'tawny stallions' riding on *fealwe stræte* 'a dusty road' in *Beowulf*, lines 865 and 916 (see **Heroic Poems**) and *fealwe blostman* 'blossoms . . . (autumnal) brown' in *The Phoenix*, line 74. Here the etymological sense 'fallow' captures (a) mud and (b) the barenness of salt (in contrast with *foldan blæd* 'glory of earth' on line 33).

51 *mod geondhweorfeð* 'feeling moves through'. On parallels for *mod* as the subject, *gemynd* as the object of this verb, see Dunning and Bliss (1969: 21–2), and compare with Alfred's *cuman on gemynd* 'come to memory' constructions in his Preface to the West Saxon translation of Gregory's *Pastoral Care* (**The Earliest English Prose**).

52 *Greteð gliwstafum* 'He greets them with (their) notes of music'. The meaning of these lines is a puzzle still waiting to be solved. For a theory that this is (a) the Wanderer observing birds for omens, and beneath that (b) Ulysses observing the Sirens (a trio of musicians according to Isidore's *Etymologies*) for what they have to offer, see North (1995: 88–91). *Gliwstafum* occurs only here. 'Joyfully' (Dunning and Bliss 1969: 58, 133) is wrong for this, given that *gliw* means 'music'.

secga geseldan. Swimmað eft on weg!
Fleotendra ferð no þær fela bringeð
cuðra cwidegiedda. Cearo bið geniwad
þam þe sendan sceal swiþe geneahhe
ofer waþema gebind werigne sefan.

Forþon ic geþencan ne mæg geond þas woruld
for hwan modsefa min ne gesweorce,
þonne ic eorla lif eal geondþence,
hu hi færlice flet ofgeafon,
modge maguþegnas. Swa þes middangeard
ealra dogra gehwam dreoseð ond fealleþ.
Forþon ne mæg weorþan wis wer, ær he age
wintra dæl in woruldrice. Wita sceal geþyldig,
ne sceal no to hatheort ne to hrædwyrde,
ne to wac wiga ne to wanhydig,

---

the companions of men always swim away.
The minds of floating ones will never in that place bring
many familiar articulate songs. Care is renewed
for the man who must very constantly send
over wave's binding a weary sense.

For this reason I cannot think through this world
why my own mind does not darken,
when I ponder all the lives of men,
how they suddenly gave up the floor,
brave young thegns. Thus this Middle World
each and every day and night declines and falls.
And so a man cannot become wise until he may possess
his share of winters in the worldly kingdom. A wise man must be patient,
never too hot-headed, nor too hasty of speech,
nor too weak a fellow, nor too reckless,

---

54 *Fleotendra ferð* 'minds of the floating ones'. Of the birds, otherwise seen here as men's companions. OE *ferð* is in the singular, but with a plural meaning. The birds are not the intelligent oracles of information which heathen augury makes them out to be, is what the poet seems to mean: they can give the Wanderer no comfort.

58 The subject switches here out of third back into the first person for the first time since line 29a. This point is also halfway through the whole poem. The emphasis on *þas woruld* 'this world' and *min* 'my', both in third-stress positions, announces the following as the poet's personal reflection, his authenticating voice, between his personae of Wanderer (line 8–29a) and Wise Man (lines 92–110).

59 *for hwan modsefa min ne gesweorce* 'why my own mind does not darken'. Optimism. The poet's mind does not darken, and he cannot think why, although it will soon become clearer that heaven is the reason for his lightening mood.

66–9 The intense *ne*-anaphora is part of homiletic discourse, in which the poet must have been trained (Klinck 1992: 119). Is he, by implication, also *wita* 'wise man', the member of an ecclesiastical or other political council? At any rate, he urges moderation in all things, as a conciliator might.

ne to forht ne to fægen, ne to feohgifre
ne næfre gielpes to georn, ær he geare cunne.
Beorn sceal gebidan, þonne he beot spriceð,
oþþæt collenferð cunne gearwe
hwider hreþra gehygd hweorfan wille.
Ongietan sceal gleaw hæle hu gæstlic bið,
þonne ealre þisse worulde wela weste standeð,
swa nu missenlice geond þisne middangeard
winde biwaune weallas standaþ,
hrime bihrorene, hryðge þa ederas.
Woriað þa winsalo, waldend licgað
dreame bidrorene, duguþ eal gecrong,
wlonc bi wealle. Sume wig fornom,
ferede in forðwege, sumne fugel oþbær
ofer heanne holm, sumne se hara wulf
deaðe gedælde, sumne dreorighleor
in eorðscræfe eorl gehydde.

---

nor too frightened, nor too relieved, nor too eager for money
nor ever too eager to boast before he sees what things are.
A man must wait when he makes a vow,
or when, stout-hearted, he may clearly see
in which direction the thoughts of his mind will tend.
A prudent man must take it in, how terrifying it will be
when the wealth of all this world stands waste,
just as now, variously throughout this middle world,
the walls stand blown upon by wind,
encrusted with frost, snow-swept the buildings.
Those wine halls crumble, their rulers lie
deprived of the good times, all the host has perished,
arrogant by the wall. Killing took some men,
carried them on the way forth, a bird bore off another
over the high seas, the hoary-coated wolf shared
another man with death, a sad-featured nobleman
hid yet another man in an earthen grave.

---

72 *hreþra gehygd* 'the thoughts of his mind'. The only other surviving example of this collocation is in *Beowulf*, line 2045, where an old mercenary probes the young Heathobard's *hreðra gehygd* for what he is really thinking (see **Heroic Poems**). This phrase thus denotes the mind in its more tangled state before concentration allows one thought to emerge.

73 *hu gæstlic bið* 'how terrifying it will be'. A parallel sense development, from 'spiritual', is found in the word *ghastly* (Dunning and Bliss 1969: 53). But a positive vision of oneself as 'ghost' proceeding to heaven on Doomsday is what the poet is also keen to promote.

81 *sumne fugel oþbær* 'a bird bore off another'. The physical entirety of this transport poses a problem if we understand a raven with flesh from the dead, as most readers do (Klinck 1992: 122). Other suggestions lie further out, including North's that this bird is a Siren carrying off a sailor figuratively (1995: 93).

Yþde swa þisne eardgeard   ælda Scyppend
oþþæt burgwara   breahtma lease
eald enta geweorc   idlu stodon.

Se þonne þisne wealsteal   wise geþohte
ond þis deorce lif   deope geondþenceð,
frod in ferðe,   feor oft gemon
wælsleahta worn,   ond þas word acwið:
'Hwær cwom mearg? Hwær cwom mago?   Hwær cwom maþþumgyfa?
Hwær cwom symbla gesetu?   Hwær sindon seledreamas?
Eala beorht bune!   Eala byrnwiga!
Eala þeodnes þrym!   Hu seo þrag gewat,
genap under nihthelm,   swa heo no wære.
Stondeð nu on laste   leofre duguþe
weal wundrum heah,   wyrmlicum fah.
Eorlas fornoman   asca þryþe,
wæpen wælgifru,   wyrd seo mære,
ond þas stanhleoþu   stormas cnyssað,

Thus Man's Creator destroyed this world's habitations,
until, bereft of the revelries of the inhabitants of their towns,
the ancient works of giants stood idle.

He then who wisely thought of this foundation
and this dark life deeply thinks through,
experienced in heart, from far back often remembers
a number of cruel slaughters, and will say these words:
'What came of the horse? Of the young man? What came of the wealth-giver?
What came of the banqueting halls? Where are the good times of the hall?
Alas the bright beaker! Alas the man in chained mail!
Alas the king's magnificence! How that time passed away,
grew dark beneath night's cover as if it had never been.
Stands now in the track of the beloved host
a wall wondrously high, painted with serpentine forms.
Warriors were taken by the strength of ashen spears,
by weapons keen to taste slaughter, by fate the infamous,
and these stone cliffs the storms do buffet,

---

85 *Yþde swa ælda Scyppend* 'thus Man's Creator destroyed' etc. An oxymoron, unless one thinks of the periodic annihilations of Genesis (which are in man's interest). The vocabulary inevitably recalls that of Cædmon's *Hymn* (see **Poems of Devotion**).

92 *Hwær cwom mearg?* 'What came of the horse?' etc. The language is homiletic, with hypermetric lines, anaphora (with *eala* also) and the use of a motif known as *ubi sunt* 'where are?' (Cross 1956). The querulous voice of this speaker, the 'Wise Man', is quite different to the dismal mood of the Wanderer earlier. If the same voice, then the speaker has become more distressed.

98 *weal wundrum heah, wyrmlicum fah* 'wall wondrously high, painted with serpentine forms'. Still a puzzle waiting to be solved. The line at any rate captures the idea of human cycles, the lost greatness of civilisations now vanished.

hrið hreosende hrusan bindeð,
wintres woma, þonne won cymeð,
nipeð nihtscua, norþan onsendeð
hreo hæglfare hæleþum on andan.
Eall is earfoðlic eorþan rice,
onwendeð wyrda gesceaft weoruld under heofonum.
Her bið feoh læne, her bið freond læne,
her bið mon læne, her bið mæg læne,
eal þis eorþan gesteal idel weorþeð!'

Swa cwæð snottor on mode, gesæt him sundor æt rune.
Til biþ se þe his treowe gehealdeþ, ne sceal næfre his torn to rycene
beorn of his breostum acyþan, nemþe he ær þa bote cunne,
eorl mid elne gefremman. Wel bið þam þe him are seceð,
frofre to fæder on heofonum, þær us eal seo fæstnung stondeð.

---

a blizzard descending binds the ground,
winter's tumult, when darkness comes,
when night-shadow grows black, from the north is dispatched
an angry hail-storm in malice against men.
All is full of hardship in the kingdom of earth,
the shaping of events changes the world beneath the heavens.
Here money is borrowed, here friend is borrowed,
here man is borrowed, here family man is borrowed,
all this earth's foundation will become empty!'

Thus spoke a man clever in mind, sat apart with himself in secret counsel.
Excellent is he who keeps his faith, nor shall a man ever reveal
grief from his breast too quickly, unless he, a gentleman, can first
carry out the cure with courage. It will be well for him who seeks grace,
solace from the Father in heaven, where security waits entirely for us.

---

102 *hrið* 'blizzard'. Not found outside *The Wanderer*. The adjective is *hryðig* 'snow-swept' on line 77. From Old Scandinavian *hríð* 'snow-storm'? Dunning and Bliss believe so (1969: 61).

107 *wyrda gesceaft* 'the shaping of events'. Providence, as opposed to 'fate' or 'what happens' in *wyrd* on lines 5, 15 and 100. The line is also hypermetric, apparently for emphasis. This speaker, unlike the Wanderer, can see through 'fate' to the Providence which fashions it. Boethius, through Lady Philosophy, comes to mind (on 'Fate and Providence' in the West Saxon *Boethius*, see **The Earliest English Prose**).

108 *Her bið feoh læne, her bið freond læne* 'Here money is borrowed, here friend is borrowed' etc. Anaphora, but within the frame of traditional wisdom, for the Norse line *deyr fé, deyja frændr* 'livestock die, kinsmen die' is clearly cut from the same cloth in *The Sayings of the High One*, stanzas 76 and 77 (see below).

111 *snottor on mode, gesæt him sundor æt rune* 'a man clever in mind, sat apart with himself in secret counsel'. This man looks like Boethius, with Lady Philosophy as his *run*. The speech in any case distils the argument of *De consolatione*, with the opening word *swa* 'thus' recalling his speech as heard.

112 *Til biþ se* 'Excellent is he' etc. This and the following hypermetric lines to the end express a proposition in syllogism: if (a) you are virtuous and (b) moderate, then (c) you will achieve grace in heaven. The poet returns to *are gebideð* on his first playful line, adding the weight of the intervening meaning in order to turn his *eardstapa* into an Everyman.

Egill's *Hard Loss of Sons*

Sonatorrek

Egill Skalla-Grímsson, *c.* 960

⁂

Personal elegy, so hard to find in northern European medieval literature, is represented in Iceland perhaps best of all in the *Sonatorrek* 'Hard Loss of Sons' of Egill Skalla-Grímsson, contextually dated to *c.* 960. Egill would thus have composed his work around when *The Wanderer* was being copied from one manuscript to another in England. Yet the sufferings that gave rise to Egill's *Hard Loss of Sons* appear to have been occasional rather than recalled from experience or recreated from older literature as in *The Wanderer*. In the saga that tells his story, *Egill's Saga* of the 1230s (ch. 78), Egill is said to have composed this elegy in memory of two sons who died before him: Gunnarr who died of fever at 14 and the young man Bǫðvarr who had just drowned off Borg (see *Egill's Saga*, **Sagas of Icelanders**). Egill's poem moves from the persona's claimed creative stasis to his expression of a keen desire for vengeance on the divine powers that drowned his son; from there to a lament for both lost sons and a reflection on the traditional but here futile (Periclean) remedy of begetting a new one; and from there to the speaker's bitter analysis of social isolation and alienation from Óðinn, his god of choice. One might say that Óðinn is the god whose failure to protect Egill's sons seems to allow their deaths. Yet Egill does not look to Óðinn for metaphysical answers about his sons, rather for the familiar mechanism of poetic composition by which he can purge himself of grief. The gift Egill always had from this god of poetry is here, in the heathen religious frame, reinterpreted as a payment of compensation that can save Egill's life.

The most contentious part of reading this poem is to call it 'heathen', as above. Many will never accept this (the latest is Torfi 2009); first because the poem's transmission gives time for invention, and second because in the minds of some critics the heathens did not have sufficient conceptual powers to engage with their gods on the level achieved here. In the first case, only the first stanza was copied into the *c.* 1350 Möðruvallabók manuscript which preserves the full saga text from the 1230s. Stanza 23 and half of 24 are also found in Snorri's *Edda*. So much for the thirteenth century. The rest of the poem was copied in the mid-seventeenth century by the clergyman Ketill Jörundarson (died 1670; ed. Chesnutt 2006) from a manuscript now lost. Despite Ketill's patent difficulties in understanding what he copied, some would treat his copy as the reflex of a thirteenth-century forgery, a cleric's clever projection of biblical or Boethian thought into the desired mindset of a tenth-century Icelandic primitive. This seems implausible, if only because Egill's cathartic mythology is so alien to Christian thought. At any rate, the jury is still out. Part of the reason for citing the text here, alongside Christian poems from England and elsewhere, will be to enable readers of this anthology to judge for themselves.

Chesnutt, M., ed., *Egils saga Skallagrímssonar, Band III. C-Redaktionen* (Copenhagen, 2006)

Gudbrand Vigfusson and F. York Powell, ed., *Corpus Poeticum Boreale I: Eddic Poetry* (Oxford, 1883)

Harris, J., 'Sacrifice and guilt in Sonatorrek', in *Studien zum Altgermanischen: Festschrift für Heinrich Beck*, ed. H. Uecker, Ergänzungsbände zum Reallexikon der Germanischen Altertumskunde 11 (Berlin, 1994), 173–96

North, R., 'The pagan inheritance of Egill's *Sonatorrek*', in *Poetry in the Scandinavian Middle Ages. Atti del 12. Congresso internazionale di studi sull'alto medioevo*, ed. T. Pàroli (Rome, 1990), 147–67

North, R., *Pagan Words and Christian Meanings*, Costerus new series 81 (Amsterdam and Atlanta, GA, 1991)

Olsen, M., 'Commentarii Scaldici. I.1. *Sonatorrek*', *Arkiv för nordisk filologi* 52 (1936), 209–55

Sigurður Nordal, ed., *Egils saga Skalla-Grímssonar*, ÍF 2 (Reykjavík, 1933)

Torfi Tulinius, 'The conversion of Sonatorrek', in *Analecta Septentrionalia: Beiträge zur nordgermanischen Kultur- und Literaturgeschichte*, ed. W. Heizmann, K. Böldl and H. Beck, Ergänzungsbände zum Reallexikon der Germanischen Altertumskunde 65 (Berlin, 2009), 701–14

Turville-Petre, E. O. G., *Scaldic Poetry* (Oxford, 1976)

1

Mjǫk erum tregt tungu at hrœra
eða loptvætt ljóðpundara;
esa nú vænligt of Viðurs þýfi,
né hógdrœgt ór hugar fylgsni.

It is hugely hard for me to stir my tongue,
The air-lift of the weigher of songs;
Not to be hoped for now is Wutherer's theft,
Not easily drawn from the hideout of mind.

'Weigher of songs': voice, whose 'air-lift' is the tongue. 'Wutherer's (Óðinn's) theft': the Mead of Poetry: poetry.

2

Esa auðþeystr, því́t ekki veldr
hǫfugligr, ór hyggju stað
fagna fundr Friggjar niðja
ár borinn ór Jǫtunheimum,

Not easily driven, for heavy-pressing grief
Causes this, from the place of opinions
Is the joyful find of Frigg's descendants,
Long ago borne from the world of the giants,

'Place of opinions': heart. 'Joyful find of Frigg's descendants': Mead of Poetry, brought by Óðinn to the gods.

3 lastalauss es lifnaði
á *Njóts* vers nǫkkva *hráki*.
Jǫtuns hals undir þjóta
Náins niðr fyr naustdurum,

Flawless when it sprang to life,
The spittle on the boat of Óðinn's fishing-grounds;
The giant's neck-wounds roar below
By the doors of King Dwarf's boat-shed,

'Fishing-grounds': sea; 'Óðinn's sea': Mead of Poetry, whose 'boat' is the vat (for this prepared by the gods), whose 'spittle' is the first poetry in the world. 'Giant's (Ymir's) neck-wounds': Ymir's blood: sea. 'King Dwarf's (Náinn's) boat-shed': cliffs, whose 'doors' are swallow holes.

4 þvít ætt mín á enda stendr,
hræbarnir sem hlynir marka;
esa karskr maðr, sás kǫggla berr
frænda hrørs af fletjum niðr.

Because my family line stands at its end,
Its men, like forest maples, crushed into wood-chips;
No hearty man he who carries down the joints
Of a kinsman's corpse from his halls.

5 Þó munk mitt ok móður hrør
fǫður fall fyrst of telja;
þat berk út ór orðhofi
mærðar timbr, máli laufgat.

Yet, besides my mother's decease,
First will I count the loss of my father;
This the timber of glory, made leafy with speech,
Which I carry out from the temple of words.

'Timber of glory': poem. 'Temple of words': heart.

6 Grimt vǫrum hlið, þats hrǫnn of braut
fǫður míns á frændgarði;
veitk ófullt ok opit standa
sonar skarð, es mér sær of vann.

Cruel to me was the gap Wave broke
In my father's family enclosure;
I know it stands open and unfilled,
The son's breach which Sea has made for me.

7 Mjǫk hefr Rǫ́n of rysktan mik,
emk ofsnauðr at ástvinum;
sleit marr bǫnd minnar ættar,
snaran þǫ́tt af sjǫlfum mér.

Goddess Robbery has shaken me hugely,
I am too much deprived of loving friends;
Ocean cut the bonds of my family,
The strong strand of me myself.

8 Veizt ef sǫk sverði rækak,
vas ǫlsmið[r] allra tíma,
[h]roða vágs brœðr, *ef* v*e*ga mættak,
fórk ægis andvígr mani.

You know that if I might avenge this crime with a sword,
Ale-brewer's time would be over;
If I could fight Wave-Pusher's brothers,
I would go against them and Ægis' mistress too.

'Ale-brewer': Ægir, the sea-god. 'Wave-Pusher': Ægir, whose 'brothers' are waves, and whose 'mistress' is the goddess Rán 'robbery'.

9 En ek ekki eiga þóttumk
sakar afl við s*onar* bana;
þvít alþjóð fyr augum verðr
gamals þegns gengileysi.

But I did not think I had the strength
For a contest with my *son's* slayers,
For the old thegn's infirmity
Is becoming clear to the eyes of everyone.

10 Mik hefr marr miklu ræntan,
grimt es fall frænda at telja,
síðans minn á munvega
ættar skjǫldr aflífi hvarf.

Me the sea has robbed of much,
Grim it is to tell of the fall of kinsmen,
Now that on the roads of joy, parted from his life,
The shield of my family has moved on.

11

Veitk þat sjalfr, í syni mínum
vas[a] ills þegns efni vaxit,
ef randviðr røskvask næði
unz her-Gauts hendr of tœki.

Myself I know that in my son
The stuff of an evil thegn had [not] grown,
If that rim-tree had managed to mature
Till War-Goth's hands might take him.

'Rim-(shield-) tree': man. 'War-Goth (-Gautr)': Óðinn.

12

Æ lét flest þats faðir mælti,
þótt ǫll þjóð annat segði;
mér upp helt of *hvárt tv*eggi
ok mitt afl mest of studdi.

Ever did he value most what father said,
Even if the whole people might say otherwise;
He upheld me whether it was right or wrong
And most was it he who kept up my strength.

13

Opt kømr mér mána bjarnar
í byrvind brœðraleysi;
hyggjumk um, es hildr þróask,
nýsumk hins ok hygg at því,

It comes to me often in the moon-bear's
Sailing breeze, my brotherlessness;
I ponder on this when battle is building,
Peer around for the other man and ponder

'Moon-bear': giant(ess), whose 'sailing-breeze (wind)' is thought: mind.

14

hverr hugaðr á hlið standi
annarr þegn við óðræði?
Þarfk þess opt við *þv*ergǫrum.
Verðk varfleygr, es vinir þverra.

What other thegn might stand brave
At my side against violent assaults?
With obstinate men I need him often,
Become wary of adventure as I lose my friends.

15

Mjǫks torfyndr, sás trúa knegum
of alþjóð Elgjar galga,
þvít niflgóðr niðja steypir
bróður hrør við baugum selr.

It's very hard to find a man we can trust
Among the nations of Óðinn's gallows,
For the man who sells his brother's body for rings
Is good only for the shades, a wrecker of relatives.

'Óðinn's gallows': the World Tree, whose 'nations' are mankind. 'The shades': the Underworld.

16

Finnk þat opt, es féar beiðir
***
***
***

I often find that when money is asked for
***
***
***

17

Þats ok mælt, at manngi getr
sonar iðgjǫld, nema sjalfr ali,
enn þann nið, es ǫðrum sé
borinn maðr í bróður stað.

It's also said that no man may get
True payment for his son, unless he himself
Begets a new heir, who, to the other men,
May be a man born in the brother's place.

18

Erumka þekt þjóða sinni,
þótt sér hverr sǫtt of haldi;
b*urr* es býskips í bœ kominn,
kvánar sonr, kynnis leita.

People's company is not pleasing to me,
Even if each man keeps the peace about him;
My boy has gone into the bee-ship's town,
Son of my wife, to call on his kin,

'Bee-ship's town': grave-mound (see note).

19 En mér fens í fǫstum þokk
hrosta hǫfundr á hendi stendr;
máka upp íarðar grímu,
rýnnis reið, rétt[r]i halda,

Whilst against me, with his mind made up,
The king of the malt-marsh stands;
My mask-surface, chariot of converse,
I haven't been able to hold up straight

'Malt-marsh': container for the Mead of Poetry, whose 'king' is Óðinn. 'Mask-surface': face. 'Chariot of converse': head.

20 síz son minn sóttar brími
heiptugligr ór heimi nam,
þanns ek veit, at varnaði
vamma vanr við vámæli.

Since the vicious fire of sickness
Took my son from this world,
Him whom I knew to be wary of disgrace,
Who held back from woeful talk.

21 Þat mank enn, es upp of hóf
í goðheim Gauta spjalli
ættar ask, þanns óx af mér,
ok kynvið kvánar minnar.

I still remember the Gautar's close friend
Raising up into the god-world
The family ash-tree which grew out of me,
Also the kin-wood of my queen.

'Gautar's close friend': Gautr: Óðinn. 'God-world': heaven: sky.

22 Áttak gótt við geirs dróttin,
gerðumk tryggr at trúa hǫnum,
áðr vinátt vagna rúni,
sigrhǫfundr, of sleit við mik.

I was on good terms with the lord of the spear,
Made myself sure that I could trust him,
Before the chariot confidant, instigator
Of victories, broke friendship with me.

'Lord of the spear': Óðinn. 'Chariot confidant': Óðinn.

23 Blœtka því bróður Vílis,
goðjaðar, at gjarn séak,
þó hefr Míms vinr mér of fengnar
bǫlva bœtr, es et betra telk. (also vs. 15)

I do not sacrifice to Vílir's brother,
Gods' guardian, because I want to;
And yet the friend of Mímir did get me
A cure for my evils, if I do a better count.

'Vílir's brother': Óðinn. 'Friend of Mímir': Óðinn.

24 Gǫfumk íþrótt ulfs of bági,
vígi vanr, vammi firða, (also vs. 16)
ok þat geð, es gerðak mér
vísa fjandr at vélǫndum.

The wolf's foe, accustomed to combat,
Has given me one skill without a flaw,
Besides that passion of soul by which I turned
Men who were my certain enemies into schemers.

'Wolf's (Fenrir's) foe': Óðinn. 'Skill without a flaw': poetry.

25 Nú erum torvelt. Tveggja bága
njǫrva nipt á nesi stendr;
skalk þó glaðr með góðan vilja
ok ó-hryggr Heljar bíða.

Now it goes hard with me, the narrow sister
Of the foe of Two-Face stands on the headland;
And yet happy, with a good will, as well as
Sorrow-free, I shall wait for goddess Hel.

'Two-Face': Óðinn, whose 'foe' is the wolf Fenrir, whose 'sister' is the goddess Hel.

Note

1 This stanza is also preserved in the manuscripts of *Egils saga*. Egill's kennings concern the myth of the Mead of Poetry, although, when their form is obscure, so is the meaning. [*hugar fylgsni* 'hide-out of mind'. Heart; but *fylgsni* may refer to a giant's rock 'refuge' such as that in which the Mead is first kept hidden by Suttungr (see **Gods of the Vikings**).

2 *fagna fundr* 'joyful find'. This word may also refer to a 'joyful reunion' such as of a family which (unlike Egill's) is reconstituted.

3 *á* Njóts *vers nǫkkva h*ráki 'spittle on the boat of Óðinn's fishing-grounds'. This is a guess, albeit of the most learned kind (Olsen 1936: 208–9). Ketill has the unintelligible *ä nǫckvers nøckva brage* (Chesnutt 2006: 143). The Mead of Poetry was spewed out by Óðinn on his return to the gods, into vats that they had prepared.

4 Egill's identification of mankind with trees, typical of the base of many 'man' kennings ('shield-tree', 'sword-tree' etc), is a leading characteristic of *Sonatorrek*.

5 *ór orðhofi mærðar timbr, máli laufgat* 'the timber of glory, made leafy with speech from the temple of words'. This is not a typical heathen kenning for poetry, so far as may be seen. Torfi suggests that the poet of *Sonatorrek* (in his view a twelfth-century Christian) bases this image on a story in the Bible, Numbers 17, in which Aaron, Moses' brother, finds himself made priest of the Israelites by the sudden sprouting of his rod within the tent of the Ark of the Covenant (2009: 709–11). The details fit; the problem, however, is the rest of *Sonatorrek* does not bear out Torfi's case that it is 'a manifesto for the use of Skaldic poetry and its resources in a Christian culture' (2009: 712). Nor is it clear why Egill's memorial poem should make him into a priest. The poem is so filled with the elements of a heathen world-view as not to be a work of Christianity as we know it in Iceland in the twelfth century.

6 Here and in stanzas 7–8 the words *hrǫnn* 'wave', *sjár* 'sea', *Rán* 'Robbery' (Ægir's wife, who plunders sailors from their ships), *marr* 'ocean', *ǫlsmið[r]* 'Ale-brewer', *[h]roða vágs brœðr* 'Wave-Pusher's brothers' and *Ægis man* 'Ægir's sweetheart' are personified on a mythological par with each other, as the *numina* or natural powers that have combined to drown Bǫðvarr. Egill describes his family like a newly abandoned shore settlement.

9 *gengileysi* 'infirmity'; but also 'lack of troops'. Ketill's *suds bana* 'ship's killer(s)' (Chesnutt 2006: 145) makes little sense, though Turville-Petre opts for it (1976: 33).

10 *á munvega* 'on the roads of joy'. Apparently a journey to the afterlife. Compare the phrase *wæs modsefa afysed on forðwege* 'my thoughts and feelings were focused on the road hence', in *The Dream of the Rood*, lines 124–5 (**Poems of Devotion**). [*ættar skjǫldr* 'shield of my family': Looking at his sons, Egill for the moment chooses Bǫðvarr, not Þorsteinn, for his biggest defence.

11 *her-Gauts hendr* 'War-Goth's (Óðinn's) hands'. 'Óðinn's hands' may be weapons. Sigurður Nordal (1933) reads this kenning as 'Óðinn of war': warrior, whose 'hands' Bǫðvarr would have acquired when he became one himself. The meaning in each case is much the same.

12 Ketill's *verbergi* (Chesnutt 2006: 145) is inexplicable on its own. It has been changed to *herbergi* 'hostel' (from a German form of French *auberge*), though Nordal rejects this as too late (1933: 250–1). The reconstruction *hvárr tveggi* 'either of two things' is guess-work. With this reading, however, the verse gives a contrast between Egill's view and the mob's, so the two things are taken to be 'right and wrong'. Bǫðvarr was more like his father than the virtuous Gunnarr, Egill's other son, who died of fever (stanza 20).

13 *mána bjarnar* 'moon-bear'. A giant, whose 'breeze' is Egill's thought or his mind. This is a variation of the 'mind' kenning *trǫllkvenna vindr* 'wind of troll-women'. 'Battle', though stylised to mean heroic combat, seems to refer to Egill's poor relations with neighbours (see *Egils saga*, chs. 79–82).

14 *varfleygr* 'wary of adventure'. A unique compound. 'Cautious in taking flight' and 'unable to fly' are less plausible meanings.

15 *Elgjar galga* 'Óðinn's (Elg's) gallows'. The World Tree, whose 'nations' are all people on earth. Compare this with the Christian image of creation beholding the Cross in *The Dream of the Rood*, lines 11–12. [*bróður hrør við baugum selr* 'sells his brother's body for rings'. This is a man who takes compensation instead of vengeance. Egill seems about to pour scorn on this option as cowardice in the incomplete stanza 16.

17 *iðgjǫld* 'True payment'. Generally impossible in monetary terms, Egill seems to be saying, and certainly so in the worst case, the loss of a son. Since he has ruled out revenge in stanza 8–9, Egill turns his mind to obtaining compensation for Bǫðvarr in a third form: neither violence, nor money, but poetry.

18 *þótt* 'Even if'. 'Because' might better express Egill's position here, as an autocrat of the old Norwegian style, now isolated because of his ways. Mss *bir er bískips* has proved almost insoluble, though the first word is doubtless *burr* 'boy'. Nordal (1933) emends *bískips* to *Bileygs*, as in 'the boy has gone to Failing-Sighted Óðinn's town': Valhǫll or Ásgarðr. The reading *býskips* is an old one (Gudbrand and York Powell 1883: 279). The most straightforward meaning for 'bee-ship' is a flower, resting the bee while he sips nectar, whose 'town' is a colony of flowers: this suggests the grave-mound in which Bǫðvarr and older members of his family have been laid to rest (*Egils saga*, ch. 78).

19 *hrosta fens* 'malt-marsh': Mead of Poetry', whose *hilmir* 'king' is Óðinn; see *Alfǫður brim hrosta* 'All-father's surf of malt' for the Mead of Poetry in *Þorfinnsdrápa* 4 (*s.a.* 1064; *SnE*, vs. 1). [*jarðar* (Mss *í áróar*) *grímu* 'mask's surface': face. [*rýnnis reið* 'chariot of converse': head.

21 *Gauta spjalli* 'the Gautar's close friend': Óðinn (Gautr). [*goðheim* 'god-world': the sky. This verse harks back to a happier time when apparently Óðinn had seemed to bless the childhood of young Bǫðvarr. Here the image of Egill's growing family as a grove is the most fully developed.

22 *vagna rúni* 'chariot confidant'. It has been suggested that Óðinn, disguised as 'Brúni' the charioteer in a story which Egill would have known, betrayed his protégé King Haraldr in the Battle of Brávellir (Harris 1994: 183). Óðinn betrays his friends as a matter of course, having the finest warriors killed for his army in Valhǫll. The cruelty of this loss, as Egill seems to admit, is that Valhǫll is not the privilege to which Bǫðvarr is entitled; although, as father of the dead, Óðinn claims him in another way.

23 *bróður Vílis* 'Vílir's brother'. Óðinn, whom Víli(r) cuckolds with Frigg (with Véi, another brother, in *Loki's Truth-Game*, stanza 26: see **Gods of the Vikings**) while the chief brother is wandering. What parallels may be intended with Egill, whose wife had been married to his brother Þórólfr, one can only imagine. [*Míms vinr* 'friend of Mímir'. Óðinn gave one of his eyes to Mímir in exchange for wisdom. This verse and half of stanza 24 are quoted separately in *Skáldskaparmál* (ch. 2). In this verse, Egill begins to reinterpret Óðinn's earlier gifts to him as an advance payment in exchange for Bǫðvarr.

24 *ulfs of bági* 'wolf's (Fenrir's) foe'. Óðinn, eaten by Fenrir at the end of the world. [*íþrótt vammi firrða* 'skill without a flaw'. Skaldic poetry, or more properly versifying, whose metre will bear no mistakes. [*þat geð* 'that passion of soul'. The Odinic turbulence that appears to characterise Egill as we know him. This term is also related to Egill's poetry, as the downside of artistic temperament, in that one gift cannot exist without the other (OE *giedd* 'song, poem' is formally the cognate of OIce *geð*; see North 1990, 1991: 56–62). [*vísa fjandr at vélǫndum* 'Men who were my certain enemies into schemers'. Others, treating the Odinic *geð* as a positive quality, emend *ad* to *af* on this line, to make 'certain enemies out of schemers': 'because of his gifts, Egill could unmask those who plotted against him' (Turville-Petre 1976: 41). It is true that Egill wises up to Gunnhildr's poison on Atli's island in *Egils saga* (ch. 44), but it is his magic, not his soul, that enables him to do this. Conversely it is his uncle Þórólfr's suddenly dark temper, in ch. 9, which causes the sons of Hildiríðr to plot against him, with fatal results. The *geð* belongs to their family.

25 *Tveggja* 'of Two-Face (Tveggi)'. Of Óðinn, whose gifts are negative as well as positive. [*njǫrva nipt* 'narrow sister'. Hel is both a goddess and the confined site of Egill's expected underworld. On the Christian hell as confinement, compare *þæs ænga styde* 'this tight place', in Satan's own description, and the hell-bound Adam and Eve, who must *þone nearwan nið niede onfon* 'be chained . . . into that close confine' *Genesis B*, line 697 (**Poems of Devotion**). [*ó-hryggr* 'Sorrow-free': by emphasising the *ó*-prefix to *hryggr*, Egill claims that his poetry has rendered him true payment for Bǫðvarr and that he is now restored to good mental health. The genre is catharsis, elegy in Icelandic style, and one fulfilled without apparent recourse to Boethian or any other Christian consolatory thought.

The Seafarer

*

'He that will learne to pray, let him goe to sea', said George Herbert, and initially it seems that *The Seafarer* simulates the same extreme dangers in verse. This poem is copied from folio 81 verso into 83 recto of the Exeter Book, separated from *The Wanderer* by *The Gifts of Men* and *Precepts*. As a poem, it is held in the same esteem as *The Wanderer* and the two of them have often been taught together. And yet although some of the sea imagery looks similar, *The Seafarer* is quite different. Its text is so corrupt or confused in places towards the end, unlike the trim form of *The Wanderer*, that some readers believe the scribe copied a different text from the end of line 109. The intellectual style is also bracingly different. Both poets seek to engage the reader with imaginative personae, but there the resemblance ends. The poet of *The Seafarer* creates a persona who changes rapidly before our eyes. He does not modify reader's views by intellectual diversion or rational persuasion, as in *The Wanderer*, but starts with the lyricism of storms and seabirds, rejecting then accepting the sea almost irrationally and then reaching a peak of spiritual ecstasy, whereupon he moves into homiletic mode in order to condition his audience into abandoning the world. His persona changes aspect from English crewman, to Irish hermit, to lonely sea-bird, to focused mind, to divested soul and then into a state of oneness with God. The sea is left behind halfway through as the poet figuratively urges each member of the audience to regulate his life, withdraw from all good or bad emotional ties and finally to surrender his identity to the state of joy. Heaven lies beyond the horizon and to get there one must leave everything behind, people as well. This image can be found more neatly expressed in the Exeter Book at the end of Cynewulf's *Christ II*, but there again *The Seafarer* is the better poem. Its poet works like an inspirational preacher, and both his language and rhetorical technique read like the sermons of active clergy. Evidence of the appropriate learning is to be found in the Bible and books of the Fathers, not in the works of Boethius or other more aureate late antique authors whose works have been seen in *The Wanderer*. Although the dialects of Old English poems are difficult to establish, *The Seafarer*, being so battered, looks older rather than younger. It seems likely also that the poem has an Anglian base, more plausibly Northumbrian than Mercian, and that it is older than *The Wanderer*. Like *The Dream of the Rood*, though a generation or two later, this poem may reflect the eighth-century era of missionary work in Germany.

Clemoes, P., '*Mens absentia cogitans* in *The Seafarer* and *The Wanderer*', in *Medieval Literature and Civilization: Studies in Memory of G. N. Garmonsway*, ed. D. A. Pearsall and R. A. Waldron (London, 1969), 62–77

Cross, J. E., '*Ubi sunt* passages in Old English – sources and relationships', *Vetenskaps-Societetens i Lund Årsbok* (Lund, 1956), 25–44

Diekstra, F. N. M., '*The Seafarer* 58–66a. The flight of the exiled soul to its fatherland', *Neophilologus* 55 (1971), 433–46

Fulk, R. D., and C. M. Cain, *A History of Old English Literature* (Oxford, 2003)

Godden, M., 'Anglo-Saxons on the mind', in *Learning and Literature in Anglo-Saxon England: Studies Presented to Peter Clemoes on the Occasion of his Sixty-Fifth Birthday*, ed. M. Lapidge and H. Gneuss (Cambridge, 1985), 271–98

Gordon, I. L., ed., *The Seafarer* (London, 1960)

Greenfield, S. B., '*Mīn, Sylf*, and dramatic voices in *The Wanderer* and *The Seafarer*', *Journal of English and Germanic Philology* 68 (1969), 212–20

Hill, J., '*Þis deade lif*: a note on *The Seafarer*, lines 64–6', *English Language Notes* 15 (1977), 95–7

Klinck, A. L., *The Old English Elegies: A Critical Edition and Genre Study* (Montreal and Kingston, 1992)

North, R., *Pagan Words and Christian Meanings*, Costerus new series 81 (Amsterdam and Atlanta, GA, 1991)

Pope, J. C., 'Second thoughts on the interpretation of *The Seafarer*', *Anglo-Saxon England* 5 (1974), 75–86

Rieger, M., 'Der *Seefahrer* als Dialog hergestellt', *Zeitschrift für deutsche Philologie* 1 (1869), 334–9

Tolley, C., *Shamanism in Norse Myth and Magic*, 2 vols, Folklore Fellows' Communications 296 (Helsinki, 2009)

Whitelock, D., 'The interpretation of *The Seafarer*', in *The Early Cultures of Northwest Europe*, ed. C. Fox and B. Dickins (Cambridge, 1950), 442–57

Mæg ic be me sylfum soðgied wrecan,
siþas secgan, hu ic geswincdagum
earfoðhwile oft þrowade,
bitre breostceare gebiden hæbbe,
gecunnad in ceole cearselda fela,
atol yþa gewealc, þær mec oft bigeat
nearo nihtwaco æt nacan stefnan,

I can sing a life-story about myself,
tell my adventures, how in days of toil
I often suffered times of hardship,
have endured breast-cares biting sharp,
in a ship got to know many shelters of care,
terrible rolling of waves where narrow night watch
has often got me at the vessel's prow

1 *soðgied wrecan* 'sing a life-story'. Lively men who *soðgied wrecað* 'sing their life-stories' are seen looking for fights in *Vainglory*, line 15. The seafaring ambience suggests a similar layman's persona at least in the poem's opening lines. On *giedd wrecan* from 'sing a poem' from 'purge the soul' see North (1991: 51–6).

5 *cearselda fela* 'many shelters of care'. Without parallel, *cearseld* literally 'care-building' has been questioned and *cearsælða* 'unhappy experiences' even proposed, but the sea-land contrast is strong enough in this poem for this compound to have been created here as an exceptional image of an anti-hall (see Klinck 1992: 127).

6–7 *mec oft bigeat nearo nihtwaco* 'narrow night watch has often got me'. His turn on watch. The persona seems to be an active crewman.

þonne he be clifum cnossað. Calde geþrungen
wæron mine fet, forste gebunden,
caldum clommum, þær þa ceare seofedun
hat ymb heortan; hungor innan slat
merewerges mod. Þæt se mon ne wat
þe him on foldan fægrost limpeð,
hu ic earmcearig iscealdne sæ
winter wunade wræccan lastum,
winemægum bidroren, [. . .]
bihongen hrimgicelum. Hægl scurum fleag!
Þær ic ne gehyrde butan hlimman sæ,
iscaldne wæg. Hwilum ylfete song
dyde ic me to gomene, ganetes hleoþor
ond huilpan sweg fore hleahtor wera,
mæw singende fore medodrince.
Stormas þær stanclifu beotan, þær him stearn oncwæð
isigfeþera. Ful oft þæt earn bigeal,

---

while she pitches past the cliffs. Crushed with cold
were my feet, bound up with frost,
with cold chains, where those cares sighed
hot around the heart. Hunger tore from within
the mind of the sea-wearied man. He does not know,
for whom on land all things work beautifully,
with what wretched care I have spent
winters on the ice-chilled sea on an exile's roads,
with friends and kinsmen fallen from me, [. . .]
hung about with frost-icicles. Hail flew by in showers!
There I heard nothing but sea resound,
the ice-cold wave. At times the swan's song
was what I made my pastime, gannet's voice
and curlew's melody instead of the laughter of men,
singing gull instead of a drink of mead.
Storms there beat the stone cliffs, where tern gave answer,
with icy wings. Very often did eagle shriek of this,

15–16 *wræccan lastum, winemægum bidroren* 'on an exile's roads, with friends and kinsmen fallen from me'. The situation may demand exile in a formulaic way, here and in line 57, which is different from that in *The Wanderer*, lines 6–7 and 20–1.

16 The second half-line is missing from the text, without a gap in the manuscript.

18 *hlimman sæ* 'sea resound'. The crash of waves may be regarded as hypnotic, in view of the poet's true longing for the sea, despite its terrors, on lines 33–8.

19 *Hwilum ylfete song* 'At times the swan's song'. The swan is the first of six solitary usually shoreline birds cited here at the rate of one per line. Their concentration prepares for the poet's sea-land contrast of lines 27–30 and marks out *The Seafarer* as an extraordinary poem. What do they know that we don't?

urigfeþra, ne ænig hleomæga
feasceaftig ferð frefran meahte.
Forþon him gelyfeð lyt, se þe ah lifes wyn
gebiden in burgum, bealosiþa hwon,
wlonc ond wingal, hu ic werig oft
in brimlade bidan sceolde.
Nap nihtscua, norþan sniwde,
hrim hrusan bond, hægl feol on eorþan,
corna caldast. Forþon cnyssað nu
heortan geþohtas, þæt ic hean streamas,
sealtyþa gelac sylf cunnige.
Monað modes lust mæla gehwylce
ferð to feran, þæt ic feor heonan
elþeodigra eard gesece.
Forþon nis þæs modwlonc mon ofer eorþan,
ne his gifena þæs god, ne in geoguþe to þæs hwæt,

---

with wings bedewed, nor was any protective kinsman
able to offer solace to the destitute heart.
And so the man who has experienced the joy of life
in towns, few times of evil, will little believe,
arrogant and flushed with wine, how often I, in weariness,
have had to suffer waiting on the ocean road.
Night's shadow grew black, from the north it snowed,
frost chained up the ground, hail fell on earth,
coldest of wheat-grains. And so now I am pitched about
by the thoughts of my heart that I should try
the high currents, the salt-waves' play by myself.
The heart's desire each season urges
the mind to sail, that far from here
I may seek the homeland of foreign people.
And so there is no man across the earth so proud in mind,
nor so generous in his gifts, nor so sharp in his youth,

---

33 *corna caldast* 'coldest of wheat-grains'. Unless OE *corn* has become a cipher for a pellet of frozen water, the poet seems to compare the harvest on land with the barrenness of storms at sea, in line with his short shrift for good living in towns.

35 *sylf cunnige* 'should try by myself'. The word *sylf* has caused problems, indicating to earlier readers a new speaker unfamiliar with the sea. This gave Rieger to believe *The Seafarer* was a dialogue between an old and young sailor (1869). For a while 'of my own accord' kept the speakers to one man, emphasising his stronger bond with the sea he has sailed on before (Greenfield 1969: 218). 'Alone', which is too strong, nonetheless gives the change that the text demands (Pope 1974: 78–80). The Seafarer wants to try the deep (relatively) on his own, like a hermit venturing into the unknown.

38 *elþeodigra eard* 'homeland of foreign people'. *Peregrinatio pro amore Dei* 'pilgrimage for love of God', and possibly the great Irish-English missionary work of the early to mid-eighth century, are invoked here (Whitelock 1950).

ne in his dædum to þæs deor, ne him his dryhten to þæs hold,
þæt he a his sæfore sorge næbbe,
to hwon hine dryhten gedon wille.
Ne biþ him to hearpan hyge ne to hringþege,
ne to wife wyn ne to worulde hyht,
ne ymbe owiht elles, nefne ymb yða gewealc,
ac a hafað longunge se þe on lagu fundað.
Bearwas blostmum nimað, byrig fægriað,
wongas wlitigað, woruld onetteð.
Ealle þa gemoniað modes fusne,
sefan, to siþe, þam þe swa þenceð
on flodwegas feor gewitan.
Swylce geac monað geomran reorde,
singeð sumeres weard, sorge beodeð

---

nor so daring in his deeds, nor his lord so loyal to him
that he may never have anxiety on his sea-journey,
to what the Lord will bring him.
He has no mind for lyre nor for receiving rings,
for joy in woman neither, nor use either for the world
or for any other thing but the rolling of the waves,
for ever has he longing who hastens on the flood.
Groves take with blossoms, towns grow beautiful,
hillsides look dazzling, the world hurries on.
All these things advise a man keen in mind,
the heart itself, to set out, so it is to the man who thinks
of moving far on the ways of the flood.
Just so mourns cuckoo with melancholy voice,
summer's guardian sings, bodes sorrows

---

42 *his sæfore sorge* 'anxiety on his sea-journey'. This still appears to be real, rather than a figure for passage to heaven. That the sea is a dangerous place, confronting us with existential questions, is perhaps why the poet has made it into his opening means of engagement with the audience.

44–7 *Ne biþ hyge ac a hafað longunge* 'He has no mind but ever has he longing'. The shift to *longung* is perhaps unexpected. We are led into this sentence with a nervous passenger forgetting all in his scrutiny of every dangerous wave, and then, against expectations, the poet shows habituation producing change: he begins to enjoy it.

48 *Bearwas blostmum nimað* 'Groves take with blossoms' etc. The poet is ambivalent towards the beauty of spring, which here merely stimulates departure to another clime (as it did for Chaucer's Pilgrims). For another such unforgiving seague into the Last Days, see the opening seven lines of *Judgement Day II*, the late-tenth-century English adaptation of Bede's poem *De die iudicii* ('On the Day of Judgement').

50–1 *modes fusne, sefan* 'man keen in mind, the heart itself'. The syntax is awkward, but may be resolved in this way (Klinck 1992: 136), with the desire to travel thus passing inwards from the man in the text to the reader.

53 *geac* 'cuckoo'. Also the subject of *Riddle* 9, the cuckoo is more often heard in medieval Welsh poetry than in Old English (Klinck 1992: 137). Here, as guardian of the summer, he is made to express the poet's longing for a better place, by auguring sorrows to come.

bitter in breosthord. Þæt se beorn ne wat,
esteadig secg, hwæt þa sume dreogað
þe þa wræclastas widost lecgað.
Forþon nu min hyge hweorfeð ofer hreþerlocan,
min modsefa mid mereflode
ofer hwæles eþel hweorfeð wide,
eorþan sceatas, cymeð eft to me
gifre ond grædig, gielleð anfloga,
hweteð on hwælweg hreþer unwearnum
ofer holma gelagu. Forþon me hatran sind
dryhtnes dreamas þonne þis deade lif,
læne on londe.

Ic gelyfe no
þæt him eorðwelan ece stondað.
Simle þreora sum þinga gehwylce,

---

bitter in the breast-hoard. That man will not know,
who is granted everything, what those rare men endure
who most widely set out the roads of their exile.
For this reason my mind now moves beyond the locker of my breast,
my imagination with the sea's flood,
over the whale's domain moves far and wide,
over earth's surfaces, comes back to me
voracious and greedy, the lone flier yells,
augurs the breast to the whale's path relentlessly,
across the waters of oceans: namely because more hot to me
are the Lord's good things than this dead life,
lent to us on land.

I will never believe
that earthly wealth stands eternal for a man.
One of three things, before he has his day,

58–66 One of the most celebrated verse passages in Old English literature, and self-consciously the climax of the first half of the poem.

58–9 *hyge* 'mind', *modsefa* 'imagination'. Much has been written on these terms (Godden 1985, North 1991: 62–93), which appear to be respectively active and passive aspects of mind, but which cannot denote the soul. They may here connote the soul, however, if this passage is an attempt to approximate to the flight of *anima* 'soul' in the more developed intellectual vocabulary of the Church Fathers (see Clemoes 1969 and especially Diekstra 1971). On such matters as the Germanic 'free soul', which is not related to Christian notions of *sawol* and *gast*, see Tolley (2009: I, 167–9). It seems likely that the 'free soul' formed a substratum to patristic ideas within this passage.

62 *gifre ond grædig, gielleð anfloga* 'voracious and greedy, the lone flier yells'. Unique here, *anfloga* appears to merge all birds into one, to give the flying mind one form as a bird auguring heaven (North 1991: 99–121).

65 *þis deade lif* 'this dead life'. An oxymoron translated from *vita mortalis* in sermons (Hill 1977). At this point the poem leaves the sea to become a sermon proper.

ær his tid aga, to tweon weorþeð;
adl oþþe yldo oþþe ecghete
fægum fromweardum feorh oðþringeð.
Forþon þæt bið eorla gehwam æftercweþendra
lof lifgendra lastworda betst,
þæt he gewyrce, ær he on weg scyle,
fremum on foldan wið feonda niþ,
deorum dædum deofle togeanes,
þæt hine ælda bearn æfter hergen,
ond his lof siþþan lifge mid englum
awa to ealdre, ecan lifes blæd,
dream mid dugeþum.

Dagas sind gewitene,
ealle onmedlan eorþan rices.

---

will always turn out dubious for him;
illness or old age or the heat of blades
squeezes out spirit from the doomed man departing.
And so for each man the praise of the living
who speak in memory of him is the best of epitaphs,
that he may create, before he should take the road,
great benefits on earth against the enmity of fiends,
daring deeds in the face of the devil,
that the sons of men may praise his memory,
and praise of him live thenceforth with the angels
for ever and eternity, the triumph of everlasting life,
a joyous living with the hosts.

Those days are past,
all the pomp of the kingdom of earth.

---

70 *adl oþþe yldo* 'illness or old age' etc. Compare Hrothgar's *adl ne yldo*, *Beowulf*, line 1736 and the same initial phrase in *Maxims I*, 10: homiletic in each case.

74–5 *gewyrce fremum wið feonda niþ* 'create benefits against the enmity of fiends'. This may be asking the individual to endow monasteries and churches as a means of winning *lof lifgendra*, posthumous fame. Beowulf's status as *lofgeornost* 'most eager to win praise' (line 3182), and the treasure he secures for his people, seem to project this pattern into an imagined heathen society.

78 *his lof siþþan lifge mid englum* 'praise of him live thenceforth with the angels'. Either while he still lives, or with *lof his* as a figure for the soul of the benefactor just mentioned.

80–93 *Dagas sind gewitene* 'Those days are past' etc. The poet moves his society into the Last Days, connecting the world's pre-apocalyptic with man's individual physical decline. The same connection is made more meditatively in *The Wanderer*, lines 73–84. These commonplaces continue in homilies of the later tenth century (Cross 1956) and have been used to claim a similar date for *The Seafarer* (Fulk and Cain 2003: 182).

82 *Næron* 'There are not'. A variant of *nearon*, which is Mercian or Northumbrian for West Saxon *ne syndon* (Klinck 1992: 141).

Næron nu cyningas   ne caseras
ne goldgiefan   swylce iu wæron,
þonne hi mæst mid him   mærþa gefremedon
ond on dryhtlicestum   dome lifdon.
Gedroren is þeos duguð eal,   dreamas sind gewitene,
wuniað þa wacran   ond þas woruld healdaþ,
brucað þurh bisgo.   Blæd is gehnæged,
eorþan indryhto   ealdað ond searað,
swa nu monna gehwylc   geond middangeard.
Yldo him on fareð,   onsyn blacað,
gomelfeax gnornað,   wat his iuwine,
æþelinga bearn,   eorþan forgiefene.
Ne mæg him þonne se flæschoma,   þonne him þæt feorg losað,
ne swete forswelgan   ne sar gefelan,
ne hond onhreran   ne mid hyge þencan.
Þeah þe græf wille   golde stregan
broþor his geborenum,   byrgan be deadum
maþmum mislicum,   þæt hine mid wille,

There are not kings, nor caesars,
nor gold-givers, such as there once were,
when among themselves they performed the greatest renown
and lived in the most courtly glory.
Fallen is all this host, good times have passed by,
weaker the men who inhabit and keep the world,
enjoy it through their toil. Triumph is brought low,
the great nobility of earth grows old and sear
just as now with each man in the middle world.
Old age comes upon him, his visage grows pale,
the grey-hair mourns, knows his friend of old,
a son of princes, given to the earth.
Nor may it then, his flesh coating, when his spirit is lost to it,
taste sweet things, or feel pain,
or move his hand, or think with his mind.
Though one brother born may want to strew with gold
the grave of another, bury with the dead man
a variety of the treasure, he will have go with him,

---

94 *se flæschoma, þonne him þæt feorg losað* 'his flesh coating, when his spirit is lost to it'. The poet's shock-tactics, in going beyond the terminus of physical decay, belong to the performance of sermons.

97 *græf wille golde stregan* 'may want to strew with gold the grave'. OE *stregan* is Anglian, possibly Northumbrian. The culture of grave-goods did not end with heathendom, but the poet's urgency does suggest that these times are not far behind. On this account, the first form of *The Seafarer* may come from the earlier eighth century.

ne mæg þære sawle þe biþ synna ful
gold to geoce for Godes egsan,
þonne he hit ær hydeð þenden he her leofað.
Micel biþ se Meotudes egsa, forþon hi seo molde oncyrreð!
Se gestaþelade stiþe grundas,
eorþan sceatas ond uprodor.
Dol biþ se þe him his Dryhten ne ondrædeþ, cymeð him se deað unþinged.
Eadig bið se þe eaþmod leofaþ, cymeð him seo ar of heofonum,
Meotod him þæt mod gestaþelað, forþon he in His meahte gelyfeð.
Stieran mon sceal strongum mode, ond þæt on staþelum healdan,
ond gewis werum, wisum clæne,
scyle monna gehwylc mid gemete healdan
wiþ leofne ond wið laþne bealo,
þeah þe he hine wille fyres fulne,
oþþe on bæle forbærnedne

---

not for the soul which is full of sins
will gold be of help against the terror of God
when he just hides it while living here.
Great is the terror of the Measurer for whom the world turns.
He established the rigid bed-rock,
earth's surfaces and the sky above.
Foolish is he who does not dread his Lord, death comes to him unappointed.
Blessed is he who lives a humble man, grace comes to him from heaven,
Measurer settles that mindset on man in return for believing in His power.
A man must restrain a strong temperament and keep it on firm footing,
and be meticulous with agreements, clean in his ways.
Each person should hold in moderation
any evil against friend or foe,
though he may want the last one filled with fire,
or burned up in the bonfire

100–1 *þære sawle . . . gold to geoce* 'for the soul . . . gold be of help'. Not only the circulation of gold, but also its endowment to the Church, seems to be urged on us here.

106–9 These hypermetric lines announce *The Seafarer*'s approaching end.

112–15 The metre appears defective, the lines therefore corrupt unless they may be presented as short lines of three stresses (as argued also for *Maxims I*, 3). These lines urge the renunciation of all emotional ties, good or bad. Love and hate are closely associated, with love betrayed prone to turn into hate: if the poet asks us to renounce both, he is continuing the transformation of the individual with which the poem starts (from crewman, to hermit, to bird, to mind, to divested soul, to being one with God in eternity).

114 *on bæle forbærnedne* 'burned up in the bonfire'. More plausibly this, as an image of hell-fire desired for a former friend, than a cremation culture at odds with the core of Christianity itself.

his geworhtne wine. Wyrd biþ swiþre,
Meotud meahtigra þonne ænges monnes gehygd.

Uton we hycgan hwær we ham agen,
ond þonne geþencan hu we þider cumen,
ond we þonne eac tilien, þæt we to moten
in þa ecan eadignesse,
þær is lif gelong in lufan dryhtnes,
hyht in heofonum. Þæs sy þam halgan þonc,
þæt he usic geweorþade, wuldres ealdor,
ece dryhten, in ealle tid. *Amen*

---

the friend he has made. Fate is stronger,
Measurer mightier, than the plans of any man.

Let us consider where we have a home,
and then think how we may get there,
and how we may then do well, that we be allowed to go
into the eternal blessedness
where life is one with love of the Lord,
hope in heaven. May the Holy One have thanks
for having honoured us, Prince of Glory,
Eternal Lord from now into all time. *Amen*

---

115 *Wyrd* 'Fate'. This stark notion is identified in the next line with *Meotud* 'Measurer', the aspect of God that the poet has introduced on lines 103 and 108, and with *gemete* 'measure, moderation', on line 111. The theme, harshly expressed in contrast to *The Wanderer*'s more benign philosophising on *wyrda gesceaft* (line 107), is self-discipline as a means of subsumption into God's eternity.

117 *Uton we hycgan* 'Let us consider' etc. These prosaic lines could be a later accretion, or even the poet's own organising measure. It hardly matters. The poet has already subsumed his unique lyricism into the communal genre of a sermon.

Vainglory

✳

Vainglory presents a world divided between good and evil, clean souls versus devil-spawn. The narrator reaches back into the past, as far as the Old Testament, to uncover the workings of the world, representing a fight in an English beer-hall as a day-to-day reflex of the war that started in heaven. The moral choices are the same; the men who make them, different; but at all times we must know which side we are on. The poet, working like a Khalil Gibran of the mid-tenth century, which is the assumed date of *Vainglory*, seems immersed in the Bible and the phrases of sermons. On this account, at least one reader thinks 'elegy' is out of the question as the poem's generic marker (McKinnell 1991: 83–9), it seems less prescriptive to treat *Vainglory* as a *giedd*, a poem on the meaning of life, just like the other 'elegies'.

The sermonic mood of this *giedd* is close to that of *The Seafarer*, the poem that it follows on folio 83 recto (to 84 verso) of the Exeter Book. It is particularly close to the mood of that poem's more battered second half. There again, the vitality of the argument in *Vainglory* also recalls passages from William Langland's *The Vision of Piers Plowman* (*c*. 1370–90). It may be for stylistic reasons that *Vainglory* is rarely read. This poem has received less attention than *The Wanderer* or *The Seafarer*, or *Widsith*, the poem that comes after it on folio 87 recto; or even lesser works in the Exeter Book such as *Resignation* and *The Order of the World. Vainglory* is missing in Anne Klinck's excellent edition of the elegies of the Exeter Book (1992), even after Tom Shippey included it in his (1976). It was a nearly a century before *Vainglory* acquired the title it has now, as given by Krapp and Dobbie in their text (1936). Although Bernard Muir has retained this in his modern edition (2000), Jane Roberts wonders whether 'The Prophet' or a similar title would connect the poem with *The Wanderer* and *The Seafarer*, works with which *Vainglory* is intellectually comparable (2008: 121).

The speaker in *Vainglory* refers to a book-learned man who has himself consulted a *witega* 'Prophet', whom it is perhaps best to think of as Isaiah in his prophecy of man's pride and God's wrath in the Book of Isaiah 2:11–19. All three men, or two if the sources are regarded as the same, are blended together in the English poem without the poet troubling to establish a clear line of transmission. It will be noted that *The Wanderer* offers a similar effect with one or two speakers to whom an equally unnamed narrator defers as he goes along. Just as the end of the Wanderer's speech is uncertainly placed, so is that of the Prophet's speech in *Vainglory* (here fixed at line 77; later in Huppé's 1970 text, however). The wicked person also, who brags and lies his way to power in *Vainglory*, lines 28–37, a catalyst for the violence to be found occasionally in English councils, is blended with his invisible sponsor, the rebel angel Satan. Conversely, a noble thegn is identified on the level of spiritual communion with Christ Himself in lines 67–74 and 79–81. The only place where the poet distinguishes between people is in the obvious division between good and bad moral character.

This delineation of examples is what *Vainglory* is about. For a poem of such modest length it drives towards its *chiaroscuro* moral with an interactive rhetoric which is angry, mocking and querulous by turn. The poet's turns of phrase differ from those in *The Wanderer* in that they seem less traditional. They seem instead to be satirically, perhaps even colloquially, condensed. The form of this poem is also straightforward. The Prophet's speech occupies centre stage in lines 50–77, whereby it is clear that the poem is structured symmetrically with the poet's placing of the narrator's voice to either side. Where other poems are concerned, it is plausible to compare *Vainglory* with Hrothgar's 'sermon' in *Beowulf*, for this heathen king's speech on pride versus eternal rewards is the thematic centre-piece to its own poem (Roberts 2008: 133; see **Heroic Poems**). However, the moral of the relatively short *Vainglory* is anti-heroic. The narrator, unlike the heroic world of Heorot, so disdains boasting as to give a negative sense to *wlonc* 'proud' in the warriors who drink in their halls, in line 14. As one scholar says, 'defeat in spiritual combat occurs at the moment these proud war-smiths boast of their heroic military exploits' (Hermann 1989: 49). And on line 70, the poet's Prophet admires men who love their enemies: not even Hrothgar comes close to him here. A less Beowulfian poem than *Vainglory* would be hard to imagine.

Hermann, J. P., *Allegories of War: Language and Violence in Old English Poetry* (Ann Arbor, MI, 1989)

Huppé, B. F., *The Web of Words: Structural Analyses of the Old English Poems 'Vainglory', 'The Wonder of Creation', 'The Dream of the Rood', and 'Judith'* (Albany, NY, 1970)

Klinck, A. L., *The Old English Elegies: A Critical Edition and Genre Study* (Montreal and Kingston, 1992)

Krapp, G. P., and E. van K. Dobbie, ed., *The Exeter Book*, The Anglo-Saxon Poetic Records, 6 vols (New York, 1931–53)

McKinnell, J. S., 'A farewell to Old English elegy: the case of *Vainglory*', *Parergon* new series 9 (1991), 67–89

Muir, B., ed., *The Exeter Anthology of Old English Poetry: An Edition of Exeter Dean and Chapter MS 3502*, 2nd ed. (Exeter, 2000)

Pickford, T. E., 'An edition of *Vainglory*', *Parergon* 10 (1974), 1–40

Roberts, J., 'A man "Boca Gleaw" and his musings', in *Intertexts: Studies in Anglo-Saxon Culture Presented to Paul E. Szarmach*, ed. V. Blanton and H. Scheck, Medieval and Renaissance Texts and Studies 334 (Tempe, AZ, 2008), 119–37

Shippey, T. A., ed., *Poems of Wisdom and Learning in Old English* (Cambridge, 1976)

Trahern, J. B., Jr., 'Caesarius, Chrodegang, and the Old English Vainglory', in *Gesellschaft, Kultur, Literatur: Beiträge Luitpold Wallach gewidmet*, ed. K. Bosl, Monographien zur Geschichte des Mittelalters 11 (Stuttgart, 1975), 167–78

Hwæt, me frod wita   on fyrndagum
sægde, snottor ar,   sundorwundra fela.
Wordhord onwreah   witgan larum
beorn boca gleaw,   bodan ærcwide,
þæt ic soðlice   siþþan meahte

Listen, a wise man learned in ancient days,
a clever herald, told me many exceptional miracles.
His wordhoard he threw open with prophet's teachings,
this man skilled in books, with a messenger's ancient precepts,
so that from then on, from his old incantation,

ongitan bi þam gealdre   Godes agen bearn,
wilgest on wicum,   ond þone wacran swa some,
scyldum bescyredne,   on gescead witan.
Þæt mæg æghwylc mon   eaþe geþencan,
se þe hine ne læteð   on þas lænan tid
amyrran his gemyndum   modes gælsan
ond on his dægrime   druncen to rice,
þonne monige beoð   mæþelh*e*gendra,
wlonce wigsmiþas   winburgum in,
sittaþ æt symble,   soðgied wrecað,
wordum wrixlað,   witan fundiaþ
hwylc æscstede   inne in ræcede
mid werum wunige.   Þonne win hweteð
beornes breostsefan,   breahtem stigeð,
cirm on corþre,   cwide scralletaþ
missenlice.   Swa beoþ modsefan
dalum gedæled,   sindon dryhtguman
ungelice.   Sum on oferhygdo

I was truly able to perceive God's own Son,
a willing guest in our village, likewise to distinguish
his contrary, separated from his sins.
Any man may easily share this thought,
who, in this borrowed hour, does not let himself
mar his rational mind with wanton heart
or drink excessively in the count of his days,
for many are the men who go to assembly,
arrogant war-smiths in wine-towns,
who sit at the banquet, sing their life-stories,
exchange words, strive to discover
what place for fighting within the building
may be among the men there. When wine stirs
a man's feelings within the breast, tumult arises,
outcry in the group, statements fly about
in various ways. Likewise, men's hearts and minds
are differently allotted, the men of a retinue
are not all the same. One man in his pride

---

6 *bi þam gealdre* 'from his old incantation'. Roberts reviews all the attempts to render OE *gealdor* in this context, favouring 'speech, recitation, teaching' (2008: 126–8, esp. 127). It seems likely that this word is chosen to capture the antiquity of the words of Isaiah.

14 *wlonce wigsmiþas* 'arrogant war-smiths'. This poet does not think much of warriors. His term looks like a mockery of a more serious use, such as Hǫgni's designation as *kumblasmið* 'craftsman of wounds' in *The Lay of Attila*, stanza 24. This poem is probably from the same period as *Vainglory*, the first half of the tenth century. The Nibelung background is briefly cited on lines 65–7 of *Widsith*, the poem that follows *Vainglory* in the Exeter Book, and Hǫgni's English counterpart, Hagena, is in *Waldere* (see **Heroic Poems**).

þrymme þringeð, þrinteð him in innan
ungemedemad mod; sindan to monige þæt!
Bið þæt æfþonca eal gefylled
feondes fligepilum, facensearwum;
breodað he ond bælceð, boð his sylfes
swiþor micle þonne se sella mon,
þenceð þæt his wise welhwam þince
eal unforcuþ. Biþ þæs oþer swice,
þonne he þæs facnes fintan sceawað.
Wrenceþ he ond blenceþ, worn geþenceþ
hinderhoca, hygegar leteð,
scurum sceoteþ. He þa scylde ne wat
fæhþe gefremede, feoþ his betran
eorl fore æfstum, læteð inwitflan
brecan þone burgweal, þe him bebead meotud
þæt he þæt wigsteal wergan sceolde,
siteþ symbelwlonc, searwum læteð

---

swells up in magnificence, pressed on from within
by an immoderate passion; too many are like that!
That is all a vexation, a man filled with
the flying darts, the criminal snares of the fiend;
he brags and sneers, boasts about himself
far more than does a man of higher class,
thinks that his manners may seem to everyone
not mean at all. The other man is afterwards betrayed
when he looks on the outcome of that malice.
The first one practises guile, pretends, thinks up a number
of wicked vexations, throws a spear of the mind,
shoots in showers. He does not see the sin
he has committed for the old feud it is, hates the gentleman,
his superior, because of an old grudge, lets envy's arrow
pierce in him that town wall with which the Measurer
commanded him to defend the apse of his church,
sits arrogant at the banquet, with malicious thoughts,

---

28 *breodað he ond bælceð* 'he brags and sneers'. The subject is the arrogant man, but the syntax lets us think of him also as the *feond* 'fiend' of the previous sentence. On line 47 this man is directly identified as a son of Satan.

34 *hygegar* 'spear of the mind'. Compare this with Macbeth's 'dagger of the mind' in *Macbeth*, Act II, Scene i, line 38.

35 *scurum sceoteþ* 'shoots in showers'. See above. The implanting of wicked thoughts as if shooting arrows is something Hrothgar attributes to the devil, in *Beowulf*, line 1744. [*þa scylde ne wat fæhþe gefremede* 'does not see that sin he has committed as the old feud it is'. 'Old' is supplied for clarity: the devil's war with God is behind every brawl.

37 *fore æfstum* 'because of an old grudge'. 'Old' supplied as above, for the same reason.

wine gewæged   word ut faran,
þræfte þringan   þrymme gebyrmed,
æfæstum onæled,   oferhygda ful,
niþum nearowrencum.   Nu þu cunnan meaht,
gif þu þyslicne   þegn gemittest
wunian in wicum.   Wite þe be þissum
feawum forðspellum   þæt þæt biþ feondes bearn
flæsce bifongen,   hafað fræte lif,
grundfusne gæst   Gode orfeormne,
Wuldorcyninge.

Þæt se witga song,
gearowyrdig guma,   ond þæt gyd awræc:
'Se þe hine sylfne   in þa sliþnan tid
þurh oferhygda   up ahlæneð,
ahefeð heahmodne,   se sceal hean wesan
æfter neosiþum   niþer gebiged,
wunian witum fæst,   wyrmum beþrungen.
Þæt wæs geara iu   in Godes rice

---

weighed down with wine he lets the words come out,
needles men ever the more, fermented with their glory,
kindled by envies, full of prideful thoughts,
with sly narrow malice. Now you can understand,
if you cross paths with a thegn of this kind
dwelling in your village. Know from these
few exhortations that this is the fiend's child
made flesh, that his will be a flash life
while his soul strives for the abyss, destitute of God,
of the King of Glory.

Of this the Prophet sang,
a man of ready words, and uttered this poem:
'The man who in this troubled time
soaks himself in prideful thoughts,
exalts himself in arrogance, shall be disgraced,
brought low after his journey to death,
stay fettered in torments, afflicted by snakes.
It was long long ago in God's kingdom

47 *feondes bearn* 'the fiend's child'. The source for this motif, the first chapter of the *Rule of Chrodegang* (Trahern 1975), might situate the poem in the Benedictine Reform, in the first half of the tenth century.

50 *se witga* 'the Prophet'. On the attempts to identify this man, see Roberts, who favours Isaiah (2:11–19), but otherwise emphasises that this is a prophet archetype: 'what is important is that all the teaching of the poem stems from his "gealdre" (6) and is passed on to us by the *ic* speaker who ruminates on what he has been taught' (2008: 123–6, esp. 126).

þætte mid englum oferhygd astag,
widmære gewin. Wroht ahofan,
heardne heresiþ, heofon widledan,
forsawan hyra sellan, þa hi to swice þohton
ond þrymcyning þeodenstoles
ricne beryfan, swa hit ryht ne wæs,
ond þonne gesettan on hyra sylfra dom
wuldres wynlond. Þæt him wige forstod
fæder frumsceafta, wearð him seo feohte to grim.
Ðonne bið þam oþrum ungelice
se þe her on eorþan eaðmod leofað,
ond wiþ gesibbra gehwone simle healdeð
freode on folce ond his feond lufað,
þeah þe he him abylgnesse oft gefremede
willum in þisse worulde. Se mot wuldres dream
in haligra hyht heonan astigan
on engla eard. Ne biþ þam oþrum swa,
se þe on ofermedum eargum dædum
leofaþ in leahtrum, ne beoð þa lean gelic
mid Wuldorcyning.'

---

that pride rose up among the angels,
a conflict of wide extent. They raised up strife,
a hard war-campaign, laid open heaven,
despised their Superior when by betrayal they thought
to rob even the mighty King of Magnificence
of his royal throne, such a violation this was,
and then to establish on their own terms
a brilliant land of joy. With war he withstood them,
Father of Creation; for them that fight became too fierce.
Unlike the first man in this case is the one
who lives here on earth with humble heart,
who constantly keeps with each of his kindred
friendship among the people and loves his enemy,
though this man has often treated him insolently
and wilfully in this world. He may from here
to the joy of saints ascend through glory's delights
into the land of angels. For the first man it is not so,
who in overweening pride with cowardly deeds
lives in vice, nor do they get quite the same reward
from the King of Glory.'

---

64 *gesettan wuldres wynlond* 'to establish a brilliant land of joy'. This refers to the rebellion dramatised in *Genesis B*, lines 259–91 and 358–60 (see **Poems of Devotion**).

Wite þe be þissum,
gif þu eaðmodne eorl gemete,
þegn on þeode, þam bið simle
gæst gegæderad Godes agen bearn
wilsum in worlde, gif me se witega ne leag.
Forþon we sculon a hycgende hælo rædes
gemunan in mode mæla gehwylcum
þone selestan sigora Waldend. *Amen.*

Know from this,
if you cross paths with a man of humble heart,
a thegn in your nation, that to him perpetually
will God's own Child be joined in spirit,
dedicated in this world, if that Prophet spoke true.
And so, thinking ever of the plan for salvation,
we must each moment in our hearts remember
the highest-ranking Commander of victories. *Amen.*

79–80 *þam gæst gegæderad Godes agen bearn* 'to him . . . God's own Child . . . joined in spirit'. That Christ is at one with the good man's soul is the antidote to the devil's fathering of the braggart in lines 28–47.

Maxims I

Wisdom poetry in Old English or Old Norse literature or elsewhere, unless it is set in a didactic framework of some kind, tends to be rambling rather than cogent, loosely associative in structure rather than the presentation of a clear line of thought. The main likely reason for this apparent lack of literary shape is that it offers readers a sura-like security in finding patterns of their own. This is especially so given that most wisdom poetry, at least in Old English, is sufficiently religious in content to invite a new pathway of contemplation each time.

The compiler of the Exeter Book, or his scribe, valued this kind of poetry quite highly, placing his great wisdom poem, *Maxims I*, third after *Vainglory* and eleventh after the start of the booklet (the second, which was copied first). Folios 88 verso to 92 verso thus contain a long poem of gnomic literature or 'wisdom' which differs from the other wisdom poems in lacking a clear line of thought. *Maxims I* is so called to distinguish it from another collection of proverbs and observations in British Library, Cotton Tiberius B.i, which scholars call *Maxims II*. Yet *Maxims I* is the longer poem. It is divided into three sections according to the scribe's initial capitals, although such initials are no sure guarantee that these three poems (often named A, B and C) were composed as separate works. The sentences that administer their wisdom in each section do so with a verb such as *biþ* 'is, will be' and *sceal* 'shall, ought to be, must be' which links one known feature of life to something else with which its association is not always obvious or known. Description sometimes also lies at the heart of *sceal* 'shall'. For instance, in *Maxims I*, B, line 103, the gnome *a mon sceal seþeah leofes wenan* 'nonetheless, a beloved shall ever be hoped for' gives us a man whose affection for his wife is returned by her in practice, not in principle; translating this 'must ever be hoped for', however, would suggest that it is a wife's duty to love her absent husband regardless. The Old English language at this point is incidentally, and sometimes deliberately, ambiguous. Below is the opening of *Maxims I*, A and the whole text of *Maxims I*, B.

Björkman, E., 'Wortgeschichtliche Kleinigkeiten' [etymological trifles], *Beiblatt zur Anglia* 30 (1919), 318–20

Bradley, S. A. J., trans., *Anglo-Saxon Poetry: An Anthology of Old English Poems in Prose Translation* (London, 1982)

Bremmer, R. H., Jr., 'Frisians in Anglo-Saxon England: a historical and toponymical investigation', *Fryske Nammen* 3 (1980), 45–94

Larrington, C., *A Store of Common Sense: Gnomic Theme and Style in Old Icelandic and Old English Wisdom Poetry* (Oxford, 1993)

North, R., *Pagan Words and Christian Meanings*, Costerus new series 81 (Amsterdam and Atlanta, GA, 1991)

North, R., *Heathen Gods in Old English Literature*, Cambridge Studies in Anglo-Saxon England 22 (Cambridge, 1997)

North, R., *The Origins of 'Beowulf': from Vergil to Wiglaf* (Oxford, 2006)

North, R., 'OE *scop* and the singing Welsh bishop', in *Northern Voices: Essays on Old Germanic and Related Topics, Offered to Professor Tette Hofstra*, ed. K. Dekker, A. A. MacDonald and H. Niebaum (Louvain, 2008), 99–121

A. The spirit of exchange

Frige mec frodum wordum! Ne læt þinne ferð onhælne,
degol þæt þu deopost cunne! Nelle ic þe min dyrne gesecgan,
3a gif þu me þinne hygecræft hylest
3b ond þine heortan geþohtas.
Gleawe men sceolon gieddum wrixlan. God sceal mon ærest hergan
fægre, fæder userne, forþon þe He us æt frymþe geteode
lif ond lænne willan. He usic wile þara leana gemonian.
Meotud sceal in wuldre, mon sceal on eorþan
geong ealdian. God us ece biþ,
ne wendað hine wyrda ne Hine wiht dreceþ,

Question me with learned words! Don't keep your mind closed,
or keep hidden what you most deeply know. I won't tell you of my secrets,
3a if you hide your skill of mind from me
3b and the thoughts of your heart.
Prudent men must exchange their poems. God is the first one must praise
in fair language, our Father, because in the beginning He drew out for us
a life and the will that we borrow. He wants to remind us of these loans.
The Measurer shall in glory, on earth a man shall
who is young, grow older. To us is God eternal,
nor do events change Him, nor does anything,

3a–b This is printed as a full line in all other modern editions, but works better as two short lines, each with three stressed syllables. In Old Norse metre, two such lines after one or more long lines qualifies as *galdralag* 'incantation measure'.

4 *gieddum wrixlan* 'exchange their poems'. Larrington treats this as a wisdom contest (1993: 122). OE *giedd* 'song, poem' defines the genre common to many of the otherwise diverse poems of the Exeter Book. Its common morphological, and semantic, origin with OIce *geð* (Björkman 1919; North 1991: 41–6) is underscored by the resemblance of this line with one in Old Norse, *geði skalt við þann blanda ok gjǫfum skipta* 'Your thoughts you must share with that man, and exchange gifts', in stanza 44 of *Sayings of the High One*. [*God sceal mon ærest hergan* 'God is the first one must praise'. Possibly the poet alludes to the injunction in Cædmon's *Hymn*, line 1, *Nu scylun hergan hefaenricaes uard* 'Now we must praise the Keep of Heaven-kingdom' (see **Poems of Devotion**).

5 *us æt frymþe geteode* 'in the beginning He drew out for us'. Cædmon's *Hymn*, again, this time in line 6–7 when God *middungeard . . . æfter tiadæ* 'afterwards drew out Middle World', may be the poet's model (Larrington 1993: 122).

8 *geong ealdian* 'who is young, grow older'. There are two meanings here, one that a young man grows older, the other that God grows older while remaining young.

adl ne yldo Ælmihtigne;
ne gomelað He in gæste, ac He is gen swa He wæs,
Þeoden geþyldig. He us geþonc syleð,
missenlicu mod, monge reorde.

---

either illness or old age, afflict the Almighty.
He does not wear out in spirit, but is still as He was,
a king of patience. He gives us thought,
diverse minds, many languages.

B. God, the world and women

Forst sceal freosan, fyr wudu meltan,
eorþe growan, is brycgian,
wæter helm wegan, wundrum lucan
eorþan ciþas. An sceal inbindan
forstes fetre felameahtig God;
winter sceal geweorpan, weder eft cuman,
sumor swegle hat. Sund unstille,
deop deada wæg, dyrne bið lengest;
holen sceal inæled, yrfe gedæled
deades monnes. Dom biþ selast.

Frost shall freeze, fire melt wood,
earth grow, ice bridge over,
water carry covering, wondrously enclose
earth's seeds. One shall unbind
frost's fetters, the God of many powers,
winter shall be cast off, good weather come back,
summer hot with sun. The unstill strait,
the dead's deep wave-way, is secret for longest.
Holly shall be kindled; divided, the inheritance
of a dead man. A good reputation is best.

---

10 *adl ne yldo* 'either illness or old age'. Forms of this homiletic doublet are found also in *Beowulf*, line 1736 (Hrothgar's words to Beowulf, see **Heroic Poems**), and in *The Seafarer*, line 70.

12 *He us geþonc syleð* 'He gives us thought'. Here the poet makes his Cædmonian injunction relevant to the intellectual theme of his introduction to the larger poem.

71–4 *Forst sceal freosan* 'Frost shall freeze' etc. The autonomy of these things is interesting (see North 1997: 204–13). No longer so lifeless, they appear to do things by themselves, until the poet makes it clear that they are not animistic powers but rather *creaturae* 'created things' controlled by God.

78 *deop deada wæg* 'the dead's deep wave-way'. The word *wæg* 'wave' is probably meant to pun with *weg* 'way', with a suggestion that only at the end of the world will the sea give up its dead.

80 *Dom biþ selast* 'A good reputation is best'. This apparently secular statement about the immortality of a good name echoes a similar line in Old Norse, *dómr um dauðan hvern* 'a good man's reputation', in *Sayings of the High One*, stanza 77.

Cyning sceal mid ceape cwene gebicgan,
bunum ond beagum; bu sceolon ærest
geofum god wesan. Guð sceal in eorle,
wig geweaxan, ond wif geþeon
leof mid hyre leodum, leohtmod wesan,
rune healdan, rumheort beon
mearum ond maþmum, meodorædenne
for gesiðmægen symle æghwær
eodor æþelinga ærest gegretan,
forman fulle to frean hond
ricene geræcan, ond him ræd witan
boldagendum bæm ætsomne.
Scip sceal genægled, scyld gebunden,
leoht linden bord, leof wilcuma
Frysan wife, þonne flota stondeð;
biþ his ceol cumen ond hyre ceorl to ham,

A king shall make payment to buy his queen,
with cups and rings. First must they both
be generous with gifts. Battle in a nobleman,
war, shall grow, and a wife shall thrive,
loved by her people, be light of mood,
keep confidences, be of open heart and hand
with horses and treasures, in mead-sessions
before the troops be constantly everywhere,
greet the king first, before she greets princes,
be sure to pass swiftly into her lord's hand
the first cup, and have knowledge of good counsel
for them both as rulers of the hall together.
Ship shall be riveted, shield bound together,
light linden-board, beloved man be welcome,
the Frisian, to his wife, when vessel docks.
His keel has come in and her churl home,

---

90 *forman fulle to frean hond* 'into her lord's hand the first cup'. To King Attila this appears to be what Guðrún is doing *með gylltum kálki* 'with gilded chalice', in *The Lay of Attila*, stanza 34 (see **Heroic Poems**).

92 *boldagendum* 'as rulers of the hall'. Beowulf receives a *bold* 'hall' from Hygelac when he comes into 7,000 hides of local governance in *Beowulf*, line 2196. On line 3112, it is as *boldagend* 'rulers of halls', that the ealdormen of Geatland are summoned to build King Beowulf's funeral pyre.

95 *Frysan wife* literally 'to the Frisian's wife' (unless *–an* is for *–um*, as 'Frisian wife'). King Alfred hired Frisian sailors for his new navy, according to the *Anglo-Saxon Chronicle, s.a.* 897 (for 896). Frisian merchants had by then settled in most major western European towns, including London and York, and were so ubiquitous in the earlier Anglo-Saxon period that forms of *Frese* 'Frisian' meant 'trader' in general (Bremmer 1980; North 2006: 20–3), as it may do here.

agen ætgeofa, ond heo hine in laðaþ,
wæsceð his warig hrægl ond him syleþ wæde niwe,
liþ him on londe þæs his lufu bædeð.
Wif sceal wiþ wer wære gehealdan, oft hi mon wommum belihð;
fela bið fæsthydigra, fela bið fyrwetgeornra,
freoð hy fremde monnan, þonne se oþer feor gewiteþ.
Lida biþ longe on siþe; a mon sceal seþeah leofes wenan,
gebidan þæs he gebædan ne mæg. Hwonne him eft gebyre weorðe,
ham cymeð, gif he hal leofað, nefne him holm gestyreð,
mere hafað mundum mægðegsan wyn.
Ceapeadig mon cyningwic þonne
leodon cypeþ, þonne liþan cymeð;
wuda ond wætres nyttað, þonne him biþ wic alyfed,
mete bygeþ, gif he maran þearf, ærþon he to meþe weorþe.
Seoc se biþ þe to seldan ieteð; þeah hine mon on sunnan læde,
ne mæg he be þy wedre wesan, þeah hit sy wearm on sumera,
ofercumen biþ he, ær he acwele, gif he nat hwa hine cwicne fede.
Mægen mon sceal mid mete fedan, morþor under eorþan befeolan,

---

her own bread-giver, and she invites him in,
washes his salt-stiff clothes and gives him fresh apparel,
grants him on shore what his love demands.
Woman with man shall keep her agreement, often falsely accused of shame.
Many are constant-minded, many are more curious,
make love to strange men while the other is away sailing.
A sailor is long on his voyage. Loved, however, he shall always be hoped for,
endure the time he cannot hasten. When a good wind rises again for him,
home he comes if alive unharmed, unless ocean restrains him,
sea holds the joy of the terror of nations in her arms.
A mercantile man then a palatial residence
for his people will buy when he comes in from sailing.
Wood and water he provides them with, when a place is granted him,
food he pays for, if he needs more, before he gets too drained.
Sick he will be, who too seldom eats. Though he is led into the sun,
he cannot remain in that good weather if the summers are hot.
Overcome he is, before dying, if he knows none to feed him when living.
Strength with food shall be fed, a murder beneath the earth consigned,

---

97 *ætgeofa* 'bread-giver'. Literally 'eat-giver'. Since *hlaford* 'lord, husband' derives from *hlaf-weard* 'loaf-keeper', *hlæfdige* 'lady' means 'loaf-kneader', we substitute 'bread' for 'eat' here.

106 *mere hafað mundum mægðegsan wyn* 'sea holds the joy of the terror of nations in her arms'. A striking instance of the personification of natural powers, consistent with a sailor's superstition on one hand, and with an earlier form of heathen animism on the other (North 1997: 216–21). Compare the image of Rán, the sea-goddess who keeps sailors, in Egill's *Hard Loss of Sons*. 'Terror of nations' for the sea is a taboo term such as a sailor might use. The 'sea's joy' kenning for the sailor is paralleled in Norse phrases such as *Friggjar angan* 'Frigg's darling' (for Óðinn her husband) in *The Sibyl's Prophecy*, stanza 51 (see **Gods of the Vikings**).

hinder under hrusan, þe hit forhelan þenceð;
ne biþ þæt gedefe deaþ, þonne hit gedyrned weorþeð.
Hean sceal gehnigan, hadl gesigan,
ryht rogian. Ræd biþ nyttost,
yfel unnyttost, þæt unlæd nimeð.
God bið genge, ond wiþ God lenge.
Hyge sceal gehealden, hond gewealden,
seo sceal in eagan, snyttro in breostum,
þær bið þæs monnes modgeþoncas.
Muþa gehwylc mete þearf, mæl sceolon tidum gongan.
Gold geriseþ on guman sweorde,
sellic sigesceorp, sinc on cwene,
god scop gumum, garniþ werum,
wig towiþre wicfreoþa healdan.
Scyld sceal cempan, sceaft reafere,
sceal bryde beag, bec leornere,
husl halgum men, hæþnum synne.
Woden worhte weos, wuldor alwalda,

---

an offence, under the ground by which one means to hide it.
Death becomes no one when it is is concealed.
Shame shall be brought low, abuse be made to sink,
justice be slandered. Good counsel is the most,
evil the least, useful option: that a wicked man takes.
The good man gets going, and belongs to God.
Mind shall be held in, hand governed,
sight shall be in the eye, wisdom in the breast,
where the thoughts of a man's heart live.
Each mouth must have meat, meals must come on time.
Gold belongs on a man's sword,
splendid victorious garments, treasure, on a queen,
a good poet with men, spear-strife with treaties
to defend inhabited precincts against war.
The champion has a shield, the poacher, an arrow,
the bride has a ring, the student, a book,
holy man has eucharist, heathen man has sin.
Woden made idols, the Almighty, glory,

---

127 *garniþ werum* 'spear-strife with treaties'. This reads *wērum* (as a variant spelling of long-vowelled *wær* 'treaty, agreement; revising North 2008: 107). The *Væringjar* 'treaty-men, covenanters' were Scandinavian mercenaries who signed up to protect the emperor of Byzantium in the tenth and eleventh centuries.

132 *Woden worhte weos* 'Woden made idols'. This is one of two brief but startling references to Woden in Old English literature. It animates the language of Psalm 95:4 (in Jerome's Hebrew version: *Omnes enim dii populorum sculptilia, Dominus autem caelos fecit* 'For all the gods of the gentiles are carved things, but the Lord made the heavens') with a heathen god whose fascination, by this token, must have been current in the poet's time (North 1997: 88–90). For an image of Óðinn dressing up 'two tree-men', see *Sayings of the High One*, stanza 49.

rume roderas; þæt is rice God,
sylf soðcyning, sawla nergend,
se us eal forgeaf þæt we on lifgaþ,
ond eft æt þam ende eallum wealdeð
monna cynne. Þæt is meotud sylfa.

---

the roomy heavens. This is a powerful god,
himself the true King, healer of souls,
who gave us everything we live on,
and again, at the end, will rule the whole
human race. The Measurer Himself is this.

Sayings of the High One

Hávamál

⁂

The stanzaic form of Old Norse and Icelandic poetry gives its gnomic verse a shape that is lacking in the Old English *Maxims*. The *ljóðaháttr* metre usually involved in *Hávamál* 'Sayings of the High One' accentuates this pattern, for each stanza is made up of two units of long-line short-line alternation which limit the length of expression. A Viking maxim must therefore be expressed in no more than one and half lines, often just in one, then perhaps reiterated. A new stanza often necessitates a new thought, although the old one may be reiterated often by repeating a line or two (as in stanzas 76 and 77). Otherwise a new stanza is created associatively by following the cue of an idea or word in the previous stanza. Sometimes the new idea reverses the previous one yet with only the slightest adjustment of words, giving a roundedness to the reflections on life which drive the poem. The effect of all this in a Norse poem is to regularise the intervals in which a new thought comes, with the poet administering his pearls of wisdom like beads on a string.

Like *Maxims I* in the Exeter Book, *Sayings of the High One* is really a collection of smaller poems. This work survives in 164 stanzas written out as prose in the Codex Regius manuscript of *c.* 1290, which is thus the poem's latest date of composition. The poem is usually first divided in two, into the Norwegian Gnomic Poem (stanzas 1–110) and *Hávamál* Proper (111–64). The scribe supports this division in the way he writes the initial M of stanza 111, but the content also makes this clear, for the *Hávamál* Proper is a distinct work. It is long and framed by stanzas of introduction (111) and farewell (164) which enclose three separate poems: the *Loddfáfnismál* 'Lay of Loddfáfnir', a didactic sequence (stanzas 112–37); the *Rúnatal* 'rune tally', a mystical composite in which the god Óðinn tells of his nine-night hanging from the World Tree, with details of initiation (stanzas 138–45); and the *Ljóðatal* 'song tally', in which the speaker promises us a list of spells for various purposes (stanzas 146–63). The *Hávamál* Proper appears to be an Icelandic confection of the twelfth or thirteenth century, which centres on Óðinn's core ritual as if protecting a battered relic in a shrine. The Norwegian Gnomic Poem, on the other hand, is less structured and more concerned with everyday life than with cooking up a cleric's idea of Viking Age paganism. Stanzas 1–79 (approximately) give us the bulk of this poem, although there are other stanzas on wisdom. Two Ovidian interludes are found as one likely twelfth-century composition in stanzas 96–110, in which Óðinn tells of his deception as suffered and practised: suffered when 'Billingr's wife' leads him on for a whole night in a vain promise of sex (stanzas 96–102); and practised when Óðinn betrays Gunnlǫð's love for him in order to steal the Mead of Poetry (stanzas 104–110). The whole *Hávamál* poem may be seen as the work of the poet of these interludes, who joined the Norwegian Gnomic Poem to the more formally framed ensemble with other gnomic stanzas and with this two-part narrative work of his own (North 1991: 136–43).

The text below comes from the Norwegian Gnomic Poem and associated stanzas, most of which were probably composed in Norway in the Viking Age. Other scholars have other opinions on this question, but the fact that Eyvindr *skáldaspillir* 'the Plagiarist' quotes from stanza 76 or 77 of this poem for the end of his own *Hákonarmál* 'Lay of King Hákon the Good', dated to *c.* 960 (see **Viking Wars**), suggests that the stanzas below were composed in one sequence before then, and probably around the time of the compilation of *Maxims I*. Their concerns may be compared, especially as poems on the meaning of life.

Clark, D. E. Martin, ed. and trans., *The 'Hávamál': With Selections from other Poems of the Edda, illustrating the Wisdom of the North in Heathen Times* (Cambridge, 1923)

Evans, D. A. H., ed., *Hávamál* (London, 1986)

Faulkes, A., *Glossary and Index* [to *Hávamál*] (London, 1987)

Larrington, C., *A Store of Common Sense: Gnomic Theme and Style in Old Icelandic and Old English Wisdom Poetry* (Oxford, 1993)

North, R., *Pagan Words and Christian Meanings* (Amsterdam and Atlanta, GA, 1991)

North, R., *Heathen Gods in Old English Literature*, Cambridge Studies in Anglo-Saxon England 22 (Cambridge, 1997)

Page, R. I., *Chronicles of the Vikings: Records, Memorials and Myths* (London, 1995)

Roesdahl, E., *The Vikings*, trans. S. Margeson and K. Williams, 2nd rev. ed. (Harmondsworth, 1998)

What it's like when you get there

1 Gáttir allar áðr gangi fram
um skoðask skyli
um skygnask skyli,
því at óvíst er at vita hvar óvinir
sitja á fleti fyrir.

All the openings, before you go forward,
must be checked,
must be studied,
For one can't know for certain where enemies
sit in wait by bench-walls.

---

1 *sitja á fleti fyrir* 'sit in wait by bench-walls'. OIce *sitja fyrir* is used also of Loki in *The Thunderclap Ballad*, when, disguised as a maid, he intercepts the giant's queries about 'Freyja'.

2 Gefendr heilir! Gestr er inn kominn.
Hvar skal sitja sjá?
Mjǫk er bráðr sá er á brǫndum skal
síns um freista frama.

Health to the givers! A guest has come in.
Where is this one to sit?
Awfully anxious, the man who in the lumber room
must try for advancement.

3 Elds er þǫrf þeims inn er kominn
ok á kné kalinn;
matar ok váða es manni þǫrf
þeims hefir um fjall farit.

A fire he needs, who has come in
and is chilled to the knees.
Food and clothing are what a man needs
who's fared across the fells.

4 Vats er þǫrf þeims til verðar kømr,
þerru ok þjóðlaðar,
góðs um œðis ef sér geta mætti,
orðs ok endrþǫgu.

Water he needs who comes to a meal,
a towel and hearty welcome,
Good cheer if he might get it,
some words and silence in return.

5 Vits er þǫrf þeims víða ratar,
dælt er heima hvat;
at augabragði verðr, sá er ekki kann
ok með snotrum sitr.

His wits he needs who roams the world,
anything passes at home.
An object of mirth he becomes, who knows nothing
and sits among the wise.

---

2 *á brǫndum* 'in the lumber room'. The meaning is uncertain, but *brandr* 'log' in this case seems to connote a log-pile in the anteroom (Evans 1986: 76–7).

6 At hyggjandi sinni skylit maðr hrœsinn vera,
heldr gætinn at geði;
þá er horskr ok þǫgull kømr heimisgarða til,
sjaldan verðr viti vǫrum,
því at óbrigðra vin fær maðr aldregi
en mannvit mikit.

About his intelligence no man should be boastful,
but watch his own nature instead.
When a clever, but silent, man arrives on the premises,
seldom is he punished by caution,
For a friend less fickle than his common sense
no man will ever get.

7 Inn vari gestr er til verðar kømr
þunnu hljóði þegir;
eyrum hlýðir, en augum skoðar:
svá nýsisk fróðra hverr fyrir.

The wary guest who comes to a meal
is silent with fine-tuned hearing,
Listening with ears, while he checks with eyes:
so the experienced spy things out.

Friendship and exchange

44 Veiztu ef þú vin átt þanns þú vel trúir
ok vill þú af honum gótt geta,
geði skalt við þann blanda ok gjǫfum skipta,
fara at finna opt.

You know, if you have an associate you well believe in
and want to get something good out of him,
Your thoughts you must share with that man, and exchange gifts,
go and see him often.

---

6 *mannvit mikit* 'his common sense'. Martin Clarke (1923) has 'a store of common sense', to render *mikit* 'big', whence the title for Larrington's book. But the play on *maðr* and *mann-* points to a person's inner mental resource as the complete object here, and 'big' may be rendered by 'his' to show this.

45 Ef þú átt annan þanns þú illa trúir
vildu af honum þó gótt geta,
fagrt skalt við þann mæla en flátt hyggja
ok gjalda lausung við lygi.

If there is another you have that you don't well believe in,
yet want to get something good out of him,
You must speak with fair language but with false mind,
repay his deception with lies.

46 Þat er enn of þann er þú illa trúir
ok þér er grunr at hans geði,
hlæja skaltu við þeim ok um hug mæla:
glík skulu gjǫld gjǫfum.

Further, with the man you do not well believe in
and have suspicion of his nature,
You must laugh with that man and speak around your thoughts:
gifts must be paid at their price.

47 Ungr var ek forðum, fór ek einn saman,
þá varð ek villr vega;
auðigr þóttumk, er ek annan fann:
maðr er manns gaman.

I was young once, went away on my own,
then found myself right off road.
I thought I was wealthy, when I met another person,
man is joy of man.

48 Mildir frœknir menn bazt lifa,
sjaldan sút ala;
en ósnjallr maðr uggir hotvetna,
sýtir æ gløggr við gjǫfum.

Generous men and brave live best,
seldom nourish sorrow,
But a man without force dreads all kinds of things,
the prudent's always sorry to get presents.

---

46 The understanding, here and in stanza 48 and elsewhere, where gifts are concerned, is that a gift is always paid for: a gift without reciprocation of some kind is not properly *gjǫf* 'a gift'. That is why, neither in Old English nor in Old Norse, no difference is made between *giefan* / *gefa* and *sellan* / *selja*, words that both mean 'give'.

47 This stanza subtly reintroduces Óðinn, whose adventure with Gunnlǫð is already retold by him in stanzas 13–14 (see *The Mead of Poetry*, **Gods of the Vikings**, Custom Version). Óðinn is the god known for his lonely wanderings across the earth.

49 Váðir mínar gaf ek velli at
tveim trémǫnnum;
rekkar þat þóttusk er þeir ript hǫfðu:
neiss er nøkkviðr halr.

I gave my clothes, for the field,
to two wooden men.
They looked like heroes when they some linen,
a naked man is despised.

50 Hrørnar þǫll, sú er stendr þorpi á,
hlýrat henni bǫrkr né barr;
svá er maðr, sá er mangi ann:
hvat skal hann lengi lifa?

The fir-tree withers that stands on a mound,
neither bark nor its needles protect it.
So it is with the man whom nobody loves,
why should he go on living?

How to get on

58 Ár skal rísa sá er annars vill
fé eða fjǫr hafa;
sjaldan liggjandi úlfr lær um getr
né sofandi maðr sigr.

Early to rise for him who will take
another man's life or his property.
Seldom lying down does a wolf get the ham
or a sleeping man victory.

---

49 These wooden men are (a) scarecrows but also (b) a memory of idols armed up for display in a heathen shrine. There is a pun here. In one way, according to the conception of the title *Hávamál* 'Sayings of the High One', it is *inn Hávi* 'the High One' or Óðinn talking; and 'Óðinn's clothes' is a well-known kenning for 'armour', i.e. chained mail and weapons. Armed idols in Norwegian shrines are worshipped in Eyvindr's *Lay of King Hákon the Good*, stanza 18, and seem to be *herþarfir* 'needed by (Earl Hákon's) army' in Einarr's *Gold-Shortage*, stanza '16' (see **Viking Wars** and **Gods of the Vikings**). Enough survives on these and other 'treemen' (see North 1997: 90–103) to show that the speaker here, if Óðinn, is saying something more than 'clothes make a man'; rather, the old idols used to make *us* men.

50 *hvat skal hann lengi lifa?* 'why should he go on living?' Perhaps he is already dead. There is a pun also here, for *þǫll* 'fir-tree' may also refer to a stripped post that stands on a grave with commemorative letters. This is so if we read the Arab envoy Ibn Fadlan's account of a funeral in Russia, in 922, for a Swedish Rus' magnate, at which the locals 'built a mound on the spot and raised a pole at its centre with the name of the chieftain and his king on it' (quoted in Roesdahl 1998: 157). Thus the stanza may also mean that the living who love the dead care for their memory, as later with the *bautarsteinar* 'memorial stone' in stanza 72.

59 Ár skal rísa sá er á yrkendr fá
ok ganga síns verka á vit;
mart um dvelr þann er um morgin sefr:
hálfr er auðr und hvǫtum.

Early to rise for the man with few workers,
and early must he go to his work.
Much slows the man who sleeps through the morning,
for keen men wealth half wins itself.

60 Þurra skíða ok þakinna næfra,
þess kann maðr mjǫt;
ok þess viðar er vinnask megi
mál ok misseri.

Dry faggots and shingles for thatching,
a man can measure out that,
As well as the wood that will be able to last him
one quarter or two.

61 Þveginn ok mettr ríði maðr þingi at
þótt hann sét væddr til vel;
skúa ok bróka skammisk engi maðr,
né hests en heldr,
þótt hann hafit góðan.

Washed and well fed a man should ride to assembly,
even if dressed not too well.
Let no man feel shame for shoes or trousers,
no more than for his horse,
though he have a poor one.

62 Snapir ok gnapir, er til sævar kømr,
ǫrn, á aldinn mar;
svá er maðr er með mǫrgum kømr
ok á formælendr fá.

With bent head he comes to it and snaps above the sea,
eagle over hoary deep.
So with a man who joins the multitude,
and has no one there to speak for him.

. . .

72 Sonr er betri þótt sé síð of alinn
ept genginn guma;
sjaldan bautarsteinar standa brautu nær
nema reisi niðr at nið.

A son is better, though he be born late,
after the man who is gone.
Seldom near the road stand memorial stones
if raised not by relatives, one for the other.

73 Tveir ru eins herjar: tunga er hǫfuðs bani;
er mér í heðinn hvern handar væni.

Two fighters kill a third: tongue does the head in,
Where in each cloak I expect to find a hand.

74 Nótt verðr feginn sá er nesti trúir,
skammar eru skips rár,
hverf er haustgríma;
fjǫlð um viðrir á fimm dǫgum,
en meira á mánuði.

Night he'll glad of who may trust his provisions,
slender are a ship's masts,
changeable the dark of autumn.
The wind whips up variously in five days,
and more so in a month.

75 Veita hinn, er vættki veit,
margr verðr af *au*rum api;
maðr er auðigr, annarr er óauðigr,
skylit þann vítka vár.

He doesn't know, who knows nothing at all,
money makes monkeys of many of us.
One man is wealthy, another not wealthy,
him one shouldn't blame for that woe.

---

72 On Scandinavian runestone memorials, some of which double as land charters for the surviving family, see Page 1995: 74–91.

73 Enigmatic, to say the least (Evans 1986: 109–10), but as a social commentary for the Viking Age, it may work. First, each part of us may be primed for survival; second, each person likewise; third, however, the head of each one of us has a tendency to self-destruction by allowing the tongue to cooperate with the armed hand of another person. The metre is *fornyrðislag* 'old story measure', possibly in preparation for the stanza 85 and following.

74 *um viðrir* 'wind whips up'. The fact that *Viðrir* 'Wutherer' is a common name for Óðinn only underlines his presence as the voice assumed to speak this poem for much of the time. Until stanza 111, where he sets about repeating his words verbatim, the speaker of *Sayings of the High One* slips in and out of impersonating Óðinn as the occasion demands (North 1991: 143–4).

76 Deyr fé, deyja frændr,
deyr sjálfr it sama;
en orðstírr deyr aldregi,
hveim er sér góðan getr.

Livestock die, kinsmen die,
one day you die yourself.
But a name, now that dies for no man
who gets a good one.

77 Deyr fé, deyja frændr,
deyr sjálfr it sama;
ek veit einn at aldri deyr:
dómr um dauðan hvern.

Livestock die, kinsmen die,
one day you die yourself.
One thing I know that never dies,
a dead man's reputation.

Love and trust

79 Ósnotr maðr, ef eignask getr
fé eða fljóðs munuð,
metnaðr honum þróask en mannvit aldregi:
fram gengr hann drjúgt í dul.

An unwise man, if he gets to possess
money or a lady's love,
His pride increases, his common sense never,
in conceit he marches on.

80 Þat er þá reynt er þú at rúnum spyrr
inum reginkunnum,
þeim er gerðu ginnregin ok fáði fimbulþulr:
þá hefir hann bazt ef hann þegir.

That's to be experienced when you ask from the runes,
the runes that come from the powers,
That the aboriginal powers made and the great titan painted:
he will do best only if silent.

---

76 The first half of this stanza and of stanza 77 was borrowed by Eyvindr the Plagiarist for his *Lay of King Hákon the Good* (see **Viking Wars**). As it appears there in the poet's farewell, it is reasonable to suppose that the first 77 stanzas, more or less, of *Sayings of the High One* pre-dated this lay, which Eyvindr composed in *c.* 961, as a separate gnomic poem (Evans 1987: 14).

80 Compare this with stanza 142, of the *Rune Tally*, and it may seem that the present stanza has been produced to bridge the old Norwegian Gnomic Poem (stanzas 1–77, more or less) with *Sayings of the High One* Proper (North 1991: 136). What the stanza means, however, is obscure, unless we accept the *hann* 'he' as a foretaste of Loddfáfnir as some kind of Odinic disciple.

81 At kveldi skal dag leyfa, konu er brennd er,
mæki er reyndr er, mey er gefin er,
ís er yfir kømr, ǫl er drukkit er.

Praise no day until evening, no wife till cremated,
No blade until tested, no maid until married,
No ice until you cross it, no ale until it's drunk.

82 Í vindi skal við hǫggva, veðri á sjó róa,
myrkri við man spjalla: mǫrg eru dags augu.
Á skip skal skriðar orka, en á skjǫld til hlífar,
mæki hǫggs, en mey til kossa!

In wind fell wood, in a breeze row out to sea,
In dark woo your mistress (many are the eyes of day).
Use a ship for fast passage, and a shield for protection,
A blade for cutting and a girl for kissing!

83 Við eld skal ǫl drekka, en á ísi skríða,
magran mar kaupa, en mæki saurgan,
heima hest feita, en hund á búi.

By the fireplace drink ale and ski on ice,
Buy the steed lean and the blade rusty,
Fatten the horse at home and the dog in your farm.

84 Meyjar orðum skyli manngi trúa
    né því er kveðr kona,
því at á hverfanda hvéli váru þeim hjǫrtu skǫpuð,
    brigð í brjóst um lagit.

No man should believe the words of a girl,
    or what a married woman says,
Because their hearts were made on a turning wheel,
    fickleness laid into their breasts.

---

84 It seems likely that this image is derived in some way from wheel of fortune in Boethius' *De consolatione Philosophiae* 'Consolation of Philosophy', which was also rendered into English with the help of King Alfred in the 890s (see **The Earliest English Prose**). If so, the verse sequence as a whole probably dates from Iceland's period of Christian literacy and learning, the twelfth or early thirteenth centuries, in keeping with the likeliest date for stanzas 97–110.

85 Brestanda boga, brennanda loga,
gínanda úlfi, galandi kráku,
rýtanda svíni, rótlausum viði,
vaxanda vági, vellanda katli,

A fracturing bow, a blazing fire,
A gaping wolf, a croaking crow,
A grunting pig, a rootless tree,
A rising wave, a boiling kettle,

86 fljúganda fleini, fallandi báru,
ísi einnættum, ormi hringlegnum,
brúðar beðmálum, eða brotnu sverði,
bjarnar leiki, eða barni konungs,

A flying arrow, a falling tide,
Ice a night old, a snake when coiled,
A bride's bed-talk or a broken sword,
A bear's play or a king's child,

87 sjúkum kálfi, sjálfráða þræli,
vǫlu vilmæli, val nýfeldum,

A sick calf, a thrall his own master,
A sibyl's pleasing prophecy, the dead just slain,

88 akri ársánum, trúi engi maðr,
né til snemma syni
(veðr ræðr akri, en vit syni,
hætt er þeira hvárt),

Crops sown early, let no man trust,
Nor too soon a son
(Wind determines the crops, his wits the son,
and both are uncertain),

89 bróðurbana sínum, þótt á brautu mœti,
húsi hálfbrunnu, hesti alskjótum,
þá er jór ónýtr ef einn fótr brotnar.
Verðit maðr svá tryggr at þessu trúi ǫllu.

Your brother's slayer if you meet him on the road,
A house half burned, the fastest stallion,
For the horse can't be useful if one leg breaks:
Let no man be so trusting as to trust any of these.

90 Svá er friðr kvenna, þeira er flátt hyggja,
sem aki jó óbryddum á ísi hálum,
teitum tvévetrum, ok sé tamr illa,
eða í byr óðum beiti stjórnlausu,
eða skyli haltr henda hrein í þáfjalli.

To have the love of women with false hearts
Is like driving an unroughshod horse on slippery ice,
A spirited two-year-old and not broken in,
Or like tacking in a violent wind with no rudder,
Or like having to catch reindeer on thawing hills when lame.

'Unroughshod': without hoof-spikes for ice.

91 Bert ek nú mæli, því at ek bæði veit:
brigðr er karla hugr konum;
þá vér fegrst mælum, er vér flást hyggjum,
þat tælir horska hugi.

Now I will speak plainly, for I have known both:
a man's heart is fickle towards women.
When we speak the fairest, our hearts are the falsest,
This deceives even clever minds.

92 Fagrt skal mæla ok fé bjóða,
sá er vill fljóðs ást fá;
líki leyfa ins ljósa mans:
sá fær er fríar.

Fair he shall speak and offer riches,
who will have all his lady's love,
Praise the shape of the beautiful mistress,
he gets his love who shows it.

93 Ástar firna skyli engi maðr
annan aldregi;
opt fá á horskan er á heimskan ne fá,
lostfagrir litir.

Make light of another man's love is what
no man should ever do.
What captivates the clever, the stupid often misses,
bewitching beauty.

---

90 The translation here, as elsewhere in this sequence, is based on that of D. E. Martin Clarke (1923: 65), which cannot be rivalled for its elegance in these stanzas, although 'love' for *friðr* here must be understood in relation to the commoner meaning of *friðr* as 'contract', or 'agreement' as in *The Lay of Skírnir*, stanza 19 (see **Gods of the Vikings**).

94 Eyvitar firna, er maðr annan skal,
þess er um margan gengr guma;
heimska ór horskum gørir hǫlða sonu
sá inn mátki munr.

Make light of another no man should do ever,
for a thing that befalls many fellows.
Mankind's clever sons are made stupid by
mighty desire.

94 This stanza prepares us for the two tales of Óðinn's adventures with women, delusion as it is suffered (the wife of Billingr, stanzas 95–102) and practised (Gunnlǫð, stanzas 103–110).

The Rhyming Poem

The Rhyming Poem claims to be the autobiography of a secular or religious lord whose youthful and political powers have now waned. His earlier strength was accompanied by popular adoration, friendships and festivity. Now he waits for the end, in uncertain times, but with his faith intact. This poem is predominantly elegiac, but it has been suggested that it refers to a real case, that of a lord (such as King Æthelwulf, Alfred's father; see *Deor*) pushed into retirement through his showing a greater interest in religion than in temporal rule (Wentersdorf 1985: 268–70). Until recently, few wished to read this poem because of its severe problems of form and meaning (Klinck 1992: 40–3). Most notably it is rhymed. Rhyme is used here and there by the half-line in Old English poetry, and often by Cynewulf, especially in his Epilogue to *Elene* (see **Poems of Devotion**). But nowhere in the surviving Old English literature, other than in the aptly named *Rhyming Poem*, is this kind of rhyme to be found as a poem's whole metrical system.

The Rhyming Poem survives in the Exeter Book, whose scribe copies the text in greater confusion the further he goes into it. As Chris Abram (2007) has observed, it seems likely that this scribe, or the scribe before, garbled parts because he was copying from a verse-lined format in the copy text before him. Verse was written with this layout in Anglo-Saxon England only if the language was Latin (O'Brien O'Keeffe 1994: 231–3). English alliterative verse was thought by scribes to be so well understood as not to need the same visual prompting. In the normal conditions of copying Old English verse, it is clear too that some scribes, including the scribe of the Exeter Book, recomposed part of their text from memory, rather than copying it minutely word for word, each time the hand approached the end of a page line (Doane 1998: 63–4). For alliterative verse this would have been easy, relative to rhymed verse, which would have severely tested the scribe's momentary improvisations. This combination of difficulties, copying lines from unfamilar verse columns while improvising rhymes rather than oral formulaic phrases, seems to have tired and confused the scribe in the poem's second half. From line 27 onwards, the rhyme scheme of *The Rhyming Poem* falls into disarray; and, with it, a quatrain format into which lines 1–26 naturally fit. Up to line 27, and in various places until the end, the poem works so well in a stanzaic format that it recalls another rhyming poem, Egill's *Head-Ransom* (*c.* 952; disputed by Klinck 1992: 239–9; but see **Viking Wars**). It is worth asking whether the end-rhymes of Latin could have inspired Anglo-Scandinavian poetry to the same, first in English and then in Norse; and whether both *The Rhyming Poem* and Egill's *Head-Ransom* were composed in assocation with Archbishop Wulfstan of York (on whom, see Keynes 1999), or with the Hiberno-Norse poetry of Ireland (Macrae-Gibson 1983: 24. A speculation, no more than that, is that *The Rhyming Poem* is the work of Wulfstan himself, composed in 954 or afterwards, after his exile fromYork and possible internment in Cornwall by King Eadred of Wessex and England. Although there is no proof for any of this, the use of a Latin verse form in two tenth-century poems, one in Old English and the other in Icelandic, remains without parallel.

Abram, C., 'The errors in the rhyming poem', *The Review of English Studies* new series 58 (2007), 1–9

Doane, A. N., 'Spacing, placing and effacing: scribal textuality and Riddle 30a/b', in *New Approaches to Editing Old English Verse*, ed. S. Larratt Keffer and K. O'Brien O'Keeffe (Cambridge, 1998), 45–65

Earl, J. W., 'A translation of *The Rhyming Poem*', *Old English Newsletter* 19, No. 1 (1985), 31–3

Earl, J. W., 'Hisperic style in the Old English rhyming poem', *Publications of the Modern Language Association* 102 (1987), 187–96

Faulkes, A., ed., *Snorri Sturluson: Edda: Skáldskaparmál*, 2 vols (London, 1998)

Keynes, S. D., 'Wulfstan I', in *The Blackwell Encyclopedia of Anglo-Saxon England*, ed. M. Lapidge, J. Blair, S. D. Keynes and D. Scragg (Oxford, 1999), 492–3

Klinck, A. L., *The Old English Elegies: A Critical Edition and Genre Study* (Montreal and Kingston, 1992)

Macrae-Gibson, O. D., ed., *The Old English Riming Poem* (Cambridge, 1983)

O'Brien O'Keeffe, K., 'Orality and the developing text of Caedmon's *Hymn*', *Speculum* 62 (1987), 1–20; also in Richards (1994), 221–50

Richards, M. P., ed., *Anglo-Saxon Manuscripts: Basic Readings* (New York and London, 1994)

Scragg, D. G., ed., *The Vercelli Homilies and Related Texts*, Early English Texts Society old series. 300 (Oxford, 1992)

Stanley, E. G., 'Notes on the text of *Christ and Satan*; and on *The Riming Poem* and *The Rune Poem*, chiefly on *wynn*, *wēn* and *wenne*', *Notes and Queries* 229 (1984), 443–53

Wentersdorf, K., 'The Old English *Rhyming Poem*: a Ruler's Lament', *Studies in Philology* 82 (1985), 265–94

1 Me lifes onlah se þis leoht onwrah,
ond þæt torhte get*ea*h, tillice onwr*ea*h.
Glæd wæs ic gliwum, glenged hiwum,
blissa bleoum, blostma hiwum.

He granted me life, who revealed this light
And drew out that bright thing, nobly revealed it.
Happy I was with music, adorned with hues,
With the colours of bliss, with blossoms' hues.

1 *geteah* and *onwreah*. The manuscript has respectively *geteoh* and *onwrah*. The rhyme improves if these acceptable variants are used in emendation.

2 Secgas mec segon (symbel ne alegon),
feorhgiefe gefegon. Frætwed *wegon*
wic[g] ofer wongum wennan gongum,
lisse mid longum leoma getongum.

Men looked upon me (the feasts did not fail),
Were glad of the gift of life. Decorated steeds
Carried me over plains, bumping in their gallops,
Joyfully with their long quickening strides.

3 Þa wæs wæstmum aweaht, world onspreht,
under roderum areaht, rædmægne oferþeaht.
Giestas gengdon, gerscype mengdon,
lisse lengdon, lustum glengdon.

Awakened with growth then was the sprightly world,
Ranging under skies, roofed with the governing power.
The guests marched in, mingled their noisy banter,
Joyfully they lingered, lustily adorned themselves.

4 Scrifen scrad, glad þurh gescad in brad,
wæs on lagustreame lad, þær me leoþu ne biglad.
Hæfde ic heanne had, ne wæs me in healle gad,
þæt þær rof weord rad. Oft þær rinc gebad,

The appointed one moved, glided on her course into the open,
On the sea's current was a road where the ship didn't deceive me.
I had a high position, nor wanted for anything in the hall,
Brave there the retinue that rode. Often a man would wait there

---

2 The manuscript has *feorhgiefe* 'gift of life' which is sometimes emended to *feohgiefe* 'gift(s) of money', tips if the *secgas* 'men' are servants (compare with line 17). But a bishop, if this is what the speaker is or was, gives the gift of spiritual life to his flock. [*wegon* 'Carried'. Emended from *wægum*, probably of the same meaning. [*wennan* 'bumping'. Stanley rules out a Kentish *wennan* for *wynnum* 'joyfully', taking *wen* 'pustule, hummock' instead as the root (1984: 450–2). The hummocks make the gallop more exciting (*lisse* as 'joyfully'), and 'bumping' captures the narrator's motion as he rides. [*mid longum leoma getongum* 'with their long quickening strides'. 'Strides' is made by reading *leoma* 'of limbs' into the meaning of *longum*.

3 Compare with Gerard Manley Hopkins, *Hurrahing in Harvest*: 'The world is charged with the grandeur of God'. [*onspreht* 'sprightly'. The connection suggested in the Bosworth-Toller dictionary between *onspreht* (only here) and OIce *sprækr* 'sprightly' still holds good, though Klinck posits 'sprouted' from (a verb created out of) OE *spræc* 'shoot' (1992: 146). [*gerscype* 'noisy banter', for *gērscipe*. OIce *gár* 'buffoonery' and OE *gyrran* 'to chatter' are both likely cognates. [*glengdon* 'adorned themselves'. This reads the verb in a middle voice. The narrator takes a dim view of his former guests' loose morals, like the Soul in hell on his former self: *he his lichoman in idelnesse glengde mid hrægle* 'in idleness he adorned his body with clothing', 'Soul and Body Dialogue', *Vercelli Homily* No. 4 (Scragg 1992: 100).

4 These lines are made obscure by the poet's combination of internal with final rhymes on *–ad*. The once-attested *leoþu* may be explained as 'ship', as related to OIce *lið* 'ship' (or as 'voyage', from OE *liþan* 'sail'; Klinck 1992: 147), and then treated as the subject. The narrator seems to assume our knowledge of a ship-metaphor for his journey through life. With preterites of the verbs *scriþan* and *glidan*, the ship 'glided'. 'Course' for *gescad* assumes a loan translation of OIce *skeið* 'course'. The word *weord* 'retinue' is Northumbrian, for West Saxon *werod*.

5 þæt he in sele sæge sincgewæge,
þegnum geþ*æge*. Þe*o*den wæs ic *wæge*,
horsce mec heredon, hilde generedon,
fægre feredon, feondon biweredon.

Until he had seen in the house a weight of treasure
Acceptable to the thegns. I was a king in my cups,
Clever men praised me, saved my life in battle,
Conveyed me with courtesy, guarded me from foes.

6 Swa mec hyhtgiefu heold, hygedryht befeold,
staþolæhtum steold, stepegongum weold;
swylce eorþe ol, ahte ic ealdorstol,
galdorwordum gol, gomelsibbe ne ofoll,

Thus joy-giving kept me, household enfolded me,
I possessed properties, men's goings I commanded,
As the earth fed me, so I owned a chieftainly throne,
Sang sweet hymns, did not reject an old family,

7 ac wæs gefest gear, gellende sner,
wuniendo wær, w*ynlic* ges*t*ær.
Scealcas wæron scearpe, scyl wæs hearpe,
hlude hlynede, hleoþor dynede.

But bountiful was the year, tuneful the chord,
Lasting the covenant, joyous my history.
Marshals were vigorous, shrill was the lyre,
Loud it resounded, my voice rang out.

---

5 Line 18, *þegnum geþyhte þenden wæs ic mægen*, is corrupt and must be emended. *þeoden* for *þenden* is relatively easy. The rhyme of *mægen* with *sæge* in the previous line justifies changing *geþyhte* to *geþæge*, the meaning of which, however, may only be found if we take this as a loan from OIce *þægr* 'acceptable'. Snorri uses *þægiligr* with 'see' and a 'gift' term, in (King Hrólfr's words): *Nú sé ek þik enga gjǫf hafa til at gefa mér . . . þá er mér sé þægilig* 'I see now that you have no gift to give me which I may find acceptable' (*Poetics* (ch. 44), ed. Faulkes 1998: 58, lines 16–17). 'Seeing acceptable treasure' makes *sæge sincgewæge þegnum geþæge* look rather Norse.

6 *hygedryht* 'household'. The *hyge*-element is not for 'mind', but for *higan* 'household' (Klinck 1992: 148), as in OIce *hý-*, in *hýbýli* 'household', or *hýnótt* 'bride-night' in *The Lay of Skírnir*, stanza 42 (see **Gods of the Vikings**). [*ealdorstol* 'chieftainly throne'. The *ealdorman* 'earl' holds an *ealdordom(scipe)*, the bishop a *bisceopstol* 'diocese'. The speaker leaves it open to which side he belongs. [*ol* 'fed'. From *alan* 'to feed', an apparently Northumbrian word, but also attested in OIce *ala* 'to bring forth'. The narrator means that his rule came to him as naturally as growing up. [*gomelsibbe ne ofoll* 'did not reject an old family'. The verb **of-alan* is not found elsewhere, but is likely here because of (a) *ol* and (b) the need for a rhyme (spoilt if we emend to *of[fe]oll* 'failed'). Perhaps *gomelsibb* 'old family' refers to the church.

7 w*ynlic* ges*tær* 'joyous my history'. This is the best guess of the best editor (Klinck 1992: 149), for *wilbec bescær* 'cut off the stream of misery'. The scribe has garbled his text. OE *stær* 'history' (from an Irish form of Latin *historia*) is not found with a *ge*-prefix, but otherwise seems good. In this 'stanza', the rhyming pattern changes markedly, for reasons unknown, but possibly because the scribe has lost his place more than once, copying in words from the wrong lines (Abram 2007: 6).

8 Sweglrad swinsade, swiþe ne minsade,
burgsele beofode, beorht hlifade.
Ellen eacnade, ead beacnade,
freaum frodade, fromum godade.

A path of melody made music, diminished hardly,
The town's hall vibrated, bright it towered.
Courage increased, wealth was a beacon,
Taught the noble, endowed the strong.

'Path of melody': lyre.

9 Mod mægnade, mine fægnade,
treow telgade, tir welgade.
Blæd blissade, [. . .]
gold gearwade, gim hwearfade,
sinc searwade, sib nearwade.

Mind strengthened, desire rejoiced,
Tree put out shoots, honour abounded,
Glory was joyful [. . .],
Gold was prepared, jewels passed around,
Treasure subtly wrought, kin became close.

10 From ic wæs in frætwum, freolic in geatwum;
wæs min dream dryhtlic, drohtað hyhtlic.
Foldan ic freoþode, folcum ic leoþode.
Lif wæs min longe, leodum in gemonge,
tirum getonge, teala gehonge.

Strong I was in adornments, noble in my trappings,
My pleasure was like a lord's, my condition delightful.
The land I protected, with local folk was gentle.
My life was a long one, in among my people,
Linked with honours, beautifully adorned.

---

8 *freaum frodade* 'Taught the noble'. The first word is from *freo* 'noble' (Middle English *fre*). The second is unique, from **frodian*, which, on analogy with OIce *frœða* 'to make wise' (perhaps its model), means 'to teach'. The narrator's wealth furnished a court, created expensive beautiful books and endowed warriors.

9 *Mod mægnade* 'Mind strengthened'. The manuscript gives *mod* a capital *M*, indicating a new start.

10 *wæs min dream dryhtlic* 'My pleasure was like a lord's'. Is the speaker a bishop then? Step forward Archbishop Wulfstan of York, removed from office by King Eadred in 954. [*folcum ic leoþode . . . leodum in gemonge* 'with local folk was gentle . . . in among my people'. He gives his own epitaph. For another, of a poet on his hero, see *leodum liðost* 'gentle with his people' on the last line of *Beowulf* (line 3182).

11 Nu min hreþer is hreoh,   heowsiþum sceoh,
nydbysgum neah;   gewiteð nihtes in fleah

Now my heart is sad, fearful of hues' going,
Pressed by compulsive cares. He flees by night

12 se ær in dæge wæs dyre.   Scriþeð nu deop feor[e]
brondhord geblowen,   breostum in forgrowen,
flyhtum toflowen.   Flah is geblowen
miclum in gemynde.   Modes gecynde
greteð ungrynde   grorn efenpynde.

Who was once esteemed by day. Spreads now deep
In life's-blood a hoard of fire, overgrown in the breast,
Dispersed to all corners. Deceitfulness spreads
Greatly in the mind. A trouble just as contained
And bottomless assails the nature of the heart.

13 Bealofus byrneð,   bittre toyrneð.
Werig winneð,   widsið onginneð,
sar ne sinniþ,   sorgum cinnið,
blæd his blinnið,   blisse linnað,
listum linneð,   lustum ne tinneð.

It burns with keen wickedness, bitterly runs wild.
Weary, he fights it, his long journey starts,
Grief does not cease, multiplies with cares,
His glory comes to an end, declines in rejoicing,
Declines artfully, does not rekindle gladly.

---

11 *Nu* 'Now'. Again, a capital letter indicates a new start. [*heowsiþum sceoh* 'fearful of hues' going'. Macrae-Gibson has 'For the hues of joy are gone' (1983: 33). Klinck follows four earlier editors in emending to *heowsiþum* 'times of lamentation', but as Macrae-Gibson points out, 'the *heow* [hues] whoe *siþ* here is clearly a journey of departure are to be seen as the same that were an emblem of rejoicing in [lines] 3–4' (1983: 48). [*gewiteð nihtes in fleah* 'He [the once esteemed man] flees by night'. An expression of weakening powers within the culture of public display: compare Egill's similar anxiety, in *alþjóð fyr augum verðr gamals þegns gengileysi* 'the old thegn's infirmity is becoming clear to the eyes of everyone', in *Hard Loss of Sons*, stanza 9.

12 *brondhord* 'hoard of fire'. This appears to be the *flah* 'deceit' of the poet's next sentence, spreading in his mind (with *geblowen* in both cases). [*grorn efenpynde* 'A trouble just as contained' (as the hoard). *Efenpynde* has been emended to *ungepynde* 'unrestrained' (Klinck 1992: 153). The poet's emphasis is on the hiddenness of his transformation.

13 *linnað*, *linnið* are Northumbrian forms of West Saxon *linneð* 'declines'.

14 Dreamas swa her gedreosað, dryhtscype gehreosað,
lif her men forleosað, leahtras oft geceosað;
treowþrag is to trag, seo untrume genag,
steapum [st]eaðole misþah, ond eal stund genag.

Delights thus crumble here, nobility falls away,
Men lose their lives here, often choose vice.
The time for believing comes late, feeble, this has withered,
Has failed in high places, and every hour has withered.

15 Swa nu world wendeþ, wyrde sendeþ,
ond hetes henteð, hæleþe scyndeð.
Wercyn gewiteð, wælgar sliteð,
flah mah fliteþ, flan mon hwiteð,
burgsorg biteð, bald ald þwiteþ.

So now the world changes, sends its fates,
And hatred it pursues, the hero it shames.
The tribe of men moves on, the death-spear pierces,
Treachery contends, the arrow whitens a man,
Town-anxiety bites, old makes less bold.

---

14 *to trag* 'comes late'. 'Evil' is *trag*'s meaning (Klinck 1992: 154), but compare OIce *tregr* 'slow' in *mjǫk erum tregt tungu at hrœra tregt* 'hugely hard is it for me to stir my tongue', in Egill's *Hard Loss of Sons*, stanza 1. [*steapum [st]eaðole misþah* 'Has failed in high places'. The form *eatole* 'terribly' in the manuscript is usually emended to give alliteration, as in the line before (see Klinck 1992: 154). Failure in the Church or royal court may here be the poet's theme. His language is much like that of the Wise Man's lament for past glories in *The Wanderer*, especially line 95, *hu seo þrag gewat* 'how that time has passed away'.

15 *Wercyn* 'tribe of men'. Compare *wifa cyn* 'tribe of women', *The Dream of the Rood*, line 94 (**Poems of Devotion**). Manuscript *wencyn* 'kind of pustule' would make little sense. [*burgsorg biteð* 'Town-anxiety bites'. Often changed to *borgsorg* 'borrowing anxiety' for the sake of perfect rhyme. [*bald ald þwiteþ* 'old makes less bold'. Compare the Norse proverb (not necessarily true) *svá ergisk hverr sem eldisk* 'each man becomes cowardly the older he becomes', in *The Saga of Hrafnkell*, ch. 8.

16 Wræcfæc wri*te*ð, wraþ að smiteþ,
singry*n* sidað, *searo*fearo glideþ.
Gro*rn* torn græfeþ, græft [hæft] hafað,
searo hwit solaþ, sumur hat colað.

Misery-time is incised, the angry man smites his oath,
Sin's net throws wide, the cunning vessel glides.
Troubled grief digs, the grave has [its prisoner],
Cunning soils the whiteness, hot summers cool.

17 Foldwela fealleð, feondscipe wealleð,
eorðmægen ealdaþ, ellen *cealda*ð.

The land's wealth falls, enmity wells up,
Earthly power grows old, courage grows cold.

18 Me þæt wyrd gewæf, ond ge*w*yr[h]t forgeaf,
þæt ic grofe græf, ond þæt grimme græf
flean flæsce ne mæg, þonne flanhred dæg
nydgrapum nimeþ, þonne seo neah[t] becymeð
seo me eðles *o*fonn ond mec her eardes onconn.

Fate wove this for me, and gave me the work
That I should dig a grave, and that grim grave
Flesh will not be able to flee when the arrow-swift day
Grips me with force, when comes the night
To cut me from inheritance and assail me in this land.

---

16 *writeð* 'is incised'. Manuscript *wriþað* 'flourishes' works well apart from the lack of rhyme. This might bring to mind the Norns incising men's fates (*skáru á skíði* 'cut marks on wood') in *The Sibyl's Prophecy*, stanza 20 (**Gods of the Vikings**), especially if we recall the poet's *wyrde* 'fates' on line 59, *wyrd* on line 70 and *se neda tan* on line 78. [*smiteþ*, probably 'smites' rather than 'smears' (Klinck 1992: 155). A famous Norse case of perjury in anger is *Þórr einn þar vá þrunginn móði* 'Þórr alone there struck, swollen with wrath', in *The Sibyl's Prophecy*, stanza 26. [searo*fearo* 'cunning vessel'. This emends the meaningless *sæcra fearo* and takes *fearo* as a feminine noun on analogy with OIce *fǫr* 'journey, ship'. In *The Sibyl's Prophecy*, stanza 48, is a death-ship in the Apocalypse, named Naglfar. In two lines, for whatever reason, three allusions here recall a Norse vision of the world's end.

17 *ellen* cealdað 'courage grows cold'. Emended from *colað*, clearly miscopied from this word above.

19 Þonne lichoma ligeð,   lima wyrm frigeþ,
ac him wenne gewigeð   ond þa wist geþygeð,
oþþæt beoþ þa ban   [................................] an,
ond æt nyhstan nan   nefne se neda tan
hæleþum her gehlote*n*.   Ne biþ se hlisa adroren.

Then the body will lie there, the worm love its limbs,
For it will try out the pustule and taste that food
Until the bones are [................................] alone,
And at last befalls nothing except the lot of necessity
Appointed here for men. Nor does fame diminish.

20 Ær þæt eadig geþenceð,   he hine þe oftor swenceð,
byrgeð him þa bitran synne,   hogaþ to þære betran wynne,
gemon morþa lisse,   *þær* sindon miltsa blisse
hyhtlice in heofona rice.   Uton nu halgum gelice

A blessed man sees that early, repents the more often,
Saves himself from bitter sins, thinks of the better joys,
Recalls the sweet rewards, where mercy's bliss lives
To hope for in heaven's kingdom. Let us now, like the saints,

21 scyldum biscyrede   scyndan generede,
wommum biwerede,   wuldre generede,
þær moncyn mot   for meotude rot
soðne God geseon,   ond aa in sibbe gefean.

Hasten separated from sins and as men saved,
Defended from defilements, be saved in glory
Where mankind may in happiness before the Measurer
See the true God and rejoice in his kindred for all time.

---

19 *frigeþ* 'will love'. Emended, for rhyme, from *friteþ* 'will eat'. [*hæleþum* 'for men'. Emended by Klinck (1992: 158) from *balawun*, which is kept and read as if *bealwum* 'evil things' by Macrae-Gibson (1983: 36).

Wulf and Eadwacer

✳

Wulf and Eadwacer is the name given to a short poem written as one prose block on folios 100 verso to 101 recto of the Exeter Book. It is a mystery what situation here we are expected to know or guess of, especially as the speaker, a woman, gives one heroic name, *Eadwacer* (line 16), and one generic name twice in *Wulf* (line 13). The woman reflects on Wulf as her lover and addresses Eadwacer apparently as her detested husband, the man who is not the real father of the 'whelp' that is her child.

There is little agreement to date on what the story could or should be. One big puzzle is that the last four lines of the poem can be set out in the Norse metre *ljóðaháttr*; not only this, but the preceding poem, which has a refrain, is divisible into four stanzas of another Norse metre, *fornyrðislag*. Old English verse is not stanzaic, but Old Norse verse is. One solution thus argued is that it is a riddle composed in the Danelaw for an English-speaking audience of Danish descent, who may have guessed the solution to be Signý of the Vǫlsungs (North 1994). Elsewhere the Exeter Book offers texts that seem to spring from York or elsewhere in the Anglo-Scandinavian north of England (*The Rhyming Poem* is one), and Sigmundr is known to Anglo-Saxons already as Sigemund, his son as Fitela, in *Beowulf*, lines 875–900. Signý is married to a man, a king naturally, who has killed her father and brothers. She safeguards her brother Sigmundr, who hides out in the woods, for a day of vengeance, yet cannot provide him with a sufficiently worthy assistant until, in disguise, she conceives this man as child from Sigmundr her own brother. Sinfjǫtli grows up to be a monster in human form, and he and his father turn into werewolves while they train in the arts of vengeance. This vengeance is about to be accomplished at the end of the poem. There are other interpretations, but as *Wulf and Eadwacer* follows *Deor* and precedes the first 59 *Riddles* of the Exeter Book, it is possible that it resembles one poem in heroic content and the other poems in riddling form.

Bouman, A. C., '*Leodum is minum*: Beadohild's Complaint', *Neophilologus* 33 (1949), 103–13

Frankis, P. J., '*Deor* and *Wulf and Eadwacer*: some conjectures', *Medium Ævum* 31 (1962), 161–75

Frese, D. Warwick, '*Wulf and Eadwacer*: the adulterous woman reconsidered', *NDEJ* 15 (1983), 1–22

Greenfield, S. B., '*Wulf and Eadwacer*: all passion pent', *Anglo-Saxon England* 15 (1986), 5–14

Klinck, A. L., *The Old English Elegies: A Critical Edition and Genre Study* (Montreal and Kingston, 1992)

North, R., 'Metre and meaning in *Wulf and Eadwacer*: Signý reconsidered', in *Loyal Letters: Studies on Mediaeval Alliterative Poetry and Prose*, ed. L. A. J. R. Houwen and A. A. MacDonald, Mediaevalia Groningana 15 (Groningen, 1994), 29–54

Orton, P., 'An approach to *Wulf and Eadwacer*', *Proceedings of the Royal Irish Academy* 85.c.9 (1986), 223–58

Schofield, W. H., 'Signý's Lament', *Proceedings of the Modern Language Association* 17 (1902), 262–95

Stanley, E. G., 'Wolf, my Wolf!', in *Old English and New: Studies in Language and Linguistics in Honor of Frederic G. Cassidy*, ed. J. H. Hall, N. Doane and D. Ringler (New York, 1992), 46–62

Tasioulas, J. A., 'The Mother's Lament: *Wulf and Eadwacer* reconsidered', *Medium Ævum* 65 (1996), 1–18

1 Leodum is minum swylce him mon lac gife;
willað hy hine aþecgan, gif he on þreat cymeð,
ungelic is us.

For my people it is as if someone might give them a game;
They will want to take him if he comes into their band,
it is not the same for us.

2 Wulf is on iege, ic on oþerre.
Fæst is þæt eglond, fenne biworpen.
Sindon wælreowe weras þær on ige;
willað hy hine aþecgan, gif he on þreat cymeð,
ungelice is us.

Wolf is on one isle, I am on another.
That island is secure, enclosed by marsh,
There are blood-thirsty savage men there on that isle;
They will want to take him if he comes into their band,
it is not the same for us.

---

1 *Leodum is minum swylce him mon lac gife*. This line, which has more than one meaning, may be taken to refer, if the speaker is Signý, to her husband's men who hunt down her brother Sigmundr, outlaw and werewolf. They do so as if for a game, perhaps like the Danes in Ælfric's *Life of St Edmund*, *swilce him to gamenes* 'as if for their own sport' (see **Writers of the Benedictine Reform**). Another meaning in line 1 may be that this whole poem is a *lac* 'game' (whence its inclusion in the Exeter Book) produced as a riddle in the Danelaw for English people of Danish descent (North 1994; compare *þe olde lorde of þat leude cowþe wel halde layk aloft* 'the old lord of that people could well hold a game aloft', *Sir Gawain and the Green Knight*, lines 1022–3).

2 *aþecgan* 'take'. The meaning of this word, as in cognate OIce *þiggja* 'take, receive, taste ' in Guðrún's invitation to Attila to eat (their sons) in *The Lay of Attila*, stanza 34, may be related to the wolf-shape of the dangerous outlaw Sigmundr, while he hides out in preparation for vengeance on the slayer of his and Signý's father. The speaker, if Signý, dreads that men will kill and eat her brother.

3 Wulfes ic mines widlastum   wenum dogode;
þonne hit wæs renig weder   ond ic reotugu sæt,
þonne mec se beaducafa   bogum bilegde,
    wæs me wyn to þon,
    wæs me hwæþre eac lað.

I availed the wide-ranging expectations of my Wolf:
When it was rainy weather and I sat weeping,
Then the battle-swift one laid his boughs about me;
    there was pleasure for me in this,
    yet it was also loathsome.

4 Wulf, min Wulf,   wena me þine
seoce gedydon,   þine seldcymas,
murnende mod,   nales meteliste.

Wolf, my Wolf, expectations of you
Have made me ill, your rare visits,
A grieving heart, not at all the lack of food.

---

3 *Wulfes ic mines wenum dogode* 'I availed the expectations of my Wolf'. On *wen* and *wulf*, see note for stanza 4. The word *dogode* may be explained, and left unemended, as a Scandinavianised past tense of *dugan* 'to avail' alternative to *dohte*, and formed in the Danelaw (the ancestor of *dawed*, as in *þat dawed but neked* 'that availed but little', *Sir Gawain and the Green Knight*, line 1805; North 1994: 38). This stanza appears to be composed in *galdralag* metre, which works better for the second short line if *hwæþre* was pronounced minus its initial aspiration. The meaning is that the speaker, if Signý, remembers her visit to Sigmundr out in the woods, when, having taken the shape of another woman, she makes as if lost in the rain, sits in his house weeping, then conceives the child which will become the *hvarleiðr* 'everywhere loathed' Sinfjǫtli (the English Fitela; the Norse reference is in *Helgakviða Hundingsbana* I 'The First Lay of Helgi Hundingsbane', stanza 36).

4 *Wulf, wena me þine* 'Wolf, expectations of you'. Aside from here and line 9 of this poem, no other collocation of OE *wen* with *wulf* exists in the Old English corpus, but two out of eight instances of OIce *ván* 'expectation' in the Old Norse poetic corpus are collocated with *úlfr* 'wolf': *ok er mér fangs ván at frekum úlfi* 'and for me is an expectation of booty from the fierce wolf' (says a bird in *Reginsmál* 'The Lay of Reginn', stanza 13); and *þar er mér úlfs ván, er ek eyru sék* 'for me there is an expectation of a wolf when I see his [young Sigurðr's] ears [listening]' (says another bird, in *Fáfnismál* 'The Lay of Fáfnir', stanza 35). The meaning is that the speaker, if Signý, is waiting for the coming of her werewolf brother Sigmundr, whose child she is carrying; the pregnancy makes her sick, while 'the lack of food' in her case refers to the two occasions when her earlier sons (by her husband) failed to bake bread and were killed by Sigmundr on her orders. The grief is for her father, to whose avenging she dedicates her life.

5 Gehyrest þu, Eadwacer? Uncerne ear[m]ne hwelp
bireð wulf to wuda;
þæt mon eaþe tosliteð þætte næfre gesomnad wæs,
uncer giedd geador.

Do you hear, Wealth-Watcher? A wolf is carrying
our cursed whelp to the wood.
That which was never composed is easily torn in two,
our passion together.

'Wealth Watcher (Eadwacer)': possibly a reference by Signý to her husband (Siggeirr).

5 *uncer giedd geador* 'our passion together'. As the use of Norse metres in this poem suggests, OE *giedd* may here be found used with the meaning of (its direct cognate) OIce *geð* 'passion, wits, sense, soul', a word that appears in the same metrical position on the short encapsulating three-stress line, in *Sayings of the High One*, stanza 12: *síns til geðs gumi*; and in stanza 14: *hverr sitt geð gumi*; in a similar position, in *The Lay of Skírnir*, stanza 31: *þik geð grípi*. The Old English short line, in line with the rest of this stanza 5, appears to contain a pun on the meanings 'song' and 'passion' which shows how the female speaker alludes to a marriage which has failed. The possibility that the speaker is meant to be (an English form of) Signý of the Vǫlsungs is strengthened if we consider Sigmundr's murders of her first and second sons by her husband, when they fail to live up to expectations.

Riddles

✳

The late Romans made up *aenigmata* 'riddles' to make each other laugh at parties, and Symposius, the late antique poet who made a collection of 100, has a name that means 'party animal'. As may be seen in the short poems below, the fun lived on, or one might say was reborn, in the Old English *Riddles* of the Exeter Book. In between lay the less saucy Latin *(a)enigmata* of Christian English poets. In the mid-seventh century Aldhelm, later bishop of Sherborne (died 709 or 710), learned Latin metre apparently by building his own collection of 100 *enigmata*. Though he based the form of his riddles on that of Symposius, the content of Aldhelm's riddles, on the universe, the church and classroom among other subjects, was devoutly Christian and educational. Aldhelm's verse style was imitated by his younger contemporaries. One was a fellow West Saxon, Boniface (*c.* 675–754), who wrote his own collection of *enigmata* more soberly with ten on the Vices and ten on the Virtues of Christian life. Another was 'Eusebius', who may or may not have been Abbot Hwætberht of Monkwearmouth-Jarrow (died 716). Eusebius wrote a collection of 60 *enigmata*, starting with 'God', 'Angel', 'Fallen Angel', 'Man' and then becoming random. Tatwine from Breedon on the Hill, later archbishop of Canterbury (731–4), complemented this number with 40 riddles of his own, which start with 'Philosophy' and move on to such things as farm tools and squirrels. If the number 100 seems essential in making riddles, it appears that the interesting person in England in the 970s, who had the Exeter Book compiled, wished to make a good collection of his own. Some 91 or 92 riddles survive in this codex, which, since it is damaged and incomplete, may have been intended to contain 100.

The present anthology seeks to retain the playful spirit of the collection in the Exeter Book. These riddles are in Old English, composed variously perhaps from the eighth century onwards. They aim to both teach and amuse. Some are on the sublime side, others are ridiculous, others use *double entendre* to mislead us with the erotic. Most ask us to guess them and none have solutions given unless by the odd runic letter in the margin here or there. In the Exeter Book the *Riddles* proceed in three sequences interrupted by other poems. The first burst is the longest, in folios 101 recto to 115 recto: the riddles below are extracted from that. After eight poems starting with *The Wife's Lament*, the second burst of riddles is briefer, with a second version of *Riddle* 30 (thus 30b) and *Riddle* 60, in folios 122 verso to 123 recto. After *The Husband's Message* and *The Ruin*, the third and last sequence of riddles runs in folios 124 verso to 130 verso: the second sequence of riddles in the Custom Version of the present anthology is extracted from that. The text is based on Williamson (1977), although the numbering of these riddles follows that of the text in Anglo-Saxon Poetic Records (III).

Blakeley, L., 'Riddles 22 and 58 of the Exeter Book', *Review of English Studies* new series 9 (1958), 241–52

Bradley, S. A. J., trans., *Anglo-Saxon Poetry: An Anthology of Old English Poems in Prose Translation* (London, 1982)

Doane, A. N., 'Spacing, placing and effacing: scribal textuality and Riddle 30a/b', in *New Approaches to Editing Old English Verse*, ed. S. Larratt Keffer and K. O'Brien O'Keeffe (Cambridge, 1998), 45–65

Erhardt-Siebold, E. von, 'The Old English Storm Riddles', *Proceedings of the Modern Language Association* 64 (1949), 884–8

Irvine, S., ed., *The Anglo-Saxon Chronicle: MS E*, The Anglo-Saxon Chronicle: A Collaborative Edition 7 (Cambridge, 2004)

Neville, J., 'Fostering the cuckoo: Exeter Book Riddle 9', *Review of English Studies* 58 (2007), 431–46

North, J. [D.], *Cosmos: An Illustrated History of Astronomy and Cosmology* (Chicago and London, 2008)

Swanton, M. J., trans., *The Anglo-Saxon Chronicle* (London, 1996)

Trautmann, M., ed., *Die altenglischen Rätsel (die Rätsel des Exeterbuchs)* (Heidelberg, 1915)

Tolley, C., *Shamanism in Norse Myth and Magic*, 2 vols, Folklore Fellows' Communications 296 (Helsinki, 2009)

Wallis, F., trans., with notes and commentary, *Bede: The Reckoning of Time*, Translated Texts for Historians 29 (Liverpool, 1999)

Williamson, Craig, *The Old English Riddles of the Exeter Book* (Chapel Hill, NC, 1977)

***Rid.* 1**

Hwylc is hæleþa þæs horsc   ond þæs hygecræftig
þæt þæt mæge asecgan,   hwa mec on sið wræce,
þonne ic astige strong,   stundum reþe,
þrymful þunie,   þragum wræce
fere geond foldan,   folcsalo bærne,
ræced reafige?   Recas stigað,
haswe ofer hrofum.   Hlyn bið on eorþan,
wælcwealm wera,   þonne ic wudu hrere,
bearwas bledhwate,   beamas fylle,

Who's the man so clever and mentally gifted
that can say who drove me on my road,
when strong I arise, sometimes cruel,
stand out mighty, from time to time in vengeance
campaign across the fields, burn people's bowers,
loot their buildings? The smoke climbs,
grey over roofs. There is tumult on earth,
cruel killing of men, when I stir the woods,
the budding groves, fell the trees,

1 Williamson (1977: 127–33) treats this *Riddle* as one piece with two more, to make one riddle ('Wind') with further sections in lines 16–30 and 31–104. The manuscript captitalisations of *H* on lines 1 and 16, however, tell us to treat this poem separately, as does the fact that the speaker asks for a solution on line 14.

holme gehrefed,   hea*h*um meahtum
wrec*e*n on waþe,   wide sended;
hæbbe me on hrycge   þæt ær hadas wreah
foldbuendra,   flæsc ond gæstas,
somod on sunde.   Saga hwa mec þecce,
oþþe hu ic hatte,   þe þa hlæst bere.

roofed by the ocean, by high powers
driven on the hunt, sent far and wide.
I have on my back what did once cover persons
who lived on earth, their flesh and souls,
together in the sea. Say who may roof me,
or what my name is, I who bear this burden.

***Rid.* 5**

Ic eom anhaga   iserne wund,
bille gebennad,   beadoweorca sæd,
ecgum werig.   Oft ic wig seo,
frecne feohtan.   Frofre ne wene,
þæt me geoc cyme   guðgewinnes,
ær ic mid ældum   eal forwurðe,
ac mec hnossiað   homera lafe,
heardecg heoroscearp,   hondweorc smiþa,
bitað in burgum;   ic a bidan sceal

I'm a lone survivor, wounded by iron,
gashed by blade, sated with war-deeds,
weary of edges. Often I see battle,
savage fighting, nor expect solace
that relief from conflict may reach me
before I perish entirely as men do,
but hammers' leavings buffet me,
cruel war-sharp edges, smiths' handiwork,
bite me in the boroughs. I must ever await

1.11 *wrecen on waþe* 'driven on the hunt'. Manuscript *wrecan* makes no sense, and must be emended. 'Hunt' for *waþ* helps us to see this line as an early reference to the Wild Hunt, part of medieval folklore in which supernatural beings were imagined to cross the stormy night sky. Such a spectacle was recorded in the Peterborough version (E) of the *Anglo-Saxon Chronicle* for the year 1127 (Swanton 1996: 258; Irvine 2004: 129).

1.12 The poet appears to refer to the Great Flood, 'in which the clouds outpoured all the waters now carried again by the air' (Erhardt-Siebold 1949: 886).

5 There is a ᛋ-rune in the lower margin, between this and the riddle that follows, one that might refer to a solution in Latin *s(cutum)* or OE *s(cyld)* 'shield' (Williamson 1977: 52 (facsimile) and 147).

5.7 *homera lafe* 'hammers' leavings': swords. This kenning is found also in *Beowulf*, line 2829, and *The Battle of Brunanburh*, line 6.

5.9 *bitað in burgum* 'bite me in the boroughs'. The fighting may be taking place either around Alfred's new *burge* 'towns', or more probably, given that it is *in* 'in' the towns, in the Danelaw 'boroughs' themselves in the early tenth century (see **Viking Wars**).

laþran gemotes. Næfre læcecynn
on folcstede findan meahte,
þara þe mid wyrtum wunde gehælde,
ac me ecga dolg eacen weorðað
þurh deaðslege dagum ond nihtum.

a meeting more hostile, could never
find the kind of medic in people's dwellings
who healed wounds with his herbs,
but cuts from blades swell out on me
from deadly strikes by day and night.

***Rid.* 7**

Hrægl min swigað, þonne ic hrusan trede,
oþþe þa wic buge, oþþe wado drefe.
Hwilum mec ahebbað ofer hæleþa byht
hyrste mine, ond þeos hea lyft,
ond mec þonne wide wolcna strengu
ofer folc byreð. Frætwe mine
swogað hlude ond swinsiað,
torhte singað, þonne ic getenge ne beom
flode ond foldan, ferende gæst.

My garments are quiet when I tread the ground,
or then settle in a place, or put to water.
Sometimes my trappings, and high up this air,
lift me over the homes of men,
and far and wide the power of clouds
carries me over people. My adornments
echo loudly and melodiously sound,
brightly sing, when I am not touching
the flood or earth, a ghost on his way.

7.7 The whooper or whistler swan gives a whistling sound in flight, yet the swan's song is also a literary motif known from antiquity. See Williamson (1977: '5', 151–3). The melody of birds' feathers is also a motif in *The Phoenix*, lines 131–9.

7.9 The whiteness of the flying creature, if a swan as the swansong motif would suggest, is best inferred if we treat the last word, *gæst*, as 'ghost' (with long vowel) rather than 'guest' (with short).

***Rid.* 9**

Mec on þissum dagum   deadne ofgeafun
fæder ond modor;   ne wæs me feorh þa gen,
ealdor in innan.   Þa mec [an] ongon,
welhold mege,   wedum þeccan,
heold ond freoþode,   hleosceorpe wrah
swa arlice   swa hire agen bearn,
oþþæt ic under sceate,   swa min gesceapu wæron,
ungesibbum wearð   eacen gæste.
Mec seo friþemæg   fedde siþþan,
oþþæt ic aweox,   widdor meahte
siþas asettan.   Heo hæfde swæsra þy læs
suna ond dohtra,   þy heo swa dyde!

Me in these days they gave up as dead,
father and mother, nor was yet blood in me,
a life within. Me then did [someone or other,]
a well faithful female relative, clothe,
love and care for, cover in a sheltering layer
as kindly as if I were her own child,
until under that sheet, as was my destiny,
against non-siblings I swelled up in spirit.
Me the adopting woman thereafter fed,
until I grew up and might further
make my journeys. She had the less sweet
sons and daughters for doing this!

9.1 *Mec* 'Me'. The *mec*-pronoun in starting position is known in other riddles. However, as the poet repeats this in lines 3 and 9, it is possible that he aims for a 'me, me, me' effect that underlines the subject's rather self-centred approach.

9.2 *feorh* 'blood'. Strictly *feorh* is for 'life's blood', the substance of living spirit.

9.3 *an* 'someone or other'. There is no word in the manuscript here, but the alliteration requires a word starting with a vowel, and *an* is the simplest choice.

9.9 *friþemæg* 'adopting woman', taking this as one word rather than two ('beautiful kinswoman'). 'Protectress of peace' (Williamson 1977: '7', 260) is not close enough to the situation, in which the child has been placed for adoption. Whether this compound was a technical term for such is unanswerable, as it is elsewhere unattested, but *freoðuwebbe* 'peace-weaver' is better known for a 'lady' in *Beowulf*, line 1942, *Widsith*, line 6 and *Elene*, line 88.

***Rid.* 12**

Fotum ic fere,   foldan slite,
grene wongas,   þenden ic gæst bere.
Gif me feorh losað,   fæste binde
swearte Wealas,   hwilum sellan men.
Hwilum ic deorum   drincan selle
beorne of bosme,   hwilum mec bryd triedeð
felawlonc fotum,   hwilum feorran broht
wonfeax Wale   wegeð ond þyð,
dol druncmennen   deorcum nihtum,
wæteð in wætre,   wyrmeð hwilum
fægre to fyre;   me on fæðme sticaþ
hygegalan hond,   hwyrfeð geneahhe,
swifeð me geond sweartne.   Saga hwæt ic hatte,
þe ic lifgende   lond reafige
ond æfter deaþe   dryhtum þeowige.

On feet I march, the soil I tear,
green hillsides, while I carry spirit.
If my life is lost, I bind fast
dark Welshmen, sometimes men of higher rank.
Sometimes I give the valiant man
a drink from my bosom, sometimes a bride treads me,
haughty, underfoot; sometimes, brought from afar,
a dark-haired Welshgirl moves and presses me,
foolish drunken maid, on dark nights,
wets me in water, warms me at times
pleasantly by the fire, the loose woman's hand
sticks me up her breast, moves me constantly,
swives me through a dark one. Say what I'm called,
I who plunder the land when living
and after death serve multitudes.

12 The first of three 'ox' riddles in the Exeter Book, the others being 38 and 72 (Williamson's 10, 36 and 70). Aldhelm (No. 83) and Eusebius (No. 37) both made riddles containing the same paradox of a thing that breaks the ground when living, binds men when dead (Williamson 1977: 166 and 255).

12.6 *of bosme* 'from my bosom'. Drinking cups were made of stiffened leather, as anyone who visits English Heritage sites will know.

12.10 *wæteð in wætre* 'wets me in water'. This and the following may be taken as a (somewhat mysterious) description of leather-tanning.

12.13 *swifeð me geond sweartne* 'swives me through a dark one'. The missing noun is *fæðm* 'breast, embrace' from two lines up, but here distinguished by *sweart* 'dark' as something other than the woman's bosom.

12.15 On the right margin is a ᛇ rune, for *e* (**eoh**) or *i* (**iw**), which Williamson interprets as the first letter of Latin *iuvencus* 'bullock' (1977: 54 (facsimile) and 167–8).

***Rid.* 22**

Ætsomne cwom sixtig monna
to wægstæþe wicgum ridan,
hæfdon endleofan eoredmæcgas
friðhengestas, feower sceamas.
Ne meahton magorincas ofer mere feolan
swa hi fundedon, ac wæs flod to deop,
atol yþa geþræc, ofras hea,
streamas stronge. Ongunnon stigan þa
on wægn weras ond hyra wicg somod

Together there came sixty men
riding steeds to a choppy ocean shore.
Eleven men of that cavalry had
beautiful horses, with four real shiners.
Nor could the young warriors pass over the sea
as they hastened, for the flood, frightening tumult
of waves, was too deep, the shores too high,
the currents too strong. So the men did
climb into a wagon, and their steeds together

---

22 'Charles' Wain', the constellation Ursa Major, accompanied by the 11 stars of Canes Venatici just beneath it, moves from SE to SW horizon in the night-time sky. This is a solution strongly endorsed by Williamson (1977). It was proposed by Blakeley (1958), who noted that the poet may have based his ideas on Aldhelm's riddle No. 53, *Arcturus* 'Arcturus' (Boötes' brightest star). The Anglo-Saxons learned the basics of astronomy in monastic schools, while studying the art of *computus* or the calculation of the correct luni-solar calendar date for Easter (Wallis 1999: xviii–xxxiv; North 2008: 234–46).

22.1 *sixtig monna* 'sixty men'. Earlier attempts to match the number exactly proved unworkable. Blakeley (1958: 244) collects similar cases of notional numbers, noting that the common use of Latin *sescenti* 'six hundred', for 'multitude', may have encouraged the use of *sixtig* for this meaning here.

22.3 *endleofan* 'Eleven'. Canes Venatici ('Hunting Dogs') has 11 stars visible to the naked eye, all beneath the 'pole' of the Wain (Blakeley 1958: 243). The name for the 'dogs' constellation was introduced in 1690 (by Johannes Hevelius; North 2008: 264), but the same pattern was doubtless observed earlier under a different name.

22.4 *friðhengestas* 'beautiful horses'. The manuscript's *fridhengestas* is left unchanged by Williamson, who proposes 'horses' only, taking *frid-* as an otherwise unattested English cognate of German *pferd* 'horse' (1977: 203). Beauty, however, is a pretty obvious quality where horses are concerned, as much as with stars. [*sceamas* 'shiners'. The meaning, this word not being found elsewhere, is obtained from the apparently cognate OE *scima* 'splendour, ray'. Canes Venatici has four especially bright stars (Blakeley 1958: 243–4).

hlodan under hrunge, þa þa hors oðbær
eh ond eorlas, æscum dealle,
ofer wætres byht wægn to lande.
Swa hine oxa ne teah, ne esna mægen,
ne fæthengest, ne on flode swom
ne be grunde wod gestum under
ne lagu drefde ne of lyfte fleag
ne under bæc cyrde. Brohte hwæþre
beornas ofre burnan ond hyra bloncan mid
from stæðe heaum þæt hy stopan up
on oþerne ellenrofe
weras of wæge ond hyra wicg gesund.

they loaded under a pole, and away then the horses,
chargers and gentlemen alike, gleaming with ash-spears,
were borne by wagon over water's bight to land.
Thus neither ox pulled the wagon, nor the strength of servants,
nor riding horse, neither did it swim in the flood,
nor travel over ground under guest-men,
nor put to sea, nor fly from the sky,
nor turn back. For all that, it brought
the men across the stream and their greys as well,
so that from one high bank they advanced
up to another, courageous fellows,
men and their mounts made safe from waves.

***Rid.* 25** Ic eom wunderlicu wiht, wifum on hyhte,
neahbuendum nyt; nængum sceþþe
burgsittendra, nymþe bonan anum.
Staþol min is steapheah, stonde ic on bedde,

I'm a wonderful creature, give women joy,
am useful if they're neighbours. I harm no one
who sits around in town, only my slayer.
In bed I stand steep, with a high foundation,

22.11 *æscum dealle* 'gleaming with their ash-spears'. The word *deall* 'bright, proud' is not common. It seems to be cognate with OIce *dallr* 'tree, burgeoner' which is used of the Norse god *Heim-dallr* 'World-tree' (Tolley 2009: 373–5, and notes 5 and 7), who leans towards the pole star (*ibid.* 385).

22.12 *ofer wætres byht* 'over water's bight'. The word *byht*, for 'bay', misleads the reader, as it is really the vault that arches over the water, rather than a sea-bay itself. 'Bight' catches the bow-shape of the vault.

22.15 *gestum under* 'under guest-men'. This appears to describe the 11 horsemen as heavily laden guests leaving a feast.

25.4 *Staþol min is steapheah* 'I stand steep, with a high foundation'. Onions are 'normally planted in loose ground raised high into mounds or rows' (Williamson 1977: 210–11).

neoþan ruh nathwær. Neþeð hwilum
ful cyrtenu ceorles dohtor,
modwlonc meowle, þæt heo on mec gripeð,
ræseð mec on reodne, reafað min heafod,
fegeð mec on fæsten. Feleþ sona
mines gemotes, seo þe mec nearwað,
wif wundenlocc. Wæt bið þæt eage.

hairy somewhere down there. At times she dares,
the churl's real pretty daughter,
spirited girl, to put her grip on me,
races me in a red one, plunders my head,
fixes me in confinement. Soon she feels
my encounter, the woman who cramps me,
a wife with braided hair. That eye will be wet.

***Rid.* 30a** Ic eom legbysig, lace mid winde,
bewunden mid wuldre, wedre gesomnad,
fus forðweges, fyres gebysgad,
bearu blowende, byrnende gled.

Flame is busy with me, I play with the wind,
encircled with glory, made one with the firmament,
focused on the road hence, troubled by fire,
blossoming in the grove, a glowing ember.

25.8 *ræseð mec on reodne* 'races me in a red one'. In her enclosed hand on the board while the other hand chops: in one sense. For the more salacious meaning, compare *swifeð me geond sweartne* 'swives me through a dark one' in *Riddle* 12, line 13. In each case what the literal translation loses in clarity, it gains in suggestiveness. Moritz Trautmann's reading 'erhebt mich an einen roten (d. i. *mūð*, den Mund)' [raises me into a red one (i.e. *mūð*, the mouth)] seems about right, at least for the noun (1915: 87).

30a The right-hand margin has an **r**-letter with a point on either side, from a later scribe, as a solution which seems to suggest *rod* 'rood, cross' (Williamson 1977: Plates XIV.a and b and 231). Moreover, this riddle is the only one in the Exeter Book to be copied out twice (see Doane 1998). *Riddle* 30b, the other text, is found much later, on folio 122 verso, after *Homiletic Fragment II* and before *Riddle* 60 (which itself precedes *The Husband's Message*); where it is partly damaged by the burn (see headnote; Williamson 1977: 228–30). Bradley more than other scholars has seen the riddle's references as consistent with the Cross, rather than with timber in general (1982: 375–6). As with *The Dream of the Rood*, however, which may be a model, this poem plays on a tree as the being from which the Cross was made (**Poems of Devotion**).

30a.2 *bewunden mid wuldre* 'encircled' (literally 'wound about') 'with glory'. Compare with *leohte bewunden* 'wound about with light', in *The Dream of the Rood*, line 5. [*wedre gesomnad* 'made one with the firmament'. Bradley's translation, with a bit of strain on *weder* 'weather, storm, wind' (1982: 376).

30a.3 *fus forðweges* 'focused on the road hence'. Compare with *wæs modsefa afysed on forðwege* 'my thoughts and feelings were focused on the road hence', in *The Dream of the Rood*, lines 124–5.

30a.4 *bearu* 'in the grove'. This reading assumes an assimilated ending from *bearwe*.

Ful oft mec gesiþas sendað æfter hondum
þæt mec weras ond wif wlonce cyssað.
Þonne ic mec onhæbbe ond hi onhnigaþ to me,
monige mid miltse, þær ic monnum sceal
ycan upcyme eadignesse.

Quite often the brothers pass me from hand to hand
that men and women arrogantly may kiss me.
When I raise myself and they bow down to me,
many with humility, there by a resurrection
shall I add to the blessedness of mankind.

***Rid.* 46** Wær sæt æt wine mid his wifum twam
ond his twegen suno ond his twa dohtor,
swase gesweostor, ond hyra suno twegen,
freolico frumbearn; fæder wæs þær inne
þara æþelinga æghwæðres mid,
eam ond nefa. Ealra wæron fife
eorla ond idesa insittendra.

A man sat at wine with his two wives
and his two sons and his two daughters,
sweet sisters, and their two sons,
noble firstborns. In there was the father
of each one of those two princelings,
uncle, nephew, grandson. Five, in all,
gentlemen and ladies were sitting within.

30a.5 *gesiþas* 'brothers'. Literally 'companions', although the lack of military context allows us to see these men's comitatus as a monastic one.

30a.6 The emotional shift from *wlonce* 'arrogantly' to *mid miltse* 'with humility' (or even from 'proudly' to 'with joy') suggests Easter, or Corpus Christi, in which the congregation gives way to a trope, or liturgical performance, like an early mystery play ('The Raising of the Cross').

30a.9 *upcyme* 'by a resurrection'. A slight liberty here, as *æriste* is the usual word for this, but the meaning is clear enough in the context, which suggests throngs in an overcrowded church at Easter.

46 No source has been found for this riddle. Barring the thought of its having some mischievous application to homes outside the monastery, this riddle was solved (in 1842) as 'Lot's family' from Genesis 19 (Williamson 1977: '44', 283–4). The poem would thus count as the earliest English pub quiz question under 'biblical knowledge'. Lot, after Sodom his city is destroyed, lives in a cave with his two daughters, who seduce him one evening in order to have children. Each has a son. Lot's daughters are thus his wives, his sons are his grandsons, and each son is both uncle and nephew to the other.

46.1 *Wær* 'man'. This form of *wer* 'man' may be Northumbrian, in which case this riddle is from the eighth or ninth century; older, at any rate, than the tenth century in which the Exeter Book was compiled.

46.6 *nefa* 'nephew, grandson'. OE *nefa* may mean both.

***Rid.* 47**

Moððe word fræt. Me þæt þuhte
wrætlicu wyrd, þa ic þæt wundor gefrægn,
þæt se wyrm forswealg wera gied sumes,
þeof in þystro, þrymfæstne cwide
ond þæs strangan staþol. Stælgiest ne wæs
wihte þy gleawra, þe he þam wordum swealg.

A moth devoured words. To me that seemed
a wondrous fate, when I heard of that miracle,
the serpent swallowing up the song of some man,
a thief in darkness ingesting a mighty utterance
and its strong foundation. The thieving guest was
by no means the wiser for swallowing those words.

---

47 The source is Symposius' riddle *Tinea* 'grub' (No. 16), a book-dwelling illiterate who confesses, as here, in the first person to eating the letters he cannot read. The English adaptor, as Williamson says, 'is less concerned with the cuteness of the paradox of the illiterate worm than he is with the mutability of songs as they pass from the traditional *wordhord* of the *scop* into the newer and strangely susceptible form of literate *memoria*' (1977: '45', 285). In other words, he is interested in the worm swallowing poetry (see note to **47**.3).

47.1 *Moððe* 'A moth'. The end-state of the grub, not found in Symposius, but here used to mislead. That the creature will later fly, however, after swallowing a man's song, is interesting if we compare with the story of Óðinn's flight in heron's or eagle's shape from the cave of Suttungr after imbibing the Mead of Poetry (see below).

47.3 *se wyrm* 'the serpent'. OE *wyrm* means this, and 'dragon' too (in *Beowulf*, line 2297), more commonly than its modern reflex 'worm'. This whole image, that of a serpent thief swallowing the *giedd* 'poem, song' that belongs to another man, recalls Óðinn drinking the Mead of Poetry in the cave of Suttungr: see his (cognate) *geð* in *Sayings of the High One*, stanzas 13–14, and 104. This is not the solution, of course, but it is possible that the poet integrates this mythological conceit with the riddle in order to mislead his audience.

47.5 *staþol* 'foundation'. The vellum on which the poem is written (or the Mead of Poetry which produces the song).

***Rid.* 54**

Hyse cwom gangan   þær he hie wisse
stondan in wincsele,   stop feorran to,
hror hægstealdmon,   hof his agen
hrægl hondum up,   hrand under gyrdels
hyre stondendre   stiþes nathwæt,
worhte his willan: wagedan buta.
Þegn onnette,   wæs þragum nyt
tillic esne,   teorode hwæþre
æt stunda gehwam   strong ær þon h*i*o,
werig þæs weorces.   Hyre weaxan ongon
under gyrdelse   þæt oft gode men
ferðþum freogað   ond mid feo bicgað.

The guy went walking to where he knew her
to be standing in a corner-room, stepped towards her
from afar, vigorous bachelor, raised his own
garment with his hands, thrust under the girdle
of her who was standing something stiff,
worked his will: the two of them rocked.
The thegn quickened pace. Useful at times was
the well-endowed servant, nonetheless he tired
each time he did this, though stronger than she,
weary of the work. In her there began to grow
under the girdle something which good men often
cherish in their hearts and buy with money.

54.2 *wincsele* (for **winclsele*) 'corner room'. *Winsele* 'wine-hall' has been suggested, but cannot work for 'churn' (Williamson 1977: '52', 299–300). [*feorran* 'from afar'. We are encouraged to think of this as a social distance, for the man is called *þegn* 'thegn' on line 7, whereas the woman, given the mention of *feo* 'money' on line 12, is probably a slave, her child potentially saleable as well. However, the distance may also be physical, and *þegn* may mean 'servant' too.

54.5 *nathwæt* 'something'. The word is used in the same coy way in *Riddle* 61.

54.12 *ferðþum freogað* 'cherish in their hearts'. Hrothgar's words are similar when he promises to 'cherish' Beowulf 'in his heart' as a son, with *freogan on ferhþe*, in *Beowulf*, line 948.

The Wife's Lament

Who is the woman? What is her story? *The Wife's Lament* has no title, like the other poems in the Exeter Book and poems in Anglo-Saxon manuscripts generally. As a meditation on love and exile, this work could have been enjoyed by some readers or listeners without need for any names, places, or dates. That is how the more sententious wisdom poems of the Exeter Book, such as *Vainglory*, or *The Order of the World*, worked with readers in their time. Less specifically, in this way, the female voice of *The Wife's Lament* has been considered generically (Belanoff 2002), whereas the use of caves and tunnels in the Anglo-Saxon period has been historically examined (Wentersdorf 1981). The fact, however, that this poem is placed directly after the first sequence of riddles in the Exeter Book (*Riddles* 1–59) draws attention to the generic meaning of its *giedd*, on line 1, as a 'riddle'. Unless the riddles themselves were intended to be enjoyed without their readers or listeners asking specific questions, this poem's lack of detail could be treated as an incitement to find a solution. Apart from textual problems that encourage this, there are no names of persons or places, nor any setting in a recognisable time, nor a linear chronology by which to find an unambiguous narrative. These omissions would allow us to call *The Wife's Lament* a riddle, albeit one of a rather different kind. Its psychology of exile has an undeniable power. Its narrative is equally gripping, scrambled as it is. The theme of marital, or pre- or extra-marital, love is rare enough. What no one will dispute is that *The Wife's Lament* is about love.

Various stories have been found to map on to this poem about love. The departed husband could be the gadabout Ecgtheow in the background of *Beowulf*, for example (Biddle 1997). The Wife may be dead, speaking from beyond the grave, as a valkyrie does in the Norse *Helgakviða Hundingsbana II* 'Second Lay of Helgi Hundingsbane' (Johnson 1983; see also Lench 1970). Or she may be the mound spirit of the old religion whose devotee, by becoming Christian, has abandoned her (Doane 1966), or an English version of Gerðr, the coerced giantess in *The Lay of Skírnir* whom Freyr is due to love and leave in nine days' time (Orton 1989; Luyster 1998; see **Gods of the Vikings**). It is even possible to match the Wife's emotions with the vehemence of Brynhildr's lost love for Sigurðr when the young prince stays with her after fighting the dragon Fáfnir. *The Wife's Lament* could thus be read as an English variant on the Germanic legend of Sigurðr's 'prior betrothal' with Brynhildr (see *The Fragmentary Lay of Sigurðr* and *The First Lay of Guðrún*). This seems less likely, but it is intriguing, nonetheless, that *The Wife's Lament* allows such possibilities. Sigurðr goes off with promises to return, which he forgets by drinking a potion from Guðrún's mother. Sigurðr's initial absence could be read into the situation of *The Husband's Message*, as is the present editor's view, but a mapping of Sigurðr's 'prior betrothal' on to *The Wife's Lament* seems less certain. This is so if we remember that the speaker meets her man before she moves to her protective enclosure.

So far the wisest approach to *The Wife's Lament* has been to read this poem as an allegory for the marriage between Jesus and Holy Church, or Jesus and the Soul (Swanton 1964; Bolton 1969; Bradley 1982: 382–4). If the erotic love of The Song of Solomon is in the Bible already under the pretext of being allegory for the same, why not in *The Wife's Lament*? Jesus' Jerusalem mission to Calvary, followed by his absence after Resurrection in the time before the Second Coming, is an attractive key to the *The Wife's Lament*, for here it is less a past narrative than an inferable situation in a 'Last Days' present. At the same time, if this allegory was true of his aims, the poet was free to express an unusual emotional range.

The most up-to-date edition is that of A. L. Klinck, *The Old English Elegies: A Critical Edition and Genre Study* (Montreal and Kingston, 1992), which may be supplemented by B. Mitchell and F. C. Robinson, ed., *A Guide to Old English*, 4th ed. (Oxford, 1986).

Belanoff, P., '"Ides . . . geomrode giddum": the Old English female lament', in *Medieval Women's Song*, ed. A. L. Klinck and A.-M. Rasmussen (Philadelphia, PA, 2002), 29–46 and 214–18

Biddle, E., '*Ecgtheow's Message*? A possible link between *The Husband's Message* and *Beowulf*', *Parergon* 15.1 (1997), 1–19

Bolton, W. F., '*The Wife's Lament* and *The Husband's Message*: a reconsideration revisited', *Archiv für das Studium der neueren Sprachen und Literaturen* 205 (1969), 337–51

Bradley, S. A. J., trans., *Anglo-Saxon Poetry: An Anthology of Old English Poems in Prose Translation* (London, 1982)

Doane, A. N., 'Heathen form and Christian function in *The Wife's Lament*', *Mediaeval Studies* 28 (1966), 77–91

Greenfield, S. B., '*The Wife's Lament* reconsidered', *Publications of the Modern Language Association* 68 (1953), 907–12

Jensen, E., '*The Wife's Lament*'s *eorðscræf*: literal or figural sign?', *Neuphilologische Mitteilungen* 91 (1990), 449–57

Johnson, W., Jr., '*The Wife's Lament* as death-song', in *The Old English Elegies: New Essays in Criticism and Research*, ed. Martin Green (Rutherford, CT, 1983), 69–81

Lench, E., '*The Wife's Lament*: a poem of the living dead', *Comitatus* 1 (1970), 3–23

Lucas, A. M., 'The narrator of *The Wife's Lament*', *Neuphilologische Mitteilungen* 70 (1969), 282–97

Luyster, R., '*The Wife's Lament* in the context of Scandinavian myth and ritual', *Philological Quarterly* 77 (1998), 243–70

Orton, P. R., '*The Wife's Lament* and *Skírnismál*: some parallels', in *Úr Dölum til Dala: Guðbrandur Vigfússon Centenary Essays*, ed. R. McTurk and A. Wawn, Leeds Texts and Monographs new series 11 (Leeds, 1989), 205–35

Rickert, E., 'The Old English Offa Saga, II', *Modern Philology* 2 (1904–5), 365–76

Rissanen, M., 'The theme of "exile" in *The Wife's Lament*', *Neuphilologische Mitteilungen* 70 (1969), 90–104

Stevens, M., 'The narrator of *The Wife's Lament*', *Neuphilologische Mitteilungen* 69 (1968), 72–90

Stevick, R. E., 'Formal aspects of *The Wife's Lament*', *Journal of English and Germanic Philology* 59 (1960), 21–5

Swanton, M. J., '*The Wife's Lament* and *The Husband's Message*: a reconsideration', *Anglia* 82 (1964), 268–90

Walker-Pelkey, F., '*Frige hwæt ic hatte*: *The Wife's Lament* as riddle', *PLL* 28 (1992), 242–66

Ward, J. A., '*The Wife's Lament*: an interpretation', *Journal of English and Germanic Philology* 59 (1960), 26–33

Wentersdorf, K., 'The situation of the narrator in the Old English *Wife's Lament*', *Speculum* 56 (1981), 492–516

Ic þis giedd wrece   bi me ful geomorre,
minre sylfre sið.   Ic þæt secgan mæg,
hwæt ic yrmþa gebad,   siþþan ic up weox,
niwes oþþe ealdes,   no ma þonne nu.
A ic wite wonn   minra wræcsiþa.
Ærest min hlaford gewat   heonan of leodum
ofer yþa gelac,   hæfde ic uhtceare
hwær min leodfruma   londes wære.
Ða ic me feran gewat   folgað secan,
wineleas wr*æ*cca,   for minre weaþearfe,
ongunnon þæt þæs monnes   magas hycgan
þurh dyrne geþoht,   þæt hy todælden unc,
þæt wit gewidost   in woruldrice
lifdon laðlicost,   ond mec longade.
Het mec hlaford min   herheard niman.
Ahte ic leofra lyt   on þissum londstede,
holdra freonda.   Forþon is min hyge geomor.
Ða ic me ful gemæcne   monnan funde,
heardsæligne,   hygegeomorne,

This lament about me I utter in misery,
a story about myself. I am able to say
what sufferings I endured since I grew up,
old ones and new, never more than now.
Ever did I fight the torment of my being exiled.
First my lord moved off from his own people
across the play of waves, and I had anguish at dawn
as to where, in which land, my prince might be.
When I went to look for his retinue myself,
a friendless exile through the woeful poverty I was in,
the kinsmen of this man, while hiding their intent,
began to plot how to part us each from other,
since when in this worldly kingdom the two of us
have lived most hatefully apart, and longing has seized me.
My lord told me to dwell in a heathen grove.
I had nobody to love in this backwoods homestead,
no loyal friends. And so my mind laments.
Back then I found myself a perfect match,
a man with cruel destiny, serious in purpose,

---

1 *bi me ful geomorre* 'about me in misery'. The *–re* ending on *geomor* 'sad', which is feminine dative singular, identifies the speaker as a woman. Rarely has grammar been so important.

18 The adverb *Ða* 'then' is doing a lot of work here, but if the time is not set in this way earlier than the story we have heard from the Wife so far, we must see the Wife accepting a new husband after she has proved unable to locate her old one: an interesting motif of infidelity, but one without match in a tale found so far.

mod miþendne, morþor hycgendne,
bliþe gebæro. Ful oft wit beotedan
þæt unc ne gedælde nemne deað ana
owiht elles. Eft is þæt onhworfen,
is nu swa hit [. . .] no wære,
freondscipe uncer. Sceal ic feor ge neah
mines felaleofan fæhðu dreogan.
Heht mec mon wunian on wuda bearwe,
under actreo in þam eorðscræfe.
Eald is þes eorðsele, eal ic eom oflongad,
sindon dena dimme, duna uphea,
bitre burgtunas, brerum beweaxne,
wic wynna leas. Ful oft mec her wraþe begeat
fromsiþ frean. Frynd sind on eorþan,
leofe lifgende, leger weardiað,
þonne ic on uhtan ana gonge
under actreo geond þas eorðscrafu.
Þær ic sittan mot sumorlangne dæg,

---

concealing his mind, plotting a murder,
with a happy expression. Full often did we vow
that nothing could part us except death itself,
and nothing else. That is now turned around,
it is now as if it had never been,
each person's love for the other. Far or near I must
endure the feud of my man whom I much love.
I was told to live in a forest clearing,
in the earth dug-out under an oak-tree.
Old is this earth-hall, my longing all obsesses me,
the valleys are dark, the downs sky-high,
the protecting hedges bite, overgrown with briars,
a home with no joy at all. Full often here am I angrily surprised
by my king's absence. There are lovers on earth,
living ones dear to each other who keep their beds,
when I, in the early dawn, walk alone
beneath the oak-tree through these dug-out caves.
There I may sit for a summer's day,

---

21 *bliþe gebæro* 'with a happy expression'. Some read this phrase as the start of a new sentence with the half-line following. This is true to the spirit of lover's vows, but it produces a sense-break more awkward than the one in mid-line, characteristic of Old English 'hook-style'. The effect of concealment, of a man plotting (if Christ, His own imminent) murder while keeping this with a smile from his intended, would also be lost.

26 *mines felaleofan* 'my man whom I much love'. This epithet resembles *margdýrr konungr* 'a king much-precious', used by Brynhildr of the dead Sigurðr in *The Fragment of The Lay of Sigurðr*, stanza 19.

þær ic wepan mæg   mine wræcsiþas,
earfoþa fela.   Forþon ic æfre ne mæg
þære modceare   minre gerestan,
ne ealles þæs longaþes   þe mec on þissum life begeat.
A scyle geong mon   wesan geomormod,
heard heortan geþoht,   swylce habban sceal
bliþe gebæro,   eac þon breostceare,
sinsorgna gedreag.   Sy æt him sylfum gelong
eal his worulde wyn,   sy ful wide fah
feorres folclondes   þæt min freond siteð
under stanhliþe   storme behrimed,
wine werigmod   wætre beflowen
on dreorsele,   dreogeð se min wine
micle modceare: he gemon to oft
wynlicran wic.   Wa bið þam þe sceal
of langoþe   leofes abidan.

---

there I may weep for the times I am in exile,
for many hardships. That is why I will never
be able to rest from these sufferings of my mind,
nor from all the longing which seized me in this life.
Ever should a young man be serious in mind,
hard his purpose of heart, and likewise he must keep
a happy expression, to go with the cares in his breast,
his rabble of constant sorrows. Be it in his own hands,
all his joy in this world, be it as a remote outcast
in a country far away that my lover sits
befrosted with the gale under a stone cliff,
my friend weary of mind, surrounded by water
in a hall of desolation, this friend of mine suffers
great anguish of mind: too often he remembers
a more joyful home. Woe for them who must
in longing await the coming of a beloved.

42–53 The Wife's parting injunction, for a young man to behave just as her husband did, is ironically altruistic, but may also show, if this is really Jesus and Holy Church, that she has intuited the reasons for her husband's prolonged absence. However, her final image of the separated lover has also been read as a curse (Greenfield 1953).

The Husband's Message

The Husband's Message was once believed to be the finishing section of *Riddle* 60 (*Ic wæs be sonde* 'I was by the sand'), the text just before it in the Exeter Book. This riddle also has seashore imagery, but is otherwise distinct and is now usually edited as a separate poem (probably for a 'reed pen'; Klinck 1992: 198; though see also Williamson 1977: '58', 315–20). As regards the poem now called *The Husband's Message*, nobody would dispute that in situation it is the story of a nobleman sending for his wife. One might add that its language tends to the legalistic, as from a messenger acting like a clerk. Some may prefer to leave it at that, to explore this poem for insights into male feelings and the rules and emotions of an aristocratic Anglo-Saxon marriage.

Yet this poem might also be read as the happy ending of *The Wife's Lament*, which is placed at the end of *Riddles* 1–59 (Howlett 1978). In tandem with this, *The Husband's Message* is argued to be 'an immutable covenant', with the message 'that, in answer to the faithful longing, love has called Jerusalem (the Church, the soul of man) to what is duly hers in heaven by virtue of espousal to Christ' (Bradley 1982: 398–9; from Swanton 1964, Bolton 1969). Such a reading works well with *The Wife's Lament*, a poem whose situation seems to have much in common with this one, and the marriage of Jesus and Holy Church was a doctrinal commonplace (through Isaiah 54:4–7). Most readers, however, would treat *The Husband's Message* as heroic, given its runes, which have no clear religious message. The speaker, the Husband's messenger, may be the stick that carries the runes that deliver the message (as a yew-stick, Pope 1978: 42–63).

The present text treats these runes as an anagram of 'Sigeweard', the Old English form of 'Sigurðr', in a story that may be connected to the Nibelung cycle in the Poetic *Edda*. It has already been suggested that the story is that of Sigurðr's love for Guðrún (Bouman 1962: 41–91). 'Brynhildr', however, works better as the woman to whom the message is sent. According to stanza 27 of the synoptic Nibelung poem *Grípisspá* 'Gríprir's Prophecy', Sigurðr meets Brynhildr at the house of her foster-father, Heimir. This meeting takes place after he slays Fáfnir and before he meets the family of Gjúki. It is the queen of the latter court who gives him the potion to forget Brynhildr and fall in love with her daughter Guðrún. Grípir, who is Sigurðr's mother's brother, foresees all of this. In stanza 29, he foretells that Brynhildr will rob Sigurðr of his happiness and life: 'no sleep will you have, nor will you care for lawsuits, you'll take no notice of anyone unless you can see the girl' (Larrington 1996: 147). When Sigurðr asks if he will marry Brynhildr, his uncle says: *It munuð alla eiða vinna, fullfastliga, fá munuð halda* 'You two will swear all your oaths very strongly, few will you keep', before revealing that Sigurðr will forget Brynhildr at Gjúki's, *mantattu horska Heimis fóstru* 'you won't recall the wise fosterling of Heimir' (stanza 31).

There is some evidence that this is this about to happen in *The Husband's Message*. The *fæhþo* 'feud' (line 19) which sent the Husband away in the first place would be Sigurðr's duty to avenge his father (*Gríprir's Prophecy*, stanza 9). In lines 25–9, the supply of gold which he has (*he genoh hafað fædan gold[es]*) could be the dragon's Nibelung hoard (if it is he, not his father Sigemund, who kills the dragon in this tradition); and the home he keeps in a foreign country (*elþeode eþel healde*) and the attendant men (*[hold]ra hæleþa*) would speak for Sigurðr's recent place as blood-brother of Gunnarr and Hǫgni in Gjúki's court in Burgundy. *The Husband's Message* seems to match the *alla eiða* 'all oaths' of the Norse tradition, in its own *aþe* 'oath' pronounced in and by the Husband's name (line 50), as well as in *wordbeotunga* 'promises' (line 15), *eald gebeot* 'old vow' (line 49) and *þa wære ond þa winetreowe* 'the agreement and the pledge of association' (line 52). And with the queen's potion in mind, we might note a dreadful irony in the runestick's claim about the Husband, that, to see his woman once more, *ne mæg him worulde willa [gelimpan] mara on gemyndum* 'no joy in this world can [befall] him greater in memory' (lines 30–1).

Bolton, W. F., '*The Wife's Lament* and *The Husband's Message*: a reconsideration revisited', *Archiv für das Studium der neueren Sprachen und Literaturen* 205 (1969), 337–51

Bouman, A. C., *Patterns in Old English and Old Icelandic Literature* (Leiden, 1962)

Bradley, S. A. J., trans., *Anglo-Saxon Poetry: An Anthology of Old English Poems in Prose Translation* (London, 1982)

Howlett, D., '*The Wife's Lament* and *The Husband's Message*', *Neuphilologische Mitteilungen* 79 (1978), 7–10

Klinck, A. L., *The Old English Elegies: A Critical Edition and Genre Study* (Montreal and Kingston, 1992)

Larrington, C., trans., *The Poetic Edda* (Oxford, 1996)

Leslie, R. F., ed., *Three Old English Elegies: 'The Wife's Lament', 'The Husband's Message' and 'The Ruin'*, 2nd ed. (Exeter, 1988)

Niles, J. D., 'The trick of the runes in *The Husband's Message*', *Anglo-Saxon England* 32 (2003), 198–233

Page, R. I., *An Introduction to English Runes*, 2nd ed. (Woodbridge, 1999)

Pope, J. C., 'Palaeography and poetry: some solved and unsolved problems of the Exeter Book', in *Medieval Scribes, Manuscripts and Libraries: Essays Presented to N. R. Ker*, ed. M. B. Parkes and A. G. Watson (London, 1978), 25–65

Swanton, M. J., '*The Wife's Lament* and *The Husband's Message*: a reconsideration', *Anglia* 82 (1964), 268–90

Williamson, Craig, *The Old English Riddles of the Exeter Book* (Chapel Hill, NC, 1977)

Nu ic onsundran þe secgan wille
[............] treocyn. Ic tudre aweox;
in mec æld[a bearn ærende] sceal
ellor londes settan [..........................]c,
sealte streamas [......................wi]sse.
Ful oft ic on bates [bosme..............] gesohte
þær mec mondryhten min [..........]
ofer heah h*a*fu; eom nu her cumen
on ceolþele, ond nu cunnan scealt
hu þu ymb modlufan mines frean
on hyge hycge. Ic gehatan dear
þæt þu þær tirfæste treowe findest.
Hwæt, þec þonne biddan het se þisne beam agrof
þæt þu sinchroden sylf gemunde
on gewitlocan wordbeotunga,
þe git on ærdagum oft gespræcon,
þenden git moston on meoduburgum
eard weardigan, an lond bugan,
freondscype fremman. Hine fæhþo adraf

Now in privacy I wish to tell you
[.................] kind of wood. With offspring I grew up;
[the son] of men on me [a message] shall
set down, [....................] in another land,
salt currents [........................knew].
Very often did I seek [..........] in the boat's [hold],
where my man and master [...............] me
over the high seas; I have now come here
on ship's deck, and now you must make known
what thoughts about my lord's heartfelt love
you may be thinking. I dare promise
that you will find there a firm and glorious pledge.
Listen, he who cut this wood told me to ask you
that you, adorned with precious things, should
in your wits-enclosure recall the promises
which in early days you both often spoke about
while still you might in towns of mead
keep the country, inhabit the same land,
show friendship. A feud drove him

2–7 The text necessary to complete these lines was destroyed in the manuscript, when the Exeter Book was damaged either by being left lying on a griddle which burned into its back, or by having a brand laid over it. The same damage accounts for the other gaps in this poem, whose meaning may only just be salvaged. Facsimile pages of the relevant folio, 123 recto and verso, are in Klinck (1992: Plates).

3 Leslie's reconstruction (1988: 59).

of sigeþeode; heht nu sylfa þe
lustum læran, þæt þu lagu drefde,
siþþan þu gehyrde on hliþes oran
galan geomorne geac on bearwe.
Ne læt þu þec siþþan siþes getwæfan,
lade gelettan lifgendne monn.
Ongin mere secan, mæwes eþel,
onsite sænacan, þæt þu suð heonan
ofer merelade monnan findest,
þær se þeoden is þin on wenum.
Ne mæg him worulde willa [gelimpan]
mara on gemyndum, þæs þe he me sægde,
þonne inc geunne alwaldend God
[þæt git] ætsomne siþþan motan
secgum ond gesiþum s[inc brytnian,]
næglede beagas; he genoh hafað
fædan gold[es þæt he................]
[geon]d elþeode eþel healde,

---

from his victorious people; he himself tells me now
joyfully to instruct you that you put to sea
as soon as on cliff's edge you have heard
a cuckoo singing sadly in his grove.
Don't let yourself be thwarted from the voyage,
hindered from travel by any living man.
Go down to seek the ocean, seagull's homeland,
board a sea-going ship, so that south from here
across the ocean road you will find a man
just where your king expects you.
No joy in this world can [befall] him
greater in memory, from what he told me,
than that Almighty God grant the two of you
the right together from this time forth
to [deal out treasure] to men and retainers,
bossed necklaces; enough store he has
of burnished gold [that he ....]
[in] foreign parts may keep a home,

---

25 *lifgendne monn* 'any living man'. If this is an English tale of Sigurðr, the irony consists of this man being the forgetful Husband himself, disguised as Prince Guthere on whose behalf he courts the woman yet again.

30 *[gelimpan]* 'befall'. There is no gap in the manuscript.

33–4 *[þæt git]* and *s[inc brytnian]* are old and clever suggestions for the manuscript gaps at these points (Leslie 1988: 50, 62–3; not taken up in Klinck 1992: 101, 203–4).

36 *[þæt he]* 'that he'. Supplied by the present editor, as required by the present third person singular subjunctive *healde* 'may keep' on line 37.

37 *[geon]d* 'in'. Supplied by Leslie (1988: 63).

fægre fold[an..........................]
hold]ra hæleþa, þeah þe her min wine
[......................................]
nyde gebæded, nacan ut aþrong,
ond on yþa gela[gu ana] sceolde
faran on flotweg, forðsiþes georn,
mengan merestreamas. Nu se mon hafað
wean oferwunnen; nis him wilna gad,
ne meara ne maðma ne meododreama,
ænges ofer eorþan eorlgestreona,
þeodnes dohtor, gif he þin beneah
ofer eald gebeot incer twega.
Ge*h*yre ic ætsomne ᛋ [***sige***l] ᚱ [***r***ad] geador,

---

a fair land [....................................]
of [loyal] men, though here my friend
[..],
driven by necessity, pushed out his vessel
and on rolling waves [alone] was forced
to sail the shipping lanes, keen to put out,
swirl the ocean currents. Now has the man
defeated his woes; he will need for no pleasure,
neither horses nor riches nor joys of drinking mead,
nor any man's treasure on the face of the earth,
O king's daughter, once he has taken you
according to the old vow that each of you made.
I hear the runes in harmony, **S**un and **R**oad together,

---

40 The manuscript gap is sufficient for one line to have been lost (so Leslie 1988: 50; Klinck 1992: 101).

44–8 The formula here is an elaborated version of *einnar mér Freyju ávant þykkir* 'I want only Freyja to think it complete', words of the giant who otherwise has everything in *The Thunderclap Ballad*, stanza 23 (see **Gods of the Vikings**).

50 *Gehyre* 'I hear'. So Klinck (1992: 102 and 206–7), who shows that the third letter in this word was erased, and argues that the scribe wrote *n* in error and erased this without putting in his desired letter. *Gehyre* is more straightforward than *gecyre* 'I might have chosen' or *genyre* 'I constrain to declare'.

49–50 The runes ᛋ ᚱ ᛠ ᚹ are undisputed, respectively for *sigel* 'sun', *rad* 'road', *eard* 'homeland' and *wynn* 'joy'; words that are needed to complete the sense. The final rune, however, ᛞ, which is clearly written for *dæg* 'day', is read by most scholars as if it were ᛗ for *monn* 'man'. But it is clearly written for 'day'. The meaning of these runes, for sun, road, homeland, joy and day, looks like a sequence of desired actions: get up in the morning, take the road, find a home, be in joy, for the rest of your days. These words also suggest terms for 'heaven above': sun-road; joy of the world; day. Third, and most importantly, they spell out a word or name. The meanings for the relevant Anglo-Saxon runes are given in Page (1999: 65–75), on the basis of the early eleventh-century *Rune Poem*. Niles (2003) departs from these guidelines for his interpretation of *The Husband's Message*, as if the runes could stand for any words alliterating with the original ones. As the runes are written, however, ᛋ ᚱ ᛠ ᚹ ᛞ, **S-R-W-E-D**, they may be read as an anagram of a name: **Sige-w-ea-r-d**, if we extend the first one, *sigel*, to almost its full extent (the final *-l* in *-el* suffixes was commonly dropped in names such as *Æþered* for *Æþelred*). *Sigeweard* is the Old English form of OIce *Sigurðr*.

ᛠᚹ [***ea***rd***w***yn] ond ᛞ [***d***æg]   aþe benemnan,
þæt he þa wære   ond þa winetreowe
be him lifgendum   læstan wolde,
þe git on ærdagum   oft gespræconn.

Ecstasy of the **W**orld and **D**ay pronounce their oath,
that he would carry out, as long as he lived to do so,
the agreement and the pledge of association
which in early days you both often spoke about.

The Lay of Hamðir

Hamðismál

*

The Lay of Hamðir, as the translator Lee M. Hollander once put it, 'enjoys the sad distinction of having been handed down in a more fragmentary condition than any other of the longer Eddic lays' (1962: 316). This poem is probably as old as *The Lay of Attila*, if not older, for *The Lay of Hamðir*, or another poem on the same theme, was used by Bragi Boddason in his *Eulogy on Ragnarr* as early as the mid-ninth century. It is closely related to another Eddic lay, *Guðrúnarhvǫt* 'The incitement of Guðrún', which also shows the lady sending off her sons, Hamðir and Sǫrli, to avenge their sister. A discussion of the relevant network of poetic and thematic relationships may be found in von See (1977) and further under *Deor* and Bragi's *Eulogy on Ragnarr* in **Heroic Poems.** There is no telling how old is the passage that is quoted from the *Lay* below, from Guðrún's final lament, in which she compares herself with a lonely tree. The situation is here less important than the suffering woman's poetic expression, which may be usefully compared with that of the Wife in *The Wife's Lament.*

The story, however, at the start of *The Lay of Hamðir* is that Svanhildr, Guðrún's daughter by Sigurðr, has been executed by the Gothic emperor Jǫrmunrekkr, to whom Guðrún's family unwisely married her off, on an unfounded suspicion of adultery with Randvér, Jǫrmunrekkr's son by an earlier marriage. Somewhat ruefully, Hamðir and Sǫrli ride to the land of the Goths to carry out their mother's vengeance, meeting Erpr on the way, who is their half-brother Jónakr's son by his previous marriage. Erpr offers his help but they cut him down instead, when he accuses them of cowardice, for having failed to understand the wording of his offer, to help them *sem fótr ǫðrum* 'as one foot to another' (stanza 13). Later (when Jǫrmunrekkr's head, the limb they leave last in their slow-paced removal of his legs and arms, divines their weakness and orders their destruction by stoning to death) the brothers come to regret not bringing Erpr, who would have started with the head. Savagely enough, the poem as it stands appears to mythologise 'family' as one entity with its members functioning as limbs. This is hardly a theme to be found in *The Wife's Lament.* Nonetheless, the position of the Wife there *under actreowe* 'under an oak tree', on line 28, does open up all kinds of possible meanings, such as the notion that the Wife, in her exiled state, is now comparable with the oak as a solitary but powerful tree, much as Guðrún comes to be with the massive aspen, or poplar, left standing high above the scrubland in a *holt* 'copse'.

Brady, C. A., *The Legends of Ermanaric* (Berkeley, 1943)

Dronke, U., ed., trans. and comm., *The Poetic Edda, vol. I: Heroic Poems* (Oxford, 1969), 161–242, especially 161–2, 168–9, 225–7

Hollander, L. M., 'The legendary form of *Hamðismál*', *Arkiv för nordisk filologi* 77 (1962), 56–62

Hollander, L. M., trans., *The Poetic Edda*, 2nd ed. (Austin, TX, 1962)

Larrington, C., trans., *The Poetic Edda* (Oxford, 1996)

von See, K., '*Guðrúnarhvǫt* und *Hamðismál*', *Beiträge zur Geschichte der deutschen Sprache und Literatur* 99 (1977), 250–58

Shippey, T. A., 'Speech and the unspoken in *Hamðismál*', in *Prosody and Poetics in the Early Middle Ages: Essays in Honour of C. B. Hieatt*, ed. M. J. Toswell (Toronto, 1995), 180–96

Guðrún's lament

1 Spruttu á tái tregnar íðir,
grœti alfa in glýstǫmu;
ár of morgin manna bǫlva
sútir hverjar sorg of kveykva.

Sprouted on the pavement deeds to be regretted,
The weeping of elves, tamed of glee.
Early in the morning, from men's wicked deeds
Every affliction kindles a new sorrow.

2 Vara þat nú né í gær,
þat hefir langt liðit síðan,
er fátt fornara, fremr var þat halfu,
er hvatti Guðrún Gjúka borin,
sonu sína unga at hefna Svanhildar:

It wasn't now nor yesterday,
A long time has passed since then,
Little is more ancient and this was twice as old,
When Guðrún, born to Gjúki, incited
Her young sons to avenge Svanhildr.

3 'Systir var ykkur Svanhildr of heitin,
sú er Jǫrmunrekkr jóm of traddi,
hvítum ok svǫrtum á hervegi,
grám, gangtǫmum Gotna hrossum.

'The sister of you two, her name was Svanhildr,
Was trodden down by Jǫrmunrekkr, with steeds
White and black on the army highway,
Grey, tamed to riding, horses of the Goths.

---

1 This sententious stanza is doubtless a new portal, built on to the older repairs of the ruin of *The Lay of Hamðir*. It resembles in that way the parting stanza of *The Lay of Attila*, which is likewise based on an old, probably tenth-century, poem.

3 Guðrún addresses Hamðir and Sǫrli, her two sons by King Jónakr, her husband after Attila, whom she wants to avenge her daughter by Sigurðr.

4 'Eftir er ykkr þrungit þjóðkonunga;
lifið einir ér þátta ættar minnar.

'Behind the two of you is a dynasty wiped out,
You alone live of the strands of my family.

5 'Einstœð em ek orðin, sem ǫsp í holti,
fallin at frændum sem fura at kvisti,
vaðin at vilja, sem viðr at laufi,
þá er in kvistskœða kemr um dag varman.'

'I am left to stand alone like the aspen in a copse,
With kinsmen fallen off me like branches of a fir-tree,
Wasted of joys like the wood of leaves
When the branch-ripping girl comes by on a warm day.'

---

4 And after the boys have been killed by Jǫrmunrekkr's men (see Bragi's *Eulogy on Ragnarr*, **Heroic Poems**), Guðrún's Burgundian 'Nibelung' line will be fully extinct.

5 Aspens, or poplars, reach 100 feet in height in the south of Norway, standing out easily from the scrub of any copse standing around them (Dronke 1969: 227). The *holt* 'copse' may refer to a birch-wood. The tree in *The Wife's Lament*, line 28, as an oak, is of different type, but may likewise stand for the lonely woman who is left to bear a burden by herself.

The Exile of the Sons of Uisliu

Longes mac n-Uislenn

✳

The two poems cited here, better known as 'Deirdre of the Sorrows', finish the longer work, 'The Exile of the Sons of Uisliu', of which the first 16 chapters are given above in **Heroic Poems**. These two elegies resolve the story of tragic love between Deirdre, the woman whose beauty is prophesied to cause wars between the men who fall in love with her, and Noisiu, nephew of King Conchobar mac Nessa of Ulster who has coveted her from her childhood. The bulk of the story was doubtless the model for the romance of Tristan and Iseult (see Thomas of Britain's *Tristan*, **Early Chivalry**).

Deirdre of the Sorrows

After Noisiu's death, the tale becomes elegiac. Deirdre is made captive in the marriage with Conchobar that the king had planned for her, then passed on by him to Eogan, his vassal, in revenge for her unrelenting coldness. The text here is slightly simplified and with the translation modernised on the basis of that by Vernam Hull (1949), some of whose scholarly doubts over some readings have respectfully been smoothed over. The *Longes mac n-Uislenn* 'The exile of the sons of Uisliu' is a poem with prose, a sort of prosimetrum rather like *The Lay of Wayland*, *The First Lay of Guðrún* and other heroic poems of the Icelandic Poetic *Edda*. As Deirdre's lament bears comparison with those of Guðrún and other tales of grieving women, so is it worth considering as an analogue of sorts with the Old English poem *The Wife's Lament*.

Hull, V., ed. and trans., *Longes Mac n-Uislenn: The Exile of the Sons of Uisliu* (New York, 1949)

17. Blíadain di-ssi trá i fail Chonchobuir ocus risin rē sin nitib gen ngāire ocus nidōid a sáith do bíud na cotluth ocus ni-tūargaib a cenn dia glún. In tan didiu dombertis na hairfiti dī, is and asbered-si in reicni sea sís:

---

17. A year now Deirdre had been with Conchobar, and during that time she didn't smile one laughing smile, nor did she take the food or sleep that she needed, nor raise her head from her knee. In this way, whenever they brought her musicians, she would utter a spontaneous lament:

---

17. *Asbered-si in reicni* 'would utter spontaneous lament'. The type of extempore poem, to which Old Irish *reicni* appears to refer, seems closely comparable to the ways in which OE *giedd wrecan* 'to compose a song, recite an elegy' is employed in the Exeter Book and elsewhere; and seems also true of the suffering latent in OIce *geð* 'soul, inclination' such as this is used in *Sonatorrek*, Egill's elegy for his sons (*c.* 960).

Cid cāin

1 Cid cāin lib ind lǽchrad lainn
cengtae i n-Emain īar tochaim,
airdiu docingtis dia taig
trí maic adlǽchda Uisnig.

Fair though you deem those keen warriors
Who stride about in Emain after a raid,
More nobly would the three high heroic sons
Of Uisliu march to their dwelling.

2 Noísi co mmid chollān chain –
folcud lim-sa dó'con tein –
arddan co ndam nó muicc mais,
asclang Aindli dar ardd-ais.

Noisiu with the good hazel mead –
His body I used to wash at the fire –
Arddan with a stag or fine pig, what a
Load that would be on Aindle's tall back!

3 Cid milis lib a mmid mas
ibes mac Nesa nīth-mas,
baīthium riäm – rén for brú –
bíäd menic ba millsiu.

Sweet though you deem the good mead
Which, glorious in battle, Mac Nessa drinks,
Time was when – across the lip of ocean –
I'd often have a meal that was sweeter.

4 Ō rosernad Noísi nár
fulocht for feda fīan-chlār,
ba millsiu cach bīud fo mil
ararālad mac Usnig.

As often as shy Noisiu would spread out
The cooking hearth on the forest's tough floor,
Sweeter than each honeyed morsel here
Was what the sons of Uisliu could contrive.

5 Cid bindi lib in cach mí
cuslennaig is cornairi,
is sí mo chobais in-diu:
rocūala céol bad bindiu.

Melodious though you deem at all times
Pipers and hornblowers to be,
This is my confession today, that
I have heard music more melodious still.

6 Bind la Conchobor for rí
cuslennaig is cornairi;
ba bindiu lem-sa – cloth n-ell –
sían nogebtis maic Uislenn.

Melodious was how your king, Conchobar,
Deemed pipers and hornblowers to be;
More melodious I, the fame of hosts, would deem
The tune which the sons of Uisliu sang.

7 Fogur tuinne toirm Noīsi;
ba cēol bind a bith-chlóisi.
Coblach Arddāin ro-po mairth,
andord Aindli dia ūar-baith.

Noisiu's voice, the sound of a wave,
To hear him was always like tuneful music.
The baritone of Arddan was good, and
Aindle's tenor on the way to his shieling.

8 Noísi, dorōnad a fert.
Ba dirsan in chomaitrecht.
Dō rodālius – drong tria alt –
in dig tonnaid dian-ērbalt.

Noisiu, his burial mound has been made.
Tragic was the accompaniment.
Through it I nourished a host, through
The deadly draught of which he died.

9 Inmain berthán áilli blai,
tuchtach duine cid dind-blai.
Ba dirsan nad[f]resco in-diu
mac Uislenn do idnaidiu.

Beloved the crop of hair with golden beauty,
Beloved the warrior, noble, very shy,
After a journey beyond the forest edge
Beloved the act of escorting at dawn.

17.9 'crop of hair with golden beauty'. Deirdre's hair, beloved of Noisiu, rather than the reverse, given that Noisiu's hair is said to be raven black in ch. 7.

10 Immain menma cobsaid cáir;
inmain óclach ard imnāir.
Īar n-imthecht dar feda fál,
inmain cosatl i tiugnár.

Beloved the blue-green eye that women would love,
Fierce it used to be against foes.
After a circuit of the forest – a noble union –
Beloved was the tenor song through the dark great wood.

11 Inmain súil glass carddais mná;
ba hamnas fri ēcrata.
Īar cúairt chaille – comul sǽr –
inmain andord tria dub-rǽd.

I don't sleep now,
Nor do I dye red my nails.
Joy, it comes not into my ken, since
It won't bring Tindell's sons back here.

12 Nicotlu trá,
ocus nicorcu m'ingne.
Fáilte, nitāet imm airi,
ōr nachtaidi mac Tindle.

I do not sleep
The half-night I lie trying.
My reason is distraught, from host to host,
Not only do I not eat, but I don't laugh.

13 Nicotlu
leth na haidche im ligiu.
Foceird mo chēill imm drungu;
sech nilungu, nitibiu.

Joy, I have no leisure for that today
In the gathering at Emain – nobles are thronged there –
Nor peace, nor delight, nor ease,
Nor big house, nor fair adornment.

17.11 'Tindell'. Mother of Noisiu and his brothers.

17.13 'gathering at Emain'. Emain Macha (Armagh), King Conchobar's palace.

18. In tan dano nobīd Conchobor oca hālgenugud-si, is and atbered-si in reicni sea sīs:

---

18. And then, whenever Conchobar mollified her, she uttered this spontaneous lament:

A Conchobuir

1 A Chonchobuir, cid notaí?
Dorurmis dam brón fo chaí,
is ed ām [i] cēin nommair,
do serc lim ni-ba romair.

Conchobar, what troubles you?
For me you have piled weeping upon sorrow.
Yes indeed, as long as I may endure
My love for you won't come to much.

2 Ní rop āilliu lim fo nim,
ocus ní rop inmainib
t[o]ucais úaim – mór in bét –
connachacciu-sa comm éc.

What I deemed most beautiful on earth,
And what of me was the most beloved,
You have carried off – great the crime –
I shan't see any of it until my death!

3 A ingnāis is toirrselem
turcht domadbat mac Uislenn.
Caurnán cir-dub dar corp ngel.
Ba sūaichnid sech ilar fer.

His absence, it grieves me
How the son of Uisliu still appears:
A jet-black crop of curls over a white body,
It was well known beyond a multitude of men.

4 Dā ngrūad corcra cāiniu srath,
bēoil deirg, abrait fo dǽl-dath;
dēitgen némanda fo lí,
amal sōer-dath snechtaidi.

Both cheeks redder than flowers of river meadow,
Scarlet the lips, eyebrows beetle-black,
A pearly row of shining teeth
Like the noble colour of snow.

5 Ba sūaichnid a eirred nglan
eter fīanaib fer n-Alban.
Fūan cāin corcra – comul cóir –
cona imthacmung derg-óir.

Well-known was his bright apparel
Among Scottish Gaels' warrior bands.
Fair purple the mantle – a fitting union –
With its border of pure gold.

6 Inar sróIda – sét co mbríg –
imbuī cét ngem – ilar mín.
Fora imdēnum is glē
coíca unga findruine.

Of satin the tunic – a treasure with substance –
On which were a hundred gems, a gentle multitude.
To adorn it, radiant it is,
Fifty ounces of purest silver.

7 Claideb ór-duirn ina láim,
dā gaī glasa co ngoth-grāin,
finden co mbil óir buidi,
ocus taul argait fuirri.

A sword with golden pommel in his hand,
Two blue spears with javelin points,
A shield with a rim of yellow gold,
And a silver boss upon that.

8 Forruīch frinn Fergus find
ar tabairt darsa mōr-lind.
Rorir a einech ar chuirm.
Dorochratar a mōr-gluinn.

Fair Fergus committed a sin against us
By bringing us over the great sea.
He sold his honour for ale,
His great deeds went into decline.

18.5 'Among Scottish Gaels' warrior bands'. The lovers spent a period of exile apparently in the Highlands, before returning to King Conchobar.

18.8 'Fair Fergus'. See further in **Heroic Poems**. Fergus mac Roig, having stood surety for protecting the lives of Noisiu and his brothers, is tricked by Conchobar into staying behind them at a feast on their way to Emain, for his honour means he has to accept, and so fails to prevent the king's betrayal of Deirdre and the sons of Uisliu.

9

Cīa nobetis forsin muig
Ulaid im gnúis Conchobuir,
dosmbēruinn uili cen chlith
ar gnāis Noīsi maic Uisnig.

Though filling the plain might be
Ulstermen around Conchobar,
I would give all of them, I tell no lie,
For Noisiu as my companion, son of Uisliu.

10

Na briss in-diu mo chride;
mosricub mo moch-lige.
Is tressiu cuma in-dā muir,
madda ēola, a Chonchobuir.

Do not break my heart today,
Soon I shall reach my early grave.
Sorrow is stronger than the sea,
If you are wise, O Conchobar.

19. 'Cid as mó miscais lat atchí?' ar Conchobor.

'Tu-ssu ám,' or-si, 'ocus Egan mac Durthacht.'

'Bia-so dano blīadain i fail Eogain,' ar Conchobor.

Dusmbert īarum for láim Eogain. Lotar īarna bárach do ōenuch Macha. Buí-si īar cúl Eogain i carput. Dorarngert-si nahaiccfiuth a dā cēile for talmain i n-ōen-fecht.

'Maith, a Derdriu,' ol Conchobor, 'súil chǽrach eter dā rethe gnīi-siu etrum-sa ocus Eogan.'

Robaí ail chloiche mór ara cinn. Dollēici a cenn immon cloich conderna brúrig dia cinn co-mbo marb.

Longas mac n-Uislenn in-sin ocus longas Fergusa ocus aided mac n-Uislenn ocus Derdrenn.

---

19. 'What do you see that you hate most?' asked Conchobar.

'You, to be sure,' she said, 'and Eogan mac Durthacht.'

'You shall be, indeed, a year with Eogan,' said Conchobar.

After that, he put her beside Eogan. On the following day they were going to the assembly at Emain Macha. She was behind Eogan in his chariot. She had vowed not to see her two consorts on one and the same occasion on earth.

'Well, Deirdre,' said Conchobar, 'it is a sheep's eye between two rams that you make between me and Eogan!'

There was a great boulder in front of her. She dashed her head against the stone until she had made a mass of fragments of her skull, and so died.

This is the exile of the Sons of Uisliu, and the exile of Fergus, and the violent death of the Sons of Uisliu, and of Deirdre.

---

19. 'Eogan mac Durthacht'. Eogan murdered Noisiu with one thrust of his spear, through the body of Fiachu mac Fergusa (Fergus' son).

The Ruin

In two areas the text of this poem is irretrievably damaged by the burn that ate into the back of the Exeter Book. The elongated burn-hole is bigger over this text than others, because *The Ruin*, as the text that follows *The Husband's Message*, is closer to the end of the book. Consequently, *The Ruin* lives up to the name it acquired when it was first edited in the nineteenth century. The poem's merits lie in the force of description, which compresses long decay into violent action rather like 'The lament of the last survivor' in *Beowulf*, lines 2247–66. The poet's focus is specific, as if he has a real town in mind, although the drama with which his civilisation falls and rises as he moves to and fro, from past to present, also owes something to the Bible, particularly Revelations. The image of a lost city is better known in two memorable vignettes from *The Wanderer*, in lines 75–80 and 86–7, but there is one clear phrasal connection with *The Seafarer* as well. Altogether the poem is thematically close to these works, albeit the other 'elegies' are intellectually more challenging. The directness of the imagery makes it easier to classify this poem as a riddle than *Wulf and Eadwacer* and *The Wanderer*, although from time to time they drift near to that definition. If a riddle, the solution of *The Ruin* may be 'Bath', which would have been visibly closer to its late imperial Roman state in the period in which the poem was composed, probably before the mid-tenth century when the baths would have silted up. The poet's dialect may have been Mercian, even from the ninth century, and it is worth noting that in two places his language resembles that of Cynewulf's *Christ II* (Klinck 1992: 16, 62).

Klinck, A. L., *The Old English Elegies: A Critical Edition and Genre Study* (Montreal and Kingston, 1992)

Wrætlic is þes wealstan,   wyrde gebræcon;
burgstede burston,   brosnað enta geweorc.
Hrofas sind gehrorene,   hreorge torras,
hri*n*g[g]eat berofen,   hrim on lime,
scearde scurbeorge   scorene, gedrorene,
ældo undereotone.   Eorðgrap hafað

Wondrous is this wall-stone, the Fates destroyed it,
shattered the town buildings, giants' work crumbles.
Roofs are fallen in, towers are falling down,
archways missing, frost in the mortar,
scarred rain-protection cut down, ruined,
age-eaten from under. Earth's clutches hold

---

2 *burgstede burston* 'shattered the town buildings'. The poet's language, here and on line 31, appears to be modelled on Cynewulf's depiction of Doomsday in his *Christ II*, lines 810–11: *wongas hreosað, burgstede berstað* 'the hills will fall, town buildings shatter' (see **Poems of Devotion**).

waldendwyrhtan forweorone, geleorene,
heardgripe hrusan, oþ hund cnea
werþeoda gewitan. Oft þæs wag gebad
ræghar ond readfah rice æfter oþrum,
ofstonden under stormum; stea[p] geap gedreas.
Wo*ra*ð giet se [.................sta]num geheapen,
felon i[...]e
grimme gegrunden [...........................]
[......................]r(e) scan heo[..................]
[....................]g orþonc ærsceaft[..........]
[...................]g[..] lamrindum beag.
Mod mo[nade, m]yne swiftne gebrægd,
hwætred in hringas, hygerof gebond
weall walanwirum wundrum togædre.
Beorht wæron burgræced, burnsele monige,
heah horngestreon, heresweg micel,
meodoheall monig **M**dreama full,
oþþæt þæt onwende wyrd seo swiþe.
Crungon walo wide, cwoman woldagas,
swylt eall fornom secgrof[ra] wera;

---

the owners and builders, rotted, deceased,
in ground's hard grip, while a hundred generations
of humanity have come and gone. Often thus the outer wall,
lichen-grey and red-stained, outlasted one empire after another,
standing in the gales. Then steep, curved, it fell.
Still totters now the [.............], heaped with [stones],
Persisted i[n...]
grimly ground [.....................................]
[.........................] it shone, hea[ven...........]
[.......................]y skill [of] ancient creation [......]
[............................] an arch with plaster coating.
The mind prompted, stimulated a swift idea,
ingenious in arches, a brilliant man tied
a wall with metal strips by a miracle together.
Bright were the town houses, many fountain-halls,
high arches in plenty, a great melody of armies,
many a mead-hall filled with joy of men,
until Fate the Mighty altered that.
Men perished far and wide, plague-days came,
death took the entirety of sword-fighting men.

---

23 **M***dreama* 'joy of men'. The **M**-rune here (in folio 124 recto) stands not for *dæg* 'day', as in *The Husband's Message*, line 52, but for *monn* 'man'. Possibly this is a miscopying, due to a confusion with the latter **M**-rune, which can be seen lying almost directly facing on the previous folio (123 verso; see Klinck 1992: Plates).

wurdon hyra wigsteal   westenstaþolas,
brosnade burgsteall.   Betend crungon,
hergas, to hrusan.   Forþon þas hofu dreorgiað,
ond þæs teaforgeapa   tigelum sceadeð
hrostbeages hrof.   Hryre wong gecrong
gebrocen to beorgum,   þær iu beorn monig
glædmod ond goldbeorht   gleoma gefrætwe*d*,
wlonc ond wingal   wighyrstum scan,
seah on sinc, on sylfor,   on searogimmas,
on ead, on æht,   on eorcanstan,
on þas beorhtan burg   bradan rices.
Stanhofu stodan,   stream hate wearp
widan wylme,   weal eall befeng
beorhtan bosme   þær þa baþu wæron,
hat on hreþre.   Þæt wæs hyðelic!
Leton þonne geotan   l[......................]
ofer harne stan   hate streamas
und[er...]

Their altars became empty foundations,
town buildings decayed. Repairers perished,
armies, to the ground. And so those courts grow dismal,
and thus the red-arched roof sheds its tiles
over the curving rafters. In ruin the site has perished,
broken up in heaps, where, formerly, many a man
gracious and gold-bright, clad in radiance,
proud and wine-flushed in war-trappings shone,
looked on treasure, on silver, on cunning jewels,
on wealth, on property, on pure gemstones,
on this bright city from the broad empire.
The stone courts stood, the hot stream cast up
its wide wave, a wall captured all
in its bright bosom where the baths were,
hot in its heart. A convenience that was!
Then they poured [..............................],
hot streams over grey stone,
und[er...]

---

34 *wlonc ond wingal* 'proud and wine-flushed'. This is the epithet also found in *The Seafarer*, line 29, to describe the soft city-dweller without knowledge of the dangers of seafaring life.

37 *on þas beorhtan burg* 'on this bright city'. A contrast is perhaps intended here with the New Jerusalem, the jewelled city in Revelations. See also *The Sibyl's Prophecy*, stanza 64, in which apparently the latter celestial city is seen in the post-millennial order (**Gods of the Vikings**). *The Ruin* supplies the part before the end of the world, as if the town were Babylon (Klinck 1992: 62).

[o]þþæt hringmere hate [..................]
[.............................] þær þa baþu wæron.
Þonne is [...]
[...........................]re; þæt is cynelic þing,
hu se [..................................] burg[........]

---

until the round pond did hotly [..........]
[............................], where the baths were.
Then is [...]
[..............] more [........]. That is the business of kings
how the [.........................] town [......].

POEMS OF DEVOTION

* * *

POEMS OF DEVOTION

* * *

This section gives a clearer picture than the previous of how Old English literature developed. The Christianity that (through the Irish) first taught the English to write was at first a hindrance as well as a help to the unwritten poems of a preliterate secular society. Cædmon's legend and poem go some way to elucidating the difficulties in adapting heroic forms, the only secular form of any moment, to the demands of Christian liturgy. Thereafter the fusion began to take place. At first this was with runes and *The Dream of the Rood* in Northumbria, where the Anglian aristocracy endowed the Cross with a new speaking part in which it (or 'he') emerges as a tragic hero, forced against his will to obey God's will in executing Christ. The Northumbrian royals, it is argued here, celebrated themselves in *Exodus* as chosen people, migrating just like the Israelites to a promised land which is at once Christian salvation and the province of Britannia, where later the necessary baptism might be offered. Christ's parents enact dramatic roles in the *Advent Lyrics* (Custom Version), while a poet named Cynewulf once more celebrates the Cross in *Elene* and *Christ II*, breaking the code of anonymity with a runic acrostic which spells his name. Then there is *Genesis B*, a poem from northern Germany, transposed into the Saxon language of England in the Junius manuscript which Milton may or may not have seen. This poem delivers like a play, with Eve taking centre stage as the forces of evil work on her to spite Adam and God. The mood of religion then matures and seems to vary. In one case, we see the poet of *Andreas* apparently mocking *Beowulf*'s great renown in a partly comic version of the Saint's Life. In another case, the poet of Judith mixes typology with political resonance as his heroine, perhaps, becomes Alfred's daughter, the Assyrians Danes. With the texts of this chapter the picture of Old English verse will look more complete.

General bibliography

Bjork, R. E., *The Old English Verse Saints' Lives: A Study in Direct Discourse and the Iconography of Style* (Toronto, 1985), 110–31

Bjork, R. E., ed., *The Cynewulf Reader* (London, 2001)

Bradley, S. A. J., trans., *Anglo-Saxon Poetry: An Anthology of Old English Poems in Prose Translation* (London, 1982)

Calder, D. G., and M. J. B. Allen, trans., *Sources and Analogues of Old English Poetry: The Major Latin Sources in Translation* (Cambridge, 1977)

Elliott, J. K., ed. and trans., *The Apocryphal New Testament* (Oxford, 1993)

Fulk, R. D., and C. M. Cain, *A History of Old English Literature* (Oxford, 2003)

Ó Carragáin, É., *Ritual and the Rood: Liturgical Images and the Old English Poems of the 'Dream of the Rood' Tradition* (London and Toronto, 2005)

Ó Carragáin, É., and R. North, '*The Dream of the Rood* and Anglo-Saxon Northumbria', *B&OS* 160–88

Orchard, A., 'Monasteries and courts: Alcuin and Offa', *B&OS* 219–45

Page, R. I., *An Introduction to English Runes*, 2nd ed. (Woodbridge, 1999)

Swanton, M. J., *English Poetry Before Chaucer*, 2nd ed. (Exeter, 2002), 93–101

Wyly, B. W., 'Cædmon the cowherd and Old English biblical verse', *B&OS* 189–218

Cædmon's *Hymn*

Cædmon was a farm-hand of Welsh descent working on the monastic estate of *Streonaeshalch* (Whitby) during the abbacy of Abbess Hild (657–79), who hosted the famous Synod or Council of Whitby in 664. Bede says that one night Cædmon had a dream, composed an English hymn on Creation without having heard the words before, recited this poem in the morning, had its moral soundness verified, and then joined the community of monks. Two generations later, Bede paraphrased the sense in Latin prose, but scribes added in a marginal English text, whether one related to the Northumbrian original or one translated (back) into English from Bede's Latin. The text is short, somewhat repetitive, and not fully meaningful unless some effort is made to understand the novelty of the form (Stanley 1995). English had not been used for poems of devotion before. Already in Bede's time there were two versions, one with *aeldu barnum* 'sons of men' (as below) and the other with *eordu barnum* 'sons of earth'. Yet the tradition valued this Hymn as the centuries passed. Though never embodied into the Latin text in manuscripts, it was sufficiently iconic to be added to the side in most of them, right into the twelfth century.

Opinions vary over which is the oldest manuscript of Bede's *Historia ecclesiastica* 'Ecclesiastical History' containing a text of Cædmon's *Hymn*, whether this is the St Petersburg manuscript, formerly known as the Leningrad Bede (St Petersburg, Saltykov-Shchedrin Public Library, Q.v.I.18) or the Moore Bede (Cambridge, University Library, Kk.5.16). The St Petersburg Bede has the edge, being from Bede's scriptorium in Jarrow. Though once put at *c.* 746, it is now believed to have been copied before *c.* 737, which is the year to which the Moore Bede is dated. There is also the Tiberius Bede which was copied from the St Petersburg Bede in the mid-eighth century, a generation after Bede's death (London, British Library, Cotton Tiberius A.xiv). An eclectic text, one that blends the early readings, has been made by O'Donnell (2005: 205), but the St Petersburg text is cited here, as probably the oldest and the closest to Bede's own scriptorium in Jarrow.

Some 15 other texts of the *Hymn* survive. Two more were copied in the second half of that century (the fragmentary Kassel, Landesbibliothek, MS. 4° Theol. 2, and the London, British Library, Cotton Tiberius C.ii). Thereafter the Northumbrian tradition moved south, through Mercia to Wessex, presumably with separate copies of the *Hymn*, for in each Latin text the vernacular *Hymn* is always added in the margin, never in the main text. Not counting manuscripts from the Continent, there are three Latin manuscripts of the early eleventh century and four from the twelfth, all with the *Hymn* added in, whether by the same or a different scribe. The West Saxon translation of Bede's *Ecclesiastical History*, which has its own West Saxon text of the *Hymn*, survives in four legible manuscripts, and one now burnt but transcribed copy, from between the tenth and the later eleventh century, of which the Tanner Bede is the oldest, from the 930s (Oxford, Bodleian Library, MS. Tanner 10; see the West Saxon *Bede*, **The Earliest English Prose**).

Cavill, P., 'The manuscripts of *Cædmon's Hymn*', *Anglia* 118 (2000), 499–530

North, R., *Heathen Gods in Old English Literature*, Cambridge Studies in Anglo-Saxon England 22 (Cambridge, 1997)

O'Donnell, D. P., 'A Northumbrian version of *Cædmon's Hymn* (*Eordu* Recension) in Brussels, Bibliothèque Royale, MS 8245–57, ff. 62r2–v1: identification, edition and filiation', in *Beda Venerabilis: Historian, Monk and Northumbrian*, ed. L. A. J. R. Houwen and A. A. MacDonald, Mediaevalia Groningana 19 (Groningen, 1996), 139–65

O'Donnell, D. P., ed., *Cædmon's Hymn: A Multimedia Study, Archive and Edition* (Cambridge, 2005)

Orchard, A., 'Poetic inspiration and prosaic translation: the making of *Cædmon's Hymn*', in *Studies in English Language and Literature: 'Doubt Wisely': Papers in Honour of E. G. Stanley*, ed. M. J. Toswell and E. M. Tyler (London and New York, 1996), 402–22

Stanley, E. G., 'New formulas for old: *Cædmon's Hymn*', in *Pagans and Christians: the Interplay between Christian Latin and Traditional Germanic Cultures in Early Medieval Europe*, ed. T. L. Hofstra, L. A. J. R. Houwen and A. A. MacDonald, Germania Latina 2 (Groningen, 1995), 131–48

Wyly, B. W., 'Cædmon the cowherd and Old English biblical verse', *B&OS* 189–218

Northumbrian text

Nu scylun herga   hefenricæs uard,
metudæs mehti   and his modgithanc,
uerc uuldurfadur,   sue he uundra gihuæs,
eci dryctin,   or astelidæ.
He ærist scop   aeldu barnum

Now we must praise the Keeper of Heaven-Kingdom,
Measurer's might and His heart's very meaning,
works of Brilliance-Father, just as for each wonder He,
Permanent Warlord, established the beginning.
He was the first, shaped for man's bairns

---

1 *scylun herga* '[we] must praise'. Bede's Latin version has *laudare debemus* of this meaning, and the early date and northern dialect might permit a first person plural meaning of *scylun* in line with OIce *skulum* 'we must'. If *scylun*, however, is read as third person plural, then the subject may be taken as *werc uuldurfadur* 'works of Brilliance-Father' on line 3: creatures praising their Creator. This is at odds with Bede's version, however.

4 *eci dryctin* 'Permanent Warlord'. The translation attempts to capture a muscular sense for a formula that soon became universal and somewhat pale. Using an early form of OE *dryhten* for the Deity here, Cædmon knew the term more with the meaning of a short-lived chieftain. His use of *eci* stabilises the meaning of this term in a novel way (Stanley 1995: 139–40).

5 *He ærist scop* 'He was the first, shaped'. These words have also been read as 'He ordained resurrection', with f. *ærest* as the noun of that meaning (Wyly: 197), but this overestimates the amount of doctrine one can embody in a creation poem (certainly *Genesis A* has nothing on the resurrection in its opening lines). [*aeldu barnum* 'for man's bairns'. This translation attempts a northern Anglian register. A variant, perhaps the second half of the eighth century, is *eordu barnum* 'earth's bairns', which persisted into West Saxon texts as well.

hefen to hrofæ, halig sceppend.
Tha middingard moncynnæs uard,
eci dryctin, æfter tiadæ
firum foldu, frea allmehtig.

---

heaven as the roof, Holy Shaping Power.
Then the Middle World did Mankind's Keeper,
Permanent Warlord, afterwards fashion
as a landscape for man, Sacral King Almighty.

6 *halig sceppend* 'Holy Shaping Power'. Once again, this formula became universal. Its novelty here, that the universe might be shaped in six days by one power, may be appreciated if one sees what Creation lore was available in Scandinavia at this time, through Snorri's *Edda* as well as *The Sibyl's Prophecy* (**Gods of the Vikings**).

7 *middingard* 'Middle World'. The location of man's world in the middle, between upper and lower worlds, pre-dated Christianity and continued to the end of the Anglo-Saxon period. Other Northumbrian examples are *The Dream of the Rood*, line 66, *Exodus*, line 2 and probably *The Seafarer*, line 90; but this phrase is commonplace. [*uard* 'Keeper'. Close to *hlaf-ward*, 'loaf-keeper' (lord), this term, with *foldu*, hints at the farming that can now take place.

9 *frea allmehtig* 'Sacral King Almighty'. The liberty of 'sacral king' in this translation is justified by the fact that the poem was composed within a generation of heathen times. This formula, in which an expendable harvest king has become all-powerful as the Lord, may be as shocking as Cædmon's others (North 1997: 266–71).

The Cross speaks

⁜

The runes on the Ruthwell Cross, which are considered 'early and Anglian' by Ray Page (1999: 148), were carved at some time between *c.* 650 and *c.* 750, probably in the first to the two campaigns in which the Ruthwell Cross was raised in the 730s. These runes deliver a speech from the borders of inhabited vinescroll, as if the standing Ruthwell Cross were indeed a World-Tree Cross that is speaking to us. From this early version of prosopopoeia, or dramatic personification, come the remarkable poems of *The Dream of the Rood* tradition.

The runes on the Ruthwell Cross are written always from left to right, but in two groups of two texts, each group on one of the narrow faces of the lower shaft, on the margins around the inhabited vinescroll. Each group is called a *titulus*. The first *titulus* on the north side runs from the top of the cross border down the right-hand margin in small groups of letters, while the second runs down from the top to bottom left-hand margin. The layout of the third and fourth *tituli* on the south side proceeds in the same style (Ó Carragáin 2005: 79–81). The runes were written in the style of the early Christian tradition in which Greek and Latin inscriptions were carved in vertical columns (Schwab 1978: 156–62). The early English runic alphabet had been in any case reformed in the seventh century under monastic supervision (Parsons 1999: 97–8). This accords with the iconography of Ruthwell, which is Italian in origin, with parallels in seventh-century Rome (Cramp 1978). The Cross was raised in two campaigns, first the lower shaft up to the cross head, then the cross head itself. The runes were carved on the lower shaft, as this lay for its carving on the ground. It would have been stupid to chisel them on when the shaft was raised upright at more than 15 feet high, and there was much more carving and writing (in Roman letters) to be done on the broad faces of the Ruthwell Cross, which carry the incipits or opening words of the liturgies that were associated with the Feast of the Annunciation and Good Friday to Easter Sunday.

Cramp, R., 'The evangelist-symbols and their parallels in Anglo-Saxon sculpture', in *Bede and Anglo-Saxon England*, British Archaeological Reports 46 (Oxford, 1978), 118–30

Ó Carragáin, É., 'Rome, Ruthwell, Vercelli: "The Dream of the Rood" and the Italian connection', in *Vercelli tra Oriente ed Occidente tra Tarda Antichità e Medioevo: Vercelli 10–11 Aprile 1997*, ed. V. Colcetti Corazza (Rome, 1997), 59–100

Ó Carragáin, É., *Ritual and the Rood: Liturgical Images and the Old English Poems of the 'Dream of the Rood' Tradition* (London and Toronto, 2005)

Ó Carragáin, É., and R. North, '*The Dream of the Rood* and Anglo-Saxon Northumbria', *B&OS* 160–88

Page, R. I., *An Introduction to English Runes*, 2nd ed. (Woodbridge, 1999)

Parsons, D. N., *Recasting the Runes: the Reform of the Anglo-Saxon 'Futhorc'* (Uppsala, 1999)

Schwab, U., 'Das Traumgesicht vom Kreuzesbaum. Ein ikonologischer Interpretationsansatz zu dem ags. "Dream of the Rood"', in *Philologische Studien. Gedenkschrift für Richard Kienast*, ed. U. Schwab and E. Stutz (Heidelberg, 1978), 131–92

The Ruthwell *Crucifixion Poem*

The community at Ruthwell knew the liturgies and probably also the *Rood* poem by heart, needing the inscriptions to trigger the right passages for recitation. The gospel story of the Crucifixion enables us to put Ruthwell's runic poem in the correct sequence of texts. To read these two columns of runes one would have had to move around the Cross from right to left, against the natural flow of reading a text, but following the clockwise movement of the sun. The first set of *tituli* would lead thus to the first side of iconography, which would have faced east; after studying this, one would have moved round to the second set of *tituli*, which led to the panels facing west. It is here that a vigil might be kept awaiting the sunrise (Ó Carragáin 2005: 83–4). The runic texts here are laid out by the half line, as this is reconstructed from Old English metre, without supplying runes for the gaps on the stone, and with the addition of spaces between words.

Bammesberger, A., 'A doubtful reconstruction in the Old English *Ruthwell Crucifixion Poem*', *Studia Neophilologica* 74 (2002), 143–5

Cassidy, B., ed., *The Ruthwell Cross: Papers from the Colloquium Sponsored by the Index of Christian Art, Princeton University, 8 December 1989*, Index of Christian Art Occasional Papers I (Princeton, NJ, 1992)

Cramp, R., 'The evangelist-symbols and their parallels in Anglo-Saxon sculpture', in *Bede and Anglo-Saxon England*, British Archaeological Reports 46 (Oxford, 1978), 118–30

Howlett, D., 'Inscriptions and design of the Ruthwell Cross', in Cassidy (1992), 71–93

North, R., *Heathen Gods in Old English Literature*, Cambridge Studies in Anglo-Saxon England 22 (Cambridge, 1997)

Runic text

North side (formerly known as the 'east side')

ᚷᛖᚱᛖᛞᚫ ᚻᛁᚾᚫ ᚸᚩᛞ ᚪᛚᛗᛖᛇᛏᛏᛁᚷ
ᚦᚪ ᚻᛖ ᚹᚪᛚᛞᛖ ᚩᚾ ᚸᚪᛚᚸᚢ ᚷᛁᛋᛏᛁᚸᚪ
ᛗᚩᛚᛁᚷ ᚠ   ᛗᛖᚾ
ᚢᚷ

ᛁᚳ ᚱᛁᛁᚳᚾᚫ ᛤᚣᚾᛁᛝ
ᚻᛠᚠᚢᚾᚫᛋ ᚻᛚᚪᚠᚪᚱᛞ ᚻᚫᛚᛞᚫ ᛁᚳ ᚾᛁ ᛞᚩᚱᛋᛏᚫ
ᛁᛋᛗᚫᚱᚫᛞᚢ ᚢᛝᛤᛖᛏ ᛗᛖᚾ ᛒᚪ ᚫᛏ ᚪᛞ
ᛁᚳ   ᛗᛁᚦ ᛒᛚᚩᛞᚫ   ᛁᛋᛏᛖᛗᛁᛞ
ᛒᛁ

South side (formerly known as the 'west side')

ᛣᚱᛁᛋᛏ ᚹᚫᛋ ᚩᚾ ᚱᚩᛞᛁ
ᚻᚹᛖᚦᚱᚫ ᚦᛖᚱ ᚠᚢᛋᚫ
ᚠᛠᚱᚱᚪᚾ ᛣᚹᚩᛗᚢ
ᚫᚦᚦᛁᛚᚫ ᛏᛁᛚ ᚪᚾᚢᛗ
ᛁᚳ ᚦᚫᛏ ᚪᛚ ᛒᛁ
ᛋᚫ ᛁᚳ ᚹ ᛋ ᛗᛁ ᛋᚫ ᚸᚢᛗ ᚷᛁᛞᚱᛟ ᛞ
ᚻ ᚪ ᚸ

ᛁᚦ ᛋᛏᚱᛖᛚᚢᛗ ᚷᛁᚹᚢᚾᛞᚪᛞ
ᚪᛚᛖᚷᛞᚢᚾ ᚻᛁᚫ ᚻᛁᚾᚫ ᛚᛁᛗᚹᛟᚱᛁᚷᚾᚫ
ᚷᛁᛋᛏᚩᛞᛞᚢ ᚻᛁᛗ ᛁᚳᚫᛋ ᚠ ᛗ
ᛠ ᛞᚢ ᛁᚦᛖ

Transcription and Modern English

North side (formerly known as the 'east side')

1 [+ *nd*]**geredæ hinæ god alme3ttig þa** ***he*** **walde on galgu gistiga**
modig **f[** ***ore*****]** [*allæ*] **men ((bug))**[an *ic ni dorstæ* . . .]

Almighty God stripped Himself. When He willed to mount the gallows, courageous before all men, [I dared not] bow . . .

2 [*Ahof*] **ic riicnæ** ***k*****yningc**
heafunæs h[*l*]afard ***h*****ælda ic ni dorstæ**
[*b*]ismær[*ad*]u ung*k*et ***m*****en ba æt[*g*]ad[*re*** ***i*****]c ((*wæs*)) [*m*]iþ b*l*odæ**
b**ist[*e*]mi[*d*]** ***bi*****[*goten of þæs gumu sida*]

I [lifted up] a powerful King,
the Lord of Heaven I dared not tilt:
they mocked the pair of us together; I was with blood
drenched, po[ured from the man's side]

---

1 ***þa he walde on galgu gistiga*** 'When He willed to mount the gallows'. Christ's 'will' is of immense importance to the poet of the original *Rood* poem and to the community that raised the Ruthwell Cross. The poet first counteracts the shock of seeing Almighty God undress, like a man, by making Him wish to do so. Second, the poet keeps to orthodoxy, the doctrine of *communicatio idiomatum* 'communication of idioms'. This was a solution to the latest crisis of Christology which was urged on the Northumbrians by the Vatican in the Council of Hatfield in 679. It gave Jesus a human will enclosed within the Divine, while acknowledging Jesus to be not man but God. Thus Almighty God wills to be crucified as part of His plan. [***modig f[ore] [allæ] men*** 'courageous before all men'. Christ's courage reflects that of Gabriel, who announces the incarnation to Mary on 25 March, the same day of the year in which the Crucifixion later took place. Gabriel's name means 'strength (or courage) of God'. In the public context the Angles were pleased to think of Christ as a warrior champion in battle against the devil.

2 **bi**[*goten of þæs gumu sida*] 'po[ured from the man's side]'. The runes are supplied by Howlett (1992: 86) on the basis of the later text in *The Dream of the Rood* (see also Bammesberger 2002).

South side (formerly known as the 'west side')

3 **[+] kris[t] wæs on rodi**
hweþræ þer fus[*æ*] fearran kw[*o*]mu
[*æ*]þþilæ til anum ic þæt al bi[*h*]((*eald*))
sa((*r*.)) ic w[*æ*]s mi[*þ*] s[*or*]gu[*m*] gidrœf[*i*]d h[*n*]ag [*ic secgum til handa*]

Christ was on the Cross.
However, eager ones came thither from afar;
the noble ones came together / to the One. I beheld all that.
I was terribly overcome with sorrows. I bowed [to the hands of the men].

4 **[*m*]iþ s[*t*]re[*l*]um giwundad**
alegdun hiæ *hinæ* limwœrignæ gistoddu[*n*] *him* [.*li*]cæs ((*hea*))f((*du*))m
((*bih*))ea((*l*))[*d*]u ((*h*))i((*æ*)) [*þ*]e(*r*) [*ond he hinæ þer hwilæ restæ*]

wounded with arrows.
They laid Him down limb-weary. They stood by His body's head.
There they looked on the Lord of Heaven [and He rested Himself there for a while].

---

3 ***mi[þ] s[or]gu[m] gidrœf[i]d*** 'terribly overcome with sorrows'. The unique perspective of this poem, which boldly relates the Crucifixion from the emotional standpoint of the Cross, unwilling slayer of his own lord. This perspective, by transferring the suffering from Jesus to the Cross, also helps the poet avoid issues of Christology (see below).

4 ***[m]iþ s[t]re[l]um*** 'with arrows'. The nails of the Crucifixion were later reputed to be used in a bridle for Emperor Constantine (324–37; see Cynewulf's *Elene*, lines 1172–95). That they are called 'arrows' here shows that the poet regards the Crucifixion as a battle between Jesus and the forces of evil, led by the devil. [***limwœrignæ*** 'limb-weary'. Here the poet describes the Crucifixion as if it were athletics, not a battle in which Christ is killed (apparently) by the enemy. Thereby he evades the heresy of referring to Jesus as a man, i.e. dead, while allowing that the physical form of Jesus is now inactive. The poem below retains other examples of this evasion. Christology was a dangerous topic in the late seventh century when the prototype of *The Dream of the Rood* was composed.

The Brussels Cross Riddle

The Brussels Cross Reliquiary, of the Cathedral of Saints Michel and Gudule, was made in England in the early eleventh century. It was designed both to contain a relic and to be used in procession, and was probably taken from England by a refugee from the civil war in the reign of King Stephen (1135–54). Containing 24 rubies and 14 diamonds, it was stripped of these by the French revolutionary army in 1793, but the inscriptions survive. They are all in Roman capitals. One of these is on the silver backing and speaks with the animation of the crosses in Ruthwell and the Vercelli poem. The Brussels Cross speaks of its maker: **DRAHMAL ME WORHTE** 'Drahmal made me'. When the Cross is bowed forward, much like the Vercelli Cross at the end of its ordeal, it also speaks the poem given below, on five silver strips. The poem clearly borrows from a version of the poem now most fully known in the Vercelli text, answering to lines 42, 44 and 48.

Ó Carragáin, É., *Ritual and the Rood: Liturgical Images and the Old English Poems of the 'Dream of the Rood' Tradition* (London and Toronto, 2005), 339–54

Ó Carragáin, É., and R. North, '*The Dream of the Rood* and Anglo-Saxon Northumbria', *B&OS* 185–7

+ ROD IS MIN NAMA GEO IC RICNE CYNING
BÆR BYFIGYNDE BLODE BESTEMED.

'Rood' is my name. Long ago a powerful King
I bore, trembling, drenched with blood.

The Dream of the Rood

Based as it is on an old Northumbrian poem with links to Italy, *The Dream of the Rood* did well to survive in the manuscript that stopped in Vercelli in the tenth century or early eleventh. Its owner may have read the book privately or to students while moving southwards over the Alps. It is possible too that he was an outcast from the period of English monastic reform, by whose standard the mid-tenth-century homilies of both Blickling and Vercelli collections had become doctrinally superseded if not a little suspect. *The Dream of the Rood* lies some way into the Vercelli Book. Beginning on the last leaf of the fourteenth quire, it continues into the fifteenth, before leading straight into Homily No. 19 (translated from the homiliary known as *St-Père de Chartres*). Here the poem was copied out just after two lesser works now known as *Soul and Body Dialogue I* and *Homiletic Fragment I*. These three poems were copied after four homilies of Mercian origin. With homilies to either side, in the heart of the Vercelli Book, it is clear that these readers of *The Dream of the Rood* considered it to be of the same genre.

The poem begins on a note of tranquility when the Dreamer, like the querulous soul of *Soul and Body I*, finds himself awake in the midnight hour. The vision that comes to him shows a tree of titanic size lit up in a bottomless darkened well, with all the universe looking on. The tree changes form and colour, from gallows to bonfire to reliquiary, with such instability that it seems to be alive. Not far into the dream, as if in response to the Dreamer's sudden flood of tears on beholding it, the tree begins to bleed and then to talk. By now we have understood that this is the Cross itself. Nonetheless, it is striking to hear the Passion narrative delivered from a new first-person witness which is not one of the four gospels, but rather the very instrument of Christ's death. The Cross is personified variously as a thegn suffering from guilt at collusion with executioners; as what looks like a war-horse refraining from trampling the legionaries and then carrying his master through a pitched battle, stung by arrows (the nails) and steaming with moisture (the blood) as the loyal warriors (disciples) take Christ's body off the saddle; as a preacher in church; and as a pendant on or even an idea within the Dreamer's breast. The effect of this whole central speech is to galvanise the man and us to become better Christians. The first half has dynamism and a strong narrative line. The second half is a sermon, as lucid as the earlier narrative and almost as dynamic, but it is unlikely the Anglo-Saxon audience saw any contradiction in modes. To them the poem was probably all a sermon, though initially lyrical in form, and *The Seafarer* proceeds in much the same way. What is remarkable is the way in which the Vercelli text conceals elements of liturgy and Christology which were active and controversial in the poet's day, at the end of the seventh century when a form of the poem was first sung, and in the 730s when four quotations from this poem were cut in runes into the narrow sides of the magnificent Ruthwell Cross.

Berkhout, C. T., 'The problem of OE *holmwudu*', *Medieval Studies* 36 (1974), 429–33

Horgan, A. D., '"The Dream of the Rood" and Christian tradition', *Neuphilologische Mitteilungen* 79 (1978), 11–20

Irvine, S., 'Adam or Christ? A pronominal pun in *The Dream of the Rood*', *Review of English Studies* new series 48 (1997), 433–47

North, R., *Heathen Gods in Old English Literature*, Cambridge Studies in Anglo-Saxon England 22 (Cambridge, 1997)

Ó Carragáin, É., 'How did the Vercelli Collector interpret *The Dream of the Rood*?', in *Studies in Language and Literature in Honour of Paul Christophersen*, ed. P. Tilling, Occasional Papers in Linguistics and Language Learning 8 (Coleraine, 1981), 63–104

Ó Carragáin, É., *The Ritual and the Rood: Liturgical Images and the Old English Poems of 'The Dream of the Rood' Tradition* (London and Toronto, 2005)

Orton, P. R., 'The technique of object personification in *The Dream of the Rood* and a comparison with the Old English *Riddles*', *Leeds Studies in English* new series 11 (1980), 1–18

Pheifer, J. D., ed., *Old English Glosses in the Épinal-Erfurt Glossary* (Oxford, 1974)

Schlauch, M., '*The Dream of the Rood* as prosopopoeia', in *Essays and Studies in Honor of Carleton Brown*, ed. P. W. Long (New York, 1940), 23–34

Swanton, M. J., ed., *The Dream of the Rood*, 2nd ed. (Exeter, 1987)

Szarmach, P. E., '*The Dream of the Rood* as ekphrasis', in *Text, Image, Interpretation: Studies in Anglo-Saxon Literature and its Insular Context in Honour of Éamonn Ó Carragáin*, ed. A. Minnis and J. Roberts, Studies in the Early Middle Ages 18 (Turnhout, 2007), 267–88

Woolf, R., 'Doctrinal influences on *The Dream of the Rood*', *Medium Ævum* 27 (1958), 13–53

Hwæt! Ic swefna cyst secgan wylle,
hwæt me gemætte to midre nihte,
syðþan reordberend reste wunedon!
Þuhte me þæt ic gesawe syllicre treow
on lyft lædan, leohte bewunden,
beama beorhtost. Eall þæt beacen wæs
begoten mid golde. Gimmas stodon
fægere æt foldan sceatum, swylce þær fife wæron
uppe on þam eaxlegespanne. Beheoldon þær engel Dryhtnes ealle,
fægere þurh forðgesceaft. Ne wæs ðær huru fracodes gealga,
ac hine þær beheoldon halige gastas,
men ofer moldan, ond eall þeos mære gesceaft.
Syllic wæs se sigebeam, ond ic synnum fah,

Listen! I wish to relate the choicest vision
that came to me in the middle of the night
when speech-bearers dwelt at rest.
It showed itself to me so that I saw a tree more splendid
leading aloft, wound about with light,
brightest of beams. All that beacon had been
poured over with gold. Jewels stood
radiant at earth's corners, likewise there were five
up on the axle-span. All things beheld the Lord's angel, all that were
radiant through space and time. Nor, indeed, was it a criminal's gallows,
for holy ghosts beheld it there,
men across earth, and all this glorious creation.
Splendid was the victory-tree, and I was stained with sins,

---

2 *me gemætte* 'that came to me (in a dream)'. Note the passivity of the Dreamer in this psychic intervention from outside.

4 *syllicre treow* 'a tree more splendid'. Add 'than any other'. So far this is no more than a tree.

6 *beama beorhtost* 'brightest of beams'. The poet puns on *beam* as is still possible, playing off 'tree' with 'ray of light'. [*beacen* 'beacon'. The bonfire on a hill-top that warns or tells distant people of great events. The runes surviving on the Bewcastle Cross of the early eighth century, not far east from Ruthwell along Hadrian's Wall, include the inscription **þis sigbecn setton hwætred** [. . .] 'Hwætred [and . . .] set up this victory beacon' (Ó Carragáin 2005: 37 and 41).

8 *þær fife wæron* 'there were five'. For the five wounds of Christ.

9 *engel Dryhtnes* 'the Lord's angel'. Not doctrinal, but apposite, this conception of the Cross works better than taking *engel* as a neuter plural subject of *beheoldon* '(they) beheld'. An angel is a messenger, a variant on the meaning of *beacen* above.

forwunded mid wommum. Geseah ic wuldres treow,
wædum geweorðode, wynnum scinan,
gegyred mid golde. Gimmas hæfdon
bewrigene weorðlice wealdendes treow.
Hwæðre ic þurh þæt gold ongytan meahte
earmra ærgewin, þæt hit ærest ongan
swætan on þa swiðran healfe. Eall ic wæs mid sorgum gedrefed,
forht ic wæs for þære fægran gesyhðe. Geseah ic þæt fuse beacen
wendan wædum ond bleom. Hwilum hit wæs mid wætan bestemed,
beswyled mid swates gange, hwilum mid since gegyrwed.
Hwæðre ic þær licgende lange hwile
beheold hreowcearig hælendes treow,
oððæt ic gehyrde þæt hit hleoðrode.

---

wounded with defilements. I saw a tree of glory,
pledge worshipped with vestments, shining with joys,
girt with gold. Jewels had
in worship covered the Commander's tree.
And yet through that gold I could perceive
a former strife of wretched men, so that only then did it
bleed on the right-hand side. I was all oppressed with sorrows,
frightened I was of the radiant sight. I saw that sparkling beacon
changing vestments and colours. Sometimes it was steamed with wetness,
soiled by the passage of blood, sometimes adorned with treasure.
And yet lying there for a long while,
grieving with repentance, I beheld the Healer's tree,
until I heard it give voice.

14–15 *wuldres treow, wædum geweorðode* 'a tree of glory, pledge worshipped with vestments'. The second main pun. OE n. *treow* is 'tree', the first meaning the opening tells us to prepare for; and f. *treow* means 'pledge', as in the Lord's covenants to the chosen people. The 'pledge' meaning is activated by the *–e* ending on *geweorðod* 'worshipped', which can be accusative feminine singular. If this were not enough, the poet reactivates the 'brilliance' sense of *wuldor* 'glory' with *treow* by having described the tree as *leohte bewunden* 'wound about with light' on line 5.

18–19 *ongytan meahte . . . þæt hit ærest ongan swætan* 'I could perceive . . . so that only then did it bleed' etc. This poem is seen as ahead of its time in presenting beauty as a compunction to tears (Szarmach 2007: 285–7). Here we have something in reverse, where the Dreamer's act of gazing on the Cross induces bleeding as its response. The communication goes two ways (see note to lines 25–6).

22–3 *Hwilum . . . hwilum* 'Sometimes . . . sometimes'. The instability of this imagery helps the poet to embody the history of the Cross from its inception to the present.

25–6 *beheold oððæt hit hleoðrode* 'beheld until it give voice'. The speech is not at once forthcoming, but after the Dreamer's grieving attention has requested it.

Ongan þa word sprecan   wudu selesta:
'Þæt wæs geara iu,   (ic þæt gyta geman),
þæt ic wæs aheawen   holtes on ende,
astyred of stefne minum.   Genaman me ðær strange feondas,
geworhton him þær to wæfersyne,   heton me heora wergas hebban.
Bæron me ðær beornas on eaxlum,   oððæt hie me on beorg asetton,
gefæstnodon me þær feondas genoge.   Geseah ic þa Frean mancynnes
efstan elne mycle   þæt He me wolde on gestigan.
Þær ic þa ne dorste   ofer Dryhtnes word
bugan oððe berstan,   þa ic bifian geseah
eorðan sceatas.   Ealle ic mihte
feondas gefyllan,   hwæðre ic fæste stod.
Ongyrede hine þa geong hæleð   (þæt wæs God ælmihtig),
strang ond stiðmod.   Gestah He on gealgan heanne,
modig on manigra gesyhðe,   þa He wolde mancyn lysan.

The highest-ranking tree did speak these words:
'It was long long ago (I still remember this)
that I was hewn down at the end of a wood,
cut off from my stem. Seized me there strong fiends,
made me there into a spectacle, commanded their outlaws to lift me.
Bore me there warriors on their shoulders, until they set me down on a hill,
fastened me there fiends enough. I saw then the King of mankind
hasten with great zeal in that it was his will to climb upon me.
There I did not dare for the Lord's word
bow down or burst, when I saw trembling
earth's corners. All of them I could have,
the fiends all felled, yet fast I stood.
Undressed himself then a young hero (that was God Almighty),
strong and stern-minded. He climbed on the high gallows,
courageous in the sight of many, when he willed the release of mankind.

---

28 *geara iu* 'long long ago'. About 670 years.

30–3 *Genaman . . . geworhton . . . heton . . . bæron . . . asetton, gefæstnodon.* The dynamism of these verbs, in hypermetric lines, turns the genre to epic, away from the lyricism of the narrative of the dream frame. The same is achieved in lines 60–8.

34 *þæt He me wolde on gestigan* 'that it was his will to climb upon me'. See *walde* in the Ruthwell poem above. The first two runic *tituli* give quotations from an earlier form of *The Dream of the Rood*, lines 40–9.

35 *ne dorste ofer Dryhtnes word* 'did not dare for the Lord's word'. The first part of this becomes a refrain, on lines 42 and 47. The Cross has to follow the divine plan.

39 *Ongyrede hine þa geong hæleð* 'Undressed himself then a young hero'. The poem proceeds as a riddle in so far as the full truth is slowly and indirectly revealed. Hereafter the policy is to show this by restoring capitals for the Deity's nouns and pronouns.

Bifode ic þa me se Beorn ymbclypte. Ne dorste ic hwæðre bugan to eorðan,
feallan to foldan sceatum, ac ic sceolde fæste standan.
Rod wæs ic aræred. Ahof ic ricne Cyning,
heofona Hlaford, hyldan me ne dorste.
þurhdrifan hi me mid deorcan næglum. On me syndon þa dolg gesiene,
opene inwidhlemmas. Ne dorste ic hira nænigum sceððan.
Bysmeredon hie unc butu ætgædere. Eall ic wæs mid blode bestemed,
begoten of þæs Guman sidan, siððan He hæfde His gast onsended.
Feala ic on þam beorge gebiden hæbbe
wraðra wyrda. Geseah ic weruda God
þearle þenian. Þystro hæfdon
bewrigen mid wolcnum Wealdendes hræw,
scirne sciman, sceadu forðeode,
wann under wolcnum. Weop eal gesceaft,
cwiðdon Cyninges fyll. Crist wæs on rode.
Hwæðere þær fuse feorran cwoman
to þam Æðelinge. Ic þæt eall beheold.
Sare ic wæs mid sorgum gedrefed, hnag ic hwæðre þam secgum to handa,
eaðmod elne mycle. Genamon hie þær ælmihtigne God,

I trembled when the warrior embraced me. Nor dared I yet bend to earth,
fall to the land's surface, for I had to stand fast.
A rood was I raised. I lifted up a powerful king,
Lord of the heavens, to lean I did not dare.
They drove me through with dark nails. On me those wounds are visible,
open gashes of evil. Nor dared I harm any one of them.
They abused us both together. I was all steamed with blood,
poured over from the man's side, after he had sent on his spirit.
Suffered have I on that hill many
cruel fates. I saw the God of hosts
severely stretched. In waves had darkness
covered with clouds the Commander's corpse,
a gleaming ray. A shadow came forth,
fought dark under clouds. All creation wept,
they lamented the King's fall. Christ was on the rood.
And yet keen men came there from afar
to the Prince. I beheld it all.
Sorely was I oppressed with sorrows, yet I sank into the arms of those men,
humble, with great zeal. They seized there Almighty God,

---

44 *Rod* 'A rood'. The poet's first use of this, the standard word for 'cross'.

53–4 *Wealdendes hræw, scirne sciman* 'Commander's corpse, a gleaming ray'. The poet's unstable imagery helps him avoid a direct description of Christ's human mortality, while steering clear of the Monophysite heresy of seeing Christ as insubstantial (Woolf 1958).

55 *wann under wolcnum* 'fought dark under clouds'. The pun is on *wann* 'fought' (from *winnan*) and 'dark'. A battle is going on in the darkness.

ahofon Hine of ðam hefian wite. Forleton me þa hilderincas
standan steame bedrifenne, eall ic wæs mid strælum forwundod.
Aledon hie ðær Limwerigne, gestodon him æt His lices heafdum,
beheoldon hie ðær heofenes Dryhten, ond He Hine ðær hwile reste,
meðe æfter ðam miclan gewinne. Ongunnon him þa moldern wyrcan
beornas on banan gesyhðe, curfon hie ðæt of beorhtan stane,
gesetton hie ðæron sigora Wealdend. Ongunnon Him þa sorhleoð galan
earme on þa æfentide, þa hie woldon eft siðian,
meðe fram þam mæran Þeodne. Reste He ðær mæte weorode.
Hwæðere we ðær greotende gode hwile
stodon on staðole, syððan stefn up gewat
hilderinca. Hræw colode,
fæger feorgbold. Þa us man fyllan ongan
ealle to eorðan. Þæt wæs egeslic wyrd!
Bedealf us man on deopan seaþe. Hwæðre me þær Dryhtnes þegnas,
freondas gefrunon, [. . .]
ond gyredon me golde ond seolfre.

---

lifted him up from the heavy torment. Me those warrior-men then left
standing driven with steam, with arrows I was all wounded.
They laid down there a limb-weary one, stood at his body's head,
beheld heaven's War-Lord there, and for a while he rested there,
exhausted after the great battle. Then they did make an earthwork building,
warriors in the slayer's sight. They carved it from bright stone,
set in there the Commander of Victories, then did sing their sorrow-chant,
wretched in the evening hour, when they wanted to journey back,
exhausted, from the glorious King. He rested there with little company.
And yet we weeping there for a good while
stood on the bedrock, when upwards passed the voice
of warrior-men. The corpse cooled,
radiant life-blood house. Then someone did fell us
all to the earth. That was a terrible fate!
A deep pit was dug for us. Yet in that place the Lord's thegns,
his friends, learned of me, [. . .]
and girt me with gold and silver.

61–2 *Forleton me standan steam bedrifenne* 'Me (they) left standing driven with steam'. This is as if the Cross is Christ's warhorse, left to cool off while the body is taken down from the saddle (North 1997: 295).

64–5 *reste, meðe* 'rested . . . exhausted'. See note for line 53–4.

66 *on banan gesyhðe* 'in the slayer's sight'. A man's third person self-reference after an act of shame is perhaps to 'remove will and agency the greatest possible distance' from what he has done, to quote a case in World War I, from Paul Fussell, *The Great War and Modern Memory* (Oxford, 1975), 177.

76 *freondas gefrunon* 'his friends, learned of me'. See *Elene* below, for the legend of Empress Helena and the Invention of the True Cross.

Nu ðu miht gehyran, hæleð min se leofa,
þæt ic bealuwara weorc gebiden hæbbe,
sarra sorga. Is nu sæl cumen
þæt me weorðiað wide ond side
menn ofer moldan, ond eall þeos mære gesceaft,
gebiddaþ him to þyssum beacne. On me Bearn Godes
þrowode hwile. Forþan ic þrymfæst nu
hlifige under heofenum, ond ic hælan mæg
æghwylcne anra, þara þe him bið egesa to me.
Iu ic wæs geworden wita heardost,
leodum laðost, ærþan ic him lifes weg
rihtne gerymde, reordberendum.
Hwæt, me þa geweorðode wuldres Ealdor
ofer holmwudu, heofonrices Weard,

Now you may hear, my dear Sir,
what pain I have endured from those who dwell in evil,
what grievous sorrows. The time has now come
that far and wide I will be worshipped
by men across the earth and all this glorious creation.
They will pray to this beacon. On me God's Child
agonised for a while. And so I, secure in my magnificence now,
do tower beneath the heavens, and I can heal
each and every person in whom there is a fear of me.
I had once become the cruellest of torments,
most hateful to the people, before a path of life for them,
a straight one, I cleared for the speech-bearers.
Listen! The Prince of Glory honoured me then
over ocean-trees, heaven-kingdom's Guardian,

---

78 The sermon starts here, for which the more lyrical and epic part of this poem was composed.

85 *ic hælan mæg* 'I can heal'. The use of relics for medicinal purposes was part of organised religion in the Middle Ages.

90–4 This comparison between the Cross and Mary has the calendar behind it. It has been suggested that John the Arch-cantator, precentor of St Peter's in Rome, who visited Northumbria around the Hatfield Council of 679, created the liturgy by which 25 March, the (Julian) spring equinox and day of the original Crucifixion, became the date for the Vatican Mass of the Annunciation (Ó Carragáin 2005: 85–91). In Northumbrian liturgy of the 680s Christ's birth and death were thus fixed on the same day, leading this poet to compare Mary with the Cross.

91 *ofer holmwudu* 'over ocean-trees'. Many emend to *holtwudu* 'woodland trees', but 'ocean-trees' as a kenning for the Cross as (a) a ship bringing the world to a safe haven (in Venantius Fortunatus' hymn *Pange linga*, and in *Christ II*, lines 850–66 below; see Berkhout 1974) and (b) as an *æsc* for Latin *navis* 'ship' (in Épinal glosses, Pheifer 1974: 11.180 and 71): *æsc* 'ash-tree' recalls the World Tree, possibly once worshipped by the Anglian culture which called the Cross a 'tree' (North 1997: 287–93).

swylce swa He His modor eac, Marian sylfe,
ælmihtig God for ealle menn
geweorðode ofer eall wifa cynn.
Nu ic þe hate, hæleð min se leofa,
þæt ðu þas gesyhðe secge mannum,
onwreoh wordum þæt hit is wuldres beam,
se ðe ælmihtig God on þrowode
for mancynnes manegum synnum
ond Adomes ealdgewyrhtum.
Deað he þær byrigde, hwæðere eft Dryhten aras
mid His miclan mihte mannum to helpe.
He ða on heofenas astag. Hider eft fundaþ
on þysne middangeard mancynn secan
on domdæge Dryhten sylfa,
ælmihtig God, ond His englas mid,
þæt He þonne wile deman, se ah domes geweald,
anra gehwylcum swa he him ærur her
on þyssum lænum life geearnaþ.
Ne mæg þær ænig *u*nforht wesan
for þam worde þe se Wealdend cwyð.

---

just as he his mother too, Mary herself,
Almighty God before all mankind
honoured over the whole tribe of women.
Now I command you, my dear Sir,
to relate this sight to humankind.
Reveal it in words that it is Glory's tree
that Almighty God agonised on
for mankind's many sins
and the old work of Adam.
Death he there tasted, buried, yet the Lord rose up again
in his great might to the aid of men.
He climbed then to the heavens. Back he will hasten here
into this middle world to seek mankind
on Judgement Day, the Lord himself,
Almighty God, and his angels with him,
that he who has the power of judgement will then judge
each person according to what back in this time here
in this borrowed life he earns for himself.
Nor can anybody there be unafraid
of the words which the Commander pronounces.

---

101 *Deað he þær byrigde* 'Death he there tasted, buried'. Adam, from line 100, 'tasted' death in Eden with the first tree, but Jesus later 'buried' death with the second. There is a skilful double pun, with *byrigan*, which has both meanings, and with the pronoun *he* which refers to both subjects (Irvine 1997). The chronology is also collapsed as with Mary and the Cross in lines 90–4.

Frineð He for þære mænige hwær se man sie,
se ðe for Dryhtnes naman deaðes wolde
biteres onbyrigan, swa He ær on ðam beame dyde.
Ac hie þonne forhtiað, ond fea þencaþ
hwæt hie to Criste cweðan onginnen.
Ne þearf ðær þonne ænig anforht wesan
þe him ær in breostum bereð beacna selest,
ac ðurh ða rode sceal rice gesecan
of eorðwege æghwylc sawl,
seo þe mid Wealdende wunian þenceð.'

Gebæd ic me þa to þan beame bliðe mode,
elne mycle, þær ic ana wæs
mæte werede. Wæs modsefa
afysed on forðwege, feala ealra gebad
langunghwila. Is me nu lifes hyht
þæt ic þone sigebeam secan mote
ana oftor þonne ealle men,
well weorþian. Me is willa to ðam
mycel on mode, ond min mundbyrd is

He will ask before the multitude where that man may be
who, for the Lord's name, wanted to taste
a bitter death just as he did on that tree before.
Then, you see, they are afraid, and few are thinking
what to Christ they may even begin to say.
In that place nobody needs to be afraid
who bears within the breast already the best of beacons,
but through that rood shall seek the kingdom
from the earthly road each soul
which thinks to dwell with the Commander.'

I prayed then to the tree with blithe spirit,
with great zeal, there where I lay, by myself,
with little company. My thoughts were
inspired on the road hence, I have been through many periods
of longing of all kinds. It is now my life's hope
that I be allowed to seek that victory-tree,
alone more often than all men
to worship it well. The will in me to this end
is great in my heart, and my safe custody is

113 *se ðe for Dryhtnes naman* 'who, for the Lord's name' etc. Missionary work in Germany?

118 *in breostum* 'within the breast'. From cosmic scale the Cross has now become an idea in the believer's heart.

geriht to þære rode. Nah ic ricra feala
freonda on foldan, ac hie forð heonon
gewiton of worulde dreamum, sohton him wuldres Cyning,
lifiaþ nu on heofenum mid Heahfædere,
wuniaþ on wuldre, ond ic wene me
daga gehwylce hwænne me Dryhtnes rod,
þe ic her on eorðan ær sceawode,
on þysson lænan life gefetige
ond me þonne gebringe þær is blis mycel,
dream on heofonum, þær is Dryhtnes folc
geseted to symle, þær is singal blis,
ond me þonne asette þær ic syþþan mot
wunian on wuldre, well mid þam halgum
dreames brucan. Si me Dryhten freond,
se ðe her on eorþan ær þrowode
on þam gealgtreowe for guman synnum.
He us onlysde ond us lif forgeaf,

---

directed to the rood. I have not many powerful
friends on earth, for out of here they have
passed on from world's delight, did seek Glory's King,
live now in heaven with High Father,
dwell in glory, and I look forward
each day to when it is me that the Lord's rood
which I once gazed on here on earth
may fetch in this life that was lent to me,
and me then may bring to where there is great bliss,
delight in heaven, to where the Lord's nation is
seated at a banquet, to where the bliss is everlasting,
and me then may set down where I may thenceforth
dwell in glory, where I may well with those saints
partake of delight. May the Lord be friend to me,
who once here on earth did agonise
on the gallows-tree for the sins of man.
He released us and gave us life,

131–2 The Dreamer's lack of living friends bothers him less now than the man in the *The Seafarer*, lines 92–3, who *wat his iuwine . . . eorþan forgiefene* 'knows his friend of old . . . given to the earth'. The Dreamer is more monastic.

138 *gefetige* 'may fetch'. That the Cross can fetch the Dreamer suggests that it is either imagined as a thegn again, as in the beginning on line 23, or as the horse it was when carrying Christ into battle in lines 34–62.

147 *He us onlysde* 'He released us'. The word *us* may refer to all good people in hell before the redemption, or to the Northumbrians who now have the chance for salvation which their heathen ancestors lacked, or to the heathens themselves, if they are recast as a pre-Mosaic tribe of Israel.

heofonlicne ham. Hiht wæs geniwad
mid bledum ond mid blisse þam þe þær bryne þolodan.
Se Sunu wæs sigorfæst on þam siðfate,
mihtig ond spedig, þa He mid manigeo com,
gasta weorode, on Godes rice,
Anwealda ælmihtig, englum to blisse
ond eallum ðam halgum þam þe on heofonum ær
wunedon on wuldre, þa heora Wealdend cwom,
ælmihtig God, þær His eðel wæs.

---

a heavenly home. Hope was renewed
with rejoicings and with bliss for those who suffered burning there.
The Son was confirmed in victory on that expedition,
mighty and triumphant, when with a multitude he came,
with a troop of ghosts into the kingdom of God,
One King Almighty, to the ecstasy of angels
of all the saints who in heaven were already
dwelling in glory when their Commander came,
Almighty God, to his promised land.

---

150 *sigorfæst on þam siðfate* 'confirmed in victory on that expedition'. Jesus is a warrior on a raid into the enemy's country, His death having been a feint. Some of the heroic imagery for the harrowing is retained in the Blickling Homily on Easter Sunday (No. 7; see **Writers of the Benedictine Reform**).

154 *eallum ðam halgum* 'all the saints' etc. How many saints were in heaven when Jesus harrowed hell? The poet's chronology is collapsed once again. The populous present-day heaven stands for the pristine heaven before the first arrival of man.

Exodus

Exodus is a rousing biblical poem, rhetorically flamboyant and typologically sophisticated. Moses and the Israelites, as they escape from Egypt across the Red Sea to the Promised Land, take part in a heroic adventure that is also a figure for good souls passing from the world through the waters of baptism to heaven. The poem is based not on the whole Book of Exodus, as the title might tell us, but selectively on Exodus 13:17–14:31, while its ideology is also shaped by digressions from Genesis on Noah and Abraham and Isaac, along with many other verses from Old and New Testaments. The poet's language, now written in a garbled West Saxon, seems to have been old and Northumbrian, and it is clear that he has mastered heroic poems. There is much in the imagery of *Exodus* to support the idea that the people who commissioned this poem, like those who had the Ruthwell *Crucifixion Poem* carved in the 730s, were members of a Northumbrian aristocracy. The Israelites are a professional army, the Egyptians an untrained family mob, and there is almost a battle before the crossing of the Red Sea. However, the poet's predominant interest is baptism as the reward for God's contract with His people. The crossing of the Red Sea was interpreted as a figure for this by St Paul in I Corinthians 10:1–2, and baptism is the means of salvation not only for the descendants of the Israelites but for the early heathen English as well. The early Northumbrians counted themselves as a chosen people like the tribes of Israel, and it has been argued that with his ship-imagery of desert crossing before the Red Sea the poet portrays Exodus as the early North-Sea migration of Angles, ancestors of his royal patrons, from Germany to Britain (Howe 1989: 92–8). With his mastery of typology, the poet of Exodus fuses the political ambition of their kings with his own liturgical need. His poem seems connected to the liturgy of Easter when catachumens were baptised, particularly the Vigil before Easter Sunday. In this light, it is reasonable to suppose that *Exodus* was a high-status royal ecclesiastical work, composed by a bishop in the early eighth century to mark the Easter in a Northumbrian court.

The manuscript that contains *Exodus* is Oxford, Bodleian Library, Junius 11, which was compiled in the later tenth century, possibly in Canterbury. This manuscript was meant to contain poems rather than homilies. *Exodus* is copied second in a line of four poems that follows the course of the Bible, *Genesis*, *Exodus*, *Daniel* and *Christ and Satan*. Its fitts (see below) are numbered with this larger sequence in mind. For a while some scholars credited Cædmon with their authorship in remembrance of Bede's story of the illiterate seventh-century cowherd who is said to have versified most of the Bible in Hild's monastery of Whitby. Junius 11 was called the 'Cædmon manuscript'. Although his authorship is no longer believed in for these poems, it is still plausible that Junius 11 was compiled in emulation of Cædmon's story, or even with the tacit claim that these were his poems. Such a tradition may have been old, for the first three poems in Junius 11 were copied in the same order out of the book's exemplar. Junius 11 itself was designed from the outset as a picture book with blank spaces set aside for illustrations at least up to *Christ and Satan*. Two artists filled these spaces, one drawing and the other colouring, five-eighths of the way into *Genesis*. Then their activity stopped, perhaps because the presumed layman who requested his lavish book ran out of money to pay for it. Indeed, staying in its monastery, the book may have survived because it was unfinished. Later it was in the hands of Bishop James Ussher of Armagh (1581–1656), who gave it to the Dutch antiquarian Franciscus Junius (1591–1677). Junius published the manuscript in 1655 and bequeathed it to the Bodleian Library in Oxford.

Bright, J. W., 'The relation of the Cædmonian *Exodus* to the liturgy', *Modern Language Notes* 27 (1912), 97–103

Calder, D. G., 'Notes on the typology of the Old English *Exodus*', *Neuphilologische Mitteilungen* 74 (1973), 85–9

Frank, R., 'What kind of poetry is *Exodus*?', in *Germania*, ed. D. G. Calder and T. Craig Christy (Wolfeboro, NH, 1988), 191–205

Godden, M., 'Biblical literature: the Old Testament', in *The Cambridge Companion to Old English Literature*, ed. M. Godden and M. Lapidge (Cambridge, 1991), 206–26

Howe, N., *Migration and Mythmaking in Anglo-Saxon England* (New Haven, CT, 1989)

Irving, E. B., Jr., ed., *The Old English Exodus*, Yale Studies in English 122 (New Haven, CT, 1953)

Irving, E. B., Jr., 'New notes on the Old English *Exodus*', *Anglia* 90 (1972), 289–324

Lucas, P. J., ed., *Exodus* (London, 1977, repr. with corrections 1994)

Swanton, M. J., *English Poetry Before Chaucer*, 2nd ed. (Exeter, 2002), 93–101

The Lord's pact with Moses

Moses in this opening is a warlord, law-giver and bishop, all in one. His education on Mount Horeb and his receiving of the Ten Commandments on Mount Sinai are here blended with his defiance of the Pharaoh and the slaying of the Egyptian firstborn, all before the Israelites ship out. The Egyptians, as an *inge[he]re* 'indigenous host' but also 'Ing-host' on line 33, are presented as idolaters of an ancient Germanic kind. Later they are known as *ingefolc* 'native people' and 'Ing-nation' (line 142). Moses' escape from their clutches may also be read as the first Northumbrian migration to religious freedom in Britain.

Ball, C., '*Incge Beow.* 2577', *Anglia* 78 (1960), 403–10

Greenfield, S. B., '"Exodus" 33a: "ingere", a new suggestion', *Notes and Queries* 224 (1979), 296–7

North, R., *Heathen Gods in Old English Literature*, Cambridge Studies in Anglo-Saxon England 22 (Cambridge, 1997)

Rosier, J. L., '*Icge gold* and *incge lafe* in *Beowulf*', *Publications of the Modern Language Association* 81 (1966), 342–46

XLII Hwæt! We feor and neah gefrigen habað
ofer middangeard Moyses domas,
wræclico wordriht wera cneorissum,
in uprodor eadigra gehwam
æfter bealusiðe bote lifes,
lifigendra gehwam langsumne ræd,
hæleðum secgan. Gehyre se ðe wille!

Þone on westenne weroda Drihten,
soðfæst Cyning, mid His sylfes miht
gewyrðode, and him wundra fela
ece Alwalda in æht forgeaf.
He wæs leof Gode, leoda aldor,
horsc and hreðergleaw, herges wisa,
freom folctoga. Faraones cyn,
Godes andsacan, gyrdwite band,
þær him gesealde sigora Waldend,
modgum magoræswan, his maga feorh,
onwist eðles, Abrahames sunum.

XLII Listen! We both far and near have heard
of Moses' judgements in the Middle World,
decrees in exile for generations of men,
for each blessed individual in heaven above,
after the feared journey a payment of Life,
long-lasting reward for each living person,
as men narrate this. Let him hear who will!

Him in the badlands did the Lord of Hosts,
righteous King, in the power of His person
show honour, and many wonders
Eternal Omnipotent gave to his keeping.
He was dear to God, a leader of the people,
clever and prescient, an army's guide,
a bold general. He bound the race of Pharaoh,
God's adversary, with rod-punishment,
when Victory Commander gave to him,
passionate young chief, the lives of his kin,
a homeland for Abraham's sons to inhabit.

---

1 *We gefrigen habað* 'We have heard'. The epic beginning is like that of *Beowulf*, nor a figure of speech. It seems that his poem is meant to be heard rather than read.

6 *langsumne ræd* 'long-lasting reward'. Hrothgar's conception of heaven is similar, *ece rædas* 'eternal rewards' in *Beowulf*, line 1760 (see **Heroic Poems**).

7 *Gehyre se ðe wille!* 'Let him hear who will!' In a poem of this quality it would be redundant if this were a mere formula. The poet claims to be dealing with a crowd of laymen, people with less interest in Bible stories.

Heah wæs þæt handlean   and him hold Frea,
gesealde wæpna geweald   wið wraðra gryre,
ofercom mid þy campe   cneomaga fela,
feonda folcriht.   Đa wæs forma sið
þæt hine weroda God   wordum nægde,
þær he him gesægde   soðwundra fela,
hu þas woruld worhte   witig Drihten,
eorðan ymbhwyrft   and uprodor,
gesette sigerice   and His sylfes naman,
ðone yldo bearn   ær ne cuðon,
frod fædera cyn,   þeah hie fela wiston.
Hæfde He þa geswiðed   soðum cræftum
and gewurðodne   werodes aldor,
Faraones feond,   on forðwegas.
Þa wæs inge[he]re   ealdum witum
deaðe gedrenced   drihtfolca mæst,

High was that hand-gift and gracious to him God,
who gave him weapon-power against hostile terror
whereby he overcame many tribes in battle, and
a jurisdiction over fiends. That was the first time
the words of the God of Hosts approached him,
when He showed him many true miracles,
how in this world the wise Lord made
earth's circumference and heaven above,
established His own victory domain and His name
which sons of man had not known before,
learned race of patriarchs, though they knew much.
By then He had strengthened with genuine powers
the leader of this host and with honour put forth
Pharaoh's enemy on the outbound highway.
The indigenous Ing-host, tribe of greatest lordship,
was then afflicted with ancient penalties, with death,

---

19 *Heah wæs þæt handlean* 'High was that hand-gift' etc. The poet's rhetorical gifts are clear here, with the balance of divine elements to either side of Moses, the man who will take on God's power.

24 *soðwundra fela* 'many true miracles'. Moses in Midian, before his return to Egypt, encountering the blazing bush (Exodus 3) and learning of the history of the world.

33–4 *inge[he]re . . . drihtfolca mæst* 'indigenous Ing-host, tribe of greatest lordship'. The manuscript, Junius 11, has *ingere*, which must be emended. Mostly commonly this is emended to *ungeare* 'soon' (Lucas 1994: 78). However, *inge[h]ere* keeps the basic letters (Greenfield 1979), and may refer to the Egyptians as 'indigenous', in line with their designation as *ingefolc* 'indigenous peoples' on line 142, *ingemen* 'indigenous men' on line 190 and *ingeðeode* 'gentile nation' on line 443 (as emended from *incaðeode* 'grudge-nation'; Rosier: 1966). The *in(c)ge*-prefix has been identified as related to OE Ing, a cognate of *ingvi* or *yngvi*, the prefix of the Norse god Freyr, with the meaning 'magical' (Ball: 1960). For a theory that keeps the connection with Ing, describing the Egyptians allegorically as heathens of the old Vanic religion of Germania, see North (1997: 58–64; see *Harvest-Long*, stanza 10, **Gods of the Vikings**).

hordwearda hryre.   Heaf wæs geniwad,
swæfon seledreamas,   since berofene.
Hæfde mansceaðan   æt middere niht
frecne gefylled,   frumbearna fela,
abrocene burhweardas.   Bana wide scrað,
lað leodhata,   land þrysmyde
deadra hræwum   (dugoð forð gewat),
wop wæs wide,   worulddreama lyt.
Wæron hleahtorsmiðum   handa belocene,
alyfed laðsið   leode gretan,
folc ferende.   F*e*ond wæs bereafod,
hergas on he[a]lle,   heof*u*n[g] þider becom,
druron deofolgyld.   Dæg wæs mære
ofer middangeard   þa seo mengeo for.
Swa þæs fæsten dreah   fela missera
ealdwerige   Egypta folc
þæs þe hie wideferð   wyrnan þohton
Moyses magum,   gif hie Metod lete,

---

its hoard-keepers ruined. Lamenting was renewed,
while, robbed of treasure, joys of hall slept through it.
Moses had at midnight savagely cut down
the perpetrators of evil, many firstborn sons,
smashed the town's inhabitants. A slayer stalked wide,
the tyrannical foe, suffocated the land
with corpses of the dead (the troop moved out),
weeping was widespread, no worldly joy this.
The hands of laughter-artesans were tied, the people
given leave to face their hateful journey,
a mob on the move. Fiend was despoiled,
altars in his hall, lamentation came there,
his idols toppled. A day renowned throughout
Middle World when that multitude went forth.
So it was that the old accursed people of Egypt
suffered for many seasons the dire straits due to them,
for constantly having thought to oppose
the kin of Moses, had the Measurer let them,

---

45 *Feond wæs bereafod* 'Fiend was despoiled'. By emendation from *freond* as in 'friend was despoiled', which makes less sense. These lines have been garbled, but the poet is clearly doing much with the Bible's brief references to the destruction of Egyptian idols on the night of Passover in Exodus 12:12 and Numbers 33:4.

46 *hergas on he[a]lle, heofun[g] þider becom* 'altars in his hall, lamentation came there'. Lucas (1994: 81) has *on helle* and *hefun* for 'altars in hell (heaven came there)'. All the plagues and sufferings of Egypt are blended here for increased effect.

on langne lust leofes siðes.
Fyrd wæs gefysed, from se ðe lædde,
modig magoræswa, mægburh heora.
Oferfor he mid þy folce fæstena worn,
land and leodweard laðra manna,
enge anpaðas, uncuð gelad,
oðþæt hie on Guðmyrce gearwe bæron.
Wæron land heora lyfthelme beþeaht,
mearchofu mor heald. Moyses ofer þa,
fela meoringa, fyrde gelædde.

---

in their long-term lust for a journey dear to them.
The militia lit out, bold the man who led,
passionate young chief, their kin-town.
He crossed, with this people, many trackless lairs,
the land and sentinels of hostile men,
narrow defiles, unknown roads,
until they were ready for the Nubians' border,
whose lands with sky-cover were roofed,
the moor held border dwellings. Through these did Moses,
through many obstacles, lead his militia.

The Israelites sail to the Red Sea

As Moses' shrine, the Ark of the Lord's Covenant, moves through the desert to the Red Sea, we are encouraged to see the story in a surreal allegorical way. The Pillar of Cloud which shields the Israelites from the sun is here described as the sail of a vast ship in the heavens, rigging and all. This is both for the Cross as the Ship of the Church and for the sailing of the Angles to Britain. The Pillar of Fire, which guides them by night, is both for the baptismal candle and the Pole Star by which seafarers set their latitude on crossings from east to west.

---

55 *mægburh heora* 'their kin-town'. This word occurs also on line 352 for 'tribes' and line 360 for 'genealogy'.

58 This line is also in *Beowulf*, line 1410, for the way to Grendel's Mere.

59–60 *Guðmyrce . . . lyfthelme beþeaht* 'Nubians' border . . . with sky-cover . . . roofed'. 'War-dark' for the first word, coupled with the idea of 'sky-cover' suggests Africans of Nubia, the etymology of which is 'cloudy' (from Latin f. *nubes* 'cloud'). The poet is playing on Latin as well as on English. Others have seen this as an early appearance of the Pillar of Cloud.

61 *mearchofu mor heald* 'the moor held border dwellings'. OE *heald* for normal *heold* is a feature of Northumbrian dialect.

XLIII Heht þa ymb twa niht   tirfæste hæleð,
siððan hie feondum   oðfaren hæfdon,
ymbwicigean   werodes bearhtme
mid ælfere   Æthanes byrig,
mægnes mæste   mearclandum on.
Nearwe genyddon   on norðwegas,
wiston him be suðan   Sigelwara land,
forbærned burhhleoðu,   brune leode
hatum heofoncolum.   Þær halig God
wið færbryne   folc gescylde,
bælce oferbrædde   byrnendne heofon,
halgan nette   hatwendne lyft.
Hæfde wederwolcen   widum fæðmum
eorðan and uprodor   efne gedæled,
lædde leodwerod,   ligfyr adranc,
hate heofontorht.   Hæleð wafedon,
drihta gedrymost.   Dægsceades hleo
wand ofer wolcnum,   hæfde witig God
sunnan siðfæt   segle ofertolden,

XLIII He ordered then his noble warriors two nights
after they had got away from the fiends
to make camp with all host's revelry
by Etham's town with their foreign force,
with company most huge in borderlands.
Dangers forced them on to northern roads,
they knew that to their south was Sun-Dwellers' land,
mountainous burnt cliffs, people made brown
by heaven's hot coals. There Holy God
shielded His people against sudden burning,
with a baulk overspread the baking heaven,
with holy webbing the withering hot sky.
That storm cloud, which had with wide embraces
divided earth and upper sky evenly in two,
led the host of people, drank up the flame-fire
heaven-radiant hot. Heroes stood staring,
most joyful of retinues. This day-shade shelter
traversed the skies, wise God from south
the route-march had so canvassed over

73–4 *bælce . . . halgan nette* 'with a baulk . . . with holy webbing'. See below.

swa þa mæstrapas   men ne cuðon,
ne ða seglrode   geseon meahton
eorðbuende   ealle cræfte,
hu afæstnod wæs   feldhusa mæst,
siððan he mid wuldre   geweorðode
þeodenholde.   Þa wæs þridda wic
folce to frofre.   Fyrd eall geseah
hu þær hlifedon   halige seglas,
lyftwundor leoht.   Leode ongeton,
dugoð Israhela,   þæt þær Drihten cwom
weroda Drihten,   wicsteal metan.
Him beforan foran   fyr and wolcen
in beorhtrodor,   beamas twegen,
þara æghwæðer   efngedælde
heahþegnunga   haliges gastes,
deormodra sið   dagum and nihtum.
Þa ic on morgen gefrægn   modes rofan
hebban herebyman   hludan stefnum,

---

that men did not know of the mast-ropes,
nor with any sailyards could it be observed
by earth's inhabitants with any skill
how the vast field-tent was fastened down,
as with this glory the King showed honour
to men of His allegiance. A third camp was
then the people's comfort. The militia all saw
how holy sails towered high in that place,
nimble sky-miracle. The people could see,
troop of Israelites, that the Lord had come,
Lord of Hosts, to mark out a campsite there.
Before them travelled fire and cloud
in the upper sky, two upright beams,
each of which shared evenly with the other
in their high service to the Holy Ghost
that journey of daring men by day and night.
In the morning I heard then that brave-hearts
raised up war-trumpets with loud voice,

82–9 *mæstrapas . . . seglrode . . . feldhusa mæst . . . halige seglas* 'mast-ropes . . . sailyards . . . vast field-tent . . . holy sails'. These nautical elements have been seen as no more than 'a figural evocation of the Cross' by way of the Pillar of Cloud (Lucas 1994: 90). Howe nonetheless sees this extraordinary image as the poet's 'desire to incorporate, in as striking a fashion as possible, the Anglo-Saxon migration into Biblical history' (1989: 98). This cloud-pillar leading the Israelites from Egypt to the Promised Land is thus a figure (a) for the Cross leading the heathen to salvation and (b) for the sea-crossing of the poet's Northumbrian ancestors, latter-day Israelites, from Germania to Britain.

wuldres woman. Werod eall aras,
modigra mægen, swa him Moyses bebead,
mære magorǣswa, Metodes folce,
fus fyrdgetrum. Forð gesawon
lifes latþeow lifweg metan.
Swegl siðe weold, sæmen æfter
foron flodwege. Folc wæs on salum,
hlud herges cyrm.

XLIV Heofonbeacen astah
æfena gehwam, oðer wundor,
syllic æfter sunnan setlrade beheold,
ofer leodwerum lige scinan,
byrnende beam. Blace stodon
ofer sceotendum scire leoman,
scinon scyldhreoðan, sceado swiðredon,
neowle nihtscuwan neah ne mihton
heolstor ahydan. Heofoncandel barn,
niwe nihtweard nyde sceolde
wician ofer weredum, þy læs him westengryre

---

gave glory's blast. All the host arose,
a force of courageous men, as Moses, renowned
ready chieftain, fired up for campaign, commanded
the Measurer's people. Onwards did they see
Life's teacher mete out a road for them to stay alive.
The sail set their course, after came the sea-men
sailing on the flood-way. People's spirits lifted,
loud the army's cry.

XLIV A bonfire in heaven,
another wonder, climbed high each evening,
resplendently occupied the road of sun's setting
to shine flames upon the men of that nation,
a blazing pillar. Brilliant the bright rays,
standing over men who could shoot high,
shield-adornments shone, shadows weakened,
nightshades of underworld could keep no refuge
in hiding nearby. Heaven's candle burned,
Need drove a new night-watchman
to dwell above the hosts, lest a horror of the wastes,

---

115 *Heofoncandel* 'Heaven's candle'. For the Pillar of Fire which leads the host by night. *Beowulf*, line 1965, has *woruldcandel* for the 'sun'. To go on with the sailing conceit, *Exodus*' *heofoncandel* may be read as the Pole Star.

har hæðbroga holmegum wederum
on ferclamme ferhð getwæfde.
Hæfde foregenga fyrene loccas,
blace beamas, belegsan hweop
in þam hereþreate, hatan lige,
þæt he on westenne werod forbærnde,
nymðe hie modhwate Moyses hyrde.
Scean scir werod, scyldas lixton,
gesawon randwigan rihte stræte,
segn ofer sweoton, oðþæt sæfæsten
landes æt ende leodmægne forstod,
fus on forðweg. Fyrdwic aras,
wyrpton hie werige, wiste genægdon
modige meteþegnas, hyra mægen beton.
Bræddon æfter beorgum, siððan byme sang,
flotan feldhusum. Þa wæs feorðe wic,
randwigena ræst, be þan Readan Sæ.

---

the hoary heath-terror in ocean storms
should strike fear into hearts with its sudden clasp.
Their guide walked in front with his locks all fiery,
with gleaming beams, menaced the war-band
with furnace terror, with white-hot flame,
that he would burn up the host in the desert
unless they set their minds to obeying Moses.
The bright host shone, shields glinted,
men at arms observed the right road,
the standard above companies, until the nation's force
was blocked by a sea-bulwark at land's edge,
ready and in their way. Campaign tents rose up,
weary men refreshed themselves, brave cook-boys
came up with meals, built up their strength.
Sailors pitched field-tents along the hills
when the trumpet sang. That was then the fourth camp,
resting-place of soldiers by the Red Sea.

---

118 *har hæðbroga holmegum wederum* 'hoary heath-terror in ocean storms'. The imagery seems to fuse the heathland predator, the wolf, with the oceanic, the shark (compare OIce *hákarl* 'grey-man', for 'shark').

Moses puts heart into the Israelites

The Israelites are first frightened to see Pharaoh's army bearing down on them. However, Moses puts heart into them by recalling God's covenant with their ancestors and also His power as enacted through Moses' hand. The rod looks like a bishop's staff of office, and his speech on the parting of the Red Sea dramatises the story as if this poem were meant to be performed in the nave of a cathedral.

Wyly, B. W., *Figures of Authority in the Old English Exodus*, Anglistische Forschungen 262 (Heidelberg, 1999)

Þa wæs handrofra   here ætgædere,
fus forðwegas.   Fana up gerad,
beama beorhtost,   bidon ealle þa gen
hwonne siðboda   sæstreamum neah
leoht ofer lindum   lyftedoras bræc.

XLVI Ahleop þa for hæleðum   hildecalla,
bald beohata,   bord up ahof,
heht þa folctogan   fyrde gestillan,
þenden modiges meðel   monige gehyrdon.
Wolde reordigean   rices hyrde
ofer hereciste   halgan stefne,
werodes wisa,   wurðmyndum spræc:
'Ne beoð ge þy forhtran,   þeah þe Faraon brohte
sweordwigendra   side hergas,
eorla unrim!   Him eallum wile

The strong-arm host was now gathered,
ready to move forward. Their standard rode high,
brightest of beams, they had all been waiting
near the sea's currents for their path-finder,
the light over linden shields, to pierce the sky's wall.

XLVI Then up leapt a war-herald before heroes,
the brave summoner lifted up his shield,
ordered the commanders to quiet down the army
while many a man listened to the brave man's address.
The kingdom's shepherd wished to speak
to the war-band's finest with holy voice,
guide of hosts, uttered words of honour:
'Do not let the broad line brought by Pharaoh
of sword-bearing war-bands, warriors beyond number,
make you more fearful! To all of them

mihtig Drihten þurh mine hand
to dæge þissum dædlean gyfan,
þæt hie lifigende leng ne moton
ægnian mid yrmðum Israhela cyn.
Ne willað eow andrædan deade feðan,
fæge ferhðlocan! Fyrst is æt ende
lænes lifes. Eow is lar Godes
abroden of breostum. Ic on[n] beteran ræd,
þæt ge gewurðien wuldres Aldor,
and eow Liffrean lissa bidde,
sigora gesynto, þær ge siðien.
Þis is se ecea Abrahames God,
frumsceafta Frea, se ðas fyrd wereð,
modig and mægenrof, mid þære miclan hand.'

Hof ða for hergum hlude stefne
lifigendra leod, þa he to leodum spræc:
'Hwæt, ge nu eagum to on lociað,
folca leofost, færwundra sum,

---

will the Mighty Lord through this my hand
grant on this day such payment for their deeds
that, while alive, they will no longer have leave
to frighten Israel with a prospect of miseries.
Nor do you want to dread companies of dead,
their bodies doomed to die! The time of their borrowed lives
is at an end. In you has God's teaching
been drawn from His heart. I give you a better plan,
that you should worship the Chief of Glory,
and pray for mercy to the Lord of Life,
for victory's salvation wherever you travel,
for it is Abraham's eternal God,
Lord of Creation, who will defend this campaign,
brave and courageous, through His great hand.'

Then before the armies did the prince of living men
raise his voice high as he spoke to the nation:
'Listen and now look with your own eyes
on a sudden wonder, you most beloved people,

262–75 *þurh mine hand . . . mid þære miclan hand* 'through this my hand . . . through His great hand'. As in the Bible, Moses promises to enact the Lord's vengeance through his own hand, but he then refers to this hand as the Lord's, as if the Lord has become manifest in him. His speech has enormous rhetorical power for just 17 lines.

hu ic sylfa sloh   and þeos swiðre hand
grene tacne   garsecges deop.
Yð up færeð,   ofstum wyrceð
wæter wealfæsten.   Wegas syndon dryge,
haswe herestræta,   holm gerymeð
ealde staðolas,   þa ic ær ne gefrægn
ofer middangeard   men geferan,
fage feldas,   þa forð heonon
in ece tid   yðe þeahton,
sælde sægrundas.   Suðwind fornam
bæðweges blæst,   brim is areafod,
sand sæcir spaw.   Ic wat soð gere
þæt eow mihtig God   miltse gecyðde,
eorlas ærglade.   Ofest is selost
þæt ge of feonda   fæðme weorðen,
nu se agend   up arærde
reade streamas   in randgebeorh.
Syndon þa foreweallas   fægre gestepte,
wrætlicu wægfaru,   oð wolcna hrof.’

---

how I myself with this right hand have struck
the spearman’s deep with a green token of life.
A breaker there moves upwards, with haste the water
is building a rampart. The road is dry,
grey the army highway, ocean is emptying from
ancient foundations on which I have never heard
before of any men moving in the Middle World,
bright-lit fields which in eternity
up to this time the waves roofed over,
a sea-floor sealed over. A south wind took off
the bath-way’s rage, ocean is stolen away,
sea’s turning has spit out sand. I can see it is true,
O gentlemen glad like none other, that Mighty God
has shown you mercy. Haste is best
for you to escape the enemies’ embrace
now that the Owner of All has reared up
the Red Streams into a fortress of shields.
Facing walls to either side of a splendid road
do cast themselves up to the cloud-roof in beauty.’

---

280 *and þeos swiðre hand* ‘with this right hand’. Moses separates his self from his right hand as if to emphasise the numinous quality that the latter now has.

Æfter þam wordum werod eall aras,
modigra mægen. Mere stille bad.
Hofon herecyste hwite linde,
segnas on sande. Sæweall astah,
uplang gestod wið Israhelum
andægne fyrst. Wæs seo eorla gedriht
anes modes, [. . .]
fæstum fæðmum freoðowære heold.

After these words the host all arose,
a force of valiant men. The sea waited still.
War-band's finest lifted white linden shields,
standards on the sand. The sea-wall climbed,
upright stood there for the sons of Israel
for the space of a day. That company of warriors
was of one mind [. . .]
kept hold of covenant in a fast embrace.

The drowning of the Egyptians

For its hurtling movement and lurid descriptive power, this passage stands comparison with St Andrew's drowning of the Mermedonians in *Andreas* below. The destructive sea is here personified in keeping with the (folk-)etymological meaning of *garsecg* 'ocean' as 'spear-man' (*gar-secg*). The Lord Himself seems to stand above the Egyptians and cut them down with a sword as they try to flee a deluge which, as the obverse of the baptism that saves the chosen people, is a figure for damnation itself.

XLIX Folc wæs afæred, flodegsa becwom
gastas geomre, geofon deaðe hweop.
Wæron beorhhliðu blode bestemed,
holm heolfre spaw, hream wæs on yðum,
wæter wæpna ful, wælmist astah.

XLIX The rabble was struck with fear, flood terror seized
the miserable souls, ocean menaced with death.
The cliff-sides were drenched with blood,
the deep spewed out gore, screaming in the waves,
water full of weapons, a mist of death arose.

---

306 *freoðowære heold* 'kept hold of covenant'. Legal metaphors are a leading motif of *Exodus* (Wyly: 1999), through the Lord's protective covenants with His chosen people in the history of Genesis. The poet emphasises these with his narrative allusions to the past and future: Noah's Flood (lines 356–79) and Abraham and Isaac (lines 380–446) on one hand and Solomon's Temple in Jerusalem (lines 389–96) on the other. He places the allusions at the critical moment when the Israelites are crossing the Red Sea.

Wæron Egypte eft oncyrde,
flugon forhtigende, fær ongeton,
woldon hereblеaðe hamas findan,
gylp wearð gnornra. Him ongen genap
atol yða gewealc, ne ðær ænig becwom
herges to hame, ac behindan beleac
wyrd mid wæge. Þær ær wegas lagon,
mere modgode, mægen wæs adrenced.
Streamas stodon, storm up gewat
heah to heofonum, herewopa mæst.
Laðe cyrmdon (lyft up geswearc)
fægum stæfnum, flod blod gewod.
Randbyrig wæron rofene, rodor swipode
meredeaða mæst, modige swulton
cyningas on corðre, cyre swiðrode
sæs æt ende. Wigbord scinon
heah ofer hæleðum, holmweall astah,
merestream modig. Mægen wæs on cwealme
fæste gefeterod, forðganges weg
searwum æsæled, sand basnodon
witodre fyrde hwonne waðema stream,
sincalda sæ, sealtum yðum
æflastum gewuna ece staðulas,

The Egyptians were turned back,
fled shaking with fear, could see the danger,
those plundering cowards wished to find their homes,
their boast now all lamentation. Towards them the air darkened
with a wave's terrible roll, nor did any man there
from their army get home, but fate cut them off
from behind with the cascade. Where the road once lay,
ocean raged, the host was drenched over.
Streams appeared, a gale whipped up
high to the heavens, a war-band's greatest weeping.
Hateful men were shrieking (the sky fully darkened)
with doomed voices, blood coursed into flood.
The shielding wall broke, heaven was lashed
by the greatest death at sea, kings within bodyguards
perished as men valiant, the sea's retreat
had finally failed. Its war-boards glinted
over heroes' heads, ocean's rampart rose,
moody stream of sea. In its own execution the host
was fettered fast, their progress out of there
tangled with harness, sands lay in ambush
for the expected army column, when waters' whirl,
the sea ever-cold with its salty waves
from off-road paths to its eternal foundations,

nacud nydboda, neosan come,
fah feðegast, se ðe feondum geneop.
Wæs seo hæwene lyft heolfre geblanden,
brim berstende blodegesan hweop,
sæmanna sið, oðþæt soð metod
þurh Moyses hand modge rymde,
wide wæðde, wælfæðmum sweop.
Flod famgode, fæge crungon,
lagu land gefeol, lyft wæs onhrered,
wicon weallfæsten, wægas burston,
multon meretorras, þa se Mihtiga sloh
mid halige hand, heofonrices Weard,
on werbeamas. Wlance ðeode
ne mihton forhabban helpendra pað,
merestreames mod, ac he manegum gesceod
gyllende gryre. Garsecg wedde,
up ateah, on sleap. Egesan stodon,
weollon wælbenna. Witrod gefeol

---

naked portender of disaster, came back prying,
a wicked footloose spirit that had stranded its foes.
The purple sky was blended with gore,
the bursting ocean menaced with bloody terror
the journey of sailors until the True Measurer,
through Moses' hand, swept away the valiant,
hunted them widely, swept them up in deadly fathoms.
The flood foamed, doomed men dropped,
waters fell upon land, air was stirred up,
fortress-walls buckled, the ramparts burst,
the sea-towers crumbled as the Mighty, the Guardian
of the Kingdom of Heaven, with holy hand struck
on the weir-struts. Proud people,
they could not block the path of helping waves,
sea-current's mood, but many men He harmed
with shrieking fury. Spear-man went mad,
drew up, slid upon them. Terror appeared,
the wounds of slaughter welled. The rod of punishment fell,

---

486 *mid halige hand* 'with holy hand'. The enactment of Moses' promise on lines 262–75.

490 *Garsecg wedde* 'Spear-man went mad'. This poet is focused on etymologies, real or imagined. For his tour-de-force account of the closing of the Red Sea, he personifies the sea as its mysterious (but transparent) OE name suggests, as an armed warrior, like Michael, sent by the Lord to slaughter the whole Egyptian army.

heah of heofonum, handweorc Godes,
famigbosma flodwearde sloh,
unhleowan wæg, alde mece,
þæt ðy deaðdrepe drihte swæfon,
synfullra sweot. Sawlum lunnon
fæste befarene, flodblac here,
siððan hie on bugon brun yppinge,
modewæga mæst. Mægen eall gedreas
ða gedrencte wæron dugoð Egypta,
Faraon mid his folcum. He onfond hraðe,
siððan grund gestah Godes andsaca,
þæt wæs mihtigra mereflodes weard,
wolde heorufæðmum hilde gesceadan,
yrre and egesfull. Egyptum wearð
þæs dægweorces deop lean gesceod,
forðam þæs heriges ham eft ne com
ealles ungrundes ænig to lafe,
þætte sið heora secgan moste,
bodigean æfter burgum bealospella mæst,
hordwearda hryre, hæleða cwenum,
ac þa mægenþreatas meredeað geswealh,
spelbodan eac. Se ðe sped ahte
ageat gylp wera. Hie wið God wunnon.

---

high out of heaven, God's handiwork,
the foam-breasted one struck his flood-guardian,
the chill wave, with an ancient sword
so that whole battalions perished by that death-blow,
legions of sinners. They lost their souls,
firmly surrounded, that flood-paled war-band,
as they bowed under the weight of the dark
moody massive wave. The company all perished,
Egyptian divisions that were inundated,
the armies of Pharaoh, who soon discovered,
God's adversary, climbing back on shore,
that the sea-flood Keeper was mightier than he,
wished with bloody fathoms to hurt him in war,
enraged and terrifying. To the Egyptians was
decreed a deep payment for that day's work,
that back home of that war-band there came
not one survivor from the whole boundless troop
who might have leave to tell their story,
to announce in the towns the greatest evil tidings,
hoard-keepers' ruin, to the ladies of these men,
but sea-death swallowed up those regiments,
their messengers too. He whose triumph it was
sacrificed the boast of those men. They were fighting God.

Þanon Israhelum ece rædas
on merehwearfe Moyses sægde,
heahþungen wer, halige spræce,
deop ærende. Dægword nemnað
swa gyt werðeode, on gewritum findað
doma gehwilcne, þara ðe him Drihten bebead
on þam siðfate soðum wordum.
Gif onlucan wile lifes wealhstod,
beorht in breostum, banhuses weard,
ginfæsten god gastes cægon,
run bið gerecenod, ræd forð gæð,
hafað wislicu word on fæðme,
wile meagollice modum tæcan
þæt we gesne ne syn Godes þeodscipes,
metodes miltsa. He us ma onlyhð,
nu us boceras beteran secgað
lengran lifwynna. Þis is læne dream,
wommum awyrged, wreccum alyfed,
earmra anbid. Eðellease

Thereupon did Moses on the sea-shore
hold forth to the Israelites on eternal rewards,
the man of high distinction, gave with sacred words
a message profound. That day's story is told
by nations still, in scriptures they will find
each of the laws which the Lord proclaimed to them
in His own words on that expedition.
If life's interpreter, keeper of the bone-dwelling
bright within the breast, should wish to unlock
long-lasting riches with the keys of the spirit,
the mystery will be told, reward will come forth,
wise words will he have in his embrace,
earnestly will he want to teach the mind
that we are not lacking in God's testimony,
the Measurer's mercy. He will grant us more,
now bookmen speak of the better, more lasting,
joys of Life. This pleasure here is lent to us,
cursed with defilements, one allowed to exiles,
the one way street of wretched men. Men of no homeland

---

525 *gastes cægon* 'with the keys of the spirit'. This well-known injunction to unlock the meaning of *Exodus* with the mind for the benefit of the soul is clearly an invitation to read this poem for allegorical meaning, and probably in more than one layer, as has been done here. As a pause before the poem's conclusion, it may be compared with the rather more playful self-interruption below in *Andreas*, lines 1478–89.

þysne gystsele   gihðum healdað,
murnað on mode,   manhus witon
fæst under foldan,   þær bið fyr and wyrm,
open ece scræf.   Yfela gehwylces
swa nu regnþeofas   rice dælað,
yldo oððe ærdeað.   Eftwyrd cymð,
mægenþrymma mæst   ofer middangeard,
dæg dædum fah.   Drihten sylfa
on þam meðelstede   manegum demeð,
þonne he soðfæstra   sawla lædeð,
eadige gastas,   on uprodor,
þær is leoht and lif,   eac þon lissa blæd.
Dugoð on dreame   drihten herigað,
weroda wuldorcyning   to widan feore.

---

occupy this guest-hall in their sorrows,
mourn in their hearts, know the torture chamber
lying fast beneath the earth, with fire and serpent,
a pit laid open for ever. All kinds of evil
share dominion, like those demonic thieves
senility and early death. Judgement will come,
the greatest force of majesty in Middle World,
a day marked by deeds. The Lord Himself
will judge many in that assembly place
when He leads the souls of the righteous,
blessed spirits, into heaven above,
where light is, and life, and pleasure in being kind.
Happily will the retinue praise the Lord,
the Glorious King of Hosts for ever more.

Cynewulf's *Elene*

⁂

Cynewulf is known from four runic signatures in the Epilogues of as many religious poems. These are *Elene* and *The Fates of the Apostles* in the Vercelli Book (*c.* 975), and *Christ II* and *Juliana* in the Exeter Book (*c.* 980). Apart from *Christ II*, they are all versified Saints' Lives. *Elene* is based on the legend of St Helena and her discovery ('Invention') of the True Cross. The story opens with her son, Emperor Constantine, just as he faces an invasion from Huns and Germans. Constantine is pagan, but dreams of the Cross the night before the invasion and takes one into battle the next day, crushing his opponents. He sends his mother to Jerusalem to find the original. Helena arrives and interrogates the elders on the Cross's whereabouts, singling out one named Judas, who eventually converts and becomes Cyriacus, Jerusalem's first bishop. He then divines the site of the nails. Cynewulf finishes with an Epilogue in which he laments the passing of years, plants the runic signature of his ownership and reflects on the Day of Judgement.

Cynewulf's source was a recension of the *Acts of St Cyriacus*, which is written with serious flaws in its chronology, placing the opening battle in 233 and making Helena a contemporary of St Stephen. Cynewulf's unemended use of this legend shows that he was a man of modest education, and he did not have to know Latin if someone paraphrased the Latin texts for him. There is a rhyming passage in his Epilogue to *Elene*, just before his signature, which has allowed his dialect to be judged as Mercian Anglian (Fulk 2001: 14). The date of his work can be judged as between the eighth and late tenth century on metrical grounds (*ibid.*, 17–18), also by finding the sources for his poems. Pat Conner's discovery that Cynewulf used the *Martyrology* of Usuardus for his *Fates* (a collection of Saints' Lives in miniature of rather inferior quality), has enabled him to put Cynewulf at the earliest in the last quarter of the ninth century, for Usuardus wrote his *Martyrology* in *c.* 875 (2001: 36–46). If Cynewulf lived in Mercia at this time, it would have had to be in the west, for the eastern half of this kingdom was overrun by Danes from the 870s to the 920s (and even later in the case of Lincolnshire). If we put all these observations together, it is a fair bet that Cynewulf lived in south-west Mercia, perhaps near Worcester, at some time between *c.* 875 and the early tenth century. It has been argued that *Elene* reflects the West Saxon campaigns in the Danelaw in the first half of the tenth century, with its celebration of Helena's drive to convert the Jews, i.e. the Danes (Estes 2006: 143–4). Yet we should remember that Helena's son Constantine is no Christian himself until he sees the Cross, nor does he try to convert his own barbarians at the beginning of the poem.

Bjork, R. E., *The Old English Verse Saints' Lives: A Study in Direct Discourse and the Iconography of Style* (Toronto, 1985)

Bjork, R. E., ed., *The Cynewulf Reader* (London, 2001)

Calder, D. G., and M. J. B. Allen, trans., *Sources and Analogues of Old English Poetry: The Major Latin Sources in Translation* (Cambridge, 1976)

Calder D. G., *Cynewulf* (Boston, MA, 1981), 105–38 (on *Elene*)

Campbell, J., 'Cynewulf's multiple revelations', *Medievalia et Humanistica* new series 3 (1972), 257–77; repr. in Bjork (2001), 229–50

Conner, P. W., 'On dating Cynewulf', in Bjork (2001), 23–56

DiNapoli, R., 'Poesis and authority: traces of an Anglo-Saxon *Agon* in Cynewulf's *Elene*', *Neophilologus* 82 (1998), 619–30

Estes, H., 'Colonization and conversion in Cynewulf's *Elene*', in *Conversion and Colonization in Anglo-Saxon England*, ed. C. E. Karkov and N. Howe, Medieval and Renaissance Texts and Studies 318 (Tempe, AZ, 2006), 133–51

Fulk, R. D., 'Cynewulf: canon, dialect, and date', in Bjork (2001), 3–21

Gardner, J., 'Cynewulf's *Elene*: sources and structure', *Neophilologus* 54 (1970), 65–76

Gradon, P. O. E., 'Constantine and the barbarians', *Modern Language Review* 42 (1947), 161–72

Gradon, P. O. E., ed., and rev. M. Swanton, *Cynewulf's 'Elene'*, 2nd ed. (Exeter, 1958, rev. ed. 1996)

Harbus, A., 'Text as revelation: Constantine's dream in *Elene*', *Neophilologus* 78 (1994), 645–53

Hermann, J. P., 'The theme of spiritual warfare in the Old English *Elene*', *Papers on Language and Literature* 11 (1975), 115–25

Constantine's vision of the Cross

The opening of this poem reveals an annalist's interest in dates. This one is in Cynewulf's source, the *Acts of St Cyriacus* (Calder and Allen 1976: 60). The date at 233 is probably a mistake for AD 333 when Constantine was fighting Goths on the Balkan frontier. His campaigns against them have here been confused with the Battle of the Milvian Bridge outside Rome in 312, six years after he was crowned by the legion in York. Doubtless the error was initiated in an older text by a miscopying of ccxxxiii for cccxxxiii, but after that it is hard to judge.

Cynewulf is no historian, and seems more at home with heroic legend. He embroiders the story of Constantine's war with a lengthy passage which is influenced by heroic poetry. The story of Constantine's nocturnal dream vision is derived from a legend near to the emperor's time. Another version is that of the contemporary historian Eusebius Pamphilus, who says that Constantine saw the Cross at noon on the field in front of his troops. The legend of Constantine was important to Anglo-Saxons, rather more so in the seventh and eighth centuries than the tenth. His vision inspired King Oswald of Northumbria to victory against Cadwalla in Heavenfield in 633, and indirectly it seems to establish a setting for *The Dream of the Rood.*

North, R., *Heathen Gods in Old English Literature*, Cambridge Studies in Anglo-Saxon England 22 (Cambridge, 1997)

Wolfram, H., *History of the Goths*, trans. T. J. Dunlap, rev. from German 2nd ed. (Berkeley, CA, 1988)

Þa wæs agangen geara hwyrftum
tu hund ond þreo geteled rimes,
swylce þritig eac, þinggemearces,
wintra for worulde, þæs þe wealdend God
acenned wearð, cyninga Wuldor,
in middangeard þurh mennisc heo,
soðfæstra Leoht. Þa wæs syxte gear
Constantines caserdomes,
þæt he Romwara in rice wearð
ahæfen, hildfruma, to hereteman.
Wæs se leodhwata lindgeborga
eorlum arfæst. Æðelinges weox
rice under roderum. He wæs riht cyning,
guðweard gumena. Hine God trymede
mærðum ond mihtum, þæt he manegum wearð
geond middangeard mannum to hroðer,
werþeodum to wræce, syððan wæpen ahof
wið hetendum. Him wæs hild boden,
wiges woma. Werod samnodan

Now was passed in the circle of years
the count of two hundred and three,
likewise a period of thirty more
winters in this world, since all-wielding God,
Glory of Kings, was born
in human form in the Middle World,
Light of the Righteous. The sixth year it was,
of the empire of Constantine, when
in the kingdom of the Romans this man,
war-prince, was raised to army commander.
This energetic leader was a protecting shield
of honour to his nobles. The chieftain's domain
grew beneath the skies. He was a just king,
keeper of his men in battle. God confirmed him
in fame and might so that to many men
he was a comfort through the Middle World,
a retribution to the nations when he raised weapons
against their attacks. To him was war offered,
the tumult of a duel. A host was gathered

2–4 *tu hund ond þreo . . . þritig eac . . . wintra* 'two hundred and three . . . likewise a period of thirty more winters'. The date of this era, 233 for AD 333.

7 *syxte gear Constantines caserdomes* 'the sixth year of the empire of Constantine'. This would date the coronation to 226, presumably 326 in source of the Acts of St Cyriac. Constantine was busy fighting Gothic tribes throughout this period (Wolfram 1988: 59–61), but the chronology is quite confused, for Constantine was crowned emperor in York in 306 and defeated his rivals six years later in 312 at the Battle of the Milvian Bridge outside Rome, where the vision took place.

Huna leode   ond Hreðgotan,
foron fyrdhwate   Francan ond Hugas.
Wæron hwate weras,   [. . .]
gearwe to guðe.   Garas lixtan,
wriðene wælhlencan.   Wordum ond bordum
hofon herecombol.   Þa wæron heardingas
sweotole gesamnod   ond eal [sib] geador.
For folca gedryht.   Fyrdleoð agol
wulf on wealde,   wælrune ne mað.
Urigfeðera   earn sang ahof,
laðum on laste.   Lungre scynde
ofer Burgen*d*a   beaduþreata mæst,
hergum to hilde,   swylce Huna cyning
ymbsittendra   awer meahte
abannan to beadwe   burgwigendra.
For fyrda mæst.   Feðan trymedon
eoredcestum,   þæt on ælfylce
deareðlacende   on Danubie,
stærcedfyrhðe,   stæðe wicedon
ymb þæs wæteres wylm.   Werodes breahtme

---

by Hunnish princes and Goths of the Baltic,
the Franks and the Hugas did march on campaign.
They were keen men [. . .]
ready to make war. The spears glinted,
mail-coats on the move. With words and shields
they lifted war-standards. The heathens now were
manifestly gathered and all their kin together.
The mob's retinue marched. The wolf in the wood who howled
his poem of campaign hid no secrets about slaughter.
With his dewy feathers the eagle lifted his song
in the track of hostile men. Hastened with speed
across Burgundy the greatest divisions
with war-bands into battle which the Hun king
to fighting could summon of city-taking warriors
from anywhere in lands round about him.
The biggest army marched. Infantry drew up
with cavalry units to make an alien nation
of javelin-tossing soldiers of hardened mind
camping out by the banks of the Danube
by the lapping water's shore. The host in its revelry

---

31 *ofer Burgenda* 'across Burgundy'. For the manuscript's *burg enta*, which Gradon emends to *burgen*de for 'over the city boundary' (1996: 27). Yet the association of Huns and Burgundians is close in *Widsith* and other lays (see **Heroic Poems**).

woldon Romwara rice geþringan,
hergum ahyðan. Þær wearð Huna cyme
cuð ceasterwarum. Þa se casere heht
ongean gramum guðgelæcan
under earhfære ofstum myclum
bannan to beadwe, beran ut þræce
rincas under roderum. Wæron Romware,
secgas sigerofe, sona gegearwod
wæpnum to wigge, þeah hie werod læsse
hæfdon to hilde þonne Huna cining.
Ridon ymb rofne, þonne rand dynede,
campwudu clynede, cyning þreate for,
herge to hilde. Hrefen uppe gol,
wan ond wælfel. Werod wæs on tyhte.
Hleopon hornboran, hreopan friccan,
mearh moldan træd. Mægen samnode,
cafe to cease.

Cyning wæs afyrhted,
egsan geaclad, siððan elþeodige,
Huna ond Hreða here sceawedon,
ðæt he on Romwara rices ende

---

wanted to push into the empire of Romans,
plunder it with war-bands. Citizens discovered
that Huns were coming. Then the emperor ordered
his old comrades in battle against the foe,
with great haste under arrows' assault
to muster for war, to bring out for attack
some soldiers under the sky. The Romans, men
brave for victory, readied without delay
to fight with weapons, although they had
a smaller host for war than the Hunnish king.
Around the valiant man they rode, when shields dinned,
battle-boards were beaten. The king in formation moved
with his army to war. Above them shrieked a raven,
shiny-black and slaughter-fierce. The host was on the march.
Trumpeters called, heralds shouted,
a stallion stepped on earth. The force was mustered,
brave men to conflict.

King Constantine took fright,
so stricken with terror when the foreigners
showed, the army of Huns and Baltic Goths,
that a host he mustered by the border

ymb þæs wæteres stæð   werod samnode,
mægen unrime.   Modsorge wæg
Romwara cyning,   rices ne wende
for werodleste,   hæfde wigena to lyt,
eaxlgestealna   wið ofermægene,
hrora to hilde.   Here wicode,
eorlas ymb æðeling,   egstreame neah
on neaweste   nihtlangne fyrst,
þæs þe hie feonda gefær   fyrmest gesægon.
Þa wearð on slæpe   sylfum ætywed
þam casere,   þær he on corðre swæf,
sigerofum gesegen   swefnes woma.
Þuhte him wlitescyne   on weres hade
hwit ond hiwbeorht   hæleða nathwylc
geywed ænlicra   þonne he ær oððe sið
gesege under swegle.   He of slæpe onbrægd,
eofurcumble beþeaht.

---

of Roman regions by the water's edge,
a force beyond numbering. Great anguish he bore,
did the king of Romans, expected no dominion
for his lack of troops, had too few front-line
warriors to match an overwhelming force, too few
roaring men for war. The army camped,
nobles about their chieftain, not far from the river-current
for a whole night long in the neighbourhood
where first they noted the enemies' invasion.
Then to the emperor's own person in sleep,
while he slumbered with entourage, was revealed
a tumultous vision for him to see who braved defeat.
Dazzling fair in a man's form there appeared to him,
white and brilliant of hue, some kind of man
displayed more peerless than any, either now or before,
whom he saw beneath the sun. He awoke from sleep,
lay beneath his boar-banner.

---

61 *Modsorge wæg* 'great anguish he bore'. This phrase is a variant of *higeþryðe wæg* 'she had passion of mind', which describes Hagar's pride against Sarah in *Genesis A*, line 2240, and *modþryþe wæg* 'passion of mind she had' in *Beowulf*, line 1931 (see **Heroic Poems**).

76 *eofurcumble beþeaht* 'lay beneath his boar-banner'. Beowulf's men have *eoforlic* 'boar-images' shining apparently from the top of their helmets, in *Beowulf*, line 303, as does the Benty Grange helmet from the eighth century. Constantine is literally 'covered' by this boar, trapped in a heathen cult of his own, but his emblem is about to change for a new one.

Him se ar hraðe,
wlitig wuldres boda, wið þingode
ond be naman nemde (nihthelm toglad):
'Constantinus, heht þe Cyning engla,
wyrda Wealdend, wære beodan,
duguða Dryhten. Ne ondræd þu ðe,
ðeah þe elþeodige egesan hwopan,
heardre hilde. Þu to heofenum beseoh
on wuldres weard, þær ðu wraðe findest,
sigores tacen.'

He wæs sona gearu
þurh þæs halgan hæs, hreðerlocan onspeon,
up locade, swa him se ar abead,
fæle friðowebba. Geseah he frætwum beorht
wliti wuldres treo ofer wolcna hrof
golde ge[g]lenged (gimmas lixtan),
wæs se blaca beam bocstafum awriten,
beorhte ond leohte: **Mid þys beacne ðu**

Speedily with him that herald,
radiant messenger from glory, came to point of order,
calling him by name (night slipped her cover):
'O Constantine, the King of Angels, Commander
of Fate, has ordered me to offer you His covenant,
Lord of Hosts He is. Be not afraid,
though foreigners with fear may menace you
with combat hard. Look into heaven above you,
towards glory, where you will find succour,
a token of victory.'

Straight off was he was ready
at the holy man's instruction, opened his heart,
looked up just as commanded by this herald,
a treaty's true weaver. Bright in its trappings, a dazzling
tree of glory he saw high above the cloud-line
adorned with gold (jewels were gleaming),
that shining tree was inscribed with Roman letters
bright and radiant: **With this beacon you**

89–90 *wliti wuldres treo . . . gimmas lixtan* 'tree of glory . . . jewels were gleaming'. Fairly close to the corresponding scene in *The Dream of the Rood*.

91 *bocstafum awriten* 'inscribed with Roman letters'. Not with runes, Cynewulf seems to say with his *boc*-prefix to *stafum*.

92 ***Mid þys beacne*** 'With this beacon'. The Bewcastle Cross calls itself a ***sigbecn*** 'victory beacon', probably with Constantine's story in mind (see the Ruthwell *Crucifixion Poem*); *beacen* is used in *The Dream of the Rood*, lines 6, 21, 83, 118; and of course Cynewulf uses *sigebeacen* for the Cross on line 1256 of *Elene*.

on þam frecnan fære feond oferswiðesð,
geletest lað werod. Þa þæt leoht gewat,
up siðode, ond se ar somed
on clænra gemang. Cyning wæs þy bliðra
ond þe sorgleasra, secga aldor,
on fyrhðsefan, þurh þa fægeran gesyhð.

II HEHT þa onlice æðelinga hleo,
beorna beaggifa, swa he þæt beacen geseah,
heria hildfruma, þæt him on heofonum ær
geiewed wearð, ofstum myclum,
Constantinus, Cristes rode,
tireadig cyning, tacen gewyrcan.
Heht þa on uhtan mid ærdæge
wigend wreccan ond wæpenþræce
hebban heorucumbul ond þæt halige treo
him beforan ferian on feonda gemang,
beran beacen Godes. Byman sungon
hlude for hergum. Hrefn weorces gefeah,
urigfeðra, earn sið beheold,
wælhreowra wig. Wulf sang ahof,

---

will overcome your enemy in the fierce invasion,
withstand the hostile host. Then the light departed,
up it moved and the herald with it
to the throng of clean beings. The king was happier for that,
and less care did the men's chief have
in his heart for that fair sight.

II Then and there the shelter of princes, warriors'
ring-giver, war-marshal of armies, commanded,
as soon as seeing the beacon, that what from heaven
was earlier revealed to Constantine,
the nobly endowed king, should with great haste
be fashioned into a sign of the Rood of Christ.
In the dawn then, in early day, did he command
soldiers to be wakened and with shock of weapons
the blood-banner to be raised and that holy tree
before him to be ferried into fiends' multitude,
God's beacon to be borne. Trumpets sang out,
loud over armies. At this deed the raven rejoiced,
dewy-feathered, the eagle beheld the expedition,
combat of men cruel to the death. Wolf lifted song,

110–13 The beasts and birds of battle turn out when needed: Cynewulf has mastered the art of heroic composition. There is a similar list in *Judith*, lines 205–12, and in *The Battle of Brunanburh*, lines 60–5 (see **Viking Wars**).

holtes gehleða. Hildegesa stod.
Þær wæs borda gebrec ond beorna geþrec,
heard handgeswing ond herga gring,
syððan heo earhfære ærest metton.
On þæt fæge folc flana scuras,
garas ofer geolorand on gramra gemang,
hetend heoro*u*grimme, hildenædran,
þurh fingra geweald forð onsendan.
Stopon stiðhidige, stundum wræcon,
bræcon bordhreðan, bil in dufan,
þrungon þræchearde. Þa wæs þuf hafen,
segn for sweotum, sigeleoð galen.
Gylden grima, garas lixtan
on her*e*felda. Hæðene grungon,
feollon friðelease. Flugon instæpes
Huna leode, swa þæt halige treo
aræran heht Romwara cyning,
heaðofremmende. Wurdon heardingas
wide towrecene. Sume wig fornam,
sume unsofte aldor generedon
on þam heresiðe, sume healfcwice
flugon on fæsten ond feore burgon
æfter stanclifum, stede weardedon

---

woodland companion. The terror of war arose.
There was the smash of boards and clash of warriors,
hard hand-swing and slaughter of war-bands,
when for the first time they encountered the arrow-storm.
Into the doomed mob whole showers of darts,
spears over shield-rim into throngs of foes,
serpents of war, did fierce bloody attackers
send forth through the power of fingers.
Stern they advanced, took vengeance from time to time,
broke through the shield-wall, plunged axes,
shock-hardened shoved. Then the standard was raised,
emblem over regiments, the chant of victory sung.
Gilded war-mask and spears alike flashed
on battle-fields. Heathens were slaughtered,
fell without ransom. As quickly as they fled,
men of the Huns, so did the king of Romans
order that the holy war-promoting tree
should be raised. Pagans found themselves
driven far and wide. Battle took some,
others with great hardship saved their lives
in that army sweep, while, half-dead, still more
fled into the wilds and protected their lives
in and out of rock cliffs, kept their place

ymb Danubie. Sume drenc fornam
on lagostreame lifes æt ende.
Đa wæs modigra mægen on luste,
ehton elþeoda oð þæt æfen forð
fram dæges orde. Daroðæsc flugon,
hildenædran, heap wæs gescyrded,
laðra lindwered, lythwon becwom
Huna herges ham eft þanon.
Þa wæs gesyne þæt sige forgeaf
Constantino Cyning ælmihtig
æt þam dægweorce, domweorðunga,
rice under roderum, þurh his rode treo.
Gewat þa heriga helm ham eft þanon,
huðe hremig (hild wæs gesceaden),
wigge geweorðod. Com þa wigena hleo
þegna þreate þryðbold secan,
beadurof cyning burga neosan.

---

on Danube's far side. Some were taken by drowning
by water's currents at their life's end.
In high spirits now was the braver company,
pursuing the foreign nation right till evening
from the start of day. Ashen darts were flying,
the serpents of war, the troop was wiped out,
shield-host of foes, few men from there
of the Huns' army came back home.
It was clear now that to Constantine
the Almighty King had given victory
in that day's work, the distinction of renown,
a kingdom under skies, through His Rood-Tree.
The helm of armies moved back home from there,
exulting in his spoil (battle was decided),
honoured in combat. Warriors' protector came then
with his troop of thegns to visit his noble seat,
a king brave in warfare, to spy out his city.

148–52 The king's triumphal homecoming is a motif not only in Æthelstan's in *The Battle of Brunanburh*, lines 57–9, but also Hygelac's in *Beowulf*, lines 2991–8.

Elene's discovery of the nails of the Cross

Empress Helena has arrived in Jerusalem with instructions to find the True Cross, source of her son's victory earlier. She tortures some local wise men until one of them, Judas, relents after a week in a pit of his own and prays to God to reveal the site of Calvary. Smoke rises from the place where three crosses are then found. Christ's cross shows itself by raising a young man from the dead. Judas converts, becomes Cyriacus and is ordained as the first bishop of Jerusalem. Helena, staying on, starts to enquire about the nails of the True Cross. Ultimately two of these three nails will be curled into bridle rings and the third straightened out for the bit of Emperor Constantine's war-horse. To find the nails, Helena asks Cyriacus to use his special power of prayer. Going to Calvary, apparently to the same open pit, the bishop prays to the Guardian of Angels to reveal the site.

North, R., 'Old English "wopes hring" and the Old Norse myth of Baldr', in *Festschrift for James Graham-Campbell*, ed. L. Webster and A. Reynolds (forthcoming)

Ða cwom semninga   sunnan beorhtra
lacende lig.   Leode gesawon
hira willgifan   wundor cyðan,
ða ðær of heolstre,   swylce heofonsteorran
oððe goldgimmas,   grunde getenge,
næglas of nearwe   neoðan scinende
leohte lixton.   Leode gefægon,
weorud willhreðig,   sægdon wuldor Gode
ealle anmode,   þeah hie ær wæron
þurh deofles spild   in gedwolan lange,
acyrred fram Criste.

Hie cwædon þus:
'Nu we seolfe geseoð   sigores tacen,

Suddenly there came, brighter than the sun,
a dancing flame. The people looked on
at their benefactor making known a miracle,
when from its dark hiding, like stars in heaven
or jewels set in gold, lying at the bottom,
nails from their confinement shining upwards
gleamed in the light. The people rejoiced,
a host exultant, said glory be to God
with hearts all in unison, although before this time
they were long heretical, devil tried to ruin them,
they had turned away from Christ.

They spoke these words:
'Now we see for ourselves the token of victory,

soðwundor Godes,   þeah we wiðsocun ær
mid leasingum.   Nu is in leoht cymen,
onwrigen, wyrda bigang.   Wuldor þæs age
on heannesse   heofonrices God!'

Ða wæs geblissod   se ðe to bote gehwearf
þurh bearn Godes,   bisceop þara leoda,
niwan stefne.   He þam næglum onfeng,
egesan geaclod,   ond þære arwyrðan
cwene brohte.   Hæfde Ciriacus
eall gefylled,   swa him seo æðele bebead,
wifes willan.   Þa wæs wopes hring,
hat heafodwylm   ofer hleor goten
(nalles for torne   tearas feollon
ofer wira gespon),   wuldres gefylled
cwene willa.   Heo on cneow sette
leohte geleafan,   lac weorðode,
blissum hremig,   þe hire brungen wæs
gnyrna to geoce.   Gode þancode,

---

the genuine wonder of God, although, in our lies,
we did earlier forsake Him. Now it has come to light,
now is fate's course revealed. For this, may the God
of Heaven's Kingdom have glory in the highest!'

Enraptured then was he who had turned to the cure
through God's own Son, the bishop of these people,
with voice all new. He received the nails,
stricken with terror, and brought them
to the venerable queen. Cyriacus had
fulfilled it all just as the noble lady commanded him,
to the woman's joy. Then did a ring of weeping,
a hot head-wave, pour out over her cheeks
(not at all for grief did the tears fall down
over the clasp of wires), gloriously fulfilled
was the queen's joy. With bright faith
she put it on her knee, worshipped the offering
with raptures, exulting, which was brought to her
in aid of sins. God she thanked,

1131 *Þa wæs wopes hring* 'Then did a ring of weeping' etc. There are three more examples of this uncertain phrase for tearful outburst: when the disciples see Christ ascend in *Christ II*, line 537; St Guthlac's young servant (Beccel), as he prepares to tell the saint's sister (Pege) of her brother's death, in *Guthlac B*, line 1339; and St Andrew, tested to the limit by a second day of flogging in *Andreas*, line 1278. For a theory that the 'ring of weeping' was a figure for (an English version of) Baldr's ring Draupnir, sight of which was meant to stimulate tears in memory of the dead, see North (forthcoming).

sigora Dryhtne, þæs þe hio soð gecneow
ondweardlice þæt wæs oft bodod
feor ær beforan fram fruman worulde,
folcum to frofre. Heo gefylled wæs
wisdomes gife, ond þa wic beheold
halig heofonlic Gast, hreðer weardode,
æðelne innoð, swa hie ælmihtig
Sigebearn Godes sioððan freoðode.

XIV Ongan þa geornlice gastgerynum
on sefan secean soðfæstnesse
weg to wuldre. Huru, weroda God
gefullæste, Fæder on roderum,
Cining ælmihtig, þæt seo cwen begeat
willan in worulde. Wæs se witedom
þurh fyrnwitan beforan sungen
eall æfter orde, swa hit eft gelamp
ðinga gehwylces. Þeodcwen ongan
þurh gastes gife georne secan
nearwe geneahhe, to hwan hio þa næglas selost
ond deorlicost gedon meahte
dugoðum to hroðer, hwæt þæs wære Dryhtnes willa.
Heht ða gefetigean forðsnotterne

Lord of Victories, for her perception of the truth
now present which had often, from time long since,
from the beginning of the world, been proclaimed
as a solace to the nations. She was filled
with a gift of wisdom, and that place was held
by the Holy Heavenly Ghost, who occupied her heart,
the noble inward part, just as the Almighty
victorious Son of God protected her later.

XIV Eagerly then in the secrets of her spirit
did she search her mind for righteousness'
path to glory. Indeed, the God of Hosts
supported her, Father in the skies,
the King Almighty, so that the queen obtained
her joy in the world. This was a prophecy
sung by ancient sages from a time before
all in correct sequence just as it later happened
in every detail. The empress began
through grace of her spirit keenly to seek out,
often with close care, to what purpose best
and most precious she could put those nails
as a comfort to her courts, what were the Lord's will in this.
She ordered them to fetch a man exceptionally wise

ricene to rune,   þone þe rædgeþeaht
þurh gleawe miht   georne cuðe,
frodne on ferhðe,   ond hine frignan ongan
hwæt him þæs on sefan   selost þuhte
to gelæstenne,   ond his lare geceas
þurh þeodscipe.

He hire þriste oncwæð:
'Þæt is gedafenlic   þæt ðu Dryhtnes word
on hyge healde,   halige rune,
cwen seleste,   ond þæs Cininges bebod
georne begange,   nu þe God sealde
sawle sigesped   ond snyttro cræft,
Nerigend fira.   Þu ðas næglas hat
þam æðelestan   eorðcyninga
burgagendra   on his bridels don,
meare to midlum.   Þæt manigum sceall
geond middangeard   mære weorðan,
þonne æt sæcce mid þy   oferswiðan mæge
feonda gehwylcne,   þonne fyrdhwate
on twa healfe   tohtan secaþ,

---

quickly to consult with her, who would keenly know
a plan for this through the power of his intellect,
a man of learned mind, and him she did ask
what seemed to his heart the best way
to proceed, and it was his teaching she chose
by the people's wish.

Boldly he answered her:
'It is proper that in your mind you keep
the word of the Lord, His holy script of mysteries,
O best of queens, and carry out with eagerness
the King's behest, now that God has granted
triumph to your soul and the skill of cleverness,
Saviour of Mankind. You command these nails,
for the noblest of earthly kings who rule cities,
to be made into a bit for the bridle
of his steed. To many this shall
become renowned across the Middle World,
for then with this bit in battle he can overcome
enemies of all kinds, when keen soldiers
of both sides come seeking a campaign,

1168 *halige rune* 'His holy script of mysteries'. OE *run* expresses both 'runes' and 'mysteries'. Cynewulf's decision to hide the letters of his name in runes, in his four surviving Epilogues, shows a desire to translate his memory into a sacred mystery of its own (see below).

sweordgeniðlan, þær hie ymb [sige] winnað,
wrað wið wraðum. He ah æt wigge sped,
sigor æt sæcce ond sybbe gehwær,
æt gefeohte frið, se ðe fonan lædeð
bridels on blancan, þonne beadurofe
æt garþræce, guman gecoste,
berað bord ond ord. Þis bið beorna gehwam
wið æglæce unoferswiðed
wæpen æt wigge. Be ðam se witga sang,
snottor searuþancum (sefa deop gewod,
wisdomes gewitt). He þæt word gecwæð:

'Cuþ þæt gewyrðeð þæt þæs cyninges sceal
mearh under modegum midlum geweorðod,
bridelshringum. Bið þæt beacen Gode
halig nemned, ond se hwæteadig,
wigge weorðod, se þæt wicg byrð.'

Þa þæt ofstlice eall gelæste
Elene for eorlum. Æðelinges heht,
beorna beaggifan, bridels frætwan,

---

men wielding swords, to where they strive for [victory],
one foe against another. He will have triumph in war,
victory in conflict and peace in all places,
his own treaty after battle, who leads this standard,
this bridle on his charger, when war-braves,
men of splendour, into the clash of spears
bring board and sword point. For all warriors this will be
against whatever rabble adversary an invincible
combat weapon. Of this the Prophet sang,
a sage of subtle thoughts (his sense moved deep,
his wise intellect). He spoke these words:

'Be it known what will pass, the king's stallion
shall be honoured beneath a proud bit
with bridle-rings. This will be named as a beacon
holy to God, and he will be fortunate,
honoured in war, whom that steed bears!'

With haste then Helena carried all this out
before her nobles. For the prince, ring-giver
of warriors, she bade a bridle be fashioned,

1188 *Be ðam se witga sang* 'Of this the Prophet sang' etc. From Zacharias 1:20, 'Holy to the Lord on that day will be what is on a horse's bridle'. The text goes on to say 'and the pots in the home will be as bowls before the altar of the Lord', but this has less relevance, clearly.

hire selfre suna   sende to lace
ofer geofenes stream   gife unscynde.
Heht þa tosomne   þa heo seleste
mid Iudeum   gumena wiste
hæleða cynnes   to þære halgan byrig
cuman in þa ceastre.   Þa seo cwen ongan
læran leofra heap   þæt hie lufan Dryhtnes,
ond sybbe swa same   sylfra betweonum,
freondræddenne,   fæste gelæston
leahtorlease   in hira lifes tid,
ond þæs latteowes   larum hyrdon,
cristenum þeawum,   þe him Cyriacus
bude, boca gleaw.   Wæs se bissceophad
fægere befæsted!   Oft him feorran to
laman, limseoce,   lefe cwomon,
healte, heorudreorige,   hreofe ond blinde,
heane, hygegeomre.   Symle hælo þær
æt þam bisceope,   bote fundon
ece to aldre.   Đa gen him Elene forgeaf
sincweorðunga,   þa hio wæs siðes fus
eft to eðle,   ond þa eallum bebead
on þam gumrice   God hergendum,
werum ond wifum,   þæt hie weorðeden

---

sent it to her own son as an offering
over ocean currents, an unblemished gift.
She commanded all the best of mankind
whom she knew to live among the men
of the Jews to come into the high keep
of that holy city. Then the queen did
teach the beloved band that the Lord's love,
likewise His peace among themselves,
all the friendship He offered, they should steadily keep
without transgression to the end of their lives,
and pay heed to this teacher's instructions,
to the Christian virtues which Cyriacus,
book-wise man, might offer them. That was an episcopate
beautifully confirmed! To him often from afar
there came the lame, sick of limb, infirm,
men paralysed, wounded, the lepers and the blind,
shamed men, depressed. Always health there
from the bishop, a cure did they find
that lasted for ever. Him moreover Helena gave
honourable treasures, when ready to leave
for her homeland back again, then bade all people
who praised God in that kingdom of man,
men and women, that they should worship

mode ond mægene   þone mæran dæg,
heortan gehigdum,   in ðam sio halige rod
gemeted wæs,   mærost beama
þara þe of eorðan   up aweoxe,
geloden under leafum.   Wæs þa lencten agan
butan syx nihtum   ær sumeres cyme
on Maias kalend.   Sie þara manna gehwam
behliden helle duru,   heofones ontyned,
ece geopenad   engla rice,
dream unhwilen,   ond hira dæl scired
mid Marian,   þe on gemynd nime
þære deorestan   dægweorðunga
rode under roderum,   þa se ricesta
ealles Oferwealdend   earme beþeahte. **Finit.**

---

in body and mind, in the thoughts of their hearts,
that celebrated day on which the holy Rood
was cut to measure, the most glorious tree
which ever grew up from the soil
with leaves luxuriant. By then Lent was advanced
to just six nights before the summer's coming
in the month of May. For each of those people
may hell's doors be shut, heaven's thrown wide,
opened eternally the kingdom of angels,
a happy state with no time to it, and a portion allotted
with Mary to all those who take to mind
the observance of the most precious day
of that Rood under skies which the most powerful
Supreme Ruler of All covered with his arms. **End.**

Cynewulf's signed Epilogue

The signature is to enable readers to pray for Cynewulf's soul, after learning some stylised information about this poet from the preliminary 21 lines. The trajectory, that of a man who gets inspiration in old age, is Cædmonian. The words from the runes in the signature do not fit with the context if read rigidly in the manner prescribed by what is known of Old English Futhorc (the runic alphabet). On the other hand, with use of homophones in the right places, a meaning does emerge which reiterates the Cynewulf-persona's autobiography earlier. (A name **sige-w-ea-r-d** in *The Husband's Message* may be read in the same pragmatic way; see **Poems on the Meaning of Life.**) The part which follows, the Day of Judgement, is the reader's parting incentive to

---

1228 *on Maias kalend* 'in the month of May'. The manuscript's *maias. kl.* is read thus by Gradon (1996: 70) in order to match the day better with 3 May, Feast of the Invention of the True Cross, or with the beginning of summer on 9 May.

remember why he should pray for Cynewulf's soul. Some day, or rather some night, the same reader may want someone else to pray for his.

Bjork, R. E., ed., *The Cynewulf Reader* (London, 2001)

Elliott, R. W. V., 'Cynewulf's runes in *Christ II* and *Elene*', in Bjork (2001), 281–91

Frese, D. W., 'The art of Cynewulf's runic signatures', in *Anglo-Saxon Poetry: Essays in Appreciation for John C. McGalliard*, ed. L. E. Nicholson and D. W. Frese (Notre Dame, IN, 1975), 312–34; repr. in Bjork (2001), 323–46

Ó Carragáin, É., 'Cynewulf's Epilogue to *Elene* and the tastes of the Vercelli compiler: a paradigm of meditative reading', in *Lexis and Texts in Early English: Studies Presented to Jane Roberts*, ed. C. J. Kay and L. M. Sylvester, Costerus new series 133 (Amsterdam and Atlanta, GA, 2001), 187–201

Page, R. I., *An Introduction to English Runes*, 2nd ed. (Woodbridge, 1999), 191–5

Rogers, H. L., 'Rhymes in the Epilogue to *Elene*: a reconsideration', *Leeds Studies in English* 5 (1971), 47–52

XV

Þus ic frod ond fus   þurh þæt fæcne hus
wordcræftum wæ*s*   ond wundrum læs,
þragum þreodude   ond geþanc reodode
nihtes nearwe.   Nysse ic gearwe
be ðære [rode] riht   ær me rumran geþeaht
þurh ða mæran miht   on modes þeaht
wisdom onwreah.   Ic wæs weorcum fah,
synnum asæled,   sorgum gewæled,

XV

Matured thus and inspired by this house of fakery
have I composed and wonders have gathered,
at times deliberated and sifted my thoughts
at night with close care. I was readily ignorant
of [Rood's] law, until wisdom was helped by
this splendid might to reveal thoughts more copious
to my heart's thinking. I was soiled by deeds,
tied up in sins, tormented by sorrows,

1236 *þurh þæt fæcne hus* 'by this house of fakery'. Cynewulf's half-line end-rhymes are crafted in imitation of Latin hymns, just as those in *The Rhyming Poem* in the Exeter Book (see **Poems on the Meaning of Life**). They prove that his dialect was Anglian, not West Saxon. The meaning of some of his tight phrases is less certain, however. 'Fake', thus 'house of fakery', is but an informed guess for OE *fæcne*. The thrust of Cynewulf's Epilogues is eternity versus mortal decay, so the whole phrase probably connotes the body, whose young needs drove his poetry a certain way: towards heroic verse, perhaps?

1237 *wordcræftum wæs* 'have I composed'. For manuscript *wæf* 'wove', of much the same meaning except that there is no rhyme with *læs* 'gathered' (from *lesan*, cognate with German *lesen* 'read'). An emendation is thus called for, although *onlag – had* on line 1245 is imperfect in a similar way.

1240–1 *riht – geþeaht, miht – þeaht, onwreah – fah*. These rhymes work better in Anglian than in West Saxon forms, i.e. *reht – geþæht, mæht – þæht, onwræh – fæh*. The form of Cynewulf's Anglian is held to be Mercian (Fulk 2001: 14). It is thus a fair bet that Cynewulf was from the Midlands.

bitrum gebunden, bisgum beþrungen,
ær me lare onlag þurh leohtne had
gamelum to geoce, gife unscynde
Mægencyning amæt ond on gemynd begeat,
torht ontynde, tidum gerymde,
bancofan onband, breostlocan onwand,
leoðucræft onleac. Þæs ic lustum breac,
willum in worlde. Ic þæs wuldres treowes
oft, nales æne, hæfde ingemynd
ær ic þæt wundor onwrigen hæfde
ymb þone beorhtan beam swa ic on bocum fand
wyrda gangum on gewritum cyðan
be ðam sigebeacne. A wæs secg oð ðæt
cnyssed cearwelmum, ᚳ [*c*en] drusende,
þeah he in medohealle maðmas þege,
æplede gold. ᚣ [*y*r] gnornode
ᚾ [*n*yd]gefera, nearusorge dreah,
enge rune, þær him ᛖ [*e*oh] fore
milpaðas mæt, modig þrægde
wirum gewlenced. ᚹ [*w*ynn] is geswiðrad,
gomen æfter gearum, geogoð is gecyrred,

---

bound up with bitterness, pressed down by cares,
until He gave me counsel in clarified form
to help an old man, a gift unflawed the King
of Power acquiring meted out for my mind,
bright He revealed it, by the hours increased it,
unbound my bone-coffer, unwound the breast-locker,
unlocked a skill in poetry. With spirit I used it,
with joy in the world. To that tree of glory
often, not just once, I gave inward mind,
before I had uncovered the miracle
of the bright beam, as in books I found
proclaimed in scriptures through history's course
the Victory Tree's story. Till that happened, the man
was ever a flickering torch (*Cen*), tossed by waves of care,
even if in meadhall he accepted treasures,
embossed gold. The bow (***yr***) pined away,
his comrade at need (***nyd***), felt straitening sorrow,
secret confines, where formerly the mettled steed (***eoh***)
measured the mile-paths, galloped powerful
in filigreed harness. Pleasure (***wynn***) has faded,
pastimes with the years, youth is changed

1257–70 Cynewulf's name is spelled in runes with medial *e* here and in the Epilogue of *Juliana* (in the Exeter Book), without it in *Christ II* (see below) and *The Fates of the Apostles*. His name can shed little light on dialect or date, as it is fairly common, but once again it seems less likely that he is Northumbrian, especially if he wrote before *c.* 850, for their spelling until then was *Cyniwulf*.

ald onmedla. ᚢ [*ur*] wæs geara
geogoðhades glæm. Nu synt geardagas
æfter fyrstmearce forð gewitene,
lifwynne geliden swa ᛚ [*lagu*] toglideð,
flodas gefysde. ᚠ [*feoh*] æghwam bið
læne under lyfte, landes frætwe
gewitaþ under wolcnum winde geliccost,
þonne he for hæleðum hlud astigeð,
wæðeð be wolcnum, wedende færeð
ond eft semninga swige gewyrðeð,
in nedcleofan nearwe geheaðrod,
þream forþrycced. [. . .]

Swa a þeos world eall gewiteð,
ond eac swa some þe hire on wurdon
atydrede, tionleg nimeð,
ðonne Dryhten sylf dom geseceð
engla weorude. Sceall æghwylc ðær
reordberendra riht gehyran
dæda gehwylcra þurh þæs Deman muð,

---

with its former pomp. Ours (***ur***) was once
the glamour of youth. Now the old days
have passed away in the fullness of time,
life's joys departed as water (***lagu***) ebbs away,
floods driven further. Wealth (***feoh***) for each man
is borrowed under heaven, landscape's adornments
vanish beneath the clouds most like the wind
when loud he climbs and high over men,
goes hunting by the clouds, raging travels
and then suddenly again falls quiet,
closely confined in his jail-cell,
violently suppressed. [. . .]

So all this world will vanish for evermore,
and likewise too, those who in her have been
nourished will be seized by flames of wrath
when the Lord Himself seeks Judgement
with His host of angels. Each person there
with a voice to speak shall hear the verdict
on each of his deeds from the Judge's mouth,

1257–76 The runes that spell Cynewulf's name provide meanings which must be worked over a little to get a sense, but such a sense is achievable: that he burned his youth away in fast living (C); that he put his hunting bow (Y) down as he grew older, because he had to (N); his horse (E) likewise; that joy (W) fell away in consequence; that ours (U) was all this youth, which has melted away like the waters (L); that all wealth (F) will vanish anyway.

ond worda swa same wed gesyllan,
eallra unsnyttro ær gesprecenra,
þristra geþonca. Þonne on þreo dæleð
in fyres feng folc anra gehwylc,
þara þe gewurdon on widan feore
ofer sidne grund. Soðfæste bioð
yfemest in þam ade, eadigra gedryht,
duguð domgeorne, swa hie adreogan magon
ond butan earfeðum eaðe geþolian,
modigra mægen. Him gemetgaþ eall
*elð*es leoma, swa him eðost bið,
sylfum geseftost. Synfulle beoð,
mane gemengde, in ðam midle þread,
hæleð higegeomre, in hatne wylm,
þrosme beþehte. Bið se þridda dæl,
awyrgede womsceaðan, in þæs wylmes grund,
lease leodhatan, lige befæsted
þurh ærgewyrht, arleasra sceolu,
in gleda gripe. Gode no syððan
of ðam morðorhofe in gemynd cumað,
Wuldorcyninge, ac hie worpene beoð
of ðam heaðuwylme in hellegrund,
torngeniðlan. Bið þam twam dælum

---

and for his words he shall likewise answer,
for all the follies once spoken by him,
his reckless intentions. At that time in three parts
in fire's grip He shall divide all people
who have ever lived now or at any time
on this broad earth. The righteous will be
uppermost in the pyre, a retinue of the blessed,
a troop eager for renown, with just enough ease
and lack of hardship for them to suffer and endure,
a company of the brave. For them He will moderate
all furnace gleams into the easiest gentlest ones
their persons may bear. Those full of sin,
mixed in with wickedness, are of the middle party,
heroes' sad at heart, in a hot burning surge
covered by suffocation. The third part,
accursed defilers, are in the fire's depths,
loose immoral tyrants, locked down in flame
for former deeds, a school who had no mercy,
in the embers' grip. To God's mind thenceforth,
from that hall of murder they will never come
to the King of Glory, but cast down they are
from that hot surge into hell's abyss,
His grievous enemies. For the two higher parts

ungelice,   moton engla Frean
geseon, sigora God.   Hie asodene beoð,
asundrod fram synnum,   swa smæte gold
þæt in wylme bið   womma gehwylces
þurh ofnes fyr   eall geclænsod,
amered ond gemylted.   Swa bið þara manna ælc
ascyred ond asceaden   scylda gehwylcre,
deopra firena,   þurh þæs domes fyr.
Moton þonne siðþan   sybbe brucan,
eces eadwelan.   Him bið engla Weard
milde ond bliðe,   þæs ðe hie mana gehwylc
forsawon, synna weorc,   ond to Suna Metudes
wordum cleopodon,   forðan hie nu on wlite scinaþ
englum gelice,   yrfes brucaþ
Wuldorcyninges   to widan feore. Amen.

---

it will be different, they will be permitted to see
the Lord of Angels, Victory God. They will be purged,
sundered from sins like refined gold
that in waves of heat, through oven's fire,
is all cleansed of every blemish,
purified and melted. Just so, each of those people
will be sheared and shed themselves of each guilt
or deep-lying wickedness through fire of Judgement.
From there they may fly up to enjoy peace,
a blessedness eternal. The Guardian of Angels
will be loving kind to them for having despised
each sin and wicked crime and for having called
on Measurer's Son aloud, for they now shine in radiance
like the angels, enjoying all the inheritance
of Glory's King for ever and ever. *Amen*

1309 *swa smæte gold* 'like refined gold'. A commonplace homiletic image from Proverbs 17:3. The ending of *Andreas*, or even that of *Judgement Day II*, is comparable though more entertaining.

Cynewulf's *Christ II*

✳

Cynewulf's Epilogue to the poem known as *Christ II* is of interest for several reasons. One is for the interpretation of the meaning of his runic signature, a variation on the theme presented in the other three extant cases. Another point of interest is the way in which Cynewulf integrates his runic persona with the purpose of his poem on the Ascension. If Christ reaches heaven by ascending through the air, Cynewulf and the rest of us will hope to get there by water, with our joys and possessions precariously enclosed in the hull of the ship of life. The fire of youth transmutes into the fire of hell should we fail, however. With water and fire in this way, Cynewulf looks forward to the theme of *Christ III*, the Day of Judgement. Neither this poem nor the *Advent Lyrics* which precede *Christ II* are Cynewulf's work, yet he seeks to join them with a poem of his own. That is so if we think of the overall thematic unity between poems, which he encourages through the letters of his name.

Bjork, R. E., ed., *The Cynewulf Reader* (London, 2001)

Elliott, R. W. V., 'Coming back to Cynewulf', in *Old English Runes and their Continental Background*, ed. A. Bammesberger, Anglistische Forschungen 217 (Heidelberg, 1991), 231–47

Frese, D. W., 'The art of Cynewulf's runic signatures', in *Anglo-Saxon Poetry: Essays in Appreciation for John C. McGalliard*, ed. L. E. Nicholson and D. W. Frese (Notre Dame, IN, 1975), 312–34; repr. in Bjork (2001), 323–46

Fulk, R. D., 'Cynewulf: canon, dialect, and date', in Bjork (2001), 3–21

Pulsiano, P., 'The sea of life and the ending of *Christ II*', *In Geardagum* 5 (1983), 1–12

Thoughts on the final harbour

Þonne ᚳ [**c**en] cwacað,   gehyreð Cyning mæðlan,
rodera Ryhtend,   sprecan reþe word
þam þe him ær in worulde   wace hyrdon,
þenden ᚣ [**y**r] ond ᚾ [**n**yd]   yþast meahtan

Then a brave man (***cen***) will quake, hear the King,
Ruler of the skies, pronounce, speak fierce words to those
who had been feeble in obeying him in this world
as long as bow (***yr***) and compulsion (***nyd***) could most easily

---

797 *Þonne [cen] cwacað* 'Then a brave man will quake'. Here Cynewulf's first rune appears to be the adjective *cēn* from which Modern English *keen* descends, rather than the short-vowelled noun for a torch, as in *Elene*, line 1257.

800 ***nyd*** 'compulsion'. A different meaning from that of the *nyd* in Cynewulf's signature in *Elene*. Here the word seems to stand for the urges that drive a young man on, in tandem with *yr*, the bow, which is Cynewulf's symbol for energetic pastimes.

frofre findan. Þær sceal forht monig
on þam wongstede werig bidan
hwæt him æfter dædum deman wille
wraþra wita. Biþ se ᚹ [***w***ynn] scæcen
eorþan frætwa. ᚢ [***u***r] wæs longe
ᛚ [***l***agu]flodum bilocen, lifwynna dæl,
ᚠ [***f***eoh] on foldan. Þonne frætwe sculon
byrnan on bæle, blac rasetteð
recen reada leg, reþe scriþeð
geond woruld wide. Wongas hreosað,
burgstede berstað, brond bið on tyhte,
æleð ealdgestreon unmurnlice,
gæsta gifrast, þæt geo guman heoldan,
þenden him on eorþan onmedla wæs.
Forþon ic leofra gehwone læran wille
þæt he ne agæle gæstes þearfe,
ne on gylp geote, þenden God wille
þæt he her in worulde wunian mote,
somed siþian sawel in lice,
in þam gæsthofe. Scyle gumena gehwylc

---

find solace. There shall many a one, terrified,
wearily await in that place on the plain
whatever harsh penalties He will adjudge him
according to his deeds. Vanished is the joy (***wynn***)
of earthly treasures. Our (***ur***) joy, our portion of life's
delights was long enclosed by water's (***lagu***-) floods,
our wealth (***feoh***) in the world. Fineries, there again, shall
burn in the blaze, sparking will it race,
the quick red flame, fiercely slide far
throughout the world. The hills will fall,
town buildings shatter, fire will be marching,
will feed without pity, most voracious of spirits,
on the ancient treasures that once men held
while they had great pomp on earth.
So I would prefer to teach each person
not to delay the needs of the spirit,
nor gush with boasting, while God still
wishes him to dwell here in the world,
his soul to go about in unison with the body
in that guest lodging. Each man should

---

806 *[lagu]flodum bilocen* 'enclosed by water's floods'. Life as one's cargo in the hull of a fast-moving ship (compare with *Sayings of the High One*, stanza 74, in **Poems on the Meaning of Life**). This phrase looks forward to the 'final harbour' simile at the end.

on his geardagum   georne biþencan
þæt us milde bicwom   meahta Waldend
æt ærestan   þurh þæs engles word.
Bið nu eorneste   þonne eft cymeð,
reðe ond ryhtwis.   Rodor bið onhrered,
ond þas miclan gemetu   Middangeardes
beofiað [. . .]   þonne Beorht Cyning leanað
þæs þe hy on eorþan   eargum dædum
lifdon leahtrum fa.   Þæs hi longe sculon
ferðwerige onfon   in fyrbaðe,
wælmum biwrecene,   wraþlic ondlean.
Þonne mægna Cyning   on gemot cymeð
þrymma mæste,   þeodegsa bið
hlud gehyred   bi heofonwoman,
cwaniendra cirm.   Cerge reotað
fore onsyne   eces Deman,
þa þe hyra weorcum   wace truwiað.
Ðær biþ oðywed   egsa mara
þonne from frumgesceape   gefrægen wurde
æfre on eorðan.   Þær bið æghwylcum
synwyrcendra   on þa snudan tid
leofra micle   þonne eall þeos læne gesceaft,

---

in his life's days think with keenness
how gently at first did the Ruler of Powers
come to us through the Angel's words.
He will be in earnest when He returns,
cruel and righteous. The sky will be insane,
and great tracts of Middle World
will tremble [. . .] when the Bright King repays them
for having lived on earth with cowardly deeds,
stained with iniquities. For this, long shall they
have to receive, exhausted in spirit in a bath of fire,
driven with waves of heat, a savage reward.
When the King of Companies comes to Assembly
in greatest majesty, then a massive terror will be
heard aloud beside the revelry of heaven,
a cry of mourners. With grief they will sob
before the face of the everlasting Judge,
those with weak faith in their own deeds.
There will be revealed a greater terror
than from the beginning of creation was heard of
ever on earth. There, for each of those
with sins behind them in that imminent hour,
much dearer than all this creation on loan to us

þær he hine sylfne   on þam sigeþreate
behydan mæge   þonne herga Fruma,
æþelinga Ord,   eallum demeð
leofum ge laðum   lean æfter ryhte,
þeoda gehwylcre.   Is us þearf micel
þæt we gæstes wlite   ær þam gryrebrogan
on þas gæsnan tid   georne biþencen.

Nu is þon gelicost   swa we on laguflode
ofer cald wæter   ceolum liðan
geond sidne sæ,   sundhengestum,
flodwudu fergen.   Is þæt frecne stream
yða ofermæta   þe we her on lacað
geond þas wacan woruld,   windge holmas
ofer deop gelad.   Wæs se drohtað strong
ær þon we to londe   geliden hæfdon
ofer hreone hrycg.   Þa us help bicwom,
þæt us to hælo   hyþe gelædde,

---

will be a place where he can hide himself
among the party of Victory when the Prince of Armies,
the Acme of Athelings, adjudges to all men
both beloved and loathed a reward that fits the law,
to each individual. For us the need is great
to think keenly of the way the spirit may look
in this fleeting time before that prodigious horror.

Now it is most as if on the water's flood
over cold waters we might sail in keels
across the wide sea, on stallions of the strait,
be ferried in flood-wood. The current is unsafe,
the waves beyond measuring on which we play here
through this weak world, storm-ridden the seas
over deep roads. Those conditions were tough
before we sailed to a shore over
the wild horizon. Then help reached us
that led us to the safety of a harbour,

---

850 *swa we on laguflode* 'as if on the water's flood' etc. See the above note. This kind of simile recalls *The Seafarer*, which Cynewulf may know, but is not unknown either in Latin writings, or in other English ones, such as in *We æthrynon mid urum arun þa yðan þæs deopan wælis* 'We have touched with our oars the waves of the deep welling water', in Byrhtferth's *Enchiridion* (see **Writers of the Benedictine Reform**, Custom Version).

Godes Gæstsunu,   ond us giefe sealde
þæt we oncnawan magun   ofer ceoles bord
hwær we sælan sceolon   sundhengestas,
ealde yðmearas,   ancrum fæste.
Utan us to þære hyðe   hyht staþelian,
ða us gerymde   rodera Waldend,
Halge on heahþu,   þa He heofonum astag.

God's Ghost-Son, and grace he has given us
to be able to recognise from ship-board
where we must tie our stallions of the strait,
old wave-steeds, fast to their anchors.
Let us fix our hope in that harbour
which the Ruler of Skies, Holy in the Height,
made free to us when He climbed to the heavens.

Genesis B

✳

In 1875 an important article appeared in which the brilliant young German grammarian Eduard Sievers (1850–1932), having noted that lines 235–851 of the 'Cædmonian' poem *Genesis* in Oxford, Bodleian Library, Junius 11, differed considerably in metre and linguistic forms from the surrounding poem, proposed that these translated an Old Saxon (i.e. early medieval North or Low German) *Genesis* poem no longer in existence. In 1894, when four fragments of an Old Saxon *Genesis* were discovered in a manuscript in the Vatican Palatine Library, Sievers was proved right. One view now held (Bremmer 2001: 383) is that *Genesis B*, as Sievers called it, was composed in *c.* 850 in a north German minster such as Fulda, Corvey or Werden, and then brought to England with Judith, daughter of Charles the Bald of Western Francia (ruled 840–79), when Æthelwulf of Wessex (ruled 839–58) married her in 856. Scholars have established that *Genesis B* was interpolated into *Genesis A* in order to complete this early biblical history; and that it had probably been translated from Old Saxon, by a Saxon from Germany less familiar with West Saxon, in the late ninth century (Doane 1991: 47–54).

Genesis B is a poem of remarkable intensity. As a piece of drama, which it well might have been in the enactment of liturgy in the nave of a church in northern Germany, *Genesis B* might at first seem ranting and unnecessarily repetitive. On further enquiry, however, this poem emerges as highly subtle and thematically rich. The poet is no theological amateur, and important questions arise from his handling of the well-known story. The issue of fate and free will is one of them. This appears to be unproblematic in *Genesis B*, for here not only Adam and Eve, but also Satan has freedom of choice. The more intricate scheme made famous by John Milton in his *Paradise Lost*, particularly Book III, that man's Fall is a predetermined prelude to Christ's Incarnation, even while Adam enjoys his (illusion of) freedom to choose, is not one to which this poet or his society have progressed. Instead, *Genesis B* seems to tell us that everyone in the foundation of the universe, the Lord God included, are actors in a history that has been written, but which is still a free play for everyone in it. The causality marks it out from *Genesis A* (Burchmore-Oldrieve 1985). Christ will eventually come because humanity falls, and this happened because Satan tried to secede from heaven, to found a bigger kingdom of his own, and this happened because he was proud.

In these conditions, with the actors unconfined by a great divine plan in the background, a certain room is made for their characterisation. God's lack of close control in this story allows the poet to cast the story as a contest between the Lord and Satan. Initially this is almost Manichean in its style of good versus evil. In the middle, quite literally in the Middle World between heaven above and hell below, stand Adam and Eve. The poet's greatest interest lies in Adam and Eve, whose part in the surviving *Genesis B* amounts to the final two-thirds. On their account, the poem may be read as a tragedy almost in Greek style, given the (natural because historical) absence of Jesus. The Lord's emotions, first love, then hate, are even more binary than in the Old Testament. Satan's are restricted to a 100 per cent belief in the justice of his cause. He makes up lies and retroactive grievances to suit his needs as he goes along. When he finishes in hell, unlike Milton's Satan he is too dangerous to God to be unfettered and so sits in an iron cage. He refers to God's infringement of law, then claims that his war was a pre-emptive strike against a new favourite. We know this conception of Adam cannot be true, because Adam formed no part of his opening speech.

Adam and Eve, in the centre of Satan's celestial grudge match with God, have lives that become pieces in the losing player's chess game. The first humans face a demon with the alarmingly human characteristics of charm and deceit combined with his own psychological damage. As they deal with him, and then fail in combating his lies, their humanity (angry, obsessive, helpful, tender and forgiving by turn) is revealed as the poem's emotional core. Eve is the lowest in rank, being under Adam who is under God's angels, including eventually Satan, who are all under God. Yet Eve's part provides the greatest, most extensive drama in this poem. The poet exonerates her from the traditional stigma by turning the cause of the Fall in his story from Eve's vanity into her falling for a low-down trick. Unique to *Genesis B* in this period is a version in which the tempter tries Adam the sentinel first, fails to impress him but thereby gains the logic against which Eve, or any one else with her limited knowledge, can have no defence: unless she persuades Adam to do what 'God's messenger' says, they run the risk of divine disfavour. Without knowing it, Eve damns humanity to save her husband. The poem becomes a tragedy, with Eve as protagonist. The play ends when Eve, under the strain of hearing Adam repudiate her, brings her husband back to her, and so saves the human race.

Bradley, S. A. J., trans., *Anglo-Saxon Poetry: An Anthology of Old English Poems in Prose Translation* (London, 1982)

Bremmer, R., 'Continental Germanic influences', in *A Companion to Anglo-Saxon Literature*, ed. P. Pulsiano and E. Treharne (Oxford, 2001), 375–87

Burchmore-Oldrieve, S., 'Traditional exegesis and the question of guilt in the Old English *Genesis B*', *Traditio* 41 (1985), 117–44

Derolez, R., 'Genesis: Old Saxon and Old English', *English Studies* 76 (1995), 133–49

Doane, A. N., ed., *The Saxon Genesis: An Edition of the West Saxon Genesis B and the Old Saxon Vatican Genesis* (Madison, WI, 1991), 232–52 (OS poem)

Fulk, R. D., and C. M. Cain, *A History of Old English Literature* (Oxford, 2003)

Langeslag, P. S., 'Doctrine and paradigm: two functions of the innovations in *Genesis B*', *Studia Neophilologica* 79 (2007), 113–18

North, R., *Pagan Words and Christian Meanings*, Costerus new series 81 (Amsterdam and Atlanta, GA, 1991), 93–8

Lucifer the rebel

In the Marlovian rant given here, Lucifer claims that his rebellion is a communal impulse and that his friends have elected him captain. There is a close parallel with Milton, who knew (of) Franciscus Junius and may have seen his manuscript. As Fulk and Cain say (2003: 114), 'it remains remarkable that the poet, like Milton, chose to narrate these events from Satan's point of view, placing God in the inscrutable distance'.

'ac niotað inc þæs oðres ealles,   forlætað þone ænne beam,
wariað inc wið þone wæstm.   Ne wyrð inc wilna gæd.'

Hnigon þa mid heafdum   Heofoncyninge
georne togenes   and sædon ealles þanc
lista and þara lara.   He let heo þæt land buan,
hwærf Him þa to heofenum   halig Drihten,
stiðferhð Cyning.   Stod His handgeweorc
somod on sande,   nyston sorga wiht
to begrornianne,   butan heo Godes willan
lengest læsten.   Heo wæron leof Gode
ðenden heo His halige word   healdan woldon.

VI
Hæfde se Alwalda   engelcynna
þurh handmægen,   halig Drihten,
tene getrimede,   þam He getruwode wel
þæt hie His giongorscipe   fyligan wolden,
wyrcean His willan,   forþon He him gewit forgeaf
and mid His handum gesceop,   halig Drihten.
Gesett hæfde He hie swa gesæliglice,   ænne hæfde He swa swiðne geworhtne,
swa mihtigne on his modgeþohte,   He let hine swa micles wealdan,
hehstne to Him on heofona rice,   hæfde He hine swa hwitne geworhtne,

---

'you enjoy everything else, but leave that one tree alone,
beware of the fruit. Your desires will want for nothing.'

They bowed their heads then to Heaven's King
eagerly towards Him, and said thanks for all
skills from Him and for that advice. He let them settle that land,
then the Holy Lord moved off to heaven,
stern-minded King. His handiwork stood there
united on the sand, knew of no sorrows
to complain of, but that God's will they were to please,
for longer than anything else. They were dear to God
as long as they willed to keep true to His holy words.

VI
The Omnipotent had of angel divisions
by the power of His hands, the Holy Lord,
fashioned ten, of whom He well trusted
that it would be their will to follow His service,
work His will, and so He gave them wits
and shaped them with His hands, did the Holy Lord.
He had set them up with such fortune, one He made so powerful,
so mighty in his intellect, so much did He let him command,
as the highest next to Him in heaven's kingdom, so white He had made him,

---

245 *healdan woldon* 'willed to keep true'. Obedience, not enforced but voluntary, is what God wants from His subjects in this poem, humans and angels alike.

swa wynlic wæs his wæstm on heofonum   þæt him com from weroda Drihtne,
gelic wæs he þam leohtum steorrum.   Lof sceolde he Drihtnes wyrcean,
dyran sceolde he his dreamas on heofonum,   and sceolde his Drihtne þancian
þæs leanes þe He him on þam leohte gescerede.   Þonne læte He his hine lange wealdan.
Ac he awende hit him to wyrsan þinge,   ongan him winn up ahebban
wið þone hehstan heofnes Waldend,   þe siteð on þam halgan stole.
Deore wæs he Drihtne urum,   ne mihte Him bedyrned weorðan
þæt His engyl ongan   ofermod wesan,
ahof hine wið his Hearran,   sohte hetespræce
gylpword ongean,   nolde Gode þeowian,
cwæð þæt his lic wære   leoht and scene,
hwit and hiowbeorht.   Ne meahte he æt his hige findan
þæt he Gode wolde   geongerdome,
Þeodne þeowian.   Þuhte him sylfum
þæt he mægyn and cræft   maran hæfde
þonne se halga God   habban mihte

---

so winsome his heavenly stature which came to him from the Lord of Hosts,
that he was like the radiant stars. His duty it was to praise the Lord,
to put the right price on his happy state in heaven, to thank the Lord
for the loan He had tendered him in that Light. Then He might let him have a long lease of it.
But he changed this into a worse deal, began to raise up strife
against heaven's highest Ruler who sits on the holy throne.
Dear he was to Our Lord, nor could it be hidden from Him
that His angel did make himself proud,
raise himself up against his Master, look for words of hate
against the terms of his boast, would not serve God,
said that his body was radiant and beautiful,
white and bright of hue. Nor could he find in his purpose
the will to serve his God, the Emperor,
with submission. To his person it seemed
that he had a greater force and quantity
of fellow soldiers than Holy God

---

256 *gelic steorrum* 'like the stars'. The poet's reference to *Lucifer* 'light-bearer', the Morning Star, the former name of Satan.

258 *þæs leanes . . . læte He his hine lange wealdan* 'for the loan . . . He might let him have a long lease of it'. God's gifts to his finest angel are not permanent, but rather a loan which Lucifer's service will repay. This loan may be taken back at any time, and after the rebellion the Lord earmarks Lucifer's holdings to give to Adam. It seems likely that Lucifer's attempt on his Master's power derives from his pique at the instability of gift-exchange.

259 *to wyrsan þinge* 'into a worse deal'. The assumption with this noun is that God has reached an agreement with His angels concerning their rights and duties.

267–8 *þæt he Gode wolde þeowian* 'the will to serve his God'. See note to line 245.

folcgestælna.   Feala worda gespæc
se engel ofermodes.   Þohte þurh his anes cræft
hu he him strenglicran   stol geworhte,
heahran on heofonum.   Cwæð þæt hine his hige speone
þæt he west and norð   wyrcean ongunne,
trymede getimbro.   Cwæð him tweo þuhte
þæt he Gode wolde   geongra weorðan.

'Hwæt sceal ic winnan?' cwæð he,   'nis me wihtæ þearf
hearran to habbanne.   Ic mæg mid handum swa fela
wundra gewyrcean.   Ic hæbbe geweald micel
to gyrwanne   godlecran stol,
hearran on heofne.   Hwy sceal ic æfter his hyldo ðeowian,
bugan him swilces geongordomes?   Ic mæg wesan god swa he.
Bigstandað me strange geneatas,   þa ne willað me æt þam striðe geswican,
hæleþas heardmode.   Hie habbað me to hearran gecorene,
rofe rincas,   mid swilcum mæg man ræd geþencean,
fon mid swilcum folcgesteallan.   Frynd synd hie mine georne,
holde on hyra hygesceaftum.   Ic mæg hyra hearra wesan,
rædan on þis rice.   Swa me þæt riht ne þinceð,
þæt ic oleccan   awiht þurfe
gode æfter gode ænegum.   Ne wille ic leng his geongra wurþan!'

---

could possibly have. Many words of pride
this angel spoke. He thought how through the power of him
alone he would build himself a stronger throne,
higher in heaven. He said that his impulse led him
to start building in the north-west quarter,
to fashion a great hall. He said he thought it doubtful
that he would submit himself to God.

'Why must I toil?' he said, 'I have no need
to have a master. With my own hands I can work
just as many wonders. Great is the power I command
to establish a more costly throne,
one higher in heaven. For what grace must I be serving him,
bowing to him with such submission? I can be a god like he is.
Strong comrades stand by me, who will not betray me in this war,
heroes of hardened courage. They have chosen me as their master,
brave men they are. With guys like these a man can think of strategy,
make it work, with soldiering mates like these. They are keen to befriend me,
loyal in their disposition. I can be their master,
rule in this kingdom. So I think it unlawful
in every way that I should need to flatter
this god for any good things. Nor will I be his subject longer!'

---

283 *Ic mæg wesan god swa he* 'I can be a god like he is'. First rivalry, then a take-over bid. Lucifer's claim to godhead recalls the polytheism of Old Saxon and other Germanic heathen religion. In this sense, Lucifer and his crew do become gods in the eyes of ignorant heathens across northern Europe. To characterise Lucifer, the poet adopts their point of view.

Satan chafes in Hell

Like World War III, but with a victor, this war is over before it starts. Lucifer and his forces are surprised by the Lord's intelligence and Lucifer is thrown down to hell where he becomes Satan. His appeal to law in these circumstances may be based on a principle that, as Lucifer did not (have time to) fight, God has no right to confiscate his lands in heaven and give these to Adam. Before long, however, Satan begins to believe that this property transfer was why he planned the rebellion in the first place.

Þa hit se Allwalda eall gehyrde,
þæt His engyl ongan ofermede micel
ahebban wið his Hearran and spræc healic word
dollice wið Drihten sinne, sceolde he þa dæd ongyldan,
worc þæs gewinnes gedælan, and sceolde his wite habban,
ealra morðra mæst. Swa deð monna gehwilc
þe wið his waldend winnan ongynneð
mid mane wið þone mæran Drihten. Þa wearð se Mihtiga gebolgen,
hehsta heofones Waldend, wearp hine of þan hean stole.
Hete hæfde he æt his Hearran gewunnen, hyldo hæfde His ferlorene,
gram wearð him se Goda on His mode. Forþon he sceolde
grund gesecean
heardes hellewites, þæs þe he wann wið heofnes Waldend.
Acwæð hine þa fram His hyldo and hine on helle wearp,

When the Omnipotent heard all this,
that His angel had begun to raise up great pride
against his Master and was speaking vaunting words
in folly against his own Lord, why, he had to pay for those deeds,
share some pain for that strife, and he should be punished for this
great of all hidden crimes. So it is for each man
who begins to contend against his ruler, and wickedly
where the Lord of Renown is concerned. Then the Mighty One, swollen
with wrath, heaven's highest Commander, cast him off the high throne.
Hatred had he won from his Master, His grace had he quite lost,
ferociously did God's heart turn against him. And so it was he was forced
to seek the cruel pain of hell's abyss, for having fought the Ruler of heaven.
He cut him out of His grace and cast him into hell,

---

297 *Swa deð monna gehwilc* 'So it is for each man' etc. This sentence relies on ambiguity of epithet to suggest that God's power is replicated on all levels beneath Him, right down to local lords.

300 *wearp hine of þan hean stole* 'cast him off the high throne'. This war in heaven is over before it has started. Milton gives his a whole book (*Paradise Lost*, Book VI).

on þa deopan dala, þær he to deofle wearð,
se feond mid his geferum eallum. Feollon þa ufon of heofnum
þurh longe swa þreo niht and dagas,
þa englas of heofnum on helle, and heo ealle forsceop
Drihten to deoflum. Forþon heo His dæd and word
noldon weorðian, forþon He heo on wyrse leoht
under eorðan neoðan, ællmihtig God,
sette sigelease on þa sweartan helle.
Þær hæbbað heo on æfyn ungemet lange,
ealra feonda gehwilc, fyr edneowe,
Þonne cymð on uhtan easterne wind.
forst fyrnum cald. Symble fyr oððe gar,
sum heard geswinc habban sceoldon.
Worhte man hit him to wite (hyra woruld wæs gehwyrfed)
forman siðe, fylde helle
mid þam andsacum. Heoldon englas forð
heofonrices hehðe, þe ær Godes hyldo gelæston.
Lagon þa oðre fynd on þam fyre, þe ær swa feala hæfdon
gewinnes wið heora Waldend. Wite þoliað,
hatne heaðowelm helle tomiddes,
brand and brade ligas, swilce eac þa biteran recas,
þrosm and þystro, forþon hie þegnscipe
Godes forgymdon. Hie hyra gal beswac,

---

into the deep gorge where he became a demon,
the fiend with all his fellows. Down then they fell from heaven,
for as long as three nights and days,
those angels from heaven to hell, and the Lord deformed
them all to demons. Because they did not want to worship
His deeds and words, so He, Almighty God,
put them into a lower-ranking world, down
beneath the earth, defeated, in black hell.
There they have of an evening, each and every fiend,
the fire surge on fire for time immeasurably long.
Then at dawn there comes an easterly wind,
a frost of wicked coldness. Whether fire or spiking chill,
some cruelly special torture must they ever have.
This was made their torment (their world was changed)
for the very first time, hell was filled
with these adversaries. Angels henceforth kept
heaven's heights who now had passed the test of loyalty to God.
The others, fiends, lay in the fire, who first had made such quantity
of strife against their Ruler. They suffer punishment,
a hot destroying wave in the midst of hell,
firebrands and broad flames, as well as acrid gases,
suffocation and darkness, all for neglecting a thegn's
attendance on God. Their lust for power betrayed them,

engles oferhygd, noldon Alwaldan
word weorþian, hæfdon wite micel,
wæron þa befeallene fyre to botme
on þa hatan hell þurh hygeleaste
and þurh ofermetto, sohton oþer land,
þæt wæs leohtes leas and wæs liges full,
fyres fær micel. Fynd ongeaton
þæt hie hæfdon gewrixled wita unrim
þurh heora miclan mod and þurh miht Godes
and þurh ofermetto ealra swiðost.

Þa spræc se ofermoda cyning, þe ær wæs engla scynost,
hwitost on heofne and his Hearran leof,
Drihtne dyre, oð hie to dole wurdon,
þæt him for galscipe God sylfa wearð
mihtig on mode yrre. Wearp hine on þæt morðer innan,
niðer on þæt niobedd, and sceop him naman siððan,
cwæð se Hehsta hatan sceolde
Satan siððan, het hine þære swеartan helle
grundes gyman, nalles wið God winnan.

---

an angel's pride, they would not worship
the Omnipotent's word, took a great punishment,
were hurled thus down to the fire's bottom
in hell the hot for want of thought, for
excess as well did they go to seek another land
devoid of light and filled with flames,
perpetual pyroclastic flow. The fiends perceived
that their side of the bargain was torments unnumbered,
through their great wilfulness, and through God's might,
and most strongly of all through their excess.

Then spoke the king of pride, formerly fairest of angels,
whitest in heaven and his Master's beloved,
dear to the Lord until they fell into folly
so that for their madness God's own heart
became mightily enraged. He cast him in that dungeon,
down into that bed of corpses, then gave him a name,
the Highest said he should be called
Satan after that, ordered him to occupy the abyss
of blackened hell, never to fight God again.

---

335 *hæfdon gewrixled* 'their side of the bargain'. The bargain promised them by Lucifer was ownership of heaven, in exchange for their loyalty. He gets their loyalty, they get hell.

338 This line marks the poet's first preparation for a speech by Satan. The second begins on line 347. The length of the first attempt may be due to the care with which the poet introduces us to 'Satan', Lucifer's new name.

Satan maðelode,   sorgiende spræc,
se ðe helle forð   healdan sceolde,
gieman þæs grundes.   Wæs ær Godes engel,
hwit on heofne,   oð hine his hyge forspeon
and his ofermetto   ealra swiðost,
þæt he ne wolde   wereda Drihtnes
word wurðian.   Weoll him on innan
hyge ymb his heortan,   hat wæs him utan
wraðlic wite.

He þa worde cwæð:
'Is þæs ænga styde   ungelic swiðe
þam oðrum ham   þe we ær cuðon,
hean on heofonrice,   þe me min Hearra onlag,
þeah we hine for þam Alwaldan   agan ne moston,
romigan ures rices.   Næfð He þeah riht gedon
þæt He us hæfð befælled   fyre to botme
helle þære hatan,   heofonrice benumen.
Hafað hit gemearcod   mid moncynne

Satan made his speech, sorrowing gave voice,
whose duty hence was to keep hell,
to occupy that abyss. He had been God's angel before,
white in heaven, until his courage misled him
and most strongly of all his excess,
in that he would not worship the word
of the Lord of Hosts. His purpose welled up
about his heart within him, hot outside him
was savage pain.

He spoke these words:
'This filthy place is very unlike
the other home we knew before,
high up in heaven, that my Master lent me,
though, thanks to the Omnipotent, we were not allowed to own it,
found our kingdom there. And it was not lawful what He did,
when He hurled us to the bottom of hell's
hot fire, when He deprived us of heaven.
He has marked it out to be settled

---

360 *Næfð He þeah riht gedon* 'And it was not lawful what He did'. To Satan, it seems that God broke His own law by revoking Lucifer's rights to the heavenly property he lived in, then by promising these to Adam. At what point this transfer takes place is left vague. Satan now believes that it happened before his rebellion. Now he makes it the reason for his rebellion.

to gesettanne. Þæt me is sorga mæst,
þæt Adam sceal, þe wæs of eorðan geworht,
minne stronglican stol behealdan,
wesan him on wynne, and we þis wite þolien,
hearm on þisse helle. Wala, ahte ic minra handa geweald
and moste ane tid ute weorðan,
wesan ane winterstunde, þonne ic mid þys werode –
Ac licgað me ymbe irenbenda,
rideð racentan sal. Ic eom rices leas,
habbað me swa hearde helle clommas
fæste befangen. Her is fyr micel,
ufan and neoðone. Ic a ne geseah
laðran landscipe. Lig ne aswamað,
hat ofer helle. Me habbað hringa gespong,
sliðhearda sal siðes amyrred,
afyrred me min feðe, fet synt gebundene,
handa gehæfte. Synt þissa heldora
wegas forworhte, swa ic mid wihte ne mæg
of þissum lioðobendum. Licgað me ymbe
heardes irenes hate geslægene
grindlas greate, mid þy me God hafað

---

by mankind. For me it is the greatest of sorrows
that Adam, who was made of earth, shall
take occupancy of my robust throne,
be happy at his ease, while we endure this punishment,
harm in this hell. O woe, if I could move my hands
and was allowed to go outside for an hour,
be there one winter's hour, then with this host I –
But around me there lie iron bonds,
a cable of chains rides over me. I am without a kingdom,
so hard are the shackles of hell that keep me
firmly caught. Here is a great fire,
above and below. I never saw
a more hostile landscape. Flames do not cease,
hot over hell. The linking of rings, a chafing
hard cable has hindered me from a journey,
removed my power of movement, my feet are bound,
my hands manacled. The roads are done for
by these doors of hell, even if I manage in some way
to slip my limbs from these bonds. About me lies
a great lattice-work frame forged hot out of
hard iron, with which God has made me

---

370 The final syntactic break is clearly intended as an emotional breakdown, an indication that this poem is to be performed as a piece of theatre. The same occurs on line 420.

gehæfted be þam healse. Swa ic wat He minne hige cuðe,
and þæt wiste eac weroda Drihten,
þæt sceolde unc Adame yfele gewurðan
ymb þæt heofonrice, þær ic ahte minra handa geweald.

VIII Ac ðoliaþ we nu þrea on helle, þæt syndon þystro and hæto,
grimme, grundlease. Hafað us God sylfa
forswapen on þas sweartan mistas. Swa He us ne mæg ænige synne gestælan,
þæt we Him on þam lande lað gefremedon, He hæfð us þeah þæs leohtes bescyrede,
beworpen on ealra wita mæste. Ne magon we þæs wrace gefremman,
geleanian Him mid laðes wihte þæt He us hafað þæs leohtes bescyrede.
He hæfð nu gemearcod anne middangeard, þær He hæfð mon geworhtne
æfter His onlicnesse, mid þam He wile eft gesettan
heofona rice mid hluttrum saulum. We þæs sculon hycgan georne,
þæt we on Adame, gif we æfre mægen,
and on his eafrum swa some, andan gebetan,
onwendan him þær willan sines, gif we hit mægen wihte aþencan.
Ne gelyfe ic me nu þæs leohtes furðor þæs þe He Him þenceð lange niotan,
þæs eades mid His engla cræfte. Ne magon we þæt on aldre gewinnan,
þæt we mihtiges Godes mod onwæcen. Uton oðwendan hit nu monna bearnum,

---

captive by the neck. So I know He was aware of my purpose,
and this the Lord of Hosts also knew,
that bad things would happen between me and Adam
concerning the kingdom of heaven, if I had the use of my hands.

VIII But we now endure correction in hell, that is to say darkness and heat,
fierce and boundless. God Himself has swept us away
into these black fogs. He cannot accuse us of any such sin
as having done harm to Him in that land, yet He has cut us out of that Light,
cast us down into the worst of all torments. We cannot do vengeance for this,
repay Him with some unfriendly act for having cut us out of that Light.
He has marked out now a Middle World, where He has made a man
in His own likeness, with whom it is His will once more to settle
heaven's kingdom with pure souls. We must eagerly plan it out,
that we on Adam, if we ever can,
and on his offspring likewise, may cure our vexation,
subvert them from their will there, if we could in some way devise this.
Nor do I believe any more in that Light which He intends them to long enjoy,
in those riches with His force of angels. There is no way we can even begin
to soften the mood of mighty God. Let us shift it away from men's sons,

þæt heofonrice, nu we hit habban ne moton, gedon þæt hie His hyldo forlæten,
þæt hie þæt onwendon þæt He mid His worde bebead. Þonne weorð He him wrað on mode,
ahwet hie from His hyldo. Þonne sculon hie þas helle secan
and þas grimman grundas. Þonne moton we hie us to giongrum habban,
fira bearn on þissum fæstum clomme. Onginnað nu ymb þa fyrde þencean!
Gif ic ænegum þægne þeodenmadmas
geara forgeafe, þenden we on þan godan rice
gesælige sæton and hæfdon ure setla geweald,
þonne he me na on leofran tid leanum ne meahte
mine gife gyldan, gif his gien wolde
minra þegna hwilc geþafa wurðan,
þæt he up heonon ute mihte
cuman þurh þas clustro, and hæfde cræft mid him
þæt he mid feðerhoman fleogan meahte,
windan on wolcne, þær geworht stondað
Adam and Eue on eorðrice
mid welan bewunden – and we synd aworpene hider

---

that kingdom of heaven, now we cannot have it, bring it about that they lose His grace,
that they subvert what He commanded them in His words. Then He will have wrath in his mind,
and remove him from His grace. Then the humans shall have to visit hell
and these grim depths. Then we may have them as our subjects,
mankind's children in these firm shackles. Now start to plan the campaign!
If, in times gone by, I might have given imperial treasures
to any thegn while in that good kingdom
we sat fortunate and had authority over our own halls,
then he could never repay the debt of my gifts
at a better time, if any one of my thegns
in turn would be willing to give
his consent to come up from here
through the barriers outside, and had the power
to be able to fly in his feathered shape,
twist into the clouds to where they stand fashioned,
Adam and Eve in the earthly domain
enveloped in wealth – while we have been cast down here

410–11 *þenden we gesælige sæton* 'while we sat fortunate'. Pehaps this was the speech of many a royal exile in England or Germany in these times.

417 *mid feðerhoman* 'in his feathered shape'. They still have their wings, even if no longer in angelic form.

on þas deopan dalo! Nu hie Drihtne synt
wurðran micle, and moton him þone welan agan
þe we on heofonrice habban sceoldon,
rice mid rihte. Is se ræd gescyred
monna cynne. Þæt me is on minum mode swa sar,
on minum hyge hreoweð, þæt hie heofonrice
agan to aldre. Gif hit eower ænig mæge
gewendan mid wihte þæt hie word Godes
lare forlæten, sona hie Him þe laðran beoð.
Gif hie brecað His gebodscipe, þonne He him abolgen wurðeþ.
Siððan bið him se wela onwended and wyrð him wite gegarwod,
sum heard hearmscearu. Hycgað his ealle,
hu ge hi beswicen! Siððan ic me sefte mæg
restan on þyssum racentum, gif him þæt rice losað.
Se þe þæt gelæsteð, him bið lean gearo
æfter to aldre, þæs we her inne magon
on þyssum fyre forð fremena gewinnan.

IX Sittan læte ic hine wið me sylfne, swa hwa swa þæt secgan cymeð
on þas hatan helle, þæt hie Heofoncyninges
unwurðlice wordum and dædum
lare [forlæten

---

into this deep gorge! To the Lord at this time they are
much worthier, and may have ownership of the wealth
which we should have had in the heavenly domain,
a kingdom by lawful title. That is the reward dispensed
for mankind. This is such a sore point in my mind!
It grieves my courage that they may own
the kingdom of heaven for ever. If any among you can
change things somehow, make them abandon the words
of God's teaching, they will at once look worse to Him.
If they break His commandment, then He will rage against them.
After that, their wealth will turn over and punishment be prepped for them,
an especially cruel share of damage. All of you think about this,
how to betray them! Then I can more gently
rest in these chains, if the kingdom is lost to them.
A reward will be ready for him who carries this out,
one to last his whole life, from whatever profits we can win
from this place inside from now on in this fire.

IX I will let him sit next to my person, whoever comes into this hot hell
with the news that these two [are quitting] the teaching
of the Heavenly King and are of no worth to Him
in words and deeds. [. . .

---

436 *æfter to aldre* 'one to last his whole life'. That much is guaranteed.

Satan's demon tempts Adam

A page has dropped out, containing all Fitt X. It is unclear how many lines have been lost, but in this part, presumably, the rebel's leading demon comes forward to volunteer for the mission. The extraordinary licence that follows (repeated in the Anglo-Norman *Le Jeu d'Adam* 'The Play of Adam' in **Early Chivalry**) is that the demon tries Adam first.

XI Angan hine þa gyrwan   Godes andsaca,
fus on frætwum   (hæfde fæcne hyge),
hæleðhelm on heafod asette   and þone full hearde geband,
spenn mid spangum.   Wiste him spræca fela,
wora worda.   Wand him up þanon,
hwearf him þurh þa helldora   (hæfde hyge strangne),
leolc on lyfte   laþwendemod,
swang þæt fyr on twa   feondes cræfte,
wolde dearnunga   Drihtnes geongran,
mid mandædum   men beswican,
forlædan and forlæran,   þæt hie wurdon lað Gode.
He þa geferde   þurh feondes cræft
oððæt he Adam   on eorðrice,
Godes handgesceaft,   gearone funde,
wislice geworht,   and his wif somed,
freo fægroste,   swa hie fela cuðon
godes gegearwigean,   þa Him to gingran self
Metod mancynnes   mearcode selfa.
And him bi twegin   beamas stodon
þa wæron utan   ofætes gehlædene,

XI God's adversary began to prepare himself then,
keen in his gear (he had a wicked aim),
set a hero's helmet on his head and tied it on hard,
drew in the flaps with clasps. He knew a lot of speeches,
many crooked words. He spun up from there,
passed through the hell-doors (had a strong sense of purpose),
danced aloft with his mind all malignant,
lashed a path through the fire with a fiend's subtle skill,
wanted in secret to deceive the Lord's
subjects, human beings, with wicked actions,
seduce and pervert them to make them ugly in God's sight.
He moved then with fiendish subtle skill
until in earth's domain Adam,
shaped by God's hands, he found ready,
him with his wife both cleverly fashioned,
and she the most dazzling lady, both just as good
as the many things they could provide, they whom as subjects
the Measurer of mankind Himself had designed.
And alongside them there stood two trees
which were hung about loaded with fruit,

gewered mid wæstme, swa hie waldend God,
heah Heofoncyning handum gesette,
þæt þær yldo bearn moste on ceosan
godes and yfeles, gumena æghwilc,
welan and wawan. Næs se wæstm gelic!
Oðer wæs swa wynlic, wlitig and scene,
liðe and lofsum, þæt wæs lifes beam.
Moste on ecnisse æfter lybban,
wesan on worulde, se þæs wæstmes onbat,
swa him æfter þy yldo ne derede,
ne suht sware, ac moste symle wesan
lungre on lustum and his lif agan,
hyldo Heofoncyninges her on worulde,
habban him to wæron witode geþingþo
on þone hean heofon, þonne he heonon wende.
Þonne wæs se oðer eallenga sweart,
dim and þystre, þæt wæs deaðes beam,
se bær bitres fela. Sceolde bu witan
ylda æghwilc yfles and godes
gewand on þisse worulde. Sceolde on wite a
mid swate and mid sorgum siððan libban,
swa hwa swa gebyrgde þæs on þam beame geweox.

---

clothed in their crop, just as God the Ruler,
High King of Heaven, planted them with His hands,
in which the sons of men might be allowed
either good or evil, each person to choose
either wealth or woe. One crop was not like the other!
One was so winsome, bright and gleaming,
soft and excellent, that was the Tree of Life.
Permission to live in eternity afterwards,
live in that world, was his who bit that fruit,
just as age would not harm him after that,
nor heavy illness, but he might live always
with quickness and energy and have his own life,
grace from the Heaven-King in this world,
and have an assured dignity pledged to him
high up in heaven when he went there hence.
The other crop was blackened all over,
dingy and dismal, that was the Tree of Death,
which bore much bitterness. Each individual
should know of both, of the fork between good
and evil in this world. He should be ever punished,
with sweat and sorrows living thereafter
whoever but tasted what grew on that tree.

---

482 *libban* 'living'. A West Saxon form, transposed from Old Saxon *libbian*. The common English form was Anglian *lif(i)gan*.

Sceolde hine yldo beniman   ellendæda,
dreamas and drihtscipes,   and him beon deað scyred.
Lytle hwile   sceolde he his lifes niotan,
secan þonne landa   sweartost on fyre.
Sceolde feondum þeowian,   þær is ealra frecna mæste
leodum to langre hwile.   Þæt wiste se laða georne,
dyrne deofles boda   þe wið Drihten wann.
Wearp hine þa on wyrmes lic   and wand him þa ymbutan
þone deaðes beam   þurh deofles cræft,
genam þær þæs ofætes   and wende hine eft þanon
þær he wiste handgeweorc   Heofoncyninges.

Ongon hine þa frinan   forman worde
se laða mid ligenum: 'Langað þe awuht,
Adam, up to Gode?   Ic eom on His ærende hider
feorran gefered,   ne þæt nu fyrn ne wæs
þæt ic wið Hine sylfne sæt.   Þa het He me on þysne sið faran,
het þæt þu þisses ofætes æte,   cwæð þæt þin abal and cræft
and þin modsefa   mara wurde,
and þin lichoma   leohtra micle,
þin gesceapu scenran,   cwæð þæt þe æniges sceattes ðearf
ne wurde on worulde.   Nu þu willan hæfst,

Age would take off him his deeds of courage,
his happiness and lordship, and death be dispensed to him.
For a little while he should enjoy his life,
then seek the blackest of lands in the fire.
Fiends he should serve there with the greatest of all evils
for people for a long, long time. This the foe keenly knew,
secret messenger of the demon who fought the Lord.
He cast himself then in serpent's form, wound himself about
the Tree of Death with a demon's subtle skill,
plucked a piece of fruit and from there turned back
to where he knew the Heaven-King's handiwork to be.

With lies the enemy then started to put a question
in these opening words: 'Is there anything you long for,
Adam, from God above? I am on His errand here,
have been travelling far, nor is it so long ago now that I sat
next to His Person. That is when He told me to come on this mission,
ordered that you ate of this fruit, declared that your strength and skill
and your mind would be greater,
and your body much lighter,
your limbs more fine, said that you would have no lack
of money in this world. Now that you have enacted

---

485 *him beon deað scyred* 'death be dispensed to him'. The apparent flaw in the case, that the good people also die, is resolved if we think of their death as a saint's departure from the world.

hyldo geworhte Heofoncyninges,
to þance geþenod þinum Hearran,
hæfst þe wið Drihten dyrne geworhtne. Ic gehyrde Hine þine dæd and word
lofian on His leohte and ymb þin lif sprecan.
Swa þu læstan scealt þæt on þis land hider
His bodan bringað. Brade synd on worulde
grene geardas, and God siteð
on þam hehstan heofna rice,
ufan Alwalda. Nele þa earfeðu
sylfa habban þæt He on þysne sið fare,
gumena Drihten, ac He His gingran sent
to þinre spræce. Nu He þe mid spellum het
listas læran. Læste þu georne
His ambyhto, nim þe þis ofæt on hand,
bit his and byrige. Þe weorð on þinum breostum rum,
wæstm þy wlitegra. Þe sende waldend God,
þin Hearra þas helpe of heofonrice.'

Adam maðelode þær he on eorðan stod,
selfsceafte guma: 'Þonne ic Sigedrihten,
mihtigne God, mæðlan gehyrde
strangre stemne, and me her stondan het,

---

the will, the friendship of Heaven's King,
with gratitude served the Lord your Master,
you have made yourself precious in His sight. I heard Him in His world
praising your deeds and words, and speaking about your life.
That is why you must do whatever His envoys are sent
in this land to ask you. Broad in this world are
the green pastures, and God sits
in the highest heavenly domain,
Omnipotent above us. He does not want
the trouble of going on this journey Himself,
Lord of Men, but sends a subject of His
to talk with you. He commands you now to learn
some skill from what I tell you. You be eager to carry out
His service, take this piece of fruit in hand,
bite it and taste. Your mind will be unbounded,
your outward form the finer. It is God the Ruler,
your Master, who has sent you this help from heaven.'

Adam spoke there where he stood on the earth,
self-determined man: 'When I heard
the Lord of Victory, Mighty God, speaking to me
in His strong voice, while he told me to stand here,

---

523 *selfsceafte guma* 'self-determined man'. As Bradley (1982: 26). Adam makes his own choices.

His bebodu healdan, and me þas bryd forgeaf,
wlitesciene wif, and me warnian het
þæt ic on þone deaðes beam bedroren ne wurde,
beswicen to swiðe, He cwæð þæt þa sweartan helle
healdan sceolde se ðe bi his heortan wuht
laðes gelæde. Nat þeah þu mid ligenum fare
þurh dyrne geþanc [oþ]þe þu Drihtnes eart
boda of heofnum. Hwæt, ic þinra bysna ne mæg,
worda ne wisna wuht oncnawan,
siðes ne sagona. Ic wat hwæt He me self bebead,
Nergend user, þa ic Hine nehst geseah.
He het me His word weorðian and wel healdan,
læstan His lare. Þu gelic ne bist
ænegum His engla þe ic ær geseah,
ne þu me oðiewdest ænig tacen
þe He me þurh treowe to onsende,
min Hearra þurh hyldo. Þy ic þe hyran ne cann,
ac þu meaht þe forð faran. Ic hæbbe me fæstne geleafan
up to þam ælmihtegan Gode þe me mid His earmum worhte,
her mid handum Sinum. He mæg me of His hean rice
geofian mid goda gehwilcum, þeah He his gingran ne sende.'

---

keep His commandments, while he gave me this bride,
my radiant beautiful wife, while He told me to guard
against any delusion in this Tree of Death or being
too much deceived by it, he was saying that black hell
would be his to hold who brought any evil out
of his heart. I do not know if you come with lies
with hidden motive, or if you really are the Lord's
messenger from the sky. Listen, I can have no way
of following your arguments, words, reasons,
conduct, or your story. I know what message He,
our Saviour, gave me Himself when I last saw Him.
He ordered me to honour His words and keep them well,
carry out His instructions. You are not like
any angel of His that I saw before,
nor have you shown me any token
which He, my Master, might send me as proof
of His trust and favour. So I don't know enough to obey you,
and you can take yourself off. I have a firm faith
in Almighty God up there who made me with His arms,
right here with His own hands. From His high kingdom He can
endow me with any good thing without sending a servant with it.'

---

538 *gelic ne bist* 'You are not like' etc. Adam is talking to a snake.

546 Adam appears to be concerned about losing his face-to-face contact with God. Perhaps this jealousy is not far removed from Satan's concerning him. In this poem it seems that God's subjects are in competition for His favour.

Satan's demon tempts Eve

The demon now has a logic to use against Eve which in other versions he lacks. Adam was rude to him, and as Adam's wife she had better repair the damage before the Lord finds out. Within the terms of Eve's knowledge, this appeal cannot be refused.

XII Wende hine wraðmod þær he þæt wif geseah
on eorðrice Euan stondan,
sceone gesceapene. Cwæð þæt sceaðena mæst
eallum heora eaforum æfter siððan
wurde on worulde: 'Ic wat, inc waldend God
abolgen wyrð, swa ic Him þisne bodscipe
selfa secge, þonne ic of þys siðe cume
ofer langne weg, þæt git ne læstan wel
hwilc ærende swa He easten hider
on þysne sið sendeð. Nu sceal He sylf faran
to incre andsware! Ne mæg His ærende
His boda beodan! Þy ic wat þæt He inc abolgen wyrð,
mihtig on mode! Gif þu þeah minum wilt,
wif willende, wordum hyran,
þu meaht his þonne rume ræd geþencan.
Gehyge on þinum breostum þæt þu inc bam twam meaht
wite bewarigan, swa ic þe wisie.
Æt þisses ofetes! Þonne wurðað þin eagan swa leoht
þæt þu meaht swa wide ofer woruld ealle
geseon siððan, and selfes stol

XII He turned away in fury to where he saw the woman
Eve standing in her earthly domain,
beautifully formed. He spoke the greatest harm
that was ever to befall any of her descendants
from then on in this world: 'I know God the Ruler
will swell with wrath against the two of you, as soon as I
tell Him this message myself when I come home
from this mission far away, that neither of you will
follow properly any instructions He sends here
on this journey westwards. Now He must come Himself
for your answer! His messenger has been unable to give
the message! So I know he will swell with rage against you,
mighty in His mood! If, however, it is your will,
willing woman, to obey these words of mine,
you can surely think of a simple solution for this.
Think within your breast of how the two of you can
both avoid punishment, just as I will guide you.
Eat this fruit! Then your eyes will become so clear
that you will then be able to see as far as
all the world extends, even to the throne itself

Herran þines, and habban His hyldo forð.
Meaht þu Adame eft gestyran,
gif þu his willan hæfst and he þinum wordum getrywð.
Gif þu him to soðe sægst hwylce þu selfa hæfst
bisne on breostum, þæs þu gebod Godes
lare læstes, he þone laðan strið,
yfel andwyrde an forlæteð
on breostcofan. Swa wit him bu tu
an sped sprecað. Span þu hine georne
þæt he þine lare læste, þy læs gyt lað Gode,
incrum Waldende, weorðan þyrfen.
Gif þu þæt angin fremest, idesa seo betste,
forhele ic incrum Herran þæt me hearmes swa fela
Adam gespræc, eargra worda.
Tyhð me untryowða, cwyð þæt ic seo teonum georn,
gramum ambyhtsecg, nales Godes engel.
Ac ic cann ealle swa geare engla gebyrdo,
heah heofona gehlidu. Wæs seo hwil þæs lang
þæt ic geornlice Gode þegnode
þurh holdne hyge, Herran minum,
Drihtne selfum. Ne eom ic deofle gelic.'

---

of your Master, while henceforth having His favour.
You will be able to manage Adam once more,
if you have his desire and he trusts your words.
If you tell him truly what precepts you have inside
your own breast, after having followed the bidding
of God as He taught it, of his own accord he will
leave this hateful strife, his evil answer, behind
in his breast-locker. The two of us to him, like this,
will speak a powerful case. Entice him eagerly
so that he follows your advice, lest it still be necessary
that the two of you turn hateful to God your Ruler.
If you follow this plan, my most noble lady,
I will hide from your Master the hurt, as big as it is,
that Adam dealt me with his shameful words.
He charges me with untruths, calls me a bloody-minded
official looking to give grief, not God's angel at all.
But I just as readily know all the families of angels,
the high gates of the skies. For a long while now
and eagerly, with a loyal resolve, I have done
thegn's service to God, my own Master,
my Lord Himself. I am nothing like a devil.'

573–4 *an forlæteð on breostcofan* 'leave behind in his breast-locker'. i.e. just keep his rudeness as a memory.

Lædde hie swa mid ligenum   and mid listum speon
idese on þæt unriht,   oðþæt hire on innan ongan
weallan wyrmes geþeaht   (hæfde hire wacran hige
Metod gemearcod),   þæt heo hire mod ongan
lætan æfter þam larum.   Forþon heo æt þam laðan onfeng
ofer Drihtnes word   deaðes beames
weorcsumne wæstm.   Ne wearð wyrse dæd
monnum gemearcod!   Þæt is micel wundor
þæt hit ece God   æfre wolde
Þeoden þolian,   þæt wurde þegn swa monig
forlædd be þam lygenum,   þe for þam larum com.
Heo þa þæs ofætes æt,   Alwaldan bræc
word and willan.   Þa meahte heo wide geseon
þurh þæs laðan læn   þe hie mid ligenum beswac,
dearnenga bedrog,   þe hire for his dædum com,
þæt hire þuhte hwitre   heofon and eorðe,
and eall þeos woruld wlitigre,   and geweorc Godes

He led her thus with lies and subtleties, enticing
the lady into the crime, until the serpent's thought
did well up inside her (the Measurer had designed
a weaker resolve for her), so that she began to let
her mood follow these instructions. And so from the foe,
against the Lord's decree, she accepted the Death-Tree's
noxious fruit. No worse deed was ever
designed for man! It is a great wonder
that God Everlasting, the Emperor above, ever
wanted to endure so many a thegn being seduced
by those lies, as happened because of those teachings.
She ate then of the fruit, broke the Omnipotent's
decree and will. Then she was able to see widely,
but through a gift of the foe who deceived her with lies,
secretly betraying her, a gift that his deeds brought to her,
so that whiter than before seemed heaven and earth,
and all this world more dazzling, and God's work

---

590 *wacran hige* 'a weaker resolve'. Not a weaker mind. Eve is acting more intelligently than Adam here. The meaning is that she was made less aggressive than the male, more open to reason.

595 *monnum gemearcod* 'designed for man'. The verb *(ge)mearcian* denotes also God's planning of the human form before the creation of Adam and Eve, on line 459, as well as that of the Middle World, on line 395. If used with the same prospective meaning, *gemearcod* here tells us that the Fall is fated or determined (but not necessarily by God). If used with a retrospective meaning, as in 'marked down later', no such (Miltonic) implication exists. [*micel wundor* 'great wonder'. With this formula, the poet does not question God's reasons but rather renders them as a mystery into which (unlike Milton) he will not enquire.

micel and mihtig, þeah heo hit þurh monnes geþeaht
ne sceawode.

Ac se sceaða georne
swicode ymb þa sawle þe hire ær þa siene onlah,
þæt heo swa wide wlitan meahte
ofer heofonrice. Þa se forhatena spræc
þurh feondscipe (nalles he hie freme lærde):
'Þu meaht nu þe self geseon, swa ic hit þe secgan ne þearf,
Eue seo gode, þæt þe is ungelic
wlite and wæstmas, siððan þu minum wordum getruwodest,
læstes mine lare. Nu scineð þe leoht fore
glædlic ongean þæt ic from Gode brohte
hwit of heofonum. Nu þu his hrinan meaht!
Sæge Adame hwilce þu gesihðe hæfst
þurh minne cime cræfta. Gif giet þurh cuscne siodo
læst mina lara, þonne gife ic him þæs leohtes genog
þæs ic þe swa Godes gegired hæbbe.
Ne wite ic him þa womcwidas, þeah he his wyrðe ne sie
to alætanne, þæs fela he me laðes spræc.'

---

great and mighty, though it was not by human mind
that she might observe it.

The destroyer, however,
who first lent her the vision whereby she could gaze
so widely across heaven's domain, was keen
to deceive her concerning the soul. In enmity did
the forsworn fiend speak (no profit did he teach her):
'You can see now, as I have no need to tell you,
good Eve, for yourself, that all brightness and shape
has looked different to you since you trusted my words,
carried out my instruction. Now shines the light before you
radiantly back which from God I brought
white from the skies. Now you can touch it!
To Adam say what powers of sight you have
from my coming. If he still carries out my teaching
with chaste conduct, then I'll give him a mass of the light
with which, as by God's wish, I have clothed you.
I will not blame him then for his filthy words, although, for speaking
much that I found evil, he is not worthy of reprieve.'

618 *þurh cuscne siodo* 'with chaste conduct'. The fiend lets Eve think that Adam swore at him earlier with sexual profanity.

Swa hire eaforan sculon   æfter lybban,
þonne hie lað gedoð,   hie sculon lufe wyrcean,
betan heora Hearran hearmcwyde   ond habban His hyldo forð.

So her descendants must live ever after,
when they do evil, they must make it up with love,
atone for their harmful words to the Master and forthwith have His grace.

Eve, deceived, deceives Adam

Eve uses both her intellectual and physical charm to persuade Adam to see reason, while the demon stands invisibly by, casting the spell of lust over the two first humans to help her. This poet exonerates Eve from her traditional guilt.

Þa gieng to Adame   idesa scenost,
wifa wlitegost   þe on woruld come,
forþon heo wæs handgeweorc   Heofoncyninges,
þeah heo þa dearnenga   fordon wurde,
forlæd mid ligenum,   þæt hie lað Gode
þurh þæs wraðan geþanc   weorðan sceolden,
þurh þæs deofles searo   dom forlætan,
Hierran hyldo,   hefonrices þolian
monige hwile.   Bið þam men full wa
þe hine ne warnað   þonne he his geweald hafað!
Sum heo hire on handum bær,   sum hire æt heortan læg,

Then went to Adam the lady most beautiful,
most dazzling of women that came into the world,
for she was the handiwork of Heaven's King,
though she had subtly been destroyed, seduced
with lies in such a way that through that angry spirit's
mind they would become hateful to God,
through that demon's cunning, lose their glory,
their Master's grace, forfeit heaven's kingdom
for many a while. Great woe betide the man
who isn't wary when he has the power to be!
One fruit she bore in her hands, another lay at her heart,

---

623 *Swa hire eaforan* 'So her descendants'. The poet's irony consists of the fact that because of the fiend's words about Adam atoning, for which there is no real need, all Adam's and Eve's descendants will have sooner or later need to atone to God with a real need for mercy.

635 *geweald* 'power'. Bradley's 'self-determination' (1982: 30) suggests, against the implication of line 523, that Adam has no choice. The meaning is rather that Adam has no knowledge on which to base a choice.

æppel unsælga, þone hire ær forbead
drihtna Drihten, deaðbeames ofet,
and þæt word acwæð wuldres Aldor,
þæt þæt micle morð menn ne þorfton
þegnas þolian, ac He þeoda gehwam
hefonrice forgeaf, halig Drihten,
widbradne welan, gif hie þone wæstman
lætan wolden þe þæt laðe treow
on his bogum bær, bitre gefylled.
Þæt wæs deaðes beam þe him Drihten forbead.
Forlec hie þa mid ligenum se wæs lað Gode,
on hete Heofoncyninges, and hyge Euan,
wifes wac geþoht, þæt heo ongan his wordum truwian,
læstan his lare, and geleafan nom
þæt he þa bysene from Gode brungen hæfde
þe he hire swa wærlice wordum sægde,
iewde hire tacen and treowa gehet,
his holdne hyge.

---

apple of disaster, which the Lord of Lords
had earlier forbidden, crop of the Death-Tree,
while Glory's Chieftain spoke the decree,
that humans, his thegns, did not need to endure
that great dungeon, but He gave heaven
to all the nations, did Holy Lord,
wealth far and wide, if their will it was
to let be the crop that the hateful tree
bore on its boughs, filled with bitterness.
That was Death's Tree the Lord forbade them.
He misled them then with lies who was God's foe,
in the hate of Heaven's King, and especially Eve's resolve,
a woman's weak purpose, so that she did trust his words,
follow his instruction, and accepted the belief
that he had brought that precept from God
which he so faithfully told her in his words,
showed her a token and promised her his pledge,
his loyal intent.

---

649 *wifes wac geþoht* 'a woman's weak purpose'. See note to line 590. Such sexism as there is here, and the poet does give women less authority than men (line 654), confines itself to taking women as less obsessive.

652 *swa wærlice* 'so faithfully'. From Eve's perspective, if the stem-vowel of *wær-* is long (as in *wærum wordum* on line 681). If short, however, 'warily', which is also the case. The poet seems to pun on these words. Eve was taken in by a fraud, as we might be.

653 *iewde hire tacen* 'showed her a token'. The demon has learned from his mistake with Adam (see line 540).

Þa heo to hire hearran spræc:
'Adam, frea min, þis ofet is swa swete,
bliðe on breostum, and þes boda sciene,
Godes engel god, ic on his gearwan geseo
þæt he is ærendsecg uncres Hearran,
Hefoncyninges. His hyldo is unc betere
to gewinnanne þonne his wiðermedo.
Gif þu him heodæg wuht hearmes gesprece,
he forgifð hit þeah, gif wit him geongordom
læstan willað. Hwæt scal þe swa laðlic strið
wið þines Hearran bodan? Unc is his hyldo þearf.
He mæg unc ærendian to þam Alwaldan,
Heofoncyninge. Ic mæg heonon geseon
hwær He sylf siteð (þæt is suð and east),
welan bewunden, se ðas woruld gesceop.
Geseo ic Him His englas ymbe hweorfan
mid feðerhaman, ealra folca mæst,
wereda wynsumast. Hwa meahte me swelc gewit gifan,
gif hit gegnunga God ne onsende,
heofones Waldend? Gehyran mæg ic rume

Then she spoke to her master:
'Adam, my lord, this fruit is so sweet,
lovely in my stomach, and this messenger so fair,
God's good angel, I see in his garments
that he is the emissary of our Master
the King of Heaven. His favour is better
for us to win than his rejection.
If you said any words of harm to him today,
he will still forgive this if we will
pay homage to him. What good is it for you, such hostility
to your Master's messenger? We need his favour.
He can intercede for us with the Omnipotent
King of Heaven. I can see from here
where God Himself sits (that is in the south east)
surrounded with wealth, He who created this world.
I see His angels circling around Him
in feathered shapes, the greatest of all companies,
the most joyous host. Who could have given me such perception
if it was not God who directly sent this,
Ruler of Heaven? I can hear things amply

---

671 *Hwa meahte me* 'Who could have' etc. The unusual perspective of this poet is clear. Eve is no less to blame than Adam. She reasons things out, and it is only due to the limits of her (and his) knowledge that the Fall can happen at all. This Fall is based on trickery, not on a woman's vanity.

and swa wide geseon   on woruld ealle
ofer þas sidan gesceaft,   ic mæg swegles gamen
gehyran on heofnum.   Wearð me on hige leohte
utan and innan,   siðþan ic þæs ofætes onbat.
Nu hæbbe ic his her on handa,   herra se goda.
Gife ic hit þe georne.   Ic gelyfe þæt hit from Gode come,
broht from His bysene,   þæs me þes boda sægde
wærum wordum.   Hit nis wuhte gelic
elles on eorðan,   buton swa þes ar sægeð,
þæt hit gegnunga   from Gode come.'

XIII   Hio spræc him þicce to   and speon hine ealne dæg
on þa dimman dæd   þæt hie Drihtnes heora
willan bræcon.   Stod se wraða boda,
legde him lustas on   and mid listum speon,
fylgde him frecne.   Wæs se feond full neah
þe on þa frecnan fyrd   gefaren hæfde
ofer langne weg.   Leode hogode
on þæt micle morð   men forweorpan,

---

and see so wide in all the world
across this vast creation that I can hear the firmament
making merry in heaven. My mind has been lit up
outside and in, since I bit this piece of fruit.
Now I have it here in my hand, generous master.
I give it you with eagerness. I believe it comes from God,
brought by His command, from what the messenger told me
with faithful words. It is like nothing
else on earth, except that, as this herald says,
it comes directly from God.'

XIII   She spoke to him often and lured him all day
into that dismal deed by which they opposed the will
of their Lord. The angry messenger stood by,
laid lusts upon them and enticed them with tricks,
followed them boldly. This fiend was close by,
who had advanced on that bold campaign
over long distance. He intended to cast down
people, human beings, into the great dungeon,

675–6 *swegles gamen* 'firmament making merry'. Apparently a derived reference to the music of the spheres.

687 *legde him lustas on* 'laid lusts upon them'. They make love, one of Eve's rhetorical devices. Compare with *Paradise Lost*, IX, lines 990–1016, for an erotic scene which, however, is negative in that it takes place after Adam has decided to eat the fruit (to keep Eve company in the punishment that will follow).

forlæran and forlædan, þæt hie læn Godes,
Ælmihtiges gife an forleten,
heofenrices geweald. Hwæt, se hellsceaða
gearwe wiste þæt hie Godes yrre
habban sceoldon and hellgeþwing,
þone nearwan nið niede onfon,
siððan hie gebod Godes forbrocen hæfdon,
þa he forlærde mid ligenwordum
to þam unrræde idese sciene,
wifa wlitegost, þæt heo on his willan spræc,
wæs him on helpe handweorc Godes
to forlæranne. [. . .]
Heo spræc ða to Adame idesa sceonost
ful þiclice, oð þam þegne ongan
his hige hweorfan, þæt he þam gehate getruwode
þe him þæt wif wordum sægde.
Heo dyde hit þeah þurh holdne hyge, nyste þæt þær hearma swa fela,
fyrenearfeða, fylgean sceolde
monna cynne, þæs heo on mod genam
þæt heo þæs laðan bodan larum hyrde,
ac wende þæt heo hyldo Heofoncyninges
worhte mid þam wordum þe heo þam were swelce
tacen oðiewde and treowe gehet,

to pervert and seduce them so that they might quite
neglect God's loan, the Almighty's gift,
power from the kingdom of heaven. Listen, the hell-demon
readily knew that they would be in for
God's rage and the crush of hell, that they would
be chained into the war of that close confine
once they had broken God's commandment,
when, with lying words, he perverted
to that disastrous course a beautiful lady,
the most dazzling woman of all, so that she spoke
according to his will, aided him in perverting
the handiwork of God. [. . .]
She then spoke to Adam, most radiant of women,
again and again, until she did turn aside
that thegn's resolve, so that he believed the promise
which the wife had said to him in her words.
She did it though with honest purpose, knew not that so many injuries,
wicked fiery hardships, would have to follow
for mankind, when in mind she apprehended
what advice from the hateful messenger she heard,
but supposed it was loyalty to Heaven's King
she was enacting, with those words she showed to her man
like a token and vowed to him like a pledge,

oðþæt Adame innan breostum
his hyge hwyrfde and his heorte ongann
wendan to hire willan. He æt þam wife onfeng
helle and hinnsið, þeah hit nære haten swa,
ac hit ofetes noman agan sceolde.
Hit wæs þeah deaðes swefn and deofles gespon,
hell and hinnsið and hæleða forlor,
menniscra morð, þæt hie to mete dædon,
ofet unfæle.

---

until she moved Adam's purpose
within his breast and began to bend
his heart to her will. He from his wife received
hell and a journey hence, though such it should not be called,
for 'the fruit' is the name it ought to have.
Yet it was the sleep of death and devil's yoke,
hell and journey hence and perdition of men,
murder of humanity, that they had for their meal,
a rotting piece of fruit.

Rejoicing and despair

Satan's demon reveals his own ambitions in these lines, as he rejoices at the forthcoming damnation of Adam and Eve. Hell will be jumping with intrigue when he comes back home. In the meantime, Adam shows his feelings about betraying the bond with God, his early feudal Lord. Eve brings his love back to her as that of the first man and wife.

Swa hit him on innan com,
hran æt heortan, hloh þa and plegode
boda bitre gehugod, sægde begra þanc
hearran sinum: 'Nu hæbbe ic þine hyldo me
witode geworhte, and þinne willan gelæst

As soon as it reached Adam's insides,
touched his heart, why then the embittered messenger
laughed and played, said thanks to his master
on two accounts: 'Now I have made sure
of your favour to me, and carried out your will

---

716 *heorte wendan to hire willan* 'bend his heart to her will'. Or turn it 'to her desire' or 'desire for her'. *Willa* 'will' is an important element of this poem, as we see Satan's will working on the messenger's, working on Eve's, working on Adam's. But Adam's 'desire' for Eve is also important here.

726–7 *þine hyldo me witode geworhte* 'made sure of your favour to me'. Here and as the demon's *wit* 'we two' dual pronoun indicates, he now regards himself as Satan's lieutenant in hell. His career has been advanced as much as the humans' prospects have fallen.

to ful monegum dæge! Men synt forlædde,
Adam and Eue! Him is unhyldo
Waldendes witod, nu hie wordcwyde His,
lare forleton. Forþon hie leng ne magon
healdan heofonrice, ac hie to helle sculon
on þone sweartan sið. Swa þu his sorge ne þearft
beran on þinum breostum, þær þu gebunden ligst,
murnan on mode, þæt her men bun
þone hean heofon, þeah wit hearmas nu,
þreaweorc þoliað, and þystre land,
and þurh þin micle mod monig forleton
on heofonrice heahgetimbro,
godlice geardas. Unc wearð God yrre
forþon wit Him noldon on heofonrice
hnigan mid heafdum halgum Drihtne
þurh geongordom, ac unc gegenge ne wæs
þæt wit Him on þegnscipe þeowian wolden.
Forþon unc Waldend wearð wrað on mode,
on hyge hearde, and us on helle bedraf,
on þæt fyr fylde folca mæste,

---

for full many a day! The humans are seduced,
Adam and Eve! The Commander's disfavour
is sure for them, now they have abandoned His
pronouncements and advice. And so no longer can they
keep the kingdom of heaven, but must take
the black road to hell. So care of this you needn't
bear in your breast, where you lie bound,
or mourn in your heart that world's men will settle
heaven on high, though you and I will now endure
injuries, pains of punishment and a land of darkness,
and have lost, through your great passion, many
high-timbered halls in heaven's domain
and well-stocked courtyards. God was angry with us both,
because we would not, when in heaven,
bow our heads to the Holy Lord
in His service, for the will to serve Him
like a thegn was not one that suited either of us.
And so our Ruler became furious at heart with us,
hardened His mind and drove us all to hell,
filled up the fire with the greatest mass of people,

---

736 *þeah wit hearmas nu* 'though you and I . . . injuries' etc. The demon fancies himself at Satan's right hand. With the dual pronoun *wit* 'we two', his soothing words are almost like a parody of Eve's to Adam, but at the same time he cannot resist nagging Satan about the grand mistake he made.

743 *unc gegenge* 'that suited either of us'. This demon is about to make his own play for power, with Satan against all the others. Hell is just as competitive as heaven in this poem.

and mid handum His eft on heofonrice
rihte rodorstolas and þæt rice forgeaf
monna cynne. Mæg þin mod wesan
bliðe on breostum, forþon her synt bu tu gedon,
ge þæt hæleða bearn heofonrice sculon
leode forlætan and on þæt lig to þe
hate hweorfan, eac is hearm Gode,
modsorg gemacod. Swa hwæt swa wit her morðres þoliað,
hit is nu Adame eall forgolden
mid Hearran hete and mid hæleða forlore,
monnum mid morðes cwealme. Forþon is min mod gehæled,
hyge ymb heortan gerume, ealle synt uncre hearmas gewrecene
laðes þæt wit lange þoledon. Nu wille ic eft þam lige near,
Satan ic þær secan wille. He is on þære sweartan helle
hæft mid hringa gesponne.'

Hwearf him eft niðer
boda bitresta, sceolde he þa bradan ligas
secan helle gehliðo, þær his hearra læg
simon gesæled.

---

and with His hands in heaven once more
He righted His sky-thrones and gave the kingdom
to mankind. The mood in your breast
can now lighten, because both things have now been done.
One is that the children of men, their people,
must quit the heavenly kingdom and move to you
into the hot flames. The other is that harm and sorrow
are caused in God's heart. Whatever murder we endure there,
both of us, Adam is now paid back for everything,
with Master's hate and the perdition of his people,
with horror of death for mankind. So my mood is healed,
my resolve near the heart is relieved, our own injuries are avenged,
all enmity we long endured. Now I will go back closer to the flames,
Satan I will visit there. He in the blackened heart of hell
lies captive within a chain of rings.'

Moved back down again
the most bitter messenger, had to find the broad flames,
seek the gates of the hell in which his master lay
sealed around with cables.

---

756 *Adame eall forgolden* 'Adam is now paid back for everything'. Satan never mentions Adam until he is in hell, where he claims man as the first cause of his rebellion. But the demon has now accepted Satan's argument. Hell from their perspective is revenge against man for being more attractive to God than His best angel.

Sorgedon þa twa,
Adam and Eue, and him oft betuh
gnornword gengdon. Godes him ondredon,
heora Herran hete, Heofoncyninges nið
swiðe onsæton. Selfe forstodon
His word onwended. Þæt wif gnornode,
hof hreowigmod (hæfde hyldo Godes,
lare forlæten), þa heo þæt leoht geseah
ellor scriðan þæt hire þurh untreowa
tacen iewde se him þone teonan geræd,
þæt hie helle nið habban sceoldon,
hynða unrim. Forþam him higesorga
burnon on breostum. Hwilum to gebede feollon
sinhiwan somed, and Sigedrihten
godne gretton and God nemdon,
heofones Waldend, and Hine bædon
þæt hie his hearmsceare habban mosten,
georne fulgangan, þa hie Godes hæfdon
bodscipe abrocen. Bare hie gesawon
heora lichaman, næfdon on þam lande þa giet
sælða gesetena, ne hie sorge wiht

Sorrowed both two of them,
Adam and Eve, and often between them
there passed mournful words. God they dreaded,
hate from their Master, Heaven-King's malevolence
they really feared. They understood that they had
transgressed His command. The woman mourned,
wailed in repentance (God's grace she had lost
by quitting His instruction) when she saw the light
slide away elsewhere that was faithlessly shown
as a token by him who devised the grief
that they should have hell's hostility, no end
of humiliations. And so their sorrows of mind
burned in the breast. At times they fell to praying,
the wedded pair in unison, greeted the generous
Lord of Victory and called Him God,
Ruler of Heaven, and begged Him
eagerly for permission to have, to undergo,
a share of harm for this, now they had broken
God's commandment. Bare they saw
their bodies, had not as yet in that country
the felicity of housing, nor knew anything

---

773 *þurh untreowa* 'faithlessly'. The devil has introduced deceit into the human world, having claimed that the Almighty deceived his faith in heaven. See note to line 258.

weorces wiston,   ac hie wel meahton
libban on þam lande,   gif hie wolden lare Godes
forweard fremman.   Þa hie fela spræcon
sorhworda somed,   sinhiwan twa.

Adam gemælde   and to Euan spræc:
'Hwæt, þu Eue, hæfst   yfele gemearcod
uncer sylfra sið.   Gesyhst þu nu þa sweartan helle
grædige and gifre?   Nu þu hie grimman meaht
heonane gehyran.   Nis heofonrice
gelic þam lige,   ac þis is landa betst,
þæt wit þurh uncres Hearran þanc   habban moston,
þær þu þam ne hierde   þe unc þisne hearm geræd,
þæt wit Waldendes   word forbræcon,
Heofoncyninges.   Nu wit hreowige magon
sorgian for þis siðe.   Forþon He unc self bebead
þæt wit unc wite   warian sceolden,
hearma mæstne.   Nu slit me hunger and þurst
bitre on breostum,   þæs wit begra ær
wæron orsorge   on ealle tid.

---

of the care of labour, but well could they have
lived in that land if it had been their will to keep
to the terms of God's teaching. Many words of sorrow
did they speak together, husband and wife.

Adam gave voice and spoke to Eve:
'Well, Eve, what an evil mark you have made against
the joint fate of both of us. Do you see black hell now,
greedy and voracious? From here now you can
hear the roaring of her. Heaven's domain is not
like that fire, but is the finest country,
which thanks to our Master we could have had,
but that you listened to him who caused us this injury,
through which we broke the command of the Ruler,
King of Heaven. Now the two of us can show
repentance for this fate. For He told us Himself
that we should guard against punishment, the greatest
harm for ourselves. Hunger now tears at me, thirst
bites me in the breast, both of which we once
had no care for in all the hours God sent us.

---

791 Lines 791–817a may be matched with Old Saxon lines close to their German original, in the *Old Saxon Genesis*, lines 1–26a (Doane 1991: 232–3).

Hu sculon wit nu libban   oððe on þys lande wesan,
gif her wind cymð,   westan oððe eastan,
suðan oððe norðan?   Gesweorc up færeð,
cymeð hægles scur   hefone getenge,
færeð forst on gemang,   se byð fyrnum ceald.
Hwilum of heofnum   hate scineð,
blicð þeos beorhte sunne,   and wit her baru standað,
unwered wædo.   Nys unc wuht beforan
to scursceade,   ne sceattes wiht
to mete gemearcod,   ac unc is mihtig God,
Waldend wraðmod.   To hwon sculon wit weorðan nu?
Nu me mæg hreowan   þæt ic bæd heofnes God,
Waldend þone godan,   þæt He þe her worhte to me
of liðum minum,   nu þu me forlæred hæfst
on mines Herran hete.   Swa me nu hreowan mæg
æfre to aldre   þæt ic þe minum eagum geseah.'

XIV   Ða spræc Eue eft,   idesa scienost,
wifa wlitegost,   hie wæs geweorc Godes,
þeah heo þa on deofles cræft   bedroren wurde:

How shall we now live or stay in this land
if wind comes from west or east,
from south or north? The gloom moves in,
a shower of hail comes near to heaven,
frost comes and joins them which is wickedly cold.
Sometimes from heaven it shines hot,
this bright sun gleams, while we stand here naked,
unprotected by clothing. There is no shelter for us
to stop the showers, nor do we have money
marked off for food, for the mind of mighty God,
our Ruler, is in fury. What shall come of us now?
Now can I repent, ever asking the God of Heaven,
the good Commander, to make you for me
out of my limbs, seeing that you misled me
into my Master's hate. So I can now rue the day
for ever in eternity that my eyes ever saw you.'

XIV   Then Eve spoke back to him, the fairest lady,
most dazzling of women, she was God's work
though she had been betrayed by demon's skill:

---

822 *wifa wlitegost, hie wæs geweorc Godes* 'most dazzling of women, she was God's work'. This poet admires beauty in women.

'Þu meaht hit me witan,   wine min Adam,
wordum þinum;   hit þe þeah wyrs ne mæg
on þinum hyge hreowan   þonne hit me æt heortan deð.'

Hire þa Adam   andswarode:
'Gif ic Waldendes   willan cuðe,
hwæt ic his to hearmsceare   habban sceolde,
ne gesawe þu no sniomor,   þeah me on sæ wadan
hete heofones God   heonone nu þa,
on flod faran,   nære he firnum þæs deop,
merestream þæs micel,   þæt his o min mod getweode,
ac ic to þam grunde genge,   gif ic Godes meahte
willan gewyrcean.   Nis me on worulde niod
æniges þegnscipes,   nu ic mines Þeodnes hafa
hyldo forworhte   þæt ic hie habban ne mæg.
Ac wit þus baru ne magon   bu tu ætsomne
wesan to wuhte.   Uton gan on þysne weald innan,
on þisses holtes hleo.'

You can blame me, Adam my associate,
with your words, though it cannot cause you worse regret
in your mind than it does me in my heart.'

Adam then gave her answer:
'If I knew the Ruler's will,
what share of harm I should have for this,
you would not at once see (though now the God of Heaven
should command me to leave and wade the seas,
fare on the flood, were it never so wickedly deep,
an ocean stream so huge) my spirit ever doubting Him,
but I would go to the bottom of the ocean to carry out
the will of God. I have no need to do a thegn's
service in this world, now I have so forfeited
that I cannot have grace from my God Emperor.
But the two of us cannot be bare like this
together in any way. Let us go inside this wood,
into the shelter of this woodland.'

826 *on þinum hyge . . . me æt heortan* 'in your mind . . . in my heart'. Eve defines mind by gender, assigning the faculty of active purpose (*hyge*) to Adam and of passive reflection (*heorte*) to herself (North 1991: 94).

Hwurfon hie þa twa,
togengdon gnorngende on þone grenan weald,
sæton onsundran, bidan selfes gesceapu
Heofoncyninges, þa hie þa habban ne moston
þe him ær forgeaf ælmihtig God.
Þa hie heora lichoman leafum beþeahton,
weredon mid ðy wealde, wæda ne hæfdon,
ac hie on gebed feollon bu tu ætsomne
morgena gehwilce, bædon Mihtigne
þæt hie ne forgeate God ælmihtig,
and him gewisade Waldend se goda,
hu hie on þam leohte forð libban sceolden.

The two of them moved off,
mournfully walked into the green forest,
sat apart to await their own destiny
from the King of Heaven, now that they were not permitted
to keep what Almighty God once gave them.
Then they covered their bodies with leaves,
dressed with the woods, had no clothing,
but fell to praying both of them together
each morning, begged the Mighty One
that He, Almighty God, would not forget them,
and that the good Ruler would guide
their steps towards survival in this world.

843 *sæton onsundran* 'sat apart'. By this the poet may show that they have no more sexual desire for each other. Their joint praying suggests a new kind of relationship.

Andreas

Andreas, a poem that survives in the Vercelli Book, Biblotheca capitolare CXVII (*c.* 975, from near Canterbury) is a Saint's Life put in Old English verse. As such it is open to the same serious figural analyses as *Juliana* or *Elene* or *Guthlac A* and *B*. *Andreas* is copied near the beginning of the second block of quires (4–17), after Homily No. 5 and before Cynewulf's shortest poem *The Fates of the Apostles*. For a while it was believed to be one poem with *The Fates*, given the lack of titles or any note for the sectional division, and thus composed by Cynewulf. This idea, however, has not lasted the various stylistic tests, which establish that the author is quite different, possibly a Mercian like Cynewulf (in the consensual view), but a poet with literary tastes which include *Beowulf*. The style of this poem has been studied in detail (Bjork 1985) and its likeness to *Beowulf* has been regarded variously as coincidental, formulaic, or a matter of concious literary borrowing. Whatever the relationship, there is no doubt that the material in St Andrew's life recommends itself to a poet with knowledge of this heroic poem.

St Andrew is working as a missionary in Achaea (Greece) when the Lord tells him to drop everything and go to save his fellow apostle St Matthew, presently detained by a nation of cannibals in Mermedonia. The opening section of *Andreas* has shown us Matthew blinded and imprisoned and awaiting a terrible death from his hosts in 30 days. The Lord, who has promised to have him freed in 27, gives the order to Andrew on the 27th day as if ('Consider it done') any command should be considered enacted as soon as given. With undue reluctance, Andrew heads out. The passages below give an idea of how. There is first a long sea-voyage to Mermedonia in which the ship's captain, the Lord in disguise, tests Andrew's faith by asking him to recall scenes from Jesus' life and works. Andrew responds well, with good stories, but fails to recognise the Lord until too late, when he has fallen asleep and been placed with his followers by angels outside the city walls. But the Lord appears again, this time as an imperious little boy, briefing Andrew on the mission in more detail. Andrew walks in to liberate Matthew, stays behind to convert the cannibals, but must undergo nearly four days of torture until, well beyond his limits and with a new access of power, he calls forth a flood from a marble pillar to drown the whole city. When nearly all have drowned and the survivors show repentance, Andrew lets the flood subside, and converts them, leaving a bishop behind to establish the diocese.

The source for this rollicking poem has been lost, but lay somewhere in between an apocryphal Greek text named the *Praxeis* 'acts' of Andrew and Matthew, and some Latin recensions of this which have come to light, the *Recensio Casanatensis*, the *Recensio Vaticana* and the Bonnet Fragment. It is more likely that the source was in Latin, but the poet may have read or been able to recognise some Greek (see note to line 1480). He adapted a source of this kind, and he may have done so in (the free west of) Mercia in the later ninth century. And yet unfortunately the story of *Andreas* is clearer to readers than what the poet's aim was in telling it. His Andrew is not the best candidate for saintly moral example, and the style of this Life is by turns vague, gaudy and outlandish. The poet is a mystery to his critics: either the inept victim of a mismatch between genres of hagiography and romance, or a comedian who can make us laugh by exploiting this; either a journeyman poet copying out lines of *Beowulf* because he cannot compose his own, or a Mercian Cervantes who mocks the fame of that great poem.

Bjork, R. E., *The Old English Verse Saints' Lives: A Study in Direct Discourse and the Iconography of Style* (Toronto, 1985), 110–31

Brooks, K. R., ed., *Andreas and the Fates of the Apostles* (Oxford, 1961)

Calder, D. G., 'Figurative language and its contexts in *Andreas*: a study in medieval expressionism', in *Modes of Interpretation in Old English Literature: Essays in Honor of Stanley B. Greenfield*, ed. P. R. Brown, G. R. Crampton and F. C. Robinson (Toronto, 1986), 115–36

Elliott, J. K., ed. and trans., *The Apocryphal New Testament* (Oxford, 1993)

Hamilton, D., '*Andreas* and *Beowulf*: placing the hero', in *Anglo-Saxon Poetry: Essays in Appreciation for John C. McGalliard*, ed. L. E. Nicholson and D. W. Frese (Notre Dame, IN, 1975), 81–98

Herbison, I., 'Generic adaptation in *Andreas*', in *Essays on Anglo-Saxon and Related Themes in Memory of Lynne Grundy*, ed. J. Roberts and J. Nelson (London, 2000), 181–211

Riedinger, A., 'The formulaic relationship between *Beowulf* and *Andreas*', in *Heroic Poetry in the Anglo-Saxon Period: Studies in Honor of Jess B. Bessinger, Jr.*, ed. H. Damico and J. Leyerle, Studies in Medieval Culture 32 (Kalamazoo, MI, 1993), 283–312

Walshe, M., 'St Andrew in Anglo-Saxon England: the evolution of an apocryphal hero', *Annuale Medioevale* 20 (1981), 97–122

Matthew and the Mermedonians

I Hwæt! We gefrunan on fyrndagum
twelfe under tunglum tireadige hæleð,
þeodnes þegnas. No hira þrym alæg
camprædenne þonne cumbol hneotan,
syððan hie gedældon, swa him Dryhten sylf,
heofona Heahcyning, hlyt getæhte.
Þæt wæron mære men ofer eorðan,
frome folctogan ond fyrdhwate,
rofe rincas, þonne rond ond hand
on herefelda helm ealgodon,

I Listen! We heard tell from ancient days
of twelve glorious heroes under the stars,
thegns of the King. Never did their power fail
in the battle-field when standards clashed,
once they had dispersed, as the Lord Himself,
High-King of heaven, showed them by lot.
These were renowned men on earth,
brave chieftains and keen for campaign,
cheerful warriors, when shield and arm
guarded helmet on the field of armies,

on meotudwange. Wæs hira Matheus sum,
se mid Iudeum ongan godspell ærest
wordum writan wundorcræfte.
Þam halig God hlyt geteode
ut on þæt igland þær ænig þa git
ellþeodigra eðles ne mihte
blædes brucan: oft him bonena hand
on herefelda hearde gesceode.
Eal wæs þæt mearcland morðre bewunden,
feondes facne, folcstede gumena,
hæleða eðel. Næs þær hlafes wist
werum on þam wonge, ne wæteres drync
to bruconne, ah hie blod ond fel,
fira flæschoman, feorrancumenra,
ðegon geond þa þeode. Swelc wæs þeaw hira
þæt hie æghwylcne ellðeodigra
dydan him to mose meteþearfendum,
þara þe þæt ealand utan sohte.

---

on the plain of doom. One of them was Matthew,
who was the first among the Jews to begin
to write the gospel in words with wondrous skill.
For him did Holy God fashion the lot
out to the island where no foreign man
as yet had been able to enjoy the happiness
of his homeland: often the hands of slayers
cruelly harmed him on the field of armies.
All that border country was steeped in murder,
with devil's crime, that tribal abode of men,
home of heroes. No loaf sustenance there was,
no drink of water, for men on that plain
to enjoy, but it was the blood and skin,
the flesh covering of men from afar
they fed on in that nation. Such was their custom,
that they made into their meal, when hungry,
each man of a foreign country
who sought that island from abroad.

---

11 *on meotudwange* 'on the plain of doom'. This is the poet's first aural indication that his 12 heroes (albeit as many as the good disciples) are Christ's followers, rather than those of a deceased earthly warlord.

15 *ut on þæt igland* 'out to the island'. Compare with *ealand* 'island', line 28. Brooks (1961: 62) considers 'land beyond the water' better for Mermedonia, but it is not clear that the poet thinks of this land as part of continental Europe, even if he calls it *mearcland* 'border country' on line 19. The border is one between civilisation and hell.

25 *Swelc wæs þeaw hira* 'Such was their custom'. Possibly a borrowing from the same half line in *Beowulf*, line 178b, in which the devil-worshipping Danes are described. Cannibalism goes further than anything the Danes do, however.

Swylc wæs þæs folces freoðoleas tacen,
unlædra eafoð, þæt hie eagena gesihð,
hettend heorogrimme, heafodgimmas
agetton gealgmode gara ordum.
Syððan him geblendan bitere tosomne,
dryas þurh dwolcræft, drync unheorne,
se onwende gewit, wera ingeþanc,
heortan on hreðre (hyge wæs oncyrred)
þæt hie ne murndan æfter mandreame,
hæleþ heorogrædige, ac hie hig ond gærs
for meteleaste meðe gedrehte.
Þa wæs Matheus to þære mæran byrig
cumen in þa ceastre. Þær wæs cirm micel
geond Mermedonia, manfulra hloð,
fordenera gedræg, syþþan deofles þegnas
geascodon æðelinges sið.
Eodon him þa togenes, garum gehyrsted,
lungre under linde (nalas late wæron)
eorre æscberend, to þam orlege.
Hie þam halgan þær handa gebundon
ond fæstnodon feondes cræfte,

Such was the uncivilised character of that people,
violence of these wretched men, that the eyesight,
head-jewels, those bloodthirsty gallows-minded
persecutors with spear-points did destroy.
Then cruelly with witchcraft the wizards
would mix a monstrous drink which changed
the reason, conscience, of the men,
the heart in each breast (the mind was overthrown),
so that they cared no longer for human joy,
men of ravenous hunger, but it was hay and grass
to torment these weary men when they wanted food.
Then it was that Matthew arrived in the city,
came to that infamous town. There was great outcry
through Mermedonia, a throng of wicked men,
a mob of the damned, when the devil's thegns
heard tell of the prince's mission.
They marched against him equipped with spears,
swiftly beneath shields (slow they were not),
angry they carried ash-spears to the war.
Then and there the saint's hands they bound
and fastened with all the devil's skill,

---

29 *freoðoleas tacen* 'uncivilised character'. OE *freoðo* stands for treaties and agreements. This epithet marks the Mermedonians out as international pariahs.

hæleð hellfuse, ond his heafdes sigl
abreoton mid billes ecge. Hwæðre he in breostum þa git
herede in heortan heofonrices Weard,
þeah ðe he atres drync atulne onfenge.
Eadig ond onmod, he mid elne forð
wyrðode wordum wuldres Aldor,
heofonrices Weard, halgan stefne,
of carcerne. Him wæs Cristes lof
on fyrhðlocan fæste bewunden.

He þa wepende weregum tearum
his Sigedryhten sargan reorde
grette, gumena Brego, geomran stefne,
weoruda Wilgeofan, ond þus wordum cwæð:
'Hu me elþeodige inwitwrasne
searonet seowað! A ic symles wæs
on wega gehwam willan þines
georn on mode, nu ðurh geohða sceal
dæde fremman swa þa dumban neat.

---

heroes hell-bound, and his head's suns
with swordblade destroyed. Yet still in his breast awhile
did he praise Heaven's Guardian within his heart,
though swallowing a terrible poison-drink.
Blessed and resolute, with courage from that moment
did he worship with words the Prince of Glory,
Heaven's Guardian, in holy singing
from the jail. For him was praise of Christ
firmly enclosed in the locker of the spirit.

Weeping, then, with weary tears,
he greeted with sorrowing tones his Victory Lord,
Chief of Men, in lamenting voice,
Joy-Giver of Hosts, and spoke these words:
'What web of malice, chains of guile,
do alien men weave against me! Ever constantly
have I been eager in heart on every road
to do your will, now in my misery
must I do things like dumb cattle.

---

50 *hæleð hellfuse* 'heroes hell-bound'. The noun is inappropriate for men such as the Mermedonians, who look more like zombies. It seems likely that the poet uses such heroic vocabulary for comic effect.

67 *dæde fremman swa þa dumban neat* 'do things like dumb cattle'. Matthew believes that he will lose his wits like all the others who have drunk the Mermedonians' brew.

Þu ana canst   ealra gehygdo,
Meotud mancynnes,   mod in hreðre.
Gif þin willa sie   wuldres Aldor
þæt me wærlogan   wæpna ecgum,
sweordum, aswebban,   ic beo sona gearu
to adreoganne   þæt ðu, Drihten min,
engla Eadgifa   eðelleasum
dugeða Dædfruma   deman wille.
Forgif me to are,   ælmihtig God,
leoht on þissum life,   þy læs ic lungre scyle,
ablended in burgum,   æfter billhete
þurh hearmcwide   heorugrædigra,
laðra leodsceaðena,   leng þrowian
edwitspræce.   Ic to anum þe,
middangeardes Weard,   mod staþolige,
fæste fyrhðlufan,   ond þe Fæder engla,
beorht Blædgifa,   biddan wille
ðæt ðu me ne gescyrige   mid scyldhetum,
werigum wrohtsmiðum,   on þone wyrrestan,
dugoða Demend,   deað ofer eorðan.'

Æfter þyssum wordum   com wuldres tacen
halig of heofenum,   swylce hadre s*i*gl

You alone know the thoughts of all,
the heart in the breast, Measurer of Mankind.
If it is your will, O Prince of Glory,
that with weapon's edges, with swords,
these warlocks slay me, I am ready straightaway
to endure whatever fate you, my Lord,
Wealth-Giver of Angels, Hosts' Benefactor,
wish to appoint for the homeless man.
As a favour, Almighty God, give me
light in this life, lest, blinded in the town,
after the heat of blades, through the harmful decree
of blood-ravening hostile enemies of humanity,
I must soon for longer suffer
words of scorn. I on you alone do
fix my heart, Guardian of the Middle World,
my firm spiritual love, and to you, Father of Angels,
bright Giver of Fame, will I pray
that you, Judge of Hosts, do not appoint
for me among evil foes, accursed artesans
of accusation, the worst death on earth.'

After these words came a sign of glory,
holy from heaven like the bright sun

to þam carcerne. Þær gecyðed wearð
þæt halig God helpe gefremede,
ða wearð gehyred Heofoncyninges stefn
wrætlic under wolcnum, wordhleoðres sweg
mæres Þeodnes.

---

towards the jail. It was known there
that Holy God was extending help
when Heaven-King's voice was heard,
marvellous, beneath the clouds, the harmony
of the King of Renown.

Andrew talks with the Lord

Andrew is forced by the Lord to undertake a journey to save Matthew within three days of his promised execution. Going to shore with his followers, he finds a small ship waiting, with a captain and two crew, and negotiates his passage. The comedy of this exchange is inherent in the analogues, and thus the lost source, for the ship's captain is the Lord in disguise and the crewmen are angels. As they sail, Andrew has a lengthy dialogue with the captain which takes up about a third of the poem. This has a serious import, for the Lord is testing Andrew for his memory of His miracles in the Holy Land and his loyalty to the faith. Nonetheless, the audience must be wondering when Andrew will work out the identity of the young, strangely gifted ship's captain who is asking him the questions.

Crowne, D. K., 'The hero on the beach: an example of composition by theme in Anglo-Saxon poetry', *Neuphilologische Mitteilungen* 61 (1960), 362–72

V Ongan ða reordigan rædum snottor,
wis on gewitte, wordlocan onspeonn:
'Næfre ic sælidan selran mette,
macræftigran, þæs ðe me þynceð,
rowend rofran, rædsnotterran,

V Then began utterance, man good at stratagems,
wise in his wits unlocked the word-store:
'Never have I met a better seafarer,
a man of greater skill, so it seems to me,
a braver mariner, one better at stratagems,

---

92 *þæt halig God helpe gefremede* 'that Holy God was extending help'. All Latin and Greek analogues, related to the lost source of *Andreas*, have the Lord give Matthew back his sight, but the poet leaves this out, either through vagueness, or because he wants us to be surprised at the lack of this expected miracle. That Matthew does regain his sight is clear when he sees Andrew later.

470 *wis on gewitte* 'wise in his wits'. Is he? We might wonder, as the dialogue unfolds.

wordes wisran. Ic wille þe,
eorl unforcuð, anre nu gena
bene biddan, þeah ic þe beaga lyt
sincweorðunga syllan mihte
fætedsinces. Wolde ic freondscipe,
þeoden þrymfæst, þinne gif ic mehte
begitan godne. Þæs ðu gife hleotest,
haligne hyht on heofonþrymme,
gif ðu lidwerigum larna þinra
este wyrðest. Wolde ic anes to ðe,
cynerof hæleð, cræftes neosan
ðæt ðu me getæhte, nu þe tir cyning
ond miht forgef, manna scyppend,
hu ðu wægflotan wære bestemdon
sæhengeste sund wisige.
Ic wæs on gifeðe iu ond nu þa
syxtyne siðum on sæbate,
mere hrerendum mundum freorig,

---

wiser in his words. From you, gentleman
without infamy, there is now just one more
request I will ask, although it is few rings
or precious adornments or plated treasure
that I could give. I would have the friendship,
powerful lord, of you if I could
get this on good terms. You will be granted grace,
holy joy in the majesty of heaven,
if you give your advice generously
to a man weary of the sea. One skill, hero
of royal birth, would I learn from you,
that you might teach me, seeing that the King,
Men's Creator, gave you the nobility and power,
how it is you keep the ocean-sprayed
wave-coaster, sea-stallion, on her course.
I have been granted now and then
to be sixteen times aboard a sea-boat,
frozen in my arms that stirred the deep,

474–8 The elaborate syntax of Andrew's request appears to be modelled on Beowulf's to Hrothgar on the king's leave to fight Grendel, in *Beowulf*, lines 426–32. Andrew thus shows politeness, but what he really wants from the captain is to learn how to steer so well.

475 *eorl unforcuð* 'gentleman without infamy'. Here, as elsewhere, the poet supplies embellishments that are not in his source. This one apparently tells us that Andrew suspects the captain might be a pirate. In line 476–8 Andrew repeats to the captain that he has no money.

490 Andrew, brother of Simon Peter, was a fisherman before joining Christ.

eagorstreamas (is ðys ane ma),
swa ic æfre ne geseah ænigne mann
þryðbearn hæleða þe gelicne
steoran ofer stæfnan. Streamwelm hwileð,
beateþ brimstæðo. Is þes bat ful scrid,
færeð famigheals fugole gelicost,
glideð on geofone. Ic georne wat
þæt ic æfre ne geseah ofer yðlade
on sæleodan syllicran cræft.
Is þon geliccost swa he on landsceare
stille stande, þær hine storm ne mæg,
wind awecgan, ne wæterflodas
brecan brondstæfne, hwæðere on brim snoweð
snel under segle. Đu eart seolfa geong,
wigendra hleo, nalas wintrum frod,
hafast þe on fyrhðe faroðlacende
eorles ondsware. Æghwylces canst
worda for worulde wislic andgit.'

---

the ocean-currents (this is one time more),
yet I have never seen one man
to equal you, mighty son of heroes,
for steering at the prow. The breaker roars,
beats the seashore. This boat is very swift,
the foamy-neck sails most like a bird,
glides on the deep. I really know
that on the wave-road I have never seen
greater skill in any sailor.
It is almost as if the boat were standing still
on a tract of land where the storm,
the wind, cannot shake her, nor water's floods
break up the stern, but she moves fast
over the sea under the sun. You are indeed young,
shelter to your warriors, in no way wintry wise,
but in your heart you hold the reply of a gentleman,
a man who sails the deep. Every word
wisely in this world you can understand.'

497 *færeð famigheals fugole gelicost* 'the foamy-neck sails most like a bird'. This line is probably lifted from *Beowulf*, line 218, with *færeð* for *flota* 'vessel'. Like Beowulf, Andrew is setting out on his big adventure.

505 *Đu eart seolfa geong* 'You are indeed young'. Not in the analogues, and apparently the poet's fulfilment of the ironies of the situation.

508–9 *Æghwylces canst worda* 'Every word you can' etc. Andrew knows not how right he is.

Him ondswarode ece Dryhten:
'Oft þæt gesæleð þæt we on sælade
scipum under scealcum, þonne sceor cymeð,
brecað ofer bæðweg brimhengestum.
Hwilum us on yðum earfoðlice
gesæleð on sæwe þeh we sið nesan,
frecne geferan. Flodwylm ne mæg
manna ænigne ofer Meotudes est
lungre gelettan: ah Him lifes geweald,
se ðe brimu bindeð, brune yða
ðyð ond þreatað. He þeodum sceal
racian mid rihte, se ðe rodor ahof
ond gefæstnode folmum sinum,
worhte ond wreðede, wuldras fylde
beorhtne boldwelan, swa gebledsod wearð
engla eðel þurh His anes miht.
Forþan is gesyne, soð orgete,
cuð oncnawen, þæt ðu Cyninges eart
þegen geþungen, Þrymsittendes,

The Eternal Lord gave him answer:
'Often it happens that on the sea-road,
when showers come, we break the bathway
with ocean-stallions, with ships under crews.
Sometimes on waves there is chance of hardship
for us on sea, though we survive the voyage,
undertake danger. Flood's surge cannot
hinder against Measurer's favour any man
from moving swiftly: He has the power of life,
who binds the oceans, crushes and rebukes
the shiny waves. He must have the right
to rule nations who raised up the sky
and fastened it with His hands,
built and sustained it, filled with glory
the bright joyous building so that angels' homeland
was blessed through the power of Him alone.
So it is obvious, a truth made evident,
known and acknowledged, that you are the King's
distinguished thegn, of Him who sits in majesty,

511–36 The captain's reply plays down his own skill and claims, instead, that the sea is smooth because it knows that Andrew is the Lord's servant.

526–8 *is gesyne þæt ðu Cyninges eart þegen geþungen* 'is obvious that you are the King's distinguished thegn'. Obvious that the Lord's power is with Andrew, or that Andrew is by nature distinguished? The captain's hyperbole, leading too easily from praise of the Lord to praise of Andrew, is a trap for the man who might be too easily flattered.

forþan þe sona sæholm oncneow,
garsecges begang, þæt ðu gife hæfdes
Haliges Gastes. Hærn eft onwand,
aryða geblond. Egesa gestilde,
widfæðme wæg (wædu swæðorodon)
seoðþan hie ongeton þæt ðe God hæfde
wære bewunden se ðe wuldres blæd
gestaðolade strangum mihtum.'

Þa hleoðrade halgan stefne
cempa collenferhð, Cyning wyrðude,
wuldres Waldend, ond þus wordum cwæð:
'Wes ðu gebledsod, Brego mancynnes,
Dryhten Hælend! A þin dom lyfað!
Ge neh ge feor is þin nama halig,
wuldre gewlitegad ofer werþeoda,
miltsum gemærsod. Nænig manna is
under heofonhwealfe, hæleða cynnes,
ðætte areccan mæg oððe rim wite
hu ðrymlice, þeoda Baldor,
gasta Geocend, þine gife dælest.

---

because the ocean, the spearman's circuit,
at once acknowledged that you had grace
from the Holy Ghost. The flood turned back,
churning of ocean rollers. The terror of wide-bosomed
waves subsided (the rigging became slack)
when it knew that the same God who founded
with strong powers heaven's brilliant vault
had also enfolded you in His covenant.'

Then with holy voice did the champion
cry out, stout of heart, worshipped the King,
Glory's Commander, and said these words:
'May you be blessed, O Chieftain of Mankind,
Healing Lord! Your fame will live for ever!
Both near and far is your name made sacred,
gloriously lit up across the nations of man,
renowned for its mercy. No person lives
of the race of men beneath heaven's vault
who can relate or know how to reckon
the power with which, Prince of Nations,
Solace of Spirits, you give out your grace.

540 *Wes ðu gebledsod, Brego mancynnes* 'May you be blessed, O Chieftain of Mankind'. The poet changes the likely source, from Andrew making an address to the captain, 'May God bless you and Himself be blessed', to his showering blessings upon God for ten fulsome lines. The effect is to make us believe that Andrew has at last realised who the captain is.

Huru is gesyne, sawla Nergend,
þæt ðu þissum hysse hold gewurde
ond hine geongne geofum wyrðodest,
wison gewitte ond wordcwidum!
Ic æt efenealdum æfre ne mette
on modsefan maran snyttro.'

Indeed it is obvious, O Saviour of Souls,
what favour you have shown to this lad,
with what gifts honoured him young as he is,
with what wise wit and eloquence!
In a man of his age I never met
greater wisdom of mind.'

Andrew frees Matthew

After being laid to rest outside the walls of Mermedonia, and waking up, Andrew realises who the captain was. His followers wake up too, having seen a dream of the future in heaven where Andrew among others stood at the Lord's right hand. Andrew appeals to the Lord for forgiveness, acknowledging His great power.

Đa him fore eagum onsyne wearð
æðeling oðywed in þa ilcan tid,
Cining cwicera gehwæs, þurh cnihtes had.
Þa He worde cwæð, wuldres Aldor:

Visibly then before his eyes appeared
the Prince revealed at that very moment,
King of all living creatures, in the form of a boy.
Chieftain of Glory, He then spoke these words:

549–50 *is gesyne þæt ðu þissum hysse hold gewurde* 'is obvious what favour you have shown to this lad'. At this point, and rather comically given the poet's repeat of the captain's formula above on lines 526–8, we realise that Andrew has still not understood.

553 *Ic æt efenealdum* 'In a man of his age' etc. This motif may owe something to the situation in *Beowulf*, lines 1842–3, when Hrothgar compliments Beowulf, saying *ne hyrde ic snotorlicor on swa geongum feore guman þingian* 'I have not heard any man with a life so young discuss affairs more wisely'. In Beowulf, the Heathobards will attack Heorot before long, burning it down. Beowulf can see this, and has just offered to help out Hrothgar if the Danes suffer an invasion. But the king cannot see, and brushes this aside. In both cases the spoken words are truer than their speakers know. In *Andreas*' case, the irony is accentuated in that the young man in question is the Lord Himself. The target of this poet's mockery is Andrew.

'Wes ðu, Andreas, hal,   mid þas willgedryht,
ferðgefeonde!   Ic þe friðe healde,
þæt þe ne moton   mangeniðlan,
grame grynsmiðas,   gaste gesceððan.'

Feoll þa to foldan,   frioðo wilnode
wordum wis hæleð,   winedryhten frægn:
'Hu geworhte ic þæt,   Waldend fira,
synnig wið seolfne,   sawla Nergend,
þæt ic Þe swa godne   ongitan ne meahte
on wægfære,   þær ic worda gespræc
minra for Meotude   ma þonne ic sceolde?'

Him andswarode   ealwalda God:
'No ðu swa swiðe   synne gefremedest
swa ðu in Achaia   ondsæc dydest,
ðæt ðu on feorwegas   feran ne cuðe
ne in þa ceastre   becuman mehte,
þing gehegan   þreora nihta
fyrstgemearces,   swa ic þe feran het
ofer wega gewinn.   Wast nu þe gearwor

'Greetings to you Andrew, and your happy band,
rejoice in your heart! I will keep my word to you
that your guilty foes, those angry ensnarers,
will not be permitted to harm your soul.'

Fell then to earth a hero wise in words, implored
his Friend and Lord for protection, asking:
'How could I do this, Commander of Men,
Saviour of Souls, so sin against your person
that I could not recognise you, as generous as you were
on the sea-voyage when I spoke more words
before God the Measurer than I should have?'

Omnipotent God gave him an answer:
'No sin did you ever commit as serious
as when you refused me in Achaea, saying
you did not know how to go to distant parts,
nor would you be able to get into the city,
set up the deal in the space of three nights
as I ordered when I told you to go
across the tumult of waves. Now you know better

---

914 *Wes ðu, Andreas, hal* 'Greetings to you Andrew' etc. The alliteration is strained, with the imperative *wes* awkwardly matching *willgedryht* in the second half line, as if expressing a strained patience from the Almighty, whose next words, expanded from the briefest greeting in the source, indirectly tell Andrew to expect the worst.

þæt ic eaðe mæg anra gehwylcne
fremman ond fyrþran freonda minra
on landa gehwylc, þær me leofost bið.
Aris nu hrædlice, ræd ædre ongit,
beorn gebledsod, swa þe beorht Fæder
geweorðað wuldorgifum to widan aldre,
cræfte ond mihte. Đu in þa ceastre gong
under burglocan, þær þin broðor is.
Wat ic Matheus þurh mænra hand
hrinen heorudolgum, heafodmagan
searonettum beseted. Þu hine secan scealt,
leofne alysan of laðra hete,
ond eal þæt mancynn þe him mid wunige
elþeodigra inwitwrasnum
bealuwe gebundene. Him sceal bot hraðe
weorþan in worulde ond in wuldre lean,
swa ic him sylfum ær secgende wæs.

IX 'Nu ðu, Andreas, scealt edre geneðan
in gramra gripe. Is þe guð weotod,

---

how easily I can advance and move
anyone who is a friend of mine
to any shore it pleases me most.
Get up now, quickly, take full note of my plan,
blessed man, in as much as you are being honoured
by Bright Father for the rest of your life with gifts of glory,
with skill and power. You go into the city
beneath the town gate to where your brother is.
I know that criminal hands have streaked
bloody wounds on Matthew, that your older kinsman
is caught in a cunning net. You shall find him,
free the dear man from the persecution of enemies,
and all that humanity who dwell alongside him
by the spiteful chains of foreigners
wickedly bound. Quickly to him shall help
be given in this world, and a reward in the next,
just as I was telling him to his face earlier.

IX 'You now, Andrew, shall at once venture
into the enemy grasp. War is assured for you,

937–8 *swa þe beorht Fæder geweorðað wuldorgifum* 'in as much as you are being honoured by Bright Father . . . with gifts of glory'. This sounds a little grudging from the imperious youth.

951 *Is þe guð weotod* 'War is assured for you' etc. Thus begins fitt IX, with news of an ordeal ahead, one that follows the example of Jesus.

heardum heoruswengum   scel þin hra dæled
wundum weorðan,   wættre geliccost
faran flode blod.   Hie þin feorh ne magon
deaðe gedælan,   þeh ðu drype ðolie,
synnigra slege.   Đu þæt sar aber,
ne læt þe ahweorfan   hæðenra þrym,
grim gargewinn,   þæt ðu Gode swice,
Dryhtne þinum.   Wes a domes georn,
læt ðe on gemyndum   hu þæt manegum wearð
fira gefrege   geond feala landa,
þæt me bysmredon   ben*d*um fæstne
weras wansælige.   Wordum tyrgdon,
slogon ond swungon,   synnige ne mihton
þurh sarcwide   soð gecyðan.
Þa ic mid Iudeum   gealgan þehte
(rod wæs aræred)   þær rinca sum
of minre sidan   swat ut forlet,
dreor to foldan.   Ic adreah feala
yrmþa ofer eorðan.   Wolde ic eow on ðon
þurh bliðne hige   bysne onstellan,
swa on ellþeode   ywed wyrðeð.
Manige syndon   in þysse mæran byrig
þara þe ðu gehweorfest   to heofonleohte

---

with harsh bloody strokes shall your body
be dealt wounds, like water most of all
will gore flood out. They cannot consign
your life to death, though you may suffer beating,
the blows of sinful men. You bear that pain,
nor let the power, the grim spear-threats,
of heathens move you to betray God,
your Lord. Be always eager for renown,
keep remembering how the fame spread
with many men through a lot of countries
how I was abused, made fast in bonds,
by unhappy men. With words they taunted,
beat and flogged, it was not truth these sinners
could prove with their words of reproach.
Among Jews then was I stretched on the gallows
(the rood was raised) where one of the warriors
let the blood flow out from my side,
gore to the ground. I endured many
wretched moments on earth. By this I wanted
with cheerful resolve to set you all an example,
such as will be shown you in this foreign land.
There are many in this infamous town
that you can turn to heaven's light

þurh minne naman, þeah hie morðres feala
in fyrndagum gefremed habban.'

Gewat him þa se Halga heofonas secan,
eallra cyninga Cining, þone clænan ham,
eaðmedum upp, þær is ar gelang
fira gehwylcum, þam þe hie findan cann.
Đa wæs gemyndig modgeþyldig,
beorn beaduwe heard, eode in burh hraðe,
anræd oretta, elne gefyrðred,
maga mode rof, Meotude getreowe,
stop on stræte (stig wisode)
swa him nænig gumena ongitan ne mihte,
synfulra geseon. Hæfde sigora Weard
on þam wangstede wære betolden
leofne leodfruman mid lofe sinum.
Hæfde þa se æðeling in geþrungen,
Cristes cempa, carcerne neh.
Geseh he hæðenra hloð ætgædere,
fore hlindura hyrdas standan,
seofone ætsomne. Ealle swylt fornam,

---

through my name, though the murders are many
they have carried out from ancient days.'

The Holy One then moved off to seek heaven,
the King of all kings, that clean homeland,
upwards in humility, where grace belongs
to each and every man who can find it.
Then the man with patient courage was inspired,
the warrior hard in battle, quickly entered the town,
a single-minded soldier sustained by valour,
a young fellow brave at heart, true to the Measurer,
marched up the street (the pavement guided him)
in such a way that none of the men with sin
might notice or see him. The Victory Keeper
had on that inhabited plain wrapped the beloved
captain in the protection of His covenant.
By then the prince had pressed on,
Christ's champion, in to near the jail.
He saw a posse of heathens together
standing as guards before the grated doors,
seven in one place. Extinction took them all,

---

982 *beorn beaduwe heard* 'warrior hard in battle'. This epithet is used of Beowulf with Grendel's Mother in *Beowulf*, line 1539 (see **Heroic Poems**).

druron domlease. Deaðræs forfeng
hæleð heorodreorige. Ða se halga gebæd
bilwytne Fæder, breostgehygdum
herede on hehðo Heofoncyninges þrym,
Godes dryhtendom. Duru sona onarn
þurh handhrine Haliges Gastes,
ond þær in eode, elnes gemyndig,
hæle hildedeor. Hæðene swæfon,
dreore druncne, deaðwang rudon.
Geseh he Matheus in þam morðorcofan,
hæleð higerofne under heolstorlocan,
secgan Dryhtne lof, domweorðinga
engla ðeodne. He ðær ana sæt
geohðum geomor in þam gnornhofe.
Geseh þa under swegle swæsne geferan,
halig haligne. Hyht wæs geniwad.
Aras þa togenes, Gode þancade
þæs ðe hie onsunde æfre moston

---

they fell without renown. Heroes blood-soaked
were snatched by sudden death. Then the saint prayed
to the Gentle Father, in the thoughts of his breast
praised to the heights Heaven-King's majesty,
God's lordship. At once the door rushed open
with a touch from the hand of the Holy Ghost,
and in there, inspired by valour, marched
a man daring in battle. Heathens were sleeping,
drunk with blood, had reddened the place of death.
He caught sight of Matthew in the murder chamber,
a hero brave and resolute, locked away in darkness,
speaking praise to the Lord, honour
to Angels' Emperor. He was sitting there alone,
mournful with cares in that court of lamentation.
In the light then he saw his own dear comrade,
one saint saw another. Hope was renewed.
He rose up to meet him, gave thanks to God
that they had ever been permitted to see one another

---

996 *hæleð heorodreorige* 'Heroes blood-soaked'. See note to line 50. This case of literary sarcasm reminds the Mermedonian heroes that death is what they signed up for.

999–1000 *Duru sona onarn þurh handhrine Haliges Gastes* 'At once the door rushed open with a touch from the hand of the Holy Ghost'. This scene mocks the literary cult of *Beowulf*. This classic poem has Grendel break into Heorot in almost the same way, when, on lines 721–2, *duru sona onarn, fyrbendum fæst, syþðan he hire folmum æthran* 'at once the door rushed open, made firm with fired bonds, when his hands touched it' (see **Heroic Poems**). Though Andrew does this with the Holy Ghost, the people inside in both cases expect to be eaten by whoever comes through that door. It is as if the poet is saying that *Beowulf* interferes with everything.

geseon under sunnan. Syb wæs gemæne
bam þam gebroðrum, blis edniwe,
æghwæðer oðerne earme beþehte,
cyston hie ond clypton. Criste wæron begen
leofe on mode. Hie leoht ymbscan
halig ond heofontorht. Hreðor innan wæs
wynnum awelled.

---

safe beneath the sun. Goodwill was shared
between both brothers, rejoicing anew,
each man covered the other with his arms,
they kissed and embraced. Both were dear
to Christ's heart. A light shone about them
holy and heaven-radiant. Their innermost hearts had
welled up with joy.

Andrew calls forth a flood

Matthew and the prisoners flee the city, while Andrew stays on to complete his heroic mission. The Mermedonians, enraged at their loss of human flesh, subject Andrew to three days and nights of torture, in and out of the jail in the city. At last Andrew can bear no more, prays to God, bitterly rebuking Him in the desperation of his cell, and then hears the divine promise that all will come right. Once again the Lord reminds Andrew of the tortures inflicted in the Passion. Presently it becomes clear that Andrew has become the tough kind of *miles Christi* 'soldier of Christ' of which the poet spoke in the poem's opening (Herbison 2000: 197). The next morning he is tormented for a fourth day. The mock epic style of this work does not detract from the devout purpose. The poet makes fun neither of God, nor really of Andrew for very long, but rather of a literary culture that must have idolised *Beowulf*.

As the following passage shows, this Cervantes-style mockery reaches its climax in what is also the climax of *Andreas*, the scene in which Andrew calls forth a flood to rout his heathen opponents. To prepare us for this, the poet restarts his work at the beginning of Fitt XIV. Here he uses the commonplace of authorial modesty to great self-deprecating effect, for he is probably better educated than he seems (*pace* Foley 1995), and he seems also to know what he is doing when he misreads a line of *Beowulf*.

Foley, J. M., 'The poet's self-interruption in *Andreas*', in *Prosody and Poetics in the Early Middle Ages: Essays in Honor of C. B. Hieatt*, ed. M. J. Toswell (Toronto, 1995), 181–207

1011–13 This sentence is based apparently on Hygelac's, when Beowulf comes home, in lines 1997–8: *Gode ic þanc secge þæs ðe ic ðe gesundne geson moste.* But even if Matthew is cast as an unlikely Hygelac to Andrew's Beowulf, their joy at reunion shines through. Andrew's tests are about to transform him into a true saint.

1016–17 *Criste wæron begen leofe on mode* 'Both were dear to Christ's heart'. The relationship between Jesus and the two saints of *Andreas* is the more sincerely given for being strengthened by the tests that fill this poem.

North, R., '"Wyrd" and "wearð ealuscerwen" in *Beowulf*', *Leeds Studies in English* New Series 25 (1994), 69–82

Rowland, J., 'OE *ealuscerwen/meoduscerwen* and the concept of "paying for mead"', *Leeds Studies in English* New Series 21 (1990), 1–12

XIV

Hwæt, ic hwile nu haliges lare,
leoðgiddinga, lof þæs þe worhte,
wordum wemde, wyrd undyrne
ofer min gemet. Mycel is to secganne,
langsum leornung, þæt he in life adreag,
eall æfter orde. Þæt scell æglæwra
mann on moldan þonne ic me tælige
findan on ferðe, þæt fram fruman cunne
eall þa earfeðo þe he mid elne adreah,
grimra guða. Hwæðre git sceolon
lytlum sticcum leoðworda dæl
furður reccan.

Þæt is fyrnsægen,
hu he weorna feala wita geðolode,

XIV

Listen, for a while now I have been pleading
words in verse ballad so as to teach what glories
the saint performed, a history which, when revealed,
lies beyond my capacity. A big task it is, a work
of time-consuming study, to say everything he suffered
in life from the start. More learned than I
is the earthly man, by my reckoning, who shall find
in his spirit the means of knowing from the beginning
every hardship that the man courageously suffered
in that fierce fighting. And yet the narration
of a few lyrics more in little snatches on this theme
must still be made.

It is a saga of ancient times,
the great number of torments he endured,

1480 *wyrd undyrne* 'a history when revealed'. This innocuous phrase alludes to the word *apocrypha*, 'revealed things', which is the Greek name for the continuation of the Acts of the Apostles on which the Acts of Saints Matthew and Andrew were based, with an admixture of Greek romance, in the second century. Perhaps Herbison is right and the surviving Greek *Praxeis* 'acts' are the closest thing to the poet's now-lost source (2000).

1488 *leoðworda dæl furður* 'a few lyrics more'. Thus the poet describes his own handling of the St Andrew theme.

1489 *fyrnsægen* 'a saga of ancient times'. The legendary quality of the genre comes through in this modern approximation to the sense of a compound resembling the sterner *ealdgesegen* in *Beowulf*, line 869 (see **Heroic Poems**).

heardra hilda, in þære hæðenan byrig.
He be wealle geseah wundrum fæste
under sælwage sweras unlytle,
stapulas standan, storme bedrifene,
eald enta geweorc. He wið anne þæra,
mihtig ond modrof, mæðel gehede,
wis, wundrum gleaw, word stunde ahof:
'Geher ðu, marmanstan, meotudes rædum,
fore þæs onsyne ealle gesceafte
forhte geweorðað, þonne hie fæder geseoð
heofonas ond eorðan herigea mæste
on middangeard mancynn secan.
Læt nu of þinum staþole streamas weallan,
ea inflede, nu ðe ælmihtig
hateð, heofona cyning, þæt ðu hrædlice
on þis fræte folc forð onsende
wæter widrynig to wera cwealme,
geofon geotende. Hwæt, ðu golde eart,
sincgife, sylla! On ðe sylf cyning
wrat, wuldres God, wordum cyðde
recene geryno, ond ryhte æ
getacnode on tyn wordum,
meotud mihtum swið! Moyse sealde,

---

what harsh assaults in that heathen town.
By the wall he saw some pillars of no mean size
wondrously firm beneath the first-floor storey,
columns standing scoured by weather,
old works of giants. He with one of them
did negotiate, mighty and brave of heart,
wise and wonder-sharp briefly made his speech:
'Hear, stone of marble, the plan of the Measurer
before whose face all things of creation
will take fright, when they see the Father
of heaven and earth with the greatest of hosts
come seeking mankind in the Middle World.
Let streams well up from your foundations,
a river in flood, now that the Almighty
King of Heaven commands you to send
rapidly forth into this trashy people
wide waters in spate to the destruction of men,
an outpouring ocean. Hear me, you are better
than gold or gifts of treasure! On you the King
Himself, Glorious God, in His words revealed
His mysteries in one instant and just laws
in ten commandments did inscribe,
Measurer wise in might! He gave them to Moses,

swa hit soðfæste syðþan heoldon,
modige magoþegnas, magas sine,
godfyrhte guman, Iosua ond Tobias.
Nu ðu miht gecnawan þæt þe cyning engla
gefrætwode furður mycle
giofum geardagum þonne eall gimma cynn.
Þurh his halige hæs þu scealt hræðe cyðan
gif ðu his ondgitan ænige hæbbe!'

Næs þa wordlatu wihte þon mare
þæt se stan togan. Stream ut aweoll,
fleow ofer foldan. Famige walcan
mid ærdæge eorðan þehton,
myclade mereflod. Meoduscerwen wearð
æfter symbeldæge, slæpe tobrugdon
searuhæb[b]ende. Sund grunde onfeng,
deope gedrefed. Duguð wearð afyrhted
þurh þæs flodes fær. Fæge swulton,

---

just as later, with truth unwavering, they were kept
by brave young thegns, kinsmen of Moses,
the God-fearing men Joshua and Tobias.
Now you may understand how the King of Angels
adorned you in ancient days with gifts far beyond
any He gave to any family of precious stones.
By His sacred order you are quickly to show
if you have any understanding of this!'

Not a jot slower than his speech did the stone
obey him, but came apart. A stream welled out,
flooded the landscape. Foamy breakers
covered the earth in the early part of day,
a sea-flood swelled. It was a serving of mead
after the feast-day, men who kept weapons
woke from their sleep. Sea enfolded ground,
stirred from the depths. The company took fright
at this flood's assault. Doomed, they died,

1526–7 *Meoduscerwen wearð æfter symbeldæge* 'It was a serving of mead after the feast-day' etc. This expression opens up an unsourced image of the deadly flood as a spontaneous and unlimited serving of beer. The mead-serving conceit continues in lines 1532–5. It may be discussed, one might say dismissed, as a case of *poculum mortis* 'the cup of death', but the humour shines through, if only because it clearly imitates and reverses (Rowland 1990 would say improves on) a famous sentence in *Beowulf*, lines 767–9: *Denum eallum wearð . . . ealuscerwen* 'to all the Danes was . . . good fortune prescribed' (see **Heroic Poems**). It is as if the poet wilfully misreads *ealu* 'good fortune' (runic **alu** – ᚨᛚᚢ) as its homophone *ealu* 'ale'. A change of fortune is signalled in both cases, but in *Andreas* the culture has changed. The audience appears willing to see some of *Beowulf*'s lines read with a cruel lack of literary nostalgia.

geonge on geofene   guðræs fornam
þurh sealtes weg.   Þæt wæs sorgb*ry*þen,
biter beorþegu.   Byrlas ne gældon,
ombehtþegnas.   Þær wæs ælcum genog
fram dæges orde   drync sona gearu.
Weox wæteres þrym.   Weras cwanedon,
ealde æscberend.   Wæs him ut myne
fleon fealone stream,   woldon feore beorgan,
to dunscræfum   drohtað secan,
eorðan ondwist.   Him þæt engel forstod,
se ða burh oferbrægd   blacan lige,
hatan heaðowælme.   Hreoh wæs þær inne
beatende brim.   Ne mihte beorna hloð
of þam fæstenne   fleame spowan.
Wægas weoxon,   wadu hlynsodon,
flugon fyrgnastas,   flod yðum weoll.
Ðær wæs yðfynde   innan burgum
geomorgidd wrecen.   Gehðo mændan
forhtferð manig,   fusleoð golon.
Egeslic æled   eagsyne wearð,
heardlic hereteam,   hleoðor gryrelic.
Þurh lyftgelac   leges blæstas
weallas ymbwurpon,   wæter mycladon.

---

young men in ocean snatched by war-charge
of salt wave. That was a brewing of sorrow,
a bitter beer-tasting. Cup-bearers did not dally,
servants and thegns. There was drink enough
at once ready for all from the start of day.
The water's might increased. Men lamented,
old spear-bearers. Their longing went outwards,
to flee the fallow stream, to save their lives,
wishing to seek refuge in mountain caves,
a lodging in earth. An angel prevented them,
overwhelming the town with gleaming fire,
with bright-hot war-surge. Savage in the town
was the pounding sea, nor did success favour
the huddle of men with escape from that city.
Waves grew higher, the deep sea roared,
fire-sparks flew, flood welled with billows.
Easy there was it to find inside the town
a performance of the blues. Bewailed their grief
many fear-stricken men, dirges they chanted.
Terrifying fire became clear to the eye,
cruel devastation, voices raised in horror.
With airborne commotion did blasts of flame
envelop the walls, the waters grew higher.

Þær wæs wop wera   wide gehyred,
earmlic ylda gedræg.

Þa þær an ongann,
feasceaft hæleð,   folc gadorigean,
hean, hygegeomor,   heofende spræc:
'Nu ge magon sylfe   soð gecnawan,
þæt we mid unrihte   ellþeodigne
on carcerne   clommum belegdon,
witebendum.   Us seo wyrd scyðeð,
heard ond hetegrim.   Þæt is her swa cuð,
is hit mycle selre,   þæs þe ic soð talige,
þæt we hine alysan   of leoðobendum,
ealle anmode   (ofost is selost)
ond us þone halgan   helpe biddan,
geoce ond frofre.   Us bið gearu sona
sybb æfter sorge,   gif we secaþ to him.'

Þa þær Andrea   orgete wearð
on fyrhðlocan   folces gebæro,
þær wæs modigra   mægen forbeged,
wigendra þrym.   Wæter fæðmedon,
fleow firgendstream,   flod wæs on luste,

Weeping of men there was widely heard,
piteous the concourse of men.

One of them then,
a destitute man, began to gather the people,
shamed, downcast, spoke in lamentation:
'Now you can understand the truth for yourselves,
that it was unjustly we did imprison
the foreigner in a jail with shackles,
torturing bonds. This fate harms us,
harsh and fierce as it is. So obvious is this
that it will be much better in my opinion
if we free him from his manacles,
being all of one mind (haste is best here)
while we pray to the saint to give us help,
aid and solace. Peace after sorrow will be
at once ready for us if we look to him.'

Then it was abundantly clear to Andrew's
mind-locker which way the people inclined,
when crushed was the vigour of passionate men,
the fighters' majesty. Waters wrapped around,
mountain rapids flowed, flood was ecstatic,

oþþæt breost oferstag brim weallende
eorlum oð exle. Þa se æðeling het
streamfare stillan, stormas restan
ymbe stanhleoðu. Stop ut hræðe
cene collenferð, carcern ageaf
gleawmod Gode leof. Him wæs gearu sona
þurh streamræce stræt gerymed.
Smeolt wæs se sigewang, symble wæs dryge
folde fram flode, swa his fot gestop.
Wurdon burgware bliðe on mode,
ferhðgefeonde. Þa wæs forð cumen
geoc æfter gyrne. Geofon swaðrode
þurh haliges hæs, hlyst yst forgeaf,
brimrad gebad. Þa se beorg tohlad,
eorðscræf egeslic, ond þær in forlet
flod fæðmian, fealewe wægas,
geotende gegrind grund eall forswealg.
Nalas he þær yðe ane bisencte,
ach þæs weorodes eac ða wyrrestan,
faa folcsceaðan, feowertyne
gewiton mid þy wæge in forwyrd sceacan
under eorþan grund. Þa wearð acolmod,
forhtferð manig folces on laste,

---

until welling seawater climbed above chest-height
to men's shoulders. The prince then commanded
the torrent to be still, storms to abate
around stone gates. He moved out quickly,
brave stout-hearted man, gave up the jail
a wise man dear to God. For him a cleared path
was at once ready through the millrace.
Pleasant the plain of victory, continually dry
of flood was the ground at each step.
The hearts of townsfolk became cheerful,
spirits were gladdened. Aid after injury
had come forth. Ocean subsided, tempest
was lost to hearing at the saint's command,
the sea-road waited. The rock then split open,
a frightening earth-trench, and let the flood,
the fallow-brown waves, sweep into it,
ground swallowed all the inundating swirl.
Not just the waves did he sink in that place,
but also the worst of that company,
people-harming criminals, fourteen
moving in haste with the sea to perdition
down to earth's core. Panicked were then
many fear-stricken men of folk remaining,

wendan hie wifa ond wera cwealmes,
þearlra geþinga ðrage hnagran,
syððan mane faa, morðorscyldige,
guðgelacan under grund hruron.

Hie ða anmode ealle cwædon:
'Nu is gesyne ðæt þe soð meotud,
cyning eallwihta, cræftum wealdeð,
se ðisne ar hider onsende
þeodum to helpe. Is nu þearf mycel
þæt we gumcystum georne hyran.'

XV Þa se halga ongann hæleð blissigean,
wigendra þreat wordum retan:
'Ne beoð ge to forhte, þeh þe fell curen
synnigra cynn. Swylt þrowode,
witu be gewyrhtum. Eow is wuldres leoht
torht ontyned gif ge teala hycgað.'

---

expected the killing of women and men,
a meaner period of severe circumstances
when, stained with crime, the murderous
war-gamers dropped into the abyss.

Of one mind then they all cried out:
'Now it can be seen that the true Measurer,
the King of All Creatures, rules in power,
He who sent this man here as herald
in aid of nations. It is now highly necessary
that we obey this noble man with eagerness.'

XV The saint then began to bless these men,
to cheer the warrior crowd with his words:
'Do not be frightened, though the sinners' kind
chose destruction. Death they have suffered,
penalties matching deeds. For you a light of glory,
if you think of virtue, will brilliantly be revealed.'

1600 *guðgelacan* 'war-gamers'. The dead in the analogues are innocents, including women and children. This poet chooses to make them people who play with people's lives in wars.

Judith

✳

The Apocryphal Book of Judith celebrates a clever widow who outwits a general of the Assyrian army. Sent by Nebuchadnezzar of Babylon to bring the remaining Hebrews to heel, Holofernes occupies Judaea, lays siege to Bethulia and cuts off the water supply. The elders make ready to give up in five days, but Judith comes out of obscurity to save the city. She dolls herself her up, goes out with a maid with their own food and water and enters the enemy camp, promising to help the general win the city. At a party on the fourth day, Holofernes becomes besotted with Judith and respectfully leaves her unmolested while he drinks his own wine. Before long he passes out alone with her. When the moment is right, Judith cuts off his head, her maid stows it in their knapsack and the two ladies make their escape. When the Assyrians find Holofernes' trunk the next morning, they flee in haste and the Bethulians take over their camp.

The Old English *Judith* tells this story rather differently. The poet has drawn elements of learned commentary into his conception of the heroine and recasts her as a virgin, either a figure for chastity or the church or a political leader. The poem, which is copied into the Nowell Codex (British Library, Cotton Vitellius A.xv) just after *Beowulf*, is missing its beginning, though how much is unknown. What survives of the rest, however, gives a vividly binary moral characterisation, with Judith portrayed as innocent of sexual wiles and Holofernes as steeped in sin. The virgin is kept in a bower until Holofernes is ready for her, then brought to his empty tent. He makes his drunken way in from the main party and falls down on his bed. Judith prays to the Trinity for strength and then cuts off his head in two blows, giving it to her maid. When the two of them return to Bethulia the citizens on the watch-tower are at first depressed, but their spirits lift when the head is displayed, and later Judith sends them out in full battle order to rout the Assyrians. When Holofernes' officers find him headless, they flee in disorder and the Bethulians cut them down from the rear, take as much spoil as they can from the corpses, and present Holofernes' full panoply to Judith as if to their general. The poem ends with the poet's celebration of divine power as something enacted through Judith.

The poet of *Judith* knows how to tell a good story, adding much comedy to the portrait of Holofernes in his drunkenness and rolling head, and in the frightened debauchery of his officers. The Assyrians are given as the inverse of heroes, too timid to see how the general got on with the maid. The Bethulians are allowed to cheerfully rout their enemies in battle. Yet the poem does not seem long. Although the poem begins in mid-ninth fitt, according to section numbering, it seems impossible that the numbering covered just this poem. That would have made *Judith* more than 1200 lines long, nearly as long as *Andreas*. The fact that Ozias the elder is neither named nor present, nor Achior the Assyrian renegade who joins the Bethulians, nor Bagoas the general's servant, nor even Nebuchadnezzar the architect of this invasion, tells us that *Judith* is selective and probably shorter than the original tale. Moreover, the Bethulians are shown to be a people occupied for some time, and Judith as filled with righteous anger as well as strategy. The poem appears to be of the tenth century, with Anglian features that would make it a Mercian, rather than West Saxon, production (Fulk 1992:

335–6, n. 147). This aspect too favours the not uncommon critical view that Judith is an allegory for Æthelflæd, the Lady of the Mercians who fought a war to 'free' the Danelaw in 909–18.

Belanoff, P. A., '*Judith*: sacred and secular heroine', in *Heroic Poetry in the Anglo-Saxon Period: Studies in Honor of Jess B. Bessinger, Jr.*, ed. H. Damico and J. Leyerle, Studies in Medieval Culture 32 (Kalamazoo, MI, 1993), 247–64

Dockray-Miller, M., 'Female community in the Old English *Judith*', *Studia Neophilologica* 70 (1998), 165–72

Fitzgerald, C. M., 'Swords, sex and revenge: teaching *Beowulf* and *Judith* with Tarantino's *Kill Bill*', *Studies in Medieval and Renaissance Teaching* 14.2 (2007), 41–55

Fulk, R. D., *A History of Old English Meter* (Philadelphia, PA, 1992), 335–6 (late Anglian)

Garner, L. A., 'The art of translation in the Old English *Judith*', *Studia Neophilologica* 73 (2001), 171–83

Griffith, M., ed., *Judith* (Exeter, 1997)

Heinemann, F., '*Judith* 236–291a: a mock-heroic approach-to-battle type scene', *Neuphilologische Mitteilungen* 71 (1970), 83–96

Lochrie, K., 'Gender, sexual violence, and the politics of war in the Old English "Judith"', in *Class and Gender in Early English Literature: Intersections*, ed. B. J. Harwood and G. R. Overing (Bloomington, IN, 1993), 1–20

Lucas, P. J., 'The place of *Judith* in the *Beowulf*-manuscript', *Review of English Studies* new series 41 (1990), 463–78

Orchard, A., *Pride and Prodigies: Studies in the Monsters of the Beowulf-Manuscript* (Woodbridge, 1995)

Swanton, M. J., *English Poetry Before Chaucer*, 2nd ed. (Exeter, 2002), 166–78

Wainwright, F. T., 'Æthelflæd, Lady of the Mercians', in *Scandinavian England: Collected Papers by F. T. Wainwright*, ed. H. P. R. Finberg (Chichester, 1975), 305–24; and in *New Readings on Women in Old English Literature*, ed. H. Damico and A. Hennessey Olsen (Bloomington, IN, 1990), 44–55

Woolf, R., 'The lost opening to the *Judith*', in *Art and Doctrine: Essays on Medieval Literature*, ed. H. O'Donoghue (London, 1986), 119–24

The feast of Holofernes

. . . ne] tweode
gifena in ðys ginnan grunde. Heo ðar ða gearwe funde
mundbyrd æt ðam mæran Þeodne, þa heo ahte mæste þearfe,
hyldo þæs hehstan Deman, þæt he hie wið þæs hehstan brogan
gefriðode, frymða Waldend. Hyre ðæs Fæder on roderum

. . .] did [not] doubt
His gifts in this wide world. Ready she found there
her protection in the renowned King, when she had the greatest need
in the loyalty of the Highest Judge, that against the highest terror
He, Ruler of Creation, would harbour her. To her then did heavenly Father,

torhtmod tiðe gefremede,   þe heo ahte trumne geleafan
a to ðam Ælmihtigan.   Gefrægen ic ða Holofernus
winhatan wyrcean georne   ond eallum wundrum þrymlic
girwan up swæsendo.   To ðam het se gumena baldor
ealle ða yldestan ðegnas.   Hie ðæt ofstum miclum
ræfndon, rondwiggende,   comon to ðam rican þeodne
feran folces ræswan.   Þæt wæs þy feorðan dogore
    þæs ðe Iudith hyne,   gleaw on geðonce,
    ides ælfscinu,   ærest gesohte.

X   Hie ða to ðam symle   sittan eodon,
    wlance to wingedrince,   ealle his weagesiðas,
    bealde byrnwiggende.   Þær wæron bollan steape
    boren æfter bencum gelome,   swylce eac bunan ond orcas
    fulle fletsittendum.   Hie þæt fæge þegon,
    rofe rondwiggende,   þeah ðæs se rica ne wende,
    egesful eorla dryhten.   Ða wearð Holofernus,
    goldwine gumena,   on gytesalum,
    hloh ond hlydde,   hlynede ond dynede,
    þæt mihten fira bearn   feorran gehyran
    hu se stiðmoda   styrmde ond gylede,
    modig ond medugal,   manode geneahhe
    bencsittende   þæt hi gebærdon wel.

---

bright of heart, answer her request because she had firm faith
ever in the Almighty. I heard then that Holofernes
eagerly threw a wine party, and that with all the wonders a magnificent
feast did he organise. To this the lord of men commanded
all the most senior thegns. This bidding the shield-toting men
carried out in great haste. There came to the powerful king
in procession the captains of that people. That was the fourth day
    after Judith, far-sighted in thinking,
    a lady elvishly fair, first visited him.

X   They then came to take their seats at the banquet,
    arrogant men to drink wine, all his companions in woe,
    bold fighters in chained mail. In that place steep bowls were
    often carried down the benches, as well as cups and glasses
    filled high for the company around the hall. Doomed did they taste,
    brave shield-men, though of this the mighty one suspected nothing,
    terrible lord of earls. That was when Holofernes,
    gold-giving friend to his men, went wild with the pouring,
    laughed and roared, shouted and dinned
    so that the sons of men from far might hear
    how that man of stiff resolve stormed and yelled,
    with passion and mead-driven lust, constantly urged
    men on the benches to make noise properly.

Swa se inwidda ofer ealne dæg
dryhtguman sine drencte mid wine,
swiðmod sinces brytta, oðþæt hie on swiman lagon,
oferdrencte his duguðe ealle, swylce hie wæron deaðe geslegene,
agotene goda gehwylces. Swa het se gumena aldor
fylgan fletsittendum, oðþæt fira bearnum
nealæhte niht seo þystre. Het ða niða geblonden
þa eadigan mægð ofstum fetigan
to his bedreste beagum gehlæste,
hringum gehrodene. Hie hraðe fremedon,
anbyhtscealcas, swa him heora ealdor bebead,
byrnwigena brego, bearhtme stopon
to ðam gysterne, þær hie Iudithðe
fundon ferhðgleawe, ond ða fromlice
lindwiggende lædan ongunnon
þa torhtan mægð to træfe þam hean,
þær se rica hyne reste on symbel
nihtes inne, Nergende lað,
Holofernus. Þær wæs eallgylden
fleohnet fæger ymbe þæs folctogan
bed ahongen, þæt se bealofulla
mihte wlitan þurh, wigena baldor,
on æghwylcne þe ðær inne com

Thus the wicked man the whole day long
drenched the men of his retinue with wine,
strong-hearted bestower of treasure, until they lay in a swoon,
overwhelmed his whole division with drink like they were struck dead,
with any good they had poured out of them. Thus did his men's chieftain
order drinks to be filled for the men on the floor, until mankind's sons
saw the dark night approach. Brewed up with badness, he then commanded
the blessed maid to be speedily fetched
to his bed, and she was loaded with necklaces,
all adorned with rings. They quickly did that,
the camp attendants, just as their chief ordered,
prince of mailed men, in revelry advanced
to the guest-lodge where Judith they
found all sharp in mind, and boldly then
the shield-men began to convey
the bright maid to the high pavilion
where the mighty, during the banquet, was to rest
in a chamber for the night, the Saviour's enemy
Holofernes. In that place an all-gold
shimmering fly-net was hung around
the general's cot, one through which the man of evil,
lord of warriors, might look
upon each man who came inside there

hæleða bearna, ond on hyne nænig
monna cynnes, nymðe se modiga hwæne
niðe rofra him þe near hete
rinca to rune gegangan. Hie ða on reste gebrohton
snude ða snoteran idese. Eodon ða stercedferhðe,
hæleð heora hearran cyðan þæt wæs seo halige meowle
gebroht on his burgetelde. Þa wearð se brema on mode
bliðe, burga ealdor, þohte ða beorhtan idese
mid widle ond mid womme besmitan. Ne wolde þæt wuldres Dema
geðafian, þrymmes Hyrde, ac he him þæs ðinges gestyrde,
Dryhten, dugeða Waldend. Gewat ða se deofulcunda,
galferhð gumena ðreate [. . .]
bealofull his beddes neosan, þær he sceolde his blæd forleosan
ædre binnan anre nihte, hæfde ða his ende gebidenne
on eorðan unswæslicne, swylcne he ær æfter worhte,
þearlmod ðeoden gumena, þenden he on ðysse worulde
wunode under wolcna hrofe. Gefeol ða wine swa druncen
se rica on his reste middan, swa he nyste ræda nanne
on gewitlocan. Wiggend stopon
ut of ðam inne ofstum miclum,
weras winsade, þe ðone wærlogan,
laðne leodhatan, læddon to bedde

---

no matter what kind of man, and upon him nobody
of man's family, unless the brave-heart might command
some cheerful war criminal to come nearer to him
for a private talk. Into this bedchamber they then brought
the clever lady without delay. The men of hardened hearts went
to let their boss know that the holy girl had been
brought to his tented bower. Then the spirits of the infamous
chieftain of the boroughs were lifted, the radiant lady he intended
to defile with filth and pollution. Nor would Glory's Judge
consent to that, Shepherd of Majesty, but from that business
the Lord, Ruler of Divisions, restrained him. Then the devil-seed came,
wanton-minded with a company of men [. . .]
the wicked man, to spy out his bed where he would lose his fame
swiftly within one night, for by then he had got coming to him
such an unsavoury end as he had worked for earlier,
cruel-minded king of men, while he dwelt beneath the cloud-roof
in this world. Fell then down so drunk with wine
the mighty one in the middle of his cot, it was as if he had no sense
in his wit-locker left. His warriors marched
out of the chamber, making great haste,
men wine-sated who had led to his bed
the truce-breaker, hostile tyrant,

---

58 *burga ealdor* 'chieftain of the boroughs'. Holofernes looks every inch the parody of a drunken Danish earl in the Five Boroughs, the Danelaw.

nehstan siðe. Þa wæs Nergendes
þeowen þrymful, þearle gemyndig
hu heo þone atolan eaðost mihte
ealdre benæman ær se unsyfra,
womfull, onwoce.

---

for the last time. Magnificent then was
the Saviour's serving maid, thoroughly mindful
of the easiest way she might deprive
the terrible man of his life, before the unclean
defiler should wake up.

Judith wields the sword

Genam ða wundenlocc
Scyppendes mægð scearpne mece,
scurum heardne, ond of sceaðe abræd
swiðran folme, ongan ða swegles Weard
be naman nemnan, Nergend ealra
woruldbuendra, ond þæt word acwæð:
'Ic ðe, frymða God ond frofre Gæst,
Bearn alwaldan, biddan wylle
miltse þinre me þearfendre,
ðrynesse Đrym. Þearle ys me nu ða
heorte onhæted ond hige geomor,
swyðe mid sorgum gedrefed. Forgif me, swegles Ealdor,
sigor ond soðne geleafan, þæt ic mid þys sweorde mote
geheawan þysne morðres bryttan. Geunne me minra gesynta,

The Creator's ringleted
maid then seized a sharp sword
forge-hardened, and drew it from its sheath
with her right hand, did call then the Guardian
of the Firmament by name, Saviour of all
who inhabit the world, and spoke these words:
'I to you, God of First Things and Spirit of Solace,
Child of the Omnipotent, wish to pray
for your mercy upon me in my need,
Three-Personed Majesty. My heart is now
extremely heated and my mind made sad,
greatly afflicted with sorrow. Give me, Chief of the Firmament,
victory as well as true faith, that with this sword I might
hew down this murder bestower. Grant me my success,

---

83 *Ic ðe, frymða God* 'I to you, God of First Things' etc. Judith's appeal to the Trinity is of course an anachronism.

þearlmod Þeoden gumena. Nahte ic þinre næfre
miltse þon maran þearfe. Gewrec nu, mihtig Dryhten,
torhtmod tires Brytta, þæt me ys þus torne on mode,
hate on hreðre minum.'

Hi ða se hehsta Dema
ædre mid elne onbryrde, swa He deð anra gehwylcne
herbuendra þe Hyne him to helpe seceð
mid ræde ond mid rihte geleafan. Þa wearð hyre rume on mode,
haligre hyht geniwod. Genam ða þone hæðenan mannan
fæste be feaxe sinum, teah hyne folmum wið hyre weard
bysmerlice, ond þone bealofullan
listum alede, laðne mannan,
swa heo ðæs unlædan eaðost mihte
wel gewealdan. Sloh ða wundenlocc
þone feondsceaðan fagum mece,
heteþoncolne, þæt heo healfne forcearf
þone sweoran him, þæt he on swiman læg,
druncen ond dolhwund. Næs ða dead þa gyt,
ealles orsawle. Sloh ða eornoste
ides ellenrof oðre siðe
þone hæðenan hund, þæt him þæt heafod wand

---

cruel-minded King of Men. I never had more need
of your generosity than now. Avenge me now, mighty Lord,
brilliant Bestower of Excellence, for there is such anger,
such hate, within my breast.'

Her then the highest Judge
swiftly inspired with courage, as He does each
person dwelling here who seeks His help
with sense and right belief. Then her heart grew stronger,
the holy woman's hope was renewed. She seized then the heathen man
firmly by his hair, pulled him towards her with her palms
to shame him and skilfully laid
the criminal down, hateful man,
the easiest way she could properly manage
the unfortunate man. Then the ringleted woman cut
the fiendish invader, the persecutor
with a bloody blade in such a way that half his neck
she carved through and he lay in a swoon,
drunk and mortally wounded. Yet he was still not dead,
totally soulless. Earnestly then she cut
the heathen hound for the second time,
lady of firm courage, so that his head rolled

---

100 *bysmerlice* 'to shame him'. The shame is Holofernes', rather than Judith's, unless the poet censures her for the technique by which she kills him.

forð on ða flore.   Læg se fula leap
gesne beæftan,   gæst ellor hwearf
under neowelne næs   ond ðær genyðerad wæs,
susle gesæled   syððan æfre,
wyrmum bewunden,   witum gebunden,
hearde gehæfted   in hellebryne
æfter hinsiðe.   Ne ðearf he hopian no,
þystrum forðylmed,   þæt he ðonan mote
of ðam wyrmsele,   ac ðær wunian sceal
awa to aldre   butan ende forð
in ðam heolstran ham,   hyhtwynna leas.

XI Hæfde ða gefohten   foremærne blæd
Iudith æt guðe,   swa hyre God uðe,
swegles Ealdor,   þe hyre sigores onleah.
Þa seo snotere mægð   snude gebrohte
þæs herewæðan   heafod swa blodig
on ðam fætelse   þe hyre foregenga,
blachleor ides,   hyra begea nest,
ðeawum geðungen,   þyder on lædde,
ond hit þa swa heolfrig   hyre on hond ageaf
higeðoncolre   ham to berenne,
Iudith gingran sinre.   Eodon ða gegnum þanonne

---

off along the floor. The foul carcass lay
empty behind, the spirit passed elsewhere
under a beetling headland where it sank down
sealed up in torments for evermore after,
wound up with serpents, bound up with punishments,
cruelly made captive in hell's burning
after his journey hence. He never needs hope,
enveloped in darkness, of being allowed out
of the serpent hall, but there he must dwell
for evermore in time without end
in that confined home, with no joy of relief.

XI A pre-eminent renown had Judith then won
by fighting in war, as God granted her,
Chief of the Firmament, who granted her victory.
Then the clever maid quickly got
the huntsman raider's head, as bloody as it was,
into the bag in which her maidservant,
the lady walking ahead of her, pale and of proven virtue,
had taken rations for both of them there,
and as gory as it now was, she gave the bag into the hand
of the resourceful woman to carry home,
did Judith to her inferior. Straight out of there

þa idesa ba   ellenþriste,
oðþæt hie becomon,   collenferhðe,
eadhreðige mægð,   ut of ðam herige,
þæt hie sweotollice   geseon mihten
þære wlitegan byrig   weallas blican,
Bethuliam.   Hie ða beahhrodene
feðelaste   forð onettan,
oð hie glædmode   gegan hæfdon
to ðam wealgate.   Wiggend sæton,
weras wæccende   wearde heoldon
in ðam fæstenne,   swa ðam folce ær
geomormodum   Iudith bebead,
searoðoncol mægð,   þa heo on sið gewat,
ides ellenrof.

---

both ladies walked with courageous boldness
until, stout-hearted and blessed with triumph,
these virgins came out of the army camp
so far they might clearly catch sight
of the shining walls of the radiant city
Bethulia. On the footpath then,
adorned with rings, they hurried along
until with exalted hearts they had come
to the wall-postern. Soldiers were sitting there,
men not sleeping did sentinel duty
in the fortress, just as Judith earlier,
maid of the cunning plan, had ordered
the miserable people when she went on her way,
courageous lady.

Vengeance on the Assyrians

Wæs ða eft cumen
leof to leodum,   ond ða lungre het
gleawhydig wif   gumena sumne
of ðære ginnan byrig   hyre togeanes gan,
ond hi ofostlice   in forlæton
þurh ðæs wealles geat,   ond þæt word acwæð

She had then returned,
beloved to her people, and the prudent woman
rapidly gave orders to one of the men
of the wide town to come towards her
and quickly allow her in
through the gate in the wall, she said these words

to ðam sigefolce: 'Ic eow secgan mæg
þoncwyrðe þing, þæt ge ne þyrfen leng
murnan on mode. Eow ys Metod bliðe,
cyninga Wuldor. þæt gecyðed wearð
geond woruld wide, þæt eow ys wuldorblæd
torhtlic toweard ond tir gifeðe
þara læðða þe ge lange drugon.'

Þa wurdon bliðe burhsittende,
syððan hi gehyrdon hu seo halige spræc
ofer heanne weall. Here wæs on lustum.
Wið þæs fæstengeates folc onette,
weras wif somod, wornum ond heapum,
ðreatum ond ðrymmum þrungon ond urnon
ongean ða Þeodnes mægð þusendmælum,
ealde ge geonge. Æghwylcum wearð
men on ðære medobyrig mod areted,
syððan hie ongeaton þæt wæs Iudith cumen
eft to eðle, ond ða ofostlice
hie mid eaðmedum in forleton.
Þa seo gleawe het, golde gefrætewod,
hyre ðinenne þancolmode
þæs herewæðan heafod onwriðan

---

to the victorious nation: 'I can tell you a thing
worth thanking me for, so you need not longer
mourn in your hearts. The Measurer likes you,
Glory of Kings. It has been made known
right across the world that glorious fame is
your bright prospect and honour is ordained
for the abuses which you have long endured.'

Then the townsmen took heart,
when they heard how the holy saint spoke
over the high wall. The war-band was in heart.
People hurried towards the fortress gate,
men and women both in groups and bands,
companies and hordes thronged and ran
towards the King's maid in their thousands,
both young and old. The heart of each
person in that mead-city was cheered
when they understood that Judith had come
back to her homeland, and quickly then
in all humility they let her in.
Then the sharp gold-ornamented woman
commanded her resourceful maidservant
to unwrap the huntsman raider's head

ond hyt to behðe blodig ætywan
þam burhleodum, hu hyre æt beaduwe gespeow.

Spræc ða seo æðele to eallum þam folce:
'Her ge magon sweotole, sigerofe hæleð,
leoda ræswan, on ðæs laðestan
hæðenes heaðorinces heafod starian,
Holofernus unlyfigendes,
þe us monna mæst morðra gefremede,
sarra sorga, ond þæt swyðor gyt
ycan wolde, ac him ne uðe God
lengran lifes, þæt he mid læððum us
eglan moste. Ic him ealdor oðþrong
þurh Godes fultum. Nu ic gumena gehwæne
þyssa burgleoda biddan wylle,
randwiggendra, þæt ge recene eow
fysan to gefeohte. Syððan frymða God,
arfæst Cyning, eastan sende
leohtne leoman, berað linde forð,

---

and brandish the bloody thing as a trophy
to the townsfolk to show how she had prospered in battle.

The noble one then spoke to all the people:
'Here, triumphant heroes, captains of the people,
you may stare clearly at the head
of the most hated heathen man of war,
Holofernes who is not alive and committed
more murders of our people than any man other,
more grievous sorrows, and still more to this
would have added, but God did not grant him
a longer life in which he might trouble us
with abuses. Myself, I pressed out his life
with God's help. Now I will bid
each man of the people in this town
who can carry a shield that you quickly
fire yourselves for a fight. As soon as the God of First Things,
merciful King, from the east does send
a gleam of light, carry out lindenshields,

---

176 *Spræc ða seo æðele to eallum þam folce* 'The noble one then spoke to all the people'. This *æðele* looks a little like *Æþel-flæd* 'noble lady' addressing her army in the 911–18 campaign of the West Midlands (Wainwright 1990); see **Viking Wars** (Custom Version), though the same epithet is used for Empress Helena in *Elene*, line 1130.

bord for breostum   ond byrnhomas,
scire helmas   in sceaðena gemong,
fyllan folctogan   fagum sweordum,
fæge frumgaras.   Fynd syndon eowere
gedemed to deaðe,   ond ge dom agon,
tir æt tohtan,   swa eow getacnod hafað
mihtig Dryhten   þurh mine hand.'

Þa wearð snelra werod   snude gegearewod,
cenra to campe.   Stopon cynerofe
secgas ond gesiðas,   bæron sigeþufas,
foron to gefeohte   forð on gerihte,
hæleð under helmum,   of ðære haligan byrig
on ðæt dægred sylf.   Dynedan scildas,
hlude hlummon.   Þæs se hlanca gefeah
wulf in walde,   ond se wanna hrefn,
wælgifre fugel.   Wistan begen
þæt him ða þeodguman   þohton tilian
fylle on fægum,   ac him fleah on last
earn ætes georn,   urigfeðera,
salowigpada   sang hildeleoð,
hyrnednebba.   Stopon heaðorincas,
beornas to beadowe,   bordum beðeahte,

---

a board at your breast and coats of mail,
glinting helmets into the mass of invaders,
cut down their generals with bloody swords,
with javelins that deal death. Your enemies have been
condemned to death, and that verdict is yours,
the honour of campaign, whose sign the mighty
Lord has given you through my hand.'

Then a host of valiant men was soon readied
keen to take the field. Brave as kings, they moved,
men and companions, carried victory banners,
marched off to battle in columns,
heroes in helmets, from the holy city
at the very break of day. Shields dinned,
loud they resounded. At this the lank wolf
in the woods rejoiced, and the shiny raven,
slaughter-hungry bird. Both of them knew
that the men of this nation meant to serve up
their fill in dead men, for in their track there flew
an eagle keen for carrion, dewy feathered,
the tawny-coated creature sang a battle song
with curved beak. Men of war advanced,
warriors into battle, covered with shields,

hwealfum lindum, þa ðe hwile ær
elðeodigra edwit þoledon,
hæðenra hosp. Him þæt hearde wearð
æt ðam æscplegan eallum forgolden,
Assyrium, syððan Ebreas
under guðfanum gegan hæfdon
to ðam fyrdwicum. Hie ða fromlice
leton forð fleogan flana scuras,
hildenædran, of hornbogan,
strælas stedehearde. Styrmdon hlude
grame guðfrecan, garas sendon
in heardra gemang. Hæleð wæron yrre,
landbuende, laðum cynne,
stopon styrnmode, stercedferhðe,
wrehton unsofte ealdgeniðlan
medowerige. Mundum brugdon
scealcas of sceaðum scirmæled swyrd,
ecgum gecoste, slogon eornoste
Assiria oretmæcgas,
niðhycgende, nanne ne sparedon

---

with hollowed boards, they who in earlier times
had suffered the insults of foreign men,
heathen men's contempt. A cruel payment
in the play of ash-spears was made for that
to all the Assyrians once the Hebrews
had marched beneath war-standards
to their army's camp. Boldly then they
let fly out showers of darts,
war-serpents, from horn-shaped bows,
smithy-hardened arrows. Loud stormed
the fierce war-braves, sent spears
into the mass of cruel men. The heroes who lived
in that land were enraged with a hated race,
advanced stern-minded with hardened hearts,
violently pursued old enemies who were
weary with mead. With hands from sheaths
the marshals drew pattern-welded longswords,
splendid in edge, earnestly struck down
the champions of the Assyrians
with battle in their minds, spared not one

214–16 *þa ðe hwile ær elðeodigra edwit þoledon, hæðenra hosp* 'they who in earlier times had suffered the insults of foreign men, heathen men's contempt'. The intensity of this goes beyond the call of duty for a biblical tale in verse, unless, as seems likely, the whole episode is an allegory for the Danish occupation of the Midlands.

þæs herefolces, heanne ne ricne,
cwicera manna þe hie ofercuman mihton.

XII Swa ða magoþegnas on ða morgentid
ehton elðeoda ealle þrage,
oðþæt ongeaton ða ðe grame wæron,
ðæs herefolces heafodweardas,
þæt him swyrdgeswing swiðlic eowdon
weras Ebrisce. Hie wordum þæt
þam yldestan ealdorþegnum
cyðan eodon, wrehton cumbolwigan
ond him forhtlice færspel bodedon,
medowerigum morgencollan,
atolne ecgplegan. Þa ic ædre gefrægn
slegefæge hæleð slæpe tobredon
ond wið þæs bealofullan burgeteldes
werigferhðe hwearfum þringan,
Holofernus. Hogedon aninga
hyra hlaforde hilde bodian,
ærðon ðe him se egesa on ufan sæte,
mægen Ebrea. Mynton ealle

man of the raiding nation, rich or poor,
of any men alive whom they might overcome.

XII Thus the young thegns in that morning hour
pursued the alien people all the while
until it was noted by those who were alert,
chief watchmen of the raiding army,
that sword-swings severe were shown them
by Hebrew men. With words they
went to tell this to the most senior
captains, shook the officers,
and frightened announced the fearful news,
a horror in the morning for mead-weary men,
a terrible play of edges. Swiftly, then, I heard
did heroes awake from sleep though doomed to be slain
and towards the wicked Holofernes'
tented bower, weary-hearted, they thronged
in groups. At once did they intend
to announce the battle to their lord,
before the terrible Hebrew force should
sit upon them. All were mindful

234 *þæs herefolces* 'the raiding nation'. Mostly, but not always, in *Judith* the words *here* 'raiding group' and *fyrd* 'militia' are used to describe Assyrian and Hebrew respectively, to a lesser degree than in the *Chronicle*, which observes this distinction almost completely.

þæt se beorna brego ond seo beorhte mægð
in ðam wlitegan træfe wæron ætsomne,
Iudith seo æðele ond se galmoda,
egesfull ond afor. Næs ðeah eorla nan
þe ðone wiggend aweccan dorste
oððe gecunnian hu ðone cumbolwigan
wið ða halgan mægð hæfde geworden,
metodes meowlan. Mægen nealæhte,
folc Ebrea, fuhton þearle
heardum heoruwæpnum, hæfte guldon
hyra fyrngeflitu fagum swyrdum,
ealde æfðoncan. Assyria wearð
on ðam dægeweorce dom geswiðrod,
bælc forbiged. Beornas stodon
ymbe hyra þeodnes træf þearle gebylde,
sweorcendferhðe. Hi ða somod ealle
ongunnon cohhetan, cirman hlude
ond gristbitian, Gode orfeorme,
mid toðon torn þoligende. Þa wæs hyra tires æt ende,
eades ond ellendæda. Hogedon þa eorlas aweccan
hyra winedryhten; him wiht ne speow.
Þa wearð sið ond late sum to ðam arod

---

that the warriors' prince and the bright maid
were together in the shining pavilion,
Judith the Noble and the wanton-minded,
terrifying and vehement man. Earl there was none,
however, who dared to rouse the fighting man
or find out how their officer had
got on with the holy virgin,
the Measurer's own girl. The force approached,
nation of the Hebrews, fought hard
with cruel bloody weapons, captives repaying
old flytings, the ancient grudge between them
with death-dealing swords. In that day's work
was the reputation and all the manly belch
of Assyrians brought low. The warriors stood
around their king's pavilion very emboldened,
with darkening minds. Together they all
started coughing, then crying aloud
and gnashing their teeth, beyond help from God,
suffering their gnawing grief. Their honour then was finished,
their wealth and deeds of valour. The earls thought to wake
their friend and lord. They had no luck.
Slowly but eventually one of the soldiers had

---

256 *Iudith seo æðele* 'Judith the Noble'. See note for line 176.

þara beadorinca, þæt he in þæt burgeteld
niðheard neðde, swa hyne nyd fordraf.
Funde ða on bedde blacne licgan
his goldgifan gæstes gesne,
lifes belidenne.

He þa lungre gefeoll
freorig to foldan, ongan his feax teran,
hreoh on mode, ond his hrægl somod,
ond þæt word acwæð to ðam wiggendum
þe ðær unrote ute wæron:
'Her ys geswutelod ure sylfra forwyrd,
toweard getacnod þæt þære tide ys
mid niðum neah geðrungen, þe we sculon nyde losian,
somod æt sæcce forweorðan. Her lið sweorde geheawen,
beheafdod healdend ure.'

Hi ða hreowigmode
wurpon hyra wæpen of dune, gewitan him werigferhðe
on fleam sceacan. Him mon feaht on last,

---

sufficient boldness that into that tented bower
the battle-hardened man drew as near as need drove him.
Found then on bed lying pale
his gold-giver bereft of spirit,
his life removed.

Quickly then he fell down
chilled to the ground, did tear his hair,
wild in mood, and his clothes as well,
and spoke these words to the warriors
who were in that place unhappily outside:
'Here is made manifest our very perdition,
a sign of our future, that the hour is at hand
when we, pressed on by battles, must needs perish,
be damned together in the strife. Here lies, by sword cut down,
our officer beheaded.'

They then repenting in mind
cast down their weapons, weary in spirit moved out
in flight to make a run for it. Their rear was engaged

288–9 *Her lið sweorde geheawen, beheafdod healdend ure* 'Here lies, by sword cut down, our officer beheaded'. The speech is an ironic inversion of the loyal retainer topos, a classic form of which may be seen in Byrhtwold's speech in *The Battle of Maldon*, line 314: *Her lið ure ealdor eall forheawen* 'here lies our chieftain all cut down' (see **Viking Wars**). The officer in question, Vagoas in other sources, now leads his men in a mass flight.

mægeneacen folc, oð se mæsta dæl
þæs heriges læg hilde gesæged
on ðam sigewonge, sweordum geheawen,
wulfum to willan ond eac wælgifrum
fuglum to frofre. Flugon ða ðe lyfdon,
laðra lindwerod. Him on laste for
sweot Ebrea sigore geweorðod,
dome gedyrsod. Him feng Dryhten God
fægre on fultum, Frea ælmihtig.
Hi ða fromlice fagum swyrdum
hæleð higerofe herpað worhton
þurh laðra gemong, linde heowon,
scildburh scæron. Sceotend wæron
guðe gegremede, guman Ebrisce,
þegnas on ða tid þearle gelyste
gargewinnes. Þær on greot gefeoll
se hyhsta dæl heafodgerimes
Assiria ealdorduguðe,
laðan cynnes. Lythwon becom
cwicera to cyððe. Cirdon cynerofe,
wiggend on wiðertrod wælscel on innan,

---

by the people swollen in size until the greatest part
of the raiding army lay brought low in war
on the victory plain, by swords cut down,
to the will of wolves and also as a solace to the birds
who raven for slaughter. Fled they who lived,
shield-host of hostiles. In their track proceeded
the Hebrew regiment with the honours of victory,
reputation enhanced. The Lord God found for them,
Almighty Prince, a beautiful reinforcement.
Boldly then with bloody swords
did these heroes valiant carve their plundering path
through the mob of foes, cut through lindenshields,
sheared through the shield-wall. Men shooting missiles
were maddened in battle, those Hebrew men,
thegns in that hour being fired up extremely
to fight with spears. There on the gravel fell
the noblest part of the chief number
of the officer corps of the hateful race
of Assyrians. Few if any got back
to their country alive. Kin-brave soldiers
wheeled about for home-march in the pile of dead,

---

310 *Lythwon becom cwicera to cyððe* 'Few if any got back to their country alive'. This topos resembles the core of the Viking rout described in *The Battle of Brunanburh*, lines 35–52 (see **Viking Wars**).

reocende hræw. Rum wæs to nimanne
londbuendum on ðam laðestan,
hyra ealdfeondum unlyfigendum
heolfrig herereaf, hyrsta scyne,
bord ond bradswyrd, brune helmas,
dyre madmas. Hæfdon domlice
on ðam folcstede fynd oferwunnen
eðelweardas, ealdhettende
swyrdum aswefede. Hie on swaðe reston,
þa ðe him to life laðost wæron
cwicera cynna. Þa seo cneoris eall,
mægða mærost, anes monðes fyrst,
wlanc, wundenlocc, wagon ond læddon
to ðære beorhtan byrig, Bethuliam,
helmas ond hupseax, hare byrnan,
guðsceorp gumena golde gefrætewod,
mærra madma þonne mon ænig
asecgan mæge searoþoncelra.
Eal þæt ða ðeodguman þrymme geeodon,
cene under cumblum on compwige
þurh Iudithe gleawe lare,
mægð modigre. Hi to mede hyre
of ðam siðfate sylfre brohton,

---

their reeking corpses. It was a moment for landsmen
to take from among the most hated
lifeless bodies of their ancient enemies
a gory war-spoil, beautiful equipment,
board and broadswords, burnished helmets,
precious treasures. They had with reputation
in that locality overwhelmed the enemy,
those guards of their homeland, put to sleep
old persecutors with swords. In a trail they were resting,
those who in life had been the most hated
race that existed. Then the whole generation,
of nations the most renowned, in the space of a month
carried and conveyed, proud and hair-plaited,
to the bright city of Bethulia
helmets and hip-swords, dark grey coats of mail,
the war-gear of men with gold appliqués on,
treasures more splendid than any clever
intellectual may be able to tell of.
All this the people's heroes performed magnificently,
keen under banner in hand-to-hand duelling
through the far-sighted teaching of Judith
the spirited maid. They to her person
did the ash-spear braves bring

eorlas æscrofe, Holofernes
sweord ond swatigne helm, swylce eac side byrnan
gerenode readum golde, ond eal þæt se rinca baldor
swiðmod sinces ahte oððe sundoryrfes,
beaga ond beorhtra maðma, hi þæt þære beorhtan idese
ageafon gearoþoncolre. Ealles ðæs Iudith sægde
wuldor weroda Dryhtne, þe hyre weorðmynde geaf,
mærðe on moldan rice, swylce eac mede on heofonum,
sigorlean in swegles wuldre, þæs þe heo ahte soðne geleafan
to ðam Ælmihtigan. Huru æt þam ende ne tweode
þæs leanes þe heo lange gyrnde. Ðæs sy ðam leofan Drihtne
wuldor to widan aldre, þe gesceop wind ond lyfte,
roderas ond rume grundas, swylce eac reðe streamas
ond swegles dreamas, ðurh His Sylfes miltse.

---

from that expedition Holofernes'
sword and bleeding helmet, also his wide coat of chained mail
forged with burnished gold, and all the treasure the arrogant
lord of men possessed, whether by private inheritance
or in rings and bright valuables, this they gave over
to the bright lady of ready mind. For all this, Judith said
glory be to the Lord of Hosts, who had given her honour,
fame in the earthly domain, as well as reward in heaven,
a payment of triumph in the glory of the firmament, for having truly
believed in the Almighty. In the end, indeed, she did not doubt
the payment she had long yearned. For this, glory be
for evermore to the Dear Lord who created wind and air,
skies and roomy territories, as well as fierce sea-currents
and sun's happy course through His generous Self.

THE EARLIEST ENGLISH PROSE

❋ ❋ ❋

THE EARLIEST ENGLISH PROSE

✳ ✳ ✳

This section explores the beginnings of English prose, mainly through King Alfred's call to the monasteries to rebuild West Saxon learning. The *Anglo-Saxon Chronicle* may be seen translating Bede's ethnogenesis in his *Ecclesiastical History of the English People*, as well as making its first true narrative outing in the revenge tragedy of Cynewulf and Cyneheard, wrongly placed in the annal for 755. Readers may consider whether or not this prose account relied on an heroic poem, and if so, how far the West Saxons used heroic poetry to celebrate historical rather than legendary achievements. Some of 'Alfred's' *Prefaces* and extracts from the works that were translated from Latin for him, possibly partially by him, after him and even before him, will then be cited to enable an understanding of what writing prose for the first time in one's language really entailed. Further into the anthology we have the flowering of these efforts with **Writers of the Benedictine Reform**, and also, indirectly, in the section that precedes that, **Sagas of Icelanders**.

When reading the earliest, often polished, attempts at English prose, it is possible to say, against all expectations, that Alfred's character as a man begins to emerge. Alfred appears to be someone brave, inquisitive and unorthodox, but always practical, to judge by the metaphors with which he must have helped others to construct the first intellectual vocabulary the English language had. This present section's extracts also illustrate some early medieval ways of reading great books. As will become clear to anyone reading the Alfredian Boethius or Augustine, Alfred and his people did not read systematically but usually with a magpie approach to the great Latin works by which they shamelessly, or one might say creatively, collected passages from different authors to blend old ideas with new ones. The extracts from the Alfredian Orosius also show (in this book's Custom Version) how King Alfred kept his eye on the topical international scene, which for him was Scandinavia, home of the Danes.

General bibliography

Irvine, S., 'Old English prose: King Alfred and his books', *B&OS* 246–71

Keynes, S. D., and M. Lapidge, trans., with introduction and notes, *Alfred the Great: Asser's 'Life of King Alfred' and Other Contemporary Sources* (Harmondsworth, 1983)

Kirby, D. P., *The Earliest English Kings* (London, 1991)

Swanton, M. J., ed. and trans., *Anglo-Saxon Prose* (London, 1993)

Swanton, M. J., trans., *The Anglo-Saxon Chronicle* (London, 1996)

Anglo-Saxon Chronicle

The *Anglo-Saxon Chronicle* is an unprecedented event, the first vernacular history to be written in western Europe. Today it survives in seven manuscripts, in versions that are lettered from A to G (although most of G was destroyed in the Cotton Library fire of 1731). These manuscripts date from the late ninth century (the time at which the annals to about 890 were written into A) to the mid-twelfth century (E continues to 1154). Version A is from Winchester, the oldest and most West Saxon in orientation. B and C are from Abingdon, closer to Mercia. D is from western Mercia, Worcester, though of course under West Saxon control. E is from Peterborough, but copied from a manuscript from (St Augustine's in) Kent. F is from Canterbury too, written in *c.* 1100, with Latin versions of each annal.

All seven manuscripts contain the 'Common Stock', which is the name for the earliest *Chronicle* that was put together from a variety of sources, including Bede's *Ecclesiastical History*, in Wessex up to the year 890. This text (which was used by Ealdorman Æthelweard, patron of Ælfric, for his Latin translation of the *Chronicle* in *c.* 975) attempted to give a coherent history of the Germanic tribes who arrived in England from the mid-fifth century, onwards. It sets this against the broader history of the island from its invasion by Julius Caesar in 60 BC. The timing of the renewal of this compilation with the writing that began in 892 and which led to the seven *Chronicle* versions, probably shows an official West Saxon response to the impending threat of Viking invasion in that year, when the great host returned to England from a spell in France (see **Viking Wars**). In the texts below, the date in square brackets is the true year. This part of the *Chronicle*, in all versions, dates events two years too early.

Bately, J., ed., *The Anglo-Saxon Chronicle: MS A*, The Anglo-Saxon Chronicle: A Collaborative Edition 3 (Cambridge, 1986)

Irvine, S., ed., *The Anglo-Saxon Chronicle: MS E*, The Anglo-Saxon Chronicle: A Collaborative Edition 7 (Cambridge, 2004)

Kirby, D. P., *The Earliest English Kings* (London, 1991)

Swanton, M. J., trans., *The Anglo-Saxon Chronicle* (London, 1996)

The coming of the Saxons

Although the language of version E, the *Peterborough Chronicle*, is of the eleventh century, the text is older and composite. The story below, of Hengest's arrival and conquest of south-east Britain, is derived from a Northumbrian adaptation of Bede's *Ecclesiastical History*, but may also, as the morphology of *Wyrtgeorn* hints, be based on the oldest Kentish vernacular poetic traditions (see *Beowulf*, 'Funeral at Finnsburh', and the *Finnsburh Fragment*, **Heroic Poems**).

Bassett, S., ed., *The Origins of Anglo-Saxon Kingdoms* (Leicester, 1989)

Brooks, N., 'The creation and early structure of the kingdom of Kent', in Bassett, ed. (1989), 55–74

Brooks, N., 'From British to English Christianity: deconstructing Bede's interpretation of the conversion', in *Conversion and Colonization in Anglo-Saxon England*, ed. C. E. Karkov and N. Howe, Medieval and Renaissance Texts and Studies 318 (Tempe, AZ, 2006), 1–30

449 (E). Her Martianus and Ualentinus onfengon rice and rixadon seofon winter, and on þeora dagum gelaðode Wyrtgeorn Angelcin hider, and hi þa coman on þrim ceolum hider to Brytene on þam stede Heopwines fleot. Se cyning Wyrtgeorn gef heom land on suðaneastan ðissum lande, wið ðan þe hi sceoldon feohton wið Pyhtas. Heo þa fuhton wið Pyhtas and heofdon sige swa hwer swa heo comon. Hy ða sendon to Angle, heton mara fultum ond heton heom secgan Brytwalana nahtscipe and þes landes cysta. Hy ða sona sendon hider mare weored þam oðrum to fultume. Đa comon þa men of þrim megðum Germanie, of Aldseaxum, of Anglum, of Iotum. Of Iotum comon Cantwara and Wihtwara, þet is seo megð þe nu eardaþ on Wiht, and þet cyn on Westsexum þe man nu git hæt 'Iutna cynn'. Of Ealdseaxum coman Eastseaxa and Suðsexa and Westsexa. Of Angle comon (se a syððan stod westig betwix Iutum and Seaxum) Eastangla, Middelangla, Mearca and ealla Norþhymbra. Heora heretogan wæron twegen gebroðra, Hengest and Horsa, þet wæron Wihtgilses suna. Wihtgils wæs Witting, Witta Wecting, Wecta Wodning. Fram þan Wodne awoc eall ure cynecynn, and Suðanhymbra eac.

---

449 (E). In this year Marcian (450–57: Eastern Empire) and Valentinian [III, actually 425–55: Western Empire] took the throne and ruled seven winters, and in their days Vortigern invited the English people here, and they came in three vessels here to Britain into the harbour called Ebbsfleet. King Vortigern have them land in the south-east of this country on condition they would fight against the Picts. They then fought against the Picts and won victories wherever they went. Then they send word to Angeln, said to ask for reinforcements and to tell them of the Britons' indolence and the virtues of the country. The others soon then sent a bigger host here to help the first group. That was when men arrived from three tribes of Germany, from Old Saxons, Angles, Jutes. From the Jutes came the Kentishmen and Wightmen, that is the nation that now lives on the Isle of Wight, and the race that in Wessex is now called to this day 'Jute kin'. From the Old Saxons came the East Saxons and South Saxons and West Saxons. From Angeln (which ever since has stood empty between Jutish and Saxon lands) came the East Angles, Middle Angles, Mercians and all kinds of Northumbrians. The commanders of these men were two brothers, Hengest and Horsa, these were the sons of Wihtgils. Wihtgils was the son of Witta, son of Wecta, son of Woden. From the same Woden awoke all our race of kings, and that of the Southumbrians as well.

Cynewulf and Cyneheard

Álvarez López, F.-J., 'The *Anglo-Saxon Chronicle*, 755: an annotated bibliography of the Cynewulf and Cyneheard episode from Plummer to Bremmer', *Journal of the Spanish Society for Medieval English and Literature* 13 (2005–6), 99–117

Bremmer, R. H., 'The Germanic context of "Cynewulf and Cyneheard" revisited', *Neophilologus* 81 (1997), 445–67

Heinemann, F. I., ' "Cynewulf and Cyneheard" and *Landnámabók*: another narrative tradition', *Leeds Studies in English* new series 24 (1993), 57–89

Scragg, D. G., '*Wifcyþþe* and the morality of the Cynewulf and Cyneheard Episode in the Anglo-Saxon Chronicle', in *Alfred the Wise: Studies in Honour of Janet Bately on the Occasion of her Sixty-Fifth Birthday*, ed. J. Roberts and J. L. Nelson, with M. Godden (Cambridge, 1997), 179–85

755 (A). [actual year 757] Her Cynewulf benam Sigebryht his rices **ond Westseaxna wiotan** for unryhtum dædum, buton Hamtunscire, ond he hæfde þa oþ he ofsloh ðone aldormon þe him **lengest wunode**. Ond hiene þa Cynewulf on Andred adræfde, ond he þær wunade, oþþæt hiene an swan ofstang æt Pryfetes flodan. Ond he wræc þone aldormon Cumbran. Ond se Cynewulf oft miclum gefeohtum feaht uuiþ Bretwalum.

[actual year 786] Ond **xxxi wintra** þæs þe he rice hæfde, he wolde adræfan ænne æþeling se wæs Cyneheard haten, ond se Cyneheard wæs þæs Sigebryhtes broþur. Ond þa geascode he þone cyning **lytle werode on**

---

755 (A). [actual year 757] Here Cynewulf deprived Sigebryht of his kingdom, Cynewulf **with the royal council of Wessex**, for unlawful deeds, all but for Hampshire, while he had held this until he slew the ealdorman who **had stayed with him the longest**. And him then Cynewulf drove into the Weald, and he dwelt there until a swineherd stabbed him at Privett's stream. And he was avengeing the ealdorman Cumbra. And this Cynewulf often fought in many battles against the Welsh.

[actual year 786] And **thirty-one winters** after he held the rule, he wished to drive out a prince whose name was Cyneheard, and this Cyneheard was that Sigebryht's brother. And

---

ond Westseaxna wiotan 'with the royal council of Wessex'. The *coup d'état* had to be sanctioned first. Apart from this, the leapfrogging word order of these sentences and the delayed revelation of detail in them (Cumbra's name for instance) tells us that they may derive from lines of verse.

lengest wunode 'stayed with him the longest'. This recalls the words *heoldon lengest* in *Widsith*, line 45, where Hrothgar and Hrothulf keep their family together 'for the longest time'.

xxxi wintra 'thirty-one winters'. The dates are all a little out, here by two years. Versions A, B and C have xxxi, 31 years, version D xxi, version E xvi. Latin numerals could easily be mistaken by scribes (the practice in our editions of text is generally to expand numbers into words, but here we have left the Roman numerals as they are). Cynewulf was assassinated in 786 (the *Chronicle* covers it briefly also under year 784).

wifcyþþe on Merantune, ond hine þær berad ond þone bur utan beeode, ær hine þa men onfunden þe mid þam kyninge wærun. Ond þa ongeat se cyning þæt, ond he on þa duru eode ond þa **unheanlice** hine werede, oþ he on þone æþeling locude, ond þa ut ræsde on hine ond hine miclum gewundode. Ond hie alle on þone cyning wærun feohtende oþþæt hie hine ofslægenne hæfdon.

Ond þa on þæs wifes gebærum onfundon þæs cyninges þegnas þa unstilnesse ond þa þider urnon swa hwelc swa þonne gearo wearþ ond radost. Ond hiera se æþeling gehwelcum feoh ond feorh gebead, ond hiera nænig hit geþicgean nolde, ac hie simle feohtende wæran oþ hie alle lægon butan anum **Bryttiscum gisle**, ond se swiþe gewundad wæs.

Þa on morgenne gehierdun þæt þæs cyninges þegnas **þe him beæftan wærun** þæt se cyning ofslægen wæs. Þa ridon hie þider, ond his aldormon Osric ond Wiferþ his þegn ond þa men þe he beæftan him læfde ær, ond þone æþeling on þære byrig metton þær se cyning ofslægen læg, ond þa gatu

---

so he asked and found out that the king would be **with a small troop visiting a woman in Merton**, and he rode after him there and surrounded the bower from without, before those men who were with the king might become aware of him. And then the king perceived this, and he went to the door and then defended himself **with no shame**, until he looked at the prince and then rushed out upon him and severely wounded him. And they all stayed fighting the king until they had slain him.

And then from the woman's cries the king's thegns perceived the disturbance and then ran to it, each as soon as he was ready and most rapidly. And the prince offered each of them money and his life, and none of them would accept this, but they stayed fighting continuously until they all lay dead, all but for a **Welsh hostage**, and he was very wounded.

Then in the morning the king's thegns **who were behind him** heard that the king had been killed. They rode there, as well as his ealdorman Osric and Wigferhth his thegn and those men he had left behind him earlier, and met the prince in the township where the

---

lytle werode on wifcyþþe 'with a small troop visiting a woman'. The first phrase may also mean 'alone'. The woman could well have been someone's wife, although not all scholars like to think of Cynewulf as immoral (Scragg 1997).

on Merantune 'in Merton'. This editor takes the Merton in question to be near Bicester, north of Oxford, on the Mercian border. In 786 Cynewulf attended an important meeting chaired by King Offa of Mercia, the Council of the Legates, with a papal emissary present (Kirby 1991: 170–1), and may have been intercepted here by Cyneheard on his way back into Wessex.

unheanlice 'with no shame'. Cynewulf is likely to have been undressed.

Bryttiscum gisle 'Welsh hostage'. Now an amicable arrangement. From this story it is clear that the Welshman had become part of Cynewulf's bodyguard.

þe him beæftan wærun 'who were behind him'. Cynewulf was on the move and had gone on ahead (see note ***on Merantune***). This larger force stayed in another hamlet, close enough for the news to get out soon after the event.

him to belocen hæfdon; ond þa þærto eodon. Ond þa gebead he him hiera agenne dom feos ond londes gif hie him þæs rices uþon, ond him cyðde þæt hiera mægas him mid wæron, þa þe him fram noldon. Ond þa cuædon hie þæt him nænig mæg leofra nære þonne hiera hlaford, ond hie næfre his banan folgian noldon. Ond þa budon hie hiera mægum þæt hie gesunde from eodon. Ond hie cuædon þæt tæt ilce hiera geferum geboden wære, þe ær mid þam cyninge wærun. Þa cwædon hie þæt hie hie þæs ne onmunden 'þon ma þe eowre geferan þe mid þam cyninge ofslægene wærun.'

Ond hie þa ymb þa gatu feohtende wæron oþþæt hie þærinne fulgon, ond þone æþeling ofslogon ond þa men þe him mid wærun, ealle butan anum, se wæs þæs aldormonnes godsunu. Ond he his feorh generede, ond þeah he wæs oft gewundad. Ond se Cynewulf ricsode an ond þritig wintra, ond his lic liþ æt Wintanceastre, ond þæs æþelinges on Ascanmynster, ond hiera **ryhtfæderencyn** gæþ to Cerdice.

---

king lay dead, and these men had shut the gate on themselves; and the king's men walked up to it. And then he offered them their own assessment of money and landed estate if they granted the rule to him, and informed them that kinsmen of theirs were with him, who would not leave him. And then the king's men declared that no kinsman would be dearer to them than their lord and they would never follow his slayer. And then they offered their kinsmen [inside] the chance to leave safely. And these men said that the same had been offered to the king's men's companions who had been with the king earlier. Then they declared that they would pay no mind to the offer 'any more than your companions did who were slain with the king'.

And they stayed fighting around the gate until they broke inside, and slew the prince and the men who were with him, all but for one, who was the ealdorman's godson. And he saved his life, although he had been wounded in many places. And this Cynewulf ruled 31 years, and his body lies at Winchester, and the prince's at Axminster, and their **family on the father's side** goes straight back to Cerdic.

---

ryhtfæderencyn 'family on the father's side'. Cynewulf and Cyneheard were cousins, as their names indicate, while Sigebryht's name shows that he was probably Cyneheard's much older half brother by a different father. The name of the next king of Wessex, Beorhtric (786–802), tells us that this incident terminated the Gewisse dynasty attributed to Cerdic, the alleged founder of Wessex (with his son Cynric) in 495.

[**755** ***cont.*** [actual year 757]] Ond **þy ilcan geare** mon ofslog Æþelbald Miercna cyning **on Seccandune**, ond his lic liþ on Hreopadune. Ond Beornræd feng to rice ond lytle hwile heold ond ungefealice. Ond þy ilcan geare Offa feng to rice ond heold nigon ond þritig wintra; ond his sunu Egferþ heold an ond feowertig daga ond hund daga. Se Offa wæs Þincgferþing, Þincgferþ Eanwulfing, Eanwulf Osmoding, Osmod Eawing, Eawa Pybing, Pybba Creoding, Creoda Cynewalding, Cynewald Cnebing, Cnebba Iceling, Icel Eomæring, Eomær Angelþ[e]owing, Angelþeow Offing, Offa Wærmunding, Wærmund Wyhtlæging, Wihtlæg Wodening.

[**755** ***cont.*** [actual year 757]] And **in the same year** Æthelbald, king of the Mercians, was slain **in Seckington**, and his body lies at Repton. And Beornred took the rule and kept it for a little while and without the love of his people. And in the same year Offa took the throne and held it for 39 winters, and his son Ecgferth held it for 141 days. This Offa was son of Thingferth, son of Eanwulf, son of Osmod, son of Eawa, son of Pybba, son of Creoda, son of Cynewald, son of Cnebba, son of Icel, son of Eomer, son of Angeltheow, son of Offa, son of Wermund, son of Wihtleg, son of Woden.

þy ilcan geare 'in the same year', i.e. 755 [truly 757]. Back to the original entry, into which the story of the king's assassination has been interpolated.

on Seccandune 'in Seckington'. Æthelbald (ruled 716–57) was killed by his bodyguard (over a woman's honour) in a lodge in the woods not far from Tamworth, in Mercia's Midlands heartland (Kirby 1991: 134–6). The Cynewulf story seems to have been drawn into the 755 annal by attraction with this one. Repton was the site of some important Mercian royal burials. King Wiglaf (ruled Mercia 827–39) is there as well (Kirby 1991: 194).

Offa's ancestry. Icel is the ancestor of Guthlac, saint of Crowland (see **Poems of Devotion** and in this section). Offa son of Wermund is the Offa of Angeln, in the far north of Germany, who is celebrated in *Beowulf*, lines 1944–62, and in *Widsith*, lines 35–44 (see **Heroic Poems**). Woden (Scandinavian Óðinn) was a heathen god to whom all important royal lines were traced in England (and in the late tenth century, through English influence, in Norway).

King Alfred's *Prefaces*

Alfred's *Prefaces*, which were written with some input from the king, give an impression of royal purpose which may also suggest something of the individuality of Alfred the Great, who was born in 849, succeeded his brothers to the throne of Wessex in 871 and died as the founder of England's first national royal dynasty in 899. Over the years the certainty of his literary input has diminished (Godden 2007), but the *Chronicle* for years 892–6 gives a powerful impression of Alfred's intelligence as a general and strategist (see **Viking Wars**, Custom Version), and Alfred's stamp on the intellectual aspect of his programme to rebuild Wessex is still accepted by most scholars. Even if reading and writing were never fully mastered by him, as they were not by his great model Emperor Charlemagne, the direction of the king's learning is still there. This appears in his expression of a national deficit in the need to bring back Latin, the European language of power; in the selection of much philosophical and historical as well as theological material for translation; and especially in Alfred's letter to Bishop Wærferth of Worcester, the Preface to the West Saxon translation of Pope Gregory's *Pastoral Care*, datable to the early 890s within the ten-year window of peace that Alfred enjoyed before the Danish great host came back in 892. Whether or not one can detect the 'voice' of Alfred in the following *Prefaces*, they are of a piece in their need to present an image of this king which is at once pious, polite and practical. In short, they are his propaganda. The deference that the king appears to show to Bishop Wærferth is but one example of this in the Preface to the West Saxon translation of Pope Gregory's *Pastoral Care*. The piety naturally follows Alfred's obedience to God as the supreme commander to whom services must be constantly made. The translations that Alfred wants represent the collaboration of advisers and other intellectuals, so the king must be polite. The scribe's turns of phrase express a king's practical pursuits, which include hunting and the command of a standing army. The impression gained from this last feature is that Alfred, constantly on the move, dictated his thoughts to advisers and scribes by his side. Some of these ideas ended up in his *Prefaces*, and all of them shaped the language of the translations that started in his reign, one which in any case needed to create a new vocabulary in English for some of the metaphors which were long part of Latin. Due to the difficulties, the following translations expand to make the sense of the original clear. Historians should note that Swanton (1996) and Keynes and Lapidge (1983) do not expand on the original text as is done here.

Abels, R., *Alfred the Great: War, Kingship and Culture in Anglo-Saxon England* (London, 1998)

Davis, R. H. C., 'Alfred the Great: propaganda and truth', *History* 56 (1971), 169–82

Godden, M., 'Anglo-Saxons on the mind', in *Learning and Literature in Anglo-Saxon England: Studies Presented to Peter Clemoes on the Occasion of his Sixty-Fifth Birthday*, ed. M. Lapidge and H. Gneuss (Cambridge, 1985), 271–98

Godden, M., 'Did Alfred ever write anything?', *Medium Ævum* 76 (2007), 1–23

Godden, M., and S. Irvine, ed., with M. Griffith and R. Jayatilaka, *The Old English Boethius: An Edition of the Old English Versions of Boethius's De Consolatione Philosophiae*, 2 vols (Oxford, 2009)

Harbus, A., 'Metaphors of authority in Alfred's Prefaces', *Neophilologus* 91 (207), 717–27

Keynes, S. D., and M. Lapidge, trans., with introduction and notes, *Alfred the Great: Asser's 'Life of King Alfred' and Other Contemporary Sources* (Harmondsworth, 1983)

Stanley, E. G., 'King Alfred's Prefaces', *Review of English Studies* 39 (1988), 349–64

Preface to the translation of Gregory's *Pastoral Care*

It has been noted that the following Preface, on education, is all of a piece with Pope Gregory's *Cura pastoralis* 'Pastoral Care' which covers the same theme. This is the fullest and most finely crafted Preface attributed to King Alfred, and appears to be written partly from dictation. The addressee marked in one copy, Bishop Wærferth of Worcester, worked there in former south-west Mercia, which lay under West Saxon jurisdiction during Alfred's wars with the Danes. Worcester was the most powerful diocese remaining from the old Mercian kingdom, and Wærferth, though not a competent Latinist, was an important member of the king's intellectual circle. Asser claims that he translated another work by Pope Gregory, the *Dialogues*.

Godden, M., 'Wærferth and King Alfred: the fate of the Old English Dialogues', in *Alfred the Wise: Studes in Honour of Janet Bately on the Occasion of her Sixty-Fifth Birthday*, ed. J. Roberts and J. L. Nelson, with M. Godden (Cambridge, 1997), 35–51

Powell, T. E., 'The "three orders of society" in Anglo-Saxon England', *Anglo-Saxon England* 23 (1994), 103–32

Ælfred kyning hateð gretan Wærferð biscep his wordum luflice ond freondlice; ond ðe cyðan hate **ðæt me com swiðe oft on gemynd**, hwelce wiotan iu wæron giond Angelcynn, ægðer ge godcundra hada ge woruldcundra; ond hu gesæliglica tida ða wæron giond Angelcynn; ond hu ða kyningas ðe ðone onwald hæfdon ðæs folces on ðam dagum Gode ond His ærendwrecum

---

King Alfred commands greetings to Bishop Wærferth in his own words with love and friendship; and to you I command it be known, **what has very often come into my memory**, what wise men there once were throughout England, both in divine and secular orders; and how fortunate were those times throughout England; and how the kings who had the dominion of the people in those days obeyed God and His messengers; and how they

---

ðæt me com swiðe oft on gemynd 'what has very often come into my memory'. Alfred's memory may have been prodigious even by the standards of a mostly illiterate secular elite. He uses versions of this formula as a refrain through the letter.

hersumedon; ond hu hie ægðer **ge hiora sibbe ge hiora siodo** ge hiora onweald innanbordes gehioldon, ond eac ut hiora eðel gerymdon; ond hu him ða speow ægðer **ge mid wige ge mid wisdome**; ond eac ða godcundan hadas hu giorne hie wæron ægðer **ge ymb lare ge ymb liornunga**, ge ymb ealle ða ðiowotdomas ðe hie Gode don scoldon; ond hu man utanbordes wisdom ond lare hieder on lond sohte, ond hu we hie nu sceoldan ute begietan, gif we hie habban sceoldan.

Swæ clæne hio wæs oðfeallenu on Angelcynne ðæt swiðe feawa wæron **behionan Humbre** ðe hiora ðeninga cuðen understondan on Englisc oððe furðum an ærendgewrit of Lædene on Englisc areccan; ond ic wene ðætte noht monige **begiondan Humbre** næren. Swæ feawa hiora wæron ðæt ic furðum anne anlepne ne mæg geðencean be suðan Temese, ða ða ic to rice feng. Gode ælmihtegum sie ðonc ðætte we nu ænigne onstal habbað lareowa! Ond for ðon ic ðe bebiode ðæt ðu do swæ ic geliefe ðæt ðu wille, ðæt ðu ðe ðissa woruldðinga to ðæm geæmetige, swæ ðu oftost mæge, ðæt ðu ðone wisdom ðe ðe God sealde ðær ðær ðu hiene befæstan mæge, befæste. Geðenc hwelc witu us ða becomon for ðisse worulde, ða ða we hit nohwæðer ne selfe

---

preserved **both their ties of kinship and their morals** as well as their dominion within the land, and extended this also outside their inherited land; and how prosperity came to them **both in war and in wisdom**; and also the divine orders, how eager they were **both in teaching and in learning**, as well as in all the services which they were to perform for God; and how people from abroad sought wisdom and teaching here in this country, and how we would have to get this teaching abroad, if we should have it.

So entire has been the decline of teaching in England that there were very few men on **this side of the river Humber** who could understand their liturgies in English or even render one letter out of the Latin into English; and I expect that there may not have been many **beyond the Humber** who could either. So few of these men there were that I cannot think of even one south of the Thames when I came to the throne. Thanks be to Almighty God that we now have any supply of teachers at all! And for this reason, I commit you to do what, so I believe, you will want to do, that you free yourself of this worldly business, as most often you can, in order to entrust the wisdom which God has given you just where you can entrust it. Think what punishments have come to us for this world, since we

---

ge hiora sibbe ge hiora siodo 'both their ties of kinship and their morals', ***ge mid wige ge mid wisdome*** 'both in war and in wisdom', ***ge ymb lare ge ymb liornunga*** 'both in teaching and in learning'. Alfred's verse helps him link ideas by alliteration.

behionan Humbre 'this side of the river Humber'. Mercian learning in the late eighth and then the ninth centuries, cultivated by King Offa (757–96), in decline in Canterbury under Archbishop Wulfred (805–32).

begiondan Humbre 'beyond the Humber'. Eighth-century Northumbrian masters of learning, such as Bede and Alcuin, gave Alfred's memory the golden age to which he refers.

ne lufodon, ne eac oðrum monnum **ne lefdon**: ðone naman anne we lufodon ðætte we Cristne wæren, ond swiðe feawe ða ðeawas.

Ða ic ða ðis eall gemunde, ða gemunde ic eac hu ic geseah, ær ðæm ðe hit eall forhergod wære ond forbærned, hu ða ciricean giond eall Angelcynn stodon maðma ond boca gefylda, ond eac micel menigeo Godes ðiowa; ond ða swiðe lytle fiorme ðara boca wiston, for ðæm ðe hie hiora nanwuht ongietan ne meahton, for ðæm ðe hie næron on hiora agen geðiode awritene. Swelce hie cwæðen: 'Ure ieldran, ða ðe ðas stowa ær hioldon, hie **lufodon wisdom**, ond ðurh ðone hie begeaton **welan, ond us læfdon**. Her mon mæg giet gesion hiora swæð, ac we him ne cunnon æfter spyrigean, ond for ðæm we habbað nu ægðer **forlæten ge ðone welan ge ðone wisdom**, for ðæm ðe we noldon **to ðæm spore mid ure mode onlutan**.'

Ða ic ða ðis eall gemunde, ða wundrade ic swiðe swiðe ðara godena wiotona ðe giu wæron giond Angelcynn, ond ða bec ealla be fullan geliornod hæfdon, ðæt hie hiora ða nænne dæl noldon on hiora agen geðiode wendan. Ac ic ða sona eft me selfum andwyrde, ond cwæð: **'Hie ne wendon þætte æfre menn sceoldon swæ reccelease weorðan ond sio lar swæ oðfeallan**: for ðære wilnunga

---

neither loved all this for its own sake, **nor left** it either for other men: the name alone that we were Christians is what we loved, and very few of the virtues.

When I called all this to memory, then I remembered also how I saw, before it was all plundered and burned, how the churches through all England stood filled with treasures and books, and also a great multitude of the servants of God; and these men knew very little sustenance from the books because they could understand nothing of them, because these were not written down in their own language. It is as if they had said, 'Our elders, who held these places before us, they **loved wisdom**, and through it they got **wealth, which they left to us**. Here one can still see where they went, but we know not how to follow their trail, and we have **lost both the wealth and the wisdom** because we would not, **with our minds, stoop to that trail**.'

When I called all this to memory, why then I wondered very hard at the wise men who were once in England, and who had fully learned all those books, that they did not want to translate any part of it into their own language. But straightaway then I answered myself, saying '**They never expected that men should ever become so reckless and that teaching**

---

ne lufedon ne lefdon 'neither loved nor left', ***lufodon wisdom . . . welan, ond us læfdon*** 'loved wisdom . . . wealth, which they left to us', ***forlæten ge ðone welan ge ðone wisdom . . . onlutan*** 'lost both the wealth and the wisdom . . . stoop'. The alliteration continues with imperfect internal rhyme (*luf-lef, luf-læt, læt-lut*), chiasmus (***l-w-w-l***, twice) and with a transposition of words (*wisdom-welan, welan-wisdom*) which not only says that wealth comes out of wisdom, but also that wisdom is a form of wealth. The second meaning continues to elude some people even today.

to ðæm spore onlutan 'stoop to that trail'. This is a hunting metaphor, one that implies the letters on the page are like little signs to lead a man to his quarry. These must be Alfred's words.

mid ure mode 'with our minds'. OE *mod* is primarily 'mood', as today, but also and mostly 'mind' (Godden 1985).

Hie ne wendon þætte æfre menn sceoldon swæ reccelease weorðan ond sio lar swæ oðfeallan 'They never expected that men should ever become so reckless and that teaching so decline'. These words have stood epitaph to many an age, and look likely to do so to ours.

hie hit forleton, ond woldon ðæt her ðy mara wisdom on londe wære ðy we ma geðeoda cuðon.'

Ða gemunde ic hu **sio æ** wæs ærest on Ebreisc geðiode funden, ond eft, ða hie Creacas geliornoden, ða wendon hie hie on hiora agen geðiode ealle, ond eac **ealle oðre bec**. Ond eft Lædenware swæ same, siððan hie hie geliornodon, hie hie wendon ealla ðurh wise wealhstodas on hiora agen geðiode. Ond eac ealla oðra Cristena ðioda sumne dæl hiora on hiora agen geðiode wendon. For ðy me ðyncð betre, gif iow swæ ðyncð, **ðæt we eac suma bec**, ða ðe nied-beðearfosta sien eallum monnum to wiotonne, **ðæt we ða on ðæt geðiode wenden** ðe we ealle gecnawan mægen; ond gedon, swæ we swiðe eaðe magon mid Godes fultume, gif we ða stilnesse habbað, ðætte eall sio giogↄuð ðe nu is on Angelcynne friora monna, ðara ðe ða speda hæbben ðæt hie ðæm befeolan mægen, sien to leornunga oðfæste, ða hwile ðe hie to nanre oðerre note ne mægen, oð ðone first ðe hie wel cunnen Englisc gewrit arædan. Lære mon siððan furður on Lædengeðiode ða ðe mon furðor læran wille ond **to hierran hade don** wille.

---

so decline: for this desire they abandoned all this, namely they would have it that the more languages we knew, the more wisdom there would be in the land.'

Then I called to memory how **the Law** was first found in the Hebrew language, and later, when the Greeks learned it, they translated all the Law into their own language, and also **all the Bible's other books**. And later, the Romans just the same, when they learned these, they translated them all, through wise interpreters, into their own language. And also all the other Christian nations translated some part of these books into their own language. And so it seems better to me, if it seems so to all of you, **that we too translate them, some of those books** which all men most need to know, **that we too translate them into the language** we can all perceive; and do, as we very easily can with the help of God, if we have the quiet times, that all the youth which is now in England of the free men who have the means to apply themselves to this, be set to learning while they can be used for no other purpose, until such time as they well know how to read what is written in English. Let the Latin language be taught as an extra to those whom one wants to teach further and **raise to holy orders**.

---

sio æ 'the Law', ***ealle oðre bec*** 'all [the Bible's] other books'. 'Bible' supplied for sense. These feminine nouns are gradually subsumed into the pronoun *hie* 'her, them', with a teleological momentum that puts the West Saxons in history as the Law's latest exponents, God's chosen people. The earlier vernacular Bible translations he refers to may have been the East Franconian (ancestor to Dutch) translation made at Fulda in *c.* 830 for the Carolingian empire, one in Old Saxon in Werden in *c.* 840 (ancestor of Plattdeutsch) and Otfried's Rhineland Gospels of 863–71 (Keynes and Lapidge 1983: 295).

ðæt we eac suma bec ðæt we ða on ðæt geðiode wenden 'that we too translate them, some of those books into the language'. As the sentence lengthens out of control, mainly through the addition of little clauses of politeness, Alfred or his scribe regains the thread by repeating the initial two words of the clause. English prose was still relatively new.

to hierran hade don 'raise to holy orders'. Literally, 'to a higher order'. There is room for Latin in the secular nobility too, as Ealdorman Æthelweard proved, as a direct consequence of this programme here, when he rendered the *Anglo-Saxon Chronicle* into Latin in *c.* 975.

Đa ic ða gemunde hu sio lar Lædengeðiodes ær ðissum afeallen wæs giond Angelcynn, ond **ðeah monige cuðon Englisc gewrit arædan**, ða ongan ic ongemang oðrum mislicum on manigfealdum bisgum ðisses kynerices ða boc wendan on Englisc ðe is genemned on Læden 'Pastoralis', ond on Englisc 'Hierdeboc', hwilum word be worde, hwilum andgit of andgiete, swæ swæ ic hie geliornode æt **Plegmunde** minum ærcebiscepe, ond æt **Assere** minum biscepe, ond æt **Grimbolde** minum mæsseprioste, ond æt **Iohanne** minum mæsseprioste. Siððan ic hie ða geliornod hæfde, swæ swæ ic hie forstod, ond swæ ic hie andgitfullicost areccean meahte, ic hie on Englisc awende; ond to ælcum biscepstole on minum rice wille ane onsendan; ond on ælcre bið **an æstel, se bið on fiftegum mancessa**. Ond ic bebiode on Godes naman ðæt nan mon ðone æstel from ðære bec ne do, ne ða boc from ðæm mynstre, uncuð hu longe ðær swæ gelærede biscepas sien, swæ swæ nu, Gode ðonc, wel hwær siendon. For ðy ic wolde ðætte hie ealneg æt ðære stowe wæren, buton se biscep hie mid him habban wille, oððe hio hwær to læne sie, oððe hwa oðre bi write.

When I called to memory how the teaching of the Latin language had declined throughout England before this time, even **though many knew how to read what was written in English**, why then I began, among the other various and manifold affairs of this kingdom, to translate into English that book which in Latin is called *Pastoralis* and in English *Herd-book*, sometimes word for word, sometimes sense for sense, just as I learned it from **Plegmund** my archbishop, and from **Asser** my bishop, and from **Grimbald** my mass-priest, and from **John** my mass-priest. When I had learned it then, as I understood it, and as I could most intelligibly render it, I translated it into English; and will to each bishop in my kingdom send one copy; and in each copy there will be **a pointer valued at fifty mancuses**. And I command in God's name that no man take the pointer from the book, nor the book from the monstery, it being unknown how long there may be bishops there so learned as now, thank God, there are nearly everywhere. And so I would that these things should always stay in the foundation, except for when the bishop wants to have the book with him, or it is somewhere on loan, or there is someone copying another one from it.

ðeah monige cuðon Englisc gewrit arædan 'though many knew how to read what was written in English'. Some charters, deeds to land, were written in English in the early ninth century; presumably other texts too, perhaps *Beowulf* and other stories in verse. Asser's *Life of Alfred* claims that Alfred's mother (this would have been in 855) gave him *quendam Saxonicum poematicae artis librum* 'a certain English book of poetic skill', after he memorised the contents at the age of six (see Abels 1998: 55–6).

Plegmund: archbishop of Canterbury (890–903), taught Alfred to read. **Asser**: monk, possibly even bishop of St David's in Dyfed, Wales, mostly resident in Wessex till his death (895–908), wrote the king's biography *The Life of Alfred* in 893. **Grimbald**: from St Bertin's monastery near St Omer in Flanders, came to England in *c.* 886. **John**: 'the Old Saxon', from Saxony in northern Germany (home of the original of *Genesis B*: see **Poems of Devotion**).

an æstel, se bið on fiftegum mancessa 'a pointer valued at fifty mancuses'. It is uncertain what this costly item is (Keynes and Lapidge 1983: 204–6). The famous Alfred Jewel may be the top end of one. A *mancus* was a gold coin worth 30 silver pieces.

Preface to the translation of Boethius' *Consolation of Philosophy*

This was almost certainly written by someone other than Alfred, and probably after his lifetime, though by a member of the court. The writer is close to the writings associated with Alfred, particularly to his Preface to the translation of Pope Gregory's *Pastoral Care*. The text is taken from the prose version (B), with omissions filled with words (through J, the transcript made by Franciscus Junius) from what was originally the same text in the prosimetrical version (C). On the relevant textual history, see the headnote under 'The West Saxon *Boethius*'.

Ælfred kuning wæs wealhstod ðisse bec and hie of boclædene on Englisc wende, swa hio nu is gedon. Hwilum he sette word be worde, hwilum andgit of andgite, swa swa he hit þa sweotolost and andgitfullicast gereccan mihte for þam mistlicum and manigfealdum [woruldbisgum] þe hine oft ægðer ge on mode ge on lichoman bisgodan. Đa bisgu us sint swiþe earfoþrime þe on his dagum on þa ricu becoman þe he underfangen hæfde, and þeah ða [he] þas boc hæfde geleornode and of Lædene to Engliscum spelle gewende, [þa geworhte he] hi eft to leoðe swa swa heo nu gedon is; and nu bit and for Godes naman he halsað ælcne þara þe þas boc rædan lyste þæt he for hine gebidde, and him ne wite gif he hit rihtlicor ongite þonne he mihte, for þam þe ælc mon sceal be his andgites mæðe and be his æmettan sprecan þæt he sprecð and don þæt þæt he deþ.

King Alfred was interpreter for this book and translated it from book-Latin into English, as has now been done. Sometimes he set down word for word, sometimes sense for sense, as he could most clearly and intelligibly tell it in the face of the various and manifold [worldly business] which often busied him in both mind and body. Those distractions, to us, are without number which in his day beset him in the kingdom which he had taken into his care, and yet when [he] had learned this book and translated it from Latin into an English story, [then he made] it again into verse, as has now been done; and now he beseeches and in God's name begs each man of those who liked to read this book, that he pray for him, and not blame him if he can make it out more clearly than Alfred did, because each man must say what he says, and do what he does, according to his measure of intellect and to the leisure which he has.

Preface to the translation of Augustine's *Soliloquies*

Alfred's reading was done for him, with him and by him (and after him, of course) in what sometimes seems to be a rather random way. The 'translation' of St Augustine's *Soliloquia* 'Soliloquies' (*c.* 420) forms only about the initial third of a free West Saxon adaptation bearing this name which is alleged to be of Alfred's court. Through this initial apparently faithful part of the translation, and especially in the composite remainder of this work, Alfred and his scholars plunder other works by Augustine, St Jerome and Boethius and others, to give a confection of wisdom that looks good to serve an outdoors monarch as a personal primer. The questions that are posed and answered via this highly medieval, but also personal, randomness of composition, must have some bearing on Alfred's own mind as a king. The impression one thereby gets of Alfred survives the persona he undoubtedly helped to develop for the propaganda of his rule. Alfred was extremely devout, though a layman. He wondered about how things work, the mind, senses and soul in particular. (In this he is accompanied by the more learned poet of *Beowulf*, a text he may have heard, used or even known by heart.) He wondered also, but with confidence, what lay in store for him in the next world. He asked scholars to help him assemble commonplace books, scrapbooks of knowledge, some or most of which ended up as the texts attributed to him in posterity. Apart from the assorted learning that helped Alfred answer questions of the existential theological kind, as he fought off the Danes, the images in the West Saxon that supplement the Latin texts are drawn from woodcraft and carpentry (see in the present *Preface*), royal vills, councils, army life and prisons. These additions are more plausibly of King Alfred than of anyone else then or later.

The language and style of this West Saxon rendition of St Augustine's *Soliloquies* have been corrupted by a long transmission of which only one manuscript survives, the Southwick Codex, which was copied in the mid-twelfth century. This codex was later sewn on to the front of the more famous Nowell Codex which contains material including *Beowulf*. Both Southwick and Nowell Codices together form British Library, MS Cotton Vitellius A.XV.

Bhattacharya, P., 'An analogue and probable source for a metaphor in Alfred's Old English Preface to Augustine's *Soliloquies*', *Notes and Queries* (1998), 1–14

Bintley, M., 'Trees and woodland in Anglo-Saxon England' (unpublished doctoral theseis, UCL, 2010)

Carnicelli, T. A., ed., *King Alfred's Version of King Alfred's Soliloquies* (Cambridge, MA, 1969)

Keynes, S. D., and M. Lapidge, trans., with introduction and notes, *Alfred the Great: Asser's 'Life of King Alfred' and Other Contemporary Sources* (Harmondsworth, 1983)

Sayers, W., 'King Alfred's timbers', *Journal of the Spanish Society for Medieval English and Literature* 15 (2008), 117–24

[... Ic] **gaderode me þonne kigclas**, and stuþansceaftas, and lohsceaftas, and hylfa to ælcum þara tola þe ic mid wircan cuðe, and bohtimbru and bol*t*imbru to ælcum þara weorca þe ic wyrcan cuðe, þa wlitegostan treowo be þam dele ðe ic aberan meihte. Ne com ic naþer mid anre byrðene ham, þe me ne lyste ealne þane wude ham brengan, gif ic hyne ealne aberan meihte. On ælcum treowo ic geseah hwæthwugu þæs þe ic æt ham beþorfte. Forþam ic lære ælcne ðara þe maga si and manigne wæn hæbbe, þæt he menige to þam ilcan wuda, þar ic ðas stuðansceaftas cearf, fetige hym þar ma and gefeðrige hys wænas mid fegrum gerdum, þat he mage windan manigne smicerne wah, and manig ænlic hus settan and fegerne tun timbrian þara, and þær murge and softe mid mæge on eardian ægðer ge wintras ge sumeras, swa swa ic nu ne gyt ne dyde.

Ac se þe me lærde, þam se wudu licode, se mæg gedon þæt ic softor eardian [mæge] ægðer ge **on þisum lænan stoclife** be þis wæge ða *hw*ile þe ic on þisse weorulde beo, ge eac on þam ecan hame ðe he us gehaten hefð þurh sanctus Augustinus and sanctus Gregorius and sanctus Ieronimus, and þurh manege oððre halie fædras; swa ic gelyfe eac þæt he gedo for heora ealra earnunge ægðer ge þisne weig gelimpfulran gedo þonne he ær þissum wes, ge huru

---

[... I] **then gathered wall-posts** and corner-posts and tie-beams, and handles for each of the tools that I knew how to work with (the timber of bough and bole) and, for each of the structures that I knew how to build, the finest wood in the quantities that I could bear away. Nor did I come home with just one burden either that I did not desire to bring home all the wood, if I could have carried all of it. In each tree I saw something that I needed at home. And so I advise each man who is vigorous and has many a wagon, that he make his way to the same wood where I cut the corner-posts, fetch himself more there and load his wagon with beautiful rods so that with these he may weave many an elegant wall, and put up many a peerless house and work up many a beautiful homestead, and with this may live merrily and comfortably both winters and summers, as I have not yet done.

But He who advised me, to whom the wood was pleasing, He can bring it about that I [may] dwell more comfortably **in this borrowed city** by this roadside, while I am in this world, and in the everlasting home which He has promised us through St Augustine and St Gregory and St Jerome and through many other Holy Fathers; as also I believe that He will, through the merits of all of them, both make this present road more convenient than it was before, and indeed will illuminate the eyes of my mind so that I can discover a straight

---

gaderode me þonne kigclas 'then gathered wall-posts' etc. The first sentence is translated by William Sayers (2008), who draws attention to the way in which carpenters chose bough and bole by their shapes for ready-made curves in their building. The woodcraft is illuminated by Mike Bintley (2010), by which coppicing and pollarding enabled houses to be built in this way. Woods were farmed as intensively as fields at the time.

on þisum lænan stoclife 'in this borrowed city'. The whole world is figured by the cottage that the man builds on leased land. Man makes his world, but on credit from the Almighty. Permanency is only possible in the heavenly home. On the term *læne* 'borrowed, on loan', hence 'transient' in poetry, see *The Wanderer*, lines 108–9 (**Poems on the Meaning of Life**) and elsewhere.

mines modes eagan to þam ongelihte þæt ic mage rihtne weig aredian to þam ecan hame, and to þam ecan are, and to þare ecan reste þe us gehaten is þurh þa halgan fæderas. Sie swa!

Nis hit nan wundor þeah man swilc ontimber gewirce eac on þare utlade ond eac on þære bytlinge; ac ælcne man lyst, siððan he ænig cotlyf in his hlafordes læne myd his fultume getimbred hæfð, þæt he hine mote hwilum þaron gerestan, and huntigan, and fuglian, and fiscian, and his on gehwilce wisan to þere lænan tilian, ægþer ge on se ge on lande, oð þone fyrst þe he **bocland and æce yrfe þurh his hlafordes miltse geearnige**. Swa gedo se wilega gifola, se ðe egðer wilt ge þissa lænena stoclife ge þara ecena hama. Se ðe ægþer gescop and ægþeres wilt, forgife me þæt me to ægðrum onhagige, ge her nytwyrðe to beonne, ge huru þider to cumane.

Agustinus, Cartaina bisceop, worhte twa bec be his agnum ingeþance. Þa bec sint gehatene 'Soliloquiorum', þæt is, be hys 'modes smeaunge and tweounga'; hu hys gesceadwisnes answarode hys mode, þonne þæt mod ymbe hwæt tweonode, oðþe hit hwæs wilnode to witanne þæs þe hit ær for sweotole ongytan ne meahte.

---

path to the everlasting home, and to the everlasting grace, and to to everlasting rest which is promised us through these Holy Fathers. May it be so!

It is no wonder that a man work with such materials both in their loading up and transport and in their building; but each man, when he has built any cottage with the help of his lord who leases him the land, likes to stay there some time and go hunting, fowling and fishing, and provide for himself in each way on that leasehold, both on water and on land, until such time as he **may earn bookland and a permanent inheritance through the generosity of his lord**. May He so grant it, the bounteous giver who wields the rule of both these leased cities of ours and our everlasting homes. May He who created and rules over both kinds of home grant that it be in my power to do both, to be of profit here and to get myself there.

Augustine, bishop of Carthage, made two books on his own meditations. These books are called *Soliloquiorum*, that is *Doubts and Reflections of his Mind*; how his reason answered his mind when his mind was in doubt about something, or when it desired to know something that it could not clearly make out before.

---

bocland and æce yrfe þurh his hlafordes miltse geearnige 'may earn bookland and a permanent inheritance through the generosity of his lord'. Bookland is land whose ownership is decided in writing, by charter. Usually it is for one lifetime, sometimes more, before reversion to the secular or ecclesiastical lord who conferred it. Permanent bookland is the founding of a monastery, whose ownership has been submitted to agents of the church, therefore to God.

Agustinus, Cartaina bisceop 'Augustine, bishop of Carthage'. This is a mistake for Hippo, which is not far from Carthage. Augustine (354–430) was regarded as the greatest Latin Father.

The West Saxon *Boethius*

✳

Boethius was an aristocrat and scholar living in northern Italy from 480 to 524. He had been educated in Greek, particularly in Plato's works. In 510 he was briefly a consul in the service of Theoderic, the Gothic prefect of Ravenna and Italy (ruled 493–526). In 523 Boethius returned to politics as a high civil servant, as Theoderic's *magister officiorum* 'master of the offices'. This was also the year in which Theoderic, who was an Arian Christian (Jesus as fully human), began to persecute Catholics and intellectuals. Theoderic had no male heir, and when his men intercepted a letter to Emperor Justin I of Byzantium on the issue of the royal succession, the author, an ex-consul named Albinus, was arrested and charged with high treason. Boethius made the mistake of defending him, saying 'if Albinus did anything, I myself and the entire Roman senate are also guilty' (Wolfram 1988: 331). Boethius' enemies at the court in Ravenna used this remark to entangle him, and a year later Boethius was dead, executed on the orders of the paranoid Goth. Whilst he sat in Pavia, awaiting execution, whether in a cell or under house arrest or in internal exile it is not clear, Boethius composed his masterpiece, *De consolatione Philosophiae* 'On the consolation of Philosophy', a rhetorical neo-Platonist dialogue in five books on the subject of fate and destiny.

In this work, Boethius' education is personified as a speaker who visits him in his cell, Lady Philosophy, who coaxes the philosopher out of self-pity back into the imperturbable world of his books. The argument proceeds playfully in prose interspersed with metres (i.e. poems) in which Philosophy sings to her pupil of the essence of her arguments, often with the examples provided by the Classical poets, 'Homer' among them. Fate and possessions are dismissed as illusions of temporary value, while the working of Providence is exalted as the only true authority and one that has the best interests of Boethius at heart. By the end of Book IV, the process is largely complete, with Boethius having come to terms with his imminent death in hope of union with the Deity. Book V consists of Philosophy's meditation on time and destiny and the place of man's free will in a predetermined universe.

This work was immensely influential and some 80 manuscripts survive in the period up to 1100. It attracted commentaries with almost each copying, which, in characteristic medieval style, were often added into the main text. The unravelling of the twelfth-century textual relationships has since become a problem of insane complexity. To begin with, however, the *De consolatione* seems to have stayed in Italy. Some northern scholars had heard of it, and in the late eighth century Alcuin, and probably other courtiers of Emperor Charlemagne (ruled 768–814), brought manuscripts of it into northern France. In the 880s King Alfred (ruled 871–99) had a version of this work adapted into West Saxon prose. Its Preface claims that he translated this himself (see 'King Alfred's *Prefaces*'). In terms of his control of the programme, this is certainly true, and it may be that he supervised the work closely enough for his preoccupations, down-to-earth expressions and boundless curiosity to influence the language. An eleventh-century copy of the entire translation, laid out in 42 prose chapters, survives in Oxford, Bodleian Library, Bodley 180 (2079) (hereafter B), although part of it (the Napier Fragment) also survived in a manuscript page used as a wrapper, transcribed by A. S. Napier in 1886, and subsequently lost (N). At some later stage, possibly also in Alfred's reign but if not in that of one of his tenth-century successors, another translation was made. This new text survives in a tenth-century copy in London, British Library, Cotton Otho A.vi (hereafter C). Its author used the original B as his main source and attempted to regain the prose-verse style of Boethius' original with poems in many relevant places. This manuscript was damaged in the Cotton Library fire of 1731, and by the restorative work in the nineteenth century. In the later seventeenth century the Dutch antiquarian Franciscus Junius copied his own version of B, adding variants from C into the margin, then added the verse sections of C with notes on the text. This late composite text (J) is preserved in Oxford, Bodleian Library, Junius 12.

As above, Alfred seems to have injected his own interests as king into the B version which his scholars prepared. Boethius' biographical sections and his more recondite philosophical arguments are often lost in favour of sections on God and His divine order and how man may comprehend this. Philosophy in this dialogue is recast as *Wisdom* 'Wisdom' (sometimes as *Wisdom ond Gesceadwisnes* 'Wisdom and Reason'). Boethius is renamed as *Mod* 'Mind', then called *Boetius* again, then represented as *ic* 'I'. The Old English texts here are based on the highly scholarly edition of Godden and Irvine: 'King Theoderic and Boethius', from B, chs. 1–2 (I, 243–4; Custom); 'Orpheus and Eurydice', from B, Prose, ch. 35 (I, 335–8); 'Ulysses and Circe', from B, ch. 38 (I, 349–51); 'Fate and Providence', from C, ch. 29 (I, 522).

Godden, M., and S. Irvine, ed., with M. Griffith and R. Jayatilaka, *The Old English Boethius: An Edition of the Old English Versions of Boethius's De Consolatione Philosophiae*, 2 vols (Oxford, 2009)

Keynes, S. D., and M. Lapidge, trans., with introduction and notes, *Alfred the Great: Asser's 'Life of King Alfred' and Other Contemporary Sources* (Harmondsworth, 1983)

North, J. [D.], *Cosmos: An Illustrated History of Astronomy and Cosmology* (Chicago and London, 2008)

Pheifer, J. D., ed., *Old English Glosses in the Épinal-Erfurt Glossary* (Oxford, 1974)

Wolfram, H., *History of the Goths*, trans. T. J. Dunlap, rev. from German 2nd ed. (Berkeley, CA, 1988)

Orpheus and Eurydice

The soul has virtue, even in a wicked man. In Boethius' text, the myth of Orpheus is about making a good end: like Orpheus ascending to the light, leaving Eurydice behind him, we must not look down, but up, however painful the parting from earthly ties. In the Alfredian adaptation of Philosophy's metre 12 in Book III, the story of Orpheus is retold so as to exemplify the need of each person to leave sin behind in constant efforts to return to the ways of God. 'God's light' was in any case a commonplace for the good Christian life (and in *Beowulf* it is even used to describe the unwitting Christian example of King Hrethel, who *Godes leoht geceas* 'chose God's light' by dying without taking vengeance in line 2469). In the West Saxon *Boethius*, this commonplace becomes active in Orpheus' return to the surface, with Eurydice becoming a rather awkward figure for sin. Along the way, there is much lively narrative which works well enough by itself before a religious use of it is made at the end. The Latin version which underlies version B, or in the contribution of the translator, relies on other texts such as Ovid's *Metamorphoses* and the *Etymologies* of Bishop Isidore of Seville.

Irvine, S., 'Wrestling with Hercules: King Alfred and the Classical past', in *Court Culture of the Early Middle Ages: the Proceedings of the First Alcuin Conference*, ed. C. Cubitt, Studies in the Early Middle Ages 3 (Turnhout, 2003), 171–88

B.35. [. . .] Wisdom: 'Þeah we nu scylon manega ond mistlice bisna ond bispell reccan, þeah **hangað ure mod ealne weg on þam ðe we æfterspiriað. Ne fo we na on þa bispell** for þara leasana spella lufian, ac for þam þe we woldan mid gebeacnian þa soðfæstnesse, ond woldon þæt hit wurde to nytte þam geherendon.

'Ic gemunde nu rihte þæs wisan Platones lara suma, hu he cwæð þæt se mon se ðe bispell secgan wolde ne sceolde fon on to ungelic bispell þære spræce þe he þonne sprecan wolde. Ac geheor nu geðyldelice hwæt ic nu sprecan wille, þeah hit gefyrn ær unnyt þuhte, hwæðer se ende a bet lician wille.' Ongan þa singan ond cwæð, 'Gesælig bið se mon þe mæg geseon þone hluttran æwellm þæs hehtan godes, ond of him selfum aweorpan mæg þa þiostro his modes. We sculon get of ealdum leasum spellum ðe sum bispell reccan.

B.35. [. . .] **Wisdom:** 'Though we must now lay out many and various examples and parables, yet **the mind of us is always bent on what we are tracking. We do not catch up those parables** for love of their fabulous stories, but because with them we would blaze a path to righteousness, and would like it to be of profit to those who are listening.

Right now I called to mind some teachings of Plato, how he said that a man who wanted to tell a parable should not catch at a parable too unlike the speech he wanted to make at that time. Still, listen now patiently to what I want to say, though it may have seemed useless before, and see whether the end will be more pleasing.' He began to sing, saying, 'Happy the man who can see the highest good's pure fountainhead, and cannot cast from him the darkness of his mind. We must still tell you a parable from old fabulous stories.

---

hangað ure mod ealne weg on þam ðe we æfterspiriað. Ne fo we na on þa bispell 'the mind of us is always bent on what we are tracking. We do not catch up those parables'. This hunting metaphor resembles Alfred's in his Preface to the West Saxon translation of the Gregory's *Pastoral Care*: *we him ne cunnon æfter spyrigean* 'we know not how to follow their trail', *we noldon to ðæm spore . . . onlutan* 'we would not . . . stoop to that trail'. See also under the Alfredian translation of St Augustine's *Soliloquies* (Custom Version).

'Hit gelamp gio þætte an hearpere was on þære þeode þe Đracia hatte, sio wæs on Creca rice. Se hearpere was swiðe ungefræglice god, þæs nama wæs Orfeus. He hæfde an swiðe ænlic wif, sio wæs gehaten Eurudice. Đa ongann mon secgan be þam hearpere, **þæt he mihte hearpian** þæt se wuda wagode ond þa stanas [hi styredon] for þam swege, ond wilde deor þær woldon to irnan and standon swilce hi tame wæron, swa stille, **þeah hi men oððe hundas wið eodon**, þæt hi na ne onscunedon!

'Þa sædon hi þæt ðæs hearperes wif sceolde acwelan, ond hire sawle mon sceolde lædan to helle. Đa sceolde se hearpere weorþan swa sarig þæt he ne mihte ongemong oðrum monnum bion, ac teah to wuda ond sæt on þam muntum ægþer ge dæges ge nihtes, weop ond hearpode þæt þa wudas bifodon ond þa ea stodon, ond nan heort ne onscunode nanne leon, ne nan hara nanne hund, ne nan neat nyste nanne andan ne nænne ege to oðrum for þære mirhðe þæs sones. Þa ðæm hearepere þa þuhte þæt hine þa nanes ðinges ne lyste on þæisse worulde, þa ðohte he þæt he wolde gesecan helle [godu] ond onginnan him oleccan mid his hearepan, ond biddan þæt hi him ageafan eft his wif.

'It happened long ago that there was a harper in the country which was called Thrace, that was in Greece. This harper, whose name was Orpheus, was very good and no one had ever heard the like. He had a most peerless wife, she was called Eurydice. Then it began to be said about the harper **that he could play** so that the woods wagged and the stones stirred because of the melody, and wild animals would run up and stand there like they were tame, so still that they would never have shied **even if men or dogs were coming at them**!

'Then people said that the harper's wife perished, and her soul was conveyed to hell. Then the harper was said to be so grief-stricken that he could not live among other men, but drew himself off to the woods and sat in the mountains both day and night, wept and played so that the woods shook and the river stood still, and not a hart shied from a lion, nor a hare from a hound, nor did one beast feel anger or fear towards another for the mirth of that sound. When the harper had thought that there was nothing he liked in this world, why then, he thought he would go visit the gods of hell and make to flatter them with his lyre, and ask them to give him back his wife.

þæt he mihte hearpian 'that he could play'. But no singing (Godden and Irvine 2009: II, 416).

þeah hi men oððe hundas wið eodon 'even if men or dogs were coming at them'. Another hunting reference, not sourced in Boethius or any other authority or glosses (Godden and Irvine 2009: II, 418).

'**Þa he ða þider com**, þa sceolde cuman þære helle hund ongean hine, þæs nama wæs [C]*e*ruerus, [se] sceolde habban þrio heafda, ond ongan fægenian mid his steorte ond pleigan wið hine for his hearpunga. Ða was þær eac swiðe egeslic geatweard, þæs nama sceolde beon Caron. Se hæfde eac þrio heafda! ond se was swiðe oreald. Ða ongon þe hearpere hine biddan þæt he hine gemundbyrde, þa hwile ðe he þær wære, ond hine gesundne eft brohte. Þa gehet he him þæt, for þam he wæs oflyst þæs seldcuþan sones.

'Ða eode he furðor, oð he gemette þa graman gydena þe folcisce men hatað "**Parcas**". Þa, hi secgað, þæt on nanum men nyton nan are ac ælcum menn wrecan be his gewyrhtum. Ða, hi secgað, þæt **wealdan ælces monnes wyrde**. Ða ongann he biddan hiora miltse, þa ongunnon hi wepan mid him.

'Ða eode he furðor, ond him urnon ealle helwaran ongean ond lædon hine to hiora cyninge, ond ongunnon ealle sprecan mid him ond biddan þæs he bæd. Ond þæt unstille hweol ðe Ixion [wæs] to gebunden, Lauita cyning, for his scilde, þæt oðstod for his hearpunga. Ond Tantalus, se cyning þe on þisse worulde ungemetlice gifre wæs ond him þær þæt yfel fyligde, þæs gifernesse he gestilde. Ond se ultor sceolde forlætan þæt he slat ða lifre Ticcies, þæs cyninges þe hine ær mid þy witnode. Ond eall hellwara witu gestildon, ða

---

'**When he arrived there**, who should come towards him but the hound of hell, whose name was Cerberus, who was said to have three heads, and began to fawn with his tail and play with him because of his harping. Then there was also a most terrifying gate-keeper, whose name was Charon. He also had three heads! and was really old. The harper then made to ask him for his protection while he was there, and to bring him back safe and sound. Charon promised him that then because he was delighted at the rare sound.

'He went further, until he met the angry goddesses that the common people call ***Parcae***. These, it is said, would show favour to no man but rather do vengeance on every man according to his deeds. These, it is said, **control the fate of each man**. When he made to ask them for mercy, they began to cry along with him.

'Then he went further, and all the people living in hell ran towards him and led him to their king, and they all began to speak to him and ask what he was asking for. And the ceaseless wheel that Ixion was tied to, king of Lavitae, for his crimes, stopped turning because of his harping. And Tantalus, the king who in this world had been greedy without measure, and that evil followed him there, he stilled the greed. And it was said the vulture gave up tearing the liver out of Tityus, the king he had punished with that before. And all the people of hell had punishments stopped while he was playing before the king. By and

---

Þa he ða þider com 'When he arrived there'. The author has an 'interest in setting up a series of narrative obstacles and meetings for Orpheus', possibly influenced by Beowulf's progress into Heorot (Godden and Irvine 2009: II, 416, 419).

'Parcas' . . . wealdan ælces monnes wyrde '*Parcae* . . . control the fate of each man'. The Épinal-Erfurt Glossary, of the eighth century, also gives 'parcae : uuyrdae' (Pheifer 1974: 41). Compare this with the three Norns in *The Sibyl's Prophecy*, stanza 20 (**Gods of the Vikings**).

hwile þe he beforan þam cyninge hearpode. Ða he ða lange ond lange hearpode, þa clipode se hellwarena cyning ond cwæð: "Uton agifan **þam esne** his wif, for þam he hi hæfð geearnod mid his hearpunga."

'Bebead him þa þæt he geara wiste þæt [he] hine næfre underbæc ne besawe, [siððan] he þononweard wære, ond sæde, gif he underbæc besawe, þæt he sceolde forlætan þæt wif. **Ond þa lufe mon mæg swiðe uneaþe forbeodan**. Wilawei! Hwæt, Orfeus þa lædde his wif mid him oð he com on þæt gemære leohtes ond ðeostro. Þa eode þæt wif æfter him. Þa he forð on þæt leoht com, þa geseah he hine underbæc wið ðæs wifes. Þa losede heo him sona.

'Ðas leasan spell lærað gehwilcne man þara ðe wilnað helle þeostra to flionne ond to þæs soðan Godes liohte to cumenne, þæt he hine ne besio [to] his ealdum yfelum swa þæt he hi eft swa fullice fullfremme swa he hi ær dyde. For þam swa hwa swa mid fullon willan his mod went to þam yflum þe he ær forlet, ond hi þonne fullfremeð ond [hi] him þonne fullice liciað, and he hi næfre forlætan ne þencð, þonne forlyst eall his ærran good, buton he hit eft gebete.'

---

by, when he had been playing for a long time, the king of hell's people called out and said: "Let's give **the mule** his wife back, he has earned her with his harping."

'Then he commanded him to be clear about never looking back behind him, when he was on the way out of there, and said, if he did look back behind him, that he would have to lose his wife. **And love is not something you can forbid very easily**. What misery! Well then, Orpheus led his wife with him until he came to the border between light and dark. Then his wife went behind him. When he came out into the light, why then, he looked back over his shoulder to his wife. Then she vanished from his sight.

'These fables teach each man who desires to flee the darkness of hell, and come to the true God's light, that he should not look to his old evils so as to carry them out again as fully as he did the first time. And so whoever turns his thoughts with all his will back to evils he left before, and then carries them out and then finds them pleasing, and does not think of leaving them ever, why then he will lose all the good he once had unless he atone for this again.'

þam esne 'the mule'. The word *esne* describes a strapping servant. It is odd to find it here, unless there is a note of admiration (Godden and Irvine 2009: II, 422), or indulgent disdain in the way the king of hell puts this.

Ond þa lufe mon mæg swiðe uneaþe forbeodan 'And love is not something you can forbid very easily'. At odds with the Alfredian moral at the end, this is from Boethius' own words *Quis legem det amantibus?* 'What law may one give lovers?' (Book III. metre 12: lines 52–8). Perhaps, in light of what Wisdom says at the outset about finding the exact parable, Alfred allows for some more warmth in this allegorical figure. The liveliness bears this out.

Ulysses and Circe

In alluding to Ulysses Boethius rendered a late Latin version of the Homeric tale of Odysseus and Circe in the *Odyssey*. Here, when Odysseus arrives on the island of Circe, an enchantress, she turns his first shore party into swine. He narrowly avoids this fate for himself, using the magic of Hermes, but then becomes her lover, using her knowledge to go to the world of the dead. In the *De consolatione*, metre 3 of Book III, Philosophy uses this story to illustrate her preceding argument that men with vices lose their human natures and become animals. Many changes have been made to this metre in the Alfredian version (Godden and Irvine 2009: II, 442–6). Alfred's Ulysses lives with Circe as her husband for some time before his men grow tired of this and ask to leave. To keep her man, Circe turns them into beasts, while they retain their human minds. The new moral message is thus that the mind is more powerful than the body; when the mind is corrupted, so is the body, and the soul is lost. In this version it is interesting, given the role of Alfred as king and naval enthusiast, that Ulysses becomes the model of royal failure: ten years from home, with 100 ships now reduced to one, be that a trireme; an attack of uxoriousness on a strange island in preference to caring for his men's well being and return; and the parting implication that he has turned himself, or been turned by Circe's magic, into a beast inside his manly form. The god Mercury, whom she mentions here as Ulysses' patron, is missing from Alfred's version (though this metre, with Mercury, may have played a role in the conception of *The Wanderer*: see **Heroic Poems**). Conversely, as regards the human spirit's endurance within beast forms, it is left to Ulysses' shipmates to illustrate the case. Circe seems to keep them as beasts indefinitely, and we never find out how, or indeed if, they ever recover their human shapes.

Grinda, K., 'The myth of Circe in King Alfred's Boethius', trans. P. Battles, in *Old English Prose: Basic Readings*, ed. P. E. Szarmach (New York and London, 2000), 237–65

Irvine, S., 'Ulysses and Circe in King Alfred's Boethius: a Classical myth transformed', in *Studies in Old English Language and Literature: 'Doubt Wisely': Papers in Honour of E. G. Stanley*, ed. M. J. Toswell and E. M. Tyler (London and New York, 1996), 387–401

B. 38. Wisdom: 'Hit gebyrede gio on Troiana gewinne þæt þær wæs an cyning þæs nama [wæs] Aulixes. Se hæfde twa þioda under þam kasere. Þa ðioda wæron hatene Iðacige ond Retie, ond þæs kaseres nama wæs Agamenon. Ða se Aulixes mid þam kasere to þam gefiohte for, þa hæfde he sume hundred scipa. Þa wæron hi sume ten gear on þam gewinne. Þa se cyning eft ham cerde from þam kasere, ond hi þæt land hæfdon gewunnen, þa næfde he þa na ma scipa þonne an. Þæt wæs þeah þrereðre.

B. 38. Wisdom: 'It happened long ago in the War of Troy that there was a king whose name was Ulysses. He had two nations to rule under the emperor. These nations were called Ithaca and Rhaetia, and the emperor's name was Agamemnon. When Ulysses went with the emperor into battle, he had some 100 ships with him. They were in this war for some ten years. When the king left the emperor to go back home, and they had conquered that land, he had no more ships than one. That had three banks of oars.

'Þa gestod hine heah weder ond stormsæ. Wearð þa fordrifen on an iglond ut **on þære Wendelsæ**. Þa wæs þær Apollines dohtor, Iobes suna. Se Iob wæs hiora cyning, ond licette þæt he sceolde bion se hehsta god, ond þæt dysige folc him gelyfde for þam ðe he wæs cynecynnes ond hi nyston nænne oðerne god on þæne timan, buton **hiora cyningas hi weorþodon for godas**. Þa sceolde þæs Iobes fæder bion eac god, þæs nama wæs Saturnus, ond his suna swa ilce ælcne hi hæfdon for god. Þa wæs hiora an **se Apollinus þe we ær ymb spræcon**. Þæs Apollines dohtor sceolde bion gydene. Þære nama wæs Kirke.

'Sio, hio sædon, sceolde bion swiðe drycræftigu, ond sio wunode on þam iglonde þe se cyning on fordrifen wearð þe we þær ymbe spræcon. Hio hæfde þær **swiðe micel werode hire ðegna** ond eac oðerra mædena.

'Then a gale blew up and stormy seas. He was driven then on to an island out **in the Vandal Sea**. Living there at this time was the daughter of Apollo, who was the son of Jove. This Jove was their king, and pretended that he was their highest god, and the silly people believed him because he was of their royal kindred and they knew of no other god at that time, except that **they worshipped their kings as gods**. Jove's father was said to be a god then as well, his name was Saturn, and they had each of his sons as a god just like he was. One of these was **the Apollo we were speaking about**. This Apollo's daughter was said to be a goddess. Her name was Circe.

'She, so people said, was very skilled in magic, and she dwelt on the island to which the king we were speaking about was driven. She had **a very big troop of thegns there** and

---

on þære Wendelsæ 'in the Vandal Sea'. The Mediterranean, so named in Germanic Europe because three generations of Vandalic kings ruled around Carthage in North Africa 430–533. See the *Hildebrandslied*, line 43, for *Wentilsęo* 'Vandal Sea' of the same meaning (**Heroic Poems**).

hiora cyningas hi weorþodon for godas 'they worshipped their kings as gods'. In Alfred's time, the same or similar could be said also of any inhabitants of Scandinavia. This is to go by Þjóðólfr's *Ynglingatal* 'Tally of the Ynglingar' (*c.* 890), in which the kings of Vestfold are traceable to the god Ingvi-freyr of Uppsala; also by *The Lay of Hákon the Good* (*c.* 960), in which Hákon, erstwhile Christian foster-son of Alfred's grandson Æthelstan, joins the Norse gods posthumously (see **Gods of the Vikings**). On the other hand, it is not clear how much Alfred knew, or cared, about this dimension to his Viking neighbours. His own ancestors could qualify, for he was alleged to come from Woden (*Anglo-Saxon Chronicle*, year 855).

se Apollinus þe we ær ymb spræcon 'the Apollo we were speaking about'. The roundabout style, repetition, and the references to an audience, make it plausible that Alfred, or someone, is improvising this story to a gathering that includes a scribe.

Apollo, Jove, Saturn. The political status of these Olympians is gathered from, among other sources, St Augustine's *De civitate Dei* 'On the City of God' (Book VII, ch. 18) and Servius' commentary on Vergil's *Aeneid* (Book VIII, line 319; see Godden and Irvine 2009: II, 444).

swiðe micel werode hire ðegna 'a very big troop of her thegns'. Apparently Circe's male retinue is an Alfredian addition.

Sona swa hio geseah þone fordrifenan cyning ðe we ær ymbe spræcon, þæs nama wæs Aulixes, þa **ongan hio hine lufian** ond hiora ægþer oðerne swiðe ungemetlice, swa þætte he for hire lufan forlet his rice eall ond his cynren, ond wunode mid hire oð ðone first þæt his ðegnas him ne mihton leng mid gewunian, ac for hiora eardes lufan ond for þære wræce tihodon hine to forlætenne.

'Ða ongunnon lease men wyrcan spell, ond sædon þæt hio sceolde mid hyre drycræftum þa men forbredan ond weorpan hi an wilde deora lic, ond siþþan slean on þa racentan ond on cospas. Sume hi sædon þæt hio sceolde forsceoppan to leon, ond þonne *h*eo sceold*on* sprecan þonne ryd*on* hio. Sume sceoldan bion eforas, ond þonne hi sceoldan hiora sar siofian, þonne grymetodan hi. Sume wurdon to wulfan, þa ðuton þonne hi sprecan sceoldon. Sume wurdon to þam deorcynne þe mon hat "tigris". Swa [wearð] eall se geferscipe forhwerfed to mistlicum deorcynnum, ælc to sumum diore, butan þam cyninge anum. Ælcne mete hi onscunedon þe men etað ond wilnodon þara þe deor etað. Næfdon hi nane anlicnesse manna, ne on lichoman ne on stemne, ond ælc wisste þeah his gewit swa swa he ær wisste. Þæt gewit wæs swiðe sorgiende for þam ermðum þe hi drogan.

---

another one of maidens too. **As soon as she saw the washed-up king** we were speaking about, whose name was Ulysses, why then **she began to love him**, and each of them the other so much beyond measure that he gave up all his kingdom for her and all his kindred, and stayed with her until such time as his thegns could stay with him no longer, but for love of their homeland, and for the state of exile they were in, they resolved to leave him.

'Then frivolous men started making up stories, and said that with her magic she transformed those men and cast them into the shapes of wild animals, and afterwards knocked them into chains and fetters. Some were said to be turned by her into lions, and when they spoke they roared. Others were said to be boars, and when they sighed over their suffering, they grunted. Some became wolves, these ones howled when they spoke. Others became the kind of beast which is called a *tigris*. In this way, all their fellowship was changed into animal species of various kinds, each man into an animal, except the king himself. Each food that people eat, they shunned, and desired the foods that animals eat. They bore no resemblance to men, neither in bodies nor in voice, and yet each man still had his wits intact as he had done before. These wits of theirs were making great sorrow for the miseries they endured.

Sona swa hio geseah þone fordrifenan cyning 'As soon as she saw the washed-up king'. In this version of the well-known tale, Ulysses' marriage to Circe is moved to a time long before his men are transformed, and the motivations are changed. Nor is Mercury, Ulysses' patron who saves him from Circe initially, to be found in this version. Susan Irvine suggests the influence of Calypso's tale on the stucture here (Godden and Irvine 2009: II, 444).

ongan hio hine lufian 'she began to love him'. Compare this with *gefeol hyre mod on his lufe* 'her mind fell into loving him': the feelings of Princess Archestrate for Apollonius, newly arrived in Cyrene, in the Old English *Apollonius of Tyre* (**Early Chivalry**). The Alfredian idea of love is more deliberate.

'Hwæt, þa menn þe ðisum leasungum gelefdon þeah wisston þæt hio mid þam drycræfte ne mihte þara monna mod onwendan, þeah hio þa lichoman onwende. Eala þæt hit is micel cræft þæs modes for þone lichoman! Be swilcum ond be swylcum, þu miht ongitan þæt se cræft þæs lichoman bið on þam mode, ond þætte ælcum men ma deriað his modes unþeawas [þonne his lichoman mettrumnes. Þa unþeawas] þæs modes tioð eallne þone lichoman to him, ond þæs lichoman mettrumnes ne mæg þæt mod eallunga to him getion.'

'Well then, the people who believed these fables still knew that she could not change the minds of those men with this magic, though she changed the bodies. Alas, what great power the mind has, in spite of the body! By such things and by others such you can see that the power of the body is in the mind, and that the vices of everyman's mind will harm him more than any weakness of his body. The mind's vices will draw the whole body their way, while the body's weakness cannot draw the mind its own way entirely.'

Fate and Providence

The following text is from the other main manuscript, London, British Library, Cotton Otho A.vi, which was damaged in the Cotton Library fire. In this version of Boethius' Book V, Alfred renders Boethius' Ptolemaic (that is pre-Copernican) vision of the universe with a more down-to-earth conceit which he and his readers could better respect as well as understand. Alfred's, or his advisers' or posterity's, underlying curiosity about mechanisms is more in line with engineering than cosmology. The system of concentric spheres which Boethius had inherited from Aristotle's *De caelo* 'on the heavens' is here transformed into a wagon wheel. Perhaps it was manuscript diagrams of these circles that encouraged the wheel (Frakes 1988: 164), but the detail is so well considered that the analogy works perfectly as a primer for understanding the divine command structure in which Alfred or his scholars wish to place us.

Frakes, J. C., *The Fate of Fortune in the Early Middle Ages: The Boethian Tradition* (New York, 1988)

C. Prose 29. [. . .] Þa ongan he sprecan swiðe fiorran ymbutan, swelce he na *þa* spræce ne mænde, ond tiohhode hit *þeah* þiderweardes, ond cwæð, 'Ealla gesceafta gesewenlica ond ungesewenlica, stillu ond unstillu, ondfoð æt þæm stillan, ond æt þam gestæððegan, ond æt þæm anfealdan God*e* endeberdnesse ond an*dwlitan* ond gemeþunge. *And for þæm hit* swa gesceapen wæs, for ðæm He wat hwy He gesceop eall þæt He gesceop. Nis Him nan whit unnyt þæs ðe He gesceop. Se God wunað symle on þære hean ceastre His anfaldnesse and

---

C. Prose 29. [. . .] Then Wisdom began to speak in a very roundabout way as if he did not mean to speak these things, and yet aimed to go in this direction, and said, 'All created things invisible and visible, still and unstill, receive from that still, stable and single God an order, appearance and governance. And it was so created because He knows why He created everything He created. Not one thing is without profit that He has created. That God dwells ever in the high fort of His singleness and simplicity, bilewitnesse, þonan He dælð manega ond misleca gemetgunga eallum His gesceaftum, ond þonan He welt eallra.

'Ac ðæt ðæt we hatað Godes foreþonc ond His foresceawung, þæt bið þa hwile þe his ðær mid Him bið on His mode ær ðæm þe hit gefremed weorðe, þa hwile ðe hit geþoht bið. Ac **siððan** hit **fullfremed** bið, **þonne** hatað we hit **wyrd**. Be þy mæg ælc mon witan þæt hit sint ægþer ge twegen naman ge twa þing, foreþonc ond wyrd. Se foreþonc is seo godcunde gesceadwisnes, sio is fæst on þæm hean Sceppende þe eall forewat, *h*u hit geweorðan sceal ær ær hit geweorðe. Ac þæt þæt He wyrd hatað, *þæt* bið Godes weorc þæt He ælce dæg wyrcð, ægþer ge þæs [ðe] we gesioð ge þæs þe us ungesewenlic bið, ac se godcunda foreþonc heaðe*rað* ealle *gesceafta þæt hi ne moton toslupan of heora* endebyrdnesse.

'Sio wyrd ðonne dælþ eallum gesceaftum andwlitan, ond stowa, ond tida, ond gemetgunga, ac sio wyrd cymð of ðæm gewitte ond of ðæm foreþonce þæs ælmehtigan Godes. Se wyrcð æfter His unasecgendlicum foreþonce swa hwæt swa [He] wile, **swa swa ælc cræftega ðencð ond mearcað his weorc on his mode** ær he hit wyrce, ond wyrcð siððan eall. Þios wandriende wyrd þe we wyrd hatað, færð æfter His foreþonce ond æfter His geþeahte, swa swa He tiohhað þæt hit sie. Þeah hit us manigfaldlic ðince, sum good, sum yfel, hit is ðeah Him anfeald good, for ðæm he hit eall to godum ende brengð, ond for gode deð ealle þæt þæt He deð. Siððan we hit hatað wyrd, syððan hit geworht bið. Ær hit wæs Godes fore*þonc* ond His foretiohhung.

---

from where He deals out many and various ordinances to all His creatures, and from where He rules all things.

'But that which we call God's forethought and His foreseeing [= providence], that lives for as long as it lives in His mind before it gets carried out, for as long as it is being intended. But **after** it has been **carried out, that is when** we call it **what's-happened** [= fate]. In this, each man can see that there are two things here, each with its name, forethought and what's-happened. "Forethought" is divine reasoning, which is fixed in the High Shaper who foreknows all, how it must happen before it does happen. But that which God calls "what's-happened" is His work which He performs each day, both the work we see and work unseen to us, for the divine forethought restrains all creatures to stop them slipping out of order.

' "What's-happened" then, or fate, deals out to all creatures appearance, and places, and times, and measure, but fate comes from the intelligence and from the providence of Almighty God. He does according to His inexpressible providence whatever He wants, **just as every craftsman thinks through and marks out his work in his mind** before he does it, and after that does it all. This fluctuating fate that we call what's-happened runs according to His providence and according to His intention, just as He plans it should do. Though it may seem of many kinds to us, some good, some bad, it is one single good fate to Him, because He brings it all to a good end, and does all He does for a good end. We call it what's-happened after it has happened. Before then, it was God's providence and His fore-ordaining.

---

siððan . . . fullfremed, þonne wyrd 'after . . . carried out, that is when . . . what's-happened'. The word *wyrd* is derived from *weorðan* 'to happen, become'.

swa swa ælc cræftega ðencð ond mearcað his weorc on his mode 'just as every craftsman thinks through and marks out his work in his mind'. *Genesis B* also has an image of God's *mearcian* in His design, in this with Adam and Eve (line 363; see **Poems of Devotion**).

'Đa wyrd He *þonne* wyrcð, oððe þurh þa goodan *eng*las, oððe þurh monna sawla, oððe þurh oðerra gesceafta lif, oððe þurh heofones tungl, oððe ðurh þara scuccena mislice lotwrencas, hwilum þurh an ðara, hwilum þurh eall ða. Ac þæt is openlice cuð, þæt sio godcunde foretiohhung is anfeald ond unawendendlic, ond welt ælces þinges endebyrdlice, ond eall þing gehiwað. Sumu þing þonne on þisse weorulde sint underðied þære wyrde, sume hire nan wuht underðied ne sint, ac sio wyrd ond eall ða þing þe hire underðied sint, sint underðied ðæm godcundan foreþonce.

'Be ðæm ic ðe mæg sum bispell secgan, þæt þu meaht þy sweotolor ongitan hwilce men bioð underðied þære wyrde, hwylce ne bioð. Eall ðios unstille gesceaft ond þios hwearfiende hwearfað on ðæm stillan Gode, ond on ðæm gestæððegan, ond on ðæm anfealdan, ond He welt eallra gesceafta swa swa He æt fruman getiohhod hæfde ond get hæfð, **swa swa on wænes eaxe hwearfiað þa hweol**, ond sio eax stint stille, ond byrð þeah ealne þone wæn, ond welt ealles þæs færeltes. Þæt h*weo*l hwerfð ymbutan ond sio nafu, nehst ðære eaxe, sio færð micle *fæstlicor* ond orsorglicor þonne ða fe*lgan don*, swelce sio eax sie þæt hehste *god þe we* nemnað *God*, ond þa selestan men farað nehste Gode, swa swa sio nafu færð neahst þære eaxe, ond þa midmestan swa swa ða spacan.

'He then performs fate, whether though the good angels, or through souls of men, or through the lives of other creatures, or through heavenly bodies, or through the various tricks of elves, sometimes through one of these, sometimes through them all. All the same, it is openly clear that divine providence is a single power and cannot be changed, that it rules everything in order and gives shape to everything. Some things then in this world are subject to fate, some are not subject to it, but both fate and everything subject to fate are subject to divine providence.

'About this, I can make up a likeness, so that you can see more clearly which men are subject to fate and which are not. All this moving and turning creation spins around the unmoving God, the stable and the single God, and He rules all creatures as He had planned in the beginning and still has planned, **just as wheels turn around the axle of a wagon**, while the axle lies rigid in position and yet bears all the wagon and controls all the movement. The wheel turns around, while the wheel-hub, closest to the axle, runs around the axle much more steadily and assured than the outer rim, as if the axle is the highest good we call God. And like the hub goes closest to the axle, so the highest-ranking men go closest to God, with the spokes being men of the middle class.

---

swa swa on wænes eaxe hwearfiað þa hweol 'just as wheels turn around the axle of a wagon'. This likeness or analogy appears to be Alfred's, one based on (perhaps an illustration of) Boethius' allusion to a reduced Aristotelian model of planets and stars revolving in concentric spheres around a fixed earth (Godden and Irvine: 2009: 466; see also North 2008: 240–49).

'For ðæm þe ælces spacan bið oðer ende fæst on ðære nafe, oðer on þære felge. Swa bið þæm midlestan monnum. Oðre hwile he smeað on his mode ymb þis eorðlice, oðre hwile ymb ðæt godcundlice, swilce he locie mid oðre eagan to heofonum, mid oðre to eorþan. Swa swa þa spacan sticiað, oðer ende on þære felge, oþer on þære nafe, middeweard se spaca bið ægðrum emn neah. Ðeah oðer ende bio fæst on þære nafe, oðer on þære felge, swa bioð þa midmestan men onmiddan þam spacan, ond þa betran near þære nafe, ond þa mætran near ðæm felgum: bioð þeah fæste on ðære nafe, ond sio nafu on ðære eaxe.

'Hwæt, þa felga þeah hongiað on þæm spacum, þeah hi eallunga wealowigen on þære eorðan. Swa doð þa mætestan men on þæm midmestum, ond þa midmestan on þæm betstum, ond þa betstan *on Gode*. Þeah þa mætestan ealle hiora lufe wenden to ðisse weorulde, *hi ne* magon þær onwunigan, ne to nauhte ne weorðað, gif hi be nanum dæle ne beoð gefæstnode to Gode, þon ma þe þæs hweoles felga magon bion on ðæm færelte, gif hi ne bioð fæste on þæm spacum, ond þa spacan on þære eaxe. Þa felgea bioð fyrrest ðære eaxe, for ðæm hi farað ungeredelicost.

'Sio nafu færð neaxst þære eaxe, for ðy hio færð gesundlicost. Swa doð ða selestan men. Swa hi hiora lufe near Gode lætað, ond swiðor þas eorðlicon þing forseoþ, swa hi beoð orsorgran, ond læs reccað hu sio wyrd wandrige, oððe hwæt hio brenge. Swa swa sio nafu bið symle swa gesund, hnæppen þa felga on þæt ðe hi hnæppen, ond þeah bið sio nafu hwæthwugu todæled from þære eaxe. Be þy þu meaht ongitan þæt se wæn bið micle leng gesund, þe læs bið todæled from þære eaxe.

'And so each spoke is fixed at one end to the hub, at the other to the outer rim. So it is with men in the middle. Sometimes the man thinks in his mind about earthly matters, sometimes about divine, like looking with one eye on heaven and with the other on earth. Just so the spokes are set, one end into the outer rim, the other into the hub, the mid-spoke being the same distance from each. If one end be fixed on the hub, the other on the rim, the middlemost men are in the mid-spoke, and the men of higher class nearer to the hub, and the men of lower class nearer to the rim: yet they are all firmly in the hub, and the hub is on the axle.

'Well then, the fellies that make up the rim, they hang off the spokes, though they wallow completely in the mud. That is how it is with the lowest men, they hang off the middle-class men, and the middle-class men off the highest, and the highest-ranking men off God. Though the lowest turn all their love to this world, they cannot stay in it for long, nor come to anything if part of them is not fastened to God, any more than the wheel's fellies can be in movement if they are not fastened to the spokes, and the spokes to the axle. The fellies are furthest from the axle and so move with the greatest abandon.

'The hub moves closest to the axle and so moves with the greatest safety. So it is with men of the highest rank. The nearer they let their love go to God, and the harder they despise the things of the world, the more assured they are therefore, and the less they care how fate may fluctuate or what it may bring. Just so the hub is constantly safe, let the fellies strike on what they strike, and yet the hub is somewhat apart from the axle. From this you can see that the wagon stays safe for much longer, the less apart it is from the axle.

'Swa bioð þa men eallra orsorgoste, ægðer ge þisses andweardan lifes earfoða, ge þæs toweardan, þa þe fæste bioð on Gode. Ac swa hi swiður bioð asyndrede fram Gode, swa hi swiður bioð gedrefde ond geswencte, ægþer ge on mode ge *on lichoman. Swylc is þæt þæt we wyrd hatað*, be þæm godcundan foreþonce. Swylce sio smeaung ond sio gesceadwisnes, is **to metanne** wið þone gearowitan, ond swylce þas lænan þing bioð **to metanne** wið ða ecan, ond swilce þæt hweol bið **to metanne** wið ða eaxe. For ðæm sio eax welt ealles þæs wænes. Swa deð se godcunda foreðonc.'

'So it is with men who are firmly with God, they are the most assuredly free of troubles both in the present life and in the life to come. But the more sundered they are from God, the more oppressed they are and afflicted, both in mind and body. Such is that which we call fate in relation to divine providence. Just so is contemplation and reason **to be measured** against perfect knowledge, and things loaned to us **to be measured** against the eternal, and the wheel **to be measured** against the axle. For the axle rules all the wagon. Likewise divine providence.'

---

to metanne 'to be measured'. Poetry's common term for God, *Me(o)tod* 'Measurer, Measured', is clearly connected with ideas of predestination on a conceptual level.

The West Saxon *Bede*

✻

The late-ninth-century West Saxon translation of Bede's *Historia ecclesiastica gentis Anglorum* 'Ecclesiastical History of the English People' (*c.* 734) became a useful adjunct to Alfred's programme to rebuild English learning. The four extant manuscripts that contain this all show, however, that the first West Saxon text was copied from a translation originally in Mercian. Which Mercian king could have wanted this great work of Bede's is less clear, although a letter from *c.* 793 to King Offa (ruled 757–96) survives in which Alcuin, Charlemagne's theologian courtier in York or Aachen, refers the old king to his own copy of Bede's *Historia ecclesiastica*, presumably in Tamworth (Lehmann 1920: 32). It is tempting to believe that either Offa or King Cenwulf (ruled 796–821) ordered the Mercian translation of Bede's work. In style this work differs from the other Alfredian translations. Although the translator has a job on his hands to keep up with Bede's polished Latin syntax, he tries valiantly with sentences that are longer and have plenty of abstract nouns, a style that must have seemed florid to the nobles around him.

Colgrave, B., and R. A. B. Mynors, ed. and trans., *Bede's Ecclesiastical History of the English People* (Oxford, 1969, repr. with corrections, 1991)

Lehmann, P., 'Ein neuer Alchvinebrief', *Holländische Reisefrüchte I–III*, Sitzungsberichte der Bayerischen Akademie der Wissenschaften, Philosophisch-philologisch-historische Klasse 13 (Munich, 1920), 29–34

Miller, T., ed. and trans., *The Old English Version of Bede's Ecclesiastical History of the English People*, Early English Texts Society old series 95 (London, 1890)

The conversion of King Edwin

To describe Coifi, the Deiran *pontifex* 'high-priest' in this tale of sudden dramatic conversion, the translator used *ealdorbiscop*, which looks like a cross between 'ealdorman', 'chieftain' and 'bishop'. Sometimes he even uses *biscop* and otherwise the ambience is alarmingly similar to the court of a Christian king. Edwin has his *biscop* Paulinus alongside him, although Paulinus appears to be the only Christian bishop there. The king's thegns debate the new faith in a civilised manner and one of their number shows an untutored gift for philosophy. Coifi's epiphany seems already to have taken place and his ride to the shrine in Goodmanham (East Riding, north of Market Weighton) draws no attention except from the peasants, who are startled in Coifi's change of dress. The fact that the translation keeps details of topography, in Goodmanham's position relative to York, itself shows that the translation was originally Mercian, for it is doubtful that the West Saxons knew or much cared what lay, in Alfred's words, *begiondan Humbre* 'beyond the Humber'. The text follows that of Oxford, Bodleian Library, MS Tanner 10, from the tenth century.

Ellis Davidson, H. R., *Gods and Myths of Northern Europe* (Harmondsworth, 1964)

Mayr-Harting, H., *The Coming of Christianity to Anglo-Saxon England*, 3rd ed. (London, 1991)
North, R., *Heathen Gods in Old English Literature*, Cambridge Studies in Anglo-Saxon England 22 (Cambridge, 1997)

Þa se cyning þa þas word gehyrde, þa andswarode he him ond cwæð þæt he æghwæþer ge wolde ge sceolde þam geleafan onfon þe he lærde. Cwæð, hwæþer, þæt he wolde mid his freondum ond mid his wytum gesprec ond geþeaht habban, þæt gif hi mid hine þæt geþafian woldan þæt hi ealle ætsomne on lifes willan Criste gehalgade wæran. Þa dyde se cyning swa swa he cwæð, ond se bisceop þæt geþafade.

Þa hæfde he gesprec ond geþeaht mid his witum, ond syndriglice wæs fram him eallum frignende, hwylc him þuhte ond gesawen wære þeos niwe lar ond þære godcundnesse bigong þe þær læred wæs.

Him þa andswarode **his ealdorbisceop, Cefi wæs haten**, 'Geseoh þu, cyning, hwelc þeos lar sie þe us nu bodad is. Ic þe soðlice andette þæt ic cuðlice geleornad hæbbe, þæt eallinga nawiht mægenes ne nyttnesse hafað sio æfestnes þe we oð ðis hæfdon ond beeodon, for ðon nænig þinra þegna neodlicor ne gelustfullicor hine sylfne underþeodde to ura goda bigange þonne ic, ond

---

When King Edwin heard these words, he answered him and said that he both would and should receive the faith that he was teaching. He said, however, that he would hold converse and deliberation with his friends and with his counsellors, to see if they, along with him, would all of them consent to being hallowed to Christ together in the joy of the Life. Then the king did what he had said, and the bishop agreed to this.

Then he held converse and deliberation with his counsellors, and was asking from each of them individually in turn how they considered and regarded this new teaching and religious worship which had been taught to them there.

His chieftain-bishop then answered him, **Coifi was his name**, 'See, my king, what this teaching may be that is now proclaimed. I confess to you truly what I have clearly learned, that there is absolutely nothing of power or profit in that religion which we have had and practised up to now, because none of your thegns subjected himself to the worship of our gods more urgently or willingly than I did, and not less many are they who received greater

---

Þa se cyning 'When King Edwin' etc. Much has happened to bring Edwin this far. Chiefly this is his memory of a vision which came to him 11 years earlier, while he was on the run from his predecessor, King Æthelfrith of Bernicia, whose men were out to kill him. The apparition in question told Edwin to repay him in the future for (a) his survival (b) his victory against enemies and (c) salvation. Since then, as if to call in the debt, the missionary bishop Paulinus has come from Italy, but cannot make the conversion work.

his ealdorbisceop, Cefi wæs haten 'His chieftain-bishop, Coifi was his name'. This term for a heathen priest is chosen on the basis of *ealdorman*. *Coifi* is the name in the tale in Bede's *Ecclesiastical History* which forms the basis of this narrative. The sound changes in *Cefi* or *Cefe* (i-mutation and palatalisation) tell us that his name has passed through an English narration older than Alfred's. The name is not found outside this story, but appears to be borrowed from late Latin *cofia* 'hood'.

noht þon læs monige syndon þa þe maran gefe ond fremsumnesse æt þe onfengon þonne ic, ond in eallum þingum maran gesynto hæfdon. Hwæt, ic wat, gif ure godo ænige mihte hæfdon, þonne woldan hie me ma fultumian, for þon ic him geornlicor þeodde ond hyrde. For þon me þynceð wislic, gif þu geseo þa þing beteran ond strangran þe us niwan bodad syndon, þæt we þam onfon.'

Þæs wordum oþer cyninges wita ond ealdormann geþafunge sealde, ond to þære spræce feng, ond þus cwæð, 'Þyslic me is gesewen, þu cyning, þis andwearde lif manna on eorðan to wiðmetenesse þære tide þe us uncuð is. Swylc þu æt swæsendum sitte mid þinum ealdormannum ond þegnum on wintertide, ond sie fyr onælæd ond þin heall gewyrmed, ond hit rine ond sniwe ond styrme ute, cume an spearwa ond hrædlice þæt hus þurhfleo, cume þurh oþre duru in, þurh oþre ut gewite. Hwæt, he on þa tid, þe he inne bið, ne bið hrinen mid þy storme þæs wintres. Ac þæt bið an eagan bryhtm ond þæt læsste fæc, ac he sona of wintra on þone winter eft cymeð. Swa þonne þis monna lif to medmiclum fæce ætyweð: hwæt þær foregange, oððe hwæt þær æfterfylige, we ne cunnun. For ðon gif þeos niwe lar owiht cuðlicre ond gerisenlicre brenge, þæs weorþe is þæt we þære fylgen.'

Þeossum wordum gelicum oðre aldormen ond ðæs cyninges geþeahteras spræcan. Þa gen toætyhte Cefi ond cwæð þæt he wolde Paulinus þone bisceop geornlicor gehyran be þam gode sprecende þam þe he bodade.

Þa het se cyning swa don. Þa he þa his word gehyrde, þa clypode he ond þus cwæð, 'Geare ic þæt ongeat, þæt ðæt nowiht wæs þæt we beeodan, for

---

favour and benefit from you than I did, and who have had more prosperity in all their affairs. Listen, I know that if our gods had any might, why then they would have helped me more for more eagerly serving and obeying them. And so it seems a wise course to me, if you see this new business which is proclaimed to us as better and stronger, that we should accept it.'

To this man's words another king's adviser and ealdorman gave his agreement, and spoke up in the assembly, saying this, 'This is how it seems to me, my king, the present life of men here on earth in comparison with that time which is unknown to us. It's as if you are sitting at the banquet with your ealdormen and thegns in winter-time, and the fire is kindled and your hall is warmed, and outside it rains and snows and storms, then comes a sparrow and quickly flies through the house, comes in through one door and goes out the other. Well then, he then in the time he is inside is not touched by the storm of winter. But that is just for the blink of an eye and the smallest interval, for straightaway he returns into the winter from the winter he came from. Just so does this life of man show itself to be a modest interval of time: what goes before it, or what follows after it, we do not know. And so if this new teaching brings anything more certain or honourable, it is worthy that we should follow it.'

The king's other ealdormen and philosophers spoke in words like these. Then Coifi again added his word and said that more eagerly would he hear Paulinus the bishop speaking about the god that he was proclaiming.

So the king then commanded. When he heard Paulinus' words, then he called out, saying this, 'Clearly do I now understand that what we practised before has been nothing, þon swa micle swa ic geornlicor on þam bigange þæt sylfe soð sohte, swa ic hit læs mette. Nu þonne ic openlice ondette þæt on þysse lare þæt sylfe soð scineð þæt us mæg þa gyfe syllan ecre eadignesse ond eces lifes hælo. For þon ic þonne nu lære, cyning, þæt þæt templ ond þa wigbedo, þa ðe we buton wæstmum ænigre nytnisse halgodon, þæt we þa hraþe forleosen ond fyre forbærnan.'

Ono hwæt, he þa, se cyning, openlice ondette þam biscope ond him eallum þæt he wolde fæstlice þam deofolgildum wiðsacan ond Cristes geleafan onfon. Mid þy þe he þa, se cyning, from þam foresprecenan biscope sohte ond ahsode heora halignesse þe heo ær bieodon, hwa ða wigbed ond þa hergas þara deofolgilda, mid heora hegum þe heo ymbsette wæron, heo ærest aidligan ond toweorpan scolde, þa ondsworede he, 'Efne ic! Hwa mæg þa nu, þa þe ic longe mid dysignesse beeode, to bysene oðerre monna gerisenlicor toweorpan þonne ic seolfa, þurh þa snytro þe ic from þam soðan Gode onfeng?'

Ond he þa sona **from him awearp þa idlan dysignesse þe he ær beeode**, ond þone cyning bæd þæt he him wæpen sealde, ond stodhors þæt he meahte on cuman ond deofolgyld toweorpan, for þon **þam biscope heora halignesse ne wæs alyfed** þæt he moste wæpen wegan ne elcor buton on myran ridan.

---

because as much the more eagerly I looked for the very truth of that worship, so much less did I find it. So now I will confess openly that in this teaching there shines the very truth which can grant us the gift of everlasting blessedness and the salvation of everlasting life. And so now I advise in this case, my king, that those temple and altars that we hallowed without increase of any profit, those we should now quickly destroy and burn in fire.'

Lo and behold, he then, the king, openly confessed to the bishop and all of them that he firmly wished to renounce the idols and accept the faith of Christ. When he, then, the king, sought and asked of the aforesaid bishop of the mysteries they had formerly practised, who would be the first to wipe out and cast down the altars and shrines of those idols along with the hedges surrounding them, why then he answered, 'I and nobody else! Who can now cast down those things, which with folly I long practised, more fittingly as an example to men than I myself, with that cleverness which I have received from the true God?'

And straightaway **he cast off the idle folly he practised before**, and asked the king to give him weapons and a stallion that he might go there and cast down the idols, because **it was not permitted that a bishop of their mysteries** might bear arms or ride otherwise

---

from him awearp þa idlan dysignesse þe he ær beeode 'he cast off the idle folly he practised before'. The central phrase, *þa idlan dysignesse*, is based on Bede's *superstitio uanitatis* 'superstition of vanity'. Possibly this use of *uanitas* was Bede's reference, through a Latin pun, to the name of Edwin's gods as *uani* (Old Norse *Vanir*; North 1997: 331).

þam biscope heora halignesse ne wæs alyfed 'it was not permitted that a bishop of their mysteries' etc. The prohibition against riding a stallion fits in with what is known of Ingvi-freyr's cult in Scandinavia, especially in *Hrafnkels saga Freysgoða* 'Saga of Hrafnkell Freyr's Chieftain'; against weapons in festivals, with the cult of Nerthus in northern Germany in Tacitus' *Germania*, ch. 40 (v. 98). Both Freyr and Nerthus belong to the Vanir, an Anglian version of which appears to have figured in Edwin's old religion (North 1997: 330–40).

Þa sealde se cyning him sweord, þæt he hine mid gyrde ond nom his spere on hond ond hleop on þæs cyninges stedan ond to þam deofulgeldum ferde. Þa þæt folc hine þa geseah swa gescyrpedne, þa **wendon** heo þæt he teola ne wiste, ac **þæt he wedde**.

Sona þæs þe he nealehte to þam herige, þa **sceat he mid þy spere**, þæt hit sticode fæste on þam herige, ond wæs swiðe gefeonde þære ongytenesse þæs soðan Godes bigonges. Ond he ða heht his geferan toweorpan ealne þone herig ond þa getimbro, ond forbærnan. Is seo stow gyt æteawed gu þara deofulgilda noht feor east from Eoforwicceastre, begeondan Deorwentan þære ea, ond gen to dæge is nemned Godmundingaham, þær se biscop þurh ðæs soðan Godes inbryrdnesse towearp ond fordyde **þa wigbed þe he seolfa ær gehalgode**.

Þa onfeng Eadwine cyning mid eallum þam æðelingum, his þeode ond mid micle folce Cristes geleafan ond fulwihte bæðe **þy endlyftan geare his rices**.

---

than on a mare. The king then gave him a sword which he girt on himself, and then he took the king's spear in hand, mounted on the king's steed and galloped off to the idols. When the people saw him so equipped, why then **they thought** that he was not in his right mind, but rather **that he had gone mad**.

As soon as he approached the shrine, **he shot with the spear** so that it stuck fast in the shrine, and constantly rejoiced at the knowledge of the worship of the true God. And then he ordered his comrades to cast down all the shrine and its timbered structure and burn them to ashes. That place of the idols can still be seen not far east of York, across the river Derwent, and still to this day the place is called Goodmanham where the bishop, through the inspiration of the true God, cast down and destroyed **the altars which he himself had once hallowed**.

Then King Edwin, together with all the princes, his nation and a multitude of people accepted faith in Christ and the bath of baptism **in the eleventh year of his rule**.

---

wendon þæt he wedde . . . sceat he mid þy spere 'they thought that he had gone mad . . . he shot with the spear'. Thought that he was Woden? OE *Woden* or OIce *Óðinn* means 'infuriated'. For Óðinn casting a spear at the Vanir in an attempt to destroy them, see *The Sibyl's Prophecy*, stanza 24: *Fleygði Óðinn ok í folk of skaut* 'Óðinn cast, and he shot into the mob' (**Gods of the Vikings**). Coifi's resemblance to Óðinn has been noted, but with the suggestion that Goodmanham featured Woden's cult, rather than one he attempted to destroy (Ellis Davidson 1964: 50–1; Mayr-Harting 1991: 26). For a suggestion that Bede knew that it was Bishop Paulinus, as 'Coifi', who impersonated Woden in his anti-Vanir role, in order to convert the locals, see North 1997: 329–30.

þa wigbed þe he seolfa ær gehalgode 'the altars which he himself had once hallowed'. Bede's phrase of the same meaning, *quas ipse sacrauerat aras*, is borrowed from Vergil's description of the shrine into which the dead King Priam falls in Book II of his *Aeneid*. The church in Goodmanham is dedicated to All Saints, or *All Hallows*, though for how long is unknown.

þy endlyftan geare his rices 'in the eleventh year of his rule'. Edwin and his people were converted in 627.

The miracle of Cædmon

As iconic as his story had clearly become by Alfred's time, it is worth noting, closer to the time in which it took place (657–79), that Cædmon's story survives only in Bede's *Historia ecclesiastica*. It is missing where we would have more cause to expect it, in the *Vita Sancti Gregorii Magni* 'The Life of St Gregory the Great', written in Whitby in *c.* 714. The period after the Council of Whitby in 664 was one of doctrinal standardisation in Northumbrian minsters, first with the calculation of Easter, then of the liturgy. Perhaps the use of English for liturgy at this time seemed heretical to the Church outside Whitby. Where the Alfredian version of Cædmon's miracle is concerned, a change has been made to the Latin original in the originally Mercian text. Abbess Hild's advisers do not learn from hearing him, but rather from their transcriptions of the religious poems which the old prodigy recites. The implication of this, if it is not added by the West Saxon scribe, is that Mercians were accustomed to transcribing English poems from performance at the time they made the translation of Bede, whether in Offa's reign or Cenwulf's or later. As above, the text follows that of Oxford, Bodleian Library, MS Tanner 10, from the tenth century. Note that this strain of the Northumbrian version gives *eorðan bearnum* 'sons of earth' where other texts have 'sons of men' (see 'Cædmon's *Hymn*', **Poems of Devotion**).

Colgrave, B., ed. and trans., *Vita Sancti Gregorii Magni: The Earliest Life of Gregory the Great* (Lawrence, KA, 1968)

Haddan, A. W., and W. Stubbs, ed., *Councils and Ecclesiastical Documents relating to Great Britain and Ireland*, 3 vols (Oxford, 1869–71)

Orchard, A., 'Monasteries and courts: Alcuin and Offa', *B&OS* 219–45

Wyly, B. W., 'Cædmon the cowherd and Old English biblical verse', *B&OS* 189–218

In ðeosse abbudissan mynstre wæs sum broðor syndriglice mid godcundre gife gemæred ond geweorðad, for þon he gewunade gerisenlice leoð wyrcan, þa ðe to æfestnisse ond to arfæstnisse belumpen, swa ðætte, **swa hwæt swa he of godcundum stafum** þurh boceras geleornode, þæt he æfter medmiclum

---

In the minster of this abbess was a monk especially famed and celebrated with a divine gift, because he was accustomed to compose honourable songs, those which pertained to religion and piety, so that, **whatever he learned of religious letters** through men of books,

---

swa hwæt swa he of godcundum stafum 'whatever he learned of religious letters' etc. The Englishness of Cædmon's composition is taken for granted by the Alfredian translator. Bede is more amazed. His text says: *quicquid ex diuinis litteris per interpretes disceret, hoc ipse post pusillum uerbis poeticis maxima suauitate et conpunctione conpositis in sua, id est Anglorum, lingua proferret* 'Whatever he learned from divine scriptures through interpreters, this, after a tiny moment, he himself brought forth in poetic words composed with the greatest sweetness and stimulus, in his own, that is the English, language' (Colgrave and Mynors 1991: 414). The wonder for him is that Christian hymns, usually composed in Latin by the literate, have been put together by an illiterate in English. In Alfred's time, the emphasis has changed. Apparently as an afterthought, the translator acknowledges Bede's wonder at vernacular hymns with the word *Engliscgereord* 'English language', but knows these in his own day too well and emphasises the idea of a *scop* 'poet', instead, with the extra verb *geglengde* in a new clause that shows Cædmon's true talent to be *scopgereord* 'poetic language'.

fæce in scopgereorde mid þa mæstan swetnisse ond inbryrdnisse geglengde ond in Engliscgereorde wel geworht forþbrohte. Ond for his leoþsongum monigra monna mod oft to worulde forhogdnisse ond to geþeodnisse þæs heofonlican lifes onbærnde wæron. Ond eac swelce monige oðre æfter him in Ongelþeode ongunnon æfeste leoð wyrcan, ac nænig hwæðre him þæt gelice don ne meahte, for þon he nalæs from monnum ne þurh mon gelæred wæs þæt he þone leoðcræft leornade, ac he wæs godcundlice gefultumod ond þurh Godes gife þone songcræft onfeng. Ond he for ðon **næfre noht leasunge ne idles leoþes wyrcan ne meahte**, ac efne þa an ða ðe to æfestnesse belumpon, ond his þa æfestan tungan gedafenode singan.

Wæs he se mon in weoruldhade geseted oð þa tide þe he wæs gelyfdre ylde, ond næfre nænig leoð geleornade. Ond he forþon oft in gebeorscipe, þonne þær wæs blisse intinga gedemed þæt heo ealle sceolden þurh endebyrdnesse be hearpan singan, þonne he geseah þa hearpan him nealecan, **þonne aras he for scome** from þam symble, ond **ham eode to his huse**. Þa he þæt þa sumre tide dyde, þæt he forlet þæt hus þæs gebeorscipes ond ut wæs

---

this after a moderate interval he adorned in poetic language with the greatest sweetness and inspiration and brought forth well composed in the English language. And because of his songs in verse, the minds of many men were often kindled into contempt of the world and into joining the heavenly life. And likewise, too, many others after him in the English nation began to compose religious songs, and yet none could do this like he could, not at all because he had been taught to learn the art of verse from hearing men or by a man, but because he was divinely aided and received the art of song through God's grace. And because of this **he could never compose fables or idle poetry**, but only those things which pertained to religion, that is if it befitted that pious tongue of his to sing it.

This man, he was established in the secular order until the time he was of advanced age, and never learned one poem. And he for this reason in beer-drinking, when for the cause of bliss it was judged fitting that they should all sing to the lyre in sequence, when he saw the lyre coming near to him, why **then he arose for shame** from the feast, and **went home to his house.** When he did this on one occasion, that he left the house of beer-drinking and was walking out to the shed of the cattle whose herdsmanship was that night commended

---

næfre noht leasunge ne idles leoþes wyrcan ne meahte 'he could never compose fables or idle poetry'. Other monks could, as is certain in the song of the hero Ingeld for which Alcuin castigates 'Bishop Speratus' in 797 (Orchard *B&OS*: 233); and likely in the case of *Beowulf*. In 747, nearly 15 years after Bede wrote this story, the Council of Clofesho, in 747, ordered bishops to ensure *ut sint monasteria juxta vocabulum nominis sui, id est, honesta silentium, quietorum, atque pro Deo laborantium habitacula, et non sint ludicrarum artium receptacula, hoc est, poetarum, citharistarum, musicorum, scurrorum* 'that minsters keep in with the designation of their name, that is, as honorable dwelling-places of quiet men in silence working for God, and not as taverns for the dramatic arts, that is, for poets, harpers, musicians, clowns' (Haddan and Stubbs 1871: III, 369). The *Riddles* of the Exeter Book also come to mind (see **Poems on the Meaning of Life**).

þonne aras he for scome 'then he arose for shame'. The last two words are added by the translator. Shame at not being able to sing, or at the ribald content of what was on offer?

ham eode to his huse 'went home to his house'. For an argument, based on this idea of a 'house', that Cædmon was a former noble in reduced circumstances, but with the necessary experience of heroic lays, see Wyly in *B&OS*.

gongende to neata scipene, þara heord him wæs þære neahte beboden, þa he ða þær in gelimplice tide his leomu on reste gesette ond onslepte, þa stod him sum mon æt þurh swefn ond hine halette ond grette ond hine be his noman nemnde, '**Cedmon, sing me hwæthwugu**.'

Þa ondswarede he, ond cwæð, 'Ne con ic noht singan, ond ic for þon of þeossum gebeorscipe ut eode ond hider gewat, for þon ic naht singan ne cuðe.'

Eft he cwæð, se ðe wið hine sprecende wæs, 'Hwæðre þu meaht me singan.'

Þa cwæð he, 'Hwæt sceal ic singan?'

Cwæð he, 'Sing me frumsceaft.'

Þa he ða þas andsware onfeng, þa ongon he sona singan in herenesse Godes Scyppendes þa fers ond þa word þe he næfre gehyrde, þara endebyrdnes þis is:

> **Nu we sculon herigean** heofonrices Weard,
> Meotodes meahte ond his modgeþanc,
> weorc Wuldorfæder, swa he wundra gehwæs,
> ece Drihten, or onstealde.
> He ærest sceop eorðan bearnum
> heofan to hrofe, halig Scyppend;
> þa middangeard monncynnes Weard,
> ece Drihten, æfter teode
> firum foldan, Frea ælmihtig.

---

to him, as he then set his limbs to rest there at a suitable time and fell asleep, there stood a man before him in his dream, hailed and greeted him and called him by name, '**Cædmon, sing me something**.'

Then he answered, saying, 'I do not know how to sing, and that is why I left this beer-drinking and came here, because I did not know how to sing.'

Again the man said, who was speaking to him, 'Yet you can sing to me.'

Then he said, 'What shall I sing?'

The man said, 'Sing to me of the first creation.'

When he received this answer, then at once he began to sing in his praising of God the Creator those verse-lines and words which he had never heard before, whose sequence this is:

> **Now we must praise** the Guardian of Heaven,
> the might of the Measurer and His purpose,
> the works of the Father of Glory, just as He,
> Eternal Lord, established each miracle's beginning.
> He first created for the children of men
> heaven as a roof, did Holy Creator;
> then the Middle World did mankind's Guardian,
> Eternal Lord, adorn afterwards
> for people of the land, Almighty King.

Cedmon, sing me hwæthwugu 'Cædmon, sing me something'. Cædmon's name is of Welsh origin, as he probably was, witness to a continuing Celtic presence in Northumbria.

Nu we sculon herigean 'Now we must praise' etc. On this poem, see one of the Northumbrian originals (**Poems of Devotion**).

Þa aras he from þam slæpe, ond eal þa þe he slæpende song fæste in gemynde hæfde, ond þam wordum sona monig word in þæt ilce gemet Gode wyrðes songes togeþeodde.

Þa com he on morgenne to þam tungerefan þe his ealdormon wæs, sægde him hwylc gife he onfeng. Ond he hine sona to þære abbudissan gelædde, ond hire þæt cyðde ond sægde. Þa heht heo gesomnian ealle þa gelæredestan men ond þa leorneras, ond him ondweardum het secgan þæt swefn ond þæt leoð singan, þæt ealra heora dome gecoren wære hwæt oððe hwonan þæt cumen wære. Þa wæs him eallum gesegen, swa swa hit wæs, þæt him wære from Drihtne sylfum heofonlic gifu forgifen. Þa rehton heo him ond sægdon sum halig spell ond godcundre lare word, bebudon him þa, gif he meahte, þæt he in swinsunge leoðsonges þæt gehwyrfde. Þa he ða hæfde þa wisan onfongne, þa eode he ham to his huse, ond cwom eft on morgenne, ond þy betstan leoðe geglenged him asong ond ageaf þæt him beboden wæs.

Ða ongan seo abbudisse clyppan ond lufigean þa Godes gife in þam men, ond heo hine þa monade ond lærde þæt he woruldhad anforlete ond munuchad onfenge, ond he þæt wel þafode. Ond heo hine in þæt mynster onfeng mid his godum, ond hine geþeodde to gesomnunge þara Godes þeowa, ond heht hine læran **þæt getæl þæs halgan stæres** on spelles. Ond he eal þa he in gehyrnesse geleornian meahte mid hine gemyndgade, ond swa swa clæne neten eodorcende in þæt sweteste leoð gehwerfde. Ond his

---

Then he arose from the sleep, and all that he sang while sleeping he held fast in mind, and straightaway added to those words many others in the same measure of song worthy to God.

When in the morning he came to the bailiff who was his boss, he told him what gift he had received. And the man led him straight to the abbess, and told and informed her about this. Then she had summoned all the most learned men and the pupils, and had the dream told and the poem sung to them there present that it might be decided in the judgement of all of them what this might be or whence this had come. Then it was seen by all, just for what it was, that to him had a heavenly gift been given from the Lord Himself. Then they narrated and said to him some holy stories and words of divine teaching, commanded him then, if he could, to turn these into the melody of poetry. When he had received the theme, then he went home to his house, and came back in the morning, and sang out and gave up to them what had been commended to him adorned in the best verse.

Then the abbess began to embrace and love the gift of God in that man, and she exhorted him then and instructed him to renounce worldly orders and to accept monastic orders, and he willingly consented to this. And she received him into the minster with his goods, and joined him to the community of the servants of God, and commanded them to teach him **the sequence of sacred history** in narrative form. And everything he could learn in hearing he committed to his memory, and like clean milch-cows chewing the cud, turned

---

þæt getæl þæs halgan stæres 'the sequence of sacred history'. The word *stær* 'history' (also in *þæt stær Genesis* later) is borrowed from Old Irish, witness that the Irish first taught the English to read and write. The Oxford, Bodleian Junius 11 manuscript, which contains the poems *Genesis*, *Exodus*, *Daniel* and *Christ and Satan*, was thought to be a repository of Cædmon's work: unlikely. However, the impulse to collect the material may owe something to Cædmon's continuing story.

song ond his leoð wæron swa wynsumu to gehyranne þætte **seolfan þa his lareowas æt his muðe wreoton ond leornodon**.

Song he ærest be middangeardes gesceape, ond bi fruman moncynnes, ond eal þæt stær Genesis, þæt is seo æreste Moyses booc. Ond eft bi utgonge Israhela folces of Ægypta londe, ond bi ingonge þæs gehatlandes, ond bi oðrum monegum spellum þæs halgan gewrites canones boca, ond bi Cristes menniscnesse, ond bi his þrowunge, ond bi his upastignesse in heofonas, ond bi þæs Halgan Gastes cyme, ond þara apostola lare, ond eft bi þam dæge þæs toweardan domes, ond bi fyrhtu þæs tintreglican wiites, ond bi swetnesse þæs heofonlecan rices, he monig leoð geworhte. Ond swelce eac oðer monig be þæm godcundan fremsumnessum ond domum he geworhte. In eallum þam he geornelice gemde þæt he men atuge from synna lufan ond mandæda, ond to lufan ond to geornfulnesse awehte godra dæda, for þon he wæs se mon swiþe æfest ond regollecum þeodscipum eaðmodlice underþeoded. Ond wið þam þa ðe in oðre wisan don woldon, he wæs mid welme micelre ellenwodnisse onbærned. Ond he for ðon fægre ende his lif betynde ond geendade.

For þon þa ðære tide nealæcte his gewitenesse ond forðfore, þa wæs he feowertynum dagum ær þæt he wæs lichomlicre untrymnesse þrycced ond hefgad, hwæðre to þon gemetlice þæt he ealle þa tid meahte ge sprecan ge gongan. Wæs þær in neaweste untrumra monna hus, in þam heora þeaw wæs þæt heo þa untruman ond þa ðe æt forðfore wæron in lædan sceoldon,

---

it into the sweetest poetry. And his songs and his poems were so winsome to hear that **his very teachers wrote it down from his mouth and learned it**.

First he sang about the shaping of the Middle World, and of mankind's beginning, and all the history of Genesis, that is the first book of Moses. And then about the exodus of the people of Israel from Egypt, and about their entry into the promised land, and about many other stories of the holy writ of the canonical Bible, and about Christ's Incarnation, and about His Passion and His Ascension into heaven, and about the coming of the Holy Ghost, and about the teaching of the Apostles, and later about the day of the future Judgement, and about the fear of tormenting punishment, and about the sweetness of the heavenly kingdom, about these things he composed many poems. And likewise, many others about the divine rewards and judgements he composed. In all these, he eagerly heeded that he should draw men away from the love of sin and wicked deeds, because this man was very pious and humbly subjected himself to the discipline of the rule. And towards those who would do things in a different manner, he was kindled with a wave of great zeal. And so he concluded and ended his life with a beautiful end.

And so when time drew near to his passing and departure, by then he had been 14 days earlier afflicted and weighed with bodily infirmity, yet moderately in so far as all that time he could both talk and walk. Nearby to there was a house for infirm people, into which it was their custom that they would lead the infirm and those who were near their departure, and serve them there together. So he asked his servant, on the eve of the night that he was

---

seolfan þa his lareowas æt his muðe wreoton ond leornodon 'his very teachers wrote it down from his mouth and learned it'. Bede has the scholars' memorisation of Cædmon's verse only. The translator adds writing to this process. Evidently the poetic culture had changed since 658–79.

ond him þær ætsomne þegnian. Þa bæd he his þegn, on æfenne þære neahte þe he of worulde gongende wæs, þæt he in þam huse him stowe gegearwode þæt he gerestan meahte. Þa wundrode se þegn for hwon he ðæs bæde, for þon him þuhte þæt his forðfor swa neah ne wære; dyde hwæðre swa swa he cwæð ond bibead. Ond mid þy he ða þær on reste eode, ond he gefeonde mode sumu þing mid him sprecende ætgædere ond gleowiende wæs, þe þær ær inne wæron, þa wæs ofer middeneaht þæt he frægn hwæðer heo ænig husl inne hæfdon. Þa ondswarodon heo ond cwædon, 'Hwylc þearf is ðe husles? Ne þinre forþfore swa neah is, nu þu þus rotlice ond þus glædlice to us sprecende eart.'

Cwæð he eft, 'Berað me husl to.'

Þa he hit þa on honda hæfde, þa frægn he hwæþer heo ealle smolt mod ond buton eallum incan bliðe to him hæfdon. Þa ondswaredon hy ealle, ond cwædon þæt heo nænigne incan to him wiston, ac heo ealle swiðe bliðemode wæron. Ond heo wrixendlice hine bædon þæt he him eallum bliðe wære. Þa ondswarade he, ond cwæð, 'Mine broðor, mine þa leofan, ic eom swiðe bliðemod to eow ond to eallum Godes monnum.' Ond swa wæs hine getrymmende mid þy heofonlecan wegneste, ond him oðres lifes ingong gegearwode.

Þa gyt he frægn, hu neah þære tide wære þætte þa broðor arisan scolden ond Godes lof ræran ond heora uhtsong singan. Þa ondswaredon heo, 'Nis hit feor to þon.'

Cwæð he, 'Teala, wuton we wel þære tide bidan.' Ond þa him gebæd, ond hine gesegnode mid Cristes rodetacne, ond his heafod onhylde to þam bolstre, ond medmicel fæc onslepte, ond swa mid stilnesse his lif geendade.

---

leaving the world, to prepare a place in that house that he might rest. Then the servant was amazed why he asked this, because it seemed to him that his departure was not so near; he did, however, as Cædmon said and commanded. And while he went to his rest there, and in that with rejoicing heart he was speaking some things and making merry together with them who were already in there, why then, it was after midnight that he asked whether they had any of the Eucharist inside. They answered then and said, 'What need do you have for the Eucharist? It is not so near to your departure, now you are speaking so cheerfully and so gladly to us.'

He said again, 'Bring me the Eucharist.'

When he held this in his hand, he asked whether they all had serene minds and were cheerful towards him without any grudge. Then they all answered, saying that they knew of no grudge against him, but were all very contented. And they in turn asked him that he should be happy with all of them. Then he answered, and said, 'My dear brothers, I am very contented with you and all men of God.' And so he stayed strengthening himself with provisions for the heavenly road, while he prepared himself for entry into the next life.

Still yet he asked how near it was to the hour that the brothers should arise and raise up God's praise and sing their matins. They answered then, 'It is not far to that time.'

He said, 'Well, let us properly wait for that hour.' And then made his prayer, and blessed himself with the sign of Christ's Rood, and inclined his head to the pillow, and in a modest interval fell asleep, and thus in stillness did he end his life.

Ond swa wæs geworden þætte swa swa he hluttre mode ond bilwiltre ond smyltre wilsumnesse Drihtne þeode, þæt he eac swylce swa smylte deaðe middangeard wæs forlætende, ond to his gesihðe becwom. Ond seo tunge, þe swa monig halwende word in þæs Scyppendes lof gesette, he ða swelce eac þa ytmæstan word in his herenisse, hine seolfne segniende ond his gast in his honda bebeodende, betynde. Eac swelce þæt is gesegen þæt he wære **gewis his seolfes forðfore**, of þam þe we nu secgan hyrdon.

And so it came to pass that, just as he served the Lord with pure heart and with an innocent and serene devotion, he was leaving the Middle World with a death just as serene, and came into His sight. And with the tongue which composed so many salutary words in the Creator's honour, he concluded likewise the very last words in His praise, blessing himself and commending his spirit into His hands. Likewise is it also clear that he was **wise to the time of his own departure**, from what we have now heard tell.

---

gewis his seolfes forðfore 'wise to the time of his own departure'. This makes Cædmon like a saint, although he has not become one.

VIKING WARS

⁂

VIKING WARS

⁂

Read to its full extent, with dates provided to lead the way, this section gives both a literary and historical tour through the two Viking Ages of Anglo-Saxon England. In the Custom Version we begin with the *Anglo-Saxon Chronicle*, with the success of Alfred's later wars against the Danes in 892–6. Thereafter another set of annals, suppressed by King Edward the Elder of the West Saxons, shows the advance through the Danelaw of his sister Æthelflæd, Lady of the Mercians (and possible model for *Judith* in the devotional poem of that name). The texts in this volume are mostly poems, heroic and eulogising works on the wars of the mid to late tenth century. Here both perspectives of Viking and Anglo-Saxon are revealed respectively through, on one side, Egill and the skalds of King Eiríkr Bloodaxe of York, and on the other, the occasional poems of the *Chronicle* which try to mark the years with West Saxon victories. The reign of Edgar the Peaceable may be juxtaposed in the Custom Version with a eulogy on King Haraldr Greycloak, son of Bloodaxe, to show the great differences between the cultures at this time. Where these cultures collided in 991, a text of *The Battle of Maldon* will hopefully bring this poem back to a widespread readership after two decades of abeyance, as a memorial whose momentum builds slowly to a crescendo at (or near) the end, where the doomed men of Essex, not their Norwegian victors, fight with the fury of berserks. A final selection of *Chronicle* and Skaldic eulogies in the Custom Version will enlarge on the role of Sveinn Forkbeard and Cnut, his half-Polish son, in and after their successful conquest of England in 1016. If a new country was being created in all this process of war and negotiation, the poems and prose of this section will show it.

General bibliography

Carroll, J., 'Viking wars and *The Anglo-Saxon Chronicle*', *B&OS* 301–23

Frank, R., 'Cnut and his skalds', in Rumble (1994), 106–24

Keynes, S. D., and M. Lapidge, trans., with introduction and notes, *Alfred the Great: Asser's 'Life of King Alfred' and Other Contemporary Sources* (Harmondsworth, 1983)

Keynes, S. D., 'Cnut's earls', in Rumble (1994), 43–88

North, R., 'Notes on the Old Norse Language', *B&OS* 323–9

Poole, R., 'Skaldic verse and Anglo-Saxon history: some aspects of the period 1009–16', *Speculum* 62 (1987), 265–98, esp. 269–80

Roesdahl, E., *The Vikings*, trans. S. M. Margesson and K. Williams, 2nd ed. (Harmondsworth, 1998)

Rumble, A. R., ed., *The Reign of Cnut: King of England, Denmark and Norway* (London and New York, 1994)

Scragg, D. G., ed., *The Battle of Maldon AD 991* (Oxford, 1991)

Swanton, M. J., trans., *The Anglo-Saxon Chronicle* (London, 1996)

Whitelock, D., ed. and trans., *English Historical Documents, vol. I: c. 500–1042* (London, 1955)

Anglo-Saxon Chronicle

⁂

In the early 880s, Ealdorman Æthelred of western (free) Mercia acknowledged Alfred as overlord. In 886 Alfred captured London and passed it into the care of Æthelred, then gave him his daughter Æthelflæd in marriage. These were the first steps in the tenth-century 'reconquest' of Scandinavian England, for thereupon all English people submitted to Alfred, who then negotiated with Guthrum, now king of East Anglia, for the Watling Street boundary with the Danelaw. Alfred's measures were tested in 892, when the Viking army returned from an extended campaign in northern France (879–91). They had failed to take Paris and in a generation some of their number would be granted lands on the peninsula later known as *Normandia*. It was at about this time that the *Chronicle* itself was first circulated, perhaps as a reflection of the war that now opened up and would last for nearly five years.

Bately, J., ed., *The Anglo-Saxon Chronicle: MS A*, The Anglo-Saxon Chronicle: A Collaborative Edition 3 (Cambridge, 1986)

Irvine, S., ed., *The Anglo-Saxon Chronicle: MS E*, The Anglo-Saxon Chronicle: A Collaborative Edition 7 (Cambridge, 2004)

The Battle of Brunanburh

937

Not long before she died in 918, Æthelflæd, Lady of the Mercians, secured pledges from the Vikings ruling York. These were Norwegians from the colony in Ireland, led by Ragnald Sigtryggsson, a grandson of of Ívarr (Ingvarr), who is known as 'Hinguar' in Ælfric's *Life of St Edmund* (see **Writers of the Benedictine Reform**), the son of Ragnarr (see *The Eulogy on Ragnarr*, **Heroic Poems** and **Gods of the Vikings**). Ragnald's Hiberno-Norse brethren had escaped Ireland after the Irish drove them out of Dubin in 902. Ragnald's brother Sigtryggr, who had ruled Dublin, regained this town in 919, and became king of York as well, on Ragnald's death in 920. Sigtryggr Sigtryggsson was known as *caoch* 'One-Eye'. The English called him Sihtric, baptising him into the faith in 925 when King Æthelstan, Æthelflæd's nephew, married him to a sister in Tamworth. Sihtric died in 927, possibly having renounced Christianity.

Sihtric's brother Guthrith then took over Dublin, and his son Anlaf (Óláfr) after him. But Dublin was not enough for Anlaf Guthfrithson, who sought to recover York for the Vikings of Ireland. In 937 Anlaf led an invasion of England across the Irish Sea. His army was annihilated by King Æthelstan and his brothers in a battle that probably took place at Bromborough in Cheshire, close to the Wirral where the Vikings would have landed. This battle is related not only in the *Chronicle*, as here, but also in *Egils saga Skalla-Grímssonar* 'Egill's Saga', chs. 50–5, in a more fabulous account which must have reached Iceland if not from Egill himself, who took part, then from Ireland (see **Sagas of Icelanders**). The saga gives most of the glory to Egill and his brother Þórólfr, while portraying the English as cunning equivocators. Anlaf survives there as Óláfr *inn rauði* 'the Red' of the Scots.

Campbell, A., ed., *The Battle of Brunanburh* (London, 1938)

Dodgson, J. McN., *The Place Names of Cheshire*, English Place-Name Society 4 (Cambridge, 1972)

Hart, C., *The Danelaw* (London, 1992)

Orton, P., 'On the transmission and phonology of *The Battle of Maldon*', *Leeds Studies in English* new series 25 (1994), 1–27

Smith, A. H., 'The site of the Battle of *Brunanburh*', *London Mediæval Studies* 1 (1937), 56–9

Smyth, A. P., *Scandinavian York and Dublin*, 2 vols (Dublin, 1987), II, 31–106

Swanton, M. J., trans., *The Anglo-Saxon Chronicle* (London, 1996)

Townend, M., 'Whatever happened to York Viking poetry? Memory, tradition and the transmission of Skaldic verse', *Saga-Book of the Viking Society* 27 (2003), 48–90

937 (A).

Her Æþelstan cyning, eorla dryhten,
beorna beahgifa, and his broþor eac,
Eadmund æþeling, ealdorlangne tir
geslogon æt sæcce sweorda ecgum
ymbe Brunanburh. Bordweal clufan,
heowan heaþolinde hamora lafan,
afaran Eadweardes, swa him geæþele wæs
from cneomægum, þæt hi æt campe oft
wiþ laþra gehwæne land ealgodon,

---

937 (A).

Here King Æthelstan, lord of earls,
warrior's ring-giver, and his brother too,
Prince Edmund, won lifelong nobility
by fighting with sword-blades in conflict
around Bromborough. Edward's offspring
split the shield-wall, hacked hammer-relics
through battle-wood, as was natural to them
from kinsmen's knee, so that often in the field
did they defend their land, hoards and homes

---

1 *eorla dryhten* 'lord of earls'. In 937 it appears that OE *eorl* 'noble warrior' now connotes the rank of OE *ealdorman*, through contact with Old Scandinavian *iarl*, Modern English 'earl'.

3 On the death of Æthelstan on 27 October 941, his brother Edmund became king, ruling until 946.

5 *ymbe Brunanburh* 'around Bromborough'. The site of *Brunanburh* has long been treated as unidentifiable (Smith 1937: 43–80; Smyth 1987: II, 31–88), or placed in Lincolnshire (the Kesteven Bourne; Hart 1992: 515–20), but it seems more sensible, given the proximity to the Wirral and the Irish Sea from whence Anlaf emerged, that the place is Bromborough in Cheshire (the names are confirmed as identical in Dodgson 1972: 237–40).

6 *hamora lafan* 'hammer-relics'. An ironic kenning for sword-blades, which hammers leave new in the smithy.

7–8 *him geæþele from cneomægum* 'natural to them from kinsmen's knee'. The *Chronicle* tells us that West Saxon royals had been fighting Vikings since the time of Æthelstan's great-grandfather, Æthelwulf (ruled 839–58).

hord and hamas. Hettend crungun,
Sceotta leoda and scipflotan
fæge feollan, feld dænnede
secga swate siðþan sunne up
on morgentid, mære tungol,
glad ofer grundas, Godes condel beorht,
eces Drihtnes, oð sio æþele gesceaft
sah to setle. Þær læg secg mænig
garum ageted, guma norþerna
ofer scild scoten, swilce Scittisc eac,
werig, wiges sæd. Wesseaxe forð
ondlongne dæg eorodcistum
on last legdun laþum þeodum,
heowan herefleman hindan þearle
mecum mylenscearpan. Myrce ne wyrndon
heardes hondplegan hæleþa nanum
þæra þe mid Anlafe ofer æra gebland

---

against all foes. Invaders perished,
men of Ireland and sea-borne marines
fell doomed, the field was darkening
with the blood of men when upwards the sun
in morning hour, the renowned star,
glided across the landscape, bright candle
of God, the eternal Lord, until the noble one
sank down to rest. There lay many a man
sacrificed by spear, many northerners
shot through their shields, and Irish too
weary and combat-sated. West Saxons onwards
the livelong day in cavalry squadrons
laid into the rear of hateful nations,
hacked hard from aft the fleeing raiders
with mill-ground blades. No Mercians withheld
harsh hand-play to any hero there
of them with Anlaf who over waves' mingling

---

12 *feld dænnede* 'the field was darkening'. The meaning of the verb is not agreed, and *dynede* 'dinned' may lie behind this (Campbell 1938).

13–17 The sun-image suggests God's approval for Æthelstan's slaughter of his Hiberno-Norse invaders.

18 *garum ageted* 'sacrificed by spear'. The poet applies this phrase to dead Norse heathens, while the verb *agetan* 'to cut open' has the sinister implication of ritual, as in cognate Norse *Gautr*, a name for Óðinn who sacrifices himself to himself in *Sayings of the High One*, stanza 138 (**Gods of the Vikings**).

24 Mercians, retaining a regional kind of status here, are given second place to West Saxons on line 20, although *Brunanburh*, certainly never in Wessex, may have been on Mercian territory (see note to line 5).

on lides bosme land gesohtun,
fæge to gefeohte. Fife lægun
on þam campstede cyningas giunge,
sweordum aswefede, swilce seofene eac
eorlas Anlafes, unrim heriges
flotan and Sceotta. Þær geflemed wearð
Norðmanna bregu, nede gebeded,
to lides stefne litle weorode.
Cread cnear on flot, cyning ut gewat
on fealene flod, feorh generede.
Swilce þær eac se froda mid fleame com
on his cyþþe norð, Costontinus,
har hilderinc, hreman ne þorfte
mæca gemanan. He wæs his mæga sceard,
freonda gefylled on folcstede,
beslagen æt sæcce, and his sunu forlet
on wælstowe wundun forgrunden
giungne æt guðe. Gelpan ne þorfte
beorn blandenfeax bilgeslehtes,
eald inwidda, ne Anlaf þy ma!

---

on ocean's bosom did seek the shore,
doomed to the fight. Bodies five, there lay
on that battlefield, of young kings
given sleep with swords, as well as seven
earls of Anlaf, and countless raiders,
of Vikings and Irish. Put to flight there was
the chief of Northmen, his need requesting his
presence at his vessel's stem and few men with him.
The tub was launched, the king sailed out
on fallow flood, he saved his life.
Likewise, too, experienced Constantine
in flight escaped northwards to his clan,
hoary-haired soldier, he need not crow
of clanging blades. He was sheared of kinsmen,
his friends felled on people's meeting ground,
slain around him in strife, while his son he lost
on the killing field, wounds having mangled
the young man in war. No boasting for that
grey-haired warrior of axe-slaughter,
crafty old fellow, any less than with Anlaf!

---

35 *cnear* 'tub'. This meaning for *cnear*, a Norse loanword, is a literary guess. Later OIce *knǫrr* refers to a high-sided ocean-going vessel suitable for traffic in the western Atlantic. The poet also uses *nægledcnearrum* 'nailed merchantmen' on line 53, as if to emphasise the Scandinavian aspect of Anlaf's rout.

Mid heora herelafum   hlehhan ne þorftun
þæt heo beaduweorca   beteran wurdun
on campstede   cumbolgehnastes,
garmittinge,   gumena gemotes,
wæpengewrixles,   þæs hi on wælfelda
wiþ Eadweardes   afaran plegodan.
Gewitan him þa Norþmen   *næ*gledcnearrum,
dreorig daraða laf,   on Dinges mere
ofer deop wæter   Difelin secan,
eft Iraland,   æwiscmode.
Swilce þa gebroþer   begen ætsamne,
cyning and æþeling,   cyþþe sohton,
Wesseaxena land,   wiges hremige,
letan him behindan   hræw bryttian
saluwigpadan,   þone sweartan hræfn,
hyrnednebban,   and þane hasewanpadan,
earn æftan hwit,   æses brucan,
grædigne guðhafoc   and þæt græge deor,
wulf on wealde.   Ne wearð wæl mare

With their remains of raiding, no need for them
to laugh of doing better in the deeds of war
on the battleground with such banner-clashing,
spears' meeting, men's assembly,
weapons' exchange as they on death's field
against the heirs of Edward played.
Northmen moved out in nailed merchantmen,
lances' bleeding leftovers, on Ding's Mere,
over watery deeps Dublin to seek,
Ireland once more, dejected in heart.
Leaving likewise, both brothers together,
king and prince, sought their country,
land of West Saxons, in combat exultant,
left behind them to share out the dead
old dusky-coat the black raven,
the curved of beak, and the tawny-coated
white-reared eagle to use the carrion,
the greedy war-hawk and grey beast,
the wolf in woodland. No greater slaughter

---

54 *Dinges mere* is unidentified, but seems to mean waters off the Wirral.

60–5 The birds and beast of battle are produced here as if the poet were shopping for them. They are coloured in with more skill in *Judith* (which just may be from *c.* 920), lines 205–12 (see **Poems of Devotion**), and in *The Battle of Maldon* (*c.* 991), lines 106–7.

on þis eiglande æfre gieta
folces gefylled beforan þissum
sweordes ecgum, þæs þe us secgað bec,
ealde uðwitan, siþþan eastan hider
Engle and Seaxe up becoman,
ofer brad brimu Brytene sohtan,
wlance wigsmiþas, Wealas ofercoman,
eorlas arhwate eard begeatan.

---

on this island ever yet happened,
no folk-felling greater before this day
with edge of sword from what books, old
sages, tell us, since from east to here
Angles and Saxons came sailing up,
over broad brim sought Britain,
proud war-smiths, overcame the Welsh,
earls keen for honour got their homeland.

Edmund's Capture of the Five Boroughs

942

The Battle of Brunanburh shows that Anlaf got away. The truth of what happened next is that he returned to England with an army of Hiberno-Norwegians two years later and took not only York in 939 but also the eastern Midlands in 940. Æthelstan's younger half-brother Edmund made peace with Anlaf in 940 after retaking the Five Boroughs. The poem below is found in all versions of the *Chronicle* except the Peterborough (E) and Canterbury (F) versions.

Mawer, A., 'The redemption of the Five Boroughs', *English Historical Review* 38 (1923), 551–7

Swanton, M. J., trans., *The Anglo-Saxon Chronicle* (London, 1996)

68–9 *bec, ealde uðwitan* 'books, old sages'. Probably a reference to Bede's *Ecclesiastical History of the English People*, rather than the *Chronicle* entry for year 449 which comes from Bede (see **The Earliest English Prose**). Gildas' *On the Ruin of Britain* (*c.* 550) is another such book. The poet by this token is a member of the clergy, one asked to fill the record with a commemorative poem.

70–3 The irony in these lines, that the Anglo-Saxons were themselves once invaders, is doubtless clear but uninteresting to this poet, who seeks to establish the West Saxons as kings of Britain by God-given right.

942 (A).

Her Eadmund cyning, Engla þeoden,
maga mundbora, Myrce geeode,
dyre dædfruma, swa Dor scadeþ,
Hwitanwyllesgeat and Humbra ea,
brada brimstream, burga fife,
Ligoraceaster and Lin[d]cylene
and Snotingaham, swylce Stanford
eac Deoraby. Dæne wæran ær
under Norðmannum nyde gebegde
on hæþenra hæfteclommum
lange þraga oþ hie alysde eft
for his weorþscipe wiggendra hleo,
afera Eadweardes, Eadmund cyning.

---

942 (A).

Here King Edmund, lord of the English,
protector of his kin, conquered Mercia,
beloved benefactor, as far as Dore divides,
to Whitwell Gap and the Humber River,
broad stream of sea, five boroughs,
Leicester and Lincoln
and Nottingham, as well as Stamford
and Derby. The Danes were earlier
under Norwegians, subjected by force
within the captive fetters of heathens
for a long time, until them he redeemed
for honour's sake, did the warrior-shield
offspring of Edward, Edmund king.

---

11 *oþ hie alysde eft* 'until them he redeemed'. The poet sails close to the wind. His language is out of the story of Jesus' harrowing of hell, as may be seen in *He us onlysde* 'he released us' in *The Dream of the Rood*, line 46. The anglicised Danes of the Boroughs fit in nicely with noble souls shackled in hell.

The English poems of Egill Skalla-Grímsson

*

Egill is a major figure in any anthology of Norse occasional poems or sagas, and his story must be considered by any historians of the English tenth century. According to the thirteenth-century *Egils saga Skalla-Grímssonar* 'Egill's Saga', Egill visited England twice, once to serve King Aðalsteinn and again, thanks to Gunnhildr's magic, when he encountered his mortal enemy King Eiríkr in York. In the first episode, Egill and his older brother Þórólfr are said to fight as mercenaries for King Æthelstan in his battle against King Óláfr of Scotland. In this likely version of the *Battle of Brunanburh*, at a place called *Vinheiðr*, Egill leads the best English troops and Þórólfr a division of Norwegians. The details of the saga are muddled by long transmission, for 'King Óláfr' here is a blend of Anlaf Guthfrithson and King Constantine of the Scots. The saga's account of negotiations between Óláfr and Aðalsteinn (i.e. Æthelstan) are a fiction. However, Scandinavian tradition has it that Hákon Haraldsson, later king of Norway (946–61), was fostered by Æthelstan in his court. He had the nickname *Aðalsteinsfóstri* ('Æthelstan's foster-son'). And Æthelstan had already married off his sister to King Sihtric of Dublin. The second story of Egill in England is equally fabulous, centring on Queen Gunnhildr with the alacrity of a misogynist Saint's Life. Eiríkr in comparison is made to withdraw into the shadows, perhaps as a shadow of his former self, and the true hero is Arinbjǫrn, who really saves Egill's life.

Hines, J., 'Scandinavian English: a Creole in context', in *Language Contact in the British Isles*, ed. P. S. Ureland and G. Broderick, Linguistische Arbeiten 238 (Tübingen, 1991), 403–27

Jesch, J., 'Skaldic verse in Scandinavian England', in *Vikings and the Danelaw: Select Papers from the Proceedings of the Thirteenth Viking Congress, Nottingham and York, 21–30 August 1997*, ed. J. Graham-Campbell, R. Hall, J. Jesch and D. N. Parsons (Oxford, 2001), 313–25

Sigurður Nordal, ed., *Egils saga Skalla-Grímssonar*, ÍF 2 (Reykjavík, 1933)

Eulogy on Æthelstan
Aðalsteinsdrápa

c. 937

Not much survives from this eulogy, for it is likely that the stanza and refrain quoted in *Egill's Saga* were extracted from the beginning of a longer poem which has not survived. Whether or not this poem was genuinely Egill's is the question. Townend takes it as Egill's (2002: 153), also Jesch (1996: 127–9), both with more circumspection than Turville-Petre (1976: 21). The opening epithet for King Æthelstan, *foldgnárr*, is unparalleled and not fully understood, but as the verse as a whole celebrates the king as a conquerer of imperial style, it seems appropriate to trust the saga on the *Brunanburh* (or Vinheiðr) context too. The reference to Æthelstan's kindred is interesting, as in England Ælle was king either of York or of Sussex. The former seems more likely, as a pointer to King Æthelstan's control of York. The number of fallen princes, three, is too easily made up from the tally of dead in *The Battle of Brunanburh*, which allows for five kings and seven earls, although Constantine's son might be one of the three. If Egill's refrain veers close to the heathen formulation for a king as the husband of his land, still there is no reference to heathen gods, whether as patrons or within kennings. That too would confirm the verse as genuine for England.

Jesch, J., 'Norse historical traditions and the *Historia Gruffud vab Kenan*: Magnús berfœttr and Haraldr hárfagri', in *Gruffudd ap Cynan: A Collaborative Biography*, ed. K. L. Maund (London, 1996), 117–47

Townend, M., *Language and History in Viking Age England: Linguistic Relations between Speakers of Old Norse and Old English*, Studies in the Early Middle Ages 6 (Turnhout, 2002)

Turville-Petre, E. O. G., *Scaldic Poetry* (Oxford, 1976)

Nú hefr foldgnárr fellda (fellr Jǫrð und nið Ellu)
hjaldrsnerrandi, harra hǫfuðbaðmr, þría jǫfra;
Aðalsteinn of vann annat, alts lægra kynfrægjum
(hér sverjum þess, hyrjar hrannbrjótr) konungmanni. (ÍF 2.21)

Now has the landscape's onslaught-stirring overtowerer (Earth falls
To Ælle's kinsman), O head-beam of warlords, felled three princes;
Æthelstan has done more, everything is lower than the kin-famed
(We swear this now, O breaker of wave-flame) man of royal birth.

'Landscape's onslaught-stirring overtowerer': England's warlord. 'Ælle's kinsman': (claimed) relative of King Ælle of Northumbria (d. 867). 'Head-beam of warlords': overlord. 'Wave-flame': gold, whose 'breaker' is a king.

Refrain Nú liggr hæst und hraustum hreinbraut Aðalsteini.

Now lies the highest deer-road beneath valiant Æthelstan!

'Deer-road': mountain.

Head-Ransom
Hǫfuðlausn

c. 952

King Æthelstan believed in royal alliances. He married off his sister to Sihtric of Dublin in 925, and he fostered young foreign nobles in his court, whose number included the infant Hákon, son of King Haraldr Finehair of Norway. Hákon was brought up an English Christian. In *c.* 945 he enlisted the support of King Edmund, Æthelstan's younger half-brother, to claim the throne of Norway from its failing ruler, his own older half-brother Eiríkr Bloodaxe Haraldsson. This mission from England was successful and Eiríkr was forced out, to England eventually where King Edmund made him ruler of York. He was confirmed as king there by Edmund's brother King Eadred in 947 and again in 948. The dates are disputed, with one scholar believing that Eiríkr was not then made king (Sawyer 1995). At any rate, in 949 Eadred undertook a punitive raid on the surrounding country, believing that the Northumbrians had betrayed him for Eiríkr. The unlucky Norwegian attacked Eadred's returning baggage train at

Castleford, on the river Aire. To stop Eadred reinvading, the Northumbrians ungratefully drove out Eiríkr and received as king, instead, another Viking from the Norse colony in Ireland.

This was the Hiberno-Norse king of Dublin, Óláfr *Cuaran* 'Sandal', who was the son of Sihtric and cousin of the same Anlaf Guthfrithson who had returned to England to take York in 939. Óláfr Cuaran was king of both York (949–52) and Dublin (until 980). He had Eiríkr's raids to contend with until 952, when Eiríkr drove him out (Townend 2003: 78–9). Eiríkr now held on to York until 954, when Óláfr chased him out to the moors and killed him at Stainmoor on the Yorkshire border with Westmorland. Although King Eadred took control of York after these events, Óláfr Cuaran was not forgotten. This Óláfr was the father of Sigtryggr *silkiskeggr* 'Silkbeard' who ruled Dublin after him, and he seems to have lived on in English folklore as Havelok the Dane. 954 was also the year when King Eadred summoned Wulfstan, Archbishop of York (pallium 931–56) from his diocese to the south-west of England. The timing of the Archbishop's house arrest, if that is what it was, suggests that he had collaborated with Eiríkr. The literary effects of this alliance, if that is what it was, may be seen in the *Head-Ransom* of the Icelander Egill Skalla-Grímsson. As a veteran of *Brunanburh* and guest at King Æthelstan's court, Egill seems to have composed the *Head-Ransom* as a result of visiting Eiríkr in York, either in his first reign in 947–9 or in his second in 952–4.

Egill's Saga, ch. 60, assigns this poem to Egill, with the story that he composed it for King Eiríkr to save his own life. The *Head-Ransom* survives in two fourteenth-century manuscripts, but not in the main text of *Egill's Saga*, Möðruvallabók. One text is from the Wolfenbüttel manuscript of the saga, and the other from a fragment (ε) with later copies (Hines 1995: 85–6). The saga tells us that Egill was drawn to York from Iceland by the magic of Queen Gunnhildr, who had a score to settle. Some years before, Egill had killed her followers and her 12-year-old son, and had cursed her and Eiríkr in such a way that they were driven out of Norway (by Hákon the Good, foster-son of King Æthelstan in *c.* 945) to Orkney and then England, where Eiríkr was allowed to rule York as a puppet for Kings Edmund and Eadred, half-brothers of the now-deceased Æthelstan. Now Gunnhildr wishes to have Egill executed in revenge. Egill's ship is wrecked by the Humber mouth and, without understanding why, he rides to York to turn himself in. When Egill takes refuge with his friend Arinbjǫrn, the king's trusty earl, Arinbjǫrn saves his life by persuading King Eiríkr to accept a *drápa* 'eulogy' in his honour instead. Egill composes this poem overnight at Arinbjǫrn's house and delivers it the next morning. Eiríkr says *Bezta er kvæðit farm flutt* 'the poem was really well presented' (ch. 62) and lets him go.

This story was developed by the author of *Egill's Saga* on the basis of Egill's poem *Arinbjarnarkviða* 'Lay of Arinbjǫrn', which he composed for his friend probably in the late 960s (ch. 78). In stanzas 3–12 of this long Skaldic poem, Egill tells how he received his life from Eiríkr, the Odinic king of York, with Arinbjǫrn's help. Some stanzas may be quoted to show this:

7 Né hamfagrt hǫlðum þótti
skaldfé mitt at skata húsum,
þás úlfgrátt við Yggjar miði
hattar staup at hilmi þák.

Not body-beautiful to those heroes seemed
My scolding fee in the warrior's courts,
When for Terrifier's mead I did receive
A wolf-grey hat-knob from the magnate.

'Scolding fee': poet's fee: reward. 'Terrifier's (Yggr's) mead': poetry. 'Hat-knob': head.

8 Við því tók, en tv*a*u fylgðu
søkk sámleit síðra brúna
ok sá muðr es mína bar
hǫfuðlausn fyr hilmis kné,

I took this in exchange, and with it my two
High-browed Sámi-featured treasures,
And the mouth which carried my
Head-ransom before the magnate's knee,

'Saami- (Lappish) featured': dark; dark 'high-browed treasures': eyes.

9 þars tannfjǫlð með tungu þák
ok hlertjǫld hlustum gǫfguð,
en sú gjǫf golli betri
hróðugs konungs of heitin vas.

Where tooth-multitude with tongue I received
And a listening tent endowed with hearing,
And better than the glorious king's gold
Was it promised this gift would be.

This story does not square exactly with *Head-Ransom* of perhaps a generation earlier. This earlier poem, as well as asking Eiríkr for cash in an obvious way, and barely referring to him as a king, mixes its praise with such potential mockery that the etymological meaning 'scold' appears more applicable to *skald* in the extract above (stanza 7, *skaldfé* 'scolding fee'), than either 'versifier' or 'eulogist'. We thus have to read Egill's own story between the lines. If we do, we might see a different story. Perhaps Egill approached Eiríkr conventionally in 952, expected gold for a new-fangled poem, but so angered the king that he was lucky to have his life. This would have been the humiliation that he embellished with the story which is now the only context for *Head-Ransom.*

The Old English *Rhyming Poem* from the Exeter Book is of Anglian, probably Northumbrian, origin, with some Scandinavian forms, and may even by divided into stanzas of the *Head-Ransom*'s type (see **Poems on the Meaning of Life**). The Norse poem's rhyming metre (*runhenda*) also derives from early medieval Latin poetry. If the *Head-Ransom* is what it is said to be, a work by Egill, this metre reached him through

Old English or possibly Irish. If Egill composed this work in York, where both were spoken, he could have been there long enough to learn the end-rhymes of Latin verse through the medium of similar English poems. It has been suggested that *Head-Ransom* survives with a few other poems through York's connection with Dublin, with a fusion of Norse, English, Irish and Latin culture which created a distinct, but now largely lost, strain of Old Icelandic poetry (Townend 2003). Below, the text is taken from Sigurður Nordal's older edition (1933), based on the Wolfenbüttel Codex, with readings from from Bjarni (ed., 2003), whose edition is based on a fragment (ε).

Bjarni Einarsson, ed., *Egils Saga* (London, 2003)

Hines, J., 'Egill's *Hǫfuðlausn* in time and place', *Saga-Book of the Viking Society* 24 (1995), 83–104

Kershaw, N., ed. and trans., *Anglo-Saxon and Norse Poems* (Cambridge, 1922)

Poole, R. G., *Viking Poems on War and Peace: A Study in Skaldic Namative* (Toronto, 1991)

Poole, R., 'Variants and variability in the text of Egill's *Hǫfuðlausn*', in *The Politics of Editing Medieval Texts*, ed. R. Frank (Toronto, 1993), 65–105

Sawyer, P., 'The last Scandinavian kings of York', *Northern History* 31 (1995), 39–44

Sigurður Nordal, ed., *Egils saga Skalla-Grímssonar*, ÍF 2 (Reykavík, 1933)

Townend, M., 'Whatever happened to York Viking poetry? Memory, tradition and the transmission of Skaldic verse', *Saga-Book of the Viking Society* 27 (2003), 48–90

1

Vestr komk of ver, en ek Viðris ber
munstrandar mar, svás mitt of far;
drók eik á flot við ísabrot;
hlóðk mærðar hlut m*un*knarrar skut.

West I came over fishing grounds, and I carry the sea
Of Wutherer's mind-beach, that's how I sail.
I pulled an oak afloat at the breaking of ice,
Loaded a glory-portion into the mind-vessel's stern.

'Wutherer's mind-beach': Óðinn's breast, whose 'sea' is the Mead of Poetry. 'Pulled an oak afloat': launched my ship. 'Breaking of ice': spring thaw. 'Glory-portion': poem.

2

Buðumk hilmir lǫð, nú ák hróðrs of kvǫð,
berk Óðins mjǫð á Engla bjǫð;
lofat vísa vann, víst mærik þann,
hljóðs biðjum hann, þvít hróðr of fann.

The magnate asked me in, I've a duty to make glory,
I bear Óðinn's mead to tracts of English land.
Praise of the prince I have finished, I surely ennoble him,
Let's ask him for a hearing, for he has found glory.

'Óðinn's mead': poetry.

3 Hygg vísi at, vel sómir þat,
hvé þylja fet, ef þǫgn of get;
flestr maðr of frá, hvat fylkir vá,
en Viðrir sá, hvar valr of lá.

Pay heed, O prince, for well it becomes you,
How I step out the chant if I get a silence.
Most men learned of the war the general fought,
And Wutherer saw where the dead lay.

4 Óx hjǫrva glǫm við hlífar þrǫm,
guðr óx of gram, gramr sótti fram;
þar heyrðisk þá, þaut mækis á,
malmhríðar spá, sús mest of lá.

The crash of swords grew against the shield's edge,
War grew about the prince, the prince advanced.
There then was heard (the sword's river roared)
Tidings of the biggest metal-blizzard overseas.

'Sword's river': blood. 'Tidings of a metal-blizzard': din of battle.

5 Vasa villr staðar vefr darraðar
fyr grams glaðar geirvangs raðar,
þars í blóði i brimils móði
vǫllr of þrumði und véum glumði.

Lance's weft did not veer off course
By the prince's shining spear-plateau rows,
Where the seal's field thundered in rage,
Roared in blood beneath the banners.

'Lance's weft': course of battle. 'Spear-plateau': shield. 'Seal's field': sea.

6 Hné ferð á fit við fleina hnit.
Orðstír of gat Eiríkr at þat.

Fyrd sank to meadow under arrow-strike.
Eiríkr got great renown from that.

7 Fremr munk segja, ef firar þegja;
frágum fleira til frama þeira;
œstu undir við iǫfurs fundi,
brustu brandar við bláar randar.

I shall speak further, if the men keep quiet,
We have heard more of their advancement.
Wounds flowed in the prince's presence,
Swords broke against the black shields.

8 Hlam heinsǫðul við hjálmrǫðul,
beit bengrefill þat vas blóðrefill;
frák at felli fyr fetilsvelli
Óðins eiki í íarnleiki.

Hone-saddle clanged on helmet-sun,
Wound-engraver bit, it used the guttering.
I heard that Óðinn's oaks fell
Before the strap-floe in the play of iron.

'Hone-saddle': thing overlaying the whetstone that sharpens it: blade. 'Helmet-sun': (here) flashing shield. 'Wound-engraver': sword-point. 'Guttering': blood-gutter on the blade: much blood flowed. 'Óðinn's oaks': (Norse as opposed to English) warriors. 'Strap-floe': ice of the sword-strap: sword. 'Play of iron': battle.

9 Þar var eggja at ok odda gnat.
Orðstír of gat Eiríkr at þat.

There was hacking of edges and clashing of spear-points.
Eiríkr got great renown from that.

10 Rauð hilmir hjǫr, þar vas hrafna gǫr,
fleinn sótti fjǫr, flugu dreyrug spjǫr;
ól flagðs gota fárbjóðr Skota,
trað nipt Nara náttverð ara.

Magnate reddened blade, there was a flock of ravens,
Arrow sought out life, the bloody spears flew.
The frightener of Scots fed the giantess' charger,
Nari's sister trod down supper for the eagle.

'Frightener of Scots': Eiríkr. 'Giantess' charger': Hyrrokkin's wolf at Baldr's funeral: wolf. 'Nari's sister': Hel, goddess of the underworld.

11 Flugu hjaldrs tranar of hræs lanar,
órut blóðs vanar benmás granar,
sleit und freki, en oddbreki
gnúði hrafni á hǫfuðstafni.

Battle-cranes flew over corpse-mounds,
Not lacking blood was the wound-gull's beak,
Ravener tore wound, and sword-point surf
Roared at the head-prow of the raven.

'Battle-cranes': ravens. 'Wound-gull': raven. 'Ravener': wolf. 'Sword-point surf': blood. 'Head-prow': beak.

12 Kom gráðar læ at gjalpar skæ;
bauð ulfum hræ Eiríkr of sæ.

Greed's poison came to Gulp's mount,
Eiríkr offered corpses to wolves over the sea.

'Greed's poison': death to greed: satiety. 'Gulp's (Gjálp's) mount': wolf (see above).

13 Lætr snót saka sverð-Freyr vaka,
en skers Haka skíðgarð braka;
brustu broddar, en bitu oddar,
báru hǫrvar af bogum ǫrvar.

The sword-Freyr had them rouse the strife lady
And crack the sea-king's skerry's wood-palisade.
Arrow-points broke, and sword-points bit,
Strings bore the arrows from bows.

'Sword-Freyr': prince of swords: battle. 'Strife lady': valkyrie. 'Sea-king's (Haki's) skerry': sea, whose 'wood' is a ship, whose 'palisade' is shields.

14 Beit fleinn floginn, þá vas friðr loginn,
vas almr dreginn, varð ulfr feginn;
stózk folkhagi við fjǫrlagi,
gall ýbogi at eggtogi.

The flown fluke bit, now the peace was a lie,
Elmwood was drawn, the wolf rejoiced.
The mob-manager withstood the laying down of his life,
Yew-bow twanged at the drawing of edges.

'Elmwood': bow. 'Mob-manager': army-general: king. 'Withstood the laying down of life': defended himself.

15 Jǫfurr sveigði ý, hrutu unda bý;
bauð ulfum hræ Eiríkr of sæ.

The chieftain drew back his yew, wound-bees hummed,
Eiríkr offered corpses to wolves over the sea.

'Wound-bees': arrows.

16 Enn munk vilja fyr verum skilja
skapleik skata, skal mærð hvata:
verpr ábrǫndum, en íǫfurr lǫndum
heldr hornklofi, hanns næstr lofi!

Still I shall be wanting to make known the warrior's
Disposition to his men, the poem must be whipped on.
He throws river-fires, whereas his lands the chieftain
Holds with hornlike cleaver: he comes closest to praise!

'River-fires': gold pieces. 'Hornlike cleaver': beak: Eiríkr holds his lands like a raven his morsels.

17 Brýtr bógvita bjóðr hrammþvita,
munat hodd-dofa hringbrjótr lofa;
mjǫks hǫnum fǫl haukstrandar mǫl,
glaðar flotna fjǫl við Fróða mjǫl.

Paw-stone offerer breaks shoulder-beacon,
Ring-breaker won't praise hoard-torpor.
Hawk-strand's shingle is hugely disposable,
Many sailors are glad to get Fróði's flour.

'Paw-stone': arm-jewel: bracelet, whose 'offerer' is a king: Eiríkr. 'Ring-breaker': the king. 'Hoard-torpor': reluctance to give treasure. 'Hawk-strand': bird's perch: arm, whose 'shingle' is gold. 'Fróði's flour': gold (according to the legend of Fróði's mill, which grinds gold).

18 Verpr broddfleti með baugseti
hjǫrleiks hvati, hanns baugskati;
þróask hér sem hvar, hugat mælik þar,
frétts austr of mar, Eiríks of far.

A sword-tip-bench he throws with his bracelet-seat,
The sword-play's inciter, he's the bracelet prince.
Here as everywhere, I say it's been thought of there,
It's been learned in Norway, Eiríkr's state flourishes.

'Sword-tip-bench': shield. 'Bracelet-seat': arm. 'Sword-play's inciter': chieftain in battle.

19 Jǫfurr hyggi at, hvé ek yrkja fat,
gótt þykkjumk þat, es þǫgn of gat;
hrœrðak munni af munar grunni
Óðins ægi of íǫru fægi.

Let the chieftain pay heed, how I stepped out the work,
I think it was generous that I got some silence.
I stirred in my mouth from my mind's shoal
Óðinn's ocean for the cultivator of battle.

'Mind's shoal': breast.'Óðinn's ocean': the Mead of Poetry: poem.

20 Bark þengils lof á þagnar rof.
Kannk mála mjǫt of manna sjǫt;
ór hlátra ham hróðr berk fyr gram,
svá fór þat fram, at flestr of nam.

A king's praise I bore into the breach of silence,
I know the measure of speech in the seats of men.
From laughter's covering I bear the prince his glory,
It came off so well that most men have heard it.

'Breach of silence': hearing. 'Laughter's covering': the breast.

21 Njóti bauga sem Bragi auga
vagna vára eðr Vili tára.

May he enjoy rings as Bragi the tears, or Vili
The eye, of the warmer of chariots.

'Warmer of chariots': Óðinn, whose 'eye' is wisdom; or Freyja, whose 'tears' are gold nuggets.

Notes

3 *hvé þylja fet* 'How I step out the chant'. This expression for recital is unique to *Head-Ransom*. OIce *feta* 'step' may be used as more than a modal 'to get', if we think of OE *fitt* 'poem'. It is possible that the exceptional end-rhyming metre is what Egill means by 'stepping'.

5 *vefr darraðar* 'Lance's weft'. The battle is described as identical with the weft of fate laid out on the loom. A similar though more gory metaphor may be found in the story of the *Darraðarljóð* 'lance's song' (in *Njáll's Saga*, ch. 156).The date of this poem has been revised to 919 (from 1014), for the victory of King Sigtryggr Caoch of Dublin over Niall Glundubh (originally by Kershaw 1922: 115–17; Poole 1991: 120–5). It has been suggested that Egill based his expression on this poem (Townend 2003: 55–7, 65). The second half of this stanza 5 has the more obscure syntax associated with Skaldic *dróttkvætt* 'court metre'. There is variant text in different manuscripts for *i brimils móði* (Nordal 1933: 187; Hines 1995: 91). What Egill appears to say in all cases is that Eiríkr fought his great battle by the sea. This, however, may have been the river Aire in Yorkshire (see below).

6 *ferð* '*Fyrd*'. This appears to be the oldest case of a loan-translation of OE *fyrd* into the Norse cognate *ferð*. Other cases are in *The Soldiers' Song*, stanza 1 (1016), and Hallvarðr's *Eulogy on King Cnut*, stanza '7' (*c.* 1030). The *Anglo-Saxon Chronicle* (D: Worcester, embodying *The Northumbrian Annals*), s.a. 948, gives 'Yryc' victory in battle at Castleford on the river Aire, against King Eadred's English *fyrde* 'militia', which was returning from a raid on Northumbria, having burned the monastery at Ripon.

7 *til frama þeira* 'of their advancement'. Egill refers to the men of Eiríkr's household, whom he has asked for silence. [*œstu undir* 'Wounds flowed'. This is the text according to the other manuscript tradition (ε). The Wolfenbüttel text has *óxu undir* 'wounds waxed big', but with defective metre for the tenth century, where *wóxu wundir* can only alliterate with *wið*, not with *iǫfurs*.

8 *hjálmrǫðul* 'helmet-sun'. Shield or sword. The other manuscript tradition (ε-group of manuscripts) has *hjaldrrǫðul* 'battle-sun', which is less ambiguously a shield (Hines 1995: 94).

10 *fárbjóðr Skota* 'frightener of Scots'. The *Chronicle*, s.a. 946, says that King Eadred got the Scots' oaths of obedience when he became king in this year; perhaps this was with Eiríkr's help.

11 The flood metaphor for blood in battle is worked into a fine conceit in this stanza, with the raven as a sea-gull cresting the wave.

12 *of sæ* 'over the sea'. As the preposition *of*, here with accusative, indicates motion not place, this cannot mean that Eiríkr had fought this battle back in Norway before coming to York (Hines 1995: 1992). The line means that the water (river, or sea-current) has washed out the dead to foreign shores. Gjálp's name (see Eilífr's *Eulogy on Þórr*, **Gods of the Vikings**) might tell us these are the shores of Norway, where Eiríkr's half-brother, Hákon the Good, might be able to see them (Hákon had helped to drive Eiríkr out of Norway a few years earlier).

13 *Lætr snót saka sverð-Freyr vaka* 'sword-Freyr had them rouse the strife lady'. This conceit appears to be based on the myth of Freyr's coercion of Gerðr in *The Lay of Skírnir* (see **Gods of the Vikings**), as if Eiríkr thereby strengthens his hold on Yorkshire.

14 *þá vas friðr loginn* 'now the peace was a lie'. Presumably the peace that Eadred had made with Wulfstan and Eiríkr in 947. The *Northumbrian Annals* (Chronicle D: Worcester), s.a. 947, say that Archbishop Wulfstan *ond ealle Norðanhymbra witan* 'all the wise men of Northumbria' made this peace, *ond binnan litlan fæce hit eall alugon* 'and within a short time belied it all'. This 'lie' became Eadred's pretext for raiding Northumbria and burning Ripon. In Egill's verse the 'lie' seems to be Eadred's. Whichever way we take this, the implication is that Wulfstan was King Eiríkr's archbishop in York. For Anglo-Scandinavian fusion in the town in this period, see Hines (1995: 101–2), whose most important evidence is the Christian devices on coins that were issued in York under heathen Scandinavian rule as early as the 890s (1991: 417–18).

16 *heldr hornklofi* 'Holds with hornlike cleaver'. The image of Eiríkr holding tracts of Yorkshire like a carrion-scavenger his scraps, coupled with *næstr lofi* 'closest to praise', suggests that his poem is a shade less than respectful.

17 All the more noteworthy, then, that this stanza begs for reward obsessively with five treasure-kennings in four lines. What was the true relationship between Egill and Eiríkr? At any rate, it seems unlikely that Egill, if the poem was his, is here begging for his life. His self-portrait as one of the *flotnar* 'sailors' at Eiríkr's court normalises his status as a visitor from out at sea, from Iceland.

18 *Eiríks of far* 'Eiríkr's state'. As in 'condition': OIce *far* means 'track' or 'style' and not any political state. The resemblance with *svás mitt of far* literally 'my voyage goes thus' in stanza 1 is striking, as if Egill compares the king with himself. For the wealth he apparently hopes to get, Egill flatters Eiríkr with the implication of *austr of mar* 'east over the sea: in Norway' that King Hákon knows his deposed older half-brother is still active in his English exile.

20 *þengils lof* 'A king's praise'. The first and last time Egill refers to Eiríkr as something higher than a chieftain (*skati, vísi, hilmir, jǫfurr*; see Hines 1995: 99–100). [*á þagnar rof* 'into the breach of silence'. It seems clear, even through the stylisation, that Egill expects Eiríkr's York retinue to have scant regard for poetry in general or his poem in particular. The other (ε) manuscript tradition, with half-stanzas in different order and some not in the Wolfenbüttel text, directs Egill's pique here more personally to Eiríkr: *svá hann of nam* 'thus he has heard it' (Bjarni 2003: 112).

21 This stanza, which is only found in the other (ε) manuscript tradition, is obscure but not very flattering. Eiríkr is apparently urged to enjoy rings like Bragi enjoys the gold of Freyja and Vili the wisdom of Óðinn: Bragi because he was a poet (like Egill); and Vili because he seduced his brother Óðinn's wife (see *Loki's Truth-Game*, stanza 26). Bragi ends up dead in Valhǫll (like Eiríkr), and Vili is chased out by his brother (like Eiríkr).

The Lay of Eiríkr Bloodaxe

Eiríksmál

c. 954

*

Eiríkr lost his rule of York to the Hiberno-Norse kings of Dublin. His chief enemies from there were Óláfr (OE *Anlaf*) Cuaran and his son Magnús (OE *Maccus*). The *Anglo-Saxon Chronicle* for 954 says simply that the Northumbrians drove 'Eric' out of York; in the twelfth century, Symeon of Durham says that 'Eiricus' was expelled and killed by Maccus Anlaf's son; and Roger of Wendover adds that he was slain by Earl 'Maccus' in a lonely place called 'Stainmore' (Swanton 1996: 94–5). Perhaps through a misreading of *Stain* in *Stainmore*, in *Ágrip* 'extracts', a brief Norwegian history written in *c.* 1190, Eiríkr is said to have died *í Spaníalandi í útlegu* 'in Spain in outlawry' (ch. 7). The Norwegian history *Fagrskinna* (*c.* 1220) has a longer account, but makes Eiríkr king of Northumbria. In this version, Eiríkr is killed on a grand raid into southern England at the head of five kings, by Óláfr, a tributary king of King Edmund (ch. 8). This is broadly in keeping with the English accounts of how Eiríkr died. The battle at Stainmore on the Yorkshire–Westmorland border, in which Óláfr Cuaran and Magnús Óláfsson killed Eiríkr in 954, is likely to have been an ambush if Eiríkr was truly *í útlegu* 'in outlawry'.

To his widow Gunnhildr, however, Eiríkr's end would not be ignominious. *Fagrskinna* says that she commissioned the poem as a memorial. Although the poem comes without title, the name *Eiríksmál* 'Lay of Eiríkr' is provided in the quotation of the first seven long lines of this poem in Snorri's *Skáldskaparmál* 'poetics', ch. 2. The poem is in poor condition, the scribes of both prose contexts having added attributions of speakers. The poem's changeable and defective metre and its varying lengths of stanza indicate that it was mauled in transmission, though for how long is unknown. On the other hand, its language has forms that show that the poet was a Scandinavian living in England. It is a fair asumption that the poet came from Eiríkr's circle in York (Townend 2003: 53). If the poem does come from *c.* 954, as the legend suggests, it is a work inferior to *Hákonarmál* 'The Lay of Hákon the Good', which Eyvindr is believed to have modelled on *The Lay of Eiríkr Bloodaxe* in *c.* 960. This inferior quality has even led one scholar to suggest that *The Lay of Eiríkr* was modelled on *The Lay of Hákon* (von See 1963). However, Eyvindr's byname *skáldaspillir* 'Plagiarist' makes the reverse more likely. The text is adapted from *Fagrskinna*, ch. 8 (ÍF 29, vss. 27–34) and (vs. 27) from *Snorra Edda*, verse no. 20, ed. Faulkes (1998).

Bjarni Einarsson, ed., *Ágrip af Nóregskonunga Sǫgum. Fagrskinna – Nóregs Konunga Tal*, ÍF 29 (Reykjavik, 1985)

Faulkes, Anthony, ed., *Snorri Sturluson: Edda: Skáldskaparmál*, 2 vols (London, 1998)

Kershaw, N., ed. and trans., *Anglo-Saxon and Norse Poems* (Cambridge, 1922)

See, K. von, 'Zwei eddische Preislieder: Eiríksmál und Hákonarmál [Two Eddic praise-poems: *Eiríksmál* and *Hákonarmál*]', in *Festgabe für Ulrich Pretzel, zum 65. Geburtstag dargebracht von*

Freunden und Schülern, ed. W. Simon, W. Bachofer and W. Dittmann (Berlin, 1963), 107–17; repr. in K. von See, *Edda. Saga. Skaldendichtung: Aufsätze zur skandinavischen Literature des Mittelalters*, Skandinavistische Arbeiten 6 (Heidelberg, 1981), 318–28 and 522–5

Swanton, M. J., trans., *The Anglo-Saxon Chronicle* (London, 1996)

Townend, M., 'Whatever happened to York Viking poetry? Memory, tradition and the transmission of Skaldic verse', *Saga-Book of the Viking Society* 27 (2003), 48–90

Williams, G., *Eirik Bloodaxe* (Kernavik, 2010)

1 [Óðinn] 'Hvats þat drauma? es ek hugðumk fyr dag lítlu
Valhǫll ryðja fyr vegnu fólki;
vakða ek Einherja, bað ek upp rísa,
bekki at stráa, bjórker at leyðra,
valkyrjur vín bera, sem vísi komi. (vs. 20)

'What dream is that, when a little before daybreak I thought
I was clearing Valhǫll for a slain host?
I awakened the Lone Warriors, ordered them to rise,
To cover the benches, to wash the beer-vats,
the Valkyries to serve wine as if a prince were coming.

2 'Es mér ór heimi hǫlða vánir,
gǫf[u]gra nǫkkurra, svá es mér glatt hjarta!'

I have hopes of seeing heroes from the world,
some worshipful men, as my heart is glad!'

3 [Bragi] 'Hvat þrymr þar, sem þúsund bifisk
eða mengi til mikit?
Braka ǫll bekkþili, sem muni Baldr koma
eptir í Óðins sali'.

'What uproar is that, as if a thousand men were moving,
or a multitude too much?
All the benchboards are creaking as if Baldr will come
back into Óðinn's hall.'

---

1 *Hvats þat drauma?* 'What dream is that'. The 'dream' sense of OIce *draumr* seems blended with the 'happy state' sense of OE *dream*. [*Einherja* 'Lone Warriors'. Óðinn's 'universal soliders', his elite division of fighting dead.

3 *sem muni Baldr koma* 'as if Baldr will come'. Baldr was killed by Hǫðr and had to stay in the world of the dead. His return from there is a figure of speech for the end of the world, a sign that Óðinn will soon be using his troops in battle. In *The Sibyl's Prophecy*, stanza 59, he returns after the world has ended (see **Gods of the Vikings**).

4 [Óðinn] ‘Heimsku mæla skalat hinn horski Bragi,
þvít þú vel hvat vitir;
fyr Eiríki glymr, es hér mun inn koma
iǫfurr í Óðins sali.

‘A folly is what the clever Bragi must not say,
for you know everything well.
The crashing is for Eiríkr, who will come in here,
a chieftain into Óðinn’s halls.

5 ‘Sigmundr ok Sinfjǫtli, rísið snarliga
ok gangið í gǫgn grami;
inn þú bjóð, ef Eiríkr sé,
hans es mér nú ván vituð.’

‘Sigmundr and Sinfjǫtli, quickly rise up
and go to greet the prince.
Ask him in, if Eiríkr it is,
my hope that it’s he is now certain.’

6 [Sigmundr] ‘Hvís þér Eiríks ván heldr en annarra konunga?’
[Óðinn] ‘Þvít mǫrgu landi hefr hann mæki roðit
ok blóðugt sverð borit.’

‘Why’s it Eiríkr you hope for, rather than other kings?’
‘Because in many a land, he has reddened his blade
and carried a bloody sword.’

7 [Sigmundr] ‘Hví namt þú hann sigri þá, es þér þótti snjallr vesa?’
[Óðinn] ‘Þvít óvíst es at vita, sér ulfr hinn hǫsvi
[greypr] á sjǫt goða.’

‘Why did you take victory off him, when you thought he was brave?’
‘Because one can’t know for certain, the grey-coated wolf looks
[fiercely] at the homes of gods.’

8 [Sigmundr] ‘Heill þú nú Eiríkr, vel skalt hér kominn
ok gakk í hǫll horskr.
Hins vilk þik fregna, hvat fylgir þér
íǫfra frá eggþrimu.’

‘Health to you now, Eiríkr, you shall be welcome here,
so wisely go into the hall.
One thing I will ask you, what chieftains follow you
from the thunder of blades?’

---

4 *Heimsku* ‘folly’. Bragi is warned not to trigger the world’s end by talking of it.

5 Sigmundr is the Sigemund of *Beowulf*, lines 884–99, the father of Sinfjǫtli, who is Fitela there (see **Heroic Poems**). Both may be the subject of Wulf and Eadwacer, which appears to be an Anglo-Scandinavian riddle from northern England in the tenth century (see **Poems on the Meaning of Life**).

9 [Eiríkr] 'Konungar eru fimm, kennik þér nafn allra,
ek em enn sétti sjalfr.'

'Kings are there five, I will teach you all their names,
I myself am the sixth.'

9 The names of Eiríkr's claimed dead vassal kings are unknown. Their number, however, adds to his fame as a proper king of Norway, in defiance of his reduced status as an outlaw.

Eyvindr's *Lay of King Hákon the Good*

Hákonarmál

Eyvindr *skáldaspillir* 'the Plagiarist', *c.* 961

⁂

While Eiríkr Bloodaxe fought for new power in the British Isles, his youngest half-brother Hákon the Good ruled Norway. Initially Hákon believed he could convert this country to Christianity. *Ágrip*, *Fagrskinna* and *Hákonar saga Góða*, the Norse and Icelandic histories of the early thirteenth century which cover his reign, tell a sad story of mutual incomprehension and failure. King Æthelstan's foster-son was king by virtue of a system he did not understand, as mediator between gods and people for the health of land and harvest. Against heathen cults in the west of Norway and particularly against the peasant farmers of Trøndelag, home of his ally Earl Sigurðr Hákonarson, Hákon was fighting a losing battle. The culture of Norway may have changed to absorb some Christianity into paganism, but if Hákon was to remain as king, he would have to enact the ceremonies as his earls advised. If we believe his eulogist Eyvindr, Hákon was a heathen when he died, having, as it were, 'gone native'. This eulogy in his memory marks the fullest expression of Valhǫll-ideology in pre-Christian Norse literature.

Fagrskinna preserves apparently the first three stanzas, then a fourth, in ch. 12; then three stanzas and finally the last three stanzas of this poem, in ch. 13 (nos. 37–9, 42; 43–5 and 52–4). *Heimskringla*, in ch. 31 of *Hákonar saga Góða*, lays out the first seven of these in sequence, then adds eleven of its own, then has the final three as in *Fagrskinna*. *Snorra Edda* quotes three stanzas, as cited below, in chs. 2 (stanzas 1 and 14) and 64 (4/5–8). The sequence is thus based on Snorri's work in *Heimskringla*.

Bjarni Einarsson, ed., *Ágrip af Nóregskonunga Sǫgum. Fagrskinna – Nóregs Konunga Tal*, ÍF 29 (Reykjavik, 1985)

Kershaw, N., ed. and trans., *Anglo-Saxon and Norse Poems* (Cambridge, 1922)

North, R., *Heathen Gods in Old English Literature*, Cambridge Studies in Anglo-Saxon England 22 (Cambridge, 1997)

See, K. von, 'Zwei eddische Preislieder: Eiríksmál und Hákonarmál [Two Eddic praise-poems: *Eiríksmál* and *Hákonarmál*]', in *Festgabe für Ulrich Pretzel, zum 65. Geburtstag dargebracht von Freunden und Schülern*, ed. W. Simon, W. Bachofer and W. Dittmann (Berlin, 1963), 107–17; repr. in K. von See, *Edda. Saga. Skaldendichtung: Aufsätze zur skandinavischen Literature des Mittelalters*, Skandinavistische Arbeiten 6 (Heidelberg, 1981), 318–28 and 522–5

1 Gǫndul ok Skǫgul sendi Gauta-týr
at kjósa of konunga, hverr Yngva ættar
skyldi með Óðni fara ok í Valhǫll vesa.

Gǫndul and Skǫgul were sent by the Gautar's deity
To choose the kings, which man of Ingvi's kindred
Was to go and join Óðinn and be in Valhǫll.

'Gǫndul and Skǫgul': valkyries. 'The Gautar's deity': Óðinn. 'Ingvi's kindred': the Norwegian royal family.

2 Bróður fundu Bjarnar í brynju fara,
konung inn kostsama, kominn und gunnfana;
drúpðu dólgáar, en darraðr hristisk,
upp vas þá hildr of hafin.

Bjǫrn's brother they found marching in mail-shirt,
The splendid king, come under war-banner.
Deadly-darts descended, and the lance shook,
battle was now begun.

'Bjǫrn's brother': Hákon the Good.

3 Hét á Háleygi sem á Holmrygi,
jarla einbani fór til orrostu,
gótt hafði inn gjǫfli gengi Norðmanna
œgir ey-Dana, stóð und árhjalmi.

He called on Hålogalanders, as well as Rogalanders,
The sole slayer of earls marched off to war,
With good Norwegian troops stood the worshipful
Terror of island-Danes, in a helmet of ancient days.

4 Hrauzk ór herváðum, hratt á vǫll brynju
vísi verðungar áðr til vígs tœki.
Lék við ljóðmǫgu, skyldi land verja,
gramr hinn glaðværi stóð und gollhjalmi.

Stripped himself of war-weeds, kicked mail-shirt to ground,
The prince of this platoon, before he started fighting.
He danced with the mob's sons, his land to defend,
The captain stood to it cheerful in a golden helmet.

5 Svá beit þá sverð ór siklings hendi
váðir Váfaðar, sem í vatn brygði.
Brǫkuðu broddar, brotnuðu skildir,
glumruðu gylfringar í gotna hausum.

From the hero's hand his sword was then biting
Swinging-One's weeds as if through water it drew.
Sword-tips shivered, shields split open,
Axe-heads clanged on warriors' skulls.

'Swinging-One's weeds': Óðinn's clothes: armour.

6 Trǫddusk tǫrgur fyr Týs ok bauga
hjalta harðfótum hausar Norðmanna.
Róma varð í eyju, ruðu konungar
skírar skjaldborgir í skatna blóði.

Targes were trodden by the hard-pommelled blade
Of the Northmen's ring-deity and skulls as well.
There was a rumble on the isle, kings reddened
The gleaming shield-walls with warriors' blood.

'Northmen's ring-deity': generous king of Norway.

7 Brunnu beneldar í blóðgum undum,
lutu langbarðar at lýða fjǫrvi,
svarraði sárgymir á sverða nesi,
fell flóð fleina í fjǫru Storðar.

Gash-fires burned in bleeding wounds,
Halberds stooped for the lives of men.
Wound-deeps thundered on sword-headland,
An arrow-flood fell on the foreshore of Storð.

'Gash-fires': swords. 'Wound-deeps': blood.

8 Blendusk við roðnum und randar himni,
Skǫglar veðr léku við ský of bauga;
umðu oddláar í Óðins veðri,
hné mart manna fyr mækis straumi.

With the rim's reddened canopy they mingled,
Skǫgul's storms danced with the buckler clouds.
In Óðinn's storm roared the sword-point torrents,
Men by the multitude dropped in the blade-stream.

'Rim's canopy', 'buckler clouds': shield-wall. 'Skǫgul's storms': engagements. 'Óðinn's storm': battle. 'Sword-point torrents', 'blade-stream': blood.

9 Sátu þá dǫglingar með sverð of togin,
með skarða skjǫldu ok skotnar brynjur;
vasa sá herr í hugum ok átti
til Valhallar vega.

Then the princes were sitting with drawn swords,
With cleft shields and shot-up coats of mail.
This was not a living army, the one that took
the road to Valhǫll.

10 Gǫndul þat mælti, studdisk geirs skapti:
'Vex nú gengi goða, es Hákoni hafa
með her mikinn heim bǫnd of boðit.'

Gǫndul then spoke (she leant on her spear-shaft):
'The gods' troop will grow, now that the bonds
Have invited Hákon with his great army home.'

'Bonds': gods.

11 Vísi þat heyrði, hvat valkyrjur mæltu
mærar af mars baki;
hyggiliga létu ok hjalmaðar sátu
ok hǫfðusk hlífar fyrir.

The leader heard what the valkyries said,
glorious women, from horseback.
Thoughtful they looked, as in helmets they sat
and held their shields before them.

12 'Hví þú svá gunni skiptir, Geirskǫgul?
órum þó verðir gagns frá goðum!'
'Vér því vǫldum, at þú velli helt,
en þínir fíendr flugu.

'Why did you decide the battle so, Spear-Skǫgul?
The gods knew us worthy to win!'
'We are the reason you mastered the field
while your foemen fled.

13 'Ríða vit skolum,' kvað in ríkja Skǫgul,
'grœnna heima goða,
Óðni at segja, at nú mun allvaldr koma
á hann sjalfan at sjá'.

'We two must ride,' said the mighty Skǫgul,
'to the green homes of gods,
Óðinn to tell that now an overlord will come
to look upon his presence.'

14 'Hermóðr ok Bragi,' kvað Hropta-týr,
'gangið í gǫgn grami,
alls konungr ferr, sás kappi þykkir,
til hallar hinig'.

'Hermóðr and Bragi,' said the god of Secrets,
'You go to meet the prince,
For it's a king, thought to be a champion, who comes
this way to our hall.'

15 Ræsir þat mælti, vas frá rómu kominn,
stóð allr í dreyra drifinn:
'Illúðigr mjǫk þykkir oss Óðinn vesa,
séumk vér hans of hugi'.

The ruler spoke, had come from the tumult,
stood all bolted in blood:
'Extremely grim we think Óðinn is looking,
we fear his intentions.'

16 'Einherja grið skalt þú allra hafa,
þigg þú at ásum ǫl.
Iarla bági, þú átt inni hér
átta brœðr' kvað Bragi.

'Quarter shall you have from all Lone Warriors,
accept some ale from the gods.
Foe of earls, you have inside here
eight brothers,' said Bragi.

17 'Gerðar órar, kvað hinn góði konungr,
viljum vér sjalfir hafa;
'hjalm ok brynju skal hirða vel,
gótt es til gǫrs at taka'.

'Our own weapons,' said the generous king,
'we want to have by us.
Helmet and mail-shirt must be carefully guarded,
it's good to have one's gear to turn to.'

18 Þá þat kynndisk, hvé sá konungr hafði
vel of þyrmt véum,
es Hákon báðu heilan koma
ráð ǫll ok regin.

Then it was made known how well this king had
respected the sanctuaries,
When Hákon they bade come in peace,
all the divine council.

19 Góðu dœgri verðr sá gramr of borinn,
es sér getr slíkan sefa,
hans aldar mun æ vesa
at góðu getit.

On a good day that prince is born who
for himself gets such good sense.
The life he has led will always be
generously mentioned.

20 Mun óbundinn á ýta sjǫt
Fenrisulfr of fara,
áðr iafngóðr á auða trǫð
konungmaðr komi.

Unbound to the homes of mankind will
the Fenris-wolf proceed,
Before, to the empty pens, so good
a royal person comes.

'Fenris-wolf': Fenrir, ending the world.

21 Deyr fé, deyja frændr,
eyðisk land ok láð;
síz Hákon fór með heiðin goð,
mǫrg es þjóð of þéuð.

Livestock die, kinsmen die,
land and lea are emptied.
Since Hákon joined the heathen gods,
many a nation is enslaved.

Notes

1 *at kjósa konunga* 'to choose the kings'. It is Hákon's performance in the Battle of Storð, not his lineage, that makes them decide to admit him to Valhǫll. Óðinn delegates the first part of this decision to his Valkyries. [*Yngva ættar* 'Ingvi's kindred'. The name Yngvi is elsewhere the prefix to the name of Freyr, the god from whom the Ynglingar kings of Uppsala, and from them Haraldr Finehair's family, claimed descent. Hákon and his inimical nephews were all members of this family.

2 *Bróður Bjarnar* 'Bjǫrn's brother'. This was Hákon's elder half-brother King Bjǫrn *farmaðr* 'the Merchant' Haraldsson of Vestfold. Eiríkr Bloodaxe treacherously killed his brother Bjǫrn just after becoming king of Norway (*The Saga of Haraldr Finehair*, ch. 35), so Hákon has also this score to settle with Eiríkr's sons. Bjǫrn's son Guðrøðr ruled Vestfold for Hákon the Good about a decade later; later, under Haraldr Greycloak, he was allowed to keep this province; it is possible that Guðrøðr's court in Vestfold is where Eyvindr has composed his *Lay of Hákon the Good*.

3 *ægir ey-Dana* 'Terror of island-Danes'. These would be the sons of Eiríkr who are trying to invade. Despite Denmark's many islands, it seems better to think of this *ey* 'island' as Orkney, from where Eiríkr's exiled sons based their attack on Norway; or even as England itself. As part of his effort to align Hákon with true Norwegians, Eyvindr identifies the sons of Eiríkr with kings of the Danelaw. They were Danish already: Haraldr Finehair was three-quarters so; his consort Ragnhildr, Eiríkr's mother, was a Dane from Jutland; thus Eiríkr was seven-eighths Danish himself and his sons still substantially so. Haraldr Greycloak, his eldest, spent most of his youth in Denmark.

4 *við ljóðmǫgu* 'with the mob's sons'. Apparently a deprecating reference to the quality of Haraldr Greycloak's men.

7 *fell flóð fleina í fjǫru* 'an arrow-flood fell on the foreshore'. Though they are part of a wild-weather conceit, the autonomous action of the weapons may be paralleled with *bogan wæron bysige* 'bows were busy' in *The Battle of Maldon*, line 110 (and similar phrases).

9 The battered equipment of this dead army is itself proof of their prowess, enough for entry into Valhǫll. Germanic weapon graves with their weapons deliberately damaged may have aimed for the same impression (North 1997: 105).

10 *með her mikinn* 'with his great army'. OE *se micele here* 'the Great Army', is how the *Anglo-Saxon Chronicle* describes the Danish host that conquered eastern England until overcome by King Alfred in Wessex in 879. Eyvindr means that Hákon and his men will now become gods in Valhǫll.

14 *Hermóðr ok Bragi* 'Hermóðr and Bragi'. The Valkyries have now delivered their message, and Óðinn makes ready to receive Hákon. Here he has two lieutenants. Hermóðr is also a stooge of Valhǫll in *Hyndluljóð* 'The Lay of Hyndla'. His English counterpart is Heremod, the bad king of the Danes in lines 901–15 of *Beowulf*, and subject of Hrothgar's speech in lines 1709–22 (**Heroic Poems**). Bragi has this role in *The Lay of Eiríkr Bloodaxe*, and he is also the gods' majordomo in *Loki's Truth-Game*, mocked for cowardice in stanza 13 (**Gods of the Vikings**). OIce *bragi*, like *bragr*, may have meant 'prince' (OE *brego*), a generic term for Valhǫll's inhabitants. Bragi thus has no connection with the poet named Bragi the Old.

15 *séumk vér hans of hugi* 'we fear his intentions'. Perhaps because Hákon has practised Christianity in his time, he is anxious about having to fight Óðinn, now looking at him from the high seat of Valhǫll.

16 *Iarla bági* 'Foe of earls'. Hákon's enemies, in this case his slayers, were Haraldr Greycloak and other sons of Eiríkr Bloodaxe and Gunnhildr. [*átta brœðr* 'eight brothers'. One of these is Eiríkr Bloodaxe, tracked down and killed by Óláfr Cuaran at Stainmore on the Yorkshire border with Westmorland. Most of the others had already been despatched by Eiríkr himself: Bjǫrn the Merchant, Óláfr Stout-Leg (father of Tryggvi, father of Óláfr who converted Iceland), Rǫgnvaldr Straight-Bone, Guðrøðr Gleam and Sigrøðr; Hálfdan the Black died suddenly at a feast.

17 *Gerðar órar viljum vér sjalfir hafa* 'Our own weapons we want to have by us'. The etiquette in *Beowulf* and elsewhere is to enter the hall with one's weapons left outside and guarded by a friend. Hákon proves his mettle to the gods by defying this courtesy. It is also possible that he is still meant to be thinking of defending himself against gods outraged by his earlier Christianity. In the long run, however, he and his men will take Óðinn's weapons as new members of his *Einherjar* 'Lone Warriors' in Valhǫll.

18 *hvé sá konungr hafði vel of þyrmt véum* 'how well this king had respected the sanctuaries'. There was clearly some doubt about that. Eyvindr here needs to prove King Hákon's heathen fervour by establishing him as a new god in Valhǫll. On becoming king in the late 940s, Hákon tried to pass on his English education to the Norwegians. The earliest Norse prose history on Hákon, *Ágrip* 'extracts' from *c.* 1190, says that his attempts at conversion failed and the men of Trøndelag in the north west bullied him into sacrificing. Given that he kept his power until *c.* 960, however, he must have willingly continued to do this. [*báðu heilan koma* 'bade come in peace'. The gods welcome Hákon. This northern match for the royal cult of martyrs so well known in England presupposes that Hákon the Good now had his own idol, one armed with weapons, in Norwegian shrines. On war-deities with weapons in *vé* 'divine sanctuaries', see Einarr Cup-Tinkle's *Gold-Shortage* (*Vellekla*), stanza '16' (*c.* 980; **Gods of the Vikings**).

20 *Fenrisulfr* 'the Fenris-wolf'. The world's-end topos places Hákon in the great kings' gallery, may also contain an understanding of the Christian Day of Judgement, but primarily refers to Hákon's imminent glory as one Óðinn's *Einherjar* 'Lone Warriors' in Ragnarǫk.

21 *Deyr fé, deyja frændr* 'Livestock die, kinsmen die'. Eyvindr 'plagiarised' this line from the end of a Norwegian gnomic poem, what is now stanzas 76 and 77 of *Sayings of the High One* (see **Poems on the Meaning of Life**). [*heiðin goð* 'heathen gods'. The OIce word *heiðinn*, OE *hæðen*, in *c.* 960 was not an old term within Norwegian society. It was a missionary term modelled on Latin *paganus* 'of the heath', which presents northern non-Christians as uncivilised. Eyvindr uses this word in reaction to the Christians around him, to vindicate Hákon's decision to go native. The enslavement to which Eyvindr alludes is first the rule of Haraldr Greycloak and Eiríkr's other sons; second, perhaps, a second wave of Christianity which he knew was on its way.

The Battle of Maldon

c. 991

⁜

The Battle of Maldon, which was fought on 10 or 11 August 991, ended in defeat for the *fyrd* of Essex as well as the death of its experienced commander, Ealdorman Byrhtnoth. This ealdorman or earl had been a rich landowner, a member of the royal council in London and an important figure in quelling the reaction on King Edgar's death, in 975, to the Benedictine or monastic Reform (Locherbie-Cameron 1991). Byrhtnoth's death was a disaster, the poem that acknowledges this, while celebrating his memory, may criticise him for this.

The Battle of Maldon was in a fragment in London, British Library, MS Cotton Otho A.xiii, between Asser's *Life of Alfred* and a series of Latin proverbs and Saints' Lives, before it was destroyed in the Cotton Library fire of 1731. Luckily a transcript had been made, by David Casley (but later assigned to John Elphinstone) some time before 1725. The eighteenth-century copy is missing both beginning and end, although not too much of either (Scragg 1991). The list of local names, however, suggests that the original text was composed within a year of the battle. When matched up to the site and what is known of the history, this poem becomes more disturbing. Maldon was the site of a royal mint; hence the reason for the Viking attack and hence, perhaps, the financial reason for Óláfr Tryggvason's accession to the throne of Norway, just four years later. The people of Maldon would have been able to see their army losing from the town, which lies a little to the west on slightly higher ground. The seaward position of Northey Island, on which the Vikings encamped, shows that they could easily get away, that Byrhtnoth had to stop them not only from entering Maldon, but also from escaping by sea to raid another eastern town. With a levy hastily assembled against fast crews of professional raiders, Byrhtnoth had little time to move. His means of holding the Vikings lay in the tides and steep muddy channel between Northey and the southern bank of the Blackwater as these things were more than 1000 years ago. Inevitably his only way of holding the Vikings would have been to invite them to his side, to keep them fighting on his bank until the tide rose again to drown them in fatal numbers. The Vikings saw the risk and played along. It was a desperate gamble on both sides. An unsentimental reading of this poem suggests that Byrhtnoth was killed by four or five Vikings at the crucial moment because the Vikings cleverly lured him out of line with a challenge to his personal honour. The fact that the poet, with *landes to fela* 'too much land' (line 90), presents the general's strategy as the grand error, rather than his temper, suggests that he was engaging with some political recrimination after the battle.

This poem thus masks what appear to be the realities with a competent array of heroic formulae. *The Battle of Maldon* is taught less than it used to be, partly because of its celebration of war, partly because of its length, but partly because it has never seemed as well finished as *Beowulf.* It was the subject of a millennial conference and celebration in Colchester in 1991, but when these were over, the fuss over the poem died down. What was *The Battle of Maldon* apart from a dutiful roll-call of dead, a string of vignettes proclaiming local loyalties, or a source book for geologists and historians charting the opening of England's second Viking Age? And yet the poem is now coming back into its own. If the style comes close to that of prose in places, we must remember that the media of poetry and prose overlapped more than before, in the time this work was composed. The poet shows himself to be clerically trained (lines 9–10), and the dying Byrhtnoth makes a good Christian end (lines 173–80), but the battle, with its speed and confusion, also gives a breathtaking sense of realism (lines 106–12).

This work also faithfully renders the heroic commonplaces of older poems such as *Beowulf*. Despite the poet's initial lack of hurry, *The Battle of Maldon* has a certain pace. It builds up momentum until we reach a furious climax at or near the end. The English general, Earl Byrhtnoth of Essex, both is and walks tall as an emblem of national pride against the ruthless invader. His speech to the Viking herald reveals a home-grown sense of humour to match the foreigner's simpering suggestion of Danegeld, i.e. payment to go away. When Byrhtnoth has died, mobbed by four or five Vikings at the same time, it is because he has *ofermod*, both 'too much courage' (if seen from the admiring warrior's point of view) and 'pride' (if from the spiritual Christian). This quality is like a coin with two faces, and it seems likely that the ambiguity was judicious. The poet admits to the cowardice of key men in Byrhtnoth's personal guard, men such as Godric who lead the flight when the English army breaks in half. At this point the poem bulges as if using heroic formulae to suppress a bitter political controversy, but thereafter *The Battle of Maldon* reaches an unusual pitch of intensity. The speeches of defiant retainers, all determined to die for their and the national honour, flow one upon the other into a longer scene of wild ferocity and carnage in which it is the English, not the Vikings, who fight with the fury of the north. And then Byrhtwold's speech, on courage hardening as one's strength wanes, seems worthy of entering the language as the quintessential statement of nobility. To read his grave words on lines 312–19 is to see the stylish praise of Cnut Sveinsson's skalds, one to two decades later, for the bragging sycophancy it really was.

Campbell, J., 'England, *c.* 991', in *The Battle of Maldon: Fiction and Fact*, ed. J. Cooper (London, 1993), 1–17; repr. in Campbell, J., *The Anglo-Saxon State* (London, 2000), 157–78

Clark, G., '*The Battle of Maldon*: a heroic poem', *Speculum* 43 (1968), 52–71

Dodgson, J. McN., 'The site of *The Battle of Maldon*', in Scragg (1991), 170–9

Keynes, S. D., 'The historical context of *The Battle of Maldon*', in Scragg (1991), 81–113

Locherbie-Cameron, M. A. L., 'The men named in the poem', in Scragg (1991), 238–49

Locherbie-Cameron, M. A. L., 'Byrhtnoth and his family', in Scragg (1991), 253–62

Lund, N., 'The Danish perspective', in Scragg (1991), 114–42

Macrae-Gibson, O. D., 'How historical is *The Battle of Maldon*?', *Medium Ævum* 39 (1970), 89–107

North, R., 'Getting to know the General in *The Battle of Maldon*', *Medium Ævum* 60 (1991), 1–15

Roesdahl, E., *The Vikings*, trans. S. M. Margesson and K. Williams, 2nd ed. (Harmondsworth, 1998)

Scragg, D. G., ed., *The Battle of Maldon* AD *991* (Oxford, 1991)

Scragg, D. G., *The Return of the Vikings* (Stroud, 2006)

Townend, M., *Language and History in Viking Age England: Linguistic Relations between Speakers of Old Norse and Old English*, Studies in the Early Middle Ages 6 (Turnhout, 2002)

Byrhtnoth and the Viking herald

[þy læs . . .] brocen wurde.
Het þa hyssa hwæne hors forlætan,
feor afysan, and forð gangan,
hicgan to handum and to hige godum.
Þa þæt Offan mæg ærest onfunde,
þæt se eorl nolde yrhðo geþolian,
he let him þa of handon leofne fleogan
hafoc wið þæs holtes, and to þære hilde stop.
Be þam man mihte oncnawan þæt se cniht nolde
wacian æt þam wige, þa he to wæpnum feng.
Eac him wolde Eadric his ealdre gelæstan,
frean to gefeohte, ongan þa forð beran
gar to guþe. He hæfde god geþanc
þa hwile þe he mid handum healdan mihte
bord and bradswurd, beot he gelæste
þa he ætforan his frean feohtan sceolde.
Ða þær Byrhtnoð ongan beornas trymian,
rad and rædde, rincum tæhte
hu hi sceoldon standan and þone stede healdan,

[lest . . .] should be broken.
Then he ordered each lad to leave his horse,
speed them off and march forwards,
think on strong arms and good heart.
When Offa's cousin first discovered
that the earl would not endure dishonour,
he let then from his arms his precious hawk
fly towards the woodland, and advanced to the war.
By that one might recognise that the boy would not
show weakness in battle when he took hold of weapons.
Eadric, too, as he wished to please his chieftain,
his lord, in fighting, did carry forth
his spear to war. He kept a good resolve
as long as he with his hands might hold
board and broadsword, this vow he fulfilled
when called upon to fight before his lord.
Then Byrhtnoth there began to line up men,
rode and reasoned, taught the ranks
how they should stand and hold position,

---

6 *se eorl* 'the earl'. OE *eorl* now means 'earl' unambiguously, thanks to the influence of Old Scandinavian *iarl* (from the people Byrhtnoth must fight). This is not the only Scandinavian aspect the English now have, as we will see with Godric son of Odda.

9 *Be þam man mihte oncnawan* 'By that one might recognise'. The poet is trained as a cleric: compare Alfred's writer in *Be þy þu meaht ongitan* 'From this you can see' in the West Saxon *Boethius*, 'Fate and Providence' (see **The Earliest English Prose**).

and bæd þæt hyra randas rihte heoldon
fæste mid folman, and ne forhtedon na.
Þa he hæfde þæt folc fægere getrymmed,
he lihte þa mid leodon þær him leofost wæs,
þær he his heorðwerod holdost wiste.

Þa stod on stæðe, stiðlice clypode
wicinga ar, wordum mælde,
se on beot abead brimliþendra
ærænde to þam eorle, þær he on ofre stod:
'Me sendon to þe sæmen snelle,
heton ðe secgan þæt þu most sendan raðe
beagas wið gebeorge, and eow betere is
þæt ge þisne garræs mid gafole forgyldon,
þon we swa hearde hilde dælon.
Ne þurfe we us spillan, gif ge spedaþ to þam.
We willað wið þam golde grið fæstnian.

---

and ordered them to hold their shield-rims right
fast against the palm, and not be frightened ever.
When he had fairly lined the people up,
he alighted then by landsmen he best liked,
where he knew his household was most loyal.

Stood then on shore, called out hard
a Viking herald, the man spoke words
who menacingly offered the seafarers'
message to the earl, where he stood on his bank:
'Bold sailors have sent me your way,
told me to tell you that you must quickly send
some rings for protection, and for you people it will
be better to buy off this spear-charge with tribute
than have us all join battle as hard as this will be.
We need not waste each other, if you can manage that.
In exchange for the gold we will confirm the truce.

---

21 *ne forhtedon na* 'not be frightened ever'. These men look like a hastily assembled local levy, of little experience.

24 *heorðwerod holdost* 'household was most loyal'. The pity of it is that some of Byrhtnoth's household, namely Godric and his brothers, prove disloyal. The poet may want to prepare us.

31 *beagas* 'some rings'. The Vikings knew of coin, minted in Denmark as well as obtained from England and France, but were still comfortable with hacking up rings and necklaces, as the *c.* 905 hoard from Cuerdale, Lancashire, shows (Roesdahl 1998: 112–14, 247). Maldon, however, was the site of a royal mint: the reason for the Vikings' arrival off this coast.

35 *grið* 'the truce'. More properly 'quarter'. The word *grið* is a Norse loanword, while *on hyra sylfra dom* 'on their own terms' may be a loan translation from *sialfdœmi* 'self-assessed compensation'. The poet seems to colour the Viking's speech with Norse terms to give a dialect impression. On Norse-English linguistic relationships at this time (each his own language mostly), see Townend 2002.

Gyf þu þat gerædest, þe her ricost eart,
þæt þu þine leoda lysan wille,
syllan sæmannum on hyra sylfra dom
feoh wið freode, and niman frið æt us,
we willaþ mid þam sceattum us to scype gangan,
on flot feran, and eow friþes healdan.'

Byrhtnoð maþelode, bord hafenode,
wand wacne æsc, wordum mælde,
yrre and anræd ageaf him andsware:
'Gehyrst þu, sælida, hwæt þis folc segeð?
Hi willað eow to gafole garas syllan,
ættrynne ord and ealde swurd,
þa heregeatu þe eow æt hilde ne deah.
Brimmanna boda, abeod eft ongean,
sege þinum leodum miccle laþre spell,
þæt her stynt unforcuð eorl mid his werode,
þe wile gealgean eþel þysne,

If you take care of this, who are the richest here,
and go so far as bailing out your countrymen,
give the sailors, on their own terms of course,
money for good will, and take our peace,
we will go with that coin to our ships,
put out to sea, and keep the peace with you.'

Byrhtnoth spoke, lifted his board,
twirled his slender spear, spoke these words,
angry and resolved gave him answer:
'You hear what these people say, swab-jockey?
They will give you spears for tribute,
poisoned points and old swords,
a death-duty no good for you in war.
Sailors' messenger, go back with this report,
tell your people a much worse piece of news,
that here stands an unshamed earl with his army,
who will defend this inheritance,

---

36 *Gyf þu þat gerædest* 'If you take care of this'. This is a local matter, and a local deal, as far as the Vikings are concerned. Byrhtnoth was a big landholder in the region, beyond it to the west, and by his marriage also in East Anglia (Locherbie-Cameron 1991 (2): 254–5)

48 *þa heregeatu þe eow æt hilde ne deah* 'a death-duty no good for you in war'. The joke is an involved one, for *heregeatu* 'heriot' signified the man's panoply which his son gave back to the lord on his decease (usually it was returned). Byrhtnoth thus presents the English weapons as all the money they have, beat-up weapons which will not help the Vikings in war; which of course (with the English still in them) will kill the Vikings in war.

Æþelredes eard, ealdres mines,
folc and foldan. Feallan sceolon
hæþene æt hilde. To heanlic me þinceð
þæt ge mid urum sceattum to scype gangon
unbefohtene, nu ge þus feor hider
on urne eard in becomon.
Ne sceole ge swa softe sinc gegangan.
Us sceal ord and ecg ær geseman,
grim guðplega, ær we gofol syllon.'

---

the homeland of Æthelred my chieftain,
his land and people. Heathen men must
fall in war. It seems too mean to me
that you should take ship with our money
without a fight, now you have
come here this far into our country.
Nor shall you get your treasure so peacefully.
Sword-point and blade will reconcile us first,
grim war-athletics, before we pay tribute.'

Byrhtnoth gives Vikings ground

Het þa bord beran, beornas gangan,
þæt hi on þam easteðe ealle stodon.
Ne mihte þær for wætere werod to þam oðrum.
Þær com flowende flod æfter ebban,
lucon lagustreamas. To lang hit him þuhte,
hwænne hi togædere garas beron.

Then he ordered men to carry shields, to march,
so that they all stood on the bank facing the river.
Nor could there for the water one host hit the other.
There came it flowing, flood after ebb-tide,
sea-streams closed it off. Too long did they think it
until the time they brought their spears together.

---

53 *Æþelredes eard* 'homeland of Æthelred'. Byrhtnoth raises the stakes: this is now a national matter, not a local one. It became national when he was killed at Maldon. Æthelred (*æþel ræd* 'noble plan') ruled England erratically (*unræd* his nickname makes his name 'noble plan no plan') from 978 to 1016.

63 Byrhtnoth's front line was further back. Now he moves it up to the river's edge. Later he will withdraw his line back to the first position. The best interpretation of his strategy suggests that Byrhtnoth always intended to let the Vikings cross to his side, hoping to cut them off when the tide came back in a few hours later (Macrae-Gibson 1970: 90–5).

Hi þær Pantan stream mid prasse bestodon,
Eastseaxena ord and se æschere.
Ne mihte hyra ænig oþrum derian
buton hwa þurh flanes flyht fyl gename.
Se flod ut gewat, þa flotan stodon gearowe,
wicinga fela, wiges georne.
Het þa hæleða hleo healdan þa bricge
wigan wigheardne, se wæs haten Wulfstan,
cafne mid his cynne, þæt wæs Ceolan sunu,
þe ðone forman man mid his francan ofsceat
þe þær baldlicost on þa bricge stop.
Þær stodon mid Wulfstane wigan unforhte,
Ælfere and Maccus, modige twegen,
þa noldon æt þam forda fleam gewyrcan,
ac hi fæstlice wið ða fynd weredon,
þa hwile þe hi wæpna wealdan moston.

Þa hi þæt ongeaton and georne gesawon
þæt hi þær bricgweardas bitere fundon,

In parade did they stand there by Pont's stream,
East Saxon vanguard and longship raiders.
Nor could men of either do harm to the other
unless someone got his from the flight of an arrow.
The flood went out, the sailors stood ready,
many Vikings keen for the combat.
The shield of heroes then bade the causeway be held
by a war-hardened man whose name was Wulfstan,
cheerful in his family, that was Ceola's son,
who with Frankish javelin shot dead the first man
so bold as to advance across the causeway.
With Wulfstan there stood warriors without fear,
Ælfhere and Magnus, two brave boys
who had no desire to flee from that ford
but firmly they fended off the enemy attack,
as long as it was given them to wield their weapons.

When they perceived this and eagerly saw
they were being bitten by the causeway's guards,

---

68 *Pantan stream* 'Pont's stream'. The Pont, or better Blackwater, is the estuary containing Northey, the Viking base for attacking Maldon, which lies on the south bank on high ground a quarter of a mile to the west, but in sight of the causeway. The sides of the channel were higher and muddier than today (Dodgson 1991: 171), not good for a heavily armed man up to his chest in water.

80 *Maccus* 'Magnus'. 'Maccus' appears to be an Irish-derived form of the Norse name Magnus (itself purloined in Norway to emulate *Carolus Magnus*, Charlemagne); proof of the Anglo-Scandinavian style of England now (Locherbie-Cameron 1991 (1): 239).

ongunnon lytegian þa   laðe gystas,
bædon þæt hi upgang   agan moston,
ofer þone ford faran,   feþan lædan.
Ða se eorl ongan   for his ofermode
alyfan landes to fela   laþere ðeode.
Ongan ceallian þa   ofer cald wæter
Byrhtelmes bearn   (beornas gehlyston):
'Nu eow is gerymed,   gað ricene to us,
guman to guþe.   God ana wat
hwa þære wælstowe   wealdan mote.'

---

the hostile guests began to practise guile,
asked if they might have passage up to land,
move across the ford, lead their troops there.
Then the earl for his over-confidence did
allow too much land to a hostile people.
He did call then over cold water,
son of Byrhthelm (the warriors listened):
'Now room is made for you, come quickly to us,
men into battle. God alone knows
who must win control of this killing ground.'

---

86 *ongunnon lytegian* 'began to practise guile'. Strictly there is no trick the Vikings could have pulled concerning their need for fighting space on the southern bank. They needed purchase; Byrhtnoth had to hold them there, lest they strike another mint town in a day or two; it was collusion between enemies, a gamble in either case (see note to line 63). The Vikings improve their chances by drawing Byrhtnoth out of his line, doubtless with some rich Norse insult (North 1991: 6–10).

87 *upgang* 'passage up to land'. This is a Norse loanword, from *uppganga* which, appropriately enough here, connotes a quick Viking raid.

89 *for his ofermode* 'for his over-confidence'. And thereby hangs a tale. Arguments have raged about this phrase, how moral it is or what criticism of Byrhtnoth it might contain. First, there is absolutely no doubt that *ofermod* means 'pride' (as in Satan's case, in *Genesis B*, lines 262 (adjective) and 272 (noun); see **Poems of Devotion**). The snag is that *The Battle of Maldon* is not a Saint's Life, but rather a war-memorial in words, and the Anglo-Saxons were alive to meanings within their compounds. So it is also clear that *mod* means 'courage' and *ofer-mod* means 'too much courage'. From a soldier's perspective, the latter is equal to 'over-confidence' (Clark 1968: 56). A religious might be right to call this 'pride'.

93 *gað ricene to us* 'come quickly to us'. Byrhtnoth's words are not as saintly as they sound: this phrase emulates a lover's 'come hither'.

96–7 *Wodon þa wælwulfas . . . wicinga werod* 'Waded the death-wolves . . . company of Vikings' etc. This image eerily echoes one for the god Þórr and his human servant wading a river, in Eilífr's *Eulogy on Þórr*, for Earl Hákon of Trøndelag in Norway, which he composed in *c.* 985: *Óðu fast fríðir eiðsvara Gauta setrs víkingar* 'Waded fast the handsome vikings of the seat of Gauti's liegemen' (pirates attacking Göteland, stanza 8; see **Gods of the Vikings**). The irony is that one of the Viking commanders in Maldon was probably Óláfr Tryggvason, a Norwegian pretender who would use the money from his Maldon campaign to oust Hákon just four years later, in 995.

Wodon þa wælwulfas (for wætere ne murnon),
wicinga werod, west ofer Pantan,
ofer scir wæter scyldas wegon,
lidmen to lande linde bæron.
Þær ongean gramum gearowe stodon
Byrhtnoð mid beornum, he mid bordum het
wyrcan þone wihagan, and þæt werod healdan
fæste wið feondum. Þa wæs feohte neh,
tir æt getohte. Wæs seo tid cumen
þæt þær fæge men feallan sceoldon.
Þær wearð hream ahafen, hremmas wundon,
earn æses georn, wæs on eorþan cyrm.
Hi leton þa of folman feolhearde speru,
gegrundene garas fleogan,
bogan wæron bysige, bord ord onfeng,
biter wæs se beaduræs, beornas feollon
on gehwæðere hand, hyssas lagon.
Wund wearð Wulfmær, wælræste geceas,
Byrhtnoðes mæg, he mid billum wearð,
his swuster sunu, swiðe forheawen.

Waded the death-wolves (for water they had no care),
company of Vikings west over Blackwater,
over shining water they carried their shields,
marines moved their war-boards to shore.
There against the enemy stood ready
Byrhtnoth with his warriors, he bade with boards
the war-hedge to be built and the host to hold
fast against the foes. The fight was now near,
glory of campaign. The hour had come
that doomed men would have to fall there.
There a scream was raised, ravens circled,
an eagle eager for carnage, there were cries on earth.
They let fly then from their hands shafts
file-hardened, as well as grimly ground spears,
bows were busy, board took point,
biting hard the battle-charge, boys were falling
on either side, young men lay dead.
Wounded was Wulfmær, chose his bed of death,
Byrhtnoth's kinsman, his sister's son,
he was with axes heavily cut down.

106–12 The chaos of fighting at close quarters (with the eye shooting up and down, the mixture of sight and sound, the weapons working by themselves, the men dropping in consequence) has rarely been imagined as well as here. It is tempting to compare this with handheld video images of modern warfare.

Þær wearð wicingum   wiþerlean agyfen:
gehyrde ic þæt Eadweard   anne sloge
swiðe mid his swurde,   swenges ne wyrnde,
þæt him æt fotum   feoll fæge cempa.
Þæs him his ðeoden   þanc gesæde,
þam burþene,   þa he byre hæfde.
Swa stemnetton   stiðhicgende
hysas æt hilde,   hogodon georne
hwa þær mid orde   ærost mihte
on fægean men   feorh gewinnan,
wigan mid wæpnum   (wæl feol on eorðan),
stodon stædefæste.   Stihte hi Byrhtnoð,
bæd þæt hyssa gehwylc   hogode to wige
þe on Denon wolde   dom gefeohtan.

Payback was given out to Vikings there:
I heard that Edward struck one of them
hard with his sword, did not withhold the stroke,
so that the doomed champion fell dead at his feet.
His lord said thank you to him for that,
to his chamberlain, when he had a moment.
So did the stern-minded men stand their ground,
young men at war, eagerly took heart at
whichever of their front line might be first
to fight for the life-blood of a doomed man,
a fighter, with his weapons (dead men dropped),
steadfast they stood. Byrhtnoth rallied them,
bade that each young fellow take heart in combat
who wanted to win glory by fighting Danes.

The Vikings take out Byrhtnoth

Wod þa wiges heard,   wæpen up ahof,
bord to gebeorge,   and wið þæs beornes stop.
Eode swa anræd   eorl to þam ceorle,
ægþer hyra oðrum   yfeles hogode.

Waded then a veteran, lifted up his weapon,
his board in defence, and advanced towards the man.
Just as resolved moved the earl to the churl,
each of them intended evil for the other.

---

130 *wiges heard* 'veteran'. This Viking, by raising his shield, challenges Byrhtnoth to single combat. We must not forget, as Byrhtnoth soon appears to, that he has ordered his men to stay in line (lines 19 and 102–3). Byrhtnoth steps out of line when he accepts the challenge. This exposes him to more attackers.

Sende ða se særinc suþerne gar,
þæt gewundod wearð wigena hlaford,
he sceaf þa mid ðam scylde, þæt se sceaft tobærst,
and þæt spere sprengde, þæt hit sprang ongean.
Gegremod wearð se guðrinc, he mid gare stang
wlancne wicing, þe him þa wunde forgeaf.
Frod wæs se fyrdrinc, he let his francan wadan
þurh ðæs hysses hals, hand wisode
þæt he on þam færsceaðan feorh geræhte.
Đa he oþerne ofstlice sceat,
þæt seo byrne tobærst. He wæs on breostum wund
þurh ða hringlocan, him æt heortan stod
ætterne ord. Se eorl wæs þe bliþra,
hloh þa, modi man, sæde Metode þanc
ðæs dægweorces þe him Drihten forgeaf.
Forlet þa drenga sum daroð of handa,
fleogan of folman, þæt se to forð gewat
þurh ðone æþelan Æþelredes þegen.
Him be healfe stod hyse unweaxen,
cniht on gecampe, se full caflice

Then the seaman sent a southern spear
so that the warrior-lord was wounded,
but shoved then with his shield to burst the shaft
and snap the lance so that it sprang back.
Enraged was our warrior, with a spear he stabbed
the arrogant Viking who gave him that wound.
Experienced was our soldier, he moved his javelin
through the fellow's neck, guided it in with his hand
so as to reach in and take the psycho's life.
Then he hastily shot another one and made his mail-coat
shatter. The other man's chest was wounded
through the ring-mail, a poisoned point
stood in his heart. That made the earl more cheerful,
he laughed then, brave man, thanked the Measurer
for the day's work the Lord had given him.
One of the mercenaries then loosed a lance,
let it fly from his hand, so that too hard did it
pass into the nobly born thegn of Æthelred.
Beside Byrhtnoth appeared a youth not fully grown,
a boy on the battlefield, who very smartly

---

143 *oþerne ofstlice* 'hastily another one'. A second Viking attacks Byrhtnoth at almost the same time.

149 *drenga sum* 'One of the mercenaries'. The third Viking to attack Byrhtnoth. The word *dreng* is loaned from Norse *drengr* 'young independent fortune-seeking man'. As it is written on Swedish and other runic memorials to describe men who died in Sveinn's later wars in England (Lund 1991: 117–130), 'mercenary' seems good here.

bræd of þam beorne blodigne gar,
Wulfstanes bearn, Wulfmær se geonga,
forlet forheardne faran eft ongean.
Ord in gewod, þæt se on eorþan læg
þe his þeoden ær þearle geræhte.
Eode þa gesyrwed secg to þam eorle,
he wolde þæs beornes beagas gefecgan,
reaf and hringas and gerenod swurd.
Þa Byrhtnoð bræd bill of sceðe,
brad and bruneccg, and on þa byrnan sloh.
To raþe hine gelette lidmanna sum,
þa he þæs eorles earm amyrde.
Feoll þa to foldan fealohilte swurd,
ne mihte he gehealdan heardne mece,
wæpnes wealdan.
Þa gyt þæt word gecwæð
har hilderinc, hyssas bylde,
bæd gangan forð gode geferan.

---

drew from his man the bleeding spear
(that was Wulfstan's child, young Wulfmær),
let the piercing dart pass back again.
The point went in, so on the ground he lay
who had hit the boy's lord hard before.
A man in armour than stepped to the earl,
wanted to fetch home our man's bracelets,
booty and rings and damascened sword.
So Byrhtnoth drew his blade from its sheath,
broad, burnished of edge, and struck his coat of mail.
Too quickly did one of the marines prevent him
in that he did cripple the earl's arm.
Fell then to earth the shiny-hilted sword,
nor could he longer hold his hard blade,
wield his weapon.
Still at that time did the grey-haired
soldier give orders, encouraged the boys,
bade his good companions move forwards.

---

159 *gesyrwed secg* 'man in armour'. The fourth Viking attacker.

164 *lidmanna sum* 'one of the marines'. The fifth Viking. A Danish *lið* 'company' implies a fleet, and is defined as operating 'under the leadership of some individual who was able to attract a following of others' (Lund 1991: 120).

170 *bæd gangan forð* 'bade move forwards'. Byrhtnoth's last order, to preserve his plan, is to move back the line, driving the Vikings into the rising tide.

Ne mihte þa on fotum leng fæste gestandan.
[. . .] He to heofenum wlat:
'Geþancie þe, ðeoda Waldend,
ealra þæra wynna þe ic on worulde gebad.
Nu ic ah, milde Metod, mæste þearfe
þæt þu minum gaste godes geunne,
þæt min sawul to ðe siðian mote
on þin geweald, Þeoden engla,
mid friþe ferian. Ic eom frymdi to þe
þæt hi helsceaðan hynan ne moton.'

Ða hine heowon hæðene scealcas
and begen þa beornas þe him big stodon,
Ælfnoð and Wulmær begen lagon,
ðа onemn hyra frean feorh gesealdon.

Nor could he on his feet stand firmly any longer.
[. . .] He gazed towards heaven:
'I thank you, Commander of Nations,
for all those joyful times I had on earth.
Now, generous Measurer, I have the greatest need
that you will grant good outcome to my ghost,
that my soul to you may journey up
into your power, O Lord of Angels,
travel in safe-keeping. Of my soul, I beseech you
that hell's warriors may not ill-treat it.'

Then heathen marshals cut him down,
along with both the men who stood by him,
Ælfnoth and Wulfmær both lay dead
who gave their lives close by their lord.

---

180 *helsceaðan* 'hell's warriors'. With this speech, Byrhtnoth makes a good Christian end, oblivious to any fiends but those of the hereafter, and hoping to enter heaven. The desecration of his body by heathen marshals may be compared to that of St Oswald by Penda's men in Ælfric's *Life of St Oswald*.

185 *þe þær beon noldon* 'who would not be there'. In other words, some elements in the Essex army were there against their will. See the following note.

186 *Oddan bearn* 'Odda's child'. Godric, who takes his brothers with him. Did they have a Scandinavian father? Odda looks like an English form of Oddi, a Norse personal name.

Englishmen fight to the end

Hi bugon þa fram beaduwe þe þær beon noldon.
Þær wearð Oddan bearn ærest on fleame,
Godric fram guþe, and þone godan forlet
þe him mænigne oft mear gesealde.
He gehleop þone eoh þe ahte his hlaford,
on þam gerædum þe hit riht ne wæs,
and his broðru mid him begen ærndon,
Godwine and Godwig, guþe ne gymdon,
ac wendon fram þam wige and þone wudu sohton,
flugon on þæt fæsten and hyra feore burgon,
and manna ma þonne hit ænig mæð wære,
gyf hi þa geearnunga ealle gemundon
þe he him to duguþe gedon hæfde.
Swa him Offa on dæg ær asæde
on þam meþelstede, þa he gemot hæfde,
þæt þær modiglice manega spræcon
þe eft æt þearfe þolian noldon.

Þa wearð afeallen þæs folces ealdor,
Æþelredes eorl. Ealle gesawon
heorðgeneatas þæt hyra heorra læg.
Þa ðær wendon forð wlance þegenas,

They sped off from the battle then who would not be there.
There Odda's child was the first to flee,
Godric from the strife, abandoning the generous man
who had often given him many a good horse.
He mounted the steed which belonged to his lord,
in the trappings which it was not right for him to have,
and his brothers both ran with him,
Godwine and Godwig, forgot the battle
but left the fighting and sought the woods,
fled into that fastness and saved their lives,
and more men too than were any decency in,
if they had recalled all those favours
he conferred on them in the battalion.
So Offa earlier that day had been saying
on the council house when he held the meeting,
that many were the men speaking bravely there
who in later need would not endure.

Now the people's chieftain was fallen,
Æthelred's earl. All the hearth-companions
could observe that their master lay dead.
Now there went forth proud thegns,

unearge men   efston georne.
Hi woldon þa ealle   oðer twega,
lif forlætan   oððe leofne gewrecan.
Swa hi bylde forð   bearn Ælfrices,
wiga wintrum geong,   wordum mælde,
Ælfwine þa cwæð,   he on ellen spræc:
'Gemunan þa mæla   þe we oft æt meodo spræcon,
þonne we on bence   beot ahofon,
hæleð on healle,   ymbe heard gewinn.
Nu mæg cunnian   hwa cene sy.
Ic wylle mine æþelo   eallum gecyþan,
þæt ic wæs on Myrcon   miccles cynnes.
Wæs min ealda fæder   Ealhelm haten,
wis ealdorman,   woruldgesælig.
Ne sceolon me on þære þeode   þegenas ætwitan
þæt ic of ðisse fyrde   feran wille,
eard gesecan,   nu min ealdor ligeð

---

men of no cowardice made eager haste.
One of two things they all wanted,
lose their lives or avenge the beloved man.
So Ælfric's child urged them forwards,
warrior young in winters, this was Ælfwine
who spoke then, with words for their courage:
'Let us recall the speeches we often made at mead,
when we lifted our boasting on the bench,
heroes in the hall, about this hard contest.
Now can be tried who is really keen.
I will declare my ancestry to everyone,
that I was of a great Mercian family.
My grandfather was called Elhhelm,
a wise ealdorman, a prosperous man.
No thegns are going to rebuke me in that country
for wanting to go away from this fyrd,
seek my homeland, now my chieftain lies

---

208 *lif forlætan oððe leofne gewrecan* 'lose their lives or avenge the beloved man'. This is the ethical ideal of Germanic warriors in Tacitus' *Germania*, ch. 14 (*c.* 98). It is also found in the ethos of the West Saxon aristocracy in the aftermath of King Cynewulf's death in 786 (see 'Cynewulf and Cyneheard', **The Earliest English Prose**).

211 Ælfwine is the highest-ranking noble after Byrhtnoth. The poet gives his father as Ælfric, but he gives his status through his maternal grandfather, Ealhhelm. His father, Ælfric Cild, married into the Mercian earldom, but disgraced himself in 983, when he inherited the earldom from Ealhhelm's son and his brother-in-law, Ælfhere, by seizing property from the latter's widow (Locherbie-Cameron 1991 (1): 241–2). Ælfhere's name is also missing. As earl of Mercia, he had been behind the anti-reform insurrection of 975, in which Byrhtnoth, championing Church privileges, became his political enemy. In 980 he made the mistake of giving proper burial to St Edward the Martyr, whom Æthelred's party has murdered two years earlier; so he fell out of favour and is not named here. In these ways, the political background was tense even before the Vikings arrived.

forheawen æt hilde.   Me is þæt hearma mæst,
he wæs ægðer min mæg   and min hlaford.'
Þa he forð eode,   fæhðe gemunde,
þæt he mid orde   anne geræhte
flotan on þam folce,   þæt se on foldan læg
forwegen mid his wæpne.   Ongan þa winas manian,
frynd and geferan,   þæt hi forð eodon.

Offa gemælde,   æscholt asceoc:
'Hwæt þu, Ælfwine, hafast   ealle gemanode
þegenas to þearfe,   nu ure þeoden lið,
eorl on eorðan.   Us is eallum þearf
þæt ure æghwylc   oþerne bylde
wigan to wige,   þa hwile þe he wæpen mæge
habban and healdan,   heardne mece,
gar and godswurd.   Us Godric hæfð,
earh Oddan bearn,   ealle beswicene!
Wende þæs formoni man,   þa he on meare rad,
on wlancan þam wicge,   þæt wære hit ure hlaford,
forþan wearð her on felda   folc totwæmed,
scyldburh tobrocen.   Abreoðe his angin,
þæt he her swa manigne   man aflymde!'

---

cut down in battle. The greatest harm in this is mine,
he was both my kinsman and my lord.'
So he went forth, remembered his feud
in that with spear-point he reached one
of the sailors so that the man lay on earth
slain with Ælfwine's weapon. His mates did then
exhort friends and comrades to go forwards.

Offa spoke, shook his ash-wood:
'Well, Ælfwine, you have admonished all the thegns
in this time of need, now our lord, the earl,
lies dead on the earth. The need is there for all of us
that each of us encourages the other
warrior to fight for as long as he may keep
and hold his weapons, his hard knife,
his spear and good sword. Godric, coward
child of Odda, has betrayed us all!
Too many men believed, when he rode the horse,
that proud charger, that it was our lord,
and so the army divided on this field,
the shieldwall broken. May his hopes die,
now he has put so many a man to flight!'

---

244 Leofsunu looks like a form of the Norse patronymic Leifsson. Possibly this was another East Saxon of Danish descent.

Leofsunu gemælde and his linde ahof,
bord to gebeorge, he þam beorne oncwæð:
'Ic þæt gehate, þæt ic heonon nelle
fleon fotes trym, ac wille furðor gan,
wrecan on gewinne minne winedrihten.
Ne þurfon me embe Sturmere stedefæste hælæð
wordum ætwitan, nu min wine gecranc,
þæt ic hlafordleas ham siðie,
wende fram wige, ac me sceal wæpen niman,
ord and iren!' He ful yrre wod,
feaht fæstlice, fleam he forhogode.

Dunnere þa cwæð, daroð acwehte,
unorne ceorl, ofer eall clypode,
bæd þæt beorna gehwylc Byrhtnoð wr*æ*ce:
'Ne mæg na wandian se þe wrecan þenceð
frean on folce, ne for feore murnan.'

Þa hi forð eodon, feores hi ne rohton,
ongunnon þa hiredmen heardlice feohtan,
grame garberend, and God bædon
þæt hi moston gewrecan hyra winedrihten
and on hyra feondum fyl gewyrcan.

Leofsunu spoke and raised his shield,
his board in defence, he spoke to this man:
'I vow to you that I will not from here
flee the pace of one foot, but will go further,
avenge in battle my friend and lord.
No steadfast men around Sturmer will need
to offer me rebukes, now my friend has fallen,
for journeying home without a lord,
fleeing combat, for a weapon will get me,
spear and blade!' In full fury he waded in,
fought without doubt, flight he despised.

Dunnere spoke then, brandished his lance,
yeoman old in years, called out to all,
bade that each boy should avenge Byrhtnoth:
'He can never flinch who means to avenge
his lord on that people, nor mourn for losing his life.'

So they marched forwards, cared not for living,
harshly did the men of the household fight,
ferocious spearmen, and prayed God
that they might avenge their friend and lord
and make great slaughter of their enemies.

Him se gysel ongan   geornlice fylstan,
he wæs on Norðhymbron   heardes cynnes,
Ecglafes bearn,   him wæs Æscferð nama.
He ne wandode na   æt þam wigplegan,
ac he fysde forð   flan genehe.
Hwilon he on bord sceat,   hwilon beorn tæsde,
æfre embe stunde   he sealde sume wunde,
þa hwile ðe he wæpna   wealdan moste.
Þa gyt on orde stod   Eadweard se langa,
gearo and geornful,   gylpwordum spræc
þæt he nolde fleogan   fotmæl landes,
ofer bæc bugan,   þa his betera leg.
He bræc þone bordweall   and wið þa beornas feaht,
oðþæt he his sincgyfan   on þam sæmannum
wurðlice wrec,   ær he on wæle *læ*ge.
Swa dyde Æþeric,   æþele gefera,
fus and forðgeorn,   feaht eornoste.
Sibyrhtes broðor   and swiðe mænig oþer
clufon cellod bord,   cene hi weredon.
Bærst bordes lærig,   and seo byrne sang
gryreleoða sum.   Þa æt guðe sloh
Offa þone sælidan,   þæt he on eorðan feoll,
and ðær Gaddes mæg   grund gesohte.

Them did the hostage eagerly support,
he was of a tough Northumbrian family,
Ecglaf's child, his name was Æscferth.
He flinched never from this war-play,
but often sped off an arrow forth. Sometimes
he shot into shields, sometimes sliced through a man,
ever at intervals he gave some wounds,
as long as he might wield his weapons.
Still at this time in the front line, ready and
alert, stood Edward the Tall, vaunted aloud
that he would not flee one foot of land,
would not turn back, now his superior lay dead.
He broke their board-wall and fought the boys,
until he had worthily avenged his giver of treasure
on the seafarers, before he lay among the dead.
Just the same did Æthelric, noble companion,
inspired and raring to go, he seriously fought.
Sigeberht's brother and many another man, cleft
the rounded shields, keenly they defended themselves.
Strap on board snapped, and the mailcoat sang
its verses of horror. Then in battle did Offa
slay the sailor so that he fell down on earth,
and there did Gadd's kinsman seek the ground.

Raðe wearð æt hilde Offa forheawen,
he hæfde ðeah geforþod þæt he his frean gehet,
swa he beotode ær wið his beahgifan
þæt hi sceoldon begen on burh ridan,
hale to hame, oððe on here crincgan,
on wælstowe wundum sweltan.
He læg ðegenlice ðeodne gehende.
Đa wearð borda gebræc. Brimmen wodon,
guðe gegremode, gar oft þurhwod
fæges feorhhus. Forð þa eode Wistan,
Þurstanes sunu, wið þas secgas feaht.
He wæs on geþrange hyra þreora bana,
ær him Wigelmes bearn on þam wæle læge.
Þær wæs stið gemot, stodon fæste
wigan on gewinne, wigend cruncon,
wundum werige. Wæl feol on eorþan.
Oswold and Eadwold ealle hwile,
begen þa gebroþru, beornas trymedon,
hyra winemagas wordon bædon
þæt hi þær æt ðearfe þolian sceoldon,
unwaclice wæpna neotan.

Quickly in the conflict was Offa cut down,
and yet he had accomplished what he promised
his lord, just as he vowed before to his ring-giver
that both of them should ride to town,
homewards safe, or perish with the raiders,
die of their wounds on the killing ground.
He lay like a thegn close to his lord.
Then there was a crack of boards. Sailors waded up,
mad with the war, often a spear pierced
a doomed man's life-house. Forth went Wistan
Thurstan's son, fought against those men.
In that throng did Wighelm's child kill
three of them before he lay among the dead.
There was a stiff encounter, warriors stood
firm in the strife, fighters perished
wearied by wounds. The dead fell on earth.
All this while did Oswold and Eadwold,
brothers both, line up the boys,
with many words asked their friends and kinsmen
that they should endure there in this need,
make unwavering use of their weapons.

---

300 *Wigelmes bearn* 'Wighelm's child'. Most take this for Wistan, whose name shows that they are probably related. The problem is Thurstan, given above as Wistan's father. Either a line has dropped out, or there was a family oddity in Wistan's background, or, as here, Wistan and Wighelm's son are two different people.

Byrhtwold maþelode, bord hafenode
(se wæs eald geneat), æsc acwehte,
he ful baldlice beornas lærde:
'Hige sceal þe heardra, heorte þe cenre,
mod sceal þe mare, þe ure mægen lytlað.
Her lið ure ealdor eall forheawen,
god on greote. A mæg gnornian
se ðe nu fram þis wigplegan wendan þenceð.
Ic eom frod feores, fram ic ne wille,
ac ic me be healfe minum hlaforde,
be swa leofan men, licgan þence.'

Swa hi Æþelgares bearn ealle bylde,
Godric to guþe. Oft he gar forlet,
wælspere windan on þa wicingas,
swa he on þam folce fyrmest eode,
heow and hynde, oðþæt he on hilde gecranc.
Næs þæt na se Godric þe ða guðe forbeah
[. . .

Byrhtwold spoke, lifted his board
(he was an old companion), brandished his ash-spear,
he very boldly instructed the warriors:
'Mind shall be the harder, heart the keener,
courage shall be the greater, though our strength grows less.
Here lies our chieftain all cut down,
a good man on the gravel. Ever can he mourn
who now intends to turn from this war-play.
I am old in my life, I will not go away,
for it is by the side of my lord, by such
a beloved man, that I think I will lie.'

Likewise did Æthelgar's child, Godric, encourage
them all in to battle. Often he let a spear,
a murderous lance spin into the Vikings,
as foremost he marched into that people,
hewed and killed until he fell in war.
Never was that the Godric who made off from battle
[. . .

---

309 Charters tell us that Byrhtwold was an endowed servant of Byrhtnoth. He later joined his household, and may be a relative (Locherbie-Cameron 1991 (1): 243). The memorable words of his final injunction (the end cannot be far away for the poem, despite the missing ending) embodies, for many, the spirit of Anglo-Saxon England.

GODS OF THE VIKINGS

* * *

GODS OF THE VIKINGS

* * *

Old Norse mythology is a popular subject, and even now a new book by Chris Abram has come out in which its essential hybridity and Christianised elements are properly observed. What this section will provide, in complement, is primary texts and annotated translations of the major works on which all scholarly judgements on the mythology are founded. This too has been done before, but in a way more limited than here. The novelty of this presentation is to introduce Skaldic poetry to readers, eulogies of complicated style, irony and surreal perspectives on the world of gods and men. These poems are usually inaccessible, but translations are here provided of the pre-Christian works which were themselves constructed out of 'Eddic' poetry, the type more commonly represented. Chapters from Snorri's expansive *Edda* are thus followed by the other half of Bragi's remaining *Eulogy on Ragnarr*, in which he shows the creation of Zealand and Þórr's fishing trip for the World Serpent. *The Lay of Skírnir* varies this presentation with a mysterious and perplexing poem on star-crossed lovers, coercion, or the planting of the land, all depending on how one approaches the dating of Norse mythology. Another more popular item from the Poetic *Edda*, that is the Codex Regius manuscript of *c.* 1290, is *The Thunderclap Ballad*, which seems to offer a thirteenth-century Christian view of Þórr, the most popular god, as he turns up in drag to marry the giant who stole his hammer. Following this comedy, however, is the real thing, a Skaldic poem in praise of Þórr in which the god is made to represent Earl Hákon, patron of the skald. If Hákon's poets fill most of the remainder of this section, that is because it was he who helped to save Norse mythology in the first place. In his brilliant but deluded reign as the last heathen ruler of Norway, Hákon stimulated the production and imitation of the richest Skaldic poetry in Icelandic literature. Hákon's archaising ideal of sacral kingship is displayed in his poems, before the Christianised elements take over, with *The Sibyl's Prophecy* from *c.* 1000 in Iceland and *Loki's Truth-Game* from (it is suggested) a generation after. This was the imaginative high-point of the culture whose armies invaded and then conquered Britain.

General bibliography

Abram, C., *Myths of the Pagan North* (London, 2010)

Faulkes, A., trans., *Snorri Sturluson: Edda* (London, 1987)

Faulkes, A., ed., *Snorri Sturluson: Edda: Skáldskaparmál*, 2 vols (London, 1998)

Frank, R., *Old Norse Court Poetry: The Dróttkvætt Stanza*, Islandica 42 (Ithaca and London, 1978)

Gunnell, T., 'Viking religion: Old Norse mythology', *B&OS* 351–75

Hollander, Lee M., *The Skalds: A Selection of Their Poems with Introduction and Notes* (Princeton, NJ, 1945)

Jónas Kristjánsson, *Eddas and Sagas: Iceland's Medieval Literature*, trans. Peter Foote (Reykjavík, 1992)

Larrington, C., trans., *The Poetic Edda* (Oxford, 1996)

Lindow, J., *Scandinavian Mythology: An Annotated Bibliography*, Garland Folklore Bibliographies 13 (New York, 1988)

Lindow, J., *Handbook of Norse Mythology* (Santa Barbara, CA, 2001)

McTurk, R., ed., *A Companion to Old Norse-Icelandic Literature* (Maldon, MA, 2005)

North, R., *Heathen Gods in Old English Literature*, Cambridge Studies in Anglo-Saxon England 22 (Cambridge, 1997)

Orchard, A., *The Cassell Dictionary of Norse Myth and Legend* (London, 1997)

Roesdahl, E., *The Vikings*, trans. S. Margeson and K. Williams, 2nd rev. ed. (Harmondsworth, 1998)

Turville-Petre, E. O. G., *Scaldic Poetry* (Oxford, 1976)

Snorri's *Edda*
Snorra Edda

c. 1220–30

✳

In early manhood Snorri Sturluson (1179–1241) began to collect poetic and mythological material and to write this up in drafts which eventually became the Prose *Edda* or *Snorra Edda*, a three-section handbook for Skaldic poets. Stories about the Norse gods form the core of *Gylfaginning* 'The Beguiling of Gylfi'. *Skáldskaparmál* 'The Language of Poetry' follows on. This treatise is a brilliant and comprehensive discussion of kennings, the intricate metaphoric tropes often drawn from the old mythology, citing examples of poems by many named skalds. The final section is a long poem called the *Háttatal* 'List of Verse Forms'. This is a catalogue of over 100 metrical verse forms composed by Snorri himself, in praise of King Hákon Hákonarson of Norway (ruled 1217–63) and the latter's enemy and father-in-law, Earl Skúli (died 1240). *The Beguiling of Gylfi* and *The Language of Poetry* were intended to provide aspiring poets in Iceland with the knowledge to compose mythological poems of their own. *The Beguiling of Gylfi* tells most of the Norse myths in prose form, within a story in which King Gylfi of Sweden, disguised as 'Gangleri', sets out to discover the magic of a mysterious race of beings called the Æsir, who had once been worshipped as gods. A welcoming committee of three beings called *Hár* 'High', *Jafnhár* 'Just-as-High' and *Þriði* 'Third' tells the disguised Gylfi, responding to his questions, everything he needs to know from the creation of the Norse cosmos to its violent end in Ragnarǫk. To help him write this, Snorri quoted some poems from a collection in his keeping. In *The Language of Poetry*, probably written earlier than *The Beguiling of Gylfi*, Snorri sets out to explain the working of the Skaldic kenning upon which Old Norse-Icelandic court poetry was based. Skaldic poetry differs from 'Eddic' in consisting of largely occasional verse produced in complex metres by poets whose names survive. In his *Edda*, Snorri quotes an abundance of pre-Christian stanzas in *The Language of Poetry*, from which much has been ascertained one way or another about the religion of his heathen ancestors in Iceland and Norway.

Below are text and translation of three passages from Snorri's *Edda*. The first describes the creation of the cosmos and man and woman. Next is the section about the death of Baldr the Good, which would lead, finally, to the catastrophic apocalypse called Ragnarǫk. Finally (in the Custom Version) is the section of *Skáldskaparmál* which tells how Óðinn managed to acquire the Mead of Poetry from the dwarves and giants for the Æsir. All of this mythological information will shed useful light on the many surprising images to be encountered in the Old Icelandic poetry in this book.

Faulkes, A., trans., *Snorri Sturluson: Edda* (London, 1987)

Gunnell, T., *The Origins of Drama in Scandinavia* (Cambridge, 1995)

Jónas Kristjánsson, *Eddas and Sagas*, trans. Peter Foote (Reykjavík, 1992)

Larrington, C., trans., *The Poetic Edda* (Oxford, 1996)

Lindow, J., *Handbook of Norse Mythology* (Santa Barbara, CA, 2001)

McTurk, R., ed., *A Companion to Old Norse-Icelandic Literature* (Maldon, MA, 2005)

North, R., *Heathen Gods in Old English Literature* (Cambridge, 1997)

Orchard, A., *Cassell's Dictionary of Norse Myth and Legend* (London, 1997)

The Old Norse myth of Creation

6. Þá mælir Gangleri, 'Hvar bygði Ymir eða við hvat lifði hann?'

'Næst var þat, þá er hrímit draup, at þar varð af kýr sú er Auðhumla hét, en fjórar mjólkár runnu ór spenum hennar, ok fœddi hon Ymi.'

Þá mælir Gangleri, 'Við hvat fœddisk kýrin?'

Hár segir, 'Hon sleikti hrímsteinana, er saltir váru. Ok hinn fyrsta dag er hon sleikti steina kom ór steininum at kveldi manns hár, annan dag manns hǫfuð, þriðja dag var þar allr maðr. Sá er nefndr Búri. Hann var fagr álitum, mikill ok máttugr. Hann gat son þann er Borr hét. Hann fekk þeirar konu er Bestla hét, dóttir Bǫlþorns jǫtuns, ok fengu þau þrjá sonu. Hét einn Óðinn, annarr Vili, þriði Vé. Ok þat er mín trúa at sá Óðinn ok hans brœðr munu vera stýrandi himins ok jarðar; þat ætlum vér at hann muni svá heita. Svá heitir sá maðr er vér vitum mestan ok ágæztan, ok vel megu þér hann láta svá heita.'

7. Þá mælir Gangleri, 'Hvat varð þá um þeira sætt, eða hvárir váru ríkari?'

Þá svarar Hár, 'Synir Bors drápu Ymi jǫtun. En er hann féll, þá hljóp svá mikit blóð ór sárum hans at með því drektu þeir allri ætt hrímþursa, nema einn komsk undan með sínu hýski. Þann kalla jǫtnar Bergelmi. Hann fór upp

---

6. Then Gangleri said, 'Where did Ymir [an ancient frost giant] live, and what did he live on?'

'The next thing, when the rime dripped, was that there appeared a cow called Auðhumla, with four rivers of milk flowing from her udders, and she fed Ymir.'

Then Gangleri said, 'What did the cow feed on?'

High said, 'She licked the rime-stones, which were salty. And the first day she licked the stones a man's hair emerged from the stones in the evening, the next day a man's head, and on the third day there was a complete man. His name was Búri. He looked beautiful, large and powerful. He had a son called Borr. He married a woman called Bestla, daughter of the giant Bǫlþorn, and they had three sons. One was named Óðinn, the second Vili, the third Vé. And it is my belief that this Óðinn and his brothers must be the rulers of the heavens and the earth; it is our opinion that this is what he must be called. This is the name of the one who is the greatest and most glorious, and you would do well to call him that too.'

7. Then Gangleri said, 'How did they get on together, and which was more powerful?'

Hár answered, 'Borr's sons killed the giant Ymir. And when he fell so much blood flowed from his wounds that with it they drowned all the race of the frost giants, except one that escaped with his household. Giants call him Bergelmir. He went up on his ark with his wife á lúðr sinn ok kona hans ok helzk þar, ok eru af þeim komnar hrímþursa ættir, svá sem hér segir:

> Ørófi vetra   áðr væri jǫrð of skǫpuð,
> þá var Bergelmir borinn;
> þat ek fyrst of man   er sá inn fróði jǫtunn
> á var lúðr of lagiðr.

8. Þá svarar Gangleri, 'Hvat hǫfðusk þá at Bors synir, ef þú trúir at þeir sé guð?'

Hár segir, 'Eigi er þar lítit af at segja. Þeir tóku Ymi ok fluttu í mitt Ginnungagap, ok gerðu af honum jǫrðina, af blóði hans sæinn ok vǫtnin. Jǫrðin var gǫr af holdinu en bjǫrgin af beinunum, grjót ok urðir gerðu þeir af tǫnnum ok jǫxlum ok af þeim beinum er brotin váru.'

Þá mælir Jafnhár, 'Af því blóði er ór sárum rann ok laust fór, þar af gerðu þeir sjá þann er þeir gerðu ok festu saman jǫrðina, ok lǫgðu þann sjá í hring útan um hana, ok mun þat flestum manni ófœra þykkja at komast þar yfir.'

Þá mælir Þriði, 'Tóku þeir ok haus hans ok gerðu þar af himin ok settu hann upp yfir jǫrðina með fjórum skautum, ok undir hvert horn settu þeir dverg. Þeir heita svá: Austri, Vestri, Norðri, Suðri. Þá tóku þeir síur ok gneista þá er lausir fóru ok kastat hafði ór Múspellsheimi, ok settu á miðjan Ginnungahimin bæði ofan ok neðan til at lýsa himin ok jǫrð. Þeir gáfu staðar ǫllum eldingum, sumum á himni, sumar fóru lausar undir himni, ok settu þó þeim

---

and was saved there, and from them are descended the families of the frost giants, as it says here:

> Countless winters before the earth was formed,
> then was Bergelmir born;
> this is the first I remember, when that wise giant
> was laid in an ark.

8. Gangleri replied, 'What did the sons of Borr do then, if you believe they were gods?'

High said, 'There is more than just a little to be told about that. They took Ymir and carried him to the middle of Ginnungagap, and made the earth out of him, and the seas and lakes from his blood. The earth was made from the flesh and the rocks from the bones, the scree and stones were made from his teeth and molars and of the bones that had been broken.'

Then Just-as-High said, 'From the blood that was flowing from his wounds unconfined they made the sea with which they surrounded and contained the earth, and they placed the sea in a circle around the outside of it, and it will seem almost an impossibility to most to get across it.'

Then Third said, 'They also took his skull and made the sky out of it and set it up over the earth with four points, and under each corner they put a dwarf. Their names are: Austri, Vestri, Norði, Suðri. They then took the molten particles and sparks that were flying without control and shooting out of the world of Muspell and set them in the middle of the firmament above and below to illuminate the heavens and the earth. They fixed all the lights, some set in the sky, some moving in a wandering course beneath the sky, but they stað ok skǫpuðu gǫngu þeim. Svá er sagt í fornum vísindum at þaðan af váru dœgr greind ok áratal, svá sem segir í Vǫluspá:

Sól þat né vissi hvar hon sali átti.
Máni þat né vissi hvat hann megins átti.
Stjǫrnur þat né vissu hvar þær staði áttu.

Svá var áðr en þetta væri of jǫrð.'

Þá mælir Gangleri, 'Þetta eru mikil tíðindi er nú heyri ek. Furðu mikil smíð er þat ok hagliga gert. Hvernig var jǫrðin háttuð?'

Þá svarar Hár, 'Hon er kringlótt útan, ok þar útan um liggr inn djúpi sjár, ok með þeiri sjávar strǫndu gáfu þeir lǫnd til bygðar jǫtna ættum. En fyrir innan á jǫrðunni gerðu þeir borg umhverfis heim fyrir ófriði jǫtna, en til þeirar borgar hǫfðu þeir brár Ymis jǫtuns, ok kǫlluðu þá borg Miðgarð. Þeir tóku ok heila hans ok kǫstuðu í lopt ok gerðu af skýin, svá sem hér segir:

Ór Ymis holdi var jǫrð of skǫpuð,
  en ór sveita sjár,
bjǫrg ór beinum, baðmr ór hári,
  en ór hausi himinn;

En ór hans brám gerðu blíð regin
  Miðgarð manna sonum,
en ór hans heila váru þau in harðmóðgu
  ský ǫll of skǫpuð.'

---

put them in position and ordered their courses. It is thus said in ancient sources that by means of this days are distinguished and also the count of years, as it says in *The Sibyl's Prophecy*:

Sun did not know where her dwelling was.
Moon did not know what might he had.
Stars did not know where their places were.

This is what it was like above the earth before this.'

Then Gangleri said: 'This is very important information that I am hearing. That is a huge construction and skilfully made. How was the earth arranged?'

High replied, 'It is circular around the edge, and around it lies the sea, and along the shore of this sea are lands to inhabit by the races of the giants. But on the inner side they made a fortification around the world against the hostility of giants, for which they used the eyelashes of the giant Ymir, and they called this fortification Miðgarð. They also took his brains and threw them into the sky to make clouds, as it says here:

From Ymir's flesh was earth formed
  and from his blood, the sea;
rocks of bones, trees of hair,
  from his skull, the sky,

And from his eyelashes made the joyous gods
  Miðgarðr for men's sons,
from his brains were those oppressive clouds
  all created.'

The death of Baldr the Beautiful

49. Þá mælir Gangleri, 'Hafa nokkvor meiri tíðindi orðit með Ásunum? Allmikit þrekvirki vann Þórr í þessi ferð.'

Hár svarar, 'Vera mun at segja frá þeim tíðindum er meira þótti vert Ásunum. En þat er upphaf þessar sǫgu at Baldr inn góða dreymði drauma stóra ok hættliga um líf sitt. En er hann sagði Ásunum draumana þá báru þeir saman ráð sín, ok var þat gert at beiða griða Baldri fyrir alls konar háska, ok Frigg tók svardaga til þess at eira skyldu Baldri eldr ok vatn, járn ok alls konar málmr, steinar, jǫrðin, viðirnir, sóttirnar, dýrin, fuglarnir, eitr, ormar.

'En er þetta var gert ok vitat, þá var þat skemtun Baldrs ok Ásanna at hann skyldi standa upp á þingum en allir aðrir skyldu sumir skjóta á hann, sumir hǫggva til, sumir berja grjóti. En hvat sem at var gert, sakaði hann ekki, ok þótti þetta ǫllum mikill frami. En er þetta sá Loki Laufeyjarson þá líkaði honum illa er Baldr sakaði ekki. Hann gekk til Fensalar til Friggjar ok brá sér í konu líki. Þá spyrr Frigg ef sú kona vissi hvat Æsir hǫfðusk at á þinginu. Hon sagði, at allir skutu at Baldri, ok þat at hann sakaði ekki.

'Þá mælir Frigg: "Eigi munu vápn eða viðir granda Baldri. Eiða hefi ek þegit af ǫllum þeim."

'Þá spyrr konan, "Hafa allir hlutir eiða unnit at eira Baldri?"

'Þá svarar Frigg, "Vex viðarteinungr einn fyrir vestan Valhǫll. Sá er mistilteinn kallaðr. Sá þótti mér ungr at krefja eiðsins."

---

49. Then Gangleri asked, 'Is there more to be told about the Æsir? It was a great feat that Þórr achieved on this journey.'

High answered, 'One can tell of an event the Æsir thought to be more significant. And the origin of this saga is that Baldr the Good dreamed great dreams which boded danger to his life. And when he told the Æsir about his dreams they took counsel together, and decided to seek immunity for Baldr from all kinds of danger, and Frigg received promises that Baldr would not be harmed by fire or water, iron and all kinds of metal, stones, earth, trees, disease, animals, birds, poisons and snakes.

'And when this was done and became known, it became an entertainment for Baldr and the Æsir that he would stand up at assemblies and the others would shoot at him; some would strike blows, and others would throw stones, and whatever they did he was unharmed, and this was thought to be a great marvel.

'But when Loki Laufeyjarson saw this he was displeased that Baldr was unharmed. He went to Frigg at Fensalir having changed himself into the likeness of a woman. Frigg asked the woman if she knew what the Æsir were doing at the assembly. She answered that everyone was shooting at Baldr and yet he suffered no injury.

'Then Frigg said, "Neither weapons nor wood will hurt Baldr. I have received oaths from them all."

'Then the woman asked, "Have all things sworn their oaths not to harm Baldr?"

'The Frigg replied, "A shoot of wood grows to the west of Vallhalla. It's called mistletoe. It seemed to me too young to demand an oath from."

'Því næst hvarf konan á braut. En Loki tók mistiltein ok sleit upp ok gekk til þings. En Hǫðr stóð útarliga í mannhringinum, þvíat hann var blindr. Þá mælir Loki við hann: ' "Hví skýtr þú ekki at Baldri?"

'Hann svarar, "Þvíat ek sé eigi hvar Baldr er, ok þat annat at ek em vápnlauss."

'Þá mælir Loki, "Gerðu þó í líking annarra manna ok veit Baldri sœmð sem aðrir menn. Ek mun vísa þér til hvar hann stendr. Skjót at honum vendi þessum."

'Hǫðr tók mistiltein ok skaut at Baldri at tilvísun Loka. Flaug skotit í gǫgnum hann ok féll hann dauðr til jarðar, ok hefir þat mest óhapp verit unnit með goðum ok mǫnnum.

'Þá er Baldr var fallinn þá fellusk ǫllum Ásum orðtǫk ok svá hendr at taka til hans, ok sá hverr til annars, ok váru allir með einum hug til þess er unnit hafði verkit. En engi mátti hefna, þar var svá mikill griðastaðr. En þá er Æsirnir freistuðu at mæla þá var hitt þó fyrr at grátrinn kom upp svá at engi mátti ǫðrum segja með orðunum frá sínum harmi. En Óðinn bar þeim mun verst þenna skaða sem hann kunni mesta skyn hversu mikil aftaka ok missa Ásunum var í fráfalli Baldrs.

'En er goðin vitkuðusk þá mælir Frigg ok spurði hverr sá væri með Ásum er eignask vildi allar ástir hennar ok hylli ok vili hann ríða á Helveg ok freista ef hann fái fundit Baldr ok bjóða Helju útlausn ef hon vill láta fara Baldr heim í Ásgarð. En sá er nefndr Hermóðr inn hvati, sveinn Óðins, er til þeirar farar varð. Þá var tekinn Sleipnir, hestr Óðins, ok leiddr fram, ok steig Hermóðr á þann hest ok hleypti braut.

'The woman disappeared immediately, but Loki took mistletoe, plucked it and went to the assembly. Hodr stood at the edge of the ring of people because he was blind.

'Then Loki said to him, "Why aren't you shooting at Baldr?"

'He said, "Because I can't see where Baldr is, and also I have no weapon."

'Then Loki said, "You should act as others, honouring Baldr as they do. I will direct you to where he is standing. Shoot at him with this twig."

'Hodr took the mistletoe and shot at Baldr, following Loki's directions. The shot went right through Baldr, and he fell dead to the ground, and this was the most unfortunate deed ever among gods and men.

'When Baldr had fallen all the Æsir were speechless and so weak in the arms that they were unable to lift him up, and they looked at one another and were of one mind towards the one who had done the killing. Yet no one could take vengeance because it was a place of such great sanctuary. When the Æsir tried to speak all that came out was weeping, so that no one could tell another in words of his or her grief. Óðinn suffered the most from this misfortune because he understood most clearly how serious the loss was, and that the death of Baldr was ruin for the Æsir. When the gods came to their senses then Frigg spoke, and asked who among the Æsir wished to earn all her love and favour by riding the road to Hel to try to find Baldr and offer Hel a ransom if she were willing to allow Baldr to go back to Ásgarðr. Hermóðr the Bold, Óðinn's son, was the one who agreed to undertake the journey. They then caught Sleipnir, Óðinn's horse, and led it forward. Hermóðr mounted the horse and galloped away.

'En Æsirnir tóku lík Baldrs ok fluttu til sævar. Hringhorni hét skip Baldrs. Hann var allra skipa mestr. Hann vildu goðin fram setja ok gera þar á bálfǫr Baldrs. En skipit gekk hvergi fram. Þá var sent í Jǫtunheima eptir gýgi þeiri er Hyrrokkin hét. En er hon kom ok reið vargi ok hafði hǫggorm at taumum þá hljóp hon af hestinum, en Óðinn kallaði til berserki fjóra at gæta hestsins, ok fengu þeir eigi haldit nema þeir feldi hann. Þá gekk Hyrrokkin á framstafn nǫkkvans ok hratt fram í fyrsta viðbragði svá at eldr hraut ór hlunnunum ok lǫnd ǫll skulfu. Þá varð Þórr reiðr ok greip hamarinn ok myndi þá brjóta hǫfuð hennar áðr en goðin ǫll báðu henni friðar. Þá var borit út á skipit lík Baldrs, ok er þat sá kona hans Nanna Nepsdóttir þá sprakk hon af harmi ok dó. Var hon borin á bálit ok slegit í eldi. Þá stóð Þórr at ok vígði bálit með Mjǫllni. En fyrir fótum hans rann dvergr nokkurr. Sá er Litr nefndr. En Þórr spyrnði fœti sínum á hann ok hratt honum í eldinn ok brann hann.

'En at þessi brennu sótti margs konar þjóð: fyrst at segja frá Óðni, at með honum fór Frigg ok valkyrjur ok hrafnar hans, en Freyr ók í kerru með gelti þeim er Gullinbursti heitir eða Slíðrugtanni. En Heimdallr reið hesti þeim er Gulltoppr heitir, en Freyja kǫttum sínum. Þar kømr ok mikit fólk hrímþursa ok bergrisar. Óðinn lagði á bálit gullhring þann er Draupnir heitir. Honum fylgði síðan sú náttúra, at hina níundu hverja nótt drupu af honum átta gullhringar jafnhǫfgir. Hestr Baldrs var leiddr á bálit með ǫllu reiði.

'En þat er at segja frá Hermóði at hann reið níu nætr døkkva dala ok djúpa svá at hann sá ekki fyrr en hann kom til árinnar Gjallar ok reið á Gjallar brúna. Hon er þǫkð lýsigulli.

'Then the Æsir took Baldr's body and carried it to the sea. Baldr's ship was called Hringhorni (Ringhorn). It was the greatest of all ships. The Æsir wanted to launch it and use it for Baldr's funeral. But the ship refused to budge. Then they sent to Giantland for a giantess called Hyrrokkin. And when she arrived, riding a wolf and using venomous snakes for reins, she jumped off her mount. Óðinn told four berserks to watch over the mount but they were unable to hold it without knocking it down. Then Hyrrokkin went to the prow of the boat and pushed it out with her first touch so that flame flew from the log rollers under the keel and the whole land quaked. Then Þórr became angry and gripped his hammer and was about to smash the head of the giantess, but the rest of the gods asked that she be left in peace. Then Baldr's body was carried out to the ship. When his wife Nanna, Nep's daughter, saw this her heart burst with grief and she died. She was carried to the funeral pyre and it was set on fire. Then Þórr stood up and blessed the pyre with Mjǫllnir. A dwarf named Litr ran in front of his feet. Þórr kicked him with his foot and the dwarf was thrust into the fire where he burned. Many kinds of beings attended the burning. First to be mentioned is Óðinn. Frigg came with him with valkyries and his ravens, but Freyr drove his chariot drawn by a boar called Gold Bristle (Gullinbursti) or Sheathed Tooth (Slíðrugtanni). Heimdallr rode his horse named Gold Top (Gulltopp) and Freyja was drawn by her cats. Many also came from among the frost-giants and the mountain-giants. Óðinn laid a gold arm-ring called Draupnir on the pyre. Afterwards it had the property that every ninth night there dripped from it eight gold rings of the same weight. Baldr's horse was led to the pyre in full harness.

'But there is this to tell of Hermóðr: he rode for nine nights through valleys so dark and deep that he could see nothing until he reached the river Gjǫll and rode on to Gjǫll Bridge. The bridge is roofed with glowing gold.

'Móðguðr er nefnd mær sú er gætir brúarinnar. Hon spurði hann at nafni eða at ætt ok sagði at hinn fyrra dag riðu um brúna fimm fylki dauðra manna, "En eigi dynr brúin minnr undir einum þér ok eigi hefir þú lit dauðra manna. Hví ríðr þú hér á Helveg?"

'Hann svarar at "ek skal ríða til Heljar at leita Baldrs. Eða hvárt hefir þú nakkvat sét Baldr á Helvegi?"

'En hon sagði at Baldr hafði þar riðit um Gjallar brú, "en niðr ok norðr liggr Helvegr."

'Þá reið Hermóðr þar til er hann kom at Helgrindum. Þá sté hann af hestinum ok gyrði hann fast, steig upp ok keyrði hann sporum. En hestrinn hljóp svá hart ok yfir grindina at hann kom hvergi nær. Þá reið Hermóðr heim til hallarinnar ok steig af hesti, gekk inn í hǫllina, sá þar sitja í ǫndugi Baldr bróður sinn, ok dvalðisk Hermóðr þar um nóttina. En at morni þá beiddisk Hermóðr af Helju at Baldr skyldi ríða heim með honum ok sagði hversu mikill grátr var með Ásum.

'En Hel sagði at þat skyldi svá reyna hvárt Baldr var svá ástsæll sem sagt er, "Ok ef allir hlutir í heiminum, kykvir ok dauðir, gráta hann, þá skal hann fara til Ása aptr, en haldask með Helju ef nakkvarr mælir við eða vill eigi gráta."

'Þá stóð Hermóðr upp, en Baldr leiðir hann út ór hǫllinni ok tók hringinn Draupni ok sendi Óðni til minja, en Nanna sendi Frigg ripti ok enn fleiri gjafar; Fullu fingrgull. Þá reið Hermóðr aptr leið sína ok kom í Ásgarð ok sagði ǫll tíðindi þau er hann hafði sét ok heyrt.

'The maiden guarding it was named Móðguðr. She asked him his name and lineage and said that the day before five battalions of dead men had ridden over the bridge, "but the bridge echoes more under you alone, and you don't have the colour of the dead. Where are you riding on the road to Hel?"

'He replied, "I am to ride to Hel to seek Baldr but have you seen anything of Baldr on the road to Hel?"

'And she said that Baldr had ridden over Gjǫll Bridge, "but lower and to the north lies the road to Hel".

'Then Hermóðr rode on until he came to Hel's gates. Then he dismounted from his horse and tightened the girth. He remounted and spurred the horse. The horse sprang forward with such force that it cleared the gate without coming near. Then Hermóðr rode up to the hall, dismounted and went inside. He saw his brother Baldr sitting in the seat of honour. Hermóðr stayed there through the night. In the morning Hermóðr begged from Hel that Baldr might ride home with him, telling her what great weeping there was among the Æsir.

'But Hel said that it must be tested whether Baldr was as beloved as people said, "If all things in the world, alive and dead, weep for him, he will be allowed to go back to the Æsir. But he will be kept in Hel if anyone objects or refuses to weep."

'The Hermóðr stood up and Baldr led him out of the hall and took the ring Draupnir and sent it to Óðinn as a reminder, and Nanna sent Frigg a linen robe and other gifts. She sent a gold finger-ring to Fulla. Then Hermóðr rode back to Ásgerd and told all the tidings of what had happened and what he had seen and heard.

'Því næst sendu Æsir um allan heim ørindreka at biðja at Baldr væri grátinn ór Helju. En allir gerðu þat, mennirnir ok kykvendin ok jǫrðin ok steinarnir ok tré ok allr málmr, svá sem þú munt sét hafa at þessir hlutir gráta þá er þeir koma ór frosti ok í hita.

'Þá er sendimenn fóru heim ok hǫfðu vel rekit sín eyrindi, finna þeir í helli nokkvorum hvar gýgr sat. Hon nefndisk Þǫkk. Þeir biðja hana gráta Baldr ór Helju. Hon segir:

"Þǫkk mun gráta þurrum tárum
Baldrs bálfarar.
Kyks né dauðs nautka ek karls sonar:
haldi Hel því er hefir."

'En þess geta menn at þar hafi verit Loki Laufeyjarson er flest hefir illt gert með Ásum.'

'After this the Æsir sent messengers all over the world to ask that Baldr be wept out of Hel. And all did this, the men and women and animals and the earth and stones and trees and all metals in the way that you have seen that these things weep when they come out of the frost and into the warmth. When the messengers were returning home having accomplished their task they found a giantess sitting in a certain cave. Her name was *Þǫkk* 'grace'. They asked her to weep Baldr out of Hel. She said:

"Þhǫkk will weep dry tears for
Baldr's funeral.
Alive or dead the old man's son gave me no joy
Let Hel keep what she has!"

'People thought that this was Loki Laufeyjarson, who has done most ill among the Æsir.'

Bragi's *Eulogy on Ragnarr*

Ragnarsdrápa

Bragi *inn gamli* 'the Old' Boddason, *c.* 850

⁕

Snorri quoted this poem in sections across his *Edda*, and the Gefjun-stanza in *Gylfaginning* and *Ynglinga saga* 'The Saga of the Ynglingar'. If it is treated as the oldest Skaldic poem surviving, that is because its alleged author, Bragi Boddason, is said in legend to have been the father of the main authors of the Danish attacks on England in the 870s (see **Viking Wars**), Ingvarr or Ívarr the Boneless and his brothers. Thus the *Eulogy on Ragnarr* is placed very approximately in the mid-ninth century. The order of stanzas in this poem is a modern convention, as it is for nearly all the others. Nonetheless, some great narratives remain, as may be seen with the story where Gefjun turns her four giant sons into oxen, yokes them to a plough and tears land from Sweden to make the new isle of Zealand; and with the story where Þórr tries to catch the World Serpent while fishing for it from Hymir's boat. For the heroic sections in this poem, which dramatise the attack on King Jǫrmunrekkr of the Goths and the endless battle of Heðinn and Hǫgni off Orkney, see the *Eulogy on Ragnarr* in **Heroic Poems**.

Gefjun drags Zealand from Sweden

12 Gefjon dró frá Gylfa glǫð djúprǫðul ǫðla,
svát af renniraukum rauk, Danmarkar auka;
bǫru øxn ok átta ennitungl þars gingu
fyr vineyjar víðri valrauf fjǫgur haufuð. (ÍF 26.1, *Gylf*, ch. 1)

Gefjun drew gleaming from Gylfi a deep-sun of heritable lands,
So that steam rose from driven draught-beasts, to Denmark's increase;
The oxen bore eight forehead moons where four heads trod
Before the wide war-spoil, seawall-breach, of meadow isle.

'Deep-sun of lands': Zealand as a big golden Brísingamen (Freyja's necklace). 'Forehead moons': eyes. 'Wide war-spoil': land ripped out of Sweden (with a pun on *vall-rauf* 'seawall-breach').

Þórr fishes for the World Serpent

13 Þat erum sýnt, at snimma sonr Aldafǫðrs vildi
afls við úri þafðan jarðar reist of freista. (vs. 24)

This is clear to me, that the son of mankind's father wanted
To try out his strength against the dew-stirred earth-rounder.

'Mankind's father': Óðinn, whose 'son' is Þórr. 'Dew-stirred': current-shifted. 'Earth-rounder': World Serpent.

14 Hamri fórsk í hœgri hǫnd, þás allra landa,
œgir Ǫflugbǫrðu, endiseiðs of kendi. (vs. 48)
Vaðr lá Viðris arfa vilgi slakr, es rakðisk,
á Eynæfis ǫndri, Jǫrmungandr at sandi. (vs. 42)

Strong-Beard's menacer, when he made out the coal-fish
Which bounds all lands, got his hammer in the right hand.
The fishing line of Wutherer's heir lay by no means slack on the sand
When Universal Spirit uncoiled on King Eynæfir's snow-shoe.

'Strong-Beard': giant, whose 'menacer' is Þórr. 'Coal-fish which bounds all lands': World Serpent. 'Wutherer's (Óðinn's) heir': Þórr. 'Universal Spirit': the World Serpent. '(King) Eynæfir': sea-king, whose 'snow-shoe' is a boat.

15 Ok borðróins barða brautar þvengr enn ljóti
á haussprengi Hrungnis harðgeðr neðan starði, (vs. 51)
þás forns Litar flotna á fangboða ǫngli
hrøkkviáll of hrokkinn hekk Vǫlsunga drekku. (vs. 153)

And the ugly encircling thong of the road of the gunwale-rowed
Prow stared with harsh spirit from below at Hrungnir's skull-splitter,
When on the hook of the wrestling-challenger of the sailors'
Old ox there hung the coiled curling-eel of Vǫlsungs' drink.

'Gunwale-rowed prow': boat, whose 'road' is the sea, whose 'encircling thong' is the World Serpent. 'Hrungnir's skull-splitter': Þórr. 'Vǫlsungs' drink': poison, whose 'coiled curling-eel' is the World Serpent. 'Sailors' old ox (Litr)': Hymir's prize ox, whose 'wrestling-challenger' is Þórr, using the ox-head for bait.

16 Vildit vrǫngum ofra vágs byrsendir œgi,
hinns mjótygil máva Mœrar skar fyr Þóri. (vs. 366)

No wish to lift up crooked bay-menacer had the wind-sender
Who cut the slender band of the gulls' Møre against Þórr's will.

'Crooked bay-menacer': World Serpent. 'Wind-sender': giant (Hræsvelgr, in *Gylfaginning*, ch. 18). 'Gulls' Møre (province)': sea, whose 'slender band' is the fishing line.

The Lay of Skírnir

Skírnismál

✳

As this poem tells an ancient – one might say 'human' – tale to do with farming and human fertility, so it seems best to place it early in the poems of **Gods of the Vikings**. To the present editors it seems likely that the poem was composed in Norway in the heathen era, in the tenth century, and thereafter brought to Iceland by Icelandic skalds. One reason for this are the borrowings that appear to have been made from *Skírnismál* in the *Hákonardrápa* 'Eulogy on Earl Hákon' which was composed by Hallfreðr Vandræðaskáld in *c.* 994 (see below). However, it should be noted that *Skírnismál* is datable at the latest to before *c.* 1290, which is the date of the manuscript Codex Regius, in which it is found (part of it survives in a fragment that is related to Codex Regius). Some scholars are reluctant to believe that the poem could be older than this.

Freyr, fertility god of the Vanir, sees the giantess Gerðr from the clouds one day and, since he cannot live without her, sends his manservant to her distant country to coerce her into meeting him for his love. Skírnir arrives and then flatters, bribes and threatens Gerðr into consent. When he comes home, Freyr shows nothing but impatience at a nine-day delay that the woman has imposed. Already controversial on moral grounds, then, this poem retains an ideology rather different from most belief systems of the present age. It can be read in many ways: as a drama for potentially star-cross'd lovers, as a case-book for feud resolution through marriage, even as the reflex of an old (or new) ritual of kingship. One or other of these ideas usually informs a reading of *Skírnismál*, a work with surprising depths, which is also the only whole surviving Norse work to celebrate Freyr. Though he speaks only at beginning and end, Freyr is the force that drives the poem. Freyr makes his manservant volunteer for a mission to the giants to ask for a young woman's 'hand in marriage', if this is what Skírnir claims to mean by *frið at kaupa* 'to buy an agreement' (stanza 19). But Freyr has no intention of marriage. To keep him happy, Skírnir turns procurer, coercing Gerðr into little more than an act of union with his master. Gerðr seems to expect a visit, as if this coercion has happened before (stanza 16). As a play with characters and plot, therefore, *Skírnismál* poses a certain ethical problem. This is as if a Norse Don Giovanni, expecting us to believe in his *mikinn móðtrega* 'great grief of heart' (stanza 4), sent his Leporello to scare the woman into compliance.

The ethical uncertainty is not just a modern response. In 995, according to later historical records, the men of Trøndelag deposed and hunted down their ruler, Earl Hákon Sigurðarson, for sending out his thralls too often to procure their wives and daughters. The stylisation of all Hákon's mistresses at this time, into his tutelary goddess 'Þór-*Gerðr*', Bride of the Men of Hordaland, suggests that the deluded earl was treating *Skírnismál* or its mythology as a template for the sexual rights of lordship (see the note to Hallfreðr's *Eulogy on Earl Hákon*). His religion would have sanctified these coercions as vital for the harvest. The lord takes a woman, the woman becomes the field, the farmer sows his barley there. Freyr's name descends from an epithet meaning 'lord', as in OE *frea*. Gerðr's name means 'plot of land', as related to OIce *gerði* 'fenced-off field'. Skírnir's name means 'brightener', as related to OIce *skírr* 'bright' and the image of bright fields of barley. The field might be hard or unyielding, as it is in 'For unfruitful land', the Old English *Metrical Charm*. Assisting magic is common to both works, and ultimately a crisis of the seed-planting kind seems to cause the dramatic tension in *The Lay of Skírnir*. As the etymologies tell us, this poem can be read as a play on the sowing of an acre.

The poet's sketches of character skilfully humanise this farming imperative. Running through the poem is a streak of fatalism, not only from the young beauty as she seems resigned to complying with Freyr's lust, but also from Skírnir himself, who threatens Gerðr only when she rebuffs two offers of payment. There is an implication that later the apples, ring and even sword are accepted anyway, but for a tryst that neither Skírnir nor Gerðr seems to want. It has to take place, indeed with Freyr it seems to happen regularly, but as Gerðr means, when she says she thought she would never *unna vaningja vel* 'yield easily to a man of the Vanir' (stanza 37), the woman has her honour too.

Dronke, U., ed., trans. and comm., *The Poetic Edda, vol. II: Mythological Poems* (Oxford, 1997)

Harris, J., 'Cursing with the thistle: "Skírnismál" 31, 6–8 and OE Metrical Charm 9, 16–17', *Neuphilologische Mitteilungen* 76 (1975), 26–33

Larrington, C., 'What does woman want? *Mær* and *Munr* in *Skírnismál*', *Alvíssmál* 1 (1992), 3–16

Mitchell, S. A., '*Fǫr Scírnis* as mythological model: *frið at kaupa*', *Arkiv för nordisk filologi* 98 (1983), 108–22

Motz, L., 'Gerðr: a new interpretation of *The Lay of Skírnir*', *Mål og Minne* (1981), 121–36

Olsen, M., 'Fra gammelnorsk myte og kultus', *Mål og Minne* (1909), 17–36

Turville-Petre, E. O. G., 'Fertility of beast and soil in Old Norse literature', in *Old Norse Literature and Mythology: a Symposium*, ed. E. C. Polomé (Austin, TX, 1969), 244–64

Freyr, sonr Njarðar, hafði einn dag setzt í Hliðskjálf, ok sá um heima alla. Hann sá í Jǫtunheima ok sá þar mey fagra, þá er hon gekk frá skála fǫður síns til skemmu. Þar af fekk hann hugsóttir miklar. Skírnir hét skósveinn Freys. Njǫrðr bað hann kveðja Frey máls. Þá mælti Skaði:

Freyr, son of Njǫrðr, had one day sat in Gateway Shelf, and was looking through all the worlds. He looked into the Land of the Giants and saw there a fair maiden walking from her father's house to her bower. From seeing her Freyr's heart fell into a great longing. Freyr's manservant was called Skírnir ('Brightener'). Njǫrðr asked him to get Freyr to talk. Then Skaði said:

1 'Rístu nú, Skírnir, ok gakk at beiða
okkarn mála mǫg,
ok þess at fregna, hveim inn fróði sé
ofreiði afi.'

'Rise up now, Brightener, and go and ask
our son for a word,
to find out with whom the mature-minded
heir is so mad.'

Skírnir kvað:

2 'Illra orða er mér ón at ykkrum syni,
ef ek geng at mæla við mǫg,
ok þess at fregna, hveim inn fróði sé
ofreiði afi.

Skírnir said:

'No hope of good words for me from your son,
if I go to speak with the boy,
to find out with whom your mature-minded
heir is so mad.

3 'Segðu mér þat, Freyr, folkvaldi goða,
ok ek vilja vita:
Hví þú einn sitr endlanga sali,
minn dróttinn, um daga?'

'Tell me this, Freyr, O ruler of divine hosts,
for I would like to know,
Why you sit alone around the halls by yourself,
my lord, from day to day?'

---

1 The verse does not reveal its speaker. Since Skaði is not Freyr's mother, the poet could have meant the speaker to be Njǫrðr. Here an adored son has become unapproachable with anger: *ofreiði* is literally 'too angry'. This situation asks for a parentally ironic use of *fróðr*, a word that means 'wise' or 'experienced' or 'learned', or even 'fertile', as Dronke shows (1997: 404). Freyr's coming sexual role supports 'fertile', though not here. The word *afi* means both 'grandfather' and 'grandson', thus 'heir' (*ibid.* 405), but the word may also convey the role of 'Yngvi-freyr' as the founder of royal dynasties in Uppsala and Trøndelag and elsewhere (Northumbria, for example: North 1997: 26–43).

3 *folkvaldi goða* 'ruler of divine hosts'. The situation calls for flattery, but the epithet, as we know from Ulfr's *Eulogy on the House*, stanza '8' (*Freyr ok fólkum stýrir* 'Freyr . . . and he guides the people'), is traditional.

Freyr kvað:

4 'Hví um segjak þér, seggr inn ungi,
mikinn móðtrega?
Því at álfrǫðull lýsir um alla daga,
ok þeygi at mínum munum.'

Freyr said:

'Why should I tell you, boy, the great grief
I have in my heart?
The elves have a disk which shines each day,
but not the way I desire it.'

Skírnir kvað:

5 'Muni þína hykka ek svá mikla vera,
at þú mér, seggr, né segir,
því at ungir saman várum í árdaga:
vel mættim tveir trúask.'

Skírnir said:

'What you want, I think, is not so great, sir,
that you can't tell me.
We were young together in olden days,
well might the two of us trust each other.'

Freyr kvað:

6 'Í Gymis gǫrðum ek sá ganga
mér tíða mey;
armar lýstu, en af þaðan
allt lopt ok lǫgr.

Freyr said:

'In Gymir's halls I saw walking
a girl just right for me.
Her arms shone, and from her arms
all the air and water.

7 'Mær er mér tíðari en manna hveim
*u*ngum í árdaga;
ása ok alfa þat vill engi maðr
at vit sa*m*t sém.'

'That girl's more right for me than for any man,
any young man who ever lived.
Of gods and elves there isn't one who wants
the two of us to be together.'

---

5 *ungir saman í árdaga* 'young together in olden days'. In stanza 4, Skírnir is classed as *seggr inn ungi* 'boy', probably because Skírnir, though old for a human, is younger than his god. Freyr, despite being forever young, is truly ancient.

7 *samt* 'together'. Codex Regius *sát*, AM 784 I 4to *sāt*. This word, if read as *sátt* 'reconciled', supports the 'warring houses' theme, at least in Freyr's mind. Moreover, Skírnir hopes for a *sætt* 'settlement' in stanza 23. Otherwise *samt* may be read as 'at one' or 'together', which provides a better focus for the selfishness of this god.

Skírnir kvað:

8 'Mar gefðu mér þá þann er mik um myrkvan beri
vísan vafrloga,
ok þat sverð, er sjalft vegisk
við íǫtna ætt.'

Skírnir said:

'Give me the horse, then, to take me through the dark
wavering flame that will know him,
And the sword which can fight by itself
against the giant kind.'

Freyr kvað:

9 'Mar ek þér þann gef, er þik um myrkvan berr
vísan vafrloga,
ok þat sverð, er sjalft mun vegask
ef sá er horskr, er hefr.'

Freyr said:

'I'll give you the horse that takes you through the dark
wavering flame that will know him,
And the sword that will fight by itself,
if he who wields it is wise.'

Skírnir mælti við hestinn:

10 'Myrkt er úti, mál kveð ek okkr fara
úrig fjǫll yfir,
þ*urs*a þjóð yfir;
báðir vit komumk, eða okkr báða tekr
sá inn ámátki jǫtunn.

Skírnir spoke to the stallion:

'It's dark outside! Time for both of us, I say, to go
over dewy fells,
over ogre-country.
Both of us will get there, or he'll get both of us,
that awesome giant!'

Skírnir reið í Jǫtunheima til Gymisgarða. Þar váru hundar ólmir ok bundnir fyrir skíðgarðs hliði, þess er um sal Gerðar var. Hann reið at þar, er féhirðir sat á haugi, og kvaddi hann:

Skírnir rode into the Land of the Giants to Gymir's Fort. There were mad dogs tied up to the gate of the palisade around the hall where Gerðr was staying. He rode up to where a herdsman sat on a mound, and greeted him:

---

8 As something *víss* 'knowing', this ring of fire has enough discernment to 'waver' so as to let some people through (Dronke 1997: 406).

11 'Segðu þat, hirðir, er þú á haugi sitr
ok varðar alla vega,
Hvé ek at an[d]spilli komumk ins unga mans
fyr greyjum Gymis.'

'Tell me, herdsman sitting on a mound
and keeping watch each way,
How to win an audience with the young mistress
past Gymir's dogs.'

[Hirðir] kvað:

12 'Hvárt ertu feigr, eða ertu framgenginn
* * *
An[d]spillis vanr þú skalt æ vera
góðrar meyjar Gymis.'

The [herdsman] said:

'Is it dying you are, or already departed?
* * *
An audience is what you will lack for all time
with the good daughter of Gymir.'

Skírnir kvað:

13 'Kostir ro betri heldr en at klǫkkva sé,
hveim er fúss er fara;
einu dœgri mér var aldr of skapaðr
ok allt líf of lagit.'

Skírnir said:

'There are better options than softness
for a man who is keen to get going.
My time here was shaped to end on one day,
and all my life laid out.'

Gerðr kvað:

14 'Hvat er þat hlymja, er ek heyri nú til
ossum rǫnnum í?
Jǫrð bifask, en allir fyrir
skjalfa garðar Gymis.'

Gerðr said:

'What is that roaring which I can hear now
in the houses of all of us here?
The earth shakes, and quaking because of it
are all Gymir's halls.'

Ambátt kvað:

15 ‘Maðr er hér úti, stiginn af mars baki,
jó lætr til jarðar taka.’

The maid said:

‘A man is outside here, dismounted from horseback,
he is having his steed put to graze.’

Gerðr kvað:

16 ‘Inn bið þú hann ganga í okkarn sal
ok drekka inn mæra mjǫð;
þó ek hitt óumk, at hér úti sé
minn bróðurbani.

Gerðr said:

‘Ask him to enter here into our hall,
to drink the glorious mead,
though I’m afraid that outside here may be
the man who killed my brother.

17 ‘Hvat er þat alfa né ása sona
né víssa vana?
Hví þú einn of komt eikinn fúr yfir
ór salkynni at sjá?’

‘What elves’ son is that, or Æsir’s,
or son of knowing Vanir?
Why have you crossed the fierce fire by yourself
to visit our family home?’

Skírnir kvað:

18 ‘Emkat ek alfa né ása sona
né víssa vana;
þó ek einn of komk eikinn fúr yfir
yður salkynni at sjá.

Skírnir said:

‘I’m not an elves’ son, or Æsir’s,
or son of the knowing Vanir,
Though I have crossed the fierce fire by myself
to visit your family home.

---

16 *minn bróðurbani* ‘the man who killed my brother’. Larrington (1992) suggests this is the herdsman, now presumed dead. More perversely, however, this stanza looks like Loki’s reproach to Iðunn, in *Loki’s Truth-Game*, stanza 17, that she embraced her *bróðurbani* after having a bath. The latter scene could be Gerðr meeting Freyr after nine days, if we treat Gerðr’s comment as an allusion to ‘the king must die’. This is an older mythologem, one otherwise inactive in *The Lay of Skírnir*. It represents the earth’s seasonal marriage with a new husband who has killed the old husband before him. As the Vanir’s idea of marriage is incestuous, each husband is a ‘brother’. The female endures, the male is replaced (North 1997: 266–71).

19 ‘Epli elli*lyfs* hér hef ek algullin,
þau mun ek þér, Gerðr, gefa,
frið at kaupa, at þú þér Frey kveðir
óleiðastan lifa.’

‘Apples of age-healing I have here all-golden,
these will I give to you, Gerðr,
To buy an agreement, that Freyr you may call your
least hateful man living.’

Gerðr kvað:

20 ‘Epli elli*lyfs* ek þigg aldregi
at mannskis munum,
né vit Freyr, meðan okkart fjǫr lifir,
byggjum bæði saman.’

Gerðr said:

‘Apples of age-healing I shall accept never
to give a man what he desires,
Nor, while we live, shall both Freyr and I
set up house together.’

Skírnir kvað:

21 ‘Baug ek þér þá gef, þann er brenndr var
með ungum Óðins syni;
átta eru jafnhǫfgir, er af drjúpa
ina níundu hverja nótt.’

Skírnir said:

‘I’ll give you the ring, then, that was burned
with Óðinn’s young son.
Eight just as heavy are they that drop off it
every ninth night.’

---

18 These words give Skírnir to be a man, perhaps in the role of the farmer who enacts the Old English *Metrical Charm* ‘For unfruitful land’.

19 ‘*Epli elli*lyfs’ ‘Apples of age-healing’. Dronke is right to emend the second word here and in stanza 20 from MS *ellifu* ‘eleven’, since Iðunn is called the *mey þás ellilyf ása kunni* ‘girl who knew the Æsir’s old-age medicine’ in Þjóðólfr’s *Harvest-Long*, stanza 9 (*c.* 900), and the number has no significance elsewhere (1997: 380 and 407). The giving of the apples, when they are accepted, seems to turn *Gerðr* into *Ið-unn*, that is the ‘plot of land’ into a ‘perennial yielder’. The Vanir preside over this process, for in stanza 10 of Þjóðólfr’s poem, when Iðunn’s apples are gone, the gods who miss their rejuvenating effects are called *allar áttir Ing[v]i-freys* ‘all the kindreds of Ingvi-freyr’.

21 ‘Draupnir’ is the ring that Óðinn puts on Baldr’s pyre, and which Hermóðr, according to Snorri (*Gylf*, ch. 29), brings back to the surface to remind all things living and lifeless to weep Baldr out of Hel. It is interesting that Skírnir can conjure it up here, five stanzas after Gerðr’s words about her ‘brother’s’ death. For a theory that Freyr and Baldr are of common origin, one for the life and one for the death of a seasonal ‘king’, see North 1997: 143–54 and 266–71. Whether or not these gods were once the same, or believed to be, the poet associates their roles.

Gerðr kvað:

22 ‘Baug ek þikkak, þótt brenndr séi
með ungum Óðins syni;
era mér gulls vant í gǫrðum Gymis,
at deila fé fǫður.’

Gerðr said:

‘I won’t accept the ring, though it may have been burned
with Óðinn’s young son.
In Gymir’s halls there’s no gold I can want for
when dealing out father’s treasure.’

Skírnir kvað:

23 ‘Sér þú þenna mæki, mær, mjóvan, málfán,
er ek hef í hendi hér?
Hǫfuð hǫggva ek mun þér hálsi af,
nema þú mér sætt segir.’

Skírnir said:

‘Girl, you see this slender, patterned, blade,
the one I have in my hand?
Cut the head off your neck with this I will,
if you don’t say you’ll settle with me.’

Gerðr kvað:

24 ‘Ánauð þola ek vil aldregi
at mannskis munum;
þó ek hins get, ef it Gymir finnizk,
vígs ótrauðir, at ykkr vega tíði.’

Gerðr said:

‘Coercion is something I will never give in to,
to give a man what he desires.
I guess, though, if you and Gymir should meet,
Neither shy of killing, you’ll both like a fight.’

Skírnir kvað:

25 ‘Sér þú þenna mæki, mær, mjóvan, málfán,
er ek hef í hendi hér?
Fyr þessum eggjum hnígr sá inn aldni jǫtunn,
verðr þinn feigr faðir.

Skírnir said:

‘Girl, you see this slender, patterned, blade
that I have in my hand?
By this sword’s edges the old giant will fall,
it’s your father who must be doomed.

26 'Tamsvendi ek þik drep, en ek þik temja mun,
mær, at mínum munum;
þar skaltu ganga, er þik gumna synir
síðan æva séi.

'With a taming-wand I'll beat you, and tame you I will,
girl, to get what I desire.
You shall go to a place where the sons of men
will never see you again.

27 Ara þúfu á skaltu ár sitja
horfa heimi ór,
snugga heljar til;
matr sé þér meir leiðr en manna hveim
inn fráni ormr með firum.

'On an eagle's mound you shall sit in the dawn,
gazing out of the world,
with hell looking out of you.
May food be more loathsome to you than the shining snake
to any in the land of the living.

28 'At undrsjónum þú verðir, er þú út kemr.
Á þik Hrímnir hari!
Á þik hotvetna stari!
Víðkunnari þú verðir en vǫrðr með goðum.
Gapi þú grindum frá!

'A sight of wonder may you be when you come of doors.
May the Frost-Man gawp at you!
May everything stare at you!
Wider may your fame be than the watchman's among gods.
May you gape from the palisade!

'The watchman': Heimdallr.

29 'Tópi ok ópi, tjǫsull ok óþoli,
vaxi þér tár með trega!
sezk þú niðr, en ek mun segja þér
sváran súsbreka
ok tvennan trega!

'Teepie and weepie, teasle and itch,
the tears may they grow with your grief!
You sit down, and I will tell you of
a heavy wave of torment
and grief to the power of two!

30 'Tramar gneypa þik skulu gerstan dag
jǫtna gǫrðum í;
til hrímþursa hallar þú skalt hverjan dag
kranga kosta laus,
kranga kosta vǫn!
Grát at gamni skaltu í gǫgn hafa
ok leiða með tárum trega.

'Demons shall pinch you the livelong day
in the courts of giants.
To the frost-ogres' hall you shall, each day,
crawl with no options new,
crawl with no options old!
For fun you will have to take crying instead,
and tire out the grief with your tears!

31 'Með þursi þríhǫfðuðum þú skalt æ nara,
eða verlaus vera!
Þik geð grípi,
þik morn morni!
Ver þú sem þistill, sá er var þrunginn
í ǫnn ofanverða.

'With a three-headed ogre you must dally for ever,
or be without a man!
May passion grip you,
withering wither you!
Be like the thistle that was crushed down
at the harvest's end!

32 'Til holts ek gekk ok til hrás viðar,
gambantein at geta,
gambantein ek gat.

'To a copse I went and to a fresh sapling,
to get a newly sprouted branch,
a newly sprouted branch I got.

---

32 *gambanteinn* 'newly sprouted branch'. The meaning of *gamban* is now obscure, but may be guessed at here through the implication of new life in *hrár viðr* 'a fresh sapling'. *Gamban* here might be described as 'the green force that drives the fuse' (Dylan Thomas), the source of regenerative Vanir magic. This branch appears to be the same as the taming-wand cited earlier, with which Skírnir (as if he were Dionysus with his 'thyrsus' and the maenads) is capable of filling Gerðr with madness.

33 'Reiðr er þér Óðinn, reiðr er þér Ásabragr,
þik skal Freyr fíask,
in firinilla mær, en þú fengit hefr
gambanreiði goða!

'Óðinn's angry with you, Prince of Æsir's angry with you,
Freyr is going to hate you,
You vicious wicked girl, for you have won
the newly sprouted anger of the gods!

'Prince of Æsir': Þórr.

34 'Heyri jǫtnar, heyri hrímþursar,
synir Suttunga, sjalfir ásliðar,
hvé ek fyrbýð, hvé ek fyrirbanna
manna glaum mani,
manna nyt mani.

'Let the giants hear, let the frost-ogres hear,
sons of the Suttungar, the Æsir's very foot-troops,
how I forbid and how I do ban
a maid from the joy of men,
a maid from the fruit of men!

35 'Hrímgrímnir heitir þurs, er þik hafa skal
fyr nágrindr neðan;
þar þér vílmegir á viðarrótum
geita hland gefi!
Œðri drykkju fá þú aldregi,
mær, *at* þínum munum,
mær, at mínum munum!

'"Frost-Mask" is the ogre called who will have you
down beneath the corpse-pens.
May the serfs in that place at the roots of the Tree
serve you goat's piss!
A better drink may you never get,
girl, the way you desire it,
girl, the way I desire it!

'The Tree': the World Tree.

33 *gambanreiði* 'newly sprouted anger'. This compound appears to be a nonce word, made to emphasise the sudden ubiquity of divine wrath.

36 'Þurs ríst ek þér ok þría stafi,
ergi ok œði ok óþola;
svá ek þat af ríst, sem ek þat á reist,
ef gørask þarfar þess.'

'"Ogre" I will cut for you and three more staves,
"Lust" and "Madness" and "Itch".
I will cut this off, the way I cut it on,
if the need for that is clear.'

Gerðr kvað:
37 'Heill ver þú nú heldr, sveinn, ok tak við hrímkálki
fullum forns mjaðar;
þó hafðak ek þat ætlat, at myndak aldregi
unna vaningja vel.'

Gerðr said:
'Welcome now instead, boy, and take this frost-chalice
filled with ancient mead,
Though I had intended that I would never in my life
yield easily to a man of the Vanir.'

Skírnir kvað:
38 'Ørendi mín vil ek ǫll vita,
áðr ek ríða heim heðan,
nær þú á þingi munt inum þroska
nenna Njarðar syni.'

Skírnir said:
'My message I want in my mind all pat
before I ride home from here,
When it will be that you dispose to meet
the vigorous son of Njǫrðr.'

Gerðr kvað:
39 'Barri heitir, er vit bæði vitum,
lundr lognfara;
en ept nætr níu þar mun Njarðar syni
Gerðr unna gamans.'

Gerðr said:
'"In the Barley" is the name, as we both know,
of a grove quite undisturbed,
And there in nine nights to Njǫrðr's son
will Gerðr yield joy.'

Þá reið Skírnir heim. Freyr stóð úti ok kvaddi hann ok spurði tíðenda:

Then Skírnir rode home. Freyr was standing outside and greeted him and asked for news:

40 'Segðu mér þat, Skírnir, áðr þú verpir sǫðli af mar
ok þú stígir feti framar:
Hvat þú árnaðir í Jǫtunheima
þíns eða míns munar?'

'Tell me, Brightener, before you throw saddle off horse
and step one foot further,
What have you procured from the Land of the Giants
that you and I both want?

Skírnir kvað:

41 'Barri heitir, er vit báðir vitum,
lundr lognfara;
en ept nætr níu þar mun Njarðar syni
Gerðr unna gamans.'

Skírnir said:

'"In the Barley" is the name, as we both know,
of a grove quite undisturbed,
And there in nine nights to Njǫrðr's son
will Gerðr yield joy.'

Freyr kvað:

42 'Lǫng er nótt, langar ro tvær,
hvé of þreyjak þrjár?
Opt mér mánaðr minni þótti
en sjá half hýnótt.'

Freyr said:

'Long is her bride-night, two of them likewise,
how can I put up with three?
Often a month seemed less time to me
than half a night like this!'

---

42 *Lǫng er nótt* 'Long is her bride-night'. The three-night pre-marital abstinence is conventional, each night called a *hýnótt* 'bride-night'. By insisting on a nine-night wait, Gerðr makes one of her 'bride-nights' equal to anyone else's three. Freyr ungratefully uses 'night' in her sense. The translation attempts to make this clearer by shifting the prefix *hý-* 'bridal' from the last to the first instance of *nótt* 'night' (Dronke 1997: 414).

Þjóðólfr's *Harvest-Long*

Haustlǫng

Þjóðólfr of Hvinir, *c.* 900

✳

The title of this poem is short for *haustlǫng drápa*, 'eulogy harvest long'. Possibly this title means that Þjóðólfr, its poet, took about a month over the composition of this work in early autumn (September to October) while staying at the house of Þorleifr, the chieftain who hired him. This magnate had given the poet an ornamental shield on which were painted scenes from Norse mythology. Þjóðólfr thanks his benefactor and retells the stories in his own deft language. The man for whom he made this poem is probably to be identified with Þorleifr *inn spaki* 'the Wise' Hǫrðu-Kárason, an adviser to King Haraldr Finehair of Norway and the chieftain who governed the western province of Hordaland. The date may thus be set at *c.* 900. This poem is preserved in the *Edda*, which Snorri wrote in order to encourage young poets in the composition of verse. *Haustlǫng* is one of several important poems preserved in the *Edda*, in two separate sequences (1–13: vs. 92–104; 14–20: 65–71) in the first half of *Skáldskaparmál* 'Poetics'. In seems probable that Þjóðólfr composed *Haustlǫng* with one or more further verse sequences which have not survived. In the text we have, it is possible to see Þjóðólfr as a poet of some character, with evidence of a dynamic sense of imagery, sardonic wit and a satirical disposition towards the gods whose cults he must have attended no less than any other social men and women of his day.

Haustlǫng opens with an image of Þjazi, a giant disguised as an eagle, flying towards Óðinn, Loki and Hœnir, as these gods prepare to roast an ox in an earth-oven cooking-fire (stanza 2). Even Loki fails to realise that the eagle is truly a giant, although Þjazi's size and ferocity become clear when he sinks down from the tree with the size and menace of a killer whale, a warlike prince of wind-dolphins. But the Æsir are too busy with their own affairs to see the danger, and Óðinn invites the eagle to share their meal. When Þjazi eats too much, Loki strikes at him with a pole but is hoisted into the sky, his life held to ransom when the eagle takes off with the pole in his clutches. Loki must beg for his life, and the price is Iðunn, a goddess of youth and renewal whose magical apples the gods need to stay forever young. A little later, the gods grow suddenly much older when they realise that Loki has kidnapped Iðunn and delivered her to Þjazi. Loki is forced by the gods to get her back. There is a hot pursuit across the sky, with Þjazi as an eagle chasing Loki who is now trasformed into a young falcon carrying Iðunn as a nut in his claws.

The second story, another episode from Norse mythology, is Þórr's duel with Hrungnir. This is a giant made of stone and whose weapon is a whetstone. In Þjóðólfr's poem Hrungnir becomes hard to distinguish from the rocks and boulders that surround him, and Þórr is similarly identified with natural phenomena, thunder and lightning, in stanzas 14–16. Gradually, however, we see the personified aspect of these figures in a way that lends them a varied characterisation equal in power to that of Óðinn, Loki and Þjazi in stanzas 1–13. Þórr, now named the son of earth and characterised as swelling up with rage, speeds towards Hrungnir. On his way, Þórr drives his clattering chariot over the moon's path, lets his billygoats kick down hail-storms which lash the ground below and, as a kinsman of Ullr, the god of brilliance, like a jagged streak of lightning, sets fire to the upper atmosphere. At the same time Þjóðólfr describes Þórr as a temple-deity, drawn forward in his easy-riding chariot as if in a procession. The duel over, Hrungnir is toppled and shattered in a ravine, while a shard from his whetstone stays lodged in Þórr's head.

Faulkes, A., trans., *Snorri Sturluson: Edda* (London, 1987), 80–1 and 86–8.

Faulkes, A., ed., *Snorri Sturluson: Edda: Skáldskaparmál*, 2 vols (London, 1998)

Hollander, Lee M., *The Skalds: A Selection of Their Poems with Introduction and Notes* (Princeton, 1945)

Holtsmark, A., 'Myten om *Idun* og *Tjatse* i Tjodolvs *Haustlǫng*', *Arkiv för nordisk filologi* 64 (1949), 1–73

North, R., ed. and trans., *The 'Haustlǫng' of Þjóðólfr of Hvinir* (Enfield Lock, 1997)

Turville-Petre, E. O. G., *Scaldic Poetry* (Oxford, 1976)

Þjazi steals Iðunn from the gods

1 Hvé skalk góðs at gjǫldum gunnveggjar brú leggja?
*** *** *** naddkleif at Þorleifi.
Týframra sék tíva trygglaust of far þriggja
á hreingǫru hlýri hildar vetts ok Þjaza.

How shall I build a bridge in payment for the good battle-wall?
*** rivet-cliff from Þorleifr. On the polished finely-wrought
Cheek of Hildr's drum I see the unsafe journey
Of three divinely prominent deities and Þjazi.

'Bridge': here, poem. 'Battle-wall', 'rivet-cliff', 'Hildr's drum': shield.

2 Segjǫndum fló sagna snótar ulfr at móti
í gemlis ham gǫmlum glamma ó- fyr -skǫmmu;
settisk ǫrn, þars æsir ár-Gefnar mar báru
(vasa byrgi-Týr bjarga bleyði vændr) á seyði.

No short time since did the gentlewoman's wolf fly with a clatter
In vulture's worn-out shape towards the tellers of tales;
The eagle settled down where the Æsir were bearing harvest-Giver's horse
(Not accused of cowardice was her rock-imprisoning titan) to the cooking fire.

'Gentlewoman's wolf': woman-snatcher: giant. 'Harvest-Giver's horse': an ox. 'Rock-imprisoning titan': Þjazi.

3 Tormiðlaðr vas tívum ta[ð]lhreinn meðal beina,
hvat, kvað hapta snytrir hjalmfaldinn, því valda;
margspakr of nam mæla már valkastar báru
(vasat Hœnis vinr hánum hollr) af fornum þolli.

Between its bones the dung-deer was divided with difficulty by the gods.
Something, said the gods' helmet-encased wisdom-teacher, is behind this;
The much-prophetic seagull of the slaughter-heap's surf began to speak
(Cockerel's friend wasn't kind to him) from the ancient fir-tree.

'Dung-deer': ox. 'Gods' helmet-encased wisdom-teacher': Óðinn. 'Much-prophetic seagull of the slaughter-heap's surf': augural bird of blood in battle: eagle. 'Cockerel's (Hœnir's) friend': Loki.

4 Fjallgylðir bað fyllar fet-Meila sér deila
(hlaut) af helgum skutli (hrafnásar vinr blása);
ving-rǫgnir lét -vǫgna vígfrekr ofan sígask,
þars vélsparir váru varnendr goða farnir.

The wolf of fell-tops (it was the lot of the raven-god's friend to blow)
Bade the stepping-Meili deal him his fill from the holy harpoon;
The combat-fierce prince of wind-dolphins let himself sink down
To where, saving on trickery, the gods' defenders had gone.

'Wolf of fell-tops': eagle. 'Raven-god's friend': Loki. 'Stepping-Meili': yard-fowl prince: Hœnir. 'Holy harpoon': trencher. 'Prince of wind-dolphins': chief eagle.

5 Fljótt bað foldar dróttinn Fárbauta mǫg vára
þekkiligr með þegnum þrymseilar hval deila,
en af breiðu bjóði bragðvíss at þat lagði
ósvífrandi ása upp þjórhluti fjóra.

Swiftly the handsome lord of the land bade Fear-Beater's boy deal out
Among the thegns the whale of the cracking traces of spring-times,
At which, furthermore, the Æsir's prank-wise disobliger
Served up four bull-portions from the broad table.

'Handsome lord of the land': Óðinn as (a) consort of Jǫrð, and (b) local lord. 'Fear-Beater's boy': Loki (Fárbauti's son). 'Cracking traces of spring-times': plough harness, whose 'whale' is an ox. 'Æsir's prank-wise disobliger': Loki.

6 Ok slíðrliga síðan svangr (vas þat fyr lǫngu)
át af eikirótum okbjǫrn faðir Mǫrna[r],
áðr djúphugaðr dræpi dolg ballastan vallar
hirði-Týr meðal herða herfangs ofan stǫngu.

And hungry then (that was long ago) the Mǫrn River's father
Ate the yoke-bear ferociously off the oak-tree's roots,
Before the deep-counselled deity watching over the war-booty struck
The very bold foe of the field down between the shoulders with a pole.

'Mǫrn River's father': giantess' father (see *Þórsdrápa* 7): giant: here Þjazi. 'Yoke-bear': ox. 'Deep-counselled deity': here Loki.

7 Þá varð fastr við fóstra farmr Sigynjar arma,
sás ǫll regin eygja, ǫndurgoðs, í bǫndum;
loddi rá við ramman reimuð Jǫtunheima,
en holls vinar Hœnis hendr við stangar enda.

Made fast then was Sigyn's arm-cargo, whom all divine powers
Glare at in his bonds, to the ski-goddess' foster-father;
The sailyard stuck to the mighty spectre of the giants' world,
And the hands of Cockerel's loyal friend to the end of the pole.

'Sigyn's arm-cargo': Sigyn's bed-companion: Loki (here described as chained underground near the end of the world). 'Ski-goddess' foster-father': Skaði's (here) foster-father: Þjazi. 'Sailyard': beam. 'Spectre of the giants' world': giant-ghost (see OE *Riddle* 7 of the 'swan' as a *ferende gæst*): Þjazi as eagle. 'Cockerel's (Hœnir's) loyal friend': Loki.

8 Fló með fróðgum tívi fangsæll of veg langan
sveita nagr, svát slitna sundr ulfs faðir mundi;
þá varð Þórs of rúni (þungr vas Loptr of sprunginn)
málunaut, hvats mátti, miðjungs friðar biðja.

With what a wise deity did the blood-nag fly happy in his spoils,
Over such a long way that the wolf's father was ready to tear asunder.
Þórr's (Lofty was heavy, near dead with exhaustion) consultant
Then had to beg a deal from the giant's meal-mate, whatever he could get.

'What a wise deity': the newly wise Loki. 'Blood-nag': old horse of blood-drinking: raven: here eagle. 'Wolf's father': Fenrir's father: Loki. 'Lofty': Loki (Loptr). 'Þórr's consultant': Loki. 'Giant's meal-mate': giant's augural bird: eagle.

9 Sér bað sagna hrœri sorgœra[n] mey fœra,
þás ellilyf ása, áttrunnr Hymis, kunni;
brunnakrs of kom bekkjar Brísings goða dísi
girðiþjófr í garða grjót-Níðaðar síðan.

The kin-branch of Hymir bade the pain-maddened tale-rouser
Bring him a girl, the one who knew the Æsir's old-age medicine.
The thief of the gods' Brísing-girdle later got the lady of the brook
Of the well-spring's cornfield into the courtyards of the rock-Níðuðr.

'Kin-branch of Hymir': giant's relative: Þjazi. 'Tale-rouser': Loki. 'Æsir's old-age medicine': Iðunn's golden apples. 'Thief of the gods' Brísing-girdle': thief of Freyja's necklace (Brísingamen): Loki. 'Well-spring's cornfield': wave (*unnr*), whose 'brook' is an eddy (*iða*), whose 'lady' is the goddess Iðunn (as in *iðu-unnar dís*). 'Rock-Níðuðr': stone-version of the legendary king who enslaved Vǫlundr: giant, whose 'courtyards' are caves.

10 Urðut bjartra barða byggvendr at þat hryggvir;
þá vas Ið- með jǫtnum -unnr nýkomin sunnan;
gættusk allar áttir Ing[v]i-freys at þingi
(váru heldr) ok hárar (hamljót regin) gamlar,

Dwellers in the bright cliff-tops did not become downcast at that;
From the south now was Eddy-Wave newly come to join the giants.
All the kin of Ingvi-Freyr (the divine skin looked rather rough)
Deliberated in the assembly, grey-haired and old,

'Dwellers in the bright cliff-tops': giants. 'Eddy-Wave': Iðunn (see stanza 9). 'All the kin of Ingvi-Freyr': all Frey's family: all gods, men and animals.

11 unz hrynsævar hræva hund ǫl-Gefnar fundu
leiðiþír ok læva lunda*r* ge*iri* bundu;
'Þú skalt véltr nema vélum,' [v]reiðr mælti svá, 'leiðir
munstœrandi mæra mey aptr, Loki, [hapta].'

Until they found the nourishment-Giver's hound of the falling sea of corpses
And bound the servant who had led her *with a spear of* the grove of venoms.
'With spells you must be spoiled of your wits', is what the angry one said,
'Unless with spells also, Loki, you lead the glorious joy-increasing girl of the gods back here.'

'Nourishment-Giver': fertility-goddess, here Iðunn, whose wolf is her kidnapper Loki. 'Falling sea of corpses': blood, whose 'hound' is a wolf. 'Servant who had led her': Loki. '*Spear of* the grove of venoms': magic wand (elsewhere known as a *læva-* or *gamban-teinn*). 'Angry one': presumably Freyr, named in stanza 10. 'Joy-increasing girl of the gods': Iðunn.

12 Heyrðak svá, þat síðan sveik ept ása leiku
hugreynandi Hœnis hauks flugbjalfa aukinn,
ok lómhugaðr lagði, leikblaðs reginn fjaðrar,
ern at ǫglis barni arnsúg faðir Mǫrnar.

Afterwards, so I heard, he who tries the heart of the Cockerel god,
Increased by a hawk's flying-fur, betrayed the playmate of the Æsir back,
And the divine king of the feather's play-leaf, the Mǫrn River's devious father,
With an eagle's vigorous wing-draft mobbed the child of the bird of prey.

'Who tries the heart of the Cockerel god: Hœnir's difficult friend: Loki. 'Increased by a hawk's flying-fur': in (Frigg's) falcon-shape. 'Playmate of the Æsir': Iðunn. 'Feather's play-leaf': bird's wing, whose 'king' is the eagle Þjazi. 'Mǫrn River's father': Þjazi. 'Child of the bird of prey': falcon fledgeling: Loki.

13 Hófu skjótt en skófu skǫpt ginnregin brinna,
en sonr biðils sviðnar (sveipr varð í fǫr) Greipar.
Þats of fátt á fjalla Finns ilja brú minni:
baugs þák bifum fáða bifkleif at Þorleifi.

Soon the shafts while the enticer-gods shaved them started to burn,
And the son of Grope's suitor (there was a flurry in his journey) singes.
A memorial of that is painted on my bridge of the footsoles of the fell-Lapp.
I have received the story-coloured rim-cliff from Þorleifr.

'Grope's (Greip's) suitor': giantess' husband: giant, here Þjazi. 'Fell-Lapp': giant, whose footsole-bridge is a shield (see stanzas 14 onwards). 'Story-coloured rim-cliff': ornamental shield.

Þórr duels with Hrungnir

14 Eðr of sér es íǫtna ótti lét of sóttan
hellis bǫr á hyrjar haugs grjót[t]úna baugi:
ók at ísarnleiki Jarðar sunr, en dunði
(móðr svall Meila blóða) Mána vegr und hánum.

And now one may see on the ring of fire where giants' dread paid a call
On the cavern-tree of the fire of the grave-mound of rock's fences:
Earth's son drove towards the play of iron, while Moon's path
(The passion of Meili's blood-kin swelled) clattered beneath him.

'Ring of fire': metal-rimmed (shield). 'Giants' dread': Þórr. 'Rock's fences': sea, whose 'grave-mound' is the sea-bed, whose 'fire', is gold: treasure: rings (*hringar*), whose 'cavern-tree', giant, is *Hrungnir* (?'ring-man'). 'Earth's son', 'Meili's blood-kin': Þórr (father of Meili). 'Moon's path': the sky.

15 Knáttu ǫll (en Ullar endilág fyr mági
grund vas grápi hrundin) ginnunga vé brinna,
þás hofregin hafrar hógreiðar fram drógu
(seðr gekk Svǫlnis ekkja sundr) at Hrungnis fundi.

All the falcon sanctuaries did burn, whilst down below,
From Brilliance's step-father, the ground was kicked with hail,
When the billy-goats drew the temple-deity of the easy-riding chariot
Forward (Svǫlnir's widow split asunder) to meet Hrungnir.

'Falcon sanctuaries': skies. 'Brilliance's (Ullr's) step-father', 'temple-deity of the easy-riding-chariot': Þórr in his chariot. 'Svǫlnir's widow': the earth (Þórr's mother).

16 Þyrmðit Baldrs of barmi (berg-) solgnum þar -dolgi
(hristusk bjǫrg ok brustu, brann upphiminn) manna;
mjǫk frák móti hrøkkva, myrkbeins Haka reinar
þás vígligan vǫgna váttr sinn bana þátti.

Baldr's bosom-brother showed no mercy in that place (mountains shook
And cliffs shattered, heaven burned above) to men's gorged mountain-foe;
Hugely, I learned, did he shrink from the meeting, the witness for the whales
Of the murk-bone of Haki's land, when he knew his killer ready for war.

'Baldr's bosom-brother': Þórr. 'Men's gorged mountain-foe': harvest-consuming giant: Hrungnir. 'Haki's land': sea-king's land: deep sea, whose 'murk-bone' is unseen rock, whose 'whales' are giants, whose 'witness' is Hrungnir.

17 Brátt fló bjarga gæti (bǫnd ollu því) randa
ímun-fǫlr und iljar íss (vildu svá -dísir);
varðat hǫggs frá hǫrðu[m] hraundrengr þaðan lengi
trjónu trolls of rúna tíðr fjǫllama at bíða.

Quickly the war-pale ice of shield-rims flew (the powers did this)
Beneath the cliff-warden's footsoles (the war-spirits wanted it so).
From that moment the eager rubble-gallant didn't have long to wait
For a many-times-mutilating blow from the the troll-snout's hard confidante.

'War-pale ice of shield-rims': metal shield-boss. 'Cliff-warden': giant. 'War-spirits': demons. 'Rubble-gallant': young man of the scree: giant. 'Troll-snout's hard confidante': the hammer Mjǫllnir kissing Hrungnir's face.

18 Fjǫrspillir lét falla fjalfrs ólágra gjalfra
bǫlverðungar Belja bolm á randar holmi;
þar hné grundar gilja gramr fyr skǫrpum hamri,
en berg-Egða bægði brjótr við jǫrmunþrjóti.

The life-spoiler of Bellower's horrific troop let fall the bear
Of the hideout of unshallow sea-swells on the island of his shield.
There sank the king of the bottom of ravines before the sharp hammer,
While the breaker of the Agder-men of mountains pushed against the titanic boor.

'Bellower's (Beli') troop': giants, whose 'life-spoiler' is Þórr. 'Unshallow sea-swells': open sea, whose 'hideout' is a cave, whose 'bear' is Hrungnir. 'Island of his shield': shield-boss. 'King of the bottom of ravines': giant. 'Agder-men of mountains': giants, whose 'breaker' is Þórr.

19 Ok harðbrotin herju heimþingaðar Vingnis
hvein í hjarna mœni hein at Grundar sveini,
þar svát, eðr í Óðins ólaus burar hausi,
stála vikr of stokkin stóð Einriða blóði,

And the hard-broken hone of the home-caller of Wind-Þórr's warrior-woman
Whizzed into the ridge of the brains of Ground's lad,
So that there, rigid in the skull of Óðinn's boy, stood soaking
The pumice stone of steel tools in Lone-Rider's blood, still

'Wind-Þórr's warrior-woman': Þórr's valkyrie (daughter or mistress: see *Þórsdrápa* 17): Þrúðr, whose 'home-caller' is Hrungnir (as peddlar). 'Ground's lad', 'Óðinn's boy': Þórr. 'Steel tools' pumice-stone': whetstone. 'Lone-Rider': Þórr.

20 áðr ór hneigihlíðum hárs ǫl-Gefjun sára
reiði-Týs et rauða ryðs hœlibǫl gœli.
Gǫrla lítk á Geitis garði þær of ferðir.
Baugs þák bifum fáða bifkleif at Þórleifi.

Waiting for the nursing-Gefjun of the chariot-deity's wounds to chant
Rust's red-boast horror out of his hair's sloping hillsides.
Clearly I behold these expeditions on the fortress of King Geitir.
I have received the story-coloured rim-cliff from Þorleifr.

'Nursing-Gefjun': Gróa, here cast as Gefjun dragging Zealand out of Sweden. 'Chariot-deity': Þórr. 'Rust's red-boast horror': the whetstone on which red rust is polished off. 'Hair's sloping hillsides': head. 'Fortress of (King) Geitir': sea-king's fortress: shield.

Notes

1 *brú leggja* 'build a bridge'. A metaphor for composing poetry, based on the idea that a poem is a monument connecting people (the living with the dead, perhaps). [*hildar vetts* 'Hildr's (battle's) drum'. The assumption may be that if Hildr, a valkyrie, fulfils the role of a witch or *vǫlva* by banging a *vett* ('drum'), the drum must be a shield.

2 *Segjǫndum sagna* 'the tellers of tales'. The gods are the narrators of their own adventures to the men on whose tradition Þjóðólfr relies. The kenning *ár-Gefnar mar* may refer to the story of *Gefjun* and her eight sons, whom the giantess or goddess Gefjun turned into oxen in order to plough land given her by King Gylfi of Sweden.

3 *ta[ð]lhreinn* 'dung-deer'. There were two ploughings in spring, one in autumn. This kenning alludes to the ox-dung from the winter stall later raked out to be spread on the fields in the spring. The irony of the claim of Óðinn's wisom here, as 'wisdom-teacher of the divine powers', is that he fails to connect the spell on his cooking-fire with the eagle in the tree.

4 *ving-rǫgnir -vǫgna* 'prince of wind-dolphins'. The eagle is thus presented as killer-whale of the sky. As Þjazi moves nearer into view, his potential for ferocity and his size become clearer.

5 *foldar dróttinn* 'lord of the land'. Óðinn's marriage with Jǫrð 'earth' is a popular type of kenning, but this scene is also presented as one with a naively festive host, lord of thegns in his hall, who cheerfully orders the guest to be served; Loki, as if a serving-boy fostered there away from his father, obeys with bad grace. [*Fárbauta mǫg* 'Fear-Beater's boy': this expression for Loki occurs elsewhere only in Úlfr Uggason's *Húsdrápa* 2. *Vára* [*þrymseilar hval* 'whale of the cracking traces of springtimes': a plough-ox making the traces crack as he shoulders forward. Ploughing, then seeding, took place in April (or May, depending on the severity of the weather).

6 *okbjǫrn* 'yoke-bear': close to *okhreinn* 'yoke-reindeer', *Ynglingatal* 16. Þjóðólfr's ox may indeed have resembled a 'bear' if the breed of cattle to which *okbjǫrn* refers was anything like the Highland Longhorn. [*faðir Mǫrna[r]* 'Mǫrn River's father': Þjazi. OIce *mǫrn* seems to mean 'giantess', but Holtsmark (1949: 24–5) identifies this word also with the wild river Månn in Mandal in Vest-Agðir at the southern end of Norway, to the east of Kvinesdal from which Þjóðólfr of *Hvinir* is likely to have come.

7 *farmr Sigynjar arma* 'Sigyn's arm-cargo': Loki. The irony of this kenning is that Loki is properly the cargo of Þjazi's arms; yet, as Þjóðólfr shows later in 7/3–4, Loki will be cradled by Sigyn, his wife, after the Æsir chain him beneath a serpent under the earth. [*í bǫndum* 'in his bonds'. Þjóðólfr conveys two images with the same expression: Óðinn and Hœnir staring at Loki as he disappears into the sky, with his staff gripped by the magical 'bonds' of Þjazi; and all the Æsir beholding Loki as this time they bind him themselves.

8 *slitna sundr ulfs faðir mundi* 'the wolf's father was ready to tear asunder'. The placing of *slitna* just before and of *sundr* just after the caesura (the break) in 8/3–4 metrically illustrates Loki's predicament. [*Þungr vas Loptr* 'Lofty was heavy': that Loki is airborne makes the name *Loptr* ('air, sky') appropriate.

9 *ellilyf ása* 'Æsir's old-age medicine'. Skírnir, Freyr's servant in *Skírnismál*, offers (by emendation) 'epli elli*lyfs*' ('eleven apples') to Gerðr in *Skí* 19–20 as part of his master's marriage gifts. [*brunnakrs bekkjar goða dísi* literally 'the gods' lady of the brook of the well-spring's cornfield', perhaps a riddle for *goða dís unnar iðu* ('gods' lady, i.e. goddess, of the wave of the eddy, i.e. (of) *Iðu-unnr*').

10 *Ið- með jǫtnum -unnr* literally 'Eddy-Wave among the giants'. Þjóðólfr splits Iðunn's compound name, then puts *-unnr* ('wave') on the headstave of 10/4, in order to emphasise his interpretation of *Iðunn* as a goddess connected with water. The words *ið(a)-* ('eddy') and *-unnr* ('wave'), placed about *með jǫtnum* ('among the giants') on 10/3–4, give us a spring-thaw image of meltwater cascading over rocks in Norway.

11 An unusual repetition of perfect internal rhymes in this half stanzas has caused scribal distortions: *-sævar hræva læva*; *hund fundu lund-bundu*. These rhyming words look incantatory, part of the Æsir's magic to drive Loki mad. [*Læva lundar geiri bundu* 'they bound [Loki] *with a spear of* the grove [branch] of venoms', with a *lævateinn* 'poison-branch'. Here we read *lundar geiri* by emendation. [*[V]reiðr* as Ingvi-freyr, 'angry'. The subject must be sought in the last unambiguous masculine proper noun, which is contained in *Ingvi-freys* in stanza 10.

12 *Heyrðak* 'I heard': an epic formula, whose use might imply that Þjazi's pursuit of Loki (and Iðunn) is not depicted on Þjóðólfr's shield.

13 This refrain is repeated at 20/7–8 and may have helped to unify *Haustlǫng* in a form even longer than that which survives in *Snorra Edda*.

14 *hellis bǫr hyrjar haugs grjót[t]úna* 'the cavern-tree of the fire of the grave-mound of rock's fences': possibly there is a playful attempt with this kenning to conceal Hrungnir's name, as if Hrungnir's stone shape, within the rocks of his dwelling.

15 *Ullar mági* 'Brilliance's (Ullr's) step-father'. Many place-names show that a god named *Ullr* or *Ullinn* was worshipped in southern and western Norway (and in Sweden) before the Viking Age. Snorri says Ullr was the son of Sif, Þórr's wife, by a previous husband. *Ullr*, if like OE *wuldor*, means 'brilliance'. With 'brilliance' and 'thunder' in the summer sky, Ullr's name portrays Þórr's duel with Hrungnir as a thunderstorm in the mountains. [*hofregin hógreiðar* 'the temple-deity of the easy-riding-chariot': Þórr. The prefix *hóg-* ('easy') emphasises the reckless speed at which Þórr travels.

17 *hǫggs frá hǫrðu[m] trjónu trolls of rúna fjǫllama* 'a many-times-mutilating blow from the troll-snout's hard confidante': from Mjǫllnir, Þórr's hammer. This is the bridal kiss that Hrungnir, here portrayed as a young man, was waiting for. In the story before his duel, he threatens to pillage Ásgarðr and take Freyja back with him. Perhaps the shield-painting on which Þjóðólfr bases stanzas 14–20 consisted of Hrungnir on his shield, Þórr, and a smaller symbol for Þórr's hammer adjacent to Hrungnir's head.

18 *berg-Egða brjótr* 'the breaker of the Agder-men of mountains': Þórr. Here, for the sake of *skothending*, *berg-Egða* must be emended from *berg-Dana* (in all manuscripts). With this kenning, Þjóðólfr of Hvinir (Kvinesdal) makes a self-deprecating allusion to the men of Agðir (Agder), his own province in south-western Norway.

19 *herju heimþingaðar Vingnis* 'the home-caller of wind-þórr's (Vingnir's) warrior-woman': Hrungnir. If Vingnir is Þórr, as some early references suggest, then his *herja* ('warrior-woman') may be Þrúðr, Þórr's girlfriend, and Þjóðólfr's kenning may allude to Hrungnir as her would-be seducer.

20 *ǫl-Gefjun sára* 'the nursing-Gefjun of wounds'. This kenning may allude to Gróa, whose chants to remove the whetstone-sherd from Þórr's head come to nothing. Þjóðólfr here probably alludes to the story in which Gefjun's plough-team drags enough land out of Sweden for a new island in the Øresund.

Einarr's *Gold-Shortage*

Vellekla

Einarr *skálaglamm* 'Cup-Tinkle' Helgason, *c.* 980

*

Einarr Cup-Tinkle, born perhaps in the mid-tenth century, came from Laxárdalr in western Iceland. His brother was the Ósvífr Helgason whose daughter Guðrún gave rise, in the climactic part of *Laxdœla saga*, to one of the greatest love-stories in medieval literature. Einarr composed many eulogies, of which only fragments survive. Two verses from a poem in honour of King Haraldr Gormsson of Denmark may tell us that Einarr spent some time in Denmark in the late 960s with his master, Earl Hákon of Hlaðir (Lade) in Trøndelag, sharing his exile while the sons of Gunnhildr and Eiríkr Bloodaxe (mis)ruled most of Norway. Einarr's greatest extant work is *Vellekla* 'Gold-Shortage'. This is the name given by posterity to one, if not more than one, poem by Einarr in honour of Earl Hákon, who eventually dominated Norway from *c.* 974 to 995. The absence of a reference in any text of this poem to the grand sea-battle of Hjǫrungavágr, in which Hákon routed the Danes and Jómsvikings in *c.* 994, dates *Vellekla* to the early 980s.

Vellekla is a broken and doubtless composite work. Its name is a term of convenience, more for the poet's penniless persona than for the grand eulogy which is now made up of stanzas and half-stanzas cited singly or in sequences in *Snorra Edda*, *Fagrskinna* (*c.* 1220), Snorri's *Haralds saga Gráfeldar* 'Haraldr Greycloak's Saga' and *Óláfs saga Tryggvasonar* 'Óláfr Tryggvason's Saga' (both from later in the 1220s). But Einarr's *Vellekla* appears to have been influential. It has been argued that the 'hydrocycle' contained in *Vellekla*'s opening stanzas, the focus on water from the ocean to the coast to the waterfalls of Norway, is emulated by Úlfr in his *Eulogy on the House*. In any case, it seems that in Scandinavia in the 980s Einarr's eulogies became the model for a new court poetry of Pindaric style. Unfortunately, *Vellekla* is incomplete; its order of sections, or stanza-sequences, is based on conjecture: with the invocation opening, with other stanzas shadowing what is known of Earl Hákon's career some time before Hjǫrungavágr, and then with a stanza of farewell. The following extract by and large keeps to this order. We have numbered stanzas according to scholarly convention and have combined some half-stanzas where there is a case for it. It should be borne in mind that some verses may belong to other poems.

Turville-Petre, E. O. G., *Scaldic Poetry* (Oxford, 1976)

Proem on the Mead of Poetry

1 (1–2) Hugstóran biðk heyra (heyr, jarl, Kvasis dreyra!)
foldar vǫrð á fyrða fjarðleggjar brim dreggjar. (vs. 27)
Ullar gengr of alla asksǫgn, þess's hvǫt magnar
byrgis bǫðvar sorgar, bergs geymi- lǫ -dverga. (vs. 28)

Earth's great-hearted guardian I bid (hear, O Earl, the blood
Of Kvasir!) hear the yeast-sea of firth-leg's front-men.
The wave of the rock of guard-dwarves floods all longship crews
Of the Brilliance who strongly whips up sorrow of war-defence.

'Earth's guardian': king: Earl Hákon. 'Blood of Kvasir': Mead of Poetry: poem. 'Firth-leg': deep (underwater) rock, whose 'front-men' are dwarves, whose 'yeast-sea (fermented liquid)' is the Mead of Poetry. 'Guard-dwarves': Fjalarr and Galarr, whose 'rock' is the tidal reef, whose 'wave' is a poem. 'Brilliance's (Ullr's) longship': shield, whose 'crews' are warriors. 'War-defence': shields, whose 'sorrow' is swords, axes, spears.

2 (3–4) Hljóta munk (ne hlítir) hertýs (of þat frýju)
fyr ǫrþeysi at ausa austr víngnoðar flausta; (vs. 18)
Þvít fjǫlkostugr flestu flestr ræðr við son Bestlu
(tekit hefk) morðs (til mærðar) mæringr an þú færa. (vs. 25)

It is I who will get to (nor need urging to) bail for the fleet's
Speed-drivers the flooding of the war-god's wine-boat;
For almost all splendid glorious men (glory) in almost all killing-exploits
(Is what I've taken on) achieve less with Bestla's son than you do.

'Fleet's speed-drivers': sailors. 'War-god': Óðinn, whose 'wine-boat' is his breast, whose 'flooding' is the Mead of Poetry (stolen from Suttungr by Óðinn), which to 'bail' is to pour out as draughts: recite verses.'Glory': eulogy. 'Bestla's (a giantess') son': Óðinn.

3 (5–6) Eisar vágr fyr vísa (verk Rǫgnis mér hagna),
þýtr Óðrøris alda aldrhafs við fles galdra. (vs. 34)
Nús þats Boðnar bára, berg-Saxa, tér vaxa,
gørvi í hǫll ok heyri hljóð-fley jǫfurs þjóðir! (vs. 35)

Crashes surf of Rǫgnir (his deeds to my advantage) before the chief,
The wave of Soul-Rouser's eternal sea roars against the flat rock of chants.
Now that Boðn's bore begins to swell, let the war-princeling's nations
Give their silence in hall and let them hear the rock-Saxon song-ferry!

'Surf of Rǫgnir (Óðinn)': the Mead of Poetry: poem. 'Soul-Rouser (Óð-[h]rørir)': container for the Mead of Poetry, whose 'sea' is the Mead, whose 'wave' is the poem. 'Flat rock of chants': (poet's) tongue. 'Boðn's bore': flood-wave of Boðn (another container for the Mead of Poetry): poem. 'Rock-Saxons': (here) dwarves, whose '(song-) ferry' is the Mead of Poetry (that brings them off the reef): poem.

Óðinn helps Earl Hákon win Norway

7 Ok oddneytir úti eiðvandr flota breiðan
glaðr í Gǫndlar veðrum (gramr svafði bil) hafði,
ok rauðmána reynir rógsegl Heðins bóga
upp hóf jǫfra kappi etju lund at setja. (ÍF 26.95)

And the oath-respecting sword-point proliferator, cheerful in Gǫndul's
Storms, kept his fleet at sea in a line amidships (the ruler wasted no time),
And impetuously did the tester of the red moon of King Heðinn's shoulder
Raise up his slander-sail to stir the fighting spirit of princes.

'Sword-point proliferator': warrior king. 'Gǫndul's (a valkyrie's) storms': battles. 'Red moon of (King) Heðinn's shoulder': shield, whose 'tester' is a warlike challenger (like King Hǫgni, pursuing Heðinn at sea). 'Slander-sail': shield.

8 Vasat ofbyrjar ǫrva odda vífs né drífu
sverða sverrifjarðar svanglýjaði at frýja;
brak-Rǫgnir skók bogna (barg óþyrmir varga)
hagl ór Hlakkar segli hjǫrs (rakkliga fjǫrvi). (ÍF 26.96)

No need to taunt the swan-gladdener of the swords' swift-firth
For giving no arrows-gale nor blizzard of a spear-points' wife;
The blade's (boldly did the outlaws' discomforter
Save his life) cracking-Óðinn shook bow-hail off Hlǫkk's sail.

'Swords' swift-firth': blood, whose 'swan' is a raven, whose 'gladdener' is a warrior: Earl Hákon. 'Spear-points' wife': valkyrie, whose 'blizzard' is battle. 'Blade's cracking-Óðinn': chief swordsman: earl. 'Outlaws' (Eiríkr's sons') discomforter': Earl Hákon. 'Bow-hail': arrows. 'Hlǫkk's (valkyrie's) sail': shield.

9 Mart varð él áðr Ála austr lǫnd at mun banda
randar lauks af ríki rœkilundr of tœki. (ÍF 26.97)

Áli's hailstorms were there many before the rim-leek's cultivator tree,
In keeping with the gods' desire, took Norway's lands by force.

'Áli': sea-king, whose 'hailstorms' are sea-battles. 'Rim-leek': shield-leek: sword, whose 'cultivator tree' (gardener) is a commander: Earl Hákon.

Earl Hákon restores the sacrifices

14 Sjau fylkjum kom silkis (snúnaðr vas þat) brúna
geymir grundar síma grandvarr und sik (landi). (ÍF 26.107)

Seven provinces did the wound-respecting silk-cord keeper
Of brow's ground (that was the country's gain) bring under him.

'Brow's ground': head, whose 'silk-cord' is a (ruler's?) head-dress, whose 'keeper' is the ruler: Earl Hákon.

15 Ǫll lét senn enn svinni sǫnn Einriða mǫnnum
herjum kunnr of herjuð hofs lǫnd ok vé banda; (ÍF 19.84)
áðr veg jǫtna vitni valfalls of sæ allan
(þeim stýra goð) geira garðs Hlórriði farði. (ÍF 26.108)

All Lone-Rider's ravaged temple lands and sanctuaries of gods
Did the wise-hearted man, famed among armies, at once make holy,
Before the Rumbler of spear's palisade ferried his death-predator
(Gods guide that man) over giant-road and all the sea.

'Lone-Rider': Þórr. 'Spear's palisade': shield, whose 'Rumbler (Þórr)' is the chief warrior: Earl Hákon. 'Death-predator': sword. 'Giant-road': mountains.

16 Ok herþarfir hverfa (Hlakkar móts) til blóta
(rauðbríkar fremsk rœkir ríkr) ásmegir (slíku).
Nú grœr jǫrð sem áðan! Aptr geirbrúar hapta
auðrýrir lætr áru óhryggva vé byggva. (ÍF 19.71, 26.109)

And the sons of Æsir, needed by the army (the red-board cultivator
Of Hlǫkk's council, mighty by such as this, wins fame) return to their sacrifices.
Now grows the earth like before! The wealth-waster lets once more
The gods' sorrow-free spear-bridge heralds inhabit their holy places.

'Sons of Æsir, needed by the army': war-gods, perhaps idols. 'Hlǫkk's (valkyrie's) council': battle, whose 'red-board' is a shield, whose 'cultivator' is the commander: Earl Hákon. 'Wealth-waster': generous king: the earl. 'Spear-bridge': shield, whose 'sorrow-free heralds' are restored warriors; gods' 'restored warriors', war-idols restored to the ravaged temples.

17 Nú liggr alt und jarli (imunborðs) fyr norðan
(veðrgœðis stendr víða) Vík (Hákonar ríki). (ÍF 19.85, 26.110)

Now beneath the earl there lies (wide extends the realm of Hákon,
The strife-board's storm-endower) everything north of Oslofjord.

'Strife-board': shield, whose 'storm' is battle, whose 'endower' is the commander: Earl Hákon.

18 Engi varð á jǫrðu ættum góðr, nema Fróði,
gæti-Njǫrðr sás gerði geirbríkar frið slíkan. (ÍF 19.72)

No spear-board's keeper-Njǫrðr of good family was there
On earth but King Fróði who made such a peace as this.

'Spear-board': shield, whose 'keeper-Njǫrðr' is the chief fertility god: here Earl Hákon.

The gods guide Earl Hákon

30 Flótta gekk til fréttar felli-Njǫrðr á velli,
draugr gat dolga Ságu dagráð Heðins váða,
ok haldboði hildar hrægamma sá ramma.
Týr vildi sá týna teinlautar fjǫr Gauta. (ÍF 19.81, 26.125)

The felling-Njǫrðr of fleeing hosts went to ask omens on the field,
The trunk of Heðinn's clothes got a choice day from the goddess of wounds,
And battle's endurance-boder saw powerful corpse-vultures.
That twig-and-bowl deity wished to wipe out the Gautar's lives.

'Felling-Njǫrðr': chief war-god; Hákon. 'Heðinn's clothes': chain-mail, whose 'trunk' is a warrior. 'Goddess (Sága) of wounds': valkyrie. 'Battle's endurance-boder': war-commander. 'Corpse-vultures': ravens. 'Twig-and-bowl deity': sacrificer: Hákon.

31 Háði jarl (þars áðan engi mannr und ranni)
hyrjar þing (at herja) hjǫrlautar (kom Sǫrla);
bara maðr lyngs en lengra loptvarðaðar barða
(alt vann gramr of gengit Gautland) frá sæ randir. (ÍF 19.82, 26.126)

The earl convened an assembly (where no man before him
Beneath Sǫrli's house had come to plunder) of blade-bowl fire;
No man bore heather-whale's loftroom-turreted (the warlord
Got to cross all Göteland) shield-rims further from the sea.

'Blade-bowl': shield, whose 'fire' is swords, whose 'assembly' is battle. 'Sǫrli's house': shield. 'Heather-whale': serpent, whose 'loft-room' is gold, which, when 'turreted', means 'gold-mounted'.

32 Valfǫllum hlóð vǫllu, varð ragna konr gagni,
hríðar áss, at hrósa (hlaut Óðinn val) Fróða. (ÍF 19.83)
Hver sé if, nema jǫfra ættrýri goð stýra?
Rammaukin kveðk ríki rǫgn Hákonar magna. (*all*: ÍF 26.127)

With slaughtered corpses he piled the field, deity of Fróði's snow-storm
(Óðinn took the slaughter), the scion of divinities must boast of victory;
What doubt but that gods guide the kindred-waster of princes?
Divinities, I declare, mightily strengthened, increase Hákon's domain.

'(King) Fróði's snow-storm': the opposite of peace: battle, whose 'deity' is the war commander. 'Kindred-waster of princes': king in battle.

33 Gullsendir lætr grundar (glaðar þengill her drengja,
hans mæti knák hljóta) hljót Yggs mjaðar njóta. (vs. 197)

Gold-sender makes ground-getter (the chieftain gladdens the host
Of heroes, I did get precious things from him) enjoy Óðinn's mead.

'Gold-sender': the generous earl. 'Ground-getter': here apparently Einarr, rewarded with (enough gold to buy an Icelandic?) estate. 'Óðinn's (Yggr's) mead': the Mead of Poetry: (making) poetry.

37 Hvar viti ǫld und einum jarðbyggvi svá liggja
(þat skyli herr of hugsa) hjarl sextían jarla?
Þess ríðr fúrs með fjórum fólkleikr Heðins reikar
logskundaðar lindar lofkenndr himins endum. (ÍF 26.142)

Where might men know of sixteen earldoms (of this an army
Should be mindful) lying thus beneath one master of his estate?
Praise of this shield-flame hastener's nation-game of the fire of Heðinn's
Hair-parting will ride high beneath the four quarters of heaven.

'Master of his estate': king: the earl. 'Shield-flame': sword, whose 'hastener' is a warrior. '(King) Heðinn's hair-parting': helmet, whose 'fire' is swords, whose 'nation-game' is an epic battle.

Notes

1 Kvasir ('man of *kvas*'') is a peripatetic wiseman whom the Æsir and Vanir liquify to provide the drink that confirms their peace, after having fought a futile war (see *The Sibyl's Prophecy*, stanzas 21–4). [*Ullar asksǫgn* 'longship crews of the Brilliance (Ullr, here standing for Earl Hákon)'. Ullr is Sif's son by her first marriage, father unknown. He is an expert bowman, his name means 'brilliance' (cognate with OE *wuldor* 'glory') and place-names indicate that he was worshipped in Norway and Sweden. [*bergs geymi- lǫ -dverga* 'wave of the rock of guard-dwarves'. Two dwarves, Fjalarr and Galarr, become guardians of the drink, now called the Mead of Poetry, but drown a giant, whose nephew Suttungr threatrens them with the same fate, rowing them to a tidal reef. They save their lives by giving Suttungr the Mead of Poetry.

7 Hákon Sigurðarson's early years were spent in uncertainty: in *c.* 962, two years after King Hákon's death in the Battle of Storð, Earl Sigurðr of Trøndelag was betrayed and killed by Grjótgarðr, his brother, on behalf of the sons of Eiríkr. Earl Hákon ruled in his father's place, in uneasy alliance with Gunnhildr, who eventually outmanoeuvred him, forcing him a few years later to take refuge with King Haraldr Gormsson in Denmark. From there Hákon conspired to recover his position, defeating King Haraldr Greycloak Eiríksson in Danish waters, and returning to deal with Gunnhildr and her remaining sons in Norway, probably in *c.* 974.

14 After driving out the sons of Gunnhildr to Orkney, the earl consolidated his power.

30 In 976 Earl Hákon obeyed a summons from his overlord, King Haraldr Gormsson of the Danes, to help defend Denmark from Emperor Otto II of Saxony on the Danevirke, the well-fortified frontier wall on the neck of the Slesvig-Holstein peninsula. The emperor's army, however, was massive: an Ottonian alliance of Saxons, Frisians and Poles. Defeated, King Haraldr agreed to convert to Christianity, into which he also forced his vassal Earl Hákon. The latter was thereafter allowed to sail home with his depleted force, but soon apostatised, turned off the priests, and for a short while plundered like a Viking in the eastern Baltic. Hákon then disembarked on the east side of Göteland, from where, after looking for omens, he marched back to Trøndelag.

32 The text for the last line of this stanza is taken from vs. 306 of Snorri's *Poetics*.

33 The end of *Vellekla* is hereafter marked or anticipated by a stanza with a tally of Norwegian and other vassals. Even before the Battle of Hjǫrungavágr, which seems to have been fought around a decade after this poem, Earl Hákon was celebrated for unifying Norway by force of arms.

The Thunderclap Ballad

Þrymskviða

⁂

This poem, the only complete Eddic poem to be found edited in Gordon's *Introduction to Old Norse*, is a good first work to read in the Norse language, as it has the deceptive simplicity of a fable or nursery rhyme. As it unknown to Snorri in any of his writings, *Gylfaginning* included, it seems unlikely that he composed it. Otherwise the poem looks sufficiently uncomplicated to be a Christian adaptation of Norse myths from the twelfth or thirteenth century. *Þrymskviða*, or 'The Thunderclap Ballad' to render its title in some way here, lacks the deeper quirks and mysteries that characterise those works on Norse mythology, such as *Harvest-Long* (*c.* 900), which are known to come from Scandinavia in the heathen age. For all that, *The Thunderclap Ballad* does give us a pace, momentum and comic burlesque similar to the best effects of Þjóðólfr's *Harvest-Long*. The poets have much in common. Perhaps the chief difference between them lies in their priorities. As it is the comedy of situation, not that of rhetorical irony, for which the poet of *The Thunderclap Ballad* is striving, his narrative is economical and above all crystal clear. The gods here are stereotypes of lovable characters, not archetypes of cruel forces. Þórr is slightly on the simple side. Until his victory, right at the end, he blunders and gives orders, forgetting his own strength. It is interesting that Óðinn is not named as present. Þórr has Loki to manage him and Freyja to remind him that there are limits, even for her. Loki for once has not abetted the giants by stealing the hammer, and his concern about losing Ásgarðr to the giants, if the hammer is not returned, is rather touching when we think of his doomsday roles in *The Sibyl's Prophecy* and *Loki's Truth-Game*. Also funny, through the mellowness of the poet's outlook, is Freyja's awareness of her reputation as something she can occasionally live down. And Heimdallr's elegant solution seems to go with his snowy white hair, as from a man who has seen too much of life to be embarrassed by anything. Other signs of more Christian times are the poet's portrait of 'Thunderclap, lord of the ogres' as materially acquisitive, rather than scarily alien, and socially ambitious; and his understanding of the giant's wedding party as relatively normal, particularly in the amusing rather than arresting way the giants' *systir* (here) 'auntie' looms into view. Anyone who doubts that *The Thunderclap Ballad* is a poem with a more detached, post-heathen, knowledge of mythology should compare these giants with Eilífr's specimens in the *Eulogy on Þórr* (*c.* 985).

Dronke, U., ed., trans. and comm., *The Poetic Edda, vol. II: Mythological Poems* (Oxford, 1997)

Gordon, E. V., ed., *An Introduction to Old Norse*, rev. A. R. Taylor (Oxford, 1957)

Gurevich, A. Ya., 'On the nature of the comic in the Elder Edda: a comment on an article by Professor Höfler', *Mediaeval Scandinavia* 9 (1976), 127–37

Höfler, O., 'Götterkomik: zur Selbstrelativierung des Mythos [Divine comedy: on the self-relativisation of myth]', *Zeitschrift für deutsches Altertum* 100 (1971), 371–89

Orchard, A., *The Cassell Dictionary of Norse Myth and Legend* (London, 1997), 165–6

Perkins, R., '*Þrymskviða*, stanza 20, and a passage from *Víglundar saga*', *Saga-Book of the Viking Society* 22 (1988), 279–84

Perkins, R., 'The Eyrarland Image – *Þrymskviða*, stanzas 30–31', in *Sagnaþing helgað Jónasi Kristjánssyni, 10. April 1994*, ed. Gísli Sigurðsson, Guðrún Kvaran and Sigurgeir Steingrímsson, 2 vols (Reykjavík, 1994), 653–64

Perkins, R., *Thor the Wind-Raiser and the Eyrarland Image* (London, 2001)

Taylor, P. B., '*Völundarkviða*, *Þrymskviða* and the function of myth', *Neophilologus* 78 (1994), 263–81

1

Vreiðr var þá Ving-Þórr er hann vaknaði
ok síns hamars of saknaði,
skegg nam at hrista, skǫr nam at dýja,
réð Jarðar burr um at þreifask.

Angry was Wind Thunder when he awakened
And felt the loss of his hammer,
His beard he did shake, his locks he did toss,
Earth's boy made to rummage around.

2

Ok hann þat orða alls fyrst of kvað:
'Heyrðu nú, Loki, hvat ek nú mæli
er eigi veit jarðar hvergi
né upphimins: áss er stolinn hamri!'

And these are the words that he first of all said:
'Hear me now, Loku, what I'm now saying,
What's known not on earth, nor up there
In heaven: the god's had his hammer stolen!'

3

Gengu þeir fagra Freyju túna,
ok hann þat orða alls fyrst of kvað:
'Muntu mér, Freyja, fjaðrhams ljá,
ef ek minn hamar mættak hitta?'

To Freyja's fair meadows they went then,
And these are the words that he first of all said:
'Will you lend me your feather-cloak, Freyja,
If my hammer I then might find?'

4

'Þó munda ek gefa þér þótt ór gulli væri,
ok þó selja, at væri ór silfri.'

'I would give it you though it were gold,
and if it were of silver I would still grant it.'

---

1 *Vreiðr var þá Ving-Þórr* 'Angry was Wind Thunder'. Þórr's chief role for the skippers who plied the northern seas was to give the right winds. It has been suggested that the heathens thought he did this by blowing into his beard (Perkins 2001: 13–23).

3 *fjaðrhams* 'feather-cloak'. In Snorri's *Skáldskaparmál* 'Poetics', ch. 18, Loki goes flying to Geirrøðr's cave in Frigg's *valshamr* 'falcon's cloak'.

5 Fló þá Loki, fjaðrhamr dunði,
unz fyr útan kom ása garða
ok fyr innan kom jǫtna heima.

Loki then flew, his feather-cloak flapped,
Until he came out of Gods' Town
And into the Land of the Giants.

6 Þrymr sat á haugi, þursa dróttinn,
greyjum sínum gullbǫnd snøri
ok mǫrum sínum mǫn jafnaði.

On a mound sat Thunderclap, lord of the ogres,
For his hounds he plaited golden bands
And trimmed the manes of his stallions.

7 'Hvat er með ásum? Hvat er með alfum?
Hví ertu einn kominn í Jǫtunheima?'
'Illt er með ásum, illt er með alfum;
hefr þú Hlórriða hamar of folginn?'

'What's with the gods? What's with the elves?
Why have you come to the Land of the Giants?'
'It's bad with the gods, it's bad with the elves,
Is it you who's hidden Rumbler's hammer?'

'Rumbler': Þórr.

8 'Ek hef Hlórriða hamar of folginn
átta rǫstum fyr jǫrð neðan;
hann engi maðr aptr of heimtir,
nema fœri mér Freyju at kvæn.'

'I have hidden Rumbler's hammer
Eight leagues beneath the earth.
No man fetches it back home
Unless he brings me Freyja for wife.'

9 Fló þá Loki, fjaðrhamr dunði,
unz fyr útan kom jǫtna heima
ok fyr innan kom ása garða.
Mœtti hann Þór miðra garða,
ok þat hann orða alls fyrst of kvað:

Loki then flew, his feather-cloak flapped,
Until he came out of Giant Land
And into the Town of the Gods.
Þórr he met in the middle of town,
And these are the words that Þórr first of all said:

---

7 *Hvat er með ásum?* 'What's with the gods?' Possibly the poet borrows this line from the more desperate situation in *The Sibyl's Prophecy*, stanza 49.

10 'Hefr þú ørendi sem erfiði?
Segðu á lopti lǫng tíðendi,
opt sitjanda sǫgur of fallask
ok liggjandi lygi of bellir.'

'Have you a message for your trouble?
Say it aloft if it's any long story.
Often a sitting man's tales begin to falter
And a man on his back makes bold with lies.'

11 'Hef ek erfiði ok ørendi;
Þrymr hefr þinn hamar, þursa dróttinn;
hann engi maðr aptr of heimtir,
nema hánum fœri Freyju at kván.

'I have trouble but a message as well.
The hammer's with Thunderclap, lord of the ogres.
No man fetches it back home
Unless he brings him Freyja for wife.'

12 Ganga þeir fagra Freyju at hitta,
ok hann þat orða alls fyrst of kvað:
'Bittu þik, Freyja, brúðar líni;
vit skulum aka tvau í Jǫtunheima.'

Freyja the fair one they then went to find,
And these are the words that Þórr first of all said:
'Bind yourself, Freyja, in bridal linen,
You and I are driving to Giant Land.'

13 Reið varð þá Freyja ok fnasaði,
allr ása salr undir bifðisk,
stǫkk þat it mikla men Brísinga:
'Mik veiztu verða vergjarnasta,
ef ek ek með þér í Jǫtunheima.'

Angry was Freyja then and snorted with rage,
All the gods' hall shook beneath her,
That great Brísing-necklace sprang off her:
'You'll know I have lost it where men are concerned
If I drive with you into Giant Land.'

---

13 *þat it mikla men Brísinga* 'That great Brísing-necklace'. Freyja's divine gift of fertility is bound up with this ancient necklace, to which Úlfr Uggason refers in stanza '2' of his *Eulogy on the House* (early 990s). The poet of *Beowulf* somehow knows of it, as the *Bresinga mene* 'necklace of the Bresings' (emended from *Brosinga*, line 1199). Here Freyja's necklace is highlighted, with *þat*, as part of her kit, as much as Mjǫllnir is part of Þórr's.

14 Senn váru æsir allir á þingi
ok ásynjur allar á máli,
ok um þat réðu ríkir tívar
hvé þeir Hlórriða hamar of sœtti.

In a trice all the gods were at the assembly,
And all the goddesses talking as well,
And they argued about this, the mighty deities,
How they might go for Rumbler's hammer.

15 Þá kvað þat Heimdallr, hvítastr ása,
vissi hann vel fram sem vanir aðrir:
'Bindum vér Þór þá brúðar líni,
hafi hann it mikla men Brísinga.

Then Heimdallr said, the god's very whitest,
The future he well knew, like other Vanir:
'Let's then bind Þórr in bridal linen,
He can wear the great Brísing-necklace.

16 Látum und hánum hrynja lukla
ok kvenváðir um kné falla,
en á brjósti breiða steina
ok hagliga um hǫfuð typpum.'

The keys from his belt we'll make jangle,
And drop a woman's skirt about his knees,
And put broad jewel-stones on his breast,
And neatly put a head-dress on his head.'

17 Þá kvað þat Þór, þrúðugr áss:
'Mik munu æsir argan kalla,
ef ek bindask læt brúðar líni!'

Then Þórr said this, powerful god:
'The gods will call me a lady-boy,
If I have myself bound in bridal linen!'

---

15 *hvítastr ása* 'the gods' very whitest'. Snorri, who knows Heimdallr more simply as *inn hvíti áss* 'the white god', may be trusted to convey the original 'whiteness' of this god's cult, which Dronke links with the white mud smeared on the bole of the World Tree (1997: 360). In this context, however, Heimdallr seems to be the god with the snowiest hair. [*Sem vanir aðrir* 'like other Vanir'. Heimdallr, though not listed as one of the Vanir in *Gylfaginning* or anywhere else, may have been part of them at one time; or this is a later error.

18 Þá kvað þat Loki Laufeyjar sonr:
'Þegi þú, Þórr, þeira orða.
Þegar munu jǫtnar Ásgarð búa,
nema þú þinn hamar þér of heimtir.'

Then Loki said this, Leaf-Isle's son:
'You be quiet, Þórr, with those words.
The Giants will soon be living in Gods' Town,
If you don't fetch your hammer home.'

19 Bundu þeir Þór þá brúðar líni
ok inu mikla meni Brísinga,
létu und hánum hrynja lukla
ok kvenváðir um kné falla,
en á brjósti breiða steina,
ok hagliga um hǫfuð typpðu.

Then they bound Þórr in bridal linen,
And with the great Brísing-necklace.
The keys from his belt they made jangle,
And dropped a woman's skirt about his knees,
And put broad jewel-stones on his breast,
And neatly put a head-dress on his head.

20 Þá kvað Loki Laufeyjar sonr:
'Mun ek ok með þér ambátt vera,
vit skulum aka tvau í Jǫtunheima.'

Then Loki said this, Leaf-Isle's son:
'I will go with you as your lady in waiting.
We shall drive, big girl, to Giant Land!'

21 Senn váru hafrar heim of reknir,
skyndir at skǫklum, skyldu vel renna;
bjǫrg brotnuðu, brann jǫrð loga,
ók Óðins sonr í Jǫtunheima.

In a trice both the goats were herded home,
Hurried into harness, they had to run well.
Mountains shattered, earth burned with flame,
Óðinn's son was driving to Giant Land.

---

18 *Þegi þú, Þórr, þeira orða* 'You be quiet, Þórr, with those words'. It seems that the poet is referring to this speaker's fearsome role in *Loki's Truth-Game.*

20 *vit skulum aka tvau* 'We shall drive, big girl'. The neuter plural form of *tvau* 'two' means that we have a male and female riding to Giant Land. Loki means himself as female (in his career he gives birth to Sleipnir, Hel, Fenrir and the World Serpent), but first we might think it is Þórr, seeing his nice frock (Perkins 1988: 280). 'Big girl' is an attempt to render this in English.

21 *bjǫrg brotnuðu, brann jǫrð loga* 'Mountains shattered, earth burned with flame'. It is worthwhile comparing this vignette with the phenomenally more spectacular image of Þórr's riding in *Harvest-Long*, stanzas 14–15.

22 Þá kvað þat Þrymr, þursa dróttinn:
'Standið upp, jǫtnar, ok stráið bekki,
nú fœra mér Freyju at kván
Njarðar dóttur ór Nóatúnum.

Then Thunderclap said, lord of the ogres:
'Get up, you giants, and cover the benches,
Now they are bringing me Freyja for wife,
Daughter of Njǫrðr from Nóa-Meadow!

23 Ganga hér at garði gullhyrndar kýr,
ǫxn alsvartir jǫtni at gamni;
fjǫlð á ek meiðma, fjǫlð á ek menja,
einnar mér Freyju ávant þykkir!'

Cows with gold horns walk here to town,
Black-coloured oxen to the joy of the giant.
I have many treasures, I have many rings,
I want only Freyja to think it complete!'

24 Var þar at kveldi of komit snemma
ok fyr jǫtna ǫl fram borit;
einn át oxa, átta laxa,
krásir allar, þær er konur skyldu,
drakk Sifjar verr sáld þrjú mjaðar.

Evening in that place came early
And ale was served to the giants.
Alone he ate an ox, eight salmon,
All the little morsels meant for women,
Sif's husband drank three barrels of mead.

25 Þá kvað þat Þrymr, þursa dróttinn:
'Hvar sáttu brúðir bíta hvassara?
Sáka ek brúðir bíta breiðara,
né inn meira mjǫð mey of drekka!'

Then Thunderclap said, lord of the ogres:
'Have you ever seen brides bite more keenly?
I have never seen brides bite more broadly,
Nor any maid drink more mead than that!'

---

22 *Njarðar dóttur ór Nóatúnum* 'Daughter of Njǫrðr from Nóa-Meadow'. The giant seems impressed by Freyja's social position.

24 Evening comes earlier here, because, if this is winter, Giant Land is in the far north (as well as east).

26 Sat in alsnotra ambátt fyrir,
er orð of fann við jǫtuns máli:
'Át vætr Freyja átta nóttum,
svá var hon óðfús í Jǫtunheima.'

Sitting in wait, the clever lady in waiting
Found words to answer the giant's remark:
'Freyja hasn't eaten for eight nights
So wild has she been for Giant Land.'

27 Laut und línu, lysti at kyssa,
en hann útan stǫkk endlangan sal:
'Hví eru ǫndótt augu Freyju?
Þykki mér ór augum eldr of brenna.'

He lifted her veil, he wished to kiss her,
But sprang back the length of the hall:
'Why are there flames in Freyja's eyes?
I think there's a fire burning from them!'

28 Sat in alsnotra ambátt fyrir,
er orð of fann við jǫtuns máli:
'Svaf vætr Freyja átta nóttum,
svá var hon óðfús í Jǫtunheima.'

Sitting in wait, the clever lady in waiting
Found words to answer the giant's remark:
'Freyja hasn't slept for eight nights
So wild has she been for Giant Land.'

29 Inn kom in arma jǫtna systir,
hin er brúðfjár biðja þorði:
'Láttu þér af hǫndum hringa rauða,
ef þú ǫðlask vill ástir mínar,
ástir mínar, alla hylli.'

In came the giants' impoverished auntie,
So bold as to beg the bride for money:
'Slip from your hands those red rings,
If you want to earn my affections,
Earn my affections, any favour from me.'

---

29 *systir* 'auntie'. Literally 'sister', but the lady seems to have this as an official title, so 'auntie' may work better. Her wheedling may be seen in the repetition of *ástir mínar* 'my affections'.

30 Þá kvað þat Þrymr, þursa dróttinn:
'Berið inn hamar brúði at vígja,
leggið Mjǫllni í meyjar kné,
vígið okkr saman Várar hendi!'

Then Thunderclap said, lord of the ogres:
'Bring in the hammer to hallow the bride,
Lay Grinder down on the maiden's knee,
Hallow the two of us to goddess Commitment!'

31 Hló Hlórriða hugr í brjósti,
er harðhugaðr hamar of þekkði;
Þrym drap hann fyrstan, þursa dróttin,
ok ætt jǫtuns alla lamði.

Rumbler's heart laughed loud in his breast
When the tough-minded fellow felt his hammer.
Thunderclap he whacked first, lord of ogres,
Then he smashed the giant's whole family.

32 Drap hann ina ǫldnu jǫtna systur,
hin er brúðfjár of beðit hafði;
hon skell of hlaut fyr skillinga,
en hǫgg hamars fyr hringa fjǫlð.
Svá kom Óðins sonr endr at hamri.

He whacked the giants' ancient auntie,
The one who begged the bride for money.
A smack she got instead of shillings,
A hammer-blow, no heap of rings.
So the son of Óðinn got his hammer back again.

---

30 *Várar hendi* 'goddess Commitment'. It seems likely that this ceremony reflects wedding customs at the time this poem was composed, probably in the twelfth or thirteenth century. Vár is an *ásynja* 'goddess', otherwise known from Snorri's list of them in *Gylfaginning*.

Eilífr's *Eulogy on Þórr*

Þórsdrápa

Eilífr Goðrúnarson, *c.* 985

*

Little is known of Eilífr except that his patron was Earl Hákon of Hlaðir (now Lade) in Trøndelag, for whom he primarily seems to have composed *Þórsdrápa* as a allegory of grand martial success. Like Þjóðólfr a century before him, Eilífr was probably Norwegian, for he is missing from Icelandic records. 'Goðrúnarson', his metronymic, claims that he was brought up without a father. As skalds go, Eilífr was a court-poet of a rare kind. His images are more complex than those of Einarr Helgason and the others: not because they test the memory for relevant but recondite myths, which they sometimes do, but because they focus on the rhetoric itself, diverting us with kennings constructed as epigrams. Eilífr's artistry is often surreal, sometimes fiendishly difficult and nearly always a subject for controversy. Unlike Einarr's more aureate eulogy *Vellekla*, Eilífr's poem shows the sensibility of an intellectual. His kennings are brilliantly abstract rather than politically apposite. A fragment of his survives in which he admires the invasive power of Christianity (see note to stanza 10), and it may be that he and the earl learned something from this religion together in Denmark on being forcibly baptised after King Haraldr's defeat to Emperor Otto in 976.

Nonetheless, it seems that Eilífr kept his old religion just as Hákon did. The gods and giants are described in *Þórsdrápa* with total sympathy. That the old heathen cults were still flourishing in Eilífr's Norway is suggested by the confidence with which he both teases and praises Þórr. The giants are named in this poem in such a way as to suggest the regions of Norway and elsewhere that Hákon, from his accession in *c.* 962 till the late 960s, and from *c.* 974 onwards, had fought, raided, overrun or wished to dominate. The best period for Eilífr to have composed *Þórsdrápa* is in the mid to late 980s; after the more obvious eulogising of Einarr's *Vellekla*, and before Earl Hákon's great victory at sea against the Danes and Jómsvikings in Hjǫrungavágr off western Norway in 994. Eilífr's poem seems to celebrate the earl before this moment of regional crisis. To show off the earl's feats of arms, the poet militarises Þórr and his human sidekick Þjálfi, allowing them to rout their giants as if taking on the world: Danes, Swedes, Gautar, provincial Norwegian rebels, even Northumbrians and various Celts from the British Isles. There seems little doubt that Earl Hákon is to be seen in Þórr, his poet Eilífr in Þjálfi. They march, fight, rob and maybe even sleep together. Through Þórr, the most popular Norse god of the Viking Age, this poem claims solidarity between Earl Hákon and his people, the men and women of Trøndelag.

Davidson, D. L., 'Earl Hákon and his poets' (unpublished D.Phil. dissertation, Oxford University, 1983)

Frank, R., 'Hand tools and power tools in Eilífr's *Þórsdrápa*', in *Structure and Meaning in Old Norse Literature*, ed. J. Lindow, L. Lönnroth and G. W. Weber (Odense, 1986), 94–109

Þórr sets off without Loki

1 Flugstalla réð felli fjǫrnets goða at hvetja
(drjúgr vas Loptr at ljúga) lǫgseims faðir heiman;
geðreynir kvað grœnar Gauts herþrumu brautir
vilgi tryggr til veggjar viggs Geirrøðar liggja. (vs. 73)

Ocean-cable's father (Lofty was big on lying) was determined to urge
The life-net feller of the gods of flight-ledges away from home;
The temper-tester of the Óðinn of war-thunder, ever so trustworthy,
Declared that green paths led to Geirrøðr's steed-wall.

'Ocean-cable's father': World Serpent's father: Loki. 'Lofty': Loki. 'Life-net feller of the gods of flight-ledges': body-killer of the mountain-dwellers: giant-killer: Þórr. 'Temper-tester of the Óðinn (Gautr) of war-thunder': one who tries Þórr's patience: Loki. 'Geirrøðr's steed-wall': his house, as a hostel.

2 Geðstrangrar lét gǫngu gammleið Þóarr skǫmmum
(fýstusk þeir at þrýsta Þorns niðjum) sik biðja,
þás gjarðvenjuðr gørðisk Gandvíkr (Skotum ríkri)
endr til Ymsa kindar (Iðja setrs) frá Þriðja. (vs. 74)

In a trice (they were eager to crush Þorn's offspring) Þórr
Let Vulture-Road ask him on a journey severe to the soul,
When the White Sea's girdle-trainer (mightier than the Irish of Iði's
Pasture-land) set off again from Þriði's place to Ymsi's kin.

'Vulture-Road': sky = 'Lofty': Loki. 'Þorn's offspring': giants. 'White Sea's girdle-trainer': World Serpent's trainer: Þórr. 'Irish of Iði's pasture-land': rock herdsmen: giants. 'From Þriði's place': from Óðinn's place: Ásgarðr. 'Ymsi's kin': giants.

3 Gǫrr varð í fǫr fyrri farmr meinsvárans arma
sóknar hapts með svipti sagna galdrs en Rǫgnir.
Þylk granstraumar Grímnis! Gall- mantælir halla
-ópnis ilja gaupnum Endils á mó spendi. (vs. 75)

Lawsuit-Shackle's arm-cargo was ready for perjury's journey
With the fable-stirrer sooner than the Rǫgnir of magic was himself.
I chant streams from the lips of Grímnir! The ladies' man of King Endill's
Shrill-shrieker's halls stretched out his footsole palms upon the heath.

'Lawsuit-Shackle's arm-cargo': bed-mate of Sif (OIce *sif*, 'family', which binds up its members with lawsuits): Þórr. 'Perjury': Loki's lie to Þórr. 'Fable-stirrer': Loki. 'Rǫgnir of magic': Óðinn of magic: probably Loki. 'Streams from the lips of Grímnir': Óðinn's draughts (of the Mead of Poetry): verses. 'King Endill': sea-king, whose 'shrill-shrieker' is a gull, whose 'halls' are cliffs, whose 'ladies' are giantesses, whose deceiver is Þórr.

4 Ok gangs vánir gengu gunnvargs himintǫrgu
fríðar, *unz* til fljóða frumseyris kom dreyra,
þás bǫlkveitir brjóta bragðmildr Loka vildi,
bræði vændr, á brúði bág sef-Grímnis mága. (vs. 76)

And the handsome hopes of the war-wolf of the course of heaven's targe
Walked *until* this got them to the blood of the first ever diminisher of women,
Where Loki's prank-generous saviour from evil, the one accused of
Intemperateness, would open hostilities with the bride of sedge-Grímnir's kin.

'Handsome hopes of the war-wolf of the course of heaven's targe': sun's orbit: sky; its wolf: eagle; eagle's hopes: princes looking for battle. 'The blood of the first ever diminisher of women': Ymir's blood: water: the river Vimur. 'Loki's prank-generous saviour from evil': Þórr. 'The bride of sedge-Grímnir's kin': of the Óðinn of marshes: Geirrøðr; the bride of his kin: one of his daughters.

Þórr and Þjalfi cross the river

5 Ok vegþverrir varra vann fetrunnar Nǫnnu
hjalts af hagli oltnar hlaupár um ver gaupu;
mjǫk leið ór stað støkkvir stikleiðar veg breiðan
urðar þrjóts, þars eitri, œstr, þjóðáar fnœstu. (vs. 77)

And the honour-diminisher of the Nanna of the puddle- or, rather, lip-pommel
Made the hail-churned jumping torrents foot-passable on the bob-cat's fishing grounds;
Furious where the mighty torrents spewed poison, the scree-boor scatterer
Moved violently forward across the stick-road's broadway.

'Nanna of the puddle- or, rather, lip- pommel': (a) goddess of the boulder: giantess; and (b) goddess of the vagina-boulder: Greip, whose 'honour-diminisher' is Þórr. 'Bob-cat's fishing grounds': hill-country. 'Scree-boor scatterer': giant-destroyer. 'Stick-road's broadway': broad river crossed by means of Gríðr's staff.

6 Þar í mǫrk fyr markar málhvettan byr settu
(né hvélvǫlur hálar) háf- skotnaðra (sváfu);
knátti hreggi hǫggvin hlymþél við mǫl glymja,
en fellihryn fjalla Feðju þaut með steðja. (vs. 78)

There they planted shooting-adders into the weir's forest (nor did the slippery
Wheel-knobs lie sleeping) against this forest's following wind keen with noise;
The banging ferule, its grooves cut by snowstorms, did crunch against the gravel,
While the falling-roar of the fells howled along the anvils of the Feðja.

'Shooting-adders': staves. 'Weir's forest': river. 'Wheel-knobs': pebbles. '(Weir-) forest's following wind': river-current. 'Falling-roar of the fells': mountain torrent. 'Anvils of the Feðja': boulders in a river in Norway.

7 Harðvaxnar lét herðir hall-lands of sik falla,
gatat maðr njótr in neytri njarð-ráð fyr sér -gjarðar;
þverrir lætr nema þyrri Þo[r]ns barna sér Mǫrnar
snerriblóð til svíra salþaks megin vaxa. (vs. 79)

The rock's shoreline-temperer let the mightily-swollen waters fall over him;
The man, helped by the power-girdle, did not guess Njǫrðr's to be the option more helpful to him;
The diminisher of Þorn's children declares that unless the blood of Mǫrn's
Onslaught dry up, his strength will grow to the height of earth's roof itself.

'Rock's shoreline': face of the rock, whose 'temperer' is Þórr, prodding with his staff. 'The man, helped by the power-girdle': Þjálfi, soon to hang from Þórr's belt of strength. 'Njǫrðr's to be the option more helpful to him': see note. 'Diminisher of Þorn's children': giant-killer: Þórr. 'Blood of Mǫrn's onslaught': of a giantess' (or river Mǫrn's) attack; giantess' waters: her urine. 'Earth's roof': heaven.

8 Óðu fast en fríðir flaut eiðsvara Gauta
setrs víkingar snotrir sv*a*rðrunn*it* fen gunnar;
þurði hrǫnn at herði hauðrs runkykva nauðar
íarðar skafls af afli áss hretviðri blásin, (vs. 80)

Waded fast, while the sward-overrunning fen flowed onwards,
The handsome vikings of the seat of Gauti's liegemen, wise in warfare;
The running-quick wave of the landscape's needs, blown by storm-gusts
Off the ridge, rushed at the earth-drift's temperer with all its power,

'Sward-overrunning fen': flooding river. 'Vikings of the seat of Gauti's liegemen': (a) pirates from Gauti's (Óðinn's) citadel: Æsir; and (b) pirates of Göteland, land of the Gautar: see note. 'Running-quick wave of the landscape's needs': quick water from the earth's toilet call: giantess' urine. 'Earth-drift': stones, whose 'temperer' is Þórr.

9 unz með ýta sinni (aflraun var þat) skaunar
á seil himinsjóla sjálflopta kom Þjálfi;
háðu stáli stríðan straum hrekk-Mímis ekkjur;
stophnísu fór steypir stríðlundr með vǫl Gríðar. (vs. 81)

Until, with mankind's help (that was a trial of strength), Þjálfi
Flew through the air of his own accord to the heaven-king's rope of defence;
The mischief-Mímir's widows made their stream as fierce as steel;
Fierce-hearted advanced the rock-porpoise destroyer with Gríðr's staff.

'With mankind's help': through human effort. 'Heaven-king's rope of defence': Þórr's belt of strength. 'Mischief-Mímir': water giant, whose 'widows' are the waves. 'Rock-porpoise destroyer': giant killer: Þórr.

10 Ne djúp- akǫrn drápu dolgs vamms firum glamma
stríðkviðjundum stǫðvar stall við rastar -falli;
ógndjarfan hlaut arfi ei*r*fjarðar hug meira.
Skálfa Þórs né Þjálfa þróttar steinn við ótta. (vs. 82)

Nor in men fiercely opposed to disgrace did the deep-planted enmity acorns
Miss a beat at the deep-fall of the howler-lair's whirlpool;
Brass-firth's heir was allotted a mind more daring in the face of terror.
Trembled with dread neither Þórr's nor Þjálfi's stone of valour.

'Men fiercely opposed to disgrace': Þórr and Þjalfi. 'Deep-planted enmity acorns': hearts. 'Howler-lair': wolf's lair: mountain. 'Brass-firth': channel for metals: the earth, whose 'heir' is Þórr. 'Stone of valour': heart.

Þórr in Geirrøðr's cave

11 Ok s[tr]*íð*v[a]na síðan sverðs liðhatar gerðu
hlífar borðs við Hǫrða harð-Gleipnis dyn barða,
áðr hylriðar hæði hrjóðendr fjǫru þjóðar
við skyld-Breta skytju skálleik Heðins reikar. (vs. 83)

And after that the haters of sword-help made the din of the Fenrir-fetter's
Hard shelter-board against the strife-worn cliff-Hordalanders,
Before the pool-crossers, these strand-folk cleansers, played the bowl-game
Of Heðinn's hair-parting with the Welshman of the grotto clan.

'Haters of sword-help': unarmed warriors: Þórr and Þjálfi. 'Fenrir-fetter's hard shelter-board': shield with an unbreakable strap, whose 'din' is battle. 'Cliff-Hordalanders': giants. 'Strand-folk cleansers': giant-killers. 'Bowl-game of Heðinn's hair-parting': warrior's head-bowl: helmet, whose '-game' is battle. 'Welshman of the grotto clan': giant: Geirrøðr.

12 Dreif með dróttar kneyfi (dolg-Svíþjóðar kolgu
sótti ferð á flótta flesdrótt) í vá nesja,
þás funhristis fasta (flóðrifs Danir) stóðu
(knáttu) Jólnis ættir (útvés fyrir lúta). (vs. 84)

The skerry courtiers of the wave-foe Sweden, driving in terror
With the crusher of the crag comitatus, sought a journey in flight,
When the kindreds of Yule-god's flame-shaker (the Danes of the flood-rib's
Outpost sanctuary did prostrate themselves) stood firm.

'Wave-foe Sweden': rock-Sweden: mountain, whose 'skerry courtiers' are outlying rock-men: giants by the river Vimur. 'Crag comitatus': giant band, whose 'crusher' is Þórr. 'Yule-god's flame-shaker': Jǫlnir's (Óðinn's) fire's shaker: swordsman, whose 'kindreds' are armies: here Þórr and Þjálfi. 'Flood-rib's outpost sanctuary': outlying rock of a mountain, whose 'Danes' are giants.

13 Þars í þróttar hersar Þornrann hugum bornir,
hlymr varð hellis Kumra hrin[g]bálkar, fram gingu;
Lista fœrðr í fasta friðsein[n] vas þar hreina
gnípu hlǫðr á greypan grán hǫtt risa kvánar. (vs. 85)

There was clamour from the ring-wall of cave-Cumbrians, when
Dukes, borne on by hearts of valour, marched into the Þorn-house;
The peak-Lister's reindeer-heaper, slow to make peace in that place,
Found himself in a tight spot on the troll-wife's dangerous hat.

'Cave-Cumbrians': giants. 'Þorn-house': giant's dwelling. 'Peak-Lister's reindeer-heaper': prolific slayer of mountain inhabitants: giant-killer: Þórr. 'Troll-wife's dangerous hat': here, chair pushed up from beneath by a giantess' head.

14 Ok hám loga himni hallfylvingum vallar
(tráðusk þær) við tróði tungls brá salar þrungu;
húfstjóri braut hváru hreggs váfreiða[r] tveggja
hlátrelliða hellis hundfornan kjǫl sprundi. (vs. 86)

And to get the high heaven of his eyelashes' flaming moon against the roof-battens
The girls pressed (were trodden down) on the rock-chamber's floor-swords;
The hull-driver of the swinging chariot of the sleet-storm broke
The centuries-old keel on the laughter-barge of each cave-mademoiselle.

'Eyelashes' flaming moon': eye, whose 'high heaven' is the top of his (Þórr's) head. 'Roof-battens': roof. 'Rock-chamber's floor-swords': stalagmites. 'Hull-driver of the swinging chariot of the sleet-storm': Þórr. 'Laughter-barge': torso, whose 'keel' is the backbone. 'Cave-mademoiselle': giantess.

15 Fátíða nam frœði (fjarðeplis) kon Jarðar
(Mœrar legs ne mýgðu menn ǫlteiti) kenna:
álmtaugar laust œgir angrþjóf sega tangar
Óðins afli soðnum áttruðr í gin Suðra. (vs. 87)

An uncommon lesson (nor did the lair-men of the fjord-apple Møre
Put their ale-mirth aside) did Earth's progeny learn:
The elm-cord's fear-twanger, kin-branch of Southerly, knocked
A forge-heated lump from his tongs into the open mouth of Óðinn's sorrow-thief.

'Fjord-apple Møre': rock-Møre, whose 'lair-men' are giants. 'Earth's progeny': Þórr. 'Elm-cord's fear-twanger': bow-string's puller: Geirrøðr. 'Kin-branch': family member. 'Southerly (Suðri)': cosmic dwarf. 'Óðinn's sorrow-thief': Þórr.

16 *** ***
*** ***
þrøngvir gein við þrungum þangs rauðbita tangar
kveldrunninna kvinna kunnleggs alinmunni, (vs. 53)

*** ***
*** ***
The mouth of the forearm of the genealogy crusher of female evening-
Travellers opened wide for the tongs' heavy red sea-weed morsel,

'Mouth of the forearm': hand. 'Genealogy crusher': exterminator. 'Female evening travellers': troll-wives. 'Tongs' heavy red sea-weed morsel': cooked newly caught fish of the tongs': molten ingot.

17 svát hraðskyndir handa hrapmunnum svalg gunnar
lyptisylg á lopti langvinr síu Þrǫngvar,
þás ǫrþrasis eisa ós Hrímnis fló drósar
til þrámóðnis Þrúðar þjóst af greipar brjósti. (vs. 88)

So that the war accelerator, Þrǫng's long-term friend, swallowed
Aloft with his hands' hasty mouths the lifted draught of molten ember,
When the wild sparking flame flew towards Þrúðr's heartfelt yearner
From the grip's breast of the passionate coveter of Hrímnir's lady.

'War accelerator': Þórr. 'Þrǫng's (Freyja's) long-term friend': Þórr. 'Hands' hasty mouths': hastily cupped palms. 'Lifted draught': cup. 'Þrúðr's yearner': Þórr (probably father (by Freyja?) of Þrúðr, a valkyrie). 'Grip's breast': palm of the hand. 'Coveter of Hrímnir's lady': giantess-wooer: Geirrøðr.

18 Bifðisk hǫll, þás hǫfði Heiðreks of kom breiðu
und fletbjarnar fornan fótlegg Þurnis veggjar;
ítr gulli laust Ullar jótrs veg- taugar þrjóti
meina niðr í miðjan mest býgyrðil nestu. (vs. 89)

The hall shook as he got the broad head of the (King) Heiðrekr
Of Þurnir's wall beneath an ancient foot-limb of the floor-bear;
Brilliance's splendid step-father knocked the injury pin right down
The middle of the honey-purse of the boor of the tooth of the path of the fishing-line.

'(King) Heiðrekr of Þurnir's wall': Heiðrekr (Gothic king of legend) of the dwarf-king's wall: mountain king: Geirrøðr. 'Ancient foot-limb of the floor-bear': an old leg of the building: a boulder. 'Brilliance's step-father': step-father of Ullr (son of Sif by another father): Þórr. 'Injury pin': the ingot, now an iron bar. 'Honey-purse': mouth. 'Path of the fishing-line': sea, whose 'tooth' is rock, whose 'boor' is Geirrøðr.

19 Glaums niðjum fór *geyma* gramr með dreyrgum hamri;
of -salvanið[s] Synjar sigr hlaut arin- bauti;
komat tvíviðar tývi tollur karms (sás harmi)
brautarliðs (of beitti bekk-) fall (jǫtuns -rekka). (vs. 90)

Furious, he moved against the offspring of Glaumr's *stable-boys* with bloody hammer;
The beater of the protest-Freyja of the hearthstone-hall frequenter was allotted victory;
Nor did the deity of the doubled woodstrip (who inflicted grief on the giant's
Benchmen) bring failure to the stave of the road-help container.

'Glaumr's *stable-boys*' (*geyma* for MS *gǫrva*): literally 'Glaumr's keepers', servants of King Attila's legendary horse: Huns, whose 'offspring' are ?(smaller) trolls. 'Hearthstone-hall frequenter': mountain-visitor: a courting giant, whose 'protest-Freyja (Syn)' is a giantess (Syn, a goddess; OIce *syn* 'denial, protest'). 'Deity of the doubled woodstrip': god of the bow: a human archer: Þjálfi. 'Giant's bench-men': serving-giants of Geirrøðr. 'Road-help container': travelling box: chariot, whose 'stave' is Þórr.

20 Herblótinn vá hneitir hógbrotningi skógar
undirfjálfrs af afli álfheims bliku kálfa;
ne liðfǫstum Lista látrvalrýg[j]ar máttu
aldrminkanda aldar Ellu steins of bella. (vs. 91)

Powerfully fighting with handy woods-fragment did the army-worshipped
Slaughterer of underground hideout-calves win the gleam of elf-realm;
Nor might the arch-wives of eyrie-falcons of the Lister range
Stand up to the well-backed life-lessener of the stone-Ælle's men.

'Handy woods-fragment': piece of bog-iron: Mjǫllnir; or piece of wood: Gríðr's staff. 'Underground hideout-calves': young giants. 'Gleam of elf-realm': elf- or dwarf-fashioned gold. 'Eyrie-falcons': eagles; 'of the Lister range': perhaps mountain giants (as in Suttungr, Þjazi), whose 'arch-wives' are giantesses. 'Stone-Ælle (Ella)': stone-version of a legendary king of Northumbria, whose 'men' are giants.

Refrain Vreiðr stóð Vrǫsku bróðir! Vá gagn faðir Magna!
skelfra Þórs né Þjálfa þróttar steinn við ótta. (vs. 44)

In wrath stood Rǫskva's brother! Magni's father struck victory!
Trembles with dread neither Þórr's nor Þjálfi's stone of valour.

'Rǫskva's brother': Þjálfi. 'Magni's father': Þórr. 'Stone of valour': heart.

Notes

1 *lǫgseims faðir* 'Ocean-cable's father'; *flugstalla fellir fjǫrnets goða* 'life-net feller of the gods of flight-ledges'; *geðreynir Gauts herþrumu* 'temper-tester of the Óðinn of war-thunder'; *vegg viggs Geirrøðar* 'Geirrøðr's steed-wall'. By stating that green paths lead to Geirrøðr's hall, Loki ensures that Þórr does not bring weapons.

2 *gjarðvenjuðr Gandvíkr* 'White Sea's girdle-trainer'. Whereas, in *The Sibyl's Prophecy* 56, the World Serpent is Þórr's last and deadliest opponent, this epithet shows them in their earlier encounter in Hymir's fishing trip. The lack of anxiety shows heathen cults to be in full swing.

3 *farmr arma sóknar hapts* 'Lawsuit-Shackle's arm-cargo'. As an *ofljóst* (recondite) kenning for Þórr as husband of Sif ('family'), this expression appears to ironise *sif* as a bond that binds up its

members in lawsuits. [*svipti sagna* 'fable-stirrer'. The last word read as genitive plural of *saga* ('tale'), appropriate to Loki's lying, rather than of *sǫgn* ('tribe'), an epithet too heroic for Loki (see *Harvest-Long*, stanza 2). [*galdrs Rǫgnir* 'Óðinn of magic'. Likely to be Loki, who, on the evidence of this line, does not accompany Þórr and Þjálfi on their expedition. [*Gall-ópnis mantælir halla Endils* literally 'ladies' man of the shrill halls of the sea-king's (Endill's) shrieker'. The poem's first mocking reference to Þórr as an attacker of giantesses.

4 *gangs vánir gunnvargs himintǫrgu fríðar* 'handsome hopes of the war-wolf of the course of heaven's targe'. For other readings, see Faulkes 1998, n. to vs. 76; this one has the virtue of treating lines 1–4 as one unit, with Þórr and Þjálfi presented as raven-friendly warriors [*fljóða frumseyris dreyri* 'the blood of the first ever diminisher of women'. As with the OIce *Runic Poem* proverb 'an ogre is torment of women' (*þurs er kvenna kvǫl*), the first one being Ymir, the primeval giant whose blood made up the waters (*Vafþrúðnismál* 'The Lay of Riddle-Weaver', stanza 21; *Grímnismál* 'The Lay of Mask-Man', stanza 40). [*bǫlkveitir bragðmildr Loka* 'Loki's prank-generous saviour from evil'. By making this journey, Þórr saves Loki from Geirrøðr, the giant who made him swear to bring the god to him without weapons; unwittingly, also, Þórr forgives this as a prank. [*brúðr sef-Grímnis mága* 'the bride of sedge-Grímnir's kin'. Eilífr's first intimation that Gulp (Gjálp), on her father's instruction, is about to add to the river's flow with her own.

5 *vegþverrir varra Nǫnnu hjalts* 'honour-diminisher of the Nanna of the puddle- or, rather, lip-pommel'. The *double entendre* in *vǫrr* ('puddle in oar's wake'; 'lips', here 'vagina') enables us to read a reference to the way in which Þórr, by lobbing a boulder at the giantess, stops the river's flow at its source; to the same end, a pun on *veg-* ('honour', but also 'road'). [*stikleiðar veg breiðan* 'stick-road's broadway'. Apparently a reference to the staff that Þórr gets from Gríðr, a giantess consort of Óðinn whose whose son Víðarr is Þórr's half-brother (she is named in stanza 9; see also stanzas 6–7).

7 This stanza is among the most vexed in *Þórsdrápa* (no mean feat). Covering the same scene, Snorri quotes a stanza from a now-lost Eddic poem (*Poetics*, ch. 18). *Harðvaxnar*, if not in agreement with a nom. fem. pl. *gjarðar* (as 'belt'), must have 'waters' supplied to make sense. Lines 3–4 appear to refer to Þjálfi having to choose: between reaching for Þórr's strength-belt (his *njarð-gjǫrð*), which he does in stanza 9; and swallowing the giantess' urine. The latter option, which is not the more useful one, would be 'Njǫrðr's advice' (*Njarð-ráð*) according to this god's deviancy with giantesses (or oceanic process with rivers) in *Loki's Truth-Game* 34. The *njarð*-element does double duty here.

8 *Óðu fríðir eiðsvara Gauta setrs víkingar snotrir gunnar* literally 'Waded the handsome vikings of the seat of Gauti's liegemen, wise in warfare'. Davidson (1983) suggests that this poem celebrates Earl Hákon's winning Norway, in which case the topography of Gautar here may refer to his march to Trøndelag from Göteland in 976. For comparison with *The Battle of Maldon*, composed in *c.* 991, lines 96–7:

> wodon þa wælwulfas (for wætere ne murnon)
> wicinga werod, west ofer Pantan
> waded the death-wolves (for water had no care),
> company of Vikings west over Blackwater.

For 'svarðrunn*it*', MSS *sverðrunnar*.

9 Þjálfi's role grows in this stanza. As the refrain suggests, the poet puts great emphasis on his help. [*hrekk-Mímis ekkjur* 'mischief-Mímir's widows'. Mímir's head lies with Óðinn, to whom he gave wisdom; this Mímir is an inversion.

10 *vamms firum stríðkviðjundum* 'in men fiercely opposed to disgrace'. In Eilífr's work of political mythology, it is perhaps surprising to see a moral attitude, one shared by Þórr and Þjálfi alike in the face of the giantess' cascade. However, this is the same poet of whom a Christian fragment (Faulkes 1998, vs. 268; *Skj* B I, 144) shows him to have engaged with Christianity, defining Christ's advance into Norway in his own mythological terms:

> Setbergs (kveða sitja suðr at Urðar brunni)
> svá hefir ramr konungr remðan Róms banda sik lǫndum.
> Thus has the powerful king of Rome (they say he sits by Fate's well
> In the south) empowered himself in the lands of the bonds' mountain seat.

11 *hlífar borðs . . . harð-Gleipnis dyn* 'din of the Fenrir-fetter's hard shelter-board'. Gleipnir is a name for a magic fetter which binds the wolf Fenrir, one made of: (a) the sound of a cat's footfall; (b) a woman's beard; (c) mountain's roots; (d) bear's sinews; (e) fish's breath; (f) bird's spittle. [*hæði skálleik Heðins reikar* 'played [subjunctive] the bowl-game of Heðinn's hair-parting'. Heðinn, having abducted Hildr, daughter of King Hǫgni, finds himself defending forever against his putative father-in-law in a battle whose combatants Hildr regenerates each day (*Poetics*, ch. 50; see Bragi's *Eulogy on Ragnarr*). These allusions stress the supernatural power, and defiance, of Þórr and Þjálfi, and of Earl Hákon, in fighting enemies who have attacked them: here a parcel of giants on the Vimur's other bank.

12 *dolg-Svíþjóðar kolgu* 'wave-foe Sweden'. Faulkes' idea (1998, 512) of this Sweden as 'Sweden the cold', Scythia, fits better with the thirteenth than with the tenth century in which this poem was composed. 'Wave-foe', as a kenning for 'rock', is relatively normal.

14 *hallfylvingum vallar (tráðusk þær) salar þrungu* 'The girls pressed (were trodden down) on the rock-chamber's floor-swords'. Rather than press for these obtrusions to be the staff by which Þórr pushes himself downwards, according to Snorri's prose version (*Poetics*, ch. 18), we have taken Eilífr to describe stalagmites as part of the furniture in Geirrøðr's hall.

15 *angrþjóf Óðins* 'Óðinn's sorrow-thief'. Apparently a reference to Óðinn's game with Þórr (in *Hárbarðsljóð* 'The Lay of Hoary-Beard'), when, disguised as a grey-bearded ferryman, he mocks his slower-witted son from the safety of the other side of a fjord. The humour here, albeit at Þórr's expense, underlines the surprise element in Geirrøðr's attack, which here, and in stanzas 16–17, is described as the surreal hospitality of madmen.

16 This half stanza is quoted separate from the main sequence, as vs. 53 (*Poetics*, ch. 4).

18 *hǫfði Heiðreks breiðu Þurnis veggjar* 'the broad head of the (King) Heiðrekr of Þurnir's wall'. The name Heiðrekr cannot stand alone as a term for a giant. With Davidson (1983), we take 'Þurnir' to be a dwarf-name, his wall the mountain, whose 'Heiðrekr' (a treacherous and maritally voracious king of the Goths in *Heiðreks saga* 'The Saga of King Heiðrekr') is Geirrøðr; this kenning leaves *hǫll* 'hall' undefined, but the cave location by now is understood. [*und fletbjarnar fornan fótlegg* 'beneath an ancient foot-limb of the floor-bear'. The latter oddity as a house-term is accepted; the 'leg of the house', however, is read by nearly all as a version of the pillar behind which, in Snorri's prose, Geirrøðr tries to save himself. The poem reads otherwise, however, with *und* 'beneath' and *niðr* 'down' making it clear that the giant's head is *under* this pillar. Thus a boulder or stalactite seems more likely, under which Þórr crams the giant's head preparatory to knocking into his mouth the molten ingot, now shaped as a big brooch-pin or iron bar. To get 'mouth', rather than 'girdle', we read an emended *bý-gyrðil* as 'purse of the bee', metonymously 'honey-purse', consonant with his head.

19 *geyma* is emended for *skothending* from MS *gǫrva* 'completely'; a less metrically regular speculation is *gumna* 'of men' (Faulkes 1998, n. 90/1–2, without change). [*komat tvíviðar tývi tollur karms brautarliðs fall* 'Nor did the deity of the doubled woodstrip bring failure to the stave of the road-help container'. Þjálfi's role as bowman is unparalleled, but necessary here (with *tývi* 'god' as a weak nominative back-formed from pl. *tívar*) so as (a) to avoid the intermingling of man and god kennings which gives *komat* no clear subject; and (b) to read *sás* 'he who' as a grammatically correct form.

20 *vá álfheims bliku* 'fighting . . . win the gleam of elf-realm'. In this reading the two adventurers cap their victory by unearthing a subterranean treasure. More importantly, thereby, Eilífr thus caps his *Eulogy* with a sly request for payment.

Úlfr's *Eulogy on the House*

Húsdrápa

Úlfr Uggason, early 990s

⁂

Laxdœla saga tells us that Kjartan's father, Óláfr *Pái* 'the Peacock' Hǫskuldsson, when he built his prestigious hall of Hjarðarholt, commissioned for his daughter's wedding there a great poem now known as the *Húsdrápa* 'Eulogy on the House' of Úlfr Uggason (probably in the early 990s). One poem to which Úlfr owes his technique in *Húsdrápa* is Einarr's *Vellekla*, and it can be argued that his emulation of this skald from Earl Hákon's court in Norway reflects a deeper rivalry between Óláfr, his patron, and the latter's distant cousin Ósvífr Helgason, who was Einarr's brother (and the father of Guðrún, whose love for Kjartan drives the climactic section of *Laxdœla saga*). Both men wished no doubt to claim a connection with the ruler of Norway, Earl Hákon of Hlaðir (ruled 978–95).

The author of *Laxdœla saga* praises *Húsdrápa* but leaves no quotations. Thirteen verses survive in Snorri's *Skáldskaparmál* 'Poetics', but these are probably a fraction of *Húsdrápa* as it was. As *Laxdœla saga* claims, Úlfr composed on 'all' the carvings of the hall, and the hall was massive. As to the order of events within *Húsdrápa*, Úlfr's verses have since been put in sequence so as to present three stories, all of them myths of Norse gods. *Húsdrápa*, stanza '2', tells of a duel between Heimdallr and Loki over Freyja's necklace, the *Brísingamen* 'necklace of the *Brísingar*'. This duel appears to start with the two gods changing shape into seals, Heimdallr a little faster, in order to catch the necklace which is sinking into the depths. The poet seems to use this dynamic scene to express ideas such as the sun sinking into the ocean west of Iceland. Stanzas '3–6', two of which are sometimes joined, relate Þórr's fishing-trip with the giant Hymir which ends in a confrontation with the World Serpent. In this version, Þórr destroys the monster as if it were a distant northern counterpart of Apollo with the Python. Stanzas '7–11' tell of the procession of Freyr, Heimdallr and Óðinn together with ravens and valkyries to Baldr's funeral pyre and the launching of his funeral ship. A half-stanza survives, which may as well cap these sequences, in which the poet appears to sum up (part of) his work as something completed (stanza '12'). This sequence of episodes could easily be changed. Baldr's death triggers the end of the world in Snorri's *Gylfaginning*, as it appears to do in *Vǫluspá*, as well as in *Lokasenna*, stanza 28; but it also falls long before the action in *Skírnismál*, in stanzas 21–2, and *Vafþrúðnismál*, stanza 54. Below Úlfr's stanzas and mainly half-stanzas are put mostly in the time-honoured order.

There is no way of telling if Norse gods were all that was carved, then painted, on the walls and ceiling of Óláfr's hall. But in their thematic groups the surviving verses of Úlfr's poem, when interpreted, help us to imagine the style, colour and function of the images that his patron put there. This hall and its wedding were climactic social events, datable to the dizzy heights of Earl Hákon's reign. Equally rare no doubt, and perhaps for reasons of expense relative to the wealth in Norwegian courts, was the composition of a long mythological Skaldic poem in Iceland.

Faulkes, A., ed., *Snorri Sturluson: Edda: Skáldskaparmál*, 2 vols, Viking Society for Northern Research (London, 1998)

Frank, R., *Old Norse Court Poetry: The Dróttkvætt Stanza*, Islandica 42 (Ithaca and London, 1978)

Graham-Campbell, J., *The Viking Age Gold and Silver of Scotland (850–1150)* (Edinburgh, 1995)

North, R., 'Image and ascendancy in Úlfr's *Húsdrápa*', in *Text, Image, Interpretation: Studies in Anglo-Saxon Literature and its Insular Context in Honour of Éamonn Ó Carragáin*, ed. A. Minnis and J. Roberts, Studies in the Early Middle Ages 18 (Turnhout, 2007), 369–404

Proem on the Mead of Poetry

1 Hjaldrgegnis telk Hildar herreifum Óleifi
(hann vilk at gjǫf Grímnis) geðfjarðar lá (kveðja). (vs. 39)

For Óláfr who is brave in war (him will I summon to the gift of Grímnir)
I recount a wave of the fjord of the soul of Battle's din-server.

Óláfr: the Peacock, Úlfr's patron, son of Hǫskuldr. 'Gift of Grímnir (Óðinn)': poem. 'Battle's din-server': Óðinn (giving business to valkyries); the 'fjord of the soul' of Óðinn is the Mead of Poetry, whose 'wave' here is *Húsdrápa*.

Heimdallr beats Loki to Freyja's necklace

2 Ráðgegninn bregðr ragna rein- at singasteini
frægr við firna slœgjan Fárbauta mǫg -vári.
Móðǫflugr ræðr mœðra mǫgr hafnýra fǫgru
(kynnik) áðr ok einnar átta (mærðar þáttum). (vs. 64)

Ready with a plan, the gods' land-warmer transforms for the blessing-jewel,
Renowned for facing the wickedly sly kinsman of Fear-Beater.
Mighty in spirit, the son of eight plus one mothers (I proclaim Óláfr
In strands of renown) is first to get control over the dazzling sea-kidney.

'Ready with a plan': (a) to regain Freyja's necklace, the Brísingamen, from Loki; (b) thereby to assist human procreation. 'Gods' land-warmer': Heimdallr, as Freyja's agent against Loki. 'Blessing-jewel': Freyja's necklace as the sun (see note). 'Kinsman of Fear-Beater (Fárbauti)': Loki, the latter's son. 'Son of eight plus one mothers': Heimdallr. 'Strands of renown': verses of a poem. 'Dazzling sea-kidney': Freyja's necklace as (a) the sun and perhaps (b) a Molucca-bean birth talisman (see note).

Þórr fishes for the World Serpent

3 Innmáni skein ennis ǫndótts vinar banda;
áss skaut œgigeislum orðsæll á men storðar. (W: *Skj* B I, 128, 4)

The inner forehead-moon of the powers' fierce friend shone;
The renowned god shot terrifying rays at the wood-realm's necklace.

'Inner forehead-moon': eye. 'The powers' fierce friend: Þórr. 'Wood-realm': earth, whose 'necklace' is the World Serpent.

4 En stirðþinull starði storðar leggs fyrir borði
fróns á fólka reyni fránleitr ok blés eitri, (vs. 316, 210)

But the taut rope of the wood-realm's leg, glittering-featured,
Stared from across the gunwale at earth-folk's adversary and blew poison.

'Wood-realm': earth, whose 'leg' is submerged rock, whose 'taut rope' is the World Serpent. 'Earth-folk': giants, whose 'adversary' is Þórr.

5 Þjokkvǫxnum kvað þykkja þikling firinmikla
hafra njóts at hǫfgum hætting megindrætti. (vs. 54)

It is said the thick-grown stumpy-legs thought he was in monstrously
Big danger from the billy-goat employer's heavy mighty haul.

'Thick-grown stumpy-legs': Hymir. 'Billy-goat employer': Þórr, whose 'haul' is the World Serpent.

6 Víðgymnir laust Vimrar vaðs af fránum naðri
hlusta grunn við hrǫnnum. Hlaut innan svá minnum. (vs. 56)

The wide-wader of the ford of Vimur struck off into the waves
the earhole's pediment
From the glittering adder of the fishing line. He got it from Norway
with images like this.

'Ford of Vimur': river on the way to Geirrøðr; its 'wide-wader' is Þórr. 'Earhole's pediment': head. 'Adder of the fishing line': World Serpent.

7 Fullǫflugr lét fellir fjall-Gauts hnefa skjalla
(ramt mein var [þat]) reyni reyrar leggs við eyra. (vs. 55)

The fully-endowed feller of the mountain-Óðinn made his fist crack
(That was a mighty injury) against the ear of the explorer of the reed's leg.

'Mountain-Óðinn (Gautr)': top giant, perhaps Hrungnir, whose 'feller' is Þórr. 'Reed's leg': rock, whose 'explorer' is Hymir.

The gods ride to Baldr's funeral pyre

8 Ríðr á bǫrg til borgar bǫðfróðr sonar Óðins
Freyr ok fólkum stýrir fyrst ok gulli byrstum. (vs. 63)

Rides in first place, and on a boar with bristles of gold,
Battle-wise Freyr to the fortress of Óðinn's son and he guides the people.

'Boar with bristles of gold': Gullinbursti (Freyr's boar). 'Fortress': unlit pyre.

9 Kostigr ríðr at kesti kynfróðs þeim er goð hlóðu
hrafnfreistaðar hesti Heimdallr at mǫg fallinn. (vs. 19)

Heimdallr rides splendid on his horse to the pyre which the gods
Have loaded for the fallen son of the strangely-wise tester of ravens.

'Strangely-wise tester of ravens': Óðinn, whose 'fallen son' is Baldr.

10 Ríðr at vilgi víðu víðfrægr (en mér líða)
Hropta-týr (of hvapta hróðrmál) sonar báli. (vs. 8)
Þar hykk sigrunni svinnum sylgs valkyrjur fylgja
heilags tafns ok hrafna. Hlaut innan svá minnum. (vs. 14)

Rides to his son's exceedingly wide bonfire (while words of glory
Flow over my jaws) the god of Secrets widely renowned.
There I think come valkyries and ravens following the
wise-at-swallowing victory-tree
To the holy sacrifice. He got it from Norway with images like this.

'Words of glory': verses. 'God of Secrets'; 'wise-at-swallowing victory-tree': Óðinn (in the latter case, drinker of the Mead of Poetry). 'Holy sacrifice': Baldr.

11 Fullǫflug lét fjalla fram haf-Sleipni þramma
Hildr, en Hropts of gildar hjálmelda mar feldu. (vs. 242)

The fully-endowed mountain-Hildr made the ocean-Sleipnir
Trundle forwards while Óðinn's helmet-fire empowerers felled her steed.

'Mountain-Hildr (-Battle)': giantess Hyrrokkin. 'Ocean-Sleipnir': sea-horse: ship. 'Helmet-fire': swords, whose 'empowerers' are warriors; Hroptr's (Óðinn's) warriors are the *einherjar* (dead 'universal soldiers') of Valhǫll. 'Her steed': a wolf.

A summation

12 Þar kømr á, en æri endr bark mærð af hendi
(ofrak svá) til sævar, sverðregns (lofi þegna). (vs. 303)

There comes a river to the sea, while once again I have delivered renown
(Thus I lift up the praise of thegns) for the herald of sword-rain.

'Praise of thegns': poetry. 'Sword-rain': blood, whose 'herald' is a warrior: here Úlfr's patron, Óláfr Hǫskuldsson.

Notes

1 *Hjaldrgegnis Hildar geðfjarðar lá* 'a wave of the fjord of the soul of Battle's din-server'. This form of the half-stanza is from the Uppsala manuscript of Snorri's *Edda*. The three other manuscripts preserve this half-stanza in a slightly less skilful form. The baroque intensity of this Mead of Poetry kenning announces a mythological praise poem such as those composed for kings of Norway. Whether or not what is left of *Húsdrápa* quite equals Einarr's *Vellekla* 'Gold-shortage' or Eilífr's *Þórsdrápa* 'Eulogy on Þórr' is for the reader to decide.

2 *rein- -vári* 'land-warmer'. The meaning of *vári* remains unclear: from the adjective *varr* 'aware'; to be linked with *verja* 'to defend' (though its long vowel fails to match with the short vowel and weak class of *verja*) as a term for Heimdallr the gods' 'defender'; the 'trusty one, the gods' confederate', as related to the feminine noun *vár* 'pledge'. The last meaning suits Heimdallr's role as the gods' watchman in the Last Days. It seems more plausible, however, that the word *vári* is related to *værr* 'comfortable, snug', hence 'warm', as someone who makes a house warm: 'land-warmer'. By recovering Freyja's necklace, the sun, Heimdallr saves the world from permanent winter. For his reward from the owner, see *Lokasenna* 'Loki's Truth-Game', stanza 20. [*singasteini* 'blessing-jewel'. It is usually thought that this word refers to a mythological place. However, no other example is found, and it is also possible to treat *singa* as a metathesised reflex of *signa* 'to bless'. This term suggests an Irish Christian admixture to Icelandic paganism, one not so easy to find in Norway, but more plausible in the British Isles. [*hafnýra fǫgru* 'dazzling sea-kidney'. The sun, bright before hitting the western wave, but perhaps also a talismanic Molucca bean washed up in Iceland by the Gulf Stream (Graham-Campbell 1995: 180).

5 *Þjokkvǫxnum þikling* 'thick-grown stumpy-legs'. The visual aspect of this poem is strong. The word *þikling* allows us to glimpse the modest size of Hymir's figure in relation to that of Þórr, who must stand close to the World-Serpent if Úlfr's description of their face-off is based on an image. With the word *þjokkvǫxnum* we also appear to see the width of the giant's limbs offsetting his smaller size.

6 *Hlaut innan svá minnum* 'he got it from Norway with images like this'. This throwaway line, also in stanza '10', is known as *hjástælt* 'abutted', and works as a refrain which may or may not have been completed in the final stanza. As a device, it is commoner in Kormákr's *Sigurðardrápa* 'Eulogy on Sigurðr' (*c.* 961). Idiomatically OIce *innan* 'from within' means from the east out of Iceland, the inverse of *útan* 'from without, from Iceland to Norway'. The saga tells us that Óláfr gets his hall-timbers from Norway, from where the myths were also derived.

10 This text joins two half-stanzas (vs. 8 and 14) to make one, on the basis of (a) content and (b) the pattern of alliteration, with s-words linking the half-stanzas in long-lines 2 and 3, as in stanza '2' above.

12 *Þar kømr á til sævar* 'There comes a river to the sea'. The water imagery in this poem, when collected, suggests a 'hydrocycle' of rain inland, cascades, water out to sea, breakers on reefs and rain again. As this has been seen in the proem of Einarr's *Vellekla* 'Gold-shortage' (Frank 1978: 60–2), from *c.* 985, it is possible that Úlfr's poem seeks to emulate the work of this man, once Earl Hákon's favourite and the brother of Ósvífr Helgason, the cousin and social rival of Úlfr's patron, Óláfr *Pái* 'the Peacock' (North 2007: 402–3).

Hallfreðr's *Eulogy on Earl Hákon*

Hákonardrápa

Hallfreðr *vandræðaskáld* 'Troublesome Poet' Óttarsson, *c.* 994

*

Hallfreðr *vandræðaskáld* 'Troublesome Poet' grew up in Vatnsdalr near Blǫnduóss on the mid-north coast of Iceland. In his late twenties he was in Norway, nursing his feelings for Kolfinna, a woman who had married another man in Iceland, while composing poems for the arch-heathen Earl Hákon of Trøndelag. His is a curious case in that he was faithful to two rulers of Norway, the second being the arch-Christian King Óláfr Tryggvason of Norway. He became close to Óláfr and converted to Christianity, but the *Saga of Hallfreðr* which works up his adulterous troubadour story (he saw Kolfinna when he could) attributes verses to Hallfreðr in which he expresses doubt over leaving his old gods behind. Whether or not these verses are genuine (they are probably not), they preserve an idea of a moody Skaldic lyricist who was unstable in religion as much as in love. King Óláfr is said to have given Hallfreðr his nickname over the mortal scrapes he got into at court. The longer extant poems said to be Hallfreðr's are more likely to be his, including his *Hákonardrápa* 'Eulogy on Earl Hákon', datable to 994, in the earl's last boisterous year. Hákon had just defeated an alliance of Danes and other Vikings in the sea-battle of Hjǫrungavágr. From what the later histories say about him, in conjunction with Hallfreðr's words here, the earl celebrated his triumph by enacting the role of Freyr in *Skírnismál* 'The Lay of Skírnir' with the wives and daughters of his subjects. Sacral kingship, the old ideology of a king marrying his land, was one he apparently revived in this practical way, but within a year of this poem the deep resentment of Hákon's subjects would lead to his ousting, his pursuit through Gaular and his death in a pig-sty, his throat cut by a slave.

Ström, F., 'Poetry as an instrument of propaganda. Jarl Hákon and his poets', in *Speculum Norroenum: Norse Studies in Memory of Gabriel Turville-Petre*, ed. U. Dronke, Guðrún P. Helgadóttir, G. W. Weber and H. Bekker-Nielsen (Odense, 1981), 440–58

Turville-Petre, E. O. G., *Scaldic Poetry* (Oxford, 1976), 70–3

Hákon the Mighty at Hjǫrungavágr

1 Askþollum stendr Ullar austr at miklu trausti
rœkilundr enn Ríki randfárs brumaðr hári. (vs. 212)

Stands out in Norway, much aided by ash-trees of Brilliance's warship,
Shield-danger's cultivator-tree, the Mighty, budded with hair.

'Brilliance's (Ullr's) warship': shield, whose 'ash-trees' are warriors. 'Shield-danger': swords, or axes, whose 'cultivator tree', making them grow, is Earl Hákon the Mighty.

2 Ólítit brestr úti unndýrs sumum runnum
hart á Hamðis skyrtum hryngráp Egils vápna. (vs. 229)
Þaðan verða fǫt fyrða (fregnk gǫrla þat) Sǫrla
rjóðask bjǫrt í blóði (benfúr) méilskúrum. (vs. 230)

Out there breaks no little crashing hailstorm of Egill's weapons
Harshly on Hamðir-tunics of the wave-deer's distinguished trees.
From those missile-showers (I am learning fully) Sǫrli's bright clothes
Are made to redden in men's blood (about that blaze of wounds).

'Egill's weapons (of Vǫlundr's brother)': arrows. 'Hamðir-tunics': (near invincible) coats of mail. 'Wave-deer': ship, whose 'trees' are warriors. 'Sǫrli's bright clothes': (near invincible) coats of mail. 'That blaze of wounds': that battle (with *benfúr* as neuter).

3 Ok geirrotu gǫtvar gagls við strengjar hagli
hungreyðundum Hanga hléðut járni séðar. (vs. 248)
Grams rúni lætr glymja gunnríkr hinns hvǫt líkar
Hǫgna hamri slegnar heiptbráðr of sik váðir. (vs. 288)

And from the string-hail no iron-linked spear-shower garments
Could shelter the hunger-annihilators of Hanged Man's gosling.
The ruler's confidant, mighty in battle, whom goading pleases,
Swift to anger, makes Hǫgni's hammer-forged garments echo about him.

'String-hail': arrows. 'Iron-linked spear-shower garments': coats of mail. 'Hanged Man (Hangi)': Óðinn, whose 'gosling' is the raven, whose 'hunger-annihilators' are Odinic warriors who wish to kill large numbers of Earl Hákon's men. 'Ruler's confidant': earl. 'Hǫgni's garments': coats of mail.

The earl goes to bed with Norway

4 Sannyrðum spenr sverða snarr þiggjandi viggjar
barrhaddaða byrjar biðkván und sik Þriðja. (vs. 10)
Því hygg fleygjanda frægjan (ferr Jǫrð und menþverri)
ítra eina [at] láta Auðs systur mjǫk trauðan. (vs. 121)

With the holy words of swords the wind-steed's brisk partaker
Entices Third-Party's barley-wimpled waiting-wife beneath him.
And so I think the famed shower-flinger (Earth lies down for the man
Who dispenses necklaces) is quite unwilling to leave Auðr's gleaming sister alone.

'Holy words of swords': hand-to-hand fighting. 'Wind-steed': ship, whose 'brisk partaker' is a captain quickly engaging an attacking fleet. 'Third-Party (Þriði)': Óðinn, whose 'barley-wimpled waiting-wife' is the sustaining lands of Norway. 'Famed shower-flinger': Earl Hákon (aided by a hail-storm from his goddess Þorgerðr; see note to stanza 2). 'Man who dispenses necklaces': earl. 'Auðr': son of Night (Nótt); his 'sister': Earth (Jǫrð): here Norway.

5 Ráð lukusk at sá síðan snjallráðr konungs spjalli
átti einga dóttur Ónars viða gróna. (vs. 118)
Breiðleita gat brúði Báleygs at sér teygða
stefnir stǫðvar hrafna stála ríkismálum. (vs. 119)

The deal closed after that in such a way that the king's eloquent intimate
Took possession of the backwoods-grown only daughter of Ónarr.
The ravens' jetty navigator has ably lured to him the broad-featured bride
Of Furnace-Eye with the kingdom-building talk of steel blades.

'King's intimate': earl. 'Ónarr': husband of Night (Nótt), whose 'only daughter' is Earth (Jǫrð): here Norway. 'Backwoods-grown': overgrown with woods; grown up in the (back)woods. 'Ravens' jetty': ship, whose 'navigator' is the captain: Earl Hákon. 'Furnace-Eye': (a jealous) Óðinn, whose 'bride' is Earth (Jǫrð): here Norway. 'Broad-featured': with massive terrain; with peasant-woman's face. 'Talk of steel blades': battle by which Hákon wins Norway as his consort.

Notes

1 *brumaðr hári* 'budded with hair'. The imagery of what is left of this poem blends, or syncretises, various cults in the Earl's religion, to do with the World Tree, the long-haired god Ingvi-freyr, *Ullr* 'brilliance', Óðinn and Þórr, in order to express the earl's combined role as warlord and sacral king.

2 *á Hamðis skyrtum* 'on Hamðir-tunics'. For the story of Hamðir and Sǫrli, here representing the earl's enemies as heroic but essentially doomed attackers, see Bragi's *Eulogy on Ragnarr*, stanzas '2–6' (**Heroic Poems**). [*hryngráp Egils vápna* 'crashing hail-storm of Egill's weapons'. Egill, brother of Vǫlundr, is the archetypal bowman (see *The Lay of Wayland*, **Heroic Poems**). Later sources, most famously *Jómsvíkinga saga* 'Saga of the Jómsvikings' of the late thirteenth century, represent the poetic commonplace of battle as a 'storm' quite literally, with the story that the earl's goddess Þorgerðr *Hǫrðabrúðr* 'bride of the men of Hordaland' helped her devotee to victory with a flash hailstorm which routed the invading Danish-Jómsviking fleet.

4 *barrhaddaða biðkván* 'barley-wimpled waiting-wife'. OIce *barr* may also mean 'pine-cone': probably trees and fields are blended in this image. Norway is two things at once: a fertile landscape covered in grain, and a bored peasant housewife who falls for the charms of Earl Hákon, the passing ship's captain. [*Þriðja* 'Third-Party'. The use of this name for Óðinn, which draws mocking attention to him as the cuckolded husband of the earth, is in keeping with the earl's new Freyr-ideology as Norway's sacral king. Later sources from the thirteenth century report that Hákon fell out with his subjects over what appears to be the enactment of this ideology: his harassment and coercion of their wives and daughters.

The Sibyl's Prophecy

Vǫluspá

⁕

The Sibyl's Prophecy is preserved in the four fourteenth-century or later manuscripts of Snorri's *Edda*, written from the 1220s onwards, in the Codex Regius from the late thirteenth century and in the *Hauksbók* manuscript of the later fourteenth. In its history, the poem, which has always commanded huge respect, was read differently by different people. The order of stanzas is still the subject of debate, as the *Hauksbók* text presents the story less coherently, particularly in the death of Baldr. Also perplexing is the fact that some stanzas occur in the *Hauksbók* text but not in Codex Regius, most notoriously stanza 62 below, which confirms the Christian apocalyptic import of earlier stanzas. To judge by the complexity of this work, which seeks to harmonise variant strains of mythology with the Revelations and with each other, the poet may have been brought up a heathen, trained in Christianity to the level of a catechumen, but brought back to heathen ways by the offensive evangelical behaviour of missionaries in Iceland. This translation is based on the indispensable readings and interpretation of Ursula Dronke, which should be followed in the first instance by anyone seeking to specialise in this poem. For the purposes of this Anthology, however, we have chosen to keep our translation more simple than hers.

Dronke, U., ed., trans. and comm., *The Poetic Edda, vol. II: Mythological Poems* (Oxford, 1997)

Faulkes, A., ed., *Snorri Sturluson: Edda: Prologue and Gylfaginning* (Oxford, 1982)

Gelling, M., *Place-Names in the Landscape: The Geographical Roots of Britain's Place-Names* (London, 1984)

North, R., 'End time and the date of *Vǫluspá*: two models of conversion', in *Conversion and Colonization in Anglo-Saxon England*, ed. C. E. Karkov and N. Howe, Medieval and Renaissance Texts and Studies 318 (Tempe, AZ, 2006), 213–36

Schach, P., 'Some thoughts on *Vǫluspá*', in *Edda: A Collection of Essays*, ed. R. J. Glendinning and Haraldur Bessason, University of Manitoba Icelandic Studies 4 (Winnipeg, 1983), 86–116

Sigurður Nordal, 'Three essays on *Vǫluspá*', trans. B. S. Benedikz and J. S. McKinnell, *Saga-Book of the Viking Society* 18 (1971), 79–135

Taylor, P. B, 'The rhythm of *Vǫluspá*', *Neophilologus* 55 (1971), 45–57

The Creation

1 Hljóðs bið ek allar helgar kindir,
meiri ok minni mǫgu Heimdallar.
Viltu at ek, Valfǫðr, vel fyr telja
forn spjǫll fira, þau er fremst of man.

A hearing I ask for from all hallowed kindreds,
Greater and lesser kinsmen of Heimdallr.
You wish me, Father of the Slain, well to narrate
The old tidings of men that I remember from furthest back.

2 Ek man jǫtna ár of borna,
þá er forðum mik fœdda hǫfðu.
Níu man ek heima, níu íviðjur,
mjǫtvið mæran fyr mold neðan.

I remember giants born early in time,
Those who had brought me up long ago.
Nine worlds I remember, nine root-ogresses,
A glorious tree of good measure beneath the soil.

3 Ár var alda, þar er Ymir byggði,
vara sandr né sær né svalar unnir.
Jǫrð fannsk æva né upphiminn,
gap var ginnunga en gras hvergi.

It was early in the ages when Ymir dwelt,
There was neither sand nor sea nor cool waves.
Earth was not to be found, nor heaven above,
It was a gap filled with voids and no grass anywhere.

4 Áðr Burs synir bjǫðum of yppðu,
þeir er Miðgarð mæran skópu.
Sól skein sunnan á salar steina,
þá var grund gróin grœnum lauki.

And then sea-beds were raised by those sons of Burr
Who shaped the glorious Middle World.
Sun shone from south on the stones of that mansion,
Then was the ground grown with green leek.

---

1 A sibyl speaks, responding to a request from Óðinn to know the future through its causes in the history of the world. Heimdallr's role as the founding father of (three classes of) mankind is the subject of *Rígr's List* (*Rígsþula*), an eleventh to thirteenth-century poem also edited in Dronke 1997.

2 *níu íviðjur* 'nine root-ogresses'. A pun on *íviðja* 'ogress' and *íviði* 'root', one which presents Heimdallr, through his fabled nine mothers, himself as the World Tree (see Dronke 1997: 109).

3 For *þar er Ymir byggði*, Snorri has *þat er ekki var* 'that there was nothing' on 3/2 (Faulkes 1982: 9), quoting this stanza before he tells of Ymir. This variant appears to be his, or of an editor after the poem was composed (Dronke 1997: 79).

5 Sól varp sunnan, sinni mána,
hendi inni hœgri um himinjǫður.
Sól þat né vissi, hvar hon sali átti,
stjǫrnur þat né vissu hvar þær staði áttu,
Máni þat né vissi, hvat hann megins átti.

Sun from the south, Moon's companion,
Cast her right hand over the rim of the sky.
Sun did not know where she had mansions,
Stars did not know where they had stations,
Moon did not know what might he had.

6 Þá gengu regin ǫll á rǫkstóla,
ginnheilǫg goð, ok um þat gættusk.
Nótt ok niðjum nǫfn of gáfu,
morgin hétu ok miðjan dag,
undorn ok aptan, árum at telja.

Walked then all powers to their thrones of judgement,
Holy aboriginal gods, and took heed of this.
To Night and her descendants they gave names,
Called them Morning and Midday,
Afternoon and Evening, how to count in years.

7 Hittusk æsir á Iðavelli,
þeir er hǫrg ok hof hátimbruðu.
Afla lǫgðu, auð smíðuðu,
tangir skópu ok tól gerðu.

Divine ancestors came together on Eddying Plain,
Who built high the outdoor and indoor shrines.
Anvils they laid down, wealth they fashioned,
Tongs they shaped and tools they made.

5–6 The heavenly bodies move without knowing the demarcations of time, which the gods provide by dividing up years into days and days into quarters, thus laying the foundations of (pre-Christian) heliacal, stellar and lunar astronomy (North 2006: 231–2). [*sunnan . . . hendi inni hœgri* 'from the south . . . her right hand'. 'Right' for 'south' is a Celtic not Germanic usage, notably an Irish one, from which it may be assumed that the poet's cultural background, if not his Christian training, was partly Irish.

8

Teflðu í túni, teitir váru,
var þeim vettergis vant ór gulli,
unz þrjár kvámu þursa meyjar
ámátkar mjǫk ór Jǫtunheimum.

They played chess in a meadow, were merry,
No want of gold was there for them,
Until there came three daughters of ogres,
Strong and huge from the land of the Giants.

9

Þá gengu regin ǫll á rǫkstóla,
ginnheilǫg goð, ok um þat gættusk,
hv*árt* skyldi dverga dróttir skepja
ór Brimis blóði ok ór Blá*in*[s] leggjum.

Walked then all powers to their thrones of judgement,
Holy aboriginal gods, and took heed of this,
Whether they should create companies of dwarves
From Brimir's blood and the limbs of Bláinn.

'Brimir': 'Brim, Sea'. 'Bláinn': 'Corpse-Blue'. Both, perhaps, are names for Ymir.

17

Unz þr*ír* kvámu ór því liði
ǫflgir ok ástgir æsir at húsi.
Fundu á landi lítt megandi
Ask ok Emblu ǫrlǫglausa.

And then from that troop there came three
Strong and affectionate gods to a house.
They found on the shore, able to do little,
Ash-tree and Elm-tree, with no destiny.

'Ash-tree and Elm-tree': man and woman.

---

8 *Teflðu* 'They played chess'. The 'chess-game' is used here for a board-game in general, whose lucky pieces amass gold in competitions by themselves for people who have no care of its value: this is a 'Golden Age'. The same pieces turn up in the grass, after the apocalypse, in stanza 58. The giantess' arrival seems to mark the loss of this gold and the gods' new (morally complicating) monetary concern.

10–16 Omitted here are two dwarf-catalogues which were interpolated at an early stage in *The Sibyl's Prophecy*'s reception, by editors who took their cue from the gods' imminent creation of dwarves, for the creation of gold, in stanza 9.

18 Ǫnd þau né áttu, óð þau né hǫfðu,
lá né læti né litu góða.
Ǫnd gaf Óðinn, óð gaf Hœnir,
lá gaf Lóðurr ok litu góða.

Breath they had not, spirit they had not,
Pulse, nor voices, nor good colour.
Breath Óðinn gave, spirit Hœnir gave,
Pulse Lóðurr gave along with good colour.

19 Ask veit ek standa, heitir Yggdrasill,
hár baðmr, ausinn hvíta auri.
Þaðan koma dǫggvar, þærs í dala falla,
stendr æ yfir grœnn Urðar brunni.

An ash I know that stands, called Yggdrasill,
A high trunk, splashed with the white mud.
From there come the dews that fall in the valleys,
It stands forever green over the well of Urðr.

'Yggdrasill': 'Terror-Packhorse'. 'Urðr': 'What's-Happened'.

20 Þaðan koma meyjar margs vitandi
þrjár ór þeim sæ, er und þolli stendr.
Urð hétu eina, aðra Verðandi
(skáru á skíði), Skuld ina þriðju;
þær lǫg lǫgðu, þær líf kuru
alda bǫrnum, ǫrlǫg seggja.

From there come maidens who know much,
Three from the lake which stands beneath the tree.
Urðr they called one, Verðandi the second
(They cut marks on wood), Skuld, the third.
The maidens laid down laws, they chose lives
For mankind's children, the destinies of men.

'Urðr': 'What's-Happened'. 'Verðandi': 'What's-Happening'. 'Skuld': 'What-has-to-Happen'.

---

18 Lóðurr: ?'fruitful'. Possibly the earliest manifestation of *Loki*, whose name could be regarded, in one way, as an abbreviation.

19 Yggdrasill: 'Terror-Packhorse'. This name for the World Tree appears to present it as a gallows, archetypally that of Óðinn when he hangs himself for greater knowledge (see *Sayings of the High One*, stanzas 138–9).

20 These Norns are traditional, yet named here as aspects of time and necessity. The poet does not need to have borrowed ideas from the Classical Parcae, for this conception to have been made.

The Æsir-Vanir cult-war

21 Þat man hon folkvíg fyrst í heimi,
er Gullveigu geirum studdu
ok í hǫll Hárs hana brenndu,
þrysvar brenndu, þrysvar borna,
opt, ósjaldan, þó hon enn lifir.

That war she remembers, the first in the world,
When Goldbrew they studded with spears
And burned her in the hall of the High One,
Thrice they burned her, a woman thrice born,
Often, not ceasing, yet she still lives.

22 Heiði hana hétu hvars til húsa kom,
vǫlu vel spá, vitti hon ganda.
Seið hon kunni, seið hon leikinn,
æ var hon angan illrar brúðar.

Heiðr they called her at the houses she came to,
A sibyl good in prophecy, she conjured spirits to help her.
Sorcery she knew; sorcery, possessed, she performed;
Ever was she the darling of an evil bride.

'Heiðr': 'Brightness'.

23 Þá gengu regin ǫll á rǫkstóla,
ginnheilǫg goð, ok um þat gættusk,
hvárt skyldu æsir afráð gjalda
eða skyldu goðin ǫll gildi eiga.

Walked then all powers to their thrones of judgement,
Holy aboriginal gods, and took heed of this,
Whether the Æsir-gods had to pay such a price,
Or whether all divinities should gain recognition.

24 Fleygði Óðinn ok í folk of skaut,
þat var enn folkvíg fyrst í heimi.
Brotinn var borðveg[g]r borgar ása,
knáttu vanir vígspá vǫllu sporna.

Óðinn cast, and he shot into the mob,
It was still the war of nations, the first in the world.
Broken was the shield-wall of the Æsir's stronghold,
Vanir by a war-charm came alive and kicking on the plain.

---

22 Heiðr's corrupting visits to family hearths may be compared with the impact of touring Dionysus, on Thebes, chiefly in Euripides' *The Bacchae*.

24 *Knáttu vanir vígspá vǫllu sporna* 'by a war-charm came alive and kicking on the plain'. The birthing-imagery has been established by Dronke (1997: 42), as a sign of the Vanir's ability, like that of the vegetation from which they draw their power, to regenerate from the dead. This is the magic that the Æsir require from them, particularly through Freyja.

Þórr's blunder and Baldr's death

25

Þá gengu regin ǫll á rǫkstóla,
ginnheilǫg goð, ok um þat gættusk,
hverr hefði lopt allt lævi blandit
eða ætt jǫtuns Óðs mey gefna.

Walked then all powers to their thrones of judgement,
Holy aboriginal gods, and took heed of this,
Who had laced all the lofty heavens with ruin
Or given Óðr's girl to the race of Giants.

'Lofty heavens': there is a pun on *loptr* ('sky') with Loptr, a name for Loki, the guilty party. 'Óðr's girl': Freyja, or a goddess like her.

26

Þórr einn þar vá þrunginn móði,
hann sjaldan sitr er hann slíkt of fregn.
Á gengusk eiðar, orð ok sœri,
mál ǫll meginlig, er á meðal fóru.

Þórr alone there struck, swollen with wrath,
He seldom stays sitting when he hears of such a thing.
One oath paid for another, the vows and sworn pledges,
All the words of weight that went between.

27

Veit hon Heimdal[l]ar hljóð of folgit
und heiðvǫnum helgum baðmi.
Á sér hon ausask aurgum forsi
af veði Valfǫðrs. Vituð ér enn eða hvat?

She knows Heimdallr's hearing to be hidden
Beneath the holy beam which frequents heaven.
A river she sees pouring itself with muddy cascade
From Slain-Father's pledge. Do you know it yet, or what?

---

26 *Á gengusk eiðar* 'One oath paid for another'. The giant-builder's death from Þórr's perjury now, and Baldr's later from the mistletoe's lack of oath, will cancel each other out.

27 *heiðvǫnum helgum baðmi* 'holy beam which frequents heaven'. World Tree's top as seen in the upper sky. [*Valfǫðrs* 'Slain-Father': Óðinn, whose 'pledge' is Urðr's well, equivalent to the eye he pledges for a drink.

28 Ein sat hon úti, þá er inn aldni kom,
Yggj*u*ngr ása, ok í augu leit.
'Hvers fregnið mik? Hví freistið mín?
Allt veit ek, Óðinn, hvar þú auga falt,
í inum mæra Mímisbrunni.
Drekkr mjǫð Mímir morgun hverjan
af veði Valfǫðrs.' Vituð ér enn eða hvat?

Alone she sat outside, when the ancient one came,
Æsir's Son of Dread, and looked into her eye.
'What do you ask me? Why do you try me?
I know it all, Óðinn, where you hid your eye,
It was in the glorious well of Mímir!
Mímir drinks mead every morning
From Slain-Father's pledge.' Do you know it yet, or what?

29 Valði henni Herfǫðr hringa ok men,
fe[kk] spjǫll spaklig ok spáganda.
Sá hon vítt ok of vítt of verǫld hverja.

Choose for her did War-Father rings and necklaces,
Sensible talk he got, along with helper-spirits of prophecy.
Far she saw, and beyond that further, through world upon world.

30 Sá hon valkyrjur vítt of komnar,
gǫrvar at ríða til goðþjóðar.
Skuld helt skildi, en Skǫgul ǫnnur,
Gunnr, Hildr, Gǫndul ok Geirskǫgul.
. . .

Valkyries she saw, come from afar,
Ready to ride to the gods' realm.
Skuld held a shield, and Skǫgul was another,
Gunnr, Hildr, Gǫndul and Spear-Skǫgul.
. . .

'Skuld': 'Had-to-Be' (see stanza 20). 'Gunnr, Hildr, Gǫndul and Spear-Skǫgul': aspects of warfare.

31 Ek sá Baldri, blóðgum tívur,
Óðins barni, ǫrlǫg folgin.
Stóð of vaxinn vǫllu[m] hæri
mjór ok mjǫk fagr mistilteinn.

I saw for Baldr, for the bleeding sacrifice,
For Óðinn's child, the hidden fate prepared.
There stood full-grown, higher than the plains,
Slender and utterly beautiful, the mistletoe.

32 Varð af þeim meiði, er mær sýndisk,
harmflaug hættlig; Hǫðr nam skjóta.
Baldrs bróðir var of borinn snemma,
sá nam Óðins sonr einnættr vega.

Came about from that stem, which seemed slender,
A perilous flight of harm; Hǫðr was taught to shoot.
Baldr's brother was born quickly,
Óðinn's son, taught to kill at one night old.

'Baldr's brother': Váli, begotten by Óðinn on Rindr to avenge Baldr on Hǫðr.

33 Þó hann æva hendr né hǫfuð kembði,
áðr á bál of bar Baldrs andskota,
en Frigg of grét í Fensǫlum
vá Valhallar. Vituð ér enn eða hvat?

He'd no time to wash his hands or comb his head
Before he bore Baldr's adversary to the pyre,
While Frigg wept in Fen Halls
For Valhǫll's woe. Do you know it yet, or what?

Visions of the End

34 Hapt sá hon liggja und Hveralundi,
lægjarns líki Loka áþekkjan.
Þar sitr Sigyn, þeygi of sínum
ver vel glýjuð. Vituð ér enn eða hvat?

A captive she saw laid out beneath Cauldrons' Grove,
Thankfully similar to the body of malign Loki.
There sits Sigyn, though surely without much
Joy in her husband. Do you know it yet, or what?

'Sigyn': Loki's wife.

35 Á fellr austan um eitrdala
sǫxum ok sverðum, Slíðr heitir sú.

From the east a river falls down poisoned dales
With knives and swords, its name is Horrible.

---

35 Two lines only in the *Hauksbók* text, which refer to a different Váli (the son of Loki with whose guts the gods bind Loki), are usually treated as stanza 35. As Dronke, however, we omit them as spurious, and give the number to the next stanza on.

36 Stóð fyr norðan á Niðavǫllum
salr ór gulli Sindra ættar,
en annarr stóð á Ókólni
bjórsalr jǫtuns, en sá Brimir heitir.

There stood to the north on Waning Moon Plains
A hall made of the gold of Sindri's race,
While there stood another on Never Cold,
The beerhall of a giant, and his name is Brimir.

'Brimir': 'Brim, Sea' (see also stanza 9). 'Sindri's race': apparently dwarves, the same who fashion Baldr's ring Draupnir.

37 Sal sá hon standa sólu fjarri
Nástrǫndu á, norðr horfa dyrr.
Fellu eitrdropar inn um ljóra.
Sá er undinn salr orma hryggjum.

A hall she saw standing, remote from the Sun
On Dead-Body Shore, its doors look north.
There fell drops of venom, in through the roof-vent.
That hall is woven of serpents' spines.

38 Sá hon þar vaða þunga strauma
menn meinsvara ok morðvarga
ok þann er annars glepr eyrarúnu.
Þar saug Niðhǫggr nái framgengna,
sleit vargr vera. Vituð ér enn eða hvat?

She saw there wading onerous streams
Men perjured and wolfish murderers
And the man who seduces another's close-trusted wife.
There Malice Striker sucked corpses of the departed,
The wolf tore men. Do you know it yet, or what?

---

38 *menn meinsvara ok morðvarga* 'Men perjured and wolfish murderers'. The poet models his language on English sermons on the Last Days, for Archbishop Wulfstan, though almost certainly not the source himself, has *mansworan and morþorwyrhtan* of similar meaning, a number of times and particularly in his *Sermo Lupi* of 1018 (see **Writers of the Benedictine Reform**; also North 2006: 218).

39 Austr sat in aldna í Járnviði
ok fœddi þar Fenris kindir.
Verðr af þeim ǫllum einna nǫkkurr
tungls tjúgari í trǫlls hami.

In the east she sat, the ancient one, in Iron Wood,
And bred there the broods of Fenrir.
There will come from them all one of that number
To be a moon-snatcher in a troll's skin.

40 Fyllisk fjǫrvi feigra manna,
rýðr ragna sjǫt rauðum dreyra.
Svǫrt *ver*ða sólskin um sumur eptir,
veðr ǫll válynd. Vituð ér enn eða hvat?

She fills herself with the life's blood of doomed men,
Paints red the powers' homes with crimson gore.
Black will be the sunshine in the summers after,
Seasons all crooked. Do you know it yet, or what?

'Powers' homes': the world of the gods, also of men.

41 Sat þar á haugi ok sló hǫrpu
gýgjar hirðir, glaðr Eggþér.
Gól of hánum í Ga*lg*viði
fagrrauðr hani, sá er Fjalarr heitir.

Sat there on a mound and struck his lyre
The giantess' herdsman, radiant Eggþér.
Crowed above him in Gallows' Wood
A cockerel dazzling red whose name is Fjalarr.

'Eggþér': 'Servant of the Blade' (see also OE *Ecgþeow*, father of Beowulf).

42 Gól of ásum Gullinkambi,
sá vekr hǫlða at Herjafǫðrs,
en annarr gelr fyr jǫrð neðan
sótrauðr hani at sǫlum Heljar.

There crowed Golden-Comb above the gods,
Who wakes up the heroes at War-Father's,
While beneath the earth there crows another,
A rust-red rooster by the halls of goddess Hel.

'At War-Father's': in Valhǫll.

39–40 This giantess is identifiable (in *The Song of Hyndla*) with Angrboða, consort of Loki, on whom he begets Fenrir and other monsters. If *fyllisk* refers to her as the last singular subject, as seems likely, she may also be seen as an image of the Whore of Babylon, the 'woman' whom 'I saw drunk with the blood of the saints and those who had borne their testimony to Jesus' in Revelations 17:1–6, esp. 6 (*vidi mulierem ebriam de sanguine sanctorum et de sanguine martyrum Iesu*; see North 2006: 220–1).

43 Geyr [nú] Garmr mjǫk fyr Gnipahelli,
festr mun slitna, en freki renna.
Fjǫlð veit hon frœða, fram sé ek lengra
um ragna rǫk rǫmm s*i*gtíva.

Garmr [now] barks loud before Looming Cave,
The fetter will break, and the ravener run free.
Much knowledge she has of things, ahead I see further,
Beyond the mighty fates of victory-divine powers.

'Garmr': like Cerberus (the names are of one root).

44 Brœðr munu berjask ok at bǫnum verðask,
munu systrungar sifjum spilla.
Hart er í heimi, hórdómr mikill,
skeggǫld, skalmǫld, skildir ro klofnir,
vindǫld, vargǫld, áðr verǫld steypisk.
Mun engi maðr ǫðrum þyrma.

Brother will fight brother and each die at the other's hands,
Siblings will ruin the bonds of kinship.
It is cruel in the world, one big whoredom,
An axe age, a sword age (shields are cloven),
A wind age, a wolf age, before the men-age crashes.
No man will have mercy on another.

Ragnarǫk: the Day of Judgement

45 Leika Míms synir, en mjǫtuðr kyndisk
at in[u] galla Gjallarhorni.
Hátt blæss Heimdallr, horn er á lopti,
mælir Óðinn við Míms hǫfuð.
Skelfr Yggdrasils askr standandi,
ymr it aldna tré, en jǫtunn losnar.

Mímir's sons play while the Fate-Wood kindles
At the shrill blast of the Horn of Resounding.
Loud blows Heimdallr, the horn is aloft,
Óðinn converses with Mímir's head.
The ash of Yggdrasill shivers as it stands,
The ancient tree groans while the Giant breaks free.

'Mímir's sons': giants, perhaps of deep wells, whose 'play' may be earthquakes. 'Fate-Wood': World Tree. 'The Giant': apparently Loki, here given as the Anti-Christ.

46 Geyr nú Garmr mjǫk fyr Gnipahelli,
festr mun slitna, en freki renna.
Fjǫlð veit hon frœða, fram sé ek lengra
um ragna rǫk rǫmm sigtíva.

Garmr now barks loud before Looming Cave,
The fetter will break, and the ravener run free.
Much knowledge she has of things, ahead I see further,
Beyond the mighty fates of victory-divine powers.

47 Hrymr ekr austan, hefisk lind fyrir,
snýsk Jǫrmungandr í jǫtunmóði.
Ormr knýr unnir, en ari hlakkar,
slítr nái niðfǫlr, Naglfar losnar.

From the east drives Hrymr, lifts his shield before him,
Mighty Wraith coils with the wrath of a giant.
The snake smacks the waves, and the eagle rejoices,
Beak-yellow, he tears corpses, Nail-Craft unmoors.

'Mighty Wraith': the World Serpent. 'Nail-Craft': the greatest ship ever known, that carries all enemies of gods and men.

48 Kjóll ferr austan, koma munu Múspells
of lǫg lýðir, en Loki stýrir.
Fara fíflmegir með freka allir,
þeim er bróðir Býleipts í fǫr.

From the east sails the ship, Múspell's levies
Will be coming across water, with Loki at the helm.
The giant's boys are all sailing with the ravener,
In company with them is Býleiptr's brother.

'The ravener': Loki. 'Býleiptr's brother': Loki.

49 Hvat er með ásum? Hvat er með alfum?
Gnýr allr Jǫtunheimr, æsir ro á þingi,
stynja dvergar fyr steindurum,
veggbergs vísir. Vituð ér enn eða hvat?

What's with the gods? What's with the elves?
All Giant-land's in uproar, the gods are in council,
Dwarves groan in rock doorways,
Wise to their mountain walls. Do you know it yet, or what?

---

46 The language here, again, appears derived from English Last Days sermons, as may be seen with the words *ne byrhð broðor oþrum* 'no brother will help another' in Wulfstan's *Secundum Marcum* (see **Writers of the Benedictine Reform**). The sentiment, though commonplace, seems rooted ultimately in Mark 13:12, 'Brother will send brother to his death, and father son' (*Tradet autem frater fratrem in mortem, et pater filium*). With his four ǫld- ('age-') compounds, the poet also reanimates the word *verǫld*, 'world', into its components *vera-ǫld* 'age of men', as this translation attempts to show.

50 Surtr ferr sunnan með sviga lævi,
skínn af sverði sól valtíva.
Grjótbjǫrg gnata, en gífr rata,
troða halir helveg, en himinn klofnar.

From the south comes Surtr with ruin of branches,
Shines from his sword the sun of death deities.
Rock-peaks clash, while hags take the road,
Men tread a hell-path, while heaven splits open.

'Ruin of branches': fire. 'Sun of death deities': volcanic fire.

51 Þá kemr Hlínar harmr annarr fram,
er Óðinn ferr við ulf vega,
en bani Belja bjartr at Surti.
Þá mun Friggjar falla angan.

Hlín's second sorrow then comes to pass
When Óðinn goes forth to fight the wolf,
And Beli's slayer, bright, to face Surtr.
That is when Frigg's darling will fall.

'Hlín's (Frigg's) second sorrow': after Baldr, the death of Óðinn. 'Beli's slayer': Freyr.

52 Þá kemr inn mikli mǫgr Sigfǫður,
Víðarr, vega at valdýri.
Lætr hann megi Hveðrungs mundum standa
hjǫr til hjarta: þá er hefnt fǫður.

Out then comes Victory-Father's great son,
Víðarr, in combat with the beast of death.
With both arms he stands his sword in the heart
Of Hveðrungr's son: father is avenged then.

'Victory-Father': Óðinn. 'Hveðrungr's (Loki's) son': the wolf Fenrir.

---

50 *helveg* 'hell-path'. As the earth erupts, the ground underfoot becomes lava, the very substance of hell for all humanity (*halir*) unlucky enough to be still alive. This *hel-* is not personified, unlike the Hel deity presiding in stanza 42.

53 Þá kemr inn mæri mǫgr Hlóðynjar,
gengr Óðins sonr við *orm* vega,
drepr af móði Miðgarðs véurr
(munu halir allir heimstǫð ryðja),
gengr fet níu Fjǫrgynjar burr
neppr frá naðri níðs ókvíðnum.

Now comes Hidden-Mother's glorious child,
Óðinn's son strides into battle with the Serpent,
Middle World's sanctifying thunder smites in wrath
(The world's homestead will be cleared of all men),
Back nine paces steps Mountain-Mother's boy,
Succumbing, from the dead adder that hadn't feared sacrilege.

54 Sól tér sortna, sígr fold í mar,
hverfa af himni heiðar stjǫrnur.
Geisar eimi við aldrnara,
leikr hár hiti við himin sjalfan.

Sun starts to blacken, earth sinks in sea,
The radiant stars fall off the heavens.
Vapours rise up against life-nourisher,
The heat licks high against heaven itself.

'Life-nourisher': fire.

55 Geyr nú Garmr mjǫk fyr Gnipahelli,
festr mun slitna, en freki renna.
Fjǫlð veit hon frœða, fram sé ek lengra
um ragna rǫk rǫmm sigtíva.

Garmr now barks loud before Looming Cave,
The fetter will break, and the ravener run free.
Much knowledge she has of things, ahead I see further,
Beyond the mighty fates of victory-divine powers.

---

53 *Hlóðynjar* 'Hidden-Mother'. Cognate with Graeco-Latin *Latona*, mother of Apollo and Diana by Zeus; probably identical with *Hludana* in Latin inscriptions in the province of Germany in the second and third centuries. [*véurr* 'sanctifying thunder'. The basis for this reading, as opposed to others such as 'sanctuary-protector' (**vé-vǫrðr*), is the name *Wigithonar* ('sanctifying thunder'), which we take to be the name ancestral to *Véurr*. [*Fjǫrgynjar* 'Mountain-Mother'. Cognate with OE *firgen-* 'hill, mountain' (North 1997: 247–50).

54 *við aldrnara* 'against life-nourisher'. Note the irony, but there is also the notion of poisonous gases stifling life. The volcanic imagery is so detailed as to make it likely that the poet is from Iceland; more so than from anywhere else in Scandinavia.

World's rebirth: the New Jerusalem

56 Sér hon upp koma ǫðru sinni
jǫrð ór ægi iðjagrœna.
Falla forsar, flýgr ǫrn yfir,
sá er á fjalli fiska veiðir.

She sees coming up a second time
Earth from ocean, once again green.
Cascades fall, an eagle flies across
Out hunting for fish in the fells.

57 Finnask æsir á Iðavelli
ok um moldþinur mátkan dœma
[ok minnask þar á megindóma]
ok á Fimbultýs fornar rúnir.

The gods find each other on Eddying Plain
And pass judgement on the awesome earth-bow
[And in that place recall momentous judgements]
And the ancient runes of the Titan God.

'Earth-bow': World Serpent. 'Titan God': probably Óðinn.

58 Þar munu eptir undrsamligar
gullnar tǫflur í grasi finnask,
þærs í árdaga áttar hǫfðu.

There once more will the wonder-working
Golden chess-pieces be found in the grass,
Those which they used to have in ancient times.

---

56 *iðjagrœna* 'once again green'. The name *Ið-unn*, that of the goddess of the apples of perpetual youth, means 'yields once again' in a microcosm of this grand conception here.

57 The third long line is found only in the *Hauksbók* text of *The Sibyl's Prophecy*. This stanza echoes stanza 7 with strange reference to the pristine conditions of before, although *finnask* here ('find each other'), for *hittusk* there ('came together'), suggests that this time the survivors, or their descendants, are out looking for each other. [*Fimbultýs* 'Titan God'. Probably Óðinn, as he is perceived in his runic aspect (as *fimbulþulr* 'titan wizard' in *Sayings of the High One*, stanzas 80 and 142).

59 Munu ósánir akrar vaxa,
bǫls mun alls batna, Baldr mun koma.
Búa þeir Hǫðr ok Baldr Hropts sigtoptir,
vé*s* valtíva. Vituð ér enn eða hvat?

Unsown the acres will begin to grow,
All evil will be cured, Baldr will come.
Hǫðr and Baldr dwell in Hroptr's triumphal ruins,
Ruins of the sanctuary of the gods of the slain. Do you know it yet, or what?

'Hroptr': 'Concealment', or similar (cognate with Greek *krypt-* 'hide'), a name for Óðinn, again in his runic aspect.

60 Þá kná Hœnir hlautvið kjósa
ok burir byggja brœðra tveggja
vindheim víðan. Vituð ér enn eða hvat?

Hœnir then knows wood for lot-casting, how to choose it,
And the two brothers' sons inhabit
The wide wind-realm. Do you know it yet, or what?

61 Sal sér hon standa sólu fegra,
gulli þakðan á Gimléi.
Þar skulu dyggvar dróttir byggja
ok um aldrdaga ynðis njóta.

A hall she sees more dazzling than the sun,
Thatched with gold in the City of Jewels.
There the worthy warrior bands shall dwell
And enjoy delight all the days of their lives.

---

59 *Hropts sigtoptir* 'Hroptr's [Concealment's] triumphal ruins'. Taking *toptir* in the sense of 'foundations' of former buildings, we read this stanza as the poet's image of the pursuit of history through archaeology and writing. This poet appears, for more than one reason, to have been trained by clergy in the Rome-based culture of Christianity.

61 *á Gimléi* 'in the City of Jewels'. The sense of *gim-* 'gem, jewel' is sufficiently well attested, as is the general meaning 'town' in the – *leah* suffix (Bintley, Stanley, Brockley) and simplex (Lee, Lea, Leigh) common in place-names across England (Gelling 1984: 198–206), for the unusual formulation *Gimlé* to be read as a nonce-word for the jewelled city of New Jerusalem in Revelations 21:9–11, esp. 11: 'It shone with the glory of God; it had the radiance of some priceless jewel, like a jasper, clear as crystal' (*habentem claritatem Dei: et lumen eius simile lapidi pretioso tanquam lapidi iaspidis, sicut crystallum*; see North 2006: 223).

62H Þá kemr inn ríki at regindómi,
ǫflugr ofan, sá er ǫllu ræðr.

Then the Mighty One comes to the court of Judgement,
Powerful from above, He who rules all.

63 Þar kemr inn dimmi dreki fljúgandi,
naðr fránn neðan, frá Niðafjǫllum.
Berr sér í fjǫðrum, flýgr vǫll yfir,
Niðhǫggr nái. Nú mun hon sǫkkvask.

There comes the dismal Dragon flying,
The glittering adder from below, from Waning Moon Fells.
Carries in his wings, as he flies across the plains,
Malice Striker, corpses. Now she will sink.

62H This stanza is not in Codex Regius, nor in Snorri's *Edda*, but only in the *Hauksbók* text of *The Sibyl's Prophecy*. Dronke rejects it as a later interpolation, made to improve the Christianised aspect of Baldr. Others see it as part of the original conception, excised by an editor older than Snorri and Codex Regius, who wished to present *The Sibyl's Prophecy* as a less ambiguously heathen work.

63 As the foreign loanword *dreki* 'dragon' (Latin *draco*) would indicate, this monster, a new World Serpent with wings, is meant to be the Dragon which, according to Revelations 20:1–3, will rise from the abyss at the end of the Thousand Years. The word *neðan* 'from below' here neatly opposes *ofan* 'from above' in the (*Hauksbók*) stanza before. For an attempt to strengthen the likelihood of an AD 1000 date for *The Sibyl's Prophecy* on the basis of some ten parallels with Revelations, see North 2006.

Loki's Truth-Game

Lokasenna

⁕

The word *senna* is cognate with OIce *sannr* 'true' (OE *soþ*), so the root idea of a *senna* 'bickering' is probably to relate home truths which, though they are insulting, may not be denied. Loki's role in his 'truth-game', *Lokasenna*, may be connected with his name: possibly 'finisher' if we link the word *loki* to OIce *lúka* 'to close, finish'. Whether or not this meaning is present among the many other etymologies that seem to empower the poem, Loki is synonymous with imminent Ragnarǫk, the end of the Norse gods' world. In *Lokasenna* he sets about unravelling the mysteries upon which the divine powers depend. In literary-critical parlance, his approach is to 'deconstruct' the gods' mysteries by moralising them as flaws of character. To give some examples, Frigg makes love to her brothers-in-law while Óðinn is away, but since her name means 'love', that may not be surprising in a goddess without whom no marriage could take place. The infidelities of other goddesses, Iðunn and Gefjun, turn out too to have a purpose; one to do with the sun, harvest and prosperity. If we think of the white mud in *The Sibyl's Prophecy*, stanza 19, Heimdallr's soiled backside becomes another way of describing the mud that the worshippers of the World Tree, which he personifies, smear on the bole of his trunk. Heimdallr holds up the universe and gives warning when it comes to an end. And Njǫrðr, for example, has imbibed the urine of giantesses, as he lay underneath them, but since he is the ocean, and 'Hymir's daughters' are rivers, what does it matter?

It is our laughter that makes it all matter, however. That is so if Loki's mocking moralisations succeed in reducing the Norse gods to the comic level of humans. When this happens, the heathen mysteries will vanish, as some gods here can see. What distinguishes this poem, then, from *The Sibyl's Prophecy* is not the time of composition, which must be a generation later in the case of *Loki's Truth-Game*, so much as the anger with which the gods in this poem are demolished one by one. The old world will end shortly in this poem, as it does in the other, but in Loki's case the demolition proceeds not through Christian history or warfare or the toppling of heathen idols, but by means of heathen ideas. The case of Hjalti Skeggjason's ditty on Freyja, which got him banished from Iceland in 997, seems similar. Hjalti's bitch-image of Freyja, a homiletic touch if there ever was one, reduces her cult to mindless sex. *Loki's Truth-Game* (all quoted here) is not far from Hjalti's way of looking at pagan cults, but its intellectual rigour is greater, for it works through sustained drama. It is possible to guess at this work as a poem made up in Iceland a generation after the conversion of 999, thus in the 1020s or 1030s. The sustained quality lets one speculate that the author was a priest who had grown up in the old religion. The poem looks like a dramatic therapy for heathens who could not let go.

Clunies Ross, M., 'Why Skaði laughed: comic seriousness in Old Norse mythic narrative', *Mål og Minne* (1989), 1–14

Dronke, U., ed., trans. and comm., *The Poetic Edda, vol. II: Mythological Poems* (Oxford, 1997)

Faulkes, A., ed., *Skáldskaparmál*, 2 vols (London, 1997)

Gunnell, T., *The Origins of Drama in Scandinavia* (Cambridge, 1995)

McKinnell, J., 'Motivation in *Lokasenna*', *Saga-Book of the Viking Society* 22.3–4 (1987–8), 234–62

Meulengracht Sørensen, P., 'Loki's *Senna* in Ægir's Hall', in *At Fortælle Historien: Studier i den gamle nordiske Litteratur. Telling History: Studies in Norse Literature*, Hesperides: Letterature e Culture Occidentali 16 (Trieste, 2001), 93–112

North, R., 'Loki's gender, or why Skaði laughed', in *Monsters and the Monstrous in Medieval Northwest Europe*, ed. K. E. Olsen and Luuk A. J. R. Houwen (Louvain, 2001), 141–51

Loki crashes the party

Ægir, er ǫðru nafni hét Gymir, hann hafði búit ásum ǫl, þá er hann hafði fengit ketil inn mikla, sem nú er sagt. Til þeirar veizlu kom Óðinn ok Frigg, kona hans. Þórr kom eigi, því at hann var í austrvegi. Sif var þar, kona Þórs, Bragi ok Iðunn, kona hans. Týr var þar. Hann var einhendr, Fenrisúlfr sleit hǫnd af honum, þá er hann var bundinn. Þar var Njǫrðr ok kona hans Skaði, Freyr ok Freyja, Víðarr, son Óðins. Loki var þar ok þjónustumenn Freys, Byggvir ok Beyla. Margt var þar ása ok alfa. Ægir átti tvá þjónustumenn, Fimafengr ok Eldir. Þar var lýsigull haft fyrir elts ljós. Sjálft barsk þar ǫl. Þar var griðastaðr mikill. Menn lofuðu mjǫk, hversu góðir þjónustumenn Ægis váru. Loki mátti eigi heyra þat, ok drap hann Fimafeng. Þá skóku æsir skjǫldu sína ok œpðu at Loka ok eltu hann braut til skógar, en þeir fóru at drekka. Loki hvarf aptr ok hitti úti Eldi. Loki kvaddi hann:

Ægir ('Ocean Man'), or Gymir by another name, he had ale made for the gods when he took delivery of the great kettle, as has just been told. Óðinn came to the party with Frigg, his wife. Þórr didn't come as he was in the east. Sif was there, Þórr's wife, Bragi and his wife Iðunn. Týr was there. He had one hand, the Fenris-wolf bit the other off for him when he was chained. Njǫrðr was there, his wife Skaði, Freyja, Freyr, and Víðarr, son of Óðinn. Loki was there along with Freyr's servants Byggvir and Beyla. There were many gods and elves. Ocean Man had two servants, Nimble-Grip and Light-a-Fire. Shining gold was used there for lighting. The ale served itself. The place was a big sanctuary. There was a lot of praise for how good Ocean Man's servants were. Loki couldn't bear to hear it, and killed Nimble-Grip. The gods then shook their shields, chanted at Loki and drove him off to the woods, then proceeded with their drinking. Loki returned and met Light-a-Fire outside. Loki addressed him:

1

'Segðu þat, Eldir, svá at þú einugi
feti gangir framar,
hvat hér inni hafa at ǫlmálum
sigtíva synir.'

'Tell me, Light-a-Fire, before you take
one step further,
What ale-talk they have inside this place,
those sons of triumphant gods.'

Eldir kvað:

2 'Of vápn sín dœma ok um vígrisni sína
sigtíva synir;
ása ok alfa er hér inni eru,
manngi er þér í orði vinr.'

Light-a-Fire said:

'They discuss their weapons and prowess in arms,
those sons of triumphant gods;
Of the gods or elves who are inside here
not one in his words is a friend to you.'

Loki kvað:

3 'Inn skal ganga Ægis hallir í
á þat sumbl at sjá;
*o*ll ok áfu fœri ek ása sonum,
ok blend ek þeim svá meini mjǫð.'

Loki said:

'An entry must be made into Ocean Man's halls
to take a look at that banquet.
Contempt and strife I will bring to sons of gods,
and so blend their mead with malice.'

Eldir kvað:

4 'Veiztu, ef þú inn gengr Ægis hallir í
á þat sumbl at sjá,
hrópi ok rógi ef þú eyss á holl regin,
á þér munu þau þerra þat.'

Light-a-Fire said:

'You know, if you go indoors into Ocean Man's halls
to take a look at that banquet,
And drench the gracious powers with catcalls and slander,
they'll towel themselves off on you.'

---

3 *oll* 'Contempt'. The scribe wrote *hropioll*, drawing *hropi* from the following stanza. Dronke removes *hropi* and reads *oll* as an English loanword from the beginning of the eleventh century (1997: 356–7). See Wulfstan, *swyþost man tæleð and mid olle gegreteð ealles to gelome þa þe riht lufiað and Godes ege habbað be ænigum dæle* 'most of all, people accuse and greet with contempt all too often those who love the right and have fear of God to any degree' (1018) in *Sermo Lupi* (**Writers of the Benedictine Reform**).

Loki kvað:

5 'Veiztu þat, Eldir, ef vit einir skulum
sáryrðum sakask,
auðigr verða mun ek í andsvǫrum,
ef þú mælir til margt.'

Loki said:

'You know, Light-a-Fire, if the two of us are to
strive at each other with wounding words,
I'll become a wealthy man in answers
if you you speak too much.'

Síðan gekk Loki inn í hǫllina. En er þeir sá, er fyrir váru, hverr inn var kominn, þǫgnuðu þeir allir.

After that, Loki went into the hall. And when the people who were there saw who had come in, they all went quiet.

Loki kvað:

6 'Þyrstr ek kom þessar hallar til,
Loptr, um langan veg,
ásu at biðja, at mér einn gefi
mæran drykk mjaðar.

Loki said:

'Thirsty I have come to this hall here,
Lofty, down a long road,
To ask the gods that one of them might give me
a glorious drink of mead.

7 'Hví þegið ér svá, þrungin goð,
at þér mæla né meguð?
Sessa ok staði velið mér sumbli at
eða heitið mik heðan.'

'Why be so silent, buttoned-up gods,
so that no words can you say?
You find me seating and a place in the banquet,
or order me out of here.'

---

5 *auðigr í andsvǫrum* 'wealthy man in answers'. Loki will (a) have lots of answers to give Light-a-Fire, but will also (b) win wealth from Eldir, servant of the sea-god Ægir, because *eldr ægis* 'fire of the sea' is a kenning for 'gold'.

Bragi kvað:

8
'Sessa ok staði velja þér sumbli at
æsir aldregi,
því at æsir vitu, hveim þeir alda skulu
gambansumbl of geta.'

Bragi said:

'Seating for you and a place in the banquet the gods
will never find,
For the gods know what people they must
make a potent party for.'

Loki kvað:

9
'Mantu þat, Óðinn, er vit í árdaga
blendum blóði saman?
Ǫlvi bergja léztu eigi mundu,
nema okkr væri báðum borit.'

Loki said:

'You remember, Óðinn, the old days, when the two of us
blended our blood together?
You said you would taste no ale at all
unless it were served to us both.'

Óðinn kvað:

10
'Rístu þá, Viðarr, ok lát ulfs fǫður
sitja sumbli at,
síðr oss Loki kveði lastastǫfum
Ægis hǫllu í.'

Óðinn said:

'Rise up then Viðarr, and let the Wolf's father
sit at the banquet right here,
Lest Loki greet us with words of blame
indoors in Ocean Man's halls.'

Loki toasts all the gods

Þá stóð Viðarr upp ok skenkði Loka. En áðr hann drykki, kvaddi hann ásuna:

Viðarr then got up and poured ale for Loki, but before he drank, he greeted the gods as follows:

11

'Heilir æsir, heilar ásynjur
ok ǫll ginnheilǫg goð,
nema sá einn áss er innar sitr,
Bragi, bekkjum á.'

'Good fortune to gods, good fortune to goddesses
and to all the holy aboriginal deities,
Save the one god who is sitting further in,
Bragi, on the benches.'

Bragi kvað:
12

'Mar ok mæki gef ek þér míns féar,
ok bœtir þér svá baugi Bragi,
síðr þú ásum ǫfund of gjaldir.
Grem þú eigi goð at þér.'

Bragi said:

'Stallion and sword from my own hoard I'll give you,
and with a ring Bragi will compensate you too,
Lest for your envy you make all the Æsir pay.
Don't make the gods mad at you.'

Loki kvað:
13

'Jós ok armbauga mundu æ vera
beggja vanr, Bragi;
ása ok alfa, er hér inni eru,
þú ert við víg varastr
ok skjarrastr við skot.'

Loki said:

'Steed and bracelets, both, are things which you
will always be wanting, Bragi.
Of gods and elves who are inside this place
you are wariest of war
and shyest of facing shots.'

Bragi kvað:

14 'Veit ek, ef fyr útan værak, svá sem fyr innan emk
Ægis hǫll of kominn,
hǫfuð þitt bæra ek í hendi mér;
lítt *er* þér þat fyr lygi.'

Bragi said:

'This I know, if I were outside, as sure as inside I have
entered Ocean Man's hall,
Your head I would carry in my hand,
a small price to pay for your lies.'

Loki kvað:

15 'Snjallr ertu í sessi, skalatu svá gøra,
Bragi bekkskrautuðr;
vega þú gakk, ef þú vreiðr séir:
hyggsk vætr hvatr fyrir.'

Loki said:

'Eloquent in your seat, that can't be how you do it,
Bragi bench-ornament.
Come and fight, if you feel angry:
a brave man thinks there's nothing in his way.'

Iðunn kvað:

16 'Bið ek [þik], Bragi, barna sifjar duga
ok allra óskmaga,
at þú Loka kveðira lastastǫfum
Ægis hǫllu í.'

Iðunn said:

'Bragi, I ask [you] to make good the kinship that binds
all our children and adopted sons,
That you don't greet Loki with words of blame
indoors in Ocean Man's hall.'

---

15 Loki's attempt to make Bragi, not himself, break the rules of sanctuary is thwarted by Iðunn's words following, in which she reminds Bragi of the children present.

Loki kvað:

17 ‘Þegi þú, Iðunn, þik kveð ek allra kvenna
vergjarnasta vera,
síztu arma þína lagðir ítrþvegna
um þinn bróðurbana.’

Loki said:

‘You be quiet, Iðunn! You of all women, I say, are
the one most eager for a man,
Since the time you laid your arms, your brightly bathed arms,
around the man who killed your brother.’

Iðunn kvað:

18 ‘Loka ek kveðka lastastǫfum
Ægis hǫllu í:
Braga ek kyrri bjórreifan;
vilkat ek, at it reiðir vegizk.’

Iðunn said:

‘I am not one to greet Loki with words of blame
in the hall of Ocean Man.
I’ll pacify Bragi, who’s gone happy with beer.
I don’t want the two of you angry and fighting.’

Gefjun kvað:

19 ‘Hví it æsir tveir skuluð inni hér
sáryrðum sakask?
Lopzki þat veit, at hann leikinn er
ok hann fjǫrg ǫll fría?’

Gefjun said:

‘Why must the two of you gods inside here
strive at each other with wounding words?
Is it not known that Loki is given to games
and all earth-deities love him?’

---

17 Iðunn’s family probity is undermined by this quip, which must be true, if it is a *senna* ‘truth-game’. However, Loki’s accusation is usually read alongside Gerðr’s concern, voiced in *The Lay of Skírnir* stanza 16, that the man arrived outside her bower is her *bróðurbani* ‘brother’s slayer’. The mythologem common to both Gerðr and *Ið-unn* (‘yields again’) appears to come from a time when the earth was seen to take a new husband in the man who had just killed her old one (North 1997: 266–71). Since Iðunn’s new marriage, seen in this light, renews the harvest, on the heathen level she is not undermined at all. Loki may thus be seen to do with Iðunn what he will do with most others, deconstruct a divine mystery by moralising it as a flaw of character.

19 *fjǫrg* ‘earth-deities’. OIce *fjarg* ‘deity’, as related to *fjǫrgyn* (OE *firgen-*) ‘mountain’, suggests that Gefjun refers particularly to earth-bound gods who might take offence at Loki’s moralisation of Iðunn. McKinnell (1987–8) argues that Gefjun steps in here to upstage Iðunn, wife of Bragi with whom Gefjun is having an affair.

Loki kvað:

20 'Þegi þú, Gefjun, þess mun ek nú geta,
er þik glapði at geði,
sveinn inn hvíti, er þér sigli gaf
ok þú lagðir lær yfir.'

Loki said:

'You be quiet, Gefjun! I'll mention him now,
the one who fooled you in your love,
The whiteboy who gave you a treasure,
and you laid your thigh over his.'

Óðinn kvað:

21 'Œrr ertu, Loki, ok ǫrviti,
er þú fær þér Gefjun at gremi,
því at aldar ǫrlǫg hygg ek, at hon ǫll of viti
jafngǫrla sem ek.'

Óðinn said:

'You're crazy, Loki, and out of your wits,
to make Gefjun mad at you,
For all the fate of the world I think she knows about
just as clearly as I do.'

Loki kvað:

22 'Þegi þú, Óðinn, þú kunnir aldregi
deila víg með verum;
oft þú gaft, þeim er þú gefa skyldira,
inum slævurum sigr.'

Loki said:

'You be quiet, Óðinn! You never knew how
to deal out the deaths among fighting men.
Often you gave to the man you shouldn't have,
victory to the more faint-hearted.'

---

20 Gefjun the whore? It is true that *Gefjun* means 'giver'. But Loki's *sveinn inn hvíti* 'whiteboy' denotes, as well as (a) the blond young man who pays Gefjun for sex, (b) the god Heimdallr (*inn hvíti áss* 'the white god' is what Snorri calls him in *Gylf*, ch. 27) whom Freyja must so reward for recovering her necklace, the Brísingamen, from Loki (after duelling with him for it in seal's shape, as in Úlfr's *Eulogy on the House*, stanza '2'; North 1997: 225–6).

22 Óðinn gives out victory in this way in order to take the better warriors for his doomsday division in Valhǫll.

Óðinn kvað:

23 'Veiztu, ef ek gaf, þeim er ek gefa né skylda,
inum slævurum, sigr,
átta vetr vartu fyr jǫrð neðan,
kýr mólkandi ok kona,
ok hefr þú þar [bǫrn of] borit,
ok hugða ek þat args aðal.'

Óðinn said:

'Know that if I did give to the man I shouldn't have,
victory to the more faint-hearted,
Eight winters you spent beneath the earth
milking cows, as a woman too,
and there you have borne children,
and I thought that was a queer thing to do.'

Loki kvað:

24 'En þik síða kóðu Sámseyu í,
ok draptu á vétt sem vǫlur;
vitka líki fórtu verþjóð yfir,
ok hugða ek þat args aðal.'

Loki said:

'And you, they said, practised witchcraft on Samsø,
and beat on a lid like the sibyls.
Like a witch you went through a nation of men,
and I thought that was a queer thing to do.'

Frigg kvað:

25 'Ørlǫgum ykkrum skylið aldregi
segja seggjum frá,
hvat it æsir tveir drýgðuð í árdaga:
firrisk æ forn rǫk firar.'

Frigg said:

'The fates you have lived with, you should never
talk about to mankind,
What you two gods got up to in the early days:
old mysteries, may men ever shun them.'

---

23 Loki's gender, as at times female, allows him to give birth (to Fenrir, Hel and the World Serpent, even if Óðinn moralises him with the allegation of being used by giants as a woman (North 2001). OIce *argr* means both 'cowardly', Loki's implication concerning Óðinn in stanza 22, and 'queer' (as in homosexual), and Óðinn plays on this sense.

24 This story, though not quite understood, is told more fully in Saxo's *History of the Danes*, III (*c.* 1200). It appears to describe the manner in which Óðinn, as Kormákr says in his *Eulogy on Sigurðr* (stanza '2', *c.* 961), 'practised witchcraft to get Rindr' (*seið Yggr til Rindar*) to beget Váli on her, who will avenge Baldr on Hǫðr at one night old: thus a sacred task.

25 As Baldr's mother, as well as Óðinn's wife, Frigg is well placed to step in, but it seems she is anxious to stop Loki and her husband unravelling the powers on which they all depend: the end of their world is fast approaching.

Loki kvað:

26 'Þegi þú, Frigg, þú ert Fjǫrgyns mær
ok hefr æ vergjǫrn verit,
er þá Véa ok Vilja léztu þér, Viðris kvæn,
báða i baðm of tekit.'

Loki said:

'You be quiet, Frigg! You are Fjǫrgynn's daughter
and have always been eager for a man,
Since you let Véi and Vili, O Wutherer's queen,
both come into your bosom.'

Frigg kvað:

27 'Veiztu, ef ek inni ættak Ægis hǫllum i
Baldri líkan bur,
út þú né kvæmir frá ása sonum,
ok væri þá at þér reiðum vegit.'

Frigg said:

'Know this, if I had here indoors inside Ocean Man's hall
a boy like Baldr was,
You wouldn't escape then from the sons of gods,
angry as you are, you'd be struck down!'

Loki kvað:

28 'Enn vill þú, Frigg, at ek fleiri telja
mína meinstafi?
ek því réð, er þú ríða sérat
síðan Baldr at sǫlum.'

Loki said:

'Do you want me, Frigg, to count up even more
of my malignancies?
It was I who decided that you shall never now see
Baldr ride again to your hall.'

Freyja kvað:

29 'Œrr ertu, Loki, er þú yðra telr
ljóta leiðstafi;
ǫrlǫg Frigg, hygg ek, at ǫll viti,
þótt hon sjalfgi segi.'

Freyja said:

'You're crazy, Loki, to count up the ugly hateful things
you did in all your forms.
Frigg, I think, knows all men's fates,
though herself she may not say so.'

---

26 As Fjǫrgynn's daughter, Frigg is essentially the 'love' (from *frjá* 'to love', OE *frige*) as earthly desire (see note to stanza 19). This story concerns Óðinn's brothers, both lovers of Frigg in her husband's absence.

Loki kvað:

30 ‘Þegi þú, Freyja, þik kann ek fullgǫrva,
era þér vamma vant:
ása ok alfa, er hér inni eru,
hverr hefir þinn hór verit.’

Loki said:

‘You be quiet, Freyja! I know all about you,
in your case there’s no want of disgrace.
Of the gods and elves who are inside here,
each one has gone whoring where you are.’

Freyja kvað:

31 ‘Flá er þér tunga, hygg ek, at þér fremr myni
ógótt of gala;
reiðir ro þér æsir ok ásynjur,
hryggr muntu heim fara.’

Freyja said:

‘You have a lying tongue, which I think will sing
no good for you either one day.
Gods and goddesses, they are angry with you,
downcast you will go home.’

Loki kvað:

32 ‘Þegi þú, Freyja, þú ert fordæða
ok meini blandin mjǫk,
síz þik at brœðr þínum s*tó*ðu blíð regin
ok myndir þú þá, Freyja, frata.’

Loki said:

‘You be quiet, Freyja! You’re a foul witch,
and much mixed up with malice,
Since the giggling powers surprised you with your brother
and then, Freyja, you must have farted!’

Njǫrðr kvað:

33 ‘Þat er válítit, þótt sér varðir vers fái,
hós eða hvárs;
hitt er undr, er áss ragr er hér inn of kominn
ok hefir sá bǫrn of borit.’

Njǫrðr said:

‘It’s hardly harmful if the ladies get a man,
a lover or two.
The real wonder is that a queer has come in here,
a god who has borne babies!’

---

30 Once again, the poet seems to draw on homilies: on English ones, if we correlate Loki’s claimed moral outrage with Wulfstan’s, in his *Sermo Lupi* (1018): *and her syndan myltestran and bearnmyrðran and fule forlegene horingas manege* ‘here are prostitutes and child-murderers and foul fornicated whorers, many of them’ (see **Writers of the Benedictine Reform**).

Loki kvað:

34 'Þegi þú, Njǫrðr, þú vart austr heðan
gíls of sendr at goðum;
Hymis meyjar hǫfðu þik at hlandtrogi
ok þér i munn migu.'

Loki said:

'You be quiet, Njǫrðr! East of here you were
sent to the gods as a hostage.
Hymir's daughters had you as a piss-trough
and made water into your mouth.'

Njǫrðr kvað:

35 'Sú erumk líkn, er ek vark langt heðan
gísl of sendr at goðum,
þá ek mǫg gat, þann er mangi fíár,
ok þykkir sá ása jaðarr.'

Njǫrðr said:

'This is my balm, when far east of here I was
sent to the gods as a hostage:
It was then I got the son who's hated by no one
and is thought to be the gods' very bastion.'

Loki kvað:

36 'Hættu nú, Njǫrðr, haf þú á hófi þik,
munka ek því leyna lengr:
við systur þinni gaztu slíkan mǫg,
ok era þó [v]ánu verr.'

Loki said:

'Stop it now, Njǫrðr! keep yourself composed,
I won't conceal it any longer:
On your sister you got such a son,
and yet that's no worse than expected.'

---

34 In line with his double perspective so far, Loki mocks Njǫrðr as a patrician deviant, moralising the fact that, as god of oceans, Njǫrðr drinks the rivers that flow from the mountains of Norway (North 1997: 214–17).

Týr kvað:

37 'Freyr er beztr allra ballriða
ása gǫrðum í;
mey hann né grœtir né manns konu
ok leysir ór hǫptum hvern.'

Týr said:

'Freyr is best of all bold riders
in the Æsir's citadels.
No girl he makes cry, nor man's wife either,
and he frees each man from his chains.'

Loki kvað:

38 'Þegi þú, Týr, þú kunnir aldregi
bera tilt með tveim;
handar innar hœgri mun ek hinnar geta,
er þér sleit Fenrir frá.'

Loki said:

'You be quiet, Týr! You never knew how
to judge fairly between two factions.
Your right hand I'll mention, the one
that Fenrir tore from you.'

Týr kvað:

39 'Handar em ek vanr, en þú Hróðrsvitnis,
bǫl er beggja þrá;
úlfgi hefir ok vel, er í ǫngum skal
bíða ragnarøkrs.'

Týr said:

'I lack a hand, and you the Lupine Glory,
a harm which causes longing for both of us.
For the wolf it's not too good either, who must in confines
wait for gods' day to darken.'

'Lupine Glory' for Hróðrsvitnir ('glorious sense-sharp'): a taboo euphemism for Fenrir.

---

37 Doubtless of common origin, Freyr resembles Dionysus in *The Bacchae* of Euripides, a young god of ecstasy who slips out of the chains put on him by King Pentheus. Like Dionysus, the Vanir play to a different set of rules.

38 Týr is cast here, one of his few surviving appearances, as a judge presiding over civil lawsuits. Though his one-handedness limits his even-handedness in this role, it should be said that his decision to lose his hand in Fenrir's mouth is good, because it prevents the early destruction of the world. In stanza 41, however, Týr is recast as the plaintiff in an unsuccessful suit.

39 *ragnarøkrs* 'gods' day to darken'. This appears to be the earliest use of *ragnarøkr* 'twilight of the gods' as a (likely Christian) variant of the more common, and more opaque, *ragnarǫk* '?purgation of the powers'. [*ǫngum* for Codex Regius *bǫndum*, which seems copied in from *bundinn* in stanza 41 (Dronke 1997: 365–6).

Loki kvað:

40 'Þegi þú, Týr, þat varð þinni konu,
at hon átti mǫg við mér;
ǫln né penning hafðir þú þess aldregi
vanréttis, vesall.'

Loki said:

'You be quiet, Týr! For your wife it came to pass
that she had a son by me.
Not one ell of cloth or penny did you ever get,
sorry fool, for that loss of rights!'

Freyr kvað:

41 'Ulfr sé ek liggja árósi fyrir,
unz rjúfask regin;
því mundu næst, nema þú nú þegir,
bundinn, bǫlvasmiðr.'

Freyr said:

'A wolf I see there, lying in the estuary mouth
till the powers are torn in two.
And you'll be bound next to him if you don't hold
your tongue now, craftsman of harm!'

Loki kvað:

42 'Gulli keypta léztu Gymis dóttur
ok seldir þitt svá sverð;
en er Múspells synir ríða Myrkvið yfir,
veizta þú þá, vesall, hvé þú vegr.'

Loki said:

'You had gold paid to buy Gymir's daughter
and likewise sold your sword,
But when Múspell's sons ride across Mirkwood,
you won't know then, fool, how you fight.'

Mirkwood: the primeval forest of central Europe.

---

42 *Múspells synir* 'Múspell's sons'. Perhaps the Four Horsemen of the Apocalypse, these sons of Múspell appear to differ from those of *The Sibyl's Prophecy*, stanza 45, whose 'play' (vb. *leika*) seems linked with earthquakes. The *Múspell* name derives from Old High German *Muspilli*, a name for the Apocalypse. Perhaps this bears witness to the presence in Iceland of Bishop Friðrekr in the 980s and Þangbrandr in 998, or to the training of Ísleifr Gizurarson, later bishop of Skálholt (1056–80), in Herford, Saxony, before 1025.

Byggvir kvað:
43 'Veiztu, ef ek eðli ættak sem Ingunar-freyr
ok svá sælligt setr,
mergi smæra mǫlða ek þá meinkráku
ok lemða alla í liðu.'

Barleyman said:
'You know, if I had estates like Ingunar-Freyr,
and such prosperous pasture-land,
Finer than marrow I would grind this evil crow
and I'd lam him in every limb.'

Loki kvað:
44 'Hvat er þat it litla er ek þat lǫggra sék
ok snapvíst snapir?
At eyrum Freys mundu æ vera
ok und kvernum klaka.'

Loki said:
'What's that little thing I can see wagging its tail
and snapping like a snuffling parasite?
At Freyr's ears you will ever be,
and chattering under the querns.'

Byggvir kvað:
45 'Byggvir ek heiti, en mik bráðan kveða
goð ǫll ok gumar;
því em ek hér hróðugr, at drekka Hropts megir
allir ǫl saman.'

Barleyman said:
'Barleyman's my name, and they say I'm hot-tempered,
all the gods and men.
I am famous here because the sons of Hroptr
are all drinking ale together.'

'Hroptr': Óðinn, with the warriors of Valhǫll.

---

44 Byggvir, like John Barleycorn of English folklore, is the personified barley. Here, and in stanzas 45–6, he is imagined to inhabit the hall floor, ale-vats, cornmill querns and even a wreath of Freyr.

Loki kvað:

46 'Þegi þú, Byggvir, þú kunnir aldregi
deila með mǫnnum mat,
ok þik í flets strái finna né máttu,
þá er vágu verar.'

Loki said:

'You be quiet, Barleyman! You never knew how
to deal out the food among men,
and in the straw on the boards they couldn't find you
when the chaps were busy fighting.'

Heimdallr kvað:

47 'ǫlr ertu, Loki, svá at þú er[t] ǫrviti,
hví né lezkaðu, Loki?
því at ofdrykkja veldr alda hveim,
er sína mælgi né manat.'

Heimdallr said:

'Drunk you are, Loki, so drunk that you're witless,
why not restrain yourself, Loki?
For overdrinking will get the better of anyone
who forgets his own prattle.'

Loki kvað:

48 'Þegi þú, Heimdallr, þér var í árdaga
it ljóta líf of lagit;
ǫrgu baki þú munt æ vera
ok vaka vǫrðr goða.'

Loki said:

'You be quiet, Heimdallr! That ugly life of yours
was ordained in the early days.
With a filthy backside you will always be,
and sleepless stand watch for the gods.'

Skaði kvað:

49 'Létt er þér, Loki; munattu lengi svá
leika lausum hala,
því at þik á hjǫrvi skulu ins hrímkalda magar
gǫrnum binda goð.'

Skaði said:

'Light-hearted Loki! You won't be for long,
making free with such a loose tail,
Because on a sword, with the guts of your frost-cold son,
the gods are going to bind you!'

Loki kvað:

50 'Veiztu, ef mik á hjǫrvi skulu ins hrímkalda magar
gǫrnum binda goð,
fyrstr ok efstr var ek at fjǫrlagi,
þars vér á Þjaza þrifum.'

Loki said:

'Know that if on a sword, with the guts of my frost-cold son,
the gods are going to bind me,
I was first at the death, and the last to leave it,
when we were thrusting at Þjazi.'

Skaði kvað:

51 'Veiztu, ef fyrstr ok efstr vartu at fjǫrlagi,
þá er ér á Þjaza þrifuð,
frá mínum véum ok vǫngum skulu
þér æ kǫld ráð koma.'

Skaði said:

'Know that if you were first at the death, and the last to leave it,
when you were thrusting at Þjazi,
From my sanctuaries and slopes shall come
cold counsel for you for ever.'

Loki kvað:

52 'Léttari í málum vartu við Laufeyjar son,
þá er þú létz mér á beð þinn boðit;
getit verðr oss slíks, ef vér gǫrva skulum
telja vǫmmin vár.'

Loki said:

'Lighter-hearted you were when talking with Leaf-Isle's son,
and you had me invited to bed with you!
Such a thing must be mentioned by us if we are completely
to count our blemishes.'

---

52 Dronke's translation for the second half cannot be surpassed (1997: 344). Loki's words appear to parody those of a priest at confession.

Enter Þórr, exit Loki

Þá gekk Sif fram ok byrlaði Loka í hrímkálki mjǫð ok mælti:

53 'Heill ver þú nú, Loki, ok tak við hrímkálki
fullum forns mjaðar;
heldr þú hana eina látir með ása sonum
vammalaus*a* vera.'

'Then Sif came forward and poured mead into a frost-chalice for Loki, and said:'

'Be welcome now, Loki, and take the frost-chalice
filled with ancient mead,
The better you may allow that at least this woman is
unblemished among sons of gods.'

Hann tók við horni ok drakk af:

54 'Ein þú værir, ef þú svá værir,
vǫr ok grǫm at veri;
einn ek veit, svá at ek vita þykkjumk,
hór ok af Hlórriða,
ok var þat sá inn lævísi Loki.'

'Loki took the horn and drained it off:'

'You at least would be, if you really were like that,
wary or fierce with a man.
One man I know, at least I think I do,
went whoring behind even Rumbler's back,
and that was crafty old Loki!'

'Rumbler (Hlórriði)': Þórr, husband of Sif.

Beyla kvað:

55 'Fjǫll ǫll skjalfa; hygg ek á fǫr vera
heiman Hlórriða;
hann ræðr ró, þeim er rœgir hér
goð ǫll ok guma.'

Cowgirl said:

'All the mountains are shaking, I think he's on his way,
the Rumbler is coming from home.
He'll make a peace here on the one who's slandering
all the gods and men.'

---

53 *Sif*, as embodying 'family' besides being the wife of Þórr, is here reserved for the most dreadful case of hypocrisy. The story is not found elsewhere, but can be 'apocryphally true'. The poet's mind, not only Loki's, which knows of double standards in unblemished housewives would appear to belong to a father confessor.

Loki kvað:

56 'Þegi þú, Beyla, þú ert Byggvis kvæn
ok meini blandinn mjǫk,
ókynjan meira koma med ása sonum;
ǫll ertu, deigja, dritin.'

Loki said:

'You be quiet, Cowgirl! You are Barleyman's wife
and really mixed up with malice.
A bigger freak never joined up with sons of gods!
Dairy-girl, you're all dirty.'

Þá kom Þórr at ok kvað:

57 'Þegi þú, rǫg vættr, þér skal minn þrúðhamarr,
Mjǫllnir, mál fyrnema;
herða klett drep ek þér halsi af,
ok verðr þá þínu fjǫrvi of farit.'

Then Þórr arrived and said:

'Be quiet, little faggot! My mighty hammer,
Grinder, will take out your talk!
That block on your shoulders I'm a-knock off its neck,
and then it'll be done with your life!'

Loki kvað:

58 'Jarðar [burr] er hér nú inn kominn,
hví þrasir þú svá, Þórr?
En þá þorir þú ekki, er þú skalt við ulfinn vega,
ok svelgr hann allan Sigfǫður.'

Loki said:

'Look who's come in now, it's Country Boy,
why big it up, Þórr, in this way?
But then you won't dare to, when you're up against the Wolf
and he's gobbling up the Father of Victories!'

'Country Boy': literally '(son) of Earth'. 'Father of Victories': Óðinn.

Þórr kvað:

59 'Þegi þú, rǫg vættr, þér skal minn þrúðhamarr,
Mjǫllnir, mál fyrnema;
upp ek þér verp ok á austrvega,
síðan þik manngi sér.'

Þórr said:

'Be quiet, little faggot! My mighty hammer,
Grinder, will take out your talk!
Up I'm a-throw you, and into eastern parts
so nobody will see you again.'

---

56 *Beyla* seems related to *baula* 'cow', as *deigja* 'dairy-maid' here would confirm but it is worth adding that the name (if from **baunilo*) would mean 'little bean', closer to 'Barleyman' for Byggvir.

Loki kvað:

60 'Austrfǫrum þínum skaltu aldregi
segja seggjum frá,
síz í hanska þumlungi hnúkðir þú einheri,
ok þóttiska þú þá Þórr vera.'

Loki said:

'Your journeys east you must never
talk about to mankind,
Since the time, great soldier, you cowered in a glove-thumb,
and didn't then think you were Þórr.'

Þórr kvað:

61 'Þegi þú, rǫg vættr, þér skal minn þrúðhamarr,
Mjǫllnir, mál fyrnema;
hendi inni hœgri drep ek þik Hrungnis bana,
svá at þér brotnar beina hvat.'

Þórr said:

'Be quiet, little faggot! My mighty hammer,
Grinder, will take out your talk!
With my right hand I'll hit you with Hrungnir's Bane
so every bone in your body is broken!'

'Hrungnir's Bane': Mjǫllnir ('Grinder'); see Þjóðólfr's *Harvest-Long*.

Loki kvað:

62 'Lifa ætla ek mér langan aldr,
þóttu hœtir hamri mér;
skarpar álar þóttu þér Skrýmis vera,
ok máttira þú þá nesti ná,
ok svalzt þú þá hungri heill.'

Loki said:

'To live my life long is what I intend,
though you threaten me with your hammer.
Tough were the straps of Skrýmir, so they seemed to you,
and you couldn't then get at your grub,
and near died of hunger, though well at the time.'

'Skrýmir': the giant in whose glove Þórr and companions stay, and to whose provision bag the 'tough straps' belong that Þórr fails to loosen.

Þórr kvað:

63 'Þegi þú, rǫg vættr, þér skal minn þrúðhamarr,
Mjǫllnir, mál fyrnema;
Hrungnis bani mun þér í hel koma
fyr nágrindr neðan.'

Þórr said:

'Be quiet, little faggot! My mighty hammer,
Grinder, will take out your talk!
Hrungnir's Bane will bring you to Hel
right below the corpse-pens.'

Loki kvað:

64 'Kvað ek fyr ásum, kvað ek fyr ása sonum,
þats mik hvatti hugr,
en fyr þér einum mun ek út ganga,
því at ek veit, at þú vegr.

Loki said:

'I have said it to gods, I have said it to gods' sons,
the things that my heart made me say.
For you alone, though, I will go from here,
for I know that you kill.

65 'Ǫl gerðir þú, Ægir, en þú aldri munt
síðan sumbl of gera;
eiga þín ǫll, er hér inni er,
leiki yfir logi,
ok brenni þér á baki!'

'Ale you brewed, Ocean Man, though never, from this time,
will you give a party again.
All your possessions that are here indoors,
may flame lick upon them,
may they burn on your back!'

65 The time in which this story is set, after Baldr's death and before Loki's capture, near the end of the world, indicates a priestly intention to focus on the Day of Judgement. The poet's culture would appear to be Christian, yet with such detailed knowledge of the old mythology that it seems likely he composed this work at the most a generation after the conversion of Iceland in 999.

En eftir þetta falsk Loki í Fránangrs forsi í lax líki. Þar tóku æsir hann. Hann var bundinn með þǫrmum sonar síns Vála, en Narfi sonr hans varð at vargi. Skaði tók eitrorm ok festi upp yfir andlit Loka. Draup þar ór eitr. Sigyn, kona Loka, sat þar ok helt munnlaug undir eitrit. En er munnlaugin var full, bar hon út eitrit, en meðan draup eitrit á Loka. Þá kippðist hann svá hart við, at þaðan af skalf jǫrð ǫll. Þat eru nú kallaðir landsskjálftar.

And after this, Loki hid himself in the falls at Fránangr in the shape of a salmon. The gods caught him there. He was tied up with the guts of his son Váli, while his son Narfi became a wolf. Skaði took a poisonous snake and fastened it over Loki's face. Poison dripped out of it. Sigyn, Loki's wife, sat there and held a hand-basin under the poison. And when the basin was full, she threw out the poison, but meanwhile the poison dripped on to Loki. Then he jerked back so hard that the whole earth shook from it. These things are now called earthquakes.

SAGAS OF ICELANDERS

* * *

SAGAS OF ICELANDERS

⁂ ⁂ ⁂

This section of the anthology will devote itself to the Old Icelandic sagas, and, in the Custom Version, histories of the Norwegian kings, and short tales and anecdotes, called *þættir* (sing, *þáttr*). This will complement the many examples of poetry already on display. If Vikings were the pirates among whom some early Icelanders, such as Egill Skalla-Grímsson, made their name, 'sagas' are the stories written about them and their descendants. These sagas were written in Old Icelandic prose and the best-known category of them is called 'Sagas of Icelanders' (modern Icelandic *Íslendinga Sögur*). In their written form, these are largely a product of the thirteenth and fourteenth centuries. During this period it became a vogue to record and elaborate upon what had been a vigorous oral tradition of telling stories about the original settlers of Iceland, their ancestors and descendants. The years in question, broadly speaking, are from 850 to 1070. Forty sagas have survived, as well as over 50 short tales (*þættir*). Many others have been lost. The writers remain anonymous.

Norwegian royal history was of interest to the early settlers from the beginning. Snorri Sturluson, parts of whose *Heimskringla* are included in the Custom Version, was a member of the powerful Sturlung clan, which gives its name to the tumultuous age of Icelandic civil war in the middle of the thirteenth century. He was fostered at Oddi, in southern Iceland, whose owners had been drawn to the Norwegian royal family since marrying into them in the twelfth century. The men of Oddi wrote royal history, Icelandic history, and poetry. As he grew up, Snorri became an active player in the politics of Iceland, and he remained so all his prolific literary life. The more equal power divisions between various *goðorð* in the earlier years of the Commonwealth, which are reported in the sagas, had become more narrowly and bitterly contested between several opposing families during the thirteenth century. Leaders like Snorri, himself lawspeaker from 1215 to 1218 and again from 1222 to 1231, courted Norwegian royalty. He and other writers of Icelandic sagas and histories display a number of narrative and stylistic features that are unique in medieval European literature. They are largely realistic. The prose is laconic, terse and succinct. What is not stated directly is often as important as what is. The plot, the events of feud and conflict, of love and loss, dominates the stories. Once introduced, characters are shown in significant action. The larger sagas range over several generations and many years. *Brennu-Njáls saga* extends for over 70 years, *Egils saga* and *Laxdæla saga* each for more than 150. Years, sometimes decades, are telescoped into a paragraph, sometimes a sentence.

What we are told in the sagas resides in the communal memory ('it was said at the time', 'people thought that', 'some say . . . others say'). It would never occur to a saga teller to describe what a character might be thinking. This approach to character is perhaps the most profound literary difference with both other medieval and later European literatures. Without access to thought patterns, the saga method suggests character in a manner just as fresh and exciting as other modes. Also notable in saga style is that characters seldom develop or change internally.

Europeans had been aware of the existence of Iceland since antiquity but the island had never been inhabited on a permanent basis. It would have been too warm and isolated for the nomadic Inuit populations, and too remote for anyone else. It was used as a summer base for some Irish hermit monks in the ninth century, who are said to have left when the Norse heathens began to arrive to settle. Ingólfr Árnarson and Hallveig Fróðadóttir established the first permanent farmstead at Reykjavík (Smokey Bay) perhaps in the 870s. Perhaps as many as 20,000 others arrived in the following decades. According to saga accounts, the settlers were mainly landed Norwegians who felt under pressure and threat during the consolidation of power in Norway of King Haraldr Finehair (*Hárfagri*) who dominated in *c.* 885–930. The emigrants travelled to Iceland from Norway and the Norse Viking strongholds in Scotland and Ireland and the North Sea Islands of Orkney, Shetland, the Faroes and the Hebrides. They brought with them their Celtic women and slaves. The settlers were dominantly heathen, although there were Christians amongst them. Some of the settlers might have been literate in Latin, Gaelic or dialects of Old English, but their own language, which we call Old Icelandic or Old Norse, did not develop a literary technology (i.e. an alphabet and grammar) until the eleventh century. That was because Christianity was not adopted as Iceland's religion until 999. With the exception of runes for certain ceremonial, memorial and graffiti inscriptions, the early Icelanders were pre-literate.

All saga chapters are from *Íslenzk Fornrit*, Hið Íslenzka Fornritfélag, Reykjavík, ongoing since 1935. The most easily available English translations of the sagas are in Penguin Classics editions. Virtually all available translations have their own strengths and points of interest. See also *The Complete Sagas of Icelanders, Including 49 Tales*, edited by Viðar Hreinsson (Reykjavík, 1997).

General bibliography

Allard, J., 'Sagas of Icelanders', *B&OS* 376–416

Andersson, T. M., *The Icelandic Family Saga: An Analytic Reading* (Cambridge, MA, 1967)

Andersson, T. M., *The Growth of the Medieval Icelandic Sagas (1180–1280)* (Ithaca, NY, 2006)

Auden, W. H., and L. MacNiece, *Letters from Iceland* (London, 1937)

Byock, J., *Feud in the Icelandic Saga* (Berkeley, CA, 1982)

Byock, J., *Viking Age Iceland* (Harmondsworth, 2001)

Clover, C., *The Medieval Saga* (Ithaca, NY, 1982)

Clunies Ross, M., ed., *Old Icelandic Literature and Society* (Cambridge, 2000)

Faulkes, A., trans., *Snorri Sturluson: Edda* (London, 1987)

Gísli Sigurðsson, *The Medieval Icelandic Saga and Oral Tradition: A Discourse on Method*, trans. N. Jones (Cambridge, MA, 2004)

Grønlie, S., trans., *Íslendingabók, Kristni Saga*, The Viking Society for Northern Research (London, 2006)

Gunnell, T., *The Origins of Drama in Scandinavia* (Cambridge, 1995)

Hines, J., and D. Slay, ed., *Introductory Essays on Egils Saga and Njáls Saga* (London, 1992)

Jónas Kristjánsson, *Eddas and Sagas*, trans. P. Foote (Reykjavík, 1992)

Jón Karl Helgason, *The Rewriting of Njál's Saga* (Clevedon, 1999)

Ker, W. P., *Epic and Romance* (London, 1897; New York, 1957)

Larrington, C., trans., *The Poetic Edda* (Oxford, 1996)

Lindow, J., *Handbook of Norse Mythology* (Santa Barbara, CA, 2001)

Lönnroth, L., *Njal's Saga, A Critical Introduction* (Berkeley, CA, 1976)

Magnusson, M., *Iceland Saga* (London, 1987)

McTurk, R., ed., *A Companion to Old Norse-Icelandic Literature* (Maldon, MA, 2005)

North, R., *Heathen Gods in Old English Literature*, Cambridge Studies in Anglo-Saxon England 22 (Cambridge, 1997)

North, R., 'Notes on the Old Norse language', *B&OS* 323–9

O'Donoghue, H., *Old Norse-Icelandic Literature: A Short Introduction* (Maldon, MA, 2004)

Orchard, A., *Cassell's Dictionary of Norse Myth and Legend* (London, 1997)

Poole, R., ed., *Skaldsagas: Text, Vocation and Desire in the Icelandic Sagas of Poets* (Berlin, 2001)

Wawn, A., *The Vikings and the Victorians* (Cambridge, 2000)

Whaley, D., *Heimskringla, An Introduction*, The Viking Society for Northern Research (London, 1991)

Ari's *Book of Icelanders*

Íslendingabók

c. 1125

*

Ari the Learned Þorgilsson (1068–1148) was a scholar and priest who compiled *The Book of Icelanders* (*Íslendingabók*) in Icelandic between 1122–33. This is a concentrated history of Iceland from the settlement to the early twelfth century. It includes a discussion of the settlement, the bringing of the laws from Norway, the establishment of the Alþingi, the settlement of Greenland by Eiríkr the Red and the journeys to *Vínland* (North America), the coming of Christianity (an account that formed the basis of the ones in *Kristni saga* and *Brennu-Njáls saga*, chs. 100–5), and brief lives of the first native-born bishops of Iceland, Ísleifr Gizurarson and his son, Gizurr Ísleifsson.

Ari's choice of the vernacular is significant for all later Icelandic literature. So, too, is his historiographical method. He used what he felt to be the most reliable informants and oral sources and always acknowledged them. His own circumspection leads him to say, in the preface to the second (and only surviving) draft, *en hvatki es missagt es í frœðum þessum, þá es skylt at hafa þat heldr, es sannara reynisk* 'whatever is wrongly reported in this history, one is duty bound to accept what proves to be more true'. Finally, Ari wrote his history from a position of living memory. His sources were informants connecting him to the past in a living chain of memory. These included his paternal uncle Þorkell Gellison, the grandson of Guðrún, heroine of *Laxdœla saga*. In other words, Guðrún was Ari's great-grandmother. The rare Icelandic word *edda*, for 'great-grandmother', is testimony that Snorri Sturluson, in the 1220s, may have chosen this as a name for his treatise to illustrate the long transmission of poetry over many generations.

Andersson, T. M., *The Growth of the Medieval Icelandic Sagas (1180–1280)* (Ithaca, NY, 2006).

Clover, C., *The Medieval Saga* (Ithaca, NY, 1982)

Gísli Sigurðsson, *The Medieval Icelandic Saga and Oral Tradition: A Discourse on Method*, trans. N. Jones (Cambridge, MA, 2004)

Grønlie, S., trans., *Íslendingabók, Kristni Saga*, The Viking Society for Northern Research (London, 2006)

Jónas Kristjánsson, *Eddas and Sagas*, trans. P. Foote (Reykjavík, 1992)

Greenland and America

This chapter tells of the discovery and settlement of Greenland in the late tenth century by Eiríkr the Red, early encounters with native Americans (pejoratively called *Skrælings*, or 'wretches') and mention of *Vínland*. The sagas about *Vínland*, or northern North America, chapters of which are included later, are a fascinating element of the old literature that has sparked a lively and ongoing debate about just when and where the Icelandic Greenlanders went in their attempts to settle in a new world.

6. Land þat, es kallat es Grœnland, fannsk ok byggðisk af Íslandi. Eiríkr inn rauði hét maðr breiðfirzkr, es fór út heðan þangat ok nam þar land, es síðan es kallaðr Eiríksfjǫrðr. Hann gaf nafn landinu ok kallaði Grœnland ok kvað menn þat myndu fýsa þangat farar, at landit ætti nafn gótt. Þeir fundu þar manna vistir bæði austr ok vestr á landi ok keiplabrot ok steinsmíði þat es af því má skilja, at þar hafði þess konar þjóð farit, es Vínland hefir byggt ok Grœnlendingar kalla Skrælinga. En þat vas, es hann tók byggva landit, fjórtán vetrum eða fimmtán fyrr en kristni kvæmi hér á Ísland, at því es sá talði fyrir Þorkeli Gellissyni á Grœnlandi, es sjálfr fylgði Eiríki enum rauða út.

---

6. The land called Greenland was discovered and settled from Iceland. A man named Eiríkr the Red from Breiðafjǫrðr went out there from here and took possession of land in a place that has since been called Eiriksfjǫrðr. He gave a name to the country and called it Greenland, and said that it would encourage people to go there if it had a good name. They found signs of human habitation there in both the east and the west of the land, the remains of skin boats and stone tools, from which we can imagine that the same kind of people had passed through there as had settled in *Vínland* and the Greenlanders call *Skrælingar*. He began to settle the country fourteen or fifteen years before Christianity came here to Iceland, according to what a man who had himself accompanied Eiríkr the Red told Þorkell Gellisson in Greenland.

The conversion of Iceland

Iceland was converted by the Norwegian King Óláfr Tryggvason, a reformed Viking who had probably been in the 991 raid which is celebrated in *The Battle of Maldon* (see **Viking Wars**). In 995 Óláfr set out to Christianise Scandinavia and the North Atlantic Viking settlements in Orkney, the Faroe Islands and Iceland. This chapter from *Íslendingabók* tells of the arrival of Óláfr's missionary priest Þangbrandr, his failure, and the renewed attempt which succeeded. The conversion took place one afternoon in the Althing, which, since 930, had been established as a national assembly meeting for two weeks in mid-summer at Thingvellir (*Þingvellir*), a plain of astonishing natural beauty, lava fields, lakes, cliffs, gorges and waterfalls. Here the lawspeaker, the only elected official in the land, would recite from memory a third of the law each year of his three-year term. Happening here, the coming of Christianity to Iceland marked a watershed. With Christianity came literacy; the development of a technology (an alphabet and grammar) with which to write the Old Icelandic language. All earlier work had been preserved and communicated in a vigorous oral tradition.

7. Óláfr rex Tryggvasonr, Óláfssonar, Haraldsonar ens hárfagra, kom kristni í Norveg ok á Ísland. Hann sendi hingat til lands prest þann, es hét Þangbrandr ok hér kenndi mǫnnum kristni ok skírði þá alla, es við trú tóku. En Hallr á Síðu Þorsteinssonr lét skírask snimhendis ok Hjalti Skeggjasonr ýr Þjórsárdali ok Gizurr enn hvíti Teitsson, Ketilbjarnarsonar frá Mosfelli, ok margir hǫfðingjar aðrir; en þeir váru þó fleiri, es í gegn mæltu ok neittu. En þá es hann hafði hér verit einn vetr eða tvá, þá fór hann á braut ok hafði vegit hér tvá menn eða þrjá, þá es hann hǫfðu nítt. En hann sagði konunginum Óláfi, es hann kom austr, allt þat es hér hafði yfir hann gingit, ok lét ørvænt, at hér mundi kristni enn takask. En hann varð við þat reiðr mjǫk ok ætlaði at láta meiða eða drepa ossa landa fyrir, þá es þar váru austr. En þat sumar et sama kvómu útan heðan þeir Gizurr ok Hjalti ok þágu þá undan við konunginn ok hétu hónum umbsýslu sinni til á nýjaleik, at hér yrði enn við kristninni tekit, ok létu sér eigi annars ván en þar mundi hlýða.

En et næsta sumar eptir fóru þeir austan ok prestr sá es Þormóðr hét, ok kvómu þá í Vestmannaeyjar, es tíu vikur váru af sumri, ok hafði allt farizk vel at. Svá kvað Teitr þann segja, es sjalfr vas þar. Þá vas þat mælt et næsta sumar áðr í lǫgum, at menn skyldi svá koma til alþingis, es tíu vikur væri af sumri, en þangat til kvómu viku fyrr. En þeir fóru þegar inn til meginlands ok síðan til alþingis ok gátu at Hjalta, at hann vas eptir í Laugardali með tolfta mann, af því at hann hafði áðr sekr orðit **fjǫrbaugsmaðr** et næsta sumar á alþingi of goðgá. En þat vas til þess haft, at hann kvað at lǫgbergi kviðling þenna:

---

7. King Óláfr Tryggvason, son of Óláfr, son of Haraldr Finehair, brought Christianity to Iceland. He sent a priest to this country called Þangbrandr and he preached Christianity and baptised all those who took the faith. And Hallr of Síða Þorsteinsson and Gizurr the White Teitsson, son of Ketilbjǫrn of Mosfell, and many other chieftans; but those who spoke against it and rejected it were in the majority. But when he had been here for one or two years he left, having killed two or three men who had slandered him. He told king Óláfr, once he had arrived in the east, everything that had happened to him here, and said it was very unlikely that Christianity might yet be accepted here. The king was very angry about this, and decided to have those from our land who were in the east maimed or killed for it. And that same summer Gizurr and Hjalti travelled out there from here and persuaded the king to release them, and promised him their fresh assistance so that Christianity might yet be accepted here, and said they expected that nothing other than this would be successful.

The next summer they left the east with a priest named Þormóðr, and arrived in the Vestmannaeyjar (Westman Islands) when ten weeks of the summer had passed, and their journey had gone very smoothly. Teitr said a man who was there at the time had said so. It had been proclaimed in the laws the previous summer that people should come to the Alþingi when ten weeks of the summer had passed; until then they had come a week earlier. They crossed to the mainland at once and proceeded to the Alþingi, and convinced Hjalti to remain behind at Laugardalr with twelve men because the previous summer he had been sentenced to **lesser outlawry** at the Alþingi for blaspheming the gods. The reason for this was he had spoken this verse at the Law Rock:

---

fjǫrbaugsmaðr 'lesser outlawry'. A three year sentence of exile. The convicted lost all rights of protection under the law and could be killed with impunity if he stayed in Iceland. Those so convicted usually went abroad. *Skóggangr* 'full outlawry', literally 'forest-going', was a life sentence.

Vik ek eigi goð geyja, grey þykki mér Freyja.

En þeir Gizurr fóru, unz þeir kvómu í stað þann í hjá Ǫlfossvatni, es kallaðr es Vellankatla, ok gørðu orð þaðan til þings, at á mót þeim skyldi koma allir fulltingsmenn þeira, af því at þeir hǫfðu spurt, at andskotar þeira vildi verja þeim vígi þingvǫllinn. En fyrr en þeir fœri þaðan, þá kom þar ríðandi Hjalti ok þeir es eptir váru með hónum. En síðan riðu þeir á þingit, ok kvómu áðr á mót þeim frændr þeira ok vinir sem þeir hǫfðu æst. En enir heiðnu menn hurfu saman með alvæpni, ok hafði svá nær, at þeir myndi berjask, at [eigi] of sá á miðli. En annan dag eptir gingu þeir Gizurr ok Hjalti til lǫgbergs ok báru þar upp erindi sín. En svá es sagt, at þat bæri frá, hvé vel þeir mæltu. En þat gørðisk af því, at þar nefndi annarr maðr at ǫðrum vátta, ok sǫgðusk hvárir ýr lǫgum við aðra, enir kristnu menn ok enir heiðnu, ok gingu síðan frá lǫgbergi.

Þá báðu enir kristnu menn Hall á Síðu, at hann skyldi lǫg þeirra upp segja, þau es kristninni skyldi fylgja. En hann leystisk því undan við þá, at hann keypti at Þorgeiri lǫgsǫgumanni, at hann skyldi upp segja, en hann vas enn þá heiðinn. En síðan es menn kvómu í búðir, þá lagðisk hann niðr Þorgeirr ok breiddi feld sinn á sik ok hvílði þann dag allan ok nóttina eptir ok kvað ekki orð. En of morguninn eptir settisk hann upp ok gørði orð, at men skyldi ganga til lǫgbergis. En þá hóf hann tǫlu sína upp, es menn kvómu þar, ok sagði, at hónum þótti þá komit hag manna í ónýtt efni, ef menn skyldi eigi hafa allir lǫg ein á landi hér, ok talði fyrir mǫnnum á marga vega, at þat skyldi eigi láta verða, ok sagði, at þat mundi at því ósætti verða, es vísa ván vas, at þær barsmíðir gørðisk á

I don't mind barking at the gods, for I think Freyja's a bitch.

But Gizurr and his men carried on until they came to a place by Ǫlfossvatn called Vellankatla, and from there they sent a message to the assembly that all their supporters should come to meet them because they had heard that their enemies meant to keep them from the assembly plain by force. Before they set off from there Hjalti came riding there with those who had stayed with him. They then rode to the assembly, and their friends and kinsmen had come to join them beforehand as they had asked. But then the heathen men thronged together with their weapons, and it came so close to fighting that no one could tell which way it would go. The next day Gizurr and Hjalti went to the Law Rock and announced their errand. And it is said that it was extraordinary how well they spoke, but what happened was that one man after another named witnesses, and each side, Christian and heathen, declared itself under separate laws from the other, and they left the Law Rock.

Then the Christian men asked Hallr of Síða to speak the law that should go with Christianity. But he avoided this responsibility by agreeing with the lawspeaker, that he, Þorgeirr, should speak the law, even though he was a heathen. Later, when everyone had returned to their booths, Þorgeirr lay down and spread a cloak over himself, and lay there all that day and the next night, and didn't speak a word. The following morning he arose and sent word that people should go to the Law Rock. Once people had arrived there, he began his address, and said that he thought men's affairs had come to a bad state if they were not all to have the same laws in the land here, and tried to persuade them in many ways that they should not let this happen, and said it would give rise to such discord that it was to be miðli manna, es **landit eyddisk af**. Hann sagði frá því, at konungar ýr Norvegi ok ýr Danmǫrku hǫfðu haft ófrið ok orrostur á miðli sín langa tíð, til þess unz landsmenn gørðu frið á miðli þeira, þótt þeir vildi eigi. En þat ráð gørðisk svá, at af stundu sendusk þeir gersemar á miðli, enda helt friðr sá, meðan þeir lifðu.

'En nú þykkir mér þat ráð,' kvað hann, 'at vér látim ok eigi þá ráða, es mest vilja í gegn gangask, ok miðlum svá mál á miðli þeira, at hvárirtveggju hafi nakkvat síns máls, ok hǫfum allir ein lǫg ok einn sið. Þat mon verða satt, es vér slítum í sundr lǫgin, at vér monum slíta ok friðinn.'

En hann lauk svá máli sínu, at hvárirtveggju játtu því, at allir skyldi ein lǫg hafa, þau sem hann réði upp at segja. Þá vas þat mælt í lǫgum, at allir menn skyldi kristnir vesa ok skírn taka, þeir es áðr váru óskírðir á landi hér; en of barnaútburð skyldu standa en fornu lǫg ok of hrossakjǫtsát. Skyldu menn blóta á laun, ef vildu, en varða fjǫrbaugsgarðr, ef váttum of kvæmi við. En síðarr fám vetrum vas sú heiðni af numin sem ǫnnur.

Þenna atburð sagði Teitr oss at því, es kristni kom á Ísland. En Ólár Tryggvason fell et sama sumar at sǫgu Sæmundar prests. Þá barðisk hann við Svein Haraldsson Danakonung ok Óláf enn sœnska, Eiríksson at Uppsǫlum Svíakonungs, ok Eirík, es síðan vas jarl at Norvegi, Hákonarson. Þat vas þremr tegum vetra ens annars hundraðs eptir **dráp Eadmundar**, en þúsundi eptir burð Krists at alþýðu tali.

---

expected that fights would take place between men by which **the land would be laid waste**. He said further that the kings of Norway and Denmark had had warfare and battles against each other for a long time, until the people in those countries made peace between them even though they didn't want it. And that policy had worked out in such a way that they were soon sending gifts to each other. And this peace lasted as long as they lived.

'And now it seems advisable to me,' he said, 'that we also do not allow those who want to oppose each other to prevail, and let us arbitrate between them, and let us all have the same law and the same faith. It will prove true that if we tear the law apart, so will we tear apart the peace.'

He ended his speech in such a fashion that both sides agreed that everyone should have the same law: the one he decided to proclaim. It was then proclaimed in the laws that all people should be Christian, and that those that had not yet been baptised should receive baptism; but the old laws about the exposure of children and the eating of horse-flesh should stand. People had the right to sacrifice in secret if they wished, but it would mean lesser outlawry if witnesses were produced. A few years later these heathen concessions were abolished, like the others.

Teitr gave this account of how Christianity came to Iceland. And Óláfr Tryggvason fell the same summer according to the priest Sæmundr. He was fighting the king of the Danes, Sveinn Haraldsson, and Óláfr the Swede, the son of Eirík at Uppsala, the king of Sweden, and Eirík Hákonarson, who was later earl in Norway. This was one hundred and thirty years after **the killing of Edmund**, and a thousand years after the birth of Christ by the accepted method of reckoning.

---

landit eyddisk af 'the land would be laid waste'. This anticipates the similar sentiment expressed by Njáll in his saga (ch. 70). Chs. 100–5 of *Njáls saga* describe the coming of Christianity and are drawn from *Ísendingabók* and the fuller account in *Kristni saga* (*c.* 1275).

dráp Eadmundar 'the killing of Edmund'. King Edmund was killed by the invading Vikings, led by Ingvarr or Ívarr *inn beinlausi* 'the Boneless', at Hoxne in Suffolk in 870 (see Ælfric's *Life of St Edmund* in **Writers of the Benedictine Reform**). He is the St Edmund of Bury St Edmunds.

The Saga of Eiríkr the Red

Eiríks saga Rauða

c. 1220

*

The two so-called *Vínland sagas* tell the story of the settlement of Greenland by Eiríkr the Red in the 980s, and the discovery, exploration and attempted settlement of North America. They are *Eiríks saga Rauða* ('Eiríkr the Red's Saga') and *Grœnlendinga saga* ('*The Saga of the Greenlanders*'). They deal with the same events but with different emphases and from different perspectives. Included here are three chapters (8, 10 and 11) from *Eiríkr the Red's Saga* which describe the early journeys of discovery and naming, then the first encounters with native Americans, whom the Norse called *Skrælingar* '(?) little leather-hides'. It is a fascinating account of one of the first European encounters with native otherness, which is predicated on misunderstanding and ends in violence. In this early instance of attempted colonisation the natives prevailed.

Gísli Sigurðsson, *The Medieval Icelandic Saga and Oral Tradition: A Discourse on Method*, trans. N. Jones (Cambridge, MA, 2004)

Jones, G., *A History of the Vikings* (Oxford, 1968)

Jónas Kristjánsson, *Eddas and Sagas*, trans. P. Foote (Reykjavík, 1992)

Magnusson, M., *Iceland Saga* (London, 1987)

Roesdahl, E., *The Vikings*, trans. S. Margeson and K. Williams, 2nd rev. ed. (Harmondsworth, 1998)

Wawn, A., *The Vikings and the Victorians* (Cambridge, 2000)

Vikings in America

8. Í Brattahlíð hófusk miklar umrœður, at menn skyldi leita Vínlands ins góða, ok var sagt, at þangat myndi vera at vitja góðra landkosta; ok þar kom, at Karlsefni ok Snorri bjuggu skip sitt at leita landsins um várit. Til þeirar ferðar réðusk þeir Bjarni ok Þórhallr með skip sitt ok þat fǫruneyti, er þeim hafði fylgt.

---

8. There were great discussions at **Brattahlíð** about going in search of Vínland the Good, where it was said that there was excellent land for the taking. The outcome was that Karlsefni and Snorri [Þorbrandsson] prepared their ship and made ready to search for Vínland. Bjarni and Þórhallr decided to accompany them on the voyage taking their own ship and companions and crew that had brought them out to Greenland.

Brattahlíð 'Steep Cliff'. Eiríkr the Red's farm in Eiríksfjǫrðr in the Eastern Settlement of Greenland. The Eastern and Western Settlements were both on the west coast. The Western Settlement was further north.

Maðr hét Þorvarðr; hann átti Freydísi, dóttur Eiríks rauða laungetna; hann fór ok með þeim ok Þorvaldr, sonr Eiríks, ok Þórhallr, er kallaðr var veiðimaðr. Hann hafði lengi verit með Eiríki, veiðimaðr hans um sumrum, en bryti um vetrum. Hann var mikill maðr ok sterkr ok svartr ok þursligr, hljóðlyndr ok illorðr, þat er hann mælti, ok eggjaði jafnan Eirík ins verra. Hann var illa kristinn. Honum var víða kunnigt í óbyggðum. Hann var á skipi með Þorvarði ok Þorvaldi. Þeir hǫfðu þat skip, er Þorbjǫrn hafði út haft.

Þeir hǫfðu alls fjóra tigu manna ok hundrað, er þeir sigldu til Vestribyggðar ok þaðan til Bjarneyjar. Þaðan sigldu þeir tvau dœgr í suðr. Þá sá þeir land ok skutu báti ok kǫnnuðu landit, fundu þar hellur stórar, ok margar tólf álna víðar. Fjǫlði var þar melrakka. Þeir gáfu þar nafn ok kǫlluðu **Helluland**.

Þaðan sigldu þeir tvau dœgr, ok brá til landsuðrs ór suðri, ok fundu land skógvaxit ok mǫrg dýr á. Ey lá þar undan í landsuðr; þar drápu þeir einn bjǫrn ok kǫlluðu þar síðan Bjarney, en landit **Markland**.

Þaðan sigldu þeir suðr með landinu langa stund ok kómu at nesi einu; lá landit á stjórn; váru þar strandir langar ok sandar. Þeir reru til lands ok fundu þar á nesinu kjǫl af skipi ok kǫlluðu þar Kjalarnes. Þeir kǫlluðu ok

---

A man named Þorvarðr was married to Freydís, Eiríkr the Red's illegitimate daughter. He went with them, along with Þorvaldr Eiríksson, and Þorhallr who was called the Hunter. He had been with Eiríkr for a long time acting as his huntsman in the summer, and was entrusted with many responsibilities. He was a large man, strong and swarthy and uncouth. He was getting on in years, bad-tempered and cunning, taciturn usually but abusive when he spoke, and always a trouble-maker. He had not had much to do with Christianity. He was not popular with most people, but he and Eiríkr had always been good friends. He was on the ship with Þorvarðr and Þorvaldr, and had considerable experience of wild regions. They had the ship that Þorbjǫrn had brought out. Altogether there were one hundred and forty people on this expedition.

They sailed first up to the Western Settlement, and then to the Bjarn-Islands. After two days at sea with a northerly wind they sighted land and rowed ashore in boats. There they found many huge slabs of stone, many twelve ells across. There were many foxes there. They gave this land a name and called it '**Slab Land**'.

From there they sailed south for two days and again sighted land, with large forests and many animals. There was an island to the south-east, off the coast, where they killed a bear and called it Bjarney, and the wooded mainland itself '**Forest Land**'.

Then they sailed south again and sighted land and approached the shore where a peninsula jutted out. It was open and harbourless, with long beaches and broad sand flats. They went ashore in boats and found a ship's keel on the headland, so they called the place

---

Helluland 'Slab Land'. Probably the south-east coast of Baffin Island or the northern coast of Labrador. Gísli Sigurðsson discusses the variety of identifications of the land sightings and landfalls over the last 160 years (2004: 277).

Markland 'Forest Land'. A heavily-wooded area between *Helluland* and *Vínland* which might be south-east Labrador or Newfoundland.

strandirnar **Furðustrandir**, því at langt var með at sigla. Þá gerðisk landit vágskorit. Þeir heldu skipunum í einn vág.

Óláfr konungr Tryggvason hafði gefit Leifi tvá menn skozka; hét karlmaðrinn Haki, en konan Hekja; þau váru dýrum skjótari. Þessir menn váru á skipi með Karlsefni.

En er þeir hǫfðu siglt fyrir Furðustrandir, þá létu þeir ina skozku menn á land ok báðu þau hlaupa suðr á landit at leita landskosta ok koma aptr, áðr þrjú dœgr væri liðin.

Þau hǫfðu þat klæði, er þau kǫlluðu kjafal; þat var svá gǫrt, at hǫttr var á upp ok opit at hliðunum ok engar ermar á ok kneppt saman milli fóta með knappi ok nezlu, en ber váru þau annars staðar.

Þeir biðuðu þar þá stund. En er þau kómu aptr, hafði annat í hendi vínberjakǫngul, en annat hveitiax sjálfsáit. Gengu þau á skip út, ok sigldu þeir síðan leiðar sinnar.

Þeir sigldu inn á fjǫrð einn. Þar lá ein ey fyrir útan; þar um váru straumar miklir; því kǫlluðu þeir hana Straumey. Svá var mǫrg æðr í eynni, at varla mátti ganga fyrir eggjum. Þeir kǫlluðu þar **Straumfjǫrð**.

Þeir báru þar farm af skipum sínum ok bjuggusk þar um. Þeir hǫfðu með sér alls konar fénað. Þar var fagrt landsleg; þeir gáðu einskis, útan at kanna landit. Þeir váru þar um vetrinn, ok var ekki fyrir unnit um sumarit. Tókusk af veiðarnar, ok gerðisk illt til matar.

Kjalarnes. They called this stretch of coast '**Marvel Strands**' because it took so long to sail past it. Then the coastline became indented with inlets and they sailed into one of them.

King Óláfr Tryggvason had given Leifr [Eiríksson] a Scottish couple, a man named Haki and a woman called Hekja. They could run faster than deer. They were on the ship with Karlsefni. When the ships had passed Marvel Strands the Scots were put ashore and told to run southwards to explore the country's resources and to return within three days. They both wore a garment called a kjafal, which had a hood at the top but no arms and open at the sides; it had no sleeves and was fastened between the legs with a button and loop. They wore nothing else.

The ships waited there at anchor. After three days the Scots came running down the shore; one was carrying some grapes and the other had self-sown wheat.

They were taken aboard and they sailed on until they reached a fjord. They sailed their ships into it. At its mouth lay an island around which flowed very strong currents, so they named it Straumey. There were so many birds there that they could hardly walk without stepping on eggs. They sailed up what they had named **Straum Fjord**, unloaded their ships and began settling in. They had brought all sorts of livestock with them and explored the land around for natural produce. There were mountains there and beautiful landscape. They paid no attention to anything but exploring it. There was tall grass everywhere.

Furðustrandir 'Marvel Strands'. Possibly southern Labrador or Nova Scotia.

Straumsfjǫrðr 'Straum Fjord'. Most recently identified as either the Strait of Belle Isle, the Bay of Fundy, or Lobster Bay.

Þá hvarf brott Þórhallr veiðimaðr. Þeir hǫfðu áðr heitit á guð til matar, ok varð eigi við svá skjótt, sem sem þeir þóttusk þurfa. Þeir leituðu Þórhalls um þrjú dœgr ok fundu hann á hamargnípu einni, hann lá þar ok horfði í lopt upp ok gapði bæði munni ok nǫsum ok þulði nǫkkut. Þeir spurðu, hví hann var þar kominn. Hann kvað þá engu þat varða. Þeir báðu hann fara heim með sér, ok hann gerði svá.

Litlu síðar kom þar hvalr, ok fóru þeir til ok skáru, ok kenndi engi maðr, hvat hvala var; ok er matsveinar suðu, þá átu þeir, ok varð ǫllum illt af.

Þá mælti Þórhallr: 'Drjúgari varð inn **rauðskeggjaði** nú en Kristr yðvarr. Hefi ek þetta nú fyrir skáldskap minn, er ek orta um Þór, fulltrúann; sjaldan hefir hann mér brugðizk.'

Ok er menn vissu þetta, báru þeir hvalinn allan á kaf ok skutu sínu máli til guðs. Batnaði þá veðrátta, ok gaf þeim útróðra, ok skorti þá síðan eigi fǫng, því at þá var dýraveiðr á landinu, en eggver í eynni, en fiski ór sjónum.

(. . .)

10. Nú er at segja af Karlsefni, at hann fór suðr fyrir landit ok Snorri ok Bjarni með sínu fólki. Þeir fóru lengi ok allt þar til, er þeir kómu at á einni, er fell af landi ofan ok í vatn eitt til sjóvar. Eyrar váru þar miklar, ok mátti eigi komask inn í ána, útan at háflœðum.

They stayed there that winter, which turned out to be a severe one. They had made no provision for it during the summer, and now they ran short of food and the hunting failed.

Meanwhile Þórhallr the Hunter had disappeared and they went to look for him. They prayed to God for something to eat, but the response was not as prompt as they would have liked. They searched for Þórhallr for three days and finally found him on the top of a cliff. He was staring up at the sky with his eyes, nose and mouth agape, scratching and pinching himself and mumbling.

They asked what he was doing there and he said that it was no concern of theirs. They asked him to come home with them, but he refused.

A little later a whale was washed up and they rushed to cut it up. No one recognised what kind of whale it was. The cooks boiled the meat, but when it was eaten it made everyone ill.

Then Þórhallr said: 'Hasn't **Old Redbeard** turned out to be more successful than your Christ? This was my reward for the poem I composed about my patron, Þór. He has seldom failed me.' When the others heard this they refused to use the whale-meat, threw it over a cliff and committed themselves to God. Then the weather improved to allow them to go out fishing and after that there were supplies in plenty. They could hunt game inland, gather eggs on the island, and fish from the sea.

(. . .)

10. Now it is said that Karlsefni sailed south around the land with Snorri and Bjarni and the rest of the company. They sailed for a long time until they came to a river that flowed down into a lake and from there into the sea. There were wide sandbars stretching out across the mouth of the river and they could only enter it at high tide.

---

rauðskeggjaði 'Old Redbeard'. The Norse god Þórr. Christianity reached Greenland slightly later than Iceland and many, like Eiríkr the Red and Þórhallr, were unimpressed.

Þeir Karlsefni sigldu í ósinn ok kǫlluðu í **Hópi**. Þeir fundu þar á landi sjálfsána hveitiakra, þar sem lægðir váru, en vínvið allt þar sem holta vissi. Hverr lœkr var þar fullr af fiskum. Þeir gerðu grafar, þar sem mættisk landit ok flóðit gekk ofast, ok þá er út fell sjórinn, váru helgir fiskar í grǫfunum. Þar var mikill fjǫlði dýra á skóginum, með ǫllu móti. Þeir váru þar hálfan mánuð ok skemmtuðu sér ok urðu við ekki varir. Fé sitt hǫfðu þeir með sér.

Ok einn morgin snimma, er þeir lituðusk um, sá þeir mikinn fjǫlða húðkeipa, ok var veift trjám á skipunum, ok lét því líkast sem í hálmþúst, ok var veift sólarsinnis.

Þá mælti Karlsefni: 'Hvað mun þetta hafa at teikna?'

Snorri Þorbrandsson svaraði honum: 'Vera kann, at þetta sé friðarmark, ok tǫkum skjǫld hvítan ok berum at móti.'

Ok svá gerðu þeir. Þá reru þeir í mót ok undruðusk þá, sem fyrir váru, ok gengu á land upp. Þeir váru svartir menn ok illiligir ok hǫfðu illt hár á hǫfði; þeir váru mjǫk eygðir ok breiðir í kinnum. Dvǫlðusk þeir of stund ok undruðusk þá, sem fyrir váru, ok reru síðan brott ok suðr fyrir nesit.

Þeir Karlsefni hǫfðu gǫrt búðir sínar upp frá vatninu, ok váru sumir skálarnir nær vatninu, en sumir firr. Nú váru þeir þar þann vetr. Þar kom enginn snjór, ok allt gekk fé þeira sjálfala fram.

Karlsefni sailed into the estuary and called the land '**Tidal Pool**'. Here they found fields of self-sown wheat in the low-lying areas and grape vines on the higher ground. Every stream was teeming with fish. They dug trenches along the high-water mark and when the water ebbed there were halibut trapped in them. In the forest there were a great number of animals of all kinds.

They stayed there a fortnight, enjoying themselves and finding nothing unusual. They had their livestock with them.

Early one morning they noticed skin-boats with people in them waving sticks which made a swishing noise as they turned them around sunwise. Karlsefni said: 'What can this mean?'

Snorri Þorbrandsson answered him: 'It might be a token of peace; we should take a white shield and lift it up in return.'

They did so.

The others then rowed towards them and were astonished at the sight of them when they landed on the shore. They were dark with ugly features and their hair was coarse. They had large eyes and broad cheekbones. They stayed there for a while, marvelling, then rowed away again south around the headland.

Karlsefni and his men had built their settlement on a slope by the lake; some of the booths near the lake, and others further inland. They remained there that winter. There was no snow at all and the livestock could fend for themselves.

Hópi 'Tidal Pool'. The area in Vínland where Karlsefni tried to settle. The mouth of the Hudson River, Miramichi Bay, eastern Newfoundland, and L'Anse aux Meadows are recent contenders.

11. En er vára tók, sá þeir einn morgin snimma, at fjǫlði húðkeipa reri sunnan fyrir nesit, svá margt sem kolum væri sáit fyrir hópit; var þá ok veift af hverju skipi trjánum.

Þeir Karlsefni brugðu þá skjǫldum upp, ok er þeir fundusk, tóku þeir kaupstefnu sín á milli, ok vildi þat fólk helzt hafa rautt skrúð. Þeir hǫfðu móti at gefa skinnavǫru ok algrá skinn. Þeir vildu ok kaupa sverð ok spjót, en þat bǫnnuðu þeir Karlsefni ok Snorri. Þeir Skrælingar tóku spannarlangt rautt skrúð fyrir ófǫlvan belg ok bundu um hǫfuð sér. Gekk svá kaupstefna þeira um hríð. Þá tók at fættast skrúðit með þeim Karlsefni, ok skáru þeir þá svá smátt í sundr, at eigi var breiðara en þvers fingrar, ok gáfu Skrælingar þó jafnmikit fyrir sem áðr eða meira.

Þat bar til, at griðungr hljóp ór skógi, er þeir Karlsefni áttu, ok gellr hátt. Þetta fælask Skrælingar ok hlaupa út á keipana ok reru síðan suðr fyrir landit. Verðr þá ekki vart við þá þrjár vikur í samt.

En er sjá stund var liðin, sjá þeir fara sunnan mikinn fjǫlða Skrælingaskipa, svá sem straumr stœði. Var þá trjánum ǫllum veift andsœlis, ok ýla upp allir mjǫk hátt. Þá tóku þeir Karlsefni rauðan skjǫld ok báru at móti.

Skrælingar hlupu af skipum, ok síðan gengu þeir saman ok bǫrðusk. Varð þar skothríð hǫrð, því at Skrælingar hǫfðu valslǫngur.

Þat sá þeir Karlsefni, at Skrælingar fœrðu upp á stǫng knǫtt stundar mikinn, því nær til at jafna sem sauðarvǫmb, ok helzt blán at lit, ok fleygðu af stǫnginni upp á landit yfir lið þeira Karlsefnis, ok lét illiliga við, þar sem niðr kom.

---

11. Then one morning as spring advanced, they saw a large number of skin-boats approaching from the south around the headland, so dense that it looked as if the estuary was strewn with charcoal, and sticks were being waved from every boat. Karlsefni and his men signalled with their shields and they began to trade.

What the visitors wanted most to buy was red cloth. They also wanted to buy swords and spears, but Karlsefni and Snorri forbade that. In exchange for the cloth they traded dark pelts and for each pelt they took a span of red cloth which they tied around their heads.

The trading went like this for a while until the cloth began to run short. They then cut the cloth into smaller pieces which were no more than a finger's breadth wide, but the Skrælings paid just as much or more for it. Then it happened that a bull belonging to Karlsefni and his men came running out of the woods bellowing loudly. The Skrælings were terrified and ran to their skin-boats and rowed away south around the headland. Three weeks passed and there was no sign of them.

Then they saw a huge number of boats approaching from the south, as thick as a torrent. They were waving their sticks counter-sunwise now and all of them were howling loudly. The men now took up their red shields and went towards them. When they clashed there was a fierce battle and a hail of missiles came flying over. The Skrælings were using catapults. Karlsefni and Snorri saw them lift up on poles a large sphere about the size of a sheep's stomach, which was dark blue in colour, which came flying in over the heads of Karlsefni and his men and made an ugly din when it landed.

Við þetta sló ótta miklum á Karlsefni ok allt lið hans, svá at þá fýsti einskis annars en flýja ok halda undan upp með ánni, því at þeim þótti lið Skrælinga drífa at sér ǫllum megin, ok létta eigi fyrr en þeir koma til hamra nǫkkurra, ok veittu þar viðtǫku harða.

Freydís kom út ok sá, at þeir Karlsefni heldu undan, ok kallaði: 'Hví renni þér undan þessum auvirðismǫnnum, svá gildir menn sem þér eruð, er mér þœtti sem þér mættið drepa niðr svá sem búfé? Ok ef ek hefða vápn, þœtti mér sem ek skylda betr berjask en einnhverr yðvar.'

Þeir gáfu engan gaum hennar orðum. Freydís vildi fylgja þeim ok varð seinni, því at hon var eigi heil; gekk hon þó eptir þeim í skóginn, en Skrælingar sœkja at henni. Hon fann fyrir sér mann dauðan; þar var Þorbrandr Snorrason, ok stóð hellusteinn í hǫfði honum. Sverðit lá bert í hjá honum; tók hon þat upp ok býsk at verja sik. Þá kómu Skrælingar at henni; hon dró þá út brjóstit undan klæðunum ok slettir á beru sverðinu. Við þetta óttask Skrælingar ok hljópu undan á skip sín ok reru í brott. Þeir Karlsefni finna hana ok lofa happ hennar.

Tveir menn fellu af þeim Karlsefni, en fjǫlði af þeim Skrælingum. Urðu þeir Karlsefni ofrliði bornir ok fóru nú heim eptir þetta til búða sinna ok bundu sár sín ok íhuga, hvat fjǫlmenni þat mundi verit hafa, er at þeim sótti af landinu ofan. Sýnisk þeim nú sem þat eina mun liðit verit hafa, er af skipunum kom, en hitt fólkit mun verit hafa sjónhverfingar.

Þeir Skrælingar fundu ok mann dauðan, ok lá øx í hjá. Einn þeira tók upp øxina ok høggr með tré ok þá hverr at ǫðrum, ok þótti þeim vera gersimi ok bíta vel. Síðan tók einn ok hjó í stein, svá at brotnaði øxin, ok þá þótti þeim engu nýt, er eigi stóðzk grjótit, ok kǫstuðu niðr.

This struck great fear into Karlsefni and his men, so much so that their only thought was to flee, and they retreated further up the river. They were sure the Skrælings were attacking them from all sides, and they didn't stop until they reached a cliff wall where they could put up a good fight.

Freydís came out of the camp and saw the retreat. She shouted: 'Why do you flee from such pitiful wretches, brave men like you? You should be able to slaughter them like sheep. I'm sure I could fight better than any of you if I had a weapon.'

The men paid no attention to what she said. Freydís wanted to go with them but could not keep up because she was pregnant. She was following them into the woods when the Skrælings caught up with her. In front of her lay a dead man, Þorbrandr Snorrason, with a flintstone buried in his head, and his sword beside him. She snatched this up and prepared to defend herself with it. When the Skrælings came rushing towards her she pulled one of her breasts out of her bodice and slapped it with the sword. The Skrælings were terrified at the sight of this and fled back to their boats and rowed away. Karlsefni and his men came over to her and praised her courage.

Even though Karlsefni and his men had been fighting against heavy odds, only two of his men had been killed, but many of the Skrælings. They returned to the booths and wondered how numerous the attackers had been who had approached them on land. It now seemed to them that the only attackers had been those in the boats, and the other attackers had only been an illusion.

The Skrælings found the other dead man with his axe lying beside him. One of them picked up the axe and chopped at a tree, and then each took his turn at it. They thought it was a real treasure that cut so well. One of them struck a stone and the axe broke.

Þeir Karlsefni þóttusk nú sjá, þótt þar væri landskostir góðir, at þar myndi jafnan ótti ok ófriðr á liggja af þeim, er fyrir bjuggu.

Síðan bjuggusk þeir á brottu ok ætluðu til síns lands ok sigldu norðr fyrir landit ok fundu fimm Skrælinga í skinnhjúpum, sofnaða, nær sjó. Þeir hǫfðu með sér stokka ok í **dýramerg, dreyra blandinn**. Þóttusk þeir Karlsefni þat skilja, at þessir menn myndi hafa verit gǫrvir brott af landinu; þeir drápu þá. Síðan fundu þeir Karlsefni nes eitt ok á fjǫlða dýra; var nesit at sjá sem mykiskán væri, af því at dýrin lágu þar um nætrnar.

Nú koma þeir Karlsefni aptr í Straumfjǫrð, ok váru þar fyrir alls gnóttir þess, er þeir þurftu at hafa.

Þat er sumra manna sǫgn, at þau Bjarni ok Guðríðr hafi þar eptir verit ok tíu tigir manna með þeim ok hafi eigi farit lengra, en þeir Karlsefni ok Snorri hafi suðr farit ok fjórir tigir manna með þeim ok hafi eigi lengr verit í Hópi en vart tvá mánuði ok hafi sama sumar aptr komit.

Karlsefni fór þá einu skipi at leita Þórhalls veiðimanns, en annat liðit var eptir, ok fóru þeir norðr fyrir Kjalarnes, ok berr þá fyrir vestan fram, ok var landit á bakborða þeim. Þar váru þá eyðimerkr einar allt at sjá fyrir þeim ok nær hvergi rjóðr í. Ok er þeir hǫfðu lengi farit, fellr á af landi ofan ór austri ok í vestr. Þeir lǫgðu inn í árósinn ok lágu við inn syðra bakkann.

Thinking it was worthless now because it could not withstand stone, they threw it away.

Karlsefni and his party then realised that although the land was excellent they could never live there in safety or free from fear of an attack by the inhabitants. So they made ready to leave the place and return home. They sailed north along the coast where they discovered five Skrælings sleeping in skin sacks. Beside them they had containers full of **deer marrow mixed with blood**. They reckoned that they must the outlaws and they killed them.

Then they came to a headland where there were numerous deer. The point looked like a huge dunghill as the deer used to spend their winters there.

Soon after they arrived at Straumfjord, where they found plenty of everything. According to some people, Bjarni and Guðríðr had stayed behind there with a hundred people and gone no farther while Karlsefni and Bjarni had sailed south with forty men and, after spending only two months south at Hóp, had returned the same summer.

The group stayed behind while Karlsefni set out with one ship to search for Þórhallr the Hunter. He sailed north around Kjarlarnes and then bore west, keeping the land on the port beam. They saw nothing but wild and desolate woodland. When they had sailed a long way they came to a river that flowed east to west into the sea. They steered into the river mouth and lay to near the south bank.

---

dýramerg, dreyra blandinn 'deer marrow mixed with blood'. This has been identified as the native American food pemmican: cakes of dried meat mixed with marrow-grease, which they used as rations on hunting trips.

The Saga of Egill Skalla-Grímsson

Egils saga Skalla-Grímssonar

c. 1230–40

*

Egill Skalla-Grímsson is one of the most memorable and colourful characters in the literature. His saga, which most scholars believe was written in the 1220s to 1230s by Snorri Sturluson (1179–1241), begins in Norway where Egill's grandfather Kveldúlfr 'evening wolf' and father Grímr (later *Skalla*-Grímr because he becomes 'bald') fall out with King Haraldr Finehair (see *B&OS*). They emigrate to Iceland where Skalla-Grímr establishes a prosperous farm at Borg in Borgarfjǫrðr. Egill's birth is reported in chapter 33, and clearly he is a handful from the off. We are told that 'as he grew up it soon became clear that he would turn out very ugly and resemble his father, with black hair. When he was three he was as big and strong as a boy of six or seven. He became very talkative at an early age and had a gift for words, but tended to be difficult to deal with in his games with other children.' When the family is invited to a feast that year Skalla-Grímr forbids Egill to join them: 'You're not coming,' said Skalla-Grímr, 'because you don't know how to behave where adults are drinking heavily. You're bad enough when you're sober.' Throughout his saga Egill is a ruthless warrior, a bit of a berserk, a prodigious drinker, a rune master, a sailor, and a first-rate Skaldic poet. Most of the individual Skaldic verses preserved in this saga are unlikely to be his, but the long poems probably are, as well as the single surviving stanza and refrain from his lost *Aðalsteinsdrápa* 'Eulogy on King Æthelstan' (see **Viking Wars**), for which, according to the saga, the king gave Egill two golden rings, each priced at half a mark of silver, and a costly cloak which had belonged to himself.

Andersson, T. M., *The Growth of the Medieval Icelandic Sagas (1180–1280)* (Ithaca, NY, 2006).

Byock, J., *Feud in the Icelandic Saga* (Berkeley, CA, 1982)

Byock, J., *Viking Age Iceland* (Harmondsworth, 2001)

Clover, C. J., *The Medieval Saga* (Ithaca, NY, 1982)

Clunies Ross, M., ed., *Old Icelandic Literature and Society* (Cambridge, 2000)

Jónas Kristjánsson, *Eddas and Sagas*, trans. P. Foote (Reykjavík, 1992)

McTurk, R., ed., *A Companion to Old Norse-Icelandic Literature* (Maldon, MA, 2005)

O'Donoghue, H., *Old Norse-Icelandic Literature: A Short Introduction* (Maldon, MA, 2004)

Poole, R., ed., *Skaldsagas: Text, Vocation and Desire in the Icelandic Sagas of Poets* (Berlin, 2001)

Egill and King Æthelstan

In this chapter we read an exceptionally vivid portrait of Egill in his mature years. He and his brother, Þórólfr, have just fought in the battle of *Brunanburh* as mercenaries for King Æthelstan. Þórólfr has been killed. The king not only richly compensates Egill for his brother, but also asks him to stay on as one of his earls. When Egill claims business prevents him, the king sends him off with a longship and a crew of 100 men, to Fjordane in Norway, where Egill stays with his friend Arinbjǫrn.

55. Aðalsteinn konungr sneri í brott frá orustunni, en menn hans ráku flóttann; hann reið aptr til borgarinnar ok tók eigi fyrr náttstað en í borginni, en Egill rak flóttann ok fylgði þeim lengi ok drap hvern mann, er hann náði. Síðan sneri hann aptr með sveitunga sína ok fór þar til, er orrustan hafði verit, ok hitti þar Þórólf, bróður sinn, látinn; hann tók upp lík hans ok þó, bjó um síðan, sem siðvenja var til. Grófu þeir þar grǫf ok settu Þórólf þar í með vápnum sínum ǫllum ok klæðum; síðan spennti Egill gullhring á hvára hǫnd honum, áðr hann skilðist við, hlóðu síðan at grjóti ok jósu at moldu. Þá kvað Egill vísu:

Gekk, sás óðisk ekki, jarlmanns bani snarla,
þreklundaðr fell, Þundar, Þórólfr í gný stórum;
Jǫrð grœr, en vér verðum, Vínu nær of mínum,
helnauð es þat, hylja harm, ágætum barma.

Ok enn kvað hann:

Valkǫstum hlóðk vestan vang fyr merkistangir,
ótt vas él þats sóttak Aðgils blǫum Naðri;
háði ungr við Engla Áleifr þrimu stála;
helt, né hrafnar sultu, Hringr á vápna þingi.

---

55. King Æthelstan left the field of battle while his men pursued those who had fled. He rode all night back to the fortress, while Egill chased the fleeing troops for a long time, killing every one of them that he caught. He then returned to the field of battle with his band of men and found his dead brother Þórólfr. He lifted his body and washed it, then prepared the corpse according to custom. They dug a grave and buried Þórólfr with all his weapons and battle armour. Egill clasped a gold ring on each of his arms before he left him. Then they piled rocks over the grave and sprinkled it with earth. Then Egill spoke a verse:

The unfearing slayer of the earl, ventured bravely forth
in the din of the thunder god; bold-hearted Þórólfr fell.
The green grass will grow over my great brother near Vín-Heath;
great as my sorrow is I must keep it to myself.

And then he spoke another verse:

Where the poles marked the battlefield, I piled body-mounds, west of where
With black Adder I smote Aðils in a heavy shower of blows.
Young Óláfr made thunder of steel with the English.
Hringr entered the weapon-fray and the ravens did not starve.

Síðan fór Egill með sveit sína á fund Aðalsteins konungs ok gekk þegar fyrir konung, er hann sat við drykkju; þar var glaumr mikill; ok er konungr sá, at Egill var inn kominn, þá mælti hann, að rýma skyldi pallinn þann hinn óœðra fyrir þeim, og mælti, at Egill skyldi sitja þar í ǫndvegi gegnt konungi.

Egill settist þar niðr ok skaut skildinum fyrir fœtr sér; hann hafði hjálm á hǫfði ok lagði sverðit um kné sér ok dró annat skeið til hálfs, en þá skelldi hann aptr í slíðrin; hann sat upprέttr ok var gneyptr mjǫk. Egill var mikilleitr, ennibreiðr, brúnamikill, nefit ekki langt, en ákafliga digrt, granstœðit vítt ok langt, hakan breið furðuliga, ok svá allt um kjálkana, hálsdigr ok herðimikill, svá að þat bar frá því, sem aðrir menn váru, harðleitr ok grimmligr, þá er hann var reiðr; hann var vel í vexti ok hverjum manni hærri, úlfgrátt hárit ok þykkt ok varð snimma skǫllóttr; en er hann sat, sem fyrr var ritat, þá hleypði hann annarri brúninni ofan á kinnina, en annarri upp í hárrœtr; Egill var svarteygr ok skolbrúnn. Ekki vildi hann drekka, þó at honum væri borit, en ýmsum hleypði hann brúnunum ofan eða upp.

Aðalsteinn konungr sat í hásæti; hann lagði ok sverð um kné sér, ok er þeir sátu svá um hríð, þá dró konungr sverðit ór slíðrum ok tók gullhring af hendi sér, mikinn ok góðan, ok dró á blóðrefilinn, stóð upp ok gekk á gólfit ok rétti yfir eldinn til Egils. Egill stóð upp ok brá sverðinu ok gekk á gólfit; hann stakk sverðinu í bug hringinum ok dró at sér, gekk aptr til rúms síns; konungr settisk í hásæti. En er Egill settisk niðr, dró hann hringinn á hǫnd sér, ok þá fóru brýnn hans í lag; lagði hann þá niðr sverðit ok hjálminn ok tók við dýrshorni, er honum var borit, ok drakk af. Þá kvað hann:

Then Egill with his band of men went to see King Æthelstan and approached him where he sat drinking. There was much revelry. When the king saw Egill arrive he ordered that the lower bench be cleared for his men and told Egill to sit in the high seat there, facing him. Egill sat down and put his shield at his feet. He was wearing a helmet and laid his sword across his knees, and now and again he would draw it halfway out of the scabbard, then thrust it back in again. He sat upright, but with his head bowed low. Egill had very distinctive features, with a wide forehead, bushy brows and a nose that was not long but extremely broad. His beard grew over a long, wide part of his face, and his chin and entire jaw were exceptionally broad. With his thick neck and broad shoulders, he stood out from other men. When he was angry, his face grew harsh and fierce. He was well built and taller than other men, with thick wolf-grey hair, although he had gone bald at an early age. When he was sitting in this particular scene, he wrinkled one eyebrow right down on to his cheek and raised the other up to the roots of his hair. Egill had dark eyes and his brows joined in the middle. He refused to drink even when he was served, but just raised and lowered his eyebrows in turn.

King Æthelstan was sitting in his high seat, with his sword lying across his knees, too. After they had been sitting there like that for some time, the king drew his sword, took a fine, large ring from his arm and slipped it over the point of his sword. He then stood up, walked across the floor, and handed it over the fire to Egill. Egill stood up, unsheathed his sword, and walked out on to the floor. He put his sword through the ring and pulled it towards him, then he went back to his place. The king sat down in his high seat. When Egill sat down he drew the ring on to his arm, and his brow went back to normal. He put down his sword and helmet, took the drinking horn that was served to him, and drank it down. Then he spoke a verse:

Hrammtangar lætr hanga hrynvirgil mér brynju
Hǫðr á hauki troðnum heiðis vingameiði;
rítmœðis knák reiða, ræðr gunnvala bræðir,
gelgju seil á galga geirveðrs, lofi at meira.

Þaðan af drakk Egill at sínum hlut ok mælti við aðra menn.

Eptir þat lét konungr bera inn kistur tvær; báru tveir menn hvára; voru báðar fullar af silfri; konungr mælti, 'Kistur þessar, Egill, skaltu hafa, ok ef þú kemr til Íslands, skaltu fœra þetta fé fǫður þínum; í sonargjǫld sendi ek honum; en sumu fé skaltu skipta með frændum ykkrum Þórólfs, þeim er þér þykkja ágætastir. En þú skalt taka hér bróðurgjǫld hjá mér, lǫnd eða lausa aura, hvárt er þú vilt heldr, ok ef þú vill með mér dveljask lengðar, þá skal ek hér fá þér sœmð ok virðing, þá er þú kannt mér sjálfr til segja.'

Egill tók við fénu ok þakkaði konungi gjafir og vinmæli; tók Egill þaðan af at gleðjask, ok þá kvað hann:

Knǫttu hvarms af harmi hnúpgnípur mér drúpa,
nú fann ek þanns ennis ósléttur þær rétti;
gramr hefr gerðihǫmrum grundar upp of hrundit,
sá's til ýgr, af augum, armsíma, mér grímu.

Síðan váru grœddir þeir menn, er sárir váru ok lífs auðit.

The god of armour hangs a jangling snare upon my arm,
the gibbet birds of prey, the play-ground of hawks.
I raise the ring, the clasp that is worn on the shield-splintering arm,
on to my rod of the battle-storm, in praise of the feeder of ravens.

From then on Egill drank his full share and spoke to others.

Afterwards the king had two chests brought in, each carried by two men. They were both full of silver.

The king said, 'These chests are for you, Egill. And when you go to Iceland you shall give this money to your father, which I am sending him in compensation for the death of his son. Share some of the money with those of Þórólfr's kinsmen who you regard as best. Take compensation for your brother from me here, wealth or land, whichever you prefer, and if you wish to stay with me longer I shall grant you any honour that you wish to name for yourself.'

Egill took the money and thanked the king for his gift and friendship. From then on he began to cheer up. Then he spoke a verse:

For grief my beetling brows drooped over my eyelids.
Now I have found one who has filled the trenches on my forehead:
the king has pushed the cliffs that grip my mask's ground,
back above my eyes. He grants bracelets no quarter.

Later the men who were thought likely to survive had their wounds dressed.

Egill dvaldisk með Aðalsteini konungi inn næsta vetr eptr fall Þórólfs, ok hafði hann allmiklar virðingar af konungi; var þá með honum lið þat allt, er áðr hafði fylgt þeim báðum brœðrum ok ór orrustu hǫfðu komist. Þá orti Egill drápu um Aðalstein konung, ok er í því kvæði þetta: [see **Viking Wars**].

Egill remained with King Æthelstan for the winter after his brother's death, and earned great respect from him. With him then was all the troop once with both brothers, who had survived the battle. Then Egill composed a eulogy in praise of the king which includes this verse: [see Egill's *Eulogy on Æthelstan* in **Viking Wars**].

Eiríkr Bloodaxe and the *Head-Ransom*

In a later chapter Egill finds himself in York as a hostage to King Eiríkr blóðøx (Bloodaxe) and Queen Gunnhildr. His ship has grounded at the mouth of the Humber and he has sought out his old friend Arinbjǫrn who lives at York with the king and queen. Matters of a bloody family history mean that the king and queen want to kill Egill. Gunnhildr, in fact, has cast the spell that has drawn Egill overseas to them in the first place. Using all his wits, Arinbjǫrn thwarts her attempt to have Egill executed on the spot, and succeeds in gaining time by proposing that Egill spend the night in his house composing a eulogy in honour of the king. They go back, with Egill strictly under house arrest, and as Egill starts to craft the verses in his head in a loft room in Arinbjǫrn's, Gunnhildr torments him from the window sill disguised as a swallow. Only when Arinbjǫrn goes on to the roof does she withdraw, and Egill is left to finish composing his poem. The following episode, when Egill arrives with Arinbjǫrn to recite it, demonstrates the power of poetry in their world. Egill's reward for his poem is his head.

For more information on the period and other works of literature associated with this, see **Viking Wars**, in which full texts and translations of Egill's extant *Eulogy on Æthelstan* and *Head-Ransom* are provided.

60. Eiríkr konungr gekk til borða at vanða sínum, ok var þá fjǫlmenni mikit með honum; ok er Arinbjǫrn varð þess varr, þá gekk hann með alla sveit sína alvápnaða í konungsgarð, þá er konungr sat yfir borðum. Arinbjǫrn krafði sér inngǫngu í hǫllina; honum var það ok heimilt gǫrt; ganga þeir Egill inn með helming sveitarinnar; annarr helmingr stóð úti fyrir durum.

Arinbjǫrn kvaddi konung, en konungr fagnaði honum vel; Arinbjǫrn mælti, 'Nú er hér kominn Egill; hefir hann ekki leitat til brotthlaups í nótt. Nú viljum vér vita, herra, hverr hans hluti skal verða; vænti ek góðs af yðr; hefi ek það gǫrt, sem vert var, að ek hefi engan hlut til þess sparat, at gera ok mæla svá,

---

60. King Eiríkr went to table with a lot of people as usual. When Arinbjǫrn saw this he took all his men, fully armed, to the hall when the king was sitting down to dine. Arinbjǫrn asked to be let in to the hall and was allowed to enter. He and Egill went in with half their men. The others waited outside the door. Arinbjǫrn greeted the king, who welcomed him.

'Egill is here, my lord,' he said. 'He didn't try to escape during the night. We would like to learn what his lot will be. I expect you to show us favour. I have acted as you deserve, sparing nothing in word or deed to enhance your renown. I have relinquished all the að yðvarr vegr væri þá meiri en áðr. Hefi ek ok látit allar mínar eigur ok frændr ok vini, er ek átta í Nóregi, ok fylgt yðr, en allir lendir menn yðrir skilðusk við yðr, ok er þat makligt, því at þú hefir marga hluti til mín stórvel gǫrt.'

Þá mælti Gunnhildr, 'Hættu, Arinbjǫrn, ok tala ekki svá langt um þetta; mart hefir þú vel gǫrt við Eirík konung, ok hefir hann þat fullu launat; er þér miklu meiri vandi á við Eirík konung en Egil; er þér þess ekki biðjanda, at Egill fari refsingalaust heðan af fundi Eiríks konungs, slíkt sem hann hefir til saka gǫrt.'

Þá segir Arinbjǫrn, 'Ef þú, konungr, ok þit Gunnhildr hafið það einráðit, at Egill skal hér enga sætt fá, þá er þat drengskapr at gefa honum frest ok fararleyfi um viku sakar, at hann forði sér; þó hefir hann at sjálfvilja sínum farit hingat á fund yðvarn ok vænti sér af því friðar; fara þá enn skipti yður sem verða má þaðan frá.'

Gunnhildr mælti, 'Sjá kann ek á þessu, Arinbjǫrn, at þú ert hollari Agli en Eiríki konungi; ef Egill skal ríða heðan viku í brott í friði, þá mun hann kominn til Aðalsteins konungs á þessi stundu. En Eiríkr konungr þarf nú ekki at dyljask í því, at honum verða nú allir konungar ofreflismenn, en fyrir skǫmmu mundi þat þykkja ekki líkligt, at Eiríkr konungr myndi eigi hafa til þess vilja ok atferð at hefna harma sinna á hverjum manni slíkum, sem Egill er.'

Arinbjǫrn segir, 'Engi maðr mun Eirík kalla at meira mann, þó at hann drepi einn bóndason útlendan, þann er gengit hefir á vald hans. En ef hann vill miklask af þessu, þá skal ek þat veita honum, at þessi tíðindi skulu heldr þykkja frásagnarverð, því at vit Egill munum nú veitask at, svá at jafnsnimma skal okkr mœta báðum. Muntu, konungr, þá dýrt kaupa líf Egils, um þat er vér erum allir at velli lagðir, ek ok sveitungar mínir; myndi mik annars vara af yðr, en þú myndir mik vilja leggja heldr að jǫrðu en láta mik þiggja líf eins manns, er ek bið.'

---

possessions and friends and kinsmen that I had in Norway to follow you, while all your other landowners turned their backs on you. I think you deserve this from me because you have treated me very well in many ways.'

Then Gunnhildr said, 'Stop going on about that, Arinbjǫrn. You have treated King Eiríkr well in many ways and he has rewarded you in full for it. You owe much more to the king than to Egill. You cannot ask for Egill to be sent away from the king unpunished, after all the wrongs he has done him.'

Arinbjǫrn said, 'If you and Gunnhildr have have already decided, King, that Egill will not be granted any reconciliation here, the noble course of action is to give him a week's grace to get away, as he came here of his own accord and expected a peaceful reception. After that your dealings may follow their own course.'

Gunnhildr replied, 'I can tell from all this that you give more loyalty to Egill than to King Eiríkr, Arinbjǫrn. If Egill is given a week to ride away from here in peace, he will have time to reach King Æthelstan. Eiríkr can't ignore the fact that every king is more powerful than he is now, even though not so long ago King Eiríkr would have seemed unlikely to lack the will and character to avenge all that he has suffered from the likes of Egill.'

'No one will think Eiríkr any the greater for killing a foreign farmer's son who has surrendered into his hands,' said Arinbjǫrn. 'If it is renown that he is seeking I can help him make this episode really memorable, because Egill and I intend to stand by each other. Everyone will have to face the two of us together. The king will pay a high price for Egill's life by killing us all, me and my men as well. I would have expected more from you than to choose to see me dead rather than grant me the life of one man when I ask for it.'

Þá segir konungr, 'Allmikit kapp leggr þú á þetta, Arinbjǫrn, at veita Agli lið; trauðr mun ek til vera at gera þér skaða, ef því er at skipta, ef þú vill heldr leggja fram líf þitt en hann sé drepinn; en œrnar eru sakar til við Egil, hvat sem ek læt gera við hann.'

Ok er konungr hafði þetta mælt, þá gekk Egill fyrir hann ok hóf upp kvæðit ok kvað hátt ok fekk þegar hljóð:

> Vestr komk of ver, en ek Viðris ber
> munstrandar mar, svás mitt of far;
> drók eik á flot við ísabrot;
> hlóðk mærðar hlut m*un*knarrar skut.
> [*etc.*; for the whole text,
> see Egill's *Head-Ransom*, **Viking Wars**]

61. Eiríkr konungr sat upþréttr, meðan Egill kvað kvæðit, ok hvessti augun á hann. Ok er lokit var drápunni, þá mælti konungr, 'Bezta er kvæðit fram flutt, en nú hefi ek hugsat, Arinbjǫrn, um mál várt Egils, hvar koma skal. Þú hefir flutt mál Egils með ákafa miklum, er þú býðr at etja vandræðum við mik. Nú skal þat gera fyrir þínar sakar, sem þú hefir beðit, at Egill skal fara frá mínum fundi heill ok ósakaðr. En þú, Egill, hátta svá ferðum þínum at síðan, er þú kemr frá mínum fundi af þessi stofu, þá kom þú aldregi í augsýn mér ok sonum mínum ok verð aldri fyrir mér né mínu liði. En ek gef þér nú hǫfuð þitt at sinni. Fyrir þá sǫk er þú gekkt á mitt vald, þá vil ek eigi gera níðingsverk á þér, en vita skaltu þat til sanns, at þetta er engi sætt við mik né sonu mína ok enga frændr vára, þá sem réttar vilja reka.'

Then the king said, 'You are staking a great deal to help Egill, Arinbjǫrn. I am reluctant to harm you if it should come to this, if you prefer to lose your own life rather than see him killed. But Egill has done me plenty of wrong, whatever I may decide to do with him.'

When the king had finished speaking, Egill went before him and performed his poem, reciting it in a loud voice. Everyone fell silent at once:

> West I came over fishing grounds, and I carry the sea
> Of Wutherer's mind-beach, that's how I sail.
> I pulled an oak afloat at the breaking of ice,
> Loaded a glory-portion into the mind-vessel's stern. [*etc.*]

61. King Eiríkr sat bolt upright while Egill recited the poem, glaring at him. And when the poem was finished, the king said, 'The poem was presented really well, and now I have been thinking, Arinbjǫrn, about the case between Egill and myself, what the verdict shall be. You have presented Egill's case with great energy, in offering to make trouble with me. For your sake now this shall happen that, as you have asked, Egill shall leave my presence in one piece safe and sound. And you, Egill, you organise your travels in such a way that from the moment you leave my presence in this chamber, never come into my sight or into my sons' sight, nor ever turn up before me or my retinue. And I will give you your head for now. Because you came into my power, I will not commit any crime against you, but be advised, this is no settlement either with me or with my sons or with any of our kinsmen who wish to seek justice of their own.'

In the backwoods: Egill and Ármóðr

Later in the saga Egill is back in Norway. He is sent on a mission to collect tribute in Vermaland, a region of backwoods bordering Sweden. Travelling through a treacherous winter landscape, Egill and his men arrive at a farm run by a man named Ármóðr. He gives them bowls of curds and a room in the barn for the night, protesting that he would give them more if he had it. What follows is an example of Viking Egill at his best. The manner, in particular, in which he takes his leave of Ármóðr and his family the next morning really conveys something of the reason the Vikings were feared throughout Europe.

71. Egill bjósk til ferðar ok þrír men aðrir hans fǫrunautar; hǫðu hesta ok sleða sem konungsmenn, þá váru snjóvar miklir ok breyttir vegar allir. Ráða þeir til ferðar, er þeir váru búnir, ok óku upp á land, ok er þeir sóttu austr til Eiða, þá var þat á einni nótt, at féll snjór mikill, svá at ógǫrla sá vegana; fórsk þeim þá seint um daginn eptir, því at kafhlaup váru, þegar af fór veginum.

Ok er á leið daginn, dvǫlðusk þeir ok áðu hestum sínum; þar var nær skógarháls einn.

Þá mæltu þeir við Egil, 'Nú skiljask hér vegar, en hér fram undan hálsinum býr bóndi sá, er heitir Arnaldur, vinr várr; munu vér fǫrunautar fara þangat til gistingar, en þér skuluð fara hér upp á hálsinn, ok þá er þér komið þar, mun brátt verða fyrir yðr bœr mikill, ok er yðr þar vís gisting; þar býr stórauðigr maðr, er heitir Ármóðr skegg. En á morgun árdegis skulu vér hittask ok fara anna kveld til Eiðaskógs, þar býr góðr bóndi, er Þorfinnr heitir.'

---

71. Egill made preparations for the journey with the three men going with him. They took horses and sleighs, and so did the king's men. There had been heavy snow by then which changed all their routes. Once they were prepared they set off and drove inland. One night on their way to Eid it snowed so heavily that it was impossible to make out where the trails were. The next day they made slow progress because they kept sinking into snowdrifts when they left the trail.

During the day they paused to rest their horses near a wooded ridge. 'The trail forks here,' they told Egill. 'The farmer who lives beneath the ridge is a friend of ours named Arnaldr. We shall go and stay with him, and you should go up on the ridge. When you get there you will soon see a large farm where you are sure of a place to stay. A very wealthy man called Ármóðr Beard lives there. We will meet up again early tomorrow morning and go on to Eideskog in the evening. A good farmer lives there named Þorfinnr.'

Then they parted. Egill and his men went up on to the ridge. As soon as they were out of Egill's sight the king's men put on the skis they had taken with them and went back as fast as they could. They travelled day and night. They went up to the Uplands and north from there across Dovrefjell, and didn't stop until they reached King Hákon and told him how things had gone.

Síðan skiljask þeir; fara þeir Egill upp á hálsinn, en frá konungsmǫnnum er þat at segja, at þegar er sýn fal í milli þeirra Egils, þá tóku þeir skíð sín, er þeir hǫfðu haft, ok stigu þar á; létu síðan ganga aptr á leið, sem þeir máttu; fóru þeir nótt ok dag ok sneru til Upplanda, ok þaðan norðr um Dofrafjall, ok léttu eigi fyrr en þeir kómu á fund Hákonar konungs ok sǫgðu um sína ferð sem farit hafði.

Egill ok fǫrunautar hans fóru um kveldit yfir hálsinn; var þat þar skjótast af at segja, at þeir fóru þegar af veginum; var snjórinn mikill; lágu hestarnir á kafi annat skeið, svá at draga varð upp. Þar váru kleifar ok kjarrskógar nǫkkurir, en um kjǫrrin ok kleifarnar var alltorsótt; var þeim þá seinkan mikil at hestunum, en mannfœrðin var in þyngsta. Mœddusk þeir þá mjǫk, en þó kómusk þeir af hálsinum ok sá þá fyrir sér bœ mikinn ok sóttu þangat til; ok er þeir kómu í túnit, þá sá þeir, at þar stóðu menn úti, Ármóðr ok sveinar hans. Kǫstuðusk þeir orðum á ok spurðusk tíðinda; ok er Ármóðr vissi, at þeir váru sendimenn konungs, þá bauð hann þeim þar gisting; þeir þekkðusk þat; tóku húskarlar Ármóðs við hestum þeirra ok reiða, en bóndi bað Egil ganga inn í stofu, ok þeir gerðu svá. Ármóðr setti Egil í ǫndvegi á inn óœðra bekk, ok þar fǫrunautar hans útar frá; þeir rœddu mart um, hversu erfilliga þeir hǫfðu farit um kveldit, en heimamǫnnum þótti mikit undr, er þeir hǫfðu fram komizk, ok sǫgðu, at þar væri engum manni fœrt, þó at snjólaust væri.

Þá mælti Ármóðr, 'Þykkir yðr eigi sá beini beztr, at yðr sé borð sett ok gefinn náttverðr, en síðan fari þér at sofa? Munu þér þá hvílask bezt.'

'Þat líkar oss allvel,' segir Egill.

Ármóðr lét þá setja þeim borð, en síðan váru settir fram stórir askar, fullir af skyri; þá lét Ármóðr, at honum þœtti þat illa, er hann hafði eigi mungát at gefa þeim. Þeir Egill váru mjǫk þyrstir af mœði; tóku þeir upp askana ok drukku ákaft skyrit, ok þó Egill miklu mest; engi kom ǫnnur vistin fram.

Egill and his companions crossed the ridge that evening and lost their way at once in the heavy snows. Their horses often sank down into drifts and had to be pulled back out. There were rocky slopes with brushwood which were difficult to negotiate. The horses caused them a long delay, and it was also extremely tough going on foot. Finally they made their way down from the ridge, exhausted, and saw a big farm and headed for it.

When they arrived in the field in front of the farmhouse they saw Ármóðr and his men standing outside. They exchanged greetings and asked each other if there was any news. When they learned that these men were envoys from the king, Ármóðr invited them to stay, and they accepted. Ármóðr's farmhands took the horses and baggage, while the farmer invited Egill into the main room. He went in with his men. Ármóðr gave Egill a seat on the lower bench and his companions were seated further down the table. They spoke at length about their hard journey that night, and the people who lived there were astonished that they had made it at all, saying that the ridge could not even be crossed when it was free of snow.

Then Ármóðr said, 'Don't you think that the best thing I can provide you with is to lay the tables and give you an evening meal, and then you can go to bed? You'll get the best night's rest that way.'

'That suits us fine,' said Egill.

Then Ármóðr had the tables laid for them, and large bowls of skyrr were brought in. Ármóðr gave the impression that he was unhappy at not having any ale to serve them. Egill and his men were so thirsty after their ordeal, they picked up the bowls and gulped down the skyrr, and Egill had more than the others. No other food was offered.

Þar var mart hjóna; húsfreyja sat á þverpalli ok þar konur hjá henni, dóttir bónda var á gólfinu, tíu vetra eða ellifu. Húsfreyja kallaði hana til sín ok mælti í eyra henna; síðan fór mærin utar fyrir borðit, þar er Egill sat. Hon kvað:

Því sendi mín móðir mik við þik til fundar
ok orð bera Agli, at ér varir skyldið;
Hildr mælti þat horna: haga svá maga þínum,
eigu órir gestir œðra nest á frestum.

Ármóðr laust meyna ok bað hana þegja – 'mælir þú þat jafnan, er verst gegnir.'

Mærin gekk á brott, en Egill skaut niðr skyraskinum, ok var þá nær tómr; váru þá ok brott teknir askarnir frá þeim. Gengu þá ok heimamenn í sæti sín, ok váru borð upp tekin um alla stofu, ok sett á vist; því næst kómu inn sendingar ok váru þá settar fyrir Egil sem fyrir aðra menn.

Því næst var ǫl inn borit, ok var þat it sterkasta mungát; var þá brátt drukkinn einmenningr; skyldi einn maðr drekka af dýrshorni; var þar mestr gaumr at gefinn, er Egill var ok sveitungar hans; skyldu drekka sem ákafast. Egill drakk ósleitilega fyrst langa hríð; en er fǫrunautar hans gerðusk ófœrir, þá drakk hann fyrir þá, þat er þeir máttu eigi. Gekk svá til þess, er borð fóru brott; gerðusk þá ok allir mjǫk drukknir, þeir er inni váru, en hvert full, er Ármóðr drakk, þá mælti hann, 'Drekk ek til þín, Egill;' en húskarlar drukku til fǫrunauta Egils ok hǫfðu inn sama formála. Maðr var til þess fenginn at bera þeim Agli hvert full, ok eggjaði sá mjǫk, at þeir skyldi skjótt drekka; Egill

---

There were many people working and living there. The farmer's wife sat on the cross-bench beside some other women. Their ten or eleven-year-old daughter was on the floor. The mother called over to her and whispered in her ear. Then the girl went over to where Egill was sitting at the table. She spoke this verse:

My mother sent me to talk to you
and bring Egill word to be very careful.
The maid of the ale horn said treat your stomach
as if you expected to be served something better.

Ármóðr slapped the girl and told her to keep quiet – 'You're always saying things at the worst of times.'

The girl went away, and Egill put down the bowl of skyrr, which was nearly empty. Then the bowls were taken and the men of the farm went to their seats as well. Tables were laid across the whole room and food was spread out on them. Choice food was then served to everyone including Egill and his men.

Then ale was brought in which was an exceptionally strong brew. Each man was given a horn to drink from, and the host made a special point of encouraging Egill and his men to drink as much as possible. Egill drank non-stop for a long time at the start, and when his companions became incapacitated, he also drank what they couldn't finish. This continued until the tables were cleared.

Everyone became very drunk, and for every toast Ármóðr drank he said, 'I drink to you, Egill,' and the men of the household drank toast to Egill's companions, with the same words. One man was given the job of keeping Egill and his men served with one toast after mælti við fǫrunauta sína, at þeir skyldi þá ekki drekka, en hann drakk fyrir þá, **þat er þeir máttu eigi annan veg undan komask**.

Egill fann þá, at honum myndi eigi svá búit eira; stóð hann þá upp ok gekk um gólf þvert, þangat er Ármóðr sat; hann tók hǫndum í axlir honum ok kneikði hann upp að stǫfum. Síðan þeysti Egill upp ór sér spýju mikla ok gaus í andlit Ármóði, í augun ok nasarnar ok í munninn; rann svá ofan um bringuna, en Ármóði varð við andhlaup, ok er hann fekk ǫndinni frá sér hrundit, þá gaus upp spýja. En allir mæltu þat, þeir er hjá váru, húskarlar Ármóðs, at Egill skyldi fara allra manna armastr ok hann væri inn versti maðr af þessu verki, er hann skyldi eigi ganga út, er hann vildi spýja, en verða eigi at undrum inni í drykkjustofunni.

Egill segir, 'Ekki er at hallmæla mér um þetta, þótt ek gera sem bóndi gerir, spýr hann af ǫllu afli, eigi síðr en ek.'

Síðan gekk Egill til rúms síns ok settisk niðr, bað þá gefa sér at drekka. Þá kvað Egill við raust:

> Títt erum verð at vátta, vætti berk at hættak
> þung til þessar gǫngu, þinn kinnalá minni;
> margr velr gestr, þars gistir, gjǫld, finnumsk vér sjaldan,
> Ármóði liggr, œðri, ǫlðra dregg í skeggi.

---

another, and urging them to drink it up at once. Egill told his companions they should not drink any more, and he drank theirs for them **when there was no avoiding it**.

Egill began to feel that he would not be able to go on like this. He stood up and crossed the floor to where Ármóðr was sitting, seized him by the shoulders and pushed him up against a wall-post. Egill then spewed a flood of vomit that gushed all over Ármóðr's face, filling his eyes, nose, and mouth and pouring down his chest. Ármóðr was nearly choking, and when he managed to exhale finally, a jet of his own vomit gushed out. All Ármóðr's men said that Egill had done a base and foul deed by not going outside when he needed to throw up, but that he had made a spectacle of himself in the drinking-room instead.

Egill said, 'Don't blame me for following the example of the master of the house. He's spewing his guts up just as much as I am.'

Then Egill went over to his place, sat down and asked for a drink. Then Egill shouted out this verse:

> With my guts' swill I repaid the compliment you served.
> I had great cause to venture my steps across the floor.
> Many guests thank favours with better-flavoured rewards.
> But we meet rarely. Ármóðr's beard is drenched with dregs of ale.

þat er þeir máttu eigi annan veg undan komask 'when there was no avoiding it'. The drinking session with Ármóðr is governed by strict rules, it seems. If toasted one must quaff the contents of the horn in one. Egill feels he must finish off the ale of his companions 'when there was no avoiding it'. Ármóðr therefore breaches rules of hospitality first by pretending that there is nothing to drink, then by forcing Egill to drink too much. Egill, of course, comes out on top.

Ármóðr hljóp upp ok út, en Egill bað gefa sér drekka; þá mælti húsfreyja við þann mann, er þeim hafði skenkt um kveldit, at hann skyldi gefa drykk, svá at þá skyrti eigi, meðan þeir vildi drekka; síðan tók hann dýrshorn mikit ok fylldi ok bar til Egils; Egill kneyfði af horninu í einum drykk. Þá kvað hann:

Drekkum ór, þótt Ekkils eykríðr beri tíðum
horna sund at hendi, hvert full, bragar Ulli;
leifik vætr, þótt Laufa leikstœrir mér fœri
hrosta tjarnar í horni, horn til dags at morgni.

Egill drakk um hríð ok kneyfði hvert horn, er at honum kom, en lítil var þá gleði í stofunni, þótt nǫkkurir menn drykki. Síðan stendr Egill upp ok fǫrunautar hans ok taka vápn sín af veggjum, er þeir hǫfðu upp fest; ganga síðan til kornhlǫðu þeirrar, er hestar þeirra váru inni; lǫgðusk þeir þar niðr í hálm ok sváfu um nóttina.

72. Egill stóð upp um morguninn, þegar er dagaði; bjuggusk þeir fǫrunautar ok fóru þegar, er þeir váru búnir, aptr til bœjarins ok leita Ármóðs. Ok er þeir kómu til skemmubúrs þess, er Ármóðr svaf í ok kona hans ok dóttir, þá hratt Egill upp hurðinni ok gekk til rekkjunnar Ármóðs; hann brá þá sverði, en annarri hendi greip hann í skegg Ármóðs ok hnykkði honum á stokk fram, en kona Ármóðs ok dóttir hljópu upp ok báðu Egil, at hann dræpi eigi Ármóð.

Egill segir, at hann skyldi þat gera fyrir þeirra sakar – 'því at þat er makligt; en hefði hann verðleika til, at ek dræpa hann.' Þá kvað Egill:

Ármóðr jumped to his feet and ran out, but Egill asked for more to drink. The farmer's wife told the man who had been serving the drinks all evening to keep pouring for them so they would not lack drink for as long as they wished. He took a large horn, filled it with drink, and carried it over to Egill. Egill quaffed the drink, then spoke this verse:

Drink every challenge down, though the rider of the waves
brings brimful horns often to the maker of verse.
I shall leave not a drop of sea-malt, even if the maker
of sword-play brings me horns until morning.

Egill went on drinking for some time, finishing off every drinking-horn that was brought to him, but there was not much merry-making in the room even though some people were still drinking there. Then Egill and his companions rose from the tables, took their weapons from the wall where they had hung them up, went to the barn where their horses were stalled, lay down in the straw, and slept the night there.

72. Egill got up at dawn the next day. He and his companions got ready to leave. When they were ready they went back into the farm to look for Ármóðr. They found the chamber where Ármóðr was sleeping with his wife and daughter and Egill threw open the door and went over to his bed. He drew his sword, seized Ármóðr by the beard with his other hand and dragged him up over to the side of the bed. Ármóðr's wife and daughter leapt up and begged Egill not to kill him.

Egill said he would spare him for their sake – 'That is the fair thing to do, but I would kill him if it were worth the bother.' Then he spoke this verse:

Nýtr illsǫgull ýtir armlinns konu sinnar,
oss's við ógnar hvessi óttalaust, ok dóttur;
þeygi munt við þenna þykkjask verðr fyr drykkju
grepp, skulum á veg vappa vítt, svágǫru hlíta.

Síðan sneið Egill af honum skeggit við hǫkuna; síðan krœkði hann fingrinum í augat, svá at úti lá á kinninni: eptir þat gekk Egill á brott ok til fǫrunauta sinna.

Fara þeir þá leið sína, koma at dagverðarmáli til bœjar Þorfinns; hann bjó við Eiðaskóg; þeir Egill krǫfðu dagverðar ok æja hestum sínum; Þorfinnr bóndi lét heimult skyldu þat; ganga þeir Egill þá inn í stofu.

Egill spurði, ef Þorfinnr hefði varr orðit við fǫrunauta hans – 'hǫfðu vér hér mælt mót með oss.'

Þorfinnr segir svá, 'Fóru hér sex menn saman nǫkkuru fyrir dag ok váru vápnaðir mjǫk.'

Þá mælti húskarl Þorfinns, 'Ek ók í nótt eptir viði, ok fann ek sex menn á leið, ok váru þat húskarlar Ármóðs, ok var þat miklu fyrir dag; nú veit ek eigi, hvárt þeir munu allir einir ok inir sex menn, er þú sagðir frá.'

Þorfinnr segir, at þeir menn, er hann hafði hitt, hǫfðu síðar farit en húskarlinn kom heim með viðarhlassit.

Ok er þeir Egill sátu ok mǫtuðust, þá sá Egill, at kona sjúk lá í þverpallinum; Egill spurði Þorfinn, hver kona sú væri, er þar var svá þungliga haldin. Þorfinnr segir, at hon hét Helga ok var dóttir hans – 'hefir hon haft langan vanmátt,' ok þat var krǫm mikil; fekk hon enga nótt svefn ok var sem hamstoli væri.

His wife and daughter save the bad-mouthing man
who binds arms with rings. I do not fear this battle-maker.
You are not to feel deserving of such dealings from the poet
for that drink you served him. Let us be gone far on our way.

Then Egill cut off his beard close to his chin, and gouged out one of his eyes with his finger, leaving it hanging on his cheek. Then Egill went off to his companions.

They went on their way and arrived at Þorfinnr's farm early in the morning. He lived in Eideskog. Egill and his men asked for breakfast and somewhere to rest their horses. Þorfinnr gave them that and Egill and his men went into the main room.

Egill asked Þorfinnr if he knew anything about his companions. 'We arranged to meet them here,' he said.

Þorfinnr replied, 'Six heavily armed men came by here before daybreak.'

One of Þorfinnr's farmhands added, 'I went out to gather timber during the night and came across six men who were going somewhere. They were Ármóðr's farmhands and it was well before daybreak. I don't know if these were the same six you refer to.'

Þorfinnr said the men he had met were travelling later than when the farmhand had brought the cartload of timber back.

When Egill and his men sat down to eat they saw a sick woman lying on the cross-bench. Egill asked Þorfinnr who she was and why she was in such a poor state.

Þorfinnr said she was his daughter Helga – 'She has been weak for a long time.'

She was suffering from a wasting sickness, and could not sleep at night because of some sort of delirium.

'Hefir nǫkkurs í verit leitat,' segir Egill, 'um mein hennar?' Þorfinnr segir, 'Ristnar hafa verit rúnar, ok er sá einn bóndason heðan skammt í brott, er þat gerði, ok er síðan miklu verr en áðr, eða kanntu, Egill, nǫkkut gera at slíkum meinum?'

Egill segir, 'Vera kann, at ekki spillisk við, þó at ek koma til.'

Ok er Egill var mettr, gekk hann þar til, er konan lá, ok rœddi við hana; hann bað þá hefja hana ór rúminu ok leggja undir hana hrein klæði, ok nú var svá gǫrt. Síðan rannsakaði hann rúmit, er hon hafði hvílt í, ok þar fann hann tálkn, ok váru þar á rúnarnar. Egill las þær, ok síðan telgði hann af rúnarnar ok skóf þær í eld niðr; hann brenndi tálknit allt ok lét bera í vind klæði þau, er hon hafði haft áðr. Þá kvað Egill:

Skalat maðr rúnar rísta, nema ráða vel kunni,
þat verðr mǫrgum manni, es of myrkvan staf villisk;
sák á telgðu talkni tíu launstafi ristna,
þat hefr lauka lindi langs ofrtrega fengit.

Egill reist rúnar ok lagði undir hœgendit í hvíluna, þar er hon hvíldi; henni þótti sem hon vaknaði ór svefni ok sagði, at hon var þá heil, en þó var hon máttlítil, en faðir hennar ok móðir urðu stórum fegin; bauð Þorfinnr, at Egill skyldi þar hafa allan forbeina, þann er hann þóttisk þurfa.

'Has anyone tried to find the cause of her illness?' Egill asked.

'We had some runes carved,' answered Þorfinnr. 'The son of a farmer who lives nearby did it. But since then she's been much worse. Do you know any remedy, Egill?'

Egill said, 'It might not do any harm if I try something.'

When Egill had eaten enough he went to where the woman was lying and spoke to her. He told them to lift her out of her bed and place clean linen underneath her, and this was done. He then examined the bed she had been lying in and found a whalebone with runes carved on to it. After reading the runes Egill shaved them off and scraped them into the fire. He burned the whalebone and had her bedclothes aired. Then he spoke this verse:

A man should never carve runes unless he can read them properly;
many go astray around those dark letters.
On the whalebone I saw ten secret letters carved,
from them the linden tree took her long harm.

Egill carved some runes and placed them under the pillow of the bed where she was lying. She felt as if she were waking from a deep sleep, and she said she was well again, but still very weak. Her father and mother were overjoyed. Þorfinnr offered Egill all the provisions he thought he might need.

Bǫðvarr and the *Hard Loss of Sons*

Later in his life, and back in Iceland, there is a family tragedy. Egill's promising young son Bǫðvarr goes to fetch wood from the Hvitá river with five farmhands. On their return a wild south-westerly gale swamps their ship and they all drown. In his grief Egill decides to starve himself to death. His wife Ásgerðr sends a messenger to their daughter Þorgerðr at Hjarðarholt. She manages to trick Egill into eating something, then insists he compose the *Sonatorrek* 'Hard Loss of Sons' (for the text and translation, see **Poems on the Meaning of Life**). This is one of the most powerful and beautiful elegies of any literature.

78. Óláfr hét maðr, sonr Hǫskulds Dala-Kollssonar ok sonr Melkorku, dóttur Mýrkjartans Írakonungs. Óláfr bjó í Hjarðarholti í Laxárdal vestr í Breiðafjarðardǫlum; Óláfr var stórauðigr at fé; hann var þeira manna friðastr sýnum, er þá váru á Íslandi; hann var skǫrungr mikill.

Óláfr bað Þorgerðar, dóttir Egils; Þorgerðr var æn kona ok kvenna mest, vitr ok heldr skapstór, en hversdagliga kyrrlát. Egill kunni ǫll deili á Óláfi ok vissi, at þat gjaforð var gǫfugt, ok fyrir því var Þorgerðr gipt Óláfi; fór hon til bús með honum í Hjarðarholt. Þeira bǫrn váru þau Kjartan, Þorbergr, Halldórr, Steindórr, Þuríðr, Þorbjǫrg, Bergþóra; hana átti Þórhallr goði Oddason; Þorbjǫrgu átti fyrr Ásgeirr Knattarson, en síðar Vermundr Þorgrímsson; Þuríði átti Guðmundr Sǫlmundarson; váru þeira synir Hallr ok Víga-Barði. Ǫzurr Eyvindarson, bróðir Þórodds í Ǫlfusi, fekk Beru, dóttir Egils.

Bǫðvarr, sonr Egils, var þá frumvaxti; hann var inn efniligsti maðr, friðr sýnum, mikill ok sterkr, svá sem verit hafði Egill eða Þórólfr á hans aldri; Egill unni honum mikir; var Bǫðvarr ok elskr at honum.

Þat var eitt sumar, at skip var í Hvítá, ok var þar mikil kaupstefna, hafði Egill þar keypt við margan ok lét flyta heim á skipi; fóru húskarlar ok hǫfðu skip áttært, er Egill átti. Þat var þá eitt sinn, at Bǫðvarr beiddisk at fara með þeim, ok þeir meittu honum þat; for hann þá inn á Vǫllu með huskǫrlum; þeir váru sex saman á áttæru skipi. Ok er þeir skyldu út fara, þá var flœðrin

---

78. There was a man called Óláfr, the son of Hǫskuldr, who was the son of Koll of the Dales. His mother was Melkorka, the daughter of the Irish king Mýrkjartan. Óláfr lived at Hjarðarholt in Laxárdal, in the dales of Breiðafjord. He was very wealthy, one of the most handsome men in Iceland, and very firm-minded.

Óláfr asked to marry Egill's daughter Þorgerðr, who was a very fine woman, clever, rather strong-willed, but usually quiet. Egill knew from Óláfr's background that this was a good offer of marriage, and so she married him and went to live at Hjarðarholt. Their children were Kjartan, Þorbergr, Halldórr, Steindórr, Þuriðr, Þorbjǫrg and Bergþóra. Bergþóra married Þorhallr Oddason the Goði. Thorbjorg was married to Asgeirr Knattarson, then later to Vermundr Þorgrímsson. Þuríð married Guðmundr, Solmund's son, and their sons were Hallr and Killer-Bard. Ozurr, the son of Eyvindr and brother of Þoroddr from Olfus, married Egill's daughter Bera.

Egill's son Bǫðvarr was grown up by this time. He was very promising and handsome, big and strong like Egill and Þórólfr at his age. Egill loved him dearly, and Bǫðvarr was likewise very fond of his father.

One summer there was a ship moored on Hvitá river and a large market was held there. Egill had bought a lot of timber and arranged for it to be shipped back to his farm. The men of his household went to fetch it from Hvitá in an eight-oared ship that Egill owned. On this occasion Bǫðvarr asked to go with them, and they allowed him to come. He went down to Vellir with the farmhands, and there were six of them on the eight-oared vessel. When síð dags, ok er þeir urðu hennar at bíða, þá fóru þeir um kveldit síð. Þá hljóp á útsynningr steinóði, en þar gekk í móti útfallsstraumr; gerði þá stórt á firðinum, sem þar kann opt verða; lauk þar svá, at skipit kafði undir þeim, ok týndusk þeir allir. En eptir um daginn skaut upp líkunum; kom lík Bǫðvars inn í Einarsnes, en sum kómu fyrir sunnan fjǫrðinn, ok rak þangat skipit; fannsk þat inn við Reykjarhamar.

Þann dag spurði Egill þessi tíðendi, ok þegar reið hann at leita líkanna; hann fann rétt lík Bǫðvars' tók hann þat upp ok setti í kné sér ok reið með út í Digranes til haugs Skalla-Gríms. Hann lét þá opna hauginn ok lagði Bǫðvar þar niðr hjá Skalla-Grími; var siðan aptr lokinn haugrinn, ok var eigi fyrr lokit en um dagsetrs skeið. Eptir þat reið Egill heim til Borgar, ok er hann kom heim, þá gekk hann þegar til lokrekkju þeirar, er hann var vanr at sofa í; hann lagðisk niðr ok skaut fyrir loku; engi þorði at krefja hann máls.

En svá er sagt, þá er þeir settu Bǫðvar niðr, at Egill var búinn: hosan var strengð fast at beini; hann haði fustanskyrtil rauðan, þrǫngvan upphlutinn ok láz at siðu; en þat eg sǫgn manna, at hann þrútnaði svá, at kyrtillinn refnaði af honum ok svá hosunar.

En eptir um daginn lét Egill ekki upp lokrekkjuna; hann hafði þá ok engan mat né drykk; lá hann þar þann dag ok nóttina eptir; engi maðr þoraði at mæla við hann.

---

they were ready to put out, high tide was in the afternoon, and since they had to wait for it they did not put out until late in the evening. A wild south-westerly gale got up, against the current of the tide, and the sea grew very rough in the fjord, as often happens. In the end their ship sank beneath them, and they were all lost at sea. The next day the bodies were washed up. Bǫðvarr's body came ashore at Einarsnes, and some of the others further south where the ship drifted to land, too; it was found washed ashore at Reykjarhamar.

Egill heard the news that day and rode off immediately to search for the bodies. He found Bǫðvarr's body, picked it up and put it across his knees, then rode with it out to Digranes to Skalla-Grímr's burial-mound. He opened the mound and laid Bǫðvarr inside by Skalla-Grímr's side. The mound was closed again, which took until sunset. After that, Egill rode back to Borg, and when he got home he went straight to his normal sleeping place in his bed-closet, lay down and locked the door. No one dared to ask to speak to him.

It is said that when Bǫðvarr was buried, Egill was wearing tight-fitting hose and a tight red fustian tunic laced at the sides. People say that he became so swollen that his tunic and hose burst off his body.

Later that day Egill kept his bed-closet locked, and took neither food nor drink. He lay there that day, and the following night. No one dared speak to him. On the third day, when it was daylight, Ásgerðr sent someone off on horseback. He galloped off westward to Hjarðarholt and when he arrived in mid-afternoon he told Þorgerðr the whole story. He also gave her a message from Ásgerðr asking her to come to Borg as quickly as possible.

En inn þriðja morgin, þegar er lýsti, þá lét Ásgerðr skjóta hesti undir mann (reið sá sem ákafligast vestr í Hjarðarholt), ok lét segja Þorgerði þessi tíðendi ǫll saman, ok var þat um nónskeið, er hann kom þar. Hann sagði ok þat með, at Ásgerðr hafði sent henni orð at koma sem fyrst syðr til Borgar.

Þorgerðr lét þegar sǫðla sér hest, ok fylgðu henni tveir menn; riðu þau um kveldit ok nóttina, til þess er þau kómu til Borgar; gekk Þorgerðr þegar inn í eldahús. Ásgerðr heilsaði henni ok spurði, hvárt þau hefði náttverð etit.

Þergerðr segir hátt, 'Engan hefi ek náttverð haft, ok engan mun ek, fyrr en at Freyju; kann ek mér eigi betri ráð en faðir minn; vil ek ekki lifa eptir fǫður minn ok bróður.'

Hon gekk at lokunni ok kallaði, 'Faðir, lúk upp hurðinni, vil ek, at vit farim eina leið bæði.'

Egill spretti frá lokunni; gekk Þorgerðr upp í hvílugólfit ok lét loku fyrir hurðina; lagðisk hon niðr í aðra rekkju, er þar var.

Þá mælti Egill, 'Vel gerðir þú, dóttir, er þú vill fylgja feðr þínum; mikla ást hefir þú sýnt við mik. Hver ván er, at ek muna lifa vilja við harm þenna?'

Síðan þǫgðu þau um hríð.

'Hvat er nú, dóttir, tyggr þú nú nǫkkut?'

'Tygg ek sǫl,' segir hon, 'því at ek ætla, at mér muni þá verra en áðr; ætla ek ella, at ek muna of lengi lifa.'

'Er þat illt manni?' segir Egill.

'Allillt,' segir hon, 'villtu eta?'

'Hvat man varða,' segir hann.

En stundu síðar kallaði hon ok bað gefa sér drekka; síðan var henni gefit vatn at drekka.

Þorgerðr had a horse saddled at once and set off with two other people. They rode that evening and into the night until they reached Borg. Þorgerðr went straight into the fire-room. Ásgerðr greeted her and asked whether they had eaten their evening meal.

Þorgerðr replied in a loud voice, 'I have had no evening meal, nor shall I do so until I go to join Freyja. I know no better course of action than my father's. I do not want to live after my father and brother are dead.'

She went to the door to Egill's bed-closet and called out, 'Father, open the door, I want both of us to go the same way.'

Egill unfastened the door. Þorgerðr walked into the bed-closet and closed the door again. Then she lay down in another bed that was there. Then Egill said, 'You do well, my daughter, in wanting to follow your father. You have shown great love for me. How can I be expected to want to live with such great sorrow?'

Then they were silent for a while.

Then Egill said, 'What are you doing, my daughter? Are you chewing something?'

'I'm chewing sea-weed,' she replied, 'because I think it will make me feel worse. Otherwise I expect I shall live too long.'

'Is it very bad for you?' asked Egill.

'Terrible,' said Þorgerðr, 'Do you want some?'

'What difference does it make?' he said.

A little later she called out for something to drink, and she was brought some water.

Þá mælti Egill, 'Slíkt gerir at, er sǫlin etr, þyrstir æ þess at meir.'

'Villtu drekka, faðir?' segir hon. Hann tók við ok svalg stórum, ok var þat í dýrshorni. Þá mælti Þorgerðr, 'Nú eru vit vélt; þetta er mjólk.'

Þá beit Egill skarð ór horninu, allt þat er tennr tóku, ok kastaði horninu síðan.

Þá mælti Þorgerðr, 'Hvat skulu vit nú til ráds taka? Lokit er nú þessi ætlan. Nú vilda ek, faðir, at vir lengðim líf okkart, svá at þú mættir yrkja erfikvæði eptir Bǫðvar, en ek mun rísta á kefli, en síðan deyju vit, ef okkr sýnisk. Seint ætla ek Þórstein son þinn yrkja kvæðit eptir Bǫðvar, en þat hlýðir eigi, at hann sé eigi erfðr, því at eigi æla ek okkr sitja at drykkjunni þeiri, at hann er erfðr.'

Egill segir, at þat var þá óvænt, at hann myndi þá yrkja mega, þótt hann leitaði við, 'en freista má ek þess,' segir hann. Egill hafði þá átt son, er Gunnarr hét, ok hafði sá ok andazk litlu áðr. Ok er þetta upphaf kvæðis:

Mjǫk erum tregt tungu at hrœra
eða loptvætt ljoðpundara;
esa nú vænligt of Viðurs þýfi
né hǫgdrœgt ór hugar fylgsni.
[*etc.*; for the whole poem,
see **Poems on the Meaning of Life**]

Then Egill said, 'That happens if you eat sea-weed, it makes you even thirstier.'

'Would you like a drink, father?' she asked. She passed him the animal horn and he took a great draught. Then Þorgerðr said, 'We've been tricked. This is milk.'

Egill bit a lump from the horn, as much as he could get his teeth into, then threw the horn away. Then Þorgerðr said, 'What shall we do now? Our plan has failed. Now I want us to stay alive, father, long enough for you to compose a poem in Bǫðvarr's memory and I shall carve it on to a rune stick. Then we can die if we want to. I doubt if your son Þorsteinn would ever compose a poem for Bǫðvarr, and it is not right if his memory is not honoured, because I don't suspect that we'll be sitting there at the feast when it is.'

Egill said it was unlikely that he would be able to compose a poem even if he tried. 'But I shall attempt it,' he said.

Another son of Egill's, named Gunnarr, had died shortly before. So Egill composed this poem:

Hugely hard is it for me to stir my tongue,
The air-lift of the weigher of songs;
Not to be hoped for now is Wutherer's theft,
Not easily drawn from the hideout of mind. [*etc.*]

The Saga of the People of Laxdale

Laxdœla saga

c. 1245

✳

This is one of the great family sagas, covering eight generations and over 150 years, from the 880s to *c.* 1060. The story begins with the Norwegian chieftain Ketill *flatnefr* 'Flat-Nose' and tells us of his migration to Ireland in the reign of the oppressor King Haraldr *hárfagri* 'Finehair', and then the settlement of his three children, Bjǫrn, Helgi and Unnr, in Iceland. It is his daughter Unnr, in particular, on whom the author dwells. Unnr *in djúpúðga* 'the Deep-Minded' is an imposing matriarch, one of the original settlers of Iceland. She leaves Norway (in around 890) with her father, the powerful and well-born lord Ketill *flatnefr* 'Flat-Nose', son of Bjǫrn Buna, when Haraldr Finehair is making life difficult for them in Norway. She settles first in Scotland with her father. Her son, Þórsteinn the Red, becomes ruler of half of the Scottish kingdom, but is then killed at Caithness. Ketill has died by now so Unnr has a cargo ship built secretly in the forest and sets off for Iceland, taking with her many notable people of good family and a number of slaves. In a remarkable genealogy en route, it transpires that Unnr fixes marriages for her grand-daughters that establish the ruling dynasties of the Orkney and the Faroe Islands. Having arrived in Iceland (in around 915), she lays claim to a large area of Breiðafjǫrðr, in the west, which becomes the setting for many later sagas.

Unnr herself settles in the *Laxaárdalr* 'salmon river valley' from which the saga takes its name. This is a district not far from Hvammr, whence Snorri Sturluson's family came, and it has been suggested that the saga was written by a member of his family, possibly his nephew Óláfr Þórðarson *hvítaskáld* 'White [viz. "blond"] Versifier' (died 1259), although there are equally strong reasons for believing that the author was a woman. There is an unusual preoccupation with fashion, particularly rich female garments, while the main events of the saga, the unfolding feud between Unnr's descendants and those of Bjǫrn, her brother, focus on another woman, Guðrún Ósvífrsdóttir. It is with Guðrún that the saga really ends. Her four husbands probably command less of her love than Kjartan Óláfsson, the curly-haired quarter-Irish grandson of Egill Skalla-Grímsson (q.v.), but Kjartan fails to marry her. Guðrún is said to be the most beautiful and intelligent woman in Iceland; Kjartan the country's most handsome and accomplished man. While Kjartan, on a trip to Norway, is kept as a hostage by King Óláfr Tryggvason because of Iceland's reluctance to accept Christianity, his cousin and foster-brother Bolli returns to Iceland and marries Guðrún. This marriage comes about almost against her will, but she consents to it because Bolli tells her that Kjartan is spending too much time with Ingibjǫrg, the king's beautiful sister. It is both the crux and tragedy of *Laxdœla saga* that Kjartan fails to marry Guðrún. Returning to Iceland after their marriage, he marries another woman, Hrefna, then treats Guðrún's family with such bitterness that in due course he drives them all to have him killed. In the text presented here, ch. 49, Kjartan is ambushed by Guðrún's brothers and their friends, the sons of another redoubtable woman named Þorhalla. Somehow Bolli is forced to join this combat and, equally reluctantly, to kill Kjartan. When Bolli reports the killing to Guðrún, her enigmatic reply is justly famous in the literature and a signal that the tale's teller has got his story from Old Norse heroic poetry, from the tale of Brynhildr's jealous slaying of Sigurðr through her husband and his brothers. The scene is especially poignant, as we have been led to believe that Kjartan and Guðrún had been ideally matched.

The text used here is derived from Einar Ólafur Sveinsson, whose text is based on the vellum Möðruvallabók codex written in *c.* 1350. The saga has long been popular in English translation. As well as Loren Auerbach's (unpublished by Virago) translation of 1990, which highlights the traits of a suggested female authorship, there have been at least six since 1899: Muriel Press, 1899; Robert Proctor, 1903; Thorstein Veblen, 1925; A. Margaret Argent, 1964; Magnús Magnússon and Hermann Pálsson, 1969; and Keneva Kunz, 1997.

Conroy, P., and T. C. S. Langen, '*Laxdœla saga*: theme and structure', *Arkiv för nordisk filologi* 100 (1988), 118–41

Dronke, U., 'Narrative insight in *Laxdœla saga*', in *J. R. R. Tolkien: Scholar and Storyteller: Essays in Memoriam*, ed. M. Salu and R. T. Farrell (Ithaca and London, 1979), 120–37

Einar Ólafur Sveinsson, ed., *Laxdœla saga*, ÍF 5 (Reykjavík, 1934)

Heinrichs, A., '*Annat er várt eðli*: the type of the prepatriarchal woman in Old Norse literature', in *Structure and Meaning in Old Norse Literature: New Approaches to Textual Analysis and Literary Criticism*, ed. John Lindow et al., Viking Collection 3 (Odense, 1986), 110–40

Jochens, J., 'The medieval Icelandic heroine: fact or fiction?', *Viator* 17 (1986), 35–50

North, R., *Pagan Words and Christian Meanings* (Amsterdam and Atlanta, GA, 1991), 159–64

Hǫskuldr buys Melkorka

Hǫskuldr is the son of Kolr, one of the original settlers of Iceland. He was a follower of Unnr the Deep-Minded (*djúpúðga*), the impressive matriarchal figure who makes the first land claim to a large area of Breiðafjǫrðr. He marries the good-looking, imperious and exceptionally intelligent Jórunn Bjarnardóttir. In the following chapter Hǫskuldr travels to Norway where he buys a slave girl.

12. Þat varð til tíðinda um sumarit ǫndvert at konungr fór í stefnuleiðangr austr í Brenneyjar ok gerði frið fyrir land sitt, eptir því sem lǫg stóðu til, it þriðja hvert sumar; sá fundr skyldi vera lagðr hǫfðingja í milli at setja þeim málum, er konungar áttu um at dœma. Þat þótti skemmtanarfǫr at sœkja þann fund, því at þangat kómu menn nær af ǫllum lǫndum þeim er vér hǫfum

---

12. It so happened early the following summer that the king went on a navel expedition east to the Brenn Islands for a royal assembly which, according to the law, had to be held every third summer to ensure continuing peace in the realm. These meetings were ordered by the northern kings to deal with matters of mutual concern. They were considered festive occasions and people flocked to them from almost every known country.

tíðindi af. Hǫskuldr setti fram skip sitt; vildi hann ok sœkja fund þenna, því at hann hafði eigi fundit konung á þeim vetri. Þangat var ok kaupstefnu at sœkja. Fundr þessi var allfjǫlmennr; þar var skemmtan mikil, drykkjur ok leikar ok alls kyns gleði; ekki varð þar til stórtíðenda. Marga hitti Hǫskuldr þar frændr sína, þá sem í Danmǫrku váru.

Ok einn dag, er Hǫskuldr gekk at skemmta sér með nǫkkura men, sá hann tjald eitt skrautligt fjarri ǫðrum búðum. Hǫskuldr gekk þangat ok í tjaldit, ok sat þar maðr fyrir í guðvefjarklæðum ok hafði gerzkan hatt á hǫfði. Hǫskuldr spurði þann mann at nafni, hann nefndisk Gilli, 'en þá kannask margir við, ef heyra kenningarnafn mitt; ek em kallaðr Gilli inn gerzki.'

Hǫskuldr kvazk opt hafa heyrt hans getit; kallaði hann þeirra manna auðgastan sem verit hǫfðu í kaupmannalǫgum.

Þá mælti Hǫskuldr, 'Þú munt hafa þá hluti at selja oss, er vér viljum kaupa.' Gilli spyrr, hvat þeir vilja kaupa fǫrunautar.

Hǫskuldr segir, at hann vill kaupa ambátt nǫkkura, 'ef þú hefir at selja.' Gilli svarar, 'Þar þykkizk þér leita mér meinfanga um þetta, er þér falið þá hluti, er þér ætlið mik eigi til hafa, en þat er þó eigi ráðit, hvárt svá ber til.'

Hǫskuldr sá, at um þvera búðina var fortjald. Þá lypti Gilli tjaldinu, ok sá Hǫskuldr, at tólf konur sátu fyrir innan tjaldit. Þá mælti Gilli, at Hǫskuldr skyldi þangat ganga ok líta á, ef hann vildi nǫkkura kaupa af þessum konum; Hǫskuldr gerir svá.

Þær sátu allar saman um þvera búðina. Hǫskuldr hyggr at vandliga at konum þessum; hann sá, at kona sat út við tjaldskǫrina; sú var illa klædd. Hǫskuldi leizk konan fríð sýnum, ef nǫkkut mátti á sjá.

Hǫskuldr launched his ship intending to go to the assembly. He had not been to see the king that winter. It was also an important trading market.

There were large crowds at the assembly that year and there was a lot of celebration, with drinking and games and every other form of entertainment. Nothing very important took place. Hǫskuldr met many of his kinsmen there who were in Denmark.

Then one day when Hǫskuldr was going out to enjoy himself with some of his companions, he saw a brightly-decorated tent standing apart from the other booths. He went over to it and entered. There he found a man dressed in costly finery and wearing a Russian hat. Hǫskuldr asked him his name. He said it was Gilli, 'and most people realise who I am when they hear my nickname: I'm called Gilli the Russian.'

Hǫskuldr said he had often heard him spoken of as he was said to be the richest man in the merchant's guild. Then Hǫskuldr said, 'So no doubt you can sell to us whatever we wish to buy.'

Gilli asked what he was looking to buy.

Hǫskuldr said he wanted to buy a slave-girl , 'if you have one for sale.'

Gilli answered, 'You're not trying to embarrass me by asking for something you don't think I have, are you? I wouldn't be too sure of that.'

Hǫskuldr could see a curtain drawn across the booth. Gilli lifted it up, and Hǫskuldr could see that there were twelve women sitting behind it. Gilli asked him to go through and see if he wanted to buy any of them. Hǫskuldr did so.

The women were sitting in a row across the booth. He inspected them carefully. He was struck by the one sitting right at the edge of the tent. She was badly dressed but Hǫskuldr thought she was beautiful, from what he could see.

Þá mælti Hǫskuldr, 'Hversu dýr skal sjá kona, ef ek vil kaupa?' Gilli svarar, 'Þú skalt reiða fyrir hana þrjár merkr silfrs.'

'Svá virði ek,' segir Hǫskuldr, 'sem þú munir þessa ambátt gera heldr dýrlagða því at þetta er þriggja verð.'

Þá svarar Gilli, 'Rétt segir þú þat, at ek met hana dýrra en aðrar; kjós nú einhverja af þessum ellefu ok gjalt þar fyrir mǫrk silfrs, en þessi sé eptir í minni eigu.'

Hǫskuldr segir, 'Vita mun ek fyrst, hversu mikit silfr er í sjóð þeim, er ek hefi á belti mér,' biðr Gilla taka vágina, en hann leitar at sjóðnum.

Þá mælti Gilli, 'Þetta mál skal fara óvélt af minni hendi, því at á er ljóðr mikill um ráð konunnar; vil ek, at þú vitir þat, Hǫskuldr, áðr vit sláum kaupi þessu.'

Hǫskuldr spyrr, hvat þat væri. Gilli svarar, 'Kona þessi er ómála; hefi ek marga vega leitat máls við hana, ok hefi ek aldrei fengit orð af henna; er þat at vísu mín ætlan, at þessi kona kunni eigi at mæla.'

Þá segir Hǫskuldr, 'Lát fram reizluna ok sjám, hvat vegi sjóðr sá, er ek hefi hér.'

Gilli gerir svá, reiða nú silfrit ok váru þat þrjár merkr vegnar. Þá mælti Hǫskuldr, 'Svá hefir nú til tekizk, at þetta mun verða kaup okkart; tak þú fé þetta til þín, en ek mun taka við konu þessi; kalla ek, at þú hafir drengiliga af máli þessu haft, því at vísu vildir þú mik eigi falsa í þessu.'

Síðan gekk Hǫskuldr heim til búðar sinnar. Þat sama kveld rekkði Hǫskuldr hjá henni. En um morguninn eptir, er menn fóru í klæði sín, mælti Hǫskuldr, 'Lítt sér stórlæti á klæðabúnaði þeim, er Gilli inn auðgi hefir þér fengit; er þat ok satt, at honum var meiri raun at klæða tólf en mér eina.'

Then Hǫskuldr said, 'How much would that woman cost, if I wanted to buy her?'

Gilli answered, 'She would cost you three marks of silver.'

'It seems to me,' said Hǫskuldr, 'that that's a high price for a slave girl. That's three times the normal price.'

Gilli answered, 'That's quite true, but I value her more highly than the others; you can buy any one of the other eleven for one mark of silver and leave this one with me.'

Hǫskuldr said, 'Let me first see how much silver I have in this purse at my belt.' He asked Gilli to get the scales while he looked in the purse.

Then Gilli said, 'I want to be fair with you about this. The woman has one major defect that I want you to know about before we finish the deal.' Hǫskuldr asked what it was. Gilli answered, 'The woman is mute. I've tried every way of trying to get her to speak, but I've never got a word out of her. I'm certain that she can't speak.'

Then Hǫskuldr said, 'Get your scales and we'll see how much there is in my purse.'

Gilli did so; and when they weighed the silver it came to three marks exactly.

Then Hǫskuldr said, 'It seems we have a deal on our hands after all. Here's the money, and I'll take the woman. You have dealt fairly over this, for you certainly didn't try to cheat me.'

Then Hǫskuldr went back home to his booth. That night Hǫskuldr slept with the woman. The next morning when they were getting dressed, Hǫskuldr said, 'Gilli the Wealthy wasn't very generous with the clothes he gave you to wear, but I suppose it was harder for him to clothe twelve than for me to clothe only one.'

Síðan lauk Hǫskuldr upp kistu eina ok tók upp góð kvenmannsklæði ok seldi henna; var þat ok allra manna mál, at henni semði góð klæði.

En er hǫfðingjar hǫfðu þar mælt þeim málum, sem þá stóðu lǫg til, var slitit fundi þessum. Síðan gekk Hǫskuldr á fund Hákonar konungs ok kvaddi hann virðuliga, sem skapligt var. Konungr sá við honum ok mælti, 'Tekit mundu vér hafa kveðju þinni, Hǫskuldr, þóttú hefðir nǫkkuru fyrr oss fagnat, ok svá skal enn vera.'

Then Hǫskuldr opened one of his chests and took some fine clothing out and gave it to her. Everyone remarked that the fine clothing suited her very well.

Later, when the rulers had finished discussing the matters that the law required, the assembly was brought to an end. Then Hǫskuldr went to find King Hákon and greet him respectfully, which was his due. The king looked at him and said, 'We would have welcomed your greeting even if it had come earlier, Hǫskuldr, but we do so now.'

The birth of Óláfr the Peacock

On her husband's return to Iceland with his timber and his slave-girl, Jórunn is understandably far from pleased. She stops him living with the young woman who, in due course, gives birth to the beautiful and promising Óláfr, nicknamed *Pái* 'peacock'. The slave woman is still thought to be deaf and dumb.

13. Eptir þetta tók konungr með allri blíðu Hǫskuldi ok bað hann ganga á sitt skip, 'ok ver með oss, meðan þú vill í Nóregi vera.'

Hǫskuldr svarar, 'Hafið þǫkk fyrir boð yðvart, en nú á ek þetta sumar mart at starfa; hefir þat mjǫk til haldit, er ek hefi svá lengi dvali at sœkja yðvarn fund, at ek ætlaða að afla mér húsaviðar.'

Konungr bað hann halda skipinu til Víkrinnar. Hǫskuldr dvalðisk með konungi um hríð; konungr fékk honum húsavið ok lét ferma skipit.

Þá mælti konungr til Hǫskulds, 'Eigi skal dvelja þik hér með oss lengr en þér líkar, en þó þykkir oss vandfengit manns í stað þitt.'

---

13. After that the king received Hǫskuldr most cordially and invited him on to his ship, 'and stay with us as long as you are in Norway'.

Hǫskuldr answered, 'Thank you for your invitation but I have much to do this summer. The reason for my long delay in coming to greet you was that I was trying to obtain some building-timber.'

The king asked him to bring his ship to Vík. Hǫskuldr spent some time there as the king's man. The king gave him building timber and had it loaded on to his ship.

Then the king spoke to Hǫskuldr, 'I shall not detain you here any longer than you wish, but I think it will be difficult to find someone to take your place.'

Síðan leiddi konungr Hǫskuld til skips ok mælti, 'At sómamanni hefi ek þik reyndan, ok nær er þat minni ætlan, at þú siglir nú it síðasta sinn af Nóregi, svá at ek sjá hér yfirmaðr.'

Konungr dró gullhring af hendi sér, þann er vá mǫrk, ok gaf Hǫskuldi, ok sverð gaf hann honum annan grip, þat er til kom hálf mǫrk gulls. Hǫskuldr þakkaði konungi gjafarnar ok þann allan soma, er hann hafði fram lagit.

Síðan stígr Hǫskuldr á skip sitt ok siglir til hafs. Þeim byrjaði vel ok kómu at fyrir sunnan land; sigldu síðan vestr fyrir Reykjanes ok svá fyrir Snæfellsnes ok inn í Breiðafjǫrð. Hǫskuldr lenti í Laxárósi; lætr þar bera farm af skipi sínu, en setja upp skipit fyrir innan Laxá, ok gerir þar hróf at, ok sér þar tóptina, sem hann lét gera hrófit; þar tjaldaði hann búðir, ok er þat kallaðr Búðardalr.

Síðan lét Hǫskuldr flytja heim viðinn, ok var þat hœgt, því at eigi var lǫng leið; ríðr Hǫskuldr eptir þat heim við nǫkkura menn ok fær viðtǫkur góðar, sem ván er; þar hafði ok fé vel haldizk síðan. Jórunn spyrr, hvat kona þat væri, er í fǫr var með honum.

Hǫskuldr svarar, 'Svá mun þér þykkja, sem ek svara þér skœtingu; ek veit eigi nafn hennar.'

Jórunn mælti, 'Þat mun tveimr skipta, at sá kvittr mun login, er fyrir mik er kominn, eða þú munt hafa talat við hana jafnmart sem spurt hafa hana at nafni.'

Hǫskuldr kvazk þess eigi þræta mundu ok segir henni it sanna ok bað þá þessi konu virkða ok kvað þat nær sínu skapi, at hon væri heima þar at vistafari.

The king then accompanied Hǫskuldr to his ship and said 'You have proved to be the most honourable of men, and now I have a feeling that this is the last time you will sail from Norway while I am ruler here.'

The king drew a gold arm-ring, which weighed one mark, from his arm and gave it to Hǫskuldr, and also to the further gift of a sword valued at half a mark of gold. Hǫskuldr thanked the king for the gifts and all the honour he had shown him. Then Hǫskuldr boarded his ship and put out to sea.

They had favourable winds and made land in the south. They then sailed west around Reykjanes, then around Snæfellsness and into Breiðafjǫrd. Hǫskuldr landed at the mouth of the Lax river and had the cargo unloaded there. He had the ship laid up further up the river, where he built a boat-shed, the remains of which are still visible. He built some booths there, so the place is called Búðardalr.

He then had the timber taken home which was an easy task as it wasn't far. He then rode home with a few companions and was given a warm welcome, as could be expected. His estate had prospered in his absence. Jórunn asked who the woman with him was.

Hǫskuldr answered, 'You'll probably think I'm kidding you, but I don't know her name.'

Jórunn said, 'Either the stories I have been hearing are lies, or else you will have talked to her long enough to ask her for her name.'

Hǫskuldr said he would not try to deny it and told her the whole story. He asked that the woman be well treated, and said he wanted her to stay there at home with them.

Jórunn mælti, 'Eigi mun ek deila við frillu þína, þá er þú hefir flutt af Nóregi, þótt hon kynni góðar návistir, en nú þykki mér þat allra sýnst, ef hon er bæði dauf ok mállaus.'

Hǫskuldr svaf hjá húsfreyju sinni hverja nótt, síðan hann kom heim, en hann var fár við frilluna. Ǫllum mǫnnum var auðsætt stórmennsku-mót á henni ok svá þat, at hon var engi afglapi.

Ok á ofanverðum vetri þeim fœddi frilla Hǫskulds sveinbarn; síðan var Hǫskuldr þangat kallaðr, ok var honum sýnt barnit; sýndisk honum sem ǫðrum, at hann þóttisk eigi sét hafa vænna barn né stórmannligra. Hǫskuldr var at spurðr, hvat sveinninn skyldi heita. Hann bað sveininn kalla Óláf, því að þá hafði Óláfr feilan andazk litlu áðr, móðurbróðir hans. Óláfur var afbragð flestra barna. Hǫskuldr lagði ást mikla við sveininn.

Um sumarit eptir mælti Jórunn, at frillan myndi upp taka verknað nǫkkurn eða fara í brott ella. Hǫskuldr bað hana vinna þeim hjónum ok gæta þar við sveins sins. En þá er sveinninn var tvævetr, þá var hann almæltr ok rann einn saman, sem fjǫgurra vetra gǫmul bǫrn.

Þá var til tíðinda einn morgun, er Hǫskuldr var genginn út at sjá um bœ sinn; veðr var got; skein sól ok var lítt á lopt komin; hann heyrði mannamál; hann gekk þangat til, sem lœkr fell fyrir túnbrekkunni; sá hann þar tvá menn ok kenndi; var þar Óláfr, sonr hans, ok móðir hans; fær hann þá skilit, at hon var eigi mállaus, því að hon talaði þá mart við sveininn. Síðan gekk Hǫskuldr at þeim ok spyrr hana að nafni ok kvað henni ekki mundu stoða at dyljask lengr.

Hon kvað svá vera skyldu; setjask þau niðr í túnbrekkuna.

Jórunn said, 'I'm not going to argue with this slave-woman you've brought back from Norway, who doesn't know how her betters behave, and who is also both deaf and dumb.'

Hǫskuldr slept with his wife every night after his return and had nothing to do with the slave-girl. Everyone noticed an air of distinction about her and realised that she was no fool.

Late that winter Hǫskuldr's slave-girl gave birth to a boy. Hǫskuldr was called and shown the child, and it seemed to him as it did to others, that he had never seen a more handsome or distinguished looking child. Hǫskuldr was asked what the child should be called. He wanted the name to be Óláfr, for his uncle Óláfr Feilan had died a short while before. Óláfr was an exceptional child, and Hǫskuldr became very fond of the boy.

Next summer Jórunn said that the slave-girl would have to do her share of the farm work, or leave. Hǫskuldr told the woman that she was to wait upon himself and Jórunn and look after her child as well. By the time the boy was two years old he could speak perfectly and was running around like a four year old.

It happened one morning that Hǫskuldr was outdoors seeing to his farm. It was a fine day, and the dawn sun was shining. He heard the sound of voices. He went over to the stream at the foot of the sloping homefield. There he saw two people he knew well: it was his son Óláfr and the boy's mother. He realised then that she was not mute at all, for she was chatting busily to the child. Hǫskuldr now went over to them and asked her what her name was, and told her there was no point in concealing it any longer. She agreed and they sat down on the slope of the homefield.

Then she said, 'If you want to know my name, it is Melkorka.'

Síðan mælti hon, 'Ef þú vill nafn mitt vita, þá heiti ek Melkorka.'

Hǫskuldr bað hana þá segja lengra ætt sína.

Hon svarar, '**Mýrkjartan** heitir faðir minn; hann er konungr á Írlandi. Ek var þaðan hertekin fimmtán vetra gǫmul.'

Hǫskuldr kvað hana helzti lengi hafa þagat yfir svá góðri ætt.

Síðan gekk Hǫskuldr inn ok sagði Jórunni, hvat til nýlundu hafði gǫrzk í ferð hans. Jórunn kvazkt eigi vita, hvat hon segði satt; kvað sér ekki um kynjamenn alla, ok skilja þau þessa rœðu; var Jórunn hvergi betr við hana en áðr, en Hǫskuldr nǫkkuru fleiri.

Ok litlu síðar er Jórunn gekk að sofa, togaði Melkorka af henni ok lagði skóklæðin á gólfit. Jórunn tók sokkana ok keyrði um hǫfuð henni. Melkorka reiddisk ok setti hnefann á nasar henna, svá at blóð varð laust. Hǫskuldr kom at ok skildi þær.

Eptir þat lét hann Melkorku í brott fara ok fékk henni þar bústað uppi í Laxárdal; þar heitir síðan á Melkorkustǫðum; þar er nú auðn; þat er fyrir sunnan Laxá. Setr Melkorka þar bú saman; fær Hǫskuldr þar til bús allt þat, er hafa þurfti, ok fór Óláfr, sonr þeirra, með henni. Brátt sér þat á Óláfi, er hann óx upp, at hann myndi verða mikit afbragð annarra manna fyrir vænleiks sakir ok kurteisi.

Hǫskuldr asked her to tell him more about her family.

She answered, 'My father is called **Mýrkjartan**; he is a king in Ireland. I was taken captive there when I was fifteen.'

Hǫskuldr said she had concealed such a noble lineage for too long.

Then Hǫskuldr went back into the house and told Jórunn what he had learned while he was out. Jórunn said there was no way of knowing if the woman was telling the truth, and she had little use for people of dubious origin. They discussed it no further. Jórunn was no better to her than before but Hǫskuldr was more friendly.

A little later, when Jórunn was going to bed, Melkorka helped her remove her socks and shoes and laid them on the floor. Jórunn picked up the socks and started beating her about the head with them. Melkorka became angry and punched her on the nose, causing it to bleed. Hǫskuldr came in and separated them.

After that he had Melkorka move to another farm further up Laxárdal, which has been called Melkorkustaðir ever since. It is now deserted. It is on the south shore of the river. Melkorka made her home there. Hǫskuldr supplied everything that she needed there, and their son Óláfr went with her.

As Óláfr grew up it was quickly apparent that he would be exceptionally handsome and courteous.

Mýrkjartan, Irish *Muircheartach*. There was no High King of Ireland called Muircheartach during the period. There were, however, several petty kings and princes of that name. Attempts to identify this Mýrkjartan have proved inconclusive.

Hjarðarholt and *Eulogy on the House*

The sword *Fótbítr* 'Leg-Biter' plays a significant role in the saga. It enters the family as a prized possession of the Norwegian Geirmundr the Noisy, who marries Óláfr the Peacock's daughter Þuríðr. At their wedding feast at Hjarðarholt, in *c.* 995, Úlfr Uggason performs his poem *Húsdrápa* (for a text and translation, see **Gods of the Vikings**). Later the marriage fails, and Geirmundr tries to flee the country, but Þuríðr boards his ship, takes Leg-Biter, and replaces it with their infant daughter Gróa. Geirmundr begs for the sword but he is refused. He then makes the curse that the sword will be responsible for the death of someone the family would least like to lose.

The heroic death is a familiar motif in the saga literature. Other heroes, like Gunnarr Hámundarson in *Brennu-Njáls saga*, and Gísli Súrsson, in *Gísla saga Súrssonar*, have memorably heroic last stands.

29. Þat er sagt eitt vár, at Óláfr lýsti því fyrir Þorgerði, at hann ætlar útan, 'vil ek, at þú varðveitir bú okkart ok bǫrn.'

Þorgerðr kvað sér lítit vera um þat, en Óláfr kvazkt ráða mundu. Hann kaupir skip, er uppi stóð vestr í Vaðli.

Óláfr fór utan um sumarit og kemr skipi sínu við Hǫrðaland. Þar bjó sá maðr skammt á land upp, er hét Geirmundr gnýr, ríkr maðr ok auðigr ok víkingr mikill; ódældarmaðr var hann og hafði nú sezk um kyrrt ok var hirðmaðr Hákonar jarls ins ríka. Geirmundr ferr til skips ok kannask brátt við Óláf, því at hann hafði heyrt hans getit; Geirmundr býðr Óláfi til sín með svá marga menn sem hann vildi; það þiggr Óláfr ok ferr til vistar með sétta mann. Hásetar Óláfs vistask þar um Hǫrðaland. Geirmundr veitir Óláfi vel. Þar var bœr risuligr ok mart manna; var þar gleði mikil um veturinn.

En er á leið vetrinn, sagði Óláfr Geirmundi skyn á um ørindi sín, at hann vill afla sér húsaviðar, kvazk þykkja mikit undir, at hann fengi gott viðaval.

---

29. It is said that one spring Óláfr told Þorgerðr that he intended to travel abroad, 'and I want you to look after the farm and our children while I'm away'. Þorgeðr said she was not in favour of the idea but Óláfr insisted. He bought a ship which was beached in the west at Vadil.

He sailed abroad that summer and made land in Hordaland. A short distance from the shore lived a man called Geirmundr the Noisy. He was a rich and powerful man and a great Viking. He was an unruly man, but had now settled down and was a retainer of earl Hákonar the Powerful.

Geirmundr went down to the ship and realised who Óláfr was, having heard stories about him. He invited Óláfr to stay with him with as many of his men as he wished. Óláfr accepted the offer and went there with five of his men; the rest of the crew got lodgings elsewhere in Hordaland. Geirmundr treated Óláfr well. He had a large farmhouse and kept a large household. There was plenty of entertainment in the winter.

At the end of winter Óláfr told Geirmundr that the purpose of his voyage was to get building timber and it was of great importance that the timber was of good quality.

Geirmundr svarar, 'Hákon jarl á bezta mǫrk, ok veit ek víst, ef þú kemr á hans fund, at þér mun sú innan handar, því að jarl fagnar vel þeim mǫnnum, er eigi eru jafnvel menntir sem þú, Óláfr, ef hann sœkja heim.'

Um várit byrjar Óláfr ferð sína á fund Hákonar jarls; tók jarl við honum ágæta vel ok bauð Óláfi með sér at vera svá lengi sem hann vildi.

Óláfr segir jarli, hversu af stózk um ferð hans, 'vil ek þess beiða yðr, herra, at þér létið oss heimila mǫrk yðra at hǫggva húsavið.'

Jarl svarar, 'Ósparat skal þat, þóttú fermir skip þitt af þeim viði, er vér munum gefa þér, því at vér hyggjum, at oss sœki eigi heim hversdagliga slíkir menn af Íslandi.'

En at skilnaði gaf jarl honum øxi gullrekna, ok var það in mesta gersemi. Skilðusk síðan með inum mesta kærleik.

Geirmundr skipar jarðir sínar á laun ok ætlar út til Íslands um sumarit á skipi Óláfs; leynt hefir hann þessu alla menn. Eigi vissi Óláfr, fyrr en Geirmundr flutti fé sitt til skips Óláfs, ok var þa mikill auðr.

Óláfr mælti, 'Eigi myndir þú fara á mínu skipi, ef ek hefða fyrr vitat, því at vera ætla ek þá munu nǫkkura á Íslandi, at betr gegndi, at þik sæi aldri; en nú er þú ert hér kominn við svá mikit fé, þá nenni ek eigi at reka þik aptr sem búrakka.'

Geirmundr segir, 'Eigi skal aptr setjask, þóttú sér heldr stórorðr, því at ek ætla at fá yðvarr farþegi.'

Geirmundr answered, 'Earl Hákon owns the best forests, and I know for certain that if you went to see him he would see you right. The earl gives a good welcome to men who are less well-accomplished than you, Óláfr.'

In the spring Óláfr set out to visit Earl Hákon. He was warmly welcomed by the earl, who invited him to to stay with him as long as he wished. Óláfr told the earl the purpose of his voyage, 'I would like your permission, my lord, to cut building timber in your forests.'

The earl answered, 'It would be an honour for me to fill your ship with timber from the forest, and you must accept it as a gift. It is not every day that we receive guests like you from Iceland.'

When they parted the earl gave him an axe inlaid with gold, a valuable treasure, and they parted the best of friends.

In the meantime Geirmundr the Noisy had secretly put others in charge in his lands as he planned to go to Iceland that summer on Óláfr's ship; but he let no one know about it. Óláfr knew nothing about it until Geirmundr had loaded all his wealth, which was no small sum, on to the ship.

Óláfr said, 'You wouldn't be travelling on my ship if I had known of this before. I think there are people in Iceland who would be better off if they never laid eyes on you. But since you're already here with so much wealth, I can hardly drive you away like some stray dog.'

Geirmundr answered, 'I'm not about to turn back despite your harsh words. I have every intention of paying for my passage.'

Stíga þeir Óláfr á skip ok sigla í haf. Þeim byrjaði vel, ok tóku Breiðafjǫrð; bera nú bryggjur á land í Laxárósi. Lætr Óláfr bera viðu af skipi ok setr upp skipit í hróf þat, er faðir hans hafði gera látit. Ólafur bauð Geirmundi til vistar með sér.

Þat sumar lét Óláfr gera eldhús í Hjarðarholti, meira ok betra en menn hefðu fyrr sét. Váru þar markaðar ágætligar sǫgur á þilviðinum ok svá á ræfrinu; var þat svá vel smíðat, að þá þótti miklu skrautligra, er eigi váru tjǫldin uppi.

Geirmundr var fáskiptinn hversdagla, óþýðr við flesta; en hann var svá búinn jafnan, at hann hafði skarlatskyrtil rauðan ok gráfeld yztan ok bjarnskinnshúfu á hǫfði, sverð í hendi; þat var mikit vápn ok gott, tannhjǫlt at; ekki var þar borit silfr á, en brandrinn var hvass, ok beið hvergi ryð á. Þetta sverð kallaði hann Fótbít ok lét þat aldregi hendi firr ganga.

Geirmundr hafði skamma hríð þar verit, áðr hann felldi hug til Þuríðar, dóttur Óláfs, ok vekr hann bónorð við Óláf, en hann veitti afsvǫr. Síðan berr Geirmundr fé undir Þorgerði, til þess at hann næði ráðinu. Hon tók við fénu, því at eigi var smám fram lagt.

Síðan vekr Þorgerðr þetta mál við Óláf; hon segir ok sína ætlan, at dóttir þeira muni eigi betr verða gefin, 'því at hann er garpr mikill, auðigr ok stórlátr.'

Þá svarar Óláfr, 'Eigi skal þetta gera í móti þér, heldr en annat, þótt ek væra fúsari at gipta Þuríði ǫðrum manni.'

Both he and Óláfr embarked and put out to sea. They had a good passage and made land in Breiðafjǫrd. They put out the gangway at the mouth of the Laxá river. Óláfr had the timber unloaded and hauled the ship to the boat-shed his father had built. He invited Geirmundr to stay at his farm.

That summer Óláfr had a fire-hall built at Hjarðarholt which was larger and finer than anyone had ever seen before. There were fine carvings depicting the old legends on the wainscoting and rafters. It was so well crafted that people thought the hall was more magnificent when the tapestries were not hung up.

Geirmundr was taciturn and brusque with most people. He usually went around with a scarlet tunic with a grey fur cloak about his shoulders, a bearskin hat on his head, and a sword in his hand. It was an impressive weapon: the pommel and guard were made from walrus ivory, without any silver, but the blade was sharp and there was never any rust on it. He called the sword Leg-Biter and never let it out of his sight.

Geirmundr hadn't been there for very long when he took a fancy to Óláfr's daughter Þuríðr. He put a proposal of marriage to Óláfr but was turned down. He then approached Þorgerðr and offered her money if she would support his suit. She accepted the money, which was no petty sum, and raised the issue with Óláfr.

She said that in her opinion, their daughter could not wish for a better match, 'He's a great warrior, rich and generous with his money.'

Óláfr replied, 'Have it your own way then, as you usually do, but I'd be happier if Þuriðr married somebody else.'

Þorgerðr gengr í brott ok þykkir gott orðit sitt ørindi; sagði nú svá skapa Geirmundi. Hann þakkaði henni sín tillǫg ok skǫrungsskap. Vekr nú Geirmundr bónorðit í annat sinn við Óláf, ok var þat nú auðsótt; eptir þat fastnar Geirmundr sér Þuríði, ok skal boð vera at áliðnum vetri í Hjarðarholti; þat boð var allfjǫlmennt, því at þá var algǫrt eldhúsit. Þar var at boði Úlfr Uggason ok hafði ort kvæði um Óláf Hǫskuldsson ok um sǫgur þær, er skrifaðar váru á eldhúsinu, ok fœrði hann þar at boðinu. Þetta kvæði er kallað Húsdrápa ok er vel ort. Óláfr launaði vel kvæðit. Hann gaf ok stórgjafar ǫllu stórmenni, er hann hafði heim sótt. Þótti Óláfr vaxit hafa af þessi veizlu.

30. Ekki var mart um í samfǫrum þeirra Geirmundar ok Þuríðar; var svá af beggja þeirra hendi. Þrjá vetr var Geirmundr með Óláfi, áðr hann fýstisk í brott ok lýsti því, at Þuríðr myndi eptir vera ok svá dóttir þeirra, er Gróa hét; sú mær var þá vetrgǫmul; en fé vill Geirmundr ekki eptir leggja. Þetta líkar þeim mœðgum stórum illa ok segja til Óláfi, en Óláfr mælti þá, 'Hvat er nú Þorgerðr, er austmaðrinn eigi jafnstórlátr nú sem um haustit, þá er hann bað þik mægðarinnar?'

Kómu þær engu á leið við Óláf, því at hann var um alla hluti samningarmaðr, kvað ok mey skyldu eptir vera, þar til er hon kynni nǫkkurn farnað. En at skilnaði þeirra Geirmundar gaf Óláfr honum kaupskipit með ǫllum reiða; Geirmundur þakkar honum vel ok sagði gefit allstórmannliga. Síðan býr hann skipit ok siglir út ór Laxárósi léttan landnyrðing, ok fellr veðrit, er þeir koma út at eyjum. Hann liggr út við Øxnaey hálfan mánuð, svá at honum gefr eigi í brott.

Þorgerðr went away highly pleased with herself, and told Geirmundr how things stood. He thanked her for her help and determination. When he approached Óláfr with his proposal a second time, he received his consent. Geirmundr was then betrothed to Þuriðr and their wedding held later that winter at Hjarðarholt. The feast was attended by many guests as the fire-hall was fully built by then. One of the guests at the feast was Úlfr Uggason who had composed a poem about Óláfr Hǫskuldsson and the carved legends depicted in the fire-hall. He recited it at the feast. It is called *Húsdrápa* [*Eulogy on the House*] and is an excellent poem.

Óláfr rewarded him handsomely for the poem. He also gave fine gifts to all the important people who had attended the feast, and gained considerable prestige as a result.

30. The marriage between Geirmundr and Þuríðr was not very happy, and they were both to blame for that. Geirmundr stayed at Óláfr's farm for three years before declaring that he wanted to go abroad and leave behind Þuríðr and their daughter Gróa, who was a year old. He refused to leave any money behind for them. Þuriðr and her mother were both angry about this and complained to Óláfr.

Óláfr said, 'Why, Þorgerðr, is your easterner not so generous now as he was in the autumn he wanted to become your son-in-law?'

They got nowhere with Óláfr as he was a peaceable man and avoided trouble whenever possible. He said that in any case the child should stay there until she was old enough to take care of herself.

In parting, Óláfr gave Geirmundr the merchant ship, completely fitted out. Geirmundr thanked him warmly and said it was a most generous gift. He made the ship ready and sailed from the mouth of the Laxá River with a light north-easterly breeze; but the wind dropped as they reached the islands. The ship lay at anchor off Øxnaey for half a month, without being able to get away.

Í þenna tíma átti Óláfur heimanfǫr at annask um **reka** sína. Síðan kallar Þuríðr, dóttir hans, til sín húskarla; bað þá fara með sér. Hon hafði ok með sér meyna; tíu váru þau saman. Hon lætr setja fram ferju, er Óláfr átti. Þuríðr bað þá sigla ok róa út eptir Hvammsfirði. Ok er þau koma út at eyjum, bað hon þá skjóta báti útbyrðis, er stóð á ferjunni. Þuríðr sté á bátinn ok tveir menn aðrir, en hon bað þá gæta skips, er eptir váru, þar til er hon kœmi aptr. Hon tók meyna í faðm sér ok bað þá róa yfir strauminn, þar til er þau mætti ná skipinu. Hon greip upp nafar ór stafnlokinu ok seldi í hendr fǫrunaut sínum ǫðrum; bað hann ganga á knarrarbátinn ok bora, svá at ófœrr væri, ef þeir þyrfti skjótt til at taka.

Síðan lét hon sik flytja á land ok hafði meyna í faðmi sér; þat var í sólarupprás. Hon gengr út eptir bryggju ok svá í skipit. Allir menn váru í svefni. Hon gekk at húðfati því, er Geirmundr svaf í. Sverðit Fótbítr hekk á hnykkistafnum. Þuríðr setr nú meyna Gró í húðfatit, en greip upp Fótbít ok hafði með sér; síðan gengr hon af skipinu ok til fǫrunauta sinna. Nú tekr mærin at gráta. Við þat vaknar Geirmundr og sezk upp ok kennir barnit ok þykkisk vita, af hverjum rifjum vera mun. Hann sprettr upp ok vill þrífa sverðit ok missir, sem ván var; gengr út á borð ok sér, at þau róa frá skipinu. Geirmundr kallar á menn sína ok bað þá hlaupa í bátinn ok róa eptir þeim. Þeir gera svá, ok er þeir eru skammt komnir, þá finna þeir, at sjár kolblár fellr at þeim; snúa nú aptr til skips. Þá kallar Geirmundr á Þuríði ok bað hana aptr snúa ok fá honum sverðit Fótbít, 'en tak við mey þinni ok haf héðan með henni fé svá mikit, sem þú vill.'

During that time Óláfr had to leave the farm to look after the **driftage** on the beaches he owned. After he left Þuriðr called some of the servants and told them to accompany her. There were ten in all, including her infant daughter whom she took along. They launched Óláfr's ferry-boat and she told them to sail or row down Hvammsfjǫrd. When they reached the islands she told them to lower the dinghy which was on board. Þuriðr got into the dinghy with two of the men, and told the others to look after the ferry until she returned.

She took the child in her arms and told the men to row across the channel to Geirmundr's ship. She then took an auger out of the locker in the prow and handed it to one of the men, telling him to make his way to the ships' tow-boat and drill a hole in it so it would be useless if it were needed in a hurry. She then had herself put ashore with the baby in her arms. It was now dawn. She walked up the gangway and on to the ship. Everyone on board was asleep. She went over to the hammock where Geirmundr was sleeping. His sword, Leg-Biter, was hanging on a peg. She laid the little girl, Gróa, in the hammock, took Leg-Biter, then left the ship and went back to her companions.

The child now began to cry, and Geirmundr woke up. He sat up, recognised the child, and realised who must be behind this. Jumping to his feet he reached for sword, but could not find it, as might be expected. He went over to the gunwale and saw Þuriðr and her companions rowing away from the ship. He called to his men to jump into the ship's boat and row after them. They did so, but hadn't gone very far when they noticed the dark-blue sea pouring in. They turned back to the ship.

Geirmundr then called out to Þuriðr to come back and return his sword Leg-Biter, 'and take your daughter with you and as much money as you want'.

'**driftage**'. The *reka* currents around Iceland, like the Gulf Stream, have always been an important source of timber for building and fuel. Driftage rights were legally defined and protected.

Þuríðr segir, 'Þykki þér betra en eigi at ná sverðinu?' Geirmundr svarar, 'Mikit fé læt ek annat, áðr mér þykkir betra at missa sverðsins.' Hon mælti, 'Þá skaltu aldrei fá þat; hefir þér mart ódrengiliga farit til vár; mun nú skilja með okkur.'

Þá mælti Geirmundr, 'Ekki happ mun þér í verða at hafa með þér sverðit.' Hon kvazk til þess mundu hætta.

'Þat læt ek þá um mælt,' segir Geirmundr, 'at þetta sverð verði þeim manni at bana í yðvarri ætt, er mestr er skaði at, ok óskapligast komi við.'

Eptir þetta ferr Þuríðr heim í Hjarðarholt. Óláfr var ok þá heim kominn ok lét lítt yfir hennar tiltekju; en þó var kyrrt. Þuríðr gaf Bolla, frænda sínum, sverðit Fótbít, því at hon unni honum eigi minna en brœðrum sínum; bar Bolli þetta sverð lengi síðan. Eptir þetta byrjaði þeim Geirmundi; sigla þeir í haf ok koma við Nóreg um haustit. Þeir sigla á einni nótt í boða fyrir Staði; týnisk Geirmundr ok ǫll skipshǫfn hans; ok lýkr þar frá Geirmundi at segja.

Þuriðr said, 'How much do you want your sword back?'

Geirmundr answered, 'I'd rather lose a fortune than lose my sword.'

'Then you shall never have it back,' said Þuriðr. 'You have treated us disgracefully, and you will never see me again.'

Geirmundr then said, 'There will be no luck for you in taking that sword.'

She said she would take that risk.

'Then I lay this curse on it,' Geirmundr said, 'that this sword will bring about the death of the man in your family who will be the greatest loss and the most missed.'

After that Þuríðr returned to Hjarðarholt. Óláfr had returned home by then and was not at all pleased by what she had done, but there the matter rested.

Þuriðr gave Leg-Biter to her cousin Bolli, as she was no less fond of him than of her own brothers. Bolli wore the sword for a long time after that.

Geirmundr and his companions now got a favourable wind and sailed out to sea, reaching Noway in the autumn. One night they ran aground on rocks near Stad and Geirmundr and all those aboard were drowned, and that's the last we hear of Geirmundr.

Bolli kills Kjartan

The following chapter is the climax of the central feud in which the heroic Kjartan Óláfsson is killed by his cousin Bolli Þorleiksson with the sword Leg-Biter. Bolli reports the killing to his wife Guðrún Ósvífrsdóttir, with tragic results.

Before their love becomes distorted with hate, Kjartan Óláfsson and Guðrún have been ideally matched. Kjartan, named for his Irish great-grandfather, grows up with his half-brother Bolli Þorleiksson whom Óláfr fosters. Kjartan is a real knock-out: 'He was the most handsome man that was ever born in Iceland. He had a broad face and regular features, the most beautiful eyes and a fair complexion. His hair was thick and as shiny as silk . . . He was a big strong man, a better fighter than other men, skilled with his hands, and a top swimmer; he could perform all the sports far and away above other men; he was the humblest of men, and so popular that every child loved him' (ch. 28). Later Kjartan falls in love with Guðrún Ósvífrsdóttir, who 'was the most beautiful woman to have grown up in Iceland, both beautiful and intelligent . . . She was the shrewdest of women and highly articulate' (ch. 32). It seems to be a match made in heaven. Before becoming engaged to marry, however, Kjartan decides to go abroad for experience of travel and to win renown. Guðrún asks to come, but Kjartan rejects her company. He asks her to wait for three years, but she refuses. They part in disagreement.

While Kjartan is kept as a hostage in Norway by King Óláfr Tryggvason because of Iceland's reluctance to accept Christianity, Bolli returns and tells Guðrún the truth, that Kjartan has spent time with Ingibjǫrg, the king's beautiful sister. Guðrún agrees to marry Bolli, but later, when Kjartan returns home, to discover what he has missed, his jealousy makes him petty and mean. One provocation leads to another, until the district is in a heightened state of tension and Guðrún has had enough. She eggs on her husband to kill her former lover and his cousin, foster-brother and best friend.

49. Nú ríðr Kjartan suðr eptir dalnum ok þeir þrír saman, Án svarti ok Þórarinn.

Þorkell hét maðr, er bjó at Hafratindum í Svínadal. Þar er nú auðn. Hann hafði farit til hrossa sinna um daginn ok smalasveinn hans með honum. Þeir sá hváratveggju, Laugamenn í fyrirsátinni ok þá Kjartan, er þeir riðu eptir dalnum þrír saman. Þá mælti smalasveinn, at þeir myndi snúa til móts við þá Kjartan; kvað þeim þat mikit happ, ef þeir mætti skirra vandræðum svá miklum, sem þá var til stefnt.

Þorkell mælti, 'Þegi skjótt,' segir hann; 'mun fóli þinn nǫkkurum manni líf gefa, ef bana verðr auðit? Er þat ok satt at segja, at ek spari hváriga til, at þeir eigi nú svá illt saman, sem þeir líkar; sýnisk mér þat betra ráð, at vit komim okkr þar, at okkr sé við engu hætt, en vit megim sem gǫrst sjá fundinn ok hafim gaman af leik þeira, því at þat ágæta allir, at Kjartan sé vígr hverjum manni betr; væntir mik ok, at hann þurfi nú þess, því at okkr er þat kunnigt, at œrinn er liðsmunr.'

Ok varð svá at vera, sem Þorkell vildi.

Þeir Kjartan rída fram at Hafragili.

---

49. Kjartan rode south down the valley with Án the Black and Þórarin.

There was a man called Þorkell who lived at Hafratindar in Svínadal; that farm is now deserted. He had gone to see to his horses that day, taking his shepherd-boy with him. They could see both parties, the men of Laugar lying in ambush, and Kjartan and his companions riding down the valley. The boy suggested that they ride to warn Kjartan for it would be good luck for them if they could prevent the terrible events that were about to happen.

Þorkell said to him:' Do hold your tongue! Are you such a fool as to think you could save the life of one fated to die? To tell you the truth, they can do as much harm to each other as they please for all I care. I think it a better idea to find a spot where we can get a good view of their meeting and enjoy the sport without any danger to ourselves. Everyone claims that Kjartan is the best fighter there is; I think he's going to need all the skill he has as the odds are heavily against him.'

Þorkell had his way, of course.

Kjartan and his companions came riding down towards Hafragil.

En í annan stað gruna þeir Ósvífrssynir, hví Bolli mun sér hafa þar svá staðar leitat, er hann mátti vel sjá, þá er menn riðu vestan. Þeir gera nú ráð sitt, ok þótti sem Bolli myndi þeim eigi vera trúr, ganga at honum upp í brekkuna ok brugðu á glímu ok á glens ok tóku í fœtr honum ok drógu hann ofan fyrir brekkuna.

En þá Kjartan bar brátt at, er þeir riðu hart, ok er þeir kómu suðr yfir gilit, þá sá þeir fyrirsátina ok kenndu mennina.

Kjartan spratt þegar af baki ok sneri í móti þeim Ósvífrssonum. Þar stóð steinn einn mikill. Þar bað Kjartan þá við taka. En áðr þeir mœttisk, skaut Kjartan spjótinu, ok kom í skjǫld Þórólfs fyrir ofan mundriðann, ok bar at honum skjǫldinn við. Spjótit gekk í gegnum skjǫldinn ok handlegginn fyrir ofan ǫlnboga ok tók þar í sundr aflvǫðvann; lét Þórólfr þá lausan skjǫldinn, ok var honum ónýt hǫndin um daginn.

Síðan brá Kjartan sverðinu, ok hafði eigi konungsnaut. Þórhǫllusynir runnu á Þórarin, því at þeim var þat hlutverk ætlat. Var sá atgangr harðr, því at Þórarinn var rammr at afli; þeir váru ok vel knáir; mátti þar ok varla í milli sjá, hvárir þar myndi drjúgari verða.

Þá sóttu þeir Ósvífrssynir at Kjartani ok Guðlaugr; váru þeir sex; en þeir Kjartan ok Án tveir. Án varðisk vel ok vildi æ ganga fram fyrir Kjartan. Bolli stóð hjá með Fótbít. Kjartan hjó stórt, en sverðit dugði illa; brá hann því jafnan undir fót sér. Urðu þá hvárirtveggju sárir, Ósvífrssynir ok Án, en Kjartan var þá enn ekki sárr.

Meanwhile, the Ósvífrssons had begun to suspect that Bolli had chosen a position where anyone approaching from the north could see him. They discussed it among themselves and felt that Bolli was not to be trusted. So they climbed up to him and started wrestling and rolling about, then took him by the legs and dragged him further down the slope.

Kjartan and his companions were riding hard and approached quickly. When they had passed south of the ravine they caught sight of the ambush and recognised the men.

Kjartan jumped off his horse immediately and turned to face the Ósvífrssons. There was huge rock standing nearby, and there Kjartan said they should stand to face the attack. As the others made for them, Kjartan hurled his spear and struck Þórólfr's shield just above the handle, forcing the shield against him. The point of the spear went through the shield and into Þórólfr's arm above the elbow where it severed the biceps. Þórólfr dropped the shield and his arm was useless for the rest of the fight.

Then Kjartan drew his sword, but he wasn't carrying the king's gift. The Þórhǫllusons set upon Þórarin, for that was the task assigned to them. It was a hard struggle for Þórarin was a strong man and the brothers were sturdy men as well. It was hard to know who would come out on top.

Guðlaugr and the Ósvífrssons attacked Kjartan so there were five of them against Kjartan and Án. Án defended himself stoutly and always tried to cover Kjartan. Bolli stood back and watched, holding Leg-Biter. Kjartan's blows were powerful but his sword was of little use, and he often had to straighten it out by standing on it. The Ósvífrssons and Án had all been wounded, but Kjartan was still untouched.

Kjartan barðisk svá snart ok hraustliga, at þeir Ósvífrssynir hopuðu undan ok sneru þá þar at, sem Án var. Þá fell Án ok hafði hann þó barizk um hríð svá, at úti lágu iðrin. Í þessi svipan hjó Kjartan fót af Guðlaugi fyrir ofan kné, ok var honum sá áverki œrinn til bana.

Þá sœkja þeir Ósvífrssynir fjórir Kjartan, ok varðisk hann svá hraustliga, at hvergi fór hann á hæl fyrir þeim.

Þá mælti Kjartan, 'Bolli frændi, hví fórtu heiman, ef þú vildr kyrr standa hjá? Ok er þér nú þat vænst, at veita ǫðrumhvárum ok reyna nú, hversu Fótbítr dugi.'

Bolli lét, sem hann heyrði eigi. Ok er Óspakr sá, at þeir myndi eigi bera af Kjartani, þá eggjar hann Bolla á alla vega, kvað hann eigi mundu vilja vita þá skǫmm eptir sér, at hafa heitit þeim vígsgengi ok veita nú ekki, 'ok var Kjartan oss þá þungr í skiptum, er vér hǫfðum eigi jafnstórt til gǫrt; ok ef Kjartan skal nú undan rekask, þá mun þér, Bolli, svá sem oss, skammt til afarkosta'.

Þá brá Bolli Fótbít ok snýr nú at Kjartani.

Þá mælti Kjartan til Bolla, 'Víst ætlar þú nú, frændi, niðingsverk at gera, en miklu þykki mér betra at þiggja banaorð af þér, frændi, en veita þér þat.'

Síðan kastaði Kjartan vápnum ok vildi þá eigi verja sik, en þó var hann lítt sárr, en ákafliga vígmóðr.

Engi veitti Bolli svǫr máli Kjartans, en þó veitti hann honum banasár. Bolli settisk þegar undir herðar honum, ok andaðisk Kjartan í knjám Bolla; iðraðisk Bolli þegar verksins ok lýsti vígi á hendr sér.

Kjartan fought with such courage and agility that the Ósvífrssons had to fall back against his force and turned on Án instead. And now Án fell, having fought for some time with his entrails spilling out.

At that moment Kjartan hacked off Guðlaugr's leg above the knee, and that killed him. The four Ósvífrssons then charged at Kjartan again, but he defended himself so bravely that he never yielded an inch to their attack.

Then Kjartan called out, 'Why did you leave home, kinsman Bolli, if you intended only to stand by and watch? You must decide whose side you are on and then see what Leg-Biter can do.'

Bolli pretended not to hear.

When Óspakr realised that they could not overcome Kjartan by themselves, he urged Bolli in every way he could, telling him that he would not want to live with the shame of having promised to help in the fight and then not given it. 'Kjartan has proved hard enough to handle, even when we had done much less to provoke him.' He added, 'and if he gets away this time you, Bolli, no less than us, will face harsh punishment before long'.

So Bolli drew Leg-Biter and turned towards Kjartan.

Then Kjartan said to Bolli, 'This is an ignoble deed, kinsman, that you are about to do, but I'd rather receive my death at your hands, cousin, than give you death at mine.'

With that Kjartan threw down his weapons, and made no further attempt to defend himself. He was only slightly wounded, but very weak with exhaustion. Bolli made no reply to Kjartan's words, but dealt him his death-blow all the same. Then Bolli caught him as he fell and Kjartan died in Bolli's arms. Immediately Bolli repented bitterly of what he had done.

Bolli sendi þá Ósvífrssonu til heraðs, en hann var eptir ok Þórarinn hjá líkunum. Ok er þeir Ósvífrssynir kómu til Lauga, þá sǫgðu þeir tíðendin. Guðrún lét vel yfir, ok var þá bundit um hǫndina Þórólfs, greri hon seint ok varð honum aldregi meinlaus.

Lík Kjartans var fœrt heim í Tungu.

Síðan reið Bolli heim til Lauga. Guðrún gekk í móti honum ok spurði, hversu framorðit væri; Bolli kvað þá vera nær nóni dags þess. Þá mælti Guðrún, 'Misjǫfn verða morginverkin; ek hefi spunnit tólf álna garn, en þú hefir vegit Kjartan.'

Bolli svarar, 'Þó mætti mér þat óhapp seint ór hug ganga, þóttú minntir mik ekki á þat.'

Guðrún mælti, 'Ekki tel ek slíkt með óhǫppum; þótti mér, sem þú hefðir meiri metorð þann vetr, er Kjartan var í Nóregi, en nú, er hann trað yðr undir fótum, þegar hann kom til Íslands; en ek tel þat þó síðast, er mér þykkir mest vert, at Hrefna mun eigi ganga hlæjandi at sæginni í kveld.'

Þá segir Bolli ok var mjǫk reiðr, 'Ósýnt þykki mér, at hon fǫlni meir við þessi tíðendi, en þú, ok þat grunar mik, at þú brygðir þér minnr við, þó at vér lægim eptir á vígvellinum, en Kjartan segði frá tíðendum.'

Guðrún fann þá, at Bolli reiddisk, ok mælti, 'Haf ekki slíkt við, því at ek kann þér mikla þǫkk fyrir verkit; þykki mér nú þat vitat, at þú vill ekki gera í móti skapi mínu.'

Bolli declared that he himself had done the killing, and sent the Ósvífrssons back to Laugar, while he and Þórarin remained behind with the bodies. When the Ósvífrssons returned home they reported what had happened. Guðrún seemed pleased at the news. Þórólfr's arm was bandaged but it took a long time to heal, and gave him trouble for the rest of his life.

Kjartan's body was taken to the farm at Tunga.

Bolli then rode to Laugar and Guðrún went out to meet him. She asked him how late in the day it was. Bolli said it was around noon of that day. Then Guðrún said, 'Morning tasks are often mixed. I have spun twelve ells of cloth and you have killed Kjartan.'

Bolli replied, 'This unfortunate deed will live long enough in my mind, even without you to remind me of it.'

Guðrún then said, 'I wouldn't consider it unfortunate. It seems to me that you were held in greater esteem the year that Kjartan was still in Norway than now in Iceland when he has walked all over you. And last of all, what I like best is that Hrefna won't go to bed tonight with a smile on her face.'

Then Bolli said in a sudden fury, 'I doubt if she will turn any paler than you at the news, and I suspect you would have been less shocked if I had been left lying there dead and Kjartan had lived to tell the tale.'

Guðrún then realised how angry Bolli was and said, 'Don't say such things, for I am very grateful for what you have done. I know now for sure that you will do anything to please me.'

Síðan gengu þeir Ósvífrssynir í jarðhús þat, er þeim var búit á laun, en þeir Þórhǫllusynir váru sendir út til Helgafells at segja Snorra goða þessi tíðendi, ok þat með, at þau báðu hann senda sér skjótan styrk til liðveizlu á móti Ólláfi ok þeim mǫnnum, er eptirmál áttu eptir Kjartan.

Þat varð til tíðenda í Sælingsdalstunga þá nótt, er vígit hafði orðit um daginn, at Án settisk upp, er allir hugðu, at dauðr væri. Urðu þeir hræddir, er vǫkðu yfir líkunum, ok þótti þetta undir mikit. Þá mælti Án til þeira, 'Ek bið yðr í guðs nafni, at þér hræðizk mik eigi, því at ek hefi lifat ok haft vit mitt allt til þeirar stundar, at rann á mik ómeginshǫfgi; þá dreymði mik in sama kona ok fyrr, ok þótti mér hon nú taka hrísit ór maganum, en lét koma innyflin í staðinn, ok varð mér gott við þat skipti.'

Síðan váru bundin sár þau, er Án hafði, ok varð hann heill ok var síðan kallaðr Án hrísmagi.

En er Óláfr Hǫskuldsson spurði þessi tiðendi, þá þótti honum mikit at um víg Kjartans, en þó bar hann drengiliga. Þeir synir hans vildu þegar fara at Bolla ok drepa hann.

Óláfr segir, 'Þat skal fjarri fara; er mér ekki sonr minn at bœttri, þó at Bolli sé drepinn, ok unna ek Kjartani um alla menn fram, en eigi mátta ek vita mein Bolla. En sé ek yðr makligri sýslu; fari þér til móts við Þórhǫllusonu, er þeir eru sendir il Helgafells at stefna liði at oss; vel líkar mér, þótt þér skapið þeim slíkt víti, sem yðr líkar.'

The Ósvífrssons went into hiding in an underground shelter which had been secretly prepared for them. The Þórhǫllusons were sent off to Helgafell to tell Snorri the Goði the news, and to ask him to send help and support against Óláfr Hǫskuldsson and others whose duty it was to take action over the slaying of Kjartan.

A remarkable thing happened at Sælingsdalstunga the night after the killings. Án the Black, whom everyone had thought to be dead, sat up.

The people keeping watch over the bodies were very frightened and thought this a great marvel. But Án said to them, 'Don't be afraid of me I beg in God's name. I have been alive all the time and only lost consciousness at the very end. Then I dreamt that this same woman came to see me as before, and now she removed the brushwood from my belly and put my entrails back instead, after which I felt much better.'

Án's wounds were now bandaged and healed well. He recovered completely and was known from then on as Án Brushwood-Belly.

When Óláfr heard of Kjartan's killing he was deeply affected, although he bore it with dignity.

His sons wanted to attack Bolli at once and kill him. 'That's the last thing I want,' said Óláfr, 'It is no compensation for my son if Bolli is slain, and though I loved Kjartan more dearly than any other person, I can't agree to Bolli being harmed. I can give you a much more fitting task: go after the Þórhǫllusons who were sent to Helgafell to gather forces against us. Anything you do to punish them will please me.'

Síðan snarask þeir til ferðar, Óláfssynir, ok gengu á ferju, er Óláfr átti; váru þeir sjau saman; róa út eptir Hvammsfirði ok sœkja knáliga ferðina. Þeir hafa vedr lítit ok hagstœtt. Þeir róa undir seglinu, þar til er þeir koma undir Skorey, ok eigu þar dvǫl nokkura ok spyrjask þar fyrir um ferðir manna. Ok litlu síðar sjá þeir skip róa vestan um fjǫrðinn, kenndu þeir brátt mennina; váru þar Þórhǫllusynir. Leggja þeir Halldórr þegar at þeim; þar varð engi viðtaka, því at þeir Óláfssynir hljópu þegar út á skipit at þeim; urðu þeir Steinn handteknir ok hǫggnir fyrir borð.

Þeir Óláfssynir snúa aptr, ok þótti þeira ferð allskǫrulig vera.

The Óláfssons set off at once. They boarded a ferry-boat that belonged to Óláfr and rowed towards the mouth of Hvammsfjord. There were seven of them and they made good progress. There was a slight breeze that favoured them and they rowed with the sail to Skor Island. They paused there briefly to ask about the movements of people in the district. Shortly after they saw a boat coming across the fjord from the west and recognized the men on board as the Þórhǫllusons. Halldórr and his companions attacked them immediately and met little resistance when the Óláfssons leapt on to their boat. Steinn was seized and beheaded over the side.

The Óláfssons then turned for home and their journey was thought to have been very capably accomplished.

The Saga of the Burned Njáll

Brennu-Njáls saga

c. 1280s

⁂

Brennu-Njáls saga 'Saga of the burned Njáll' was composed about a generation after Iceland had agreed to come under the legal control of Norway in 1261–2. The Commonwealth founded at Þingvellir in 930 with the establishment of the Alþingi had now come under increasing pressure and menace during the thirteenth century Sturling Age (named for Snorri Sturluson's family) when increasingly brutal feuds and battles were pursued by an ever smaller, and more powerful, group of families. This was leading to such chaos and the breakdown of the law that the Alþingi decided to cede power to Norway between 1262 and 1264. *Brennu-Njáls saga* is a vast and moving work composed by someone with a deep fascination with the law.

The first half of the saga concerns the fate of Gunnarr Hámundarson of Hliðarendi. Like Kjartan Óláfsson, he is strong, skilled in arms and sport, handsome and popular. He is a great friend of Njáll Þorgeirsson of Bergþórshvol, a prescient man highly skilled in the law. After an exciting and successful journey abroad, fighting Vikings in the service of King Haraldr Gormsson of Denmark and Earl Hákon of Norway, Gunnarr returns in splendour to the Alþingi, where he sees a beautiful, long-haired woman. She is Hallgerðr, Hǫskuldr's daughter, early said to be 'a woman of great beauty. She was very tall, which earned her the name Long-Legs, and her lovely hair was now so long that it could veil her whole body. She was extravagant and quick-tempered' (ch. 9). Of course they fall in love.

Andersson, Theodore M., *The Growth of the Medieval Icelandic Sagas (1180–1280)* (Ithaca, NY, 2006).

Byock, J., *Feud in the Icelandic Saga* (Berkeley, CA, 1982)

Byock, J., *Viking Age Iceland* (Harmondsworth, 2001)

Clover, C., *The Medieval Saga* (Ithaca, NY, 1982)

Clunies Ross, M., ed., *Old Icelandic Literature and Society* (Cambridge, 2000)

Dronke, U., *The Role of Sexual Themes in Njáls Saga*, The Dorothea Coke Memorial Lecture (London, 1980)

Einar Ól. Sveinsson, *Njáls saga: A Literary Masterpiece*, trans. P. Schach (Lincoln, NA, 1971)

Grønlie, S., trans., *Íslendingabók*, *Kristni Saga*, The Viking Society for Northern Research (London, 2006)

Jochens, J., *Old Norse Images of Women* (Philadelphia, PA, 1996)

Jón Karl Helgason, *The Rewriting of Njál's Saga* (Clevedon, 1999)

Lönnroth, L., *Njal's Saga, A Critical Introduction* (Berkeley, CA, 1976)

McTurk, R., ed., *A Companion to Old Norse-Icelandic Literature* (Maldon, MA, 2005)

O'Donoghue, H., *Old Norse-Icelandic Literature: A Short Introduction* (Maldon, MA, 2004)

Hallgerðr wins Gunnarr

Hallgerðr's character and temper are, indeed, *blandin mjǫk* 'awfully mixed'. She is 34 when she meets Gunnarr. She has been married twice. Both husbands have been killed by her sinister foster-father Þjóstólfr, (who cohabited with her in her childhood), because both husbands slapped her (for pretty good reason in each case). She is regarded as trouble, yet she is beautiful, and before Gunnarr knows what has happened, he has proposed to her.

In the following, note that booths at Þingvellir were semi-permanent structures where the people of the various districts stayed during the Alþingi. The floors and walls were stone-built and they were temporarily tented for the event. The remains of many of the regional and family booths have been identified and are still visible.

33. Gunnarr reið, ok þeir allir, til þings. En er þeir kómu á þing, þá váru þeir svá vel búnir, at engir váru þeir þar, at jafnvel væri búnir, ok fóru menn út ór hverri búð at undrask þá. Gunnarr reið til búðar Rangæinga ok var þar með frændum sínum. Margr maðr fór at finna Gunnar ok spyrja hann tíðenda; hann var við alla menn léttr ok kátr ok sagði ǫllum slíkt, er vildu.

Þat var einn dag, er Gunnarr gekk frá lǫgbergi; hann gekk fyrir neðan Mosfellingabúð; þá sá hann konur ganga í móti sér ok váru vel búnar. Sú var í ferðarbroddi konan, er betzt var búin. En er þau fundusk, kvaddi hon þegar Gunnar.

Hann tók vel kveðju hennar ok spurði, hvat kvenna hon væri; hon nefndisk Hallgerðr ok kvazk vera dóttir Hǫskulds Dala-Kollssonar. Hon ælti til hans djarfliga ok bað hann segja sér frá ferðum sínum, en hann kvazk ekki mundu varna henni máls; settusk þau þá niðr ok tǫluðu. Hon var svá búin at hon var í rauðum kyrtli, ok var á búningr mikill; hon hafði yfir sér skarlatsskikkju, ok var búin hlǫðum ískaut niðr; hárit tók ofan á bringu henni ok var bæði mikit ok fagrt. Gunnarr var í tignarklæðum þeim, er Haraldr konungr Gormsson gaf honum; hann hafði ok hringinn á hendi, Hákonarnaut.

---

33. Gunnarr and all his companions rode to the Alþingi. When they arrived they were all so well dressed that no one there could compare with them, and people came out of every booth to admire them. Gunnarr rode to the Rangarvellir booth and stayed there with his kinsmen. Many people came to see him and ask him his news. He was light-hearted and cheerful with everyone and told them everything they wanted to hear.

One day, as he was walking from the Law Rock, Gunnar passed down by the Mosfell booth. He saw there some well-dressed women coming towards him; the one in front was the best dressed of them all. When they met, she greeted Gunnarr at once.

He made a friendly reply and asked her who she was. She said that her name was Hallgerðr, and that she was the daughter of Hǫskuldr Dala-Kollssonar. She spoke to him boldly, and asked him to tell her about his travels. Gunnarr replied that he would not refuse her this, and they sat down to talk. She was dressed like this: she had on a red, richly-decorated gown, under a scarlet cloak trimmed with lace down to the hem. Her beautiful, thick hair flowed down over her bosom. Gunnarr was wearing the robes given him by King Haraldr Gormsson, with the gold bracelet from Earl Hákon.

Þau tǫluðu lengi hátt. Þar kom, er hann spurði, hvárt hon væri ógefin. Hon segir, at svá væri, 'ok er þat ekki margra at hætta á þat,' segir hon.

'Þykki þeir hvergi fullkosta?' segir hann.

'Eigi er þat,' segir hon, 'en mannvǫnd mun ek vera.'

'Hversu munt þú því svara ef ek bið þín?' segir Gunnarr.

'Þat mun þér ekki í hug,' segir hon.

'Eigi er þat,' segir hann.

'Ef þér er nǫkkurr hugr á,' segir hon, 'þá finn þú fǫður minn.' Siðan skilðu þau talit.

Gunnarr gekk þegar til búðar Dalamanna ok fann menn úti fyrir búðinni ok spurði, hvárt Hǫskuldr væri í búð, en þeir sǫgðu, at hann var þar; gekk þá Gunnarr inn.

Hǫskuldr ok Hrútr tóku vel við Gunnarri; hann settisk niðr í meðal þeira, ok fannsk þat ekki í tali þeira, at þar hefði nǫkkur misþykkja í meðal verit. Þar kómu niðr rœður Gunnars, hversu þeir brœðr myndi þvi svara, ef hann bæði Hallgerðar.

'Vel,' segir Hǫskuldr, 'ef þer er þat alhugat.' Gunnarr segir sér þat alvǫru, 'en svá skilðu vér næstum, at mǫrgum myndi þat þykkja líkligt, at hér myndi ekki samband verða.'

'Hversu lízk þér, Hrútr frændi?' segir Hǫskuldr.

Hrútr svaraði: 'Ekki þykki mér þetta jafnræði.'

'Hvat finnr þú til þess?' segir Gunnarr.

They talked for a long time, and at last he asked her if she were unmarried. She said that she was, 'and marrying me is not a risk that many would take'.

'Do you think there is no one good enough for you?' he asked.

'Not at all,' said Hallgerðr, 'but I am very particular when it comes to men.'

'How would you answer if I were to ask for your hand?' said Gunnarr.

'You can't be thinking of that,' she replied.

'But I am,' he said.

'If you have any wish to do that,' she said, 'then you must go and speak with my father.' With this they ended their conversation.

Gunnarr went at once to the booth of the people of Dalir. There were men in front of the booth and he asked them if Hǫskuldr were inside. They said he was, and Gunnarr went in.

Hǫskuldr and Hrútr gave him a good welcome. Gunnarr sat down between them, and there was no hint from their conversation that there had ever been differences between them. Gunnarr finally asked how the brothers would answer if he were to ask to marry Hallgerðr.

'With good will,' said Hǫskuldr, 'if your mind is set on this.' Gunnarr said that it certainly was, 'but from the way we last parted, most people would think it unlikely that such a bond of kinship might be formed'.

'What do you think of this, brother Hrútr?' asked Hǫskuldr.

Hrútr replied, 'This doesn't seem an even match to me.'

'What makes you say that?' asked Gunnarr.

Hrútr mælti, 'Þvi mun ek svara þér um þetta, er satt er: þú ert maðr vaskr ok vel at þér, en hon er blandin mjǫk, ok vil ek þik í engu svíkja.'

'Vel mun þér fara,' segir Gunnarr, 'en þó mun ek þat fyrir satt hafa, at þér virðið í fornan fjandskap, ef þér vilið eigi gera mér kostinn.'

'Eigi er þat,' segir Hrútr, 'meir er hitt, at ek sé, at þú mátt nú ekki við gera. En þó at vér keyptim eigi, þá vildim vit þó vera vinir þínir.'

'Ek hefi talat við hana, ok er þat ekki fjarri hennar skapi,' segir Gunnarr.

'Veit ek, at svá mun vera, at ykkr er báðum girndarráð, ok hættið þit mestu til, hversu ferr.'

Hrútr segir Gunnari allt um skaplyndi Hallgerðar ófregit, ok þótti Gunnari þat fyrst œrit mart, er áfátt var, en þar kom um síðir, at saman fell kaupmáli þeira. Var þá sent eptir Hallgerði, ok var þá um talat svá, at hon var við. Létu þeir nú enn sem fyrr, at hon festi sik sjálf. Skyldi þetta boð vera at Hlíðarenda ok skyldi fara fyrst leyniliga, en þó kom þar, er allir vissu.

Gunnarr reið heim af þingi ok til Bergþórshváls ok sagði Njáli kaup sín. Hann tók þungt á kaupum hans. Gunnarr spurði, hvat hann fyndi til, at honum þótti slíkt svá óráðligt.

'Af henni mun standa allt it illa, er hon kemr austr hingat,' segir Njáll.

'Aldri skal hon spilla okkru vinfengi,' segir Gunnarr.

'Þat mun þó svá nær leggja,' segir Njáll, 'en þó munt þú jafnan bœta fyrir henni.' Gunnarr bauð Njáli til boðs ok ǫllu því þaðan, sem hann vildi, at fœri; Njáll hét at fara. Síðan reið Gunnarr heim ok reið um heraðit at bjóða mǫnnum.

Hrútr replied, 'I will give you a truthful answer. You are a valiant and accomplished man, but Hallgerðr is rather a mixture. I don't want to deceive you in any way.'

'Good fortune go with you,' said Gunnarr, 'but I will take it to mean that you are keeping up our old enmity if you are not willing to make this match.'

'That is not so,' said Hrútr, 'but rather that I can see you cannot help yourself at present. Even if we did not make this marriage deal, we would still wish to be your friends.'

'I have been speaking with Hallgerðr,' said Gunnarr, 'and she is not averse to it.'

'I can see that you are infatuated with one another,' said Hrútr, 'and you are the ones who will have to face the consequences.'

Without being asked, Hrútr told Gunnarr all about Hallgerðr's character. At first Gunnarr thought the faults were more than enough, but they finally came to terms about the marriage contract. Then Hallgerðr was sent for, and the arrangements were discussed in her presence. As before, Hallgerðr was allowed to betroth herself. The wedding-feast was to be held at Hliðarendi. For the time being it was to be kept a secret, but soon everybody knew about it.

Gunnarr rode home from the Alþingi and went to Bergþórshvol to tell Njáll about the marriage contract. Njáll showed heavy disapproval. Gunnarr asked him why he found it so unwise.

'She will be the source of nothing but trouble when she comes east,' said Njáll.

'She will never spoil our friendship,' said Gunnarr.

'She will very nearly do so,' said Njáll, 'but you will always make amends for her.' Gunnarr invited Njáll to the wedding-feast with as many of his household as he cared to bring along with him. Njáll promised to come. Then Gunnarr rode home and then rode around the district to invite more guests.

Gunnarr's last stand

Feuds and tensions slowly engulf Gunnarr. There is a plot on his life devised by two men both named Þorgeirr. They become subject to arbitration that will be decided by Njáll. Chapter 70 gives a taste of legal proceeding on a small scale. It contains Njáll's famous statement *með lǫgum skal land várt byggja, en með ólǫgum eyða* 'with law our land shall rise, but be laid waste by lawlessness', which is today the motto of the Icelandic police force. This chapter also describes Gunnarr's visit to Óláfr the Peacock at Hjarðarholt, and Óláfr's gift to Gunnarr of the Irish wolf hound Sámr which had been given to him in Ireland. After this, Gunnarr's enemies close in.

Despite Njáll's warning and advice, Gunnarr kills twice in the same family. He is sentenced at the Alþingi to the lesser outlawry, a three-year loss of all rights under the law during which most (as Eiríkr the Red) left the country. On his way to the ship, his horse stumbles and he looks back to the sloping fields of his farm at Hlíðarendi. His response has an understandably iconic status in the Icelandic imagination: 'How lovely the slopes are: more lovely than they have ever seemed to me before, pale cornfields and new-mown hay. I am going back home, and I will not go away' (ch. 75). Soon after this, Gunnarr is besieged by his enemies at his house, but can keep the attackers at bay with his bow and arrows. One of his enemies manages to slash his bowstring. He asks Hallgerðr for locks of her famously long hair to make repairs. She refuses. He had slapped her once, she reminds him. He is overcome and killed.

At the moment this chapter begins, Gunnarr's attackers are sneaking up to Hlíðarendi. One lures Sámr away but the hound becomes aware of danger and bites him in the groin. Ǫnundr ór Trǫllaskógi drives an axe into the animal's head, all the way to the brain, and 'The hound let out a loud howl, the like of which none had ever heard before, and fell down dead'.

77. Gunnarr vaknaði í skálanum ok mælti, 'Sárt ertú leikinn, Sámr fóstri, ok búð svá sé til ætlat, at skammt skyli okkar í meðal.'

Skáli Gunnars var gǫrr af viði einum ok súðþakiðr utan ok gluggr hjá brúnásunum ok snúin þar fyrir speld. Gunnarr svaf í lopti einu í skálanum ok Hallgerðr ok móðir hans.

Þá er þeir kómu at, vissu þeir eigi, hvárt Gunnarr myndi heima vera ok báðu, at einn hverr mundi fara heim fyrir ok forvitnask um, en þeir settusk niðr á vǫllinn. Þorgrímur Austmaðr gekk upp á skálann; Gunnar sér, at

---

77. Inside the house Gunnarr woke up and said, 'You have been cruelly treated Sámr, my fosterling. It may well mean that my turn is coming soon.'

Gunnarr's house was built entirely of timber, clinker-built on the outside. There were windows near the roof-beams fitted with shutters. Gunnarr slept in a loft above the main room with Hallgerðr and his mother.

When the attackers came near they were not sure if Gunnarr was at home, and wanted someone to go right up to the house and find out. They sat down on the ground and Þorgrímur the Norwegian climbed on to the roof. Gunnarr caught sight of a red tunic at rauðan kyrtil berr við glugginum, ok leggr út með atgeirinum á hann miðjan. Austmanninum varð lauss skjldrinn, ok spruttu honum fœtrnir, ok hrataði hann ofan af þekjunni; gengr síðan at þeim Gizuri, þar er þeir sátu á vellinum.

Gizurr leit við honum ok mælti, 'Hvárt er Gunnarr heima?'

Þorgrímr svarar, 'Vitið þér þat, en hitt vissa ek, at atgeirr hans var heima.' Siðan féll hann niðr dauður.

Þeir sóttu þá at húsunum. Gunnarr skaut út ǫrum að þeim ok varðisk vel, og gátu þeir ekki at gǫrt. Þá hljópu sumir á húsin upp ok ætluðu þaðan at at sœkja. Gunnarr kom þangat at þeim ǫrunum, ok gátu þeir ekki at gǫrt, ok fór svá fram um hríð. Þeir tóku hvíld ok sóttu at í annat sinn; Gunnarr skaut enn út ǫrunum, ok gátu þeir enn ekki at gǫrt ok hrukku frá í annat sinn.

Þá mælti Gizurr hvíti, 'Sœkjum at betr, ekki verðr af oss.' Gerðu þeir þá hríð ina þriðju ok váru við lengi; eptir þat hrukku þeir frá.

Gunnarr mælti, 'Ǫr liggr þar úti á vegginum, ok er sú af þeirra ǫrum, ok skal ek þeirri skjóta til þeirra; er þeim þat skǫmm, ef þeir fá geig af vápnum sínum.'

Móðir hans mælti, 'Ger þú eigi þat, at þú vekir nú við þá, er þeir hafa áðr frá horfi.' Gunnarr þreif ǫrina ok skaut til þeirra, ok kom á Eilíf Ǫnundarson, ok fékk hann af sár mikit; hann hafði staðit einn saman, ok vissu þeir eigi, at hann var særðr.

'Hǫnd kom þar út,' segir Gizurr, 'ok var á gullhringr, ok tók ǫr, er lá á þekjunni; ok mundi eigi út leitat viðfanga ef gnógt væri inni, ok skulu vér nú sœkja at.'

---

the window and made a thrust with his halberd and hit the middle of it. The Norwegian dropped his shield, lost his footing, and he fell off the roof. He walked to where Gizurr and the others were sitting.

Gizurr looked up at him and asked, 'Is Gunnarr at home?'

'That's for you to find out,' replied Þorgrímur, 'but I know that his halberd certainly is.' With that he fell dead.

The others then made for the house, but Gunnarr warded them off with a shower of arrows, and they could not make any progress. Some climbed on to the roofs of other buildings but Gunnarr could reach them with his arrows and fought them off. After a while they took a rest, and then attacked again; but again they could do nothing in the face of Gunnarr's arrows and they fell back a second time.

Gizurr the White said 'We must attack with more spirit, we're making no headway.' They made a third attack and kept it up for a long time, but once again they drew back.

Gunnarr said, 'There is an arrow lying on the roof there, one of theirs. I'm going to shoot it back at them. It will be humiliating for them to be hurt by one of their own weapons.'

His mother said, 'Don't stir them up again when they have just withdrawn.' But Gunnarr reached out for the arrow and shot it at them. It struck Eilífr Ǫnundarson and wounded him badly. He was standing by himself off to one side, and the others didn't realise he had been hit.

'An arm reached out over there,' said Gizurr, 'with a gold bracelet around it, and it grabbed an arrow that was lying on the roof. He would not be looking out here if he had enough inside. Let us attack again.'

Mǫrðr mælti, 'Brennu vér hann inni.'

'Þat skal verða aldrei,' segir Gizurr, 'þó at ek vita, at líf mitt liggi við. Er þér sjálfrátt at leggja til ráð þau, er dugi, svá slœgr maðr sem þú ert kallaðr.'

Strengir lágu á vellinum ok váru hafðir til at festa með hús jafnan. Mǫrðr mælti, 'Tǫku vér strengina ok berum um ásendana, en festum aðra endana um steina ok snúum í vindása ok vindum af ræfrit af skálanum.'

Þeir tóku strengina ok veittu þessa umbúð alla, ok fann Gunnarr eigi fyrr en þeir hǫfðu undit allt ræfrit af skálanum. Gunnarr skýtr þá af boganum, svá at þeir komask aldri at honum. Þá mælti Mǫrðr í annat sinn, at þeir myndi brenna Gunnar inni.

Gizurr svarar, 'Eigi veit ek, hví þú vill það mæla, er engi vill annarra, ok skal þat aldrei verða.'

Í þessu bili hleypr upp á þekjuna Þorbrandr Þorleiksson ok høggr í sundr bogastrenginn Gunnars. Gunnarr þrífr báðum hǫndum atgeirinn ok snýsk at honum skjótt ok rekr í gegnum hann ok kastar honum af þekjunni. Þá hljóp upp Ásbrandr, bróðir hans; Gunnarr leggr til hans atgeirinum, ok kom hann skildi fyrir sik; atgeirinn renndi í gegnum skjǫldinn ok meðal handleggjanna; snaraði Gunnarr þá atgeirinn, svá at skjǫldurinn klofnaði, en brotnuðu handleggirnir, ok féll hann út af þekjunni.

Áðr hafði Gunnarr særða átta men, en vegit tvá; þá fekk Gunnarr sár tvau, ok segja þat allir men, at hann brygði sér hvárki við sár né við bana. Hann mælti til Hallgerðar, 'Fá mér leppa tvá ór hári þínu, ok snúið þit móðir mín saman til bogastrengs mér.'

'Liggr þér nǫkkut við?' segir hon.

Mǫrðr said, 'Let's burn him to death inside.'

'That must never happen,' said Gizurr, 'even if I knew that my life depended on it. But surely a man as clever as you are said to be would be able to come up with a plan that works.'

There were some ropes lying on the ground, used for anchoring the buildings. Mǫrðr said, 'Let us tie these ropes around the ends of the roof-beams and fasten them to boulders. Then we can winch the roof off with winding-poles.'

They took the ropes and and rigged them in this way, and before Gunnarr was aware of it they had pulled off the whole roof. He kept shooting with his bow so they could not get at him. Then Mǫrðr again suggested they should burn Gunnarr to death inside.

Gizurr replied, 'I don't know why you keep talking about something that no one else wants. That must never happen.'

At that moment Þorbrandr Þorleiksson leapt up on the roof and cut through Gunnarr's bow-string. Gunnarr grasped his halberd with both hands, whirled round on Þorbrandr and drove the halberd through him and hurled him off the roof. Then Ásbrandr, Þorbrandr's brother, leapt up; Gunnarr lunged again with his halberd and Ásbrandr thrust his shield in the way. The halberd went right through the shield and between the upper arm and forearm. Gunnarr then twisted the halberd so violently that the shield split and and both his arm bones were shattered. He, too, toppled from the roof.

By this time, Gunnarr had wounded eight men and killed two. Now he received two wounds himself, but everyone agreed that he flinched at neither wounds nor death. Gunnarr spoke to Hallgerðr, 'Give me two locks of your hair, and help my mother twist them into a bow-string for me.'

'Does anything depend on it?' asked Hallgerðr.

'Líf mitt liggr við,' segir hann, 'því at þeir munu mik aldri fá sóttan, meðan ek kem boganum við.'

'Þá skal ek nú,' segir hon, 'muna þér kinnhestinn, ok hirði ek aldri, hvárt þú verr þik lengr eða skemr.'

'Hefir hver til síns ágætis nǫkkut,' segir Gunnarr, 'ok skal þik þessa eigi lengi biðja.'

Rannveig mælti, 'Illa ferr þér, ok mun þín skǫmm lengi uppi.'

Gunnarr varði sik vel ok frœknliga ok særir nú aðra átta menn svá stórum sárum, at mǫrgum lá við bana. Gunnarr verr sik, þar til er hann fell af mœði. Þeir særðu hann þá mǫrgum stórum sárum, en þó komsk hann þá enn ór hǫndum þeim ok varði sik þá enn lengi, en þó kom þar, at þeir drápu hann.

Um vǫrn hans orti Þorkell Elfaraskáld í vísu þessi:

> Spurðu vér, hvé varðisk vígmóðr kjalar slóða
> glaðstýrandi geiri, Gunnarr, fyrir Kjǫl sunnan.
> Sóknrýrir vann sára sextán viðar mána
> hríðar herðimeiða hauðrmens, en tvá dauða.

Gizurr mælti, 'Mikinn ǫldung hǫfu vér nú at velli lagit, ok hefir oss erfitt veitt, ok mun hans vǫrn uppi, meðan landit er byggt.'

Síðan gekk hann til fundar við Rannveigu ok mælti, 'Villtú veita mǫnnum várum tveimr jǫrð, er dauðir eru, at þeir sé hér heygðir?'

'At heldr tveimr, at ek munda veita yðr ǫllum,' segir hon.

'Várkunn er þér til þess, er þú mælir,' segir hann, 'því at þú hefir mikils misst,' ok kvað á, at þar skyldi engu ræna ok engu spilla; fóru á braut síðan.

'My life depends on it,' he replied, 'for they will never be able to get me as long as I can use my bow.'

'Then I'll remind you,' she said, 'of the slap on my face you once gave me. I don't care in the least if you hold out for a long time or not.'

'To each his own way of earning fame,' said Gunnarr. 'You shall not be asked again.'

Rannveig said, 'You are an evil woman, and your shame will be long remembered.'

Gunnarr defended himself with great courage and wounded eight more so badly that many of them barely lived. He kept on fighting until he fell from exhaustion. His enemies dealt him many wounds but even then he got away from them and held them at bay for a long time. But at last they killed him.

This is what Þorkell Elfaraskáld said about his defence:

> We have heard how, in the south Gunnarr, warrior of many seas,
> Greedy for gore in battle, wielded his mighty halberd,
> Waves of foemen broke on the cliffs of his defence;
> He wounded sixteen men and brought death to two others.

Gizurr the White said, 'We have felled a great warrior, and it has been hard for us. His last defence will be remembered for as long as this land is lived in.'

Then he went over to Rannveig and said, 'Will you give us land to bury our two dead men in?'

'Willingly for these two,' she said, 'but even more gladly if it were for all of you.'

'You cannot be blamed for saying that,' said Gizurr, 'for you loss has been great,' and he gave orders that there was to be no looting or pillaging. Then they went away.

The burning of Njáll

Many chapters, and years, later the feuds and killings have raised the tension and temperature remorselessly. The Alþingi and the law have been unable to calm the various factions in the disputes. Finally a band of 100 enemies, led by Flosi Þórðarsson of Svínafell, attack Njáll and his family at Bergþórshvol, where they set the house alight and burn to death those inside. Eleven people die in the blaze, including Njáll and Bergþóra, their sons Grímr, and Skarpheðinn, Kári's five-year old boy Þórðr, who refuses to leave his grandmother, old Sæunn, Þórdr Freedman (*leysingja*) and four others. Only Kári manages to escape the conflagration, later to wreak terrible revenge on the Burners.

129. Síðan tóku þeir eld ok gerðu bál mikit fyrir dyrunum. Þá mælti Skarpheðinn, 'Eld kveykvið þér nú, sveinar! Hvárt skal nú búa til seyðis?'

Grani svaraði, 'Svá skal þat vera, ok skaltú eigi þurfa heitara at baka.'

Skarpheðinn mælti, 'Því launar þú mér, sem þú ert maðr til, er ek hefnda fǫður þíns, ok virðir þat meira, er þér er óskyldara.'

Þá báru konur sýru í eldinn ok sløkktu niður fyrir þeim.

Kolr Þorsteinsson mælti til Flosa, 'Ráð kemr mér í hug. Ek hefi sét lopt í skálanum á þvertrjám, ok skulu vér þar inn bera eldinn ok kveykva við arfasátuna, þá er hér stendr fyrir ofan húsin.'

Síðan tóku þeir arfasátuna ok báru þar í eldinn, ok fundu þeir eigi, er inni váru, fyrr en logaði ofan allr skálinn, gerðu þeir Flosi þá stór bál fyrir ǫllum dyrum. Tók þá kvennaliðit illa at þola, þat er inni var.

Njáll mælti til þeirra, 'Verðið vel við ok mælið eigi æðru, því at él eitt mun vera, en þó skyldi langt til annars slíks. Trúið þér ok því, at guð er miskunnsamr, ok mun hann oss eigi bæði láta brenna þessa heims ok annars.'

Slíkar fortǫlur hafði hann fyrir þeim ok aðrar hraustligri.

---

129. Then they kindled a fire and made a great blaze in front of the doors. Skarpheðinn said, 'So you're making a fire now lads! Are you thinking of doing some cooking?'

Grani answered, 'That's right, and it'll be as hot as you need for roasting.'

Skarpheðinn spoke, 'So this is your way of rewarding me for avenging your father; you value more highly the duty that has a lesser claim on you.'

The women threw whey on the flames and doused the fire.

Kolr Þorsteinsson said to Flosi, 'I have an idea. I have noticed that there is a loft above the cross-beams of the main room. This is where we should start the fire, and use the pile of chickweed behind the house as kindling.'

They took the chickweed and set fire to it, and before those inside knew what was happening, the ceiling of the room was ablaze from end to end. Then Flosi's men started big fires in front of all the doors. At this the women who were inside began to panic.

Njáll said to them, 'Be brave and speak no words of fear, for this is just a passing storm and it will be a long time before we have another like it. Have faith that God is merciful, and that he will not let us burn both in this world and the next.'

Such were the words of comfort he had for them, and others even more reassuring.

Nú taka ǫll húsin at loga. Þá gekk Njáll til dyra ok mælti, 'Er Flosi svá nær, at hann megi heyra mál mitt?'

Flosi kvezk heyra.

Njáll mælti, 'Villt þú nǫkkut taka sættum við sonu mína eða leyfa nǫkkurum mǫnnum útgǫngu?'

Flosi svarar, 'Eigi vil ek taka sættum við sonu þína, ok skal nú yfir lúka með oss ok eigi frá ganga, fyrr en þeir eru allir dauðir. En þó vil ek lofa útgǫngu konum ok bǫrnum ok huskǫrlum.'

Njáll gekk þá inn ok mælti við fólkit, 'Út skulu þeir nú allir ganga, er leyft er. Ok gakk þú út Þórhalla Ásgrímsdóttir, ok allr lýðr með þér, sá er lofat er.'

Þórhalla mælti, 'Annarr verðr skilnaðr okkarr Helga en ek ætlaða um hríð, en þó skal ek eggja fǫður minn ok bræðr, at þeir hefni þessa mannskaða, er hér er gǫrr.'

Njáll mælti, 'Vel mun þér fara, því at þú ert góð kona.' Síðan gekk hon út ok mart lið með henni.

Ástríðr af Djúpárbakka mælti við Helga, 'Gakk þú út með mér, ok mun ek kasta yfir þik kvenskikkju ok falda þér við hǫfuðdúki.'

Hann taldisk undan first, en þó gerði hann þetta fyrir bæn þeirra. Ástríðr vafði hǫfuðdúki at hǫfði honum, en Þórhildr lagði yfir hann skikkjuna, ok gekk hann út á meðal þeirra. Þá gekk út Þorgerðr Njálsdóttir ok Helga, systir hennar, ok mart annat fólk.

En er Helgi kom út, þá mælti Flosi, 'Sú er há kona ok mikil um herðar; takið þér hana ok haldið henni!'

Now the whole house began to blaze.

Njáll went to the door and said, 'Is Flosi near enough to hear my words?' Flosi said that he could hear him.

Njáll said, 'Would you consider making a settlement with my sons, or letting some people leave the house?'

Flosi answered, 'I will come to no settlement with your sons. We shall settle matters now, once and for all, and we are not leaving here until they are all dead. But I shall allow the women, children and servants to come out.'

Njáll went back inside and said to the household, 'All those with permission to go must do so now. Leave the house now, Þórhalla Ásgrímsdóttir, along with all those who are allowed to leave.'

Þórhalla said, 'This is not the parting from Helgi that I ever expected, but I shall urge my father and brothers to avenge the killings that are committed here.'

Njáll said, 'You will do well, for you are a good woman.'

She went out taking many people with her.

Ástríðr of Djúpárbaki said to Helgi, 'Come out with me, I'll put a woman's cloak on you and wrap a scarf around your head.'

Helgi refused at first, but finally went along with their request. Ástríðr wrapped a scarf around his head and Þórhildr laid the cloak over his shoulders. Then he walked out between them, along with his sisters Þorgerdr and Helga and several other people.

When Helgi came outside, Flosi said, 'That woman there is very tall and broad-shouldered, seize her.' When Helgi heard this he threw off the cloak. He was carrying a

En er Helgi heyrði þetta, kastaði hann skikkjunni; hann hafði haft sverð undir hendi sér ok hjó til manns, ok kom í skjǫldinn, ok af sporðinn ok fótinn með. Þá kom Flosi at ok hjó á háls Helga, svá at þegar tók af hǫfuðit.

Flosi gekk þá at dyrum ok mælti, at Njáll skyldi ganga til máls við hann ok svá Bergþóra; þau gerðu svá.

Flosi mælti, 'Útgǫngu vil ek bjóða, því at þú brennr ómakligr inni.' Njáll mælti, 'Eigi vil ek út ganga, því at ek em maðr gamall ok lítt til búinn at hefna sona minna, en ek vil eigi lifa við skǫmm.'

Flosi mælti þá til Bergþóru, 'Gakk þú út, húsfreyja, því ak eg vil þik fyrir engan mun inni brenna.'

Bergþóra mælti, 'Ek var ung gefin Njáli, ok hefi ek því heitit honum, at eitt skyldi ganga yfir okkr bæði.'

Síðan gengu þau inn bæði. Bergþóra mælti, 'Hvat skulum vit nú til ráða taka?'

Njáll svarar, 'Ganga munu vit til hvílu okkarrar og leggjask niðr.' Síðan mælti hon við sveininn Þórð Kárason, 'Þik skal bera út, ok skalt þú eigi inni brenna.'

'Hinu hefir þú mér heitit, amma,' segir sveinninn, 'at við skyldim aldri skilja, ok skal svá vera, því at mér þykkir miklu betra at deyja með ykkr.'

Síðan bar hon sveininn til hvílunnar.

Njáll mælti við brytja sinn, 'Nú skaltú sjá, hvar vit leggjumsk niðr ok hversu ek býg um okkr, því at ek ætla mér hvergi héðan at hrœrask, hvárt sem mér angrar reykr eða bruni, munt þú þá næst geta, hvar beina okkarra er at leita.'

---

sword under his arm, and struck out at one of the men, slicing off the bottom of his shield and severing his leg as well. Then Flosi came up and struck at Helgi's neck, cutting off his head with one blow.

Flosi went up to the door and called for Njáll and Bergþóra to come and talk with him. When they came he said, 'I want to offer you the chance to come out, for you do not deserve to be burned.'

Njáll answered, 'I do not wish to leave, as I am an old man and hardly fit to avenge my sons; and I do not want to live in shame.'

Flosi spoke to Bergþóra, 'You come out, Bergþóra, for by no means do I want you to burn in your house.'

Bergþóra replied, 'I was given to Njáll in marriage when I was young, and I promised him that we would share the same fate.'

Then they both went back inside.

Bergþóra asked, 'What should we do now?'

Njáll answered, 'Let us go to our bed and lie down.'

Then she said to the boy Þórðr Kárason, 'You are to be taken out. You are not to be burned.'

The boy replied, 'You promised me, grandmother, that we would never be parted, and so it must be, for I would much prefer to die beside you both.'

Then she carried the boy to the bed.

Njáll said to his steward, 'Now you must see where we lay ourselves down and how we dispose ourselves, for I shall not move from here no matter how much the smoke and fire distress me. Then you will know where to find our remains.' The steward said he would.

Hann sagði, at svá skyldi vera. Uxa einum hafði slátrat verit ok lá þar húðin. Njáll mælti við brytjann, at hann skyldi breiða húðina yfir þau; hét hann því. Þau leggjask niðr bæði í rúmit ok lǫgðu sveininn í millum sín. Þá signdu þau sik bæði ok sveininn ok fálu ǫnd sína guði á hendi ok mæltu þat síðast, svá at menn heyrði. Þá tók brytinn húðina ok breiddi yfir þau ok gekk út síðan. Ketill ór Mǫrk tók í mót honum ok kippti honum út ok spurði vandliga at Njáli, mági sínum; hann sagði allt it sanna.

Ketill mælti, 'Mikill harmr er at oss kveðinn, er vér skulum svá mikla ógæfu saman eiga.' Skarpheðinn hafði sét, er faðir hans hafði niðr lagizk ok hversu hann hafði um sik búit, ok mælti þá, 'Snimma ferr faðir várr í hvilu, ok er þat sem ván er, hann er maðr gamall.' Þá tóku þeir Skarpheðinn ok Kári ok Grímr brandana jafnskjótt sem ofan duttu, ok sløngðu út á þá, ok gekk þat um hríð. Þá skutu þeir spjótum inn at þeim, ok tóku þeir ǫll á lopti ok sendu út aptr.

Flosi bað þá hætta at skjóta, 'því at oss munu ǫll vápnaskipti þungt ganga við þá. Meguð þér vel bíða þess, er eldurinn vinnr þá.'

Þeir gerðu svá. Þá fellu ofan stórviðirnir ór ræfrinu.

Skarpheðinn mælti 'Nú mun faðir minn dauðr vera, ok hefir hvárki heyrt til hans styn né hósta.'

Síðan gengu þeir í skálaendann; þar var fallit ofan þvertréit ok var brunnit mjǫk í miðju.

Kári mælti til Skarpheðins, 'Hlaup þú hér út, ok mun ek beina at mér þér, en ek mun hlaupa þegar eptir, ok munu vit báðir í braut komask, ef vit breytum svá, því at hingat leggr allan reykinn.'

An ox had recently been slaughtered, and its hide was lying nearby. Njáll told the steward to spread the hide over them, and he said he would. Njáll and Bergþóra lay down on the bed and placed the boy between them. Then they crossed themselves and the boy, and commended their souls to God. These were the last words that people heard them speak. The steward took the hide and spread it over them, and then left the house. Ketill of Mǫrk seized his arm and dragged him clear and questioned him closely about his father-in-law Njáll, and the steward told him everything that had happened.

Ketill said, 'A great sorrow has been given us, that we should all share such terrible luck.' Skarpheðinn had seen his father go to lie down and the preparations he had made. 'Our father is going to bed early,' he said, 'which is only to be expected as he is an old man.'

Then Skarpheðinn, Kári and Grímr snatched up the burning brands as soon as they fell and hurled them at those outside. After a while the attackers threw spears at them, which they caught in flight and hurled back.

Flosi told his men to stop, 'for we shall always come off worse in any exchange of blows with them. We should be wiser to wait until the fire overwhelms them.'

They did as he said.

Then the main beams fell down from the roof. Skarpheðinn said, 'My father must be dead by now, and not a groan or cough has been heard from him.'

Then they went to the far end of the room. The end of one cross-beam had fallen there, and it was almost burned through at the centre. Kári said to Skarpheðinn, 'Use that beam to run out on, and I shall give you a hand and run out right behind you. That way we can both escape because the smoke is all drifting in this direction.

Skarpheðinn mælti, 'Þú skalt hlaupa fyrri, en ek mun þegar eptir.'

'Ekki er þat ráð,' segir Kári, 'því at ek mun komask annars staðar, þótt hér gangi eigi.'

'Eigi vil ek þat,' segir Skarphéðinn; 'hlaup þú út fyrri, en ek mun þegar íhæla þér.' Kári mælti, 'Þat er hverjum manni boðit at leita sér lífs, ok skal ek svá gera. En þó mun nú sá skilnaðr með okkr verða, at vit munum aldri sjásk síðan; ef ek hleyp út ór eldinum, þá mun ek eigi hafa skap til at hlaupa inn aptr til þín í eldinn, ok mun þá sína leið fara hvárr okkarr.' Skarpheðinn mælti, 'Þat hlœgir mik, ef þú kemsk á braut, mágr, at þú munt hefna vár.'

Þá tók Kári einn stokk loganda í hǫnd sér ok hleypur út eptir þvertrénu, sløngvir þá stokkinum út af þekjunni, ok fellr hann ofan at þeim, er úti váru fyrir; þeir hljópu þá undan. Þá loguðu klæðin ǫll á Kára ok svá hárit. Hann steypir sér út af þekjunni ok stiklar þá með reykinum.

Þá mælti maðr einn, er úti var, 'Hvárt hljóp þar maðr út af þekjunni?' 'Fjarri fór þat,' sagði annarr, 'ok kastaði Skarpheðinn þar eldistokki at oss.' Síðan grunuðu þeir ekki.

Kári hljóp, til þess er hann kom at lœk einum, ok kastaði sér í ofan ok sløkkti á sér eldinn. Þaðan hljóp hann með reykinum í gróf nǫkkura ok hvíldi sik, ok er þat síðan kǫlluð Káragróf.

'You go first and I will follow you at once,' said Skarpheðinn.

'That is not a good plan,' said Kári, 'because I can get out somewhere else if I don't make it here.'

'No,' said Skarpheðinn, 'you go out first, and I shall be right on your heels.' Kári said, 'It is every man's instinct to save his own life, and I shall do so now. But this parting now means that we'll never meet again. Once I leap out of the flames, I won't feel inclined to run back into the fire to you. Then each of us must go his own way.'

Skarpheðinn said, 'I shall laugh, brother-in-law, if you escape, because you will avenge us all.'

Then Kári took a blazing brand and ran up the sloping cross-beam. He threw the brand down from the wall at those in his way outside and they scattered. By now Kári's clothes and hair were on fire, as he threw himself down off the wall and dodged away in the thick of the smoke.

Someone said, 'Was that a man jumping down from the roof?' 'Far from it,' said someone else, 'that was Skarpheðinn throwing another brand at us.' After that no one suspected anything.

Kári ran until he reached a small stream. He threw himself into it and extinguished his blazing clothes. From there he ran under cover of smoke until he reached a hollow, where he rested. That place has been called Kári's Hollow ever since.

The Saga of Grettir the Strong

Grettis saga

c. 1400

⁜

The Saga of Grettir the Strong is usually counted as the last of the great *Sagas of Icelanders*. Scholars had commonly thought the saga was composed in the middle decades of the fourteenth century but recent arguments suggest the later date of 1400. This would make it contemporary with Geoffrey Chaucer and the literature of Renaissance Europe. The saga's author is fully aware of the entire saga tradition and makes direct references to several. The final section of the saga is set in Byzantium, in which Grettir's half-brother, Þorsteinn *drómundr* 'Galley', avenges his killing and becomes the lover of the courtly and romantic Spes. Here is evidence of the author's acquaintance with the full flourish of continental romance, given that the story is based on that of Tristan when, disguised as a leper, he rescues Iseult (see Thomas of Britain's *Tristan*, **Early Chivalry**). Intriguingly, in addition, there is also a close similarity with *Beowulf* in two chapters. Had the author, or an author before him, seen a manuscript of *Beowulf*?

Grettir Ásmundarson is Iceland's most famous strong man and outlaw. Like Egill he has an unruly childhood and a gift for poetry. He is, however, ill-starred. During his life he spends a total of 18 years as an outlaw. The first term of outlawry is for killing Skeggi, in 1011, when he is 15. This is a sentence of lesser outlawry for three years. The second, which is for the (accidental) burning of Þórir's sons in Norway in 1015, is of full outlawry. In either case the outlaw loses all legal rights and protection and can be killed with impunity. This is, indeed, a life sentence. Grettir is 35, in the fifteenth year of the second sentence, when he is killed by his enemies, with the help of sorcery and witchcraft, on Drangey Island in Skagafjǫrðr in 1031.

Grettir's fight with Glámr

Grettir is an archetypal ghost-buster. Early in his life he enters a burial mound in Norway and has to sort out the revenant Kárr the Old (*Kárs in gamla*), an undead dwelling in a mound. Grettir is 16 years old at the time (in 1011). Two years later he kills the revenant Glámr in the north of Iceland in the Valley of the Shadows (*Forsæludal*) but is cursed by Glámr with a change of his luck, the threat of outlawry and, most chillingly, fear of the dark. This encounter will haunt him for the rest of his life. The following chapters describe that encounter.

34. Nú er þar til at taka, at Grettir Ásmundarson sat heima at Bjargi um haustit, síðan þeir Víga-Barði skilðu á Þóreyjargnúpi. Ok er mjǫk var komit at vetrnóttum, reið Grettir heiman norðr yfir hálsa til Víðidals ok gisti á Auðunarstǫðum. Sættusk þeir Auðunn til fulls, ok gaf Grettir honum ǫxi góða, ok mæltu til vináttu með sér. Auðunn bjó lengi á Auðunarstǫðum ok var kynsæll maðr; hans sonr var Egill, er átti Úlfheiði, dóttur Eyjólfs Guðmundarsonar, ok var þeira sonr Eyjólfr, er veginn var á alþingi; hann var faðir Orms, kapiláns Þorláks byskups.

Grettir reið norðr til Vatnsdals ok kom á kynnisleit í Tungu. Þar bjó þá Jǫkull Bárðarson, móðurbróðir Grettis. Jǫkull var mikill maðr ok sterkr ok inn mesti ofsamaðr; hann var siglingamaðr ok mjǫk ódæll, en þó mikilhœfr maðr. Hann tók vel við Gretti, ok var hann þar þrjár nætr. Þá var svá mikit orð á aptrgǫngum Gláms, at mǫnnum var ekki jafntíðrœtt sem þat. Grettir spurði inniliga at þeim atburðum, er hǫfðu orðit.

Jǫkull kvað þar ekki meira af sagt en til væri hœft, 'eða er þér forvitni á, frændi, at koma þar?'

Grettir sagði, at þat var satt.

Jǫkull bað hann þat eigi gera, 'því at þat er gæfuraun mikil, en frændr þínir eigu mikit í hættu, þar sem þú ert,' sagði hann; 'þykkir oss nú engi slíkr af ungum mǫnnum sem þú, en illt mun af illum hljóta, þar sem Glámr er; er ok miklu betra at fásk við mennska menn en við óvættir slíkar.'

Grettir kvað sér hug á at koma á Þórhallsstaði ok sjá, hversu þar væri um gengit.'

Jǫkull mælti: 'Sé ek nú, at eigi tjáir at letja þik, en satt er þat, sem mælt er, at sitt er hvárt, gæfa eða gǫrvigleikr.'

---

34. The story now turns to Grettir Ásmundarson who stayed at home at Bjarg the autumn after he had left Killer-Barði at Þóreyjargnúp. Just before the Winter Nights, Grettir rode north across the ridges to Viðidalr and stayed at Auðunarstaðir. He and Auðunn made a full reconciliation. Grettir gave him a fine axe, and they pledged each other their friendship. Auðunn lived at Auðunarstaðir for a long time and had many descendants. His son was Egill who married Ulfheiðr, the daughter of Eyjólfr Guðmundarson. Their son Eyjólfr, who was killed at the Alþingi, was the father of Ormr, chaplain to Bishop Þorlákr.

Grettir rode north to Vatnsdal and paid a visit to Tunga. His maternal uncle, Jǫkull Bárðarson, was living there at that time. Jǫkull was a tall, strong man, and exceptionally arrogant. He was a merchant and was very overbearing, but a man of considerable importance. He welcomed Grettir, who stayed with him for three nights. Glámr's hauntings had become so notorious that people hardly talked about anything else. Grettir enquired closely about all the incidents that had taken place. Jǫkull said the stories were no exaggeration. 'Would you be curious about having a look in there, kinsman?'

Grettir said that he was, but Jǫkull warned him not to, 'for that would be tempting fate. You are an important man in your family. We do not consider any other young man a match for you, but evil begets evil as far as Glámr is concerned. And it's much better to tackle human beings than such monstrous creatures.'

Grettir said he was still interested in calling at Þórhallsstaðir and seeing what had been going on there. Jǫkull said, 'I can see there's no point in trying to dissuade you. The old saying is true, that great ability and good luck do not always go hand-in-hand.'

'Þá er ǫðrum vá fyrir durum, er ǫðrum er inn um komit, ok hygg at, hversu þér mun fara sjálfum, áðr lýkr,' kvað Grettir.

Jǫkull svarar: 'Vera kann, at vit sjáim báðir nǫkkut fram, en hvárrgi fái við gǫrt.'

Eptir þat skilðu þeir, ok likaði hvárigum annars spár.

35. Grettir reið á Þórhallsstaði, ok fagnaði bóndi honum vel. Hann spurði, hvert Grettir ætlaði at fara, en hann segisk þar vilja vera um nóttina, ef bónda líkaði, at svá væri.

Þórhallr kvazk þǫkk fyrir kunna, at hann væri þar, 'en fám þykkir slœgr til at gista hér um tíma; muntu hafa heyrt getit, um hvat hér er at væla, en ek vilda gjarna, at þú hlytir engi vandræði af mér. En þó at þú komisk heill á brott, þá veit ek fyrir víst, at þú missir hests þíns, því at engi heldr hér heilum sínum fararskjóta, sá er kemr.'

Grettir kvað gott til hesta, hvat sem af þessum yrði.

Þórhallr varð glaðr við, er Grettir vildi þar vera, ok tók við honum báðum hǫndum; var hestr Grettis læstr í húsi sterkliga. Þeir fóru til svefns, ok leið svá af nóttin, at ekki kom Glámr heim.

Þá mælti Þórhallr: 'Vel hefir brugðit við þína kvámu, því at hverja nótt er Glámr vanr at ríða húsum eða brjóta upp hurðir, sem þú matt merki sjá.'

Grettir mælti: 'Þá mun vera annaðhvárt, at hann mun ekki lengi á sér sitja, eða mun af venjask meir en eina nótt; skal eg vera nótt aðra ok sjá, hversu ferr.'

'Disaster waits at a man's door, though another goes in before,' said Grettir. 'You should be thinking about what fate you yourself will meet in the end.'

Jǫkull replied, 'We both may have some insight into the future, but neither of us can do anything about it.'

After that they parted, and neither of them liked the other's predictions.

35. Grettir rode to Þórhallsstaðir and the farmer welcomed him warmly. He asked Grettir where he was heading, and the farmer was pleased when he replied that he wanted to stay there for the night.

Þórhallr said he would be grateful if Grettir would stay 'for there aren't many people who feel they stand to gain from staying here at present. You must have heard of our trouble here, and I wouldn't like you to come to grief on my account. Even if you leave here in one piece, I know for certain that you will lose your horse, because no one who comes here manages to keep his horse safe.'

Grettir said that horses were easy enough to come by, whatever might happen to his. Þórhallr was delighted that Grettir wanted to stay and welcomed him with open arms. Grettir's horse was firmly locked indoors, then they went to bed and the night passed without Glámr turning up. Then Þórhallr said, 'Things have changed for the better since you arrived, because Glámr usually rises every night and straddles the roof or breaks down the doors, as you can see for yourself.'

Grettir said, 'Either he will resume his old ways soon, or he will give up for more than a single night. So I'm going to stay another night and see what happens.'

Síðan gengu þeir til hests Grettis, ok var ekki við hann glezk; allt þótti bónda at einu fara.

Nú er Grettir þar aðra nótt, ok kom ekki þrællinn heim. Þá þótti bónda mjǫg vænkask; fór hann þá at sjá hest Grettis. Þá var upp brotit húsit, er bóndi kom til, en hestrinn dreginn til dura útar, ok lamit í sundr í honum hvert bein.

Þórhallr sagði Gretti, hvar þá var komit, ok bað hann forða sér, 'þvi at víss er dauðinn, ef þú bíðr Gláms.'

Grettir svarar: 'Eigi má ek minna hafa fyrir hest minn en at sjá þrælinn.'

Bóndi sagði, at þat var eigi bati, at sjá hann, 'því at hann er ólíkr nǫkkurri mannligri mynd; en góð þykki mér hver sú stund, er þú vill hér vera.'

Nú líðr dagrinn, ok er menn skyldu fara til svefns, vildi Grettir eigi fara af klæðum ok lagðist niðr í setit gegnt lokrekkju bónda; hann hafði rǫggvarfeld yfir sér ok hneppði annat skautit niðr undir fœtr sér, en annat snaraði hann undir hǫfuð sér ok sá út um hǫfuðsmáttina. Setstokkr var fyrir framan setit mjǫg sterkr, ok spyrndi hann þar í. Duraumbúningrinn allr var frá brotinn útidurunum, en nú var þar fyrir bundinn hurðarflaki ok óvendiliga um búit. Þverþilit var allt brotit frá skálanum, þat sem þar fyrir framan hafði verit, bæði fyrir ofan þvertréit ok neðan. Sængr allar váru ór stað fœrðar; heldr var þar óvistuligt. Ljós brann í skálanum um nóttina.

Ok er af myndi þriðjungr af nótt, heyrði Grettir út dynur miklar; var þá farit upp á húsin ok riðit skálanum ok barit hælunum, svá at brakaði í hverju tré; því gekk lengi. Þá var farit ofan af húsunum ok til dura gengit; ok er upp var lokit hurðunni, sá Grettir, at þrællinn rétti inn hǫfuðit, ok sýndisk honum

---

Then they went to inspect Grettir's horse, which had not been touched. The farmer thought everything was pointing in the same way.

Grettir stayed a second night and the wretch did not come to the house. The farmer thought the outlook was much more promising. Then he went to look at Grettir's horse, but this time the stable had been broken into when he arrived, and the horse had been dragged outdoors, and every bone in its body was broken. Þórhallr told Grettir what had happened and told him to leave, 'because you're sure to die if you wait for Glámr'.

Grettir answered, 'A glimpse of that wretch is the least I can ask in return for my horse.'

The farmer said it would do him no good to see Glámr, 'for he is different from any human being. But I feel better for every hour you are willing to stay here.'

The day passed, and when the people went to bed, Grettir did not get undressed, but lay down on the bench opposite the farmer's bed-closet. He covered himself with a shaggy fur cloak, tucking one end under his feet and the other around his head, so that he could see out through the opening at the neck. In front of the seat was a very strong bed-frame, and he braced his feet against it. The entire frame of the outer door to the house had been smashed right away and some makeshift boards had been put in its place. The wooden partition which separated the hall from the entrance passage had also been broken away, both above and below the cross-beam. All the beds had been moved out of place and the house was hardly fit for habitation. A light was left burning in the living-room that night.

When a third of the night had passed, Grettir heard a great din outside. Someone climbed up on to the house and straddled the roof of the hall, kicking against it with its heels so that every beam in the house creaked. This went on for a long time. Then it climbed down from the roof and came to the door. When the door opened, Grettir watched the afskræmiliga mikit ok undarliga stórskorit. Glámr fór seint ok réttisk upp, er hann kom inn í dyrrnar; hann gnæfði ofarliga við rjáfrinu, snýr at skálanum ok lagði handleggina upp á þvertréit ok gnapði inn yfir skálann. Ekki lét bóndi heyra til sín, því at honum þótti œrit um, er hann heyrði, hvat um var úti. Grettir lá kyrr ok hrœrði sik hvergi.

Glámr sá, at hrúga nǫkkur lá setinu, ok rézk nú innar eptir skálanum ok þreif í feldinn stundar fast. Grettir spyrndi í stokkinn, ok gekk því hvergi. Glámr hnykkði í annat sinn miklu fastara, ok bifaðisk hvergi feldrinn. Í þriðja sinn þreif hann í með báðum hǫndum svá fast, at hann rétti Gretti upp ór setinu; kippðu nú í sundr feldinum í millum sín. Glámr leit á slitrit, er hann hélt á, ok undraðisk mjǫk, hverr svá fast myndi togask við hann. Ok í því hljóp Grettir undir hendr honum ok þreif um hann miðjan ok spennti á honum hrygginn sem fastast gat hann, ok ætlaði hann, at Glámr skyldi kikna við; en þrællinn lagði at handleggjum Grettis svá fast, at hann hǫrfaði allr fyrir orku sakar. Fór Grettir þá undan í ýmis setin; gengu þá frá stokkarnir, ok allt brotnaði, þat sem fyrir varð. Vildi Glámr leita út, en Grettir fœrði við fœtr, hvar sem hann mátti, en þó gat Glámr dregit hann fram ór skálanum. Áttu þeir þá allharða sókn, því at þrællinn ætlaði at koma honum út ór bœnum; en svá illt, sem at eiga var við Glám inni, þá sá Grettir, at þó var verra at fásk við hann úti, ok því brauzk hann í móti af ǫllu afli at fara út. Glámr fœrðisk í aukana ok hneppði hann að sér, er þeir kómu í anddyrit. Ok er Grettir sér, at hann fekk eigi við spornat, hefir hann allt eitt atriðit, at hann hleypr sem harðast í fang þrælnum ok spyrnir báðum fótum í jarðfastan stein, er stóð í durunum. Við þessu bjósk þrællinn eigi; hann hafði þá togazk við at

---

wretch stick its head inside, which looked hideously huge with grotesque features. Glámr moved slowly and stood up straight once he was through the door. He towered up to the rafters, rested his arm on the cross-beam, and turned to the hall. The farmer did not make a single sound, for he had already had quite enough just hearing what went on outside. Grettir lay there completely still.

When Glámr noticed a heap lying on the seat, he moved along inside the hall and gave the cloak a sharp tug. Grettir braced his feet against the bed-frame, and did not budge. Glámr yanked at it again, much harder, yet the cloak still would not move. The third time he tugged so hard with both hands that he sat Grettir up on the bench, and they ripped the cloak in two between them. Glámr looked at the strip he was left holding, astonished that someone could have pulled so hard against him. At that moment Grettir leapt under Glámr's arms and clutched him around the waist, clasped him with all his might hoping to topple him. But the wretch gripped Grettir's arms so tightly that he was forced to break away. Grettir backed away into one seat after another. All the benches were torn loose and everything in their way was smashed. Glámr tried to make it to the door, while Grettir struggled for a foothold. Finally Glámr managed to drag him out of the hall. A fierce struggle ensued, because the wretch intended to take him outside. But difficult as Glámr was to deal with indoors, Grettir saw he would be even worse in the open, so he struggled with all his might to keep from going out. Using all his power Glámr pulled Grettir towards him when they reached the entrance hall. When Grettir realised that he could not hold him back, he suddenly thrust himself as hard as he could into the wretch's arms and pressed both his feet against a rock that was buried in the ground in the doorway. The wretch was draga Gretti at sér, ok því kiknaði Glámr á bak aptr ok rauk ǫfugr út á dyrrnar, svá at herðarnar námu uppdyrit, ok ræfrit gekk í sundr, bæði viðirnir ok þekjan frǫrin; fell hann svá opinn ok ǫfugr út ór húsunum, en Grettir á hann ofan. Tunglskin var mikið úti ok gluggaþykkn; hratt stundum fyrir, en stundum dró frá.

Nú í því er Glámr fell, rak skýit frá tunglinu, en Glámr hvessti augun upp í móti, ok svá hefir Grettir sagt sjálfr, at þá eina sýn hafi hann sét svá, at honum brygði við. Þá sigaði svá at honum af ǫllu saman, mœði ok því, er hann sá, at Glámr gaut sínum sjónum harðliga, at hann gat eigi brugðit saxinu ok lá náliga í milli heims og heljar.

En því var meiri ófagnaðarkraptr með Glámi en flestum ǫðrum aptrgǫngumǫnnum, at hann mælti þá á þessa leið:

'Mikit kapp hefir þú á lagit, Grettir,' sagði hann 'at finna mik, en þat mun eigi undarligt þykkja, þó at þú hljótir ekki mikit happ af mér. En þat má ek segja þér, at þú hefir nú fengit helming afls þess ok þroska, er þér var ætlaðr, ef þú hefðir mik ekki fundit; nú fæ ek þat afl eigi af þér tekit, er þú hefir áðr hreppt, en því má ek ráða, at þú verðr aldri sterkari en nú ertu, ok ertu þó nógu sterkr, ok at því mun mǫrgum verða. Þú hefir frægr orðit hér til af verkum þínum, en héðan af munu falla til þín sekðir ok vígaferli, en flest ǫll verk þín snúask þér til ógæfu ok hamingjuleysis.

'Þú munt verða útlægr gǫrr ok hljóta jafnan úti at búa einn samt. Þá legg ek þat á við þik, at þessi augu sé þér jafnan fyrir sjónum, sem ek ber eptir, ok mun þér þá erfitt þykkja einum at vera, ok þat mun þér til dauða draga.'

---

caught unawares, and as he had been straining to pull Grettir towards him, Glámr fell over backwards and crashed through the door. His shoulders took the door-frame with him and the rafters were torn apart, the wooden roofing and the frozen turf on it. Glámr fell out of the house on to his back, face upwards, and Grettir landed on top of him. The moon was shining strongly but thick patches of clouds covered and uncovered it in turns.

Just as Glámr fell, the clouds drifted away and Glámr glared up at the moon. Grettir himself once said that this was the only sight that ever frightened him. Suddenly Grettir's strength deserted him, from exhaustion and also because of the fierce way Glámr was rolling his eyes. Unable to draw his sword, he lay there closer to death than to life.

Glámr was endowed with more evil force than any other ghost, as he spoke these words: 'You have gone to great lengths to meet me, Grettir,' he said, 'and it won't seem surprising if you do not earn much good luck from me. I can tell you that you have attained only half the strength and manhood allotted to you had you not met me. I cannot take away from you the strength you already have, but I can ordain that you will never become any stronger than you are now, strong enough as you may be, as many people will find to their cost. You have become famous until now for your deeds, but henceforth outlawry and killings will come your way, and most of your deeds will bring you misfortune and ill-luck. You will be made an outlaw and be forced to live alone and outdoors. And this curse I lay on you: my eyes will always be before your sight and this will make your solitude unbearable, and this shall drag you to your death.'

As the wretch finished saying this, the helplessness that had come upon Grettir left him. He drew his short-sword, chopped off Glámr's head and placed it against the buttocks.

Ok sem þrællinn hafði þetta mælt, þá rann af Gretti ómegin þat, sem á honum hafði verit. Brá hann þá saxinu ok hjó hǫfuð af Glámi ok setti þat við þjó honum. Bóndi kom þá út ok hafði klæzk, á meðan Glámr lét ganga tǫluna, en hvergi þorði hann nær at koma, fyrr en Glámr var fallinn. Þórhallr lofaði guð fyrir og þakkaði vel Gretti, er hann hafði unnit þenna óhreina anda. Fóru þeir þá til ok brenndu Glám at kǫldum kolum. Eptir þat báru þeir ǫsku hans í eina hít ok grófu þar niðr, sem sízt váru fjárhagar eða mannavegir; gengu heim eptir þat, ok var þá mjǫk komit at degi. Lagðisk Grettir niðr, því at hann var stirðr mjǫk.

Þórhallr sendi menn á næstu bœi eptir mǫnnum, sýndi ok sagði, hversu farit hafði. Ǫllum þótti mikils um vert um þetta verk, þeim er heyrðu; var þat þá almælt, at engi væri þvílíkr maðr á ǫllu landinu fyrir afls sakar ok hreysti ok allrar atgǫrvi sem Grettir Ásmundarson.

Þórhallr leysti Gretti vel af garði ok gaf homun góðan hest ok klæði sœmilig, því at þau váru ǫll sundr leyst, er hann hafði áðr borit; skilðu þeir með vináttu. Reið Grettir þaðan í Ás í Vatnsdal, ok tók Þorvaldr við honum vel ok spurði inniliga at sameign þeira Gláms, en Grettir segir honum viðskipti þeira ok kvazk aldri í þvílíka aflraun komit hafa, svá langa viðreign sem þeir hǫfðu saman átt.

Þorvaldr bað hann hafa sik spakan, 'ok mun þá vel duga, en ella mun þér slysgjarnt verða.'

Grettir kvað ekki batnat hafa um lyndisbragðit ok sagðisk nú miklu verr stilltr en áðr, ok allar mótgǫrðir verri þykkja. Á því fann hann mikla muni, at hann var orðinn maðr svá myrkfælinn, at hann þorði hvergi at fara einn saman, þegar myrkva tók; sýndisk honum þá hvers kyns skrípi, ok þat er haft

---

The farmer came outside, having dressed while Glámr delivered his speech; he had not dared to approach until Glámr was laid low. Þórhallr praised God and thanked Grettir warmly for having overcome this unclean spirit. Þórhallr set to work and burned Glámr to ashes, gathered them in a skin bag and buried them as far away as possible from grazing land or paths. After that they went back home; it was close to daybreak by then. Grettir lay down to rest, for he was very stiff.

Þórhallr sent for men from the neighbouring farms in order to show them and tell them what had happened. All who heard of this exploit were greatly impressed by it, and said that in the entire country no man was a match for Grettir Ásmundarson in strength, courage and all accomplishments.

Þórhallr sent Grettir on his way with generous gifts, giving him a good horse and splendid clothes, because those he had been wearing were all torn to shreds. They parted the best of friends.

Grettir rode over to Ás in Vatnsdal. Thorvaldr welcomed him warmly and asked in detail about his encounter with Glámr. Grettir told him about their dealings, and said that he had never before been through such a test of strength, so long had they grappled together.

Thorvaldr warned him to keep his temper in check, 'and everything will turn out well. Otherwise, you will be prone to much bad luck.'

Grettir said his temperament had not improved. And that he had much more trouble restraining himself and was much quicker to take offence than before. He also said he could notice one change: he had grown so afraid of the dark that he did not dare go anywhere síðan fyrir orðtœki, at þeim ljái Glámr augna eða gefi glámsýni, er mjǫk sýnisk annan veg en er.

Grettir reið heim til Bjargs, er hann hafði gǫrt ǫrendi sín, ok sat heima um vetrinn.

---

alone after nightfall – he thought he could see all kinds of phantoms. It has since become a common saying about people who suffer hallucinations that Glámr lends them his eyes, or they see things with Glámr's eyes.

Grettir rode back home to Bjarg when he had finished his business, and stayed there for the rest of the winter.

Grettir fights the cave-trolls

In the eleventh year of his outlawry, in 1027–8, Grettir spends the winter on a farm in Bárðardalr in the north. The area has been plagued by trolls and Grettir is the man to sort out the problem. The following chapters recount his defeat of the troll-woman and then his battle with the troll-man beneath the waterfall. It is this episode, in ch. 66, that bears such striking echoes of the *Beowulf.* Not only does Grettir fight the monster in a cave after diving through the waterfall, like the Geatish hero of *Beowulf*, but his normal weapon of choice is a *sax*, the sort of sword that gave the Saxons their name. The cave-troll attacks him with a *heptisax*, a pike or shafted sword. This is the only occurance of the word in Old Icelandic literature. The hilted sword named Hrunting, which Beowulf borrows from Umferth to kill Grendel's Mother, is called a *hæftmece* (line 1457).

65. Nú er frá Gretti þat að segja, a þá er dró at miðri nótt, heyrði hann út dynur miklar. Því næst kom inn í stofuna trollkona mikil; hon hafði í hendi trog, en annarri skálm heldr mikla. Hon litask um, er hon kom inn, ok sá, hvar Gestr lá, ok hljóp at honum, en hann upp í móti, ok réðusk á grimmliga ok sóttusk lengi í stofunni. Hon var sterkari, en hann fór undan kœnliga, en allt þat, sem fyrir þeim varð, brutu þau, jafnvel þverþilit undan stofunni. Hon dró hann fram yfir dyrrnar ok svá í anddyrit; þar tók hann fast í móti. Hon vildi draga hann út ór bœnum, en þat varð eigi, fyrr en þau leystu frá allan útiduraumbúninginn ok báru hann út á herðum sér; þœfði hon þá ofan til árinnar ok allt fram at gljúfrum.

---

65. To return to Grettir, it is said that towards midnight he heard a great noise. Then a large troll-woman came into the room; she held a trough in one hand and a big knife in the other. She looked around as she entered, and seeing Gestr lying there she rushed at him; he jumped up to confront her, and they attacked each other fiercely and struggled for a long time in the room. She was stronger, but he dodged her skilfully. They broke everything that got in their way, even the partition between the entry-way and the main room. She managed to drag him out through the door and towards the front door, where he stood his ground against her. She wanted to drag him out of the farm house, but could not manage it until they had broken the entire outer door-frame and took it with them on their shoulders. Then she dragged him off down to the river, right up to the edge of the chasm.

Þá var Gestr ákafliga móðr, en þó varð annaðhvárt at gera, at herða sik, ella myndi hon steypa honum í gljúfrin. Alla nóttina sóttusk þau. Eigi þóttisk hann hafa fengizk við þvílíkan ófagnað fyrir afls sakar. Hon hafði haldit honum svá fast at sér, at hann mátti hvárigri hendi taka til nǫkkurs, útan hann helt um hana miðja, kvinnuna; ok er þau kómu á árgljúfrit, bregðr hann flagðkonunni til sveiflu. Í því varð honum laus hin hœgri hǫndin; hann þreif þá skjótt til saxins, er hann var gyrðr með, ok bregðr því, høggr þá á ǫxl trollinu, svá at af tók hǫndina hœgri, ok svá varð hann lauss, en hon steyptisk í gljúfrin ok svá í fossinn.

Gestr var þá bæði stirðr ok móðr ok lá þar lengi á hamrinum. Gekk hann þá heim, er lýsa tók, ok lagðisk í rekkju; hann var allr þrútinn ok blár.

Ok er húsfreyja kom frá tíðum, þótti henni heldr raskat um híbýli sín; gekk hon þá til Gests ok spurði, hvat til hefði borit, er allt var brotit ok bœlt. Hann sagði allt, sem farit hafði. Henni þótti mikils um vert, ok spurði, hverr hann var. Hann sagði þá til it sanna ok bað sœkja prest ok kvazk vildu finna hann; var og svá gǫrt.

En er Steinn prestr kom til Sandhauga, varð hann brátt þess víss, at þar var kominn Grettir Ásmundarson, er Gestr nefndisk. Prestr spurði hvat hann ætlaði af þeim mǫnnum myndi vera orðit, er þar hǫfðu horfit. Grettir kvazk ætla, at í gljúfrin myndi þeir hafa horfit. Prestr kvazk eigi kunna at leggja trúnað á sagnir hans, ef engi merki mætti til sjá. Grettir segir, at síðar vissi þeir þat gørr; fór prestr heim. Grettir lá í rekkju margar nætr. Húsfreyja gerði við hann harðla vel; ok leið svá af jólin.

Gestr was out of breath, but knew either he had to fight on or she would hurl him into the chasm. They fought all night long and he felt he had never fought such a powerful monster before. She held him so close against her that he could do nothing with either of his arms except to clutch at her waist. When they were at the edge of the chasm he lifted her off her feet and swung her off balance, freeing his right hand. He grabbed for the short sword he was wearing and drawing the sax, he swung it at her shoulder and chopped off her right arm. In this way he broke free and she plunged into the chasm and under the waterfall.

Gestr was both stiff and exhausted and lay for a long time on the edge of the cliff. He went back at daybreak and got into bed both swollen and bruised.

When the farmer's wife returned from Mass she saw the shambles of her house and asked Gestr what had happened there as everything was broken and smashed. He told her about everything that had happened. She found it remarkable and asked him his name. He told her his real name and asked her to fetch the priest, saying he wished to talk with him. This was done.

When Steinn the priest arrived at Sandhaugar he realised at once that it was Grettir Ásmundarson who called himself Gestr. He asked Grettir what he thought might have happened to the men who had disappeared, and Grettir said he assumed they had vanished into the chasm. The priest said he could not believe Grettir's stories without seeing any evidence, but Grettir said they would find out later for sure. The priest returned home. Grettir lay in bed for many days, and the farmer's wife treated him very well; and Christmas went by.

Þetta er sǫgn Grettis, at trollkonan steypðisk í gljúfrin við, er hon fekk sárit, en Bárðardalsmenn segja, at hana dagaði uppi, þá er þau glímdu, sprungit, þá er hann hjó af henni hǫndina, ok standi þar enn í konulíking á bjarginu. Þeir dalbúarnir leyndu þar Gretti um vetrinn.

Eptir jól var þat einn dag, at Grettir fór til Eyjardalsár, ok er þeir Grettir fundusk ok prestr, mælti Grettir: 'Sé eg þat, prestr,' segir hann, 'at þú leggr lítinn trúnað á sagnir mínar. Nú vil ek, at þú farir með mér til árinnar ok sjáir, hver líkendi þér þykkir á vera.'

Prestr gerði svá; en er þeir kómu til forsins, sá þeir skúta upp undir bergit; það var meitilberg svá mikit, at hvergi mátti upp komask, ok nær tíu faðma ofan at vatninu. Þeir hǫfðu festi með sér.

Þá mælti prestr: 'Langt um ófœrt sýnisk mér þér niðr að fara.'

Grettir svarar: 'Fœrt er víst, en þeim mun bezt þar sem áræðismenn eru. Mun ek forvitnask, hvat í forsinum er, en þú skalt geyma festar.'

Prestr bað hann ráða ok keyrði niðr hæl á berginu ok bar at grjót ok sat þar hjá.

66. Nú er frá Gretti að segja, at hann lét stein í festaraugat ok lét svá síga ofan at vatninu.

'Hvern veg ætlar þú nú,' segir prestr, 'at fara?'

'Ekki vil ek vera bundinn,' segir Grettir, 'þá er ek kem í forsinn; svá boðar mér hugr um.'

According to Grettir, the troll-woman plunged into the chasm when she was wounded but the people of Barðardal claim she turned into stone at daybreak while they wrestled and she died when he chopped off her arm, and she is still standing there on the cliff, as a rock in the shape of a woman. The people of the valley hid Grettir there that winter.

One day after Christmas Grettir went to Eyjardalsá and when he saw the priest he said, 'I can see that you don't have much faith in my account. Now I want you to go down to the river with me and see how likely you think it is.'

The priest agreed. When they reached the waterfall they saw a cave in the cliff-face which was so sheer that no one could climb it. It was nearly ten fathoms down to the water. They had a rope with them.

The priest said, 'It looks well beyond what you can manage to go down there.'

Grettir replied, 'Certainly there is a way, and all the greater for great men. I shall have a look at what is in the cave while you stay here and guard the rope.'

The priest said it was up to him, and drove a peg into the top of the cliff and piled stones around it.

66. Now this is said about Grettir: he looped the ends of the rope around a stone and lowered it down to the water.

'How do you plan to get down?' asked the priest.

'I don't want to be tied to anything when I enter the waterfall,' said Grettir, 'I've had an intuition.'

Eptir þat bjó hann sik til ferðar ok var fáklæddr ok gyrði sik með saxinu, en hafði ekki fleiri vápn; síðan hljóp hann af bjarginu ok niðr í forsinn. Sá prestr í iljar honum ok vissi síðan aldri, hvat af honum varð. Grettir kafaði undir forsinn, ok var þat torvelt, því at iða var mikil, ok varð hann allt til grunns at kafa, áðr en hann kœmisk upp undir forsinn. Þar var forberg nǫkkut, ok komsk hann inn þar upp á. Þar var hellir mikill undir forsinum, ok féll áin fram af berginu.

Hann gekk þá inn í hellinn, ok var þar eldr mikill á brǫndum. Grettir sá, at þar sat jǫtunn ógurliga mikill; hann var hræðiligr at sjá. En er Grettir kom at honum, hljóp jǫtunninn upp og greip flein einn ok hjó til þess, er kominn var, því at bæði mátti hǫggva ok leggja með því; tréskapt var í; þat kǫlluðu menn þá heptisax, er þann veg var gǫrt. Grettir hjó á móti með saxinu, ok kom á skaftit, svá at í sundr tók. Jǫtunninn vildi þá seilask á bak sér aptr til sverðs, er þar hekk í hellinum. Í því hjó Grettir framan á brjóstit, svá at náliga tók af alla bringspelina ok kviðinn, svá at iðrin steypðusk ór honum ofan í ána, og keyrði þau ofan eptir ánni.

Ok er prestr sat við festina, sá hann, at slyðrur nǫkkurar rak ofan eptir strengnum, blóðgar allar. Hann varð þá lauss á velli ok þóttisk nú vita, at Grettir myndi dauðr vera; hljóp hann þá frá festarhaldinu ok fór heim. Var þá komit at kveldi, ok sagði prestr víslega, at Grettir væri dauðr, ok sagði, at mikill skaði væri eptir þvílíkan mann.

Nú er frá Gretti at segja; hann lét skammt hǫggva í milli þar til er jǫtunninn dó. Gekk Grettir þá innar eptir hellinum; hann kveikði ljós ok kannaði

---

After that he prepared himself to set off. He took off most of his clothes and girded on the sax, but he did not take any other weapons. Then he plunged off the side of the cliff and down into the waterfall. The priest watched as the soles of his feet disappeared, then had no idea what had become of him. Grettir dived under the waterfall, which was no easy task because to avoid the swirling current he had to dive down to the bottom before he could rise to the surface on the other side. There was a ledge that he climbed on to. There was a large cave behind the waterfall where the river plunged over the cliff.

Grettir entered the cave where a great log fire was burning. Grettir saw a giant lying there, monstrous in size and terrifying to look at. As Grettir approached, the giant grabbed a pike and swung a blow at the intruder; with such a pike one can both slice and thrust. It had a wooden shaft and men call this sort of weapon a *heptisax*. Grettir returned the blow with his sax, striking the shaft and cutting through it. Now the giant tried to reach behind him for a sword that was hanging on the cave wall, but as he did so Grettir struck him on the chest, slicing his lower ribs and belly straight off so that his guts gushed out of him and into the river where they were swept away.

As the priest sat beside the rope he saw some bloody pieces of flesh floating in the current and he lost his nerve. He was convinced that Grettir was dead, so he abandoned the rope and went home. It was evening by then. The priest announced that Grettir was certainly dead and described it as a great loss.

Now this is said about Grettir: he kept raining blows on the giant until he was dead, then went inside the cave. He lit a flame and searched around. It is not told how much treasure hellinn. Ekki er frá því sagt, hversu mikit fé hann fékk í hellinum, en það ætla men, að verit hafi nǫkkut; dvalðisk honum þar fram á nóttina. Hann fann þar tveggja manna bein ok bar þau í belg einn. Leitaði hann þá ór hellinum ok lagðisk til festarinnar ok hristi hana ok ætlaði, at prestr myndi þar vera, en er hann vissi, at prestr var heim farinn, varð hann þá at handstyrkja upp festina, ok komsk hann svá upp á bjargit.

Fór hann þá heim til Eyjardalsár ok kom í forkirkju belginum þeim, sem beinin váru í, ok þar með rúnakefli því, er vísur þessar váru forkunnliga vel á ristnar:

> Gekk eg í gljúfr et døkkva, gein veltiflug steina
> við hjǫrgœði hríðar hlunns úrsvǫlum munni;
> fast lá framan at brjósti flugstraumr í sal Naumu;
> heldr kom á herðar skáldi hǫrð fjón Braga kvánar.

Ok enn þessi:

> Ljótr kom mér í móti mellu vinr ór helli;
> Hann fékksk heldr at sǫnnu harðfengr við mik lengi;
> harðeggjat létk hǫggvit heptisax af skepti;
> Gangs klauf brjóst ok bringu bjartr gunnlogi svarta.

Þar sagði svá, at Grettir hafi bein þessi ór hellinum haft. En er prestr kom til kirkju um morguninn, fann hann keflit ok þat, sem fylgði, ok las rúnarnar; en Grettir hafði farit heim til Sandhauga.

---

he found there, but people assume it was a great hoard. He stayed there through the night, found the bones of two men and put them into a bag. Then he made his way out of the cave, swam back to the rope and shook it, expecting the priest to be there. When he realised the priest had gone, he had to climb up the rope with his hands, and finally he made it to the cliff-top.

Then he headed back to Eyjardalsá, where he placed the bag with the bones on the church-porch, and a rune-stick beautifully carved with this verse:

> I entered the black gorge where the plummeting rock face gaped
> with its cold spouting mouth at me, the maker of sword-showers.
> The plunging current pressed hard at my chest in the troll-woman's hall;
> the wife of the god of poets came down hard on my shoulders.

And also this one:

> The troll-woman's ugly mate came at me from his cave,
> made his long and bold struggle with me.
> I snapped his hard-edged pike from its shaft, my sword
> ablaze with battle, split open his chest and black belly.

The runes also said that Grettir had taken these bones from the cave. When the priest went to the church the next morning he found the stick and all the rest and read the runes. By then Grettir had gone back to Sandhaugar.

WRITERS OF THE BENEDICTINE REFORM

* * *

WRITERS OF THE BENEDICTINE REFORM

✻ ✻ ✻

The reform of monasteries in Anglo-Saxon England, which was inspired by the Benedictine monastic rule, had its roots in the Alfredian 890s, its first flowering in the mid-tenth century and its fruits in the late tenth century, progressing into the early eleventh. In Winchester and other schools, the West Saxon dialect of Old English was taught to the level of a new literary standard. As the public face of a movement to ensure religious orthodoxy, one which came from the Continent, this tendency to teach good writing in English with Latin stylistic models allowed the creation of the finest prose in the English language, not to be equalled until the sixteenth-century English Renaissance. As will be seen in this section, the Latin *Alexander's Letter to Aristotle* received its earliest vernacular translation perhaps a generation or two after Alfred, during the reign of King Edmund (939–46), from whom the first reforming impetus came. The translator appears to have used *Beowulf* to help him construct the megalomania of his all-conquering Macedonian hero, whose paranoia emerges convincingly in the extracts below. Thereafter a renewed surge of doctrinal reform during the reign of King Edgar the Peaceable (959–75) allowed the composition of homilies which explored themes such as compassion, pagan idolatry, and here in the extracts from Blickling Homily No. 16, a chapel in Apulia in the south of Italy. *Beowulf*, once again, is connected to this homily, probably by virtue of having used the same source for a description of hell.

King Edgar had Dunstan ordained as archbishop of Canterbury (959–88), Æthelwold as bishop of Winchester (963–84), and Oswald as bishop of Worcester (961–92) and then archbishop of York (971–92). Through these men, inheritors of Alfred's kingdom, the Reform produced a wealth of prose that might be called respectively early (Vercelli and Blickling Homilies) and late (Ælfric, Byrhtferth and Wulfstan). This vernacular literature was without parallel elsewhere in Europe. Some of its textual highlights are given below, in the limpid prose of Ælfric who sought to avoid the florid 'hermeneutic' style, which may be seen in Byrhtferth (in the Custom Version), and in the arresting sermons of Archbishop Wulfstan of York, who lambasted the English for their sins while negotiating the necessary treaties with King Cnut (1016–35). The fact, however, that one of the manuscripts preserving Wulfstan's homilies also contains a prose romance or early novel, *The Apollonius of Tyre* from *c.* 1050, shows that not all was doom and gloom in England at this time, and that, to the extent of this light relief from savage reforming sermons, some English tastes were beginning to change (see Early Chivalry).

General bibliography

Adam, A., *The Liturgical Year* (New York, 1981)

Attwater, D., with C. R. John, *The Penguin Dictionary of Saints*, 3rd ed. (Harmondsworth, 1995)

Baker, P. S., 'The Old English Canon of Byrhtferth of Ramsey', *Speculum* 55 (1980), 22–37

Baker, P. S., 'The Old English language', *B&OS* 272–300

Brookes, S., 'Prose writers of the English Benedictine Reform', *B&OS* 417–54

Clemoes, P., 'Ælfric', in *Continuations and Beginnings: Studies in Old English Literature*, ed. E. G. Stanley (London, 1966), 1–36

Gneuss, H., 'The origin of standard Old English and Æthelwold's school at Winchester', *Anglo-Saxon England* 1 (1972), 63–83

Godden, M., ed., *Ælfric's Catholic Homilies: The Second Series*, Early English Texts Second Series 5 (Oxford, 1979)

Hofstetter, W., 'Winchester and the standardization of Old English vocabulary', *Anglo-Saxon England* 17 (1988), 139–61

Orchard, A., 'Wulfstan as reader, writer and rewriter', in *The Old English Homily: Precedent, Practice and Appropriation*, ed. A. J. Kleist, Studies in the Early Middle Ages 17 (Turnhout, 2007), 311–41

Swanton, M. J., ed. and trans., *Anglo-Saxon Prose* (London, 1993)

Wright, C. D., 'Old English homilies and Latin sources', in *The Old English Homily: Precedent, Practice and Appropriation*, ed. A. J. Kleist, Studies in the Early Middle Ages 17 (Turnhout, 2007), 15–66

Alexander's Letter to Aristotle

⁕

The Old English *Alexander's Letter to Aristotle* is found in MS BL Cotton Vitellius A.xv, folios 107 recto to 131 verso, where it ends just before the opening page of *Beowulf*. It has the distinction of being the oldest surviving vernacular translation of the fourth-century Latin *Epistola Alexandri ad Aristotelem* (of the same meaning). The Latin work was a forgery, but popular, surviving in many manuscripts. Alexander, who inspired a wealth of literature in the Middle Ages, including the *Alexandreis* of Walter of Châtillon (of the late eleventh century), died famously at the age of 33 in 323 BC, having conquered much of the known world. His empire then began to break up immediately. He had lost the love of his tribe by becoming a new Persian potentate rather than remaining the young prodigy of Macedon. But his fame magnified with each century, each time a despot used his model as a path to power. Arguments about the morally or intellectually attractive character of Alexander continue until this day, both passionately for (Renault 1975) and carefully against (Worthington 2004). Philosopher king, or alcoholic war-monger? This fierce division of opinion started, on the positive side, with contemporary biographers such as General Ptolemy, and later with Plutarch (second century AD). On the negative side, there was Cicero, a failed politician whose anxieties were focused on Julius Caesar (50s BC); Seneca (50s AD); and even the opening verses of the First Book of the Maccabees (Orchard 1995: 116–19; Worthington 2004: 2–7). The Church Fathers took Alexander as a model of tyrannical pride. St Jerome's dim view was further darkened by Orosius in his *History Against the Pagans in Seven Books* (of the fifth century). Since this work was translated into West Saxon, probably in the 890s as part of Alfred's programme to rebuild learning in England, it is likely that it has influenced the Old English translation of the *Epistola*, in whose sparse Latin Alexander is generally admired.

The author of the English translation, amplifying the Latin as may be seen below, accordingly gives an impression of Alexander as imperious, self-centred, magnetic but increasingly paranoid. The artistry of this adaptation begs the question of which version of English society at what time provided the translator with a living model. The epic hero Beowulf seems to have helped the translator, however (Orchard 2003: 25–39). This, when combined with the fact that *Beowulf* the poem directly follows *Alexander's Letter to Aristotle* in the same manuscript, which is dated roughly to *c.* 1000, suggests that the two works existed in an exemplar perhaps one or two generations earlier. On this basis it may be suggested that the translation was made as early as the middle of the tenth century.

Marsden, R., ed., *The Cambridge Old English Reader* (Cambridge, 2004), 239–44 (edits ch. 34 (ahead of the excerpt below) some way into ch. 38)

Orchard, A., *Pride and Prodigies: Studies in the Monsters of the Beowulf-Manuscript* (Woodbridge, 1995)

Orchard, A., *A Critical Companion to Beowulf* (Woodbridge, 2003)

Renault, M., *The Nature of Alexander* (London, 1975)

Worthington, I., *Alexander the Great: Man and God* (Harlow, 2004)

Alexander's address to Aristotle

1. HER IS SEO GESETENIS Alexandres epistoles þæs miclan kyninges ond þæs mæran Macedoniscan, þone he wrat ond sende to Aristotile his magistre **be gesetenisse** Indie þære miclan þeode ond be þære widgalnisse his siðfato ond his fora þe he geond Middangeard ferde. Cwæþ he þus sona ærest in fruman þæs epistoles.

2. Simle ic beo gemindig þin ge efne betweoh tweondan frecennisse ura gefeohta, þu min se leofesta lareow, ond efne to minre meder ond geswystrum þu me eart se leofesta freond. Ond for þon þe ic þe wiste wel getydne in wisdome, þa geþohte ic for þon to þe to writanne be þam þeodlonde Indie, ond be heofenes gesetenissum, ond be þam unarimdum cynnum nædrena ond monna ond wildeora, to þon þæt hwæthwygo to þære ongietenisse þissa niura þinga þin gelis ond gleawnis to geþeode.

Þeoh to þe seo gefylde gleawnis ond snyttro ond naniges fultumes abædeð sio lar þæs rihtes, hwæþere ic wolde þæt þu mine dæde ongeate, þa þu lufast, ond **þa þing þe ungesewene mid þe siond, þa ic in Indie geseah** þurh monigfeald gewin ond þurh micle frecennisse mid Greca herige.

---

1. HERE IS THE TEXT of the letter of Alexander the great king and renowned Macedonian, which he wrote and sent to Aristotle, his schoolmaster, **concerning the disposition** of the great nation of India and the vast range of his expeditions and the travels which he made through the Middle World. He says it this way at the beginning of the letter:

2. Constantly am I mindful of you in between the unsettling dangers of our battles, my dearest teacher, and next to my mother and sisters you are my dearest friend. And because I have known you to be well instructed in wisdom, on this account I thought to write to you concerning the huge land of India, the disposition of the heavens and the unnumbered species of serpents and people and wild animals, namely that your great reading and sagacity might add in some way to the understanding of these new things.

Though in you the consummate sagacity, cleverness and teaching of what is right require no aid, yet I would have you take note of my deeds, which you will love, as well as **those things unseen where you are which I have seen in India** through manifold wars and great dangers in company with the army of the Greeks.

---

be gesetenisse 'concerning the disposition'. Latin *de statu* 'on the status' (Orchard 1995: 204). OE *gesetenis* may mean 'ordinance, constitution, law', as well as 'text' just above. The English language is now at home with the intellectual vocabulary of Latin (and Greek), relative to the first outings of this in the Alfredian period (see **The Earliest English Prose**).

þa þing þe ungesewene mid þe siond, þa ic in Indie geseah 'those things unseen where you are which I have seen in India'. The translator makes a contrast by repeating *geseon* 'to see', one which the Latin does not, by which Alexander appears to measure himself against Aristotle, his former teacher.

3. Þa ic write ond cyþe. Ond æghwylc þara is wyrðe synderlice in gemyndum to habbanne æfter þære wisan þe ic hit oferseah. Ne gelyfde ic æniges monnes gesegenum swa fela wundorlicra þinga þæt hit swa beon mihte ær ic hit self minum eagum ne gesawe. Seo eorðe is to wundrienne, hwæt heo ærest oþþe godra þinga cenne oððe eft þara yfelra þe heo þam sceawigendum is æteowed. Hio is cennende þa fulcuþan wildeora ond wæstma ond wecgan oran, ond **wunderlice wyhta**, þa þing eall **þam monnum þe hit geseoð ond sceawigað wæron uneþe to gewitanne** for þære missenlicnisse þara hiowa.

4. Ac þa ðing, þe me nu in gemynd cumað, ærest þa ic þe write, þy læs on me mæge idel spellung oþþe scondlic leasung beon gestæled. Hwæt, þu eac sylfa const þa gecynd mines modes, mec a gewunelice healdon þæt gemerce soðes ond rihtes. Ond ic sperlicor mid wordum sægde þonne hie mid dædum gedon wærun. Nu ic hwæþre gehyhte ond gelyfe þæt þu þas þing ongete swa þu me ne talige owiht gelpan ond secgan be þære micelnisse ures gewinnes ond compes. For ðon ic oft wiscte ond wolde þæt hyra læs wære swa gewinfulra.

---

3. These things I write and make known. And each one of them is especially worth keeping in memory according to the way I surveyed it. Nor would I have believed any man's stories that so many wondrous things could be just so, before I had seen this with my own eyes. The earth is to be wondered at, first of all for what good things she brings forth, but then also for the evil things by which she is revealed to those who observe her. She goes on bringing forth fully, known wild animals and fruits and minerals and metal ores, and **wondrous creatures**, all the things which, for their variety of forms, **have not been easy to understand for the men who see and observe them**.

4. But the things which now come to my memory, first I will write to you of these, lest I am charged with empty fables or shameful lies. Listen, you yourself know the kind of mind I have, that it is ever my custom to keep within the bounds of truth and accuracy. And I have told things more sparingly in words than they were done in deeds. Now, however, I hope and believe that you will so understand these things as not to count me boastful in any way when I speak of the greatness of our warfare and campaign. For it was often my wish and desire, regarding these things, that fewer of them brought so much war.

---

wunderlice wyhta 'wondrous creatures'. *The Wonders of the East* is another text in MS BL Cotton Vitellius A.xv, derived from the *Epistola Alexandri* but also influencing the Old English *Alexander's Letter to Aristotle* (Orchard 1995: 117–19).

þam monnum þe hit geseoð ond sceawigað wæron uneþe to gewitanne 'have not been easy to understand for the men who see and observe them'. The Latin is expanded from its statement of general wonder to suggest that Alexander feels superior to other people for being able to observe marvels more intelligently than they can.

5. Ic ðæs þoncunge do Greca herige ond swyðost þam mægene þære iuguþe ond þam unforswyþdum urum weorode, for þon on ieþum þingum hie me mid wæron ond on þam earfeðum no from bugon. Ac hie on þære geþylde mid me a wunedon þæt ic wæs nemned ealra kyninga kyning.

Þara weorðmynta blissa þu, min se leofa Lareow! Ond ic nu þas þing write to þe gemænelice, ond to Olimphiade, minre meder, ond minum geswustrum, for þon incer lufu sceal beon somod gemæne. Ond gif hit oþor bið, þonne æteawest þu læsson þonne ic nu ær to þe gelyfde.

6. On þam ærrum gewritum þe ic þe sende, ic þe cyþde **ond getacnode** be þære asprungnisse Sunnan ond Monan, ond be tungla rynum ond gesetenissum, ond be lyfte tacnungum. Þa ðing eall ne magon elcor beon buton micelre gemynde swa geendebyrded ond fore stihtod. Ond nu þas niwan spel ic þe ealle in cartan awrite. Ðonne þu hie ræde, þonne wite þu þæt his ealle swylce wæron **swa þam gemyndum gedafenode þines Alexandres** þe to sendanne.

---

5. I give thanks therefore to the Greek army, and mostly to the vigour of that division of young men and to that unconquered host of ours for being with me through the easy things and for never leaving me through the hardships we faced. With patience, rather, did they ever remain with me, so that I was named king of all kings.

Rejoice in these honours, my dear Teacher! And now I write of these things to you jointly with Olympias my mother and my sisters, for the love which each of you holds shall be of the same kind. And if it is otherwise, you show yourself less a man than I once took you for.

6. In the earlier letters I sent you, I informed you **with drawings** of the eclipse of Sun and Moon, and of the courses and dispositions of heavenly bodies, and of heavenly signs. None of these things can be so arranged and ordained unless by a great mind. And all these new tidings of mine I shall now write for you in a missive. When you read it, know that all these things were of such kind **as the mind of your own Alexander considered appropriate** to send to you.

---

ond getacnode 'with drawings'. The Latin has *significaueram* 'I had explained the meanings of' (Orchard 1995: 205), which *getacnode* literally translates. The text is strewn with doublets of this kind. But the additional use of *cyþde* 'informed' here might suggest that the translator, perhaps mindful of Byrhtferth of Ramsey and his ilk, introduces the idea of astronomical diagrams as well.

swa þam gemyndum gedafenode þines Alexandres 'as the mind of your own Alexander considered appropriate'. Note how soon this follows after *buton micelre gemynde* 'unless by a great mind'. The Latin has *cura* 'care' in both cases (Orchard 1995: 205). The English translator, by rendering this word *gemynd*, appears to accord Alexander an Alfredian style whilst letting him compare himself with the Almighty (see the 'Preface to the translation of Gregory's *Pastoral Care*', **The Earliest English Prose**).

A meeting with King Porus

22. Þa hit ða on morgen dæg wæs, ða het ic ealle mine ladþeowas, þe mec **on swelc earfeðo** gelæddon, het hie þa gebindan ond him þa ban ond sconcan forbrecan, ðæt hie on niht wær*o*n from þam wyrmum asogene þe þæt wæter sohton. Ond ic him het eac þa honda of aheawan, þæt hie be gewyrhtum þes wites wite drugon þe hie ær hiora þonces us on gelæddon ond gebrohton.

23. Het þa blawan mine byman ond þa fyrd faran forð þy wege þe we ær ongunnen hæfdon. Foran we ða þurh ða fæstlond ond þurh þa ungeferenlican eorþan. Þa wæs þær eft gesomnad micel fyrd Indiscra monna ond þæra elreordigra þe ða lond budon, ond we þa wið þam gefuhton.

Mid þy we þa us eft ongeaton maran gefeoht toweard ond mara gewin, ða forleton we þa frecnan wegas ond siðfato ond þa þam selran we ferdon. Ond swa mid mine werode onsunde in Patriacen þæt lond we becwoman mid golde ond oþrum weolum swiðe gewelgode, ond hie us þær fremsumlice ond luflice onfengon. Mid þy we þa eft of þam londe foron of Patriacen, ða becwoman we on þa londgemæro Medo ond Persa. Þa we ðær eft ednio-wunga hæfdon micle gefeoht, ond twintig daga **ic þær mid minre fyrde wið him wicode**.

---

22. When day broke the next morning, I summoned all my guides who had led me **into such difficulties**, ordered them to be bound and their bones and legs to be broken, that they might be swallowed by the pythons that sought the water in the night. And I had their hands cut off too, that they themselves might be on the receiving end of the torment to which their efforts had led and conveyed us earlier.

23. Then I had my trumpets blown and the army move out along the road which we had started on before. We marched through the fastnesses and territory which could not be crossed. There again, when a great army was gathered of men from India and other barbarians who dwelt in that land, we fought against them.

When we realised that bigger battles and more wars lay ahead of us, we gave up the dangerous roads and missions and proceeded on to better ones. And thus safely with my host did we arrive in the land of Patriacen, and greatly enriched with gold and other wealth, and they received us there with gifts and love. When we once more headed out, leaving the land of Patriacen, we came to the frontier of Medes and Persians. There we renewed our progress with another great battle, and twenty days **with my army was I encamped there** by that frontier.

---

on swelc earfeðo 'into such difficulties'. The local guides had failed to mention the scorpions, serpents, a rhino, pestilential vapours and giant rats by the drinking water to which they led the Greeks a few days earlier (chs. 16–21).

ic þær mid minre fyrde wicode . . . þær Porrus se cyning mid his fyrde wicode 'with my army was I encamped there . . . where King Porus was encamped with his army'. The repetition in the Old English (of chapter 24 on page 124) is an addition. The Latin has no such parallel construction (Orchard 1995: 213). Once more, it seems that the English Alexander is matching himself up to a worthy adversary, even before he has met him face to face.

24. Sioðþan we þa þonon ferdon, þa wæs hit on seofon nihta fæce þæt we to þam londe ond to þære stowe becwoman **þær Porrus se cyning mid his fyrde wicode**. Ond he swið*or* þæs londes fæstenum truwode þonne his gefeohte ond gewinne.

Þa wilnade he þæt he me cuðe ond mine þegnas. Þa he þæs frægen ond axsode from þam ferendum minra wicstowa, þa wæs þæt me gesæd þæt he wilnade me to cun[ni]enne ond min werod. Đa alede ic minne kynegyrlan, ond me mid uncuþe hrægle ond mid lyþerlice gerelan me gegerede swelce ic wære hwelc folclic mon ond **me wære metes ond wines þearf**. Þa ic wæs in þam wicum Porres, swa ic ær sæde, **ða sona swa he me þær geahsode** ond him mon sægde þæt þær mon cymen wæs of Alexandres herewicum, þa het he me sona to him lædan.

Mid þy ic þa wæs to him gelæded, þa frægn he me ond ahsode hwæt Alexander se cyning dyde, ond huilc mon he wære, ond in hwylcere yldo. Đa bysmrode ic hine mid minum ondswarum, ond him sæde þæt he forealdod wære ond to þæs eald wære þæt he ne mihte elcor gewearmigan buton æt fyre ond æt gledum. Þa wæs he sona swiðe glæd, ond gefeonde þara minra ondswaro ond worda for þon ic him sæde þæt he swa forealdod wære, ond ða cwæð he eac, 'Hu mæg he la ænige gewinne wið me spowan, swa forealdod mon? For þon ic eom me self geong ond hwæt.'

---

24. When we marched off from there, it was after an interval of seven nights that we arrived in the country and to the place **where King Porus was encamped with his army**. And he trusted more in the fastnesses of that land than in making his own battle and war.

It was then that he desired to know me and my thegns. As he asked questions and learned things from the people travelling through my encampments, it was told me that he desired to get to know me and my troop. So I put off my royal garments and girt myself in unfamiliar costume and shabby clothes, as if I were a man of the common people and **had need of food and wine**. When I was in Porus' camp, as I just said, **as soon as he learned that I was there** with a man having told him that someone had come from Alexander's barracks, he commanded me to be led before him.

When I was led before him, he asked questions about what King Alexander was doing, and what kind of man he was, and at what time of life. So I mocked him with my answers, and told him that Alexander was ancient and so old that he could not warm himself other than by the fire and its embers. He was glad about that at once, relieved to hear my answers and the words with which I told him Alexander was so ancient, and then he added, 'Look, how can he win any fight against me, a man so ancient? For I myself am young and keen.'

---

me wære metes ond wines þearf 'had need of food and wine'. Compare a less cosmopolitan idiom for travellers in Old Norse, *matar ok váða es manni þǫrf þeims hefir um fjall farit* 'Food and clothing are what a man needs who's fared across the fells', in *Sayings of the High One*, stanza 3 (see **Poems on the Meaning of Life**). This is the type of traveller Alexander is going to appear as before Porus.

ða sona swa he me þær geahsode 'as soon as he learned that I was there'. The Latin is expanded into this phrase and one following, in which Alexander, having given the impression that Porus knew his true identity, corrects himself with a statement about a man telling the king of a new arrival.

Þa he ða geornlicor me frægn be his þingum. Đa sæde ic þæt ic his þinga feola ne cuþe ond hine seldon gesawe, ðone cyning, for þon þe ic wære his þegnes mon ond his ceapes heorde, ond wære his feohbigenga. Þa he ðas word gehyrde, ða sealde me an gewrit ond ænne epistolan, and me bæd þæt ic hine Alexandre þam kyninge ageafe, ond me eac mede gehet gif ic hit him agyfan wolde. Ond ic him gehet þæt ic swa don wolde swa he me bæd.

Swa ic ða þonon gewiten wæs, ond eft cwom to minum herewicum, þa ægþer ge ær ðon þe ic þæt gewrit rædde, ge eac æfter þon, þæt ic wæs swiðe mid hleahtre onstyred. Đas þing ic for þon þe secge, Magister, on Olimphiade minre meder, ond minum geswustrum, þæt ge gehyrdon ond ongeaton **þa oferhygdlican gedyrstignesse þæs elreordigan kyninges**.

25. Hæfde ic þa þæs kyninges wic ond his fæstenu gesceawod þe he mid his fyrde in gefaren hæfde. Đa sona on morgne þæs, **ða eode Porus se kyning me on hond** mid ealle his ferde ond dugoþe. Þa he hæfde ongieten þæt he wið me gewinnan ne meahte!

Ond of þam feondscipe þe us ær betweonum wæs, þæt he me seoðþan wæs me freond ond eallum Greca herige ond min gefera ond gefylcea, ond ic him ða eft his rice ageaf. Ond þa ðære unwendan are þæs rices þe he him seolfa næniges rices ne wende, þæt he ða me eall his goldhord æteowde, ond he þa ægþer ge mec ge eac eall min werod mid golde gewelgode.

Then he asked me about Alexander's business even more eagerly. So I told him that I did not know much about his business and that I seldom saw him, the king, because I was his thegn's man and herded his cattle and ran errands for him for money. When he heard these words, he gave me a document and in it a letter, asking me to give it to King Alexander and also promising me payment if I would give it to him. And I promised him I would do as he asked.

So I left that place and came back to my barracks, and both before I read that letter, and after I did so, I was in real fits of laughter. I tell these things to you, Schoolteacher, and to my mother Olympias and my sisters, so you can all understand with your own ears **the outrageous cheek of this barbarian king**.

25. By now I had observed the king's camp and the fastness into which he had gone with his army. As soon as it was morning, **King Porus walked** with his whole army and division **right into my hands**. He had understood by then that he could not fight against me!

And from the enmity which had been between us before, straightaway he became friends with me and with all the Greek host, and my companion and ally, and I gave him back his kingdom. And then, by the unexpected favour of a kingdom where himself he had expected no kingdom at all, straightaway he revealed to me his whole goldhoard and enriched both me and all my troop with gold.

þa oferhygdlican gedyrstignesse þæs elreordigan kyninges 'the outrageous cheek of this barbarian king'. Enough said, here as in the Latin (*superbam inclinatamque barbari temeritatem* 'the barbarian's proud and self-indulgent audacity'; Orchard 1995: 213). We learn more about Alexander than Porus.

ða eode Porus se kyning me on hond 'King Porus walked right into my hands' etc. Orchard punctuates differently, having Porus surrender before any attempt on Alexander (1995: 240), although the Latin, *contuli cum Indis manum* 'I came to close quarters with the Indians', makes it clear there is a battle (1995: 214). Thanks to Alexander's brilliance the battle is quickly over, however.

Ond Herculis gelicnesse ond Libri, ðara twegea goda, he buta of golde gegeat ond geworhte ond hie butu asette in þam eastdæle Middangeardes. Ða wolde ic witan hwæþer ða gelicnessa wæron gegotene ealle, swa he sæde, het hie þa þurhborian. Þa wæron hie buta of golde gegotene. Ða het ic eft þa ðyrelo, þe hiora mon þurh cunnode, mid golde forwyrcean ond afyllon, ond het þa ðæm godum bæm **onsægdnisse onsecgan**.

And likenesses of both Hercules and Bacchus, those two gods, he made by pouring gold into moulds for them and set them both up in the eastern end of the Middle World. I wished to see then whether these likenesses were solid gold, as he said, so had them drilled through. They turned out to be both of solid gold. So I had the holes which had been bored through them stopped up and filled with gold, and then had **sacrifices offered** to both of those gods.

The Prophecy of the trees of Sun and Moon

34. Mid þy we þa nealehtan ðæm þeodlonde, þa gesawon we ægþer ge wif ge wæpnedmen mid panthera fellum ond tigriscum þara deora hydum gegyryde, ond nanes oðres brucon. Mid þy ic þa frægn hie ond ahsode hwelcre ðeode kynnes hie wæron, ða ondswarodon hie mec, ond sægdon on hiora geþeode þæt hie wæran Indos. Wæs seo stow rum ond wynsumo, ond balzamum ond recels ðær wæs genihtsumnis, ond þæt eac of þæra treowa telgan weol, ond þa men þæs londes bi ðy lifdon ond þæt æton. Mid þy, we ða geornlicor þa stowe sceawedon ond betwih þa bearwas eodon, ond ic ða wynsumnese ond fægernesse þæs londes wundrade.

---

34. When we approached the inhabited country, we could see both women and men girt in the skins of panthers and with the hides of beasts called tigers, and they used nothing else. When I asked questions of them about the kind of people they were, they answered me in their language, saying they were Indians. The place was spread out and delightful, and with an abundance of balsam and incense there, which also welled out of the branches of the trees, and the people of that land lived off it by eating it. Meanwhile we looked more eagerly into this place and walked in amongst the groves, and I wondered at how delightful and beautiful this country was.

---

onsægdnisse onsecgan 'sacrifices offered'. The vocabulary follows the Latin without anxiety, here with *deiectis victimis* 'by presenting victims', and earlier by rendering *simulacra* 'likenesses' with *gelicnesse* (Orchard 1995: 214). This translation seems moved on from the heights of the Benedictine Reform, since it needs no emotive terms such as *wigbed*, *gield* or *deofolgield* 'idols', such as in *Beowulf*, lines 175–8 (the Danes worshipping the devil), *Exodus*, line 47 (the Egyptians; see **Poems of Devotion**), or 'The Conversion of King Edwin' (the Northumbrians; see **The Earliest English Prose**).

35. Ða cwom **se bisceop þære stowe** us togeanes. Wæs he se bisceop tyn fota upheah ond eall him wæs se lichoma sweart, buton þam toþum, ða wæron hwite. Ond þa earan him þurh þyrelode, ond earhringas onhongedon of mænigfealdan gimcynne geworhte, ond he wæs mid wildeora fellum gegerwed. Þa se bisceop to me cwom, ða gegrette he me sona ond halette his leodþeawe. Frægn he eac me to hwon ic þider cwome ond hwæt ic þær wolde. Þa ondswarode ic him þæt mec lyste geseon **þa halgan trio Sunnan ond Monan**.

Ða ondswarode he, '**Gif þine geferan beoð clæne from wifgehrine**, þonne moton hie gongan in þone godcundan bearo.' Wæs minra geferana mid me þrio hund monna.

Þa het se bisceop mine geferan þæt hie hiora gescie ond ealne heora gerelan him of adyden, ond het ic æghwæt swa don swa he us bebead. Wæs hit þa **sio endlefte tid dæges**. Ða bæd se socerd Sunnan setlgonges, for þone Sunnan trio agefeð ondsware æt þam upgone ond eft æt setlgonge, ond þæt Monan triow gelice swa on niht dyde.

36. Ða ongon ic geornlicor þa stowe sceawigan, ond geond þa bearwas ond treowu gongan. Þa geseah ic þær balzamum þæs betstan stences genoh of

---

35. Then **the bishop of this place** came towards us. This bishop was ten feet tall and his whole body was black, but for his teeth, which were white. And the ears on him were bored through, and earrings hung off them made of manifold kinds of jewels, and he was decorated with the skins of wild animals. When the bishop came to me, he greeted me at once with a salutation customary in his land. He also asked me why I had come to this place and what I would do there. My answer to him was I was keen to see **the holy trees of Sun and Moon**.

Then he answered, '**If your companions are clean from woman's touch**, then they may go into the divine grove.' I had three hundred companions with me.

Then the bishop told my companions to take off their shoes and all their clothes, and I told them to do everything the way he commanded us. It was then **the eleventh hour of the day**. Then the priest waited for Sun to go down, the tree of the Sun gives answers at sunrise and again at sunset, and the tree of the Moon did so at moonrise and moonset at night.

36. Then I began to examine the place more eagerly and to walk through the groves and trees. I saw enough balsam to make the finest perfume welling up out of the trees there. You

---

se bisceop þære stowe 'the bishop of this place'. Alexander, returning to Persia via Ethiopia (!), has made a detour, leaving the bulk of his army with King Porus in Fasiacen while he seeks out a remote oracle. On this term as a translation of *oraculi antistes* 'overseer of the oracle' (Orchard 1995: 218), compare the use of *ealdorbiscop* for Coifi in Goodmanham in 'The conversion of King Edwin' (**The Earliest English Prose**).

þa halgan trio Sunnan ond Monan 'the holy trees of Sun and Moon'. Alexander's opening declaration to Aristotle considers Sun and Moon in such a way as to pre-empt what will be the climactic episode of *Alexander's Letter to Aristotle*.

Gif þine geferan beoð clæne from wifgehrine 'If your companions are clean from woman's touch'. Note that he does not consider Alexander to be part of this group.

sio endlefte tid dæges 'the eleventh hour of the day'. 5 p.m., so evening.

þam treowum ut weallan. Þæt balzamum ægþer ge ic ge mine geferan þær betwih þam rindum noman þæra trio. Þonne wæron ða halgan trio Sunnan ond Monan on middum þam oðrum treowum. Meahton hie beon hundteontiges fota upheah, ond eac þær wæron oþre treow wunderlicre heanisse, ða hatað Indeos 'Bebronas'.

Þara triowa heanisse ic wundrade, ond cwæð þæt ic wende þæt hie for miclum wætan ond regnum swa heage weoxon. Ða sægde se bisceop þæt þær næfre in þam londum regnes dropa ne cwome, ne fugel, ne wildeor, ne ænig ætern wyrm þæt her dorste gesecean ða halgan gemæro Sunnan ond Monan. Eac þonne he sægde se bisceop, þonne þæt 'eclypsis' wære (þæt is þonne ðæs Sunnan asprungnis oðþe þære Monan), þæt ða halgan triow swiðe wepen ond mid micle sare onstyred wæron, for þon hie ondredon þæt hie hiora godmægne sceoldon beon genumene.

Ða þohte ic þæt ic wolde onsægdnisse þær onsecgan, ac þa forbead me se bisceop, ond sægde þæt ðæt nære alyfed ænigum men þæt he þær ænig nyten cwealde oþþe blodgyte worhte. Ac mec het þæt ic me to þara triowa fotum gebæde, þæt Sunna ond Mone me soþre ondsware **geondwyrdum** þara þinga ðe ic frune, sioððan þas þing þus gedon wæron. Þa gesawon we westan þone leoman Sunnan, ond se leoma gehran þam treowum ufonweardum.

Ða cwæð se sacerd, 'Lociað nu ealle up. Ond be swa hwylcum þingum swa ge willon frinan, þence on his heortan deagollice ond nænig mon his geþoht openum wordum ut ne cyðe.'

---

see the holy trees of Sun and Moon were in the centre of the other trees. They could have been one hundred feet high, and there were also other trees of wonderful height which the Indians call 'Bebronas'.

I wondered at the height of these trees, saying that I believed they grew so high for the great wet and the rains. That is when the bishop said that not one drop of rain ever came in those regions, nor was there any bird or wild animal or poisonous snake that dared visit the holy precincts of Sun and Moon. He also said, did the bishop, that when it was an 'eclipse' (in this case that is a waning of either Sun or Moon), the holy trees would weep greatly, being stirred with great anguish because they feared their divine powers would be taken from them.

Then I thought I would offer sacrifices there, but the bishop forbade me, saying that it would never be allowed for any man to kill any animals there or cause bloodshed. Rather he ordered me to pray at the foot of those trees, that Sun and Moon **might reply** with a truthful answer to the things I should ask, after these things had been done. Then from the west we saw the last gleam of Sun, and the gleam touched the tops of the trees.

Then the priest said, 'All of you look up now. And concerning such things as you would like to ask, let each man think secretly in his heart and let no man make known his thoughts in open words.'

---

geondwyrdum 'might reply'. As regards the state of the Old English spelling system at the time of this manuscript, MS BL Cotton Vitellius A.xv of *c.* 1000 (it is the younger of two scribes), this *–um* ending (normally dative plural on a noun or adjective) is a hypercorrection for *–en* (the subjunctive plural ending on a verb). The two endings now sound the same, and the scribe tries too hard to show how well he can spell.

37. Mid þy we þa wel neah stodan þam bearwum ond þam godsprecum, þa ðohte ic on minum mode hwæþer ic meahte ealne Middangeard me on onweald geslean, ond þonne sioþþan, mid þam siogorum geweorþad, ic eft meahte becuman in Macedoniam to Olimphiade, minre meder, ond minum geswustrum.

Ða ondswarode me þæt triow Indiscum wordum, ond þus cwæð, 'Ða unoferswyðda Alexander in gefeohtum, þu weorðest cyning ond hlaford ealles Middangeardes. Ac hwæþre ne cymst þu on þinne eðel, ðonan þu ferdest ær, for þon þin wyrd hit swa be þinum heafde ond fore hafað aræded.'

Ða wæs ic ungleaw þæs geþeodes þara Indiscra worda þe þæt triow me to spræc. Ða rehte hit me se bisceop ond sægde. Mid þy hit mine geferan gehyrdon, þæt ic eft cwic ne moste in minne eþel becuman, ða wæron hie swiðe unrote for þon. Þa wolde ic eft on þa æfentid ma ahsian, ac þa næs se Mona þa gyt uppe.

Mid þy we þa eft eodon in þone halgan bearo, ond we þa eft be þam treowum stodan, gebædon us þa sona to þam treowum swa we ær dydon. Ond ic eac in mid mec gelædde mine þrie ða getreowestan frynd, ða wæron mine syndrige treowgeþoftan, þæt wæs ærest Perticam ond Clitomum ond Pilotan. For þon ic me ne ondred þæt me þæra ænig beswice, **for þon þær næs riht on þære stowe** ænigne to acwellanne for þære stowe weorþunge.

---

37. As we were standing very close to the groves and the oracles, I thought to myself in my mind whether I would be able to quell the whole Middle World into my power, and then, honoured with those triumphs, come home again into Macedonia to Olympias, my mother, and to my sisters.

Then the tree replied to me in Indian words, saying 'O Alexander, unconquered in any battle, you will become king and overlord of all the Middle World. However, you will not come into your homeland from whence you journeyed previously, for your fate has so determined it, on your head and before your time.'

I was unclear then about the meaning of the Indian words which the tree spoke to me. The bishop explained it to me in words I understood. When my companions heard that I must not come back alive into my homeland, they were very unhappy. I wanted then to find out more later that evening, for the Moon was still not up yet at this time.

When we walked back into the sacred grove, and were once again standing by those trees, we prayed immediately to the trees as we had done before. And I had also led in with me my three most trusted friends, these were my special confidants, first Perticas, then Clitomus and Pilotas. I had no fear that any of them would betray me, **for the reverence due to that place made it unlawful** to kill anyone there.

---

for þon þær næs riht on þære stowe 'for the reverence due to that place made it unlawful'. This is to say that Alexander trusts nobody. The Latin also says that 'none' of his friends 'had cause to fear me' either (*nec me quisquam timebat*), but that element is redundant here.

38. Ða þohte ic on minum mode ond on minum geþohte on hwelcre stowe ic sweltan scolde. Mid þy ða ærest se Mona upeode, þa gehran he mid his sciman þam triowum ufeweardum.

Ond þæt triow ondswarode þam minum geþohte, ond þus cwæð, 'Alexander, fulne ende þines lifes þu hæfst gelifd, ac þys æftran geare þu swyltst on Babilone, on Maius monðe, from þam þu læst wenst from þam þu bist beswicen.'

Ða wæs ic swiðe sariges modes, ond þa mine frynd swa eac, þa me þær mid wæron. Ond hie weopon swiðe **for þon him wære min gesynto leofre þonne hiora seolfra hælo**. Ða gewiton we to urum geferum eft, ond hie woldon to hiora swæsendum sittan, ond ic wolde for þam bysegum mines modes me gerestan. Ac þa bædon mec mine geferan þæt ic on swa micelre modes unreto ond nearonisse mec selfne mid fæstenne ne swencte. Þigde ða tela medmicelne mete wið mines modes willan ond þa tidlice to minre reste eode, for þon ic wolde beon gearo æt Sunnan upgonge þæt ic eft in geeode.

39. Ða on morgne mid þy hit dagode, þa onbræd ic ond þa mine getreowestan frynd aweahte, þæt ic wolde in þa halgan stowe gan. Ac þa reste hine se bisceop þa giet, ond mid wildeora fellum wæs gegerwed ond bewrigen. Ond irenes ond leades þa men on þam londum wædliað, ond goldes genihtsumiað, ond be ðæm balzamum þa men in þam londe lifgeað. Ond of ðæm neahmunte

---

38. Then I thought, in my mind and in my reason, of what place I should have to die in. As soon as the Moon had risen, he touched the tops of the trees with his rays.

And the tree replied to this thought of mine, saying 'Alexander, you have lived your life fully to its end, for later this year you will die in Babylon, in the month of May, from what or whom you least expect to be betrayed.'

Then I was cast into great depression, and those friends of mine also who were there with me. And they wept greatly, **for all that my safety were dearer to them than their own good fortune**. Then we went back to our companions, and they wanted to sit down to their banquet, and I wanted to rest myself on account of the cares of my mind. But my companions prayed me not to afflict myself with fasting in such great distress and unhappiness of mind. So I had a very small portion of food, against the will of my heart, and then went to bed at a good hour, for I wanted to be ready to go back in there when the Sun rose.

39. Then in the morning, when day broke, I awoke, and wakened my most trusty friends in that I wanted to go into that holy place. But the bishop was still sleeping at this time, and was adorned and covered in the skins of wild animals. And the people in those regions, who are poor in iron and lead, have a quantity of gold and of the balsam that people live by in that land. And from the nearby mountain there wells pure water and fair, and that very

---

for þon him wære min gesynto leofre þonne hiora seolfra hælo 'for all that my safety were dearer to them than their own good fortune'. Alexander is surprised at his friends, perhaps even touched, but still not sure whether he should trust them. The Latin (Orchard 1995: 220) makes him trust them now: *Nullumque ab his dolum aut scelus resurrecturum aestimabam, sed magis pro mea salute more paratos* 'and no treachery or villainy did I think would come from them, but rather, from their manner, that they were disposed towards my safety'. The English Alexander, in contrast, has become paranoid.

wealleð hluter wæter ond fæger, ond þæt swiðe swete. Þonne drincað þa men þæt ond by lifigeað. Ond þonne hie restað, þonne restað hie buton bedde ond bolstre, ac on wildeora fellum on bedding bið.

Ða awehte ic þone bisceop. Hæfde se bisceop þreo hund wintra on yldo.

40. Mid þy he þa se bisceop aras, ða eode ic on þa godcundan stowe ond þa þriddan siðe þæt Sunnan treow ongon frinan, þurh hwelces monnes hond min ende wære getiod oððe hwelcne endedæg min modor oþðe min geswuster nu gebidan scoldon.

Þa ondswarode me þæt treow on Grecisc, ond þus cwæð, '**Gif ic þe þone [mon ond þone ende] gesecge þines feores**, yþelice þu ða wyrde oncyrrest ond his hand befehst.

'Ac soð ic þe secge, þæt ymb anes geares fyrst ond eahta monað þu swyltst in Babilone, nalles mid iserne acweald, swa ðu wenst, ac mid atre. Ðin modor gewiteð of weorulde þurh scondlicne deað ond unarlicne, ond heo ligeð unbebyrged in wege, fuglum to mete ond wildeorum. Þine sweostor beoð longe gesæliges lifes.

'Ðu ðonne, þeah þu lytle hwile lifge, hweþre ðu geweorðest an cyning ond hlaford ealles Middangeardes. Ac ne frign ðu unc nohtes ma ne axa, for þon wit habbað oferhleoðred þæt gemære uncres leohtes, ac to Fasiacen ond Porre þam cyninge eft gehworf ðu!'

---

sweet. People drink it and live off it, you see. And when they sleep, then they sleep without bed or bolster, but their bedding is made up of the skins of wild animals.

Then I wakened the bishop. The bishop was three hundred winters old.

40. When the bishop had risen, I went into the divine place and for the third time I began to ask questions of the tree of the Sun, by what man's hand my end was cast or on what day my mother or my sisters should now meet their end.

Then the tree replied to me in Greek, saying, '**If I tell you [who the man is who will end] your life**, easily then will you avert the fate and stay his hand.

'But it is true what I say to you, that within the period of a year and eight months you will die in Babylon, not killed with iron, as you think, but with poison. Your mother will pass from the world by a shameful deed and dishonourable, and she will lie unburied on the wayside as food for birds and wild animals. Your sisters will live long and fortunate lives.

'And you, though you live but a little while, still you will become the one king and overlord of the whole Middle World. Do not ask the two of us any more questions now, for we have spoken beyond the limit of our light, but get back to Fasiacen and King Porus!'

Gif ic þe þone [mon ond þone ende] gesecge þines feores 'If I tell you [who the man is who will end] your life' etc. The Latin (Orchard 1995: 221) is probably *Si mortis [B] tuae tibi insidiatorem prodidero* 'if I betray to you the lurking agent of your death', so some Old English text seems to be lost here, where isolated *þone* makes little sense. The other thing to note is the ease with which it is assumed that knowledge will give Alexander the means to avert his fate. This is not the conception of fate that we know of, for example, in *The Wanderer*, line 5: *Wyrd bið ful aræd* 'Fate is fully determined', even though the Sun Tree's language is similar, in ch. 37: *þin wyrd hit swa . . . hafað aræded* 'your fate has so determined it'.

Ond fer ðy þa weopon mine geferan for þon ic swa lytle hwile lyfigan moste. Ac þa forbead hit se bisceop þæt hi ne weopon, þy læs þa halgan treow þurh heora wop ond tearas abulgen.

41. Ond ne geherde ða ondsware þara treowa ma manna þonne þa mine getreowestan freond. Ond hit nænig mon ut cyþan ne moste, þy læs þa elreordegan kyningas, ðe ic ær mid nede to hyrsumnesse gedyde, þæt hie on þæt fægon þæt ic swa lytle hwile lifgean moste. Ne hit eac ænig mon þære ferde ðon ma ut mæran moste, þy læs hie for ðon ormode wæron ond þy sænran mines willan ond weorðmyndo ðæs hie mid mec to fromscipe geferan scoldon.

Ond me næs se hrædlica ende mines lifes swa miclum weorce, swa me wæs þæt ic læs mærðo gefremed hæfde þonne min willa wære. Ðas þing ic write to þon, min se leofa Magister, þæt þu ærest gefeo in þam fromscipe mines lifes, ond eac blissige in þam weorðmyndum, ond eac swelce ecelice min gemynd stonde ond hleouige oðrum eorðcyningum to bysne, ðæt hie witen þy gearwor þæt min þrym ond min weorðmynd maran wæron þonne ealra oþra kyninga þe in Middangearde æfre wæron.

And my companions wept that I must have such little time to live. But the bishop forbade them to weep, lest the holy trees should be angered at their weeping and tears.

41. And no man heard the trees' answers other than my most trusted friends. And none of them was permitted to tell the story, in case the barbarian kings whom I had forced into obedience to me should rejoice that I must have such little time to live. Nor, too, was anyone permitted to broadcast this further to the army, in case they were dispirited and became the slower to enact such will and worship of me as they must have in order to carry me to success.

And for me the swift end of my life was not as great a pain as the thought that I had achieved less renown than I desired. These things I write of to you, my dear Schoolteacher, that you first take pleasure in the success of my life, and also rejoice in the honours, and likewise, that the memory of me shall stand for ever and tower over other earthly kings as their example, that they may the more keenly see that my majesty and my worship were greater than those of all other kings who ever lived in the Middle World.

Ond me næs se hrædlica ende mines lifes 'And for me the swift end of my life' etc. Alexander refers to himself as if from the grave, but without concern, as he says, because his mind is set on future renown. This is the time-defeating heathen ethos of *dom* 'reputation', one which is otherwise known from *Beowulf*, other heroic poetry and *Sayings of the High One*, stanzas 76–7 (see **Heroic Poems** and **Poems on the Meaning of Life**). So it is no surprise to see it in Alexander here. But the author of this *Letter*, who seems to have used *Beowulf* to help him translate the *Epistola*, has gone further, removing references to India, Hercules and Bacchus here so that Alexander may focus entirely on himself (Orchard 2003: 25–39, esp. 39). These closing words, as Orchard says (1995: 138), 'must have had for Christian ears a distinctly chilling ring'.

The Blickling Homilies

*

Although the existence of English homilies in the vernacular before Ælfric and Wulfstan in the mid-tenth century is impossible to prove, the unique status of English as a language used politically from the late sixth century makes it quite plausible that early preachers in England wrote their sermons down not always in Latin, but often in the language in which they spoke. Sermons must have been written in Old English, and if these have not survived from the earlier period, it seems likely that this is because they were being constantly rewritten, sometimes renewed, and when it came to it, replaced. An active preaching culture had to keep itself up to date. In these circumstances, we are lucky to have the Vercelli and Blickling collections, both of which are late copies of homilies that date from the first active phase of the English Reform in about the mid-tenth century. The style of these writings is less rigorous than that of either of the two great writers of the end of the century, and their sources were often insular and heterodox rather than validated and continental. The fact that the Vercelli manuscript was discovered in Italy suggests that the collection was heading out of England because the owner and his culture were no longer welcome in the height of monastic reform. The Blickling Homilies, though they were placed in Blickling Hall in Norfolk before they moved to Princeton University Library, were in the same undefined category as the collection that finished in Vercelli.

Within their manuscript, which is a fragment of *c.* 1000, the Blickling Homilies were ordered so as to follow the liturgical year. On this basis it can be judged that the homilies in the five quires now missing from the manuscript dealt with the season preceding the Ascension. The homilies that remain proceed through temporal (i.e. moveable) feasts for the first 13, thereafter sanctoral (i.e. fixed) feasts for the last five. The latter are accordingly Saints' Lives, for St John the Baptist, Peter and Paul, Michael, Martin and Andrew. The phrases of public address in some of these homilies suggests that the collection was intended to be used in preaching to laymen during the Mass, and the structure resembles that of the *St-Père de Chartres* collection from France in the early ninth century, which was used for this purpose. The two sections from Homily No. 16 below, for the Feast of St Michael the Archangel, are of relevance to *Beowulf*-studies as well as being engagingly written. Space did not permit the quotation of the whole homily on the grotto chapel of St Michael in Gargano, Apulia, but the two passages that are quoted appear to rely on sources as old as the eighth or ninth century. The descriptive language of both the herd on Mount Garganus at the beginning, and the Pauline vision of hell at the end, resembles certain phrases in Hrothgar's speeches on Grendel's Mere and in his 'sermon', so closely that for a while it was thought that *Beowulf* relied on Blickling No. 16, or vice versa. More recently, however, it has been argued that these texts both rely on a common source (see below).

Gatch, M. McC., 'The unknowable audience of the Blickling Homilies', *Anglo-Saxon England* 18 (1989), 99–115

Kabir, A. J., *Paradise, Death and Doomsday in Anglo-Saxon Literature* (Cambridge, 2001)

Kleist, A. J., ed., *The Old English Homily: Precedent, Practice and Appropriation*, Studies in the Early Middle Ages 17 (Turnhout, 2007)

Thompson, N. M., 'The Carolingian *De festiuitatibus* and the Blickling Book', in Kleist, ed. (2007), 97–119

Toswell, M. J., 'The codicology of Anglo-Saxon homiletic manuscripts, especially the *Blickling Homilies*', in Kleist, ed. (2007), 209–26

Tristram, H. L. C., 'Stock descriptions of heaven and hell in Old English prose and poetry', *Neuphilologische Mitteilungen* 79 (1978), 102–113

No. 16 'The Feast of St Michael the Archangel'

This homily is not as well written as others in the Blickling collection, showing as it does the strains of many successive adaptations in a homily on St Michael originally from southern Italy in the eighth century, one that had reached England via Ireland probably in the ninth century. Parts of this homily are of real interest, however, in the argument that an earlier vernacular version seems to have been used by the poet of *Beowulf*, in conjunction with the hell-imagery of *Visio sancti Pauli* 'the vision of St Paul', for Hrothgar's 'sermon' and his description of the haunted Mere (see **Heroic Poems**). The church that is celebrated in this homily, the grotto chapel of Mont'Angelo on Monte Gargano in Apulia, southern Italy, was also a major destination for English pilgrims on their way to Rome. This is known from some Anglo-Saxon names that the pilgrims left behind them in runic graffiti on the walls. This aspect of history transforms the genre of the work potentially from that of homily to tourist brochure.

Brown, C., '*Beowulf* and the *Blickling Homilies* and some textual notes', *Proceedings of the Modern Language Association* 53 (1938), 905–16

Clemoes, P., *Interactions of Thought and Language in Old English Literature*, Cambridge Studies in Anglo-Saxon England 12 (Cambridge, 1995)

Collins, R. I., 'Blickling Homily XVI and the dating of *Beowulf*', in *Medieval Studies Conference, Aachen, 1983*, ed. W.-D. Bald and H. Weinstock, Bamberger Beiträge zur Englischen Sprachwissenschaft 15 (Frankfurt, 1984), 61–9

Godden, M., ed., *Ælfric's Catholic Homilies: The Second Series*, Early English Texts second series 5 (Oxford, 1979)

Healey, A. diP., ed., *The Old English Vision of St Paul*, Speculum Anniversary Monographs 2 (Cambridge, MA, 1978)

Johnson, R. F., *Saint Michael the Archangel in Medieval English Legend* (Woodbridge, 2005)

Page, R. I., *An Introduction to English Runes*, 2nd ed. (Woodbridge, 1999)

Silverstein, T., *Visio S. Pauli: The History of the Apocalypse in Latin Together with Texts* (London, 1935)

Wright, C. D., *The Irish Tradition in Old English Literature*, Cambridge Studies in Anglo-Saxon England 6 (Cambridge, 1993)

Mount Garganus and the bull

Men ða leofestan, manaþ us ond myngaþ seo ar ond seo eadignes þæs hean ond þæs ha[l]gan Heahengles tid þæt we hwæthwugu [*sc.* asecgen] be þære his eadgan gemynde se þe is on ealra ymbhwyrfte to weorþienne ond to wuldrienne his Ciricean, gehweþer ge his agen geweorc ge on his naman gehalgod, ond þus ærest mannum æteawde ond gecyþde.

Heo þonne nalles on goldes wlite ond on seolfres ne scineþ, ac on sundorweorþunge þurh godcundra mægen heo gewuldrad stondeþ. Heo is eac on onsyne utan yfeles heowes, ac heo is innan mid ece mægene geweorþod. Swa hit eaþe beon mæg þæt se halga Heahengel of heofenum cumen wære, ond wære gemyndig manna tyddernesse, þæt he hine geeaðmedde þæt he hie mid his sylfes handum gesette and geworhte, to þam þæt he wolde þæt þær mihten deaþlice men gyrnan þara uplicra burhwara on þæs ecean geferscipes.

Þonne is seo halige cirice Michaeles geseted on þam hean cnolle sumes muntes, on scræfes onlicnesse wæs æteowed. Þonne is seo cirice on Campania þæs landes gemæro. Ðonne is þær on neaweste sum swiþe mære burh betwih þære sæ, seo is genemned Adriaticus, on þam munte Garganus geseted, se is haten Sepontus. Þonne syndon from þære burge weallum twelf mila ametene up to þam hean cnolle, þe ic ær big sægde, þæs Hean Engles ciricean, ond heo mid gefean ond mid blisse growende standeþ.

Ðas ciricean heo þonne þus æteowde ond gecyþde æt fruman, seo ilce boc seo on þære ciricean funden wæs ond gemeted. Segeþ þæron þæt sum rice man and for worlde æhtspedig wære on þære burh, þæs nama wæs Garganus. Se welega man þam munte gesette þone ilcan naman swa swa he hatte.

My dearest people, we are admonished and reminded by the grace and blessedness of the high and holy Archangel's festival [to tell] something concerning the blessed memory of him who is to be worshipped and glorified through the circumference of this world in his Church, hallowed both by his own work and in his own name, and who first revealed and proclaimed himself to men in the following way.

His church shines not at all in the glow of gold or silver, but rather she stands glorified at a special worth of her own through power of the Divine. In her appearance as seen from outside she is of a poor shape, but inside she is honoured with eternal virtue. We can easily see in this way that the holy Archangel came from heaven and was mindful of the infirmity of men, in humbling himself so far as to establish and build our Church with his own hands, from his desire that in that place mortal men might yearn for an everlasting fellowship with citizens of the celestial.

Michael's holy church, you see, was established on the high knoll of a mountain, and was revealed in the likeness of a cave. This church is on the border of the land of Campania. In the neighbouring region by the sea called the Adriatic, on Mount Garganus, there is established a most famous city by the name of Siponto. From the walls of that city it is a distance of twelve miles up to the high knoll where the Archangel's church is that I just spoke of, and there she stands flourishing in joy and bliss.

This church was thus first revealed and proclaimed by a book which turned up in the church and was encountered there. It says in the book that there was a powerful man, prosperous in possessions of the world, in that city, whose name was Garganus. This

Se man ahte mycelne welan, mid þy þe þas welegan mannes ungeendod w[e]or[o]d ond unarimed mengeo on hryþrum ond on manigfealdum ceapum **geweox ond gewridode**, to þon þæt he wæs geond þæs muntes feld mid þy feo oferbræded ond beþeaht.

Þa gelamp þæt sum fearhryþer þæs oþres ceapes geferscipe oferhogode, ond him gewunode þæt he wæs geond þæt westen sundorgenga, ond þa æt nehstan eft hwyrfende wæs to þam yrfe ond to þam ceape ond to heora gesetum. He þa, se fear þæs hyrdes drafe forhogode ond him on þæt westen gewunode to sumes scræfes duna. Đa þæt se hlaford geahsode þæt þæt hryþer swa on wlencu geond þæt westen ferde, þa forbealh he hine for þon þe þæt hryþer him þuhte on wedenheorte þe þær swa ferde geond þone widgillan munt. Þa gesamnode he mycel weorod his manna ond hwearf æfter wegum ge buton geond þone wudu, ond sohton þæt forwlenctan hryþær. Đa gemette he hit æt nehstan on þæs muntes cnolle, ond geseah þæt hit stod an sumes scræfes dura. Þa wæs he mid yrre swiðlice onstyred, for ðon þe hit swa wedende eode ond swa ofermodlice ferde. Þa genam he his bogan ond hine gebende, ond ða mid geættredum stræle ongan sceotan wiþ þæs þe he geseah þæt hryþer stondan.

Đa sona, mid þan þe se stræl on flyge wæs, þa com swiðe mycel windes blæd foran ongean þæt seo stræl instepe wearð eft gecyrred, ond ða þone welegan mon, þe heo ær from sended wæs, he[o] sceat þæt he sona dead wæs. Đa þæt gesawon ða burgware, ða wurdon hie swiðe forhte for ðæm fære þe heo næfre swylc wundor ne gesawon, ond þa ne dorstan hie þære stowe genealæcan þe hie þæt hryþer gesawon æt stondan.

---

wealthy man put the same name to the mountain that he had. The man had great wealth, for the endless herds and countless oxen and all kinds of cattle of this wealthy man **increased and flourished** right until the mountain plain was covered and roofed with that livestock.

It befell then that a bull among the oxen became too proud to keep company with the rest of the herd, became a loner throughout that wilderness and finally vanished from the oxen, the cattle and their pastures. This bull, then, he scorned the herdsman's droving and dwelt in the wilderness at the door of a cave. When the lord found out that the ox had thus in its arrogance moved off through the wilderness, he grew angry in thinking that the ox there which was thus wandering over the vast mountain had lost its mind. So he mustered his men into a big platoon and moved up the roads and also through the woods about them, and they looked for the arrogant ox. At last he found it on the knoll of the mountain, and could see that it was standing at the door of some cave. By then he was powerfully stirred up with wrath, so madly had it gone and so proudly it had wandered. So he took his bow, bent it back, and then with a poisoned arrow he made to shoot at where he could see the ox standing.

Just then, as the arrow was in flight, there came a really big gust of wind against it, so that the arrow was instantly turned back and shot the wealthy man from whom it had just been sent, and he died on the spot. When the citizens saw that, they became most afraid of the sudden event, for never having seen such wonders before, and from then on did not dare to approach the place where they had seen this ox standing.

---

geweox ond gewridode 'increased and flourished'. This phrase for the herd resembles Hrothgar's expression in his 'sermon', *Beowulf*, line 1741, for a man's pride which *weaxeð ond wridað* 'increases and flourishes'. The bull is the animal with pride (*oferhogian*), as is the owner, whose fate is to be shot with an arrow; rather like the man of whom Hrothgar tells.

Đa wæs on þa ilcan tid, on þære heora byrig, se wæs haten Sepontus, halig biscep. Þa gesohtan hie hine ond him þæt wundor sægdon, ond hie hine lare beahsodan hwæt him þæs to donne wære. Þa lærde he hie, ond him to ræde fand þæt hie þry dagas fæston, ond to Sancte Michaele þæt hie wilnodan þæt God gecyþde þæt mannum bemiðen wæs ond bedigled. Þa hie þæt gedon hæfdon, ge on fæstenne ge on sealmsange ge on ælmessan, ða wæs þam ilcan biscepe ætiewed on niht se hea ond se halga Heahengel Michahel.

Ond him þa eaðmodlice ond luflice tospræc ond þus cwæð, 'Weoroldlice ond wislice ge dyde þætte mannum bedigled wæs on eorðan, þæt ge þæt on heofenas to Gode sohtan. Wite þu eac þæt se mon se þær mid his agenum stræle ofsceoten wæs, þa þæt wæs mid minum willan gedon. Ond min nama is Michael. Ic eom heahengel Heofoncyninges ond ic on his gesihþe simle stonde. Secgge ic þe nu eac þæt ic onsundrum þa stowe her on eorðan lufige. Ond ofer ealle oþre ic hie geceas, ond eac gecyþe on eallum ðæm tacnum þe þær gelimpeð, þæt ic eom ðære stowe onsundran scyppend ond hyrde.'

Đa þæt wæs þus gesprecen ond gecyðed, hie þa, þa burgware, swiþe bliþe ond gefeonde mid heora halgan bisceope þa stowe sohtan ond þa æfter heora gewunon þær þone lifgendan God ond þone halgan Heahengel Michael meagollice gebædon, ond God þær eaðmodlice lac onsægdon. Ond hie þa ðær twa dura sceawodan on þære ciricean, ðær wæs seo suðduru hwæthwega hade mare. Ond þa gyt hie ne mihton ofer þæt scræf, swa swæðhlype þær hi gongan, ærðon hie gerymdon þone upgang ond geworhtan. Ac hie daga gehwylce geornlice þær ute heora gebedum æt fulgon.

At the same time there was a holy bishop living in that city of theirs who was called Sepontius. They sought him out and told him of the wonder, and they asked him for instruction on what their options were. He instructed them then, and the advice he found was that they should fast for three days and should beg St Michael that God make it known to men what was hidden and kept secret from them. When they had done this, with fasting and psalm-singing and alms, then the same bishop had a revelation in the night of the high and holy Archangel Michael.

And humbly and lovingly did he speak to him, saying, 'Practically and prudently did you all behave in seeking from God in heaven what was kept secret from men on earth. You yourself should know, too, that the man who was shot there with his own arrow, well, that was done by my will. And my name is Michael. I am archangel of the King of Heaven and I constantly stand in His sight. I tell you now too that this place on earth is one I have a special love for. And I chose it above all the others, and I will also make known in all the signs which appear there that I am this place's special creator and guardian.'

When these words had accordingly been spoken and made known, they then, the citizens, very happy and relieved, went to find the place with their holy bishop, and then, in keeping with their holy custom, earnestly prayed there to the living God and to the Archangel, and to God did they humbly make offerings there. And there they beheld two doors in what was really the church, of which the south door was of a somewhat bigger order. And still they could not get up to the cave, so precipitous was the path they should follow, until they had cleared the way up to it and built this into a road. For they committed themselves eagerly to their prayers each and every day outside there.

St Paul's vision of hell

Heavily studied because of its resemblance to part of *Beowulf*, this small concluding section of the homily on Archangel Michael represents a popular rather than doctrinally sound topic, one in keeping with the early part of the tenth century. It is derived from an originally Irish collection of homilies which are themselves indebted to the *Visio sancti Pauli* 'vision of St Paul', and also to the latter's source, the apocryphal Gospel of Nicodemus. One generation after the Blickling compilation, Ælfric would mock the *Visio* as unorthodox (Godden 1979: 190). That the *Visio* was rendered directly into English, however, shows how widespread the interest in the harrowing of hell had become since its early exposure in *The Dream of the Rood*. It was an interest shared by the poet of *Beowulf*, who seems to have drawn from the same (Irish-derived) vernacular version of the *Visio* as was used by the author of this (part of) Blickling Homily No. 16. Even if some other relationship is proposed, whereby for instance the poet of *Beowulf* borrowed directly from the homily, this passage remains a fascinating proof of the eclectic reading that was possible in the monastic culture of Anglo-Saxon England.

Ac uton nu biddan þone Heahengel Sanctus Michahel, ond ða nigen endebyrdnessa ðara haligra engla, þæt hie us syn on fultume wið helsceaðum. Hie wæron þa halgan [. . .?] on onfeng manna saulum. Swa Sanctus Paulus wæs geseonde on norðanweardne þisne middangeard, þær ealle wætero niðergewitað, ond he þær geseah ofer ðæm wætere sumne harne stan, ond wæron norð of ðæm stane awexene swiðe **hrimige bearwas**. Ond ðær wæron þystrogenipo, ond þær under þam stane wæs nic*e*ra eardung ond wearga. Ond he geseah þæt on ðæm clife hangodan on ðæm isigean bearwum manige swearte saula be heora handum gebundne. Ond þa fynd þara on nicra onlicnese heora gripende wæron, swa swa grædig wulf. Ond þæt wæt*er* wæs sweart under þam clife neoðan. Ond betuh þam clife on ðæm wætre wæron

---

So let us now pray to the Archangel St Michael, and the nine orders of holy angels, that they may give us aid against the assailants of hell. These were the saints [. . .?] in the receiving of men's souls. So was St Paul looking out in the northern quarter of this Middle World, where all the waters pass down, and there he saw over the water a grey rock, and north of the rock were grown up very **rimy groves**. And there were dark headlands, and under the rock was where sea-monsters and wolves did dwell. And he saw that on the cliff there hung in the icy groves many blackened souls bound by their hands. And the fiends grasping them were in the likeness of sea-monsters, each one like a ravenous wolf. And the water down

---

hrimige bearwas 'rimy groves' etc. This passage, anticipated earlier in the homily (see Custom) is celebrated for its close resemblance to the words of Hrothgar in *Beowulf*, lines 1357–64, when he describes the haunted Mere of Grendel and his Mother. It has been argued that *Beowulf* is based on the homily (Collins 1984), that the homily was based on *Beowulf* (Brown 1938), and that both authors relied on the same source, possibly the early ninth-century Irish 'Redaction XI' of the *Visio sancti Pauli* 'Vision of St Paul' on which this part of the Blickling Homily is based (Wright 1993; Clemoes 1995: 25).

twelf mila, ond ðonne ða twigo forburston þonne gewitan þa saula niðer þa þe on ðæm twigum hangodan, ond him onfengon ða nicras. Ðis, ðonne, wæron ða saula, þa ðe her on worlde mid unrihte gefyrenode wæron ond ðæs noldan geswican ær heora lifes ende. Ac uton nu biddan Sanctus Michael geornlice þæt he ure saula gelæde on gefean, þær he motan blissian a buton ende on ecnesse. Amen.

---

beneath the cliff was black. And from the cliff-top down to the water it was twelve miles, and when the twigs snapped, then the souls passed downwards that hung off these and the sea-monsters received them. These, then, were the souls that were fired up with wrongdoing and would not desist from this before the end of their lives. So let us now pray eagerly to St Michael that he convey our souls into joy, where he may rejoice for ever into eternity without end. Amen.

Abbot Ælfric of Eynsham

⁂

Ælfric (*c.* 950–1010) was a Benedictine monk and then in 1005 the abbot of Eynsham outside Oxford. Having been educated at Winchester as a student of Bishop Æthelwold in the 960s and 970s, he became the most prolific and versatile author of the whole period. His surviving works include translations of the Bible, stories of saints, a treatise on astronomy, a Latin grammar, texts on the duties of monks and priests, an assortment of letters, and about 130 sermons. The sermons consist of two series of 40 homilies each, *Catholic Homilies* (*Sermones Catholici*) I and II, which he completed in 995, as well as *The Lives of Saints* which followed on from there. There are also many *Supplementary Homilies* ascribed to Ælfric, whose prose is marked out from that of other homilists for a lively and attractive style in which complex ideas are expressed with remarkable clarity. Ælfric modelled his style consciously on Latin literature so as to bring such long-developed rhetorical techniques of this as repetition and parallelism into the English language. In his later work he went further, this time employing the alliteration of Old English poetry in tandem with the rhythms of ordinary English speech. It was still prose, nor did it baffle its audiences with the traditional vocabulary of Old English verse, but Ælfric now wrote sentences that could be set out as lines of poetry.

Clemoes, P., 'Ælfric', in *Continuations and Beginnings: Studies in Old English Literature*, ed. E. G. Stanley (London, 1966), 1–36

Godden, M., ed., *Ælfric's Catholic Homilies: The Second Series*, Early English Texts second series 5 (Oxford, 1979)

Lapidge, M., 'The saintly life in Anglo-Saxon England', in *The Cambridge Companion to Old English Literature*, ed. M. Godden and M. Lapidge (Cambridge, 1991), 243–63

Pope, J. C., ed., *Homilies of Ælfric: A Supplementary Collection*, Early English Texts Society old series (Oxford, 1967–8), 259–60

Skeat, W. W., ed., *Ælfric's Lives of Saints*, Early English Texts Society old series 94 and 114 (Oxford, 1890 and 1900, repr. as one vol., 1966)

Preface to Genesis

In this Preface, Ælfric is concerned with orthodoxy in circumstances that suggest that the laymen around him took the Bible rather literally. He carefully refers to three periods: the Jewish law before Moses, the Old Law (i.e. the Old Testament laws which start with the Ten Commandments) and the New Law (the New Testament precepts of the Gospels and particularly the Sermon of Jesus on the Mount). His approach to the Bible is the model from which the present-day art of literary criticism developed. This is exegesis, repeated endlessly in all the religions of the book to this day. The summary and analysis of detail for greater meaning is what Ælfric did for his living. He does this with his trademark lucidity in the following passage. Quite apart from the validity of its spiritual meaning, this passage may be read as an introduction to the art of metaphor for a layman who is presumably unaccustomed to think too often on figurative lines. As it happened, Ealdorman Æthelweard was educated, and had translated an early version of the *Anglo-Saxon Chronicle* into Latin in *c.* 975, but he was essentially a historian, not an early literary critic; and so Ælfric attempts to redress the balance. The section on translation is integrally connected with literary criticism. Anyone who thinks that the mastery of foreign languages has nothing to do with critical analysis should read this.

Incipit prefatio Genesis Anglice

Ælfric munuc gret Æðelwærd ealdormann eadmodlice. Þu bæde me, leof, þæt ic sceolde ðe awendan of Ledene on Englisc þa boc Genesis. Þa þuhte me hefigtime þe to tiðienne þæs, and þu cwæde þa þæt ic ne þorfte na mare awendan þære bec buton to Isaace, Abrahames suna, for þam þe sum oðer man þe hæfde awend fram Isaace þa boc oð ende. Nu þincð me, leof, þæt þæt weorc is swiðe pleolic me oððe ænigum men to underbeginnenne, for þan þe ic ondræde, gif sum dysig man þas boc ræt oððe rædan gehyrð, þæt he wille wenan þæt he mote lybban nu on þære niwan æ swa swa men leofodon under Moyses æ.

Hwilon ic wiste þæt sum mæssepreost, se þe min magister wæs on þam timan, hæfde þa boc Genesis, and he cuðe be dæle Lyden understandan; þa cwæð he be þam heahfædere Iacobe, þæt he hæfde feower wif, twa geswustra and heora twa þinena. Ful soð he sæde, ac he nyste, ne ic þa git, hu micel todal ys betweox þære ealdan æ and þære niwan. On anginne þisere worulde nam se broðor hys swuster to wife, and hwilon se fæder tymde bi his agenra dehter, and manega hæfdon ma wifa to folces eacan, and man ne mihte þa æt fruman wifian buton on his siblingum. Gyf hwa wyle nu swa lybban æfter Cristes tocyme swa swa men leofodon ær Moises æ oððe under Moises æ, ne byð man na Cristen, ne he furðon wyrðe ne byð þæt him ænig Cristen man mid ete.

Here begins the *Preface* to the English *Genesis*

Ælfric the Monk greets Æthelweard the Ealdorman with humility. You requested of me, Sir, that I should translate the Book of Genesis for you from Latin into English. At that time it seemed a burden to grant this, and you said then that I would not need to translate this book any further than Isaac, Abraham's son, because some other man had translated the book from Isaac to the end. Now, Sir, it seems to me that this is a risky piece of work to undertake for me or any man, because I fear that if some foolish man reads this book or hears it read, he will believe that he is permitted to live at this time in the New Law just as men lived by the Law of Moses.

I once knew that a mass-priest who was my Latin master at the time, had the book of Genesis, and had a partial understanding of Latin; he used to say then of the Patriarch Jacob that he had four wives, that is two sisters and their two handmaids. He spoke the whole truth, but he did not know, nor I yet at the time, how great the difference is between the Old Law and the New. In the beginning of this world a brother took his sister to wife, and on one occasion a father bred offspring off his own daughter, and many had more wives for the increase of the people, and a man could not then, at the start, take a wife unless with a woman of his family. If there is anyone now, after Christ's coming, who wishes to live as men lived before Moses' Law or under Moses' Law, that man is no Christian nor even worthy to eat in the same company as a Christian.

Þa ungelæredan preostas, gif hi hwæt litles understandað of þam Lydenbocum, þonne þincð him sona þæt hi magon mære lareowas beon; ac hi ne cunnon swa þeah þæt gastlice andgit þær to, and hu seo ealde æ wæs getacnung toweardra þinga oððe hu seo niwe gecyðnis æfter Cristes menniscnisse wæs gefillednys ealra þæra þinga, þe seo ealde gecyðnis getacnode towearde be Criste and be hys gecorenum. Hi cwæðað eac oft be Paul, hwi hi ne moton habban wif swa swa Petrus se apostol hæfde, and hi nellað gehiran ne witan þæt se eadiga Petrus leofede æfter Moises æ oð þæt Crist þe on þam timan to mannum com and began to bodienne his Halige Godspel and geceas Petrum ærest him to geferan: þa forlet Petrus þær rihte his wif and ealle þa twelf apostolas, þa þe wif hæfdon, forleton ægðer ge wif ge æhta, and folgodon Cristes lare to þære niwan æ and clænnisse þe he silf þa arærde. Preostas sindon gesette to lareowum þam læwedum folce. Nu gedafnode him þæt hig cuðon þa ealdan æ gastlice understandan and hwæt Crist silf tæhte and his apostolas on þære niwan gecyðnisse, þæt hig mihton þam folce wel wissian to Godes geleafan and wel bisnian to godum weorcum.

We secgað eac foran to þæt seo boc is swiðe deop gastlice to understandenne, and we ne writað na mare buton þa nacedan gerecednisse. Þonne þincð þam ungelæredum þæt eall þæt andgit beo belocen on þære anfealdan gerecednisse; ac hit ys swiðe feor þam. Seo boc ys gehaten Genesis, þæt ys 'gecyndboc', for þam þe heo ys firmest boca and spricð be ælcum gecinde (ac heo ne spricð na be þæra engla gesceapenisse). Heo onginð þus: *In principio creauit Deus celum and terram*, þæt ys on Englisc, '**On anginne gesceop** God heofenan and eorðan'.

These unlearned priests, if they understand something or other of Latin books, think then that they can be great teachers immediately; however, they know not the spiritual meaning that pertains, and how the Old Law was a tokening of things to come, or how, after Christ's Incarnation, the New Testament was a fulfilment of all the things which the Old Testament prefigured concerning Christ and His disciples. They often speak of Paul, why they are not permitted to have a wife like Peter the Apostle did, and they will not hear or see that the blessed Peter lived by Moses' Law until in that time Christ came to mankind and began to preach His Holy Gospel and first chose Peter as His companion: Peter then and there left his wife, and all the twelve apostles, those who had wives, left both their wives and their property, and followed Christ's teaching of the New Law and the chastity which He Himself then established. Priests are appointed to teach the unlearned. It would be right for them now to know how to understand the Old Law spiritually, and, as to what Christ Himself taught as well as His apostles in the New Testament, that they might guide the people properly to faith in God and set good examples to them in their own deeds.

We also said, earlier on the subject, that this book is very deep to understand spiritually, and we will never write more than the bare narrative. Now the uneducated think that all the sense is enclosed in that simple narrative; but that is very far from being the case. The book is called Genesis, that is 'book of origins', because it is the first book and speaks of every origin (though it never speaks of the creation of the angels). It begins thus: *In principio creauit Deus celum and terram*, in English that is '**In the beginning God created** heaven and earth'.

On anginne gesceop God 'In the beginning God created' etc. Genesis 1:1.

Hit wæs soðlice swa gedon þæt God ælmihtig geworhte on anginne þa þa he wolde gesceafta. Ac swa þeah æfter gastlicum andgite þæt anginn ys Crist, swa swa he sylf cwæð to þam Iudeiscum: '**Ic eom angin**, þe to eow sprece.' Ðurh þis angin worhte God Fæder heofenan and eorðan, for þan þe he gesceop ealle gesceafta þurh þone Sunu se þe was æfre of him acenned wisdom of þam wisan Fæder. Eft stynt on þære bec on þam forman ferse: *Spiritus dei ferebatur super aquas*, þæt is on Englisc, '**And Godes Gast** wæs geferod ofer wæteru'.

Godes Gast ys se Halga Gast þurh þone geliffæste se Fæder ealle þa gesceafta þa he gesceop þurh þone Sunu, and se Halga Gast færð geond manna heortan and silð us synna forgifenisse, ærest þurh wæter on þam fulluhte and siððan þurh dædbote; and gif hwa forsihð þa forgifenisse þe se Halga Gast sylð, þonne bið his synn æfre unmyltsiendlic on ecnysse.

Eft ys seo Halige Þrinnys geswutelod on þisre bec, swa swa ys on þam worde þe God cwæð: 'Uton wircean mannan to ure anlicnisse.' Mid þam þe he cwæð, 'Uton wyrcean,' ys seo þrinnys gebicnod; mid þam þe he cwæð, 'to ure anlicnysse,' ys seo soðe annis geswutelod; he ne cwæð na menigfealdlice to urum anlicnissum, ac anfealdlice to ure anlicnisse. **Eft comon þri englas to Abrahame** and he spræc to him eallum þrim swa swa to anum. Hu clipode **Abeles blod** to Gode buton swa swa ælces mannes misdæda wregað hine to Gode butan wordum? Be þisum litlan man mæg understandan hu deop seo boc ys on gastlicum andgite, þeah þe heo mid leohtlicum wordum awriten sig.

It was truly done so that God Almighty in the beginning made the creatures He wanted to make. Nonetheless, however, in the spiritual sense, that beginning is Christ; just as He Himself said to the Jews: '**I am the beginning**, who speak to you'. Through this beginning God the Father made heaven and earth, because He created all created things through the Son from whom the Wise Father's wisdom was ever brought forth. Later in the book it is said in the first verse: *Spiritus dei ferebatur super aquas*, that is in English '**And God's Spirit** was carried over the waters'.

God's Spirit is the Holy Ghost, through which the Father brought to life all the created things which He had made by the Son, and the Holy Ghost moves through the hearts of men and gives us forgiveness for sins, first through water in baptism and then through atonement; and if anyone despises the forgiveness which the Holy Ghost gives, then his sin is unforgivable for ever into eternity.

Later the Holy Trinity is manifested in this book, as it is in the words which God says: 'Let Us make man in Our likeness'. When he says 'Let *Us* make', the Trinity is indicated; when He says 'in Our likeness', the true Oneness of Person is manifested; He does not speak in the plural of 'Our likenesses', but in the singular of 'Our likeness'. **Later three angels came to Abraham** and he spoke to all three as to one person. How could **the blood of Abel** call to God except as each man's misdeeds betray him to God without words? By this little thing one may understand how deep this book is in the spiritual sense, though it be written down with deceptively simple words.

Ic eom angin 'I am the beginning'. Revelations 1:8, 21:6, 22:13: 'I am the Alpha and the Omega'.

And Godes Gast 'And God's Spirit' etc. Genesis 1:2.

Eft comon þri englas to Abrahame 'Later three angels came to Abraham'. Genesis 18:1–5.

Abeles blod 'the blood of Abel'. Abel, slaughtered by Cain, yet his blood called for vengeance. Genesis 4:10.

Eft Iosep, þe wæs geseald to Egipta lande and he ahredde ðæt folc wið þone miclan hunger, hæfde Cristes getacnunge þe wæs geseald for us to cwale and us ahredde fram þam ecan hungre hellesusle. **Þæt micele geteld** þe Moises worhte mid wundorlicum cræfte on þam westene, swa swa him God sylf gedihte, hæfde getacnunge Godes gelaðunge þe he silf astealde þurh his apostolas mid menigfealdum frætewum and fægerum þeawum. To þam geweorce brohte þæt folc gold and seolfor and deorwurðe gimstanas and menigfealde mærða; sume eac brohton gatehær, swa swa seo æ bebead. Þæt gold getacnode urne geleafan and ure gode ingehid, þe we Gode offrian sceolon; þæt seolfor getacnode Godes spræca and þa halgan lare, þe we habban sceolon to Godes weorcum; þa gimstanas getacnodon mislice fægernissa on Godes mannum; þæt gatehær getacnode þa stiðan dædbote þæra manna, þe heora sinna behreowsiað. Man offrode eac **fela cinna orf Gode to lace** binnan þam getelde, be þam is swiðe menigfeald getacnung, and wæs beboden þæt se tægel sceolde beon gehal æfre on þam nytene æt þære offrunge, for þære getacnunge þæt God wile þæt we simle wel don oð ende ures lifes: þonne bið se tægel geoffrod on urum weorcum.

Nu ys seo foresæde boc on manegum stowum swiðe nearolice gesett, and þeah swiðe deoplice on þam gastlicum andgite, and heo is swa geendebyrd swa swa God silf hig gedihte þam writere Moise, and we durron na mare awritan on Englisc þonne þæt Leden hæfð, ne þa endebirdnisse awendan buton þam anum, þæt þæt Leden and þæt Englisc nabbað na ane wisan on þære spræce fadunge. Æfre se þe awent oððe se þe tæcð of Ledene on Englisc,

---

Later Joseph, when he was given to the land of Egypt and he saved the people from the great hunger, was a prefiguration of Christ who was given to die for us and saved us from the great hunger of hell's torment. **The great Tabernacle tent** that Moses made with wondrous skill in the desert, as God Himself directed, was a prefiguration of God's congregation which He Himself established through His apostles with manifold ornaments and beautiful virtues. To that work the people brought gold and silver and precious gemstones and manifold glories; some also brought goat-hair, as the Law commanded. The gold betokened our faith and our conscience, which we must offer to God; the silver betokened God's utterances and the holy doctrine we must have for God's works; the gemstones betokened various kinds of excellence in the men of God; the goat-hair betokened the stern atonement which men make who repent their sins. Also **cattle of many kinds** was sacrificed **as an offering to God**, concerning which the prefiguration is very manifold, and it was commanded that the tail should always be left intact in the animal at the offering, the prefigured meaning being that God wishes that we constantly do well until the end of our lives: then the tail will be offered in our deeds.

Now in many places the aforesaid Book of Genesis is set down very densely, and yet very profoundly in the spiritual sense, and it is arranged as God Himself directed to the writer, to Moses, and we dare not write down more in English than the Latin has, nor change the arrangement, except for the simple fact that Latin and English do not have the same way of ordering language. He who translates or teaches from Latin into English, ever shall he order

---

Þæt micele geteld 'The great Tabernacle tent'. Exodus 35–9.

fela cinna orf Gode to lace 'cattle of many kinds . . . as an offering to God', Leviticus 3:9.

æfre he sceal gefadian hit swa þæt þæt Englisc hæbbe his agene wisan, elles hit bið **swiðe gedwolsum to rædenne** þam þe þæs Ledenes wisan ne can.

Is eac to witene þæt **sume gedwolmen** wæron þe woldon awurpan þa ealdan æ, and sume woldon habban þa ealdan and awurpan þa niwan, swa þa Iudeiscean doð; ac Crist sylf and His apostolas us tæhton ægðer to healdenne þa ealdan gastlice and þa niwan soðlice mid weorcum. God gesceop us twa eagan and twa earan, twa nosðirlu, twegen weleras, twa handa and twegen fet, and He wolde eac habban twa gecyðnissa on þissere worulde gesett, þa ealdan and þa niwan; for þam þe He deð swa swa Hine silfne gewyrð, and He nænne rædboran næfð, ne nan man ne þearf Him cweðan to, 'Hwi dest Ðu swa?'

We sceolon **awendan urne willan** to His gesetnissum, and we ne magon gebigean his gesetnissa on urum lustum. Ic cweðe nu þæt ic ne dearr ne ic nelle **nane boc** æfter þissere of Ledene **on Englisc awendan**; and **ic bidde þe**, leof ealdorman, þæt **þu me** þæs na leng **ne bidde**, þi læs þe ic beo þe ungehirsum, oððe leas gif ic do. God þe sig milde a on ecnisse. **Ic bidde nu on Godes naman**, gif hwa þas boc awritan wylle, þæt he hig gerihte wel be þære bysne, for þan þe ic nah geweald, þeah þe hig hwa to woge bringe þurh lease writeras, and hit byð þonne his pleoh na min: mycel yfel deð se unwritere, gif he nele his woh gerihtan.

---

it so that the English follows its own idiom, otherwise it will be **very misleading** for anyone **to read it** who does not know the idiom of the Latin.

It should also be seen that there have been **some heretics** who wished to cast down the Old Law, and some would have the Old and cast down the New, as the Jews do; but Christ Himself and His apostles taught us both to keep the Old Law spiritually and the New Law truly in our deeds. God created us with two eyes and two ears, two nostrils, two lips, two hands and two feet, and he would also have two Testaments established in this world, the Old and the New; because he does as it suits Him to do, and He has no counsellor, nor need any man speak to Him, asking 'Why do You do it this way?'

We must **change our will** to His decrees, and we cannot bend His decrees to our desires. I say now that I do not dare, **nor** do I wish, to **translate any book** after this one from Latin **into English**; and **I ask you**, dear Ealdorman, **not to bid me** do that any longer, in case I am disobedient to you, or in case I am not. May God be merciful to you for ever and ever. **I pray now in God's name**, if anyone wishes to write down this book, that he correct it well according to the copy text, for I do not have the power to stop someone bringing the book into error through false scribes, and it will be then his risk and never mine: much evil the bad copyist does if he will not correct his error.

---

swiðe gedwolsum to rædenne 'very misleading to read it', ***sume gedwolmen*** 'some heretics'; ***awendan urne willan*** 'change our will', ***nane boc on Englisc awendan*** 'nor translate any book into English'; ***ic bidde þe*** 'I ask you', ***þu me ne bidde*** 'not to bid me', ***Ic bidde nu on Godes naman*** 'I pray now in God's name'. These are three cases of paronomasia, in which Ælfric repeats a word each time with an incrementally different sense, in order to suggest fundamental relationships between, respectively: silly mistakes and heresy; changing things and translating texts; and request, order and entreaty.

The Life of St Edmund

St Edmund was a king executed by Danish invaders, reputedly by a son of Ragnarr to whom Bragi's *Eulogy* was dedicated (see **Heroic Poems, Gods of the Vikings**), in either 869 or 870. His cult grew stronger until, in 987 or 988, Abbo of Fleury wrote the first *Passio Sancti Eadmundi* 'Passion of St Edmund' in Latin for the monks of Ramsey (incuding the young Byrhtferth), with whom he had been staying for two years. Like a good historian, Abbo dedicated this long work to Archbishop Dunstan, who had told him some of the details, as he had heard these from King Æthelstan, whose own informant had been Edmund's sword-bearer. Ælfric translated Abbo's Life into English soon after, in *c.* 990. He included his translation in his *Lives of Saints*, which he dedicated to Ealdorman Æthelweard. Ælfric does not add anything substantial to Abbo's account of events, but writes in a beautifully limpid English which may be set out as verse. His concern with this style was to produce clear and unpretentious writing, however powerful the rhetoric. In this, he went against the stylistic fashion of the time, a remnant of which may be seen in Byrhtferth's *Enchiridion* 'manual' (in the Custom Version). This kind of writing was a showy Benedictine favourite, developed from (Aldhelm's) Latin. The monks favoured flamboyant metaphors, obscure and recondite words, flowery language and convoluted syntax. Ælfric had probably learned to write like this in Winchester, but now abandoned this in favour of plain English, because he was writing for the 'unlearned'. The text below sets out a small number of lines in verse, in order to show the novelty of Ælfric's composition.

Grundy, L., *Books and Grace: Ælfric's Theology* (London, 1991)

Szarmach, P., ed., *Holy Men and Holy Women: Old English Prose Saints' Lives and their Contents* (Albany, NY, 1996)

SVM SWYÞE GELÆRED MUNUC com suþan ofer sæ fram Sancte Benedictes stowe on Æþelredes cynincges dæge to **Dunstane ærcebisceope**, þrim gearum ær he forðferde, and se munuc hatte Abbo. Þa wurdon hie æt spræce, oþ þæt Dunstan rehte be Sancte Eadmunde swa swa Eadmundes swurdbora hit rehte **Æþelstane cynincge**, þa þa Dunstan iung man wæs and se

---

A MOST LEARNED MONK came from south over the sea from St Benedict's foundation in King Æthelred's day to **Archbishop Dunstan**, three years before he departed this life, and the monk was called Abbo. They talked then one to the other, until Dunstan told the story of King Edmund just as Edmund's swordbearer had told it to **King Æthelstan**,

---

SVM SWYÞE GELÆRED MUNUC 'A MOST LEARNED MONK'. The capitalisation of the manuscript is here preserved. Abbo of Fleury stayed at Ramsey 985–7, where he taught the young Byrhtferth. His book is the *Vita et passio sancti beati Eadmundi* 'Life and Passion of the Blessed St Edmund'. Ælfric abridges it.

Dunstane ærcebisceope 'Archbishop Dunstan'. Lived *c.* 909–88; credited (along with Bishop Æthelwold (died 984) of Winchester) by Ælfric with restoring the knowledge of Latin to England, and one of the exponents of the tenth-century Reform.

Æþelstane cynincge 'King Æthelstan'. Son of Edward the Elder; ruled 924–39. The human chain of informants is thus neatly established, from the swordbearer who was a young man in 870 (presumably the survivor mentioned below), to Dunstan in *c.* 930, to Abbo in 985, to Ælfric (in *c.* 1000).

swurdbora wæs forealdod man. Þa gesette se munuc ealle þa gereccednysse on anre bec, and eft, ða þa seo boc com to us binnan feawum gearum, þa awendon we hit on Englisc swa swa hit heræfter stent. Se munuc þa Abbo binnan twam gearum gewende ham to his mynstre, and wearð sona to abbode geset on þam ylcan mynstre.

EADMUND SE EADIGA, EASTENGLA CYNINCG,
wæs snotor and wurðfull, and wurðode symble
mid æþelum þeawum þone ælmihtigan God.
He wæs eaþmod and geþungen, and swa anræd þurhwunode
þæt he nolde abugan to bysmorfullum leahtrum,
ne on nawþre healfe he ne ahielde his þeawas,
ac wæs symle gemyndig þære soþan lare:
'[Gif] þu eart to heafodmen geset, ne ahefe þu ðe,
ac beo betwux mannum swa swa an man of him.'
He wæs cystig wædlum and widewum swa swa fæder,
and mid welwillendnysse gewissode his folc
symle to rihtwisnysse, and þam reþum styrde,
and gesæliglice leofode on soþum geleafan.

---

when Dunstan was a young man and the swordbearer was an aged man. Then the monk set down the whole narrative in a book, and later, when the book came to us wthin a few years, we translated it into English just as it stands after this. Abbo the monk then within two years went home to his minster, and was straightaway appointed abbot of the same minster.

EADMUND THE BLESSED, KING OF EAST ANGLES,
was wise and honourable and honoured constantly
with noble virtues the Almighty God.
He was humble and distinguished, and continued so resolute
that he would never yield to shameful vices,
nor to either side did he incline his virtues,
but was constantly mindful of the true teaching:
'If you are made the captain, do not exalt yourself
but be to the people as a man like any other.'
He gave choice gifts to beggars and was like a father to widows,
and with benevolence guided his people
constantly to righteousness, and held back the cruel,
and lived in the true faith in a state of grace.

EADMUND SE EADIGA, EASTENGLA CYNINCG 'EADMUND THE BLESSED, KING OF EAST ANGLES'. The capitalisation gives the reader a cue to note the shift from ordinary to alliterative prose. The latter is now Ælfric's predominant style.

Hit gelamp ða æt nextan þæt þa Deniscan leode ferdon mid sciphere, hergiende and sleande wide geond land swa swa hiera gewuna is. On þam flotan wæron þa fyrmestan **heafodmen** Hinguar and Hubba, **geanlæhte þurh deofol**; and hie on Norðhymbralande gelendon mid æscum and aweston þæt land, and þa leoda ofslogon. Þa gewende Hinguar east mid his scipum, and Hubba belaf on Norðhymbralande, **gewunnenum sige mid wælhreownysse**.

Hinguar þa becom to Eastenglum rowende, on þam geare þe Ælfred æþeling an and twentig geara wæs, se þe Westsexena cynincg siþþan wearþ mære. And se foresæda Hinguar færlice swa swa wulf on lande bestalcode and þa leode sloh, weras and wif and þa ungewittigan cild, and to bysmore tucode þa bilewitan Cristenan. He sende ða sona syððan to þam cynincge beotlic ærende, þæt he abugan sceolde to his mannrædene gif he rohte his feores.

Se ærendraca com þa to Eadmunde cynincge, and Hinguares ærende him arodlice abead, 'Hinguar ure cynincg, cene and sigefæst on sæ and on lande, hæfð fela þeoda geweald, and com nu mid fyrde færlice her to lande þæt he her wintersetl mid his werode hæbbe. Nu hætt he þe dælan þine digelan goldhordas, and þinra yldrena gestreon arodlice wið hine, and þu beo his underkyning gif ðu cucu beon wylt, for ðan þe ðu næfst þa mihte þæt þu mage him wiðstandan.'

It happened at last that the Danish people came raiding with a fleet, harrying and slaying far across the land just as their custom is. In that fleet the foremost **captains** were Ingvarr and Ubbi, **united by the devil**; and they landed in Northumbria with warships and laid waste to the land, and slew the people. Then Ingvarr went east with his ships, while Ubbi stayed on in Northumbria, **victory having been won with murderous cruelty**.

Ingvarr then rowed his ships to East Anglia, in the year that Prince Alfred was twenty-one years old, he who later became the renowned king of Wessex. And the aforesaid Ingvarr suddenly, like a wolf, stole up on the land and slew the people, husbands and wives and the unwitting children, and mocked and abused the innocent Christians. He then at once sent to the king a threatening message that Edmund should submit to his authority if he cared for his life.

The messenger then came to King Edmund, and boldly announced to him Ingvarr's message, 'Ingvarr our king, keen and victorious on sea and on land, has power over many peoples, and has now come with his army suddenly to this land that he may have winter-quarters here with his host. Now he commands you to share out your secret goldhoards and ancestral treasures smartly with him, and you to be his under-king if you wish to stay alive, because you do not have the might with which you may withstand him.'

---

heafodmen 'captains'. See Ælfric's earlier use of this word, in Edmund's resolution to be a good king. Their style of leadership is thus up for comparison. Ingvarr's messenger's speech gives his style to be pompous, pretentious and despotic.

geanlæhte þurh deofol 'united by the devil'. *Ragnars saga Loðbrókar* 'Saga of Ragnarr Shaggy-Breeches', of the thirteenth century, says that these invaders, as well as Ívarr *inn beinlausi* 'the Boneless', were sons of Ragnarr (for whom, apparently in the mid-ninth century, Bragi composed his *Ragnarsdrápa* 'Eulogy on Ragnarr'; see **Heroic Poems** and **Gods of the Vikings**).

gewunnenum sige mid wælhreownysse 'victory having been won with murderous cruelty'. This is a dative absolute construction, not natural to English but modelled on the Latin ablative absolute in order to achieve an elegant brevity by avoiding the normal subordinate clause.

Hwæt þa, Eadmund clipode anne bisceop þe him þa gehendost wæs, and wið hine smeade hu he **þam reþan Hinguare** andwyrdan sceolde. Þa forhtode se bisceop for þam færlican gelimpe, and for þæs cynincges life, and cwæþ þæt him ræd þuhte þæt he to þam gebuge þe him bead Hinguar.

Þa swigode se cynincg and beseah to þære eorþan, and cwæþ þa æt nextan cynelice him to, 'Eala þu bisceop, to bysmore sind getawode þas earman landleoda, and me nu leofre wære þæt ic on gefeohte feolle, wið þam þe min folc moste heora eardes brucan.'

And se bisceop cwæþ, 'Eala þu leofa cynincg, þin folc lið ofslagen, and þu næfst þone fultum þæt þu feohtan mæge, and þas flotmen cumað and þe cucenne gebindaþ butan þu mid fleame þinum feore gebeorge, oððe þu þe swa gebeorge þæt þu buge to him.'

Þa cwæþ Eadmund cynincg, swa swa he ful cene wæs, 'Þæs ic gewilnige and gewysce mid mode, þæt ic ana ne belife æfter minum leofum þegnum, þe on heora bedde wurdon mid bearnum and wifum færlice ofslægene fram þissum flotmannum. Næs me næfre gewunelic þæt ic worhte fleames, ac ic wolde swiðor sweltan, gif ic þorfte, for minum agenum earde; and se ælmihtiga God wat þæt ic nylle abugan fram His biggengum æfre, ne fram His sofan lufe, swelte ic, lybbe ic.'

Æfter þissum wordum he gewende to þam ærendracan þe Hinguar him to sende, and sæde him unforht, 'Witodlice þu wære wyrðe sleges nu, ac ic nelle afylan on þinum fulum blode mine clænan handa, for þan þe ic Criste folgie, þe us swa gebysnode; and ic bliðelice wille beon ofslagen þurh eow, gif hit swa

---

Well then, Edmund called to him a bishop who was the closest at hand to him then, and discussed with him how he should answer **the cruel Ingvarr**. The bishop was then frightened of the sudden event, and for the king's life, and said it seemed advisable to him that he yield to what Ingvarr had commanded.

Then the king fell silent and looked at the earth, and at last spoke to him regally, 'O my bishop, with shame are the people of this country afflicted, and I would find it preferable to fall in battle provided that my common people might have the use of their homeland.'

And the bishop said, 'O my beloved king, your people lie slain, and you do not have the support with which you may fight, and these Vikings will come and bind you alive unless you save your life by fleeing, or so save yourself that you surrender to them.'

Then said King Edmund, so entirely brave he was, 'This is my will and the wish of my heart, that I do not remain alive after the death of my beloved thegns, who in their beds with their women and children were suddenly slain by these Vikings. It was never my custom to take flight, but I would rather die, if I needed to, for my country; and the Almighty God knows that I will not turn from His examples at any time, nor from His true love, whether I live or die.'

After these words he turned to the messenger whom Ingvarr had sent to him, and said to him without fear, 'Surely it would be worth killing you now, but I will not befoul my clean hands with your foul blood, because I follow Christ, who set us such an example; and

---

þam reþan Hinguare 'the cruel Ingvarr'. With this epithet, Ælfric shows us that Edmund's decision is motivated by what we saw in him earlier, his habit of 'restraining the cruel' (*þam reþum styrde*).

God foresceawað. Far nu swiþe hraþe, and sege þinum reþan hlaforde, "Ne abihð næfre Eadmund Hinguare on life, hæþen*ra* heretogan, buton he to Hælende Criste ærest mid geleafan on þyssum lande gebuge." '

Þa gewende se ærendraca arodlice aweg, and gemette be wæge þone wælhreowan Hinguar mid ealre his fyrde fuse to Eadmunde, and sægde þam arleasan hu him geandwyrd wæs. Hinguar þa bebead mid byldu þam sciphere þæt hie þæs cynincges anes ealle cepan sceoldon, þe his hæse forseah, and hine sona bindan.

Hwæt þa, Eadmund cynincg, mid þam þe Hinguar com, stod innan his healle þæs Hælendes gemyndig, and **awearp his wæpnu**, wolde geæfenlæcan Cristes gebysnungum, þe forbead Petre mid wæpnum to winnenne wið **þa wælhreowan Iudeiscan**. Hwæt, þa arleasan þa Eadmund gebundon, and gebysmrodon huxlice, and beoton mid saglum, and swa syððan læddon þone geleaffullan cyning to anum eorðfæstum treowe, and tigdon hine þærto mid heardum bendum and hine eft swuncgon langlice mid swipum. And he symle clypode betwux þara swinglum mid soþum geleafan to Hælende Criste, and þa hæþenan þa for his geleafan wurdon wodlice yrre, for þam þe he clipode Crist him to fultume. Hi scuton þa mid gafelucum swilce him to gamenes to, oð þæt he eall wæs beset mid heora scotungum swilce igles byrsta, swa swa Sebastianus wæs.

I will cheerfully be slain by all of you, if that is what God foresees. Go now most quickly, and tell your cruel lord, "Edmund will never surrender to Ingvarr alive, to the duke of heathen men, unless he first submit to Christ the Healer in the faith of this land." '

Then the messenger boldly went away, and met on the way there the murderously cruel Ingvarr hastening to Edmund with all his army, and told the man of no mercy how he had been answered. Ingvarr then with arrogance gave orders to the ships' host that they should all keep an eye out just for Edmund, who had despised his commands, and bind him straightaway.

Well then, King Edmund, as Ingvarr arrived, stood within his hall, mindful of the Healer, and **threw down his weapons**, wishing to imitate the examples of Christ, who forbade Peter to fight with weapons against **the murderously cruel Jews**. Well then, the merciless men then bound Edmund and violently mocked him, and beat him with rods, and likewise after that they led the devout king to an earth-fast tree, and tied him thereto with harsh bonds and swung at him once more for a long time with whips. And he constantly cried out between the strokes with true faith to Christ the Healer, and then the heathens became furiously angry because of his faith, that he cried on Christ for aid. They shot then with javelins as if for their amusement at him, until their missiles covered him completely like the bristles of a hedgehog, just as was the case with St Sebastian.

---

awearp his wæpnu 'threw down his weapons'. The *Chronicle*'s brief note on King Edmund makes it clear that he was captured or surrounded before he had time to go into battle. The following narrative styles his death on that of Christ, whom he is said to imitate (*wolde geæfenlæcan*).

þa wælhreowan Iudeiscan 'the murderously cruel Jews'. Ælfric follows his sources, who take their line on the Jews from St Augustine. Had Ælfric met any Jews in person? It is unlikely that he had: although there may have been individual Jews in England at this time, it seems unlikely that there were yet Jewish communities living here. Ælfric's view of Jews is here spiritually rather than ethnically dismissive. For this reason, it seems wiser to define his denunciation here as 'anti-Judaeic' than 'anti-Semitic'.

Þa geseah Hingwar se arleasa flotman þæt se æþela cyning nolde Criste wiðsacan, ac mid anrædum geleafan Hine æfre clipode. Het hine þa beheafdian and þa hæðenan swa dydon. Betwux þam þe he clipode to Criste þa git, þa tugon þa hæþenan þone halgan to slæge, and mid anum swencge slogon him of þæt heafod, and his sawol siþode gesælig to Criste. Þær wæs **sum man gehende** gehealden þurh God, behyd þam hæþenum, þe þis gehyrde eall and hit eft sæde swa swa we hit secgað her.

Hwæt ða, se flothere ferde eft to scipe, and behyddon þæt heafod þæs halgan Eadmundes on þam þiccum bremelum þæt hit bebyrged ne wurde. Þa æfter fyrste, syððan hie afarene wæron, com þæt landfolc to, þe þær to lafe wæs þa, þær heora hlafordes lic læg butan heafde, and wurdon swiþe sarige for his slege on mode, and huru þæt hie næfdon þæt heafod to þam bodige. Þa sæde se sceawere, þe hit ær geseah, þæt þa flotmen hæfdon þæt heafod mid him; and wæs him geðuht, swa swa hit wæs ful soð, þæt hie behyddon þæt heafod on þam holte forhwega.

Hi eodon þa ealle endemes to þam wuda, secende gehwær geond þyfelas and bremelas gif hie ahwær mihton gemeton þæt heafod. Wæs eac micel wundor þæt an wulf wearð asend, þurh Godes wissunge, to bewerigenne þæt heafod wið þa oþre deor ofer dæg and niht.

Hi eodon þa secende, and symble clypigende, swa swa hit gewunelic is þam ðe on wuda gaþ oft, 'Hwær eart þu nu, gefera?' And him andwyrde þæt heafod, 'Her! her! her!' and swa gelome clypode andswariende him eallum, swa oft swa heora ænig clypode, oþ þæt hie ealle becomen þurh ða clypunga him to.

Then Ingvarr the merciless Viking could see that the noble king would not forsake Christ, but rather cried ever out to Him with single-minded belief. He ordered him to be beheaded then and the heathens did so. While he was still calling upon Christ, the heathens dragged the saint to execution, and with one swing they struck off the head, and his soul journeyed to Christ in a state of grace. There was **a man nearby** preserved by God, hidden from the heathens, who could hear all this and said it again as we say it here.

Well then, the Viking host went back to their ships, and hid the head of Edmund the holy in the thick brambles so that it might not be buried. Then, after some time, when they had gone away, the peasantry, what there was left of it by then, came to where their lord's body lay without a head, and felt great pain in their hearts for his slaying, and indeed that they did not have the head for the body. Then the observer said who had seen it before that the Vikings had kept the head with them; and it had seemed to him, just as proved fully true, that they hid the head somewhere in the woodland.

They went then all of them together to the woods, searching everywhere through thickets and brambles to see if they might find the head anywhere. A great wonder also transpired, that a wolf was sent through God's guidance to guard the head from the other animals through day and night.

They went then searching, and constantly calling as is the custom for those who often go in the woods, 'Where are you now, mate?' And the head answered, 'Here I am! Here I am! Here I am!' and called to them thus frequently answering them all as often as any of them called, until through that calling they all came to it.

---

sum man gehende 'a man nearby'. This may be the swordbearer, the first link in the chain of narrative connecting Ælfric with Edmund's death in *c.* 870.

Þa læg se græga wulf, þe bewiste þæt heafod, and mid his twam fotum hæfde þæt heafod beclypped, grædig and hungrig; and for Gode ne dorste þæs heafdes abyrian, ac heold hit wið deor. Þa wurdon hie ofwundrode þæs wulfes hyrdrædenne, and þæt halige heafod ham feredon mid him, þancigende þam Ælmihtigan ealra His wundra. Ac se wulf folgode forð mid þam heafde, oþ þæt hie to tune comon, swylce he tam wære, and gewende eft siþþan to wuda ongean.

Þa landleode þa siþþan legdon þæt heafod to þam halgan bodige, and bebyrigdon hine swa swa hie selost mihton on swylcere hrædinge, and ciricean arærdan sona him onuppon. Eft þa on fyrste, æfter fela gearum, þa seo hergung geswac and sibb wearþ forgifen þam geswenctan folce, þa fengon hie togædere and worhton ane cyricean wurþlice þam halgan, for þam þe gelome wundra wurdon æt his byrgenne, æt þam gebædhuse þær he bebyrged wæs. Hi woldon þa ferian mid folclicum wurðmynte þone halgan lichaman, and læcgan innan þære cyrcan. Þa wæs micel wundor þæt he wæs eall swa gehal swylce he cucu wære, mid clænum lichaman, and his swura wæs gehalod, þe ær wæs forslagen; and wæs swylce an seolcen þræd embe his swuran, ræd, mannum to sweotolunge hu he ofslagen wæs. Eac swilce þa wunda, þe þa wælhreowan hæþenan mid gelomum scotungum on his lice macodon, wæron gehælde þurh þone heofonlican God, and he liþ swa ansund oþ þisne andweardan dæg, andbidigende æristes and þæs ecan wuldres. His lichama us cyð, þe lið unformolsnod, þæt he butan forligre her on worulde leofode, and mid clænum life to Criste siþode.

The grey wolf lay there, who protected the head, and with his two paws had embraced the head, ravenous and hungry; and for God did not dare to taste the head, but kept it from the animals. Then were they amazed at the wolf's guardianship, and ferried the holy head home with them, thanking the Almighty for all His wonders. And the wolf led the way with the head until they came to town, as if he were tame, and then after that went back to the woods again.

The peasants then afterwards laid the head to the holy body, and buried them as best they could in such haste, and raised up a church straightaway above this. Some time later then, after many years, when the plundering ceased and peace was granted to the afflicted people, they pooled their resources and built a church with worship for the saint, because there had often been miracles at his tomb, at the praying-house where he was buried. They wanted to ferry the holy body there with popular veneration and lay him inside the church. A great miracle had taken place by then, that he was all as whole as if he were alive, with his body clean, and his neck was healed, which had once been cut through; and it was like a silken thread around his neck, a red one, as a clear sign to men of how he was slain. Likewise, too, the wounds which the murderously cruel heathens with frequent shots had made on his body were healed by the God of heaven, and he lies there as well and entire to this present day, awaiting the resurrection and the eternal glory. His body tells us, which lies uncorrupted, that he lived in this world without fornication, and that he journeyed to Christ with a clean life.

Sum wudewe wunode, Oswyn gehaten, æt þæs halgan byrgenne, on gebedum and fæstennum manigu gear syððan. Seo wolde efsian ælce geare þone sanct, and his næglas ceorfan syferlice mid lufe, and on scryne healdan to haligdome on weofode. Þa wurðode þæt landfolc mid geleafan þone sanct, and Þeodred bisceop þearle mid giefum on golde and on seolfre þam sancte to wurðmynte.

Þa comon on sumne sæl ungesælige þeofas, eahta on anre nihte, to þam arwurðan halgan, woldon stelan þa maðmas þe men þyder brohton, and cunnodon mid cræfte hu hie in cumon mihton. Sum sloh mid slecge swiðe þa hæpsan, sum heora mid feolan feolode ymbutan, sum eac underdealf þa duru mid spade, sum heora mid hlæddre wolde unlucan þæt ægðyrl. Ac hi swuncon on idel, and earmlice ferdon, swa þæt se halga wer hi wundorlice geband, ælcne swa he stod strutigende mid tole, þæt heora nan ne mihte þæt morð gefremman, ne hie þanon astyrian, ac stodon swa oð mergen.

Men þa þæs wundrodon hu þa weargas hangodon, sum on hlæddre, sum leat to gedelfe, and ælc on his wurce wæs fæste gebunden. Hi wurdon þa gebrohte to þam bisceope ealle, and he het hi hon on heagum gealgum ealle. Ac he næs na gemyndig hu se mildheorta God clypode þurh His witegan þas word þe her standaþ, *Eos qui ducuntur ad mortem eruere ne cesses*, 'þa þe man læt to deaðe alys hie ut symble'. And eac þa halgan canones gehadodum forbeodaþ, ge bisceopum ge preostum, to beonne ymbe þeofas, for þam þe hit ne gebyraþ þam þe beoð gecorene Gode to þegnigenne þæt hie geþwærlæcan sceolon on æniges mannes deaðe, gif hie beoð Drihtnes þegnas. Eft þa Ðeodred bisceop sceawode his bec syððan, [he] behreowsode mid geomrunge

---

There dwelt a widow, named Oswyn, at the saint's shrine, in prayers and fasts many years afterwards. She would barber the saint once each year, and cleanly cut his nails with love, and keep them in the shrine as a relic on the altar. The peasants then devoutly worshipped the saint, and Bishop Theodred endowed the saint richly with gifts in gold and silver in his honour.

One time there came some misbegotten thieves, eight in one night, to the saint worthy of grace, wished to steal the treasures which people brought there, and tested ways in which they might get in there. One struck the lock hard with a sledgehammer, another of them filed around it with a file, another also dug under the doorway with a spade, another wanted to unlock the casement from a ladder. But they toiled in vain, and fared wretchedly, in such a way that the sainted man miraculously bound them, each man with his tool struggling as he stood, that none of them could carry out the crime, nor stir from there, but stood like that until morning.

People then wondered at how those criminals hung there, one on a ladder, one stooped to digging, and each was bound fast at his work. They were all brought to the bishop, and he had them all hanged on high gallows. But he was not mindful at any time of how merciful God called out through His prophet these words which stand here, *Eos qui ducuntur ad mortem eruere ne cesses*, 'those who are being led to death, be constant in releasing them'. And also the sacred canons forbid men of the clergy, both bishops and priests, to be near thieves, because it does not befit those who are chosen to serve God that they should consent to any man's death, if they are servants of the Lord. Later, when Bishop Theodred looked afterwards at his books, he repented with lamentation of having passed so cruel þæt he swa reðne dom sette þam ungesæligum þeofum, and hit besargode æfre oð his lifes ende; and þa leode bæd georne þæt hie him mid fæsten fullice þry dagas, biddende þone Ælmihtigan þæt He him arian scolde.

On þam lande wæs sum man, Leofstan gehaten, rice for worulde and unwittig for Gode. Se rad to þam halgan mid riccetere swiþe, and het him æteowian orhlice swiþe þone halgan sanct, hwæþer he gesund wære; ac swa hraðe swa he geseah þæs sanctes lichaman, þa awedde he sona and wælhreowlice grymetede, and earmlice geendode yfelum deaðe. Þis is ðam gelic þe se geleaffulla Papa Gregorius sæde on his gesetnysse be ðam halgan Laurentie, ðe lið on Romebyrig, þæt menn woldon sceawian symle hu he læge, ge gode, ge yfele; ac God hi gestilde, swa þæt þær swulton on þære sceawunge ane seofon menn ætgædere. Þa geswicon þa oþre to sceawigenne þone martyr mid menniscum gedwylde.

Fela wundra we gehyrdon on folclicre spræce be þam halgan Eadmunde þe we her nellaþ on gewrite settan, ac hi wat gehwa. On þyssum halgan is swutel, and on swilcum oþrum, þæt God Ælmihtig mæg þone man aræran eft on Domesdæg ansundne of eorþan, Se þe hylt Eadmunde halne his lichaman oð þone micclan dæg, þeah ðe he of moldan come. Wyrðe is seo stow for þam wurðfullan halgan þæt hie man wurþige and wel gelogige mid clænum Godes þeowum to Cristes þeowdome, for þam þe se halga is mærra þonne men magon asmeagan.

---

a sentence on those misbegotten thieves, and grieved for this ever until his life's end; and prayed eagerly to the people that they would fast without remission with him for three days, praying to the Almighty that He would have mercy on him.

In the land was a man called Leofstan, a man of worldly power and ignorant of God. He rode to the saint with strong presumption, quite arrogantly ordering them to reveal the holy saint, to see whether he might be in one piece; but as soon as he could see the saint's body, he went mad at once and roared with murderous cruelty, and ended miserably with an evil death. This is just like what devout Pope Gregory said in his text about St Lawrence, who lies in the city of Rome, that people would constantly observe how he was lying, both good people and bad; but God restrained them in such a way that there died in one showing seven men all at once together. Then the others ceased observing the martyr in their human folly.

Many miracles have we heard of in folk-tale hearsay concerning St Edmund which we will not set down in witing, for everyone knows them. In this saint it is manifest, and in others like him, that Almighty God can raise up a man once more on Doomsday uncorrupted from the earth, He who keeps Edmund's body whole until that great day, though he may have come from dust. That place is worthy of being worshipped on account of the worshipful saint and of being well stocked with God's clean-living servants for service to Christ, because that saint is more splendid than men may conceive.

Nis Angelcynn bedæled Drihtnes halgena, þonne on Englalande licgaþ swilce halgan swylce þæs halga cyning, and Cuþberht se eadiga, and Sancte Æþelþryð on Elig and eac hire sweostor, ansunde on lichaman geleafan to trymminge. Synd eac fela oðre on Angelcynne halgan þe fela wundra wyrcað, swa swa hit wide is cuð þam Ælmihtigan to lofe þe hi on gelyfdon. Crist geswutelaþ mannum þurh His mæran halgan þæt He is Ælmihtig God þe macað swilce wundra, þeah þe þa earman Iudei Hine eallunga wiðsocen, for þam þe hi synd awyrgede swa swa hi wiscton him sylfum. Ne beoð nane wundru geworhte æt heora byrgenum, for ðan þe hi ne gelyfað on þone lifigendan Crist, ac Crist geswutelað mannum hwær se soða geleafa is, þonne He swylce wundra wyrcð þurh His halgan wide geond þas eorþan. Þæs Him sy wuldor a mid His heofonlican Fæder, and þam Halgan Gaste, a buton ende. *Amen*

The English people are not deprived of the Lord's saints, when in England there lie such saints as this holy king, and the blessed Cuthbert, and St Audrey of Ely and also her sister, uncorrupted in body as a confirmation of belief. There are in England many other saints as well who work many wonders, as is widely known to the praise of the Almighty in Whom they believed. Christ makes manifest to men through His renowned saint that He is Almighty God who performs such wonders, though the poor Jews entirely forsook Him, for their being as accursed as they wished upon themselves. No miracles are performed at their tombs, because they do not believe in the living Christ, but Christ makes it manifest to men where the true faith lies, when He works such wonders through His saint widely across the earth. For this let there be glory to Him ever with His Father in heaven, and to the Holy Ghost, ever without end. *Amen*

Nis Angelcynn bedæled Drihtnes halgena 'The English people are not deprived of the Lord's saints'. Not thanks to Ælfric, whose later *Catholic Sermons, Second Series* (990s) celebrate St Cuthbert, and whose *Lives of Saints*, begun in *c.* 998, include several other English saints including Edmund, Oswald and Æthelthryth (Audrey) of Ely. It has been noted that, conversely, Ælfric does not mention a number of French and Flemish saints whose cults were popular in his time (Lapidge 1991: 257).

Archbishop Wulfstan of York

⁂

Wulfstan, possibly a native of the fenlands around Ely, was bishop of London from 996 to 1002. Thereafter he was bishop of Worcester and simultaneously archbishop of York until 1016, when he delegated Worcester and continued in York until his death on 28 May 1023. As time goes on, and more research is done, ever fewer of the 26 homilies attributed to him are reconfirmed as his. This diminishing status of authorship nonetheless reveals how influential Wulfstan's own prose-style, a strongly rhythmical use of words in alliterative pairs, was to his active preaching contemporaries. His style began as a product of its time, and proof of this is found in the most unlikely place, in *The Sibyl's Prophecy*, an Icelandic poem of *c.* 1000, which contains echoes of the Christian formulae in general English use. Indeed the relationship with Scandinavians defined Wulfstan's career. In 1016, when the Danes succeeded in turning England into part of a Danish empire under Cnut, son of Sveinn Forkbeard, Wulfstan normalised the regime change. Cnut, who ruled 1016–35, let Wulfstan draft a new set of laws, promoted English Christianity internationally with his journeys to Rome across Ottonian Europe, resided in Winchester rather than in Denmark, and in short became more English than the dynasty he had supplanted.

Wulfstan was an organiser; a poltician within and sometimes without the English Church whose canons he spent much of his life reforming, sometimes with the help of Abbot Ælfric of Eynsham. Temperamentally he was quite unlike Ælfric, however. Wulfstan was a writer of thunderously brilliant but often bitterly sardonic rhetorical prose. As above, if the canon of his work is shrinking, this is because his work spawned imitations which then became identified with the master's own work. The Ælfrician prose style was imitated too, but never courted by contemporaries or successors in quite the same way. Selected below are two sermons from what is known to be Archbishop Wulfstan's work: the first probably from 1002, when he moved up from bishop of London to bishop of Worcester; and the second sermon, which he wrote in three drafts, the third being around Cnut's accession in 1016 on to 1018.

Bethurum, D., ed., *The Homilies of Wulfstan* (Oxford, 1952), 134–41 (V: *Secundum Marcum*), 267–75 (XX: *Sermo Lupi*)

Bethurum, D., ed., *The Homilies of Wulfstan* (Oxford, 1957)

Bethurum, D., 'Wulfstan', in *Continuations and Beginnings: Studies in Old English Literature*, ed. E. G. Stanley (London, 1966), 210–46

Dance, R., *Words Derived from Old Norse in Early Middle English: Studies in the Vocabulary of the South-West Midland Texts*, Medieval and Renaissance Texts and Studies 246 (Tempe, AZ, 2003)

Orchard, A., 'Crying wolf: oral style and the *Sermones Lupi*', *Anglo-Saxon England* 21 (1992), 239–64

Orchard, A., 'Wulfstan as reader, writer and rewriter', in *The Old English Homily: Precedent, Practice and Appropriation*, ed. A. J. Kleist, Studies in the Early Middle Ages 17 (Turnhout, 2007), 311–41

Pons-Sanz, S. M., *Norse-Derived Vocabulary in Late Old English Texts: Wulfstan's Works: A Case Study*, North-Western European Language Evolution Supplement 22 (Odense, 2007)

Wilcox, J., 'The dissemination of Wulfstan's Homilies: the Wulfstan tradition in eleventh-century vernacular preaching', in *England in the Eleventh Century: Proceedings of the 1990 Harlaxton Symposium*, ed. C. Hicks (Stamford, 1992), 199–217

Wormald, P., 'Archbishop Wulfstan: eleventh-century state-builder', in *Wulfstan, Archbishop of York: The Proceedings of the Second Alcuin Conference*, ed. M. Townend (Turnhout, 2004), 9–27

De Falsis Deis

Once archbishop of York, Wulfstan may have noticed that he had a past namesake. At any rate, he is not to be confused with the first Archbishop Wulfstan of York, who was in and out of office in this frontier town from 931 to 956 (see Egill's *Head-Ransom* in **Viking Wars**). Both Wulfstans, however, adapted to Scandinavian conditions. The later Wulfstan turned his writing increasingly to political use. As archbishop of York, he drafted legal essays and law-codes and used the resources of Worcester to rebuild the northern archdiocese after half a century of Scandinavian conquest and rule. It was probably during a period of consultation with Norse settlers, as well as English scholars, that Wulfstan wrote his short text *De Falsis Deis*, of which an extract is given here. Wulfstan based his text on the *De Falsis Diis* of Ælfric who was perhaps the greatest writer of English of the time (see above in this section). Ælfric, writing in the 990s, used as his source the text *De correctione rusticorum* 'On the Correction of Pagans', written by Bishop Martin of Braga (in what is now Portugal) in the sixth century. Ælfric, however, added topical names to Martin's biblical and Classical list, in 'Óðon', 'Þór' and 'Fricg'. The idea at this time with all heathen gods, to pass them off as as wrongly deified ancestors, is now called 'euhemerism'. Wulfstan, who remains faithful to this learned part of Ælfric's text, nonetheless shapes it better to Norse mythology, as we know it from sources in Scandinavia.

Pons-Sanz, S. M., *Norse-Derived Vocabulary in Late Old English Texts: Wulfstan's Works: A Case Study*, North-Western European Language Evolution Supplement 22 (Odense, 2007)

Pope, J. C., ed., *Homilies of Ælfric: a Supplementary Collection*, Early English Texts Society old series 259–60 (Oxford, 1967–8)

Skeat, W. W., ed., *Ælfric's Lives of Saints*, Early English Texts Society old series 94 and 114 (Oxford, 1890 and 1900, repr. as one vol., 1966)

An man wæs on geardagum eardiende on þam iglande þe Creta hatte, se wæs Saturnus gehaten, and se wæs swa wælhreow þæt he fordyde his agene bearn, alle butan anum, and unfæderlice macode heora lif to lyre sona on geogoðe. He læfde swaþeah uneaðe ænne to life, þeah ðe he fordyde þa broðra elles;

There was a man living on the island called Crete, whose name was Saturn, and he was so deadly cruel that he did away with his own children, all save one, and in an unfatherly manner thus made evil work of their lives in their immediate youth. He left one child just about still living, though he otherwise did away with its brothers; and this one was called

An man wæs 'There was a man' etc. Mid-section from Bethurum (1957: 221–4 (Homily XII)).

and se wæs Iouis gehaten and se wearð hetol feond. He aflymde his agene fæder eft of ðam ylcan foresædan iglande, þe Creta hatte, and wolde hine forfaran georne gif he mihte. And se Iouis wearð swa swyðe gal þæt he on his agenre swyster gewifode, seo wæs genamod Iuno, and heo wearð swyðe healic gyden æfter hæðenscype geteald. Heora twa dohtra wæron Minerua and Uenus.

Þas manfullan men þe we ymbe specað wæron getealde for ða mærostan godas þa on ðam dagum, and þa hæðenan wurðodon hy swyðe þurh deofles lare. Ac se sunu wæs swaþeah swyðor on hæðenscype gewurðod þonne se fæder wære, and he is geteald eac arwurðost ealra þæra goda þe þa hæðenan on ðam dagum for godas hæfdon on heora gedwylde. And he hatte Þor oðrum naman betwux sumum þeodum, ðone Denisca leoda lufiað swyðost and on heora gedwylde weorðiaþ geornost.

His sunu hatte Mars, se macode æfre gewinn and wrohte, and saca and wraca he styrede gelome. Ðysne yrming æfter his forðsiðe wurðodon þa hæðenan eac for healicne god, and swa oft swa hy fyrdedon oððe to gefeohte woldon, þonne offrodon hy heora lac on ær to weorðunge þissum gedwolgode. And hy gelyfdon þæt he miclum mihte heom fultumian on gefeohte forðan þe he gefeoht and gewinn lufude on life. Sum man eac wæs gehaten Mercurius on life, se wæs swyðe facenfull and ðeah full snotorwyrde swicol on dædum and on leasbregdum. Ðone macedon þa hæðenan be heora getæle eac heom to mæran gode, and æt wega gelætum him lac offrodon oft and gelome þurh deofles lare, and **to heagum beorgum** him brohton oft mistlice

---

Jove and became a hostile fiend. Jove put his own father to flight from the same aforesaid island which is called Crete, and eagerly would have destroyed him if he could. And this Jove became so very wanton that he took his own sister as a wife, whose name was Juno, and she was counted a very high goddess in heathen custom. Their two daughters were Minerva and Venus.

These criminals we are speaking of were counted as the most renowned gods of their day, and through the devil's instruction the heathens worshipped them devoutly. The son, however, was worshipped more in heathen custom than the father was, and he is also counted as the most venerable of all those gods which the heathens in their error held to be gods. And the son's name, as he was otherwise named in some nations, was Þor, whom the Danish people love most of all and in their error worship most eagerly.

Jove's son was Mars, who made and performed much strife, and frequently did he stir up battles and vengeance. This wretch, after his decease, the heathens also worshipped as a high god, and as often as they went on campaign or wanted to join battle, so often did they first make their offerings in worship of this false god. And they believed that he could greatly support them in battle because he had loved fighting and strife in his lifetime. There was also a man called, while he lived, Mercury, who had been very treacherous and yet also completely clever in deceiving in his deeds and frauds. This man, too, the heathens made into their god who, by their reckoning, was famous, and at cross-roads they often and repeatedly made offerings at the devil's instruction, and **on high hill-tops** often brought

---

to heagum beorgum 'on high hill-tops'. This feature, not of Mercury's but of Óðinn's worship (Bethurum 1957: 338), is paralleled in *The Lay of Atli*, stanza 30: *at Sigtýs bergi* 'by the mountain of the Victory-Deity (Óðinn)'.

loflac. Đes gedwolgod wæs arwurðe eac betwux eallum hæðenum on þam dagum, and he is Oðon gehaten oðrum naman **on Denisce wisan**.

Nu secgað sume þa Denisce men on heora gedwylde þæt se Iouis wære, þe hy Þor hatað, Mercuries sunu, þe hi Oðon namiað; ac hi nabbað na riht, forðan þe we rædað on bocum ge on hæþenum ge on Cristenum þæt se hetula Iouis to soðan is Saturnes sunu. And **sum wif hatte Uenus**. Seo wæs Ioues dohtor, and seo wæs swa ful and swa fracod on galnysse þæt hyre agen broðor wið hy gehæmde, þæs þe man sæde, þurh deofles lare. And ða yfelan wurðiað þa hæðenan eac for healice fæmnan.

---

him various tokens of praise. This false god was also honoured among all heathens in those days, and another name for him is Oðon, **in the Danish way**.

Now some of the Danish men say in their error that this Jove, whom they call Þor, was the son of Mercury, whom they name Oðon; but they are not correct, because we read in books, both pagan and Christian, that this fierce Jove is really the son of Saturn. And **there was a woman called Venus**. She was Jove's daughter, and she was so foul and so wicked in wantonness that her own brother had sexual intercourse with her, at the devil's instruction, according to what was said. And that evil one the heathens also worship as a female of high station.

Secundum Marcum

The End of the World is foretold across the Bible variously in the Book of Daniel 11–13, St Paul's 1 Thessalonians 4:13–5:11 and 2 Thessalonians 2, St Peter's 1 Peter 4:17 and 2 Peter 3:10–11, and in the 'Little Apocalypse' from Mark 13, Matthew 24–5 and Luke 21. Taken together, these other texts show the Day of Judgement prophesied at an undisclosed time, after the blowing of a heavenly trumpet, the Lord's descent from heaven and the resurrection of the dead. This orderly view of the future is somewhat blurred in the text attributed to St John, the Apocalypse (Book of Revelations), which has nonetheless gathered more fame. One reason for this fame is the chiliasm, or doctrine of the thousand years, which was based on the reading of AD 1000 as the date for world's end. Byhrtferth's mentor Abbo of Fleury, in his *Apologeticus* of *c.* 995, says that when he was a young man he heard a sermon on the End of the World in the cathedral in Paris, 'according to which, as soon as the number of a thousand years was completed, the Antichrist would come and the Last Judgement would follow in a brief time'. Wulfstan, newly archbishop of York in 1002, refers to this date as having passed in the text below, 'according to Mark'.

---

on Denisce wisan 'in the Danish way'. The use of 'Danish' as a term for Scandinavian culture in general is attested in Old Icelandic, as *dǫnsk tunga* 'the Danish (i.e. Old Norse) tongue'.

sum wif hatte Uenus 'there was a woman called Venus'. Ælfric in his *De Falsis Diis*, Wulfstan's source, adds the words *and Fric[g] on Denisc* 'and in Danish Fricg' when he cites Venus as the origin of the name for the sixth day (Friday); he also names Venus *Fricg* in his *Life of St Martin of Tours* (Pope, 1967–8: 685; Skeat, 1966: 265). According to Ælfric, Venus also slept with her father, but Wulfstan, probably thinking of the West Norse *Freyja* with whom *Frigg* was easily confused, confines Venus' incest to her brother.

Jenks, G. C., *The Origin and Early Development of the Antichrist Myth* (Berlin, 1991)

McGinn, B., *Visions of the End: Apocalyptic Traditions in the Middle Ages*, 2nd ed. (New York, 1998)

North, R., 'End time and date of *Vǫluspá*: two models of conversion', in *Conversion and Colonization in Anglo-Saxon England*, ed. C. E. Karkov and N. Howe, Medieval and Renaissance Texts 318 (Tempe, AZ, 2006), 213–36

***Interrogatus Iesus** a discipulis de consummatione seculi, dixit eis: Cum uideritis abhominationem desolationis, & reliqua. Væ pregnantibus & nutrientibus in illis diebus. Erunt enim tribulationes tales quales non fuerunt ab initio creature quam condidit deus usque nunc neque fient, & reliqua.*

Leofan men, Ures Drihtnes apostolas ahsadan hwilum Hine sylfne ymbe þisre worulde geendunge. Ða sæde He heom þæt swilce earfoðnessa and swylce gedrecednessa sculan on worulde ær þam ende geweorðan swylce næfre ær ne gewurdan ne næfre eft ne geweorðað. And þæt godspel cwæð, 'Wa ðam wifum þe þonne timað and on þam earmlican timan heora cild fedað.'

La, nyde hit sceal eac on worulde for folces synnan yfelian swyðe. Forðam nu is se tima þe Paulus se Apostol gefyrn foresæde. He sæde hwilum þam biscope Tymothee þæt on ðam endenyhstan dagum þissere worulde beoð frecenlice tida for manna synnum, and men þonne lufiað, he cwæð, ealles to swyðe þas swicolan woruld and beoð ofergrædige woruldgestreona, and to

---

***Jesus, questioned by His disciples** on the ending of the age, said to them: [Mark 13:14] 'When you see the abomination of desolation, and so on* [: usurping a place which is not his (let the reader understand), then those who are in Judaea must take to the hills. [Mark 13:15] If anyone is on the roof he must not go down into the house to fetch anything out; [Mark 13:16] if anyone is in the field, he must not turn back for his coat.] *[Mark 13:17] Woe for women with child in those days, and for those who have children at the breast!* [[Mark 13:18] Pray that it may not come in winter.] *[Mark 13:19] For those days will bring such distress as there has never been before since the beginning of the world which God created, and will never be again, and so on.* [: [Mark 13:20: If the Lord had not cut short that time of troubles, no living thing could survive. However, for the sake of His own, whom He has chosen, He has cut short the time.]

Dear people, the Apostles of Our Lord at one time asked Himself about the end of this world. Then He told them that such troubles and such afflictions were to take place in the world before the end as had never happened before nor ever would again. And the gospel says, 'Woe to the women who bear children at that time and who in that wretched time put their children to the breast'.

Look, it is because of the sins of the people that things shall of necessity become very bad in this world. For now is the time of which Paul the Apostle foretold long ago. He once told Bishop Timothy that the Last Days of this world will be dangerous times because of the sins of man, and men will then love, he said, all too powerfully this deceitful world, and will be

---

Interrogatus Iesus 'Jesus, questioned by His disciples' etc. After Wulfstan's opening, which quotes verses from Mark 13.

manege weorðaþ to wlance and ealles to rance and **to gylpgeorne**, and sume weorþað egeslice godcundnessa hyrwende and boclare leande and unriht lufiende, and sume weorðað swicole and swæslice ficole and butan getrywðum forscyldgode on synnan. And gecnawe se ðe cunne, nu is se tima þæt ðeos woruld is gemæncged mid mænigfealdan mane and mid felafealdan facne, and ðæs hit is þe wyrse wide on worulde, ealswa þæt godspel cwæð, ***Quoniam abundabit*** *iniquitas refrigescat caritas multorum*. Ðæt is on Englisc, 'forðam þe unriht weaxeð ealles to wide, soð lufu colað'. Ne man God ne lufað swa swa man scolde. Ne manna getrywða to ahte ne standað, ac unriht ricsað wide and side, and tealte getrywða syndon mid mannum, and þæt is gesyne on mænigfealde wisan, gecnawe se ðe cunne.

Eala, eala, ac þa wæs mycel blis and bot seo betste mannum towerd þa Crist com on ðas woruld þurh mennisce gebyrde, and þæt com us eallan to helpe þam mæstan and to frofre þam betstan. And mycel is seo þwyrnes þe nu is towerd, gebide ðære yrmðe se þe hit gebide, þæt Antecrist geboren beo. Crist wæs ealra bearna betst geboren þe æfre geboren wurde, and Antecrist bið ealra þæra bearna wyrst on þas woruld geboren þe ær oððe æfter æfre gewurde oððe geweorðe. Nu sceal hit nyde yfelian swyðe, for ðam þe hit nealæcð georne his timan, ealswa hit awriten is and gefyrn wæs gewitegod, *Post mille Annos soluetur satanas*. Þæt is on Englisc, 'Æfter þusend gearum bið satanas unbunden'.

---

voracious for the treasures of this world, and too many will become proud and all too showy and **too eager to make a boast**, and some will end up deriding divine things, defaming the teaching of the Bible and loving injustice, and others will become deceitful and sweetly fickle and steeped in sins without any loyalty at all. And let him know this who can, now is the time that this world is mixed up with manifold crime and with multiple wickedness, and for this reason things are worse widely in the world, just as the gospel says, ***Quoniam abundabit*** *iniquitas refrigescat caritas multorum*. In English that is 'because injustice grows all too widely, true love will cool'. Nor do people love God as they should. Nor do the loyalties between men stand for anything, but injustice rules far and wide, and flimsy is the loyalty between men, and that is visible in manifold ways, let him know this who can.

O look, look at this, you can see that great bliss and a cure of the best kind was in the offing when Christ came into this world through a human birth, and this came to us as the greatest help and the best solace. And great crookedness is now in the offing for us, let him await the misery who can await this, when Antichrist is born. Christ was born the best of all bairns that ever was born, and Antichrist will be of all children the worst one born into the world that ever was before or ever will be since. Now of necessity it shall get much worse, because it is drawing near to his time, just as is written and was prophesied long ago, *Post mille Annos soluetur satanas*. In English that is 'After a thousand years Satan will be let loose'.

---

to gylpgeorne 'too eager to make a boast'. This theme is also familiar to the poet of *The Wanderer*, line 69, who urges his reader to be *næfre gielpes to georn, ær he geare cunne* 'nor ever too eager to boast before he sees what things are' (see **Poems on the Meaning of Life**). The end of the world is part of that poem's frame too.

Quoniam abundabit etc. From Matthew 24:12.

Þusend geara and eac ma is nu agan syððan Crist wæs mid mannum on menniscan hiwe, and nu syndon Satanases bendas swyðe toslopene, and Antecristes tima is wel gehende, and ðy **hit is on worulde a swa leng swa wacre**. Men syndon swicole and woruld is þe wyrse, and þæt us dereð eallum. And huru hit sceal hefegian heonanforð þearle rihtwisan þearfan and ðam unbealafullum. Nu ða yfelan and ða swicelan swa oferlice swyðe brædað on worulde ongean þæt mæste yfel þe mannum is towerd. Ðæt is se þeodfeond Antecrist sylfa.

Eala, mycel wæs seo ehtnes þe Cristene þoledon iu ær on worlde oft and gelome þurh wælhreowe manswican wide and side, and huru hit sceal heonanforð mænigfealdre weorðan, nu **deofol sylf** his mægnes mot wealdan, and deofles bearn swa swiðlice motan Cristene bregean. And oft ær wæs mænigfeald ehtnes, næfre þeah þam gelic þe æfter ðysan gyt bið. Forðam hit wæs oft ær þæt Godes halgan fela wundra þurh Godes mihta openlice worhtan on gemang þam þe hy ehtnesse þoledon, and ðurh þæt mænigne man gebettan, ac hit ne bið na swa on Antecristes timan. Ne magan þonne halige men on

---

A thousand years and also more has now passed since Christ was among men in human form, and now Satan's bonds are very frayed, and the time of Antichrist is very close, and so **the longer the world goes on the worse it is**. People are treacherous and the world is the worse for it, and that damages us all. And henceforth, indeed, things are going to become seriously heavy for the righteous, the needy and the innocent. Now are the evil and the treacherous breeding extremely fast in this world in preparation for the greatest evil intended for mankind. That is the arch-enemy Antichrist himself.

Well now, great was the persecution which Christians endured in former times in this world often and repeatedly through murderously cruel treacherous deceivers far and wide, and henceforth, indeed, this shall grow more manifold, now **the devil himself** may wield his power, and now the devil's children are permitted to terrorise Christians so severely. And often before was there a persecution of manifold kinds, but never to equal the one there will yet be after this time. For before now it was often the case that God's saints worked many wonders through God's might openly during the time they suffered persecution, and through this made many people atone, but in Antichrist's time it will not be so.

Þusend geara and eac ma is nu agan 'A thousand years and also more has now passed' etc. The quotation is from Revelations 20:7, whence the doctrine of chiliasm or the 1000-year extent of this world from Christ's birth to the Second Coming (McGinn 1998: 14–20; North 2006: 226–7). On the dating of this sermon, see Bethurum, who places it just after Wulfstan became archbishop of York in 1002 (1957: 291). No date is given for the End elsewhere in Wulfstan's work. The Roman Church was reluctant to fix a date for the Apocalypse on the basis of the 'thousand years' in Revelations, preferring, instead, to see the End as possible at any time. As the end of the millennium approached, however, at a subcultural level the anxiety grew. *The Sibyl's Prophecy*, whose poet has heard English-inspired sermons on the Last Days, gives an insight into the effects of this anxiety on heathen Icelanders (see **Gods of the Vikings**).

hit is on worulde a swa leng swa wacre 'the longer the world goes on, the worse it is'. This form is also present in *The Seafarer*, lines 87–90 (see **Poems on the Meaning of Life**).

deofol sylf 'the devil himself'. One of the hallmarks of Wulfstan's style is his use of *deofol* 'devil' without a definite article, as if to stress his terms of familiarity with this figure as his enemy on a daily basis.

þam timan ænige tacna openlice wyrcan, ac sculan þolian eal þæt heom man to deð. Ne God þonne ane hwile His mihta ne His wundra Sylf nele cyðan, swa He oft ær dyde, ac læt þone deofol Antecrist rabbian and wedan sume hwile and þa ðe him fylstað.

He bið mennisc man geboren, ac he bið þeah mid deofles gaste eal afylled. And se gesewenlica feond wyrcð þurh deofles cræft fela wunderlicra tacna and þurh drycræft mænigfealde gedwimera. And feorðehealf gear he ricsað ofer mancynn and mid his scincræftum mæst manna beswicð þe æfre ær ðurh ænig ðing beswicen wurde. And þa ðe he elles mid his lotwrencum bepæcan ne mæg, þa he wile þreatian and ægeslice wyldan and earmlice pinian on mænigfealde wisan and neadunga nydan þæt hy gebugan to his unlaran. He aginð leogan deoflice swyðe and ætsæcð Cristes ac cweð þæt he sylf sy Godes agen bearn, and gebringð on gedwylde ealles to manege. And God him geðafað þæt for manna gewyrhtum þæt he sume hwile mot swa wodlice derian, forðam þe men beoð þurh synna swa swyðe forwyrhte þæt deofol mot openlice þonne heora fandian hu fela he forspanan mæge to ecan forwyrde.

And þa ðe swa gesælige þonne weorþað þæt hi Godes lage healdað on an swyðe georne and on rihtan geleafan anrædlice þurhwunian willað, þa sculon þolian ehtnesse þa mæstan þe æfre ær on worulde ænige men þoledon, and eac mycle maran þonne æfre ær ahwar gewurdan oððon æfter þam æfre eft weorðan. Ac se bið gesælig þe þonne ne awacað, forðam raðe æfter þam witod him bið towerd þurh Godes mihte ece frofer. La, hwylc wunder bið þeah se mennisca deofol synfullum mote heardlice derian, þonne God geþafað

Then no holy people will be able to perform any signs openly in that time, but rather will have to suffer everything that is done to them. Nor will God then Himself at any time wish to make known His powers or His miracles as often as He did before, but rather He will let the devil Antichrist rage and foam for a while as well as those who aid him.

Antichrist will be born human, but will be all filled up with the devil's spirit. And the visible fiend through devil's power will perform many more wondrous signs and through witchcraft manifold illusions. And three and half years he will rule over mankind and will deceive with his magical powers the greatest part of humanity that was before now ever deceived by anything. And the people whom he cannot otherwise trick with his arts and dodges, those people he will threaten and terribly subdue, and wretchedly torment in manifold ways, and with violence compel them to submit to his anti-doctrine. In real diabolical fashion he will begin to lie and will deny Christ, saying rather that he himself is God's own child, and will bring into heresy all too many people. And God for the deeds of mankind will consent to Antichrist being permitted at times to do such insane damage, because people are so extremely obstructed through sin that the devil may openly test them in this case to see how many of them he can lure into everlasting damnation.

And those people who are then so fortunate as to keep God's laws each one the same very keenly, and to desire to continue resolutely in the true faith, those people shall suffer the biggest persecution that ever any people ever suffered in the world before, and greater too than ever happened anywhere or will ever happen anywhere after this time. For happy the man who then does not awake, for soon after that shall everlasting solace be ordained for him through the might of God. Look, what wonder is it though the devil in human shape may cruelly damage people filled with sin, when God consents to working such þæt He mot on His agenum halgum swylc wundor gewyrcan þæt Enoh and Elias þurh þone þeodfeond gemartrode weorðaþ, þe God sylfa fela hund wintra mid saule and lichaman geheold ær to þam anan, þæt hi þonne scoldan mid heora lare folce gebeorgan, þæt hit eal ne forwurde endemes ætgædere þurh þone deofol þe ealle men bregeð and ealle woruld drefeð?

Nis se man on life þe mæge oððe cunne swa yfel hit asecgan swa hit sceal geweorðan on þam deoflican timan. **Ne byrhð þonne broðor oðrum** hwilan, ne fæder his bearne, ne bearn his agenum fæder, ne gesibb gesibban þe ma þe fremdan. And þeodscypas winnað and sacað heom betweonan foran to þam timan þe þis sceal geweorþan. Eac sceal aspringan wide and side **sacu and clacu, hol and hete** and rypera reaflac, here and hunger, bryne and blodgyte and styrnlice styrunga, stric and steorfa and fela unglimpa. And mænigfealde tacna beoð wide gesawene on sunnan and on monan and on mistlican tunglan, and fela cynna egesan geweorþað on eorðan folce to heortgryre and to egeslican fære on mænigfealde wisan. And eal hit forwurde gyf God ne gescyrte **þæs þeodscaðan** lifdagas þe raþor ðurh His mihta. Ac for þæra gebeorge þe Him syn gecorene and ðe He habban wyle gehealdan and geholpen, He fordeð þæne þeodfeond and on helle grund þananforð

---

wonders through His own saints that Enoch and Elijah were martyred by the archfiend, saints whom God Himself had formerly kept in body and soul for many hundreds of years so that they should save the people with their teaching, [what wonder] that things do not all perish at once together through the devil who terrorises all people and afflicts the whole world?

There is no man alive who is either so capable or wise as to tell things as bad as they shall become in that diabolical time. Sometimes **no brother will save another**, nor father his child, nor a child his own father, nor one member of a family the other any more than he would a stranger. And nation will fight and war against nation before the time that all this shall take place. Far and wide there shall also spring up **war and anarchy**, **collapse and hatred** and the despoliation of plunderers, raiding and starvation, burning and bloodshed and inexorable riots, plague and pestilence and many disasters. And manifold signs will be widely seen in the sun and the moon and in various planets, and many kinds of terrors will appear to horrify the hearts and to frighten into being the fear of the people of this earth. And everything would perish if God did not shorten the living days of **the arch-assailant** all the sooner through His powers. Rather, for the protection of those whom He has elected and wishes to keep preserved and helped, He will destroy the archfiend and will sink him into hell's abyss from that time forth with all the gang that once followed him and too

---

Ne byrhð þonne broðor oðrum 'no brother will save another'. Wulfstan used the same list (from Mark 13:12) later in the 1014–18 *Sermo Lupi*, though in the past tense, as disasters that had been carried out: *Ne bearh nu foroft gesib gesibban* 'Neither did one member of the same family too often save the other'.

sacu and clacu, hol and hete 'war and anarchy, collapse and hatred'. 'Anarchy' for *clacu* is a guess, for this is one of Wulfstan's racy usages from contemporary speech, of the type that lasts but a short time.

þæs þeodscaðan 'the arch-assailant'. Antichrist.

besenceð mid eallum þam gegenge þe him ær fyligde and his unlarum to swyðe gelyfde. Đonne wurð Godes dom rihtlice toscaden, and ða þonne witodlice þe nu God lufiað and Godes lagum fylgeað and Godes lare georn-lice hlystað and hy wel healdað and anrædlice þurhwuniað on rihtan geleafan forð oð heora ende, þa scylan habban ece edlean on heofonlicre myrhðe mid Gode Sylfum æfter þam dome and mid His halgum þananforð æfre, **ðær is ece blis** and æfre bið in ealra worulda woruld a butan ende, Amen.

---

much believed in his anti-doctrine. Then God's Judgement will become justly distinguished, and those people who surely do love God now and follow God's laws and eagerly listen to God's doctrine and keep them well and resolutely continue in righteous faith from this time forth until the end, those people shall have everlasting repayment in heavenly ecstasy with God Himself according to the Judgement and shall then on dwell with His saints for ever, **where there is everlasting bliss** and ever will be in the world or all worlds ever without end, Amen.

Sermo Lupi

It has been surmised from the manuscripts of Wulfstan's sermons that he wrote his most famous work, his 'sermon of the Wolf' (his pen-name), in successive drafts from 1013 to 1018, altering according to political circumstance and the needs of performance. Many of the formulae he had deployed before, those catalogues of crimes and abuses which he tries to prevent happening in *Secundum Marcum* and other sermons of the Last Days kind, but in this one Wulfstan refers to these crimes of humanity as things that have already happened. Although the world had not yet ended, Wulfstan's *Sermo Lupi* gives the impression that he thought it soon would, if only for the evil abroad. Nonetheless, the pounding rhythmical alliteration of his sermon makes his message sustained and intensely cogent. Wulfstan begins by playing on individuals' bickering sense of outrage, connects this alliteratively with others' misdemeanours, returns to the mishaps and then upgrades these to the status of calamities, moves back to sin and the outright evils being committed and returns to God's punishments in the shape of runaway Viking terror. Some of the scenes he portrays are as horrific as anything more recent world history has seen, yet the use Wulfstan makes of these things, as for example when he connects sex-trade trafficking with Christ's devalued sacrifice, becomes extraordinary. As the focus finally narrows to religion, the sufferings of the English are connected to their crimes in a straight quid pro quo. Personal grievances then vanish in the face of the communal need to set things right; all of course, as Wulfstan makes clear, under the auspices of the Church. This, in the words of a man who actually knew what he was talking about, is the politician's 'Big Society' of a millennium ago.

ðær is ece blis 'where there is everlasting bliss'. Although this sermon seems to date to 1002, the Old English formulae stay constant for this from the time of *The Dream of the Rood*, lines 139–44, possibly as early as the late seventh century.

Godden, M., 'Apocalypse and invasion in late Anglo-Saxon England', in *From Anglo-Saxon Society to Early Medieval English: Studies Presented to Eric Gerald Stanley*, ed. M. Godden, D. Gray and T. Hoad (Oxford, 1994), 130–62

North, R., 'End time and the date of *Vǫluspá*: two models of conversion', in *Conversion and Colonization in Anglo-Saxon England*, ed. C. E. Karkov and N. Howe, Medieval and Renaissance Texts and Studies 318 (Tempe, AZ, 2006), 213–36

Pelteret, A. A. E., *Slavery in Early Medieval England from the Reign of Alfred until the Twelfth Century* (Woodbridge, 1995)

Roesdahl, E., *The Vikings*, trans. S. M. Margesson and K. Williams, 2nd ed. (Harmondsworth, 1998)

Sermo Lupi ad Anglos, quando Dani maxime persecuti sunt eos quod fuit anno millesimo XIIII ab incarnatione domini nostri Iesu Cristi

Leofan men, gecnawað þæt soð is: ðeos worolde is on ofste and hit nealæcð þam ende. And þy hit is on worolde aa swa leng swa wyrse, and swa hit sceal nyde for folces synnan fram dæge to dæge, ær Antecristes tocyme, yfelian swyþe. And huru hit wyrð þænne egeslic and grimlic wide on worolde. Understandað eac georne þæt deofol þas þeode nu fela geara dwelode to swyþe, and þæt lytle getreowþa wæran mid mannum, þeah hy wel spræcan. And unrihta to fela ricsode on lande, and næs a fela manna þe smeade ymbe þa bote swa georne swa man scolde, ac dæghwamlice man ihte yfel æfter oðrum, and unriht rærde and unlaga manege ealles to wide gynd ealle þas þeode. And we eac forþam habbað **fela byrsta and bysmara gebiden**, and gif we

---

Semon of the Wolf to the English, when the Danes were most persecuting them, which was in the year 1014 from the Incarnation of Our Lord Jesus Christ

Dear people, know what is true: this world is in haste and things are drawing near to the end. And so ever the longer it goes on in this world, the worse it is, and so it is necessity, for the sins of the people, from day to day until the coming of Antichrist, that things shall grow much worse. And indeed it will all become terrible and cruel widely in the world. Understand also eagerly this, that the devil has tricked this nation too much now for many years, and that little is the loyalty there has been among people though they spoke well. And too much injustice has ruled in this land, and there were not many people who considered the remedy for this as eagerly as one should, but on a daily basis one evil was added to another, and wrong was raised up as well as many violations of law all too widely through all this nation. And also because of that, we have **suffered many injuries and insults**, and if we are

---

fela byrsta and bysmara gebiden 'suffered many injuries and insults'. Wulfstan returns to *byrst and bysmer* further down, by then making it clear that *byrst* 'injury', as one we inflict rather receive, is the direct cause of the *bysmer* 'insult' we suffer from the Vikings (God's punishment). There is a play on *gebidan* 'suffer, experience' as well.

ænige bote gebidan scylan þonne mote we þæs to Gode **ernian bet** þonne we ær þysan dydan. Forþam **mid miclan earnungan we geearnedan** þa yrmða þe us on sittað and **mid swyþe micelan earnungan we þa bote** motan æt Gode **geræcan**, gif hit sceal heonanforð godiende weorðan.

La hwæt, we witan ful georne þæt to miclan bryce sceal micel bot nyde, and **to miclan bryne** wæter unlytel, gif man þæt fyr sceal to ahte acwencan. And micel is nydþearf eac manna gehwilcum þæt he **Godes lage gyme** heonanforð georne bet þonne he ær dyde, and **Godes gerihta mid rihte gelæste**. **On hæþenum þeodum** ne dear man forhealdan lytel, ne micel, þæs þe gelagod is to gedwolgoda weorðunge, and we forhealdað æghwær Godes gerihta ealles to gelome. And ne dear man gewanian on hæþenum þeodum, inne ne ute,

---

to **experience any remedy** then we will have to **earn this** from God **better** than we have done before this time. For **with great deserts did we earn** the miseries which oppress us, and **with very great merits we must reach the remedy** from God, if things are going to improve from this time on.

Look here and listen, we can see very eagerly that for a great breach a great repair is needed, and **for a great burning** some water in no small supply, if that fire is to be quenched in any way. And great is the dire necessity also for each man, that he eagerly **pay heed to God's laws** from now on, better than he did before, and **uphold God's rights in the right way**. **Among heathen peoples** a man dares not withhold little, or much, of the tax that is appointed for the worship of foolish gods, and we withhold God's rights everywhere all too frequently. And a man dares not curtail among heathen peoples, in private or in public, any

---

ænige bote gebidan . . . ernian bet 'experience any remedy . . . earn this better', ***mid miclan earnungan we geearnedan . . . mid swyþe micelan earnungan we þa bote geræcan*** 'with great deserts did we earn . . . with very great merits we must reach the remedy'. There are two rhetorical devices at work here. One is a type of chiasmus, an A-B-A-B-A sequence of elements which is *bot – earnung – bet – earnung – bot*, with 'any' at the start becoming 'the' at the end, and with *bet* 'better' in the middle playing on the root-meaning of *bot* 'bettering, improvement, remedy, atonement'. The other device is paronomasia, in which meanings are artfully shifted from one to another in the same word as this is repeated: *bot – earnung – bet – earnung – bot* as 'remedy – deserts – (earn) better – merit – improvement'. The aim is apparently to remind people, through the meanings of their everyday words, that there is not one thing without the other, no quick fix without repentance, and within that, no merits without earning them first. This is inductive rhetoric in its early stages, however: the 'atonement' meaning of *bot* has not yet come into view.

to miclan bryne 'for a great burning'. As a surreptitious incentive to understanding responsibility for others, Wulfstan reminds his audience of hell.

Godes lage gyme . . . Godes gerihta mid rihte gelæste 'pay heed to God's laws . . . uphold God's rights in the right way'. The two-for-one nature of English vocabulary has started here, with Old Scandinavian *lagu* being borrowed into English (our 'law') in place of *geriht*, which here means 'rights, privileges'. The figure of speech *mid rihte* is so placed as to revive the sense of 'duties' which the word *geriht* also contains.

On hæþenum þeodum 'Among heathen peoples'. What Wulfstan says here may be taken with a pinch of salt. The Danes in England and Scandinavia were generally Christian in *c.* 1016, though Norwegians and Icelanders less so (for the Christian purging of kennings for Cnut, see Hallvarðr Háreksblesi's *Eulogy on King Cnut*, 1028; **Viking Wars**, Custom Version). The Swedes, however, stayed heathen in an organised way for more than a century after. There is a lively description of their Uppsala temple in Adam of Bremen's 1080s *Deeds of the Church and Bishops of Hamburg* claims (Roesdahl 1998: 150–2).

ænig þæra þinga þe gedwolgodan broht bið and to lacum betæht bið. And we habbað Godes hus, inne and ute, clæne berypte ælcra gerisena, and Godes þeowas syndan mæþe and munde gewelhwær bedælde. And sume men secgað þæt **gedwolgoda þenan** ne dear man misbeodan on ænige wisan mid hæþenum leodum, swa swa man Godes þeowum nu deð to wide, þær Cristene scoldan Godes lage healdan and Godes þeowas griðian.

Ac soð is þæt ic secge: þearf is þære bote, for þam Godes gerihta wanedan to lange innan þysse þeode on æghwylcan ænde, and folclaga wyrsedan ealles to swyþe, **syððan Eadgar geendode**. And halignessa syndan to griðlease wide and Godes hus syndan to clæne berypte ealdra gerihta and innan bestrypte ælcra gerisena. And wydewan syndan wide fornydde on unriht to ceorle and to mænege foryrmde and gehynede swyþe, and earme men syndan sare beswicene and hreowlice besyrwde, and ut of þysan earde wide gesealde swyþe unforworhte fremdum to gesealde, and cradolcild geþeowede þurh wælhreowe unlaga, forlytelre þyfþe, wide gynd þas þeode, and freoriht fornumene and þrælriht genyrwde and ælmæsriht gewanode, and hrædest is

---

of those things which are brought and entrusted as offerings to foolish gods. And we have picked clean God's houses both inside and out of all their fittings, and God's servants are deprived of respect and protection just about everywhere. And some men say that no man dares mistreat the **thegns of foolish gods** among heathen people, as is now done too widely to God's servants in cases where Christians should keep God's laws and give sanctuary to God's servants.

For it is true what I say: the remedy is necessary, because God's rights have been curtailed too long within this nation from one end to the other, and public laws have deteriorated all too badly **since King Edgar met his end**. And sanctuaries are too unprotected widely, and God's houses are picked too clean of ancient privileges and stripped from the inside out of each and every fitting. And widows are widely forced wrongly into marriage with churls and too many are impoverished and humiliated badly, and poor men are grievously betrayed and ruefully defrauded, and sold widely to foreigners out of this country quite unconvicted of any crime, and children barely out of the cradle are enslaved in cruel violation of law, for a tiny theft here and there, widely throughout this nation, and freemen's rights seized off them and thralls' rights restricted and the rights to alms curtailed, and to put it in the shortest way, God's laws hated and His teachings despised, and for this

---

gedwolgoda þenan 'thegns of foolish gods'. The Viking religion was without priests, but by chance the middle of this phrase echoes Norse *goðar* 'chieftains, brokers', the nearest Scandinavian term for a people's representative to heathen gods. Wulfstan carefully distinguishes between the religions by using *þegnas* 'officers' and *þeowas* 'servers' for heathens and Christians respectively.

syððan Eadgar geendode 'since King Edgar met his end'. King Edgar the Peaceable, king of Mercia and Northumbria (957–9), thereafter king of England (959–75), patron of the English Benedictine Reform. Wulfstan added these words in 1016 in what is now Bodley, MS Hatton 113 (E).

to cweþenne, Godes laga laðe and lara forsawenne, and þæs we habbað ealle **þurh Godes yrre bysmor** gelome, gecnawe se þe cunne. And **se byrst wyrð gemæne**, þeh man swa ne wene, eallre þysse þeode butan God beorge.

Forþam hit is on us eallum swutol and gesene þæt we ær þysan oftor bræcan þonne we bettan, and þy is þysse þeode fela onsæge. Ne dohte hit nu lange inne ne ute: ac wæs here and hungor, bryne and blodgyte on gewelhwylcan ende oft and gelome, ad us stalu and cwalu, **stric** and steorfa, orfcwealm and uncoþu, **hol** and hete, and rypera reaflac derede swyþe þearle. And us ungylda swyðe gedrohtan, and us unwedera foroft weoldan unwæstma; forþam on þysan earde wæs, swa hit þincan mæg, nu fela geara unrihta fela and tealte getrywða æghwær mid mannum. **Ne bearh nu foroft gesib gesibban** þe ma þe fremdan, ne fæder his bearne, ne hwilum bearn his agenum fæder, ne broþor oþrum. Ne ure ænig his lif ne fadode swa swa he scolde, ne gehadode regellice, ne læwede lahlice, ac **worhtan lust us to lage** ealles to

---

we all have **insult heaped upon us through the wrath of God**, let him understand who can. And **the injury will become a shared one**, though people do not think so, to this whole nation except God save us.

For it is manifest and visible to us all that before this time we broke rules more often than we bettered any state of affairs, and much attacks the people as a result of this. It has been no good for a long time neither here nor abroad: for there has been raiding and starvation, burning and bloodshed just about everywhere both often and repeatedly, and stealing and slaying, **plague** and pestilence, cattle fever and pandemic, **collapse** and hatred and the destitution of robbers have harmed us most severely. And we have been taxed to death, and bad seasons have too often spoiled the harvest; for in this country there has been, as can be imagined, for many years now much injustice and flimsy loyalty everywhere among the people. **Neither did one member of the same family too often save the other**, any more than he would a stranger, nor a father his child, nor sometimes even a child his own father, nor one brother another. Nor did any of us order his own life as he should have done, neither the clergy by the rule, nor laymen by the law, but **we have made lust into our law** all too frequently, and neither doctrine nor laws of either God or man have we kept, as

---

þurh Godes yrre bysmor . . . se byrst wyrð gemæne 'insult heaped upon us through the wrath of God . . . the injury will become a shared one'. Here is the reprise of the *byrst and bysmer* of Wulfstan's first paragraph, but this time making the injuries Englishmen inflict on each other into the direct cause of the insults we all suffer. By and by Wulfstan thus dissolves the dog-eat-dog indifference of his people to others by reminding them of the Vikings, their common affliction from God.

stric . . . hol 'plague . . . collapse'. These meanings are guesses. The meaning is lost, probably because Wulfstan got these elsewhere unattested words from the street, racy but soon dated. See similarly *clacu* '?anarchy' in Wulfstan's *Secundum Marcum*.

Ne bearh nu foroft gesib gesibban 'Neither did one member of the same family too often save the other'. Ultimately the commonplace of this sentence is from Mark 13:12: *Tradet autem frater fratrem in mortem, et pater filium suum* 'Brother will send brother to his death, and father his son'. Wulfstan uses this also in *Secundum Marcum* (above) and elsewhere; here however in the past tense, by which Wulfstan gives these horrors a reality (noted in Godden 1994: 147).

worhtan lust us to lage 'we have made lust into our law'. Ælfric tries to deter us from the same when he says *we ne magon gebigean his gesetnissa on urum lustum* 'we cannot bend His decrees to our desires' at the end of his *Preface to Genesis*. The difference between writers is not only in tense (Wulfstan says that this has now happened), but in expression (Wulfstan's is alliteratively direct and violent).

gelome, and naþor ne heoldan ne lare ne lage Godes ne manna, swa swa we scoldan. Ne ænig wið oþerne getrywlice þohte swa rihte swa he scolde, ac mæst ælc swicode and oþrum derede wordes and dæde, and huru unrihtlice mæst ælc oþerne æftan heaweþ mid sceandlican onscytan **and mid wrohtlacan**, do mare gif he mæge.

Forþam her syn on lande ungetrywþa micle for Gode and for worolde, and eac her syn, on earde, on mistlice wisan hlafordswican manege. And ealra mæst hlafordswice se bið on worolde þæt man his hlafordes saule beswice, and ful micel hlafordswice eac bið on worolde þæt man his hlaford of life forræde, oððon of lande lifiendne drife, and ægþer is geworden on þysan earde: **Eadweard man forrædde**, and syððan acwealde and æfter þam forbærnde. And godsibbas and godbearn to fela man forspilde wide gynd þas þeode, toeacan oðron ealles to manegan þe man unscyldige forfor, ealles to wide. And ealles to mænege halige stowa wide forwurdan þurh þæt þe man sume men ær þam gelogode swa man na ne scolde, gif man on Godes griðe mæþe witan wolde, and cristenes folces to fela man gesealde ut of þysan earde, nu ealle hwile, and eal þæt is Gode lað, gelyfe se þe wille. Eac we witan georne hwær seo yrmð geweard and scandlic is to specenne þæt geworden is

---

we should have done. Nor did any one man mean to be loyal to another as rightly as he should, rather almost everyone betrayed and harmed the other in word and deed, and wrongly indeed did almost everyone each man stab the other in the back with shameful attacks **and with wrongful accusations**, do more if he may.

For here in this land there is much disloyalty towards God and the world, and here in this country, too, are in various ways many betrayals of lords. And the greatest betrayal of one's lord of all such kinds that there is in this world is when a man betrays his lord's soul, and very much betrayal of lords is also found in this world when a man treacherously kills his lord, or drives him out of the land alive, and both have happend in this homeland: **Edward was betrayed**, and then killed and afterwards burned. And sponsors at baptism and godchildren too many have been destroyed widely throughout this people, to add to all too many others that were ruined as innocents, all too far and wide. And all too many holy places far and wide came to grief because some people were appointed to them before now who should never have been, if one wished to show any respect to God's sanctuary, and too many Christian folk were sold out of this country for a long while now, and all of these things are hateful to God, let him believe who will. We can also eagerly see where that misery has happened, and shameful is it to speak of what has happened too widely, and terrible

---

and mid wrohtlacan 'and with wrongful accusations'. Wulfstan added this in the E text of 1016 or later (see note to *syððan Eadgar geendode*).

Eadweard man forrædde 'Edward was betrayed' etc. In 978, after three years of rule, St Edward the Martyr was murdered at Corfe Castle in Dorset by agents of his halfbrother Æthelred's mother, then burned so that his body should not be the focus of a saint's cult. The two oldest texts of the *Sermo Lupi*, which are Corpus Christi College, Cambridge, MS 419 (B) and Bodley MS 343 (H), have a clause (*and Æþelred mon dræfde ut of his earde* 'and Æthelred was driven out of his country') which Wulfstan cut out of the later drafts because his king was now Cnut, whose father Sveinn Forkbeard had helped to expel the unpopular King Æthelred to Normandy for a year in 1013–14 (ruled 978–1016).

to wide, and egeslic is to witanne þæt oft doð to manege, þe dreogað þa yrmþe, þæt sceotað togædere and **ane cwenan gemænum ceape** bicgað gemæne and wið þa ane fylþe adreogað, an æfter anum and ælc æfter oðrum hundum geliccast þe for fylþe ne scrifað, and syððan wið weorðe syllað of lande feondum to gewealde Godes gesceafte and his agenne ceap þe He deore gebohte.

Eac we witan georne hwær seo yrmð gewearð þæt fæder gesealde bearn wið weorþe, and bearn his modor, and broþor sealde oþerne fremdum to gewealde, and ut of ðisse þeode. Eal þæt syndan micle and egeslice dæda, understande se þe wille. And gyt hit is mare and eac mænigfealdre þæt dereð þysse þeode: mænige synd forsworene and swyþe forlogene, and wed synd to brocene oft and gelome, and þæt is gesyne on þysse þeode þæt us Godes yrre hetelice on sit, gecnawe se þe cunne. And la! Hu mæg mare scamu þurh Godes yrre mannum gelimpan þonne us deð gelome for agenum gewyrhtum? Ðeh þræla hwylc hlaforde æthleape and of Cristendom to wicinge weorþe, and hit æfter þam eft geweorþe þæt wæpngewrixl weorðe gemæne þegene and þræle: gif þræl þæne þegen fullice afylle, licge ægylde ealre his mægðe, and, gif se þegen þæne þræl þe he ær ahte fullice afylle, gylde þegengylde. Ful earhlice laga and scandlice nydgyld þurh Godes yrre us syn gemæne, understande se þe cunne.

---

is it to know what often too many men do, those who perform the misery of pooling their money, buying **a woman in one joint purchase for common use**, and practising that filth upon just her, one after another and each man after the other most like dogs who have no care for filth, and then selling on abroad for a price into the power of fiends that creature of God, that very purchase that he dearly paid for with Himself.

Also we can eagerly see where such misery has happened as a father having sold his child for a price, and a child his mother, and one brother having sold another into the power of strangers, and out of this nation. All these are huge and terrible deeds, let him understand who will. And yet there are greater and also more manifold things that harm this people: many men are forsworn and badly perjured, and contracts are too much broken often and repeatedly, and it is obvious in this people that God's hot anger sits heavily upon us, let him know this who can. And look at this! How can more shame befall the people through God's wrath than it frequently does through our own actions? If a thrall runs off from his lord and leaves Christendom to become a Viking, and it afterwards later happens that an exchange of weapons takes place between the thegn and his ex-thrall: if the thrall kills the thegn outright, the thegn's body lies unpaid for to his whole people, and if the thegn kills outright the thrall that was once his property, he may be paying the wergild of a thegn. Very cowardly laws and shameful tributes are common amongst us through the wrath of God, let him understand who can.

---

ane cwenan gemænum ceape 'a woman in one joint purchase for common use'. The reality behind the dealings of Vikings and Englishmen in the traffic of women out of here to Europe. Gilli the Russian in *Laxdœla saga*, ch. 13, is the euphemistic literary example. Wulfstan's humanity is never more evident, in the way he turns the young female victim into the hypostasis of Christ, thus reviving the meaning of Calvary for those who have forgotten.

And fela ungelimpa gelimpð þysse þeode oft and gelome: ne dohte hit nu lange inne ne ute, ac wæs here and hete on gewelhwilcan ende, oft and gelome, and Engle nu lange eal sigelease and to swyþe geyrigde þurh Godes yrre, and flotmen swa strange þurh Godes þafunge, þæt oft on gefeohte an feseð tyne, and twegen oft twentig, and hwilum læs hwilum ma, eal for urum synnum. And oft tyne oððe twelfe, ælc æfter oþrum, scendað to bysmore þæs þegenes cwenan and hwilum his dohtor oððe nydmagan, **þær he on locað**, þe læt hine sylfene rancne and ricne and genoh godne ær þæt gewurde. And oft þræl þæne þegen þe ær wæs his hlaford cnyt swyþe fæste and wyrcð him to þræle þurh Godes yrre. Wala þære yrmðe and wala þære woroldscame þe nu habbað Engle eal þurh Godes yrre! Oft twegen sæmæn, oððe þry hwilum, drifað þa drafe Cristenra manna fram sæ to sæ, ut þurh þas þeode, gewelede togædere, us eallum to woruldscame, gif we on eornost ænige cuþon ariht understandan. Ac ealne þæne bysmor þe we oft þoliað, we gyldað mid weorðscype þam þe us scendað. We him gyldað singallice and hy us hynað dæghwamlice, hy hergað and hy bærnað, rypaþ and reafiað, and to scipe lædað.

And la, hwæt is ænig oðer on eallum þam gelimpum butan Godes yrre ofer þas þeode swutol and gesæne? Nis eac nan wundor þeah us mislimpe: forþam we witan ful georne þæt nu fela geara mænn na ne rohtan foroft hwæt hy worhtan wordes oððe dæde. Ac wearð þes þeodscipe, swa hit þincan

---

And many misfortunes befall this people often and repeatedly: for a long time it has been no good either here or abroad, but there has been raiding and persecution in nearly every part, often and repeatedly, with English people for a long time now totally defeated and too much disheartened through God's wrath, with Vikings as strong as they are with God's consent, so that often one of them in a battle drives off ten of ours, and two often twenty, and sometimes fewer against more, all for our sins. And often ten or twelve, each man after the other, abusively put to shame the thegn's wife and sometimes his daughter or close kinswoman, **there where he looks on**, who considered himself proud and powerful and a good enough householder before that happened. And often a thrall ties up the thegn who was once his lord really hard and makes him into a thrall through God's wrath. O woe for the misery and woe for the shame in this world which the English now have all through the wrath of God! Often two sailors, or three sometimes, drive these droves of Christian people from sea to sea, out across this country, huddled together, to the shame in this world of us all, if we in earnest knew how to understand any part of this. But all the insult which we often endure we pay for, with interest, to the men who shame us. We pay them constantly and they humiliate us daily, they raid and they burn, they plunder and they rob, and they take it all to their ships.

And look here, what else is any of this in all these incidents except God's wrath made manifest and visible over this people? It is no wonder if we have misfortunes: for we know quite eagerly that for many years now, and all too often, no man could care less what he did in either word or deed. But rather this nation, as can be imagined, has been badly corrupted

---

þær he on locað 'there where he looks on'. With this photographic image of anarchy, Wulfstan seems to come as close as he can to portraying the householder himself, the untouchable male element of his congregation, as the joint victim of rape.

mæg, swyþe forsyngod þurh mænigfealde synna and þurh fela misdæda: þurh morðdæda and þurh mandæda, þurh gitsunga and þurh gifernessa, þurh stala and þurh strudunga, þurh mannsylena and þurh hæþene unsida, þurh swicdomas and þurh searacræftas, þurh lahbrycas and þurh æswicas, þurh mægræsas and þurh manslyhtas, þurh hadbrycas and þurh æwbrycas, þurh siblegeru and þurh mistlice forligru and eac syndan wide, swa we ær cwædan, þurh aðbricas and þurh wedbrycas, and þurh mistlice leasunga forloren, and forlogen ma þonne scolde, and freolsbricas and fæstenbrycas wide geworhte oft and gelome!

And eac her syn on earde **Godes wiðersacan**, apostatan abroþene and cyrichatan hetole, and leodhatan grimme ealles to manege, and oferhogan wide godcundra rihtlaga and Cristenra þeawa, and hocorwyrde dysige æghwær on þeode oftost of þa þing þe Godes bodan beodaþ and swyþost on þa þing þe æfre to Godes lage gebyriað mid rihte. And þy is nu geworden wide and side to ful yfelan gewunan þæt menn swyþor scamað nu for goddædan þonne for misdædan, forþam to oft man mid hocere goddæda hyrweð and godfyrhte lehtreð ealles to swyþe and swyþost man tæleð and mid olle gegreteð ealles to gelome þa þe riht lufiað and Godes ege habbað be ænigum dæle. And þurh þæt þe man swa deð þæt man eal hyrweð þæt man scolde heregian and to forð laðet þæt man scolde lufian, þurh þæt man gebringeð ealles to manege on yfelan geþance and on undæde, swa þæt hy ne scamað

---

by sin in manifold sins and through many misdeeds: through murderous deeds and criminal deeds, through greed and through avarice, through stealing and through despoliation, through enslavement and sale of slaves and through heathen vices, through betrayals and through frauds, through breaches of law and through swindling, through attacks on kinsmen and through manslaughters, through offences against clergy and through offences against marriage, through incest and through various fornications and also far and wide, as we said before, people have been damned and perjured more than should have been, through forsworn oaths and through forsworn pledges and through lies of all kinds, and offences against church festivals and offences against fasting have widely been committed often and repeatedly!

And here in this country are **God's adversaries**, degenerate apostates and vindictive persecutors of the Church, and ferocious tyrants all too many, and despisers far and wide of divine laws and Christian virtues, and foolish sarcastic mockers everywhere among the people, most often in the things God's messengers preach and most awfully in the things that rightfully belong to God's law. And so a practice quite too evil has arisen far and wide that people are more badly ashamed now of doing good than of doing wrong, for too often are good deeds derided with sarcasm and God-fearing people reviled all too much, and most awfully are accusation and scornful greeting made all too frequently against those who love justice and have fear of God to any degree. And because it so often happens that shame is felt for all that should be praised and hate is felt too continually for all that should be loved, because of this all too many people are turned to evil thoughts and to crime, so

---

Godes wiðersacan 'God's adversaries' etc. In this interlude, almost a lull in the storm of crimes and criminals, Wulfstan turns from the outward appearance of his long list of sins to the nature of the sinners themselves, what makes them tick. In a few lines his focus narrows to individuals' choices and the prospect of their damnation in the Day of Judgement.

na þeh hy syngian swyðe and wid God sylfne forwyrcan hy mid ealle, ac for idelan onscytan hy scamað þæt hy **betan heora misdæda**, swa swa bec tæcan, gelice þam dwæsan þe **for heora prytan lewe** nellað beorgan ær hy na ne magan, þeh hy eal willan.

Her syndan þurh synleawa, swa hit þincan mæg, sare gelewede to manege **on earde**. Her syndan, swa we ær sædon, mannslagan and mægslagan and mæsserbanan and mynster hatan **and hlafordswican and æbere apostatan**, and her syndan **mansworan and morþorwyrhtan**, and her syndan hadbrecan and æwbrecan, **and ðurh siblegeru and ðurh mistlice forligeru forsyngode swyðe**, and her syndan myltestran and bearnmyrðran and fule forlegene horingas manege, and her syndan wiccan and **wælcyrian**, and her syndan ryperas and reaferas and woruldstruderas and ðeofas and þeodscaðan, and wedlogan and wærlogan, and hrædest is to cweþenne mana and misdæda

---

that they have no shame if they sin an awful lot and entirely do wrong against God Himself, but for vain attacks made on them grow ashamed of **atoning for their misdeeds**, as books teach, like idiots who, **for the blemish of their pride**, will not save themselves until they cannot, though then they all may want to.

Here through the blemishes of sin, as can be imagined, too many are grievously injured **in the land**. Here there are, as we said before, manslayers and manslaughterers and killers of mass-priests and persecutors of monasteries **and betrayers of their lords and notorious apostates**, and here there are **perjurers and murderers**, and here offenders against the clergy and offenders against marriage, **and men greatly corrupted by sin through incest and all kinds of fornication**, and here there are prostitutes and infanticides and many foully mislaid fornicators, and here there are witches and **sorceresses**, and here are plunderers and robbers and despoliators of the world and thieves and monstrous enemies of the people, and pledge breakers and truce breakers, and to say it most briefly, a countless

---

betan heora misdæda 'atoning for their misdeeds'. Here we arrive at the 'atoning' sense of *betan* and *bot*, words that up to now were more selfishly concerned with 'repairing' damage or misfortune.

for heora prytan lewe 'for the blemish of their pride'. The prestige word *pryte* is saved for last. As it is loaned from French *prute* 'proud', so Wulfstan shows the beginning of a reorientation of English culture away from Scandinavia towards Europe.

Her . . . on earde 'Here . . . in the land'. A panoptic view. Wulfstan effortlessly encloses the English people within the borders of his sentence, before repeating *her . . . her . . . her* in order to enclose them further, to narrow his focus to within the walls of the room in which he delivers the sermon. The spotlight falls inexorably on the individual.

and hlafordswican and æbere apostatan 'and betrayers of their lords and notorious apostates', ***and ðurh siblegeru and ðurh mistlice forligeru forsyngode swyðe*** 'and men greatly corrupted by sin through incest and all kinds of fornication'. Additions in Bodley MS Hatton 113, these phrases are proof that Wulfstan could spoil the flow of what he wrote by too much improvement.

mansworan and morþorwyrhtan 'perjurers and murderers'. This formula, used doubtless many times before Wulfstan, was transposed into the Icelandic *menn meinsvara ok morðvarga* 'men perjured and wolfish murderers' in a vision of hell in *The Sibyl's Prophecy*, stanza 38 (*c.* 1000; see **Gods of the Vikings**).

wælcyrian 'sorceresses'. A loan from Norse *valkyriur* 'choosers of the slain'. Evidently the valkyrie-term had been used as an ironic nickname for women whose voodoo claimed to cause the death of men.

ungerim ealra. And þæs us ne scamað na, ac þæs us scamað swyþe þæt we bote aginnan, swa swa bec tæcan, and þæt is gesyne on þysse earman forsyngodan þeode. Eala! Micel magan manege git hertoeacan eaþe beþencan þæs þe an man ne mehte on hrædinge asmeagan, hu earmlice hit gefaren is nu ealle hwile wide gynd þas þeode! And smeage huru georne gehwa hine sylfne, and þæs na ne latige ealles to lange. Ac la, on Godes naman, **utan don swa us neod is**, beorgan us sylfum swa we geornost magan, þe læs we ætgædere ealle forweorðan!

An þeodwita wæs on Brytta tidum, Gildas hatte. Se awrat be heora misdædum, hu hy mid heora synnum swa oferlice swyþe God gegræmedan, þæt He let æt nyhstan **Engla here** heora eard gewinnan, and Brytta dugeþe forðon mid ealle. And þæt wæs geworden þæs þe he sæde, þurh gelæredra regolbryce and ðurh læwedra lahbryce, þurh ricra reaflac and þurh gitsunge wohgestreona, ðurh leode unlaga and þurh wohdomas, ðurh biscopas asolcennesse and unsnotornesse, and þurh lyðre yrhðe Godes bydela, þe soþes geswugedan ealles to gelome and clumedan mid ceaflum þær hy scoldan clypian. Þurh fulne eac folces gælsan and þurh oferfylla and mænigfealde synna heora eard hy forworhtan and selfe hy forwurdan. Ac wutan don swa

---

number of crimes and misdeeds of all kinds. And that will never shame us, but rather it shames us badly to make a start on atonement, as books may teach us, and this is visible in this wretched people corrupted in sin. O look at us! Much can many men still easily think of besides, that one man cannot investigate in haste, to what wretched pass things have come now for all this time widely across this people! And indeed let each man eagerly look into himself, nor let him ever delay all too long in doing that. For look at us, in God's name, **let us do as the need tells us**, save ourselves as we most eagerly can, lest together we all go down in perdition!

There was a great scholar in the time of the Britons, called Gildas. He wrote about their misdeeds, how with their sins they angered God so excessively badly that He finally let the **raiding host of the English** win their homeland and had the troop of the Britons completely destroyed. And it happened just as Gildas said, through clerics' breaches of the monastic rule and through laymen's breaches of public law, through power-brokers' robberies and through an avarice for ill-gotten gains, through bad laws in the nation and through unjust sentencing, through bishops' sloth and stupidity, and through the base cowardice of God's beadles, who kept quiet about the truth all too frequently and mumbled with their jaws when they should have cried out. Through the people's foul wantonness too, through surfeit and manifold sins they forfeited their homeland and did their souls in.

---

utan don swa us neod is 'let us do as the need tells us'. Here Wulfstan succeeds in instilling a feeling of guilt in each person among his audience, then of uniting his congregation in the common purpose of making amends (through the Church, of course).

An þeodwita wæs on Brytta tidum, Gildas hatte 'There was a great scholar in the time of the Britons, called Gildas'. This uncharacteristic Ælfrician touch is soon overwhelmed in Wulfstan's return to rhetoric. The reference is to the Welsh Gildas' *De excidio Britanniae* 'On the Ruin of Britain' (*c.* 550), a major source for Bede's *Ecclesiastical History of the English People* (*c.* 734).

Engla here 'raiding host of the English'. Irony of ironies, that the first English people were like Vikings themselves.

us þearf is, warnian us be swilcan, and soþ is þæt ic secge, **wyrsan dæda we witan mid Englum** þonne we mid Bryttan ahwar gehyrdan. And þy us is þearf micel þæt we us beþencan and wið God sylfne þingian georne. And utan don swa us þearf is, gebugan to rihte and be suman dæle unriht forlætan, and **betan swyþe georne þæt we ær bræcan**. And utan God lufian and Godes lagum fylgean, and gelæstan swyþe georne þæt þæt we behetan þa þe fulluht underfengan, oððon þa þe æt fulluhte ure forespecan wæran, and utan word and weorc rihtlice fadian, and ure in geþanc clænsian georne, and að and wed wærlice healdan, and sume getrywða habban us betweonan butan uncræftan. And utan gelome understandan þone miclan Dom þe we ealle to sculon and beorgan us georne wið þone weallendan bryne helle wites, and **geearnian us þa mærþa and þa myrhða** þe God hæfð gegearwod þam þe his willan on worolde gewyrcað. God ure helpe, Amen.

So let us do as the need arises, warn ourselves by such things, and what I say is true, **worse deeds we have known among the English** than we ever heard of anywhere among the Britons. And so the need is great for us to take stock and eagerly to intercede with God Himself. And let us do as the need tells us, turn to what is right and in some way relinquish wrong, and **atone most eagerly for the offences we have committed**. And let us love God and follow God's laws, and carry out most eagerly what we did promise when we received baptism, or what they did who were our sponsors at baptism, and let us organise word and deed in the right way, and cleanse ourselves eagerly in thought, and keep oaths and pledges carefully, and keep at least some loyalty among us without deceits. And let us frequently understand the great Judgement to which we all must go and eagerly save ourselves from the welling burning of hell's torment, and **deserve those splendours and ecstasies** which God has prepared for those who work his will in the world. God help us, Amen.

---

wyrsan dæda we witan mid Englum 'worse deeds we have known among the English'. As archbishop of York and bishop of Worcester, and with connections in Canterbury, Wulfstan was in a position to know everything that might be passed up to him from clergy across most of England.

betan swyþe georne þæt we ær bræcan 'atone most eagerly for the offences we have committed'. Wulfstan regains the wordplay of his opening paragraphs, repeating the words that now have so much more meaning.

geearnian us þa mærþa and þa myrhða 'deserve those splendours and ecstasies'. Wulfstan repeats the 'earn' sense of *geearnian*, this time with a welcome new *m-m* alliterative doublet with which to offset his *byrst and bysmor* 'injury and insult' of the opening.

EARLY CHIVALRY

❋ ❋ ❋

EARLY CHIVALRY

* * *

The Old English *Apollonius of Tyre*, the first extant English novel, was written in the mid-eleventh century. It features a princess who falls in love with a young nobleman of dashing skill, a father who steers the couple towards marriage, and a helter-skelter seafaring plot whose twists and turns are rendered also by Shakespeare in *Pericles, Prince of Tyre*. The English were already on their way towards chivalry, as well as what followed, the love poetry of *fin'amor* 'refined loving' in troubadour lyrics and verse and then prose romances. Novels came out of this, despite the later attempt, implicit in the term *novel* 'new', to claim a Classical epic ancestry for extended English prose fiction. The Modern French, German and Russian word *roman* 'novel', which derives from the French word *roman* 'romance', is a more honest indicator of the developments that led to the nineteenth-century psychological novels which so define any literary study today. The roots of this are on display here.

There are the prose accounts of *Chronicle* and Icelandic saga which first show the change of the political tide, away from Scandinavia towards Norman France. The *Apollonius* was part of this, and after the Conquest, even when the culture stratified into extremes of domination and power, as seen in the *Roland*, an interest in love continued. Through Gaimar's *Estoire des Engleis*, the *Anglo-Saxon Chronicle* became a new repository of resistance fighters and lovers of secret royal birth. As international as England now was in the mid-twelfth century, the heart of a new Angevin empire from Scotland to the Pyrenees, so this anthology is able to show extracts from the chivalric literature of related cultures. We have one from the Castillian *Poem of My Cid* as well as the story about a Scandinavian troubadour in Narbonne, Earl Rǫgnvaldr kali of Orkney, who modified Skaldic poetry to serve the partly Arabic influenced Occitan genre of Duke William IX of Aquitaine. Through Wace's *Brut*, readers will see King Arthur emerging from Latin into this varied vernacular light. In the early *Tristan* poem, of Thomas of Britain, appears a reflex of the story in the Irish tale of Deirdre and Noisiu, which we saw in the first and second sections of this anthology. Past Marie de France's poem, *Laüstic* 'The Nightingale' on illicit love which influenced *The Owl and the Nightingale*, we read scenes from *Le Jeu d'Adam*, a play on Adam and Eve, which seems to have inherited the Eve-exonerating theme of the originally Old Saxon poem *Genesis B*. As Eve says here, holding the apple to Adam, 'Eat! Don't be afraid!'

General bibliography

Andersson, T. M., *Early Epic Scenery: Homer, Virgil, and the Medieval Legacy* (Ithaca, NY, 1976)

Ashe, L., *Fiction and History in England, 1066–1200* (Cambridge, 2007)

Calin, W., *The French Tradition and the Literature of Medieval England* (Toronto, 1994)

Chibnall, M., *The Normans* (Oxford, 2000)

Crane, S., *Insular Romance: Politics, Faith and Culture in Anglo-Norman and Middle English Literature* (Berkeley, CA, 1986)

Crouch, D., *The Birth of Nobility: Constructing Aristocracy in England and France 900–1300* (Harlow, 2005)

Dean, R. J., with M. B. M. Boulton, *Anglo-Norman Literature: A Guide to Texts and Manuscripts* (London, 1999)

Fletcher, R., *The Quest for El Cid* (Oxford, 1989)

Gillies, P., 'Anglo-Norman literature: the road to Middle English', *B&OS* 454–88

Golding, B., *Conquest and Colonization; The Normans in Britain, 1066–1100* (London, 1994)

Harper-Bill, C., and N. Vincent, ed., *Henry II: New Interpretations* (Woodbridge, 2007)

van Houts, E., *Memory and Gender in Medieval Europe 900–1200* (London, 1999)

Johns, S. M., *Noblewomen, Aristocracy and Power in the Twelfth-Century Anglo-Norman Realm* (Manchester, 2003)

Krueger, R. L., ed., *The Cambridge Companion to Medieval Romance* (Cambridge, 2000)

Legge, M. D., *Anglo-Norman Literature and Its Background* (Oxford, 1963)

Pope, M., *From Latin to Modern French With Especial Consideration of Anglo-Norman* (Manchester, 1961)

Short, I., 'Literary culture at the court of Henry II', in Harper-Bill (2007), 335–61

Weiss, J., *The Birth of Romance: An Anthology* (London, 1992)

Apollonius of Tyre

✳

This story is the prose romance of Apollonius, an 'ealdorman' of Tyre (in Lebanon). His adventures begin when he sets out to win the hand of a princess of Antioch (Asia Minor) by solving a riddle with which her father, King Antiochus, keeps her secure. Unfortunately the riddle hides the truth about Antiochus, that he is already an incestuous abuser of his own daughter and will kill all suitors who solve the riddle, and some who do not. To save himself from publicity, Antiochus gives Apollonius 30 days for another solution, but makes plans to have him bumped off privately. Apollonius returns to Tyre to get his money, closely pursued by the king's hired assassin, then loses all but his life when his ship goes down off Libya. He crawls ashore naked, to be clothed by a poor fisherman who gives him half his cloak. By now we know that Ealdorman Apollonius has a decent moral character, but are surprised to learn more about him: that he is a ball-player (football? the OE word for 'ball' is *þoðer*). Apollonius so rejuvenates Arc(h)estrates, the local king, with this sport in the bathhouse courtyard that he is later summoned to the palace, clothed in a good cloak, and invited to a banquet. Princess Arc(h)estrate comes in just where the extract starts.

The princess falls in love with the stranger as he reveals his other skills, at the lyre, singing, and acting out theatrical roles, and before long she has contrived to have Apollonius richly endowed, housed, and taken on as her teacher, all by her father. This is as far as a girl can go in one day. Throughout the scene it looks as if her father, the devoted but apparently absent-minded Archestrates, has no idea of the love that is growing in his daughter. However, it turns out that this king knows more than he lets on, is mischievous rather than oblivious, and secretly steers the young people towards marriage in a politically sensitive way of his own. Our chief surprise may be how slowly the *lareow* 'teacher' Apollonius becomes aware of the princess's love for him. In later works on this theme, of the *roman courtois* 'romance' of medieval France, it is usually the courtier who first succumbs to pangs of love. However, the Old English *Apollonius* still bears witness to an English interest in love stories which would presumably give the tradition of Eleanor of Aquitaine its own crucial footing in England a century later.

Thus far the prelude. The story that follows the marriage of Apollonius with Princess Archestrate is more moving, because it is even more disrupted. It is disrupted first because at some stage the manuscript of the Old English *Apollonius* was maimed by a censor (on the lacuna, see Kobayashi 1979). It happens that our only text of the *Apollonius* was copied in alongside a large collection of Archbishop Wulfstan's homilies in the first (mid-eleventh-century) codex of the two that make up Cambridge, Corpus Christi College 201. Evidently the compiler needed some relief, or was less anxious about the morals of his collection than its later owner was. The content of the offending pages is known from the many Latin versions (Goolden 1958: 59–60). The couple proceeds to Tyre on the death of Antiochus, but at sea Princess Archestrate seems to die in childbirth and is thrown overboard in a coffin, to wash up in Ephesus (western Asia Minor) where she revives and becomes high priestess of the temple of Diana. Her daughter Thasia is committed by Apollonius to a couple in Tarsus, who try to kill her when she comes of age. Instead, the beautiful young woman is abducted by pirates and sold to a brothel in Mytilene on Lesbos, where, however, she remains a virgin by moving any visitors to tears with her story. So in young Thasia her father's performance skills live on. After returning to Tarsus, Apollonius finds evidence to believe his daughter dead, comes to Lesbos in grief and is introduced unwittingly to his daughter Thasia by the local governor in an attempt to cheer him up. The revelations and reunions follow, including one with Archestrate in Ephesus. This is where the vandalism ends and the Old English text resumes.

The long-lost original of this story was a Greek prose romance from Asia Minor, probably dating from the third century, which was adapted into Latin in the same period, and thereafter embellished until reaching a stable form in the fifth century. There are still well over 50 manuscripts of Latin versions, of which two have been treated as the closest versions to the Old English *Apollonius*, thus representative of its source. Peter Goolden, the editor, reconstructs a source from these (called 'G': 1958: xiv–vii), which the English translator slightly abbreviated, paraphrased and very occasionally mistranslated, playing down any hint of eroticism in favour of the soulful aspects of love between Apollonius and Archestrate. The transmission of this story therefore has certain parallels with that of *The Legend of St Matthew and St Andrew in the Land of the Cannibals*, originally from the New Testament *Apocrypha* but soon rendered into a number of Greek and Latin versions, which formed the basis of Old English works in prose and chiefly in the verse *Andreas* (Riedinger 1990; see **Poems of Devotion**). The *Apollonius of Tyre* was a popular story in the early Middle Ages. There is a reference to it in a poem of Venantius Fortunatus in the sixth century, as well as a citation in the book inventory of Abbot Wando of the monastery of St Wandrille (north-west Francia) in 742–9 (Goolden 1958: x–xii). There were many later uses, including in John Gower's *c.* 1360s *Confessio Amantis* 'The Lover's Confession' (Book 8) and Shakespeare's early-seventeenth-century play *Pericles, Prince of Tyre* (Archibald 1991).The Old English *Apollonius* is preserved in the first of the two codices that comprise MS Cambridge, Corpus Christi College 201. The work is thus datable to the mid-eleventh century, around the time of Earl Godwin's dispute with King Edward the Confessor (ruled 1042–66; see 'Flashpoint at Dover', *The Anglo-Saxon Chronicle* in the Custom Version). If it fills a literary need, this is one of a sophisticated secular class where English literacy was the norm. In the absence of an Alcinous, Odysseus and Nausicaa in any text of the *Odyssey* with which to fill the hours, the readership is happy instead to enjoy Archestrates, Archestrate and Apollonius.

Archibald, E., *Apollonius of Tyre: Medieval and Renaissance Themes and Variations* (Cambridge, 1991)

Brookes, S., 'Prose writers of the English Benedictine Reform', *B&OS*, 417–53, esp. 446–52

Goolden, P., ed., *The Old English Apollonius of Tyre* (Oxford, 1958)

Kobayashi, E., 'On the "lost" portions in the Old English *Apollonius of Tyre*', in *Explorations in Linguistics: Papers in Honor of Kazuko Inoue*, ed. G. Bedell et al. (Tokyo, 1979), 244–50

Marsden, R., ed., *The Cambridge Old English Reader* (Cambridge, 2004), 233–8 (edits ch. 15 to the end of ch. 18)

Riedinger, A. R., 'The Englishing of Arcestrate: women in *Apollonius of Tyre*', in *New Readings on Women in Old English Literature* , ed. H. Damico and A. Hennessey Olsen (Bloomington, IN, 1990), 292–306

The Princess falls in love

15. Mid þi ðe se cyning þas word gecwæð, ða færinga þar eode in ðæs cyninges iunge dohtor, and cyste hyre fæder and ða ymbsittendan. Þa heo becom to Apollonio, þa gewænde heo ongean to hire fæder and cwæð, 'Ðu goda cyningc, and min se leofesta fæder, hwæt is þes iunga man þe ongean ðe on swa wurðlicum setle sit mit sarlicum andwlitan? Nat ic hwæt he besorgað.'

Ða cwæð se cyningc, 'Leofa dohtor, þes iunga man is forliden and he gecwemde me manna betst on ðam plegan, forðam ic hine gelaðode to ðysum urum gebeorscipe. Nat ic hwæt he is, ne hwanon he is, ac gif ðu wille witan hwæt he sy, axsa hine, forðam þe gedafenað þæt þu wite.'

Ða eode þæt mæden to Apollonio, and mid forwandigendre spræce cwæð, 'Ðeah ðu still*e* sy and unrot, þeah ic þine æðelborennesse on ðe geseo. Nu þonne, gif ðe to hefig ne þince, sege me þinne naman and þin gelymp arece me.'

Ða cwæð Apollonius, 'Gif ðu for neode axsast æfter minum namon, ic secge þe ic hine forleas on sæ. Gif ðu wilt mine æðelborennesse witan, wite ðu þæt ic hig forlet on Tharsum.'

Ðæt mæden cwæð, 'Sege me gewislicor, þæt ic hit mæge understandan.'

16. Apollonius þa soðlice hyre arehte ealle his gelymp and æt þare spræcan ende him feollon tearas of ðam eagum. Mid þy þe se cyngc þæt geseah, he bewænde hine ða to ðare dohtor and cwæð, 'Leofa dohtor, þu gesingodest. Mid þy þe þu woldest witan his naman and his gelimp, þu hafast nu geedniwod his ealde sar. Ac ic bidde þe þæt þu gife him swa hwæt swa ðu wille.'

---

15. When the king had said these words, suddenly the king's young daughter came in, and kissed her father and those sitting around the table. When she arrived at Apollonius, she turned back to her father and said, 'Good my liege and dearest father, what is this young man that sits with a pained expression in such an honoured seat? I have no idea what troubles him.'

Then the king said, 'Dear daughter, this young man has been shipwrecked, and pleased me more than the other men there in the games, so I invited him to this party of ours. I don't know who he is, or where he is from, but if you want to know what he is, ask him, because it is right that you should know.'

The girl then went to Apollonius, and said to him in respectful words, 'You may be quiet and unhappy, but still I can see the nobility of your birth in you. So then, if it doesn't seem too heavy to you, tell me your name and relate your circumstances to me.'

Apollonius said then, 'If you really have to ask me for my name, I can tell you that I lost it at sea. If you want to know the nobility of my birth, you should know that I left that behind in Tarsus.'

The girl said, 'Tell me this more clearly, so I can understand.'

16. Apollonius then related the truth of all his circumstances to her and at the end of his speech the tears were rolling out of his eyes. When the king saw this, he turned to the daughter and said, 'Dear daughter, you did wrong there. When you wanted to know his name and circumstances, you ended up opening his old wounds. Therefore I bid you give him whatever you want.'

Đa ða þæt mæden gehirde þæt hire wæs alyfed fram hire fæder þæt heo ær hyre sylf gedon wolde, ða cwæð heo to Apollonio, 'Apolloni, soðlice þu eart ure. Forlæt þine murcnunge and nu ic mines fæder leafe habbe, ic gedo ðe weligne.'

Apollonius hire þæs þancode, and se cyngc blissode on his dohtor welwillendnesse, and hyre to cwæð, 'Leofa dohtor, hat feccan þine hearpan and gecig ðe to þin*e* inum frynd, and afirsa fram þam iungan his sarnesse.'

Đa eode heo ut and het feccan hire hearpan, and sona swa heo hea[r]pian ongan, heo mid winsumum sange gemægnde þare hearpan sweg. Đa ongunnon ealle þa men hi herian on hyre swegcræft, and Apollonius ana swigode. Đa cwæð se cyningc, 'Apolloni, nu ðu dest yfele, for ðam þe ealle men heriað mine dohtor on hyre swegcræft and þu ana hi swigende tælst.'

Apollonius cwæð, 'Eala ðu goda cyngc, gif ðu me gelifst, ic secge þæt ic ongite þæt soðlice þin dohtor gefeol on swegcræft, ac heo næfð hine na wel geleornod. Ac hat me nu sillan þa hearpan. Þonne wast þu þæt þu nu git nast.'

Arcestrates se cyning cwæð, 'Apolloni, ic oncnawe soðlice þæt þu eart on eallum þingum wel gelæred!' Đa het se cyng sillan Apollonige þa hearpan.

Apollonius þa ut eode and hine scridde, and sette ænne cynehelm uppon his heafod and nam þa hearpan on his hand, and in eode, and swa stod þæt se cyngc and ealle þa ymbsittendan wendon þæt he nære Apollonius, ac þæt he wære Apollines ðara hæðenra god.

Đa wearð stilnes and swige geworden innon ðære healle, and Apollonius his hearpenægl genam and he þa hearpestrengas mid cræfte astirian ongan, and þare hearpan sweg mid winsumum sange gemægnde. And se cyngc silf

---

When the girl heard that her father had allowed her to do what she herself had wished to do, she said to Apollonius, 'Apollonius, truly you are one of us now. Leave your grief, and now I have my father's leave, I will make you a rich man.'

Apollonius thanked her for this, and the king rejoiced in his daughter's benevolence, saying to her, 'My dear daughter, tell them to fetch your lyre, call your friends round and take this young man's suffering away.'

Then she went out and ordered them to fetch her lyre, and as soon as she began to play, she mingled the melody of the lyre with sweet song. All the people began to praise her musical skill, while only Apollonius kept silent. The king then said, 'Apollonius, now you do wrong, because everyone is praising my daughter for her musical skill and you, by keeping silent, are the only one to blame her.'

Apollonius said, 'Well, my liege, if you believe me, I will tell you how I see it, that truly your daughter has got the knack of music, but learned it well she has not. So tell them now to give me the lyre. Then you will know something you haven't known before.'

King Archestrates said, 'Apollonius, I can really see that you have been well taught in every way!' Then the king ordered the lyre to be given to Apollonius.

Apollonius went out and cloaked himself, set up a royal crown on his head and took the lyre in his hand, and came back in, standing in such a way that the king and all the people around the table believed that it was not Apollonius but Apollo, a god of the pagans.

Then a stillness and silence fell within the hall, and Apollonius took his plectrum and began to move the strings with skill, and mingled the melody of the lyre with sweet song. And the king himself and all who were present called out with great voice and praised him.

and ealle þe þar andwearde wæron micelre stæfne cliopodon and hine heredon. Æfter þisum forlet Apollonius þa hearpan **and plegod[e]**, and fela fægera þinga þar forð teah þe þam folce ungecnawe[n] wæs and ungewunelic, and heom eallum þearle licode ælc þara þinga ðe he forð teah.

17. Soðlice, mid þy þe þæs cynges dohtor geseah þæt Apollonius on eallum godum cræftum swa wel wæs getogen, þa **gefeol hyre mod on his lufe**. Đa, æfter þæs gebeorscipes geendunge, cwæð þæt mæden to ðam cynge, 'Leofa fæder, þu lyfdest me litle ær þæt ic moste gifan Apollonio swa hwæt swa ic wolde of þinum goldhorde.'

Arcestrates se cyng cwæð to hyre, 'Gif him swa hwæt swa þu wille.' Heo ða sweoðe bliðe ut eode, and cwæð, 'Lareow Apolloni, ic gife þe be mines fæder leafe twa hund punda goldes and feower hund punda gewihte seolfres and þone mæstan dæl deorwurðan reafes and twentig ðeowa manna.' And heo þa þus cwæð to ðam þeowum mannum, 'Berað þas þingc mid eow þe ic behet Apollonio minum lareowe, and lecgað innon bure, beforan minum freondum.'

Þis wearð þa þus gedon æfter þare cwene hæse, and ealle þa men hire gife heredon ðe hig gesawon. Đa soðlice geendode þe gebeorscipe, and þa men ealle arison and gretton þone cyngc and ða cwene and bædon hig gesunde

---

After this, Apollonius left the lyre **and acted**, and played many roles which were unknown and unusual to the people, and they all sincerely liked all the roles he put on.

17. Truly, when the king's daughter saw that Apollonius was so well educated in all good things, **her mind fell into loving him**. Then, after the party had ended, the girl said to the king, 'Dear father, a little earlier you granted me permission to give Apollonius whatever I wanted from your goldhoard.'

King Archestrates said to her, 'Give him whatever you want.' Overjoyed, she went out and said, 'Apollonius, my teacher, I give you by my father's leave two hundred pounds of gold and four hundred pounds of weighed silver and the greatest share of expensive clothing and twenty servants.' And so she said to the servants, 'Carry with you those things I have promised my teacher Apollonius and put them inside his chamber, in front of my friends.'

This was then done just as the princess commanded, and all the men who saw them praised her gifts. The party ended properly at that point, and the people all arose and greeted the king and princess and bade them be well, and went home. Likewise, too, did

---

and plegod[e] 'and acted'. This version leaves genres undefined, whereas the Latin source specifies both comic and tragic roles. Acting in England in the eleventh century was sanctioned only in the 'tropes' of liturgical speaking parts in the church nave during religious festivals, such activities which led to the Corpus Christi guild plays of the later Middle Ages (see *Christ I*: 'Advent Lyrics', in **Poems of Devotion**, Custom Version).

gefeol hyre mod on his lufe 'her mind fell into loving him'. 'She is the first lady in English literature to *fall in love*' (Goolden 1958: 55). Not quite, if we think of Circe for Ulysses in the Alfredian Boethius (see **The Earliest English Prose**). Compare also with Irish literature, one day to become English, for the different latitude given to Deirdre with Noisiu in *The Exile of the Sons of Uisliu* (see **Heroic Poems**). Ultimately in *Apollonius*' Latin source, the falling in love is borrowed from Queen Dido's response to Aeneas' telling of his adventures, at the beginning of Book IV of Vergil's *Aeneid*, but in its own way it looks forward to the revolution in love-poetry which defines the literature of the later twelfth century.

beon, and ham gewændon. Eac swilce Apollonius cwæð, 'Đu goda cyngc and earmra gemiltsigend, and þu cwen, lare lufigend, beon ge gesunde!'

He beseah eac to ðam þeowum mannum þe þæt mæden him forgifen hæfde, and heom cwæð to, 'Nimað þas þing mid eow þe me seo cwen forgeaf, and gan we secan ure gesthus þæt we magon us gerestan.'

Đa adred þæt mæden þæt heo næfre eft Apollonium ne gesawe swa raðe swa heo wolde, and eode þa to hire fæder and cwæð, 'Đu goda cyningc, licað ðe wel þæt Apollonius, þe þurh us todæg gegodod is, þus heonon fare and cuman yfele men and bereafian hine?'

Se cyngc cwæð, 'Wel þu cwæde, hat him findan hwar he hine mæge wurðlicost gerestan.'

Đa dide þæt mæden swa hyre beboden wæs, and Apollonius onfeng þare wununge ðe him getæht wæs, and ðar in eode, Gode þancigende ðe him ne forwyrnde cynelices wurðscipes and frofres.

18. Ac þæt mæden hæfde unstille niht, mid þare lufe onæled þara worda and sanga þe heo gehyrde æt Apollonige, and na leng heo ne gebad ðonne hit dæg wæs, ac eode sona swa hit leoht wæs and gesæt beforan hire fæder bedde. Đa cwæð se cyngc, 'Leofa dohtor, for hwi eart ðu þus ær wacol?'

Đæt mæden cwæð, 'Me awehton þa gecnerdnessan þe ic girstandæg gehyrde. Nu bidde ic ðe forðam þæt þu befæste me urum cuman Apollonige to lare.'

Đa wearð se cyningc þearle geblissod, and het feccan Apollonium and him to cwæð, 'Min dohtor girnð þæt heo mote leornian æt ðe ða gesæligan lare ðe þu canst, and gif ðu wilt þisum þingum gehyrsum beon, ic swerige ðe þurh

---

Apollonius say, 'Good my liege and generous giver to the poor, and my princess, lover of learning, may you live in good health!'

He looked also at the serving men whom the girl had given him, and said to them, 'Take with you those things the princess has given me, and let's go to find our lodgings so we can rest.'

Then the girl feared that she would not see Apollonius again as soon as she would like, and went to her father and said, 'Good my liege, do you really like the idea of Apollonius, who is enriched by us today, going off from here like this and meeting bad men and being robbed by them?'

The king said, 'Well said, have a place found for him where he can rest himself in the most honourable state.'

Then the girl did as she was commanded, and Apollonius accepted the residence which was assigned to him, and went inside, thanking God for not refusing him royal honour and solace.

18. But the girl had a restless night, inflamed by her love for the words and songs which she had heard from Apollonius, and never the longer did she wait than daybreak, but straightaway going out as soon as it was light, sat down by her father's bed. Then the king said, 'Dear daughter, why are you awake so early?'

The girl said, 'I was kept awake by the accomplishments I heard yesterday. So I ask you now to commit me to the instruction of our houseguest Apollonius.'

The king then was overjoyed, and had Apollonius brought in and said to him, 'It is my daughter's desire that she may learn from you the outstanding things you can teach, and mines rices mægna þæt swa hwæt swa ðu on sæ forlure, ic ðe þæt on lande gestaðelige.'

Ða ða Apollonius þæt gehyrde, he onfengc þam mædenne to lare and hire tæhte **swa wel swa he silf geleornode**.

19. Hyt gelamp ða æfter þisum **binnon feawum tidum**, þæt Arcestrates se cyngc **heold Apollonius hand on handa** and eodon swa ut on ðare ceastre stræte. Þa æt nyhstan comon ðar ongean hy þry gelærede weras and æþelborene, þa lange ær girndon þæs cyninges dohtor. Hi ða ealle þry togædere anre stæfne gretton þone cyngc. Ða smercode se cyng, and him to seah and þus cwæð, 'Hwæt is þæt, þæt ge me anre stæfne gretton?'

Ða andswerode heora an, and cwæð, 'We bædon gefirn þynre dohtor and þu us oftrædlice mid elcunge geswænctest. Forðam we comon hider todæg þus togædere. We syndon þyne ceastergewaran, of æðelum gebyrdum geborene. Nu bidde we þe þæt þu geceose þe ænne of us þrym, hwilcne þu wille þe to aðume habban.'

Ða cwæð se cyngc, 'Nabbe ge na godne timan aredodne. Min dohtor is nu swiðe bisy ymbe hyre learnunga, ac þe læs þe ic eow a leng slæce, awritað

---

if you will be obedient in these matters, I swear to you by the powers invested in me that whatever you may have lost on the sea, I will restore for you on land.'

When Apollonius heard this, he accepted the girl as his pupil and taught her everything **as well as he himself had learned it**.

19. It happened then, **some time after this**, that King Archestrates **was holding Apollonius' hand in his** while the two of them were walking on the city's street. Suddenly there came towards them three learned men and nobly born, who had desired the king's daughter for a long time. They all greeted the king together with one voice in unison. The king smirked, looked at them, and said, 'Why do you greet me with one voice?'

Then one of them answered, and said, 'We have been asking for your daughter's hand for ages, and you have habitually tormented us with delay. So we have come here today together in this way. We are your citizens, born of noble family. Now we would ask you to choose the man you would like as your son-in-law from among the three of us.'

Then the king said, 'You never did hit on a good time. My daughter is awfully busy at her studies now, but in case I hold you up any longer, each of you write down your name in a

---

swa wel swa he silf geleornode 'as well as he himself had learned it'. The Latin versions of the Apollonius legend, which are closer to the Old English version (as edited in Goolden 1958: 31), have at this point about five lines of extra narrative, in which the princess falls ill with a sickness which doctors, after bleeding her, find to be without cause.

binnon feawum tidum 'some time after this'. Goolden believes that this is a mistranslation, for the Latin has *post paucos dies* 'after a few days' (1958: 57), whereas the Old English better matches the beginning of the section missing (above), *Interposito pauci temporis spacio* 'After an interval of little time'. However, it is possible that the adapter has shortened things in order to give Archestrate a stronger character and to move the love story between her and Apollonius more speedily towards marriage.

heold Apollonius hand on handa 'was holding Apollonius' hand in his'. Not only a Middle Eastern custom, but apparently an eleventh-century Anglo-Saxon one too.

eowre naman on gewrite and hire **morgengife**. Þonne asænde ic þa gewrita minre dohtor, þæt heo sylf geceose hwilcne eowerne heo wille.'

Ða didon ða cnihtas swa, and se cyngc nam ða gewrita and geinseglode hi mid his ringe and sealde Apollonio, þus cweðende, 'Nim nu, lareow Apolloni, swa hit þe ne mislicyge, and bryng þinum lærincgmædene.'

20. Ða nam Apollonius þa gewrita and eode **to ðare cynelican healle**. Mid þam þe þæt mæden geseah Apollonium, þa cwæð heo, 'Lareow, hwi gæst ðu ana?'

Apollonius cwæð, 'Hlæfdige, næs git yfel wif, nim ðas gewrita ðe þin fæder þe sænde, and ræd.'

Ðæt mæden nam and rædde þara þreora cnihta naman, ac heo ne funde na þone naman þaron þe heo wolde. Ða heo þa gewrita oferræd hæfde, ða beseah heo to Apollonio and cwæð, 'Lareow, ne ofþingð hit ðe gif ic þus wer geceose?'

Apollonius cwæð, 'Na, ac ic blissige swiðor ðæt þu miht ðurh ða lare þe þu æt me underfenge þe silf on gewrite gecyðan hwilcne heora þu wille. Min willa is þæt þu ðe wer geceose þar ðu silf wille.'

Þæt mæden cwæð, 'Eala lareow, gif ðu me lufodest, þu hit besorgodest!'

Æfter þisum wordum heo mid modes anrædennesse awrat oðer gewrit, and þæt geinseglode and sealde Apollonio. Apollonius hit þa ut bær on ða stræte and sealde þam cynge. Ðæt gewrit wæs þus gewriten: 'Þu goda cyngc

---

letter and what her **morning gift** shall be. Then I will send the letters to my daughter so that she herself may choose which man she wants from among you.'

The young men then did this, and the king took the letters, sealed them with his ring and gave them to Apollonius, saying, 'Take these now, Teacher Apollonius, if you don't mind, and take them to the girl your pupil.'

20. Then Apollonius took the letter and went **to the royal hall**. When the girl saw Apollonius, she said, 'Teacher, why do you come alone?'

Apollonius said, 'My Lady, who are not yet a bad woman, take these letters that your father has sent you, and read them.'

The girl took them and read the names of the three men, but she could not find the name there that she wanted. When she had read over these letters, she looked at Apollonius and said, 'Teacher, doesn't it displease you to see me choose a husband in this way?'

Apollonius said, 'No, but I rejoice far more that you are able to make known in your own writing, through the teaching you have received from me, which man you would like from among them. What I desire is that you should choose a man anywhere you yourself want.'

The girl said, 'O my teacher, if you loved me, you would care about this!'

After these words she wrote another letter with her mind made up, sealed it and gave it to Apollonius. Apollonius carried it out then on to the street and gave it to the king. The letter was written thus, 'Good my liege and my most dear father, now that your mercy has

---

morgengife 'morning gift'. A gift from groom to bride the day after the first wedding night, and part of the financial settlement. The Latin is *dotis quantitatem* 'size of marriage-portion'.

to ðare cynelican healle 'to the royal hall'. The Latin has *ad domum regiam* of the same meaning, but there the girl's following words are more explicit: *Quid . . . magister . . . singularis cubiculum introisti?* 'Why, teacher, have you entered my bedroom alone?' The English translator here has quietly dropped *cubiculum*, removing any eroticism in favour of the love of the heart.

and min se leofesta fæder, nu þin mildheortnesse me leafe sealde þæt ic silf moste ceosan hwilcne wer ic wolde, ic secge ðe to soðan þone forlidenan man ic wille, and gif ðu wundrige þæt swa scamfæst fæmne swa unforwandigendlice ðas word awrat, þonne wite þu þæt ic hæbbe **þurh weax aboden**, ðe nane scame ne can, þæt ic silf ðe for scame secgan ne mihte.'

21. Ða ða se cyningc hæfde þæt gewrit oferræd, þa **niste he hwilcne forliden[n]e heo nemde**. Beseah ða to ðam þrim cnihtum and cwæð, 'Hwilc eower is forliden?'

Ða cwæð heora an, se hatte Ardalius, 'Ic eom forliden.'

Se oðer him andwirde and cwæð, 'Swiga ðu! Adl þe fornime þæt þu ne beo hal ne gesund. Mid me þu boccræft leornodest and ðu næfre buton þare ceastre geate fram me ne come. Hwar gefore ðu forlidennesse?'

Mid ði þe se cyngc ne mihte findan hwilc heora forliden wære, he beseah to Apollonio and cwæð, 'Nim ðu, Apolloni, þis gewrit and ræd hit. Eaðe mæg gewurðan þæt þu wite þæt ic nat, ðu ðe þar andweard wære.'

Ða nam Apollonius þæt gewrit and rædde, and sona swa he ongeat þæt he gelufod wæs fram ðam mæden, his andwlita eal areodode. Ða se cyncg þæt geseah, þa nam he Apollonies hand and hine hwon fram þam cnihtum gewænde, and cwæð, 'Wast þu þone forlidenan man?'

---

given me leave to choose of my own free will which man I would have, I say to you truly that I want the man who is shipwrecked, and if you wonder that so modest a woman wrote these words so without shame, then know that it is **through wax**, which knows no shame, that I have **announced** what I cannot for shame say myself.'

21. When the king read over the letter, he **could not see which man she was calling shipwrecked**. He looked at the three young men then and said, 'Which of you has been shipwrecked?'

One of them, whose name was Ardalius, said, 'I have.' The second man answered him and said, 'Be quiet! Plague take you, do not live long or prosper. You learned your letters with me, and have never gone further than the city's gates. Where did you suffer shipwreck?'

When the king could not find out which of them had been shipwrecked, he looked at Apollonius and said, 'Take this letter, Apollonius, and you read it. It can easily be that you know something I don't, you who were present there yourself.'

Then Apollonius took the letter and read it, and as soon as he understood that he was loved by the girl, his face went all red. When the king saw this, he took Apollonius' hand, turned away from the young men, and said, 'Do you know who the shipwrecked man is?'

þurh weax aboden 'through wax announced'. Archestrate's letter is incised on a wax tablet, as those of the three men. It seems likely that OE *gewrit* 'letter' covers this meaning, for wax tablets were still used in Anglo-Saxon times. The problem lies with *geinseglian* 'to seal': whether the seal indicates the royal source only or whether it has closed the letter from being read. The answer to this question affects how we see Apollonius' awareness or otherwise of the girl's interest in him.

niste he hwilcne forliden[n]e heo nemde 'could not see which man she was calling shipwrecked'. Archestrate's man has told him of Apollonius' shipwrecked status in ch. 14, before this extract, so we know that he knows that the teacher might qualify. But the king is still playing his game with the three suitors, and pretends not to show an interest in the teacher.

Apollonius cwæð, 'Ðu goda cyning, gif þin willa bið, ic hine wat.'

Ða geseah se cyngc þæt Apollonius mid rosan rude wæs eal oferbræded, þa ongeat he þone cwyde and þus cwæð to him, 'Blis[s]a, blissa, Apolloni, for ðam þe min dohtor gewilnað þæs ðe min willa is. Ne mæg soðlice on þillicon þingon nan þinc gewurðan buton Godes willan.'

Arcestrates beseah to ðam þrym cnihtum and cwæð, 'Soð is þæt ic eow ær sæde þæt ge ne comon on gedafenlicre tide mynre dohtor to biddanne, ac **þonne heo mæg hi fram hyre lare geæmtigan**, þonne sænde ic eow word!' **Ða gewændon hie ham mid þissere andsware**.

22. And Arcestrates se cyngc heold for ðon Apollonius hand, and hine lædde ham mid him, na swilce he cuma wære, ac swilce he his aðum wære.

Ða æt nyxstan forlet se cyng Apollonius hand and eode ana into ðam bure þar his dohtor inne wæs, and þus cwæð, 'Leofe dohtor, hwæne hafast þu ðe gecoren to gemæccan?'

Ðæt mæden þa feol to hyre fæder fotum and cwæð, 'Ðu arfæsta fæder, gehyr þinre dohtor willan! Ic lufige þone forlidenan man ðe wæs þurh ungelymp beswicen, ac þi læs þe þe tweonige þare spræce, Apollonium ic wille, minne lareow, and gif þu me him ne silst, þu forlætst ðine dohtor!'

Apollonius said, 'Good my liege, if it is your will, I know who it is.'

Then the king could see that Apollonius was all overspread with a rose-coloured blush, knew his words to be true, and said to him, 'Rejoice, rejoice, Apollonius, because my daughter's desire is my will too. In such matters nothing can happen unless it is God's will.'

Archestrates looked at the three young men and said, 'It is true what I said to you before that you did not come at a more fitting time to ask for my daughter's hand, but **when she may free herself from her study**, then I will send you word!' **So this is the answer they went home with**.

22. And so King Archestrates held Apollonius' hand, and led him home with him, not as if he were a guest, but as if he were his son-in-law.

Straight after that, King Archestrates let go Apollonius' hand and walked alone into the bower inside which his daughter was, and said, 'Dear daughter, what man have you chosen to marry you?'

The girl then fell to her father's feet and said, 'My gracious father, hear your daughter's will! I love the shipwrecked man who was cheated by misfortune, but lest my words give you any doubt, it is Apollonius I want, my teacher, and if you don't give him to me, then you will lose your daughter!'

þonne heo mæg hi fram hyre lare geæmtigan 'when she may free herself from her study'. This phrase, which expands on the Latin *tempus adfuit* 'when there has been time', recalls Alfred's words to Bishop Wærferth in his Preface to the West Saxon translation of Pope Gregory's *Pastoral Care* (although away from learning rather than towards it) *ðæt ðu ðe ðissa woruldðinga . . . geæmetige* 'that you free yourself of this worldly business' (see **The Earliest English Prose**).

Ða gewændon hie ham mid þissere andsware 'So this is the answer they went home with'. The king plays a trick on them, for they will now have to discover the princess's marriage to Apollonius for themselves. Perhaps going too far, in view of several places in the verse *Andreas* (see **Poems of Devotion**), Goolden calls this 'the first comedy scene in the English language' (1958: xxvii).

Se cyng ða soðlice ne mihte aræfnian his dohtor tearas, ac arærde hi up and hire to cwæð, 'Leofe dohtor, ne ondræt þu ðe æniges þinges. Þu hafast gecoren þone wer þe me wel licað.'

Eode ða ut, and beseah to Apollonio and cwæð, 'Lareow Apolloni, ic smeade minre dohtor modes willan. **Ða arehte heo me** mid wope, betweox oðre spræce, þas þingc, þus cweðende, "Þu geswore Apollonio, gif he wolde gehirsumian minum willan on lare, þæt þu woldest him geinnian swa hwæt swa seo sæ him ætbræd. Nu for ðam þe he gehyrsum wæs þinre hæse and minum willan, ic for æfter him [. . .]"'

Truly the king then could not endure his daughter's tears, but raised her up and said to her, 'Dear daughter, don't fear a thing. The man you have chosen pleases me well.'

He went out then, looked at Apollonius and said, 'Teacher Apollonius, I have looked into my daughter's heart's desire. **She just now related to me** with weeping, among other words, these matters, saying, "You swore to Apollonius, if he would obey my will in his teaching, that you would replace whatever the sea took from him. Now because he was obedient to your command and to my will, I have followed him [. . .]"'

Ða arehte heo me 'She just now related to me'. This fine tale is made up, of course, to save his daughter's blushes before Apollonius. The censor starts his work shortly afterwards.

The Song of Roland

La Chanson de Roland

⁕

Somewhere between the Norman Conquest and the early twelfth century, a version of that continental celebration of heroism in defeat was copied down, one which was curiously suitable to Norman victor and English subject as both sides began to forge a new hybrid culture and language. This became what we know as the Oxford *Roland*, the unique manuscript of a unique version of *La Chanson de Roland* 'Song of Roland'. Roland's death in 778 was likely much sung about, following on a disastrous defeat of King Charlemagne's rearguard in the Pyrenees. We are aware of this song tradition, because it surfaces in accounts of the 1066 Norman Conquest. If the events and associated poetic constructions are continental, the singing of Roland's heroism comes to England with the Norman forces. Early twelfth-century chroniclers and Gaimar's *Estoire des Engleis* 'History of the English' tell us that William of Normandy's troops advanced at Hastings singing a song about Roland after a night of righteous praying in which Anglo-Saxon drinking songs provided an echoing counterpoint. William of Poitiers (*c.* 1070) presents the Normans attacking with cries and exhortations. He finds great classical epics such as the *Aeneid* and the *Iliad* suitable for singing the heroic actions of King Harold and Duke William.

The Song of Roland, as preserved in the Oxford *Roland*, tells the tale of Charlemagne's great hero, who dies with his friend Oliver and the rest of the rearguard in the Pyrenees, all of them betrayed by Ganelon. In form, this feudal epic consists of 4002 decasyllabic or ten-syllable verses divided in two hemistichs with a strong caesura or cut (stop) after the fourth syllable. These are distributed over 291 assonanced stanzas. The verses do not rigorously match the metre, nor are the stanzas of uniform length. Where rhyme relies on similarity in vowel and consonant together, the construction of assonanced stanzas highlights the agreement in sound of the last stressed vowels in the line. In length, organisation and roots in oral composition and Germanic warrior tradition, *The Song of Roland* has affinities with *Beowulf.* Whereas it is sometimes thought that *Beowulf* may be divided into three parts suggesting performance over three evenings, the Oxford *Roland* divides into three principal parts and a closing (also transitional) episode: the betrayal of Ganelon; the death of Roland and rearguard; Charlemagne's battle with Emir Baligant; and the trial of Ganelon. There are also continental versions of *The Song of Roland* from the thirteenth and fourteenth centuries (the Chateauroux and Venice versions). These are similar, but copied in *laisses monorimes.* The Oxford *Roland* is consistent with the latter with its marked preferences for certain sounds such as 'i' (in some 40 laisses). However, increasingly elaborate and stylistically varied versions of *The Song of Roland* began to surface and spread rapidly through continental society. Paradoxically, therefore, in the Oxford *Roland* we have a unique version of a text that was to become a site of cultural elaboration throughout Europe. This paradox and the way it joins to other unique Anglo-Norman texts such as the *Jeu d'Adam* (not a mystery play about the Fall of Adam, but something much more individual) speak for a creative cultural interplay quite at odds with the meticulous spirit of accounting in the Domesday Book of the 1080s.

The First Crusade took place in 1095–1102. *The Song of Roland*, which is naturally of this political background, joins the older Germanic values of warfare with the new crusade ethos in order to construct an ethical system of war, identity and death. However, the apparent certainty of this new ethos in the poem is shot through with some ambiguous hesitations and lamentations which place these values in question. The trial episode, excerpted below, displays how legal rituals can reassert order amid competing ethical claims, and yet a sense of disjuncture persists, with doughty Pinabel representing a strong and brave family in defence of Ganelon, their traitorous and clandestine relative. Championed by the frail Thierry, Charlemagne's royal right, his law, prevails over the robust loyalties of the clan system. While the mysteries of divinely ordained monarchic justice may be exhibited here, echoes of Germanic family feud and revenge narratives contest the apparent resolution of these conflicts. The Oxford *Roland* ends as Emperor Charlemagne weeps at the Angel Gabriel's call to further battle against pagan enemies.

Brault, G. J., ed., *The Song of Roland; An Analytical Edition, vol. I: Introduction and Commentary* (Pennsylvania, PA, 1978)

Crane, S., *Insular Romance: Politics, Faith and Culture in Anglo-Norman and Middle English Literature* (Berkeley, CA, 1986)

Crouch, D., *The Birth of Nobility: Constructing Aristocracy in England and France 900–1300* (Harlow, 2005)

Dean, R. J., with M. B. M. Boulton, *Anglo-Norman Literature: A Guide to Texts and Manuscripts* (London, 1999)

van Emden, W., *La Chanson de Roland*, Critical Guides to French Texts (London, 1995)

Jones, G. F., *The Ethos of the Song of Roland* (Baltimore, MD, 1963)

Pratt, K., *Roland and Charlemagne in Europe: Essays on the Reception and Transformation of a Legend* (London, 1996)

Whitehead, F., ed., *La Chanson de Roland*, 2nd ed. (Oxford, 1975)

The dreams of Charlemagne

Charlemagne experiences the poem's first pair of ambiguous dreams below in laisses 56–7, just before the controversial naming of Roland to the rearguard by his stepfather, the secretly treacherous Count Ganelon (laisse 58). These dreams are enigmatic in their symbolic beasts, especially leopards, unless we think of the crisis in the Anglo-Norman rulership which lies behind the Oxford *Roland*'s unique presence in Britain. The leopard represents England in Geoffrey of Monmouth's section on the prophecies of Merlin (Book VII, ch. 3) in his *History of the Kings of Britain* (*c.* 1135). That text and its link to constructing kingship otherwise surfaces again to articulate English monarchic and religious independence in *When Rome is Removed*, which is a poem that dates to the turbulent fourteenth century.

Reeve, M. D. ed., and N. Wright, trans., *Geoffrey of Monmouth: The History of the Kings of Britain: an Edition and Translation of the De Gestis Britonum [Historia Regum Britanniae]*, Arthurian Studies 69 (Woodbridge, 2007)

Spearing, A. C., *Medieval Dream Poetry* (London, 1976)

56 Tresvait le jur, la noit est aserie,
Carles se dort, li empereres riches;
Sunjat qu'il eret al greignurs porz de Sizer,
Entre ses poinz teneit sa hanste fraisnine.
Guenes li quens l'ad sur lui saisie,
Par tel air l'at crullee e brandie
Qu'envers le cel en volent les escicles.
Carles se dort, qu'il ne s'esveillet mie.

57 Aprés iceste altre avisiun sunjat:
Qu'il ert en France a sa capele ad Ais.
El destre braz li morst uns vers si mals.

---

56 The day vanishes, the night grows dark.
Charles sleeps, the powerful emperor,
Dreams that he is at the higher pass of Cize,
In his grasp he holds his spearshaft in ashwood,
Ganelon the Count had seized it from him.
With such violence he shakes and brandishes,
That up to the heavens fly the splinters from it.
Charles sleeps, he wakes not at all.

57 After this he dreams another vision
That he is in France, at his chapel, at Aix.
On the right arm such a fierce boar bites him.

---

718 *li empereres riches* 'the powerful emperor'. Charles, king of the Franks, is called emperor here, even though he did not become emperor of the Holy Roman Empire until crowned by the Pope Leo III in 800.

719 *greignurs porz de Sizer* 'the higher pass of Cize'. Most likely this indicates the higher or western Pass or Port of Cize, located between the lower and the higher Pyrenees, part of the medieval pilgrimage route to the great shrine of St James by the sea in Galicia, Santiago de Compostela. The Port of Cize connects St-Jean-Pied-de-Port with Pamplona. Looking from this greater height, Charlemagne sees the battle of Roncevaux where the rearguard will die.

720 *sa hanste fraisnine* 'his spearshaft in ashwood'. This is likely to refer to Charlemagne's nephew and finest warrior, Roland.

726 *en France a sa capele ad Ais* 'in France at his chapel, at Aix'. Aix-la-Chapelle, Charlemagne's capital, is no longer in France, the land of the Franks, but in Germany. Now called Aachen, it borders on Belgium and the Netherlands. It was called *Aquis-Granum* for its hot sulphur springs by the Romans. Such attractions must have been valued by the Carolingian court, but the chill does not bring them to the king's mind, so terrible this night is. The chapel of Charlemagne's palace is now part of the cathedral. In any case, it was not yet built in 778 when the events presaged by these dreams occurred. Construction began in 792. The chapel was consecrated to the Blessed Virgin Mary in 805 by Pope Leo III. Charlemagne died in Aachen in 814.

727 *uns vers si mals* 'such a fierce boar'. The ferocious boar is probably the traitor Ganelon.

Devers Ardene vit venir uns leuparz,
Sun cors demenie mult fierement asalt.
D'enz de [la] sale uns veltres avalat
Que vint a Carles le[s] galops e les salz,
La destre oreille al premer ver trenchat,
Ireement se cumbat al lepart.
Dient Franceis que grant bataille i ad,
Il ne sevent li quels d'els la veintrat.
Carles se dort, mie ne s'esveillat. AOI.

58 Tresvait la noit e apert la clere albe.
Par mi cel host sunent . . . graisles.
Li empereres mult fierement chevalchet.
'Seignurs barons,' dist li emperere Carles,
'Veez les porz e les destreiz passages,

From the Ardenne he sees approach a leopard,
His very own body the leopard attacks with great ferocity.
From the castle hall a hound comes down
That runs towards Charles by leaps and bounds,
The right ear he severs first from the boar,
Furiously he fights the leopard.
The French say that there is a great battle,
They do not know which of them will win.
Charles sleeps, he wakes not at all. AOI.

58 The night vanishes and the day dawns clear;
throughout the army the . . . horns resound.
The emperor rides out in fierce pride.
'Noble warriors,' says the Emperor Charles,
'Look at the Ports and the narrow passes,

---

728 *Devers Ardenne . . . uns leuparz* 'From the Ardenne . . . a leopard'. A region of old mountains, hills, forests and mists, the Ardenne is another border area, much fought over, now incorporated in Belgium, Luxembourg and France. The leopard that comes from the Ardenne possibly foreshadows Pinabel, Ganelon's kinsman, who will later fight for him in judicial combat at Aix (laisses 280-93). The leopard reappears in Charlemagne's dreams prior to the battle with Emir Baligant in laisses 135-6 and especially in 145, a laisse which is meant to echo the terrifying animal life of the Apocalypse.

730 *uns veltres* 'a hound'. The hound may be Charlemagne's much slighter champion Thierry, a kind of David to the Goliaths of the Ganelon clan. But like the Pinabel figuration, Thierry belongs to the trial section that closes the poem.

732 *trenchat* 'he severs'. The referent is likely to be Charlemagne, who remains a powerful warrior despite his age.

736 *AOI.* Perhaps these letters represent a cry or a musical indication that may have links with the sung versions of this textual copy. It may also be an abbreviation. The letters occur from time to time in the manuscript at the end of laisses.

Kar me jugez, ki ert en la rereguarde.'
Guenes respunt: 'Rollant, cist miens fillastre:
N'avez baron de si grant vasselage.'
Quant l'ot li reis, fierement le reguardet,
Si li ad dit: 'Vos estes vifs diables.
El cors vos est entree mortel rage.
E ki serat devant mei en l'ansguarde?'
Guenes respunt: 'Oger de Denemarche,
N'avez barun, ki mielz de lui la facet.'

---

because it's you who appoint my rearguard.'
Ganelon answers: 'Roland, this man my stepson.
You have no warrior of greater valour.'
When the king looked at him fiercely,
so he said to him: 'You are a devil from Hell.
In your body is a mortal fury.
And who will be before me in the vanguard?'
Ganelon answers: 'Ogier of Denmark:
You have no warrior better than he to accomplish it.'

The trial of Ganelon

When Roland and Oliver and the rearguard are dead, Ganelon's treachery is revealed and his fate decided in council. In this episode, 'The trial of Ganelon', the defendant's family pledges 30 hostages and defends his honour in the person of the noble Pinabel, who fights Charlemagne's champion Thierry in a trial by combat. If the great battle of Charlemagne's army with Emir Baligant is a reprise of the Battle of Rencesvals on a grander scale, to inscribe the heroic deaths and the conflict itself into a universal history, the trial of Ganelon emerges as an intriguing showpiece of the ambiguities of medieval justice. Ganelon's case emphasises that the Anglo-Saxon need for vengeance does not correspond to actual judicial procedures. In the trial by combat of Anglo-Scandinavian England, Ganelon would have fought for himself rather than be represented by a family member. Charlemagne, on the other hand, cannot rely on his feudal barons to support him, despite the feudal validity of his case, that his family has lost the service of Roland and Oliver. In the end, the emperor is represented in judicial combat by the slender Thierry of Provence (Occitan area), the only noble to argue in favour of supporting him. Thierry then fights in defence of the emperor's case against the big Pinabel in a scene that resembles the biblical motif of David and Goliath. The judgement by combat is an archaic feature of a judicial form which was already falling into disuse.

749 *Oger de Denemarche* 'Ogier of Denmark'. Although Ogier occurs in numerous epics throughout the European tradition, usually as an exceptionally brave and accomplished warrior, his appellation may originally have referred to the Ardenne.

Like Roland, Pinabel ends up with his brains on the ground. The family hostages are hanged but, as befits a traitor, Ganelon is stretched between four horses and torn to pieces. Marsile's Saracen queen Bramimonde turns into the Christian convert Juliana, baptised at Aix after all. Oliver's sister and Roland's betrothed, the very Christian Aude, falls dead at the news of his death. Nuns take her body to a convent and receive a gift of land for their trouble. Everyone is paid off in some way, but with room in the narrative for us to consider the logic of the rewards. At the very end of this epic poem, the Archangel Gabriel calls on white-haired Charlemagne to go on a new crusade. The emperor, now a kind of Christian Baligant, weeps at the prospect of endless war that opens before him. Or is he weeping about something else?

276 Li emperere est repairét ad Ais.
Guenes li fels en caienes de fer
En la citét est devant le paleis.
A un'estache l'unt atachét cel serf,
Les mains li lient a curreies de cerf,
Tres ben le batent a fuz e a jamelz.
N'ad deservit que altre ben i ait,
A grant dulur iloec atent sun plait.

277 Il est escrit en l'anciene geste
Que Carles mandet humes de plusurs teres;
Asemblez sunt ad Ais a la capele,
Halz est li jurz, mult est grant la feste,

---

276 The emperor has repaired to Aix.
Wicked Ganelon stands in iron chains
He is in the city, in front of the palace.
The lowest of servants have bound him to a post,
His hands tied by straps of deerskin.
They beat him hard with clubs and cudgels.
He doesn't deserve any better.
In great suffering he awaits his trial.

277 It is written in the old song of these heroic deeds
That Charles sent for men from many lands.
They gathered at the Chapel at Aix.
It is a high holy day, a solemn observance,

3735–9 *en caienes de fer . . . a fuz e a jamelz* 'Wicked Ganelon . . . clubs and cudgels'. Ganelon is treated by ignoble servants, perhaps even slaves, as a captured wild animal, likely a bear in the urban sport of bear-baiting. But there is also a perverse parallel in the scourging or beating of Christ before his trial and judgement by Pontius Pilate and the citizens of Jerusalem. Note also that the animal reference recalls the beast symbolism of the dreams in the laisses above and thus asserts the connection of the dreams to the events now in train.

3744 *ad Ais a la capele* 'at the Chapel at Aix'. Built by Charlemagne, 796–805, in Romanesque style, arguably to assert his connection to Rome and to the imperial court at Byzantium.

Dient alquanz, del baron seint Silvestre.
Des ore cumencet le plait e les noveles
De Guenelun ki traïsun ad faite.
Li emperere devant sei l'ad fait traire. AOI.

278 'Seignors barons', dist Carlemagnes li reis,
'De Guenelun car me jugez le dreit!
Il fut en l'ost tresque en Espaigne od mei,
Si me tolit .xx. milie de mes Franceis
E mun nevold que ja mais ne verreiz,
E Oliver, li proz e li curteis;
Les .xii. pers ad traït por aveir.'
Dist Guenelon: 'Fel seie, se jo.l ceil!
Rollanz me forfist en or e en aveir,
Pur que jo quis sa mort e sun destreit;

Some say that it is the Feast of Saint Sylvester.
At this point begins the trial and verification of the facts
About Ganelon who committed treason.
The emperor has Ganelon brought before him. AOI.

278 'Noble barons', says King Charlemagne,
'You must judge the case about Ganelon according to the law!
All the way to Spain, Ganelon was in the army at my side.
He deprived me of twenty thousand of my French warriors
And of my nephew whom I will never see again,
And he took from me Oliver, valiant and noble warrior.
He betrayed the twelve Peers of the Realm for riches.'
Ganelon says: 'I'd be wicked to conceal such a thing!
Roland did wrong to me, for my gold and my wealth.
For that I sought his death and his destruction.

3746 *seint Sylvestre* 'Saint Sylvester'. Commemorated 31 December; in this situation a somewhat ambiguous figure, since, as a Roman citizen, he protected St Timothy, who preached Christianity in Rome until his martyrdom. Thereupon Sylvester took up this mission in a time of official persecution of Christianity, thus contravening Roman law. Eventually Sylvester became Pope (314–35). Traditionally Pope Sylvester I is associated with the conversion of Emperor Constantine and the building of the great churches in Rome during his reign.

3756 *.xii.pers* 'twelve Peers'. Charlemagne's elite warriors, and counsellors, among his inner circle but not exclusively so. The names vary from epic to epic, version to version.

Mais traïsun nule nen i otrei.'
Respundent Franc: 'Ore en tendrum cunseill.'

279 Devant le rei la s'estut Guenelun.
Cors ad gaillard, e.l vis gente color.
S'il fust leials, ben resemblast barun,
Veit cels de France e tuz les jugeürs,
De ses parenz .xxx. ki od lui sunt.
Puis s'escriat haltement e a grant voeiz:
'Por amor Deu, car m'entendez, barons!
Seignors, jo fui en l'ost avoec l'empereür,
Serveie le par feid e par amur.
Rollant sis nies me coillit en haür,
Si me jugat a mort e a dulur.
Message fui al rei Marsiliun,
Par mun saveir vinc jo a guarisun;
Jo desfiai Rollant le poigneor
E Oliver e tuiz lur cumpaignun,

But I do not admit to committing treason in any way.'
The Franks answer, 'Now we'll hold a council.'

279 Ganelon stands before the king.
He has a strong body and a handsome face.
If he were loyal, he would look like a noble baron.
He looks at all the men of France and all his judges,
He looks at thirty men of his kinship who support him.
Then he shouts out loud, powerful in voice:
'For the love of God, listen to me, barons!
Lords, I was in the army at the emperor's side.
I served him with loyalty and love.
Charlemagne's nephew, Roland developed a hatred for me.
He appointed me to death and suffering.
I was named the messenger to King Marsile.
By my skill I returned safely.
I repudiate Roland the warrior
and I repudiate Oliver and all their companions.

3760 *traïsun* 'treason'. Interestingly enough in this setting, it is Ganelon who first uses the word treason, defined here as a crime of violence against the ruler.

3761 *Franc* 'The Franks'. Somewhat mythical ancestors of the French people, the historical Franks stem from West Germanic tribes that shifted into numerous small kingdoms after the collapse of the Roman Empire. They formed Charlemagne's power base when he became king of the Franks in 768.

3773 *rei Marsiliun* 'King Marsile'. King of the Saracens. When not in battle, he resides in his palace at Zaragoza. He had previously killed messengers from Charlemagne.

Carles l'oïd e si nobilie baron;
Vengét m'en sui, mais n'i ad traïsun.'
Respundent Francs: 'A conseill en irums.'

280 Quant Guenes veit que ses granz plaiz cumencet,
De ses parenz ensemble od li out trente,
Un en i ad a qui li altre entendent:
Ço est Pinabel del Castel de Sorence;
Ben set parler e dreite raisun rendre,
Vassals est bons por ses armes defendre. AOI

Emperor Charles hears him and his noble barons
I have taken just vengeance but have committed no treason.'
The Franks answer, 'We will hold a council.'

280 When Ganelon sees that his great trial is about to begin,
He gathers thirty of his relatives with him.
There is one to whom all the others listen.
That man is Pinabel of Castel de Sorence.
He knows how to speak well and argue clearly.
He is valiant and skilful in using arms. AOI

Thierry closes the battle, defeating the great champion Pinabel of Sorence.

291 Ço dist Tierri: 'Pinabel, mult ies ber,
Granz ies e forz e tis cors ben mollez;
De vasselage te conoissent ti per.
Cest bataille, car la laisses ester!
A Carlemagine te ferai acorder.
De Guenelun justise ert faite tel,
Jamais n'ert jur que il n'en seit parlét.'

---

291 Thierry says, 'Pinabel, you are very brave.
You are tall and strong. Your body is well formed.
Your equals know how courageous you are.
But leave this fight.
I will negotiate your case with Charlemagne.
Justice will be done about Ganelon.
The day will never pass when the story will not be told.'

3783 *Castel de Sorence.* Pinabel's fiefdom. Mighty warrior and skilful speaker, Pinabel becomes Ganelon's designated champion in the following judicial combat to decide Ganelon's guilt and the fate of his relatives who would live or die with him.

3889 *Tierri* 'Thierry'. Charlemagne's designated champion, the average man of courtliness and courage, brother of Duke Geoffrey of Anjou, who is standard-bearer to the emperor.

Dist Pinabel: 'Ne placet Damnedeu!
Sustenir voeill trestut mun parentét,
N'en recrerrai pur nul hume mortel;
Mielz voeill murir que il me seit reprovét.'
De lur espees cumencent a capler
Desur cez helmes ki sunt a or gemez;
Cuntre le ciel en volet li fous tuz clers.
Il ne poet estre qu'il seient desevrez.
Seint hume mort ne poet estre afinét. AOI.

Pinabel says, 'God forbid!
I want to uphold the right of my whole family.
I will never give up for the sake of any man living.
I would rather die than anyone be able to reproach me with that.'
With their swords, Pinabel and Thierry start to strike blows
on their helmets, studded with jewels in gold.
Hot sparks fly brightly into the sky.
Not a single warrior could separate them.
The combat can only end in a man's death. AOI.

By divine will, the monarchy triumphs and Roland is judicially avenged.

293 Ço veit Tierris que el vis est ferut,
Li sancs tuz clers en chiet el pred herbus.
Fiert Pinabel sur l'elme d'acer brun,
Jusqu'al nasal li ad f[r]ait e fendut,
Del chef li ad le cervel espandut,
Brandit sun colp si l'ad mort abatut.
A icest colp est l'esturs vencut.
Escrient Franc: 'Deus i ad fait vertut.
Asez est dreiz que Guenes seit pendut
E si parent ki plaidét unt pur lui.' AOI.

---

293 Thierry sees that Pinabel is wounded in the face.
Bright blood falls on the green meadow.
He strikes Pinabel on his helmet of burnished steel.
Thierry breaks and splits it down to the noseguard.
Pinabel's brains spill out of his skull.
Thierry lifts his blade and strikes him dead.
With this blow the combat is won.
The Franks shout: 'God has shown his power!
It is just that Ganelon be hanged
and all his relatives that supported him.' AOI.

Gaimar's *History of the English*

L'Estoire des Engleis

Whereas the Oxford *Roland* is an epic from the Continent, transplanted into the new and more complex culture of Island Conquest, Gaimar's *L'Estoire des Engleis* is an Anglo-Norman verse chronicle which was written and revised in 1136–8, some 50 years later. Partially based on the 'Northern Recension' of the *Anglo-Saxon Chronicle* (which lies behind the Worcester (D), Peterborough (E) and Canterbury Bilingual (F) versions), Gaimar's verse chronicle attests to the political strains of the day, particularly a continuing historical rupture and multi-cultural tension. Rooting English history in an area other than what we have seen in the earlier *Chronicle*, Gaimar's retells the history of Britain from the arrival of the Trojans to the present day, the interests of his provincial court in Lincoln. Geography plays a leading role. Indeed Gaimar's material on local history became an important source for later narratives about Havelok the Dane and Hereward the Wake. England in his day was self-consciously a multi-cultural society, rather than 'Norman' at the top and 'English' below.

Havelok the Dane

Not all of Gaimar's *Estoire* survives. It begins with the struggles of British peoples and the conquering continental invaders, Saxon and Danish, but the list of names and battles first takes real narrative shape in the story of Havelok the Dane. The story spotlights the genealogy of his wife, the powerful and argumentative Argentille, daughter of the Danish king Adelbriht, master of four earldoms in Denmark and conqueror of King Cole in Britain. As if he were an avatar of King Cnut the Mighty, Adelbriht's domain stretches from ancient Celtico-Roman Colchester to Holland in Lincolnshire, and includes Norfolk and Thetford (the Celtic seat of Queen Boudicca, leader of the Iceni in their revolt against Rome and the burner of their British capital at Colchester). In keeping with this weave of ancient British cultures, Adelbriht dies in Thetford but is buried in Colchester. His daughter is then raised in Lincolnshire by a treacherous royal stepfather, King Edelsi, who hopes to defraud her of her rights by marrying her to Cuheran the scullery boy. Sleeping with Cuheran, Argentille has prophetic dreams of great battles among beasts great and small, which echo Charlemagne's dreams about the struggle for his royal power and domains. Argentille also notices a flame that comes out of Cuheran's mouth when he sleeps. Inspired by the dreams and fiery breath, Argentille and Cuheran take off for his birth town of Grimsby, much to the delight of her scheming royal stepfather.

In Grimsby, a major town that is itself linked to royal Danish genealogy through its founder, the sailor Grim, it turns out that Cuheran is actually Havelok, a royal son of Denmark, dispossessed in the conquest of his country by King Arthur. Proving himself the royal heir by both flame and horn blowing, Havelok turns the hatred of the Danes for those who had conquered them into the joy of conquest as he regains the kingdom from Colchester to Holland for his wife, the legitimate heir, and himself. Yet while the conquest itself starts out with a fleet and army as might be expected, it soon turns into a trickster story. Argentille devises a stratagem where those slaughtered in battle are restored to an image of life, and bloodshed is turned into a bloodless victory. Before Gaimar, this fabulous tale has roots stretching back to Norse mythology and Óláfr *Cuaran* 'sandal', the Hiberno-Norse king of York and Dublin in the mid-tenth century (see Egill's *Head-Ransom*, **Viking Wars**), from whom the names *Cuheran* and *Havelok* are both derived (*Alave-cua* > *Aveleke* > *Havelok*). The Middle English romance *Havelok the Dane*, which is still a major part of Grimsby's identity today, is derived from Gaimar's *History of the English*, among other sources, with stylistic parallels (Smithers 1988).

Bradbury, N. M., 'The traditional origins of *Havelok the Dane*', *Studies in Philology* 90 (1993), 115–42

Herzmann, R. B., G. Drake and E. Salisbury, ed. and introduction and notes, *Four Romances of England* (Kalamazoo, MI, 1999)

Kretzschmar, W. A., Jr., 'Three stories in search of an author: the narrative versions of *Havelok*', *Allegorica* 5 (1980), 21–97

Reiss, E., '*Havelok the Dane* and Norse mythology', *Modern Language Quarterly* 27 (1966), 115–24

Sands, D. B., ed., *Middle English Verse Romances* (New York, 1966)

Smithers, G. V., ed., *Havelok*, rev. ed. (Oxford, 1987)

Smithers, G. V., 'The style of *Havelok*', *Medium Ævum* 57 (1988), 190–218

Aprés sumond tut son navire,
de son rëalme tut l'empire,
od sa grant ost la mer passa,
rei Edelsi donc deffia:
ço li manda k'il le defie
s'il ne li rend le drait s'amie.
Reis Edelsi li remandat
ke cuntre lui se combaterat.

At that point Havelok calls for all his ships,
for the whole military might of his kingdom,
and with his great force he crossed the sea
finally to confront King Edelsi.
Havelok sends Edelsi a message that he would dispute
if he did not give her back her rights.
King Edelsi sends a message in return
that he would meet him in battle.

---

764 *s'il ne li rend le drait s'amie* 'if he did not give her back her rights'. Argentille is the daughter of King Edelsi's sister, Orwain, who married Adelbriht, king of the Danes. Edelsi is a Briton, king of Lindsey or Lincolnshire.

Combatirent sei en un plain
dés le matin tresk'al serain:
mult i out homes afolez
d'ambedous parz e mort rüez,
quant naire nuit les desevra
tresk'al demain k'il ajurna.
Mes par conseil de la reïne,
ki enseignat une mescine,
remist le mal e[n] la bataille;
son regne out sanz grei[gnur contraille]:
tute nuit fist enficher pels
plus gros e greignurs de tinels;
les morz homes ensus ficherent
e tute nuit sus les drecerent;
dous escheles en firent granz,
ki veirement estait semblant
k'il fuissent combatanz e vifs –
le jor devant erent ocis!
Home ki de loinz les esguardout,
tute la char l'en heriçout.

They fought on open land
from early in the morning until nightfall.
Many men were killed
and slaughtered on both sides
when dark of night drove them apart
until dawn of the next day.
But according to the queen's strategy,
who showed them a way out,
the damage of battle was avoided
and she gained her kingdom without [further conflict].
All night long she had stakes fixed,
stakes thicker and bigger than long heavy staffs.
She had the dead men thrust on the stakes
and throughout the night the soldiers stood them up straight.
They made them into two large battle groups in close formation.
The dead looked like warriors
who were fighting fit and eager.
But they had been killed the day before!
Men who looked at them from afar,
all their flesh began to creep,

---

773 *par conseil de la reïne* 'according to the queen's strategy'. Argentille's activity seems to share the motif in Bragi's *Eulogy on Ragnarr* in which Hildr regularly revives the dead in an endless battle between her lover Heðinn and father Hǫgni and their men (Reiss 1966; see **Heroic Poems**). Her stratagem also recalls that of Bǫðvarr bjarki in *Hrólfs saga kraka* 'The Saga of Hrólfr Pole-Ladder', when Bǫðvarr sets up the beast he has killed to look as though it is attacking; also that of the Etruscan king Mezentius, in *Aeneid*, Book VIII, lines 481–8, who binds up the living to the dead in order to terrify his enemies.

Ambure de loinz e de près,
hydus semblent morz desconfés.
Lendemain se reparillerent,
de combatre mult s'aficherent.
Le veors vindrent devant,
veher la gent dan Cuherant.
Quant unt veu que tant en i a,
tute la char l'en heriça:
car encontre un hom k'il aveient,
de l'altre part set en vaient.
Arere en vont al rei nuncier:
'Li combatre n'i ad mester:
rende [à] la dame son dreit,
e fasce peis ainz ke pis seit!'
Li reis ne poit par el aler,
donc li estut ço granter,
car [si] baron li ont löé.
Rendu li fu tut li regné,
dés Hoiland tresk'a Colecestre.

---

both from far and near
the unconfessed corpses seemed hideous.
The next day they drew up again
and put themselves in order for battle.
The scouts went in front
to see Lord Cuheran's men.
When they saw he had so many
it made all their flesh creep,
for against each one of theirs
they saw seven on the other side.
Back they came to the king:
'It is no use fighting.
Give the lady back her rights
and make peace before it all gets worse!'
The king could not help it,
so he determined to grant this,
for so the barons advised him.
The entire kingdom was handed back to Havelok
all the way from Holland to Colchester.

---

805 *Colecestre* 'Colchester'. This town in Essex is some 50 miles from London. It was first a port and stronghold of the Celtic war god called Camulus by the Romans. As *Camulodunum*, Colchester became the capital of the new Roman colony, Britannia, in the mid-first century. It was the reputed seat of 'Old King Cole' of nursery rhyme fame. Camulodunum was looted, burned and destroyed in the great Celtic revolt of Queen Boudicca ten years after its founding. Later Colchester was a considerable Saxon town. After 1066, a major Norman castle was built at Colchester on the foundation of the great Roman Temple to Emperor Claudius.

Rei Haveloc la tin[t] sa feste;
les homages de ses barons
reçuz partut ses regïons.
Puis aprés ço, ke quinz[e] dis
ne vesqui li reis Edelsis.
Il n'out nul eir si dreiturel
com Haveloc e sa muiller.

King Havelok held great celebrations.
Homage from his nobles
throughout the realm was received by Havelok.
Then after all that, only another two weeks
was left to live for King Edelsi.
He had no heir that had a greater right to his realm
than Havelok and Argentille.

Hereward the Wake

Hereward the Wake (*c.* 1035–1072) was an Anglo-Saxon leader in the resistance to the Norman Conquest. His base, according to legend, was the Isle of Ely. He and his men roamed the fens, which stretched from north Cambridgeshire, south Lincolnshire and Norfolk, leading popular resistance to William the Conqueror, otherwise known as 'the Bastard'. 'Wake', which means 'watcher', was popularly added to Hereward's name many years after his death. Some stories about Hereward the Wake were later incorporated into the Robin Hood legends, including issues such as the interaction of land-ownership with lineage and vengeance. William the Bastard is a more powerful but equally oppressive version of the Sheriff of Nottingham. There is later historical evidence that Hereward survived and went to live in the Low Countries.

Aprés comanda ço li reis
ke hom feïst punt ultre maries,
si dist ke tuz les destruereit
ja nus [d'els] ne l'eschapereit
Quant cil le surent en Ely,

Next King William commanded
that a raised pathway be constructed to bridge over the fen.
The king said that he would destroy all the outlaws
and that not a single man would escape his power.
When the people of the town of Ely found this out,

5497 *Ely*. A town in East Cambridgeshire, famous for its magnificent cathedral, 'the ship of the fens'. An Anglo-Saxon monastery was founded at Ely in 673 and then re-established in 970. Ely became the site of a Norman bishopric in 1109. After the Norman Conquest and the quelling of Hereward's rebellion, the Norman abbot began a great rebuilding programme that resulted in the thirteenth-century cathedral now largely present.

si se sunt mis en sa merci:
tuz alerent merci crïer,
fors Hereward ki mult fu ber,
Il eschapat od poi de gent,
Geri od lui, un son parent;
Od els ourent cinc compaignons.

Uns hom qui amenout peissons
as gardeürs long le mareis,
fist ke prodom e ke curteis:
en son batel les recuilli,
de ros, de glai tut les covri,
vers les gardeins prist a nager
Sicom, un seir, dust anu[i]ter,
vint pres des loges od sa nef,
Franceis estaient en un tref,
Gui le vesconte en ert seignur,
bien conisseit le pesc[e]ür
e bien surent k[ë] il veneit,
de lui nul d'els guarde n'aveit
le pesc[e]ür virent nager,
nuit ert, si sistrent al manger.
Fors de la nef ist Hereward,

---

they trusted in the king's mercy.
All of them went out to shout for mercy
except Hereward who was very brave.
He escaped with a few men.
One of his relatives, Geri, went with him.
They had five companions in all.

There was a fellow who brought fish
to the soldiers on guard along the marshland.
That man was honourable and noble in his actions,
for he received the outlaws into his boat,
covered them all over with reeds and sedges.
Then he started rowing towards the guards.
Just as evening turned to night,
he approached their camp by boat.
The French soldiers were in their tent.
Their leader was Sheriff Gui.
All were familiar with the fisherman
and all knew that he was coming.
They suspected nothing
when they saw the fisherman row towards them.
It was nightfall, so they sat eating their meal.
First out of the boat is Hereward.

de hardement semblout leupart.
Ses compaignons aprés issirent,
desuz un bois le tref choisirent,
od els ala le pescheür.
Hereward ert ainz son seignur.
K'en dirraie? Li chivaler
furent suppris a lur manger
cil entrent od haches es mains,
de bien ferir ne sunt vilains.
Normans oscistrent vint e sis
e dusze Engleis i out oscis.
Grant fu l'effrei par les ostels
de la fuite sunt communels.
chevals leissent tuz enselez
Les udlages i sunt montez
tut a leisir e sainement,
unc n'i ourent desturbement
a us erent de fere mal
chescon choisi tresbon cheval.
Li bois ert pres, enz sunt entrez,
il n'alerent pas esguarez
bien saveient tut cel païs
mult i aveit de lur amis.

He leapt out bold as a leopard.
His companions follow on after him.
They pick out the tent overhung by trees.
The fisherman also goes with them
because Hereward had been his lord.
What more can I tell? The knights
were surprised as they ate.
Hereward and his men entered the tent, axes in hand.
They were no peasants when it comes to striking hard.
The outlaws killed twenty-six Normans
and twelve English collaborators.
Great fright went through the camp,
All the other men took to flight,
even leaving the horses saddled up.
The outlaws mounted the horses,
at their leisure and in safety
None of them were troubled at all.
They had the knack of crime now:
each man chose a fine horse.
The woods were near so in they went
and they didn't go wandering around.
Hereward and his men knew the whole countryside well.
Among their supporters were many local people.

A une vile u sunt turnez
troverent dis de lur privez
a Hereward cil se sunt pris.
Ainz furent huit, or plus de dis.
Dis e huit sunt li compaignon.
Ainz k'il passasent Huntedon,
urent cent homes bien armez,
des Hereward liges privez.
Si home erent e si fedeel.
Ainz k'el demain levast soleil
seit cenz [en] sunt a li venuz,
en Bruneswald l'consecüz.

When they came to a town,
they discovered ten of their most trusted men
who joined up with Hereward.
Once there were eight, now there are ten more –
eighteen companions in all.
Before they got beyond Huntingdon,
they had a hundred strongly armed men,
who acknowledged Hereward as their liege lord.
They were his men and loyal to him alone.
Before the sun rose on the following day,
there were seven hundred men who came to Hereward
and they accompanied him into the Forest of Bourne.

5550 *liges privez* 'loyal to him alone'. To owe loyalty is a feudal relation.

5554 *Bruneswald* 'Forest of Bourne'. Near Bourne, an ancient market town on the western edge of the fens in Lincolnshire.

The Poem of My Cid

El Poema de Mio Cid

✻

Rodrigo Díaz de Vivar, otherwise known as 'the Cid' (*c.* 1043–1099), was a knight initially in the service of two kings, Sancho II of Castille and then his brother Alfonso VI of Leon and Castille. He was born in Vivar, near the city of Burgos in north-west Castille. Don Rodrigo served Sancho as standard-bearer until this king's death at the siege of Zamora in 1072, then fell out with Alfonso, who banished him in 1081–7 and again in 1089–92. In his first exile Rodrigo served Mu'taman, the Moorish emir of Zaragoza, in war against the emir's brother Emir al-Hayyib of neighbouring Lerida and also against Count Ramón II of Barcelona. In 1092 Rodrigo turned his attention southwards, laying siege to Valencia, which fell to him in 1094. In the last five years of his life, Rodrigo defended this city from the Almoravids, an army of puritan zealots from North Africa (Fletcher 1989: 147–51). This defence forms the romantic climax to the Charlton Heston film (directed by Anthory Mann, 1961) by which the story is now most widely known. During his service to Emir Mu'taman, Rodrigo gained his title *mio Cid* from the Arabic *sayyidi* 'my lord'; hence the title of the epic. He was also known as *el Campeador* 'the Battler' (perhaps from *campi ductor* 'leader of the battle-field'), which was his preferred designation in General Franco's Spain (1939–75). Neither term is easy to translate, and both are here left in their original form. Rodrigo's attitude to the religion of his patrons and enemies alike is worth noting, for the healthy indifference he displays to this question was a characteristic of Spain in the eleventh century. Duke William IX of Aquitaine, who perfected the genre of *fin'amor* 'refined loving' in his lyrics while on campaign to take Cordoba in 1120–3, also socialised with Moorish allies. The complexity of this background sets *El Poema de Mio Cid* apart from the straightforward anti-Muslim crusade mentality of *La Chanson de Roland* 'The Song of Roland', which belongs to a culturally less hybrid society.

The poem, divided into three *cantares*, is written for a later age. The poet not only celebrates Rodrigo's skill as a knight and reluctant outlaw, but connects him eventually, through the fictitious marriages of his daughters to princes, to two royal dynasties. Earlier in the epic, though by far the better man, el Cid continues to serve his king Alfonso from exile, from where he sends sufficient treasures and tokens of loyalty to be reconciled to him at the climax of the second *cantar*. The third *cantar* consolidates el Cid's forthcoming royal status in a trial scene in which he gains legal redress for the repudiation and abuse of his daughters at the hands of their first husbands, the low-life *infantes* 'barons' of Carrión, with their second marriages to the princes of Navarre and Aragon. Soon they become queens and the character of their father gains the status it deserves. The poem thus adumbrates el Cid's fairness and sense of duty to royal institutions with conflicts that show how kings and other royals are often inferior people to their subjects.

El Poema de Mio Cid is the only medieval Castillian epic to survive in near complete form (Michael 1975: 2). As seen below, it is missing the opening, but not too much is lost. The rugged metre, grand narrative fusion of *cantares* or episodes and the resulting length of this epic poem encourage a broad comparison with *La Chanson de Roland* 'The Song of Roland', but there the resemblance ends. The Spanish poem suggests a background in line with the mixed Moorish, Christian and Jewish culture of Spain in the twelfth and thirteenth centuries. The later end of this period is appropriate to the time in which the poem was copied. *El Poema de Mio Cid* was copied into its sole surviving manuscript, Biblioteca Nacional, Madrid, MS Vitr. 7–17, by one Per Abbat in May 1207, according to a concluding rubric. Earlier scholars followed the great Hispanist Ramón Menéndez Pidal (adviser to the Heston film) in seeing this as an epic composed in 1140 (1961). Later Pidal believed that *El Poema de Mio Cid*, though finished then, was inititiated by another poet in *c.* 1110, a view that placed the poem even closer to the historical person, to within a couple of decades of the height of Rodrigo's career (Menéndez Pidal 1969). Yet there are sufficient historical inventions and topographical inaccuracies to doubt this as wishful thinking. It has been argued that the copyist Per Abbat was the author, or at least the last man to draft this poem (Smith 1973). Such questions always wait for evidence, but the likelihood that the poet was a native of Vivar remains strong. It was in Vivar that the manuscript first turned up in the late sixteenth century. Just as Rodrigo was a son of the province of Burgos in Castille, so it seems likely that the poet was too. It has been suggested that the work was written as part of a recruiting drive for the decisive Christian advance into Moorish Spain which started from this region in 1212.

Fletcher, R., *The Quest for El Cid* (Oxford, 1989)

Fletcher, R., *Moorish Spain* (Berkeley, CA, 1992)

Hamilton, R., and J. Perry, trans., with introduction and notes by I. Michael, *The Poem of the Cid: A Bilingual Edition with Parallel Text* (Harmondsworth, 1975)

Menéndez Pidal, R., 'Dos Poetas el el *Cantar de Mio Cid*', *Romania* 82 (1961), 135–200

Menéndez Pidal, R., *La España del Cid*, 7th ed., *Obras Completas*, vols 6–7 (Madrid, 1969)

Michael, I., introduction and notes to Hamilton and Perry (1975)

Smith, C., 'Per Abbat and the *Poema de Mio Cid*', *Medium Ævum* 42 (1973), 1–17

Whitehead, F., '*Ofermod* et *desmesure*', *Cahiers de civilisation médiévale* 3 (1960), 115–17

Exile of the Campeador

. . .]

1 De los sos oios   tan fuerte mientre lorando
tornaua la cabeça   e estaua los catando:
vio puertas abiertas   e vços sin cannados,
alcandaras uazias   sin pielles e sin mantos,
e sin falcones   e sin adtores mudados.
Sospiro Myo Çid   ca mucho auie grandes cuydados.
Ffablo Myo Çid   bien e tan mesurado:
'Grado a ti Sennor   Padre que estas en alto,
esto me an buelto   myos enemigos malos!'

2 Alli pienssan de aguiiar,   alli sueltan las rriendas:
a la exida de Biuar   ouieron la corneia diestra,
e entrando a Burgos   ouieron la siniestra.
Meçio Myo Çid los ombros   e engrameo la tiesta:
'Albricia Albar Ffanez   ca echados somos de tierra.'

3 Myo Çid Rruy Diaz   por Burgos entraua,
en su conpanna   sessaenta pendones leuaua:
exien lo ver   mugieres e uarones.

. . .]

1 With the weeping coming so heavy from his eyes,
he turned his head and stood looking at them.
He saw gates open and doors unbolted,
empty pegs without fur kirtles or cloaks,
without falcons or moulted hawks.
My Cid heaved a sigh, for he had many great cares.
My Cid spoke properly and with such measure:
'I thank you Lord Father that are on high,
it is my wicked enemies who have done this to me!'

2 There they make ready to leave, there they slacken the reins:
on leaving Vivar they saw a crow fly from right,
and entering Burgos they saw one from left.
My Cid shrugged his shoulders and nodded his head:
'Be of good cheer, Álvar Fáñez, for we are exiled from the land.'

3 My Cid Ruy Díaz came into Burgos,
in his company he took with him sixty knights:
there come out to see him women and men.

---

7 *tan mesurado* 'with such measure'. The term *mesura*, Old French *mesure*, as the ideal of a feudal warrior or knight, is not far from what seems to be expected of Ealdorman Byrhtnoth before his *ofermod* in *The Battle of Maldon* (see **Viking Wars**; Whitehead 1960: 115).

Burgeses e burgesas por las finiestras son,
plorando de los oios, tanto auyen el dolor.
De las sus bocas todos dizian una rrazon:
'Dios, que buen vassalo si ouiesse buen sennor!'

4 Conbidar le yen de grado, mas ninguno non osaua,
el rrey don Alfonso tanto auye la grand sanna;
antes de la noche en Burgos del entro su carta
con grande rrecabdo e fuerte mientre sellada:
que a Myo Çid Rruy Díaz que nadi nol diessen posada
e aquel que ge la diesse sopiesse vera palabra
que perderie los aueres e mas los oios de la cara
e aun demas los cuerpos e las almas.
Grande duelo auyen las yentes cristianas,
ascondense de Myo Çid, ca nol osan dezie nada.
El Campeador adelinno a su posada,
assi como lego a la puerta, falo la bien cerrada
por miedo del rrey Alfonso, que assi lo auyen parado
que si non la quebrantas por fuerça, que non ge la abriesse nadi.
Los de Myo Çid a altas vozes laman,
los de dentro non les quieren tornar palabra.
Aguiio Myo Çid, a la guerra se legaua,
saco el pie del estribera, una feridal daua;

Townsmen and townswomen are at the windows,
weeping from the eyes, such grief they have.
From their mouths they all spoke one idea:
'My God, what a good vassal. Had he but a good lord!'

4 Indeed they would have invited him in, but no one dared,
of the King don Alfonso's anger they held such dread.
From him the night before his letter had entered Burgos
with great secrecy and heavily sealed,
that no man should give shelter to My Cid Ruy Díaz
and any who did should know for certain
that he would lose his wealth, the eyes in his face,
and what is more his body and his soul as well.
Great grief the Christian folk have in them,
they hide from My Cid for they dare not address him.
The Campeador went to the lodging he was used to,
when he came to the door, he found it well closed,
for fear of King don Alfonso they had agreed
that if he did not force it, no one would open it to him.
My Cid's men call out in loud voices,
the people inside have no wish to answer.
My Cid spurred on, he bore himself to war,
drew his foot from the stirrup, gave a great kick;

non se abre la puerta,   ca bien era cerrada.
Vna ninna de nuef annos   a oio se paraua:
'Ya Campeador,   en buen ora cinxiestes espada!
El rrey lo ha uedado,   a noch del e[n]tro su carta
con grant rrecabdo   e fuerte mientre sellada.
Non uos osariemos   abrir nin coger por nada;
si non, perderiemos   los aueres e las casas
e demas – los oios de las caras.
Çid, en el nuestro mal   vos non ganades nada,
mas el Criador vos vala   con todas sus vertudes sanctas.'
Esto la ninna dixo   e tornos pora su casa.
Ya lo ver el Çid   que del rrey non auie gr[azi]a;
partios de la puerta,   por Burgos aguiiaua.

---

the door does not open for it is well closed.
A girl nine years old appeared before his eyes:
'Hey now, Campeador, knighted in a fortunate hour!
The king has forbidden it, his letter came in last night
with great secrecy and heavily sealed.
We would not dare to open up or take you in for anything.
If we did, we would lose our wealth and our homes
and more – the very eyes in our face.
Cid, from our misfortune you will gain nothing,
but may the Creator save you with all His holy powers!'
So the girl said and turned back to her house.
Now the Cid can see that he does not have the king's favour,
he moves from the door, through Burgos spurs on his way.

Lyrics of William IX

William, ninth duke of Aquitaine (1071–1126), was the first troubadour of whom records survive, both a noble and a lyric poet who employed his own romance vernacular, 'Occitan'. He was twice divorced, twice (nearly three times) excommunicated and is remembered in an anonymous thirteenth-century *vida* 'life' as 'one of the most courtly men in the world and one of the greatest deceivers of women. He was a fine knight at arms, liberal in his womanising, and a fine composer and singer of songs. He travelled much through the world, seducing women.'

William's escapades started early, with marriage at the age of 16 to Ermengard, daughter of Count Fulk 'the Contrary' of Anjou. William was too carefree for Ermengard, who divorced him after four years and married the duke of Brittany. Later she retired to the Abbey of Fontevrault in the Loire, where a generation later she could comfort William's second wife Philippa. William married Philippa three years later in 1094, partly to help her recover her father's county of Toulouse. In 1099 William organised his own expedition to join the First Crusade, whose beginning he had missed in 1096. He witnessed the Seljuk Turks wipe out his army in Asia Minor and escaped to recuperate in the Christian city of Antioch, which was now ruled by Tancred, nephew of Bohemund I. While staying there in 1101–2, William learned something of Arabic songs and poetry. Back in Aquitaine, he started to experiment on the themes of love, women, sex, his own literary and sexual prowess and feudal politics. Much of the poetry was already in place. Literary people read Ovid, and outside, the local Goliards, often unfrocked priests, were busy turning the older rhyming Latin verse forms into modern Latin love lyrics (see also the Old English *Rhyming Poem*, **Poems on the Meaning of Life**). William and contemporaries added Arabic poetry to the mix, having learned of this in translation through Castillian and related dialects. At the core of William's lyrics was the shocking idea that women should be free to choose to love as and when and whom they pleased, in or out of marriage. The result was the heady culture of *fin'amor* in the first (extant) troubadour lyrics and then in the *romans courtois* 'court romances'.

In trouble with the Church over tax evasion, William was excommunicated by Bishop Peter of Poitiers in 1114. He arrived in the cathedral in time to hear the bishop begin the anathema, raised his sword and said 'I will kill you if you don't absolve me.' The bishop finished the anathema, bowed his head and said 'Go on, strike!' William replied 'No, I don't love you enough to send you to Paradise' and sheathed his sword. The Church repealed the sentence, but in 1116, when William's wife Philippa came home to Poitiers, from a visit to Toulouse, to find another woman installed in her place, William was excommunicated again. The new lady was Dangereuse, wife of one of William's vassals, and this time the sentence lasted four years. By this time, the first wife Ermengard had returned. She had comforted William's second wife in Fontevrault, and when Philippa died there in 1118 Ermengard returned to be reinstated as duchess. William refused, staying with Dangereuse. Ermengard tried and failed to have William excommunicated for a third time.

To escape from all this and enrich himself in a new local 'crusade', William took his army to Spain, where he joined the kings of Castille and Leon in their campaign to take Cordoba from its new North African rulers, the puritan Almoravids. The Castillians had Muslim allies, some of whom acquainted him with translated versions of Arabic love-poetry (Menocal 1987: 33–8). An outstanding example of this is *The Dove's Neck-Ring*, which was written by the Maghrebi poet Ibn Hazm in the 1030s under the partial influence of Ovid. William returned to Poitiers in 1123 and died of ill health three years later. Through Philippa's son William X, he was the grandfather of Eleanor of Aquitaine (1122–1204), later wife of Henry II, queen of England, and the driving force behind the northern French and English romance literature of the twelfth and thirteenth centuries. William IX is one of the founders of this tradition, one which would culminate in Dante, Chaucer, Petrarch, Malory and ultimately the nineteenth-century European psychological novel. His lyrics, two of which are given (from eclectic texts) below, are usually known by their first lines, but new titles have been created here.

Bec, P., *Le Comte de Poitiers, Premier Troubadour: A l'Aube d'un Verbe et d'un Erotique*, Centre d'Etudes de l'Université de Montpellier 3 (Montpellier, 2004)

Bond, G. A., ed., *The Poetry of William VII, Count of Poitiers, IX Duke of Aquitaine* (New York, 1982)

Chayter, H. J., *The Troubadours* (Cambridge, 1912)

Dronke, P., *Medieval Latin and the Rise of the European Love Lyric*, 2 vols (Oxford, 1965–6)

Gaunt, S., and S. Kay, ed., *The Troubadours: An Introduction* (Cambridge, 1999)

Menocal, M. R., *The Arabic Role in Medieval Literary History: A Forgotten Heritage* (Philadelphia, PA, 1987)

Pasero, N., ed., *Guglielmo IX. Poesie: Edizione Critica* (Modena, 1973)

Paden, W. D., *An Introduction to Old Occitan* (New York, 1998)

Paden, W. D., and F. Freeman Paden, trans., *Troubadour Poems From the South of France* (Cambridge, 2007)

Topsfield, L. T., *Troubadours and Love* (Cambridge, 1975)

A suitable poem

1 Companho farai un vers [qu' èr] covinen,
et aura.i mais de foudatz no i a de sen
et èr totz mesclatz d'amor e de joi e de joven.

Friends, I shall make a suitable poem
and it will have more foolery than good sense.
Aspects of love, joy and youth will be all stirred up too.

2 E tenhatz lo per vilan, qui no l'enten
qu'ins en son cor voluntiers, res non l'apren:
greu partir si fai d'amor qui la trob a son talen.

And I'll take him for a peasant who doesn't understand it
or if he doesn't learn it gladly deep in his heart.
It is hard to part from love for those who find love's part to their liking.

3 Dos cavals ai a ma sselha ben e gen;
bon son ez ardit per armas e valen;
ma no.ls puesc tener amdos, que l'uns l'autre non consen.

I have two horses to my saddle, fine and well bred.
They are pleasing and agile for war and brave too.
But I can't hold on to both of them because one won't accept the other.

4 Si.ls pogues adomesgar a mon talen
ja no volgr'aillors mudar mon garnimen,
que meils for'encavalguatz de nuill home [en mon] viven.

If I could domesticate them to suit my desire
I would never take my equipment anywhere else,
for I would be better horsed than any man as long as I live.

5 Launs fo dels montanhiers lo plus corren,
mas aitan fer'estranhez'ha longuamen
ez es tan fers e salvatges, que del bailar si defen.

One is the swiftest runner of the mountain breed
But so much playing the rough stranger for a long time,
that horse is just so fierce and wild that it resists all control.

6 L'autre fo noiritz sa jos, pres Cofolen;
ez anc no'n vis belazor, mon essien:
aquest non er ja camjatz, ni per aur ni per argen.

The other was brought up over around Confolens
And you'll never see a more beautiful one, to my way of thinking.
This one I will never exchange, neither for gold nor for silver.

7 Qu'ie.l donei a son senhor poilli paisen,
pero si.m retinc ieu tan de covinen
que, s'il lo tenia un an, ieu lo tengues mais de cen.

For I gave the horse to her master as a filly still feeding
But I held out for one promise,
that for every year he kept the horse, I would keep it more than a hundred.

8 Cavalier, datz mi conseill d'un pensamen:
anc mais no fui eissarratz de causimen:
re no sai ab cal me tenha, de N'Agnes o de Arsen.

Knights, give me advice about this debate.
for I never was so awkward about choosing
I don't know which one I should keep, whether Lady Agnes or Lady Arsen.

---

6 Confolens is in the Charente in the area of Poitevin and Limousin.

9 De Gimel ai lo castel e.l mandamen
e per Niol fauc ergueill a tota gen:
c'ambedui me son jurat e plevit per sagramen.

I have Gimel and its rights
and everyone knows I take pride in Niol
For both are sworn to me and pledged by oath.

Feeling sleepy

1 Farai un vers, pos mi sonelh,
e'm vauc e m'estauc al solelh;
donnas i a de mal conselh,
et sai dir cals;
cellas c'amor de chevaler
tornon a mals.

I will make a poem, because I am feeling sleepy
and I move along and I linger in the sun.
There are ladies with evil plans.
I know how to tell which ones:
they are those ladies who
turn the love of a knight in the wrong direction.

2 Donna non fai pechat mortau
que ama chevaler leau;
mas s'ama monge o clergau
non a raizo:
per dreg la deuria hom cremar
ab un tezo.

A lady does not commit a mortal sin
who loves a knight loyally.
But if she loves a monk or a clerk
she can't justify herself.
By rights one should burn her
with a brand.

---

9 Gimel is in the Corrèze, on the Montane river, where there is a waterfall. Niol is probably today's Nieul in the Charente, about 15 miles south-west of Confolens.

2 *pechat mortau* 'mortal sin'. This always merits eternal flaming punishment in hell.

3 En Alvernhe, part Lemozi,
m'en aniei totz sols a tapi:
trobei la moiller d'en Guari
e d'En Bernart;
saluderon mi sinplamentz,
per saint Launart.

In Auvergne, beyond the Limousin
I went alone, on the quiet.
I met up with wife of Sir Garin
and the wife of Sir Bernart;
they greeted me openly,
by Saint Leonard.

4 La una.m diz en son lati:
'O, Deus vos salf, don peleri!
Mout mi senblatz de bel aizi,
mon escient;
mas trop vezem anar pel mon
de folla gent.

One of the two said in her kind of talk
O, God save you, Honourable Pilgrim!
You look like a well-bred man,
to my way of thinking;
but we see going through the world too many
of the foolish kind.

5 Ar auziretz qu'ai respondut:
anc no li diz ni 'bat' ni 'but'.
Ni fer ni fust no ai mentagutz
mas sol aitan:
'Barbariol, barbariol,
barbarian'.

Now listen to what I said:
Never did I say our words sounding 'bat' nor 'but'.
Nor did I celebrate tool or handle
but only said so much as
'Barbariol, barbariol,
barbarian.'

---

3 *En Alvernhe, part Lemozi* 'In Auvergne, beyond the Limonsin'. In the region of Limoges. [*per sain Launart* 'by Saint Leonard'. A popular saint who was known for breaking chains; a saint with special appeal for prisoners.

5 *Barbariol barbariol* 'barbarian'. These sounds may encode words comprehensible in a foreign language (probably Arabic, which was not so foreign to Provence and Catalonia) as yet another level of the linguistic and semantic irony.

6 ‘Sor’, diz N’Agues a N’Ermessen,
‘trobat avem que anam queren!’
‘Sor, per amor Deu l’alberguem,
que ben es mutz,
e ja per lui nostre conselh
non er saubutz’.

‘Sister,’ said Lady Agnes to Lady Ermessen,
‘We have discovered what we have been searching for!’
‘Sister, for the love of God, let’s give him shelter,
for he has no tongue
and never through him will our project
be known.’

7 La una.m pres sotz son mantel
et mes m’en sa cambra, el fornel:
sapchatz qu’a mi fo bon e bel,
e.l foc fo bos,
et eu calfei me volenter
al gros carbos.

One of them took me under her cloak
and brought me to their room by the fireplace.
You know that was all well and good to me.
And the fire was good.
Willingly too I warmed myself up
by the big hot coals.

8 A manjar mi deron capos,
e sapchatz aig i mais de dos;
et no.i ac cog ni cogastros,
mas sol nos tres;
e.l pans fo blancs e.l vins fo bos
e.l pebr’espes.

They gave me capons to eat.
You know too that I had more than one.
There was neither cook nor kitchen boys
just the three of us alone.
And the bread was fine white and the wine was good,
plenty of pepper too.

9 'Sor, s'aquest hom es enginhos
e laissa lo parlar per nos,
nos aportem nostre gat ros
de mantenent,
que.l fara parlar ad estros,
si de re.nz ment'.

'Sister, if this man is a cheater
and if he takes leave of his speech just for us,
Let's bring out our big, red cat
quick smart.
For the cat will make him talk at once,
if this fellow is lying about anything at all.'

10 N'Agnes, anet per l'enois:
et fo granz, et ac loncz guinhos:
et eu, can lo vi entre nos,
aig n'espavent,
qu'a pauc no.n perdei la valor
e l'ardiment.

Lady Agnes went to get the troublemaker.
He was big too and he had long whiskers.
And I, when I saw him among us,
I had such fear
that I nearly lost my valour
and my daring.

11 Quant aguem begut e manjat,
e.m despoillei per lor grat;
detras m'aporteron lo chat
mal e felon:
la una.l tira del costat
tro al talon.

When we had eaten and drunk our fill
and when I stripped off to please them,
from the rear, they brought the cat
an evil and criminal creature.
One of the ladies dragged the cat along my side
down to my heels.

12 Per la coa de mantenen
tirr'el chat, et el escoisen:
plajas mi feron mais de cen
aquella ves;
mas eu no.m mogra ges enguers
qui m'aucizes.

By the tail, all of a sudden,
she pulled the cat and he skinned me alive.
The ladies and their cat gave me more than a hundred wounds
that time.
But I wouldn't have moved
even if they had killed me.

[/12] Monet, tu m'iras al mati,
mo vers portaras el borssi
dreg a la molher d'En Guari
e d'En Bernat:
e diguas lor que per m'amor
aucizo.l cat.

Monet, you will go in the morning.
You will bring my song in your purse
straight to the wife of Sir Garin,
and to the wife of Sir Bernart.
And tell them, for my own sake, kill the cat!

13 'Sor,' diz N'Agnes a N'Ermessen,
'mutz es, que ben es conoissen'.
'Sor, del bainh nos apaireillem
e del sojorn'.
Ueit jorn ez ancar mais estei
az aquel torn.

'Sister', said Lady Agnes to Lady Ermessen,
He cannot speak, that's very evident.'
'Sister, let's get ready for our amusement
and our pleasure.'
Another eight days and even more went by
at that occupation.

14

Tant las fotei com auziretz:
cent et quatre-vinz et ueit vetz,
que q pauc no.i rompei mos corretz
e mos arnes:
e no.us puesc dir lo malavegz,
tan gran m'en pres.

You will hear how I goaded them so much
One hundred and eighty-eight times,
for I nearly broke all my reins
and my equipment.
And I cannot tell you how painful it was,
so great did the pain come upon me.

Fin'amor from Orkney: Rǫgnvaldr kali

✳

According to *Orkneyinga saga* 'Saga of the Orcadians' (ch. 86), whose first draft was written in Iceland in *c.* 1200, Earl Rǫgnvaldr kali Kolsson of Orkney sailed to the Holy Land to join the Second Crusade (in 1147). On the way, he put in to Narbonne in southern France. The local count had died, and his kinsmen invited Rǫgnvaldr and some of his men to the castle to become acquainted with their new queen, the count's daughter Ermengard ('Ermingerðr'). Rǫgnvaldr took two other poets with him, Icelanders named Ármóðr and Oddi *inn lítli* 'the Little'. Some formal influence either here in 1150, or later elsewhere, seems to have flowed from the Occitan courtly love lyric (*fin'amor*) to the old Skaldic genre of Icelandic poetry. The cultural ambience also suggests Galicia and Spain, proof of the interest that the Scandinavian culture of northern Britain was beginning to show in the love-lyrics of the courtly south.

Cheyette, F. L., *Ermengard of Narbonne and the World of the Troubadours* (Ithaca, NY, 2001)

Finlay, A., 'Skalds, troubadours and sagas', *Saga-Book of the Viking Society* 29.2–3 (1995), 105–53

Finlay, A., '*Skaldsagas* in their literary context, 2: possible European contexts', in *Skaldsagas: Text, Vocation, and Desire in the Icelandic Sagas of Poets*, ed. R. Poole (Berlin, 2000), 232–71

Þat var einn dag, er jarl at veizlunni, at drottning gekk inn í hǫllina ok margar konur með henni; hon hafði borðker í hendi af gulli. Hon var klædd inum beztum klæðum, hafði laust hárit, sem meyjum er títt at hafa, ok hafði lagt gullhlað em enni sér. Hon skenkti jarli, en meyjarnar léku fyrir þeim. Jarl tók hǫnd hennar með kerinu ok setti hana í kné sér, ok tǫluðu mart um daginn. Þá kvað jarl vísu:

Víst er at frá berr flestu   Fróða meldrs at góðu
vel skúfaðra vífa   vǫxtr þinn, konan svinna.
Skorð lætr hár á herðar   haukvallar sér falla,
átgjǫrnum rauðk erni   ilka, gult sem silki.   (no. 55)

One day, when the earl was at the feast, the queen walked into the hall, and many women with her; she was carrying a cup from the table, one made of gold. She was dressed in the best clothes, had let her hair down the way girls do, and was wearing a lace hairband embroidered with gold. She served the cup to the earl while the girls played music before them. The earl took her hand along with the cup, and put her on his knee, and all day long they had much to speak of. This was when the earl made up a verse:

It is certain, noble woman, that your locks' abundance stands good
Comparison with that of nearly all wives tasselled with King Fróði's grain.
The prop of the hawk's plain lets hair fall down to her shoulders
(The ravenous eagle's footsole have I reddened) yellow as silk.

'(King) Fróði's grain': gold. 'Hawk's plain': forearm, whose 'prop' is a noble lady.

Jarl dvalðisk þar mjǫk lengi í allgóðum fagnaði. Staðarmenn fýstu jarl at staðfestask þar ok mæltu mjǫk á veðr um, at þeir myndi gipta honum frúna. Jarl kvazk fara vilja ferð þá, er hann hafði ætlat, en kvazk koma mundu þar, er hann fœri aptr, ok myndi þau þá gera ráð sín, sem þeim líkaði. Eptir þat býsk jarl á brot þaðan með fǫruneyti sínu. Ok er þeir sigldu vestr fyrir Þrasnes, hǫfðu þeir byr góðan; sátu þeir þá ok drukku ok váru allkátir. Þá kvað jarl vísu:

Orð skal Ermingerðar ítr drengr muna lengi;
brúðr vill rǫkk, at ríðim Ránheim til Jórðánar.
En er aptr fara runnar unnviggs of haf sunnan,
rístum, heim at hausti, hvalfrón til Nerbónar. (no. 56)

Þetta kvað Ármóðr:

Ek mun Ermingerði, nema ǫnnur skǫp verði
(margr elr sorg of svinna) síðan aldri finna.
Værak sæll ef ek svæfa (sýn væri þat gæfa,
brúðr hefr allfagrt enni) eina nótt hjá henni. (no. 57)

The earl stayed there for a very long time, enjoying the finest hospitality. The local people urged the earl to settle down there, with broad hints that they would marry him to the lady. The earl said he wished to make the journey he had intended, but said he would come back on his return and then he and the lady would make such arrangements as they pleased. After that, the earl and his company make ready to leave. And as they sailed west before Cadaqués(?), they got a good wind; so they rested, began to drink and became quite merry. The earl then made this verse:

Ermengard's glorious words the gallant shall long remember;
The upright bride will have us ride Rán's world to River Jordan.
But when back from southern parts the wave-steed's trees cross oceans
In autumn home, we'll carve a path on whale-country to Narbonne.

'Rán's (sea-goddess') world': sea. 'Wave-steed': ship, whose 'trees' are sailors. 'Whale-country': sea.

This was Ármóðr's:

Ermengard, unless other fates intervene (many a man nurses
Sorrow over a wise woman) will I never be meeting more.
I were a blessed man to be sleeping (that were evident good fortune,
The bride has a perfect face) with her for just one night.

Oddi inn lítli kvað vísu:

> Trautt erum vér, sem ek vætti, verðir Ermingerðar,
> veitk at horsk má heita hlaðgrund konungr sprunda,
> þvít sómir Bil bríma bauga stalls, at ǫllu
> hon lifi sæl und sólar setri, miklu betra. (no. 58)

Oddi the Little made up this:

> Scarcely, I expect, are we worthy of Ermengard, for I know
> The clever lace-terrain must be called the very king of ladies;
> To the Heart-Sink Goddess of ring-platform's flame (in all ways
> Blessed may she live beneath sun's halls) much more is due.

'Lace-terrain': woman. 'King of ladies': noblest of noblewomen (the use of a 'king' epithet for a lady is matched by that of *sayyidi* 'lord' for a woman in Arabic poetry from the twelfth-century culture of al-Andalus). 'Ring-platform': arm, whose 'flame' is gold, whose 'Heart-Sink (Bil from OIce *bila* 'to pause, fail') Goddess' is a lady. 'Sun's halls': sky.

Wace's *Brut*

King Arthur never dies: that is the unifying value of his legend. Arthur lives on in Wace's Anglo-Norman adaptation of Geoffrey of Monmouth's *History of the Kings of Britain*. The poet Wace, from the Channel Islands, composed the *Roman de Brut* 'The Story of Brut' in *c.* 1155. Writing less than 20 years after Geoffrey, he could already draw on other historical narratives that referred briefly to Arthur's struggle against the Saxons. Wace expanded his Arthurian narrative over that of the other kings in order to satisfy the craze for this king which had grown up in the meantime. He famously summed up his common-sense view of the magical kingship of Arthur as *ne tut mençunge, ne tut veir, tut folie ne tut saveir* 'not all lies, not all truth, neither total folly nor total wisdom' (lines 9793–4). In the passage below, Arthur fights chivalrously for Helen, a lady who has been kidnapped by the giant and and held on the smoky top of St Michel in Brittany. This fight may be compared with Beowulf's against Grendel or Grendel's Mother.

Blacker, J., with G. S. Burgess, *Wace: A Critical Bibliography* (St Helier, 2008)

Glowka, A. W., trans., *Wace. Le Roman de Brut: The French Book of Brutus* (Tempe, AZ, 2005)

Baumgartner, E., and I. Short, ed. and trans., *La Geste du Roi Arthur selon le Roman de Brut de Wace* et *l'Historia Regum Britanniae de Geoffrey of Monmouth* (Paris, 1993)

Le Saux, F. H. M., *A Companion to Wace* (Cambridge, 2005)

Weiss, J., *Wace's Roman de Brut: The History of the British: Text and Translation*, rev. ed. (Exeter, 2002)

Arthur fights the giant of Mont St Michel

De Eleyne fud mult dolenz.
mes ne fud pas cuarz ne lenz . . .
al flot retraiant de la mer
ad fait ses cumpaignuns munter
al greinur munt vindrent tant tost

Arthur was suffering much over Helen
but he wasn't cowardly or slow to act.
When the sea was at ebbtide
He ordered his companions to mount up.
Soon they arrived at the larger mountain.

2633 *Eleyne*. Helen, niece of Hoel, Arthur's nephew and himself king of Cornwall. She is carried off, raped and murdered by the giant Dinabuc, arrived from Spain and now established on Mont St Michel ('St Michael's Mount'), which is about a kilometre from the Brittany coast, and approached by a tidal causeway. Dinabuc is reminiscent of the Cyclops in his cannibal tastes.

cume la mer le munt desclost
Lur palefreiz e lur destriers
cumanderent as escuiers
cuntremunt sunt alé tuit trei
Arthur e Bedüer e Key.

'Jo irrai', dist Arthur, 'avant,
jo me cumbatrai al jaiant.
Vus vendrez aprés mei ariere
mes bien guardez que nul n'i fiere
tant cum jo me purrei aidier
ne ja si jo n'en ai mestier
cuardie resemblereit
si nuls fors mei s'i cumbatreit
E nequedent si vus vëeiz
mun busuin si me sucurreiz.'

Ço qu'il quist cil unt otrié
puis unt tuit trei le munt puié
Li jaianz al feu se sëeit
char de poirc al feu rostiseit

When the sea uncovered the mountain,
their saddle-horses and warhorses
they entrusted to the squires.
Alongside the mountain three of them went,
Arthur, Bedoer and Kay.

'I will go,' said Arthur, 'in front,
I will fight the giant myself.
You will come after me in the rear.
But take care that no one strikes there
as long as I can take care of myself,
no one strikes as long as I am not in danger.
I would look like a coward
if anyone besides me would do battle there.
But nevertheless, if you could see
my difficulty, then you could assist me.'

That which the king asked, the others agreed.
Then all three climbed up the mountain.
The giant was sitting at his fire.
He was roasting pig meat on the fire,

2642 *Bedüer e Key*. Bedivere is Arthur's cupbearer, count of Normandy. Kay is Arthur's seneschal, count of Angers, known for his irascible temper and violence.

en espeiz en ot quit partie
e partie es charbuns rostie
La barbe aveit e les gernuns
suilliez de char quit es charbuns
Arthur le quida ainz supprendre
qu'il pëust sa maçue prendre,
mes li jaianz Arthur choisi
merveilla sei, en piez sailli
sa maçue ad el col levee
ki mult esteit grosse e quarree
dui païsant ne la portassent
ne de terre ne la levassent
Arthur le vit en piez ester
e de ferir bien acesmer
s'espee traist, l'escu leva
sun chief covri, le cop duta
e li jaianz tel li duna
que tut li munz en resuna
e Arthur tut en estuna
mes fort fu pas ne chancela
Arthur senti le cop pesant
s'espee tint leva le brand
le braz halça e estendi

---

he cooked a portion on the spit
and part of it roasted down in the coals.
He had a beard and a moustache
dirtied from the meat cooked in the charcoal.
Arthur intended to surprise him
before he could take up his bludgeon,
but the giant saw Arthur.
In amazement, he jumped to his feet.
He lifted up to his neck the club
that was very thick and squared off.
Two peasants couldn't have carried it
or lifted it up from the ground.
Arthur saw that the giant was on his feet
and, eager to strike hard,
the king draws his sword, raises his shield,
protects his head, he fears the blow
and the giant gives him such a blow
that the whole mountain echoes with it.
And Arthur was completely stunned from it,
but he was brave, he didn't stumble.
Arthur felt the heavy blow.
He held his sword, he lifts the blade.
The king raises his arm and stretches it out.

le jaiant sus el frunt feri
les deus surcilz li entama
li sancs es oilz li devala
escervelé e mort l'ëust
ja recuvrier n' estëust
mes li jaianz ad la maçue
cuntre le cop en halt tenue
guenchi le chief en halt s'estut
e nequedent tel cop reçut
que tut lu vis ensanglanta
e la vëue li trubla.
Quant il senti ses oilz trubbler
dunc veïssiez jaiant desver
cume sengliers parmi l'espié
quant les chiens l'unt lunges chacié
s'enbat cuntre le venëur
tut ensement par grant irrur
curut al rei si l'enbraça
unc pur l'espee nel laissa
Granz fu e fors, parmi le prist
a genuilluns venir le fist
mes cil primes s'esvertua
en piez revint si se dresça

He strikes the giant high on the forehead.
Arthur opens a wound in his eyebrows.
Blood drips down into his eyes.
He might have knocked his brains out and killed him,
he would never have recovered
but the giant had the club
lifted high up to parry the blow.
He ducked his head and stayed on his feet.
but nonetheless he took such a hit
that his whole face ran with blood
and obscured his sight.
When he felt his eyes grow dim,
then you could have seen the giant go mad.
Just like a boar that's been speared,
after the hounds have chased him for a long time,
then the boar charges the huntsman,
in just the same way, in a great rage,
the giant rushes at the king then seizes on him,
even for fear of Arthur's sword, the giant won't relax his grip.
The giant was huge and strong, took the king around the middle,
he made the king go down on his knees,
but before all else the king exerted himself hard,
so he got back on his feet and stood up.

Arthur fud forment aïrus
e merveilles fud engignus
curusciez fud e pöur ot
esforça sei tant cum il pot
a sei traist e de sei empeinst
de maltalent nerci e teinst
en saillant guenchi en travers
de l'enemi s'est desäers.
Desqu'il se fu de lui estuers
e delivre senti sun curs
mult fud ignels entur ala
ore ert deça ore ert dela
od s'espee suvent ferant
e cil alot as meins tastant
les oilz aveit tut plein de sanc
ne cunuisseit ne neir ne blanc
Tant ala Arthur guandissant
suvent detriés, suvent devant
que de Calibuerne l'alemele
l'enbati en la cervele
traist e enpeinst e cil chaï
eschalcela si fist un cri

Arthur was powerfully enraged,
he was also wondrously clever
The king was angry and frightened.
He struggled as hard as he could
to get himself away and he thrust himself back from the giant
blackened with anger and discoloured,
with a leap Arthur escaped sideways,
from his enemy the king gets himself free.
As soon as Arthur was safe from the giant
and realised that his body was set free,
he ran swiftly, all around the giant,
now he was here, now over there,
striking often with his sword.
And the giant went feeling his way with his hands,
his eyes were full of blood.
The giant couldn't tell black from white.
So much did Arthur go bobbing and weaving
sometimes behind him, at other times in front
that the king drove Calibuerne's blade
into the giant's brain.
He pulled the sword and pushed it back and that giant fell
staggered as he shouted out.

2721 *Calibuerne.* Arthur's sword, Caliburn or Excaliber.

tel escrius fist el chäement
cume cheisnes ki chiet par vent
Dunc cumença Arthur a rire
kar dunc fud trespassee sa ire
de luin s'estut si l'esgarda
a sun buteillier cumanda
que al jaiant lu chief trenchast
a un escuier le livrast
a l'ost le volt faire porter
pur faire a merveille mustrer
'Eu ai' dist Arthur 'grant pöur
n'en oi mes de jaiant greinur
fors de Riton tant sulement
ki fait aveit maint rei dolent.'
Riton aveit maint rei cunquis
e tant vencuz que morz que vifs
de barbes que de reis ot escorcees
ot unes peals apareillie[e]s
pels en ot fait pur afubler
Bien dëust l'em Riton tuer

In his collapse he made such a thunderous noise
like an oak tree that falls down in the wind.
Then Arthur began to laugh
because now his anger was spent.
The king stood and looked at the giant from a distance.
He told his cupbearer
that he should cut off the giant's head,
that he should give it to a squire.
The king wants it to be carried to the army
to be displayed as a wonder.
'I have', said Arthur, 'great fear
greater than I have ever had about a giant,
except for Riton alone
who had made many kings suffer.'
Riton had conquered many kings
and so defeated them that, whether dead or alive,
he stripped the beards from the kings
and he had a skin cloak prepared,
a skin that he had made to wrap himself in.
Riton surely had to be killed.

2734 *pur faire a merveille mustrer* 'to be displayed as a wonder'. This might remind us of Hrothgar's decision to nail Grendel's arm to the gable of Heorot.

ant orguil e par fierté
al rei Arthur aveit mandee
que la sue barbe escorçast
e bonement li envëast
e sicum plus forz esteir
des altres reis valeit
la sue barbe honurrereit
e a ses pels urle en fereit
e si Arthur cuntrediseit
ço que Rithon li requereit
cors a cors ensemble venissent
e cors a cors se cumbatissent
e li quels d'els l'autre ocireit
u ki vif veintre le purreit
la barbe ëust, preïst les pels
si feist urle e tassels.
Arthur a lui se cumbati,
el munt d'Aravie le venqui
les pels ot, la barbe escorça
unques puis Arthur ne trova
qui fust d'itel vigur
ne dunt il ëust tel pöur.

By great pride and out of arrogance,
Riton had ordered that King Arthur
should scrape off his own beard
and willingly send it to him
and since Arthur was braver
and worth more than the other kings,
he would respect his beard
and he would place it at the cloak's hem.
And if Arthur denied
what Riton demanded from him,
they would come together body to body
and they would fight body on body
and whichever of them killed the other
or could defeat him alive
would have the beard, the victor would take the skin
and he would make the hem and tassels.
Arthur fought with him
on the Mount of Aravie he defeated him.
He had the skin, he scraped off his beard
never more did Arthur find
any giant who was of such strength
nor one who made him so afraid.

2754 Riton is a giant especially famous for hating kings.

Quant Arthur ot le munstre ocis
e Bedüer ot le chief pris
joius e lié del munt turnerent
et revindrent e si cunterent
u e purquei orent esté
puis unt lu chief a tuz mustré.
Hoel fu dolenz de sa niece
grant marrement en ot piece
hunte ot que si esteit perie.
De ma dame sainte Marie
fist faire el munt un chapele
que l'um ore Tumbe Eleyne apele
del tumbel u Eleyne jut
Tumbe Eleyne cest nun reçut
de la tumbe u li cors fud mis
as Tumbe Eleyne est nun pris.

When Arthur had killed the monster
and Bedoer had taken the head
they returned joyous and celebrating from the Mount.
They went back to the army and they told the story there,
where and for what reason they had been there.
Then they showed the head to everyone.
Hoel was suffering about his niece.
He endured great distress for a long time.
Hoel felt shame that she had perished in such circumstances.
For my lady Sainte Mary
he had a chapel built on the Mount
which is now called Helen's Tomb
on account of the tombstone that marked where Helen lay buried.
It received the name Helen's Tomb
from the tomb in which the body was placed,
from Helen's Tomb is the name derived.

Thomas of Britain's *Tristan*

⁂

The *Tristan* of Thomas of Britain (or Brittany), from *c.* 1173, has the reputation of being the greatest, or at least probably the most influential, work of Anglo-Norman literature. Thomas' preface dedicates his poem to Queen Eleanor of England and Aquitaine. The legend on which he based his poem was developed on the Celtic fringes of the British Isles, in Ireland and also Wales. It has analogues, probably also of common ancestry, in the Welsh *Culhwch* and the story of Deirdre and Noisiu in the *Longes mac n-Uislenn* 'Exile of the Sons of Uisliu' (see **Heroic Poems** and **Poems on the Meaning of Life**). Tristan, nephew of King Mark of Cornwall, sets off to Ireland to escort Princess Iseult back to Cornwall as his uncle's new bride. Their ship is becalmed, they play chess in the hot sun and look for a drink. Unfortunately the bottle they find contains the love-potion which Iseult's maid, Brengain, brought with her for the wedding night with Mark. Tristan and Iseult fall hopelessly in love. Their affair continues after Iseult weds Mark on arrival in Cornwall, and the lovers use various tricks to escape detection as Mark's advisers seek to catch them out. When Mark finds out about the lovers, he sends Iseult to live in a leper house and has Tristan led to the stake. Tristan, escaping by a great leap from a chapel, returns disguised as a leper in a successful bid to rescue his lover (see the second passage below). They hide out in the Wild Wood of Cornwall. In the earthier version of Béroul, from about the same time as Thomas' *Tristan*, the potion wears off three years to the day after its ingestion while the lovers are in hiding. In Thomas' version, however, the potion stays effective and continues to absolve Tristan and Iseult of responsibility even to the end of their destructive affair. Mark finds the lovers again and reconciles with Iseult on condition Tristan leave the kingdom. Having left, and at a loose end in Brittany, unhappily married to another woman named Iseult (of the White Hands), Tristan is wounded by a poisoned lance while trying to rescue a young woman from six knights. He sends his brother-in-law and friend Kahedin to Cornwall to fetch the first Iseult to heal him, with instructions to hoist a white sail if she is coming, a black sail if not. Tristan's wife overhears. As the ship heaves into view with a white sail, she lies to him about the colour and the man dies, to be followed shortly after by his lover Iseult, who passes out for ever over his dead body.

Thomas adapted an allegedly Cornish or Breton poem on Tristan which is now lost. In his own poem he deals with themes of reason versus passion, kingship and secret love, and socio-political tension and crisis. His poem now exists in some 3300 lines in a series of eight fragments which may be put together from different manuscripts. Enough of it survives, however, together with material from thirteenth-century translations and adaptations, to show that Thomas' original work would have been much longer. His work stresses the importance of emotion, but it is repressed emotion and hidden action in the face of society and authority. This kind of love is very much a reflection of the Anglo-Norman world, but times were changing and Thomas dedicates this work to the young Queen Eleanor. The first selection given here evokes the beginning of their love at sea as Tristan, King Mark of Cornwall's nephew, accompanies his uncle's bride-elect, Iseut, daughter of the King of Ireland, from her homeland.

Sailing towards England

Car ambedeus sunt en esseir.
Dient lur bon e lur voleir,
Baisent et enveisent e acolent.
A Branguain de l'amur parolent.
Tant ly promettent, tant li dient
Que par fïance s'entrelïent
E ele lur voleir consent.
Tuz lur bons font privément
E lur joië e lur deduit,
Quant il pöent e jur e nuit.

Delitablë est le deport
Qui de sa dolur ad confort.
Car c'est costume d'amur
De joie aveir aprés dolur.
Pus qu'il se sunt descovert,
Que plus s'astient e plus i pert.

Vont s'en a joie li amant
La haute mer a plein siglant
Vers Engleterre a plein tref.
Tere ont vëue cil de la nef.

For Tristan and Iseult each expect much from the other.
They tell each other what is pleasing and what they desire
Tristan and Iseult kiss and embrace and press each other closely.
They talk to Brengain about their love.
So much do they promise her, so much do they tell her
that they pledge loyalty to one another
and she consents to their desires.
All their pleasures take place in secret,
and their joy and their delight,
as much as possible both day and night.

Delightful is the happiness
which includes solace in its grief.
For it is the way of love
that grief follows joy.
Once Tristan and Iseult opened themselves to each other
the more they kept apart from each other, the more they lost there.

The lovers travelled in joy
sailing straight across the high seas
towards England at full sail.
The ship's sailors saw the land.

Il en sunt tuit lié e joius
Fors sul Tristan l'amerous.
Car s'il alast par son voleir
Grant tens ne la vousis vëer.
Mielz en amat Ysolt en mer,
Ses enveisures demener.
Vers la terre vont nequedent:
A la wëue de la gent
La nef Tristan est conue.
Ainz que ele seit a terre venue,
Est esmëu un damoisel
Vers le rey sur cheval ignel.
En bois le trove si li dit
Que la nef Tristan ariver vit.
Quant li reis l'ot, molt lié se vait.
Del damoysel chevaler fait
Pur ce qu'il li dit la novele
De Tristan e de la pucele.
Encuntre vient tresqu'el rivage
Pus mande pur tut son barnage.

They are happy and joyous,
except for Tristan in love.
If he could have done whatever he wished,
he would not have seen land for a very long time.
He preferred to love Iseult out on the sea,
to continue with his close coupling.
Towards the land they go nevertheless.
In the sight of everyone watching
Tristan's ship is recognised.
Before the ship came to port
a young gentleman takes off
on a swift horse to reach the king.
The young courtier finds him in the woods to tell him
that he saw Tristan's ship arrive.
When the king hears this, he becomes very happy.
King Mark makes the young gentleman a knight
because he announced the news
that Tristan and the young lady
have just arrived at the shore.
Then the king sends for his assembly of noblemen.

Tristan disguised as a leper [MS Douce/Bodleian]

E returne tut le chemin
E jur que ja mais n'ert liez
Si avrad lur estre assaiez.
Mult fud Tristan suspris d'amur
Ore s'turne de povre atur
De povre atur, de vil abit
Que nuls ne que nule quit
Ne aparceive que Tristan seit.
Par un herbe tut les deceit.
Sun vis em fait tut eslever
Cum se malade fust, emfler
Pur sei seürement covrir
Ses pez e ses mains fait vertir.
Tut se apareille cum fust lazre
E puis prent un hanap de mazre
Que la reine li duna
Le primer an que il l'amat.
Met i de buis un gros nüel,
Si s'apareille un flavel.
A la curt le rei s'en vait
E près des entrees se trait
E desire mult a saver

Tristan goes back the way he came.
He swears that he will never be happy
until he has put King Mark's court off the test.
Tristan was much overtaken by love.
Now he puts on a poor man's appearance,
a poor man's outfit, peasant clothing
so that no one would know
nor recognise that man for Tristan.
By a herbal stratagem he fools them all.
He makes his face puff up all over
as though he were diseased, to swell
to disguise himself more effectively
he makes his feet and his hands twist.
In every way he takes on a leper's look.
Tristan takes a maplewood cup
that Queen Iseult gave him
during the first year that he loved her.
He put inside a big ball of boxwood,
so equipped himself with a leper's rattle.
Tristan went to King Mark's court
and drew himself up near the entrance
and wanted greatly to know

L'estre de la curt e veer.
Sovent prie, sovent flavele,
N'en puet oïr nule novele
Dunt en sun cuer plus liez en seit.
Li reis un jur feste teneit,
Sin alat a la halte glise
Pur oïr le grant servise.
Eissuz en ert hors des palés,
E la reïne vent aprés.
Tristan la veit, del sun li prie
Mais Ysolt nel reconut mie.
Et il vait après, si flavele
A la halte vuiz vers li apele
Del sun requiert pur Deu amur
Pitusement par grant tendrur.
Grant eschar en unt li serjant
Cum la reine vait si avant.
Li uns l'empeinst, l'altre le bute,
E sil metent hors de la rute.
L'un manace, l'altre le fert
Il vait après, si lur requiert
Que pur Deu alcun ben li face.
Ne s'en returne pur manace.

---

the habits and sights of the court.
Often he begs, and often shakes his rattle,
but he doesn't hear any news
that makes his heart any happier than it is.
The king was celebrating a holy day.
He went with his retinue to the great church
to hear a solemn High Mass.
He processed out from the palace precinct
and the queen came after him.
Tristan saw her. He begs her for alms,
But Iseult doesn't recognise him at all.
And he goes after her, he shakes his rattle.
He shouts in her direction in a loud voice
for the alms sought for the love of God
piteously in a deeply touching voice.
The servants treated him with great scorn
once the queen went on ahead.
Some pushed him, other knocked him
and they shoved him out of the procession.
Some threaten him, others beat him.
He follows after them, so he seeks them out,
to ask that for God's sake something good might be done for him.
He doesn't turn back in spite of their threats.

Tuit le tenent pur ennuius
Ne sevent cum est besuignus.
Suit les tresqu'enz en la capele
Crie e del hanap flavele.
Ysolt en est tut ennuée
Regarde le cum feme irée
Si se merveille que il ait
Ki pruef de li itant se trait
Veit le hanap qu'ele cunuit
Que Tristan ert buen s'aparçut
Par sun gent cors, par sa faiture
par la furme de s'estature.
En sun cuer en est esfrée
E el vis teinte e colurée
Kar ele ad grant poür del rei.
Un anel d'or trait de sun dei
Ne set cum li puisse duner,
En sun hanap le volt geter.
Si cum le teneit en sa main
Aparceüe en est Brengvein.
Regarde Tristan sil conut
De sa cuintise s'aparçut.
Dit li qu'il est fols e bricuns

Everyone considers him an annoyance
They don't know how needy really he is.
He follows them all the way into the chapel.
Tristan shouts and rattles his cup.
Iseult is greatly annoyed by his behaviour.
She looks at him like a woman in a rage.
So she wonders what possesses him,
the leper who draws so near to her.
She sees the cup that she can recognise.
That the man is Tristan, she realises,
by his noble body, by his build
by the proportions of his stature.
In her heart this frightens her,
and her face pales and blushes
because she has great fear of the king.
A gold ring she takes from her finger,
but knows not how to give it to him.
Into his cup she wants to throw the ring.
As she holds it in her hand,
Brengain takes notice of it.
She looks at Tristan in recognition
She notices his trickery.
Brengain says that he is a madman and a rogue

Ki si embat sur les baruns.
Les serjanz apele vilains
Qui le suffrent entre les seins,
E dit a Ysolt qu'ele est feinte
'Des quant avez esté si seinte
Que dunisez si largement
A malade u a povre gent?
Vostre anel doner li vulez.
Par ma fei, dame, nun ferez.
Ne donez pas a si grant fès
Que vus repentez en après
E si vus or li dunisez
Encor ui vus repentirez.'
As serjanz dit qu'illuques veit
Que hors de le glise mis seit
E cil le metent hors ad l'us
E il n'ose preier plus.
Or veit Tristan e ben le set
Que Brengvein li e Ysolt het.

---

who attacks the barons themselves.
Brengain calls the servants low fellows
who allow him to be among their noble company.
And she says to Iseult that she is deceitful.
'Since when have you been so devout
that you give so generously
to lepers and to poor people?
You want to give him your ring.
By my faith, lady, you will not do it.
You do not give at such a great price
in order to regret it afterwards.
And if you give him the gold ring
Yet this very day you will regret it.'
To the servants she says that the man she sees there
should be put out of the church.
And those men put him out of the door.
And he did not dare beg any more.
But now Tristan knows and understands well
that Brengain hates him and Iseult.

Love and images [MS de Turin]

When love lets in suspicion, the hell may be of one's own making, and few poets have expressed this irrational state of mind in a lover's absence as well as Thomas, in his account here of Tristan's physical and mental wanderings after being forced to leave Iseult in the court of King Mark. Unfortunately for Tristan, he has made images of

Iseult and her maid Brengain for use in his exile. His adoration of the first one, then appeal to the second, suggests a parody of the worship of icons of the Virgin and the saints. The theme of *la folie de Tristan* 'Tristan's madness' was later developed from these lines, which survived for a while in the Turin fragment. This went missing in the early twentieth century. Luckily, however, it had been transcribed by the great Breton scholar Joseph Bédier (1864–1938), whose text is given below.

Bédier, J., trans., *Le Roman de Tristan et Iseult*, 2 vols, Societé des Anciens Textes Français (Paris, 1902–5)

E les deliz des granz amors
E lor travaus et lor dolurs
E lor paignes et lor ahans
Recorde a l'himage Tristans
Molt la baise quant est haitez.
Corrusce soi, quant est irez,
Que par penser, que par songes
Que par craire en son cuer mençoinges.
Qu'ele mette lui en l'obli
Ou qu'ele ait acun autre ami:
Qu'ele ne se pusse consirrer
Que li n'estoce autre amer,
Que mieuz a sa volunté l'ait.
Hiceste penser errer le fait.
Errance son corage debote.
Del biau Cariados se dote
Qu'ele envers lui ne turne s'amor.

And the delight of grand passions,
And their torment and their grief,
And their suffering and their weariness
Tristan remembers, as he looks at Iseult's image.
Many times he kisses it when he feels hot desire.
He responds to rage when he feels it,
in his thoughts, in his dreams,
for believing lies in his heart,
that she would forget him,
or that she would have some other lover,
that she could not do without
wanting to love another man
who could better match her desire.
The very thought made him roam about.
Such roamings attacked his ability to think.
He feared handsome Cariados,
that she might turn her love his way.

16 Cariados is a count at King Mark's court who also loves Iseult.

Entur li est e nuit e jor.
E si la sert e si la losange
E sovent de lui la blestange.
Dote quant n'a son voler
Qu'ele se preigne a son poer.
Por ce qu'ele ne puet avoir lui
Que son ami face d'autrui.
Quant il pense de tel irur,
Donc mustre a l'image haiur,
Vient l'autre a esgarder,
Mais ne volt ne seoir ne parler.
Hidonc enparole Brigvain,
E dist donc: 'Bele a vos me plain
Del change e de la trischerie
Que envers moi fait Ysode m'amie.'
Quanqu'il pense a l'image dit.
Poi s'en desserve un petit,
Regarde en la main Ysodt,
L'anel d'or doner li volt,
Vait la chere e le senblant
Qu'au departir fait son amant.
Menbre lui de la covenance
Qu'il ot a la desevrance.

Cariados is round about her day and night.
He serves her and he flatters her,
often speaks abusively to her about Tristan.
Tristan fears that when Iseult does not have the man she desires,
then she will take the man available to her.
Since she cannot have Tristan,
Iseult could make someone else her beloved.
When Tristan thinks about such enraging thoughts,
then he acts out his hatred to the image.
He starts to look at Brengain's image,
because he does want to linger or speak to Iseult any more.
Next he addresses Brengain.
And he says then: 'Lovely lady, it is to you that I complain
about the change of heart and betrayal
that Iseult has committed towards me.'
Whatever he thinks about, he tells to the image.
Then Tristan steps back a bit,
he looks at Iseult's hand,
at the gold ring that he wants to give her.
He sees the face and her expression
at parting from her beloved Tristan.
He remembers the agreement
that he made with her at their separation.

Hidonc plure e merci crie
De ce que pensa folie
E siet bien que il est deceü
De la fole irur que il a eü
Por iço fist il ceste image
Que dire li volt son corage,
Son bon penser et sa fole errur
Sa paigne, sa joie d'amor
Car ne sot vers cui descoverir
Ne son voler, ne son desir.

Then he weeps and begs for mercy
for having thought such madness.
And he knows well that he has given way
to the mad anger that he had.
For Tristan himself made this image
because he wanted to speak his heart to it,
his good thoughts and his mad wanderings,
his suffering, his joy in love,
because he knew no one to whom he could reveal
his desire or his passion.

49 *Car ne sot* 'because he knew no one' etc. For an illustration of the changes wrought by chivalry since the tenth century, compare these lines with the same construction, yet with such different object of love, in *The Wanderer*, lines 9–11 (**Poems on the Meaning of Life**).

Marie de France's *The Nightingale*

Laüstic

✳

Whereas much is known about the charismatic Eleanor of Aquitaine, little survives concerning the Marie who wrote her *Lays* in Anglo-Norman. Even the choice of title (*Lays*, suggesting music and song) is elusive because Marie uses verbs of speaking and writing to express the making of her stories in verses. Yet we can only hear Marie's voice echo through the writing of the tale of *Guigemar* that begins: *Oëz, seignurs, ke dit Marie, Ki en sun tens pas ne s'oblie* 'Hear, gentlemen, what Marie says, she who does not want to be forgotten in her own time' (lines 3–4). Like Marie herself and the sound of her voice, the music remains beyond our grasp. What we can see of her style is poetry, which is narrative verse composed in octosyllabic (eight-syllabled) couplets. Research into her romance sources tells many scholars that Marie wrote her stories in England in the first two decades after *c.* 1150. The earliest and most reliable manuscript dates from the thirteenth century (Harley 978 in the British Library). This was the period of Angevin rule, a watershed when a secular culture, one that has much in common with our own, began to gain power in society and expression by questioning religious concepts and values. Queen Eleanor, granddaughter of Duke William IX of Aquitaine, was no exception. In the 1160s, when Marie de France was writing her *Lays* or 12 short stories translated from Breton sources in verse (more or less 500 lines each), somewhere in England, Eleanor was active in court life. It is thought that Eleanor's interests inspired Marie. The *nobles reis* 'noble king', who is addressed in the prologue to Marie's story *Guigemar*, is probably Eleanor's second husband, Henry II. Marie tells us that *E en ki quoer tuz biens racine* 'All good things take root in his heart' (line 46). The compliment is a double-edged reference to the fact that Henry's Angevin stock, calling itself *Planta-genet*, had only recently 'taken root' in England.

Marie's texts are filled with fables that prompt debate and questions about the role of women, the position of a young foreign queen such as Eleanor, and the compromises sometimes made by married partners abroad. References to birds and bird song are linked to the general themes of love, nature and memory. In *Laüstic* 'The Nightingale' (also known as *Le Rossignol*) the link between the lovers and languages is in the song of a nightingale:

Une aventure vus dirai
Dunt li bretun firent un lai.
Laüstic ad nun, ceo m'est vis,
Si l'apelent en lur pais:
Ceo est 'rossignol' en franceis
E 'nuhtegale' en dreit engleis. (lines 1–6)

I'll tell you an adventure
that the Bretons made into a lay.
Laüstic is the title, that's what I think,
that's how they call it in their land;
that is *rossignol* in French
and *nihtegale* in proper English.

The woman stands by the window each night waiting to exchange words with her lover. She tells her husband that it is to listen to a songbird. When the woman's jealous husband brutally kills the nightingale, the bird's death marks the end of the lovers' contact. To commemorate their loss, the wife wraps the body of the bird in fine brocade, on which she has embroidered the story of their love in gold letters. When her servant tells the lover his lady's story and gives him the little corpse wrapped in the embroidered version of her story, he has a little coffer made of pure gold, adorned with jewels. Therein he places the dead nightingale, and seals him within it. The box remains always with him. What first seems an amusing story of a sudden taste for birdsong used to fool a gullible husband becomes a story where the nightingale is both contained in the love-story and embodies it at the same time. So the forbidden yet conventional love of two human beings becomes a secret mating with another kind of being. The creation of this hybrid union perhaps marks the release of some magical harmony in the universe. The story does not stay sealed, in the end, but circulates in a Breton lay, unheard by us until released by Marie. From her, in turn, it was passed down into *The Owl and the Nightingale*, a poem from southern England in the early thirteenth century.

Cartlidge, N., ed., *The Owl and the Nightingale: Text and Translation* (Exeter, 2001)

Gaunt, S., *Retelling the Tale: An Introduction to Medieval French Literature* (London, 2001)

Micha, A., ed. and trans., *Lais de Marie de France* (Paris, 1994)

Weir, A., *Eleanor of Aquitaine: By the Wrath of God, Queen of England* (London, 2000)

The husband finds the nightingale

Les nuiz, quant la lune luseit
E ses sires cuché esteit,
De juste lui sovent levot
E de sun mantel se afublot;
A la fenestre ester veneit
Pur sun ami qu'ele saveit
Que autreteu vie demenot
E le plus de la nuit veillot.
Delit aveient al veer,
Quant plus ne poeient aver.
Tant i estut, tant i leva
Que ses sires s'en curuça
E meintefeiz li demanda
Pur quei levot e u ala.

'Sire, la dame li respunt,
Il nen ad joïe en cest mund
Ki n'ot le laüstic chanter.

On those nights, when the moon was shining
and her husband had gone to sleep,
she often got up from her bed
and wrapped her cloak around her.
She would go to the window
for the sake of her beloved whom she knew
did exactly the same thing
and she watched at the window much of the night.
They delighted to see each other
though they could never have more of each other than eyes could hold.
So many times did she stand there, so many times did she get up,
that her husband grew angry
and numerous times did he ask
why she got up and where she went.

'My lord,' she answered him,
'there is no real joy in this world
for anyone who has not heard the nightingale sing.

---

85 *laüstic* 'nightingale'. Breton for nightingale, compare Middle English *nihtingale*, female night singer. Although stories about nightingales often ascribe the singing to the female, Marie de France's tale seems to get right the bird's gender and purpose, as an unpartnered male singing often at night and especially near dawn to attract a mate. This may also link Marie's story to the lyric genre of the troubabour *alba* or 'dawn song' where a husband and watching servants pose a deadly menace to wide-awake lovers.

Pur ceo me vois ici ester.
Tant ducement l'i oi la nuit
Que mut me semble grant deduit.
Tant me delit e tant le voil
Que jeo ne puis dormir de l'oil.'

Quant li sires ot que ele dist,
De ire e de maltalent en rist.
De une chose se purpensa:
Le laüstic enginnera.
Il n'ot vallet en sa meisun
Ne face engin, reis u laçun
Puis les mettent par le verger
N'i ot codre ne chastainier
U il ne mettent laz u glu.
Tant que pris l'unt e retenu.
Quant le laüstic eurent pris
Al seigner fu rendu tut vis.
Mut en fu liez, quant il le tint
As chambres a la dame vint.

For this reason I go to just this place.
So much sweetness I listen to over there at night
that it seems ravishing to me.
So much it pleasures me and so much do I desire it
that I cannot shut my eyes in sleep.'

When her husband heard what she said
he laughed out of anger and wickedness.
He thought about a scheme
to snare the nightingale.
There was not a servant in the house
that didn't make a trap, a net or a loop.
Then they placed them around the garden.
There was not a hazel tree or a chestnut tree
where they did not put a snare or birdlime,
so many traps they set that they took and captured the nightingale.
When the nightingale was taken,
the bird was handed over alive to the master.
He was very pleased, when he held him.
The husband went to his lady's chamber.

---

99 *glu* 'birdlime'. A sticky adhesive preparation usually applied to twigs with a little stick to catch small birds.

'Dame,' fet il, 'u estes vus?
Venez avant, parlez a nus!
J'ai le laüstic enginnié
Pur quei vus avez tant veillié.
Des or poëz gisir en peis.
Il ne vus esveillerat meis.'

Quant la dame l'ad entendu,
Dolente e cureçuse fu.
A sun seigneur l'ad demandé,
E il l'ocist par engresté.
Le col li rumpt a ses deus meins.
De ceo fist il ke trop vileins.
Sur la dame le cors geta,
Si que sun chainse ensanglanta
Un poi desur le piz devant.
De la chambre s'en ist atant.
La dame prent le corps petit;
Durement plure e si maudit
Ceus ki le laüstic traïrent
Et les engins e laçuns firent,
Kar mut li unt toleit grant hait.

'Lady', he says, 'Where are you?
Come near, talk to us both!
I have trapped the nightingale
for which you stayed up late for so long.
From now on you can rest in peace.
He won't keep you awake ever again.'

When the lady listened to him,
she suffered and grew angry.
The lady asked her husband for the bird
and he killed it in rough cruelty:
he broke its neck with both hands.
What he did was too vile for a nobleman:
he threw the little corpse on the lady
so that her linen dress was bloodied
just a bit over her breast.
From the chamber he then departed.
The lady takes the little body,
weeps and weeps and curses those
who had betrayed the nightingale
and had made the traps and snares,
for taking so much joy from her.

'Lasse,' fet ele, 'male m'estait!
Ne purrai mes la nuit lever
Ne aler a la fenestre ester,
U jeo suil mun ami veer.
Une chose sai jeo de veir:
Il quidera ke jeo me feigne;
De ceo m'estuet que cunseil preigne.
Le laüstic li trametrai,
L'aventure li manderai.'

En une piece de samit
A or brusdé e tut escrit
Ad l'oiselet envolupé.
Un son vaslet ad apelé
Sun message li ad chargié
A sun ami l'ad enveié.
Cil est la chevalier venuz;
De sa dame li dist saluz,
Tut sun message li cunta,
La laüstic li presenta.

'Alas,' she said, 'ill fortune is mine,
no more will I be able to get up at night
or go to stand by the window
where I used to see my friend.
One thing I know is true,
he will think I am faint-hearted,
therefore I have to take action.
I shall send him the nightingale
and let him know what has happened.'

It was in a piece of samite
that she embroidered in gold thread and wrote the whole story.
The lady wrapped up the tiny bird.
She called for one of her own servants.
The lady explained her message to him.
To her beloved she sent him on his way.
This man came to the knight.
He gave the nobleman his lady's greetings.
The servant recounted all her message.
He presented the knight with the nightingale.

---

135 *samit* 'samite'. A silk twill cloth with a smooth and shining surface much valued in the Middle Ages. The warp threads are hidden by the weft threads suggesting that the way the cloth is made could be linked to the narrative codes of this story about fetishised love.

Quant tut li ad dit e mustré
E il l'aveit bien escuté,
De l'aventure esteit dolenz,
Mes ne fu pas vileins ne lenz
Un vaisselet ad fet forger.
Unques n'i ot fer ne acer,
Tut fu de or fin od bones pieres
Mut precïuses e mut cheres;
Covercle i ot tres bien asis
Le laüstic ad dedenz mis.
Puis fist la chasse enseeler.
Tuz jors l'ad fete od lui porter.

When he had said all he had to show and tell
and when the knight had listened to him closely,
the knight suffered over what had happened.
But he was not vile or slow to act.
He had a container worked in metal,
not at all in iron or steel
but completely made from fine gold and good gemstones,
Very precious and great in worth.
A cover fitted with precision.
The nightingale was placed within,
then the knight had the casket sealed.
All the days of his life the knight carried it with him.

149 *Un vaisselet ad fet forger* 'He had a container worked in metal'. A reliquiary, one might say, if this were the end of a saint's life. There is humour as well as pathos in the situation.

The Play of Adam

Le Jeu d'Adam

⁎

Le Jeu d'Adam counts as one of the earliest texts that is written in a vernacular language and is indisputably a work of drama. As we have seen with the Advent Lyrics of *Christ I*, and the Old Saxon *Genesis B*, both of the ninth century (see **Poems of Devotion**, with the former in the Custom Version), some poems are based on liturgy and lend themselves to dramatic performance. There is no doubt of this, however, with *Le Jeu d'Adam* (sometimes known as *Le Mystère d'Adam* 'Adam's Mystery Play'). This work, *The Play of Adam*, is preserved in Old French in one manuscript from *c.* 1225–50 (Tours, Bibliothèque Municipale, 927), which was copied in the first half of the thirteenth century. Yet various Anglo-Norman forms are so prominent that it seems likely the play was originally composed in that language in northern France in the second half of the twelfth century. The play is not part of a cycle of mystery plays, but was rather a kind of music hall show in three parts, where Latin liturgy is dramatised in the vernacular through octosyllabic verse, mime and music in order to convey: (a) the Fall of Man, (b) its murderous consequence in the conflict of Cain and Abel and (c) the Latin Procession of Prophets (Abraham, Moses, Isaiah and Nebuchadnezzar), whose words prophesy Christ and the Redemption.

The stage directions are in Latin, and the liturgical framework of this play is the Latin responses of the Septuagesima Mass (for the ninth Sunday before Easter), but in the first part there is also a highly secular focus on the personality and thoughts of Adam and Eve in temptation, contrition and repentance. Eve's independence and wit suggest an Anglo-Norman culture where misogynistic attitudes towards women were not accepted without irony or challenge. Her characterisation places her alongside other strong-minded women, such as those to be found in Gaimar's *Estoire des Engleis* and in Old English and Old Icelandic literatures too. Most remarkable of all, however, is the fact that this version of the Fall allows the devil to approach Adam first, to fail in persuading him to eat the apple, then to succeed at the same with Eve. As we have seen in **Poems of Devotion**, this order of temptation is a feature of *Genesis B*, from which the Anglo-Norman tradition may even be descended. In this much older poem, however, Eve eats the apple in order to shield Adam and herself from the divine punishment that the devil has told her to expect as a result of Adam's refusal. In *The Play of Adam*, the devil presents Adam's stubborn loyalty to God as a lack of ambition, to which Eve responds by coveting the promised godlike power as a means of social advancement for both of them.

Beadle, R., ed., *The Cambridge Companion to Medieval English Theatre* (Cambridge, 1994)

van Emden, W., ed., *Le Jeu d'Adam*, 2nd ed., Société Rencesvals: British Branch Publications 1 (Edinburgh, 1999)

Enders, J., *The Medieval Theatre of Cruelty: Rhetoric, Memory, Violence* (Ithaca, NY, 1999)

Enders, J., *Death by Drama and Other Medieval Urban Legends* (Chicago and London, 2002)

Grace, F., *The Medieval French Drama* (Oxford, 1954)

Harris, J. W., *Medieval Theatre in Context: An Introduction* (London, 1992)

Solterer, H., *The Master and Minerva: Disputing Women in French Medieval Culture* (Berkeley and Los Angeles, CA, 1995)

The devil talks to Eve

In this scene, part of the first 'act' of *The Play of Adam*, the devil enters with the charm of an amatory deceiver. Entering into Eve's confidence, he finds out and then plays on her reservations about Adam her 'rough' husband, until she has almost made a compact with him. The devil compliments Eve on having a greater intelligence than Adam. However, he does not promise her an enhanced vision, as in *Genesis B*, lines 564–7 (although she receives this on line 307). He offers her the forbidden fruit instead as a means of achieving a power so far denied to her.

Diabolus: Or me mettrai en ta creance:
ne voil de toi altre fiance.
Eva: Bien te pois creire a ma parole.
Diabolus: Tu as esté en bone escole!
Jo vi Adam, mais trop est fols.
Eva: Un poi est durs.
Diabolus: Il serra mols!
Il est plus dors que n'est emfers.
Eva: Il est mult francs!
Diabolus: Ainz est mult serf!

Devil: Now I place myself in your trust
I don't want any other promise from you.
Eve: You can certainly trust in my word.
Devil: You have been well polished!
I saw Adam, but he is too foolish . . .
Eve: He is a bit rough.
Devil: Adam will soften,
But he is tougher than hell is.
Eve: He is very noble-minded.
Devil: Rather, he is very much a peasant.

---

217 *en ta creance* 'in your trust'. This devil appears quite friendly and relaxed.

221 *Jo vi Adam, mais trop est fols* 'I saw Adam, but he is too foolish'. The alternative version of the story, as presented in *Genesis B*, also seems to be remembered in some way here: that the devil tries to deceive Adam first. In this play, however, the devil seeks to divide Eve from her husband as if she knows that she might go her own way.

222 *plus dors que n'est emfers* 'tougher than hell is'. How would this visitor know? The dramatist re-animates a figure of speech as a sign of the speaker's place of origin.

224 *est mult serf* 'he is very much a peasant'. There are already class distinctions in this Garden of Eden. Like the guild plays of later medieval England, this play is meant to be of the present world.

Cure nen voelt prendre de soi,
Car la prenge sevsals de toi!
Tu es fieblette e tendre chose,
e es plus fresche que n'est rose;
tu es plus blanche que cristal,
que neif que chiet sor glace en val.
Mal cuple em fist li criator;
tu es trop tendre, e il trop dur!
Mais neporquant tu es plus sage:
en grant sens as mis tun corrage:
por ço fait bon trairë a toi.
Parler te voil!
Eva: Ore i ait fai!
Diabolus: N'en sache nuls!
Eva: Ke le deit saver?
Diabolus: Neïs Adam?
Eva: Nenil, par veir.
Diabolus: Or te dirrai, e tu m'ascute.
N'a que nus dous en ceste rote,
e Adam la, qu'il ne nus ot.

If he doesn't want to think about himself,
at least he should think about you.
You are a fragile and delicate creature
and also fresher than a rose,
you gleam brighter than rock crystal.
You are whiter than the snow that falls on the ice in the valley.
A bad pairing did the Creator make of you two.
You are too delicate and he is too rough,
But nevertheless you are the wiser of the two.
The Creator has put great good sense in your heart.
For that reason it is good to turn to you.
I want to talk with you!
Eve: Now I trust you on that.
Devil: But no one must know.
Eve: Who ought to know about it?
Devil: Not even Adam?
Eve: No, truly.
Devil: Now I'll tell you and you listen to me.
There are only two of us on this path.
And Adam over there who can't hear us.

---

228 *plus fresche que n'est rose* 'fresher than a rose'. The devil knows the language of *fin'amor*, a dimension to his wiles that comes too late for the ninth-century Saxon play in *Genesis B*, particularly lines 551–87 (see **Poems of Devotion**).

230 *en val* 'in the valley' etc. The similies are based on gardens in north-west Europe, but with *val* the devil sketches out a setting that resembles the *lilium convallium* 'lily in the valley' of the Song of Songs 2:1.

Eva: Parlez en halt, n'en savrat mot.
Diabolus: Jo vus acoint d'un grant engin
que vus est fait en cest gardin:
le fruit que Deus vus ad doné
nen a en soi gaires bonté.
Cil qu'il vus ad tant defendu.
il ad en soi grant vertu
En celui est grace de vie,
de poëste e de seignorie,
de tut saver, [e] bien e mal.
Eva: Quel savor a?
Diabolus: Celestial!
A ton bel cors, a ta figure
bien covendreit tel aventure
que tu fusses dame del mond
del soverain e del parfont
e seüsez quanquë a estre,
que de tuit fuissez bone maistre.

Eve: Speak up, he won't know a thing about it.
Devil: I am telling you about a great trick
that has been played on the two of you in this garden.
The fruit that God has given you
has hardly any nourishing strength in it.
The fruit that he has forbidden so strictly to you,
that fruit has great power.
In that fruit is the gift of life,
the gift of power, and the gift of rulership,
the gift of all knowledge, good and evil.
Eve: What does it taste like?
Devil: Heaven itself!
For your beautiful body, for your face
such good fortune would be suitable,
that you would be Queen of the World,
of the heights and the depths,
Queen over whatever has been and whatever will be,
that you would be the powerful ruler over everything.

---

243 *n'en savrai mot* 'he won't know a thing about it'. Eve uses the language of clandestine love. The devil has wooed her successfully, though to a more serious end.

252 *Celestial* 'Heaven itself'. There again, the speaker knows what it means to be in heaven. This figure of speech takes on its original meaning.

255 *dame del mond* 'Queen of the World'. The devil promises Eve a place that will be filled by Mary, her descendant, having sensed that Eve has aspirations to a power all of her own. In the second half of the twelfth century, it is hard not to think of Eleanor's presence in the mind of playwright and audience alike.

Eva: Est tel li fruiz?
Diabolus: Oïl, par voir.

Tunc diligenter intuebitur Eva fructum vetitum, quo diucius intuito dicet:

Eva: Ja me fait bien sol le veer.
Diabolus: Si tu le mangues, que feras?
Eva: E jo que sai?
Diabolus: Ne me crerras?
Primes le pren e a Adam le done:
del ciel averez sempres corone,
al creator serrez pareil,
ne vus purra celer conseil.
Puis que del fruit avrez mangié
sempres vus iert le cuer changié.
O Deus, serrez, sanz faillance,
de egal bonté, de egal puissance.
Guste del fruit!

Eve: Is it such a fruit as that?
Devil: Oh yes, truly.

Then Eve shall be looking cautiously at the fruit and once she has looked at the fruit for a long time, she shall say:

Eve: It does me good just to look at it.
Devil: If you eat it, what could you achieve?
Eve: But how would I know that?
Devil: Don't you trust me?
First you take it and then give it to Adam
You will wear the Crown of Heaven.
You will be just like the Creator.
He will not be able to keep any knowledge from you
because you will have eaten the fruit.
Right away you will have your heart transformed.
Without any weakness, you will be like God,
equal in strength, equal in power.
Taste the fruit!

---

260 *Ja me fait bien* 'It does me good' etc. This is developed from Genesis 3:6, *Vidit igitur mulier quod bonum esset lignum ad vescendum, et pulchrum oculis* 'So the woman saw that the fruit of the tree was good to eat, and pleasing to the eye'.

Adam takes the apple

Adam: E tu coment?
Eva: Car l'asaiai
De ço quen chat me del veer?
[Adam:] Il te ferra changer saver.
Eva: Nel f[e]ra pas, car nel crerai
de nule rien tant que l'asai.
Adam: Nel laisser mais venir sor toi
Car il est mult de pute foi!
Il volst traïr ja son seignor
e so[i] poser al des halzor.
Tel paltonier qui ço ad fait
ne voil que vers vus ait nul retrait.

Tunc serpens artificiose compositus ascendit iuxta stypitem arboris vetite, cui Eva propius adhibebit aurem, quasi ipsius ascultans consilium. De hinc accipiet Eva pomum, porriget Ade; ipse vero nondum eam accipiet. Et Eva dicet ei:

Eva: Manjue, Adam! Ne sez que est.
Prenum ço bien que nus est prest!
Adam: Est il tant bon?

Adam: And how do you know?
Eve: Because I trusted him.
What can happen to me from just seeing it?
[Adam:] He will make you change your understanding.
Eve: He wouldn't do that, because I will trust nothing
at all that I haven't put to the test.
Adam: Don't let him approach you any more,
for he is so evil-minded:
long ago he betrayed his own Lord
and tried to place himself in the highest seat.
Such a rogue who did something like that,
I don't want him finding refuge at your side.

Then the snake, calm, climbs artfully about the trunk of the forbidden tree, and Eve gives ear to him more closely as if listening to his advice. From there Eve will take the apple, and will extend it to Adam; he will not take it yet, however. And Eve will say:

Eve: Eat, Adam! You know not what it is.
Make good use of what has been prepared for us!
Adam: Is it so good then?

285–6 *tant que l'asai* 'that I haven't put to the test'. Eve has the empiricism of a Marie Curie, not believing something unless she has tested it for herself. For Eve, the whole thing has become an experiment to verify which of their two interlocutors, God or the devil, is telling them the truth.

Eva: Tu le saveras.
Nel poez saver si'n gusteras.
Adam: J'en duit.
Eva: Lai le!
Adam: Nen frai pas!
Eva: Del demorer fai tu que las.
Adam: E je le prendrai.
Eva: Manjue! Ten!
Par ço saveras e mal e bien.
Jo en manjerai premirement.
Adam: E jo aprés.
Eva: Seürement!

Tunc commedet Eva partem pomi, et dicet Ade:

Gusté en ai. Deus, quele savor!
Unc ne tastai d'itel dolçor!
D'itel savor est ceste pome . . .
Adam: De quel?

Eve: You will know.
You won't know if you don't taste.
Adam: I'm scared.
Eve: Leave your fear!
Adam: I won't do it!
Eve: You are quite wretched to delay.
Adam: I will share it too.
Eve: Eat it! Take it!
By this fruit you will know good and evil.
I will eat it first.
Adam: And I will eat it afterwards.
Eve: Absolutely.

Then Eve shall eat part of the apple and she shall say to Adam:

I have tasted it. God, what a flavour.
I have never tasted anything of such sweetness.
Of such flavour in this apple . . .
Adam: Flavour of what?

306 *nen gusta home* 'as human beings have never tasted'. That is to say at this point, neither Eve nor Adam (or just Adam, if home is taken to mean just 'man').

Eva: D'itel nen gusta home.
Or sunt mes oil tant cler veant,
je semmble Deu le tuit puissant!
Quanque fu, quanque doit estre
sai jo trestut, bien en sui maistre!
Manjue, Adam! Ne faz demore!
Tu le prendras en mult bon' ore.

Tunc accipiet Adam pomum de manu Eve, dicens:

Adam: Jo t'en crerra: tu es ma per.
Eva: Manjue! Nen pöez doter!

Eve: Of such a flavour as human beings have never tasted.
Now my eyes see with such brightness
I feel like God the all powerful.
Whatever has been, whatever will be
I know everything, I am in charge of it all.
Eat, Adam! Don't waste time!
You will share it in an hour of great profit to us.

Then Adam shall receive the apple from Eve while saying:

Adam: I will trust you on that. You are my mate.
Eve: Eat! Don't be afraid!

---

313 *Jo t'en crerra* 'I will trust you on that'. The devil has won her trust, and now she has won Adam's. This play treats the Fall as an essay on deceptive reasoning.

INDEX

* * *

This includes works in the Custom Version (CV). Definite articles (*The*, *Le*/*La*) are retained in the entry. Works, unless with labels indicating excerpts, are given complete.

Aðalsteinsdrápa, *see* Egill Skalla-Grímsson

Advent Lyrics, *see Christ I*

Ælfric, 740: The Preface to Genesis, 740; The Life of St Edmund, 746; The Sermon of Judith, CV; The Life of St Oswald, CV

Alexander's Letter to Aristotle, 719: Alexander to Aristotle (chapters 1–6), 720; A meeting with King Porus (chapters 22–25), 723; The Prophecy of the Trees of Sun and Moon (chapters 34–41), 726

Alfred, *see King Alfred's Prefaces, The West Saxon Boethius, The West Saxon Augustine, The West Saxon Bede, The West Saxon Orosius*

Andreas, 376: Matthew and the Mermedonians (lines 1–94), 377; Andrew talks with the Lord (lines 469–554), 382; Andrew frees Matthew (lines 910–1019), 387; Andrew calls forth a flood (lines 1478–1612), 393

The Anglo-Saxon Chronicle, 424, 470: The coming of the Saxons (449), 424; Cynewulf and Cyneheard (755 [for 786]), 426; Alfred's early wars with the Danes (871–8), CV; Alfred's later wars with the Danes (892–6), CV; Æthelflæd, Lady of the Mercians (910–19), CV; *The Battle of Brunanburh* (937), 470; *Edmund's Capture of the Five Boroughs* (942), 470; *The Coronation of King Edgar* (973), CV; *The Death of King Edgar* (975), CV; The martyrdom of Archbishop Ælfheah (1012), CV; The battle for England (1016–17), CV; Flashpoint at Dover (1051), CV; The Norman Conquest (1066), CV

Apollonius of Tyre, 781: The Princess falls in love (chapters 15–22), 783

Ari Þorgilsson, *Book of Icelanders* (*Íslendingabók*), 638: Greenland and America (chapter 6), 638; The conversion of Iceland (chapter 7), 639

Atlakviða, *see The Lay of Attila*

Augustine, *see The West Saxon Augustine*

The Battle of Brunanburh (937), 470

The Battle of Maldon (*c.* 991), 499

Bede, *see The West Saxon Bede*

Beowulf, 5: Scyld Scefing's funeral (lines 1–52), 6; Beowulf and the Danish coastguard (lines 217–300), 10; Beowulf greets King Hrothgar (lines 405–490), 15; Beowulf's fight with Grendel (lines 710–828), 20; Funeral at Finnsburh: Hildeburh and Wealhtheow (lines 1063–1191), 27; Future foretold: the fall of Hygelac (lines 1192–1231), 35; King Hrothgar on Grendel's Mere (1345–1376), 37; Beowulf's fight with Grendel's Mother (lines 1473–1572), 39; King Hrothgar's Sermon (lines 1677–1784), 45; Beowulf on Princess Freawaru (lines 2014–2072), 52; The lament of the last survivor (lines 2231–2270), 56; King Beowulf fights the Dragon (lines 2529–2599), 59; Wiglaf helps King Beowulf (lines 2599–2711), 63; History related: the rise of Hygelac (lines 2922–2998), 69; King Beowulf's funeral (lines 3058–3182), 74

Blickling Homilies, 733; No. 16 'The Feast of St Michael the Archangel', 734 (Mount Garganus and the Bull, 735; St Michael and the Neapolitans, CV; The consecration of St Michael's church, CV; A pilgrim's guide to the chapel on Monte Gargano, CV; St Paul's Vision of Hell, 738)

Boethius, *see The West Saxon Boethius*
Bragi the Old, *Eulogy on Ragnarr* (*Ragnarsdrápa, c.* 850): 128 (stanzas '1–11'); 532 (stanzas '12–16')
Brennu-Njáls saga, see The Saga of the Burned Njáll
Brot, see Fragment of the Lay of Sigurðr
Brussels Cross Riddle, 283; *see also Dream of the Rood* tradition
Brut, see Wace
Byrhtferth, *Enchiridion* 'handbook', CV: Teaching aims and outcomes, CV; On the joy of Easter (III.1), CV; Poetic genres and rhetorical figures (III.3), CV

Cædmon, *Hymn*, 276 (Northumbrian text); 459 (West Saxon text); *see also The West Saxon Bede*
Christ I (*Advent Lyrics*), CV: No. 5 'O Dayspring', CV; No. 7 'O my own Joseph', CV; No. 9 'O splendid woman of Middle World', CV
Christ II, see Cynewulf
Companho farai un vers, see William IX
The Coronation of King Edgar (973), CV
Cynewulf, *Elene*, 314: Constantine's Vision of the True Cross (lines 1–152), 315; Elene's discovery of the Nails of the Cross (lines 1109–1235), 324; Cynewulf's signed Epilogue (lines 1236–1321), 330; *Christ II*, 336: Thoughts on the final harbour (lines 797–866), 336
'Cynewulf and Cyneheard', *see The Anglo-Saxon Chronicle*

The Death of King Edgar (975), CV
De falsis deis, see Wulfstan
Deor, 101
The Dream of the Rood, 283; *see also Dream of the Rood* tradition
Dream of the Rood tradition, 279: The Ruthwell *Crucifixion Poem*, 280; The Brussels Cross Riddle, 283; *The Dream of the Rood*, 283

Edmund's Capture of the Five Boroughs (942), 470
Egill Skalla-Grímsson, *Eulogy on Æthelstan* (*Aðalsteinsdrápa*, 937), 477; *Head-Ransom* (*Hǫfuðlausn, c.* 952), 478; *Hard Loss of Sons* (*Sonatorrek*), 176; *see also The Saga of Egill Skalla-Grímsson*
Egils saga Skalla-Grímssonar, see The Saga of Egill Skalla-Grímsson
Eilífr Goðrúnarson, *Eulogy on Þórr* (*Þórsdrápa, c.* 985), 573
Einarr Cup-Tinkle, *Gold-Shortage* (*Vellekla, c.* 985), 558; Proem on the Mead of Poetry (stanzas '1–6'), 559; Óðinn helps Earl Hákon win Norway (stanzas '7–9'), 560; Earl Hákon restores the sacrifices (stanzas '14–18'), 560; The gods guide Earl Hákon (stanzas '30–33', '37'), 562
Eiríks saga Rauða, see The Saga of Eiríkr the Red
Eiríksmál, see The Lay of Eiríkr Bloodaxe
El Poema de Mio Cid, see The Poem of My Cid
Elene, see Cynewulf
Eulogies on King Cnut, see Óttarr the Black, Hallvarðr háreksblesi, Sighvatr Þórðarson
Exeter Book *Riddles, see Riddles*
The Exile of the Sons of Uisliu (*Longes Mac n-Uislenn*), 134, 262; The flight of Deirdre and Noisiu (chapters 1–16), 135; Deirdre of the Sorrows (chapters 17–19), 262
Exodus, 295: The Lord's pact with Moses (lines 1–62), 296; The Israelites sail to the Red Sea (lines 63–134), 300; Moses puts heart into the Israelites (lines 247–306), 305; The drowning of the Egyptians (lines 447–548), 308
Eyvindr the Plagiarist, *Lay of King Hákon the Good* (*Hákonarmál, c.* 961), 492

Farai un vers, pos mi sonelh, see William IX
Finnsburh Fragment, 82
Fragment of The Lay of Hildebrand (*Hildebrandslied*), 122
Fragment of the Lay of Sigurðr (*Brot*), CV

Gaimar, *History of the English* (*L'Estoire des Engleis*), 802: Havelok the Dane (lines 759–812), 802; Hereward the Wake (lines 5493–5554), 806

Genesis B (The Saxon *Genesis*; = *Genesis* (A), lines 235–851), 341
Glúmr Geirason, *Eulogy on Greycloak* (*Gráfeldardrápa*, *c.* 970), CV
Gododdin, *see Y Gododdin*
Gráfeldardrápa, *see* Glúmr
Grettis saga, *see The Saga of Grettir the Strong*
Guthlac B, CV; Guthlac retires to the wilderness (lines 878–999), CV; The dying Guthlac with his thegn (lines 1134–1304), CV; The thegn tells Guthlac's sister (lines 1305–1379), CV
Gylfaginning, *see* Snorri

Hákonardrápa, *see* Hallfreðr Troublesome Poet
Hákonarmál, *see* Eyvindr the Plagiarist
Hallfreðr Óttarsson, *Eulogy on Earl Hákon* (*Hákonardrápa*, *c.* 994), 588
Hallvarðr háreksblesi, *Eulogy on King Cnut* (*Knútsdrápa*, 1028), CV
Hamðismál, *see The Lay of Hamðir*
Haralds saga Harðráða, *see* Snorri Sturluson
Haustlǫng, *see* Þjóðólfr of Hvinir
Hávamál, *see Sayings of the High One*
Hildebrandslied, *see Fragment of The Lay of Hildebrand*
The Husband's Message, 253
Húsdrápa, *see* Úlfr Uggason
Hǫfuðlausn, *see* Egill Skalla-Grímsson

Íslendingabók, *see* Ari Þorgilsson

Judith, 401

King Alfred's Prefaces, 431: To the translation of Gregory's *Pastoral Care*, 431; To the translation of Boethius' *Consolation of Philosophy*, 436; To the translation of Augustine's *Soliloquies*, 437
Knútsdrápur (*Eulogies on King Cnut*), *see* Óttarr the Black, Hallvarðr háreksblesi, Sighvatr Þórðarson
Kormákr Ǫgmundarson, *Eulogy on Earl Sigurðr* (*Sigurðardrápa*, *c.* 961), CV

L'Estoire des Engleis, *see* Gaimar
La Chanson de Roland, *see The Song of Roland*
Laüstic, *see* Marie de France
Laxdœla saga, *see The Saga of the People of Laxdale*
The Lay of Attila (*Atlakviða*), 150
The Lay of Eiríkr Bloodaxe (*Eiríksmál*, *c.* 954), 488
The Lay of Hamðir (*Hamðismál*), 259; Guðrún's lament (stanzas 1–5), 260
The Lay of Skírnir (*Skírnismál*), 534
The Lay of Wayland (*Vǫlundarkviða*), 106
Le Jeu (Mystère) d'Adam, *see The Play of Adam*
The Life of St Edmund, *see* Ælfric
The Life of St Oswald, *see* Ælfric
Liðsmannaflokkr, *see The Soldiers' Song*
Lokasenna, *see Loki's Truth-Game*
Loki's Truth-Game (*Lokasenna*), 609
Longes Mac n-Uislenn, *see The Exile of the Sons of Uisliu*

Marie de France, *The Nightingale* (*Laüstic*), 845: The husband finds the nightingale (lines 69–156), 847
Maxims I, 203: A. The spirit of exchange (lines 1–13), 204; B. God, the world and women (lines 71–137), 205
The Mercian Life of St Guthlac (Vercelli Homily, No. 23), CV (Demons in the wilderness)

Njáls saga, *see The Saga of the Burned Njáll*

'Ohthere and Wulfstan', *see The West Saxon Orosius*
Orosius, *see The West Saxon Orosius*
Óttarr the Black, *Eulogy on King Cnut* (*Knútsdrápa*, *c.* 1026), CV

The Play of Adam (*Le Jeu (Mystère) d'Adam*), 852: The devil talks to Eve (lines 217–271), 853; Adam takes the apple (lines 282–314), 857
The Poem of My Cid, 810: Exile of the Campeador (cantos 1–4, or lines 1–52), 812
Prefaces, see *King Alfred's Prefaces*

Rǫgnvaldr kali, Lyrics (*Saga of the People of Orkney*, chapter 86), 824
Ragnarsdrápa, *see* Bragi the Old
The Rhyming Poem, 223
Riddles (of the Exeter Book), 236: No. 1 'Wind', 237; No. 5 'Shield', 238; No. 7 'Swan', 239; No. 9 'Cuckoo', 240; No. 12 'Ox', 241; No. 22 'Wagon of stars', 242; No. 25 'Onion', 243; No. 30a 'The Cross', 244; No. 46 'Lot and family', 245; No. 47 'Bookworm', 246; No. 54 'Churn', 247; No. 61 'Helmet', CV; No. 66 'Creation', CV; No. 74 'Bone', CV; No. 80 'Horn', CV; No. 95 'Book', CV
Roman de Brut, *see* Wace
The Ruin, 269
Ruthwell *Crucifixion Poem*, 280; *see also Dream of the Rood* tradition

The Saga of Egill Skalla-Grímsson (*Egils saga Skalla-Grímssonar*), 651: Egill and King Æthelstan (chapter 55), 651; Eiríkr Bloodaxe and the *Head-Ransom* (chapters 60–61), 655; In the backwoods: Egill and Ármóðr (chapters 71–72), 658; Bǫðvarr and the *Hard Loss of Sons* (chapter 78), 664 (*see also* Egill)
The Saga of Eiríkr the Red (*Eiríks saga Rauða*), 643: Vikings in America (chapters 8, 10–11), 643
The Saga of Grettir the Strong (*Grettis saga*) 702: Grettir's fight with Glámr (chapters 34–35), 702; Grettir fights the cave-trolls (chapters 65–66), 709
The Saga of the Burned Njáll (*Brennu-Njáls saga*), 689: Hallgerðr wins Gunnarr (chapter 33), 690; Gunnarr's last stand (chapter 77), 693; The burning of Njáll (chapter 129), 697
The Saga of the People of Laxdale (*Laxdœla saga*), 669: Hǫskuldr buys Melkorka (chapter 12), 670; The birth of Óláfr the Peacock (chapter 13), 673; Hjarðarholt and *Eulogy on the House* (chapters 29–30; *see also* Úlfr), 677; Bolli kills Kjartan (chapter 49), 682
The Saxon *Genesis*, *see Genesis B*
Sayings of the High One (*Hávamál*), 118, 210: What it's like when you get there (stanzas 1–7), 210; Friendship and exchange (stanzas 44–50), 213; How to get on (stanzas 58–62, 72–77), 215; Love and trust (stanzas 79–94), 218; Óðinn and Billingr's wife (stanzas 95–102), 118; Gunnlǫð and the Mead of Poetry (stanzas 13–14, 103–110), CV; *The Rune Tally* (stanzas 138–145), CV
The Seafarer, 186
Secundum Marcum, *see* Wulfstan
Sermo Lupi, *see* Wulfstan
The Sermon of Judith, *see* Ælfric
The Sibyl's Prophecy (*Vǫluspá*), 591
Sighvatr Þórðarson, *Eulogy on King Cnut* (*Knútsdrápa*, 1035), CV
Sigurðarbrot, *see Fragment of the Lay of Sigurðr*
Sigurðardrápa, *see* Kormákr Ǫgmundarson
Skáldskaparmál, *see* Snorri Sturluson
Skírnismál, *see The Lay of Skírnir*, 534
Snorri Sturluson (1178–1241), *Edda*, 523: The Old Norse myth of Creation (*Gylfaginning*, chapters 6–8), 524; The death of Baldr the Beautiful (*Gylfaginning*, chapter 49), 527; The myth of the Mead of Poetry (*Skáldskaparmál* (*Gylfaginning*, chapters 57–8)), CV; *Saga of Haraldr Harsh-Ruler* (*Haralds saga Harðráða*), CV; The Battle of Stamford Bridge (1066; chapters 90–92), CV
The Soldiers' Song (*Liðsmannaflokkr*, 1016), CV
Sonatorrek, *see* Egill Skalla-Grimsson
The Song of Roland, 792: The dreams of Charlemagne (laisses 56–58, or lines 717–750), 793; The trial of Ganelon (laisses 276–280, 291–3, or lines 3734–3785, 3899–3933), 796

Thomas of Britain, *Tristan*, 835: Sailing towards England (lines 75–114), 836; Tristan disguised as a leper (lines 500–586), 838; Love and images (MS de Turin, lines 1–50), 840
The Thunderclap Ballad (*Þrymskviða*), 564
Tristan, *see* Thomas of Britain

Þjóðólfr of Hvinir, *Harvest-Long* (*Haustlǫng*, *c.* 900), 548
Þórsdrápa, *see* Eilífr Goðrúnarson
Þrymskviða, *see The Thunderclap Ballad*

Úlfr Uggason, *Eulogy on the House* (*Húsdrápa*, early 990s), 583

Vǫlundarkviða, *see The Lay of Wayland*
Vǫluspá, *see The Sibyl's Prophecy*
Vainglory, 196
Vellekla, *see* Einarr Cup-Tinkle
Vercelli Homilies, CV: No. 23, *see The Mercian Life of St Guthlac*

Wace, *Brut* (*Roman de Brut*), 827; Arthur fights the giant of Mont St Michel (lines 2633–2782), 827
Waldere, 145
The Wanderer, 167
The West Saxon Augustine, CV: Many are the ways to find a king, CV; Life in the world to come, CV
The West Saxon Bede, 454: King Edwin's conversion (*HE* II.13), 454; The miracle of Cædmon (*HE* IV.24(22)), 459 (*see also* Cædmon)
The West Saxon Boethius, 440: Orpheus and Eurydice (B. Prose, chapter 36), 441; Ulysses and Circe (B. Prose, chapter 38), 446; Fate and Providence (C. Prose, chapter 29, 449)
The West Saxon Orosius, CV: The voyages of Ohthere, CV; The voyage of Wulfstan, CV
Widsith, 91
The Wife's Lament, 248
William IX, duke of Aquitaine, *Lyrics*, 815; A suitable poem (*Companho farai un vers*), 816; Feeling sleepy (*Farai un vers, pos mi sonelh*), 818
Wulf and Eadwacer, 232
Wulfstan, 756; *De falsis deis*, 757 (excerpt); *Secundum Marcum*, 759; *Sermo Lupi*, 765

Y Gododdin, The Fight at Catterick (verses 8–13), 86

CONTENTS OF THE CUSTOM VERSION

⁜

(in **bold** within the (abbreviated) contents of the present volume)

Heroic Poems

From *Beowulf*
Finnsburh Fragment
From *Y Gododdin*
Widsith
Deor
The Lay of Wayland
From *Sayings of the High One*
Fragment of The Lay of Hildebrand
From Bragi's *Eulogy on Ragnarr*
From *The Exile of the Sons of Uisliu*
Fragment of the Lay of Sigurðr
Brynhildr lies to Gunnarr
Brynhildr tells Gunnarr the truth
Waldere
The Lay of Attila

Poems on the Meaning of Life

The Wanderer
Egill's *Hard Loss of Sons*
The Seafarer
Vainglory
From *Maxims I*
From *Sayings of the High One*
The Rhyming Poem
Wulf and Eadwacer
From *Riddles*
The Wife's Lament
The Husband's Message
From *The Lay of Hamðir*
From *The Exile of the Sons of Uisliu*
The Ruin

More *Riddles*
No. 61 'Helmet'
No. 66 'Creation'
No. 74 'Bone'
No. 80 'Horn'
No. 95 'Book'

Poems of Devotion

Cædmon's *Hymn* (Northumbrian text)
The Cross Speaks
The Ruthwell *Crucifixion Poem*
The Brussels Cross Riddle
The Dream of the Rood
From *Exodus*
Christ I: Advent Lyrics
No. 5 'O Dayspring'
No. 7 'O my own Joseph'
No. 9 'O splendid woman of Middle World'
From Cynewulf's *Elene*
From Cynewulf's *Christ II*
Guthlac B
Guthlac retires to the wilderness
The dying Guthlac with his thegn
The thegn tells Guthlac's sister
Genesis B
From *Andreas*
Judith

The Earliest English Prose

The Anglo-Saxon Chronicle
The coming of the Saxons
Cynewulf and Cyneheard
Alfred's early wars with the Danes
The Mercian Life of St Guthlac
Demons in the wilderness
King Alfred's Prefaces
From *The West Saxon Boethius*
The West Saxon Augustine
Many are the ways to find a king
Life in the world to come
From *The West Saxon Bede*

The West Saxon Orosius
The voyages of Ohthere
The voyage of Wulfstan

Viking Wars

The Anglo-Saxon Chronicle
Alfred's later wars with the Danes (892–6)
Æthelflæd, Lady of the Mercians (910–19)
The Battle of Brunanburh (937)
Edmund's Capture of the Five Boroughs (942)
The English poems of Egill Skalla-Grímsson
Eulogy on Æthelstan (937)
Head-Ransom (*c.* 952)
The Lay of Eiríkr Bloodaxe (*c.* 954)
Eyvindr's *Lay of King Hákon the Good* (961)
Eulogies on the sons of Edmund and Eiríkr
1. *The Anglo-Saxon Chronicle*
***The Coronation of King Edgar* (973)**
***The Death of King Edgar* (975)**
2. Glúmr's *Eulogy on Greycloak* (*c.* 970)
The Battle of Maldon (*c.* 991)
King Sveinn's big invasion
1. *The Anglo-Saxon Chronicle*
The martyrdom of Archbishop Ælfheah (1012)
The battle for England (1016–17)
2. *The Soldiers' Song* (1016)
Eulogies on King Cnut
Óttarr the Black (*c.* 1026)
Hallvarðr háreksblesi (1028)
Sighvatr Þórðarson (1035)

Gods of the Vikings

Snorri's *Edda*
The Old Norse myth of Creation
The death of Baldr the Beautiful
The myth of the Mead of Poetry
From Bragi's *Eulogy on Ragnarr* (*c.* 850)
The Lay of Skírnir
Þjóðólfr's *Harvest-Long* (*c.* 900)
Sayings of the High One
Gunnlọð and the Mead of Poetry
The Rune Tally

Kormákr's *Eulogy on Earl Sigurðr* (*c.* 961)
From Einarr's *Gold-Shortage* (*c.* 985)
The Thunderclap Ballad
Eilífr's *Eulogy on Þórr* (*c.* 985)
Úlfr's *Eulogy on the House* (early 990s)
Hallfreðr's *Eulogy on Earl Hákon* (*c.* 994)
The Sibyl's Prophecy
Loki's Truth-Game

Sagas of Icelanders

From Ari's *Book of Icelanders*
From *The Saga of Eiríkr the Red*
From *The Saga of Egill Skalla-Grímsson*
From *The Saga of the People of Laxdale*
From *The Saga of the Burned Njáll*
From *The Saga of Grettir the Strong*

Writers of the Benedictine Reform

From *Alexander's Letter to Aristotle*
Blickling Homilies
No. 16 'The Feast of St Michael the Archangel'
Mount Garganus and the bull
St Michael and the Neapolitans
The consecration of St Michael's church
A pilgrim's guide to the chapel on Monte Gargano
St Paul's Vision of Hell
From Abbot Ælfric of Eynsham
The Preface to Genesis
The Sermon of Judith
The Life of St Edmund
The Life of St Oswald
Byrhtferth of Ramsey
***Enchiridion* ('handbook')**
Teaching aims and outcomes
On the joy of Easter
Poetic genres and rhetorical figures
From Archbishop Wulfstan of York

Early Chivalry

From *Apollonius of Tyre*
The Anglo-Saxon Chronicle
Flashpoint at Dover (1051)

Snorri's *Saga of Haraldr Harsh-Ruler*
The battle of Stamford Bridge (1066)
The Anglo-Saxon Chronicle
The Norman Conquest (1066)
From *The Song of Roland*
From Gaimar's *History of the English*
From *The Poem of My Cid*
From *Lyrics* of William IX
Fin'amor from Orkney: Rǫgnvaldr kali
From Thomas of Britain's *Tristan*
From Marie de France's *The Nightingale*
From *The Play of Adam*